# *Guide to* **Understanding Financial Statements**

*Interpretation, Application and Analytics*

# *Guide to* **Understanding Financial Statements**

*Interpretation, Application and Analytics*


B.D. Chatterjee

B.Com (Hons), FCA, ACMA, ACS, Dip IFR (ACCA - UK)



BLOOMSBURY

NEW DELHI • LONDON • OXFORD • NEW YORK • SYDNEY

First published in India 2022


ISBN 978-93-54358-14-2

10 9 8 7 6 5 4 3 2 1

Bloomsbury Publishing India Pvt. Ltd
DDA Complex, LSC Building No.4
Second Floor, Pocket C–6 & 7, Vasant Kunj
New Delhi 110070
Phone: +91-11-40574957, 40574954
www.bloomsbury.com
CIN: U22130DL2012PTC232353

***To provide feedback, please mail at professionalbooks@bloomsbury.com***

Printed and bound in India by Thomson Press (India) Ltd.

# About the author

B D Chatterjee is a finance leader with over 35 Years of rich industry experience in overall business and finance function. He is a Chartered Accountant with CS and CMA qualifications and holds a diploma in IFRS from UK.

During his long and enriching career he has handled many high-profile leadership positions like CFO/VP/Director Finance assignments in global Multinationals (BOC Gases, DuPont, and Kelly Services) both in India and abroad and large Indian conglomerates (Mother Dairy group, Max India) in India. In handling the above positions, he acquired extensive knowledge and experience in industries like industrial gases, engineering polymers, agro chemicals, FMCG and dairy products, health care and manpower services, among others.

Apart from above, he also has deep consulting experience in managing CFO solutions including Enterprise Resource Planning Systems projects in various industries spanning from food and beverage (PepsiCo franchisee), telecom, auto ancillary industries, and Quick Serve Restaurant chain (McDonalds) to name a few.

He possesses expertise in implementation of best practices in finance, corporate governance, change management through corporate restructuring, business process and financial re-engineering and enterprise Risk Management. He has rich experience in Mergers and Acquisitions including financial due diligence and business valuation.

He had also been associated with an International Institute as a visiting faculty and taught finance professionals Diploma in IFRS as well as certificate courses of IFRS organized by ACCA Global (UK).

Currently, he is associated with a reputed International Think Tank ACCESS Health International Inc as their global CFO for the past four and half years. The operation of the organization spans across countries like the United States, India, China, Middle East, and Southeast Asia. This stint has provided him invaluable experience in handling global finance and administration in digital space, intricate compliance management prevailing in various countries, risk management and international governance processes like global Audit and Assurance process including Audit Committee and international Board Meetings.

He is an established author, and his books include wide range of contemporary business and finance topics like International Financial Reporting Standards (IFRS), Indian Accounting Standards (Ind AS), Business Valuation, Financial Due Diligence, The CFO

Guide to Understanding Financial Statements

Handbook, Enterprise Risk Management and Corporate Governance published by reputed publishers.

*Linked in profile: in.linkedin.com/pub/biswajeet-chatterjee/2/5a9/b6/*

Address:
121/105 Silver Oaks Apartments
DLF Phase I
Gurgaon 122002.
HARYANA
Mobile: 9810119275

# Preface

As is conventionally known, Financial Statements are a set of reporting templates which provide snap shot financial results of an organization along with the financial performance for a certain period under reference. The financial information is generated using these templates as conduit based on accounting principles known as International Financial Reporting Standards. These templates are designed in prescribed format through legislations to generate relevant and fairly representative financial information related to an organization to the users.

The makers of these Financial Statements have an onerous responsibility to ensure that, accounting information is fair and represent the firm's economic performance, financial position, and risk. At the same time, these Financial Statements should provide relevant and credible information to forecast the firm's expected future earnings and cash flows in order that the users can take informed business decisions based on the reported numbers. Accordingly, the quality of financial reporting needs to articulate fair and accurate economic information contained in the income statement, the balance sheet, the statement of cash flows and notes to the Financial Statements.

To be honest, approach to quality of Financial Reporting through the conduit of Financial Statements go far beyond the compliance of related statutory provisions and International Financial Reporting Standards and an unqualified opinion of the independent auditors. Hence the importance of interpretation of Financial Statements in its application and analytics cannot be underscored.

Also, the qualified users like bankers, financial institutions and prospective investors use Analytics extensively and apply it to reported financial statements to determine whether they provide useful information that is relevant and reliable for understanding the firm's financial position, performance, growth, and risk and assists in projection of the firm's future earnings and cash flows.

To bring about a simplified approach to the above, I have conceived this body of work, wherein I have made an attempt to bring forth to the reader a simplified understanding of Financial Statements, its interpretation, application to various areas like business and corporate restructuring, consolidated financial reporting and specific reporting under Non-banking Financial Companies together with Analytics for better understanding and interpretation of the myriad of numbers.

Accordingly, the book has been structured in three sections as explained below.

Section A discusses the *building blocks of developing, presentation and interpretation* of Financial Statements. These are as follows:

- Financial Statements – an overview.
- Classification of current and non-current assets and liabilities.
- Shareholders' funds.
- Non-current liabilities.
- Current liabilities.
- Non-current Assets.
- Current Assets.
- Statement of Profit and Loss and other Comprehensive Income.
- Contingent Liabilities and Assets.
- Other Notes on Accounts.
- Statement of Cash Flows.

Section B highlights the *application* of Financial Statements as under:

- Corporate Restructuring, including merger and acquisitions and demergers and internal reconstruction,
- Consolidated Financial Statements for group reporting purposes
- Financial Statements related Non-Banking Finance Companies (NBFCs)

Section C addresses the *analytics* related to health and hygiene of the business, and these are covered as under:

- Business / Financial Analysis,
- Comparative Financial Statements,
- Common size Statements,
- Trend Ratios,
- Forecasting Techniques,
- Ratio Analysis,
- Return on Capital Employed including DuPont Analysis,
- Case studies related to Financial Health and Hygiene Analysis.

Considerable effort has been put in to explain the concepts in simplified and lucid form with many charts, illustrations and case studies some of which are from the Author's personal experience.

In developing this body of work, references have been made on various pronouncements made by the Institute of Chartered Accountants of India through its Guidance Notes published from time to time.

I believe the book will be useful for all financial professionals and students, who would like to use this book as a working guide in understanding the concepts and effectively handle the challenges while finalizing Financial Statements.

I would like to take this opportunity to mention that while considerable care has been taken to ensure that the contents of the book are accurate a few errors and omissions might have crept in, for which I seek with all humility to my readers to bear with me.

I would also like to take this opportunity to thank my publishers Bloomsbury professionals in providing me this opportunity to publish the book.

I would like to dedicate this book to my wife Debika, my daughter Bidyut and my son Badri for their constant inspiration in developing this body of work.

121/105 Silver Oaks Apartments

DLF Phase I

Gurgaon 122002

Email: bdchatterjee105@gmail.com

B D Chatterjee

# Contents at a glance

## SECTION V
# Health and Hygiene of the Businesses Emanating from Financial Statements

# Table of contents



## SECTION I
## OVERVIEW

## SECTION II
## Building Blocks of developing, presentation and interpretation

## SECTION III
## Financial Statements in Corporate Restructuring and Consolidated Financial Statements

## SECTION IV
# Financial Reporting of Non-Banking Financial Companies

## SECTION V
## Health and Hygiene of the Businesses Emanating from Financial Statements

# SECTION I

# OVERVIEW

# Chapter 1

# Financial Statements: An Overview

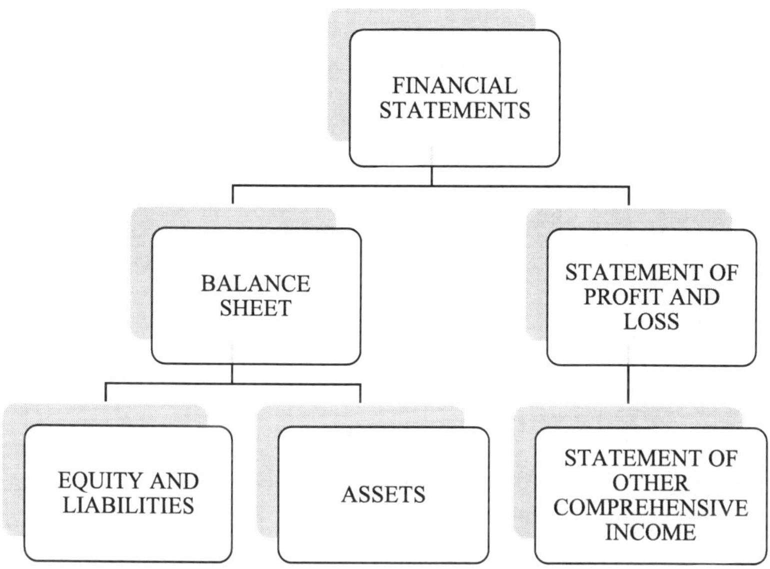


## 1.1 INTRODUCTION

Financial statements are a set of reporting formats which are prepared to provide financial information about the reporting entity's assets, liabilities, equity, income, and expenses that is useful to users of financial statements in assessing the prospects for future net cash inflows to the reporting entity and in assessing management's stewardship of the entity's economic resources. These statements can be a thought of as a mechanism which provides to the world at large the financial results in a standard and uniform template understandable by the stakeholders and users.

According to section 2(40) of the Companies Act 2013, *financial statement* in relation to a company includes,

| *financial statement* | (i) a Balance Sheet as at the end of financial year,<br>(ii) a Profit & Loss Account, or in the case of a company carrying on any activity not for profit, an income and expenditure account for the financial year,<br>(iii) cash flow statement for the financial year,<br>(iv) a statement of change in equity, if applicable and<br>(v) any explanatory note annexed to or forming part of any document referred to in sub-clause (i) to sub-clause (iv) |
|---|---|

Provided that the financial statement, with respect to One Person Company, small Company and dormant company, may not include the cash flow statement.

**(i)** **Balance Sheet**: This statement represents the financial position which discloses short term and long-term solvency, which is the ability to meet the liability in the short as well as long term. According to framework Liquidity represents the availability of sufficient funds to meet the deposit withdrawals and other financial commitments as they fall due. Solvency is the availability of cash over the longer term to meet the financial commitments as they fall due.

**(ii)** **Statement of Profit and Loss**: This statement reflects net financial results of an entity

**(iii)** **Cash flow statement**: This statement manifests sources from where cash has been acquired and the utilisation of the same and also helps the entity to predict future cash flows.

**(iv)** **Statement of changes in Equity:** Depicts movement in shareholder's equity and includes net profit or loss during the accounting period, increase or decrease in reserves and dividend payments to shareholders.

**(v)** **Notes and schedules forming part of Accounts**: These represent a summary of accounting policies, explanations and assumptions forming integral part of Accounts. Proper disclosures ensure meaning interpretation of the financial statements for users of financial statements.

The Financial statements are borne out of Books of Accounts.

In accordance the Companies Act 2013, every company to prepare and keep at its registered office -

(a) books of account and

(b) other relevant books and papers and

(c) financial statement for every financial year

which give *a true and fair view* of the state of affairs of the company including that of its branch office or offices, if any, and explain the transactions effected both at the registered office and its branches and such books are kept on *accrual basis* and according to the *double entry system of accounting.* (Section 128 (1))

As per section 2(13) *Books of account* includes records maintained in respect of:

| *Books of account* | |
|---|---|
| | (i) all sums of money received and expended by a company and matters in relation to which the receipts and expenditures take place,<br>(ii) all sales and purchases of goods and services by the company,<br>(iii) the assets and liabilities of the company, and<br>(iv) the items of cost as may be prescribed under section 148 in the case of a company which belongs to any class of companies specified under that section |

As per section 2(14) *books and papers* include books of account, deeds, vouchers, writings, documents, minutes and registers maintained on paper or in electronic form,

The financial statements shall

(a) Give a *true and fair* view of the state of affairs of the Company or companies,

(b) Comply with the accounting standards notified under section 133 and

(c) Shall be in the form as may be provided for different class or classes of Companies under Schedule III

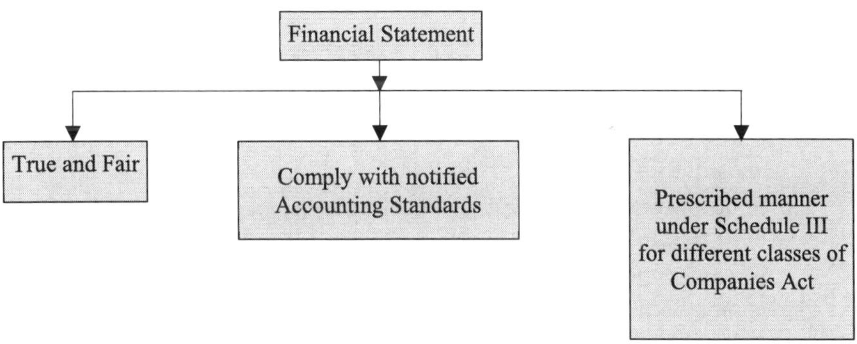


## 1.2 ACCOUNTING QUALITY

At this stage, we need to have a broad understanding of Accounting Quality. It presupposes the following:

- Accounting information should be a fair and complete representation of the firm's economic performance, financial position, and risk.
- Accounting information should provide relevant information to forecast the firm's expected future earnings and cash flows.

Accounting quality encompasses the economic information contained in the income statement, the balance sheet, the statement of cash flows and notes to the financial statements. Each of these financial statements and supplemental disclosures integrates and articulates with the others, and each aids financial statement users in the assessment of profitability, growth, risk, and value. Actually, approach to accounting quality goes beyond the compliance of related statutory provisions and International Financial Reporting Standards and an unqualified opinion of the independent auditors.

Through Analytics rigorous test is applied to reported financial statements to determine whether

- they provide users with useful information that is relevant and reliable for understanding the firm's financial position, performance, growth, and risk, and
- that aids the projection of the firm's future earnings and cash flows.

It is imperative to realize that even correctly applied accounting rules may, on occasions, fail to indicate future earnings potential and limit the balance sheet's usefulness in assessing financial position and risk because even the best accounting standards and principles in the world cannot perfectly measure and report each firms' financial position and performance. In this chapter and the future chapters we have made an attempt to highlight the tools and techniques which will assist in bringing about the credibility of financial statements to the extent possible through analytics.

## 1.3 SCOPE OF FINANCIAL STATEMENTS

According to the *Framework*, that information is provided:

(a) in the statement of financial position, by recognizing assets, liabilities, and equity.

(b) in the statement(s) of financial performance, by recognizing income and expenses; and

(c) in other statements and notes, by presenting and disclosing information about:

  (i) recognized assets, liabilities, equity, income, and expenses, including information about their nature and the risks arising from those recognized assets and liabilities.

  (ii) assets and liabilities that have not been recognized including information about their nature and the risks arising from them.

  (iii) cash flows.

  (iv) contributions from holders of equity claims and distributions to them; and

  (v) the methods, assumptions, and judgments used in estimating the amounts presented or disclosed, and changes in those methods, assumptions, and judgments.

## 1.4 ELEMENTS OF FINANCIAL STATEMENTS AS DEFINED IN THE FRAMEWORK

The elements of financial statements defined in the *Conceptual Framework* are:

(a) assets, liabilities, and equity, which relate to a reporting entity's financial position; and

(b) income and expenses, which relate to a reporting entity's financial performance.

The table explains this further:

| Item | Element | Description |
|---|---|---|
| ***Economic resource*** | Asset | A present economic resource controlled by the entity as a result of past events.<br>An economic resource is a right that has the potential to produce economic benefits. |
| ***Claim*** | a) Liability<br>b) Equity | A present obligation of the entity to transfer an economic resource as a result of past events.<br>The residual interest in the assets of the entity after deducting all its liabilities. |
| ***Changes in economic resources and claims, reflecting financial performance*** | a) Income<br>b) Expenses | Increases in assets, or decreases in liabilities, that result in increases in equity, other than those relating to contributions from holders of equity claims.<br>Decreases in assets, or increases in liabilities, that result in decreases in equity, other than those relating to distributions to holders of equity claims. |
| ***Other changes in economic resources and claims*** | a) Contributions<br>b) Exchanges | Contributions from holders of equity claims, and distributions to them.<br>Exchanges of assets or liabilities that do not result in increases or decreases in equity. |

## 1.5 GOING CONCERN ASSUMPTION

The financial statements are normally prepared on the assumption that an enterprise is a going concern and will continue in operation for the foreseeable future. Going concern concept indicates that assets are kept for generating benefit in the future, not for immediate sale, the current change in the asset value is not realizable and so it should not be counted.

## 1.6 QUALITATIVE CHARACTERISTICS OF FINANCIAL REPORTING ACCORDING TO FRAMEWORK

The qualitative characteristics involve Fundamental and Enhancing characteristics are explained in the chart below.

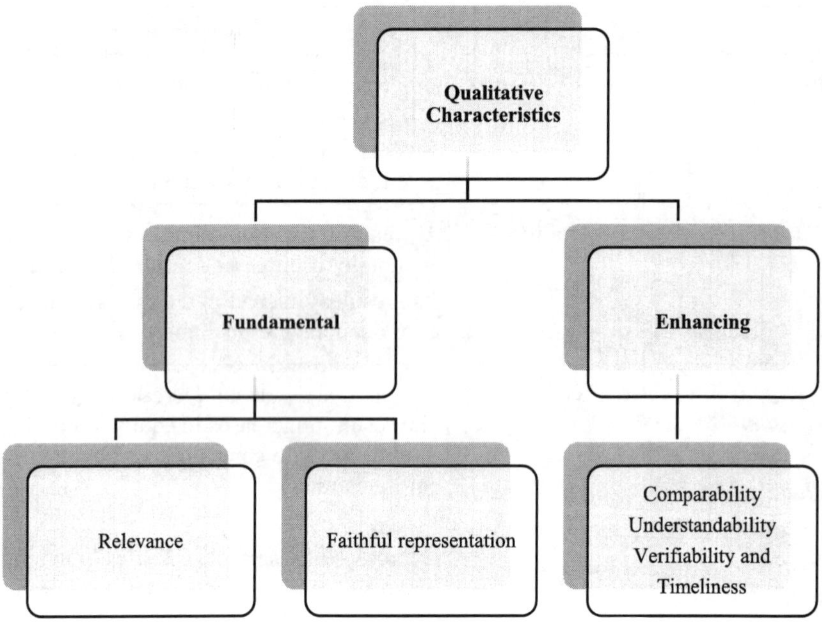

The qualitative characteristics of financial statements are explained further in the table below:

| | | |
|---|---|---|
| **Fundamental** | **Relevance**<br>The financial statements need to ensure relevance for the decision-making needs of the users. According to the *framework* information has the quality of relevance when it influences the economic decisions of users by assisting them to evaluate past, present, or future events or confirming or correcting their past evaluations. | **A) Predictive value**<br>With the help of relevant financial information, the users can arrive at reasonable estimate of the foreseeable future.<br><br>**B) Confirmatory value**<br>Relevance ensures confirmation of current events through facts and figures. |
| | **Faithful representation**<br>The word faithful or "true and fair" signifies truthfulness and fairness in the representations. The characteristics that lead to faithful representation are: | **a) Completeness**<br>Financial information must ensure completeness, within the restrictions of materiality and costs to be reliable. Any material omission may result in misrepresentation of information.<br>**b) Neutrality**<br>Information needs to be free from bias to be reliable. Neutrality is lost if the financial statements are prepared with a view to influencing the user to make a judgement or decision to achieve a predetermined outcome.<br>**c) Free from errors**<br>This would mean that there are no errors or omissions in the description of the phenomenon and the process used to produce the reported information has been selected and applied with no errors in the process |

| | | |
|---|---|---|
| **Enhancing** | **Comparability:** The financial statements need to stand on robust and consistent accounting policies to ensure that these are comparable between accounting periods within the entity as also between entities in the same industry.<br>Users must be able to compare the financial statements-<br>i) through time to identify trends<br>ii) with other enterprise's statements, to evaluate their relative financial position, performance, and changes in financial position.<br>**Verifiability:** Financial statements should be verifiable to be comparable and understandable.<br>**Timeliness:** it is very critical to ensure that financial statements are released within timelines to ensure that these are made use of and are not out of date.<br>**Understandability**: One of the principal characteristics of the financial statements is to ensure understandability such that these documents are comprehensible by various user communities like investors, government agencies, etc. | |

## 1.7 ELEMENTS OF STATEMENT OF FINANCIAL POSITION

The elements of the Statement of Financial Position are enumerated as under:

A) Assets
B) Liabilities
C) Equity

### 1.7.1 How is Asset defined under the Framework?

An asset is a present economic resource controlled by the entity as a result of past events. An economic resource is a right that has the potential to produce economic benefits.

The above definition stresses three elements as shown below:

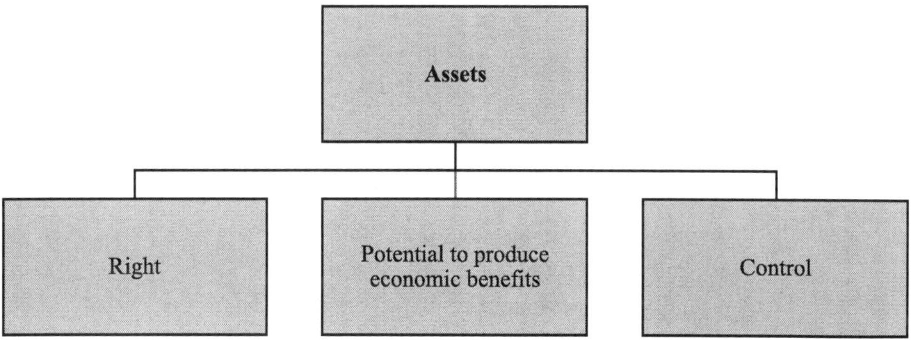


## Right

Rights that have the potential to produce economic benefits take many forms, including:

(a) rights that correspond to an obligation of another party,

For example:

(i) rights to receive cash.

(ii) rights to receive goods or services.

(iii) rights to exchange economic resources with another party on favourable terms. Such rights include, for example, a forward contract to buy an economic resource on terms that are currently favourable or an option to buy an economic resource.

(iv) rights to benefit from an obligation of another party to transfer an economic resource if a specified uncertain future event occurs.

(b) rights that do not correspond to an obligation of another party,

For example:

(i) rights over physical objects, such as property, plant and equipment, or inventories. Examples of such rights are a right to use a physical object or a right to benefit from the residual value of a leased object.

(ii) rights to use intellectual property.

### Economic Benefits

An economic resource is a right that has the potential to produce economic benefits. For that potential to exist, it does not need to be certain, or even likely, that the right will produce economic benefits.

An economic resource could produce economic benefits for an entity by entitling or enabling it to do, for example, one or more of the following:

(a) receive contractual cash flows or another economic resource,

(b) exchange economic resources with another party on favourable terms,

(c) produce cash inflows or avoid cash outflows by, for example:

- (i) using the economic resource either individually or in combination with other economic resources to produce goods or provide services,
- (ii) using the economic resource to enhance the value of other economic resources; or
- (iii) leasing the economic resource to another party,

(d) receive cash or other economic resources by selling the economic resource; or

(e) extinguish liabilities by transferring the economic resource.

### Control

Control links an economic resource to an entity. Assessing whether control exists helps to identify the economic resource for which the entity accounts.

An entity controls an economic resource if it has the present ability to direct the use of the economic resource and obtain the economic benefits that may flow from it. Control includes the present ability to prevent other parties from directing the use of the economic resource and from obtaining the economic benefits that may flow from it. It follows that, if one party controls an economic resource, no other party controls that resource.

## 1.7.2 How is liability defined under the Framework?

According to *Framework,* a liability is a present obligation of the entity to transfer an economic resource as a result of past events.

The above definition stresses three elements as shown below:

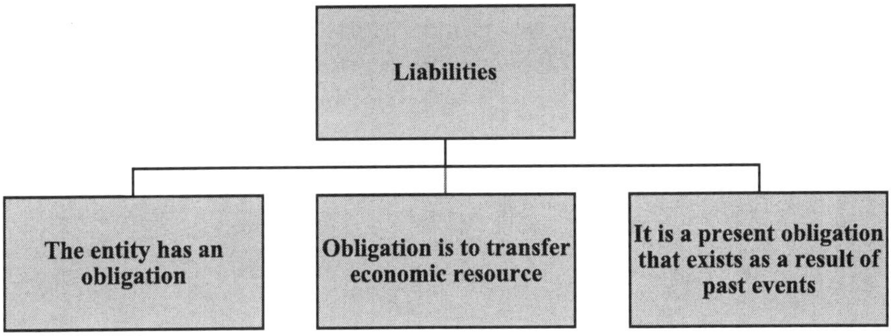


**Obligation**

**Obligation, as defined in Framework, is as under:**

> **An obligation is a duty or responsibility that an entity has no practical ability to avoid.**
> **An obligation is always owed to another party (or parties).**
> **The other party (or parties) could be a person or another entity, a group of people or other entities, or society at large.**
> *Framework*

### 1.7.3 How is equity defined under the Framework?

The residual interest in the assets of the enterprise after deducting all its liabilities.

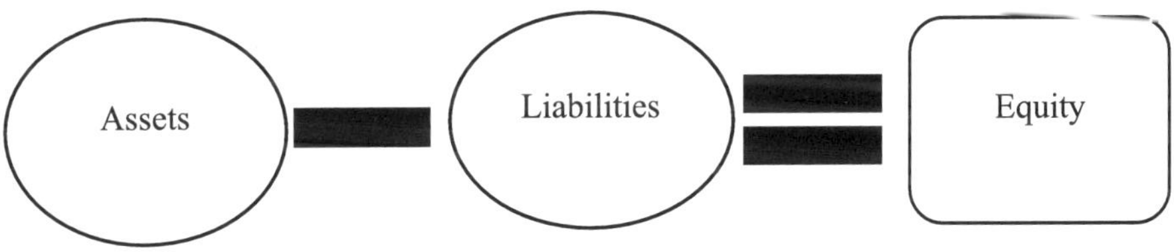


### 1.7.4 How is income defined under the Framework?

Income is increases in assets, or decreases in liabilities, that result in increases in equity, other than those relating to contributions from holders of equity claims.

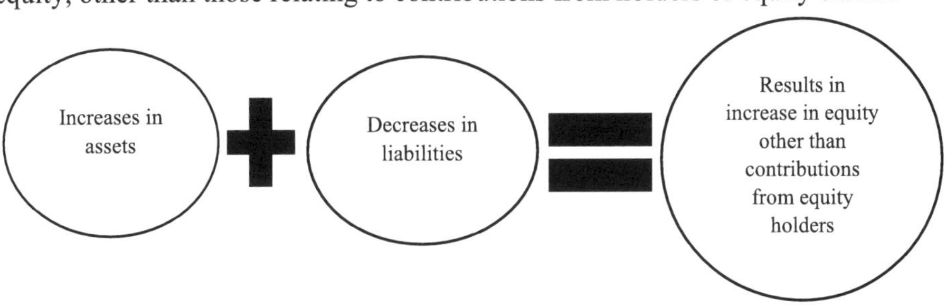

### 1.7.5 How are expenses defined under the Framework?

Expenses are decreases in assets, or increases in liabilities, that result in decreases in equity, other than those relating to distributions to holders of equity claims.

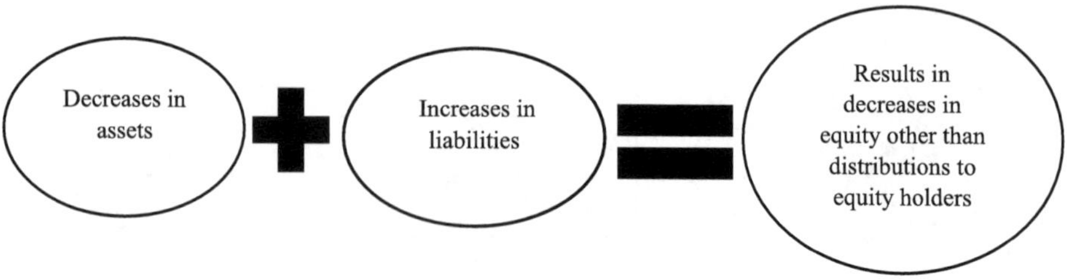


## 1.8 PROCESS OF RECOGNITION OF FINANCIAL STATEMENTS ENUNCIATED BY THE FRAMEWORK

According to *Framework*, recognition is the process of capturing for inclusion in the statement of financial position or the statement(s) of financial performance an item that meets the definition of one of the elements of financial statements—an asset, a liability, equity, income, or expenses.

Recognition links the elements; the statement of financial position and the statement(s) of financial performance as follows:

(a) in the statement of financial position at the beginning and end of the reporting period, total assets minus total liabilities equal total equity, and

(b) recognized changes in equity during the reporting period comprise:

   (i) income minus expenses recognised in the statement(s) of financial performance; plus

   (ii) contributions from holders of equity claims, minus distributions to holders of equity claims.

| Recognition | Explanation |
|---|---|
| ***Income*** | (i) the initial recognition of an asset, or an increase in the carrying amount of an asset; or<br>(ii) the derecognition of liability, or a decrease in the carrying amount of liability. |
| ***Expense*** | (i) the initial recognition of a liability, or an increase in the carrying amount of liability; or<br>(ii) the derecognition of an asset, or a decrease in the carrying amount of an asset. |

This is further explained in the diagram below.

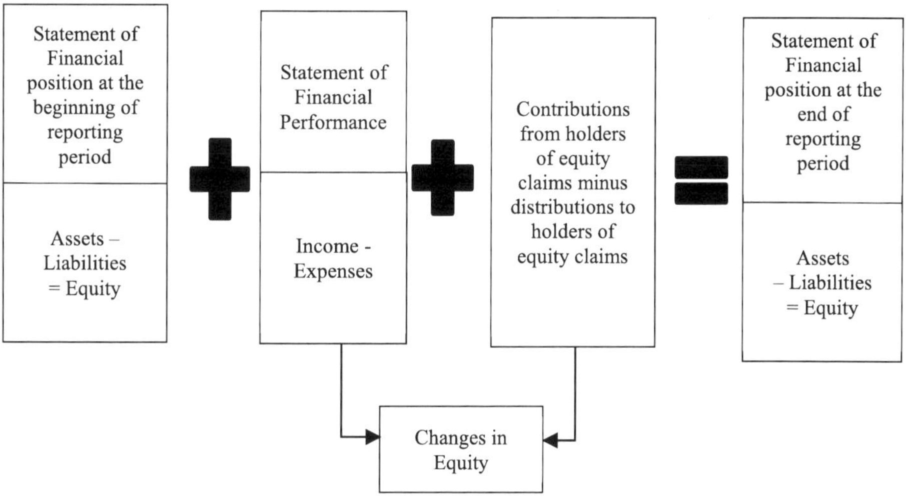


The above diagram explains the flow of information incorporated under the Financial Statements.

A Balance Sheet at the commencement of the reporting period provides a snapshot of Assets minus Liabilities and the resultant difference is reflected under Equity.

During the reporting period, a statement financial performance which is the Statement of Profit & Loss depicts Income and deduct therefrom all the expenses to arrive at Surplus if any. Together with this the contributions from the holders of equity (share capital) less distributions to holder of equity claims and both add up to generate Change in Equity. This is termed as Statement of Changes in Equity. Hence it is clear that Statement of Profit and Loss and Statement of changes in Equity are closely interwoven.

Once we consolidate the financial position in the beginning of the year and add the Statement of changes in Equity, we arrive at closing Statement of Financial Position or Balance Sheet as at the end of the reporting period.

### 1.8.1 Recognition criteria

As per *Framework* recognition criteria are:

An asset or liability is recognized only if recognition of that asset or liability and any resulting income, expenses, or changes in equity provides users of financial statements with information that is useful, i.e. with:

(a) relevant information about the asset or liability and any resulting income, expenses, or changes in equity; and

(b) a faithful representation of the asset or liability and any resulting income, expenses, or changes in equity.

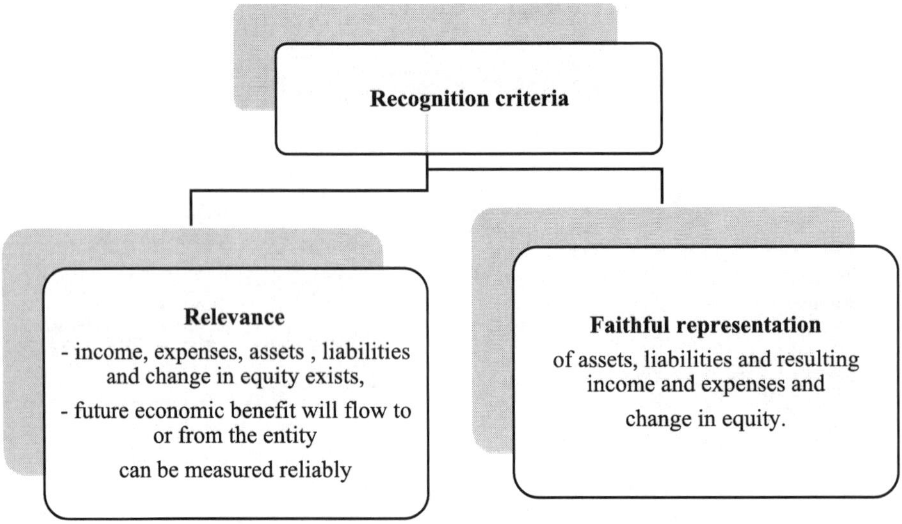


## 1.8.2 Relevance

Information about assets, liabilities, equity, income, and expenses is relevant to users of financial statements. However, recognition of a particular asset or liability and any resulting income, expenses, or changes in equity may not always provide relevant information. That may be the case if, for example:

(a) it is uncertain whether an asset or liability exists; or

(b) an asset or liability exists, but the probability of an inflow or outflow of economic benefits is low.

Hence, in other words, relevance takes effect only if:

a) If the assets, liability, income, expenses, or changes in equity exists,

b) it is probable that any future economic benefit associated with the item will flow to or from the entity and

c) the item in consideration has a cost or value which can be measured reliably.

## 1.8.3 Faithful representation

Recognition of a particular asset or liability is appropriate if it provides not only relevant information, but also a faithful representation of that asset or liability and any resulting income, expenses, or changes in equity. Whether a faithful representation can be provided may be affected by the level of measurement uncertainty associated with the asset or liability or by other factors.

For an asset or liability to be recognized, it must be measured.

## 1.9 MEASUREMENT OF EQUITY UNDER THE FRAMEWORK

According to the *Framework*, the total carrying amount of equity (total equity) is not measured directly. It equals the total of the carrying amounts of all recognized assets less the total of the carrying amounts of all recognized liabilities. But the *Framework* makes it clear that, because general purpose financial statements are not designed to show an entity's value, the total carrying amount of equity will not generally equal:

(a) the aggregate market value of equity claims on the entity,

(b) the amount that could be raised by selling the entity as a whole on a going concern basis; or

(c) the amount that could be raised by selling all of the entity's assets and settling all of its liabilities.

## 1.10 ACCRUAL ACCOUNTING

When the accrual basis of accounting is used, an entity recognizes items as assets, liabilities, equity, income, and expenses (the elements of financial statements) when they satisfy the definitions and recognition criteria for those elements in the *Conceptual Framework.*

## 1.11 INFORMATION ELEMENTS THE FINANCIAL STATEMENTS NEED TO PROVIDE

Financial statements must provide information about the following aspects:

- Assets
- Liabilities
- Equity
- Income & Expenses (including gains and losses)
- Contributions by and contributions to owners in their capacity as owners
- Cash flows

## 1.12 BALANCE SHEET

The Statement of Financial Position or Balance Sheet depicts the short term and long-term solvency of the organization and depicts the following:

- Assets
- Liabilities and
- Equity of the organization.

A Balance Sheet shall include line items that present the following amounts:

| | |
|---|---|
| (a) | property, plant and equipment. |
| (b) | investment property; |
| (c) | intangible assets. |
| (d) | financial assets (excluding amounts shown under (e), (h) and (i)); |
| (da) | Insurance contracts |
| (e) | investments accounted for using the equity method. |
| (f) | biological assets within the scope of Ind AS 41 *Agriculture*; |
| (g) | inventories. |
| (h) | trade and other receivables; |
| (i) | cash and cash equivalents; |
| (j) | the total of assets classified as held for sale and assets included in disposal groups classified as held for sale following Ind AS 105 *Non-current Assets Held for Sale and Discontinued Operations*. |
| (k) | trade and other payables. |
| (l) | provisions. |
| (m) | financial liabilities |
| (n) | liabilities and assets for current tax, as defined in Ind AS 12 *Income Taxes*. |
| (o) | deferred tax liabilities and deferred tax assets, as defined in Ind AS 12; |
| (p) | liabilities included in disposal groups classified as held for sale following Ind AS 105; |
| (q) | non-controlling interests, presented within equity; and |
| (r) | issued capital and reserves are attributable to owners of the parent. |

## 1.13 COMPONENTS UNDER ASSETS

The broad components under assets are:

- **Property, Plant and Equipment** are disaggregated by class as described in *Ind AS 16 Property, Plant and Equipment*
- **Receivables** are disaggregated between amounts receivables from trade customers, other members of the group, receivables from related parties, prepayments, and other amounts
- **Inventories** are disaggregated as per Ind AS 2 Inventories into merchandise, production supplies, materials, work in progress, and finished goods.

## 1.14 COMPONENTS UNDER EQUITY AND RESERVES

For each class of share capital:

- Number of shares authorized
- Number of shares issued and fully-paid, and issued but not fully paid
- Par value per share or that the shares have no par value
- Reconciliation of number of shares outstanding at the beginning and the end of the year
- Rights, preferences, and restrictions attaching to that class including restrictions on the distribution of dividends and the repayment of capital
- Shares in the entity held by the entity itself or by related group companies
- Shares reserved for issuance under options and sales contracts, including terms and amounts
- Description of the nature and purpose of each reserve within owners' equity

## 1.15 FINANCIAL STATEMENTS UNDER SCHEDULE III OF Companies Act 2013

### 1.15.1 Financial Statements under Schedule III: Division I (For non Ind AS entities)

#### *1.15.1.1 Applicability*

Schedule III, Division I, applies to all companies, except for those companies where Division II and Division III of the Schedule III is applicable, for the Financial Statements to be prepared for the financial year commencing on or after April 1, 2014.

The requirements of Schedule III, however, do not apply to companies as referred to in the proviso to section 129(1) of the Companies Act 2013, i.e., any insurance or banking company, or any company engaged in the generation or supply of electricity or to any other class of company for which a form of Balance Sheet and Statement of Profit and Loss has been specified in or under any other Act governing such class of company.

According to the Guidance Note of ICAI (Revised January, 2022 Edition) on Schedule III Division I, Section 1(4)(d) of the Companies Act, 2013 states that the Companies Act will apply to electricity companies, to the extent it is not inconsistent with the provisions of the Electricity Act. Keeping this in view, Schedule III may be followed by such companies till the time any other format is prescribed by the relevant statute.

In accordance with the ICAI Guidance Note (Revised January, 2022 Edition), all companies that prepare, either voluntarily or mandatorily, Financial Statements in compliance with the Companies (Accounts) Rules, should consider Schedule III. Additionally, preparers of financial statements should also consider requirements of the Act as well as other Statutes, Notifications, Circulars issued by various Regulators.

Also, with respect to interim financial reporting, AS 25, Interim Financial Reporting states that, if a company is presenting condensed interim Financial Statements, its format should also going forward conform to that used in the company's most recent annual Financial Statements, i.e., the Schedule III of Companies Act, 2013.

### 1.15.1.2 Structure of Schedule III, Division I

| S/L No. | Narrative |
|---|---|
| I | General Instructions for Preparation of Balance Sheet and Statement of Profit and Loss. |
| II | Part I – Format of Balance Sheet |
| III | Part I – Notes - General Instructions for preparation of Balance Sheet |
| IV | Part II – Format of Statement of Profit and Loss |
| V | Part II – Notes – General Instructions for preparation of Statement of Profit and Loss |
| VI | Part III – General Instructions for preparation of Consolidated Financial Statements |

### 1.15.1.3 Rounding off

(i) Depending upon the **Total Income** of the company, the figures appearing in the Financial Statements **shall** be rounded off as given below:

| Total Income | Rounding off |
|---|---|
| (a) less than ***one hundred crore*** rupees | To the nearest hundreds, thousands, lakhs or millions or decimals thereof |
| (b) ***one hundred crore rupees or more*** | To the nearest lakhs, millions or crores or decimals thereof |

(ii) Once a unit of measurement is used, it shall be used uniformly in the Financial Statements.

### 1.15.1.4 Reporting of comparatives for immediately preceding reporting period

Except in the case of the first Financial Statements laid before the company (after its incorporation) the corresponding amounts (comparatives) for the immediately preceding reporting period for all items shown in the financial statements including notes shall also be given.

#### *1.15.1.5 Definitions of Terminologies used*

For the purpose of Schedule III, the terms used herein shall be as per the applicable Accounting Standards.

---

Note: The Schedule sets out minimum requirements for disclosure on the face of the Balance Sheet and the Statement of Profit and Loss (hereinafter referred to as "Financial Statements" for the purposes of this Schedule) and Notes, Line items, sub-line items and Sub-totals shall be presented as an addition or substitution on the face of the Financial Statements when such presentation is relevant to an understanding of the company's financial position or performance or to cater to industry / sector-specific disclosure requirements or when required for compliance with the amendments to the Companies Act or under the Accounting Standards.

---

### 1.15.2 Financial Statements under Schedule III: Division II (For Ind AS entities)

#### *1.15.2.1 Applicability*

Financial Statements for a company whose financial statements are drawn up in compliance with the Companies (Indian Accounting Standards) Rules, 2015 and as amended from time to time.

According to Rule 4(1) of these Rules,

(*i*) Any company and its holding, subsidiary, joint venture or associate company may comply with the Indian Accounting Standards (Ind AS) for financial statements for accounting periods beginning on or after 1st April, 2015, with the comparatives for the periods ending on 31st March, 2015, or thereafter;

(*ii*) The following companies shall comply with the Indian Accounting Standards (Ind AS) for the accounting periods beginning on or after 1st April, 2016, with the comparatives for the periods ending on 31st March, 2016, or thereafter, namely:

   (*a*) companies whose equity or debt securities are listed or are in the process of being listed on any stock exchange in India or outside India and having net worth of rupees **five hundred crore** or more;

   (*b*) companies other than those covered by sub-clause (*a*) of clause (*ii*) of sub-rule (1) and having net worth of rupees **five hundred crore** or more;

   (*c*) holding, subsidiary, joint venture or associate companies of companies covered by sub-clause (*a*) of clause (*ii*) of sub-rule (1) and sub-clause (*b*) of clause (*ii*) of sub-rule (1) as the case may be; and (*iii*) The following companies shall comply with the Indian Accounting Standards (Ind AS) for the accounting periods beginning on or after 1st April, 2017, with the comparatives for the period ending on 31st March, 2017, or thereafter, namely:

(*a*) companies whose equity or debt securities are listed or are in the process of being listed on any stock exchange in India or outside India and having net worth of less than rupees **five hundred crore;**

(*b*) companies other than those covered in clause (*ii*) of sub-rule (1) and sub-clause (*a*) of clause (*iii*) of sub-rule (1), that is, unlisted companies having net worth of rupees **two hundred and fifty crore or more but less than rupees five hundred crore;**

(*c*) holding, subsidiary, joint venture or associate companies of companies covered under sub-clause (*a*) of clause (*iii*) of sub- rule (1) and sub-clause (*b*) of clause (*iii*) of sub- rule (1), as the case may be.

### 1.15.2.2 Structure of Schedule III, Division II

| S/L No. | Narrative |
|---|---|
| I | General Instructions for Preparation of Financial Statements that is required to comply with Ind AS ('General Instructions for Preparation of Financial Statements') |
| II | Part I – Format of Balance Sheet and Statement of Changes in Equity |
| III | Part I – Notes - General Instructions for preparation of Balance Sheet |
| IV | Part II – Format of Statement of Profit and Loss |
| V | Part II – Notes – General Instructions for preparation of Statement of Profit and Loss |
| VI | Part III – General Instructions for preparation of Consolidated Financial Statements |

According to Guidance note of ICAI (Revised January, 2022 Edition), Financial Statements would include the following:

- Balance Sheet,
- Statement of Changes in Equity for the period,
- Statement of Profit and Loss for the period and Notes.
- Cash Flow Statement.

| ***Balance Sheet*** | • Division II provides a format of the balance sheet and sets out the minimum requirements of disclosure on the face of the balance sheet.<br>• Items presented in the balance sheet are to be classified as current and non-current.<br>• It does not permit to avail of the option of presenting assets and liabilities in the order of liquidity, as provided by Ind AS 1, *Presentation of Financial Statements*. |
|---|---|

| | |
|---|---|
| ***Statement of changes in Equity*** | • The statement of changes in equity would reconcile opening to closing amounts for each component of equity including reserves and surplus and items of other comprehensive income.<br>• Additionally, the conditions or restrictions for distribution attached to statutory reserves have to be separately disclosed in the notes as stipulated by the relevant statute. |
| ***Statement of Profit & Loss*** | • The division provides a format of the statement of profit and loss and sets out the minimum requirements of disclosure on the face of the statement of profit and loss.<br>• Items comprising 'revenue from operations' and 'other comprehensive income' have to be disclosed on the face of the statement of profit and loss. |
| ***Cash flow statement*** | • shall be prepared in accordance with the requirements of the relevant Ind AS. |

### 1.15.2.3 Rounding off

Depending upon the total income of the company, the figures appearing in the Financial Statements may be rounded off as below:

| Total Income | Rounding off |
|---|---|
| (i) less than one hundred crore rupees | To the nearest hundreds, thousands, lakhs or millions, or decimals thereof. |
| (ii) one hundred crore rupees or more | To the nearest, lakhs, millions or crores, or decimals thereof. |

Once a unit of measurement is used, it should be used uniformly in the Financial Statements.

### 1.15.2.4 Reporting of comparatives related to immediately preceding reporting period

Financial Statements shall contain the corresponding amounts (comparatives) for the immediately preceding reporting period for all items shown in the Financial Statements including Notes except in the case of first Financial Statements laid before the company after incorporation.

### 1.15.2.5 Materiality

Financial Statements shall disclose all 'material' items, i.e., the items if they could, individually or collectively, influence the economic decisions that users make based on the financial statements. Materiality depends on the size and nature of the item judged in particular circumstances.

### 1.15.2.6 Definition of Accounting terms

For the purpose of this Schedule, the terms used herein shall be as per the Indian Accounting Standards. For any terms which are not specifically defined in Ind AS, attention may also be drawn to the Framework for the Preparation and Presentation of Financial Statements in accordance with Indian Accounting Standards ('Ind AS Framework') issued by ICAI. However, if any term is not defined in the Ind AS Framework, the entity may consider the principles described in paragraph 10 to paragraph 12 of Ind AS 8 for developing and applying an accounting policy.

## 1.16 FORMAT OF BALANCE SHEET UNDER SCHEDULE III of Companies Act 2013

Format of Balance Sheet for two separate divisions prescribed under Schedule III of Companies Act 2013 are highlighted below.

With respect to Division I of Schedule III of the Companies Act 2013 (non Ind AS) the format is as under:

### 1.16.1 Balance Sheet: (Schedule III: Division I – Part I)

Name of Company...........

Balance Sheet as at..........

| Particulars | Note no. | Figures as at the end of current reporting period (in Rs.)<br>(DD/MM/YYYY) | Figures as at the end of previous reporting period (in Rs.)<br>(DD/MM/YYYY) |
|---|---|---|---|
| 1 | 2 | 3 | 4 |
| **I. EQUITY AND LIABILITIES** | | | |
| (1) **Shareholders' funds** | | | |
| (a) Share capital | | | |
| (b) Reserve and surplus | | | |
| (c) Money received against share warrants | | | |
| (2) **Share application money pending allotment** | | | |
| (3) **Non-current liabilities** | | | |
| (a) Long term borrowings | | | |
| (b) Deferred tax liabilities (net) | | | |

| Particulars | Note no. | Figures as at the end of current reporting period (in Rs.)<br>________<br>(DD/MM/YYYY) | Figures as at the end of previous reporting period (in Rs.)<br>________<br>(DD/MM/YYYY) |
|---|---|---|---|
| 1 | 2 | 3 | 4 |
| (c) Other long-term liabilities | | | |
| (d) Long term provisions and | | | |
| (4) **Current liabilities** | | | |
| (a) Short term borrowings | | | |
| (b) Trade payables | | | |
| (A) total outstanding dues of micro enterprises and small enterprises; and | | | |
| (B) total outstanding dues of creditors other than micro enterprises and small enterprises. | | | |
| (c) Other current liabilities | | | |
| (d) Short term provisions | | | |
| TOTAL | | | |
| **II. ASSETS** | | | |
| **Non-current assets** | | | |
| (1) (a) Property, Plant and Equipment and Intangible Assets | | | |
| (i) Property, Plant and Equipment | | | |
| (ii) Intangible assets | | | |
| (iii) capital work-in-progress | | | |
| (iv) Intangibles under development | | | |

| Particulars | Note no. | Figures as at the end of current reporting period (in Rs.)<br>______<br>(DD/MM/YYYY) | Figures as at the end of previous reporting period (in Rs.)<br>______<br>(DD/MM/YYYY) |
|---|---|---|---|
| 1 | 2 | 3 | 4 |
| (b) Non-current investments<br>(c) Deferred tax assets (net)<br>(d) Long term loans and advances<br>(e) other non-current assets<br>(2) **Current assets**<br>(a) Current investments<br>(b) Inventories<br>(c) Trade receivables<br>(d) Cash and cash equivalents<br>(e) Short term loans and advances<br>(f) Other current assets<br>TOTAL | | | |

## 1.16.2 Balance Sheet: (Schedule III: Division II – Part II)

*Name of the Company……………………….*

*Balance Sheet as at ………………………*

(Rupees in…………)

| | Particulars | Note no. | Figures as at the end of current reporting period | Figures as at the end of the previous reporting period |
|---|---|---|---|---|
| | 1 | 2 | 3 | 4 |
| **(1)** | **ASSETS**<br>**Non-current assets**<br>(a) Property, Plant and Equipment<br>(b) Capital work-in-progress<br>(c) Investment Property | | | |

| | Particulars | Note no. | Figures as at the end of current reporting period | Figures as at the end of the previous reporting period |
|---|---|---|---|---|
| | 1 | 2 | 3 | 4 |
| | (d) Goodwill | | | |
| | (e) Other Intangible assets | | | |
| | (f) Intangible assets under development | | | |
| | (g) Biological Assets other than bearer plants | | | |
| | (h) Financial Assets | | | |
| | (i) Investments | | | |
| | (ii) Trade receivables | | | |
| | (iii) Loans | | | |
| | (iv) Others (to be specified) | | | |
| | (i) Deferred tax assets (net) | | | |
| | (j) Other non-current assets | | | |
| **(2)** | **Current assets** | | | |
| | (a) Inventories | | | |
| | (b) Financial Assets | | | |
| | (i) Investments | | | |
| | (ii) Trade receivables | | | |
| | (iii) Cash and cash equivalents | | | |
| | (iv) Bank balances other than (iii) above | | | |
| | (v) Loans | | | |
| | (vi) Others (to be specified) | | | |
| | (c) Current Tax Assets (Net) | | | |
| | (d) Other current assets | | | |
| | **Total assets** | | | |
| | **Equity and Liabilities** | | | |
| | **Equity** | | | |
| | (a) Equity Share capital | | | |
| | (b) Other Equity | | | |
| | **LIABILITIES** | | | |
| **(1)** | **Non-current liabilities** | | | |
| | (a) Financial Liabilities | | | |
| | (i) Borrowings | | | |
| | (ia) Lease liabilities | | | |
| | (ii) Trade payables | | | |

| | Particulars | Note no. | Figures as at the end of current reporting period | Figures as at the end of the previous reporting period |
|---|---|---|---|---|
| | 1 | 2 | 3 | 4 |
| (2) | (iii) Other financial liabilities (other than those specified in (b) below, to be specified)<br>(b) Provisions<br>(c) Deferred tax liabilities (Net)<br>(d) Other non-current liabilities<br>**Current liabilities**<br>(a) Financial Liabilities<br>(i) Borrowings<br>(ia) Lease liabilities"<br>(ii) Trade payables<br>(iii) Other financial liabilities (other than those specified in (c) below)<br>(b) Other current liabilities<br>(c) Provisions<br>(d) Current Tax Liabilities (Net)<br>**Total equity and liabilities** | | | |

Along with the Balance Sheet there needs to be accompanying notes to the Financial Statements which have been enunciated in detail in Schedule III.

## 1.17 STATEMENT OF PROFIT & LOSS

The statement of Profit & Loss depicts the net financial results of the organization represented by income and expenses and would include all items of income and expense in a period in profit or loss unless an IFRS requires or permits otherwise.

## 1.18 STATEMENT OF OTHER COMPREHENSIVE INCOME

The Statement of other comprehensive income would include amounts of other comprehensive income in the period, classified by nature (including share of the other comprehensive income of associates and joint ventures accounted for using the equity method) and grouped into those that, by other IFRSs-

(a) will not be reclassified subsequently to profit or loss; and

(b) will be reclassified subsequently to profit or loss when specific conditions are met.

## 1.19 COMPONENTS UNDER THE STATEMENT OF PROFIT & LOSS AND OTHER COMPREHENSIVE INCOME

The minimum disclosures are as under:

(a) The Statement of Profit & Loss shall present in Statement of Profit & Loss and other comprehensive income sections:

- (a) profit or loss;
- (b) total other comprehensive income;
- (c) comprehensive income for the period, being the total of profit or loss and other comprehensive income.

(b) An entity shall present the following items, in addition to the profit or loss and other comprehensive income sections, as allocation of profit or loss and other comprehensive income for the period:

- (a) profit or loss for the period attributable to:
  - (i) non-controlling interests, and
  - (ii) owners of the parent.
- (b) comprehensive income for the period attributable to:
  - (i) non-controlling interests, and
  - (ii) owners of the parent.

(c) In addition to requirements by other IFRSs the profit & loss section of the Statement of Profit & Loss shall include line items that present the following amounts for the period:

- (a) revenue presenting separately interest revenue calculated using the effective interest method;
- (aa) gains and losses arising from the derecognition of financial assets measured at amortized cost;
- (ab) insurance service expenses from contracts issued;
- (ac) income or expenses from reinsurance contracts held;
- (b) finance costs;
- (ba) impairment losses (including reversals of impairment losses or impairment gains) of Financial Assets determined by Ind AS 109;
- (bb) insurance finance income or expenses from contracts issued;
- (bc) finance income or expenses from reinsurance contracts held;
- (c) share of the profit or loss of associates and joint ventures accounted for using the equity method;
- (ca) if a financial asset is reclassified out of the amortized cost measurement category so that it is measured at fair value through profit or loss, any gain or loss arising from a difference between the previous amortized cost of the financial asset and its fair value at the reclassification date (as defined in Ind AS 109);

(cb) if a financial asset is reclassified out of the fair value through other comprehensive income measurement category so that it is measured at fair value through profit or loss, any cumulative gain or loss previously recognized in other comprehensive income that is reclassified to profit or loss;

(d) tax expense;

(ea) a single amount comprising the total of discontinued operation;(Ind AS 105)

(d) The other comprehensive income section shall present line items for amounts of other comprehensive income in the period, classified by nature (including share of the other comprehensive income of associates and joint ventures accounted for using the equity method) and grouped into those that, by other IFRSs

(i) will not be reclassified subsequently to profit or loss; and

(ii) will be reclassified subsequently to profit or loss when specific conditions are met.

(e) the share of the other comprehensive income of associates and joint ventures accounted for using the equity method, separated into the share of items that, following other IFRSs:

(i) will not be reclassified subsequently to profit or loss; and

(ii) will be reclassified subsequently to profit or loss when specific conditions are met.

**(f) Profit or loss for the period**

An entity shall recognize all items of income and expense in a period in profit or loss unless an IFRS requires or permits otherwise.

Some IFRSs specify circumstances when an entity recognizes particular items outside profit or loss in the current period.

Ind AS 8 specifies two such circumstances, namely,

(a) the correction of errors and

(b) the effect of changes in accounting policies.

Other IFRSs require or permit components of other comprehensive income that meet the *Framework*'s definition of income or expense to be excluded from profit or loss.

**(g) Other comprehensive income for the period**

An entity shall disclose the amount of income tax relating to each item of other comprehensive income, including reclassification adjustments, either in the statement of profit and loss or in the notes.

An entity may present items of other comprehensive income either:

(a) net of related tax effects, or

(b) before related tax effects with one amount shown for the aggregate amount of income tax relating to those items.

If an entity elects alternative (b), it shall allocate the tax between the items that might be reclassified subsequently to the profit or loss section and those that will not be reclassified subsequently to the profit or loss section.

An entity shall disclose reclassification adjustments relating to components of other comprehensive income.

## 1.20 SPECIMEN FORMAT OF STATEMENT OF PROFIT AND LOSS

Specimen format of Statement of Profit and Loss in line with Division I and Division II of Schedule III of the Companies Act 2013 are shown below.

### 1.20.1 Statement of Profit and Loss (Schedule III, Division I, Part I) of the Companies Act 2013

Name of Company............

Profit & Loss statement for the year ended ...

| S/No | Particulars | Note no. | Figures as at the end of current reporting period | Figures as at the end of previous reporting period |
|---|---|---|---|---|
| 1 | 2 | 3 | | |
| I | REVENUE FROM OPERATION | | | |
| II | OTHER INCOME | | | |
| **III** | **(TOTAL INCOME (I + II)** | | | |
| IV | EXPENSES: | | | |
| | (a) Cost of material consumed | | | |
| | (b) Purchase of stock-in-trade | | | |
| | (c) Changes in inventories of finished goods, work-in-progress and stock-in-trade | | | |
| | (d) Employees benefit expenses | | | |
| | (e) Finance cost | | | |
| | (f) Depreciation and amortisation expenses | | | |

| S/No | Particulars | Note no. | Figures as at the end of current reporting period | Figures as at the end of previous reporting period |
|---|---|---|---|---|
| 1 | 2 | 3 | | |
| | (h) Other expenses | | | |
| | **TOTAL EXPENSES** | | | |
| V | PROFIT BEFORE EXCEPTIONAL AND EXTRA- | | | |
| | ORDINARY ITEMS AND TAX (III - IV) | | | |
| VI | EXCEPTIONAL ITEMS | | | |
| VII | PROFIT BEFORE EXTRAORDINARY ITEMS AND | | | |
| | TAX (V-VI) | | | |
| VIII | EXTRAORDINARY ITEMS | | | |
| IX | PROFIT BEFORE TAX (VII - VIII) | | | |
| X | TAX EXPENSES: | | | |
| | (a) Current tax | | | |
| | (b) Deferred tax | | | |
| XI | PROFIT/(LOSS) FOR THE PERIOD FROM | | | |
| | CONTINUING OPERATIONS (IX - X) | | | |
| XII | Profit / (loss) from discontinuing operations | | | |
| XIII | Tax expenses from discontinuing operations | | | |
| XIV | Profit/(loss) from discontinuing operations (after tax) (XII-XIII) | | | |
| XV | PROFIT/(LOSS) FOR THE PERIOD | | | |

| S/No | Particulars | Note no. | Figures as at the end of current reporting period | Figures as at the end of previous reporting period |
|---|---|---|---|---|
| 1 | 2 | 3 | | |
| | (XI + XIV) | | | |
| XVI | Earning per equity share: | | | |
| | (1) Basic | | | |
| | (2) Diluted | | | |

### 1.20.2 Statement of Profit and Loss (Schedule III, Division II, Part II) of the Companies Act 2013

*Name of the Company……………………….*

*Statement of Profit and Loss for the period ended ………………………*

(Rupees in…………)

| S/No | Particulars | Note no. | Figures for the current reporting period | Figures for the previous reporting period |
|---|---|---|---|---|
| 1 | 2 | 3 | | |
| I | Revenue from Operations | | | |
| II | Other Income | | | |
| **III** | **Total Income (I + II)** | | | |
| IV | EXPENSES: | | | |
| | Cost of material consumed | | | |
| | Purchases of stock-in-trade | | | |
| | Changes in inventories of finished goods, stock-in-trade and work-in-progress | | | |
| | Employees benefit expenses | | | |
| | Finance cost | | | |

| S/No | Particulars | Note no. | Figures for the current reporting period | Figures for the previous reporting period |
|---|---|---|---|---|
| 1 | 2 | 3 | | |
| | Depreciation and amortisation expenses | | | |
| | Other expenses | | | |
| | **Total expenses (IV)** | | | |
| V | Profit/(loss) before exceptional items and tax (I- IV) | | | |
| VI | Exceptional items | | | |
| VII | Profit/(loss) before tax (V-VI) | | | |
| VIII | Tax expenses: | | | |
| | (a) Current tax | | | |
| | (b) Deferred tax | | | |
| IX | Profit (Loss) for the period from continuing operations (VII-VIII) | | | |
| X | Profit / (loss) from discontinued operations | | | |
| XI | Tax expenses from discontinued operations | | | |
| XII | Profit / (loss) from discontinued operations (X-XI) | | | |
| XIII | Profit/(loss) for the period (IX+XII) | | | |
| XIV | Other Comprehensive Income<br>A (i) Items that will not be reclassified to profit or loss<br>(ii) Income tax relating to items that will not be reclassified to profit or loss<br>B (i) Items that will be | | | |

| S/No | Particulars | Note no. | Figures for the current reporting period | Figures for the previous reporting period |
|---|---|---|---|---|
| 1 | 2 | 3 | | |
| | reclassified to profit or loss<br>(ii) Income tax relating to items that will be reclassified to profit or loss | | | |
| XV | Total Comprehensive Income for the period (XIII+XIV)(Comprising Profit (Loss) and Other Comprehensive Income for the period) | | | |
| XVI | Earning per equity share (for continuing operations):<br>(1) Basic<br>(2) Diluted | | | |
| XVII | Earning per equity share (for discontinued operations):<br>(1) Basic<br>(2) Diluted | | | |
| XVIII | Earnings per equity share(for discontinued & continuing operations)<br>(1) Basic<br>(2) Diluted | | | |

## 1.21 STATEMENT OF CHANGES IN EQUITY

(i) An entity shall present a statement of changes in equity as a part of Balance Sheet as required by the Ind AS. The statement of changes in equity includes the following information:

(a) total comprehensive income for the period, showing separately the total amounts attributable to owners of the parent and non-controlling interests.

(b) for each component of equity, the effects of retrospective application or retrospective restatement recognized per Ind AS 8;

(c) for each component of equity, a reconciliation between the carrying amount at the beginning and the end of the period, separately disclosing each change resulting from:

(i) profit or loss;

(ii) other comprehensive income.

(iii) transactions with owners in their capacity as owners, showing separately contributions by and distributions to owners and changes in ownership interests in subsidiaries that do not result in a loss of control and

(iv) any item recognized directly in equity such as amount recognized directly in equity as capital reserve under provisions of Ind AS 103.

Information to be presented in the statement of changes in equity which is a part of the Statement of Financial Position or in the notes

(ii) For each component of equity an entity shall present, either in the statement of changes in equity or in the notes, an analysis of other comprehensive income by item.

(iii) An entity shall present, either in the statement of changes in equity or in the notes, the number of dividends recognized as distributions to owners during the period and the related amount of dividends per share.

***Specimen format of Statement of Changes in Equity is given in the table below.***

***Name of the Company……………………..***

A. Equity Share Capital

(1) Current reporting period

| **Balance at the beginning of the current reporting period** | **Changes in Equity Share Capital due to prior period errors** | **Restated balance at the beginning of the current reporting period** | **Changes in equity share capital during the current year** | **Balance at the end of the current reporting period** |
|---|---|---|---|---|
| | | | | |

(2) Previous reporting period

| **Balance at the beginning of the previous reporting period** | **Changes in Equity Share Capital due to prior period errors** | **Restated balance at the beginning of the previous reporting period** | **Changes in equity share capital during the previous year** | **Balance at the end of the previous reporting period** |
|---|---|---|---|---|
| | | | | |

B. Other Equity

(1) Current reporting period

| | **Share application money pending allotment** | **Equity component of compound financial instruments** | **Reserves & surplus - Capital Reserve** | **Reserves & surplus - Securities premium** | **Reserves & Surplus – Other reserves (specify nature)** | **Reserves & surplus - Retained earnings** |
|---|---|---|---|---|---|---|
| Balance at the beginning of the current reporting period | | | | | | |
| Changes in accounting policy or prior period errors | | | | | | |
| Restated balance at the beginning of the current reporting period | | | | | | |
| Total Comp-rehensive Income for the current year | | | | | | |
| Dividends | | | | | | |
| Transfer to retained earnings | | | | | | |

| | **Share application money pending allotment** | **Equity component of compound financial instruments** | **Reserves & surplus - Capital Reserve** | **Reserves & surplus - Securities premium** | **Reserves & Surplus – Other reserves (specify nature)** | **Reserves & surplus - Retained earnings** |
|---|---|---|---|---|---|---|
| Any other change (to be specified) | | | | | | |
| Balance at the end of the current reporting period | | | | | | |

| **Debt instruments through Other Comprehensive Income** | **Equity Instruments through Other Comprehensive Income** | **Effective portion of Cash Flow Hedges** | **Revaluation Surplus** | **Exchange differences on translating the financial statements of a foreign operation** | **Other items of Other Comprehensive Income (specify nature)** | **Money received against share warrants** | **Total** |
|---|---|---|---|---|---|---|---|
| | | | | | | | |
| | | | | | | | |
| | | | | | | | |
| | | | | | | | |
| | | | | | | | |

(2) Previous reporting period

| | **Share application money pending allotment** | **Equity component of compound financial instruments** | **Reserves & surplus - Capital Reserve** | **Reserves & surplus - Securities premium** | **Reserves & Surplus – Other reserves (specify nature)** | **Reserves & surplus - Retained earnings** |
|---|---|---|---|---|---|---|
| Balance at the beginning of the current reporting period | | | | | | |
| Changes in accounting policy or prior period errors | | | | | | |
| Restated balance at the beginning of the current reporting period | | | | | | |
| Total Comprehensive Income for the current year | | | | | | |
| Dividends | | | | | | |
| Transfer to retained earnings | | | | | | |
| Any other change (to be specified) | | | | | | |
| Balance at the end of the current reporting period | | | | | | |

| Debt instruments through Other Comprehensive Income | Equity Instruments through Other Comprehensive Income | Effective portion of Cash Flow Hedges | Revaluation Surplus | Exchange differences on translating the financial statements of a foreign operation | Other items of Other Comprehensive Income (specify nature) | Money received against share warrants | Total |
|---|---|---|---|---|---|---|---|
| | | | | | | | |
| | | | | | | | |
| | | | | | | | |
| | | | | | | | |
| | | | | | | | |
| | | | | | | | |
| | | | | | | | |

*Note*: Re-measurement of defined benefit plans and fair value changes relating to own credit risk of financial liabilities designated at fair value through profit or loss shall be recognised as a part of retained earnings with separate disclosure of such items along with the relevant amounts in the Notes or shall be shown as a separate column under Reserves and Surplus".

## 1.22 NOTES TO ACCOUNTS

- Present information about the basis of preparation of financial statements and specific accounting policies used
- disclose any information required by IFRSs not presented elsewhere in the financial statements and
- provide additional information that is relevant for the understanding of the financial statements not presented elsewhere in the financial statements

For details, please refer Chapter 11.

## 1.23 ACCOUNTING STANDARDS

### 1.23.1 Applicability of Accounting Standards

Financial Statements shall comply with the accounting standards notified by the Central Government as recommended by the Institute of Chartered Accountants of

India in consultation with and after examination of the recommendations made by the National Financial Reporting Authority.

## 1.23.2 Precedence of Companies Act and Accounting Standards over Schedule III

According to Paragraph I, of general instructions of preparation of Balance Sheet and Statement of Profit and Loss of a Company, where compliance with the requirements of the Act including Accounting Standards as applicable to the companies require any change in treatment or disclosure including addition, amendment, substitution, or deletion in the head or sub-head or any changes, inter se, in the financial statements or statements forming part thereof, the same shall be made and the requirements of this Schedule shall stand modified accordingly.

In accordance with Paragraph 2, the disclosure requirements specified in this Schedule are in addition to and not in substitution of the disclosure requirements specified in the Accounting Standards prescribed under the Companies Act 2013. Additional disclosures specified in the Accounting Standards shall be made in the notes to accounts or by way of additional statement unless required to be disclosed on the face of the Financial Statements. Similarly, all other disclosures as required by the Companies Act shall be made in the notes to accounts in addition to the requirements set out in this schedule.

According to Clause (1) of Annexure A, Indian Accounting Standards, which are notified, are intended to be in conformity with the provisions of applicable laws. However, if due to subsequent amendments in the law, a particular Indian Accounting Standard is found to be not in conformity with such law, the provisions of the said law shall prevail and the financial statements shall be prepared in conformity with such law.

**Illustration 1.1**

One of the line items to be presented on the face of the Balance Sheet under current assets is" Cash and cash equivalents". The break-up of these items required to be presented by Schedule III comprises of items such as balances with banks held as margin money or security against borrowings, guarantees etc and bank deposits with more than 12 months maturity.

According to ***AS 3 Cash flow statements,*** cash is defined to include cash on hand and demand deposits with banks. Cash equivalents are defined as short term, highly liquid investments that are readily convertible into known amounts of cash and which are subject to an insignificant risk of changes in value. The standard further explains that an investment normally qualifies as a cash equivalent only when it has a short maturity of three months or less from the date of acquisition. Hence, normally, deposits with original maturity of three months or less only should be classified as cash equivalents.

*Indian Accounting Standards Ind AS 7: Cash flow statements attributes the same definition.*

Further, bank balances held as margin money or security against borrowings are neither in the nature of demand deposits, nor readily available for use by the company, and accordingly, do not meet the aforesaid definition of cash equivalents.

Thus, this is an apparent conflict between the requirements of Schedule III and the Accounting Standards (both AS 3 and Ind AS 7) with respect to which items should form part of Cash and Cash equivalents.

As laid down in the general instructions, para 1 of Schedule III, requirements of the Accounting Standards would prevail over Schedule III and the company should make necessary modification in the Financial Statements which may include addition, amendment, substitution or deletion in the head / sub-head or any other changes inter se.

Accordingly, the conflict should be resolved by changing the caption "cash and cash equivalents" to "cash and bank balances", which may have two sub-headings e.g. (a) Cash and cash equivalents and (b) Other bank balances. The former should include only the items that constitute cash and cash equivalents defined in accordance with AS 3 and Ind AS 7(and not Schedule III), while the remaining line items may be included under the latter.

*(Source : Guidance Note of the Institute of Chartered Accountants of India – Adapted)*

Also para 2 of the General Instructions to the Schedule III states that the disclosure requirements of the Schedule are in addition to and not in substitution of the disclosure requirements specified in the notified Accounting Standards. They further clarify that the additional disclosures specified in the Accounting Standards shall be made in the Notes to Accounts or by way of an additional statement unless required to be disclosed on the face of the Financial Statements.

All other disclosures required by the Act are also required to be made in the Notes to Accounts in addition to the requirements set out in Schedule III.

**Illustration 1.2**

*AS 24 Discontinuing Operations* requires that specific disclosure be given on the face of the Statement of Profit and Loss. The disclosure pertains to the pre-tax gain or loss recognised on disposal of assets or settlement of liabilities attributable to discontinuing operation.

According to Ind AS 105: Non-current assets held for sale and discontinued operations, (para 33), an entity shall disclose:

(a) a single amount in the statement of profit and loss comprising the total of:

  (i) the post-tax profit or loss of discontinued operations and

  (ii) the post-tax gain or loss recognised on the measurement to fair value less costs to sell or on the disposal of the assets or disposal group(s) constituting the discontinued operation.

(b) an analysis of the single amount in (a) into:

  (i) the revenue, expenses and pre-tax profit or loss of discontinued operations;

  (ii) the related income tax expense as required by paragraph 81(h) of Ind AS 12; and

  (iii) the gain or loss recognised on the measurement to fair value less costs to sell or on the disposal of the assets or disposal group(s) constituting the discontinued operation.

  (iv) the related income tax expense as required by paragraph 81(h) of Ind AS 12.

  The analysis may be presented in the notes or in the statement of profit and loss. If it is presented in the statement of profit and loss it shall be presented in a section identified as relating to discontinued operations, i.e. separately from continuing operations.

(c) The net cash flows attributable to the operating, investing and financing activities of discontinued operations. These disclosures may be presented either in the notes or in the financial statements. These disclosures are not required for disposal groups that are newly acquired subsidiaries that meet the criteria to be classified as held for sale on acquisition.

(d) The amount of income from continuing operations and from discontinued operations attributable to owners of the parent. These disclosures may be presented either in the notes or in the statement of profit and loss.

An entity shall represent the disclosures in paragraph 33 for prior periods presented in the financial statements so that the disclosures relate to all operations that have been discontinued by the end of the reporting period for the latest period presented. (Para 34)

Such disclosures are specifically covered on the face of either the Statement of Profit and Loss or Balance Sheet as prescribed under Schedule III.

Also, though not mandated by Schedule III, disclosures required by other Act or legal requirements will have to be made in the Financial Statements.

### Illustration 1.3

The Micro, small and Medium Enterprises Development (MSMED) Act 2006 stipulates that specified disclosures are required to be made in the annual Financial Statements of the buyer wherever such Financial Statements are required to be audited under any law. Accordingly, such disclosures are necessary for the buyer company's Financial Statements.

*(Source: Guidance Note of The Institute of Chartered Accountants of India)*

### Illustration 1.4

(a) Disclosure required under Clause 32 to the Listing Agreement

(b) ICAI pronouncement on disclosure related to derivatives and unhedged foreign currency exposures

(c) Disclosures related to employee share-based payments as per Guidance Note of ICAI

These disclosures to continue in addition to the disclosures specified under Schedule III.

### Illustration 1.5

**A company is preparing its financial statements in accordance with Schedule III for the first time. For certain information required to be disclosed in the notes, the current year amounts are nil. For example, let us assume that there is no default in repayment of loan and interest existing as at the end of current year. Is the company required to present previous year figures for such notes? Alternatively, can it omit the previous year information since no disclosure is required in the current year?**

**Solution**

Schedule III requires that "Except in the case of the first financial statements laid before the company (after its incorporation), the corresponding amounts (comparatives) for the immediately preceding reporting period for all items shown in the financial statements including notes shall also be given."

The objective of presenting comparative information is to help users of financial statements in understanding the trends and key changes vis-à-vis the previous period financial statements. The inter-period comparability of information assists users in taking their economic decisions. Hence, a company needs to present comparative information for disclosures required under Schedule III even if their current period amount is nil.

**Illustration 1.6**

**Schedule III of Companies Act 2013 requires a balance to be maintained between excessive detail and too much aggregation. Can a company use this principle to avoid giving disclosures specifically required by Schedule III / Guidance Note on the Revised Schedule VI, say, security details for each loan?**

**Solution**

A company should not use this principle to avoid making material disclosures, which are specifically required under Schedule III, accounting standards, guidance notes and so on. Since disclosure regarding security for each loan is required by Schedule III (Revised Schedule VI) and Guidance Note on the Revised Schedule VI, a company cannot avoid making this disclosure.

## 1.24 INCOME COMPUTATION AND DISCLOSURE STANDARDS

Income Computation and Disclosure Standard is applicable for computation of income chargeable under the head "Profits and gains of business or profession" or "Income from other sources" and not for the purpose of maintenance of books of accounts.

In the case of conflict between the provisions of the Income-tax Act, 1961 ('the Act') and this Income Computation and Disclosure Standard, the provisions of the Act shall prevail to that extent.

## 1.25 COMPARATIVE SUMMARY OF ACCOUNTING STANDARD (AS) INDIAN ACCOUNTING STANDARDS (IND AS) AND INCOME COMPUTATION AND DISCLOSURE STANDARDS (ICDS)

| AS | Ind AS | ICDS |
|---|---|---|
| AS 1: Disclosure of Financial Statements | Ind AS 1: Presentation of Financial Statements | ICDS 1: Accounting policies |
| AS 2: Inventories | Ind AS 2: Inventories | ICDS II: Valuation of inventories |
| AS 3: Statement of Cash Flows | Ind AS 7: Statement of Cash flows | - |
| AS 4: Post Balance Sheet event | Ind AS 10: Events after the reporting date | - |
| AS 5: Accounting policies, change in accounting | Ind AS 8: Accounting policies, | - |

| AS | Ind AS | ICDS |
|---|---|---|
| estimates and errors | change in accounting estimates and errors | |
| AS 7: Construction contracts | Ind AS 115: Revenue from contract with Customers | ICDS III: Construction contracts |
| AS 9: Revenue Recognition | ------------do----------- | ICDS IV: Revenue Recognition |
| AS 10: Property, Plant and Equipment | Ind AS 16: Property, Plant and Equipment | ICDS V: Tangible Fixed Assets |
| AS 11: Effects of changes in Foreign Exchange rates | Ind AS 21: Effects of changes in Foreign Exchange rates | ICDS VI: Effects of changes in foreign exchange rates |
| AS 12: Accounting for Government grants | Ind AS 20: Accounting for Government grants | ICDS VII: Government grants |
| AS 13: Accounting for Investments | Ind AS 32: Financial Instruments – presentation | ICDS VIII: Securities |
| | Ind AS 109: Financial Instruments | |
| | Ind AS 107: Financial Instruments – disclosures | |
| AS 14: Accounting for amalgamations | Ind as 103: Business Combinations | - |
| AS 15: Employee Benefits | Ind AS 19: Employee Benefits | - |
| AS 16: Borrowing costs | Ind AS 23: Borrowing costs | ICDS IX: Borrowing costs |
| AS 17: Segment Reporting | Ind AS 108: Operating Segments | - |
| AS 18: Related Party Disclosures | Ind AS 24: Related Party Disclosures | - |

| AS | Ind AS | ICDS |
|---|---|---|
| AS 19: Leases | Ind AS 116: Leases | - |
| AS 20: Earnings per share | Ind AS 33: Earnings per share | - |
| AS 21: Consolidated Financial Statements | Ind AS 110: Consolidation of Financial Statements | - |
| | Ind AS 27: Separate Financial Statements | - |
| AS 22: Accounting for taxes on income | Ind AS 12: Income Taxes | - |
| AS 23: Accounting for investment in Associates in Consolidated Financial Statements | Ind AS 28: Investment in Associates and Joint Ventures | - |
| AS 24: Discontinuing Operations | Ind AS 105: Non-current assets held for sale and discontinuing operations | - |
| AS 25: Interim Financial Reporting | Ind AS 34: Interim Financial Reporting | - |
| AS 26: Intangible Assets | Ind AS 38: Intangible Assets | - |
| AS 27: Financial Reporting of interests in Joint Ventures | Ind AS 111: Joint Arrangements | - |
| - | Ind AS 112: Disclosure of interests in other Entities | - |
| AS 28: Impairment of Assets | Ind AS 36: Impairment of Assets | - |
| AS 29: Provisions, Contingent Liabilities and | Ind AS 37: Provisions, Contingent Liabilities and | ICDS X: Provisions, Contingent Liabilities |

| AS | Ind AS | ICDS |
|---|---|---|
| Contingent Assets, | Contingent Assets, | and Contingent Assets |
| - | Ind AS 40: Investment Properties | - |
| - | Ind AS 41: Agriculture | - |
| - | Ind AS 101: First time adoption of international financial reporting standards | - |
| - | Ind AS 102: Share based payments | - |
| - | Ind AS 104: Insurance contracts | - |
| - | Ind AS 106: Exploration and evaluation of mineral resources | - |
| - | Ind AS 113: Fair Value Measurement | - |
| - | Ind AS 114: Regulatory Deferral Accounts | - |

## 1.26 INTERIM FINANCIAL STATEMENTS

An interim financial report needs to include at a minimum the following components in line with AS 25 and Ind AS 34:

(a) condensed balance sheet;
(b) condensed statement of profit and loss;
(c) condensed cash flow statement; and
(d) selected explanatory notes.

### 1.26.1 Form and content of Interim Financial Statements

| |
|---|
| • If an enterprise prepares and presents a complete set of financial statements in its interim financial report, the form and content of those statements should conform to the requirements as applicable to annual complete set of financial statements. |
| • If an enterprise prepares and presents a set of condensed financial statements in its interim financial report, those condensed statements should include, at a minimum, each of the headings and sub-headings that were included in its most recent annual financial statements and the selected explanatory notes as required by this Standard. Additional line items or notes should be included if their omission would make the condensed interim financial statements misleading. |
| • If an enterprise presents basic and diluted earnings per share in annual financial statements in accordance with AS 20, Earnings Per Share, basic and diluted earnings per share should be presented in accordance with AS 20 on the face of the statement of profit and loss, complete or condensed, for an interim report |

### 1.26.2 Minimum financial information to be provided in interim financial statements

An enterprise should include the following information, as a minimum, in the notes to its interim financial statements, if material and if not disclosed elsewhere in the interim financial report:

(a) a statement that the same accounting policies are followed in the interim financial statements as those followed in the most recent annual financial statements or, if those policies have been changed, a description of the nature and effect of the change;

(b) explanatory comments about the seasonality of interim operations;

(c) the nature and amount of items affecting assets, liabilities, equity, net income, or cash flows that are unusual because of their nature, size, or incidence

(d) the nature and amount of changes in estimates of amounts reported in prior interim periods of the current financial year or changes in estimates of amounts reported in prior financial years, if those changes have a material effect in the current interim period;

(e) issuances, buy-backs, repayments and restructuring of debt, equity and potential equity shares;

(f) dividends, aggregate or per share (in absolute or percentage terms), separately for equity shares and other shares;

(g) segment revenue, segment capital employed (segment assets minus segment liabilities) and segment result for business segments or geographical segments, whichever is the enterprise's primary basis of segment reporting (disclosure of segment information is required in an enterprise's interim financial report only if the enterprise is required, in terms of AS 17, Segment Reporting, to disclose segment information in its annual financial statements);

(h) material events subsequent to the end of the interim period that have not been reflected in the financial statements for the interim period;

(i) the effect of changes in the composition of the enterprise during the interim period, such as amalgamations, acquisition or disposal of subsidiaries and long-term investments, restructurings, and discontinuing operations; and

(j) material changes in contingent liabilities since the last annual balance sheet date.

The above information should normally be reported on a financial year-to-date basis. However, the enterprise should also disclose any events or transactions that are material to an understanding of the current interim period.

### 1.26.3 Periods for which Interim Financial Statements are required to be presented

Interim reports should include interim financial statements (condensed or complete) for periods as follows:

(a) balance sheet as of the end of the current interim period and a comparative balance sheet as of the end of the immediately preceding financial year;

(b) statements of profit and loss for the current interim period and cumulatively for the current financial year to date, with comparative statements of profit and loss for the comparable interim periods (current and year-to-date) of the immediately preceding financial year;

(c) cash flow statement cumulatively for the current financial year to date, with a comparative statement for the comparable year to- date period of the immediately preceding financial year.

In deciding how to recognise, measure, classify, or disclose an item for interim financial reporting purposes, materiality should be assessed in relation to the interim period financial data. In making assessments of materiality, it should be recognised that interim measurements may rely on estimates to a greater extent than measurements of annual financial data.

### 1.26.4 Recognition and measurement of interim financial statements

| | |
|---|---|
| ***Same accounting policies as annual*** | (except for accounting policy changes made after the date of the most recent annual financial statements that are to be reflected in the next annual financial statements) |

| | |
|---|---|
| ***Revenue received seasonally or occasionally*** | within a financial year should not be anticipated or deferred as of an interim date if anticipation or deferral would not be appropriate at the end of the enterprise's financial year. (e.g. dividend, royalties and Government grants) |
| ***Costs incurred unevenly during the year*** | should be anticipated or deferred for interim reporting purposes if, and only if, it is also appropriate to anticipate or defer that type of cost at the end of the financial year. |
| ***Use of estimates*** | the resulting information is reliable and that all material financial information that is relevant to an understanding of the financial position or performance of the enterprise is appropriately disclosed. |
| ***Restatement of previously reported interim periods*** | A change in accounting policy, other than one for which the transition is specified by an Accounting Standard, should be reflected by restating the financial statements of prior interim periods of the current financial year. |

**Illustration 1.7: Specimen formats**

**(A) Condensed Balance Sheet**

| | **Figures at the end of the current interim period** | **Figures at the end of the previous accounting year** |
|---|---|---|
| **I. Sources of Funds** | | |
| 1. Capital | | |
| 2. Reserve and surplus | | |
| 3. Minority interests (in case of consolidated financial statements) | | |
| 4. Loan funds: | | |
| (a) Secured loans | | |
| (b) Unsecured loans | | |
| **Total** | | |
| **II. Application of Funds** | | |
| 1. Non-current assets | | |
| (a) Tangible assets | | |
| (b) Intangible assets | | |
| 2. Investments | | |

| | Figures at the end of the current interim period | Figures at the end of the previous accounting year |
|---|---|---|
| 3. Current assets, loans and advances<br>(a) Inventories<br>(b) Sundry debtors<br>(c) Cash and bank balances<br>(d) Loans and advances<br>(e) Others<br>Less: Current liabilities and provisions<br>(a) Liabilities<br>(b) Provisions<br>Net Current assets<br>4. Miscellaneous expenditure to the extent not written off or adjusted<br>5. Profit and loss account<br>**Total** | | |

**(B) Condensed Statement of Profit and Loss**

| | Three months ended | Corresponding three months of the previous accounting year | Year-to-date figures for current period | Year-to-date figures for the previous year |
|---|---|---|---|---|
| 1. Turnover<br>2. Other Income<br>**Total**<br>3. Changes in inventories of finished goods and work in progress | | | | |

| | Three months ended | Corresponding three months of the previous accounting year | Year-to-date figures for current period | Year-to-date figures for the previous year |
|---|---|---|---|---|
| 4. Cost of raw materials and consumables used | | | | |
| 5. Salaries, wages and other staff costs | | | | |
| 6. Other expenses | | | | |
| 7. Interest | | | | |
| 8. Depreciation and amortisations | | | | |
| 9. Profit or loss from ordinary activities before tax | | | | |
| **Total** | | | | |
| 10. Extraordinary items | | | | |
| 11. Profit or loss before tax | | | | |
| 12. Tax expense | | | | |
| 13. Profit or loss after tax | | | | |
| 14. Minority Interests (in case of consolidated financial statements) | | | | |
| **15. Net profit or loss for the period** | | | | |
| Earnings Per Share | | | | |
| 1. Basic Earnings Per Share | | | | |
| 2. Diluted Earnings Per Share | | | | |

### (C) Condensed Cash Flow Statement

| | Year-to-date figures for the current period | Year-to-date figures for the previous year |
|---|---|---|
| 1. Cash flows from operating activities<br>2. Cash flows from investing activities<br>3. Cash flows from financing activities<br>4. Net increase/(decrease) in cash and cash equivalents<br>5. Cash and cash equivalents at beginning of period<br>6. Cash and cash equivalents at end of period | | |

**Illustration 1.8**

Intelligent corporation deals in seasonal products. The quarterly sales pattern of the product is given below.

| Quarter I | Quarter II | Quarter III | Quarter IV |
|---|---|---|---|
| 31st March | 30th June | 30th September | 31st December |

For the first quarter ending 31st March 2021, the company gives you the following information:

| | Rs Crores |
|---|---|
| Sales | 50 |
| Salary and other expenses | 30 |
| Advertisement expenses (routine) | 02 |
| Administrative and selling expenses | 08 |

While preparing the interim financial report for the first quarter the company wants to defer Rs. 21 crores expenditure to third quarter on the argument that third quarter is having more sales, therefore third quarter should be debited by higher expenditure, considering the seasonal nature of business. The expenditures are uniform throughout all quarters.

Calculate the result of first quarter and comment on the company's view.

**Solution**

**Result of the first quarter ended**
**31st March 2021**

| | | Rs in crores |
|---|---|---|
| Turnover | | 50 |
| Add: Other income | | Nil |
| Total | | 50 |
| Less: Changes in inventories | nil | |
| Salaries and other cost | 30 | |
| Administrative and selling expenses (8+2) | 10 | 40 |
| Profit | | 10 |

In accordance with AS 25 "Interim Financial Reporting" the income and expenditure should be recognised when they are earned and incurred respectively. As per para 38 of AS 25, the Costs should be anticipated or deferred only when

(a) It is appropriate to anticipate that type of cost at the end of financial year and

(b) Costs are incurred unevenly during the financial year of an enterprise

Therefore, the argument given by Intelligent corporation relating to deferment of Rs. 21 crores is not tenable as expenses are uniform during the financial year of an enterprise.

**Illustration 1.9**

Alpha Ltd presents interim financial report (IFR) quarterly, earns Rs. 450 lakhs pre-tax profit in the first quarter ending 30.06.21 but expect to incur losses of Rs.150 lakhs in each of the three remaining quarters, which will result zero income during the financial year. Effective income tax rate expected to be 35%. Calculate the income tax expense to be reported in each quarter as per AS 25.

**Solution**

Statement of calculation of income tax expenses

| Quarter | Particulars | Tax calculator | Rs/ lakhs |
|---|---|---|---|
| | Pre-tax profit/ (loss) | | |
| I | Rs.450 lakhs | 450 x 40% | 180 |
| 2 | (Rs.150 lakhs) | -150 x 40% | -60 |
| 3 | (Rs.150 lakhs) | -150 x 40% | -60 |

| 4 | (Rs.150 lakhs) | -150 x 40% | -60 |
|---|---|---|---|
| | Annual tax expenses | | nil |

**Illustration 1.10**

XYZ Ltd presents interim financial report quarterly on 1.4.2020. XYZ Ltd has carried forward losses of Rs.400 lakhs for income tax purposes for which deferred tax has not been recognized. XYZ Ltd earns Rs.500 lakhs in each of the quarters ending on 30.6.2020, 31.12.2020 and 31.3.2021 excluding the loss carried forward. Income tax rate is expected to be 40%. Calculate the amount of tax expense to be reported in each quarter.

**Solution**

**Statement of calculation of tax expense**

| Particulars | Rs/lakhs |
|---|---|
| Total earnings for the year | 2000 |
| Carried forward loss | 400 |
| Net earnings | 1600 |
| Tax rate 40% | 640 |
| Average annual effective tax rate (640 / 2000) x 100 | 32% |
| Tax expense for each quarter (Rs.500 lakhs x 32%) | 160 |

**Illustration 1.11**

An enterprise reports quarterly estimates of annual income of Rs.10 lakhs. Assume tax rates on 1st Rs. 5,00,000 30% and the balance income at 40%. The estimated quarterly income are Rs.75,000, Rs. 2,50,000, Rs. 3,75,000 and Rs. 3,00,000.

Calculate the tax expenses to be recognized each quarter.

**Solution**

In accordance with *para* 29 of AS 25 "*Interim financial reporting*" , income tax expense is recognised in each interim period based on the best estimate of the weighted average annual income tax rate expected for the full financial year.

| Particulars | | Amount Rs. |
|---|---|---|
| Estimated annual income | | 10,00,000 |
| 30% on Rs.5,00,000 | Rs.1,50,000 | |
| 40% on balance of Rs. 5,00,000 | Rs. 2,00,000 | 3,50,000 |

| | | |
|---|---|---|
| Weighted average income tax rate (Rs.3,50,000 x Rs.10,00,000) x 100 | | 35% |
| Tax expense to be recognised quarterly is as under: | | |
| Quarter I | Rs.75,000 × 35% | Rs. 26,250 |
| Quarter II | Rs.2,50,000 × 35% | Rs. 87,500 |
| Quarter III | Rs.3,75000 × 35% | Rs. 1,31,250 |
| Quarter IV | Rs.3,00,000 × 35% | Rs. 1,05,000 |
| | | Rs. 3,50,000 |

## 1.27 CONTINGENCIES AND EVENTS OCCURRING AFTER THE BALANCE SHEET DATE

### 1.27.1 AS 4: Contingencies and events occurring after the Balance Sheet date

According to AS 4, the main principles as under:

| | |
|---|---|
| ***Contingencies*** | The amount of a contingent loss should be provided for by a charge in the statement of profit and loss if:<br>(a) it is probable that future events will confirm that, after taking into account any related probable recovery, an asset has been impaired or a liability has been incurred as at the balance sheet date, and<br>(b) a reasonable estimate of the amount of the resulting loss can be made.<br>The existence of a contingent loss should be disclosed in the financial statements if either of the conditions in paragraph 10 is not met, unless the possibility of a loss is remote.<br>Contingent gains should not be recognised in the financial statements. |
| ***Events Occurring after the Balance Sheet Date*** | Assets and liabilities should be adjusted for events occurring after the balance sheet date that provide additional evidence to assist the estimation of amounts relating to conditions existing at the balance sheet date or that indicate that the fundamental accounting assumption of going concern (i.e., the continuance of existence or substratum of the enterprise) is not appropriate.<br>**If an enterprise declares dividends to shareholders after the balance sheet date, the enterprise should not recognise those dividends as a liability at the balance sheet date unless a statute requires otherwise. Such** |

| | **dividends should be disclosed in notes.**<br>Disclosure should be made in the report of the approving authority of those events occurring after the balance sheet date that represent material changes and commitments affecting the financial position of the enterprise. |
|---|---|

## 1.27.2 Ind AS 10: Events after the reporting period

Events after the reporting period are those events, favourable and unfavourable, that occur between the end of the reporting period and the date when the financial statements are approved by the Board of Directors in case of a company, and, by the corresponding approving authority in case of any other entity for issue. Two types of events can be identified:

(a) those that provide evidence of conditions that existed at the end of the reporting period (*adjusting events after the reporting period); and*

(b) those that are indicative of conditions that arose after the reporting period (*non- adjusting events after the reporting period).*

### *Adjusting events after the reporting period*

An entity shall adjust the amounts recognised in its financial statements to reflect adjusting events after the reporting period.

The Standard highlights examples of adjusting events after the reporting period that require an entity to adjust the amounts recognised in its financial statements.

| ***Examples of adjusting events*** | (a) The settlement after the reporting period of a court case that confirms that the entity had a present obligation at the end of the reporting period. The entity adjusts any previously recognised provision related to this court case in accordance with *Ind AS 37 Provisions, Contingent Liabilities and Contingent Assets* or recognises a new provision<br>(b) The receipt of information after the reporting period indicating that an asset was impaired at the end of the reporting period, or that the amount of a previously recognised impairment loss for that asset needs to be adjusted, e.g.<br>(I) The bankruptcy of a customer that occurs after the reporting period usually confirms that a loss existed at the end of the reporting period on a trade receivable and that the entity needs to adjust the carrying amount of the trade receivable and<br>(II) The sale of inventories after the reporting period may give evidence about their net realisable value at the end of the reporting period |
|---|---|

| | |
|---|---|
| | (c) The determination after the reporting period of the cost of assets purchased, or the proceeds from assets sold, before the end of the reporting period |
| | (d) The determination after the reporting period of the amount of profit-sharing or bonus payments, if the entity had a present legal or constructive obligation at the end of the reporting period to make such payments as a result of events before that date (refer *Ind AS 19: Employee Benefits*) |
| | (e) The discovery of fraud or errors that show that the financial statements are incorrect |

### *Non-adjusting events after the reporting period*

An entity shall not adjust the amounts recognised in its financial statements to reflect non-adjusting events after the reporting period.

### Illustration 1.12

> An example of a non-adjusting event after the reporting period is a decline in fair value of investments between the end of the reporting period and the date when the financial statements are approved for issue.
>
> The decline in fair value does not normally relate to the condition of the investments at the end of the reporting period, but reflects circumstances that have arisen subsequently. Therefore, an entity does not adjust the amounts recognised in its financial statements for the investments. Similarly, the entity does not update the amounts disclosed for the investments as at the end of the reporting period, although it may need to give additional disclosures.

A decision tree related to the use of Adjusting and Non-adjusting events related to those events arising after the reporting date is explained in the chart below.

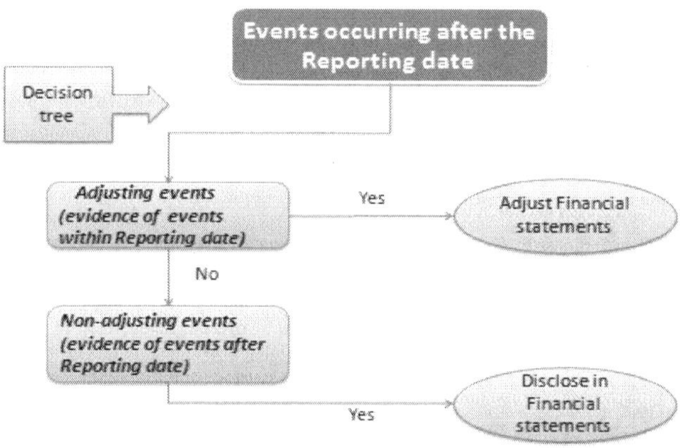

### Dividends

If an entity declares dividends to holders of equity instruments (as defined in Ind AS 32 Financial Instruments: Presentation) after the reporting period, the entity shall not recognise those dividends as a liability at the end of the reporting period.

If dividends are declared after the reporting period but before the financial statements are approved for issue, the dividends are not recognised as a liability at the end of the reporting period because no obligation exists at that time. Such dividends are disclosed in the notes in accordance with *Ind AS 1 Presentation of Financial Statements.*

### Going concern

- An entity shall not prepare its financial statements on a going concern basis if management determines after the reporting period either that it intends to liquidate the entity or to cease trading, or that it has no realistic alternative but to do so.
- Deterioration in operating results and financial position after the reporting period may indicate a need to consider whether the going concern assumption is still appropriate. If the going concern assumption is no longer appropriate, the effect is so pervasive that this Standard requires a fundamental change in the basis of accounting, rather than an adjustment to the amounts recognised within the original basis of accounting.
- Ind AS 1 specifies required disclosures if:
  - (a) the financial statements are not prepared on a going concern basis; or
  - (b) management is aware of material uncertainties related to events or conditions that may cast significant doubt upon the entity's ability to continue as a going concern. The events or conditions requiring disclosure may arise after the reporting period.
  - (b) an estimate of its financial effect, or a statement that such an estimate cannot be made.

### Non-adjusting events after the reporting period – examples

| | | |
|---|---|---|
| ***Examples of non-adjusting events*** | (a) | a major business combination after the reporting period Ind AS 103 Business Combinations requires specific disclosures in such cases) or disposing of a major subsidiary; |
| | (b) | announcing a plan to discontinue an operation; |
| | (c) | major purchases of assets, classification of assets as held for sale in accordance with Ind AS 105, Non-current Assets Held for Sale and Discontinued Operations, other disposals of assets, or expropriation of major assets by government; |

(d) the destruction of a major production plant by a fire after the reporting period;

(e) announcing, or commencing the implementation of, a major restructuring (see Ind AS 37);

(f) major ordinary share transactions and potential ordinary share transactions after the reporting period Ind AS 33 Earnings per Share requires an entity to disclose a description of such transactions, other than when such transactions involve capitalisation or bonus issues, share splits or reverse share splits all of which are required to be adjusted under Ind AS 33);

(g) abnormally large changes after the reporting period in asset prices or foreign exchange rates;

(h) changes in tax rates or tax laws enacted or announced after the reporting period that have a significant effect on current and deferred tax assets and liabilities (see Ind AS 12 Income Taxes);

(i) entering into significant commitments or contingent liabilities, for example, by issuing significant guarantees; and

(j) commencing major litigation arising solely out of events that occurred after the reporting period.

## 1.28 ACCOUNTING POLICIES, CHANGES IN ACCOUNTING ESTIMATES AND ERRORS

### 1.28.1 AS 5: Accounting policies, changes in accounting estimates and errors

This Standard should be applied by an enterprise in presentation and disclosures related to Items mentioned in the chart below.

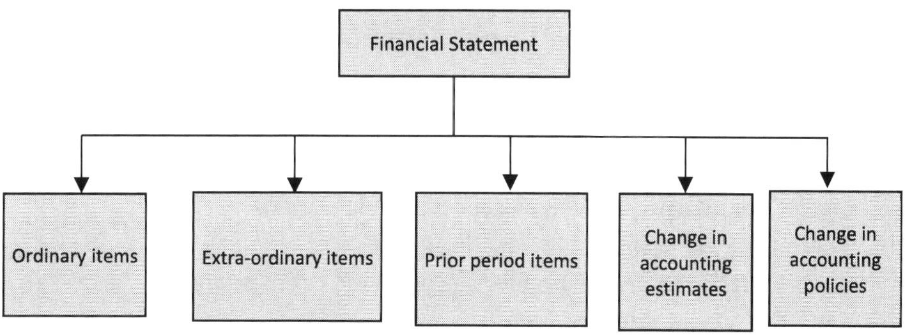

### 1.28.1.1 Components of Profit and Loss

| | |
|---|---|
| ***Profit or loss from ordinary activities*** | When items of income and expense within profit or loss from ordinary activities are of such size, nature or incidence that their disclosure is relevant to explain the performance of the enterprise for the period, the nature and amount of such items should be disclosed separately. |
| ***Extra-ordinary Items*** | Extraordinary items should be disclosed in the statement of profit and loss as a part of net profit or loss for the period.<br>The nature and the amount of each extraordinary item should be separately disclosed in the statement of profit and loss in a manner that its impact on current profit or loss can be perceived. |
| ***Prior period items*** | The nature and amount of prior period items should be separately disclosed in the statement of profit and loss in a manner that their impact on the current profit or loss can be perceived |

### 1.28.1.2 Change in accounting estimates

- The effect of a change in an accounting estimate should be included in the determination of net profit or loss in:
  - (a) the period of the change, if the change affects the period only; or
  - (b) the period of the change and future periods, if the change affects both.
- The effect of a change in an accounting estimate should be classified using the same classification in the statement of profit and loss as was used previously for the estimate
- The nature and amount of a change in an accounting estimate which has a material effect in the current period, or which is expected to have a material effect in subsequent periods, should be disclosed. If it is impracticable to quantify the amount, this fact should be disclosed.

### 1.28.1.3 Changes in accounting policies

- A change in an accounting policy should be made only if the adoption of a different accounting policy is required
  - (a) by statute or
  - (b) for compliance with an accounting standard or
  - (c) if it is considered that the change would result in a more appropriate presentation of the financial statements of the enterprise.
- The following are not changes in accounting policies:

(a) the adoption of an accounting policy for events or transactions that differ in substance from previously occurring events or transactions, e.g., introduction of a formal retirement gratuity scheme by an employer in place of ad hoc ex-gratia payments to employees on retirement; and

(b) the adoption of a new accounting policy for events or transactions which did not occur previously or that were immaterial.

### 1.28.1.4 *Examples*

**AS 5: Net profit or loss for the period, prior period Items and changes in accounting policies – Examples**

| | |
|---|---|
| • A change in the method of depreciation from SLM to WDV or WDV to SLM | • *Change in accounting policy* |
| • Useful life reduced based on new management estimates, depreciation method unchanged, but depreciation rate increased | • *Change in an accounting estimate* |
| • Error in computing depreciation in the previous year detected in the current year | • *Prior period item* |
| • Depreciation not corrected added | • *Prior period item* |
| • Fixed Assets destroyed in earthquake | • *Extra-ordinary item* |
| • Major disposal of Fixed Assets | • *Ordinary activity (exceptional item to be disclosed separately applying materiality concept)* |

## 1.28.2 Ind AS 8: Accounting policies, changes in accounting estimates and errors

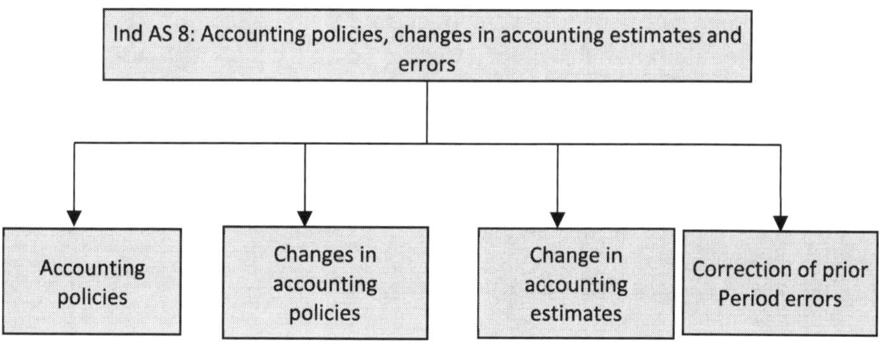

### 1.28.2.1 Accounting policies

| ***Accounting policies are specific principles, bases, conventions rules and practices applied by an entity in preparing and presenting Financial Statements*** |
|---|

Para 7. When an Ind AS specifically applies to a transaction, other event or condition, the accounting policy or policies applied to that item shall be determined by applying the Ind AS.

According to para 10, in the absence of an Ind AS that specifically applies to a transaction, other event or condition, management shall use its judgement in developing and applying an accounting policy that results in information that is:

| | |
|---|---|
| ***(a) relevant*** | to the economic decision-making needs of users; and |
| ***(b) reliable, in that the financial statements:*** | (i) represent faithfully the financial position, financial performance and cash flows of the entity;<br>(ii) reflect the economic substance of transactions, other events and conditions, and not merely the legal form;<br>(iii) are neutral, i.e. free from bias;<br>(iv) are prudent; and<br>(v) are complete in all material respects. |

In making the judgement described above management shall refer to, and consider the applicability of, the following sources in descending order:

(a) the requirements in Ind ASs dealing with similar and related issues; and

(b) the definitions, recognition criteria and measurement concepts for assets, liabilities, income and expenses in the *Framework.*

In making the judgement described above, management may also first consider the most recent pronouncements of International Accounting Standards Board and in absence thereof those of the other standard-setting bodies that use a similar conceptual framework to develop accounting standards, other accounting literature and accepted industry practices, to the extent that these do not conflict with the sources above.

**Major areas for which disclosures of accounting policies are made are:**

- Revenue recognition
- Expenses e.g. research and development expenses
- Impairment of assets
- Depreciation and amortization
- Investments
- Inventories
- Accounts receivables

### Consistency of accounting policies

According to para 13, an entity shall select and apply its accounting policies consistently for similar transactions, other events and conditions, unless an Ind AS specifically requires or permits categorisation of items for which different policies may be appropriate. If an Ind AS requires or permits such categorisation, an appropriate accounting policy shall be selected and applied consistently to each category.

## *1.28.2.2 Changes in Accounting policies*

An accounting policy can be changed only if the change:

***(a) is required by an Ind AS; or***
***(b) results in the financial statements providing reliable and more relevant information about the effects of transactions, other events or conditions on the entity's financial position, financial performance or cash flows. (Para 14)***

Users of financial statements need to be able to compare the financial statements of an entity over time to identify trends in its financial position, financial performance and cash flows. Therefore, the same accounting policies are applied within each period and from one period to the next unless a change in accounting policy meets one of the criteria above.

According to para 16, the following are not changes in accounting policies:

***(a) the application of an accounting policy for transactions, other events or conditions that differ in substance from those previously occurring; and***
***(b) the application of a new accounting policy for transactions, other events or conditions that did not occur previously or were immaterial.***

The initial application of a policy to revalue assets in accordance with Ind AS 16 *Property, Plant and Equipment* or Ind AS 38 *Intangible Assets* is a change in an accounting policy to be dealt with as a revaluation in accordance with Ind AS 16 or Ind AS 38, rather than in accordance with this Standard (para 17).

### Applying changes in accounting policy

According to para 19, subject to paragraph 23:

(a) an entity shall account for a change in accounting policy resulting from the initial application of an Ind AS in accordance with the specific transitional provisions, if any, in that Ind AS; and

(b) when an entity changes an accounting policy upon initial application of an Ind AS that does not include specific transitional provisions applying to that change, or changes an accounting policy voluntarily, it shall apply the change retrospectively

For the purpose of this Standard, early application of an Ind AS is not a voluntary change in accounting policy.

### Retrospective application

*Para 22.* Subject to paragraph 23, when a change in accounting policy is applied retrospectively in accordance with paragraph 19(a) or (b), the entity shall adjust the opening balance of each affected component of equity for the earliest prior period presented and the other comparative amounts disclosed for each prior period presented as if the new accounting policy had always been applied.

### Limitations on retrospective application

*Para 23* When retrospective application is required by paragraph 19(a) or (b), a change in accounting policy shall be applied retrospectively except to the extent that it is impracticable to determine either the period-specific effects or the cumulative effect of the change.

*Para 24* When it is impracticable to determine the period-specific effects of changing an accounting policy on comparative information for one or more prior periods presented, the entity shall apply the new accounting policy to the carrying amounts of assets and liabilities as at the beginning of the earliest period for which retrospective application is practicable, which may be the current period, and shall make a corresponding adjustment to the opening balance of each affected component of equity for that period.

*Para 25* When it is impracticable to determine the cumulative effect, at the beginning of the current period, of applying a new accounting policy to all prior periods, the entity shall adjust the comparative information to apply the new accounting policy prospectively from the earliest date practicable.

**Illustration 1.13**

Alpha Co follows the accounting policy of depreciating its plant & machinery using the straight line method. The company feels that the WDV method of depreciation is more realistic. Accordingly, it intends to change its accounting policy to apply depreciation under WDV method. Comment giving reasons for your answer.

**Solution**

The WDV method of depreciation is permitted by Ind AS 16. Also, the company feels that this method of depreciation is more realistic under the circumstances and makes the financial statements more reliable. Hence, the change in accounting policy is acceptable.

This signifies that the company is permitted to change its accounting policy and make appropriate disclosures in the financial statements.

**Illustration 1.14**

Beta Co has reported depreciation in its expenses. However, the directors are of the opinion that, to ensure meaningful reporting, they should split the depreciation in two parts, i.e. depreciation on factory equipment should be reported under cost of sales, whereas depreciation on office furniture should be reported under administrative expenses. Comment whether this is an acceptable change.

**Solution**

The problem should be approached as under:

Step 1

Is the change prescribed by a standard : The answer is NO

Step 2

Is the change required by law : The answer is NO

Step 3

Will the change result in greater accuracy and meaningful disclosure : The answer is YES

Therefore the decision should be : The change is acceptable

**Illustration 1.15**

Gamma Co is in the process of finalisation of its financial statements for 2011. The management intends to change the valuation of its inventory from FIFO method to weighted average method. Comment whether this is possible and whether this would require a prior period adjustment.

**Solution**

The above change falls under the purview of change in accounting policy. Hence, this would entail a prior period adjustment.

### *1.28.2.3 Accounting estimates*

- ***The effect of change in an accounting estimate shall be recognised prospectively by including it in the profit or loss of the year of change or also in the future periods, if the change affects both***
- ***If the extent of the change impacts assets and liabilities or relates to any item of equity it is recognised by adjusting the carrying amount of the related asset, liability or equity item in the period of the change.***

There are many items in the financial statements which cannot be measured with precision. An entity has to make a judgment to estimate the value of such items

Some items that require estimation are:

- bad debts
- inventory obsolescence
- the fair value of financial assets or financial liabilities
- the useful lives of, or expected pattern of consumption of, the future economic benefits in depreciable assets and
- warranty obligations

***The effect of change in accounting estimate is applied prospectively i.e. from the date of the change in estimate by including it in profit or loss in:***
***(a) the period of the change, if the change affects that period only; or***
***(b) the period of the change and future periods, if the change affects both.***

**Illustration 1.16**

An equipment has been purchased at a cost of Rs. 1,00,000 and an estimated useful life of ten years with nil residual value. It is depreciated on a straight line method and the annual depreciation works out to Rs.10,000 p.a. The carrying amount of the equipment after four years works out to Rs. 60,000. It was decided in the fifth year that the remaining useful life of the equipment is only three years and not six years.

Please state the accounting treatment of the equipment in the books.

**Solution**

Since the estimated useful has been shortened to three years from six years, the carrying amount of Rs. 60,000 is to be divided in three years i.e. Rs.60,000 / 3 = Rs. 20,000.

Hence, depreciation charged in the past three years will not be changed, additional depreciation of Rs.10,000 over and above the past three years need to be charged to Statement of Profit & Loss and disclosed in the financial statements.

### 1.28.2.4 Accounting Errors

- ***The general principle is that the entity must correct all material prior period errors retrospectively as soon as they are discovered by***
- ***restating the comparative amounts for the prior period(s) presented in which the error occurred or***
- ***if the error occurred before the earliest prior period presented, restate the opening balances of assets, liabilities and equity for the earliest period presented.***

**Illustration 1.17**

The financial statements of Delta Co for 2010 has shown inventory at Rs. 2,50,000. However, the inventory statement erroneously missed out couple of pages the amount working out to Rs. 55,000, which was lying outside the premises of the Company with a consignment stock agent. The error was detected in 2011 after the financial statements were approved.
In such a scenario, the correction of the error in the financial statements would be made retrospectively from 2010.

## 1.29 COMPARATIVE SUMMARY OF AS, IFRS, US GAAP AND IND AS

### 1.29.1 Constituents of financial statements

| AS | IFRS | US GAAP | Ind AS |
|---|---|---|---|
| **Constituents of financial statements**<br>- Balance sheet<br>- Statement of profit and loss or income and expenditure account<br>- Statement of changes in equity is disclosed as notes to financial statements as a part of the Balance Sheet.<br>- Cash flow statements (exempted for SMC)<br>- Accounting policies Notes to financial Statements | - Statement of Financial position<br>- Statement of Profit & Loss and Other comprehensive income<br>- Statement of changes in equity<br>- Cash flow statement<br>- Notes to financial statements and accounting policies as a part thereof | For US Companies and SEC Registrants (public companies)<br>- Balance Sheet<br>- Income Statements<br>- Cash flow statement<br>- Statement of changes in equity<br>- Accounting policies and notes<br>Non-US companies with registered securities in US have an option to prepare their financial statements either based on US GAAPs or on IFRS along-with | - Balance Sheet<br>- Statement of Profit & Loss and Other comprehensive income<br>- Statement of changes in equity<br>- Cash flow statement<br>- Notes to financial statements and accounting policies as a part thereof<br>- Entities are permitted classification of expenses only by nature |

| AS | IFRS | US GAAP | Ind AS |
|---|---|---|---|
| | | reconciliation of net income and equity to US GAAP, as disclosure to note | |
| **Comparatives**<br>1 year of comparatives are required (except in certain circumstances wherein 5 year comparatives (bonus shares, buy back, etc.) are required as per Revised Schedule VI of Companies Act, 1956/ Schedule III of Companies Act, 2013). | One year of comparatives are required (except in certain circumstances where more than 1 year comparative disclosures are required). | Comparatives are not required. (except SEC requirements which require 1 year comparatives for balance sheet and 2 year comparatives for other statements). | One year of comparatives are required (except in certain circumstances where more than 1 year comparative disclosures are required). |
| **Reclassification of comparatives**<br>Disclosures regarding reclassification of comparatives are required. | Disclosures regarding reclassification of comparatives are required. | Permitted in certain circumstances. | Disclosures regarding reclassification of comparatives are required. |
| **Deviation from Standards**<br>Deviations from standards are permitted only in case of any regulation. In such cases proper disclosures are required. | Deviations from standards are permitted only if complying with the standards will make the financial statements misleading. In case there is difference between IFRS | Deviations are generally not permitted. | Deviations from standards are permitted only if complying with the standards will make the financial statements misleading.<br>In case there is difference between Ind AS and any other statute, then the legal statute will take |

| AS | IFRS | US GAAP | Ind AS |
|---|---|---|---|
| | and any other regulation, IFRS should be applied. | | precedence. |

## 1.29.2 Balance-sheet

| AS | IFRS | US GAAP | Ind AS |
|---|---|---|---|
| **Format**<br>Provides format of Balance Sheet under Revised Schedule VI of Companies Act 1956 and Schedule III of Companies Act 2013 | IFRS does not prescribe any format, but stipulates minimum line items like PPE, Investment property, intangible assets, financial assets, biological assets, inventory, receivables, etc. | US GAAP also does not prescribe any format, but Rule S-X of SEC stipulates for listed companies minimum line items to be disclosed either on face of Balance Sheet or Note to Accounts | Ind AS does not prescribe any format, but stipulates minimum line items like PPE, Investment property, intangible assets, financial assets, biological assets, inventory, receivables, etc.<br>However, the reporting is complemented by Schedule III of Companies Act 2013 |
| **Order**<br>The line items are presented in increasing order of liquidity | Under IFRS line items are presented in increasing order of liquidity | Under US GAAP, items in assets and liabilities are presented in decreasing order of liquidity | Similar to IFRS |
| **Consolidation**<br>It is not mandatory for companies to prepare CFS under AS 21.<br>However, listed enterprises are mandatorily required by listing agreement of SEBI | Consolidated basis. However, an entity voluntarily or in certain circumstances may prepare standalone financials. | Under US GAAP, consolidation of results of subsidiaries and variable interest entity (FIN 46R) is compulsory | Consolidated basis. However, an entity voluntarily or in certain circumstances may prepare standalone financials. |

| AS | IFRS | US GAAP | Ind AS |
|---|---|---|---|
| to prepare and present CFS | | | |
| **Current/non-current**<br>No such requirement | An entity has an option to adopt Current or Non-current classification of assets and liabilities | Bifurcation into current and non-current is compulsorily required | An entity has an option to adopt Current or Non-current classification of assets and liabilities |

## 1.29.3 Income statement

| AS | IFRS | US GAAP | Ind AS |
|---|---|---|---|
| **Format**<br>Provides format of Statement of Profit & Loss under Revised Schedule VI of Companies Act 1956 and Schedule III of Companies Act 2013 | IFRS does not prescribe any standard format, but stipulates minimum disclosure which includes revenue, finance costs, share of post-tax results of associates and joint arrangements using Equity method<br>Suggests two alternative i.e. disclosure of expenses by functions or elements | US GAAP also does not prescribe any format, but Rule S-X of SEC stipulates for listed companies minimum line items to be disclosed on face of Income statement and suggests two alternatives<br>(a) Single step format where expenses are classified by function and<br>(b) Multi step format where cost of sales is deducted from sales | Similar to IFRS.<br>However, this is complemented by Schedule III of Companies Act 2013.<br>The format suggests disclosure of expenses by elements. |
| **Bifurcation of cost**<br>Based on format provided in Schedule III of Companies Act, 2013 | Total cost is required to be split based on two alternatives e.g. by | Total cost is required to be | Total cost is split by elements based on format provided in |

| AS | IFRS | US GAAP | Ind AS |
|---|---|---|---|
| | functions and by elements | shown separately under:<br>(a) cost of sales<br>(b) selling and administration<br>(c) R&D | Schedule III of Companies Act, 2013. |
| **Prior period items**<br>Requires separate disclosure of prior period in the current financial statement and no restatement of retained earnings is required | A prior period item / error should be corrected by retrospective effect by restatement of opening balance of assets , liabilities or equities | Mandates retrospective application of errors and requires restatement of comparative opening balance with suitable footnote disclosure | A prior period item / error should be corrected by retrospective effect by restatement of opening balance of assets , liabilities or equities |
| **Discounting**<br>There is no concept of discounting under AS | In cases where inflow or outflow of cash is delayed through deferred settlement, then the income or expense is discounted to present value to comply with the basis of "cash or cash equivalent".<br>Unwinding of discount is charged to finance cost or credited to finance income in later years in Statement of Profit or loss (SOPL) | Permits discounting in certain cases e.g. loans, debentures, bonds and upfront fees | In cases where inflow or outflow of cash is delayed through deferred settlement, then the income or expense is discounted to present value to comply with the basis of "cash or cash equivalent".<br>Unwinding of discount is charged to finance cost or credited to finance income in later years in Statement of Profit or loss (SOPL) |
| **Extra-ordinary items**<br>The nature and amount of each extra-ordinary item should be separately | Disclosure is prohibited | Nature should be both<br>(a) Infrequent<br>(b) Unusual<br>Disclosed separately | Disclosure is prohibited |

| AS | IFRS | US GAAP | Ind AS |
|---|---|---|---|
| disclosed in the Statement of P&L in a manner that its impact on current profit & loss can be perceived | | on the face of the income statement net of taxes after results from operations | |

### 1.29.4 Statement of changes in Equity

| AS | IFRS | US GAAP | Ind AS |
|---|---|---|---|
| **Disclosure**<br>Disclosure for two years.<br>This statement is not applicable, share capital and reserves and surplus are disclosed by way of Notes to Accounts to Balance Sheet | Disclosure for two years. Primary statement shows capital transactions with owners, movement in accumulated profits and reconciliation of equity. This is linked to Other comprehensive income, which is a part of the Income statement | Disclosure for three years. May be shown as a part of notes to accounts and shows capital transactions with owners, movement in accumulated profits and reconciliation of equity. Other comprehensive income may be shown as a part of it. | Same as IFRS |
| **Repurchase of own shares**<br>An entity may purchase its own shares provided it is in consonance with the complex legal requirements stipulated in the Companies Act and SEBI guidelines | Similar to US GAAP<br>Repurchased stock is shown as a deduction from equity | Repurchased for retiring stock, excess of cost over par value may be charged entirely to retained earnings; or allocated between retained earnings and additional paid-in-capital (APIC), or charged entirely to APIC | Similar to IFRS subject to compliance of provisions of Companies Act, 2013 |

| AS | IFRS | US GAAP | Ind AS |
|---|---|---|---|
| **Dividend on equity shares**<br>Presented as an appropriation of profits<br>Dividends are accounted for in the year when it is proposed | Presented as a deduction in the Statement of Changes in Shareholders equity.<br>Dividends are accounted for in the year when it is declared. | Presented as a deduction in the Statement of Changes in Shareholders equity.<br>Dividends are accounted for in the year when it is declared. | Presented as a deduction in the Statement of Changes in Shareholders equity.<br>Dividends are accounted for in the year when it is declared. |

### 1.29.5 Change in Accounting policies and accounting estimates and errors

| AS | IFRS | US GAAP | Ind AS |
|---|---|---|---|
| **Change in Accounting policies**<br>In the year of change, the effect of change is included in income statement of the year and also impact of change disclosed | Retrospective effect of change in accounting policy is accounted and comparative figures restated | Similar to IFRS from the date of adoption and of FAS 154 | Retrospective effect of change in accounting policy is accounted and comparative figures restated |
| **Change in Accounting estimates**<br>Change is accounted in the income statement of the current year when identified.<br>In general no retrospective effect is accounted for such change. | Change is accounted for in the income statement of the current year when identified. In general no retrospective effect is accounted for such change | Similar to IFRS | Similar to IFRS |
| **Prior period errors**<br>Reported as a prior period adjustment in current year results.<br>Comparatives are not | Prior period errors are to be corrected retrospectively and restate the opening | Similar to IFRS | Prior period errors are to be corrected retrospectively and restate the opening |

| AS | IFRS | US GAAP | Ind AS |
|---|---|---|---|
| required to be restated | balances of assets, liability and equity | | balances of assets, liability and equity |

### 1.29.6 Events occurring after the reporting date

| AS | IFRS | US GAAP | Ind AS |
|---|---|---|---|
| Financial statements are adjusted for events after the reporting date, providing evidence of conditions at balance sheet date and materially affecting amounts in financial statements (adjusting events) except non-adjusting events which are not required to be disclosed in financial statements but are disclosed in report of approving authority e.g. directors report. | Financial statements are adjusted for events after the reporting date, providing evidence of conditions at balance sheet date and materially affecting amounts in financial statements (adjusting events) Non-adjusting events which are required to be disclosed in financial statements | Similar to IFRS | Financial statements are adjusted for events after the reporting date, providing evidence of conditions at balance sheet date and materially affecting amounts in financial statements (adjusting events) Non-adjusting events which are required to be disclosed in financial statements |

## 1.30 WHAT IS FAIR VALUE?

In accordance with Indian Accounting Standards, *Ind AS 113, Fair value measurement* is defined as under:

| ***the price that would be received to sell an asset or paid to transfer a liability in an orderly transaction between market participants at the measurement date.*** |
|---|

If we break down the above definition the following attributes surface:

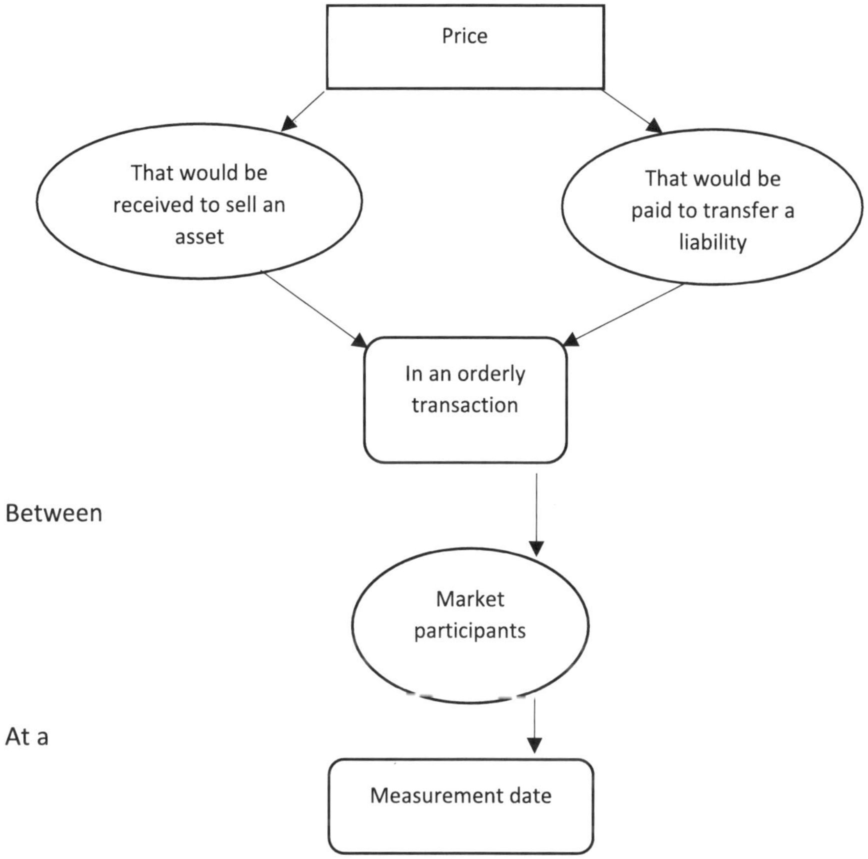


## 1.31 FAIR VALUE MEASUREMENT OF ASSETS AND LIABILITIES

When measuring fair value for an asset or a liability, an entity shall take into account the characteristics of the asset or liability if market participants would take those characteristics into account when pricing the asset or liability at the measurement date. Such characteristics include, for example, the following:

(a) the condition and location of the asset; and

(b) restrictions, if any, on the sale or use of the asset.

The asset or liability measured at fair value might be either of the following:

(a) a stand-alone asset or liability (e.g. a financial instrument or a non-financial asset); or

(b) a group of assets, a group of liabilities or a group of assets and liabilities (e.g. a cash-generating unit or a business).

### 1.31.1 Transaction

A fair value measurement assumes that the asset or liability is exchanged in an orderly transaction between market participants to sell the asset or transfer the liability at the measurement date under current market conditions.

A fair value measurement assumes that the transaction to sell the asset or transfer the liability takes place either:

(a) in the *principal market* for the asset or liability; or

(b) in the absence of a principal market, in the *most advantageous market* for the asset or liability.

### 1.31.2 Price

(a) Fair value is the *price* that would be received to sell an asset or paid to transfer a liability in an orderly transaction in the principal (or most advantageous) market at the measurement date under current market conditions (i.e. an exit price) regardless of whether that price is directly observable or estimated using another valuation technique.

(b) *Transaction costs*

The price in the principal (or most advantageous) market used to measure the fair value of the asset or liability shall not be adjusted for *transaction costs.* Transaction costs shall be accounted for in accordance with other Ind ASs. Transaction costs are not a characteristic of an asset or a liability; rather, they are specific to a transaction and will differ depending on how an entity enters into a transaction for the asset or liability.

(c) *Transport costs*

Transaction costs do not include *transport costs.* If location is a characteristic of the asset (as might be the case, for example, for a commodity), the price in the principal (or most advantageous) market shall be adjusted for the costs, if any, that would be incurred to transport the asset from its current location to that market.

### 1.31.3 Application to non-financial assets

A fair value measurement of a non-financial asset takes into account a market participant's ability to generate economic benefits by using the asset in its *highest and best use* or by selling it to another market participant that would use the asset in its highest and best use.

The highest and best use of a non-financial asset takes into account the use of the asset that is physically possible, legally permissible and financially feasible, as follows:

(a) A use that is physically possible takes into account the physical characteristics of the asset that market participants would take into account when pricing the asset (e.g. the location or size of a property).

(b) A use that is legally permissible takes into account any legal restrictions on the use of the asset that market participants would take into account when pricing the asset (e.g. the zoning regulations applicable to a property).

(c) A use that is financially feasible takes into account whether a use of the asset that is physically possible and legally permissible generates adequate income or cash flows (taking into account the costs of converting the asset to that use) to produce an investment return that market participants would require from an investment in that asset put to that use.

### 1.31.4 Application to liabilities and an entity's own equity instruments – general principles

A fair value measurement assumes that a financial or non-financial liability or an entity's own equity instrument (e.g. equity interests issued as consideration in a business combination) is transferred to a market participant at the measurement date. The transfer of a liability or an entity's own equity instrument assumes the following:

(a) A liability would remain outstanding and the market participant transferee would be required to fulfil the obligation. The liability would not be settled with the counterparty or otherwise extinguished on the measurement date.

(b) An entity's own equity instrument would remain outstanding and the market participant transferee would take on the rights and responsibilities associated with the instrument. The instrument would not be cancelled or otherwise extinguished on the measurement date.

### 1.31.5 Liabilities and equity instruments held by other parties as assets

When a quoted price for the transfer of an identical or a similar liability or entity's own equity instrument is not available and the identical item is held by another party as an asset, an entity shall measure the fair value of the liability or equity instrument from the perspective of a market participant that holds the identical item as an asset at the measurement date. In such cases fair value will be measured as under:

(a) using the quoted price in an *active market* for the identical item held by another party as an asset, if that price is available.

(b) if that price is not available, using other observable inputs, such as the quoted price in a market that is not active for the identical item held by another party as an asset.

(c) if the observable prices in (a) and (b) are not available, using another valuation technique, such as:

   (i) an *income approach* (e.g. a present value technique that takes into account the future cash flows that a market participant would expect to receive from holding the liability or equity instrument as an asset,

   (ii) a *market approach* (e.g. using quoted prices for similar liabilities or equity instruments held by other parties as assets;

### 1.31.6 Liabilities and equity instruments not held by other parties as assets

When a quoted price for the transfer of an identical or a similar liability or entity's own equity instrument is not available and the identical item is not held by another party as an asset, an entity shall measure the fair value of the liability or equity instrument using a valuation technique from the perspective of a market participant that owes the liability or has issued the claim on equity.

### 1.31.7 Non-performance risk

The fair value of a liability reflects the effect of *non-performance risk.* Non-performance risk includes, but may not be limited to, an entity's own credit risk (as defined in Ind AS 107, *Financial Instruments: Disclosures).* Non-performance risk is assumed to be the same before and after the transfer of the liability.

### 1.31.8 Restriction preventing the transfer of a liability or an entity's own equity instrument

When measuring the fair value of a liability or an entity's own equity instrument, an entity shall not include a separate input or an adjustment to other *inputs* relating to the existence of a restriction that prevents the transfer of the item. The effect of a restriction that prevents the transfer of a liability or an entity's own equity instrument is either implicitly or explicitly included in the other inputs to the fair value measurement.

### 1.31.9 Financial liability with a demand feature

The fair value of a financial liability with a demand feature (eg a demand deposit) is not less than the amount payable on demand, discounted from the first date that the amount could be required to be paid.

### 1.31.10 Application to financial assets and financial liabilities with offsetting positions in market risks or counterparty credit risk

(a) An entity that holds a group of financial assets and financial liabilities is exposed to market risks (as defined in Ind AS 107) and to the credit risk (as defined in Ind AS 107) of each of the counterparties.

(b) If the entity manages that group of financial assets and financial liabilities on the basis of its net exposure to either market risks or credit risk, the entity is permitted to apply an exception to this Ind AS for measuring fair value.

(c) That exception permits an entity to measure the fair value of a group of financial assets and financial liabilities on the basis of the price that would be received to sell a net long position (i.e. an asset) for a particular risk exposure or paid to transfer a net short position (i.e. a liability) for a particular risk exposure in an orderly transaction between market participants at the measurement date under current market conditions.

(d) Accordingly, an entity shall measure the fair value of the group of financial assets and financial liabilities consistently with how market participants would price the net risk exposure at the measurement date.

## 1.32 FAIR VALUE AT INITIAL RECOGNITION

(a) When an asset is acquired or a liability is assumed in an exchange transaction for that asset or liability, the transaction price is the price paid to acquire the asset or received to assume the liability (an *entry price).* In contrast, the fair value of the asset or liability is the price that would be received to sell the asset or paid to transfer the liability (an exit price).

(b) Entities do not necessarily sell assets at the prices paid to acquire them. Similarly, entities do not necessarily transfer liabilities at the prices received to assume them.

(c) In many cases the transaction price will equal the fair value (e.g. that might be the case when on the transaction date the transaction to buy an asset takes place in the market in which the asset would be sold).

## 1.33 VALUATION TECHNIQUES

An entity shall use valuation techniques that are appropriate in the circumstances and for which sufficient data are available to measure fair value, maximising the use of relevant observable inputs and minimising the use of unobservable inputs.

Three widely used valuation techniques are the *market approach*, the *cost approach* and the *income approach*. These are summarised below.

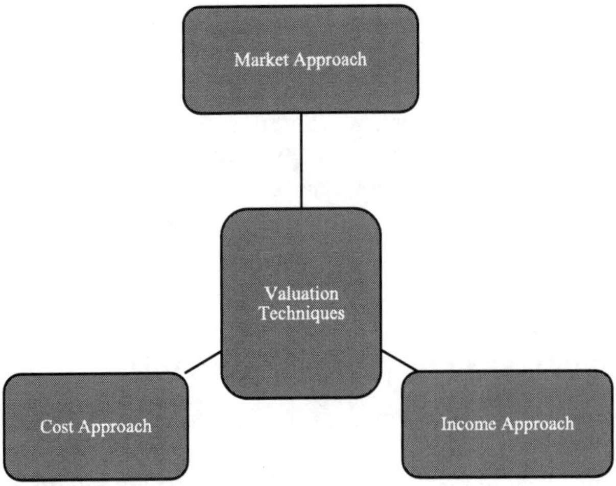


| **Valuation techniques** | **Description** |
|---|---|
| ***Market approach*** | (a) The market approach uses prices and other relevant information generated by market transactions involving identical or comparable (i.e. similar) assets, liabilities or a group of assets and liabilities, such as a business. (Para B5)<br>(b) Valuation techniques consistent with the market approach often use market multiples derived from a set of comparables.<br>(c) Multiples might be in ranges with a different multiple for each comparable. The selection of the appropriate multiple within the range requires judgement, considering qualitative and quantitative factors specific to the measurement. (Para B6)<br>(d) Valuation techniques consistent with the market approach include matrix pricing. Matrix pricing is a mathematical technique used principally to value some types of financial instruments, such as debt securities, without relying exclusively on quoted prices for the specific securities, but rather relying on the securities' relationship to other benchmark quoted securities. (Para B7) |
| ***Cost approach*** | The cost approach reflects the amount that would be required currently to replace the service capacity of an asset (often referred to as current replacement cost). |

| | |
|---|---|
| ***Income approach*** | The income approach converts future amounts (e.g. cash flows or income and expenses) to a single current (i.e. discounted) amount. When the income approach is used, the fair value measurement reflects current market expectations about those future amounts.<br>Valuation techniques include, for example, the following:<br>(a) present value techniques;<br>(b) option pricing models, such as the Black-Scholes-Merton formula or a binomial model (i.e. a lattice model), that incorporate present value techniques and reflect both the time value and the intrinsic value of an option; and<br>(c) the multi-period excess earnings method, which is used to measure the fair value of some intangible assets. |

Valuation techniques used to measure fair value shall be applied consistently.

However, a change in a valuation technique or its application (e.g. a change in its weightage when multiple valuation techniques are used or a change in an adjustment applied to a valuation technique) is appropriate if the change results in a measurement that is equally or more representative of fair value in the circumstances. That might be the case if, for example, any of the following events take place:

(a) new markets develop;

(b) new information becomes available;

(c) information previously used is no longer available;

(d) valuation techniques improve; or

(e) market conditions change.

## 1.34 PRESENT VALUE TECHNIQUES

(i) Present value (i.e. an application of the income approach) is a tool used to link future amounts (e.g. cash flows or values) to a present amount using a discount rate. A fair value measurement of an asset or a liability using a present value technique captures all the following elements from the perspective of market participants at the measurement date:

(a) an estimate of future cash flows for the asset or liability being measured.

(b) expectations about possible variations in the amount and timing of the cash flows representing the uncertainty inherent in the cash flows.

(c) the time value of money, represented by the rate on risk-free monetary assets that have maturity dates or durations that coincide with the period covered by the cash flows and pose neither uncertainty in timing nor risk of default to the holder (i.e. a risk-free interest rate).

(d) the price for bearing the uncertainty inherent in the cash flows (i.e. a *risk premium*).

(e) other factors that market participants would take into account in the circumstances.

(f) for a liability, the non-performance risk relating to that liability, including the entity's (i.e. the obligor's) own credit risk.

(ii) Also, all the following general principles govern the application of any present value technique used to measure fair value:

(a) Cash flows and discount rates should reflect assumptions that market participants would use when pricing the asset or liability.

(b) Cash flows and discount rates should take into account only the factors attributable to the asset or liability being measured.

(c) To avoid double-counting or omitting the effects of risk factors, discount rates should reflect assumptions that are consistent with those inherent in the cash flows.

For example, a discount rate that reflects the uncertainty in expectations about future defaults is appropriate if using contractual cash flows of a loan (i.e. a discount rate adjustment technique).

That same rate should not be used if using expected (i.e. probability-weighted) cash flows (i.e. an expected present value technique) because the expected cash flows already reflect assumptions about the uncertainty in future defaults; instead, a discount rate that is commensurate with the risk inherent in the expected cash flows should be used.

(d) Assumptions about cash flows and discount rates should be internally consistent. For example, nominal cash flows, which include the effect of inflation, should be discounted at a rate that includes the effect of inflation. The nominal risk-free interest rate includes the effect of inflation.

Real cash flows, which exclude the effect of inflation, should be discounted at a rate that excludes the effect of inflation. Similarly, after-tax cash flows should be discounted using an after-tax discount rate.

Pre-tax cash flows should be discounted at a rate consistent with those cash flows.

(e) Discount rates should be consistent with the underlying economic factors of the currency in which the cash flows are denominated.

## 1.35 INPUT TO VALUATION TECHNIQUES

(i) Valuation techniques used to measure fair value shall maximise the use of relevant observable inputs and minimise the use of unobservable inputs.

(ii) To increase consistency and comparability in fair value measurements and related disclosures, this Ind AS establishes a fair value hierarchy that categorises into three levels, the inputs to valuation techniques used to measure fair value. The fair value hierarchy gives the highest priority to quoted prices (unadjusted) in active markets for identical assets or liabilities (Level 1 inputs) and the lowest priority to unobservable inputs (*Level 3 inputs).*

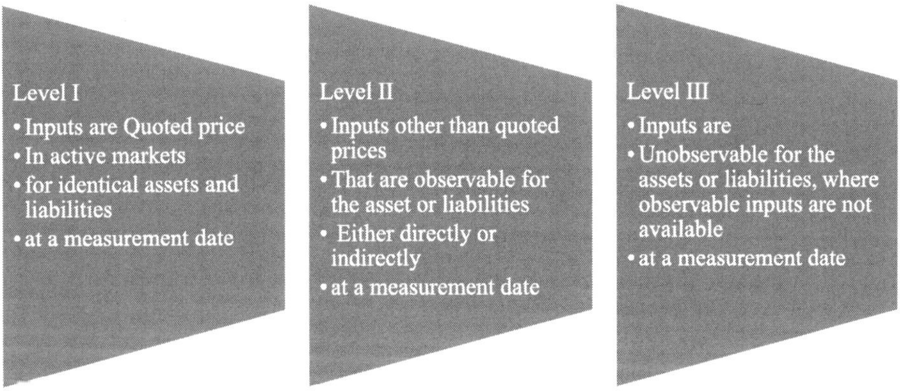


(iii) **Level 1**

Level 1 inputs are quoted prices (unadjusted) in active markets for identical assets or liabilities that the entity can access at the measurement date. A quoted price in an active market provides the most reliable evidence of fair value and shall be used without adjustment to measure fair value whenever available. The emphasis within Level 1 is on determining both of the following:

(a) the principal market for the asset or liability or, in the absence of a principal market, the most advantageous market for the asset or liability; and

(b) whether the entity can enter into a transaction for the asset or liability at the price in that market at the measurement date.

(iv) **Level 2**

Level 2 inputs are inputs other than quoted prices included within Level 1 that are observable for the asset or liability, either directly or indirectly. If the asset or liability has a specified (contractual) term, a Level 2 input must be observable for substantially the full term of the asset or liability. Level 2 inputs include the following:

(a) quoted prices for similar assets or liabilities in active markets.

(b) quoted prices for identical or similar assets or liabilities in markets that are not active.

(c) inputs other than quoted prices that are observable for the asset or liability, for example:

(i) interest rates and yield curves observable at commonly quote intervals;

(ii) implied volatilities; and

(iii) credit spreads.

(d) *market-corroborated inputs.*

Adjustments to Level 2 inputs will vary depending on factors specific to the asset or liability. Those factors include the following:

(a) the condition or location of the asset;

(b) the extent to which inputs relate to items that are comparable to the asset or liability (including those factors described in paragraph 39); and

(c) the volume or level of activity in the markets within which the inputs are observed.

(v) **Level 3**

Level 3 inputs are unobservable inputs for the asset or liability.

Unobservable inputs shall be used to measure fair value to the extent that relevant observable inputs are not available, thereby allowing for situations in which there is little, if any, market activity for the asset or liability at the measurement date.

However, the fair value measurement objective remains the same, i.e. an exit price at the measurement date from the perspective of a market participant that holds the asset or owes the liability. Therefore, unobservable inputs shall reflect the assumptions that market participants would use when pricing the asset or liability, including assumptions about risk.

## 1.36 HIERARCHY OF FINANCIAL STATEMENTS

Broad hierarchy under Financial Statements is shown in the charts below. This is developed at a conceptual level and does not necessarily follow the reporting requirements under Schedule III of Companies Act 2013 and nomenclature therein.

### 1.36.1 Equity and Liabilities

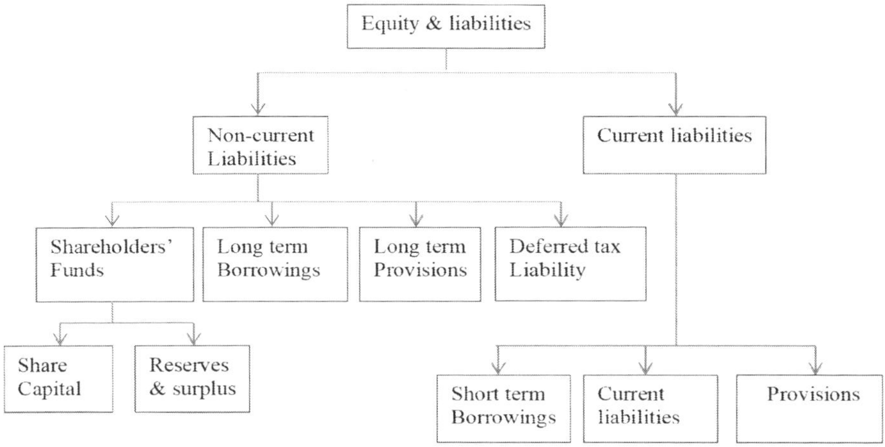


### 1.36.2 Assets

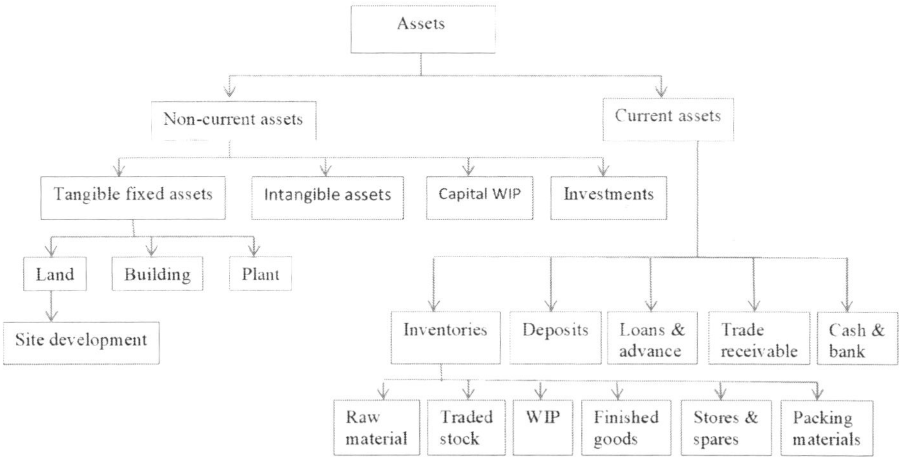

### 1.36.3 Income

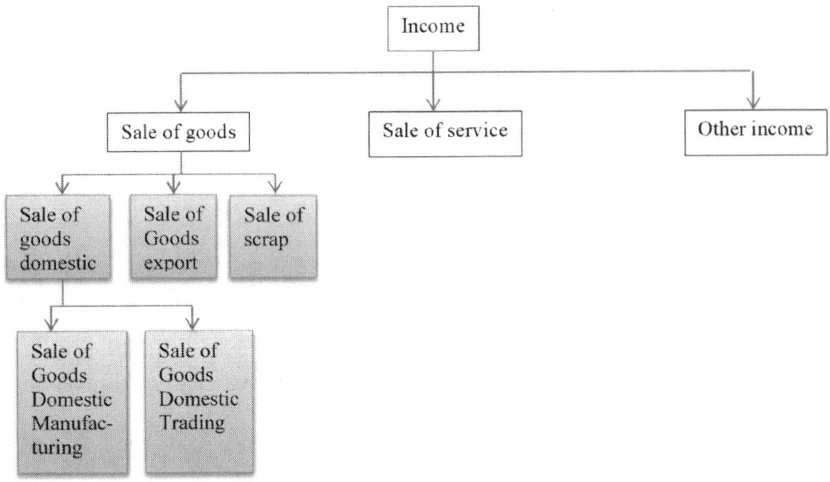


### 1.36.4 Expenses

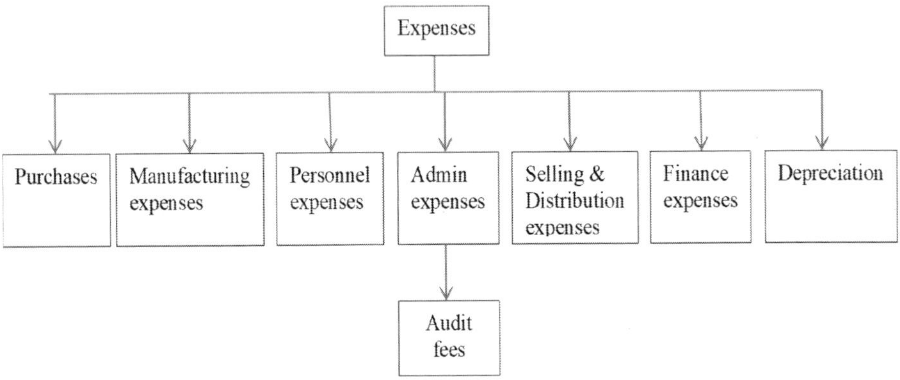

*Chapter 2*

# Classification of Current and Non-Current Assets and Liabilities

## 2.1 CLASSIFICATION OF ASSETS OF BETWEEN CURRENT AND NON-CURRENT

An asset should be classified as a current asset when it:

(a) it expects to realize the asset, or intends to sell or consume it, in its normal ***operating cycle,***

(b) it holds the asset primarily for trading,

(c) it expects to realize the asset within twelve months after the reporting period; or

(d) the asset is cash or a cash equivalent (as defined in Ind AS 7) unless the asset is restricted from being exchanged or used to settle a liability for at least twelve months after the reporting period.

An entity shall classify all other assets as non-current.

## 2.2 CLASSIFICATION OF LIABILITIES CLASSIFIED BETWEEN CURRENT AND NON-CURRENT

An entity shall classify a liability as current when:

(a) it expects to settle the liability in its normal ***operating cycle***;

(b) it holds the liability primarily for trading;

(c) the liability is due to be settled within twelve months after the reporting period; or

(d) it does not have an unconditional right to defer settlement of the liability for at least twelve months after the reporting period.

Terms of a liability that could, at the option of the counterparty, result in its settlement by the issue of equity instruments do not affect its classification.

An entity shall classify all other liabilities as non-current.

According to ICAI Guidance Note on Division I of Schedule III (Revised January, 2022 Edition), Schedule III defines "current assets" and "current liabilities", with the non-current category being the residual. It is therefore necessary that the balance pertaining to each item of assets and liabilities contained in the Balance Sheet be split into its current and non-current portions and be classified accordingly as on the reporting date.

## 2.3 OPERATING CYCLE

An operating cycle is the time between the acquisition of assets for processing and their realisation in cash or cash equivalents. Where the normal operating cycle cannot be identified. It is assumed to have a duration of 12 months.

In accordance with ICAI Guidance Note, where a company is engaged in running multiple businesses, the operating cycle could be different for each line of business. Such a company will have to classify all the assets and liabilities of the respective businesses into current and non-current, depending upon the operating cycles for the respective businesses.

A diagrammatic representation of typical Operating cycle would be as under:

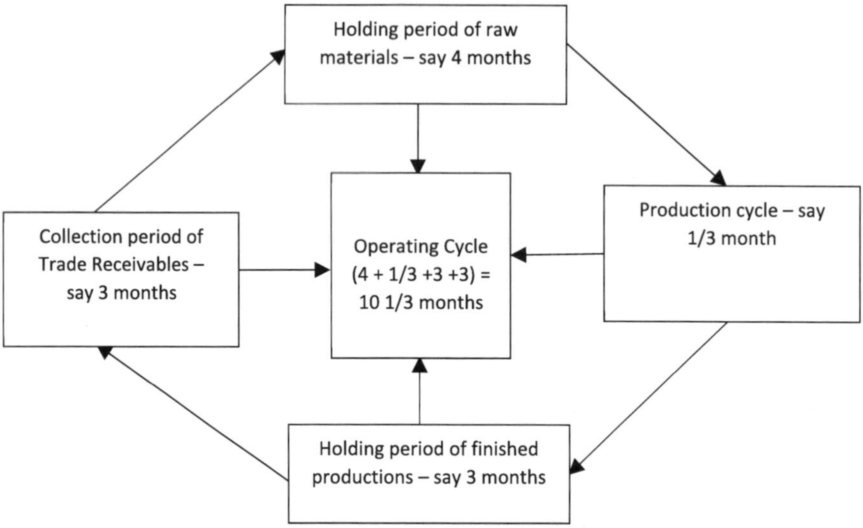


| Under AS | Under Ind AS |
|---|---|
| 2. An operating cycle is the time between the acquisition of assets for processing and their realisation in cash or cash equivalents. Where the normal operating cycle cannot be identified. It is assumed to have a duration of 12 months. | 2. The operating cycle of an entity is the time between the acquisition of assets for processing and their realisation in cash or cash equivalents. When the entity's normal operating cycle is not clearly identifiable, it is assumed to be twelve months. |

According to *ICAI Guidance Note on Division I and II: Schedule III*, current assets include assets such as raw material and stores which are intended for consumption or sale in the course of the company's normal operating cycle. Items of inventory, or trade receivables which may be consumed or realized within the company's normal operating cycle should be classified as current even if the same are not expected to be so consumed or realised within twelve months after the reporting date.

Current assets would also include assets held primarily for the purpose of being traded and the current portion of non-current financial assets.

Similarly, current liabilities would include items such as trade payables, employee salaries payable and other operating costs that are expected to be settled in the company's normal operating cycle or due to be settled within twelve months from the reporting date. Such operating liabilities are normally part of the working capital of the company used in the company's normal operating cycle and hence, should be classified as current even if they are due to be settled in more than twelve months after the end of the reporting date.

Further, unless the liability carries an unconditional right to defer its settlement beyond twelve months from the reporting date, it will be construed and classified as a current liability.

**Illustration 2.1**

A company has excesss finished goods inventory that it does not expect to realise within the company's operating cycle of fifteen months. Since such finished goods inventory is held primarily for the purpose of bcing traded, the same should be classified as "current".

**Illustration 2.2**

A company has sold 10,000 tonnes of steel to its customer. The sale contract provides for a normal credit period of three months. The company's operating cycle is six months. However, the company does not expect to receive payment within twelve months from the reporting date. Therefore, the same should be classified as "non-current" in the Balance Sheet. In case, however, if the company expects to realise the amount upto 12 months from the Balance Sheet date (though beyond the operating cycle), the same should be classified as "current".

**Illustration 2.3**

In manufacturing industries holding period of spares are not included in Operating Cycle. These inventory items are considered insurance spares and do not have regular consumption pattern.

**Illustration 2.4**

| In case of high seas sales, the operating cycle would start when the goods are delivered FOB on ships from port of embarkation till these are taken delivery, sold and converted to cash or cash equivalents in the receiving country |
|---|

**Illustration 2.5**

| A company engaged in milk and dairy manufacturing would have operating cycle starting from paying producer price to milk unions till the time the milk is processed and packed for delivery to end customers and customer pays for it. |
|---|

**Illustration 2.6**

| In case of software development companies building bespoke software systems, operating cycle starts from time spent on study of Functional Requirements Definition, system design, designing prototype and final delivery and billing to customers and when finally when the customers would pay on achieving the respective milestones. This would be in line with Percentage completion method in accordance with AS 7. |
|---|

## 2.4 HOW DO WE DISCLOSE AN OPERATING CYCLE

As a matter of best practice, a company may disclose the same, especially if the same is more than 12 months. This disclosure will be particularly helpful to the users of financial statements, where determination of the operating cycle involves significant judgment and it is more than 12 months.

## 2.5 SHOULD THE OPERATING CYCLE BE CALCULATED FOR EACH ITEM SEPARATELY, SAY FOR DEBTORS, INVENTORY OR FOR THE COMPANY AS A WHOLE?

Operating cycle should not be considered for each component separately but, at the same time, it may not be so for the company as a whole. It will have to be calculated for each business line separately.

## 2.6 IS THE OPERATING CYCLE TO BE CONSIDERED CUSTOMER WISE, ESPECIALLY WHERE A LARGE CUSTOMER IS PROVIDED A SIGNIFICANTLY DIFFERENT CREDIT PERIOD?

The Schedule III and the Guidance Note on the Revised Schedule VI contemplates the company to identify its operating cycle for each of its businesses and not based on each of its customers. Hence, the operating cycle must be defined in terms of each business.

### Illustration 2.7

**What will be the basis for determining the operating cycle, where say the private sector clients and government sector clients have a significantly different credit period? Can the operating cycle be determined on the basis of customer category?**

**Solution**

The Revised Schedule VI and the Guidance Note on the Revised Schedule VI contemplates that the company identify its operating cycle for each of its business and not based on each customer. Hence, the operating cycle must be defined in terms of each business and not customer category wise. The company needs to suitably determine the normal operating cycle for the business considering the significance of the different credit periods, among other matters.

### Illustration 2.8

**Is the lead-time for procuring raw material (time taken by the supplier from the order to delivery) included in the operating cycle?**

**Solution**

Operating cycle of a business should comprise the normal time required to complete its processes of (i) Acquiring raw material, (ii) Processing the same into finished goods, (iii) Making the sale, and (iv) Realising the sale proceeds in cash. Hence, in the given case, the normal lead -time to acquire raw material should be included in determining the operating cycle.

### Illustration 2.9

**Is the credit period allowed by supplier reduced when determining the operating cycle?**

**Solution**

In accordance with ICAI Guidance on Schedule III, operating cycle is the time between the acquisition of assets for processing and their realisation in cash or cash equivalents. This suggests that the operating cycle should comprise the normal time spent on various activities, starting from purchase of raw material till realisation of cash and there is no need to reduce the credit period allowed by supplier from the same.

Further, though the company has not paid for the raw material during the first six months, it might have started incurring expenses on other items such as labour and overhead costs.

Hence, the credit period allowed by the supplier need not be reduced when determining the operating cycle.

When the entity's normal operating cycle is not clearly identifiable, it is assumed to be twelve months.

**Illustration 2.10**

**A company has classified the loan as non-current liability in the previous year. The loan becomes a current liability in the current year's financial statements. Is the company required to reclassify the loan as current liability in previous year also to match the current year classification?**

**Solution**

Current/non -current classification of assets/liabilities is determined on a particular date, viz., the balance sheet date. Thus, the company should have determined the current/non-current classification of previous year balances based on the position existing as at the end of the previous year. If there is any change in the position at the end of current year resulting in different classification of assets/liabilities in the current year, it will not impact the classification made in the previous year. In other words, the company will continue to classify the loan as non -current liability in the figures of the previous period.

**Illustration 2.11**

**A company is preparing its financial statements in accordance with Schedule III for the first time. When identifying current/non -current assets /liabilities at the end of previous year, can a company apply hindsight based on the development that happened in the current year?**

**Solution**

Current/non -current classification of assets/liabilities is determined on a particular date, viz., the balance sheet date. If there is any new development in the current period, it should not impact the classification of assets and liabilities for the previous year. Hence, a company is not allowed to use hindsight in arriving at the current/non-current classification of assets or liabilities at the end of previous year.

However, in our view, it is important to distinguish from hindsight the facts existing at the previous balance sheet date. In certain cases, the events happening in the current period may not be new developments. Rather, they may merely be an additional evidence of conditions existing as at the previous year balance sheet.

Obviously, these events need to be incorporated in arriving at current/non –current classification of assets or liabilities at the end of previous year. In many cases, identification of the two events separately may not be straightforward and would require exercise of significant judgment.

**Illustration 2.12**

**How should "fixed assets held for sale" be classified in the balance sheet?**

**Solution**

They should be classified as a current asset since the intent of the company to sell is established.

**Illustration 2.13**

**How will a company classify its investment in preference shares, which are convertible into equity shares within one year from the balance sheet date? Will it classify the investment as a current asset or a non-current asset?**

**Solution**

In accordance with Schedule III, an investment realisable within 12 months from the reporting date is classified as a current asset. Such realisation should be in the form of cash or cash equivalents, rather than through conversion of one asset into another non-current asset. Hence, the company must classify such an investment as a non-current asset, unless it expects to sell the preference shares or the equity shares on conversion and realise cash within 12 month

**Illustration 2.14**

**Schedule III of the Companies Act 2013 requires that a company present trade receivables in the following format:**

| **Trade receivable** | |
|---|---|
| **Secured, considered good** | **XX,XXX** |
| **Unsecured, considered good** | **XX,XXX** |
| **Doubtful** | **X,XXX** |
| **Total** | **XX,XXX** |
| **Less: Provision for bad and doubtful debts** | **X,XXX** |
| **Trade receivables** | **XX,XXX** |

**A company needs to disclose trade receivables under "current" and "non - current" assets depending on Schedule III criteria. Should the company divide the "provision for bad and doubtful debts" also on the same basis?**

**Solution**

Yes, a company needs to disclose trade receivables under "current" and "non - current" assets depending on Schedule III criteria. The company also needs to divide the "provision for bad and doubtful debts" on the same basis.

**Illustration 2.15**

**How should a slow-moving stock of stores and spares be classified when it will neither be consumed within the normal operating cycle nor will be sold within 12 months from the balance sheet date?**

**Solution**

Inventory should always be categorised as a current asset even if the normal operating cycle extend beyond 12 months.

**Illustration 2.16**

**There is a breach of a major debt covenant as on the balance sheet date related to long-term borrowing. This allows the lender to demand immediate repayment of loan. However, the lender has not demanded repayment till authorisation of financial statements for issue. Can the company continue to classify the loan as non-current? Will the classification be different if the lender has waived the breach before authorisation of financial statements for issue?**

**Solution**

As per the ICAI Guidance Notes on Schedule III, a breach is considered to impact the non-current nature of the loan only if the loan has been irrevocably recalled. Hence, in the Indian context, long-term loans, which have a minor or major breach in terms, will be considered as current only if the loans have been irrevocably recalled before authorisation of the financial statements for issue.

## 2.7 COMPARATIVE POSITION ON CURRENT VS NON-CURRENT CLASSIFICATION

The table below explains the comparative provisions clearly.

| Schedule III of Companies Act 2013 | Ind AS 1: Disclosure of Accounting policies | AS 1: Disclosure of Accounting policies |
|---|---|---|
| In line with the disclosure requirements in IFRS between current and non-current classification. Schedule III under the Companies Act requires classification of assets and liabilities between current and non-current. | Para 60 of Ind AS 1 states that an entity shall present current and non-current assets, and current and non-current liabilities, as separate classifications in its balance sheet in accordance with paragraphs 66–76 except when a presentation based on liquidity provides information that is reliable and more relevant. When that exception applies, an entity shall present all assets and liabilities in order of liquidity.<br>Whichever method of presentation is adopted, an entity shall disclose the amount expected to be recovered or settled after more than twelve months for each asset and liability line item that combines amounts expected to be recovered or settled:<br>(a) no more than twelve months after the reporting period, and<br>(b) more than twelve months after the reporting period.<br>According to para 56, when an entity presents current and non-current assets, and current and non-current liabilities, as separate classifications in its balance sheet, it shall not classify deferred tax assets (liabilities) as current assets (liabilities). | No such provision has been stipulated in AS 1 |

## 2.8 TREATMENT ON CURRENT AND NON-CURRENT RELATED TO INVESTMENTS

The comparative position is explained as under:

| Schedule III of Companies Act 2013 | Ind AS 1 | AS 13: Securities |
|---|---|---|
| Schedule III of Companies Act, 2013 requires investments to be classified as current and non-current. | In accordance with Ind AS 1, distinction between current and non-current will hold good as well. | AS 13: Accounting for investments requires to classify investments as current and long-term. As per AS 13, current investment is an investment that is by its nature readily realisable and is intended to be held for not more than one year from the date on which such investment is made. A long term investment is an investment other than a current investment.<br>Accordingly, in accordance with AS 13: Accounting for investments, the assessment of whether an investment is "long term" has to be made with respect to the date of investment whereas, as per Schedule III, "Non-current" investment has to be determined with respect to the Balance Sheet date.<br>It is pertinent to note at this stage that though Schedule III clarifies that the Accounting Standards would take precedence over itself in case of any inconsistency between the two, AS 13 does not prescribe presentation norms, though it requires disclosures to be made for current and long-term investments.<br>Accordingly, presentation for all investments in the Balance Sheet should be made based on Current/Non-current classification as defined in the Schedule III. |

| Schedule III of Companies Act 2013 | Ind AS 1 | AS 13: Securities |
|---|---|---|
| | | The portion of long term investment as per AS 13 which is expected to be realised within 12 months from the Balance Sheet date needs to be shown as Current Investment under the Schedule III. |

## 2.9 TREATMENT OF DEFERRED TAX ON CURRENT/NON-CURRENT CLASSIFICATION

Comparative position is highlighted in the table below:

| Schedule III of Companies Act, 2013 | Ind AS 1 | AS 22 |
|---|---|---|
| In accordance with the classification in Schedule III and in line with the ICAI's earlier announcement with regard to the presentation and classification of net deferred tax asset or liability, the same should always be classified as "non-current". | According to para 56 of Ind AS 1, when an entity presents current and non-current assets, and current and non-current liabilities, as separate classifications in its balance sheet, it shall not classify deferred tax assets (liabilities) as current assets (liabilities). | According to AS 22, Deferred tax assets and liabilities should be distinguished from assets and liabilities representing current tax for the period.<br>Deferred tax assets and liabilities should be disclosed under a separate heading in the balance sheet of the enterprise, separately from current assets and current liabilities. However, it does not highlight bifurcation between current and non-current. |

**Illustration 2.17**

**What will be the scenario if a long-term loan has been classified as a nonperforming asset by the bank/financial institution? Can it still be classified as non-current?**

**Solution**

The situation in case of a loan being classified as a non-performing asset will also be the same as the case of a performing asset. The essential ingredient to impair the long-term nature of the loan would be irrevocable recall of the loan by the lender.

### Illustration 2.18

**How would a rollover/refinance arrangement entered for a loan, which was otherwise required to be repaid in six months, impact current/non-current classification of the loan? Consider three scenarios: (a) Rollover is with the same lender on the same terms, (b) Rollover is with the same lender but on substantially different terms, and (c) Rollover is with a different lender on similar/different terms.**

**Solution**

In general, the classification of the loan will be based on the tenure of the loan. Thus, in all the above cases, if the original term of the loan is short term, the loan would be treated as only current, irrespective of the rollover/refinance arrangement. However, in exceptional cases, there may be a need to apply significant judgment on substance over form. In such cases, categorisation could vary as appropriate.

### Illustration 2.19

**A company has taken a three-year loan specifically for a business whose operating cycle is four years. Hence, it needs to classify the three -year loan as current liability. This gives rise to the following issues:**

**(a) Should the loan be classified in the balance sheet under the head "long-term borrowing", "short-term borrowing" or "current maturities of long-term debt"?**

**(b) Does the company need to make all the disclosures required for long-term borrowings for this loan also?**

**Solution**

Any borrowing whose repayment falls within the operating cycle will be only a current liability. Hence, it will be included under short-term borrowings. Disclosures will also be required accordingly.

### Illustration 2.20

**Fixed deposits have a maturity of more than 12 months from the balance sheet date. Will they be classified as current or non-current?**

**Solution**

They will be classified as non-current.

## Illustration 2.21

**In case there is lien over FDs, thereby making it impossible to convert them into cash before the agreed period, how will the FDs be presented in the balance sheet? Moreover, will the interest accrued over such FDs be also classified as current and non-current?**

**Solution**

Such fixed deposits will be coterminous with the liability. Current or non-current distinction will be applied based on the expectation to be realised within 12 months after the reporting date. Interest accrued on such deposit will also be treated on the same basis.

## Illustration 2.22

**What would be treatment of settlement of a liability by issuing of equity in current/non-current classification?**

**Solution**

According to the Schedule III, the terms of a liability that could, at the option of the counterparty, result in its settlement by the issue of equity instruments do not affect its classification.

A consequence of this is that if the conversion option in convertible debt is exercisable by the holder at any time, the liability cannot be classified as "current" if the maturity for cash settlement is greater than one year. A question therefore arises as to how does the aforesaid requirement affect the classification of items for say,

(a) convertible debt where the conversion option lies with the issuer, or

(b) mandatorily convertible debt instrument

Based on the specific exemption granted only to those cases where the conversion option is with the counterparty, the same should not be extended to other cases where such option lies with the issuer or is a mandatorily convertible instrument. For all such cases, conversion of a liability into equity should be considered as a means of settlement of the liability as defined in the Framework for preparation and presentation of Financial Statements issued by ICAI.

Accordingly, the timing of such settlement would also decide the classification of such liability in terms of current or non-current as defined under Schedule III.

### Illustration 2.23

**The company has received security deposit from its customers/dealers. Either the company or the customer/dealer can terminate the agreement by giving two months' notice. The deposits are refundable within one month of termination. However, based on past experience, it is noted that deposits refunded in a year are not material, with 1% to 2% of the amount outstanding. The intention of the company is to continue long-term relationship with its customers /dealers. Can the company classify such security deposits as non-current liability?**

**Solution**

As per Schedule III, a liability is classified as current if the company does not have an unconditional right to defer its settlement for at least 12 months after the reporting date. This will apply generally. However, in specific cases, based on the commercial practice, say for example electricity deposit collected by the department, though stated on paper to be payable on demand, the company's records would show otherwise as these are generally not claimed in short term. Treating them as non-current may be appropriate and may have to be considered accordingly.

A similar criterion will apply to other deposits received, for example, under cancellable leases.

### Illustration 2.24

**The company has taken premises on operating leases for which it has paid a security deposit to the lessor. The lease term is five years. However, both parties can terminate the agreement after giving a three months' notice. The deposits are refundable immediately on termination of agreement. The intention of the company is to continue the lease agreement for 5 years. Further, the company has taken electricity connection for which it has paid security deposits. These deposits are repayable on demand on surrender of the electricity connection. Can the company classify these security deposits as current assets?**

**Solution**

Classification of deposits paid depends on the expectation of its realisation. Hence, a company will classify lease/electricity deposits given as a non-current asset, unless it expects to recover the same within 12 months after the reporting date, that is, by cancelling the lease contract or surrendering the electricity connection.

### Illustration 2.25

**For funded defined benefit plans, Guidance Note on Schedule III requires that amount due for payment to the fund within next 12 months be treated as current liability. Since a company will also recognise service cost in the next year, how should it determine the component of net deficit in the fund to be classified as current liability? For example, deficit is 500 and the LIC is expected to demand a pay-out of 300 in the next year. The expected cost for the next year is 200.**

**Solution**

Current/non-current classification will depend on the relevant provisions of the Contract Act and Arrangement with LIC. If the LIC demand is known, then that portion will be reflected as a current liability. If the actuarial valuation is higher, then the difference between the actuarial valuation and the LIC demand will be treated as a long term provision.

### Illustration 2.26

**In case of Provision for Gratuity and Leave Encashment, can current and noncurrent portions are bifurcated on the basis of Actuarial valuation?**

**Solution**

The actuary should be specifically requested to indicate the current and non-current portions, based on which the disclosure is to be made.

### Illustration 2.27

**Guidance Note on Division II – Ind AS - Schedule III requires deferred tax assets/liabilities to be classified as non-current. Does it imply that the provision for tax (net of advance tax)/advance tax (net of provision) also be classified as noncurrent?**

**Solution**

Current year tax provision (net of advance tax) will generally be treated as current liability, as this will become due in the short term. Current year advance tax (net of provision) as well as past year's advance tax (net of provision) shall generally be classified as non-current as these are not likely to arise in the short term. Advance tax against which refund orders have been passed, and if not adjusted towards other liabilities, will only be treated as a current asset.

### Illustration 2.28

**The Reserve Bank of India (RBI), vide its notification No. DNBS.223/CGM (US)-2011dated 17 January 2011, has issued directions to all NBFCs to make a provision of 0.25% on standard assets. The RBI requires this provision to be shown as a liability and not netted from loan balance. Will the NBFC have to split the provision into "current" and "non-current" portions?**

**Solution**

An NBFC creates provision on the standard assets at the rate prescribed by RBI. In accordance with Schedule III, it will classify these standard assets into current and non-current portions. Since the provision is closely linked to the underlying asset, we believe that an NBFC should split the standard asset provision also into current and noncurrent portions by using the same criterion.

### Illustration 2.29

**The issue is whether NCI (Minority Interest) must be broken up and classified as current and non-current. To the extent of the share of provision of dividend to subsidiary, should it be current?**

**Solution**

The non-controlling interest is not subject to current and non-current distinction as it forms a part of the shareholders' funds.

### Illustration 2.30

**Company X has taken a five year loan. The loan contains certain debt covenants, e.g., filing of quarterly information, failing which the bank can recall the loan and demand repayment thereof. The company has not filed such information in the last quarter; as a result of which the bank has the right to recall the loan. However, based on the past experience and/or based on the discussions with the bank the management believes that default is minor and the bank will not demand the repayment of loan. Will this be treated as Current Liability?**

**Solution**

According to the definition of Current Liability, what is important to note is, whether a borrower has an unconditional right at the Balance Sheet date to defer the settlement irrespective of the nature of default and whether or not a bank can exercise its right to recall the loan. If the borrower does not have such right, the classification would be "current."

Hence, considering that the practical implications of a minor breach are negligible in the Indian scenario, an entity could continue to classify the loan as "non-current" as on the Balance Sheet date since the loan is not actually demanded by the bank at any time prior to the date on which the Financial Statements are approved. However, in case a bank has recalled the loan before the date of approval of the financial statements on breach of a loan covenant that occurred before the year-end, the loan will have to be classified as current.

Above situation should not be confused with a loan which is repayable on demand from day one. For such loans, even if the lender does not demand repayment of the loan at any time, the same would have to be continued to be classified as "current".

*(Source: ICAI Guidance Note on Schedule III)*

# SECTION II

## Building Blocks of developing, presentation and interpretation

# *Chapter 3*

# Shareholders' funds

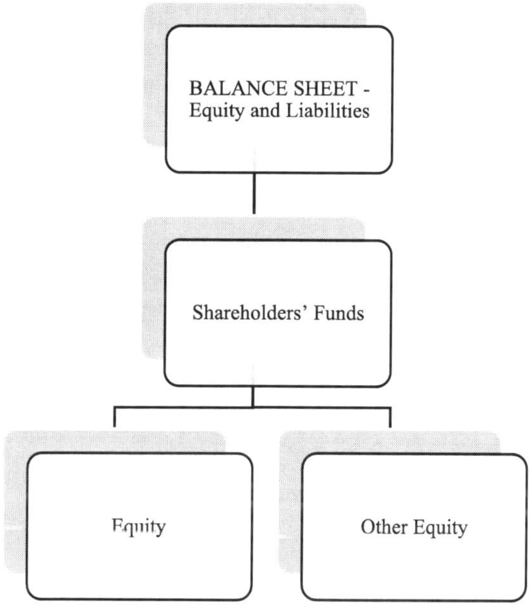


## 3.1 DEFINITION OF SHAREHOLDERS' FUNDS

Shareholders' Funds has been defined in ICAI Guidance Note on terms used in Financial Statements as:

"The excess of the book value of assets (other than fictitious assets) of an enterprise over its liabilities."

Shareholders' Equity has been defined as the interest of the shareholders in the net assets of a corporate enterprise. However, in the case of liquidation it is represented by the residual assets after meeting prior claims.

## 3.2 COMPONENTS OF SHAREHOLDERS' FUNDS

Comparative summary of Equity is shown in the table below.

| Under AS[1] | Under Ind AS[2] |
|---|---|
| **A. Share Capital**<br>For each class of share capital (different classes of preference shares to be treated separately) | **D. Equity**<br>**I. Equity Share Capital**<br>for each class of equity share capital: |
| (a) the number of amount of shares authorised | (a) the number and amount of shares authorised; |
| (b) the number of shares issued, subscribed and fully paid up and subscribed and not fully paid up | (b) the number of shares issued, subscribed and fully paid, and subscribed but not fully paid; |
| (c) par value of shares | (c) par value per share; |
| (d) a reconciliation of number of shares outstanding at the beginning and at the end of the reporting period | (d) a reconciliation of the number of shares outstanding at the beginning and at the end of the period; |
| (e) the rights, preferences and restrictions attaching to each class of shares including restrictions on the distribution of dividend and repayment of capital | (e) the rights, preferences and restrictions attaching to each class of shares including restrictions on the distribution of dividends and the repayment of capital; |
| (f) shares in respect of each class in the company held by its holding company or its ultimate holding company including shares held by or by subsidiaries or associates of the holding or its ultimate holding company in aggregate | (f) shares in respect of each class in the company held by its holding company or its ultimate holding company including shares held by or by subsidiaries or associates of the holding company or the ultimate holding company in aggregate; |
| (g) shares in the company held by each shareholder holding more than 5% shares specifying the number of shares held | (g) shares in the company held by each shareholder holding more than 5 percent shares specifying the number of shares held; |
| (h) shares reserved for issue under options and contracts/commitments for the sale of shares/disinvestment including terms and amounts | (h) shares reserved for issue under options and contracts/commitments for the sale of shares/disinvestment, including the terms and amounts; |
| (i) for the period of five years immediately preceding the date as at which the Balance Sheet is | (i) For the period of five years immediately preceding the date as at which the Balance Sheet is prepared: |

1 General Instructions for Preparation of Balance Sheet, Part I, Division I of Schedule III of the Companies Act, 2013.

2 General Instructions for Preparation of Balance Sheet, Part I of Division II of Schedule III of the Companies Act, 2013.

| Under AS[1] | Under Ind AS[2] |
|---|---|
| prepared :<br>– aggregate number and class of shares allotted as fully paid up pursuant to contracts without payment being received in cash<br>– aggregate number and class of shares allotted as fully paid up by way of bonus shares<br>– aggregate number and class of shares Bought back | • Aggregate number and class of shares allotted as fully paid up pursuant to contract(s) without payment being received in cash.<br>• Aggregate number and class of shares allotted as fully paid up by way of bonus shares.<br>• Aggregate number and class of shares bought back. |
| (j) Terms of any securities convertible into equity/preference shares issued with the earliest date of conversion in descending order starting from the farthest | (j) Terms of any securities convertible into equity shares issued along with the earliest date of conversion in descending order starting from the farthest such date. |
| (k) calls unpaid (showing aggregate value of calls unpaid by directors and officers ) | (k) Calls unpaid (showing aggregate value of calls unpaid by directors and officers) |
| (l) forfeited shares (amount originally paid up) | (l) Forfeited shares (amount originally paid up) |
| **B. Reserves and surplus**<br>(i) Reserves and Surplus shall be classified as:<br>(a) Capital reserve,<br>(b) Capital redemption reserve,<br>(c) Securities premium reserve,<br>(d) Debenture redemption reserve<br>(e) Revaluation Reserve;<br>(f) Share Options Outstanding Account ;<br>(g) Other Reserves – (specify the nature and purpose of each reserve and the amount in respect thereof)<br>(h) Surplus i.e. balance in Statement of Profit & Loss disclosing allocations and appropriations such as dividend, bonus shares and transfer to/from reserves etc. (Additions and deductions since last balance sheet to be | **II. Other Equity**<br>(i) 'Other Reserves' shall be classified in the notes as:<br>(a) Capital Redemption Reserve;<br>(b) Debenture Redemption Reserve;<br>(c) Share Options Outstanding Account;<br>(d) Others– (specify the nature and purpose of each reserve and the amount in respect thereof);<br>(Additions and deductions since last balance sheet to be shown under each of the specified heads)<br>(ii) Retained Earnings represents surplus i.e. balance of the relevant column in the Statement of Changes in Equity.<br>(iii) A reserve specifically represented by earmarked investments shall disclose the fact that it is so represented.<br>(iv) Debit balance of Statement of Profit and Loss shall be shown as a negative figure under the head 'retained earnings'. |

| Under AS[1] | Under Ind AS[2] |
|---|---|
| shown under each of the specific heads)<br>(ii) A reserve specifically represented by earmarked investments shall be termed as a "fund"<br>(iii) Debit balance of Statement of Profit and Loss shall be shown as a negative figure under the head "surplus". Similarly balance of "Reserves and surplus" after adjusting the negative balance of surplus. If any, shall be shown under the head "Reserves and surplus" even if the resulting figure is in the negative. | Similarly, the balance of 'Other Equity', after adjusting negative balance of retained earnings, if any, shall be shown under the head 'Other Equity' even if the resulting figure is in the negative.<br>(v) Under the sub-head 'Other Equity', disclosure shall be made for the nature and amount of each item. |

## 3.3 SHARE CAPITAL

### 3.3.1 Equity Share capital

For each class of equity share capital:

**(a) the number and amount of shares authorised;**

**(b) the number of shares issued, subscribed, and fully paid, and subscribed but not fully paid;**

According to ICAI Guidance Glossary of Terms Used in Financial Statements, the definitions related to Equity Share Capital are summarised as under:

| | |
|---|---|
| *Capital* | Under a financial concept of capital, such as invested money or invested purchasing power, capital is synonymous with the net assets or equity of the enterprise. Under a physical concept of capital, such as operating capability, capital is regarded as the productive capacity of the enterprise based on, for example, units of output per day. |
| *Share Capital* | Aggregate amount of money paid or credited as paid on the shares and/or stocks of a corporate enterprise. |
| *Authorised Share Capital* | The number and par value, of each class of shares that an enterprise may issue in accordance with its instrument of incorporation. This is sometimes referred to as nominal share capital. |
| *Subscribed Share Capital* | That portion of the issued share capital which has actually been subscribed and allotted. This includes any bonus shares issued to the shareholders. |

| *Paid-up Share Capital* | That part of the subscribed share capital for which consideration in cash or otherwise has been received. This includes bonus shares allotted by the corporate enterprise. |
|---|---|

Section 2(84) of the Indian Companies Act, 2013 defines "share" as "a share in the share capital of a company and includes stock".

Section 2(30) of the Act defines "debenture" to "include debenture stock, bonds or any other instrument of a company evidencing a debt, whether constituting a charge on the assets of the company or not".

Further, section 43 of the Act gives two kinds of share capital of a company limited by shares viz.,

(a) Equity share capital;

(b) Preference share capital

According to Ind AS 32, an equity instrument is "any contract that evidences a residual interest in the assets of an entity after deducting all of its liabilities. In respect of Equity Share Capital, it may be with voting rights or with differential voting rights as to dividend, voting or otherwise in accordance with such rules and subject to such conditions as may be prescribed under Companies (Share Capital and Debentures) Rules, 2014.

Accordingly, all instruments (including convertible preference shares and convertible debentures) that meet the definition of 'Equity' as per Ind AS 32 in its entirety and when they do not have any component of liability, should be considered as having the nature of 'Equity' for the purpose of Ind AS Schedule III. Such instruments shall be termed as 'Instruments entirely equity in nature as per ICAI Guidance Note on Division II – Ind AS Schedule III.

### 3.3.2 Whether Preference share capital would be classified as Share Capital

Pursuant to the ICAI Guidance Note on Terms Used in Financial Statements, the expression 'Preference Share Capital' means "that part of the share capital of a corporate enterprise which enjoys preferential rights in respect of payments of fixed dividend and repayment of capital. Preference shares may also have full or partial participating rights in surplus profits or surplus capital."

With respect to Preference Shares, the rights include

(a) with respect to dividend, a preferential right to be paid a fixed amount or at a fixed rate and,

(b) with respect to capital, a preferential right of repayment of amount of capital on winding up.

Disclosure requirements related to Share Capital, Schedule III of Companies Act prescribes that" different classes of preference share capital to be treated separately".

### 3.3.3 Treatment on presentation of uncalled share capital under Schedule III of the Companies Act, 2013

As per Schedule III, though there is no stipulation to disclose the amount per share called, if shares are not fully called, it would be appropriate to state the amount per share called.

In accordance with Old Schedule VI, debit balance on the allotment or call account is presented in the Balance Sheet not as an asset but by way of deduction from Called-up capital. However, as required by Clause (k) of Note 6A of the Schedule III, calls unpaid are to be disclosed separately as per the Schedule III of Companies Act 2013.

The unpaid amount towards shares subscribed by the subscribers of the Memorandum of Association should be considered as "subscribed and paid-up capital" in the Balance Sheet and the debts due from the subscriber should be appropriately disclosed as an asset in the Balance Sheet.

### 3.3.4 What are par value per share as highlighted under Share capital

Par value per share is the face value of a share as indicated in the capital clause of the Memorandum of Association of a company. It is also referred to as "face value" per share. In the case of a company having share capital, (unless the company is an unlimited company), the Memorandum shall also state the amount of share capital with which the company is registered and their division thereof into shares of fixed amount as required under clause (e) to the sub-section (1) of section 4 of the Companies Act, 2013. In the case of a company limited by guarantee, Memorandum shall state that each member undertakes to contribute to the assets of the company in the event of winding-up while he is a member or within one year after he ceases to be a member, for payment of debts and liabilities of the company, as the case may be.

There is no specific mention for the disclosure by companies limited by guarantee and having share capital, and companies limited by guarantee and not having share capital. Such companies need to consider the requirement so as to disclose the amount each member undertakes to contribute as per their Memorandum of Association.

This disclosure is recommended for instruments entirely equity in nature as well as for compound instruments that have an equity component, to the extent applicable. (*Source: ICAI Guidance Note Division II, Ind AS Schedule III*)

**Illustration 3.1: Specimen format of Share Capital**

| | As at 31st March 2021 | As at 31st March 2020 |
|---|---|---|
| Authorised Share Capital: | | |
| Equity shares of Rs. each | xxx | xxx |
| Preference shares of Rs. Each | xxx | xxx |
| Total | xxx | xxx |
| Issued, subscribed and paid-up: | | |
| Equity shares of Rs. each | xxx | xxx |
| Preference shares of Rs. Each | xxx | xxx |
| Less: Calls in arrears (Rs. (Previous Year Rs.)) | xxx | xxx |
| Total | xxx | xxx |

## 3.3.5 Reconciliation of the number of shares outstanding at the beginning and at the end of the reporting period

In accordance with Schedule III, opening number of shares outstanding, shares issued, shares bought back, other movements etc. during the year and closing number of outstanding shares should be shown. Though the requirement is only for a reconciliation of the number of shares, as given for the disclosure of issued, subscribed capital etc. (clause (b) of Note 6A) above, to make the disclosure relevant for understanding the company's share capital, the reconciliation is to be given even for the amount of share capital.

Reconciliation for the comparative previous period is also to be given. Further, the above reconciliation should be disclosed separately for both equity and preference shares and for each class of share capital within equity and preference shares.

With respect to Ind AS, the disclosure requirements are similar as mentioned above. According to ICAI Guidance Note, Division II, Ind AS, Schedule III, This disclosure is recommended for instruments entirely equity in nature. Also, for compound instruments having both equity and liability components, the reconciliation should be given for total number of shares/debentures outstanding, which will facilitate understanding the movement of compound instrument upon either redemption or conversion or when both occur partly.

**Illustration 3.2: Reconciliation of number of shares outstanding**

| Particulars | As at 31st March 2021 No. of shares | As at 31st March 2021 Amount (Rs) | As at 31st March 2020 No. of shares | As at 31st March 2020 Amount (Rs) |
|---|---|---|---|---|
| Equity shares at the beginning of the year | X | X | X | X |
| Add: Shares issued on exercise of employee stock Option | X | X | X | X |
| Less: Shares cancelled on buy back of equity Shares | X | X | X | X |
| Equity shares at the end of the year | X | X | X | X |

### 3.3.6 The rights, preferences and restrictions attaching to each class of shares including restrictions on the distribution of dividends and the repayment of capital

Preference Share Capital would mean, that part of the share capital of a corporate enterprise which enjoys preferential rights in respect of payments of fixed dividend and repayment of capital. Preference shares may also have full or partial participating rights in surplus profits or surplus capital. The rights, preferences and restrictions attached to shares are based on the classes of shares, terms of issue etc, whether equity or preference.

With respect to equity share capital, it may be with voting rights or with differential voting rights as to dividend, voting or otherwise in accordance with such rules and subject to such conditions as may be prescribed under Companies (Share Capital and Debentures) Rules, 2014.

As mentioned in 3.3.2. above, with respect to preference shares, the rights would include:

(a) with regard to dividend, a preferential right to be paid a fixed amount or at a fixed rate and

(b) with regard to capital, a preferential right of repayment of amount of capital on winding up.

Further, preference shares can be cumulative, non-cumulative, redeemable, convertible, non-convertible etc.

All such rights, preferences and restrictions attached to each class of preference shares, terms of redemption etc. have to be disclosed separately under Schedule III.

This disclosure is recommended for instruments entirely equity in nature as well as for compound instruments that have an equity component, to the extent applicable.

**Illustration 3.3: Disclosure of rights,preferences and restrictions to each class of shares**

**A company has a single class of equity shares. Is the company still required to disclose rights, restrictions and preferences with respect to the same?**

**Solution**

Schedule III requires disclosures of rights, preferences and restrictions attached to each class of shares. If a company has only one class of equity shares, it is still required to make this disclosure.

**Illustration 3.4: Disclosure for ADR/GDR issued**

**Is a company required to make this disclosure separately for the ADR/GDR issued?**

**Solution**

In case of ADR/GDR, a company typically issues its shares to a bank in a foreign country.

Against such shares, the foreign bank issues depository receipts to investors in the foreign country. Hence, from the perspective of the company, it has issued shares for which disclosure of rights, preferences, restrictions and so on are already disclosed. If there are any additional rights/restrictions attached to ADR/GDR, those rights and restrictions need to be disclosed. If there are no additional rights /restrictions attached to ADR/GDR, it will not be required to make a separate disclosure for rights, preferences and restrictions attached to the ADR/GDR. In any case, it will disclose the fact of ADR/GDR issued by way of an appropriate note.

### 3.3.7 Shares of each class in the company held by its holding company or its ultimate holding company including shares held by or by subsidiaries or associates of the holding company or the ultimate holding company in aggregate

According to ICAI Guidance Note on Division I of Schedule III, the requirement is to disclose shares of the company held by –

- Its holding company;
- Its ultimate holding company;
- Subsidiaries of its holding company;

- Subsidiaries of its ultimate holding company;
- Associates of its holding company; and
- Associates of its ultimate holding company.

Aggregation should be done for each of the above categories. The terms 'subsidiary', 'holding company' and 'associate' should be understood as defined under AS-21, Consolidated Financial Statements and Guidance Note on Division I – Non Ind AS Schedule III to the Companies Act, 2013 20 AS-18, Related Party Disclosures. Based on the above, shares held by the entire chain of subsidiaries and associates starting from the holding company and ending right up to the ultimate holding company would have to be disclosed. Further, all the above disclosures need to be made separately for each class of shares, both within Equity and Preference Shares.

With respect to Ind AS, the terms 'subsidiary' and 'associate' should be understood as defined under *Ind AS 110 : Consolidated Financial Statements, Ind AS 111 Joint Arrangements, Ind AS 28 Investments in Associates and Joint Ventures and Ind AS 24: Related Party Disclosures*. The term 'holding company' is not defined in Ind AS, therefore, it may be referred from the definition as per Section 2 (46) of the Act. However, the equivalent term 'parent' is defined in Ind AS 110. Based on the aforesaid definitions, for the purposes of the above disclosures, shares held by the entire chain of subsidiaries and associates starting from the holding company and going right up to the ultimate holding company would have to be disclosed.

In case of a joint arrangement viz., a joint venture or a joint operation conducted through a separate legal entity, disclosure may be made for shares of such joint arrangement held by its venturers.

This disclosure is recommended for instruments entirely equity in nature, to the extent applicable. (*Source: ICAI Guidance Note Division II, Ind AS Schedule III*).

### 3.3.8 Shares in the company held by each shareholder holding more than 5 percent shares specifying the number of shares held

With respect to the above disclosure, in the absence of any specific indication of the date of holding, the date of computing such percentage should be taken as the Balance Sheet date.

If during the year, any shareholder held more than 5% equity shares but does not hold as much at the Balance Sheet date, disclosure is not required.

Though it is not specified as to whether the disclosure is required for each class of shares or not, companies should disclose the shareholding for each class of shares within equity and preference shares.

Accordingly, such percentage should be computed separately for each class of shares outstanding with equity and preference shares. This disclosure would also be required for the comparative previous period as well.

This disclosure is recommended for instruments entirely equity in nature, to the extent applicable.

**Illustration 3.5: Specimen format of details of shareholders holding more than 5% shares**

| Name of the shareholder | As at 31st March 2021 No. of % Shares held | As at 31st March 2020 No. of % Shares held |
|---|---|---|
| Share holder A | x x | x x |
| Share holder B | x x | x x |
| Share holder C | x x | x x |

**Illustration 3.6: Disclosure based on legal or beneficial ownership**

**Is a company required to make disclosure regarding shareholders holding more than 5% shares based on legal or beneficial ownership? Can a company include information regarding beneficial ownership on a selective basis?**

**Solution**

Disclosure is to be on the basis of legal ownership, except where beneficial ownership is clearly available from the depositories. For instance, beneficial ownership of GDR/ADR may not be available.

### 3.3.9 Shares reserved for issue under options and contracts/commitments for the sale of shares/ disinvestment, including terms and amounts under Schedule III

Shares under options generally arise under promoters or collaboration agreements, loan agreements or debenture deeds (including convertible debentures), agreement to convert preference shares into equity shares, ESOPs or contracts for supply of capital goods etc. The disclosure would be required for the number of shares, amounts and other terms for shares so reserved. Such options are related to unissued portion of share capital.

With respect to Division II, Ind AS of Schedule III, this disclosure is recommended for instruments entirely equity in nature as well as for compound instruments that has an equity component and liability component, to the extent applicable.

### 3.3.10 Disclosure of allotment of shares

This would be for a period of five years immediately preceding the balance sheet date information such as, aggregate number and class of shares

(a) Allotted as fully paid up pursuant to contract(s) without payment being received in cash,

(b) Allotted as fully paid up by way of bonus shares, and

(c) Bought back.

According to sub-clause (i) of Schedule III Division I and II, the disclosure requirements are as under:

| | |
|---|---|
| ***(a) Aggregate number and class of shares allotted as fully paid up pursuant to contract(s) without payment being received in cash*** | The following allotments are considered as shares allotted for payment being received in cash and not as without payment being received in cash and accordingly, the same are not to be disclosed under this clause:<br>(a) if the subscription amount is adjusted against a bona fide debt payable in money at once by the company<br>(b) conversion of loan into shares in the event of default in repayment |
| ***(b) Aggregate number and class of shares allotted as fully paid up by way of bonus shares*** | According to Guidance Note on terms used in Financial Statements "bonus shares" are defined as shares allotted by capitalisation of the reserves or surplus of a corporate enterprise. The requirement of disclosing the source of bonus shares has been omitted in Schedule III. |
| ***(c) Aggregate number and class of shares bought back*** | The total number of shares bought back for each class of shares need to be disclosed. |

The disclosures as above would be necessary only if such event has occurred during a period of five years immediately preceding the Balance Sheet date.

Since disclosure is for the aggregate number of shares, it is not necessary to give the year-wise break-up of the shares allotted or bought back, but the aggregate number for the last five years needs to be disclosed.

This disclosure is recommended for instruments entirely equity in nature, to the extent applicable.

**Illustration 3.7: Disclosure requirements on allotment of shares**

**Schedule III requires that a company disclose for a period of five years immediately preceding the balance sheet date information such as, aggregate number and class of shares (a) Allotted as fully paid up pursuant to contract(s) without payment being received in cash, (b) Allotted as fully paid up by way of bonus shares, and (c) Bought back. In accordance with Guidance Note on Schedule III, a company is not required to give year-wise break-up of the shares allotted or bought back. Rather, the aggregate number for the last five financial years needs to be disclosed. Is a company required to give**

**comparative information for this disclosure? If yes, how will the comparative information be presented?**

**Solution**

Schedule III is clear that except for the first financial statements laid before a company (after its incorporation), it will disclose the corresponding (comparative) amounts for the immediately preceding reporting period for all items shown in the financial statements, including notes. The application of this principle requires the company to disclose corresponding figures for information related to shares allotted /bought back during the period of five years.

Typically, the comparative information disclosed in the current period financial statements is the figure disclosed in the previous period financial statements. Hence, the same information will be disclosed as the comparative number in the current period.

Thus, the current year figure will be for the current year and previous four years while the previous year figure will be for the previous five financial years.

### 3.3.11 Terms of any securities convertible into equity/preference shares issued along with the earliest date of conversion in descending order starting from the furthest such date

According to sub clause (j) above, this disclosure would cover securities such as Convertible Preference Shares, Convertible Debentures/Bonds etc.- optionally or otherwise into equity.

With respect to this clause, disclosure is required for any security, when it is either convertible into equity or preference shares. In such cases, terms of such securities and the earliest date of conversion, disclosure is to be made in the descending order of conversion. If the option can be exercised in different periods then earlier date in that period is to be considered.

In case of compulsorily convertible securities, where conversion is done in fixed tranches, all the dates of conversion have to be considered. Terms of convertible securities are required to be disclosed under this clause. However, in case of convertible debentures/bonds etc. for the purpose of simplification, reference may also be made to the terms disclosed under the note on long term borrowings where these are required to be classified in the Balance Sheet, rather than disclosing the same again under this clause.

With respect to Schedule III Division II related to Ind AS, in case of Convertible debentures/bonds, etc., reference may also be made to the terms disclosed under the note on non-current borrowings where these are required to be classified in the Balance Sheet, rather than disclosing the same again under this clause. This disclosure is recommended for instruments entirely equity in nature and compound instruments that have an equity component and a liability component. In other words, this disclosure is not required for instruments entirely liability in nature (for e.g., those instruments which entirely meet the definition of a financial liability as per para 11 of Ind AS 32) since similar disclosure needs to be provided as a part of 'Borrowings'.

(*Source: ICAI Guidance Note Division II Ind AS Schedule III*)

### 3.3.12 Calls unpaid (showing aggregate value of calls unpaid by directors and officers)

According to ICAI Guidance Note on Schedule III, a separate disclosure is required for the aggregate value of calls unpaid by directors and also officers of the company. However, the unpaid amount towards shares subscribed by the subscribers of the Memorandum of Association should be considered as 'subscribed and paid-up capital' in the Balance Sheet and the debts due from the subscriber should be appropriately disclosed as an asset in the balance sheet. This disclosure is recommended for instruments entirely equity in nature, to the extent applicable.

**Illustration 3.8: An example of disclosure of Share capital under Schedule III**

| | **As at 31st March 2021 (No of shares)** | **As at 31st March 2021 (Rs in crores)** | **As at 31st March 2020 (No of shares)** | **As at 31st March 2020 (Rs in crores)** |
|---|---|---|---|---|
| **Share capital** | | | | |
| **Authorised** | | | | |
| Ordinary Shares of Rs.1.00 each | 10,00,00,00,000 | 1000.00 | 10,00,00,00,000 | 1000.00 |
| **Issued and Subscribed** | | | | |
| Ordinary Shares of Rs 1.00 each, fully paid | 7,81,84,24,300 | 781.84 | 7,73,81,44,280 | 773.81 |
| **(A) Reconciliation of number of Ordinary Shares outstanding** | | | | |
| As at beginning of the year | 7,73,81,44,280 | 773.81 | 3,81,81,76,790 | 381.82 |
| Add: Issue of Bonus Shares | – | – | 3,82,67,01,530 | 382.67 |
| Add: Issue of Shares on exercise of Options | 8,02,80,020 | 8.03 | 9,32,65,960 | 9.32 |
| As at end of the year | 7,81,84,24,300 | 781.84 | 7,73,81,44,280 | 773.81 |

**(B) Shareholders holding more than 5% of the Ordinary Shares in the Company**

| | As at 31st March 2021 (No of shares) | As at 31st March 2021 % | As at 31st March 2020 (No of shares) | As at 31st March 2020 % |
|---|---|---|---|---|
| XYZ Manufacturers (India) Limited | 1,98,55,64,880 | 25.39 | 1,98,55,64,880 | 25.66 |
| Life Insurance Corporation of India | 93,87,40,442 | 12.01 | 1,00,01,60,528 | 12.92 |
| Specified Undertaking of the Unit Trust of India | 89,67,22,590 | 11.47 | 89,67,21,090 | 11.59 |

**(C) Ordinary Shares allotted as fully paid-up Bonus Shares for the period of five years immediately preceding 31st March**

| | 2021 (No of shares) | 2020 (No of shares) |
|---|---|---|
| Bonus Shares issued in 2020-21 | 3,82,67,01,530 | 3,82,67,01,530 |

**(D) Rights, preferences and restrictions attached to the Ordinary Shares**

The Ordinary Shares of the Company, having par value of Rs. 1.00 per share, rank *pari-passu* in all respects including voting

Rights and entitlement to dividend.

**(E) Shares reserved for issue under Options**

| | As at 31st March 2021 (No of shares) | As at 31st March 2020 (No of shares) |
|---|---|---|
| Ordinary Shares of Rs. 1.00 each | 27,20,11,920 | 29,76,07,800 |

**Terms and Conditions of Options Granted**

Each Option entitles the holder thereof to apply for and be allotted ten Ordinary Shares of the Company of Rs.1.00 each upon payment of the exercise price during the exercise period. The exercise period commences from the date of vesting of the Options and expires at the end of five years from (i) the date of grant in respect of Options granted under the XYZ Employee Stock Option Scheme (introduced in 2001) and (ii) the date of vesting in respect of Options granted under the XYZ Employee Stock Option Scheme -2006 & the XYZ Employee Stock Option Scheme -2020

The vesting period for conversion of Options is as follows:

On completion of 12 months from the date of grant of the Options: 30% vests

On completion of 24 months from the date of grant of the Options: 30% vests

On completion of 36 months from the date of grant of the Options: 40% vests

The Options have been granted at the 'market price' as defined from time to time under the Securities and Exchange Board of India (Employee Stock Option Scheme and Employee Stock Purchase Scheme) Guidelines, 1999.

### 3.3.13 Forfeited shares

This represents forfeiture of shares of amount originally paid up.

### 3.3.14 Shareholding of promoters

Shareholding of promoters need to be disclosed in the lines of the format highlighted below.

| Shares held by promoters at the end of the year | | | | % Change during the year*** |
|---|---|---|---|---|
| S. No. | Promoter name | No of shares ** | % of total shares | |
| | | | | |

* Promoter here means promoter as defined in the Companies Act, 2013.

** Details shall be given separately for each class of shares

*** Percentage change shall be computed with respect to the number at the beginning of the year or if issued during the year for the first time then with respect to the date of issue.

According to ICAI Guidance Note on Schedule III, the definition of promoter should be considered as per the Companies Act, 2013. The prescribed format shown above requires disclosure only in respect of shares held at the end of the year, however, companies should also disclose number and percentage of shares at the beginning of the year as additional columns in order to facilitate an understanding of the percentage change during the year since percentage change during the year needs to be computed with respect to shares held at the beginning of the year.

Where shares have been issued for the first time during the reporting period, such percentage change needs to be computed from date of such issuance.

## 3.4 RESERVES AND SURPLUS

In accordance with Schedule III, Division I related to non Ind AS entities, Reserves and Surplus shall be classified as:

(*a*) Capital reserve,

(*b*) Capital redemption reserve,

(*c*) Securities premium,

(*d*) Debenture redemption reserve,

(*e*) Revaluation Reserve,

(*f*) Share Options Outstanding Account,

(*g*) Other Reserves – (specify the nature and purpose of each reserve and the amount in respect thereof) (*h*) Surplus i.e. balance in Statement of Profit & Loss disclosing allocations and appropriations such as dividend, bonus shares and transfer to/from reserves etc.

(Additions and deductions since last balance sheet to be shown under each of the specific heads)

(*ii*) A reserve specifically represented by earmarked investments shall be termed as a "fund"

(*iii*) Debit balance of Statement of Profit and Loss shall be shown as a negative figure under the head "surplus". Similarly balance of "Reserves and surplus" after adjusting the negative balance of surplus. If any, shall be shown under the head "Reserves and surplus" even if the resulting figure is in the negative.

## 3.5 OTHER EQUITY

According to Schedule III, Division II with respect to Ind AS entities, Schedule III, Part I – Format of Balance Sheet includes along with the format of Balance Sheet comprising (A) Equity Share Capital and (B) Other Equity.
The section under Other Equity would include the following:

(i) 'Other Reserves' shall be classified in the notes as:

(a) Capital Redemption Reserve;

(b) Debenture Redemption Reserve;

(c) Share Options Outstanding Account;

(d) Others– (specify the nature and purpose of each reserve and the amount in respect thereof);

(Additions and deductions since last balance sheet to be shown under each of the specified heads)

(ii) Retained Earnings represents surplus i.e. balance of the relevant column in the Statement of Changes in Equity.

(iii) A reserve specifically represented by earmarked investments shall disclose the fact that it is so represented.

(iv) Debit balance of Statement of Profit and Loss shall be shown as a negative figure under the head 'retained earnings'. Similarly, the balance of 'Other Equity', after adjusting negative balance of retained earnings, if any, shall be shown under the head 'Other Equity' even if the resulting figure is in the negative.

(v) Under the sub-head 'Other Equity', disclosure shall be made for the nature and amount of each item.

## 3.6 STATEMENT OF CHANGES IN EQUITY

In the ***Statement of Changes in Equity***, the portion for 'Equity Share Capital' provides reconciliation for current/previous reporting periods:

| | |
|---|---|
| (a) | Balance at the beginning of the current/previous reporting period; |
| (b) | Changes in Equity Share Capital due to prior period errors; |
| (c) | Restated balance at the beginning of the current/previous reporting period |
| (d) | Changes in equity share capital during the current/previous year; |
| (e) | Balance at the end of the current/previous reporting period |

According to ICAI Guidance Note on Schedule III, Division II, as a part of Statement of Changes in Equity, the portion for 'Other Equity' requires an entity to provide a reconciliation during a particular reporting period, as a part of one single statement, of all items other than equity share capital, that are attributable to the holders of equity instruments of an entity.

The items included in columnar form are listed as under:

(a) Share application money pending allotment;

(b) Equity component of compound financial instruments;

(c) Reserves and Surplus:

- (i) Capital Reserve;
- (ii) Securities Premium;
- (iii) Other Reserves (specify nature);
- (iv) Retained Earnings;

(d) Debt instruments at fair value through other comprehensive income;

(e) Equity instruments at fair value through other comprehensive income;

(f) Effective portion of Cash Flow Hedges;

(g) Revaluation Surplus;

(h) Exchange differences on translating the financial statements of a foreign operation;

(i) Other items of other comprehensive income (specify nature);

(j) Money received against share warrants;

(k) Non-controlling interests (for Statement of Changes in Equity of Consolidated Financial Statements.

### 3.6.1 Reconciliation of Statement of changes in Equity

| | |
|---|---|
| *The reconciliation for current/previous reporting period by way of the* | (i) Balance at the beginning of the current/previous reporting period;<br>(ii) Changes in accounting policy or prior period errors;<br>(iii) Restated balance at the beginning of the current/previous reporting period; |

| | |
|---|---|
| *following line items:* | (iv) Total comprehensive income for the current/previous year;<br>(v) Dividends;<br>(vi) Transfer to retained earnings;<br>(vii) Any other change (to be specified);<br>(viii) Balance at the end of the current/previous reporting period. |

### 3.6.2 Restatement owing to prior period error

With respect to restatement owing to prior period error the 'balance at the beginning of the current reporting period/previous reporting period' in the statement of changes in equity shall include:

- The balances as originally presented in the previous years' financial statements.
- The adjustments on account of correction of prior period errors in the 'changes due to prior period errors'
- to arrive at restated balance at the beginning of respective period.

### 3.6.3 Presentation of remeasurement of defined benefit plans and fair value changes

Schedule III Division II provides two options for presentation of remeasurement of defined benefit plans and fair value changes relating to own credit risk of financial liabilities designated at fair value through profit or loss. These are highlighted as under:

(i) recognise as a part of retained earnings with separate disclosure of such items along with the relevant amounts in the Notes,

(ii) shown as a separate column under Reserves and Surplus,

The above two items are initially taken to Other Comprehensive Income in the Statement of Profit and Loss.

Prescribed format of Statement of Changes in Equity is shown in 1.21 of Chapter 1.

## 3.7 RESERVES

Reserves shall be classified in the notes as:

According to Guidance Note from ICAI on terms used in financial statements defines the term "Reserve" as the portion of earnings, receipts or other surplus of an enterprise (whether capital or revenue) appropriated by the management for a general or a specific purpose other than a provision for depreciation of diminution in the value of assets or for a known liability.

### 3.7.1 Capital Redemption Reserve

Under the Companies Act 2013, Capital Redemption Reserve is required to be created in the followings situations:

(a) Under the provisions of section 55 of the Act, where the redemption of preference shares is out of profits, an amount equal to nominal value of shares redeemed is to be transferred to a reserve called capital redemption reserve

(b) Under section 69 of the Act, if the buy-back of shares is out of the free reserves, the nominal value of the shares so purchased is required to be transferred to capital redemption reserve from distributable profit.

In relevant cases this should be disclosed separately under Reserves and Surplus as per Schedule III.

### 3.7.2 Debenture Redemption Reserve

Where a company issues debenture after the commencement of the Act, it is required to create a debenture redemption reserve for the redemption of such debentures. The company is required to credit adequate amounts, from out of its profits every year to debenture redemption reserve, until such debentures are redeemed.

On redemption of the debentures for which the reserve is created, the amounts no longer necessary to be retained in this account need to be transferred to the General Reserve.

In relevant cases this should be disclosed separately under Reserves and Surplus as per Schedule III.

### 3.7.3 Share Options Outstanding Account

**Ind AS 102: Share based payments**

An entity shall apply this Standard in accounting for all share-based payment transactions, whether or not the entity can identify specifically some or all of the goods or services received, including

(a) equity settled share-based payment transactions

(b) cash settled share-based payment transactions and

(c) transactions in which the entity receives or acquires goods or services and the terms of the arrangement provide either the entity or the supplier of those goods or services with a choice of whether the entity settles the transaction in cash (or other assets) or by issuing equity instruments.

## Recognition

An entity shall recognise the goods or services received or acquired in a share-based payment transaction when it obtains the goods or as the services are received. The entity shall recognise a corresponding increase in equity if the goods or services were received in an equity-settled share-based payment transaction, or a liability if the goods or services were acquired in a cash-settled share-based payment transaction.

When the goods or services received or acquired in a share-based payment transaction do not qualify for recognition as assets, they shall be recognised as expenses.

## Equity-settled share-based payment transaction

For equity-settled share-based payment transactions, the entity shall measure the goods or services received, and the corresponding increase in equity, directly, at the fair value of the goods or services received, unless that fair value cannot be estimated reliably. If the entity cannot estimate reliably the fair value of the goods or services received, the entity shall measure their value, and the corresponding increase in equity, indirectly, by reference to the fair value of the equity instruments granted.

With respect to transactions with *employees and others providing similar services*, the entity shall measure the fair value of the services received by reference to the fair value of the equity instruments granted, because typically it is not possible to estimate reliably the fair value of the services received. The fair value of those equity instruments shall be measured at *grant date.*

Typically, shares, share options or other equity instruments are granted to employees as part of their remuneration package, in addition to a cash salary and other employment benefits. Usually, it is not possible to measure directly the services received for particular components of the employee's remuneration package. It might also not be possible to measure the fair value of the total remuneration package independently, without measuring directly the fair value of the equity instruments granted.

Furthermore, shares or share options are sometimes granted as part of a bonus arrangement, rather than as a part of basic remuneration, e.g. as an incentive to the employees to remain in the entity's employment or to reward them for their efforts in improving the entity's performance. By granting shares or share options, in addition to other remuneration, the entity is paying additional remuneration to obtain additional benefits. Estimating the fair value of those additional benefits is likely to be difficult. Because of the difficulty of measuring directly the fair value of the services received, the entity shall measure the fair value of the employee services received by reference to the fair value of the equity instruments granted.

**Cash-settled share-based payment transactions**

For cash-settled share-based payment transactions, the entity shall measure the goods or services acquired and the liability incurred at the fair value of the liability. Until the liability is settled, the entity shall re-measure the fair value of the liability at the end of each reporting period and at the date of settlement, with any changes in fair value recognised in profit or loss for the period.

The entity should recognise an asset or an expense and a liability if the goods and services were received in a cash-settled share-based payment transaction until the ability is settled the entity should re-measure the fair value of the liability at each reporting date and the date of settlement, with any changes in fair value recognised in profit or loss for the period.

**Share-based payment transactions with cash alternatives**

For share-based payment transactions in which the terms of the arrangement provide either the entity or the counterparty with the choice of whether the entity settles the transaction in cash (or other assets) or by issuing equity instruments, the entity shall account for that transaction, or the components of that transaction, as a cash settled share-based payment transaction if, and to the extent that, the entity has incurred a liability to settle in cash or other assets, or as an equity-settled share-based payment transaction if, and to the extent that, no such liability has been incurred.

For share based payment transactions in which the terms of the arrangement provide either the entity or the counterparty with the choice of whether the entity settles the transaction in cash or by issuing equity instruments, the entity should account that transaction as **a cash-settled share-based payment transaction**, if the entity has incurred liability to settle in cash or other assets. If no such liability is incurred, it should be **equity-settled share-based payment transaction.**

**Share-based payment transactions among group entities**

(a) For share-based payment transactions among group entities, in its separate or individual financial statements, the entity receiving the goods or services shall measure the goods or services received as either an equity-settled or a cash-settled share-based payment transaction by assessing:

    (a) the nature of the awards granted, and

    (b) its own rights and obligations.

    The amount recognised by the entity receiving the goods or services may differ from the amount recognised by the consolidated group or by another group entity settling the share-based payment transaction.

(b) The entity receiving the goods or services shall measure the goods or services received as an equity-settled share-based payment transaction when:

    (a) the awards granted are its own equity instruments, or

(b) the entity has no obligation to settle the share-based payment transaction.

The entity shall subsequently re-measure such an equity-settled share-based payment transaction only for changes in non-market vesting conditions in accordance with the Standard. In all other circumstances, the entity receiving the goods or services shall measure the goods or services received as a cash-settled share-based payment transaction.

(c) The entity settling a share-based payment transaction when another entity in the group receives the goods or services shall recognise the transaction as an equity-settled share-based payment transaction only if it is settled in the entity's own equity instruments. Otherwise, the transaction shall be recognised as a cash-settled share-based payment transaction.

(d) Some group transactions involve repayment arrangements that require one group entity to pay another group entity for the provision of the share-based payments to the suppliers of goods or services. In such cases, the entity that receives the goods or services shall account for the share-based payment transaction in accordance with paragraph 43B regardless of intragroup repayment arrangements.

**Accounting for Share-based payment transactions**

(a) Journal entry for cash settled transactions:

| | | | |
|---|---|---|---|
| Dr. | Expenses/Asset | x | |
| | Cr. | Asset/Liability | x |

---

(b) Journal entry for equity settled transactions

| | | | |
|---|---|---|---|
| Dr. | Expenses/Asset | x | |
| | Cr. | Equity | x |

Equity settled share-based payments – measured at fair value at grant date

**Illustration 3.9: Cash-settled share-based payments**

J Ltd grants 50 share appreciation rights to each of its 100 employees to be settled in cash on the condition that the employees will remain in employment for the next three years.

Required:

Does the transaction qualify as a cash-settled share-based payment transaction?

**Solution:**

Here the transaction involves exchange of "services" and the amount of consideration is based on the value of the shares of J Ltd. Hence, this qualifies as a cash-settled share-based payment transaction.

**Illustration 3.10: Equity-settled share-based payments**

XYZ ltd offers 200 shares to each of its 1000 staff if they stay for 3 years.

FV of the option at grant date is Rs. 30. At the end of the 1st year 15 employees leave and the entity estimates 25% will have left at the end of the vesting period. During the 2nd year a further 15 employees leave and the entity revises its estimate of total departures over the vesting period from 25% to 27%. During the 3rd year a further 15 employees leave.

Required:

Calculate the amounts are to be recognised in the financial statements.

**Solution**

**Step I : Fair value on grant date :**

= 200 X 1000 X Rs.30 = Rs.60,00,000

**Step II : Cumulative charge to statement of comprehensive income**

Year I : 200 shares x Rs.30 x (1000x75%) x 1/3 = Rs.15,00,000

Year II: 200 shares x Rs.30 x (1000x73%) x 2/3 = Rs. 29,20,000

Year III: 200 shares x Rs.30 x 955 x 3/3 = Rs. 57,30,000 **(W1)**

**Step III: Expenses for the vesting period**

Year I : Rs.15,00,000 - 0 = Rs. 15,00,000

Year II: Rs.29,20,000 – Rs. 15,00,000 = Rs. 14,20,000

Year III: Rs. 57,30,000 – Rs.29,20,000 = Rs. 28,10,000

**W1** = Total employees in the beginning – total employees left during 3 years

= 1000 – (15 (yr-1) + 15 (yr-2) +15 (yr-3))

= 955

### 3.7.4 Others (specify the nature and purpose of each reserve and the amount in respect thereof)

Additions and deductions since last balance sheet to be shown under each of the specified heads.

### 3.7.5 Capital Reserve

The term Capital reserve has not been defined under Schedule III. However, under Guidance Note on Terms Used in Financial Statements, the expression capital reserve is defined as a "reserve of a corporate enterprise which is not available for distribution as dividend". Though Schedule III does not have the requirement of transferring capital profit on reissue of forfeited shares to capital reserve, since profit on reissue of forfeited shares is basically profit of a capital nature, hence it should be credited to Capital reserve. This is to be disclosed separately under Reserve and Surplus as per Schedule III.

### 3.7.6 Securities Premium Reserve

According to the Guidance Note of ICAI on Terms Used in Financial Statements, Share Premium is the "excess of the issue price of shares over their face value". Though the terminology used in the Schedule III is " Securities Premium Reserve", the nomenclature used in the Act as "Securities Premium Account" is to be synonymously used.

In relevant cases, this should be disclosed separately under Reserves and Surplus as per Schedule III.

### 3.7.7 Gain/Loss on changes in the proportion held by non-controlling interests

Paragraph B96 of Ind AS 110, stipulates that an entity shall recognize directly in 'Equity' any difference between the amount by which the non-controlling interests are adjusted and the fair value of the consideration paid or received, and attribute it to the owners of the parent.

It is pertinent to note that paragraph 106(d)(iii) of Ind AS 1, prescribes for each component of equity, a reconciliation between the carrying amount at the beginning and the end of the period, separately disclosing changes resulting from changes in ownership interests in subsidiaries that do not result in a loss of control.

For such difference, which is the gain/loss on changes in the proportion held by non-controlling interests, Ind AS does not specify whether such gain/loss should be presented separately under 'Capital Reserve' or under 'Other Reserves'.

Ind AS Schedule III also does not specify anything in this regard. Hence according to ICAI Guidance Note, an entity may present such gain/loss separately as 'Gain/Loss on change in proportion held by non-controlling interests' shown under 'Other Reserves' by specifying the nature of such gain/loss.

### 3.7.8 Retained earnings

Retained Earnings represents surplus i.e. balance of the relevant column in the Statement of Changes in Equity.

Appropriations to the profit for the year (including carried forward balance) is to be presented under the main head "Reserves and surplus". Unlike the current prevalent practice, under Schedule III, the Statement of Profit and Loss will no longer reflect any appropriations like dividends transferred to reserves, bonus shares etc.

### 3.7.9 Reserve earmarked by investments

A reserve specifically represented by earmarked investments shall disclose the fact that it is so represented.

### 3.7.10 Debit balance of Statement of Profit and Loss

Debit balance of Statement of Profit and Loss shall be shown as a negative figure under the head 'retained earnings'. Similarly, the balance of 'Other Equity', after adjusting negative balance of retained earnings, if any, shall be shown under the head 'Other Equity' even if the resulting figure is in the negative.

### 3.7.11 Share application money pending allotment

Share Application money pending allotment is to be disclosed as a separate line item under Other Equity. Note 8 of General Instructions for Preparation of Balance Sheet states that share application money pending allotment shall be classified into equity or liability in accordance with relevant Ind AS. Share application money to the extent not refundable shall be shown in this line item.

Share application money to the extent refundable shall be separately shown under 'other financial liabilities'

### 3.7.12 Equity component of compound financial instruments

Pursuant to *Ind AS 32*, equity component is required to be presented as a part of 'Other Equity' under this head. On the other hand, the 'liability component of compound financial instrument' is required to be presented as a part of 'Borrowings'.

### 3.7.13 Debt instruments through other comprehensive income

According to *Ind AS 109*, investments are subsequently measured at FVOCI based on the company's business model for managing the portfolio of debt instruments as well as the debt instruments' contractual cash flow characteristics. Any fair value gain or loss on debt instruments measured at FVOCI is presented as a part of Other Equity under this heading until the debt instrument is derecognised.

### 3.7.14 Equity instruments through other comprehensive income

Pursuant to *Ind AS 109*, companies have an option to designate investments in equity instruments to be measured at FVOCI. For such instruments, the cumulative fair value gain or loss is presented as a part of Other Equity under this heading.

### *3.7.15* Effective portion of Cash Flow Hedges

With respect to cash flow hedges, this component of Other Equity associated with the hedged item (i.e. cash flow hedge reserve) is adjusted to the lower of the cumulative change in the fair value of the hedging instrument and the cumulative change in the fair value of the hedged item attributable to the hedged risk.

The portion of the gain or loss on the hedging instrument that is determined to be an effective hedge (i.e. the portion that is offset by the change in the cash flow hedge reserve) is recognised in Other Comprehensive Income.

Also, *Ind AS 109* requires that exchange differences on monetary items that qualify as hedging instruments in a cash flow hedge are recognised initially in other comprehensive income to the extent that the hedge is effective.

### 3.7.16 Revaluation surplus

In accordance with *Ind AS 16, Property, Plant and Equipment* if an asset's carrying value is increased as a result of revaluation, such increase shall be recognised in other comprehensive income and accumulated in equity under the heading of revaluation surplus. However, such increase shall be recognised in profit or loss to the extent that it reverses a revaluation decrease of the same asset previously recognized in profit or loss.

### 3.7.17 Exchange differences on translating the Financial Statements of a foreign operation

Pursuant to *Ind AS 21 The Effects of Changes in Foreign Exchange Rates*, the exchange differences arising on translation of the financial statements of foreign operation from functional currency to presentation currency needs to be included in this head of Other Comprehensive Income.

### 3.7.18 Other items of Other Comprehensive Income (specific nature)

Any other items that need to be presented in Other Comprehensive Income as per the relevant Ind AS shall be included under this head of OCI. Example - presentation of remeasurement of defined benefit plans under *Ind AS 19.*

### 3.7.19 Money received under Share Warrants

Ind AS 33 Earnings per Share defines 'warrants' as "financial instruments which give the holder the right to acquire equity shares". Generally, in case of listed companies, share warrants are issued to promoters and others in terms of the Guidelines for preferential issues viz., SEBI (Issue of Capital and Disclosure Requirements), Guidelines, 2009.

Since shares are yet to be allotted against the same, these are not reflected as part of Share Capital but as a separate line item – 'Money received against share warrants

(*Source: ICAI Guidance Note Division II Ind AS Schedule III*)

**Illustration 3.11: Other Equity: Specimen format**

| | As at 31st March 2022 | As at 31st March 2021 |
|---|---|---|
| **Capital Redemption Reserve** | | |
| As per last Balance Sheet | xxx | xxx |
| Add: Transferred from Profit & Loss Account on buy back of equity shares | xxx | xxx |
| Sub-total | xxx | xxx |
| **Debenture redemption reserve** | | |
| As per last Balance Sheet | xxx | xxx |
| Sub-total | xxx | xxx |
| **Revaluation Reserve** | | |
| As per last Balance Sheet | xxx | xxx |
| Less: Transferred to Profit and Loss Account | (xxx) | (xxx) |
| Less: Utilised on demerger adjustments | (xxx) | (xxx) |
| Sub-total | xxx | xxx |
| **Capital Reserve** | | |
| As per last Balance Sheet | xxx | xxx |
| Sub-total | xxx | xxx |
| **Share Application money pending allotment** | | |
| As per last Balance Sheet | xxx | xxx |
| Add: Issue of Share/Application money received | xxx | xxx |

| | As at 31st March 2022 | As at 31st March 2021 |
|---|---|---|
| Sub-total | xxx | xxx |
| **Securities Premium** | | |
| As per last Balance Sheet | xxx | xxx |
| Add: On issue of shares | xxx | xxx |
| | xxx | xxx |
| Less: Redemption of debentures/bonds | (xxx) | (xxx) |
| Less: Buy back of equity shares | (xxx) | (xxx) |
| Less: Calls in arrears – others | (xxx) | (xxx) |
| Sub-total | xxx | xxx |
| **Share based payments reserve** | | |
| As per last Balance Sheet | xxx | xxx |
| Less: On Employee Stock Options | (xxx) | (xxx) |
| Sub-total | xxx | xxx |
| **Special Economic Zone Reinvestment Reserve** | | |
| As per last Balance Sheet | xxx | xxx |
| Add: Transferred from Retained Earnings | xxx | xxx |
| Sub-total | xxx | xxx |
| **General Reserve** | | |
| As per last Balance Sheet | xxx | xxx |
| Add: Transfer from Profit and Loss Account | xxx | xxx |
| Sub-total | xxx | xxx |
| **Retained Earnings** | | |
| As per last Balance Sheet | xxx | xxx |
| Add: Profit for the year | xxx | xxx |
| | xxx | xxx |
| Less: Appropriations | | |
| Transfer to General Reserve | (xxx) | (xxx) |
| Transfer to Capital Redemption reserve on buy | (xxx) | (xxx) |

| | As at 31st March 2022 | As at 31st March 2021 |
|---|---|---|
| Back of equity shares | (xxx) | (xxx) |
| Proposed dividend on equity shares | (xxx) | (xxx) |
| (Dividend per share Rs. (Previous Year Rs.)) | (xxx) | (xxx) |
| Tax on dividend | (xxx) | (xxx) |
| Transferred to Special Economic Zone Reinvestment Reserve | (xxx) | (xxx) |
| Transferred to Debenture Redemption Reserve | (xxx) | (xxx) |
| **Sub-total** | xxx | xxx |
| **Other Comprehensive Income**<br>As per last Balance Sheet | xxx | xxx |
| Add: Movement in OCI (Net) during the year | xxx | xxx |
| **Sub-total** | xxx | xxx |
| **Total** | xxx | xxx |

**Illustration 3.12: Accounting Policy: Shared based payment**

Equity-settled share-based payments to employees and others providing similar services are measured at the fair value of the equity instruments at the grant date. Details regarding the determination of the fair value of equity-settled share-based payments transactions.

The fair value determined at the grant date of the equity-settled share-based payments is expensed on a straight-line basis over the vesting period, based on the Company's estimate of equity instruments that will eventually vest, with a corresponding increase in equity. At the end of each reporting period, the Company revises its estimate of the number of equity instruments expected to vest. The impact of the revision of the original estimates, if any, is recognised in Statement of Profit and Loss such that the cumulative expenses reflects the revised estimate, with a corresponding adjustment to the Share Based Payments Reserve.

The dilutive effect of outstanding options is reflected as additional share dilution in the computation of diluted earnings per share.

# *Chapter 4*

# Non-current liabilities

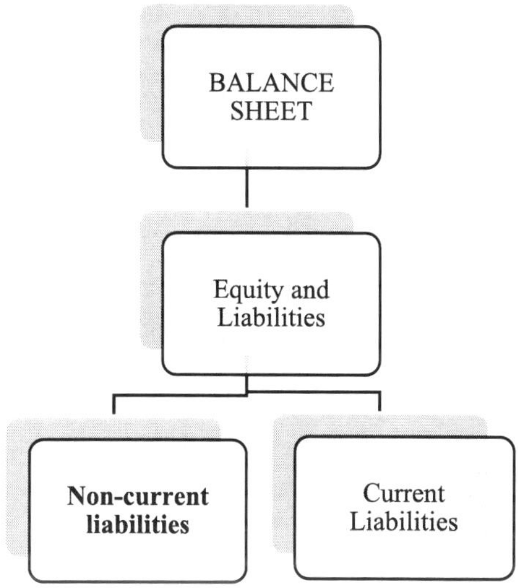


## 4.1 DEFINITION OF NON-CURRENT LIABILITIES

Non-current liabilities have not been defined. However, under Guidance Note of ICAI on Terms used under Financial Statements, Long-term Liability has been defined as liability which does not fall due for payment in a relatively short period, i.e., normally a period not more than twelve months.

According to Ind AS non-current liabilities have been defined by default as under:

An entity shall classify a liability as non-current if it belongs to any category apart from the ones categorized below.

(a) it expects to settle the liability in its normal ***operating cycle***;
(b) it holds the liability primarily for trading;
(c) the liability is due to be settled within twelve months after the reporting period; or
(d) it does not have an unconditional right to defer settlement of the liability for at least twelve months after the reporting period.

Terms of a liability that could, at the option of the counterparty, result in its settlement by the issue of equity instruments do not affect its classification.

## 4.2 COMPONENTS OF NON-CURRENT LIABILITIES

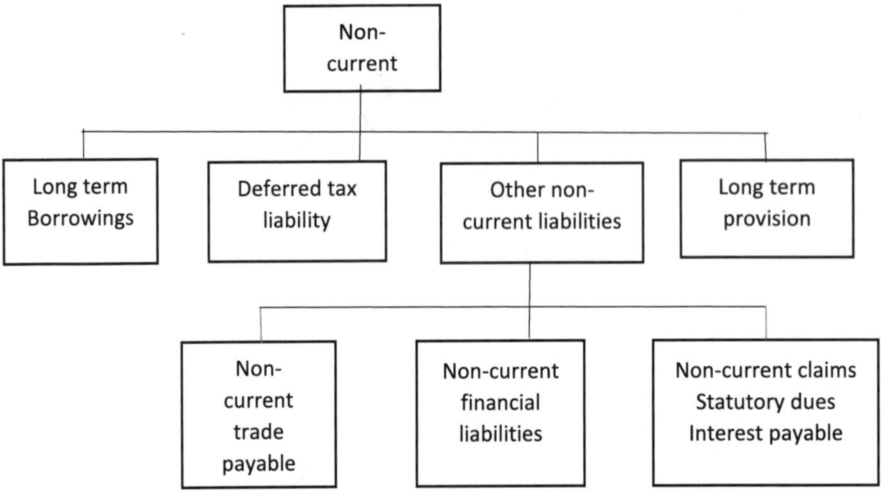


| Under AS[1] | Under Ind AS[2] |
|---|---|
| **C. Long-term borrowings**<br>(i) Long-term borrowings shall be classified as:<br>(a) Bonds/debentures<br>(b) Term loans<br>• From banks<br>• From other parties<br>(c) Deferred payment liabilities<br>(d) Deposits<br>(e) Loans and advances from related parties<br>(f) Long term maturities of finance lease obligations<br>(g) Other loans and advances (specify nature)<br>(ii) Borrowings shall further be sub-classified as secured and unsecured. Nature of security shall be specified separately in each case. | **E. Non-Current Liabilities**<br>**I. Borrowings**<br>(i) Borrowings shall be classified as:<br>(a) Bonds/debentures<br>(b) Term loans<br>I from banks.<br>II from other parties.<br>(c) Deferred payment liabilities.<br>(d) Deposits.<br>(e) Loans from related parties.<br>(f) Long term maturities of finance lease obligations<br>(g) Liability component of compound financial instruments<br>(h) Other loans (specify nature).<br>(ii) Borrowings shall further be sub-classified as secured and unsecured. Nature of security shall be specified separately in each case. |

1 General Instructions for Preparation of Balance Sheet, Part I, Division I of Schedule III of the Companies Act, 2013.

2 General Instructions for Preparation of Balance Sheet, Part I of Division II of Schedule III of the Companies Act, 2013.

| Under AS[1] | Under Ind AS[2] |
|---|---|
| (iii) Where loans have been guaranteed by directors and others, the aggregate amount of such loans under each head shall be disclosed.<br>(iv) Bonds/debentures alongwith rate of interest and particulars of redemption or conversion as the case may be) shall be stated in descending order of maturity or conversion starting from farthest date of redemption or conversion as the case may be. Where bonds/debentures are redeemable by instalments, the date of maturity for this purpose,must be reckoned as the date on which the first instalment becomes due.<br>(v) Particulars of any redeemed bonds/debentures which the company has the power to reissue shall be disclosed.<br>(vi) Terms of repayment of term loans and other loans shall be stated<br>(vii) Period and amount of continuing default as on the balance sheet date in repayment of loans shall be specified separately in each case | (iii) Where loans have been guaranteed by directors or others, the aggregate amount of such loans under each head shall be disclosed.<br>(iv) Bonds/debentures (along with the rate of interest, and particulars of redemption or conversion, as the case may be) shall be stated in descending order of maturity or conversion, starting from farthest redemption or conversion date, as the case may be. Where bonds/debentures are redeemable by instalments, the date of maturity for this purpose must be reckoned as the date on which the first instalment becomes due.<br>(v) Particulars of any redeemed bonds/ debentures which the company has power to reissue shall be disclosed.<br>(vi) Terms of repayment of term loans and other loans shall be stated.<br>(vii) Period and amount of default as on the balance sheet date in repayment of borrowings and interest shall be specified separately in each case. |
| **D. Other long-term liabilities**<br>Other long term liabilities to be classified as :<br>(a) Trade payables<br>(b) Others | **II. Other non-current liabilities**<br>(a) Advances<br>(b) Others (specify nature) |
| **E. Long term provisions**<br>The amount shall be classified as :<br>(a) Provision for long term benefits<br>(b) Others ( specify nature) | **III. Provisions**<br>The amounts shall be classified as:<br>(a) Provision for employee benefits.<br>(b) Others (specify nature). |

## 4.3 LONG TERM BORROWINGS

According to Guidance Note on Schedule III by ICAI, the phrase "long term" has not been defined. However, the definition of "non-current liability" in Schedule III may be used as long term liability for the above disclosure. Also the phrase "term loan" has not been defined under Schedule III. Term loans normally have a fixed or pre-determined maturity period or a repayment schedule.

Also, in accordance with paragraph 62(a) of the ICAI Guidance Note on Companies (Auditor's Report) Order, 2020, in the banking industry, loans with repayment period beyond thirty-six months are usually known as "term loans". Cash credit, overdraft and call money accounts/deposit are, therefore, not covered by the expression "term loans". Term loans are generally provided by banks and financial institutions for acquisition of capital assets which then become the security for the loan, i.e., end use of funds is normally fixed.

The current maturities of all long term borrowings will be disclosed under "other current liabilities" and not under long-term borrowings and short-term borrowings. Hence, it is possible that the same bonds/debentures. Term loans may be bifurcated under both long term borrowings as well as other current liabilities.

At the same time long-term borrowings are to be sub-classified as secured and unsecured giving the nature of the security for the secured position.

Ind AS Schedule III further stipulates that under the head "Borrowings," period and amount of default as on the Balance Sheet date in repayment of borrowings and interest shall be specified separately in each case.

Ind AS 107, further stipulates that, an entity needs to disclose only those breaches made during the reporting period, which permitted the lender to demand accelerated repayment and, were not remedied on or before the end of the reporting period. Also it requires that, if there was a default during the reporting period, an entity shall provide a disclosure even if the default was remedied before the financial statements were approved for issue.

Terms of repayment of term loans and other loans shall be disclosed. The term 'other loans' is used in general sense and should be interpreted to mean all categories listed under the heading 'Non – Current borrowings' as per Ind AS Schedule III.

Disclosure of repayment terms should include:

(i) period of maturity with respect to the Balance Sheet date,

(ii) number and amount of instalments due,

(iii) the applicable rate of interest and

(iv) other significant relevant terms, if any.

## 4.4 LEASE LIABILITIES

Lease liabilities under non-current liabilities represent principal amount of such lease liability payable (as recognised and measured in accordance with Ind AS 116, Leases) beyond a period of 12 months from the reporting date. Lease liabilities are to be presented under non-current financial liabilities as a line item separately from borrowings. The disclosure requirements stated above for borrowings shall not be applicable to lease liabilities.

## 4.5 DEFERRED PAYMENT LIABILITIES

According to Guidance Note, deferred payment liabilities would include any liability for which payment is to be made on deferred credit terms, e.g. deferred sales tax liability, deferred payment for acquisition of Property, Plant and Equipment etc.

## 4.6 LIABILITY COMPONENT OF COMPOUND INSTRUMENTS

With respect to Ind AS, disclosure requirements as applicable to 'Borrowings' should be given for compound instruments with liability component in nature (for e.g., those instruments which entirely meet the definition of a financial liability as per Ind AS 32).

## 4.7 DISCLOSURE OF SECURITY

Also according to ICAI Guidance Note on Ind AS, Schedule III also stipulates that the nature of security shall be specified separately in each case. A blanket disclosure of different securities covering all loans classified under the same head such as 'All Term loans from banks' will not suffice. However, where one security is given for multiple loans, the same may be clubbed together for disclosure purposes with adequate details.

Disclosure about the nature of security should also cover the type of asset given as security e.g. inventories, plant and machinery, land and building, etc. When promoters, other shareholders or any third party have given any personal security for any borrowing, such as shares or other assets held by them, disclosure should be made thereof.

## 4.8 DEPOSITS ACCEPTED FROM PUBLIC

Deposits classified under Borrowings would include deposits accepted from public and inter corporate deposits which are in the nature of borrowings.

## 4.9 LOANS FROM RELATED PARTIES

Loans from related parties are required to be disclosed. Definition of related parties would be as per Accounting Standards AS 18 and Ind AS 24. All the disclosure requirements of non-current borrowings would be applicable to such loans from related parties according to ICAI Guidance Note on Schedule III.

## 4.10 SECURITY AND GUARANTEE BY PROMOTERS, DIRECTORS OR OTHERS RELATED TO BORROWINGS

Where loans have been guaranteed by directors or others, the aggregate amount of such loans under each head need to be disclosed. The word "others" used in the phrase "directors or others" would mean any person or entity other than a director. Therefore, this is not restricted to mean only related parties. Also, in cases where promoters, other shareholders or any third party have given any personal security for any borrowing, such as shares or other assets held by them, disclosure should be made thereof, though such security does not result in the classification of such borrowing as secured.

## 4.11 REDEMPTION OF DEBENTURES AND BONDS

According to ICAI Guidance Note on Schedule III, bonds/debentures (along with the rate of interest and particulars of redemption or conversion, as the case may be) shall be stated in descending order of maturity or conversion, starting from farthest redemption or conversion date, as the case may be. Where bonds/debentures are redeemable by instalments, the date of maturity for this purpose must be reckoned as the date on which the first instalment becomes due. Particulars of any redeemed bonds/ debentures which the company has power to reissue shall be disclosed

**Illustration 4.1: Specimen format for long term borrowings**

| | **As at 31$^{st}$ March 2021** | | **As at 31$^{st}$ March 2020** | |
|---|---|---|---|---|
| | Non-current | Current | Non-current | Current |
| **Secured** | | | | |
| Non-convertible debentures | xxx | xxx | xxx | xxx |
| Term loans from banks | xxx | xxx | xxx | xxx |
| Long term maturities of finance lease obligations | xxx | xxx | xxx | xxx |

| **Unsecured** | | | | |
|---|---|---|---|---|
| Bonds | xxx | xxx | xxx | xxx |
| Term loans from banks | xxx | xxx | xxx | xxx |
| Deferred payment liabililies | xxx | xxx | xxx | xxx |
| **Total** | xxx | Xxx | xxx | xxx |

**Illustration 4.2: Specimen format of Maturity profile and rate of interest of Debentures and bonds**

| Rate of interest | 2016-17 | 2017-18 | 2018-19 | 2019-20 | 2020-21 |
|---|---|---|---|---|---|
| Xxx | xxx | xxx | xxx | xxx | xxx |
| Xxx | xxx | xxx | xxx | xxx | xxx |
| Xxx | xxx | xxx | xxx | Xxx | xxx |
| Xxx | xxx | xxx | xxx | Xxx | xxx |

Applicable for unsecured term loans as well.

## 4.12 DEFERRED TAX LIABILITIES (NET)

### 4.12.1 Differences between taxable income and accounting income

- Taxable income is calculated in accordance with tax laws. In some circumstances, the requirements of these laws to compute taxable income differ from the accounting policies applied to determine accounting income.
- The effect of this difference is that the taxable income and accounting income may not be the same.
- The differences between taxable income and accounting income can be classified into
  - (a) permanent differences and
  - (b) timing differences

| | |
|---|---|
| ***(a) Permanent differences are*** | those differences between taxable income and accounting income which originate in one period and do not reverse subsequently.<br>For instance, if for the purpose of computing taxable income, the tax laws allow only a part of an item of expenditure, the disallowed amount would result in a permanent difference. |
| ***(b) Timing differences are*** | those differences between taxable income and accounting income for a period that originate in one period and are capable of reversal in one or more subsequent periods. |

| | Timing differences arise because the period in which some items of revenue and expenses are included in taxable income do not coincide with the period in which such items of revenue and expenses are included or considered in arriving at accounting income. |
|---|---|
| ***Recognition: Tax expense for the period, comprising current tax and deferred tax, should be included in the determination of the net profit or loss for the period*** | |

Taxes on income are considered to be an expense incurred by the enterprise in earning income and are accrued in the same period as the revenue and expenses to which they relate. Such matching may result into timing differences. The tax effects of timing differences are included in the tax expense in the statement of profit and loss and as deferred tax assets (subject to the consideration of prudence as set out in paragraphs 15-18) or as deferred tax liabilities, in the balance sheet.

***Permanent differences do not result in deferred tax assets or deferred tax liabilities.***

**Principles of Deferred tax liabilities have been detailed in the following Accounting Standards:**

- AS 22: Accounting for taxes on Income
- Ind AS 12: Income taxes

**Examples of tax effect on timing difference**

**Illustration 4.3: Tax effect of deferred tax assets**

An expense provided in the statement of profit and loss but not allowed as a deduction under Section 43B of the Income-tax Act, 1961. This timing difference will reverse when the deduction of that expense is allowed under Section 43B in subsequent year(s)

**Illustration 4.4: Tax effect of deferred tax liabilities**

Higher charge of depreciation allowable under the Income-tax Act, 1961, compared to the depreciation provided in the statement of profit and loss. In subsequent years, the differential will reverse when comparatively lower depreciation will be allowed for tax purposes.

## 4.12.2 Principle of recognition of deferred tax

Recognition of deferred tax for all the timing differences is based on the principle that the financial statements for a period should recognise the tax effect, whether current or deferred, of all the transactions occurring in that period.

### 4.12.3 Taxable temporary differences

A deferred tax liability shall be recognised for all taxable temporary differences, except to the extent that the deferred tax liability arises from:

(a) the initial recognition of goodwill; or

(b) the initial recognition of an asset or liability in a transaction which:

   (i) is not a business combination; and

   (ii) at the time of the transaction, affects neither accounting profit nor taxable profit (tax loss).

However, for taxable temporary differences associated with investments in subsidiaries, branches and associates, and interests in joint ventures, a deferred tax liability shall be recognised.

Deferred tax assets should be recognised and carried forward only to the extent that there is a reasonable certainty that sufficient future taxable income will be available against which such deferred tax assets can be realised.

Deferred tax assets are recognised and carried forward only to the extent that there is a reasonable certainty of their realisation. This reasonable level of certainty would normally be achieved by examining the past record of the enterprise and by making realistic estimates of profits for the future.

Where an enterprise has unabsorbed depreciation or carry forward of losses under tax laws, deferred tax assets should be recognised only to the extent that there is virtual certainty supported by convincing evidence that sufficient future taxable income will be available against which such deferred tax assets can be realised.

### 4.12.4 Deductible temporary differences

A deferred tax asset shall be recognised for all deductible temporary differences to the extent that it is probable that taxable profit will be available against which the deductible temporary difference can be utilised, unless the deferred tax asset arises from the initial recognition of an asset or liability in a transaction that:

(a) is not a business combination; and

(b) at the time of the transaction, affects neither accounting profit nor taxable profit (tax loss).

However, for deductible temporary differences associated with investments in subsidiaries, branches and associates, and interests in joint ventures, a deferred tax asset shall be recognised

### 4.12.5 Unused tax losses and unused tax credits

A deferred tax asset is recognised for the carry forward of unused tax losses and unused tax credits to the extent that it is probable that future taxable profit will be available against which the unused tax losses and unused tax credits can be utilised.

### 4.12.6 Reassessment of unrecognised deferred tax assets

At the end of each reporting period, an entity reassesses unrecognised deferred tax assets. The entity recognises a previously unrecognised deferred tax asset to the extent that it has become probable that future taxable profit will allow the deferred tax asset to be recovered. For example, an improvement in trading conditions may make it more probable that the entity will be able to generate sufficient taxable profit in the future for the deferred tax asset to meet the recognition criteria. Another example is when an entity reassesses deferred tax assets at the date of a business combination or subsequently.

### 4.12.7 Investments in subsidiaries, branches and associates and interests in joint Arrangements

An entity recognises a deferred tax liability for all taxable temporary differences associated with investments in subsidiaries, branches and associates, and interests in joint arrangements, except to the extent that both of the following conditions are satisfied:

(a) the parent, investor, joint venturer or joint operator is able to control the timing of the reversal of the temporary difference; and

(b) it is probable that the temporary difference will not reverse in the foreseeable future.

An entity recognises a deferred tax asset for all deductible temporary differences arising from investments in subsidiaries, branches and associates, and interests in joint arrangements, to the extent that, and only to the extent that, it is probable that:

(a) the temporary difference will reverse in the foreseeable future; and

(b) taxable profit will be available against which the temporary difference can be utilised.

### 4.12.8 Measurement

Current tax liabilities (assets) for the current and prior periods shall be measured at the amount expected to be paid to (recovered from) the taxation authorities, using the tax rates (and tax laws) that have been enacted or substantively enacted by the end of the reporting period.

Deferred tax assets and liabilities shall be measured at the tax rates that are expected to apply to the period when the asset is realised or the liability is settled, based on tax rates (and tax laws) that have been enacted or substantively enacted by the end of the reporting period.

The measurement of deferred tax liabilities and deferred tax assets shall reflect the tax consequences that would follow from the manner in which the entity expects, at the end of the reporting period, to recover or settle the carrying amount of its assets and liabilities.

## Illustration 4.5

Z Ltd presents the following information for the year ending 31.03.2020 and 31.03.2021 from which you are required to calculate the Deferred tax asset/liability assuming tax rate of 30% and state how the same would be dealt with as per relevant accounting standard.

| | 31.03.2020 | 31.03.2021 |
|---|---|---|
| | Rs/Lakhs | Rs/Lakhs |
| Depreciation as per books | 4,010.10 | 4,023.54 |
| Unabsorbed carry forward business losses and Depreciation allowance | 2,016.50 | 4,110.00 |
| Disallowance under Section 43B of Income tax Act 1961 | 518.35 | 611.45 |
| Deferred Revenue expenses | 4.88 | - |
| Provision for doubtful debts | 282.51 | 294.35 |

Z Ltd had incurred a loss of Rs.504 lakhs for the year ended 31.03.2021 before providing for current tax of Rs.26.0 lakhs.

**Solution**

**Statement of calculation of deferred tax asset/liability**

| | **31.03.2020** | **31.03.2021** |
|---|---|---|
| | Rs/Lakhs | Rs/Lakhs |
| Carried forward business loss and depreciation allowance | 2,016.60 | 4,110.00 |
| Add: Disallowance under section 43 B of Income tax Act 1961 | 518.35 | 611.45 |
| Provision for doubtful debts | 282.51 | 294.35 |
| | 2,817.46 | 5,015.80 |
| Less: Depreciation | 4010.10 | 4023.54 |
| | (1,192.64) | 992.26 |
| Less: Deferred Revenue Expenditure * | 4.88 | ------ |
| Timing difference | (1,197.52) | 992.26 |
| Deferred tax liability | | 359.26 |
| Deferred tax asset | | 297.68 |

Where an enterprise has unabsorbed depreciation or carry forward of losses under tax laws, deferred tax assets should be recognised only to the extent that there is virtual certainty supported by convincing evidence that future taxable income will be available against which such deferred tax assets can be realised. The existence of unabsorbed depreciation or carry forward of losses is strong evidence that future taxable income may not be available. Deferred tax asset of Rs.297.68 lakhs should not be recognised as an asset as per *para* 17 of AS 22 on "Accounting for taxes on income". Deferred tax liability of Rs.359.26 lakhs should be disclosed under a separate heading in the balance sheet of Z Ltd. Separately from current assets and current liabilities.

**Illustration 4.6**

The following particulars are stated in the Balance Sheet of M/s Exe Ltd as on 31.03.2021:

| | Rs/Lakhs |
|---|---|
| Deferred tax liability (Cr) | 20.00 |
| Deferred tax assets (Dr) | 10.00 |

The following transactions were reported during the year 2003-04:

| | | |
|---|---|---|
| (i) | Tax | rate 50% |
| (ii) | Depreciation – as per books | 50.00 |
| | Depreciation – for tax purposes | 30.00 |
| | There was no addition to fixed assets during the year | |
| (iii) | Items disallowed in 2020-21 and allowed for tax purposes in 2021-22 | 10.00 |
| (iv) | Interest to financial institutions accounted in the books on accrual basis, but actual payment was made on 30.09.2022 | 20.00 |
| (v) | Donations to private trusts made in 2021-22 | 10.00 |
| (vi) | Share issued expenses allowed under 35D of the IT Act, 1961 for the year 2021-22 (1/10th of Rs. 50 lakhs incurred in 2017-2018) | 5.00 |
| (vii) | Repairs to Plant and Machinery Rs.100 lakhs were spread over the period 2021-22 and 2022-23 equally in the books. However, the entire expenditure was allowed for income tax purposes. | |

Indicate clearly the impact of above items in terms of Deferred Tax Liability/Deferred Tax Assets and the balances of Deferred Tax Liability/Deferred Tax Asset as on 31.03.2022.

**Solution**

**Impact of various items in terms of deferred tax liability/deferred tax asset.**

| Transactions | Analysis | Nature of Difference | Effect | Amount Rs |
|---|---|---|---|---|
| Difference in depreciation | Generally, written down method of depreciation is adopted under | Responding Time difference | Reversal of DTL | Rs.20 lakhs x 50% = Rs.10lakhs |

| | | | | |
|---|---|---|---|---|
| | IT Act which leads to higher depreciation in earlier years of useful life of the asset in comparison to later years | | | |
| Disallowances as per IT Act, of earlier years | Tax payable for the earlier year was higher on this account | Responding Timing difference | Reversal of DTA | Rs.10 lakhs x 50% = Rs.5 lakhs |
| Interest to financial institutions | It is allowed as deduction under section 43B of the IT Act, if the payment is made before the due date of filing the return of income (i.e.31st October 2022) | No timing difference | Not applicable | Not applicable |
| Donation to private trusts | Not an allowable expenditure under IT Act | Permanent difference | Not applicable | Not applicable |
| Share issue expenses | Due to disallowance of full expenditure under IT Act, tax payable in the earlier years was higher | Responding Timing difference | Reversal of DTA | Rs.5 lakhs x 50% = Rs.2.5 lakhs |
| Repairs to plant and machinery | Due to allowance of full experience under IT Act, tax payable of | Originating timing difference | Increase in DTL | Rs.50 lakhs x 50% = Rs.25 lakhs |

| | the current year will be less | | | |
|---|---|---|---|---|

**Dr. Deferred Tax Liability Account Cr**

| | Rs/lakhs. | | Rs/lakhs |
|---|---|---|---|
| 31.3.2022 To Profit & Loss A/c (Depreciation) | 10.00 | 1.4.2021 By Balance b/d | 20.00 |
| | | By P& L A/c (Repairs to Plant) | 25.00 |
| To Balance c/d | 35.00 | | |
| | 45.00 | | 45.00 |
| | | By Balance b/d | 35.00 |

**Dr. Deferred Tax Asset Account Cr**

| | Rs/lakhs. | | Rs/lakhs |
|---|---|---|---|
| 1.04.2021To Balance b/d | 10.00 | 31.03.2022 By Profit & Loss A/c Items disallowed in 2020-21 and allowed As per IT Act in 2021-22 | 5.00 |
| | | Share issue expenses | .50 |
| | | By Balance c/d | 2.50 |
| | 10.00 | | 10.00 |
| To Balance b/d | 2.50 | | |

## Measurement of deferred tax asset or liabilities on non-depreciable assets

If a deferred tax liability or deferred tax asset arises from a non-depreciable asset measured using the revaluation model in Ind AS 16, the measurement of the deferred tax liability or deferred tax asset shall reflect the tax consequences of recovering the carrying amount of the non-depreciable asset through sale, regardless of the basis of measuring the carrying amount of that asset.

Accordingly, if the tax law specifies a tax rate applicable to the taxable amount derived from the sale of an asset that differs from the tax rate applicable to the taxable amount derived from using an asset, the former rate is applied in measuring the deferred tax liability or asset related to a non-depreciable asset.

### 4.12.9 Cases where income taxes are paid at higher or lower rate of tax when dividend is paid out of retained earnings

(a) In some jurisdictions, income taxes are payable at a higher or lower rate if part or all of the net profit or retained earnings is paid out as a dividend to shareholders of the entity. In some other jurisdictions, income taxes may be refundable or payable if part or all of the net profit or retained earnings is paid out as a dividend to shareholders of the entity. In these circumstances, current and deferred tax assets and liabilities are measured at the tax rate applicable to undistributed profits.

(b) In the circumstances described above, the income tax consequences of dividends are recognised when a liability to pay the dividend is recognised. The income tax consequences of dividends are more directly linked to past transactions or events than to distributions to owners.

### 4.12.10 Deferred tax on business combination

Temporary differences may arise in a business combination. In accordance with Ind AS 103, an entity recognises any resulting deferred tax assets or deferred tax liabilities as identifiable assets and liabilities at the acquisition date.

Consequently, those deferred tax assets and deferred tax liabilities affect the amount of goodwill or the bargain purchase gain the entity recognises. However, an entity does not recognise deferred tax liabilities arising from the initial recognition of goodwill.

### 4.12.11 Current and deferred tax on share-based payments

In some tax jurisdictions, an entity receives a tax deduction (i.e. an amount that is deductible in determining taxable profit) that relates to remuneration paid in shares, share options or other equity instruments of the entity. The amount of that tax deduction may differ from the related cumulative remuneration expense, and may arise in a later accounting period. For example, in some jurisdictions, an entity may recognise an expense for the consumption of employee services received as consideration for share options granted, in accordance with Ind AS 102, *Share-based Payment*, and not receive a tax deduction until the share options are exercised, with the measurement of the tax deduction based on the entity's share price at the date of exercise.

### 4.12.12 Offset of current tax assets and liabilities

An entity shall offset current tax assets and current tax liabilities if, and only if, the entity:

(a) has a legally enforceable right to set off the recognised amounts; and

(b) intends either to settle on a net basis, or to realise the asset and settle the liability simultaneously.

### 4.12.13 Offset of deferred tax assets and liabilities

An entity shall offset deferred tax assets and deferred tax liabilities if, and only if:

(a) the entity has a legally enforceable right to set off current tax assets against current tax liabilities; and

(b) the deferred tax assets and the deferred tax liabilities relate to income taxes levied by the same taxation authority on either:

   (i) the same taxable entity; or

   (ii) different taxable entities which intend either to settle current tax liabilities and assets on a net basis, or to realise the assets and settle the liabilities simultaneously, in each future period in which significant amounts of deferred tax liabilities or assets are expected to be settled or recovered.

### 4.12.14 Exchange differences on deferred foreign tax liabilities or assets

Ind AS 21 requires certain exchange differences to be recognised as income or expense but does not specify where such differences should be presented in the statement of profit and loss. Accordingly, where exchange differences on deferred foreign tax liabilities or assets are recognised in the statement of profit and loss, such differences may be classified as deferred tax expense (income) if that presentation is considered to be the most useful to financial statement users.

**Illustration 4.7: Deferred Tax liabilities – specimen format**

| | **As at 31st March 2022** | **As at 31st March 2021** |
|---|---|---|
| At the beginning of the year | xxx | xxx |
| Charge to Statement of Profit & Loss | xxx | xxx |
| Charge to Other comprehensive income | xxx | xxx |
| At the end of the year | xxx | xxx |

**Components of Deferred Tax liabilities – specimen format**

| | As at 31st March 2021 | Charge/(credit) to Statement of Profit & Loss | Charge/ (Credit) to Other Comprehensive Income | As at 31st March 2021 |
|---|---|---|---|---|
| Property, Plant & Equipment | xxx | xxx | xxx | xxx |
| Intangible Assets | xxx | xxx | xxx | xxx |
| Financial Assets | xxx | xxx | xxx | xxx |
| Loans and advances | xxx | xxx | xxx | xxx |
| **Total** | xxx | xxx | xxx | xxx |

## 4.13 OTHER NON-CURRENT LIABILITIES

### 4.13.1 Non-current Trade Payables

A payable is classified as "Trade Payable" if it is in respect of amount due on account of goods purchased or services received in the normal course of business. In accordance with Old Schedule VI, the term "sundry creditors" included amounts due in respect of goods purchased or services received or in respect of other contractual obligations as well. Hence, amount due under contractual obligations can no longer be included within Trade Payables. Such items may include dues payable in respect of statutory obligations like contribution to provident fund, purchase of fixed assets, contractually reimbursable expenses, interest accrued on trade payables etc. Such payables should be classified as "others" and each such item should be disclosed nature-wise.

However, acceptances should be disclosed as part of trade payables in terms of Schedule III.

Ind AS Schedule III requires presenting 'Trade Payables' as a separate line item on the face of the Balance Sheet under 'Financial Liabilities'.

#### *4.13.1.1 Trade Payable ageing schedule*

The format provided by Schedule III is as under:

(Amount in Rs.)

| Particulars | Outstanding for following periods from due date of payment# | | | | |
|---|---|---|---|---|---|
| | Less than one year | One to two years | Two to three years | More than three years | Total |
| (i) MSME<br>(ii) Others | | | | | |
| (iii) Disputed dues - MSME<br>(iv) Disputed dues - others | | | | | |

# similar information shall be given where no due date of payment is specified in that case disclosure shall be from the date of the transaction.

Unbilled dues shall be disclosed separately"

For ICAI Guidance Note related to interpretation and clarifications regarding reporting requirements please refer Chapter 5.

### 4.13.2 Non-current Trade Payables related to The Micro, Small and Medium Enterprises Development (MSMED) Act, 2006

Pursuant to Section 22 of MSMED Act, 2006, following disclosures are required in Financial Statements related to delayed payments of MSMEs:

(a) the principal amount and the interest due thereon (to be shown separately) remaining unpaid to any supplier as at the end of each accounting year;

(b) the amount of interest paid by the buyer under MSMED Act, 2006 along with the amounts of the payment made to the supplier beyond the appointed day during each accounting year;

(c) the amount of interest due and payable for the period of delay in making payment (which has been paid but beyond the appointed day during the year) but without adding the interest specified under the MSMED Act, 2006);

(d) The amount of interest accrued and remaining unpaid at the end of accounting year; and

(e) The amount of further interest remaining due and payable even in the succeeding year, until such date when the interest dues as above are actually paid to the small enterprise, for the purpose of disallowance as a deductible expenditure under section 23 of MSMED Act 2006.

### 4.13.3 Non-current Other Financial Liabilities

Ind AS Schedule III requires disclosure of 'Other Financial Liabilities' as a separate line item on the face of the Balance Sheet under 'Financial Liabilities'. Items which meet the definition of financial liabilities as per Ind AS 32 are contingent consideration, derivative contracts, financial guarantee contracts issued, contractually reimbursable expenses etc. and these should be presented under other financial liabilities.

### 4.13.4 Contract Liabilities

In accordance with Ind AS 115 Revenue from contract with customers, contract liability needs to be presented in Balance Sheet, when either party has performed, a contract liability related to a contract with customers. Contract liability occurs if a customer pays consideration, or an entity has a right to an amount of consideration that is unconditional (i.e. a receivable), before the entity transfers a good or service to the customer, the entity shall present the contract as a contract liability when the payment is made or the payment is due (whichever is earlier).

A company shall apply the requirements of Ind AS 1 and Ind AS 32 to determine whether it is appropriate to offset contract assets and liabilities against other balance sheet items (e.g., receivables).

Unless a company presents its balance sheet on a liquidity basis, it will need to apply current and non-current classification against these contract liabilities arising from contracts within the scope of Ind AS 115.

### 4.13.5 Other Non-current Liabilities

All advances that are not financial liabilities as defined in Ind AS 32 should be classified under 'Other non-current liabilities'. Examples are:

(i) amount received in advance against goods to be sold or services to be provided,

(ii) statutory dues payable,

(iii) legal claims outstanding,

(iv) interest payable on unpaid amount to supplier as per MSMED Act, 2006, if such interest payable is not a contractual obligation as per the MSMED Act, 2006

## 4.14 LONG TERM PROVISIONS

Under Schedule III, Division I, Long term provisions need to be classified into provision for employee benefits and others specifying the nature.

Provision for employee benefits should be bifurcated into long term (non-current) and other current and the long-term portion is disclosed under this section. All long-term provisions, other than those related to employee benefits should be disclosed separately based on their nature.

Examples are provisions for warranties etc.

With respect to *AS 15: Employee Benefits,* the measurement of various employee benefit obligations, their classifications as current and non-current liability will be governed by the criteria laid down in the Schedule III.

Accordingly, a liability is classified as non-current if a company has an unconditional right as on the Balance Sheet date to defer its settlement beyond 12 months after the reporting date. Each company will need to apply these criteria to its specific facts and circumstances and decide an appropriate classification for its employee benefit obligations.

## 4.15 NON-CURRENT PROVISIONS

According to Ind AS 19, this should be classified into 'provision for employee benefits' and 'others' specifying the nature. Provision for employee benefits, mainly unfunded defined post-employment benefits, are bifurcated into non-current and current of which the non-current portion shall be disclosed under this section. All non-current provisions, other than those related to employee benefits should be disclosed separately based on their nature. Such items would include provision for warranties, etc.

## 4.16 COMPARATIVE SUMMARY OF NON-CURRENT PROVISIONS

Comparative summary of non-current provisions is highlighted in the table below.

| AS | Ind AS | ICDS | ICAI Guidance Note |
|---|---|---|---|
| As per *AS 29: Provisions, contingent liabilities and contingent assets*, a "provision" is a liability which can be measured only by using a substantial degree of | According to *Ind AS 37: Provisions, contingent liabilities and contingent assets*, a "*provision*" is a liability of uncertain timing or amount.<br>A liability is a | (a) "***Provision***" is a liability which can be measured only by using a substantial degree of estimation.<br>(b) "***Liability***" is a present obligation of the person arising from past events, the settlement of which | According to Guidance Note on Schedule III by ICAI, the phrase "long term" has not been defined. However, the definition of "non-current liability" in Schedule III may be used as long term liability for the above |

| AS | Ind AS | ICDS | ICAI Guidance Note |
|---|---|---|---|
| estimation. A liability is a present obligation of the enterprise arising from past events, the settlement of which is expected to result in an outflow from the enterprise of resources embodying economic benefits. | present obligation of the entity arising from past events, the settlement of which is expected to result in an outflow from the entity of resources embodying economic benefits.<br>An "*obligating event*" is an event that creates a legal or constructive obligation that results in an entity having no realistic alternative to settling that obligation. | is expected to result in an outflow from the person of resources embodying economic benefits.<br>(c) "***Obligating event***" is an event that creates an obligation that results in a person having no realistic alternative to settling that obligation. | disclosure. |

As mentioned above the definition of current and non-current liabilities will apply to long term provisions as well.

## 4.17 QUALITY OF ACCOUNTING OF NON-CURRENT LIABILITIES

Accounting quality of non-current liabilities needs to be addressed through the following components:

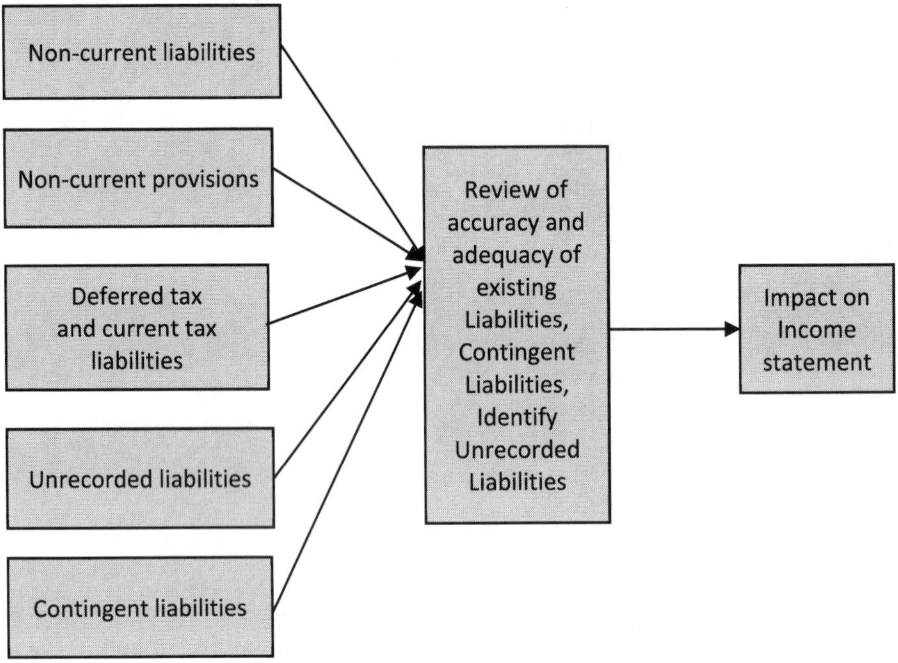


Some of the focus areas which would ensure Accounting quality have been highlighted in the table below.

| Item |
|---|
| Whether there is periodic review of debt covenants are carried out |
| Whether detailed records of all long-term debts are maintained |
| Whether all long-term debts are approved by the board of directors |
| Whether adequate records of all collaterals are maintained |
| Whether register of charges are regularly updated |
| Whether all provisions of the Companies Act 2013 have been complied with |
| Whether all records related to debt components of the compound financial instruments are properly maintained and tied up with financial statements |
| Whether all deferred tax liabilities have been properly computed and reflected in the books of accounts and financial statements |

# Chapter 5

# Current Liabilities

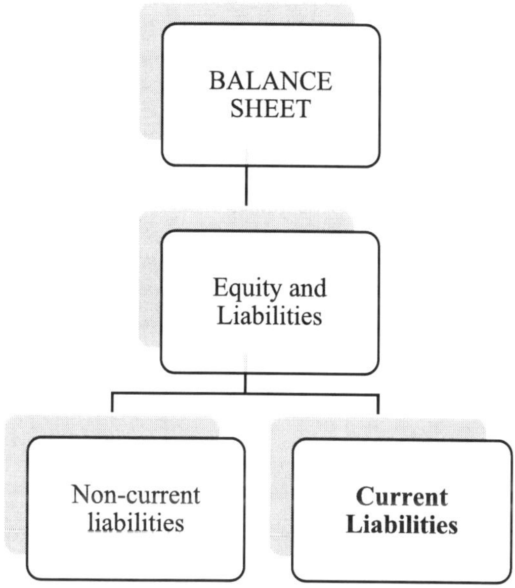


## 5.1 DEFINITION OF CURRENT LIABILITIES

According to ICAI Guidance Note on definitions Current Liability has been defined as,

"Liabilities including loans, deposits and bank overdraft which falls due for payment in a relatively short period, normally not more than twelve months."

As mentioned in Chapter 2 under IFRS and Ind AS, an entity shall classify a liability as current when:

(a) it expects to settle the liability in its normal ***operating cycle***;

(b) it holds the liability primarily for trading;

(c) the liability is due to be settled within twelve months after the reporting period; or

(d) it does not have an unconditional right to defer settlement of the liability for at least twelve months after the reporting period.

Terms of a liability that could, at the option of the counterparty, result in its settlement by the issue of equity instruments do not affect its classification.

## 5.2 COMPONENTS OF CURRENT LIABILITIES

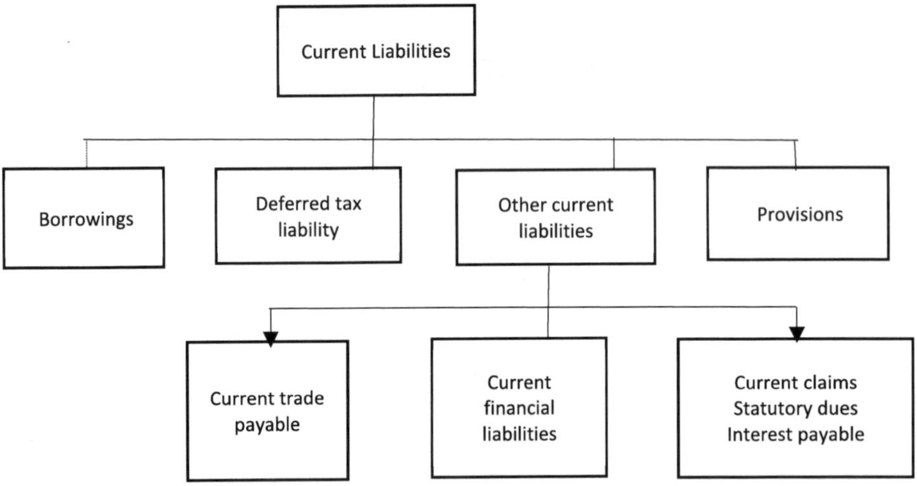


| Under AS[1] | Under Ind AS[2] |
|---|---|
| **F. Short-term borrowings**<br>(i) Short term borrowings shall be classified as:<br>(a) loans repayable on demand<br>• From banks<br>• From other parties<br>(b) Loans and advances from related parties<br>(c) Deposits<br>(d) Other loans and advances (specify nature)<br>(ii) Borrowings shall further be sub-classified as secured and unsecured. Nature of security shall be specified separately in each case.<br>(iii) Where loans have been guaranteed by directors or others, the aggregate amount of | **F. Current Liabilities**<br>**I. Borrowings**<br>(i) Borrowings shall be classified as:<br>(a) Loans repayable on demand<br>(I) from banks.<br>(II) from other parties.<br>(b) Loans from related parties.<br>(c) Deposits.<br>(d) Other loans (specify nature).<br>(ii) Borrowings shall further be sub-classified as secured and unsecured. Nature of security shall be specified separately in each case.<br>(iii) Where loans have been guaranteed by directors or others, the aggregate amount of such loans under each head shall be disclosed. |

1 General Instructions for Preparation of Balance Sheet, Part I, Division I of Schedule III of the Companies Act, 2013.

2 General Instructions for Preparation of Balance Sheet, Part I of Division II of Schedule III of the Companies Act, 2013.

| Under AS[1] | Under Ind AS[2] |
|---|---|
| such loans under each head shall be disclosed.<br>(iv) Period and amount of default as on the balance sheet date in repayment of loans and Interest, shall be specified separately in each case. | (iv) Period and amount of default as on the balance sheet date in repayment of borrowings and interest, shall be specified separately in each case. |
| | **II. Other Financial Liabilities**<br>Other Financial liabilities shall be classified as:<br>(a) Current maturities of long-term debt;<br>(b) Current maturities of finance lease obligations;<br>(c) Interest accrued;<br>(d) Unpaid dividends;<br>(e) Application money received for allotment of securities to the extent refundable and interest accrued thereon;<br>(f) Unpaid matured deposits and interest accrued thereon;<br>(g) Unpaid matured debentures and interest accrued thereon;<br>(h) Others (specify nature).<br>'Long term debt' is a borrowing having a period of more than twelve months at the time of origination |
| **G. Other current liabilities:**<br>The amounts shall be classified as:<br>(a) Current maturities of long-term debt ;<br>(b) Current maturities of finance lease obligations;<br>(c) Interest accrued but not due on borrowings<br>(d) Interest accrued and due on borrowings<br>(e) Interest received in advance<br>(f) Unpaid dividends<br>(g) Application money received from allotment of securities and due for | **III. Other current liabilities**<br>The amounts shall be classified as:<br>(a) Revenue received in advance;<br>(b) Other advances (specify nature);<br>(c) Others (specify nature); |

| Under AS[1] | Under Ind AS[2] |
|---|---|
| refund and interest accrued thereon.<br>(h) Unpaid matured deposits and interest accrued thereon<br>(i) Unpaid matured debentures and interest accrued thereon<br>(j) Other payables (specify nature) | |
| **H. Short term provisions**<br>The amounts shall be classified as :<br>(a) Provision for employee benefits<br>(b) Others ( specify nature ) | **IV. Provisions**<br>The amounts shall be classified as:<br>(i) Provision for employee benefits.<br>(ii) Others (specify nature). |
| | **G.** The presentation of liabilities associated with group(s) of assets classified as held for sale and non-current assets classified as held for sale shall be in accordance with the relevant Indian Accounting Standards (Ind ASs). |

### 5.2.1 Borrowings

(i) Borrowings shall be classified as:
- (a) Loans repayable on demand
  - (A) from banks.
  - (B) from other parties.
- (b) Loans from related parties.
- (c) Deposits.
- (d) Other loans (specify nature).

(ii) Borrowings shall further be sub-classified as secured and unsecured. Nature of security shall be specified separately in each case.

(iii) Where loans have been guaranteed by directors or others, the aggregate amount of such loans under each head shall be disclosed.

(iv) Period and amount of default as on the balance sheet date in repayment of borrowings and interest, shall be specified separately in each case.

(v) Current maturities of Long-term borrowings shall be disclosed separately

### 5.2.2 Loans payable on demand

According to ICAI Guidance Note on Schedule III, loans payable on demand should be treated as part of current borrowings. Current borrowings will include all loans payable within a period of 12 months from the date of the loan.

In the case of current borrowings, the period and amount of defaults existing as at the date of the Balance Sheet needs to be disclosed (item-wise).

### 5.2.3 Current maturities of long-term borrowings

Ind AS Schedule III prescribes presenting 'current maturities of long-term borrowings' under 'current borrowings'. Long-term debt is specified in Ind AS Schedule III as a borrowing having a period of more than twelve months at the time of origination. The portion of non-current borrowings, which is due for payments within twelve months of the reporting date is required to be classified under "current borrowings" while the balance amount should be classified under non-current borrowings.

**Illustration 5.1: Borrowings –Current – specimen format**

| | **As at 31st March 2022** | **As at 31st March 2021** |
|---|---|---|
| **SECURED – Amortized cost** | | |
| Working capital loans | | |
| (A) from banks. | xxx | xxx |
| (B) from other parties. | xxx | xxx |
| Deferred payment liabilities. | xxx | xxx |
| Deposits. | xxx | xxx |
| Loans from related parties. | xxx | xxx |
| Liability component of compound financial instruments | xxx | xxx |
| Other loans (specify nature). | xxx | xxx |
| Sub-total | xxx | xxx |
| **UNSECURED – Amortized cost** | | |
| Other loans and advances | | |
| From banks | | |
| - Foreign currency loans | xxx | xxx |
| - Rupee loans | xxx | xxx |
| From other parties. | | |
| - Commercial paper | xxx | xxx |
| Deferred payment liabilities. | xxx | xxx |
| Loans from related parties. | xxx | xxx |
| Other loans (specify nature). | | |
| Sub-total | xxx | xxx |
| Total | xxx | xxx |

## 5.2.4 Other Financial Liabilities

Other Financial liabilities shall be classified as:

(a) Interest accrued;

(b) Unpaid dividends;

(c) Application money received for allotment of securities to the extent refundable and interest accrued thereon;

(d) Unpaid matured deposits and interest accrued thereon;

(e) Unpaid matured debentures and interest accrued thereon;

(f) Others (specify nature).

## 5.2.5 Interest accrued

According to ICAI Guidance Note on Schedule III related to Ind AS, Interest accrued on financial liabilities shall form part of its carrying amount whether it is at amortized cost (i.e. as per effective interest method), or at fair value. Accordingly, an entity may not be required to present 'Interest Accrued' separately from the related financial liability.

**Illustration 5.2 Other Financial Liabilities –Current – specimen format**

| | **As at 31st March 2022** | **As at 31st March 2021** |
|---|---|---|
| Interest accrued. | xxx | xxx |
| Unpaid dividends; | xxx | xxx |
| Application money received for allotment of securities to the extent refundable and interest accrued thereon; | xxx | xxx |
| Unpaid matured deposits and interest accrued thereon; | xxx | xxx |
| Unpaid matured debentures and interest accrued thereon; | xxx | xxx |
| Others (specify nature). | xxx | xxx |
| Total | Xxx | xxx |

### 5.2.6 Trade Payables

The following details relating to micro, small and medium enterprises shall be disclosed in the notes:

(a) the principal amount and the interest due thereon (to be shown separately) remaining unpaid to any supplier at the end of each accounting year,

(b) the amount of interest paid by the buyer in terms of section 16 of the Micro, Small and Medium Enterprises Development Act, 2006 (27 of 2006), along with the amount of the payment made to the supplier beyond the appointed day during each accounting year,

(c) the amount of interest due and payable for the period of delay in making payment (which has been paid but beyond the appointed day during the year) but without adding the interest specified under the Micro, Small and Medium Enterprises Development Act, 2006;

(d) the amount of interest accrued and remaining unpaid at the end of each accounting year; and

(e) the amount of further interest remaining due and payable even in the succeeding years, until such date when the interest dues above are actually paid to the small enterprise, for the purpose of disallowance of a deductible expenditure under section 23 of the Micro, Small and Medium Enterprises Development Act, 2006.

Explanation- The terms 'appointed day', 'buyer', 'enterprise', 'micro enterprise', 'small enterprise' and 'supplier', shall have the same meaning as assigned to them under clauses (b), (d), (e), (h), (m) and (n) respectively of section 2 of the Micro, Small and Medium Enterprises Development Act, 2006.

**Illustration 5.3: Trade Payables –Current – specimen format**

| | **As at 31st March 2022** | **As at 31st March 2021** |
|---|---|---|
| Micro and small enterprise | xxx | xxx |
| Other than Micro and small enterprise | xxx | xxx |
| Total | Xxx | xxx |

### 5.2.6.1 Trade Payables Aging schedule

(Amount in Rs.)

| Particulars | Outstanding for following periods from due date of payment# | | | | |
|---|---|---|---|---|---|
| | Less than one year | One to two years | Two to three years | More than three years | Total |
| (i) MSME<br>(ii) Others | | | | | |
| (iii) Disputed dues - MSME<br>(iv) Disputed dues - others | | | | | |

# similar information shall be given where no due date of payment is specified in that case disclosure shall be from the date of the transaction.

Unbilled dues shall be disclosed separately"

According to ICAI Guidance Note on Division I and II of Schedule III (Revised January, 2022 Edition) on ageing of trade payables due for payment, the entity needs to provide details of ageing of trade payables due for payment as on the balance sheet date as per the prescribed format shown above. In order to tie-up the amounts presented in the 'total' column with the amounts presented in the financial statements or notes, the ICAI Guidance Note suggests two additional columns with heading 'Unbilled' and the heading 'Not due' to be added before the ageing columns to separately disclose the amount for unbilled payables and the amount of trade payables which are not due, respectively. The ageing requirement shall not apply to these trade payables not due for payment.

Now we come to the explanation of trade payables. According to AS 29, trade payables are liabilities to pay for goods or services that have been received or supplied and have been invoiced or formally agreed with the supplier.

In accordance with ICAI Guidance Note, unbilled trade payables shall include accruals which are not classified as provisions under AS 29. Also, it is clarified that a "provision" shall not be considered as unbilled trade payables.

The amounts to be presented under:

(i) MSME and

(ii) Others shall include those trade payable dues that are undisputed.

Here the ICAI Guidance Note adequate clarifies the interpretation of "*due date*" and the term "*dispute*".

According to the Guidance Note, *due date* shall be the date by when a buyer should make payment to the supplier as per terms agreed upon between the buyer and supplier.

In case if the *due date* is re-negotiated or the invoice is revised, *due date* shall be considered from the original due date or revised due date based on the agreed terms between buyer and seller, as the case may be. In case if the *due date* is neither agreed in writing nor oral, then the disclosure needs to be prepared from the *transaction date.*

Transaction date shall be the date on which the liability is recognised in the books of accounts as per the requirement of applicable standards.

The term "*dispute*" would be as defined under Insolvency and Bankruptcy code, 2016. Dispute means a disagreement between two parties demonstrated by some positive evidence which supports or corroborates the fact of disagreement and will depend on facts and circumstances of the individual case.

### 5.2.7 Other Current Liabilities

Under Division I of Schedule III, the other current liabilities have been classified as:

(a) Current maturities of finance lease obligations;

(b) Interest accrued but not due on borrowings;

(c) Interest accrued and due on borrowings;

(d) Income received in advance;

(e) Unpaid dividends;

(f) Application money received for allotment of securities and due for refund and interest accrued thereon;

(g) Unpaid matured deposits and interest accrued thereon;

(h) Unpaid matured debentures and interest accrued thereon;

(i) Other payables (specify nature)

**Application money received for allotment of securities and due for refund**

Division I of Schedule III explains Application money received for allotment of securities and due for refund and interest accrued thereon as under:

Share application money includes advances towards allotment of share capital. The terms and conditions including number of shares proposed to be issued, the amount of premium, if any, and the period before which shares shall be allotted should be disclosed.

It shall also be disclosed whether the company has sufficient authorised capital to cover the share capital amount resulting from allotment of shares out of such share applicatio money.

Further the period for which share application money has been pending beyond the period of allottment as mentioned in the document inviting application of shares along with the reason for such share application money being pending shall be disclosed. Share application money not exceeding the issued capital and to the extent not refundable shall be shown under the head Equity and share application money to the extent refundable i.e. the amount in excess of subscription or in case the requirements of minimum subscription are not met shall be separately shown under "other current liabilities.

Under Division II of Schedule III, the other current liabilities have been classified as follows:

(a) Revenue received in advance.

(b) Other advances (specify nature);

(c) Others (specify nature);

### 5.2.8 Other Advances

Other advances, that satisfy the requirements for being classified as current and that are not financial liabilities as defined in Ind AS 32, should be classified under 'Other current liabilities. For example, amount received in advance from customers or other parties against sale of investments or immovable property.

### 5.2.9 Others

Others should include items under other current liabilities for example, statutory dues payable, legal claims outstanding.

According to ICAI Guidance Note on Schedule III on Ind AS, trade Deposits and Security Deposits, which do not meet the definition of financial liabilities, should be classified as 'Others' grouped under this head. Others may also include liabilities in the nature of statutory dues such as Withholding taxes, Service Tax, VAT, Excise Duty, Goods and Services Tax (GST), etc.

**Illustration 5.4: Other Current liabilities – specimen format**

| | As at 31st March 2022 | As at 31st March 2021 |
|---|---|---|
| Revenue received in advance. | xxx | xxx |
| Other advances (specify nature); | xxx | xxx |
| Others (specify nature); | xxx | xxx |
| Total | xxx | xxx |

## 5.2.10 Provisions

The amounts shall be classified as:

(i) Provision for employee benefits.

(ii) Others (specify nature).

**Illustration 5.5: Provisions –Current – specimen format**

| | As at 31st March 2022 | As at 31st March 2021 |
|---|---|---|
| Provision for employee benefits. | xxx | xxx |
| Others (specify nature). | xxx | xxx |
| Total | xxx | xxx |

### *5.2.10.1 AS 29: Provisions, Contingent Liabilities and Contingent Assets*

The relevant extracts of AS -29 is provided below for reference purposes.

**Recognition**

***Para 14. A provision should be recognised when:***

- ***(a) an enterprise has a present obligation as a result of a past event;***
- ***(b) it is probable that an outflow of resources embodying economic benefits will be required to settle the obligation; and***
- ***(c) a reliable estimate can be made of the amount of the obligation.***

***If these conditions are not met, no provision should be recognised.***

***Para 26. An enterprise should not recognise a contingent liability.***

Para 27. A contingent liability is disclosed, as required by paragraph 68, unless the possibility of an outflow of resources embodying economic benefits is remote.

***Para 30. An enterprise should not recognise a contingent asset.***

According to Para 33, a contingent asset is not disclosed in the financial statements. It is usually disclosed in the report of the approving authority (Board of Directors in the case of a company, and, the corresponding approving authority in the case of any other enterprise), where an inflow of economic benefits is probable.

**Measurement**

**Para 35. The amount recognised as a provision should be the best estimate of the expenditure required to settle the present obligation at the balance sheet date. The amount of a provision should not be discounted to its present value except in case of decommissioning, restoration and similar liabilities that are recognised as cost of Property, Plant and Equipment. The discount rate (or rates) should be a pre-**

**tax rate (or rates) that reflect(s) current market assessments of the time value of money and the risks specific to the liability. The discount rate(s) should not reflect risks for which future cash flow estimates have been adjusted. Periodic unwinding of discount should be recognised in the statement of profit and loss.**

Para 38. The risks and uncertainties that inevitably surround many events and circumstances should be taken into account in reaching the best estimate of a provision.

Para 41. Future events that may affect the amount required to settle an obligation should be reflected in the amount of a provision where there is sufficient objective evidence that they will occur.

Para 44. Gains from the expected disposal of assets should not be taken into account in measuring a provision.

Para 46. Where some or all of the expenditure required to settle a provision is expected to be reimbursed by another party, the reimbursement should be recognised when, and only when, it is virtually certain that reimbursement will be received if the enterprise settles the obligation. The reimbursement should be treated as a separate asset. The amount recognised for the reimbursement should not exceed the amount of the provision.

Para 47. In the statement of profit and loss, the expense relating to a provision may be presented net of the amount recognised for a reimbursement.

**Disclosure**

Para 66. For each class of provision, an enterprise should disclose:

(a) the carrying amount at the beginning and end of the period;

(b) additional provisions made in the period, including increases to existing provisions;

(c) amounts used (i.e. incurred and charged against the provision) during the period; and

(d) unused amounts reversed during the period.

Provided that a Small and Medium-sized Company, as defined in the Notification, may not comply with paragraph 66 above.

Para 67. An enterprise should disclose the following for each class of provision:

(a) a brief description of the nature of the obligation and the expected timing of any resulting outflows of economic benefits.

(b) an indication of the uncertainties about those outflows. Where necessary to provide adequate information, an enterprise should disclose the major assumptions made concerning future events, as addressed in paragraph 41; and

(c) the amount of any expected reimbursement, stating the amount of any asset that has been recognised for that expected reimbursement.

Provided that a Small and Medium-sized Company, as defined in the Notification, may not comply with paragraph 67 above.

Para 68. Unless the possibility of any outflow in settlement is remote, an enterprise should disclose for each class of contingent liability at the balance sheet date a brief description of the nature of the contingent liability and, where practicable:

(a) an estimate of its financial effect, measured under paragraphs 35-45;

(b) an indication of the uncertainties relating to any outflow; and

(c) the possibility of any reimbursement.

Para 69. In determining which provisions or contingent liabilities may be aggregated to form a class, it is necessary to consider whether the nature of the items is sufficiently similar for a single statement about them to fulfil the requirements of paragraphs 67 (a) and (b) and 68 (a) and (b). Thus, it may be appropriate to treat as a single class of provision amounts relating to warranties of different products, but it would not be appropriate to treat as a single class amounts relating to normal warranties and amounts that are subject to legal proceedings.

Para 70. Where a provision and a contingent liability arise from the same set of circumstances, an enterprise makes the disclosures required by paragraphs 66-68 in a way that shows the link between the provision and the contingent liability.

Para 71. Where any of the information required by paragraph 68 is not disclosed because it is not practicable to do so, that fact should be stated.

Para 72. In extremely rare cases, disclosure of some or all of the information required by paragraphs 66-70 can be expected to prejudice seriously the position of the enterprise in a dispute with other parties on the subject matter of the provision or contingent liability. In such cases, an enterprise need not disclose the information, but should disclose the general nature of the dispute, together with the fact that, and reason why, the information has not been disclosed.

**Illustration 5.6: Tables - Provisions, Contingent Liabilities and Reimbursements**

*The purpose of this illustration is to summarise the main requirements of the Accounting Standard. It does not form part of the Accounting Standard and should be read in the context of the full text of the Accounting Standard.*

| **Where, as a result of past events, there may be an outflow of resources embodying future economic benefits in settlement of: (a) a present obligation the one whose existence at the balance sheet date is considered probable; or (b) a possible obligation the existence of which at the balance sheet date is considered not probable.** |
|---|

| **There is a present obligation that probably requires an outflow of resources and a reliable estimate can be made of the amount of obligation.** | **There is a possible obligation or a present obligation that may, but probably will not, require an outflow of resources.** | **There is a possible obligation or a present obligation where the likelihood of an outflow of resources is remote.** |
|---|---|---|
| Provision is recognised (paragraph 14).<br>Disclosures are required for the provision (paragraphs 66 and 67) | No provision is recognised (paragraph 26).<br>Disclosures are required for the contingent liability (paragraph 68). | No provision is recognised (paragraph 26).<br>No disclosure is required (paragraph 68). |

**Reimbursements**

| **Some or all of the expenditure required to settle a provision is expected to be reimbursed by another party.** | | |
|---|---|---|
| **The enterprise has no obligation for the part of the expenditure to be reimbursed by the other other party.** | **The obligation for the amount expected to be reimbursed remains with the enterprise that reimbursement will be received if the enterprise settles the provision.** | **The obligation for the amount expected to be reimbursed remains with the enterprise and the reimbursement is not virtually certain if the enterprise settles the provision** |
| The enterprise has no liability for the amount to be reimbursed (paragraph 50). | The reimbursement is recognised as a separate asset in the balance sheet and may be offset against the expense in the statement of profit and loss. The amount recognised for the expected reimbursement does not exceed the liability (paragraphs 46 and 47). | The expected reimbursement is not recognised as an asset (paragraph 46). |

| | | |
|---|---|---|
| No disclosure is required. | The reimbursement is disclosed together with the amount recognised for the reimbursement (paragraph 67(c)). | The expected reimbursement is disclosed (paragraph 67(c)). |

### *5.2.10.2 Ind AS 37: Provisions, Contingent Liabilities and Contingent Assets*

The objective of the Standard is to ensure that appropriate recognition criteria and measurement bases are applied to provisions, contingent liabilities and contingent assets and that sufficient information is disclosed in the notes to enable users to understand their nature, timing and amount

The Standard shall be applied by all entities in accounting for provisions, contingent liabilities and contingent assets, except:

(a) Those resulting from executory contracts, except where the contract is onerous and

(a) Those covered by another Standard

This Standard does not apply to financial instruments including guarantees that are within the scope of *Ind AS 109 Financial Instruments.*

Executory contracts are contracts under which neither party has performed any of its obligations or both parties have partially performed their obligations to an equal extent. The Standard does not apply to executory contracts unless they are onerous

According to Para 5, when another Standard deals with a specific type of provision, contingent liability or contingent asset, an entity applies that Standard instead of this Standard.

**Definitions**

*A provision* is a liability of uncertain timing or amount

*A liability* is a present obligation of the entity arising from past events, the settlement of which is expected to result in an outflow from the entity of resources embodying economic benefits.

*An obligating event* is an event that creates a legal or constructive obligation that results in an entity having no realistic alternative to settling that obligation

*A legal obligation* is an obligation that derives from:

(a) A contract (through its explicit or implicit terms)

(b) Legislation or

(c) Other operation of law

*A constructive obligation* is an obligation that derives from an entity's actions were:

(a) By an established pattern of past practice, published policies or a sufficiently specific current statement, the entity has indicated to other parties that it will accept certain responsibilities and

(b) As a result, the entity has created a valid expectation on the part of those other parties that will discharge those responsibilities

*A contingent liability is:*

(a) A possible obligation that arises from past events and whose experience will be confirmed only by the occurrence or non-occurrence of one or more uncertain future events not wholly within the control of the entity or

(b) A present obligation that arises from past events but is not recognised because:

(i) it is not probable that an outflow of resources embodying economic benefits will be required to settle the obligation; or

(ii) the amount of the obligation cannot be measured with sufficient reliability

*A contingent asset* is a possible asset that arises from past events and whose existence will be confirmed only by the occurrence or non-occurrence of one or more uncertain future events not wholly within the control of the entity

*An onerous contract* is a contract in which the unavoidable costs of meeting the obligations under the contract exceed the economic benefits expected to be received under it.

*A restructuring* is a programme that is planned and controlled by management, and materially changes either:

(a) The scope of a business undertaken by an entity or

(b) The manner in which that business is conducted

**Recognition of provisions**

According to the Standard, a provision is recognised when

(a) an entity has a present obligation (legal or constructive) as a result of a past event

(b) it is probable that an outflow of economic benefits will be required to settle the obligation, and

(c) a reliable estimate can be made of the obligation

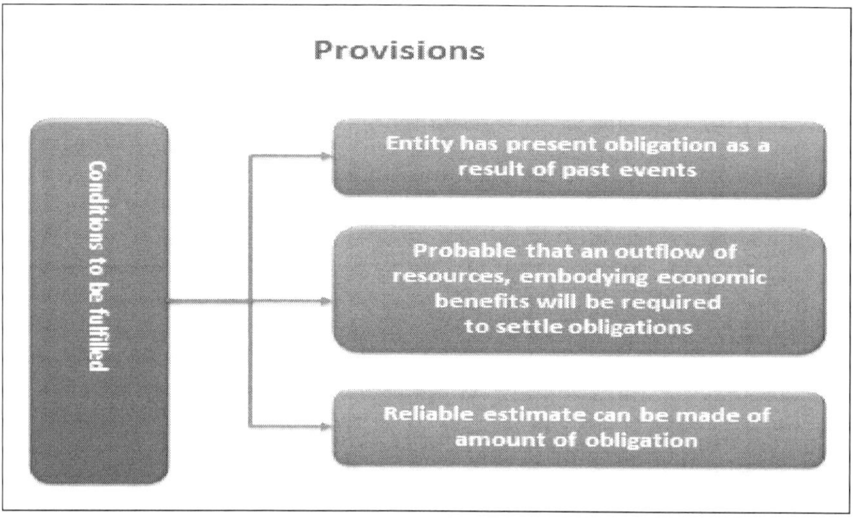


**Measurement of provisions**

The amount recognised as a provision shall be the best estimate of the expenditure required to settle the present obligation at the end of the reporting period.

**Illustration 5.7: Provision for warranty**

An entity sells goods with a warranty under which customers are covered for the cost of repairs of any manufacturing defects that become apparent within the first six months after purchase. If minor defects were detected in all products sold, repair costs of Rs 1 million would result. If major defects were detected in all products sold, repair costs of Rs 4 million would result.

The entity's past experience and future expectations indicate that, for the coming year, 75 per cent of the goods sold will have no defects, 20 per cent of the goods sold will have minor defects and 5 per cent of the goods sold will have major defects. In accordance with paragraph 24, an entity assesses the probability of an outflow for the warranty obligations as a whole.

The expected value of the cost of repairs is:

(75% of nil) + (20% of 1m) + (5% of 4m) = Rs 4,00,000

In accordance with Para 42, the risks and uncertainties that inevitably surround many events and circumstances shall be taken into account in reaching the best estimate of a provision.

**Present value**

(a) Where the effect of the time value of money is material, the amount of a provision shall be the present value of the expenditures expected to be required to settle the obligation

(b) The discount rate (or rates) shall be a pre-tax rate (or rates) that reflect(s) current market assessments of the time value of money and the risks specific to the liability. The discount rate(s) shall not reflect risks for which future cash flow estimates have been adjusted.

**Future operating losses**

(a) Provisions shall not be recognised for future operating losses.

(b) Future operating losses do not meet the definition of a liability and the general recognition criteria.

(c) An expectation of future operating losses is an indication that certain assets of the operation may be impaired. An entity tests these assets for impairment under Ind AS 36, *Impairment of Assets*.

**Onerous contracts**

Liabilities derived from onerous contract have to be provided for as they fulfil all the three recognition criteria related to provisions.

**Restructuring**

A provision for restructuring costs is recognised only when the general recognition criteria for provisions set out in paragraph 14 are met.

The following are examples of events that may fall under the definition of restructuring:

- (a) sale or termination of a line of business;
- (b) the closure of business locations in a country or region or the relocation of business activities from one country or region to another;
- (c) changes in management structure, for example, eliminating a layer of management; and
- (d) fundamental reorganisations that have a material effect on the nature and focus of the entity's operations.

A constructive obligation to restructure arises only when an entity:

- (a) has a detailed formal plan for the restructuring identifying at least:
  - (i) the business or part of a business concerned;
  - (ii) the principal locations affected;
  - (iii) the location, function, and approximate number of employees who will be compensated for terminating their services;
  - (iv) the expenditures that will be undertaken; and
  - (v) when the plan will be implemented; and
- (b) has raised a valid expectation in those affected that it will carry out the restructuring by starting to implement that plan or announcing its main features to those affected by it.

A restructuring provision shall include only the direct expenditures arising from the restructuring, which are those that are both:

(a) necessarily entailed by the restructuring; and

(b) not associated with the ongoing activities of the entity.

A restructuring provision does not include such costs as:

(a) retraining or relocating continuing staff;

(b) marketing; or

(c) investment in new systems and distribution networks.

These expenditures relate to the future conduct of the business and are not liabilities for restructuring at the end of the reporting period. Such expenditures are recognised on the same basis as if they arose independently of a restructuring.

Identifiable future operating losses up to the date of a restructuring are not included in a provision, unless they relate to an onerous contract.

**Illustration 5.8**

**In accordance with ICAI Guidance Note on Schedule III of Companies Act 2013, a payable is classified as "trade payable" if it pertains to amount due towards goods purchased or services received in the normal course of business. Based on this principle, can a company include in trade payables the liability towards employees, leases or other contractual liabilities? What is the treatment for amounts due towards capital goods purchased?**

**Solution**

Pursuant to Guidance Note on the Schedule III of Companies Act 2013 provides the following information with regard to identification of trade payables:

"A payable shall be classified as trade payable if it is in respect of amount due on account of goods purchased or services received in the normal course of business. As per the old Schedule VI, the term sundry creditors included amounts due in respect of goods purchased or services received or in respect of other contractual obligations as well. Hence, amounts due under contractual obligations can no longer be included within trade payables and only commercial dues can be included under trade payables.

Amounts due towards purchase of capital goods should also not be included in trade payables. They must be disclosed under other current liabilities with a suitable description.

**Illustration 5.9**

| **If a third party gives a personal security for any borrowings and creates, by means of a legal deed, a charge on the assets held by such third party, can such borrowings be described as 'secured' instead of 'unsecured'?**<br>**Solution**<br>If the deed properly conveys a security, it can be suitably disclosed in the terms of the loan. However, the loan itself is disclosed under unsecured loan because the assets of the company are not provided as a security for the loan. |
|---|

**Illustration 5.10: Provisions, Contingent Liabilities and Contingent Assets**

| **Provisions, Contingent Liabilities and Contingent Assets**<br>Provisions involving substantial degree of estimation in measurement are recognised when there is a present obligation as a result of past events and it is probable that there will be an outflow of resources. Contingent Liabilities are not recognised but are disclosed in the notes. Contingent Assets are neither recognised nor disclosed in the financial statements. |
|---|

**Illustration 5.11: Provision for current and deferred tax**

| **Provision for Current and Deferred Tax**<br>Provision for current tax is made after taking into consideration benefits admissible under the provisions of the Income-tax Act, 1961. Deferred tax resulting from "timing difference" between taxable and accounting income is accounted for using the tax rates and laws that are enacted or substantively enacted as on the balance sheet date.<br>Deferred tax asset is recognised and carried forward only to the extent that there is a virtual certainty that the asset will be realised in future. |
|---|

**Illustration 5.12: Specimen format of Trade payables**

| | **As at 31st March 2021** | **As at 31st March 2020** |
|---|---|---|
| Micro, small and medium enterprises<br>Others | xxx<br>xxx | Xxx<br>Xxx |
| Total | xxx | xxx |

The details of amounts outstanding to Micro, Small and Medium Enterprises based on available information with the Company are as under:

| **Particulars** | **As at 31st March 2021** | **As at 31st March 2020** |
|---|---|---|
| Principal amount due and remaining unpaid | xxx | xxx |
| Interest due on above and the unpaid interest | xxx | xxx |
| Interest paid | xxx | xxx |
| Payment made beyond the appointed day during the year | xxx | xxx |
| Interest due and payable for the period of delay | xxx | xxx |
| Interest accrued and remaining unpaid | xxx | xxx |
| Amount of further interest remaining due and payable in succeeding years | xxx | xxx |
| Total | xxx | xxx |

**Illustration 5.13: Specimen format: Other current liabilities**

| | **As at 31st March 2021** | **As at 31st March 2020** |
|---|---|---|
| Current maturities of long-term debt | xxx | xxx |
| Current maturities of finance lease obligations | xxx | xxx |
| Interest accrued but not due on borrowings | xxx | xxx |
| Unclaimed Dividends | xxx | xxx |
| Application money received and due for refund | xxx | xxx |
| Unpaid matured debentures and interest accrued thereon | xxx | xxx |
| Creditors for Capital Expenditure | xxx | xxx |
| Advance for Transfer of Participating Interest | xxx | xxx |
| Other Payables * | xxx | xxx |
| Total | xxx | xxx |

* Includes statutory dues, security deposit and advance from customers.

**Illustration 5.14: Specimen format: Short-term provisions**

| - | As at 31st March 2021 | As at 31st March 2020 |
|---|---|---|
| Provisions for Superannuation/Gratuity/Leave Encashment | xxx | xxx |
| Proposed Dividend | xxx | xxx |
| Tax on Dividend | xxx | xxx |
| Provision for Taxes | xxx | xxx |
| Other Provisions | xxx | xxx |
| Total | xxx | xxx |

**Illustration 5.15: Provisions for indirect taxes**

**Goods and Services Tax**

Goods and Service tax is accounted on the basis of both, payments made in respect of goods cleared/services provided as also provision made for goods lying in bonded warehouses. Goods and Services tax/Value added tax paid is charged to Profit and Loss account.

## 5.3 ACCOUNTING QUALITY OF CURRENT LIABILITIES

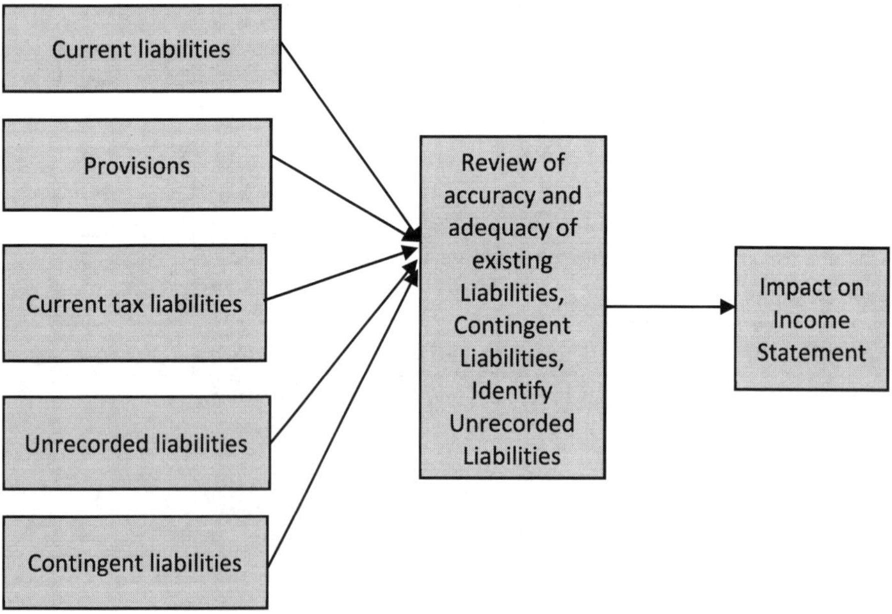

Key focus areas to ensure Accounting Quality of current liabilities may be highlighted in the table below.

| Item |
|---|
| Whether new vendors are investigated and approved before being added to the vendor master list. |
| Whether there is segregation of duties between purchases, receiving and payment. |
| Whether there is a proper request for proposal process followed before creating vendor contract. |
| Whether vendors no longer used are inactivated or purged from the vendor master list. |
| Whether vendors are properly evaluated when purchases are made. Whether competitive prices are obtained. |
| Whether duplicate vendor numbers and names appear in the vendor master file |
| Whether purchases are made that exceed the approved budget. |
| Whether purchases are made without proper approval.<br>Whether in some case purchase orders are not prepared or authorized. |
| Whether receipt of goods is documented and updated in the system. |
| Whether Trade Payable duties are effectively segregated to minimize the risk of fraud. |
| Whether disbursements are made without proper approval. |
| Whether prices charged on invoice match the purchase order or pricing program. |
| Whether amounts recorded / paid match the approved invoices. |
| Whether payment terms are established for each vendor so that discount and payment dates are automatically calculated. |
| Whether the system provides a three-way match between PO, Goods receipt note and invoice |
| Whether duplicate invoices are recorded and prevented from payment |
| Whether the system allows an invoice to be paid more than once. |
| Whether outstanding credit memos are applied to current or future invoices. |
| Whether invoices are coded to the appropriate account. |
| Whether payments are incorrectly recorded but not made. |
| Whether payment is recorded in the proper period. |

| Item |
|---|
| Where purchases made are not recorded / paid or not recorded / paid timely. |
| Whether payment to vendor is made but not recorded. |
| Whether The Trade Payable detail is not properly summarized / posted to the General Ledger |
| Whether disbursements are not properly summarized/posted to the General Ledger. |
| Whether there is audit trail of payables or purchasing related activities. |
| Whether all Trade Payables records are reconciled with sub-ledger, general ledger and financial statements. |

# Chapter 6

# Non-Current Assets

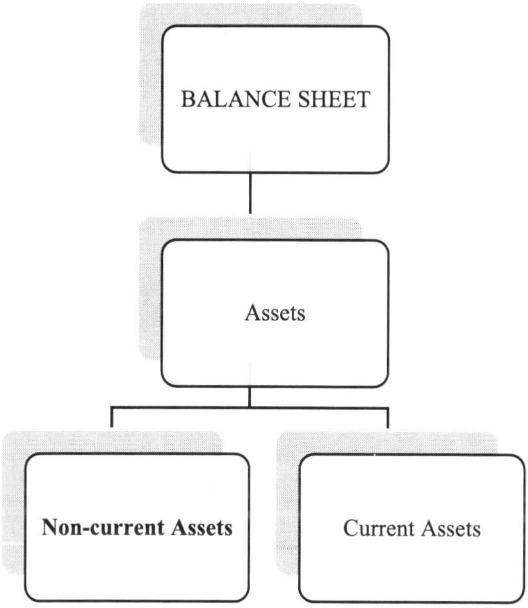


## 6.1 DEFINITION OF NON-CURRENT ASSETS

Non-current has not been defined. However, as per ICAI Guidance Note on Terms used under Financial Statements, Fixed Assets has been defined as under:

"Asset held for the purpose of providing or producing goods or services and that is not held for resale in the normal course of business."

In accordance with IFRS and Ind AS, non-current assets have been defined by default as under:

Any asset which does not fall within the categories of assets highlighted below are treated as non-current assets.

(a) it expects to realize the asset, or intends to sell or consume it, in its normal ***operating cycle,***

(b) it holds the asset primarily for trading,

(c) it expects to realize the asset within twelve months after the reporting period; or

| | |
|---|---|
| (d) | the asset is cash or a cash equivalent (as defined in Ind AS 7) unless the asset is restricted from being exchanged or used to settle a liability for at least twelve months after the reporting period. |

## 6.2 COMPONENTS OF NON-CURRENT ASSETS

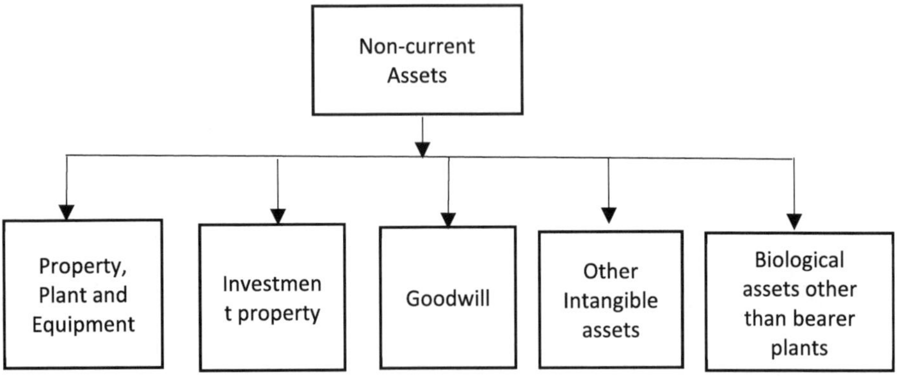


Comparative classification of Non-Current Assets as provided in Schedule III Division I and Division II of Companies Act, 2013 is shown in table below.

| Under AS | Under Ind AS |
|---|---|
| **I. Tangible Assets**<br>(i) Classification shall be given as:<br>(a) Land<br>(b) Buildings<br>(c) Plant and Equipment<br>(d) Furniture and fixtures<br>(e) Vehicles<br>(f) Office equipment<br>(g) Others (specify nature)<br>(ii) Assets under lease shall be separately specified under each class of asset.<br>(iii) A reconciliation of the gross and net carrying amounts of each class of assets at the beginning and end of the reporting period showing additions, disposals, acquisitions through business combinations, amount of change due to revaluation (if change is 10% or more in the aggregate of the net carrying value of each | **A. Non-Current Assets**<br>**I. Property, Plant and Equipment**<br>(i) Classification shall be given as:<br>(a) Land.<br>(b) Buildings.<br>(c) Plant and Equipment.<br>(d) Furniture and Fixtures.<br>(e) Vehicles.<br>(f) Office equipment.<br>(g) Bearer Plants<br>(h) Others (specify nature).<br>(ii) Assets under lease shall be separately specified under each class of assets.<br>(iii) A reconciliation of the gross and net carrying amounts of each class of assets at the beginning and end of the reporting period showing additions, disposals, |

| Under AS | Under Ind AS |
|---|---|
| class of Property, Plant and Equipment) and other adjustments and the related depreciation and impairment losses/reversals shall be disclosed separately.<br>(iv) Where sums have been written off on a reduction of capital or revaluation of assets or where sums have been added on revaluation of assets, every balance sheet subsequent to date of such write-off, or addition shall show the reduced or increased figures as applicable and shall by way of a note also show the amount of the reduction or increase as applicable together with the date thereof for the first five years subsequent to the date of such reduction or increase. | acquisitions through business combinations, amount of change due to revaluation (if change is 10% or more in the aggregate of the net carrying value of each class of Property, Plant and Equipment) and other adjustments and the related depreciation and impairment losses or reversals shall be disclosed separately. |
| | **II. Investment Property**<br>A reconciliation of the gross and net carrying amounts of each class of property at the beginning and end of the reporting period showing additions, disposals, acquisitions through business combinations and other adjustments and the related amortisation and impairment losses/reversals shall be disclosed separately. |
| | **III Goodwill**<br>A reconciliation of the gross and net carrying amount of goodwill at the beginning and end of the reporting period showing additions, impairments, disposals and other adjustments. |
| **J. Intangible Assets**<br>(i) Classification shall be given as:<br>(a) goodwill<br>(b) brand/trademarks<br>(c) computer software | **IV. Other Intangible assets**<br>(i) Classification shall be given as:<br>(a) Brands /trademarks.<br>(b) Computer software.<br>(c) Mastheads and publishing |

| Under AS | Under Ind AS |
|---|---|
| (d) mastheads and publishing titles<br>(e) Mining rights<br>(f) Copyrights, patents and other intellectual property rights, services and operating rights<br>(g) recipes, formulae, models, designs and prototypes<br>(h) licenses and franchise<br>(i) Others (specify nature)<br>(ii) A reconciliation of the gross and net carrying amounts of each class of assets at the beginning and end of the reporting period showing additions, disposals, acquisitions through business combinations, amount of change due to revaluation (if change is 10% or more in the aggregate of the net carrying value of each class of intangible assets) and other adjustments and the related depreciation and impairment losses or reversals shall be disclosed separately.<br>(iii) Where sums have been written off on a reduction of capital or revaluation of assets, every balance sheet subsequent to date of such write-off, or addition, shall show the amount of reduction or increase as applicable together with the date thereof for the first five years subsequent to the date of such reduction or increase | titles.<br>(d) Mining rights.<br>(e) Copyrights, patents, other intellectual property rights, services and operating rights.<br>(f) Recipes, formulae, models, designs and prototypes.<br>(g) Licenses and franchises.<br>(h) Others (specify nature).<br><br>(ii) A reconciliation of the gross and net carrying amounts of each class of assets at the beginning and end of the reporting period showing additions, disposals, acquisitions through business combinations, amount of change due to revaluation (if change is 10% or more in the aggregate of the net carrying value of each class of intangible assets) and other adjustments and the related amortization and impairment losses or reversals shall be disclosed separately. |
| | **V. Biological Assets other than bearer plants**<br>A reconciliation of the carrying amounts of each class of assets at the beginning and end of the reporting period showing additions, disposals, acquisitions through |

| Under AS | Under Ind AS |
|---|---|
| | business combinations and other adjustments shall be disclosed separately. |

## 6.3 PROPERTY, PLANT AND EQUIPMENT

### 6.3.1 Classification under Schedule III, Division I (non-Ind AS)

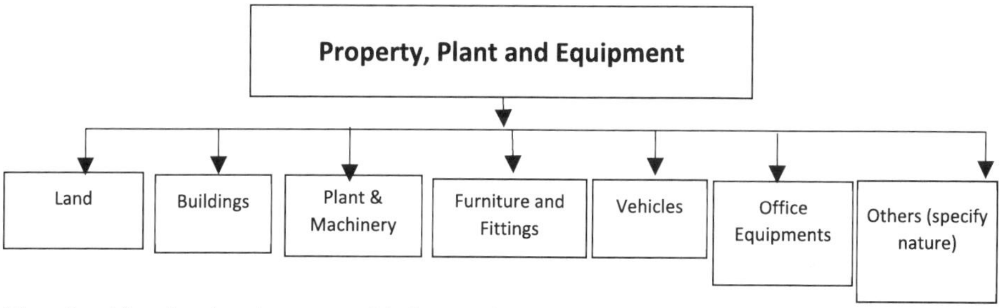


The classification has been provided as under:

(a) Land;

(b) Buildings;

(c) Plant and Equipment;

(d) Furniture and Fixtures;

(e) Vehicles;

(f) Office equipment;

(g) Others (specify nature).

Some salient points related to presentation under Schedule III Division for non-Ind AS entities are highlighted below.

**Precedence of Accounting Standards over Schedule III**

Schedule III is clear that the disclosure requirements of the Accounting Standards are in addition to disclosures required under the Schedule, and in case of any conflict, the Accounting Standards will prevail over the Schedule. Keeping this in view, the companies should make disclosures required by Schedule III only for five years. However, details required by AS 10 (Revised 2016) will have to be provided as long as the asset is held by the company.

**Presentation of lease hold and free hold land**

Schedule III does not prescribe any particular classification/presentation for leasehold land. *AS 19 Leases* excludes land leases from its scope. According to ICAI Guidance Note on Schedule III for non-Ind AS entities, the accounting treatment for leasehold land should be continued to be presented as a separate asset class under

Tangible Assets as is currently being followed under prevailing Indian generally accepted accounting principles and practices. Also freehold land should continue to be presented as a separate asset class.

**Revaluation of Property, Plant and Equipment**

With respect to revaluation of Property, Plant and Equipment, AS-10 (Revised 2016) Property, Plant and Equipment requires an entity to disclose details such as

- effective date of the revaluation,
- whether an independent valuer was involved,
- the methods and significant assumptions applied in estimating fair value of the items,
- the extent to which fair values of items were determined directly by reference to observable prices in an active market or recent market transactions on arm's length terms or were estimated using other valuation techniques, and
- the revaluation surplus, indicating the change for the period and any restrictions on the distribution of the balance of shareholders.

## 6.3.2 Classification under Schedule III, Division II (Ind AS)

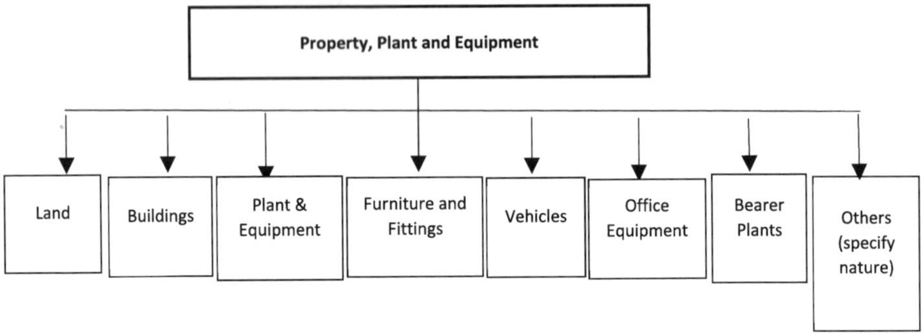


(i) Classification shall be given as:

(a) Land.

(b) Buildings.

(c) Plant and Equipment.

(d) Furniture and Fixtures.

(e) Vehicles.

(f) Office equipment.

(g) Bearer Plants

(h) Others (specify nature).

**Grouping of Land and Building as separate classes of non-current assets**

According to ICAI Guidance Note on Schedule III related to Ind AS, land and building are presented as two separate classes of property, plant and equipment under Schedule III, Division II on Ind AS as mentioned above. In contrast, paragraph 37 of Ind AS 16 gives an example of grouping land and building under same class for revaluation purposes. However, companies should continue to present land and building separately as given in Ind AS Schedule III and such presentation needs to be followed consistently.

**Separate disclosure of change owing to revaluation of each class of Property, Plant and Equipment**

Also, Ind AS Schedule III requires separate disclosure of the amount of change due to revaluation, where change is 10% or more in the aggregate of the net carrying value of each class of Property, Plant and Equipment as mentioned in the table above. In contrast, paragraph 73 of Ind AS 16 requires reconciliation of the carrying amount at the beginning and end of the period showing increases or decreases resulting from revaluations, irrespective of the percentage change. According to ICAI Guidance Note, separate presentation of the amount of change due to revaluation should be continued, irrespective whether such a change is 10% or more, in order to comply with a broader presentation requirement of Ind AS 16 and such presentation needs to be followed consistently.

**Capital work-in-progress**

According to ICAI Guidance Note, under Ind AS Schedule III, capital advances/ advances for purchase of capital assets should be included under other non- current assets and hence, should not be included under capital work-in-progress.

### 6.3.3 AS 10: Property, Plant and Equipment

The relevant extracts of AS 10 have been summarized below for reference purposes.

**Recognition**

***Para 7. The cost of an item of property, plant and equipment should be recognised as an asset if, and only if:***

***(a) it is probable that future economic benefits associated with the item will flow to the enterprise; and***

***(b) the cost of the item can be measured reliably.***

Para 8. Items such as spare parts, stand-by equipment and servicing equipment are recognised in accordance with this Standard when they meet the definition of property, plant and equipment. Otherwise, such items are classified as inventory.

Para 10. An enterprise evaluates under this recognition principle all its costs on property, plant and equipment at the time they are incurred. These costs include costs incurred:

(a) initially to acquire or construct an item of property, plant and equipment; and

(b) subsequently to add to, replace part of, or service it.

## Measurement

### Initial Measurement

***Para 16. An item of property, plant and equipment that qualifies for recognition as an asset should be measured at its cost.***

Para 17. The cost of an item of property, plant and equipment comprises:

| **Elements of cost** | (a) its purchase price, including import duties and non –refundable purchase taxes,, after deducting trade discounts and rebates.<br>(b) any costs directly attributable to bringing the asset to the location and condition necessary for it to be capable of operating in the manner intended by management.<br>(c) the initial estimate of the costs of dismantling, removing the item and restoring the site on which it is located, referred to as 'decommissioning, restoration and similar liabilities', the obligation for which an enterprise incurs either when the item is acquired or as a consequence of having used the item during a particular period for purposes other than to produce inventories during that period. |
|---|---|

Para 18. Examples of directly attributable costs are:

(a) costs of employee benefits (as defined in AS 15, Employee Benefits) arising directly from the construction or acquisition of the item of property, plant and equipment;

(b) costs of site preparation;

(c) initial delivery and handling costs;

(d) installation and assembly costs;

(e) costs of testing whether the asset is functioning properly, after deducting the net proceeds from selling any items produced while bringing the asset to that location and condition (such as samples produced when testing equipment); and

(f) professional fees.

Para 19. An enterprise applies AS 2, Valuation of Inventories, to the costs of obligations for dismantling, removing and restoring the site on which an item is located that are incurred during a particular period as a consequence of having used the item to produce inventories during that period. The obligations for costs accounted for in accordance with AS 2 or AS 10 are recognised and measured in accordance with AS 29, Provisions, Contingent Liabilities and Contingent Assets.

Para 20. Examples of costs that are not costs of an item of property, plant and equipment are:

(a) costs of opening a new facility or business, such as, inauguration costs;

(b) costs of introducing a new product or service (including costs of advertising and promotional activities);

(c) costs of conducting business in a new location or with a new class of customer (including costs of staff training); and

(d) administration and other general overhead costs.

Para 21. Recognition of costs in the carrying amount of an item of property, plant and equipment ceases when the item is in the location and condition necessary for it to be capable of operating in the manner intended by management. Therefore, costs incurred in using or redeploying an item are not included in the carrying amount of that item. For example, the following costs are not included in the carrying amount of an item of property, plant and equipment:

(a) costs incurred while an item capable of operating in the manner intended by management has yet to be brought into use or is operated at less than full capacity.

(b) initial operating losses, such as those incurred while demand for the output of an item builds up; and

(c) costs of relocating or reorganising part or all of the operations of an enterprise.

**Subsequent measurement**

Para 32. An enterprise should choose either the cost model in paragraph 33 or the revaluation model in paragraph 34 as its accounting policy and should apply that policy to an entire class of property, plant and equipment.

**Cost model**

Para 33. After recognition as an asset, an item of property, plant and equipment should be carried at its cost less any accumulated depreciation and any accumulated impairment losses.

**Revaluation model**

Para 34. After recognition as an asset, an item of property, plant and equipment whose fair value can be measured reliably should be carried at a revalued amount, being its fair value at the date of the revaluation less any subsequent accumulated depreciation and subsequent accumulated impairment losses. Revaluations should be made with sufficient regularity to ensure that the carrying amount does not differ materially from that which would be determined using fair value at the balance sheet date.

Para 39. If an item of property, plant and equipment is revalued, the entire class of property, plant and equipment to which that asset belongs should be revalued.

***Para 42. An increase in the carrying amount of an asset arising on revaluation should be credited directly to owners' interests under the heading of revaluation surplus However, the increase should be recognised in the statement of profit and loss to the extent that it reverses a revaluation decrease of the same asset previously recognised in the statement of profit and loss.***

***Para 43. A decrease in the carrying amount of an asset arising on revaluation should be charged to the statement of profit and loss. However, the decrease should be debited directly to owners' interests under the heading of revaluation surplus to the extent of any credit balance existing in the revaluation surplus in respect of that asset.***

**Depreciation**

***Para 52. The depreciable amount of an asset should be allocated on a systematic basis over its useful life.***

***Par 53. The residual value and the useful life of an asset should be reviewed at least at each financial year-end and, if expectations differ from previous estimates, the change(s) should be accounted for as a change in an accounting estimate in accordance with AS 5, Net Profit or Loss for the Period, Prior Period Items and Changes in Accounting Policies.***

***Para 62. The depreciation method used should reflect the pattern in which the future economic benefits of the asset are expected to be consumed by the enterprise.***

***Para 63. The depreciation method applied to an asset should be reviewed at least at each financial year-end and, if there has been a significant change in the expected pattern of consumption of the future economic benefits embodied in the asset, the method should be changed to reflect the changed pattern. Such a change should be accounted for as a change in an accounting estimate in accordance with AS 5.***

**Changes in existing decommissioning, restoration and other liabilities**

Para 66. The cost of property, plant and equipment may undergo changes subsequent to its acquisition or construction on account of changes in liabilities, price adjustments, changes in duties, changes in initial estimates of amounts provided for dismantling, removing, restoration and similar factors and included in the cost of the asset in accordance with paragraph 16. Such changes in cost should be accounted for in accordance with paragraphs 67–68 below.

Para 67. If the related asset is measured using the cost model:

(a) subject to (b), changes in the liability should be added to, or deducted from, the cost of the related asset in the current period.

(b) the amount deducted from the cost of the asset should not exceed its carrying amount. If a decrease in the liability exceeds the carrying amount of the asset, the excess should be recognised immediately in the statement of profit and loss.

(c) if the adjustment results in an addition to the cost of an asset, the enterprise should consider whether this is an indication that the new carrying amount of the asset may not be fully recoverable. If it is such an indication, the enterprise should test the asset for impairment by estimating its recoverable amount, and should account for any impairment loss, in accordance with AS 28.

Para 68. If the related asset is measured using the revaluation model:

(a) changes in the liability alter the revaluation surplus or deficit previously recognised on that asset, so that:

(i) a decrease in the liability should (subject to (b)) be credited directly to revaluation surplus in the owners' interest, except that it should be recognised in the statement of profit and loss to the extent that it reverses a revaluation deficit on the asset that was previously recognised in the statement of profit and loss;

(ii) an increase in the liability should be recognised in the statement of profit and loss, except that it should be debited directly to revaluation surplus in the owners' interest to the extent of any credit balance existing in the revaluation surplus in respect of that asset.

(b) in the event that a decrease in the liability exceeds the carrying amount that would have been recognised had the asset been carried under the cost model, the excess should be recognised immediately in the statement of profit and loss.

(c) a change in the liability is an indication that the asset may have to be revalued in order to ensure that the carrying amount does not differ materially from that which would be determined using fair value at the balance sheet date. Any such revaluation should be taken into account in determining the amounts to be taken to the statement of profit and loss and the owners' interest under (a). If a revaluation is necessary, all assets of that class should be revalued.

Para 69. The adjusted depreciable amount of the asset is depreciated over its useful life. Therefore, once the related asset has reached the end of its useful life, all subsequent changes in the liability should be recognised in the statement of profit and loss as they occur. This applies under both the cost model and the revaluation model.

**Impairment**

Para 70. To determine whether an item of property, plant and equipment is impaired, an enterprise applies AS 28, Impairment of Assets. AS 28 explains how an enterprise reviews the carrying amount of its assets, how it determines the recoverable amount of an asset, and when it recognises, or reverses the recognition of, an impairment loss.

**Retirement**

Para 73. Items of property, plant and equipment retired from active use and held for disposal should be stated at the lower of their carrying amount and net realisable value. Any write-down in this regard should be recognised immediately in the statement of profit and loss.

**Derecognition**

Para 74. The carrying amount of an item of property, plant and equipment should be derecognised

(a) on disposal; or

(b) when no future economic benefits are expected from its use or disposal.

Para 75. The gain or loss arising from the derecognition of an item of property, plant and equipment should be included in the statement of profit and loss when the item is derecognised (unless AS 19, Leases, requires otherwise on a sale and leaseback). Gains should not be classified as revenue, as defined in AS 9, Revenue Recognition.

Para 76. However, an enterprise that in the course of its ordinary activities, routinely sells items of property, plant and equipment that it had held for rental to others should transfer such assets to inventories at their carrying amount when they cease to be rented and become held for sale. The proceeds from the sale of such assets should be recognised in revenue in accordance with AS 9, Revenue Recognition.

Para 79. The gain or loss arising from the derecognition of an item of property, plant and equipment should be determined as the difference between the net disposal proceeds, if any, and the carrying amount of the item.

**Disclosure**

***Para 81. The financial statements should disclose, for each class of property, plant and equipment:***

***(a) the measurement bases (i.e., cost model or revaluation model) used for determining the gross carrying amount;***

***(b) the depreciation methods used;***

***(c) the useful lives or the depreciation rates used. In case the useful lives or the depreciation rates used are different from those specified in the statute governing the enterprise, it should make a specific mention of that fact;***

***(d) the gross carrying amount and the accumulated depreciation (aggregated with accumulated impairment losses) at the beginning and end of the period; and***

***(e) a reconciliation of the carrying amount at the beginning and end of the period showing:***

*(i) additions;*

*(ii) assets retired from active use and held for disposal;*

*(iii) acquisitions through business combinations;*

*(iv) increases or decreases resulting from revaluations under paragraphs 34, 42 and 43 and from impairment losses recognised or reversed directly in revaluation surplus in accordance with AS 28;*

*(v) impairment losses recognised in the statement of profit and loss in accordance with AS 28;*

*(vi) impairment losses reversed in the statement of profit and loss in accordance with AS 28;*

*(vii) depreciation;*

*(viii) the net exchange differences arising on the translation of the financial statements of a non-integral foreign operation in accordance with AS 11, The Effects of Changes in Foreign Exchange Rates; and*

*(ix) other changes.*

***Para 82. The financial statements should also disclose:***

*(a) the existence and amounts of restrictions on title, and property, plant and equipment pledged as security for liabilities;*

*(b) the amount of expenditure recognised in the carrying amount of an item of property, plant and equipment in the course of its construction;*

*(c) the amount of contractual commitments for the acquisition of property, plant and equipment;*

*(d) if it is not disclosed separately on the face of the statement of profit and loss, the amount of compensation from third parties for items of property, plant and equipment that were impaired, lost or given up that is included in the statement of profit and loss; and*

*(e) the amount of assets retired from active use and held for disposal.*

***Para 85. If items of property, plant and equipment are stated at revalued amounts, the following should be disclosed:***

*(a) the effective date of the revaluation;*

*(b) whether an independent valuer was involved;*

*(c) the methods and significant assumptions applied in estimating fair values of the items;*

*(d) the extent to which fair values of the items were determined directly by reference to observable prices in an active market or recent market*

| | |
|---|---|
| | ***transactions on arm's length terms or were estimated using other valuation techniques; and*** |
| *(e)* | ***the revaluation surplus, indicating the change for the period and any restrictions on the distribution of the balance to shareholders.*** |

### 6.3.4 Ind AS 16: Property, Plant and Equipment

Salient points related to the Ind AS 16 are summarized below.

**Recognition of non-current assets**

Now recognition criteria for non-current assets are highlighted as under:

An item is recognised as non-current assets if:

(a) it is probable that future economic benefit will flow to the entity.

(b) cost of an item can be measured reliably.

**Initial Measurement**

Property, Plant and equipment is initially recognised at historical cost.

The elements of cost are highlighted below.

| | |
|---|---|
| ***Purchase price*** | Considered after deducting ***trade discounts*** and ***rebates*** and adding ***duties and non-refundable taxes***<br>The price to be considered is the cash price equivalent at the recognition date. If the asset is acquired on deferred credit i.e. credit beyond the normal credit period, then the difference between the cash price and the total payment is treated as ***interest*** and recognised over the credit period unless such interest is capitalised in accordance with Ind AS 23.<br>The cost of assets involved in the exchange is determined at fair value (of asset received or the asset given up) unless:<br>(a) the transaction lacks commercial substance; or<br>(b) the fair value of neither of the two assets is reliably measured<br>In such a scenario the cost of the asset acquired is measured at the carrying amount of the asset given up. |
| ***Costs directly attributable to bringing the asset to its location and in the condition so as to make it available for its intended use*** | (a) Costs of employee benefits (as per Ind AS 19 Employee benefits), arising from construction or acquisition of property, plant and equipment<br>(b) Costs of preparing the site<br>(c) Initial delivery and handling costs (freight and delivery charge)<br>(d) Installation and assembly costs (e.g. wages to install machinery) |

| | |
|---|---|
| | (e) Testing costs net of revenue generated, such as sale proceeds of material produced during a test run<br>(f) Professional fees (architect's fees) |
| ***Initial estimate of the costs of dismantling and removing the item and restoration of site on which it is located*** | The obligation for which for which the entity incurs either:<br>(a) When the item is acquired or<br>(b) As a consequence of having used the item during a particular period for purposes other than to produce inventories during that period<br>These are recognised and measured in accordance with Ind AS 37, *Provisions, Contingent Liabilities and Contingent Assets*. |

Initial measurement of Property, Plant and Equipment at historical cost is depicted in the chart below.

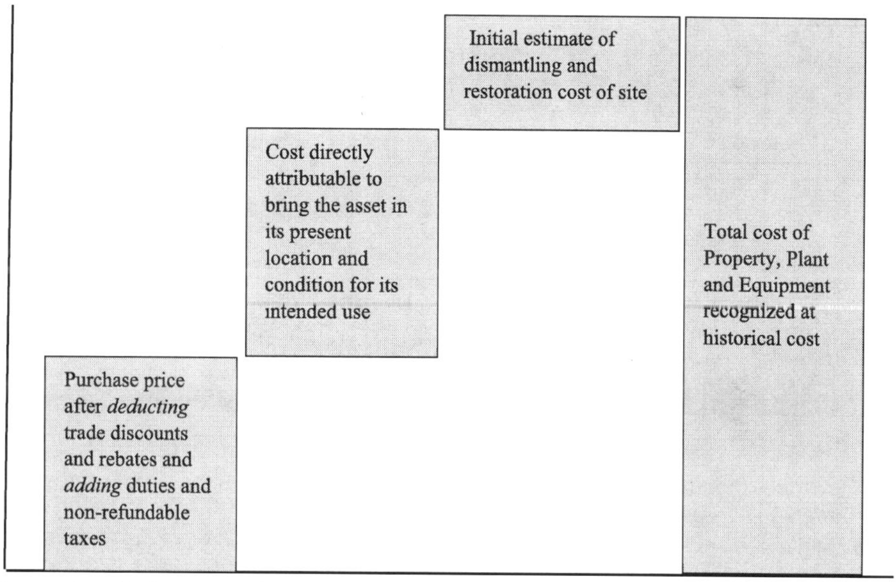


Examples of elements of cost not to be included are:

(a) Cost of opening a new facility

(b) Administration and general overhead

(c) Cost of launching a new product or service (including costs of advertising and promotional activities);

(d) Expenses on opening a new business facility or expenses related to an inaugural function

(e) Cost of relocating – shifting factory consequent to statutory order

(f) Initial losses when the asset operates at lower capacity

| | |
|---|---|
| (g) | Costs of incidental operations not necessary to bring the asset to its required condition and location. |

**Subsequent measurement**

The treatment of subsequent expenditure would be as under:

| | |
|---|---|
| ***Capital expenditure*** | Expenditure which ***enhances the revenue generating capacity*** of the asset so that it works more efficiently or the useful life is extended |
| ***Revenue expenditure*** | Expenditure which ***maintains the existing capacity of the asset,*** in order that it can work effectively |
| ***Subsequent costs – capital and revenue expenditure*** | (a) Cost of ***day-to-day servicing of an asset*** is treated as revenue expenditure and charged to SOPL and not included in carrying amount of the asset<br>(b) Cost of ***replacements***:<br>– at regular intervals<br>– at less frequent intervals<br>– at occasional intervals – i.e. non-recurring replacements<br>These are recognised as capital expenditure and added to carrying value of asset<br>Once the new parts are recognised, the old parts are replaced and de-recognised and removed from Balance Sheet<br>Certain plant and equipment (e.g. aircraft, engines, turbines etc) are required to carry out major inspection and overhauling expenses on a periodic basis. The above principle would apply to these cases as well. |

With respect to subsequent measurement, we have two models viz, the cost model and revaluation model as explained below:

| | |
|---|---|
| **(a) Cost model** | After recognition as an asset, an item of property, plant and equipment shall be carried at its cost less any accumulated depreciation and any accumulated impairment losses. |
| **(b) Revaluation model** | After recognition as an asset, an item of property, plant and equipment whose fair value can be measured reliably shall be carried at a revalued amount, being its fair value at the date of the revaluation less any subsequent accumulated depreciation and subsequent accumulated impairment losses. Revaluations shall be made with sufficient regularity to ensure that the carrying amount does not differ materially from that which would be determined using fair value at the end of the reporting period. |

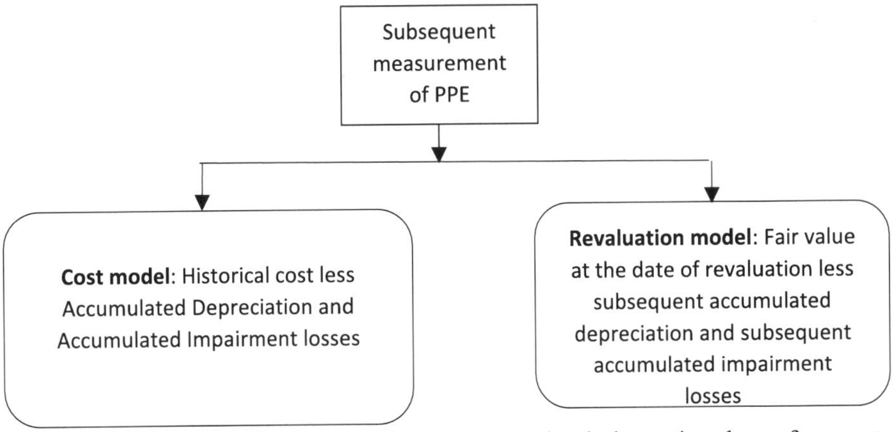


If an item of property, plant and equipment is revalued, the entire class of property, plant and equipment to which that asset belongs shall be revalued.

A class of property, plant and equipment is a grouping of assets of a similar nature and use in an entity's operations.

The following are examples of separate classes:

(a) land;

(b) land and buildings;

(c) machinery;

(d) ships;

(e) aircraft;

(f) motor vehicles;

(g) furniture and fixtures;

(h) office equipment; and

(i) bearer plants.

**Revaluation model**

| ***Salient points of revaluation model are:*** | ***The fair value of an asset*** is required to be determined under the revaluation model. Ind AS 16 provides guidance on how to determine the fair value:<br>(a) If there is market-based evidence:<br>Land & Buildings – derived from market-based values as appraised By professionally qualified valuers<br>Plant & Equipment-based on market value determined by experts<br>(b) If there is no market-based evidence: |
|---|---|

| | |
|---|---|
| | estimate fair value using an income or a depreciated replacement cost method<br>Frequency of valuation should be annual in those class of assets where the fair value is materially different from carrying value based on volatile conditions – otherwise every three to five years would be sufficient.<br>***Accounting for revaluation adjustment***<br>(a) If an asset's carrying amount is increased – it should be recognised ***in other comprehensive income and accumulated in equity*** under the heading revaluation surplus. However, if there is a revaluation decrease of the same asset earlier – *which was recognised in profit or loss as per Ind AS 16* – then the increase should be credited in profit or loss to the extent it reverses the revaluation decrease<br>(b) If an asset's carrying amount is decreased – it should be recognised in ***profit or loss*** (income statement). However, if there is a balance in the revaluation surplus under equity for the same asset based on revaluation performed earlier, such decrease is recognised in other comprehensive income.<br>If an item of property, plant and equipment is revalued, the entire class of assets to which the asset belongs should be revalued. A class is a group of assets of a similar nature and use in an entity's business operation.<br>***Treatment of revaluation reserve and profit or loss on sale***<br>When the assets is derecognised (sold), the revaluation surplus included in equity should be transferred directly to retained earnings. Profit or loss on sale will be calculated in the usual manner i.e. sale proceeds less carrying value (revalued) |

**De-recognition of Property, Plant and Equipment**

PPE is derecognised (eliminated) from Balance Sheet when PPE is disposed of or withdrawn from use & no future economic benefits expected from its disposal.

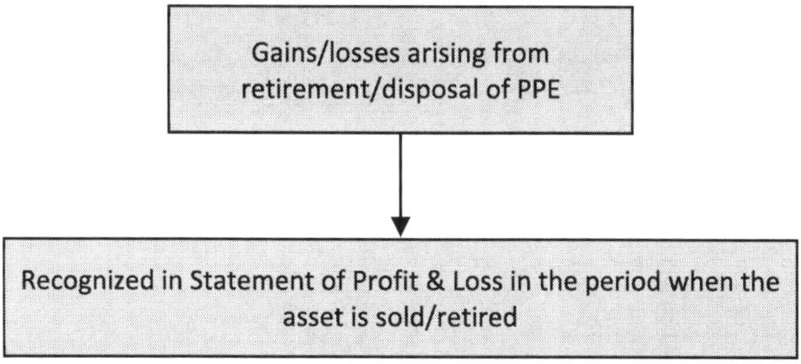


**Changes in existing decommissioning, restoration and similar liabilities**

**Background**

Many entities have obligations to dismantle, remove and restore items of property, plant and equipment. In this Appendix such obligations are referred to as "decommissioning, restoration and similar liabilities". Under Ind AS 16, the cost of an item of property, plant and equipment includes the initial estimate of the costs of dismantling and removing the item and restoring the site on which it is located, the obligation for which an entity incurs either when the item is acquired or as a consequence of having used the item during a particular period for purposes other than to produce inventories during that period. Ind AS 37 contains requirements on how to measure decommissioning, restoration and similar liabilities. This Appendix provides guidance on how to account for the effect of changes in the measurement of existing decommissioning, restoration, and similar liabilities.

This Appendix applies to changes in the measurement of any existing decommissioning, restoration or similar liability that is both:

(a) recognised as part of the cost of an item of property, plant and equipment in accordance with Ind AS 16; and

(b) recognised as a liability in accordance with Ind AS 37.

For example, a decommissioning, restoration, or similar liability may exist for decommissioning a plant, rehabilitating environmental damage in extractive industries, or removing equipment.

**Accounting principle**

**(i) Cost model**

(a) subject to (b), changes in the liability shall be added to, or deducted from, the cost of the related asset in the current period.

(b) the amount deducted from the cost of the asset shall not exceed its carrying amount. If a decrease in the liability exceeds the carrying amount of the asset, the excess shall be recognised immediately in profit or loss.

(c) if the adjustment results in an addition to the cost of an asset, the entity shall consider whether this is an indication that the new carrying amount of the asset may not be fully recoverable. If it is such an indication, the entity shall test the asset for impairment by estimating its recoverable amount, and shall account for any impairment loss, in accordance with Ind AS 36.

**(ii) Revaluation model**

(a) changes in the liability alter the revaluation surplus or deficit previously recognised on that asset, so that:

(i) a decrease in the liability shall (subject to (b)) be recognised in other comprehensive income and increase the revaluation surplus within equity, except that it shall be recognised in profit or loss to the extent that it reverses a revaluation deficit on the asset that was previously recognised in profit or loss;

(ii) an increase in the liability shall be recognised in profit or loss, except that it shall be recognised in other comprehensive income and reduce the revaluation surplus within equity to the extent of any credit balance existing in the revaluation surplus in respect of that asset.

(b) in the event that a decrease in the liability exceeds the carrying amount that would have been recognised had the asset been carried under the cost model, the excess shall be recognised immediately in profit or loss.

The adjusted depreciable amount of the asset is depreciated over its useful life. Therefore, once the related asset has reached the end of its useful life, all subsequent changes in the liability shall be recognised in profit or loss as they occur. This applies under both the cost model and the revaluation model.

The periodic unwinding of the discount shall be recognised in profit or loss as a finance cost as it occurs. Capitalisation under Ind AS 23 is not permitted.

**Stripping costs in the production phase of a surface mine**

In surface mining operations, entities may find it necessary to remove mine waste materials ('overburden') to gain access to mineral ore deposits. This waste removal activity is known as 'stripping'.

During the development phase of the mine (before production begins), stripping costs are usually capitalised as part of the depreciable cost of building, developing and constructing the mine.

Those capitalised costs are depreciated or amortised on a systematic basis, usually by using the units of production method, once production begins.

A mining entity may continue to remove overburden and to incur stripping costs during the production phase of the mine.

The material removed when stripping in the production phase will not necessarily be a total waste; often it will be a combination of ore and waste. The ratio of ore to waste can range from uneconomic low grade to profitable high grade.

Removal of material with a low ratio of ore to waste may produce some usable material, which can be used to produce inventory. This removal might also provide access to deeper levels of material that have a higher ratio of ore to waste. There can therefore be two benefits accruing to the entity from the stripping activity: usable ore that can be used to produce inventory and improved access to further quantities of material that will be mined in future periods.

**Issue**

The following issues are addressed:

(a) recognition of production stripping costs as an asset;

(b) initial measurement of the stripping activity asset; and

(c) subsequent measurement of the stripping activity asset.

**Accounting principles**

**(a) Recognition of production stripping costs as an asset**

(i) To the extent that the benefit from the stripping activity is realised in the form of inventory produced, the entity shall account for the costs of that stripping overburden removal activity in accordance with the principles of Ind AS 2, Inventories.

(ii) To the extent the benefit is improved access to ore, the entity shall recognise these costs as a non-current asset, say, Stripping Activity Asset, if and only if, all of the following are met:

(a) it is probable that the future economic benefit (improved access to the ore body) associated with the stripping activity will flow to the entity;

(b) the entity can identify the component of the ore body for which access has been improved; and

(c) the costs relating to the stripping activity associated with that component can be measured reliably.

The stripping activity asset will be accounted for as *part* of an existing asset. The stripping activity asset's classification as a tangible or intangible asset is the same as the existing asset.

**(b) Initial measurement of the stripping activity asset**

The entity shall initially measure the stripping activity asset at cost, this being the accumulation of costs directly incurred to perform the stripping activity that improves access to the identified component of ore, plus an allocation of directly attributable overhead costs.

When the costs of the stripping activity asset and the inventory produced are not separately identifiable, the entity shall allocate the production stripping costs between the inventory produced and the stripping activity asset by using an allocation basis that is based on a relevant production measure. This production measure shall be calculated for the identified component of the ore body, and shall be used as a benchmark to identify the extent to which the additional activity of creating a future benefit has taken place. Examples of such measures include:

(a) cost of inventory produced compared with expected cost;

(b) volume of waste extracted compared with expected volume, for a given volume of ore production; and

(c) mineral content of the ore extracted compared with expected mineral content to be extracted, for a given quantity of ore produced.

**(c) Subsequent measurement of the stripping activity asset**

After initial recognition, the stripping activity asset shall be carried at either its cost or its revalued amount less depreciation or amortisation and less impairment losses, in the same way as the existing asset of which it is a part.

The stripping activity asset shall be depreciated or amortised on a systematic basis, over the expected useful life of the identified component of the ore body that becomes more accessible as a result of the stripping activity.

The units of production method shall be applied unless another method is more appropriate.

The expected useful life of the identified component of the ore body that is used to depreciate or amortise the stripping activity asset will differ from the expected useful life that is used to depreciate or amortise the mine itself and the related life-of-mine assets.

## 6.4 AGRICULTURE

### 6.4.1 Ind AS 41 Agriculture

The salient features of this Ind AS 41 is highlighted below.

This Standard shall be applied to account for the following when they relate to agricultural activity:

(a) biological assets;

(b) agricultural produce at the point of harvest; and

(c) government grants

This Standard does not apply to:

(a) land related to agricultural activity (see Ind AS 16 *Property, Plant and Equipment* and Ind AS 40 *Investment Property*);

(b) bearer plants related to agricultural activity (see Ind AS 16). However, this Standard applies to the produce on those bearer plants.

(c) government grants related to bearer plants (see Ind AS 20 *Accounting for Government Grants and Disclosure of Government Assistance*).

(d) intangible assets related to agricultural activity (See Ind AS 38 *Intangible Assets*).

The Standard explains its application to agricultural produce, which is the harvested produce of the entity's biological assets, at the point of harvest. Thereafter, Ind AS 2 *Inventories* or another applicable Standard is applied. Accordingly, this Standard does not deal with the processing of agricultural produce after harvest; for example, the processing of grapes into wine by a vintner who has grown the grapes. While such processing may be a logical and natural extension of agricultural activity, and the events taking place may bear some similarity to biological transformation, such processing is not included within the definition of agricultural activity in this Standard.

The Standard explains biological assets, agricultural produce and products that are the result of processing after harvest enumerated in a table below:

| **Biological assets** | **Agricultural produce** | **Products that are the result of processing after harvest** |
|---|---|---|
| Sheep | Wool | Yarn, carpet |
| Trees in a timber plantation | Felled Trees | Logs, lumber |
| Dairy Cattle | Milk | Cheese |
| Pigs | Carcass | Sausages, cured hams |
| Cotton plants | Harvested cotton | Thread, clothing |
| Sugarcane | Harvested cane | Sugar |
| Tobacco plants | Picked leaves | Cured tobacco |
| Tea bushes | Picked leaves | Tea |
| Grape vines | Picked grapes | Wine |
| Fruit trees | Picked fruit | Processed fruit |
| Oil palms | Picked fruit | Palm oil |
| Rubber trees | Harvested latex | Rubber products |
| Some plants, for example, tea bushes, grape vines, oil palms and rubber trees, usually meet the definition of a bearer plant and are within the scope of Ind AS 16. However, | | |

| Biological assets | Agricultural produce | Products that are the result of processing after harvest |
|---|---|---|
| the produce growing on bearer plants, for example, tea leaves, grapes, oil palm fruit and latex, is within the scope of Ind AS 41. | | |

**Definitions**

**(a) Agriculture based definitions**

***Agricultural activity*** is the management by an entity of the biological transformation and harvest of biological assets for sale or for conversion into agricultural produce or into additional biological assets.

***Agricultural produce*** is the harvested product of the entity's biological assets.

***A bearer plant*** is a living plant that:

(a) is used in the production or supply of agricultural produce;

(b) is expected to bear produce for more than one period; and

(c) has a remote likelihood of being sold as agricultural produce, except for incidental scrap sales.

***A biological asset*** is a living animal or plant.

***Biological transformation*** comprises the processes of growth, degeneration, production, and procreation that cause qualitative or quantitative changes in a biological asset.

***Costs to sell*** are the incremental costs directly attributable to the disposal of an asset, excluding finance costs and income taxes.

***A group of biological assets*** is an aggregation of similar living animals or plants.

***Harvest*** is the detachment of produce from a biological asset or the cessation of a biological asset's life processes.

The following are not bearer plants:

(a) plants cultivated to be harvested as agricultural produce (for example, trees grown for use as lumber);

(b) plants cultivated to produce agricultural produce when there is more than a remote likelihood that the entity will also harvest and sell the plant as agricultural produce, other than as incidental scrap sales (for example, trees that are cultivated both for their fruit and their lumber); and

(c) annual crops (for example, maize and wheat).

When bearer plants are no longer used to bear produce they might be cut down and sold as scrap, for example, for use as firewood. Such incidental scrap sales would not prevent the plant from satisfying the definition of a bearer plant.

Produce growing on bearer plants is a biological asset.

Agricultural activity covers a diverse range of activities; for example, raising livestock, forestry, annual or perennial cropping, cultivating orchards and plantations, floriculture and aquaculture (including fish farming). Certain common features exist within this diversity:

(a) ***Capability to change*** Living animals and plants are capable of biological transformation;

(b) ***Management of change*** Management facilitates biological transformation by enhancing, or at least stabilising, conditions necessary for the process to take place (for example, nutrient levels, moisture, temperature, fertility, and light).

Such management distinguishes agricultural activity from other activities. For example, harvesting from unmanaged sources (such as ocean fishing and deforestation) is not agricultural activity; and

(c) ***Measurement of change*** The change in quality (for example, genetic merit, density, ripeness, fat cover, protein content, and fibre strength) or quantity (for example, progeny, weight, cubic metres, fibre length or diameter, and number of buds) brought about by biological transformation or harvest is measured and monitored as a routine management function.

Biological transformation results in the following types of outcomes:

(a) asset changes through (i) growth (an increase in quantity or improvement in quality of an animal or plant), (ii) degeneration (a decrease in the quantity or deterioration in quality of an animal or plant), or (iii) procreation (creation of additional living animals or plants); or

(b) production of agricultural produce such as latex, tea leaf, wool, and milk.

**(b) General Definitions**

***Carrying amount*** is the amount at which an asset is recognised in the balance sheet.

*Fair value* is the price that would be received to sell an asset or paid to transfer a liability in an orderly transaction between market participants at the measurement date. (See Ind AS 113 *Fair Value Measurement*.)

***Government grants*** are as defined in Ind AS 20.

**Recognition and measurement**

An entity shall recognise a biological asset or agricultural produce when, and only when:

(a) the entity controls the asset as a result of past events;

(b) it is probable that future economic benefits associated with the asset will flow to the entity; and

(c) the fair value or cost of the asset can be measured reliably.

In agricultural activity, control may be evidenced by, for example, legal ownership of cattle and the branding or otherwise marking of the cattle on acquisition, birth, or weaning. The future benefits are normally assessed by measuring the significant physical attributes.

Biological asset shall be measured on initial recognition and at the end of each reporting period at its fair value less costs to sell, except where the fair value cannot be measured reliably.

Agricultural produce harvested from an entity's biological assets shall be measured at its fair value less costs to sell at the point of harvest. Such measurement is the cost at that date when applying Ind AS 2 Inventories or another applicable Standard.

Entities often enter into contracts to sell their biological assets or agricultural produce at a future date. Contract prices are not necessarily relevant in measuring fair value, because fair value reflects the current market conditions in which market participant buyers and sellers would enter into a transaction. As a result, the fair value of a biological asset or agricultural produce is not adjusted because of the existence of a contract. In some cases, a contract for the sale of a biological asset or agricultural produce may be an onerous contract, as defined in Ind AS 37 *Provisions, Contingent Liabilities and Contingent Assets*. Ind AS 37 applies to onerous contracts.

Cost may sometimes approximate fair value, particularly when:

(a) little biological transformation has taken place since initial cost incurrence (for example, for seedlings planted immediately prior to the end of a reporting period or newly acquired livestock); or

(b) the impact of the biological transformation on price is not expected to be material (for example, for the initial growth in a 30-year pine plantation production cycle).

Para 25. Biological assets are often physically attached to land (for example, trees in a plantation forest). There may be no separate market for biological assets that are attached to the land but an active market may exist for the combined assets, that is, the biological assets, raw land, and land improvements, as a package. An entity may use information regarding the combined assets to measure the fair value of the biological assets. For example, the fair value of raw land and land improvements may be deducted from the fair value of the combined assets to arrive at the fair value of biological assets.

**Gains and losses**

A gain or loss arising on initial recognition of a biological asset at fair value less costs to sell and from a change in fair value less costs to sell of a biological asset shall be included in profit or loss for the period in which it arises.

A loss may arise on initial recognition of a biological asset, because costs to sell are deducted in determining fair value less costs to sell of a biological asset. A gain may arise on initial recognition of a biological asset, such as when a calf is born.

A gain or loss arising on initial recognition of agricultural produce at fair value less costs to sell shall be included in profit or loss for the period in which it arises.

A gain or loss may arise on initial recognition of agricultural produce as a result of harvesting.

**Inability to measure fair values reliably**

There is a presumption that fair value can be measured reliably for a biological asset. However, that presumption can be rebutted only on initial recognition for a biological asset for which quoted market prices are not available and for which alternative fair value measurements are determined to be clearly unreliable.

In such a case, that biological asset shall be measured at its cost less any accumulated depreciation and any accumulated impairment losses.

Once the fair value of such a biological asset becomes reliably measurable, an entity shall measure it at its fair value less costs to sell. Once a non-current biological asset meets the criteria to be classified as held for sale (or is included in a disposal group that is classified as held for sale) in accordance with Ind AS 105 *Noncurrent Assets Held for Sale and Discontinued Operations*, it is presumed that fair value can be measured reliably.

**Government Grants**

(a) An unconditional government grant related to a biological asset measured at its fair value less costs to sell shall be recognised in profit or loss when, and only when, the government grant becomes receivable.

(b) If a government grant related to a biological asset measured at its fair value less costs to sell is conditional, including when a government grant requires an entity not to engage in specified agricultural activity, an entity shall recognise the government grant in profit or loss when, and only when, the conditions attaching to the government grant are met.

In accordance with ICAI Guidance Note on Schedule III, for biological assets, the guidance note applicable to Property, Plant and Equipment, to the extent relevant, would also to be used for Biological Assets other than bearer plants.

### 6.4.2 Biological Assets other than bearer plants

According to Clause V of Schedule III, Division II, a reconciliation of the carrying amounts of each class of assets at the beginning and end of the reporting period showing additions, disposals, acquisitions through business combinations and other adjustments shall be disclosed separately.

According to Ind AS 41, the reconciliation would be as shown in the illustration below.

**Illustration 6.1: Biological assets other than bearer plants: Specimen format**

| Particulars | Current Reporting Period | Previous Reporting Period |
|---|---|---|
| Beginning of the reporting period | xxx | Xxx |
| Add: Additions<br>Increases due to purchases | xxx | xxx |
| Add: Acquisitions through Business Combinations | xxx | xxx |
| Less: Disposal<br>Decreases attributable to sales and biological assets classified as held for sale (or included in a disposal group that is classified as held for sale) in accordance with Ind AS 105;<br>Decreases due to harvest | (xxx)<br>(xxx) | (xxx)<br>(xxx) |
| Add/Less Other adjustments<br>Gain or loss arising from changes in fair value less costs to sell<br>Net exchange differences arising on the translation of financial statements into a different presentation currency, and on the translation of a foreign operation into the presentation currency of the reporting entity;<br>Other changes | xxx<br>xxx<br>xxx | xxx<br>xxx<br>xxx |
| End of the reporting period | xxx | xxx |

## 6.5 ASSETS UNDER LEASE

### 6.5.1 Schedule III Division I (Non Ind AS entities)

Assets under lease shall be separately specified under each class of asset.

The term "under lease" should be taken to mean assets given on operating lease in the case of lessor and assets held under finance lease in the case of lessee. Further, leasehold improvements should continue to be shown as a separate asset class.

**Illustration 6.2: Assets under lease: Specimen format**

| Description | Land | Buildings | Plant and Equipment | Furniture and Fixtures | Vehicle | Office Equipment | Others | Total |
|---|---|---|---|---|---|---|---|---|
| **Gross Block**<br>**As at 1.04.2021** | | | | | | | | |
| Add:<br>Additions<br>Acquisitions through business combinations<br>Change due to revaluation*<br>Other adjustments | | | | | | | | |
| Less:<br>Disposals<br>Change due to revaluation*<br>Other adjustments | | | | | | | | |
| **Gross Block as at 31.03.2022** | | | | | | | | |
| **Depreciation**<br>As at 1.04.2021<br>Add: For the year<br>Less:<br>Deduction/adjustments/ reversals<br>As at 31.03.2022 | | | | | | | | |
| **Impairment losses**<br>As at 1.04.2021<br>Add: For the year<br>Less:<br>Deduction/adjustments/ reversals<br>As at 31.03.2022 | | | | | | | | |
| **Net Block as at 31.03.2021** | | | | | | | | |

| Description | Land | Buildings | Plant and Equipment | Furniture and Fixtures | Vehicle | Office Equipment | Others | Total |
|---|---|---|---|---|---|---|---|---|
| Net Block as at 31.03.2022 | | | | | | | | |

*if change is 10% or more in the aggregate of the net carrying value of each class of Property, Plant and Equipment.

## Accounting Standard (AS 19 : Leases)

A lease is classified as ***finance lease*** or ***operating lease*** at its inception (i.e. when the agreement of commitment is made).

***Finance leases*** are those leases that transfer substantially the risks and rewards incidental to ownership to the lessee.

All other leases are ***operating lease***, which signifies that substantially all the risks and rewards incidental to ownership are not transferred

| ***In case of land & buildings the treatment is as follows:*** | – Land – normally treated as operating leases unless the title passes to the lessee at the end of the lease term<br>– Building- treated as operating or finance lease applying classification criteria in AS 19 |
|---|---|

### Illustration 6.3. Finance Lease

Colmax Co, a mining company, takes on lease a dumper from Transporter Co at an annual lease rent of Rs.6000. Colmax Co is to make minimum lease payments for five years. The present value of annual lease rentals is Rs.23956. The fair value of the dumper is Rs.25000. Since the present value of minimum lease payments work out to Rs.23956 and the fair value is Rs.25000, the present value of the minimum lease payments amounts to substantially all of the fair value of the dumper, the lease is classified as *finance lease.*

### Illustration 6.4: Finance Lease

Gigabyte hotel Co, a large five-star hotel takes a 100 KVA generator on lease from Kirloskar Co. The terms of the lease state that Gigabyte hotel will pay an annual lease rent of Rs. 25000 for the next five years. At the end of the 5$^{th}$ year the title will be transferred to Gigabyte.

Since the transfer of title of the asset would move from Kirloskar to Gigabyte by the end of the lease term, this lease becomes a *finance lease.*

**Illustration 6.5: Operating Lease**

Kingfisher Co has leased an equipment to Crow Co. Crow Co has to pay an annual lease of Rs. 5000 to Kingfisher Co for a period of 5 years. The estimated useful life of the equipment is 12 years.

A lease is classified as finance lease if the lease term is for the major part of the economic life of the asset even if the title is not transferred. In this case less than half of the estimated useful life is used up as lease term. If this lease does not satisfy any other term which will classify this as finance lease, it will be classified as an *operating lease.*

**Minimum Lease payments**

Minimum lease payments are the payments over the lease term that the lessee is or can be required to make, excluding contingent rent, costs for services and taxes to be paid by and reimbursed to the lessor, together with:

(a) for a lessee, any amounts guaranteed by the lessee or by a party related to the lessee; or

(b) for a lessor, any residual value guaranteed to the lessor by:

(i) the lessee;

(ii) a party related to the lessee; or

a third party unrelated to the lessor that is financial capable of discharging the obligations under the guarantee.

However, if the lessee has an option to purchase the asset at a price that is expected to be sufficiently lower than fair value at the date the option becomes exercisable for it to be reasonably certain, at the inception of the lease, that the option will be exercised, the minimum lease payments comprise the minimum payments payable over the lease term to the expected date of exercise of this purchase option and the payment required to exercise it.

**Characteristics of Finance Lease**

As explained earlier in this chapter, a lease is classified as finance lease if it transfers substantially all the risks and rewards incidental to ownership. Title may or may not eventually be transferred. A lease is classified as operating lease if risks and rewards incidental to ownership are not transferred substantially.

Whether a lease is a finance lease or an operating lease would depend on the substance rather than legal form, some characteristics of which are explained as under:

| | |
|---|---|
| ***Characteristics which define*** | (a) The lease transfers ownership of the asset to the lessee by the end of the lease term. |

| *substance over legal form* | (b) The lessee has the option to purchase the asset at a price that is expected to be sufficiently lower than the fair value of the asset, at the date the option becomes exercisable.<br>(c) The lease term is for the major part of the economic life of the asset even if the title is not transferred<br>(d) At the inception of the lease the present value of the minimum lease payments amounts to at least substantially all of the fair value of the leased asset<br>(e) The leased assets are of such a specialised nature that only the lessee can use them without major modifications<br>(f) If the lessee can cancel the lease, then the lessor's losses associated with the cancellation are borne by the lessee<br>(g) Gains or losses from the fluctuation in the fair value of the residual accrue to the lessee<br>(h) The lessee has the ability to continue the lease for a secondary period at a rent that is substantially lower than the market rent. |
|---|---|

**Illustration 6.6: Finance Lease**

Parakeet Dental Company takes a dental chair on lease specially developed for it by Toothpick Co. The leased dental chair cannot be sold or leased to any other person unless major modifications are made to it.

Since the dental chair is of a very special nature which cannot be used by anyone other than Parakeet Dental Company, the lease is treated as *finance lease.*

**Illustration 6.7: Finance Lease**

Crow Co has leased out machinery to Spear Co at an annual lease rental of Rs. 5000. The lease agreement stated that this lease is for a minimum period of 10 years. If Spear Co wishes to cancel the lease at an earlier date, then Spear Co has to compensate Crow Co for the losses that it will incur because of cancellation of the lease.

Since in this case Spear Co has to indemnify Crow Co of all the losses related to the foreclosure of the lease it becomes a *finance lease*.

## Accounting treatment of Finance Lease

<table>
<tr><td>(a) Accounting by lessees</td><td>• At the inception of the lease Finance lease is recognised as an asset and a liability in the lessee's balance sheet at the lower of<br>– the fair value of the leased asset and<br>– the present value of the minimum lease payments<br>• Any initial direct costs are added to the amount recognised as an asset.<br>• The minimum lease payments are apportioned between finance charge and reduction of outstanding liability.<br>• Finance charge signifies constant periodic rate of interest on the outstanding liability.<br>• The leased asset is depreciated in accordance with AS 6.<br>• The asset is fully depreciated over the shorter of lease term and the asset's useful life, if there is no reasonable certainty of eventual ownership.</td></tr>
<tr><td>(b) Accounting by lessors</td><td>• At the inception of the lease Finance lease is recorded as receivable at an amount equal to net investment of the lease. It is the present value of<br>– minimum lease payments and<br>– any unguaranteed residual value accruing to the lessor<br>• Includes initial direct costs incurred by the lessors ( other than manufacturer or dealer lessors)<br>• Finance income is recognised to produce a constant periodic rate of return on the lessors' net investment in the lease.<br>• According to policy of outright sales, manufacturer or dealer lessors recognise selling profit or loss</td></tr>
<tr><td>(c) Disclosures (Lessors): Finance Lease</td><td>(a) a reconciliation between the gross investment in the lease at the end of the reporting period, and the present value of minimum lease payments receivable at the end of the reporting period. In addition, an entity shall disclose the gross investment in the lease and the present value of minimum lease payments receivable at the end of the reporting period, for each of the following periods:<br>(i) not later than one year;<br>(ii) later than one year and not later than five years;<br>(iii) later than five years.<br>(b) unearned finance income.<br>(c) the unguaranteed residual values accruing to the benefit of the lessor.</td></tr>
</table>

| | |
|---|---|
| | (d) the accumulated allowance for uncollectible minimum lease payments receivable.<br>(e) contingent rents recognised as income in the period.<br>(f) a general description of the lessor's material leasing arrangements. |

**Accounting treatment of Operating Lease**

| | |
|---|---|
| ***(a) Accounting by lessees*** | Operating lease payments are recognised over the lease term as an expense on a straight-line basis. |
| ***(b) Accounting by lessors*** | Operating lease income is recognised on a straight-line basis over the period of lease.<br>AS 19 specifies the accounting treatment of for sale and leaseback transactions, which would depend on the classification of the lease back as either finance or operating |

**A sale and leaseback transaction involves**

***(a) the sale of an asset by the vendor and***

***(b) the leasing of the same asset back to the vendor.***

The lease payments and the sale price are usually interdependent as they are negotiated as a package.

Accounting treatment of sale and leaseback transaction is depicted as under:

| | |
|---|---|
| ***Finance lease*** | Any excess or deficiency of sale proceeds over the carrying amount should not be immediately recognised as income or loss in the financial statements of a seller – lessee. Instead it should be deferred and amortised over the lease term in proportion to the depreciation of the leased asset |
| ***Operating lease*** | If the transaction is established at fair value, any profit or loss should be recognised immediately.<br>If the sale price is *below* fair value, any profit or loss should be recognised immediately except that, if the loss is compensated by future lease payments at below market price, it should be deferred and amortised in proportion to the lease payments over the period for which the asset is expected to be used.<br>If the sale price is *above* fair value, the excess over fair value should be deferred and amortised over the period for which the asset is expected to be used. |

| | |
|---|---|
| | If the fair value at the time of a sale and leaseback transaction is less than the carrying amount of the asset, a loss equal to the amount of the difference between carrying amount and fair value should be recognised immediately. |

### 6.5.2 Schedule III Division II (Ind AS entities)

According to Schedule III on Ind AS, Assets under lease shall be separately specified under each class of assets.

In accordance with Ind AS 116, a lessee shall either present in the balance sheet or disclose in the notes: right-of-use assets separately from other assets (except those meeting the definition of investment property).

If a lessee does not present right-of-use assets separately in the balance sheet, the lessee shall:

(i) include right-of-use assets within the same line item as that within which the corresponding underlying assets would be presented if they were owned; and

(ii) disclose which line items in the balance sheet include those right-ofuse assets.

For assets obtained under lease, and accounted as right-of-use (ROU) assets, an entity shall apply the presentation and disclosure requirements under Ind AS 116 in addition to the requirements of Ind AS Schedule III

For assets given on lease, an entity shall apply the presentation and disclosure requirements under Ind AS 116 in addition to the requirements of Ind AS Schedule III.

Salient points related to Ind AS 116, Leases are summarized below for the understanding of readers.

**Recognition exemptions**

A lessee may elect not to apply the requirements to:

(a) *short-term* leases; and

(b) leases for which the underlying asset is of low value.

If a lessee elects not to apply the requirements to either short-term leases or leases for which the underlying asset is of low value, the lessee shall recognize the *lease payments* associated with those leases as an expense on either a straight-line basis over the *lease term* or another systematic basis. The lessee shall apply another systematic basis if that basis is more representative of the pattern of the lessee's benefit.

If a lessee accounts for short-term leases, the lessee shall consider the lease to be a new lease for the purposes of this Standard if:

(a) there is a *lease modification*; or

(b) there is any change in the lease term (for example, the lessee exercises an option not previously included in its determination of the lease term).

The election for short-term leases shall be made by class of underlying asset to which the right of use relates. A class of underlying asset is a grouping of underlying assets of a similar nature and use in an entity's operations. The election for leases for which the underlying asset is of low value can be made on a lease-by-lease basis.

## Identifying a lease

At inception of a contract, an entity shall assess whether the contract is, or contains, a lease. A contract is, or contains, a lease if the contract conveys the right to control the use of an identified asset for a period of time in exchange for consideration.

This is explained in the chart below with the help of a decision tree.

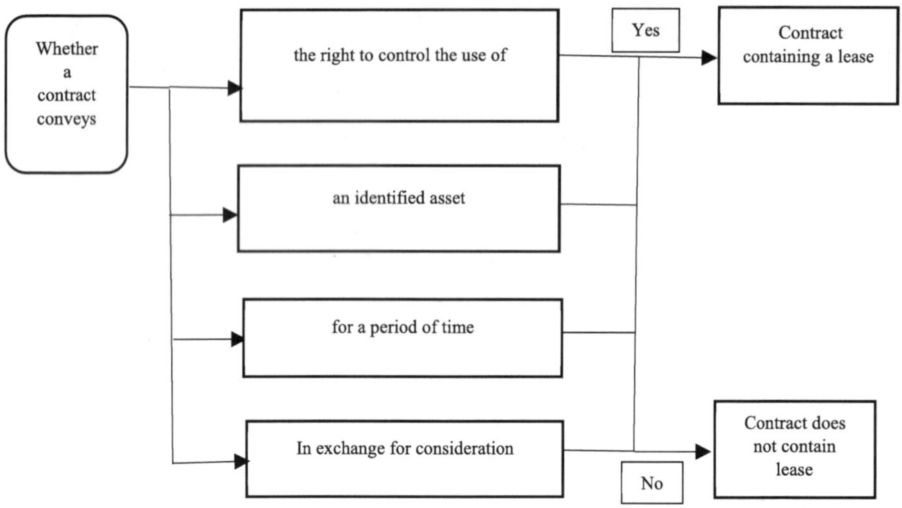


A period of time may be described in terms of the amount of use of an identified asset (for example, the number of production units that an item of equipment will be used to produce).

An entity shall reassess whether a contract is, or contains, a lease only if the terms and conditions of the contract are changed.

## Separating components of a contract

For a contract that is, or contains, a lease, an entity shall account for each lease component within the contract as a lease separately from non-lease components of the contract, unless the entity applies the practical expedient specified in the Standard.

## Lessee

### Recognition

At the *commencement date*, a lessee shall recognize a right-of-use asset and a lease liability.

### Measurement

### Initial measurement

*Initial measurement of the right-of-use asset*

**At the commencement date, a lessee shall measure the right-of-use asset at cost.**

The cost of the right-of-use asset shall comprise:

(a) the amount of the initial measurement of the lease liability;
(b) any lease payments made at or before the commencement date, less any *lease incentives* received;
(c) any *initial direct costs* incurred by the lessee; and
(d) an estimate of costs to be incurred by the lessee in dismantling and removing the underlying asset, restoring the site on which it is located or restoring the underlying asset to the condition required by the terms and conditions of the lease, unless those costs are incurred to produce inventories. The lessee incurs the obligation for those costs either at the commencement date or as a consequence of having used the underlying asset during a particular period.

A lessee shall recognize the costs as part of the cost of the right-of-use asset when it incurs an obligation for those costs. A lessee applies Ind AS 2, *Inventories,* to costs that are incurred during a particular period as a consequence of having used the right-of-use asset to produce inventories during that period. The obligations for such costs accounted for applying this Standard or Ind AS 2 are recognised and measured applying Ind AS 37, *Provisions, Contingent Liabilities and Contingent Assets*.

### Initial measurement of the lease liability

**At the commencement date, a lessee shall measure the lease liability at the present value of the lease payments that are not paid at that date. The lease payments shall be discounted using the *interest rate implicit in the lease*, if that rate can be readily determined. If that rate cannot be readily determined, the lessee shall use the *lessee's incremental borrowing rate.***

At the commencement date, the lease payments included in the measurement of the lease liability comprise the following payments for the right to use the underlying asset during the lease term that are not paid at the commencement date:

(a) *fixed payments* (including in-substance fixed payments), less any lease incentives receivable;

(b) *variable lease payments* that depend on an index or a rate, initially measured using the index or rate as at the commencement date;

(c) amounts expected to be payable by the lessee under *residual value guarantees*;

(d) the exercise price of a purchase option if the lessee is reasonably certain to exercise that option; and

(e) payments of penalties for terminating the lease, if the lease term reflects the lessee exercising an option to terminate the lease.

Variable lease payments that depend on an index or a rate described in paragraph 27(b) include, for example, payments linked to a consumer price index, payments linked to a benchmark interest rate (such as LIBOR) or payments that vary to reflect changes in market rental rates.

## Subsequent measurement

*Subsequent measurement of the right-of-use asset*

After the commencement date, a lessee shall measure the right-of-use asset applying a cost model, unless it applies the other measurement model described below.

## Cost model

To apply a cost model, a lessee shall measure the right-of-use asset at cost:

**(a)** less any accumulated depreciation and any accumulated impairment losses; and

**(b)** adjusted for any remeasurement of the lease liability.

A lessee shall apply the depreciation requirements in Ind AS 16, *Property, Plant and Equipment,* in depreciating the right-of-use asset.

If the lease transfers ownership of the underlying asset to the lessee by the end of the lease term or if the cost of the right-of-use asset reflects that the lessee will exercise a purchase option, the lessee shall depreciate the right-of-use asset from the commencement date to the end of the *useful life* of the underlying asset. Otherwise, the lessee shall depreciate the right-of-use asset from the commencement date to the earlier of the end of the *useful life* of the right-of-use asset or the end of the lease term.

A lessee shall apply Ind AS 36, *Impairment of Assets,* to determine whether the right-of-use asset is impaired and to account for any impairment loss identified.

## Other measurement models

If right-of-use assets relate to a class of property, plant and equipment to which the lessee applies the revaluation model in Ind AS 16, a lessee may elect to apply that revaluation model to all of the right-of-use assets that relate to that class of property, plant and equipment.

*Subsequent measurement of the lease liability*

After the commencement date, a lessee shall measure the lease liability by:

(a) increasing the carrying amount to reflect interest on the lease liability;

(b) reducing the carrying amount to reflect the lease payments made; and

(c) remeasuring the carrying amount to reflect any reassessment or lease modifications, or to reflect revised in-substance fixed lease payments.

Interest on the lease liability in each period during the lease term shall be the amount that produces a constant periodic rate of interest on the remaining balance of the lease liability. The periodic rate of interest is the discount rate, or if applicable the revised discount rate.

After the commencement date, a lessee shall recognize in profit or loss, unless the costs are included in the carrying amount of another asset applying other applicable Standards, both:

(a) interest on the lease liability; and

(b) variable lease payments not included in the measurement of the lease liability in the period in which the event or condition that triggers those payments occurs.

## Reassessment of the lease liability

After the commencement date, a lessee shall to remeasure the lease liability to reflect changes to the lease payments. A lessee shall recognize the amount of the remeasurement of the lease liability as an adjustment to the right-of-use asset. However, if the carrying amount of the right-of-use asset is reduced to zero and there is a further reduction in the measurement of the lease liability, a lessee shall recognize any remaining amount of the remeasurement in profit or loss.

A lessee shall remeasure the lease liability by discounting the revised lease payments using a revised discount rate, if either:

(a) there is a change in the lease term, as described in paragraphs 20–21. A lessee shall determine the revised lease payments on the basis of the revised lease term; or

(b) there is a change in the assessment of an option to purchase the underlying asset, assessed considering the events and circumstances in the context of a purchase option. A lessee shall determine the revised lease payments to reflect the change in amounts payable under the purchase option.

In applying the above provisions, a lessee shall determine the revised discount rate as the interest rate implicit in the lease for the remainder of the lease term, if that rate can be readily determined, or the lessee's incremental borrowing rate at the date of reassessment, if the interest rate implicit in the lease cannot be readily determined.

A lessee shall remeasure the lease liability by discounting the revised lease payments, if either:

(a) there is a change in the amounts expected to be payable under a residual value guarantee. A lessee shall determine the revised lease payments to reflect the change in amounts expected to be payable under the residual value guarantee.

(b) there is a change in future lease payments resulting from a change in an index or a rate used to determine those payments, including for example a change to reflect changes in market rental rates following a market rent review. The lessee shall remeasure the lease liability to reflect those revised lease payments only when there is a change in the cash flows (ie when the adjustment to the lease payments takes effect). A lessee shall determine the revised lease payments for the remainder of the lease term based on the revised contractual payments.

In applying the provisions mentioned above a lessee shall use an unchanged discount rate, unless the change in lease payments results from a change in floating interest rates. In that case, the lessee shall use a revised discount rate that reflects changes in the interest rate.

*Lease modifications*

A lessee shall account for a lease modification as a separate lease if both:

(a) the modification increases the scope of the lease by adding the right to use one or more underlying assets; and

(b) the consideration for the lease increases by an amount commensurate with the stand-alone price for the increase in scope and any appropriate adjustments to that stand-alone price to reflect the circumstances of the particular contract.

For a lease modification that is not accounted for as a separate lease, at the *effective date of the lease modification* a lessee shall:

(a) allocate the consideration in the modified contract;

(b) determine the lease term of the modified lease; and

(c) remeasure the lease liability by discounting the revised lease payments using a revised discount rate. The revised discount rate is determined as the interest rate implicit in the lease for the remainder of the lease term, if that rate can be readily determined, or the lessee's incremental borrowing rate at the effective date of the modification, if the interest rate implicit in the lease cannot be readily determined.

For a lease modification that is not accounted for as a separate lease, the lessee shall account for the remeasurement of the lease liability by:

(a) decreasing the carrying amount of the right-of-use asset to reflect the partial or full termination of the lease for lease modifications that decrease the scope of the lease. The lessee shall recognise in profit or loss any gain or loss relating to the partial or full termination of the lease.

(b) making a corresponding adjustment to the right-of-use asset for all other lease modifications.

## Presentation

A lessee shall either present in the balance sheet, or disclose in the notes:

(a) right-of-use assets separately from other assets. If a lessee does not present right-of-use assets separately in the balance sheet, the lessee shall:

  (i) include right-of-use assets within the same line item as that within which the corresponding underlying assets would be presented if they were owned; and

  (ii) disclose which line items in the balance sheet include those right-of-use assets.

(b) lease liabilities separately from other liabilities. If a lessee does not present lease liabilities separately in the balance sheet, the lessee shall disclose which line items in the balance sheet include those liabilities.

The requirement in paragraph 47(a) does not apply to right-of-use assets that meet the definition of investment property, which shall be presented in the balance sheet as investment property.

In the statement of profit and loss, a lessee shall present interest expense on the lease liability separately from the depreciation charge for the right-of-use asset. Interest expense on the lease liability is a component of finance costs specified under Ind AS 1, *Presentation of Financial Statements,* which requires it to be presented separately in the statement of profit and loss.

In the statement of cash flows, a lessee shall classify:

(a) cash payments for the principal portion of the lease liability within financing activities;

(b) cash payments for the interest portion of the lease liability within financing activities applying the requirements in Ind AS 7, *Statement of Cash Flows,* for interest paid; and

(c) Short-term lease payments, payments for leases of low-value assets and variable lease payments not included in the measurement of the lease liability within operating activities.

## Lessor

### Classification of leases

**A lessor shall classify each of its leases as either an *operating lease or a finance lease.***

**A lease is classified as a finance lease if it transfers substantially all the risks and rewards incidental to ownership of an underlying asset. A lease is classified as an operating lease if it does not transfer substantially all the risks and rewards incidental to ownership of an underlying asset.**

Whether a lease is a finance lease or an operating lease depends on the substance of the transaction rather than the form of the contract. Examples of situations that individually or in combination would normally lead to a lease being classified as a finance lease are:

(a) the lease transfers ownership of the underlying asset to the lessee by the end of the lease term.

(b) the lessee has the option to purchase the underlying asset at a price that is expected to be sufficiently lower than the *fair value* at the date the option becomes exercisable for it to be reasonably certain, at the *inception date*, that the option will be exercised;

(c) the lease term is for the major part of the *economic life* of the underlying asset even if title is not transferred;

(d) at the inception date, the present value of the lease payments amounts to at least substantially all of the fair value of the underlying asset; and

(e) the underlying asset is of such a specialised nature that only the lessee can use it without major modifications.

Indicators of situations that individually or in combination could also lead to a lease being classified as a finance lease are:

(a) if the lessee can cancel the lease, the lessor's losses associated with the cancellation are borne by the lessee;

(b) gains or losses from the fluctuation in the fair value of the residual accrue to the lessee (for example, in the form of a rent rebate equalling most of the sales proceeds at the end of the lease); and

(c) the lessee has the ability to continue the lease for a secondary period at a rent that is substantially lower than market rent.

The examples and indicators are not always conclusive. If it is clear from other features that the lease does not transfer substantially all the risks and rewards incidental to ownership of an underlying asset, the lease is classified as an operating lease. For example, this may be the case if ownership of the underlying asset transfers at the end of the lease for a variable payment equal to its then fair value, or if there are variable lease payments, as a result of which the lessor does not transfer substantially all such risks and rewards.

Lease classification is made at the inception date and is reassessed only if there is a lease modification. Changes in estimates (for example, changes in estimates of the economic life or of the residual value of the underlying asset), or changes in circumstances (for example, default by the lessee), do not give rise to a new classification of a lease for accounting purposes.

**Finance leases**

**Recognition and measurement**

**At the commencement date, a lessor shall recognize assets held under a finance lease in its balance sheet and present them as a receivable at an amount equal to the *net investment in the lease.***

**Initial measurement**

The lessor shall use the interest rate implicit in the lease to measure the net investment in the lease. In the case of a sublease, if the interest rate implicit in the sublease cannot be readily determined, an intermediate lessor may use the discount rate used for the head lease (adjusted for any initial direct costs associated with the sublease) to measure the net investment in the sublease.

Initial direct costs, other than those incurred by manufacturer or dealer lessors, are included in the initial measurement of the net investment in the lease and reduce the amount of income recognised over the lease term. The interest rate implicit in the lease is defined in such a way that the initial direct costs are included automatically in the net investment in the lease; there is no need to add them separately.

**Initial measurement of the lease payments included in the net investment in the lease**

At the commencement date, the lease payments included in the measurement of the net investment in the lease comprise the following payments for the right to use the underlying asset during the lease term that are not received at the commencement date:

(a) fixed payments (including in-substance fixed payments), less any lease incentives payable;

(b) variable lease payments that depend on an index or a rate, initially measured using the index or rate as at the commencement date;

(c) any residual value guarantees provided to the lessor by the lessee, a party related to the lessee or a third party unrelated to the lessor that is financially capable of discharging the obligations under the guarantee;

(d) the exercise price of a purchase option if the lessee is reasonably certain to exercise that option; and

(e) payments of penalties for terminating the lease, if the lease term reflects the lessee exercising an option to terminate the lease.

### Manufacturer or dealer lessors

At the commencement date, a manufacturer or dealer lessor shall recognize the following for each of its finance leases:

(a) revenue being the fair value of the underlying asset, or, if lower, the present value of the lease payments accruing to the lessor, discounted using a market rate of interest;

(b) the cost of sale being the cost, or carrying amount if different, of the underlying asset less the present value of the *unguaranteed residual value*; and

(c) selling profit or loss (being the difference between revenue and the cost of sale) in accordance with its policy for outright sales to which Ind AS 115 applies. A manufacturer or dealer lessor shall recognize selling profit or loss on a finance lease at the commencement date, regardless of whether the lessor transfers the underlying asset as described in Ind AS 115.

Manufacturers or dealers often offer to customers the choice of either buying or leasing an asset. A finance lease of an asset by a manufacturer or dealer lessor gives rise to profit or loss equivalent to the profit or loss resulting from an outright sale of the underlying asset, at normal selling prices, reflecting any applicable volume or trade discounts.

Manufacturer or dealer lessors sometimes quote artificially low rates of interest in order to attract customers. The use of such a rate would result in a lessor recognizing an excessive portion of the total income from the transaction at the commencement date. If artificially low rates of interest are quoted, a manufacturer or dealer lessor shall restrict selling profit to that which would apply if a market rate of interest were charged.

A manufacturer or dealer lessor shall recognize as an expense, costs incurred in connection with obtaining a finance lease at the commencement date because they are mainly related to earning the manufacturer or dealer's selling profit. Costs incurred by manufacturer or dealer lessors in connection with obtaining a finance lease are excluded from the definition of initial direct costs and, thus, are excluded from the net investment in the lease.

### Subsequent measurement

**A lessor shall recognize finance income over the lease term, based on a pattern reflecting a constant periodic rate of return on the lessor's net investment in the lease.**

A lessor aims to allocate finance income over the lease term on a systematic and rational basis. A lessor shall apply the lease payments relating to the period against the *gross investment in the lease* to reduce both thc principal and the *unearned finance income.*

A lessor shall apply derecognition and impairment requirements in Ind AS 109 to the net investment in the lease. A lessor shall review regularly estimated unguaranteed residual values used in computing the gross investment in the lease. If there has been a reduction in the estimated unguaranteed residual value, the lessor shall revise the income allocation over the lease term and recognize immediately any reduction in respect of amounts accrued.

A lessor that classifies an asset under a finance lease as held for sale (or includes it in a disposal group that is classified as held for sale) applying Ind AS 105, *Non-current Assets Held for Sale and Discontinued Operations,* shall account for the asset in accordance with that Standard.

**Lease modifications**

A lessor shall account for a modification to a finance lease as a separate lease if both:

(a) the modification increases the scope of the lease by adding the right to use one or more underlying assets; and

(b) the consideration for the lease increases by an amount commensurate with the stand-alone price for the increase in scope and any appropriate adjustments to that stand-alone price to reflect the circumstances of the particular contract.

For a modification to a finance lease that is not accounted for as a separate lease, a lessor shall account for the modification as follows:

(a) if the lease would have been classified as an operating lease had the modification been in effect at the inception date, the lessor shall:

  (i) account for the lease modification as a new lease from the effective date of the modification; and

  (ii) measure the carrying amount of the underlying asset as the net investment in the lease immediately before the effective date of the lease modification.

(b) otherwise, the lessor shall apply the requirements of Ind AS 109.

**Finance leases**

A lessor shall provide a qualitative and quantitative explanation of the significant changes in the carrying amount of the net investment in finance leases.

A lessor shall disclose a maturity analysis of the lease payments receivable, showing the undiscounted lease payments to be received on an annual basis for a minimum of each of the first five years and a total of the amounts for the remaining years. A lessor shall reconcile the undiscounted lease payments to the net investment in the lease. The reconciliation shall identify the unearned finance income relating to the lease payments receivable and any discounted unguaranteed residual value.

**Sale and leaseback transactions**

If an entity (the seller-lessee) transfers an asset to another entity (the buyer-lessor) and leases that asset back from the buyer-lessor, both the seller-lessee and the buyer-lessor shall account for the transfer contract and the lease applying paragraphs 99–103.

**Assessing whether the transfer of the asset is a sale**

An entity shall apply the requirements for determining when a performance obligation is satisfied in Ind AS 115 to determine whether the transfer of an asset is accounted for as a sale of that asset.

**Transfer of the asset is a sale**

If the transfer of an asset by the seller-lessee satisfies the requirements of Ind AS 115 to be accounted for as a sale of the asset:

(a) the seller-lessee shall measure the right-of-use asset arising from the leaseback at the proportion of the previous carrying amount of the asset that relates to the right of use retained by the seller-lessee. Accordingly, the seller-lessee shall recognize only the amount of any gain or loss that relates to the rights transferred to the buyer-lessor.

(b) the buyer-lessor shall account for the purchase of the asset applying applicable Standards, and for the lease applying the lessor accounting requirements in this Standard.

If the fair value of the consideration for the sale of an asset does not equal the fair value of the asset, or if the payments for the lease are not at market rates, an entity shall make the following adjustments to measure the sale proceeds at fair value:

(a) any below-market terms shall be accounted for as a prepayment of lease payments; and

(b) any above-market terms shall be accounted for as additional financing provided by the buyer-lessor to the seller-lessee.

The entity shall measure any potential adjustment on the basis of the more readily determinable of:

(a) the difference between the fair value of the consideration for the sale and the fair value of the asset; and

(b) the difference between the present value of the contractual payments for the lease and the present value of payments for the lease at market rates.

**Transfer of the asset is not a sale**

If the transfer of an asset by the seller-lessee does not satisfy the requirements of Ind AS 115 to be accounted for as a sale of the asset:

(a) the seller-lessee shall continue to recognize the transferred asset and shall recognize a financial liability equal to the transfer proceeds. It shall account for the financial liability applying Ind AS 109.

(b) the buyer-lessor shall not recognize the transferred asset and shall recognize a financial asset equal to the transfer proceeds. It shall account for the financial asset applying Ind AS 109.

**Illustration 6.8: Assets under lease: Specimen format**

| Description | Land | Buildings | Plant and Equipment | Furniture and Fixtures | Vehicle | Office Equipment | Others | Total |
|---|---|---|---|---|---|---|---|---|
| **Gross Block As at beginning of reporting period** | | | | | | | | |
| Add:<br>Additions<br>Acquisitions through business combinations<br>Change due to revaluation*<br>Other adjustments | | | | | | | | |
| Less:<br>Disposals<br>Change due to revaluation*<br>Other adjustments | | | | | | | | |
| **Gross Block as at end of reporting period** | | | | | | | | |
| **Depreciation**<br>As at beginning of reporting period<br>Add: For the year<br>Less: Deduction/adjustments/<br>reversals<br>As at end of reporting period | | | | | | | | |
| **Impairment losses**<br>As at beginning of reporting period<br>Add: For the year<br>Less: Deduction/adjustments/ | | | | | | | | |

| **Description** | **Land** | **Buildings** | **Plant and Equipment** | **Furniture and Fixtures** | **Vehicle** | **Office Equipment** | **Others** | **Total** |
|---|---|---|---|---|---|---|---|---|
| reversals<br>As at end of reporting period | | | | | | | | |
| **Net Block as at end of previous reporting period** | | | | | | | | |
| **Net Block as at end of current reporting period** | | | | | | | | |

*if change is 10% or more in the aggregate of the net carrying value of each class of Property, Plant and Equipment.

### Illustration 6.9: Right-of-use assets under Ind AS 116: (Specimen format)

| | **Right-of-use land** | **Right-of-use Building** | **Right-of-use Plant & Machinery** | **Right-of-use Vehicles** | **Right-of-use railway sidings** | **Total** |
|---|---|---|---|---|---|---|
| Cost as at April 1, 2020<br>Addition on account of transition to Ind AS 116 "Leases"<br>Additions<br>Disposals<br>Other re-classifications<br>Cost as at March 31.2021 | | | | | | |
| Accumulated impairment as at 31st March 2021 | | | | | | |
| Accumulated depreciation as at April 1, 2020<br>Charge for the year<br>Disposals<br>Other reclassifications<br>Accumulated depreciation as at 31st March 2021 | | | | | | |
| **Total accumulated depreciation and impairment as at March 31, 2021** | | | | | | |
| **Net carrying value as at April 1, 2020** | | | | | | |
| **Net carrying value as at March 31, 2021** | | | | | | |

## 6.6 RECONCILIATION OF GROSS AND NET CARRYING AMOUNT OF EACH CLASS OF ASSETS

A reconciliation of the gross and net carrying amounts of each class of assets at the beginning and end of the reporting period showing:

- additions,
- disposals,
- acquisitions through business combinations,
- amount of change due to revaluation (if change is 10% or more in the aggregate of the net carrying value of each class of Property, Plant and Equipment) and

other adjustments and the related depreciation and impairment losses or reversals shall be disclosed separately.

According to ICAI Guidance Note on Division I and Division II of Schedule III, since reconciliation of gross and net carrying amounts of Property, Plant and Equipment, Investment Property and Other Intangible assets is required, the corresponding depreciation/amortisation for each class of asset should be disclosed in terms of Opening Accumulated Depreciation, Depreciation/amortisation for the year, Deductions/Other adjustments and Closing Accumulated Depreciation/ Amortisation. Similar disclosures should also be made for Impairment, if any, as applicable. A proposed format is shown as under:

| **Particulars** | **Amount** |
|---|---|
| ***Gross:*** | |
| Opening balance | |
| **Additions** | |
| Acquisitions through business combination | |
| Other adjustments | |
| Sub-total | |
| **Less:** Disposals | |
| Gross Block at year end | |
| **Less:** | |
| Depreciation/Amortisation | |
| Depreciation/Amortisation for the year | |
| Impairment loss/reversal of impairment loss for the year | |
| Total depreciation at year end | |
| Net carrying value | |

In case if and entity wants to disclose information regarding gross block of assets, accumulated depreciation and provision for impairment under previous GAAP, the same may only be disclosed as an additional information by way of a note forming part of the financial statements.

All acquisitions, whether by way of an asset acquisition or through a business combination are to be disclosed as part of the reconciliation in the note on Property, Plant & Equipment Acquisitions through 'Business Combinations' need to be disclosed separately for each class of assets. According to ICAI Guidance Note, it is advisable that asset disposals through demergers, etc. may also be disclosed separately for each class of assets.

Also according to Ind AS Division II Schedule III land and building should be presented as two separate classes of property, plant and equipment on a consistent basis.

Further, pursuant to Ind AS Schedule III, capital advances are required to be included under other non- current assets and hence, cannot be included under capital work-inprogress.

With respect to Investment Property, Ind AS Schedule III stipulates that a reconciliation of the gross and net carrying amounts of each class of property at the beginning and end of the reporting period showing additions, disposals, acquisitions through business combinations and other adjustments and the related depreciation and impairment losses or reversals shall be disclosed separately.

According to ICAI Guidance Note on Schedule III, guidance note related to Property, Plant and Equipment, to the extent applicable, is also to be made applicable for Investment Property.

**Illustration 6.10: Property, Plant and Equipment: Specimen format**

| Description | Land | Buildings | Plant and Equipment | Furniture and Fixtures | Vehicle | Office Equipment | Others | Total |
|---|---|---|---|---|---|---|---|---|
| **Gross Block As at beginning of reporting period** | | | | | | | | |
| Add:<br>Additions<br>Acquisitions through business combinations<br>Change due to revaluation*<br>Other adjustments | | | | | | | | |

| Description | Land | Buildings | Plant and Equipment | Furniture and Fixtures | Vehicle | Office Equipment | Others | Total |
|---|---|---|---|---|---|---|---|---|
| Less:<br>Disposals<br>Change due to revaluation*<br>Other adjustments | | | | | | | | |
| **Gross Block as at end of reporting period** | | | | | | | | |
| **Depreciation**<br>As at beginning of reporting period<br>Add: For the year<br>Less: Deduction/adjustments/<br>reversals<br>As at end of reporting period | | | | | | | | |
| **Impairment losses**<br>As at beginning of reporting period<br>Add: For the year<br>Less: Deduction/adjustments/<br>reversals<br>As at end of reporting period | | | | | | | | |
| **Net Block as at end of previous reporting period** | | | | | | | | |
| **Net Block as at end of** | | | | | | | | |

| Description | Land | Buildings | Plant and Equipment | Furniture and Fixtures | Vehicle | Office Equipment | Others | Total |
|---|---|---|---|---|---|---|---|---|
| current reporting period | | | | | | | | |

*if change is 10% or more in the aggregate of the net carrying value of each class of Property, Plant and Equipment.

### Illustration 6.11: Accounting policy: Property, Plant and Equipment

**Property, Plant and Equipment**

Property, Plant and Equipment are stated at cost, net of recoverable taxes, trade discount and rebates less accumulated depreciation and impairment losses, if any. Such cost includes purchase price, borrowing cost and any cost directly attributable to bringing the assets to its working condition for its intended use, net charges on foreign exchange contracts and adjustments arising from exchange rate variations attributable to the assets. In case of land the Company has availed fair value as deemed cost on the date of transition to Ind AS.

Subsequent costs are included in the asset's carrying amount or recognized as a separate asset, as appropriate, only when it is probable that future economic benefits associated with the item will flow to the entity and the cost can be measured reliably.

Property, Plant and Equipment which are significant to the total cost of that item of Property, Plant and Equipment and having different useful life are accounted separately.

Other Indirect Expenses incurred relating to project, net of income earned during the project development stage prior to its intended use, are considered as pre-operative expenses and disclosed under Capital Work-in-Progress.

Depreciation on Property, Plant and Equipment is provided using written down value method on depreciable amount except in case of certain assets from Refining and Petrochemical segment & SEZ units/developer which are depreciated using straight-line method. Depreciation is provided based on useful life of the assets as prescribed in Schedule II to the Companies Act, 2013 except in respect of the following assets, where useful life is different than those prescribed in Schedule II;

| Particular | Depreciation |
|---|---|
| Fixed Bed Catalyst (useful life: 2 years or more) | Over its useful life as technically assessed |
| Fixed Bed Catalyst (useful life: up to 2 years) | 100% depreciated in the year of addition |

| | |
|---|---|
| Premium on Leasehold Land (range up to 99 years) | Over the period of lease term |
| Plant and Machinery (useful life: 25 to 40 years) | Over its useful life as technically assessed |
| ***(Source: Reliance Industries Limited: Annual Report: 2019-20)*** | |

**Illustration 6.12: Accounting policy: Property, Plant and Equipment**

**Property, Plant and Equipment**

An item of property, plant and equipment is recognized as an asset if it is probable that future economic benefits associated with the item will flow to the Company and its cost can be measured reliably. This recognition principle is applied to costs incurred initially to acquire an item of property, plant and equipment and also to costs incurred subsequently to add to, replace part of, or service it. All other repair and maintenance costs, including regular servicing, are recognized in the statement of profit and loss as incurred. When a replacement occurs, the carrying value of the replaced part is derecognized.

Where an item of property, plant and equipment comprises major components having different useful lives, these components are accounted for as separate items.

Property, plant and equipment is stated at cost or deemed cost applied on transition to Ind AS, less accumulated depreciation and impairment. Cost includes all direct costs and expenditures incurred to bring the asset to its working condition and location for its intended use. Trial run expenses (net of revenue) are capitalized. Borrowing costs incurred during the period of construction is capitalized as part of cost of qualifying asset.

The gain or loss arising on disposal of an item of property, plant and equipment is determined as the difference between sale proceeds and carrying value of such item and is recognized in the statement of profit and loss.

(*Source: Tata Steel: Annual Report 2019-20*)

**Illustration 6.13: Accounting policy: Property, Plant and Equipment**

**Property, plant and equipment (PPE)**

PPE is recognized when it is probable that future economic benefits associated with the item will flow to the Company and the cost of the item can be measured reliably. PPE is stated at original cost net of tax/duty credits availed, if any, less accumulated depreciation and cumulative impairment, if any. All directly attributable costs related to the acquisition of PPE and borrowing costs in case of qualifying assets are capitalized in accordance with the Company's accounting policy.

Own manufactured PPE is capitalized at cost including an appropriate share of overheads. Administrative and other general overhead expenses that are specifically attributable to construction or acquisition of PPE or bringing the PPE to working condition are allocated and capitalised as a part of the cost of the PPE.

Subsequent costs are included in the asset's carrying amount or recognised as a separate asset, as appropriate, only when it is probable that future economic benefits associated with the item will flow to the Company and the cost can be measured reliably.

PPE not ready for the intended use on the date of the Balance Sheet are disclosed as "capital work-in-progress". (Also refer to policy on leases, borrowing costs, impairment of assets and foreign currency transactions infra).

Depreciation is recognised using straight-line method so as to write off the cost of the assets (other than freehold land and properties under construction) less their residual values over their useful lives specified in Schedule II to the Companies Act, 2013, or in the case of assets where the useful life was determined by technical evaluation, over the useful life so determined.

Depreciation method is reviewed at each financial year end to reflect the expected pattern of consumption of the future economic benefits embodied in the asset. The estimated useful life and residual values are also reviewed at each financial year end and the effect of any change in the estimates of useful life/residual value is accounted on prospective basis.

Where cost of a part of the asset ("asset component") is significant to total cost of the asset and useful life of that part is different from the useful life of the remaining asset, useful life of that significant part is determined separately, and such asset component is depreciated over its separate useful life.

Depreciation on additions to/deductions from, owned assets is calculated pro rata to the period of use.

Depreciation charge for impaired assets is adjusted in future periods in such a manner that the revised carrying amount of the asset is allocated over its remaining useful life.

Freehold land is not depreciated.

PPE is derecognized upon disposal or when no future economic benefits are expected from its use or disposal. Any gain or loss arising on derecognition is recognised in the Statement of Profit and Loss in the same period.

*(Source: Larsen & Toubro Annual Report 2019-20)*

**Illustration 6.14: Accounting policy: Leases**

**Leases**

The Company, as a lessee, recognizes a right-of-use asset and a lease liability for its leasing arrangements, if the contract conveys the right to control the use of an identified asset.

The contract conveys the right to control the use of an identified asset, if it involves the use of an identified asset and the Company has substantially all of the economic benefits from use of the asset and has right to direct the use of the identified asset. The cost of the right-of-use asset shall comprise of the amount of the initial measurement of the lease liability adjusted for any lease payments made at or before the commencement date plus any initial direct costs incurred. The right-of-use assets is subsequently measured at cost less any accumulated depreciation, accumulated impairment losses, if any and adjusted for any remeasurement of the lease liability. The right-of-use assets is depreciated using the straight-line method from the commencement date over the shorter of lease term or useful life of right-of-use asset.

The Company measures the lease liability at the present value of the lease payments that are not paid at the commencement date of the lease. The lease payments are discounted using the interest rate implicit in the lease, if that rate can be readily determined. If that rate cannot be readily determined, the Company uses incremental borrowing rate.

For short term and low value leases, the Company recognizes the lease payments as an operating expense on a straight-line basis over the lease term.

(*Source: Reliance Industries Limited: Annual Report: 2019-20*)

**Illustration 6.15: Accounting policy: Leases**

**Leases**

Ind AS 116 "Leases" replaces Ind AS 17 "Leases" with effect from April 1, 2019.

The adoption of this new Standard has resulted in the Company recognizing a right-of-use asset and related lease liability in connection with all former operating leases except for those identified as low-value or having a remaining lease term of less than 12 months from the date of initial application.

The new Standard has been applied using the modified retrospective approach, with the right-of-use asset recognised at an amount equal to the present value of lease liability, adjusted by the amount of any prepaid or accrued lease payments relating to those leases. Prior periods have not been restated.

For contracts in place at the date of initial application, the Company has elected not to carry forward the definition of leases as per Ind AS 17 and has therefore, applied the definition of a lease as per Ind AS 116 to all such arrangements.

On transition, for leases previously accounted for as operating leases with a remaining lease term of less than 12 months and for leases of low-value assets the Company has applied the optional exemptions to not recognise right-of-use assets but to account for the lease expense on a straight-line basis over the remaining lease term.

For those leases previously classified as finance leases, the right-of-use asset and lease liability are measured at the date of initial application at the same amounts as under Ind AS 17 'Leases' immediately before the date of initial application.

**The Company as lessee**

The Company accounts for each lease component within the contract as a lease separately from non-lease components of the contract and allocates the consideration in the contract to each lease component on the basis of the relative stand-alone price of the lease component and the aggregate stand-alone price of the non-lease components. The Company recognizes right-of-use asset representing its right to use the underlying asset for the lease term at the lease commencement date.

The cost of the right-of-use asset measured at inception comprises of the amount of initial measurement of the lease liability adjusted for any lease payments made at or before the commencement date.

Certain lease arrangements include options to extend or terminate the lease before the end of the lease term. The right-of- use assets and lease liabilities include these options when it is reasonably certain that such options would be exercised.

The right-of-use assets is subsequently measured at cost less any accumulated depreciation, accumulated impairment losses, if any and adjusted for any remeasurement of the lease liability. The right-of-use assets is depreciated using the straight-line method from the commencement date over the shorter of lease term or useful life of right-of-use asset.

Right-of-use assets are tested for impairment whenever there is any indication that their carrying amounts may not be recoverable. Impairment loss, if any, is recognised in the statement of profit and loss.

Lease liability is measured at the present value of the lease payments that are not paid at the commencement date of the lease. The lease payments are discounted using the interest rate implicit in the lease, if that rate can be readily determined.

If that rate cannot be readily determined, the Company uses incremental borrowing rate. The lease liability is subsequently remeasured by increasing the carrying amount to reflect interest on the lease liability, reducing the carrying amount to reflect the lease payments made and remeasuring the carrying amount to reflect any reassessment or lease modifications.

The Company recognizes the amount of the remeasurement of lease liability as an adjustment to the right-of-use asset. Where the carrying amount of the right-of-use asset is reduced to zero and there is a further reduction in the measurement of the lease liability, the Company recognizes any remaining amount of the remeasurement in statement of profit and loss.

Variable lease payments not included in the measurement of the lease liabilities are expensed to the statement of profit and loss in the period in which the events or conditions which trigger those payments occur.

The Company accounts for sale and lease back transaction, recognizing right-of-use assets and lease liability, measured in the same way as other right-of-use assets and lease liability.

Gain or loss on the sale transaction is recognized in statement of profit and loss.

**The Company as lessor**

(i) **Operating lease** – Rental income from operating leases is recognized in the statement of profit and loss on a straight-line basis over the term of the relevant lease unless another systematic basis is more representative of the time pattern in which economic benefits from the leased asset is diminished. Initial direct costs incurred in negotiating and arranging an operating lease are added to the carrying value of the leased asset and recognised on a straight-line basis over the lease term.

(ii) **Finance lease** –When assets are leased out under a finance lease, the present value of minimum lease payments is recognised as a receivable. The difference between the gross receivable and the present value of receivable is recognized as unearned finance income. Lease income is recognised over the term of the lease using the net investment method before tax, which reflects a constant periodic rate of return.

(*Source: Tata Steel: Annual Report 2019-20*)

**Illustration 6.16: Accounting policy: Leases**

**Leases**

Leases are accounted as per Ind AS 116 which has become mandatory from April 1, 2019. Assets taken on lease are accounted as right-of-use assets and the corresponding lease liability is accounted at the lease commencement date.

Initially the right-of-use asset is measured at cost which comprises the initial amount of the lease liability adjusted for any lease payments made at or before the commencement date, plus any initial direct costs incurred and an estimate of costs to dismantle and remove the underlying asset or to restore the underlying asset or the site on which it is located, less any lease incentives received.

The lease liability is initially measured at the present value of the lease payments, discounted using the Company's incremental borrowing rate. It is remeasured when there is a change in future lease payments arising from a change in an index or a rate, or a change in the estimate of the guaranteed residual value, or a change in the assessment of purchase, extension, or termination option. When the lease liability is remeasured in this way, a corresponding adjustment is made to the carrying amount of the right-of-use asset, or is recorded in the Statement of Profit and Loss if the carrying amount of the right-of-use asset has been reduced to zero.

The right-of-use asset is measured by applying cost model i.e. right-of-use asset at cost less accumulated depreciation and cumulative impairment, if any. The right-of-use asset is depreciated using the straight-line method from the commencement date to the end of the lease term or useful life of the underlying asset whichever is earlier. Carrying amount of lease liability is increased by interest on lease liability and reduced by lease payments made.

Lease payments associated with following leases are recognised as expense on straight-line basis:

Low value leases; and

Leases which are short-term.

Assets given on lease are classified either as operating lease or as finance lease. A lease is classified as a finance lease if it transfers substantially all the risks and rewards incidental to ownership of an underlying asset. Initially asset held under finance lease is recognised in balance sheet and presented as a receivable at an amount equal to the net investment in the lease. Finance income is recognised over the lease term, based on a pattern reflecting a constant periodic rate of return on Company's net investment in the lease. A lease which is not classified as a finance lease is an operating lease. The Company recognizes lease payments in case of assets given on operating leases as income on a straight-line basis. The Company presents underlying assets subject to operating lease in its balance sheet under the respective class of asset. (*Source: Larsen & Toubro Annual Report 2019-20*)

**Illustration 6.17: Stripping costs**

**Stripping costs**

The Company separates two different types of stripping costs that are incurred in surface mining activity:

- developmental stripping costs and
- production stripping costs

Developmental stripping costs which are incurred in order to obtain access to quantities of mineral reserves that will be mined in future periods are capitalised as part of mining assets.

Capitalization of developmental stripping costs ends when the commercial production of the mineral reserves begins.

A mine can operate several open pits that are regarded as separate operations for the purpose of mine planning and production. In this case, stripping costs are accounted for separately, by reference to the ore extracted from each separate pit. If, however, the pits are highly integrated for the purpose of mine planning and production, stripping costs are aggregated too.

The determination of whether multiple pit mines are considered separate or integrated operations depends on each mine's specific circumstances. The following factors normally point towards the stripping costs for the individual pits being accounted for separately:

- mining of the second and subsequent pits is conducted consecutively with that of the first pit, rather than concurrently
- separate investment decisions are made to develop each pit, rather than a single investment decision being made at the outset
- the pits are operated as separate units in terms of mine planning and the sequencing of overburden and ore mining, rather than as an integrated unit
- expenditures for additional infrastructure to support the second and subsequent pits are relatively large
- the pits extract ore from separate and distinct ore bodies, rather than from a single ore body.

The relative importance of each factor is considered by the management to determine whether, the stripping costs should be attributed to the individual pit or to the combined output from the several pits.

Production stripping costs are incurred to extract the ore in the form of inventories and/or to improve access to an additional component of an ore body or deeper levels of material.

Production stripping costs are accounted for as inventories to the extent the benefit from production stripping activity is realized in the form of inventories.

The Company recognizes a stripping activity asset in the production phase if, and only if, all of the following are met:

- it is probable that the future economic benefit (improved access to the ore body) associated with the stripping activity will flow to the Company

- the Company can identify the component of the ore body for which access has been improved and
- the costs relating to the improved access to that component can be measured reliably.

Such costs are presented within mining assets. After initial recognition, stripping activity assets are carried at cost/deemed cost less accumulated amortization and impairment.

The expected useful life of the identified component of the ore body is used to depreciate or amortize the stripping asset.

(*Source: Tata Steel: Annual Report 2019-20*)

## 6.7 INVESTMENT PROPERTY

According to Clause H of Schedule III, Division II, with respect to Investment Property, a reconciliation of the gross and net carrying amounts of each class of property at the beginning and end of the reporting period showing additions, disposals, acquisitions through business combinations and other adjustments and the related amortisation and impairment losses/reversals shall be disclosed separately.

### 6.7.1 Ind AS 40: Investment Property

Para 7 of the above Ind AS defines Investment Property as the property (land or a building—or part of a building—or both) held (by the owner or by the lessee as a right-of-use asset) to earn rentals or for capital appreciation or both, rather than for:

(a) use in the production or supply of goods or services or for administrative purposes; or

(b) sale in the ordinary course of business.

Therefore, an investment property generates cash flows largely independently of the other assets held by an entity.

This distinguishes investment property from owner-occupied property. The production or supply of goods or services (or the use of property for administrative purposes) generates cash flows that are attributable not only to property, but also to other assets used in the production or supply process.

According to ICAI Guidance Note on Schedule III (Revised January, 2022 Edition), Right-of-use assets that meet the definition of investment property must be presented in the balance sheet as investment property.

Following examples show which of these properties are owner-occupied or investment properties:

**Illustration 6.18: Examples of Investment Property**

| | |
|---|---|
| (a) | land held for long-term capital appreciation rather than for short-term sale in the ordinary course of business. |
| (b) | land held for a currently undetermined future use. (If an entity has not determined that it will use the land as owner-occupied property or for short-term sale in the ordinary course of business, the land is regarded as held for capital appreciation.) |
| (c) | A building owned by the entity (or held by the entity under a finance lease) and leased out under one or more operating leases. |
| (d) | A building that is vacant but is held to be leased out under one or more operating leases. |
| (e) | Property that is being constructed or developed for future use as investment property. |

**Illustration 6.19: Examples which are not Investment Property**

| | |
|---|---|
| (a) | property intended for sale in the ordinary course of business or in the process of construction or development for such sale (see Ind AS 2, Inventories), for example, property acquired exclusively with a view to subsequent disposal in the near future or for development and resale. |
| (b) | owner-occupied property (see Ind AS 16), including (among other things) property held for future use as owner-occupied property, property held for future development and subsequent use as owner-occupied property, property occupied by employees (whether or not the employees pay rent at market rates) and owner occupied property awaiting disposal. |
| (c) | property that is leased to another entity under a finance lease. |

**Recognition**

According to para 16 of the Standard, Investment property shall be recognised as an asset when, and only when,

(a) it is probable that the future economic benefits that are associated with the investment property will flow to the entity and

(b) the cost of the investment property can be measured reliably

**Measurement**

**Initial measurement**

(i) Investment property is initially recognised at cost comprising the purchase price and directly attributable transaction costs (e.g. legal services, transfer services)

(ii) The cost of a purchased investment property comprises its purchase price and any directly attributable expenditure. Directly attributable expenditure includes, for example, professional fees for legal services, property transfer taxes and other transaction costs.

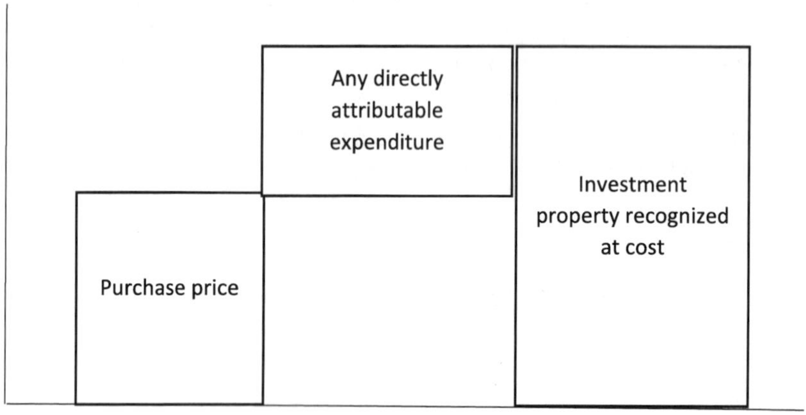


(iii) The cost of an investment property is not increased by:

(a) start-up costs (unless they are necessary to bring the property to the condition necessary for it to be capable of operating in the manner intended by management),

(b) operating losses incurred before the investment property achieves the planned level of occupancy, or

(c) abnormal amounts of wasted material, labour or other resources incurred in constructing or developing the property.

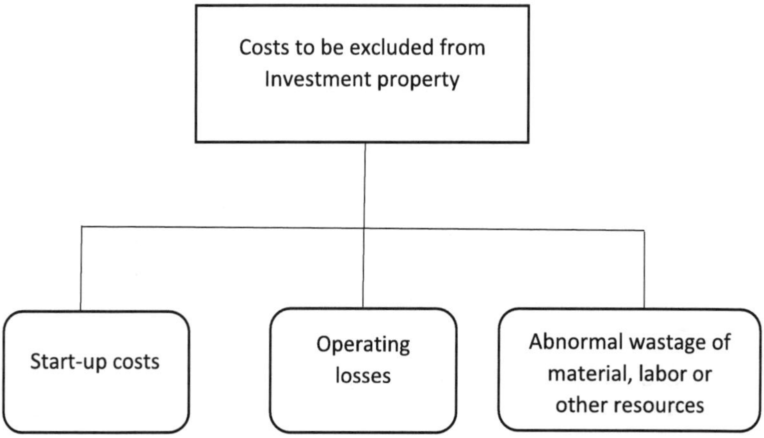

(iv) If payment for an investment property is deferred, its cost is the cash price equivalent. The difference between this amount and the total payments is recognised as interest expense over the period of credit.

(v) The initial cost of a property interest held under a lease and classified as an investment property shall be as prescribed for a finance lease, i.e. the asset shall be recognised at the lower of the fair value of the property and the present value of the minimum lease payments. An equivalent amount shall be recognised as a liability in accordance with the Standard.

(vi) Any premium paid for a lease is treated as part of the minimum lease payments for this purpose, and is therefore included in the cost of the asset, but is excluded from the liability. If a property interest held under a lease is classified as investment property, the item accounted for at fair value is that interest and not the underlying property. Guidance on measuring the fair value of a property interest is set out by the Standard as well as in Ind AS 113. That guidance is also relevant to the measurement of fair value when that value is used as cost for initial recognition purposes.

(vii) Under the recognition principle, an entity does not recognise in the carrying amount of an investment property the costs of the day-to-day servicing of such a property. Rather, these costs are recognised in profit or loss as incurred. Costs of day-today servicing are primarily the cost of labour and consumables and may include the cost of minor parts. The purpose of these expenditures is often described as for the 'repairs and maintenance' of the property.

(viii) Parts of investment properties may have been acquired through replacement. For example, the interior walls may be replacements of original walls. Under the recognition principle, an entity recognises in the carrying amount of an investment property the cost of replacing part of an existing investment property at the time that cost is incurred if the recognition criteria are met. The carrying amount of those parts that are replaced is derecognised in accordance with the derecognition provisions of this Standard.

**Subsequent measurement**

**Cost model**

(a) Subsequently investment property is carried at cost model, which is cost less accumulated depreciation and any accumulated impairment losses – in similar lines of Ind AS 16, other than those that meet the criteria to be classified as held for sale (or are included in a disposal group that is classified as held for sale) in accordance with Ind AS 105 Non-current Assets held for sale and discontinued operations.

(b) Subsequent expenditures on investment property are capitalized when it is probable that economic benefits in excess of the original standards will flow to the entity, otherwise it is charged to P&L

(c) According to Para 56, after initial recognition, an entity shall measure all of its investment properties in accordance with Ind AS 16's requirements for cost model, other than those that meet the criteria to be classified as held for sale (or are included in a disposal group that is classified as held for sale) in accordance with Ind AS 105, *Non-current Assets Held for Sale and Discontinued Operations*. Investment properties that meet the criteria to be classified as held for sale (or are included in a disposal group that is classified as held for sale) shall be measured in accordance with Ind AS 105.

Revaluation model as per Ind AS 16, is not permitted under Ind AS 40.

**Transfers**

Transfers to or from, investment property shall be made when, and only when, there is a change in use, evidenced by:

(a) commencement of owner-occupation, for a transfer from investment property to owner occupied property

(b) commencement of development with a view to sale, for a transfer from investment property to inventories

(c) end of owner-occupation, for a transfer from owner-occupied property to investment property; or

(d) commencement of an operating lease to another party, for a transfer from inventories to investment property

**Disposals**

In accordance with para 66, an investment property shall be derecognised (eliminated from Balance Sheet) on disposal or when the investment property is permanently withdrawn from use and no future economic benefits are expected from its disposal.

Gains or losses arising from the retirement or disposal of investment property shall be determined as the difference between the net disposal proceeds and the carrying amount of the asset and shall be recognised in profit or loss (unless Ind AS 17 requires otherwise on a sale and leaseback) in the period of the retirement or disposal.

**Illustration 6.20: Investment Property: Specimen format**

| Description | Land | Buildings | Others | Total |
|---|---|---|---|---|
| **Gross Block**<br>**As at beginning of reporting period** | | | | |

| Description | Land | Buildings | Others | Total |
|---|---|---|---|---|
| Add:<br>Additions<br>Acquisitions through business combinations<br>Other adjustments | | | | |
| Less:<br>Disposals<br>Other adjustments | | | | |
| **Gross Block as at end of reporting period** | | | | |
| **Depreciation**<br>As at beginning of reporting period<br>Add: For the year<br>Less: Deduction/adjustments/ reversals<br>As at end of reporting period | | | | |
| **Impairment losses**<br>As at beginning of reporting period<br>Add: For the year<br>Less: Deduction/adjustments/ reversals | | | | |

| Description | Land | Buildings | Others | Total |
|---|---|---|---|---|
| As at end of reporting period | | | | |
| **Net Block as at end of previous reporting period** | | | | |
| **Net Block as at end of current reporting period** | | | | |

**Illustration 6.21: Investment properties**

**Investment property**

Properties, including those under construction, held to earn rentals and/or capital appreciation are classified as investment property and are measured and reported at cost, including transaction costs and borrowing cost capitalised for qualifying assets, in accordance with the Company's accounting policy

Depreciation is recognised using straight-line method so as to write off the cost of the investment property less their residual values over their useful lives specified in Schedule II to the Companies Act, 2013 or in the case of assets where the useful life was determined by technical evaluation, over the useful life so determined. Depreciation method is reviewed at each financial year end to reflect the expected pattern of consumption of the future benefits embodied in the investment property. The estimated useful life and residual values are also reviewed at each financial year end and the effect of any change in the estimates of useful life/ residual value is accounted on prospective basis. Freehold land and properties under construction are not depreciated. An investment property is derecognised upon disposal or when the investment property is permanently withdrawn from use and no future economic benefits are expected from the disposal. Any gain or loss arising on derecognition of property is recognised in the Statement of Profit and Loss in the same period.

**(*Source: Larsen & Toubro: Annual Report 2019-20*)**

## 6.8 BORROWING COST

### 6.8.1 Borrowing Cost: AS 16 (For non Ind AS entities)

Capitalisation of borrowing costs as carried out in accordance with *AS 16 Borrowing costs* needs to be disclosed separately for each class of assets as per Schedule III as specified in the Guidance Note published by ICAI. Accounting policy may be disclosed in the Financial statements as shown in the illustrations below.

**Recognition**

Borrowing costs that are directly attributable to the acquisition, construction or production of a qualifying asset should be capitalised as part of the cost of that asset. The amount of borrowing costs eligible for capitalisation should be determined in accordance with this Standard.

Other borrowing costs should be recognised as an expense in the period in which they are incurred.

To the extent that funds are borrowed specifically for the purpose of obtaining a qualifying asset, the amount of borrowing costs eligible for capitalisation on that asset should be determined as the actual borrowing costs incurred on that borrowing during the period less any income on the temporary investment of those borrowings.

To the extent that funds are borrowed generally and used for the purpose of obtaining a qualifying asset, the amount of borrowing costs eligible for capitalisation should be determined by applying a capitalisation rate to the expenditure on that asset.

The capitalisation rate should be the weighted average of the borrowing costs applicable to the borrowings of the enterprise that are outstanding during the period, other than borrowings made specifically for the purpose of obtaining a qualifying asset.

The amount of borrowing costs capitalised during a period should not exceed the amount of borrowing costs incurred during that period.

The disclosure requirements would include the following:

(a) The accounting policy adopted for borrowing costs and

(b) The amount of borrowing costs capitalised during the year

## 6.8.2 Borrowing Cost: Ind AS 23

Salient features related to the Ind AS 23 are highlighted below.

Prescribes the accounting treatment of borrowing costs, which are defined as interest and other costs incurred by an entity in connection with the borrowing of funds.

**Borrowing costs** include

- Interest on bank overdrafts and borrowings
- Finance charges on finance leases and
- Exchange differences on foreign currency borrowings where they are regarded as an adjustment to interest costs

**A qualifying asset** is an asset that takes a substantial period of time to get ready for its intended use. It can be property, plant and equipment and investment property during the construction period, intangible assets during the development period, or "made-to-order" inventories.

Depending on the circumstances, any of the following may be qualifying assets:

(a) inventories

(b) manufacturing plants

(c) power generation facilities

(d) intangible assets

(e) investment properties

(f) bearer plants.

Financial assets, and inventories that are manufactured, or otherwise produced, over a short period of time, are not qualifying assets. Assets that are ready for their intended use or sale when acquired are not qualifying assets.

According to para 6A, with regard to exchange difference required to be treated as borrowing costs, the manner of arriving at the adjustments stated therein shall be as under:

(i) the adjustment should be of an amount which is equivalent to the extent to which the exchange loss does not exceed the difference between the cost of borrowing in functional currency when compared to the cost of borrowing in a foreign currency

(ii) where there is an unrealised exchange loss which is treated as an adjustment to interest and subsequently there is a realised or unrealised gain in respect of the settlement or translation of the same borrowing, the gain to the extent of the loss previously recognised as an adjustment should also be recognised as an adjustment to interest

**Recognition of borrowing cost**

According to para 8, an entity shall capitalise borrowing costs that are directly attributable to the acquisition, construction or production of a qualifying asset as part of the cost of that asset.

Other borrowing costs should be recognised as an expense in the period in which they are incurred.

**Borrowing costs eligible for capitalization**

To the extent that funds are borrowed specifically for the purpose of obtaining a qualifying asset, the amount of borrowing costs eligible for capitalisation on that asset should be determined as the actual borrowing costs incurred on that borrowing during the period less any income on the temporary investment of those borrowings.

To the extent that funds are borrowed generally and used for the purpose of obtaining a qualifying asset, the amount of borrowing costs eligible for capitalisation should be determined by applying a capitalisation rate to the expenditure on that asset.

The capitalisation rate should be the weighted average of the borrowing costs applicable to the borrowings of the enterprise that are outstanding during the period, other than borrowings made specifically for the purpose of obtaining a qualifying asset.

The amount of borrowing costs capitalised during a period should not exceed the amount of borrowing costs incurred during that period.

**Commencement of capitalization**

(a) expenditure for the acquisition, construction or production of a qualifying asset is being incurred;

(b) borrowing costs are being incurred; and

(c) activities that are necessary to prepare the asset for its intended use or sale are in progress.

**Suspension of capitalization**

Capitalisation of borrowing costs should be suspended during extended periods in which active development is interrupted.

**Cessation of capitalization**

Capitalisation of borrowing costs should cease when substantially all the activities necessary to prepare the qualifying asset for its intended use or sale are complete.

When the construction of a qualifying asset is completed in parts and a completed part is capable of being used while construction continues for the other parts, capitalisation of borrowing costs in relation to a part should cease when substantially all the activities necessary to prepare that part for its intended use or sale are complete. The process of capitalisation is explained in the chart below.

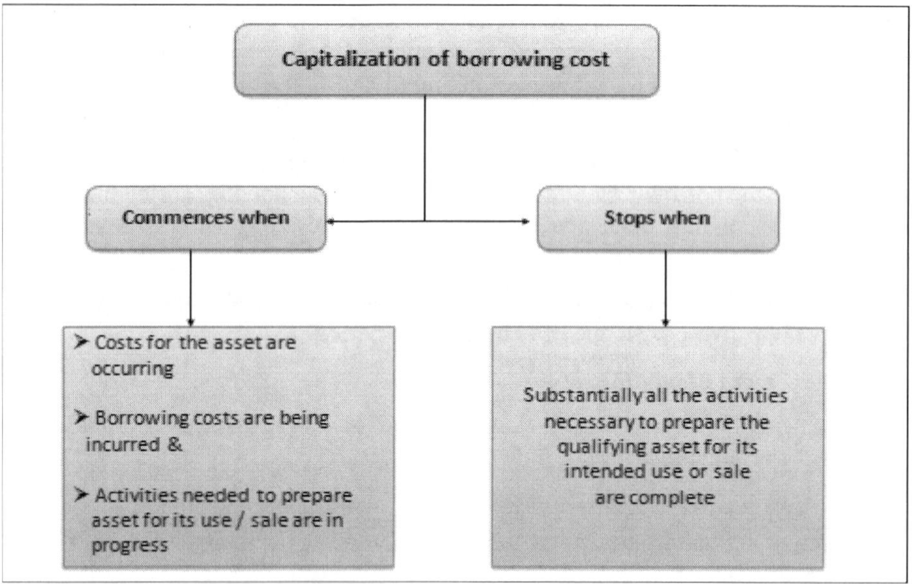


**Accounting of borrowing costs**

Borrowing costs defined as interest and other costs incurred by an entity in connection with the borrowing of funds. Ind AS 23 allows two methods of accounting borrowing costs:

(a) Borrowing costs should be recognised as expense in the period it is incurred or

(b) Borrowing costs directly attributable to acquisition, construction or production of a qualifying asset can be capitalised when

- it is probable that they will result in future economic benefits of the entity and
- the costs can be measured reliably (effective interest rate method as per Ind AS 109)

## 6.9 GOVERNMENT GRANTS

### 6.9.1 Accounting for Government grants – AS 12 (For non Ind AS entities)

Treatment of Government grants would be as follows:

| | |
|---|---|
| *(a) Government grants related to revenue* | Government grants related to revenue should be recognised on a systematic basis in the profit and loss statement over the periods necessary to match them with the related costs which they are intended to compensate.<br>Such grants should either be shown separately under 'other income' or deducted in reporting the related expense. |
| *(b) Government grants related to Promoters contribution* | Government grants of the nature of promoters' contribution should be credited to capital reserve and treated as a part of shareholders' funds. |
| *(c) Government grants related to Fixed Assets* | Government grants related to specific fixed assets should be presented in the balance sheet by showing the grant as a deduction from the gross value of the assets concerned in arriving at their book value.<br>Where the grant related to a specific fixed asset equals the whole, or virtually the whole, of the cost of the asset, the asset should be shown in the balance sheet at a nominal value.<br>Alternatively, government grants related to depreciable fixed assets may be treated as deferred income which should be recognised in the profit and loss statement on a systematic and rational basis over the useful life of the asset, i.e., such grants should be allocated to income over the periods and in the proportions in which depreciation on those assets is charged.<br>Grants related to non-depreciable assets should be credited to capital reserve under this method. However, if a grant related to a non-depreciable asset requires the fulfilment of certain obligations, the grant should be credited to income over the same period over which the cost of meeting such obligations is charged to income. The deferred income balance should be separately disclosed in the financial statements. |
| *(d) non-monetary Government Grants* | Government grants in the form of non-monetary assets, given at a concessional rate, should be accounted for on |

| | |
|---|---|
| | the basis of their acquisition cost. In case a non-monetary asset is given free of cost, it should be recorded at a nominal value. |
| ***(e) Government Grants that are receivable as compensation for expenses or losses incurred in previous accounting period*** | Government grants that are receivable as compensation for expenses or losses incurred in a previous accounting period or for the purpose of giving immediate financial support to the enterprise with no further related costs, should be recognised and disclosed in the profit and loss statement of the period in which they are receivable, as an extraordinary item if appropriate (see Accounting Standard (AS) 5, Net Profit or Loss for the Period, Prior Period Items and Changes in Accounting Policies). |

A contingency related to a government grant, arising after the grant has been recognised, should be treated in accordance with Accounting Standard (AS) 4, Contingencies and Events Occurring after the Balance Sheet Date.

The following should be disclosed:

(i) the accounting policy adopted for government grants, including the methods of presentation in the financial statements.

(ii) the nature and extent of government grants recognised in the financial statements, including grants of non-monetary assets given at a concessional rate or free of cost.

## 6.9.2 Accounting for Government grants – Ind AS 20

Salient features of this Ind AS 20 are summarized below.

Government grants, including non-monetary grants at fair value shall not be recognised until there is a reasonable assurance that:

(a) the entity will comply with the conditions attaching to them and

(b) the grants will be received

The manner in which a grant is received does not affect the accounting method to be adopted in regard to the grant. Thus a grant is accounted for in the same manner whether it is received in cash or as a reduction of a liability to the government.

A forgivable loan from government is treated as a government grant when there is reasonable assurance that the entity will meet the terms for forgiveness of the loan.

The benefit of a government loan at a below-market rate of interest is treated as a government grant. The loan shall be recognised and measured in accordance with Ind AS 109, *Financial Instruments*. The benefit of the below market rate of interest shall be measured as the difference between the initial carrying value of the loan determined in accordance with Ind AS 109, and the proceeds received. The benefit is accounted for in accordance with this Standard.

Government grants are of two types

(a) Grant related to assets

(b) Grant related to income

**Non-monetary government grants**

A government grant may take the form of a transfer of a non-monetary asset, such as land or other resources, for the use of the entity. In these circumstances, the fair value of the non-monetary asset is assessed and both grant and asset are accounted for at that fair value.

**Presentation of grants related to assets**

Government grants related to assets, including non-monetary grants at fair value, shall be presented in the balance sheet by setting up the grant as deferred income.

The grant set up as deferred income is recognised in profit or loss on a systematic basis over the useful life of the asset.

The purchase of assets and receipt of related grants can cause major movements in the cash flow of an entity. Hence in order to show the gross movement in assets, such movements are disclosed as separate items in the statement of cash flows.

**Presentation of grants related to income**

Grants related to income are sometimes presented as a credit in the statement of profit and loss, either separately or under a general heading such as "other income" ; alternatively they are deducted in reporting the related expense.

**Repayment of Government grants**

A government grant that becomes repayable shall be accounted for as a change in accounting estimate (see Ind AS 8 *Accounting Policies, Changes in Accounting Estimates and Errors*).

Repayment of a grant related to income shall be applied first against any unamortised deferred credit recognised in respect of the grant. To the extent that the repayment exceeds any such deferred credit, or when no deferred credit exists, the repayment shall be recognised immediately in profit or loss.

Repayment of a grant related to an asset shall be recognised by reducing the deferred income balance by the amount repayable.

## 6.10 IMPAIRMENT OF ASSETS

### 6.10.1 Impairment of Assets (AS 28): For non Ind AS entities

An asset is impaired when the carrying amount of the asset exceeds its recoverable amount.

An enterprise should assess at each balance sheet date whether there is any indication that an asset may be impaired. If any such Indication exists, the enterprise should estimate the recoverable amount of the asset.

Impairment loss may be in the following areas:

(a) Impairment loss on a specific asset

(b) Impairment loss for a cash generating unit. A Cash Generating Unit (CGU) is a smallest group of assets for which cash flows can be determined independently

(c) Impairment loss for discontinuing operations. In this situation, the impairment loss shall depend on the way the discontinuing operation is disposed of:

    (i) Substantially in its entirety

    (ii) as piecemeal sales

    (iii) by abandonment

**Impairment loss = Carrying amount of the asset – Recoverable amount**

Carrying amount is the amount at which an asset is carried in the Balance Sheet

Recoverable amount of an asset is higher of:

(a) Net selling price

(b) Value-in-use

**Net Selling Price = Expected realisable value of an asset – cost of disposal**

- The best evidence of an asset's net selling price is a price in a binding sale agreement in an arm's length transaction, adjusted for incremental costs that would be directly attributable to the disposal of the asset
- If there is no binding sale agreement but an asset is traded in an active market, net selling price is the asset's market price less the costs of disposal. The appropriate market price is usually the current bid price

**Value-in-use** = Present value of estimated future cash flows arising from the use of asset + residual value at the end of its useful life. Present value is calculated by applying discount rate to future cash flows.

A simple example explaining impairment of an asset is shown below.

**Recognition and measurement of impairment loss**

- If the recoverable amount of an asset is less than its carrying amount, the carrying amount of the asset should be reduced to its recoverable amount. That reduction is an impairment loss.
- An impairment loss should be recognised as an expense in the statement of profit and loss immediately, unless the asset is carried at revalued amount in

accordance with another Accounting Standard (see Accounting Standard (AS) 10, Property, Plant and Equipment), in which case any impairment loss of a revalued asset should be treated as a revaluation decrease under that Accounting Standard.

- When the amount estimated for an impairment loss is greater than the carrying mount of the asset to which it relates, an enterprise should recognise a liability if, and only if, that is required by another Accounting Standard.
- After the recognition of an impairment loss, the depreciation (amortisation) charge for the asset should be adjusted in future periods to allocate the asset's revised carrying amount, less its residual value (if any), on a systematic basis over its remaining useful life.

**Cash generating Unit**

- If there is any indication that an asset may be impaired, the recoverable amount should be estimated for the individual asset.
- If it is not possible to estimate the recoverable amount of the individual asset, an enterprise should determine the recoverable amount of the cash generating unit to which the asset belongs (the asset's cash- generating unit).
- The recoverable amount of an individual asset cannot be determined if:
    - (a) the asset's value in use cannot be estimated to be close to its net selling price (for example, when the future cash flows from continuing use of the asset cannot be estimated to be negligible); and
    - (b) the asset does not generate cash inflows from continuing use that are largely independent of those from other assets. In such cases, value in use and, therefore, recoverable amount, can be determined only for the asset's cash-generating unit.

**Impairment loss of Cash Generating Unit**

| | |
|---|---|
| **Calculation of impairment loss of a Cash Generating Unit** | • An impairment loss should be recognised for a cash-generating unit if, and only if, its recoverable amount is less than its carrying amount.<br>• The impairment loss should be allocated to reduce the carrying amount of the assets of the unit in the following order:<br>(a) first, to goodwill allocated to the cash-generating unit (if any); and<br>(b) then, to the other assets of the unit on a pro-rata basis based on the carrying amount of each asset in the unit.<br>• These reductions in carrying amounts should be treated as impairment losses on individual assets and recognised accordingly<br>• In allocating an impairment loss, the carrying amount of |

| | an asset should not be reduced below the highest of:<br>(a) its net selling price (if determinable);<br>(b) its value in use (if determinable); and<br>(c) zero. |
|---|---|

**Disclosure requirements**

For each class of assets, the financial statements should disclose:

(a) the amount of impairment losses recognised in the statement of profit and loss during the period and the line item(s) of the Statement of profit and loss in which those impairment losses are included;

(b) the amount of reversals of impairment losses recognised in the statement of profit and loss during the period and the line item(s)of the statement of profit and loss in which those impairment losses are reversed.

(c) the amount of impairment losses recognised directly against revaluation surplus during the period; and

(d) the amount of reversals of impairment losses recognised directly in revaluation surplus during the period.

An enterprise that applies AS 17, Segment Reporting, should disclose the following for each reportable segment based on an enterprise's primary format (as defined in AS 17):

(a) the amount of impairment losses recognised in the statement of profit and loss and directly against revaluation surplus during the period; and

(b) the amount of reversals of impairment losses recognised in the statement of profit and loss and directly in revaluation surplus during the period.

If an impairment loss for an individual asset or a cash-generating unit is recognised or reversed during the period and is material to the financial statements of the reporting enterprise as a whole, an enterprise should disclose:

(a) the events and circumstances that led to the recognition or reversal of the impairment loss;

(b) the amount of the impairment loss recognised or reversed;

(c) for an individual asset:

(i) the nature of the asset; and

(ii) the reportable segment to which the asset belongs, based on the enterprise's primary format (as defined in AS 17, Segment Reporting);

(d) for a cash-generating unit:

  (i) a description of the cash-generating unit (such as whether it is a product line, a plant, a business operation, a geographical area, a reportable segment as defined in AS 17 or other);

  (ii) the amount of the impairment loss recognised or reversed by class of assets and by reportable segment based on the enterprise's primary format (as defined in AS 17); and

  (iii) if the aggregation of assets for identifying the cash-generating unit has changed since the previous estimate of the cash generating unit's recoverable amount (if any), the enterprise should describe the current and former way of aggregating assets and the reasons for changing the way the cash generating unit is identified;

(e) whether the recoverable amount of the asset (cash-generating unit) is its net selling price or its value in use;

(f) if recoverable amount is net selling price, the basis used to determine net selling price (such as whether selling price was determined by reference to an active market or in some other way); and

(g) if recoverable amount is value in use, the discount rate(s) used in the current estimate and previous estimate (if any) of value in use.

If impairment losses recognised (reversed) during the period are material in aggregate to the financial statements of the reporting enterprise as a whole, an enterprise should disclose a brief description of the following:

(a) the main classes of assets affected by impairment losses (reversals of impairment losses)

(b) the main events and circumstances that led to the recognition (reversal) of these impairment losses

## 6.10.2 Impairment of Assets (Ind AS 36)

Impairment of Assets relate to procedures that an entity applies to ensure that its assets are carried at no more than their recoverable amount. An asset is carried at more than its recoverable amount if its carrying amount exceeds the amount to be recovered through use or sale of the asset. In such an event, the asset is described as impaired and the Standard requires the entity to recognise an impairment loss. The Standard specifies when an entity should reverse an impairment loss and prescribes disclosures.

**Identification of assets that may be impaired**

An asset is impaired when the carrying amount of the asset exceeds its recoverable amount.

An entity shall assess at the end of each reporting period whether there is any indication that an asset may be impaired. If any such indication exists, the entity shall estimate the recoverable amount of the asset.

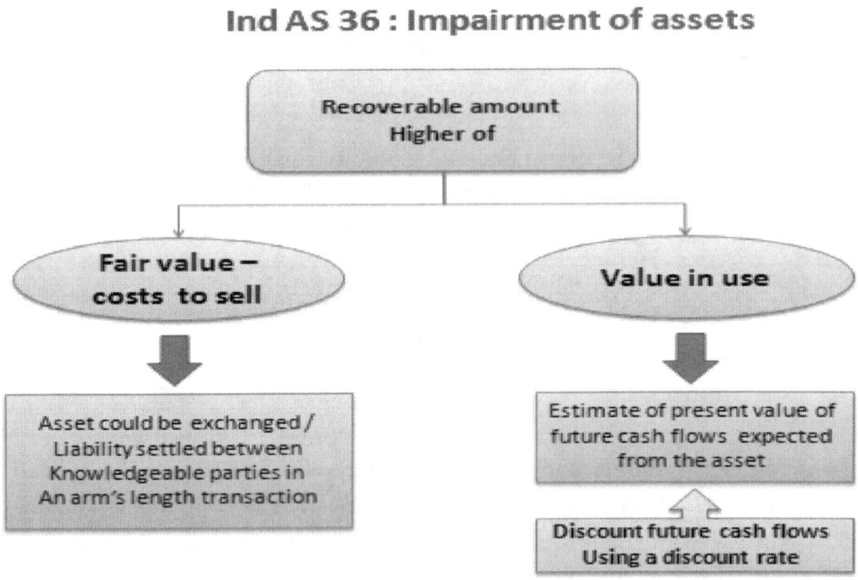


According to the Standard irrespective of whether there is any indication of impairment, an entity shall also:

(a) test an intangible asset with an indefinite useful life or an intangible asset not yet available for use for impairment annually by comparing its carrying amount with its recoverable amount. This impairment test may be performed at any time during an annual period, provided it is performed at the same time every year. Different intangible assets may be tested for impairment at different times. However, if such an intangible asset was initially recognised during the current annual period, that intangible asset shall be tested for impairment before the end of the current annual period.

(b) test goodwill acquired in a business combination for impairment annually in accordance with paragraphs 80–99 of the Standard.

**Measurement of recoverable amount**

The Standard defines recoverable amount as the higher of an asset's or cash generating unit's fair value less costs of disposal and its value in use. Paragraphs 19–57 of the Standard set out the requirements for measuring recoverable amount. These requirements use the term 'an asset' but apply equally to an individual asset or a cash-generating unit.

**Measurement of recoverable amount of an intangible asset with indefinite useful life**

The Standard requires an intangible asset with an indefinite useful life to be tested for impairment annually by comparing its carrying amount with its recoverable amount, irrespective of whether there is any indication that it may be impaired.

However, the most recent detailed calculation of such an asset's recoverable amount made in a preceding period may be used in the impairment test for that asset in the current period, provided all of the following criteria are met:

(a) if the intangible asset does not generate cash inflows from continuing use that are largely independent of those from other assets or groups of assets and is therefore tested for impairment as part of the cash-generating unit to which it belongs, the assets and liabilities making up that unit have not changed significantly since the most recent recoverable amount calculation;

(b) the most recent recoverable amount calculation resulted in an amount that exceeded the asset's carrying amount by a substantial margin; and

(c) based on an analysis of events that have occurred and circumstances that have changed since the most recent recoverable amount calculation, the likelihood that a current recoverable amount determination would be less than the asset's carrying amount is remote.

**Fair value less cost of disposal**

Costs of disposal, other than those that have been recognised as liabilities, are deducted in measuring fair value less costs of disposal. Examples of such costs are legal costs, stamp duty and similar transaction taxes, costs of removing the asset, and direct incremental costs to bring an asset into condition for its sale.

However, termination benefits (as defined in Ind AS 19) and costs associated with reducing or reorganising a business following the disposal of an asset are not direct incremental costs to dispose of the asset.

**Value-in-use**

(a) The following elements shall be reflected in the calculation of an asset's value in use:

  (a) an estimate of the future cash inflows the entity expects to derive from the asset

  (b) expectations about possible variations in the amount or timing of those future cash flows

  (c) the time value of money, represented by the current market risk-free rate of interest

  (d) the price for bearing the uncertainty inherent in the asset and

(e) other factors, such as illiquidity, that market participants would reflect in pricing the future cash flows the entity expects to derive from the asset

(b) Estimating the value in use of an asset involves the following steps:

(a) estimating the future cash inflows and outflows to be derived from continuing use of the asset and from its ultimate disposal; and

(b) applying the appropriate discount rate to those future cash flows

**Estimating future cash flows**

(a) base cash flow projections should be based on reasonable and supportable assumptions that represent management's best estimate of the set of economic conditions that will exist over the remaining useful life of the asset. Greater weight should be given to external evidence;

(b) base cash flow projections should be based on the most recent financial Budgets/ forecasts that have been approved by management. Projections based on these budgets/forecasts should cover a maximum period of five years unless a longer period can be justified. But it shall exclude estimated future cash inflows or outflows expected to arise from future restructurings or from improving or enhancing the asset's performance.

(c) cash flow projections beyond the period covered by the most recent budgets/forecasts should be estimated by extrapolating the projections based on the budgets/forecasts using a steady or declining growth rate for subsequent years unless an increasing rate can be justified. This growth rate should not exceed the long-term average growth rate for the products, industries, or country or countries in which the enterprise operates, or for the market in which the asset is used, unless a higher rate can be justified.

**Discount rate**

The discount rate(s) should be a pre-tax rate(s) that reflect(s) current market assessments of

(a) the time value of money and

(b) the risks specific to the asset. The discount rate(s) should not reflect risks for which future cash flow estimates have been adjusted.

As a starting point, the enterprise may take into account the following rates:

(a) the enterprise's weighted average cost of capital determined using techniques such as the Capital Asset Pricing Model;

(b) the enterprise's incremental borrowing rate; and

(c) other market borrowing rates.

These rates are adjusted:

(a) to reflect the way that the market would assess the specific risks associated with the projected cash flows; and

(b) to exclude risks that are not relevant to the projected cash flows. Consideration is given to risks such as country risk, currency risk, price risk and cash flow risk.

**Recognition and measurement of impairment loss**

If the recoverable amount of an asset is less than its carrying amount, the carrying amount of the asset should be reduced to its recoverable amount. That reduction is an impairment loss.

An impairment loss should be recognised as an expense in the statement of profit and loss immediately, unless the asset is carried at revalued amount in accordance with another Accounting Standard (*see Ind AS 16 Property, Plant and Equipment*) in which case any impairment loss of a revalued asset should be treated as a revaluation decrease under that Ind AS.

When the amount estimated for an impairment loss is greater than the carrying amount of the asset to which it relates, an enterprise should recognise a liability if, and only if, that is required by another Accounting Standard.

After the recognition of an impairment loss, the depreciation (amortisation) charge for the asset should be adjusted in future periods to allocate the asset's revised carrying amount, less its residual value (if any), on a systematic basis over its remaining useful life.

**Illustration 6.22: Impairment loss**

B Ltd has a machine that originally cost Rs.3,50,000. Its accumulated depreciation is Rs. 50,000. The market value of the machine is Rs.3,00,000 the cost of dismantling is Rs. 10000 and the direct selling cost is Rs. 20,000. The costs of restructuring the Co if the machine is sold is Rs.1,00,000. The value in use as determined by the management is Rs.2,75,000. The remaining estimated life of the asset is 5 years and estimated residual value at the end of this life is Rs.25,000.

Account for the loss on impairment. Also calculate the depreciation charge on the machine after the impairment loss has been recognised.

**Solution**

**Calculation of recoverable amount**

| | Rs | Rs. |
|---|---|---|
| Carrying amount | | 3,50,000 |
| Less: Accumulated depreciation | | 50,000 |
| Carrying amount (A) | | 3,00,000 |

| | | |
|---|---|---|
| Recoverable amount<br>(fair value less cost of disposal) | | 3,00,000 |
| Market value | | |
| Less: Cost of dismantling | 10,000 | |
| Direct selling cost (B) | 20,000 | 30,000 |
| | | 2,70,000 |
| Value-in-use as determined by management (C) | | 2,75,000 |
| Recoverable amount higher of B and C = (D) | | 2,75,000 |

**Loss on impairment = Carrying amount – recoverable amount**

| | Rs | Rs |
|---|---|---|
| Carrying amount (A) | | 3,00,000 |
| Less: Recoverable amount (D) | | 2,75,000 |
| (A – D) = (E) | | 25,000 |

**Calculation of depreciation**

| | Rs | Rs |
|---|---|---|
| Depreciation charge | | |
| Revised carrying amount of machine | | 2,75,000 |
| Less: Estimated residual level | | 25,000 |
| Amount to be depreciated | | 2,50,000 |
| Estimated useful life | | 5 |
| Depreciation charge (250000/5) | | 50,000 |

**Cash Generating Unit**

A Cash Generating Unit (CGU) is the smallest identifiable group of assets that generates cash inflows that are largely independent of the cash inflows from other assets or group of assets

**Identification of Cash-Generating Unit to which an asset belongs**

- If there is any indication that an asset may be impaired, the recoverable amount should be estimated for the individual asset.
- If it is not possible to estimate the recoverable amount of the individual asset, an enterprise should determine the recoverable amount of the cash generating unit to which the asset belongs (the asset's cash- generating unit).
- The recoverable amount of an individual asset cannot be determined if:
  - (a) the asset's value in use cannot be estimated to be close to its net selling price(for example, when the future cash flows from continuing use of the asset cannot be estimated to be negligible); and
  - (b) the asset does not generate cash inflows from continuing use that are largely independent of those from other assets. In such cases, value in

use and, therefore, recoverable amount, can be determined only for the asset's cash-generating unit.

**Illustration 6.23: Cash Generating Unit**

A mining enterprise owns a private railway to support its mining activities. The private railway could be sold only for scrap value and the private railway does not generate cash inflows from continuing use that are largely independent of the cash inflows from the other assets of the mine.

*It is not possible to estimate the recoverable amount of the private railway because the value in use of the private railway cannot be determined and it is probably different from scrap value. Therefore, the enterprise estimates the recoverable amount of the cash-generating unit to which the private railway belongs, that is, the mine as a whole.*

**Illustration 6.24: Cash Generating Unit**

A bus company provides services under contract with a municipality that requires minimum service on each of five separate routes. Assets devoted to each route and the cash flows from each route can be identified separately. One of the routes operates at a significant loss.

*Because the enterprise does not have the option to curtail any one bus route, the lowest level of identifiable cash inflows from continuing use that are largely independent of the cash inflows from other assets or groups of assets is the cash inflows generated by the five routes together. The cash-generating unit for each route is the bus company as a whole.*

**Recoverable amount and carrying amount of a cash generating unit**

The recoverable amount of a cash-generating unit is the higher of the cash-generating unit's fair value less cost to sell and value in use

The carrying amount of a cash-generating unit should be determined consistently with the way the recoverable amount of the cash-generating unit is determined.

The carrying amount of a cash-generating unit:

(a) includes the carrying amount of only those assets that can be attributed directly, or allocated on a reasonable and consistent basis, to the cash-generating unit and that will generate the future cash inflows estimated in determining the cash-generating unit's value in use; and

(b) does not include the carrying amount of any recognised liability, unless the recoverable amount of the cash-generating unit cannot be determined without consideration of this liability. This is because net selling price and value in use of a cash-generating unit are determined excluding cash flows that relate to assets that are not part of the cash-generating unit and liabilities that have already been recognised in the financial statements.

Steps to be followed to ascertain impairment loss of a Cash Generating Unit (CGU) is explained in the chart below.

**Goodwill**

According to para 80, for the purpose of impairment testing, goodwill acquired in a business combination shall, from the acquisition date, be allocated to each of the acquirer's cash generating units or groups of cash generating units, that is expected to benefit from the synergies of the combination, irrespective of whether other assets or liabilities of the acquiree are assigned to those units or groups of units.

Each unit or group of units to which the goodwill is so allocated shall:

(a) represent the lowest level within the entity at which the goodwill is monitored for internal management purposes; and

(b) not be larger than an operating segment as defined by paragraph 5 of *Ind AS 108 Operating Segments* before aggregation

In accordance with para 86, if goodwill has been allocated to a cash-generating unit and the entity disposes of an operation within that unit, the goodwill associated with the operation disposed of shall be:

(a) included in the carrying amount of the operation when determining the gain or loss on disposal and

(b) measured on the basis of the relative values of the operation disposed of and the portion of the cash-generating unit retained, unless the entity can demonstrate that some other method better reflects the goodwill associated with the operation disposed of.

**Corporate Assets**

In testing a cash-generating unit for impairment, an enterprise should identify all the corporate assets that relate to the cash-generating unit under review. If a portion of the carrying amount of a corporate asset:

(a) can be allocated on a reasonable and consistent basis to that unit, the entity shall compare the carrying amount of the unit, including the portion of the carrying amount of the corporate asset allocated to the unit, with its recoverable amount. Any impairment loss shall be recognised.

(b) Cannot be allocated on a reasonable and consistent basis to that unit, the entity shall:

    (i) compare the carrying amount of the unit, excluding the corporate asset, with its recoverable amount and recognise any impairment loss.

(ii) identify the smallest group of cash-generating units that includes the cash-generating unit under review and to which a portion of the carrying amount of the corporate asset can be allocated on a reasonable and consistent basis,

(iii) compare the carrying amount of that group of cash-generating units, including the portion of the carrying amount of the corporate asset allocated to that group of units, with the recoverable amount of the group of units. Any impairment loss shall be recognised.

**Impairment loss of a cash generating unit**

An impairment loss should be recognised for a cash-generating unit if, and only if, its recoverable amount is less than its carrying amount.

The impairment loss should be allocated to reduce the carrying amount of the assets of the unit in the following order:

(a) first, to goodwill allocated to the cash-generating unit (if any); and

(b) then, to the other assets of the unit on a pro-rata basis based on the carrying amount of each asset in the unit.

These reductions in carrying amounts should be treated as impairment losses on individual assets and recognised accordingly.

In allocating an impairment loss, the carrying amount of an asset should not be reduced below the highest of:

(a) its net selling price (if determinable);

(b) its value in use (if determinable); and

(c) zero.

The amount of the impairment loss that would otherwise have been allocated to the asset should be allocated to the other assets of the unit on a pro-rata basis.

**Reversal of impairment loss**

An enterprise shall assess at each balance sheet date whether there is any indication that an impairment loss recognised for an asset in prior accounting periods may no longer exist or may have decreased. If any such indication exists, the enterprise should estimate the recoverable amount of that asset.

An impairment loss recognised for an asset in prior accounting periods should be reversed if there has been a change in the estimates of cash inflows, cash outflows or discount rates used to determine the asset's recoverable amount since the last impairment loss was recognised.

Accordingly, the carrying amount of the asset should be increased to its recoverable amount. That increase is a reversal of an impairment loss.

### Reversal of impairment loss of an individual asset

The increased carrying amount of an asset due to a reversal of an impairment loss should not exceed the carrying amount that would have been determined (net of amortisation or depreciation) had no impairment loss been recognised for the asset in prior accounting periods.

Reversal of an impairment loss for an asset should be recognised as income immediately in the statement of profit and loss, unless the asset is carried at revalued amount in accordance with another. Accounting Standard (Ind AS 16, Property, Plant and Equipment) in which case any reversal of an impairment loss on a revalued asset should be treated as a revaluation increase under that Accounting Standard.

### Reversal of impairment loss of a cash generating unit

Reversal of an impairment loss for a cash-generating unit should be allocated to increase the carrying amount of the assets of the unit in the following order:

(a) first, assets other than goodwill on a pro-rata basis based on the carrying amount of each asset in the unit; and

(b) then, to goodwill allocated to the cash-generating unit (if any),

These increases in carrying amounts should be treated as reversals of impairment losses for individual assets. In allocating a reversal of an impairment loss for a cash-generating Unit, the carrying amount of an asset should not be increased above the lower of:

(a) its recoverable amount (if determinable); and

(b) the carrying amount that would have been determined (net of amortisation or depreciation) had no impairment loss been recognised for the asset in prior accounting periods.

The amount of the reversal of the impairment loss that would otherwise have been allocated to the asset should be allocated to the other assets of the unit on a pro-rata basis.

### Reversal of impairment loss related to goodwill

An impairment loss recognised for goodwill shall not be reversed in a subsequent period.

Ind AS 38, *Intangible Assets,* prohibits the recognition of internally generated goodwill. Any increase in the recoverable amount of goodwill in the periods following the recognition of an impairment loss for that goodwill is likely to be an increase in internally generated goodwill, rather than a reversal of the impairment loss recognised for the acquired goodwill.

**Illustration 6.25: Accounting policy: Impairment of Non-financial assets**

The Company assesses at each reporting date as to whether there is any indication that any Property,

Plant and Equipment and Intangible Assets or group of Assets, called Cash Generating Units (CGU) may be impaired. If any such indication exists, the recoverable amount of an asset or CGU is estimated to determine the extent of impairment, if any. When it is not possible to estimate the recoverable amount of an individual asset, the Company estimates the recoverable amount of the CGU to which the asset belongs.

An impairment loss is recognized in the Statement of Profit and Loss to the extent, asset's carrying amount exceeds its recoverable amount. The recoverable amount is higher of an asset's fair value less cost of disposal and value in use. Value in use is based on the estimated future cash flows, discounted to their present value using pre-tax discount rate that reflects current market assessments of the time value of money and risk specific to the assets.

The impairment loss recognized in prior accounting period is reversed if there has been a change in the estimate of recoverable amount.

**(*Source: Reliance Industries Limited: Annual Report: 2019-20*)**

**Illustration 6.26: Accounting policy: Impairment of Non-financial assets**

**Impairment**

At each balance sheet date, the Company reviews the carrying value of its property, plant and equipment and intangible assets to determine whether there is any indication that the carrying value of those assets may not be recoverable through continuing use. If any such indication exists, the recoverable amount of the asset is reviewed in order to determine the extent of impairment loss, if any. Where the asset does not generate cash flows that are independent from other assets, the Company estimates the recoverable amount of the cash generating unit to which the asset belongs.

Recoverable amount is the higher of fair value less costs to sell and value in use. In assessing value in use, the estimated future cash flows are discounted to their present value using a pre-tax discount rate that reflects current market assessments of the time value of money and the risks specific to the asset for which the estimates of future cash flows have not been adjusted. An impairment loss is recognised in the statement of profit and loss as and when the carrying value of an asset exceeds its recoverable amount.

Where an impairment loss subsequently reverses, the carrying value of the asset (or cash generating unit) is increased to the revised estimate of its recoverable amount so that the increased carrying value does not exceed the carrying value that would have been determined had no impairment loss been recognised for the asset (or cash generating unit) in prior years. A reversal of an impairment loss is recognised in the statement of profit and loss immediately.

*(Source: Tata Steel: Annual Report 2019-20)*

## 6.11 NON-CURRENT ASSETS HELD FOR SALE AND DISCONTINUED OPERATIONS

Salient points related to Ind AS 105 are summarized below.

This Ind AS prescribes accounting for assets held for sale and presentation and disclosure of discontinued operations. This Standard stipulates that:

(a) assets that meet the criteria to be classified as held for sale to be measured at the lower of carrying amount and *fair value* less *costs to sell*, and depreciation on such assets to cease; and

(b) assets that meet the criteria to be classified as held for sale to be presented separately in the balance sheet and the results of discontinued operations to be presented separately in the statement of profit and loss.

The classification and presentation requirements of this Standard apply to all recognised *non-current assets*[1] and to all *disposal groups* of an entity. The measurement requirements of this Ind AS apply to all recognised non-current assets and disposal groups, except for those assets listed below which shall continue to be measured in accordance with the respective Standards noted.

Assets classified as non-current in accordance with Ind AS 1, *Presentation of Financial Statements,* shall not be reclassified as *current assets* until they meet the criteria to be classified as held for sale in accordance with this Ind AS.

Assets of a class that an entity would normally regard as non-current that are acquired exclusively with a view to resale shall not be classified as current unless they meet the criteria to be classified as held for sale in accordance with this Ind AS.

According to this Standard, the measurement provisions of this Ind AS do not apply to the following assets, which are covered by the Ind ASs listed, either as individual assets or as part of a disposal group:

(a) deferred tax assets (Ind AS 12, *Income Taxes*).

(b) assets arising from employee benefits (Ind AS 19, *Employee Benefits).*

(c) financial assets within the scope of Ind AS 109, *Financial Instruments.*

(e) non-current assets that are measured at fair value less costs to sell in accordance with Ind AS 41, *Agriculture.*

(f) contractual rights under insurance contracts as defined in Ind AS 104, *Insurance Contracts.*

**Classification of non-current assets (or disposal groups) held for sale or as held for distribution to owners**

(a) According to this Standard, an entity shall classify a non-current asset (or disposal group) as held for sale if its carrying amount will be recovered principally through a sale transaction rather than through continuing use.

(b) In such cases, the asset (or disposal group) must be available for immediate sale in its present condition subject only to terms that are usual and customary for sales of such assets (or disposal groups) and its sale must be *highly probable*. Thus, an asset (or disposal group) cannot be classified as a non-current asset (or disposal group) held for sale, if the entity intends to sell it in a distant future.

(c) For the sale to be highly probable,

(i) the appropriate level of management must be committed to a plan to sell the asset (or disposal group), and

(ii) an active programme to locate a buyer and complete the plan must have been initiated.

(iii) the asset (or disposal group) must be actively marketed for sale at a price that is reasonable in relation to its current fair value.

(iv) In addition, the sale should be expected to qualify for recognition as a completed sale within one year from the date of classification, and

(v) actions required to complete the plan should indicate that it is unlikely that significant changes to the plan will be made or that the plan will be withdrawn.

The probability of shareholders' approval (if required in the jurisdiction) should be considered as part of the assessment of whether the sale is highly probable.

(d) According to the Standard, an entity that is committed to a sale plan involving loss of control of a subsidiary shall classify all the assets and liabilities of that subsidiary as held for sale when the criteria set out in paragraphs 6–8 are met, regardless of whether the entity will retain a non-controlling interest in its former subsidiary after the sale.

(e) According to the Standard, events or circumstances may extend the period to complete the sale beyond one year. An extension of the period required to complete a sale does not preclude an asset (or disposal group) from being classified as held for sale if the delay is caused by events or circumstances beyond the entity's control and there is sufficient evidence that the entity remains committed to its plan to sell the asset (or disposal group). This will be the case when the criteria in Appendix B are met.

### Non-current asset to be abandoned

An entity shall not classify as held for sale a non-current asset (or disposal group) that is to be abandoned. This is because its carrying amount will be recovered principally through continuing use. However, if the disposal group to be abandoned meets the criteria enumerated in the Standard, the entity shall present the results and cash flows of the disposal group as discontinued operations in accordance with the Standard at the date on which it ceases to be used.

Non-current assets (or disposal groups) to be abandoned include non-current assets (or disposal groups) that are to be used to the end of their economic life and non-current assets (or disposal groups) that are to be closed rather than sold.

An entity shall not account for a non-current asset that has been temporarily taken out of use as if it had been abandoned.

### Measurement of non-current assets (or disposal groups) classified held for sale

An entity shall measure a non-current asset (or disposal group) classified as held for sale at the lower of its carrying amount and fair value less costs of disposal.

> Measurement of assets held for sale is at lower of:
>
> Carrying amount.
>
> Fair value less costs of disposal.
>
> It can be seen that this method of valuation is similar to valuation of inventories rather than property, plant and equipment. The reason is that the nature of these assets is now similar to inventory which is a current asset expected to be sold in the near future.

An entity shall measure a non-current asset (or disposal group) classified as held for distribution to owners at the lower of its carrying amount and fair value less costs to distribute.

If a newly acquired asset (or disposal group) meets the criteria to be classified as held for sale, will result in the asset (or disposal group) being measured on initial recognition at the lower of its carrying amount had it not been so classified (for example, cost) and fair value less costs to sell. Hence, if the asset (or disposal group) is acquired as part of a business combination, it shall be measured at fair value less costs to sell.

When the sale is expected to occur beyond one year, the entity shall measure the costs to sell at their present value. Any increase in the present value of the costs to sell that arises from the passage of time shall be presented in profit or loss as a financing cost.

Immediately before the initial classification of the asset (or disposal group) as held for sale, the carrying amounts of the asset (or all the assets and liabilities in the group) shall be measured in accordance with applicable Ind ASs.

On subsequent re-measurement of a disposal group, the carrying amounts of any assets and liabilities that are not within the scope of the measurement requirements of this Ind AS, but are included in a disposal group classified as held for sale, shall be re-measured in accordance with applicable Ind ASs before the fair value less costs to sell of the disposal group is re-measured.

**Recognition of impairment losses and reversals**

An entity shall recognise an impairment loss for any initial or subsequent write-down of the asset (or disposal group) to fair value less costs to sell, to the extent that it has not been recognised.

An entity shall recognise a gain for any subsequent increase in fair value less costs to sell of an asset, but not in excess of the cumulative impairment loss that has been recognised either in accordance with this Ind AS or previously in accordance with Ind AS 36, Impairment of Assets.

**Change to a plan of sale or distribution to owners**

If an entity has classified an asset (or disposal group) as held for sale or as held for distribution to owners, but the criteria mentioned in the Standard are no longer met, the entity shall cease to classify the asset (or disposal group) as held for sale or held for distribution to owners (respectively).

The entity shall measure a non-current asset (or disposal group) that ceases to be classified as held for sale or as held for distribution to owners (or ceases to be included in a disposal group classified as held for sale or as held for distribution to owners) at the lower of:

> *its carrying amount before the asset (or disposal group) was classified as held for sale or as held for distribution to owners, adjusted for any depreciation, amortisation or revaluations that would have been recognised had the asset (or disposal group) not been classified as held for sale or as held for distribution to owners, and*
>
> *its recoverable amount at the date of the subsequent decision not to sell or distribute.*

**Note**: If the non-current asset is part of a cash-generating unit, its recoverable amount is the carrying amount that would have been recognised after the allocation of any impairment loss arising on that cash-generating unit in accordance with Ind AS 36.

**Presentation**

An entity shall present and disclose information that enables users of the financial statements to evaluate the financial effects of discontinued operations and disposals of non-current assets (or disposal groups).

A discontinued operation is a component of an entity that either has been disposed of, or is classified as held for sale, and

(a) represents a separate major line of business or geographical area of operations,

(b) is part of a single co-ordinated plan to dispose of a separate major line of business or geographical area of operations or

(c) is a subsidiary acquired exclusively with a view to resale.

In accordance with the Standard an entity shall disclose:

(a) a single amount in the statement of profit and loss comprising the total of:

  (i) the post-tax profit or loss of discontinued operations and

  (ii) the post-tax gain or loss recognised on the measurement to fair value less costs to sell or on the disposal of the assets or disposal group(s) constituting the discontinued operation.

(b) an analysis of the single amount in (a) into:

  (i) the revenue, expenses and pre-tax profit or loss of discontinued operations;

  (ii) the related income tax expense as required by Ind AS 12; and

  (iii) the gain or loss recognised on the measurement to fair value less costs to sell or on the disposal of the assets or disposal group(s) constituting the discontinued operation.

  (iv) the related income tax expense as required by Ind AS 12.

  The analysis may be presented in the notes or in the statement of profit and loss. If it is presented in the statement of profit and loss it shall be presented in a section identified as relating to discontinued operations, i.e. separately from continuing operations.

(c) The net cash flows attributable to the operating, investing and financing activities of discontinued operations. These disclosures may be presented either in the notes or in the financial statements. These disclosures are not required for disposal groups that are newly acquired subsidiaries that meet the criteria to be classified as held for sale on acquisition.

(d) The amount of income from continuing operations and from discontinued operations attributable to owners of the parent. These disclosures may be presented either in the notes or in the statement of profit and loss.

An entity shall re-present the above disclosures for prior periods presented in the financial statements so that the disclosures relate to all operations that have been discontinued by the end of the reporting period for the latest period presented.

An entity that is committed to a sale plan involving loss of control of a subsidiary shall disclose the information required, when the subsidiary is a disposal group that meets the definition of a discontinued operation.

**Illustration 6.27: Accounting policy: Non-current assets held for sale**

Non-current assets are classified as held for sale if their carrying amount will be recovered principally through a sale transaction rather than through continuing use and sale is considered highly probable.

A sale is considered as highly probable when decision has been made to sell, assets are available for immediate sale in its present condition, assets are being actively marketed and sale has been agreed or is expected to be concluded within 12 months of the date of classification.

Non-current assets held for sale are neither depreciated nor amortized.

Assets and liabilities classified as held for sale are measured at the lower of their carrying amount and fair value less cost of sale and are presented separately in the Balance Sheet.

(***Source: Reliance Industries Limited: Annual Report: 2019-20***)

**Illustration 6.28: Accounting policy: Non-current assets held for sale**

**Non-current assets held for sale and discontinued operations**

Non-current assets and disposal groups classified as held for sale are measured at the lower of their carrying value and fair value less costs to sell. Assets and disposal groups are classified as held for sale if their carrying value will be recovered through a sale transaction rather than through continuing use. This condition is only met when the sale is highly probable and the asset, or disposal group, is available for immediate sale in its present condition and is marketed for sale at a price that is reasonable in relation to its current fair value. The Company must also be committed to the sale, which should be expected to qualify for recognition as a completed sale within one year from the date of classification.

Where a disposal group represents a separate major line of business or geographical area of operations or is part of a single co-ordinated plan to dispose of a separate major line of business or geographical area of operations, then it is treated as a discontinued operation. The post-tax profit or loss of the discontinued operation together with the gain or loss recognised on its disposal are disclosed as a single amount in the statement of profit and loss, with all prior periods being presented on this basis.

***(Source: Tata Steel: Annual Report: 2019-20)***

## 6.12 GOODWILL

With respect to Goodwill, a reconciliation of the gross and net carrying amount of goodwill at the beginning and end of the reporting period showing additions, impairments, disposals, and other adjustments.

In accordance with AS 28 (for non Ind AS entities) and *Ind AS 38: Intangible Assets*, goodwill is an asset representing the future economic benefits arising from other assets acquired in a business combination that are not individually identified and separately recognised.

As shown in the flow diagram above Goodwill can be internally developed or purchased.

Internally generated goodwill cannot be recognised and valued.

Purchased goodwill is to be recognised and valued.

Calculation of purchased goodwill is the difference between the amount paid by the acquirer plus value of non-controlling interest and net assets (assets less liabilities).

| Goodwill = amount paid by acquirer + value of NCI – (assets – liabilities) |
|---|

According to *Ind AS 103, Business Combinations* (Para 32), the acquirer shall recognise goodwill as of the acquisition date measured as the excess of (a) over (b) below:

(a) the aggregate of:

- (i) the consideration transferred measured in accordance with this Ind AS, which generally requires acquisition-date fair value;
- (ii) the amount of any non-controlling interest in the acquiree measured in accordance with this Ind AS; and
- (iii) in a business combination achieved in stages, the acquisition-date fair value of the acquirer's previously held equity interest in the acquiree.

(b) the net of the acquisition-date amounts of the identifiable assets acquired and the liabilities assumed measured in accordance with this Ind AS.

In extremely rare circumstances where the fair value of net assets exceeds acquirer's interest, the resultant gain called "bargain purchase" shall be recognized by the acquirer in other comprehensive income on the acquisition date and accumulate the same in equity as capital reserve. The gain shall be attributed to the acquirer.

**Illustration 6.29: Goodwill: Specimen format**

| Particulars | Current Reporting Period | Previous Reporting Period |
|---|---|---|
| Beginning of the reporting period | xxx | xxx |
| Add: Additions | xxx | xxx |

| Particulars | Current Reporting Period | Previous Reporting Period |
|---|---|---|
| Less: Impairment Disposal | (xxx) | (xxx) |
| Add/Less Other adjustments | xxx | xxx |
| End of the reporting period | xxx | xxx |

## 6.13 OTHER INTANGIBLE ASSETS

### 6.13.1 Intangible Assets: AS 26 (for non Ind AS entities)

**An intangible asset** is an identifiable non-monetary asset, without physical substance held for production or supply of goods and services for rental to others or for administrative purposes. Examples are, patents, copyrights, license, brand name, import quota, computer software, leasehold right, marketing rights, technical know-how etc.

**Characteristics determining intangible assets**

*(A)* ***Identifiability***: Need to be separable

*(B)* ***Control:*** An enterprise has the power to obtain future economic benefits, and restrict access of others from the same

*(C)* ***Future economic benefits:*** An enterprise need to assess the probability of future economic benefits using best estimate of the set of economic conditions that will exist during the useful life of the asset based on external evidence available at the time of initial recognition

*(D)* ***Cost can be measured reliably:*** Initially measured at cost i.e. purchase price, taxes and duties and other directly attributable expenses to make the asset ready for its intended use.

**Intangible assets are acquired through**

(a) purchase of assets e.g. acquisition of patent rights

(b) business combination e.g. purchased goodwill on acquisition of business

(c) Government grant

(d) Internally generated: these are not recognised in the financial statements as intangible assets, except for research and development expenses, if it meets criteria for recognition

**Internally generated intangible assets**

**(a) Research phase**

| No intangible asset arising from research (or from the research phase of | **Examples** of research activities are:<br>(a) activities aimed at obtaining new |
|---|---|

| | |
|---|---|
| an internal project) should be recognised.<br>Expenditure on research (or on the research phase of an internal project) should be recognised as an expense when it is incurred. | knowledge;<br>(b) the search for, evaluation and final selection of, applications of research findings or other knowledge;<br>(c) the search for alternatives for materials, devices, products, processes, systems or services; and<br>(d) the formulation, design, evaluation and final selection of possible alternatives for new or improved materials, devices, products, processes, systems or services. |

### (b) Development phase

| | |
|---|---|
| An intangible asset arising from development (or from the development phase of an internal project) should be recognised if, and only if, an enterprise can demonstrate all of the following: | (a) the technical feasibility of completing the intangible asset so that it will be available for use or sale;<br>(b) its intention to complete the intangible asset and use or sell it;<br>(c) its ability to use or sell the intangible asset;<br>(d) how the intangible asset will generate probable future economic benefits. Among other things, the enterprise should demonstrate the existence of a market for the output of the intangible asset or the intangible asset itself or, if it is to be used internally, the usefulness of the intangible asset;<br>(e) the availability of adequate technical, financial and other resources to complete the development and to use or sell the intangible asset; and<br>(f) its ability to measure the expenditure attributable to the intangible asset during its development reliably.<br>**Examples of development activities**<br>(a) the design, construction and testing of pre-production or pre-use prototypes and models;<br>(b) the design of tools, jigs, moulds and dies involving new technology;<br>(c) the design, construction and operation of a pilot plant that is not of a scale economically feasible for commercial |

| | |
|---|---|
| | production; and<br>(d) the design, construction and testing of a chosen alternative for new or improved materials, devices, products, processes, systems or services.<br>***Internally generated brands, mastheads, publishing titles, customer lists and items similar in substance should not be recognised as intangible assets.*** |

## Amortisation of intangible assets

| | |
|---|---|
| ***Amortisation period*** | The depreciable amount of an intangible asset should be allocated on a systematic basis over the best estimate of its useful life. There is a rebuttable presumption that the useful life of an intangible asset will not exceed ten years from the date when the asset is available for use. Amortisation should commence when the asset is available for use.<br>In some cases, there may be persuasive evidence that the useful life of an intangible asset will be a specific period longer than ten years. In these cases, the presumption that the useful life generally does not exceed ten years is rebutted and the enterprise:<br>(a) amortises the intangible asset over the best estimate of its useful life;<br>(b) estimates the recoverable amount of the intangible asset at least annually in order to identify any impairment loss and<br>(c) discloses the reasons why the presumption is rebutted and the factor(s) that played a significant role in determining the useful life of the asset. |
| ***Amortisation method*** | The amortisation method used should reflect the pattern in which the asset's economic benefits are consumed by the enterprise. If that pattern cannot be determined reliably, the straight-line method should be used. The amortisation charge for each period should be recognised as an expense unless another Accounting Standard permits or requires it to be included in the carrying amount of another asset. |
| ***Residual Value*** | The residual value of an intangible asset should be assumed to be zero unless:<br>(a) there is a commitment by a third party to purchase the asset at the end of its useful life; or<br>(b) there is an active market for the asset and:<br>(i) residual value can be determined by reference to that |

| | |
|---|---|
| | market; and<br>(ii) it is probable that such a market will exist at the end of the asset's useful life. |
| ***Review of Amortisation Period and Amortisation Method*** | • The amortisation period and the amortisation method should be reviewed at least at each financial year end.<br>• If the expected useful life of the asset is significantly different from previous estimates, the amortisation period should be changed accordingly.<br>• If there has been a significant change in the expected pattern of economic benefits from the asset, the amortisation method should be changed to reflect the changed pattern.<br>• Such changes should be accounted for in accordance with AS 5, Net Profit or Loss for the Period, Prior Period Items and Changes in Accounting Policies. |

**Disclosure Requirements**

The financial statements should disclose the following for each class of intangible assets, distinguishing between internally generated intangible assets and other intangible assets:

(a) the useful lives or the amortisation rates used;

(b) the amortisation methods used;

(c) the gross carrying amount and the accumulated amortisation (aggregated with accumulated impairment losses) at the beginning and end of the period;

(d) a reconciliation of the carrying amount at the beginning and end of the period showing

  (i) additions, indicating separately those from internal development and through amalgamation;

  (ii) retirements and disposals;

  (iii) impairment losses recognised in the statement of profit and loss during the period (if any);

  (iv) impairment losses reversed in the statement of profit and loss during the period (if any);

  (v) amortisation recognised during the period; and

  (vi) other changes in the carrying amount during the period.

A class of intangible assets is a grouping of assets of a similar nature and use in an enterprise's operations. Examples of separate classes may include:

(a) brand names;

(b) mastheads and publishing titles;

(c) computer software;

(d) licences and franchises;

(e) copyrights, and patents and other industrial property rights, service and operating rights;

(f) recipes, formulae, models, designs and prototypes; and

(g) intangible assets under development.

The classes mentioned above are disaggregated (aggregated) into smaller (larger) classes if this results in more relevant information for the users of the financial statements.

The financial statements should also disclose:

(a) if an intangible asset is amortised over more than ten years, the reasons why it is presumed that the useful life of an intangible asset will exceed ten years from the date when the asset is available for use. In giving these reasons, the enterprise should describe the factor(s) that played a significant role in determining the useful life of the asset;

(b) a description, the carrying amount and remaining amortisation period of any individual intangible asset that is material to the financial statements of the enterprise as a whole;

(c) the existence and carrying amounts of intangible assets whose title is restricted and the carrying amounts of intangible assets pledged as security for liabilities, and the amount of commitments for the acquisition of intangible assets.

## 6.13.2 Intangible Assets: Ind AS 38 (for non Ind AS entities)

With respect to other intangible assets the classification shall be as shown in the chart below.

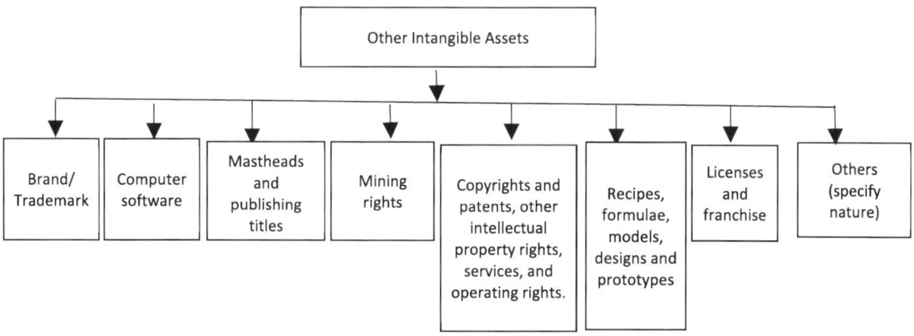

Classification shall be given as:

(a) Brands /trademarks.

(b) Computer software.

(c) Mastheads and publishing titles.

(d) Mining rights.

(e) Copyrights, patents, other intellectual property rights, services and operating rights.

(f) Recipes, formulae, models, designs and prototypes.

(g) Licenses and franchises.

(h) Others (specify nature).

The classes mentioned above are disaggregated (aggregated) into smaller (larger) classes if this results in more relevant information for the users of the financial statements.

**Principles of recognition**

An asset is classified as intangible if it satisfies the following recognition criteria:

(a) it is possible that future economic benefit flows to the entity

(b) Cost/value measured reliably

Conditions to be satisfied by an item to be called Intangible asset are:

| | |
|---|---|
| ***(i) The asset is identifiable, if it is,*** | (a) is separable, i.e. is capable of being separated or divided from the entity and sold, transferred, licensed, rented or exchanged, either individually or together with a related contract, identifiable asset or liability, regardless of whether the entity intends to do so; or<br>(b) arises from contractual or other legal rights, regardless of whether those rights are transferable or separable from the entity or from other rights and obligations. |
| ***(ii) There must be adequate control over the concerned item.*** | This would be represented by<br>– power to obtain future economic benefits and<br>– power to restrict access of others to those benefits |
| ***(iii) Existence of future economic benefits.*** | This could be substantiated by<br>– revenue from sale of products/services<br>– cost savings or<br>– other benefits resulting from use of an asset |

**Categories of intangible assets**

Intangible assets belong to the following categories:

(a) Purchased intangibles

(b) Internally generated intangibles e.g. development expenses and

(c) Intangibles acquired through business combination

are the principal components which account for as intangible assets.

The decision tree on intangible assets is shown below.

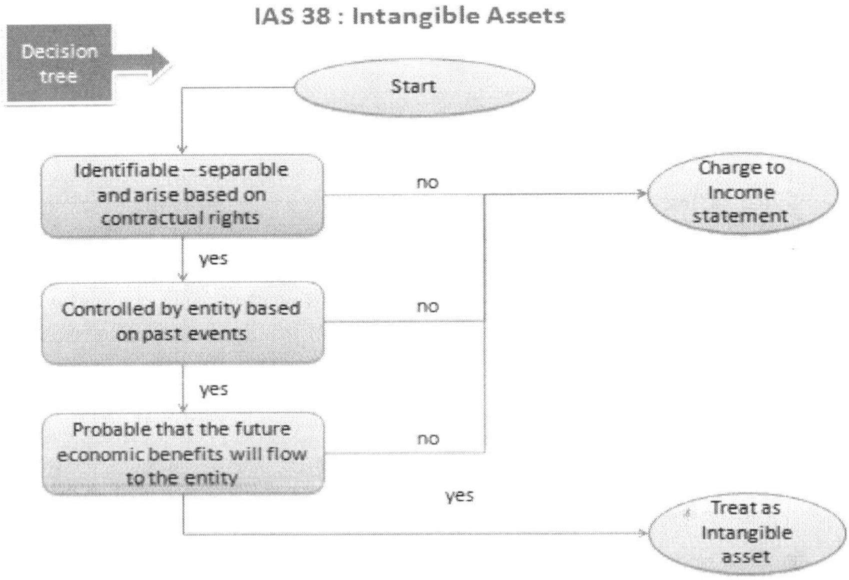


**Initial measurement**

According to this Standard, an intangible asset shall be measured initially at cost.

**Separate acquisition**

Normally, the price an entity pays to acquire separately an intangible asset will reflect expectations about the probability that the expected future economic benefits embodied in the asset will flow to the entity.

The cost of a separately acquired intangible asset comprises:

(a) its purchase price, including import duties and non-refundable purchase taxes, after deducting trade discounts and rebates; and

(b) any directly attributable cost of preparing the asset for its intended use.

**Examples of directly attributable costs**

(a) costs of employee benefits (as defined in Ind AS 19) arising directly from bringing the asset to its working condition.

(b) professional fees arising directly from bringing the asset to its working condition; and

(c) costs of testing whether the asset is functioning properly.

**Examples of expenditure that are not a part of intangible assets**

(a) costs of introducing a new product or service (including costs of advertising and promotional activities);

(b) costs of conducting business in a new location or with a new class of customer (including costs of staff training); and

(c) administration and other general overhead costs.

**Illustration 6.30: Recognition of production process as Intangible asset**

An enterprise is developing a new production process. During the year 20X1, expenditure incurred was Rs. 10 lakhs, of which Rs. 9 lakhs was incurred before 1 December 20X1 and 1 lakh was incurred between 1 December 20X1 and 31 December 20X1. The enterprise is able to demonstrate that, at 1 December 20X1, the production process met the criteria for recognition as an intangible asset. The recoverable amount of the know-how embodied in the process (including future cash outflows to complete the process before it is available for use) is estimated to be Rs. 5 lakhs.

**Solution**

At the end of 20X1, the production process is recognised as an intangible asset at a cost of Rs. 1 lakh (expenditure incurred since the date when the recognition criteria were met, that is, 1 December 20X1). The Rs. 9 lakhs expenditure incurred before 1 December 20X1 is recognised as an expense because the recognition criteria were not met until 1 December 20X1. This expenditure will never form part of the cost of the production process recognised in the balance sheet.

**Illustration 6.31: Recognition of intangible assets**

During the year 20X2, expenditure incurred is Rs. 20 lakhs. At the end of 20X2, the recoverable amount of the know-how embodied in the process (including future cash outflows to complete the process before it is available for use) is estimated to be Rs. 19 lakhs.

**Solution**

At the end of the year 20X2, the cost of the production process is Rs. 20 lakhs (i.e. Rs. 20 lakhs expenditure recognised in 20X2). The enterprise recognises an impairment loss of Rs. 1 lakh to adjust the carrying amount of the process before impairment loss (Rs. 20 lakhs) to its recoverable amount (Rs. 19 lakhs). This impairment loss will be reversed in a subsequent period if the requirements for the reversal of an impairment loss in Accounting Standard on Impairment of Assets, are met.

**Acquisition as a part of business acquisition**

In accordance with Ind AS 103, *Business Combinations*, if an intangible asset is acquired in a business combination, the cost of that intangible asset is its fair value at the acquisition date. The fair value of an intangible asset will reflect market participants' expectations at the acquisition date about the probability that the expected future economic benefits embodied in the asset will flow to the entity.

**Acquisition by a Government grant**

In some cases, an intangible asset may be acquired free of charge, or for nominal consideration, by way of a government grant. This may happen when a government transfers or allocates to an entity intangible asset such as airport landing rights, licences to operate radio or television stations, import licences or quotas or rights to access other restricted resources. In accordance with Ind AS 20, *Accounting for Government Grants and Disclosure of Government Assistance*, an entity recognises both the intangible asset and the grant initially at fair value.

**Exchange of assets**

One or more intangible assets may be acquired in exchange for a non-monetary asset or assets, or a combination of monetary and non-monetary assets.

The cost of such an intangible asset is measured at fair value unless

(a) the exchange transaction lacks commercial substance or

(b) the fair value of neither the asset received nor the asset given up is reliably measurable.

The acquired asset is measured in this way even if an entity cannot immediately derecognise the asset given up. If the acquired asset is not measured at fair value, its cost is measured at the carrying amount of the asset given up.

**Internally generated intangible assets**

(i) According to Para 66 of the Standard, the cost of an internally generated intangible asset comprises all directly attributable costs necessary to create, produce, and prepare the asset to be capable of operating in the manner intended by management. Examples of directly attributable costs are:

   (a) costs of materials and services used or consumed in generating the intangible asset;

   (b) costs of employee benefits (as defined in Ind AS 19) arising from the generation of the intangible asset;

   (c) fees to register a legal right; and

   (d) amortisation of patents and licences that are used to generate the intangible asset.

Ind AS 23 specifies criteria for the recognition of interest as an element of the cost of an internally generated intangible asset.

(ii) However, according to para 67, the following are not components of the cost of an internally generated intangible asset:

(a) selling, administrative and other general overhead expenditure unless this expenditure can be directly attributed to preparing the asset for use;

(b) identified inefficiencies and initial operating losses incurred before the asset achieves planned performance; and

(c) expenditure on training staff to operate the asset.

(iii) Internally generated brands, mastheads, publishing titles, customer lists and items similar in substance shall not be recognised as intangible assets

**Research phase**

No intangible asset arising from research (or from the research phase of an internal project) should be recognised. Expenditure on research (or on the research phase of an internal project) should be recognised as an expense when it is incurred

Examples of research activities are:

(a) activities aimed at obtaining new knowledge.

(b) the search for, evaluation and final selection of, applications of research findings or other knowledge.

(c) the search for alternatives for materials, devices, products, processes, systems or services; and

(d) the formulation, design, evaluation, and final selection of possible alternatives for new or improved materials, devices, products, processes, systems or services.

**Development phase**

An intangible asset arising from development (or from the development phase of an internal project) should be recognised if, and only if, an enterprise can demonstrate all of the following:

(a) the technical feasibility of completing the intangible asset so that it will be available for use or sale;

(b) its intention to complete the intangible asset and use or sell it;

(c) its ability to use or sell the intangible asset;

(d) how the intangible asset will generate probable future economic benefits. Among other things, the enterprise should demonstrate the existence of a market for the output of the intangible asset or the intangible asset itself or, if it is to be used internally, the usefulness of the intangible asset;

(e) the availability of adequate technical, financial and other resources to complete the development and to use or sell the intangible asset; and

(f) its ability to measure the expenditure attributable to the intangible asset during its development reliably.

**Examples of development activities**

(a) the design, construction and testing of pre-production or pre-use prototypes and models;

(b) the design of tools, jigs, moulds and dies involving new technology;

(c) the design, construction and operation of a pilot plant that is not of a scale economically feasible for commercial production; and

(d) the design, construction and testing of a chosen alternative for new or improved materials, devices, products, processes, systems or services.

**Recognition of expenses**

Expenditure on an intangible item should be recognised as an expense when it is incurred unless:

(a) it forms part of the cost of an intangible asset that meets the recognition criteria or

(b) the item is acquired in a business combination and cannot be recognised as an intangible asset. If this is the case then It forms part of the amount recognised as goodwill at the date of acquisition.

**Examples of expenses are**

(a) Research costs

(b) expenditure on start-up activities (start-up costs), unless this expenditure is included in the cost of an item of fixed asset under AS 10. Start-up costs may consist of preliminary expenses incurred in establishing a legal entity such as legal and secretarial costs, expenditure to open a new facility or business (pre-opening costs) or expenditures for commencing new operations or launching new products or processes (pre-operating costs);

(c) expenditure on training activities.

(d) expenditure on advertising and promotional activities; and

(e) expenditure on relocating or re-organising part or all of an enterprise.

**Subsequent measurement**

Subsequent expenditure on an intangible asset after its purchase or its completion should be recognised as an expense when it is incurred unless:

(a) it is probable that the expenditure will enable the asset to generate future economic benefits in excess of its originally assessed standard of performance; and

(b) the expenditure can be measured and attributed to the asset reliably.

If these conditions are met, the subsequent expenditure should be added to the cost of the intangible asset.

According to the Standard, an entity shall choose either the cost model or the revaluation model as its accounting policy. If an intangible asset is accounted for using the revaluation model, all the other assets in its class shall also be accounted for using the same model, unless there is no active market for those assets.

**Cost model**

After initial recognition, an intangible asset shall be carried at its cost less any accumulated amortisation and any accumulated impairment losses.

**Revaluation Model**

(a) After initial recognition, an intangible asset shall be carried at a revalued amount, being its fair value at the date of the revaluation less any subsequent accumulated amortisation and any subsequent accumulated impairment losses. For the purpose of revaluations under this Standard, fair value shall be measured by reference to an active market. Revaluations shall be made with such regularity that at the end of the reporting period the carrying amount of the asset does not differ materially from its fair value.

(b) An intangible asset can only be carried at revalued amount if there is an active market for the asset.

(c) If an intangible asset in a class of revalued intangible assets cannot be revalued because there is no active market for this asset, the asset shall be carried at its cost less any accumulated amortisation and impairment losses.

(d) If the fair value of a revalued intangible asset can no longer be measured by reference to an active market, the carrying amount of the asset shall be its revalued amount at the date of the last revaluation by reference to the active market less any subsequent accumulated amortisation and any subsequent accumulated impairment losses.

**Accounting principles under Revaluation model**

(a) If an intangible asset's carrying amount is increased as a result of a revaluation, the increase shall be recognised in other comprehensive income and accumulated in equity under the heading of revaluation surplus.

(b) However, the increase shall be recognised in profit or loss to the extent that it reverses a revaluation decrease of the same asset previously recognised in profit or loss.

(c) If an intangible asset's carrying amount is decreased as a result of a revaluation, the decrease shall be recognised in profit or loss.

(d) However, the decrease shall be recognised in other comprehensive income to the extent of any credit balance in the revaluation surplus in respect of that asset. The decrease recognised in other comprehensive income reduces the amount accumulated in equity under the heading of revaluation surplus.

**Useful life**

An entity shall assess whether the useful life of an intangible asset is finite or indefinite and, if finite, the length of, or number of production or similar units constituting, that useful life. An intangible asset shall be regarded by the entity as having an indefinite useful life when, based on an analysis of all of the relevant factors, there is no foreseeable limit to the period over which the asset is expected to generate net cash inflows for the entity.

Following factors determine useful life of an intangible asset:

| | | |
|---|---|---|
| ***Factors determine useful life of an intangible asset*** | (a) | the expected usage of the asset by the entity and whether the asset could be managed efficiently by another management team; |
| | (b) | typical product life cycles for the asset and public information on estimates of useful lives of similar assets that are used in a similar way; |
| | (c) | technical, technological, commercial or other types of obsolescence; |
| | (d) | the stability of the industry in which the asset operates and changes in the market demand for the products or services output from the asset; |
| | (e) | expected actions by competitors or potential competitors; |
| | (f) | the level of maintenance expenditure required to obtain the expected future economic benefits from the asset and the entity's ability and intention to reach such a level; |
| | (g) | the period of control over the asset and legal or similar limits on the use of the asset, such as the expiry dates of related leases; and |
| | (h) | whether the useful life of the asset is dependent on the useful life of other assets of the entity. |

**Intangible Assets with finite useful lives**

(a) According to the Standard, the depreciable amount of an intangible asset with a finite useful life shall be allocated on a systematic basis over its useful life. Amortisation shall begin when the asset is available for use, i.e. when it is in the location and condition necessary for it to be capable of operating in the manner intended by management.

(b) Amortisation shall cease at the earlier of the date that the asset is classified as held for sale (or included in a disposal group that is classified as held for sale) in accordance with Ind AS 105 and the date that the asset is de-recognised. The amortisation method used shall reflect the pattern in which the asset's future economic benefits are expected to be consumed by the entity. If that pattern cannot be determined reliably, the straight-line method shall be used.

(c) The amortisation charge for each period shall be recognised in profit or loss unless this or another Standard permits or requires it to be included in the carrying amount of another asset.

(d) The residual value of an intangible asset with a finite useful life shall be assumed to be zero unless:

   (a) there is a commitment by a third party to purchase the asset at the end of its useful life; or

   (b) there is an active market (as defined in Ind AS 113) for the asset and:

      (i) residual value can be determined by reference to that market; and

      (ii) it is probable that such a market will exist at the end of the asset's useful life.

(e) The amortisation period and the amortisation method for an intangible asset with a finite useful life shall be reviewed at least at each financial year-end. If the expected useful life of the asset is different from previous estimates, the amortisation period shall be changed accordingly. If there has been a change in the expected pattern of consumption of the future economic benefits embodied in the asset, the amortisation method shall be changed to reflect the changed pattern. Such changes shall be accounted for as changes in accounting estimates in accordance with Ind AS 8.

**Intangible assets with indefinite useful lives**

(a) Para 107 - An intangible asset with an indefinite useful life shall not be amortised.

(b) Para 108 - In accordance with Ind AS 36, an entity is required to test an intangible asset with an indefinite useful life for impairment by comparing its recoverable amount with its carrying amount:

   (a) annually, and

   (b) whenever there is an indication that the intangible asset may be impaired.

(c) According to Para 109, the useful life of an intangible asset that is not being amortised shall be reviewed each period to determine whether events and circumstances continue to support an indefinite useful life assessment for that asset. If they do not, the change in the useful life assessment from indefinite to finite shall be accounted for as a change in an accounting estimate in accordance with Ind AS 8.

**Recoverability of the carrying amount – impairment losses**

- To determine whether an intangible asset is impaired, an enterprise applies

  Accounting Standard on Impairment of Assets. That Standard explains how an enterprise reviews the carrying amount of its assets, how it determines the recoverable amount of an asset and when it recognises or reverses an impairment loss.
- If an impairment loss occurs before the end of the first annual accounting period commencing after acquisition for an intangible asset acquired in an amalgamation in the nature of purchase, the impairment loss is recognised as an adjustment to both the amount assigned to the intangible asset and the goodwill (capital reserve) recognised at the date of the amalgamation.
- In addition to the requirements of Accounting Standard on Impairment of Assets, an enterprise should estimate the recoverable amount of the following intangible assets at least at each financial year end even if there is no indication that the asset is

  (a) an intangible asset that is not yet available for use; and

  (b) an intangible asset that is amortised over a period exceeding ten years from the date when the asset is available for use.

  The recoverable amount should be determined under Accounting Standard on Impairment of Assets and impairment losses recognised accordingly.

**Retirements and disposals**

An intangible asset should be derecognised (eliminated from the balance sheet) on disposal or when no future economic benefits are expected from its use and subsequent disposal.

Gains or losses arising from the retirement or disposal of an intangible asset should be determined as the difference between the net disposal proceeds and the carrying amount of the asset and should be recognised as income or expense in the statement of profit and loss.

**Intangible Assets – website costs**

**Issue**

(i) An entity may incur internal expenditure on the development and operation of its own web site for internal or external access. A web site designed for external access may be used for various purposes such as to promote and advertise an entity's own products and services, provide electronic services, and sell products and services. A web site designed for internal access may be used to store company policies and customer details, and search relevant information.

(ii) The stages of a web site's development can be described as follows:

(a) Planning – includes undertaking feasibility studies, defining objectives and specifications, evaluating alternatives and selecting preferences.

(b) Application and Infrastructure Development – includes obtaining a domain name, purchasing and developing hardware and operating software, installing developed applications and stress testing.

(c) Graphical Design Development – includes designing the appearance of web pages.

(d) Content Development – includes creating, purchasing, preparing and uploading information, either textual or graphical in nature, on the web site before the completion of the web site's development. This information may either be stored in separate databases that are integrated into (or accessed from) the web site or coded directly into the web pages.

(iii) Once development of a web site has been completed, the Operating stage begins.

During this stage, an entity maintains and enhances the applications, infrastructure, graphical design and content of the web site.

(iv) When accounting for internal expenditure on the development and operation of an entity's own web site for internal or external access, the issues are:

(a) whether the web site is an internally generated intangible asset that is subject to the requirements of Ind AS 38; and

(b) the appropriate accounting treatment of such expenditure.

## Accounting Principles

(a) An entity's own web site that arises from development and is for internal or external access is an internally generated intangible asset that is subject to the requirements of Ind AS 38.

(b) A web site arising from development shall be recognised as an intangible asset if, and only if, in addition to complying with the general requirements described in paragraph 21 of Ind AS 38 for recognition and initial measurement, an entity can satisfy the requirements in paragraph 57 of Ind AS 38.

(c) In particular, an entity may be able to satisfy the requirement to demonstrate how its web site will generate probable future economic benefits in accordance with paragraph 57 (d) of Ind AS 38 when, for example, the web site is capable of generating revenues, including direct revenues from enabling orders to be placed.

(d) An entity is not able to demonstrate how a web site developed solely or primarily for promoting and advertising its own products and services will generate probable future economic benefits, and consequently all expenditure on developing such a web site shall be recognised as an expense when incurred.

(e) Any internal expenditure on the development and operation of an entity's own web site shall be accounted for in accordance with Ind AS 38. The nature of each activity for which expenditure is incurred (e.g. training employees and maintaining the web site) and the web site's stage of development or post-development shall be evaluated to determine the appropriate accounting treatment.

**Illustration 6.32: Intangible Assets: Specimen format**

| Description | Brand / Trademark | Computer software | Mastheads / Publishing titles | Mining rights | Copyrights, patents and intellectual | Recipe, formulae, Models, | Licenses and Franchise | Total |
|---|---|---|---|---|---|---|---|---|
| **Gross Block As at beginning of current reporting period** | | | | | | | | |
| Add:<br>Additions<br>Acquisitions through business combinations<br>Change due to revaluation*<br>Other adjustments | | | | | | | | |
| Less:<br>Disposals<br>Change due to revaluation*<br>Other adjustments | | | | | | | | |

| **Description** | **Brand / Trademark** | **Computer software** | **Mastheads / Publishing titles** | **Mining rights** | **Copyrights, patents and intellectual** | **Recipe, formulae, Models,** | **Licenses and Franchise** | **Total** |
|---|---|---|---|---|---|---|---|---|
| **Gross Block as at end of current reporting period** | | | | | | | | |
| **Amortization**<br>As at beginning of current reporting period<br>Add: For the year<br>Less: Deduction/adjustments/ reversals<br>As at end of current reporting period | | | | | | | | |
| **Impairment losses**<br>As at beginning of current reporting period<br>Add: For the year<br>Less: Deduction/adjustments/ reversals<br>As at end of current reporting period | | | | | | | | |
| **Net Block as at end of previous reporting period** | | | | | | | | |
| **Net Block as at end of current reporting period** | | | | | | | | |

*if change is 10% or more in the aggregate of the net carrying value of each class of intangible assets.

**Illustration 6.33: Accounting policy on Intangible assets**

Intangible Assets are stated at cost of acquisition net of recoverable taxes, trade discount and rebates less accumulated amortization/depletion and impairment losses, if any. Such cost includes purchase price, borrowing costs, and any cost directly attributable to bringing the asset to its working condition for the intended use, net charges on foreign exchange contracts and adjustments arising from exchange rate variations attributable to the Intangible Assets.

Subsequent costs are included in the asset's carrying amount or recognised as a separate asset, as appropriate, only when it is probable that future economic benefits associated with the item will flow to the entity and the cost can be measured reliably.

Other Indirect Expenses incurred relating to project, net of income earned during the project development stage prior to its intended use, are considered as pre-operative expenses and disclosed under Intangible Assets Under Development.

Gains or losses arising from derecognition of an Intangible Asset are measured as the difference between the net disposal proceeds and the carrying amount of the asset and are recognised in the Statement of Profit and Loss when the asset is derecognized.

The Company's intangible assets comprise assets with finite useful life which are amortised on a straight-line basis over the period of their expected useful life.

| **Particular** | **Depreciation** |
|---|---|
| Technical Know-How | Over the useful life of the underlying assets ranging from 5 years to 35 years. |
| Computer Software | Over a period of 5 years. |
| Development Rights | Depleted using the unit of production method. The cost of producing wells along with its related facilities including decommissioning costs are depleted in proportion of oil and gas production achieved vis-à-vis Proved Developed Reserves. The cost for common facilities including its decommissioning costs are depleted using Proved Reserves. |
| Others | In case of Jetty, the aggregate amount amortised to date is not less than the aggregate rebate availed by the Company. |

(*Source: Reliance Industries Limited: Annual Report: 2019-20*)

**Illustration 6.34: Accounting policy on Intangible assets**

**Intangible assets**

Patents, trademarks, and software costs are included in the balance sheet as intangible assets when it is probable that associated future economic benefits would flow to the Company. In this case they are measured initially at purchase cost and then amortized on a straight-line basis over their estimated useful lives. All other costs on patents, trademarks and software are expensed in the statement of profit and loss as and when incurred.

Expenditure on research activities is recognized as an expense in the period in which it is incurred. Costs incurred on individual

development projects are recognized as intangible assets from the date when all of the following conditions are met:

(i) completion of the development is technically feasible.

(ii) it is the intention to complete the intangible asset and use or sell it.

(iii) ability to use or sell the intangible asset.

(iv) it is clear that the intangible asset will generate probable future economic benefits.

(v) adequate technical, financial, and other resources to complete the development and to use or sell the intangible asset are available.

(vi) it is possible to reliably measure the expenditure attributable to the intangible asset during its development.

Recognition of costs as an asset is ceased when the project is complete and available for its intended use, or if these criteria are no longer applicable.

Where development activities do not meet the conditions for recognition as an asset, any associated expenditure is treated as an expense in the period in which it is incurred.

Subsequent to initial recognition, intangible assets with definite useful lives are reported at cost or deemed cost applied on transition to Ind AS, less accumulated amortization and accumulated impairment losses.

(*Source: Tata Steel Annual Report 2019-20)*

**Illustration 6.35: Accounting policy on Intangible assets**

Intangible assets

Intangible assets are recognized when it is probable that the future economic benefits that are attributable to the asset will flow to the Company and the cost of the asset can be measured reliably. Intangible assets are stated at original cost net of tax/duty credits availed, if any, less accumulated amortization and cumulative impairment. Administrative and other general overhead expenses that are specifically attributable to acquisition of intangible assets are allocated and capitalized as a part of the cost of the intangible assets. Research and development expenditure on new products:

(i) Expenditure on research is expensed under respective heads of account in the period in which it is incurred.

(ii) Development expenditure on new products is capitalized as intangible asset, if all of the following can be demonstrated:

A. the technical feasibility of completing the intangible asset so that it will be available for use or sale;

B. the Company has intention to complete the intangible asset and use or sell it;

C. the Company has ability to use or sell the intangible asset;

D. the manner in which the probable future economic benefits will be generated including the existence of a market for output of the intangible asset or intangible asset itself or if it is to be used internally, the usefulness of intangible assets;

E. the availability of adequate technical, financial and other resources to complete the development and to use or sell the intangible asset; and

F. the Company has ability to reliably measure the expenditure attributable to the intangible asset during its development. Development expenditure that does not meet the above criteria is expensed in the period in which it is incurred. Intangible assets not ready for the intended use on the date of the Balance Sheet are disclosed as "intangible assets under development".

Intangible assets are amortized on straight-line basis over the estimated useful life. The method of amortization and useful life are reviewed at the end of each financial year with the effect of any changes in the estimate being accounted for on a prospective basis.

Amortization on impaired assets is provided by adjusting the amortization charge in the remaining periods so as to allocate the asset's revised carrying amount over its rcmaining useful life.

(*Source: Larsen & Toubro Annual Report: 2019-20*)

**Illustration 6.36: Accounting policy: Research and Development expenses**

Revenue expenditure pertaining to research is charged to the Statement of Profit and Loss as and when incurred.

Development costs are capitalized as an intangible asset if it can be demonstrated that the project is expected to generate future economic benefits, it is probable that those future economic benefits will flow to the entity and the costs of the asset can be measured reliably, else it is charged to the Statement of Profit and Loss.

***(Source: Reliance Industries Limited: Annual Report: 2019-20)***

## 6.14 INVESTMENTS, TRADE RECEIVABLES, LOANS, BANK DEPOSITS MORE THAN TWELVE MONTHS AND OTHER NON-CURRENT ASSETS

The comparative summary of non-current investments between Division I and Division II of Schedule III is depicted below.

| Schedule III Part I under AS (Division 1) | Schedule III Part I under Ind AS (Division 2) |
|---|---|
| **K. Non-current investments**<br>(i) Non-current investments shall be classified as trade investments and other investments and further classified as:<br>(a) investment property ;<br>(b) investment in equity instruments;<br>(c) Investments in preference shares<br>(d) Investments in government or trust securities<br>(e) Investments in debentures or bonds;<br>(f) Investments in mutual funds ;<br>(g) Investments in partnership firms<br>(h) Other non-current investments (specify nature) | **VI. Investments**<br>(i) Investments shall be classified as:<br>(a) Investments in Equity Instruments;<br>(b) Investments in Preference Shares;<br>(c) Investments in Government or trust securities;<br>(d) Investments in debentures or bonds;<br>(e) Investments in Mutual Funds;<br>(f) Investments in partnership firms;<br>(g) Other investments (specify nature). |
| Under each classification, details shall be given of names of the bodies corporate (indicating separately whether such bodies are<br>(i) subsidiaries,<br>(ii) associates,<br>(iii) joint ventures or<br>(v) controlled special purpose entities) in whom investments have been made | Under each classification, details shall be given of names of the bodies corporate that are<br>(i) subsidiaries,<br>(ii) associates,<br>(iii) joint ventures, or<br>(iv) structured entities, in whom investments have been made and the nature and extent of the investment |

| Schedule III Part I under AS (Division 1) | Schedule III Part I under Ind AS (Division 2) |
|---|---|
| and the nature and extent of the investment so made in such body corporate (showing separately investments which are partly paid). In regard to investments in the capital of partnership firms, the names of the firms (with the names of all their partners, the total capital and shares of each partner) shall be given.<br>(ii) Investments carried at other than at cost should be separately stated specifying the basis of valuation thereof.<br>(iii) The following shall also be disclosed:<br>(a) Aggregate amount of quoted investments and market value thereof,<br>(b) Aggregate amount of unquoted investments ,<br>(c) Aggregate provision of dimunition in value of investments | so made in each such body corporate (showing separately investments which are partly-paid). Investments in partnership firms along with names of the firms, their partners, total capital and the shares of each partner shall be disclosed separately.<br>(ii) The following shall also be disclosed:<br>(a) Aggregate amount of quoted investments and market value thereof;<br>(b) Aggregate amount of unquoted investments;<br>(c) Aggregate amount of impairment in value of investments. |
| | **VII. Trade Receivables**<br>(i) Trade receivables shall be sub-classified as:<br>(a) Secured, considered good;<br>(b) Unsecured considered good;<br>(c) Doubtful.<br>(ii) Allowance for bad and doubtful debts shall be disclosed under the relevant heads separately.<br>(iii) Debts due by directors or other officers of the company or any of them either severally or jointly with any other person or debts due by firms or private companies respectively in which any director is a partner or a director or a member should be separately stated. |
| **L. Long-term loans and advances**<br>(i) Long-term loans and advances shall be classified as: | **VIII. Loans**<br>(i) Loans shall be classified as:<br>(a) Security Deposits; |

| Schedule III Part I under AS (Division 1) | Schedule III Part I under Ind AS (Division 2) |
|---|---|
| (a) Capital advances ;<br>(b) Security deposits ;<br>(c) Loans and advances to related parties (giving details thereof)<br>(d) Other loans and advances (specify nature)<br>(ii) The above should be separately sub-classified as:<br>(a) Secured considered good<br>(b) Unsecured considered good<br>(c) Doubtful<br>(iii) Allowance for bad and doubtful loans and advances shall be disclosed under relevant heads separately<br>(iv) Loans and advances due by directors and other officers of the company or any of them whether severally or jointly with any other persons or amounts due by firms or private companies respectively in which any director is a partner or a director or a member should be separately stated | (b) Loans to related parties (giving details thereof);<br>(c) Other loans (specify nature).<br>(ii) The above shall also be separately sub-classified as:<br>(a) Secured, considered good;<br>(b) Unsecured, considered good;<br>(c) Doubtful.<br>(iii) Allowance for bad and doubtful loans shall be disclosed under the relevant heads separately.<br>(iv) Loans due by directors or other officers of the company or any of them either severally or jointly with any other persons or amounts due by firms or private companies respectively in which any director is a partner or a director or a member should be separately stated. |
| | **IX. Bank deposits with more than 12 months maturity shall be disclosed under 'Other financial assets';** |
| **M. Other non-current assets**<br>Other non-current assets shall be classified as:<br>(i) Long term trade receivables (including trade receivables on deferred credit terms)<br>(ii) others (specify nature)<br>(iii) Long term trade receivables, shall be sub-classified as:<br>(i) (a) Secured , considered good ;<br>(b) Unsecured, considered good ;<br>(c) considered doubtful<br>(ii) Allowance for bad and doubtful | **X. Other non-current assets**<br>Other non-current assets shall be classified as-<br>(i) Capital Advances;<br>(ii) Advances other than capital advances;<br>1. Advances other than capital advances shall be classified as:<br>(a) Security Deposits;<br>(b) Advances to related parties (giving details thereof);<br>(c) Other advances (specify nature). |

| Schedule III Part I under AS (Division 1) | Schedule III Part I under Ind AS (Division 2) |
|---|---|
| debts shall be disclosed under relevant heads separately<br>(iii) Debts due by directors and other officers of the company or any of them whether severally or jointly with any other persons or amounts due by firms or private companies respectively in which any director is a partner or a director or a member should be separately stated | 2. Advances to directors or other officers of the company or any of them either severally or jointly with any other persons or advances to firms or private companies respectively in which any director is a partner or a director or a member should be separately stated. In case advances are of the nature of a financial asset as per relevant Ind AS, these are to be disclosed under 'other financial assets' separately.<br>(iii) Others (specify nature). |

## 6.15 CLASSIFICATION OF NON-CURRENT INVESTMENTS

(a) Investments in Equity Instruments.

(b) Investments in Preference Shares;

(c) Investments in Government or trust securities;

(d) Investments in debentures or bonds;

(e) Investments in Mutual Funds;

(f) Investments in partnership firms;

(g) Other investments (specify nature).

The Schedule III provides for certain disclosures where the company is a partner in partnership firms. In the Balance Sheet, under the sub-heading "Non-current Investments", separate disclosure is to be made of any investment in the capital of partnership firm by the company. In addition, in the Notes to Accounts separate disclosure is required with regard to the names of the firms in which the company is a partner, along with the names of their partners, total capital and the shares of each partner.

Under each classification, details shall be given of names of the bodies corporate that are

(i) subsidiaries,

(ii) associates,

(iii) joint ventures, or

(iv) Controlled special purpose entities or structured entities, in whom investments have been made and the nature and extent of the investment so made in each such body corporate (showing separately investments which are partly-paid). Investments in partnership firms along with names of the firms, their partners, total capital and the shares of each partner shall be disclosed separately.

(ii) The following shall also be disclosed:

(a) Aggregate amount of quoted investments and market value thereof.

(b) Aggregate amount of unquoted investments.

(c) Aggregate amount of impairment in value of investments.

**Controlled special purpose entities**

According to ICAI Guidance Note under Schedule III of Non Ind AS entities, under investments, there is also a requirement to disclose the names of bodies corporate, including separate disclosure of investments in "controlled special purpose entities" in addition to subsidiaries, etc. The expression "controlled special purpose entities" however, has not been defined either in the Act or in the Schedule III or in the Accounting Standards. Accordingly, no disclosures would be additionally required to be made under this caption. If and when such terminology is explained/ introduced in the applicable Accounting Standards, the disclosure requirement would become applicable.

**Structured Entities**

ICAI Guidance Note under Schedule III on Ind AS entities specifies that, in addition to investment in subsidiaries, associates, joint ventures, there is also a requirement to disclose the names of bodies corporate, including separate disclosure of investments in "structured entities". According to *Ind AS-112 Disclosure of Interests in Other Entities*, a "structured entity" is an entity that has been designed so that voting or similar rights are not the dominant factor in deciding who controls the entity, such as when any voting rights are related to administrative tasks only and the relevant activities are directed by means of contractual arrangements. As per Ind AS Schedule III, investments in all structured entities need to be given, irrespective of whether controlled or not.

Ind AS Schedule III also requires disclosure of the 'nature and extent' of the investment so made. In case of a Structured Entity, rights are mainly established by way of contractual arrangements and therefore as a part of 'nature and extent', a brief description of the nature of contracts may be provided along with the rights held in such entities as evidenced by such contracts.

**Basis of Valuation of non-current investments**

Investments carried at other than at cost should be separately stated specifying the basis for valuation thereof.

Schedule III requires disclosure of the "basis of valuation" of non-current investments which are carried at other than cost.

As per ICAI Guidance Note on Schedule III related to non Ind AS entities the same has been interpreted in the following manner:

(a) One view is that basis of valuation would mean the market value, or valuation by independent valuers, valuation based on the investee's assets and results, or valuation based on expected cash flows from the investment, or management estimate etc. Hence, for all investments carried at other than cost, the basis of valuation for each individual investment should be disclosed.

(b) The other view is that, disclosure for basis of valuation should be either of:

   - at cost,
   - at cost less provision for other temporary diminution
   - lower of cost and fair value

However, making disclosures in line with the latter view would be sufficient compliance with the disclosure requirements.

**Investments in equity instruments**

According to ICAI Guidance Note on Ind AS Schedule III, para 11A of Ind AS 107 requires, entities to disclose which investments in equity instruments have been designated to be measured at FVOCI along with the fair value of each such investment at the end of the reporting period.

Hence, over and above the requirements of Ind AS Schedule III, companies will be required to disclose the names, number of equity instruments held and the face value of such instrument of all other bodies corporate for which they have designated the investments in equity instruments at FVOCI.

However, apart from investments in equity instruments designated at FVOCI and investments in subsidiaries, associates, joint ventures and structured entities, if a company intends to provide such additional disclosure, it may choose to do so.

**Sub-classification of investments**

Schedule III under Ind AS, requires that, under each sub-classification of Investments, disclosure is required on details of investments including names and the nature and extent of the investment in each body corporate which is a subsidiary, associate, joint venture and structured entity.

The nature and extent of the disclosure would imply the number of such instruments held and the face value of such instrument. There is also a requirement to disclose separately, investments which are partly-paid. It is advisable to clearly disclose whether investments are fully paid or partly paid.

### Aggregate amount of quoted investments at fair value

Ind AS Schedule III further requires disclosure of the aggregate amount of quoted investments and market value thereof and the aggregate amount of unquoted investments. Disclosure under aggregate amount of such investments would include aggregate amount of carrying value of these investments as at the reporting date as included in the financial statements. This disclosure would need to be made separately for non-current investments and current investments.

Where the investments are measured at either FVTPL or FVOCI, as per Ind AS 109, the carrying amount and the market value of such investments are expected to be same subject to considerations of fair value as per the above paragraph and should be disclosed accordingly.

The market value of quoted investments would, generally, mean disclosure of the 'fair value' of quoted investments as at each reporting date. Ind AS 113 defines fair value and also stipulates that the fair value of assets might be affected when there has been a significant decrease in the volume or level of activity for that asset in relation to normal market activity for that asset.

However, according to ICAI Guidance Note, based on evaluation, if the reporting entity determines that a quoted price does not represent fair value, then the entity shall disclose the market value of quoted investments based on the quoted price which would be different from the investment's fair value.

### Impairment in the value of investments

In accordance with Ind AS Schedule III, impairment in value of investments is required to be disclosed separately. As per Ind AS 109, the company is required to recognize a loss allowance (i.e. impairment) for expected credit losses on investments measured at amortized cost. Such loss allowance should be presented as an adjustment to the amortized cost of the investment.

To give effect to disclosure of aggregate provision for impairment in the value of investments, an entity shall disclose an amount equal to the aggregate amount of impairment recognized and measured in accordance with Ind AS 109.

The aggregate provision for impairment in the value of investments may be either presented in totality for all the investments or separately for each class of investments (e.g., 'Investment at amortized cost', 'Investment in debt instruments at FVOCI') disclosed in the financial statements.

### Classification of investments

Division II of Schedule III does not specify whether the Investments should first be categorized as above or should be first classified as per the nature (e.g., investment in equity instruments, investment in preference shares, investment in debentures or bonds, etc.).

Accordingly, the companies may disclose Investments by grouping them in the following manner:

(i) Broad Categories as per Ind AS 107

(a) Measured at amortized cost;

(a) Investments in Redeemable Preference Shares

(b) Investments in Redeemable Debentures

(c) Investments in Redeemable Bonds

(d) Investments in Government Securities

(b) Mandatorily measured at FVTPL;

(a) Investments in Equity Instruments

(b) Investments in Redeemable Preference Shares

(c) Investments in Optionally Convertible Preference Shares

(d) Investments in Optionally Convertible Debentures

(e) Investments in Redeemable bonds

(f) Investments in Government Securities

(c) Designated at FVTPL – as in (b) above

(d) Measured at FVOCI;

(a) Investments in Equity Instruments

(b) Investments in Redeemable Preference Shares

(c) Investments in Redeemable Debentures

(d) Investments in Redeemable Bonds

(e) Investments in Government Securities

(e) Designated at FVOCI (e.g., investments in equity instruments).

(ii) Under each board categorization, nature-based classification as per Ind AS Schedule III; (for e.g., Investment in Equity Instruments, Investments in Preference Shares, etc.)

(iii) Under each nature-based classification, grouping based on the relationship of bodies corporate (viz., subsidiaries, associates, joint ventures, and structured entities) as required by Ind AS Schedule III; and

(iv) Under each grouping of bodies corporate, details giving names of bodies corporate and nature and extent of investments in bodies corporate as required by Ind AS Schedule III. (for e.g., details are required for investments at FVOCI, investment in subsidiary, etc.).

**Investment in Partnership firms, in which company has invested (under non-current investments in the Balance Sheet)**

The Schedule III provides for certain disclosures where the company is a partner in partnership firms. In the Balance Sheet, under the sub-heading "Non-current Investments", separate disclosure is to be made of any investment in the capital of partnership firm by the company. In addition, in the Notes to Accounts separate disclosure is required with regard to the names of the firms in which the company is a partner, along with the names of their partners, total capital and the shares of each partner.

**Application money toward securities**

Any application money paid towards securities, where security has not been allotted on the date of the Balance Sheet, shall be disclosed as a separate line item under 'other non- current financial assets'. If the amount is material, details about the date of allotment or when the allotment is expected to be completed may also be disclosed.

**Illustration 6.37: Non-current Investments: Specimen format**

| **Particulars** | **As at 31st March 2022** | | **As at 31st March 2021** | |
|---|---|---|---|---|
| **Investment-Non-current** | Units | Amount | Units | Amount |
| **Investments measured at amortized cost**<br>In debentures of other companies-unquoted fully paid-up<br>In Government securities – unquoted | | | | |
| **Total investment at amortized cost** | | | | |
| **Investments measured at cost**<br>In Equity shares of Associate companies-quoted fully paid-up<br>In Equity shares of Associate companies<br>Unquoted fully paid-up<br>In Equity shares of Joint Ventures<br>Unquoted fully paid-up<br>In Equity shares of subsidiary companies | | | | |

| Particulars | As at 31st March 2022 | | As at 31st March 2021 | |
|---|---|---|---|---|
| Unquoted fully paid-up<br>In Preference shares of subsidiary companies<br>Unquoted fully paid-up<br>Unquoted partly paid-up<br>In Debentures of subsidiary companies<br>Unquoted fully paid-up<br>In corpus of Trust<br>Unquoted | | | | |
| **Total of investments measured at cost** | | | | |
| **Investments measured at Fair value Through other comprehensive income (FVTOCI)**<br>In Equity shares of other companies<br>Unquoted fully paid-up<br>In Preference shares of other companies<br>Unquoted fully paid-up<br>Other investments | | | | |
| **Total of Investments measured at Fair Value Through Other Comprehensive Income** | | | | |
| **Investments measured at Fair value through profit & loss (FVTPL)**<br>In Equity Shares of Other Companies<br>– Quoted, fully paid up<br>In Equity Shares of Other Companies<br>– Unquoted, fully paid up<br>In Preference Shares of Other Companies<br>– Unquoted, fully paid up | | | | |

| Particulars | As at 31st March 2022 | | As at 31st March 2021 | |
|---|---|---|---|---|
| **Total of Investments measured at Fair Value Through Profit and Loss** | | | | |
| **Total Investments – Non-Current** | | | | |
| Aggregate amount of Quoted Investments<br>Market Value of Quoted Investments<br>Aggregate amount of Unquoted Investments<br>Aggregate provision for impairment in value of Investments | | | | |

## 6.16 ACCOUNTING STANDARDS RELATED NON-CURRENT INVESTMENTS

### 6.16.1 Accounting for investments: AS 13 (As amended) for non Ind AS entities

Main principles are summarized as under:

| | |
|---|---|
| ***Classification of Investments*** | Para 26. An enterprise should disclose current investments and long-term investments distinctly in its financial statements.<br>Para 27. Further classification of current and long-term investments should be as specified in the statute governing the enterprise. In the absence of a statutory requirement, such further classification should disclose, where applicable, investments in:<br>(a) Government or Trust securities<br>(b) Shares, debentures or bonds<br>(c) Investment properties<br>(d) Others—specifying nature. |
| ***Cost of Investments*** | Para 28. The cost of an investment should include acquisition charges such as brokerage, fees and duties.<br>Para 29. If an investment is acquired, or partly acquired, by the issue of shares or other securities, the acquisition cost should be the fair value of the securities issued (which in appropriate cases may be indicated by the issue price as determined by statutory authorities). The fair value may not necessarily be |

| | |
|---|---|
| | equal to the nominal or par value of the securities issued. If an investment is acquired in exchange for another asset, the acquisition cost of the investment should be determined by reference to the fair value of the asset given up. Alternatively, the acquisition cost of the investment may be determined with reference to the fair value of the investment acquired if it is more clearly evident. |
| ***Investment Properties*** | Para 30. An enterprise holding investment properties should account for them in accordance with cost model as prescribed in AS 10, Property, Plant and Equipment. |
| ***Carrying Amount of Investments*** | Para 31. Investments classified as current investments should be carried in the financial statements at the lower of cost and fair value determined either on an individual investment basis or by category of investment, but not on an overall (or global) basis.<br>Para 32. Investments classified as long term investments should be carried in the financial statements at cost. However, provision for diminution shall be made to recognise a decline, other than temporary, in the value of the investments, such reduction being determined and made for each investment individually. |
| ***Changes in Carrying Amounts of Investments*** | Para 33. Any reduction in the carrying amount and any reversals of such reductions should be charged or credited to the profit and loss statement. |
| ***Disposal of Investments*** | Para 34. On disposal of an investment, the difference between the carrying amount and net disposal proceeds should be charged or credited to the profit and loss statement. |
| ***Disclosure*** | 35. The following information should be disclosed in the financial statements:<br>(a) the accounting policies for determination of carrying amount of investments;<br>(b) classification of investments as specified in paragraphs 26 and 27 above;<br>(c) the amounts included in profit and loss statement for:<br>(i) interest, dividends (showing separately dividends from subsidiary companies), and rentals on investments showing separately such income from long term and current investments. Gross income should be stated, the amount of income tax deducted at source being included under Advance Taxes Paid; |

| | |
|---|---|
| | (ii) profits and losses on disposal of current investments and changes in the carrying amount of such investments; and<br>(iii) profits and losses on disposal of long term investments and changes in the carrying amount of such investments;<br>(d) significant restrictions on the right of ownership, realisability of investments or the remittance of income and proceeds of disposal;<br>(e) the aggregate amount of quoted and unquoted investments, giving the aggregate market value of quoted investments;<br>(f) Other disclosures as specifically required by the relevant statute governing the enterprise. |

### 6.16.2 Ind AS 32: Financial Instruments – Presentation

The standard prescribes requirements for the presentation of financial instruments and identifies information that should be disclosed about them.

It applies to all types of financial instruments both recognized and unrecognized and should be applied to contracts to buy or sell a non-financial item that can be settled:

- In cash
- By another financial instrument or
- By exchanging financial instruments, as if the contracts were financial instruments

Financial instruments are classified, from the perspective of the issuer, as

- financial assets,
- financial liabilities and
- equity instruments.

Compound financial instruments may contain both a liability and an equity component.

Interest, dividends, losses and gains relating to financial liabilities are recognized as income or expense in profit or loss.

Distributions to holders of equity instruments are debited directly to equity, net of any related income tax benefit.

Financial assets and financial liabilities are offset when there is a legally enforceable right to set off and the entity intends to settle on a net basis,

### 6.16.3 Ind AS 109: Financial Instruments

**Classification and measurement**

The Ind AS deals with the classification and measurement of financial assets and liabilities. This Ind AS enunciates three classification categories:

amortized cost

fair value through profit or loss and

fair value through other comprehensive income.

Classification under this Ind AS is driven by the entity's business model for managing the financial assets and the contractual characteristics of the financial assets.

A financial asset is measured at amortized cost if two criteria are met:

- The objective of the business model is to hold the financial asset for the collection of the contractual cash flows; and
- The contractual cash flows under the instrument solely represent payments of principal and interest.

This Standard requires a hybrid contract to be classified in its entirety at either amortised cost or fair value through profit or loss.

Ind AS 109 prohibits reclassifications except in rare circumstances when the entity's business model changes.

There is specific guidance for contractually linked instruments that create concentrations of credit risk, which is often the case with investment tranches in a securitization.

Ind AS 109's classification principles indicate that all equity investments should be measured at fair value. However, management has an irrevocable option to present in other comprehensive income unrealized and realized fair value gains and losses on equity investments that are not held for trading.

**Hedge accounting**

The standard provides two kinds of hedge accounting:

- Cash flow hedge - possibility of changes in cash flow
- Fair value hedge - possibility of changes in fair value conditions to be met before hedge accounting is applied:
  - There is formal designation and documentation of a hedge at inception
  - The hedge is expected to be highly effective (i.e. the hedging instrument is expected to almost fully offset changes in fair value or cash flows of the hedged item that are attributable to the hedged risk)
- Any forecast transaction being hedged is highly probable

- Hedge effectiveness is reliably measurable (*i.e.* fair value or cash flows of the hedged item and the fair value of the hedging instrument can be reliably measured)
- The hedge must be assessed on an ongoing basis and be highly effective.

When a fair value hedge exists, the fair value movements on the hedging instrument and the corresponding fair value movements on the hedged item are recognized in profit or loss.

When a cash flow hedge exists, the fair value movements, on the part of the hedging instrument, that is effective, are recognized in equity until such time as the hedged item affects profit or loss.

## 6.17 TRADE RECEIVABLES

According to Schedule III, Division II, Clause VII. Trade Receivables are classified as under:

(i) Trade receivables shall be sub-classified as:

(a) Secured, considered good.

(b) Unsecured considered good;

(c) Doubtful.

(ii) Allowance for bad and doubtful debts shall be disclosed under the relevant heads separately.

(iii) Debts due by directors or other officers of the company or any of them either severally or jointly with any other person or debts due by firms or private companies respectively in which any director is a partner or a director or a member should be separately stated.

(i) For trade receivables outstanding, following ageing schedule shall be given:

**Trade Receivables ageing schedule**

(Amount in Rs.)

| **Particulars** | **Outstanding for following periods from due date of payment#** | | | | | |
|---|---|---|---|---|---|---|
| | **Less than six months** | **Six months to one year** | **One to two years** | **Two to three years** | **More than three years** | **Total** |
| (i) Undisputed trade receivable considered good<br>(ii) Undisputed Trade Receivables – | | | | | | |

| | | | | | | |
|---|---|---|---|---|---|---|
| which have significant increase in credit risk<br>(iii) Undisputed Trade Receivables – credit impaired<br>(iv) Disputed Trade Receivables– considered good<br>(v) Disputed Trade Receivables – which have significant increase in credit risk<br>(vi) Disputed Trade Receivables – credit impaired | | | | | | |

# similar information shall be given where no due date of payment is specified in that case disclosure shall be from the date of the transaction.

Unbilled dues shall be disclosed separately

According to ICAI Guidance Note on Schedule III, Divison II-Ind AS, a receivable shall be classified as 'trade receivable' if it is in respect of the amount due on account of goods sold or services rendered in the normal course of business.

Hence, amounts due under contractual rights, other than arising out of sale of goods or rendering of services, cannot be included within Trade Receivables.

Such items may include dues in respect of insurance claims, sale of Property, Plant and Equipment, contractually reimbursable expenses, etc. Such receivables should be classified as "other financial assets" and each such item should be disclosed nature-wise. While disclosing a trade receivable as 'doubtful', the company shall disclose the amount of credit loss that is expected on that trade receivable. According to Ind AS 109, 'credit loss' has been defined as 'the difference between all contractual cash flows that are due to an entity in accordance with the contract and all the cash flows that the entity expects to receive (i.e. cash shortfalls), including cash flows from the sale of collateral held.'

**Impairment on Trade Receivables**

In accordance with Ind AS 109, an entity is required to recognize a loss allowance (i.e., Impairment) for expected credit losses on financial assets including trade receivables.

The impairment requirements in Ind AS 109 are based on application of one of the following approaches:

(a) *The general approach*, where an entity recognises ECLs in the following stages viz.,
   - credit exposures for which there has not been a significant increase in credit risk since initial recognition;
   - credit exposures for which there has been a significant increase in credit risk since initial recognition but not credit-impaired;
   - credit exposures that are credit impaired;

(b) *The simplified approach* where an entity does not separately track changes in credit risk.

(c) *The purchased or originated credit-impaired approach*

**Trade Receivable and Contract Assets**

Ind AS 115 stipulates in case of a contract with customer, when either party has performed, to present a contract asset in the balance sheet as a line item separate from trade receivables. Contract asset arises if an entity performs by transferring goods or services to a customer before the customer pays consideration or before payment is due. It excludes any amounts presented as a receivable.

According to ICAI Guidance Note on Schedule III on Ind AS, with respect to trade receivables and contract assets under Ind AS 115 that do not contain a significant financing component, it is a requirement to apply a simplified approach while for trade receivables and contract assets under Ind AS 115 that contain a significant financing component, and for lease receivables, a choice between a general approach or a simplified approach is available.

Ind AS 115 also stipulates impairment of contract assets to be measured presented and disclosed on the same basis as a financial asset that is within the scope of Ind AS 109.

**Illustration 6.38: Non-current trade receivable**

An entity XYZ Ltd has a trade receivable of Rs. 1,50,000 at the reporting date of which the amount of credit loss expected in line with Ind AS 109 is Rs. 25,000. Accordingly, the company shall disclose trade receivables as below, assuming entire amount is unsecured:

| Non-current trade receivables | Amount |
|---|---|
| Secured, considered good | - |
| Unsecured, considered good | 125,000 |
| Doubtful | 25,000 |
| Sub-total | 150,000 |

| Non-current trade receivables | Amount |
|---|---|
| Less: Allowance for bad and doubtful debts | 25,000 |
| Total | 125,000 |

## 6.18 LOANS

Loans are classified as under:

(i) Loans shall be classified as:

(a) *Omitted,*

(b) Loans to related parties (giving details thereof);

(c) Other loans (specify nature).

(ii) The above shall also be separately sub-classified as:

(a) Secured, considered good.

(b) Unsecured, considered good;

(c) Doubtful.

(iii) Allowance for bad and doubtful loans shall be disclosed under the relevant heads separately.

(iv) Loans due by directors or other officers of the company or any of them either severally or jointly with any other persons or amounts duc by firms or private companies respectively in which any director is a partner or a director or a member should be separately stated.

**Loans to related parties**

Details of loans to related parties need to be disclosed. Since Ind AS Schedule III states that the terms used therein shall have the same meanings assigned to them in applicable Ind AS, the term "details" shall mean the disclosure requirements contained in *Ind AS-24 Related Parties Disclosures*. Other loans may include loans given to parties other than related parties, for e.g., loans to employees, which are not expected to be realized within the next twelve months from the Balance Sheet date. Please refer *Ind AS Related Parties Disclosures* below.

**Sub-classification of loans and advances**

Each item of loans should be further sub-classified as:

(a) Secured, considered good;

(b) Unsecured, considered good; and

(c) Doubtful

According to ICAI Guidance Note under Schedule III – Division II – Ind AS, while disclosing a loan as 'doubtful', the company shall disclose the amount of credit loss that is expected on that loan. The balance amount of loan other than the amount considered as doubtful shall be disclosed as 'good'.

As in case of receivables, Ind AS 109 defines 'credit loss' as 'the difference between all contractual cash flows that are due to an entity in accordance with the contract and all the cash flows that the entity expects to receive (i.e. cash shortfalls), including cash flows from the sale of collateral held.'

**Illustration 6.39: Non-current loans and advances**

An entity has given a loan with outstanding amount of Rs. 385,000 at the reporting date. The amount of credit loss expected in line with Ind AS 109 is Rs. 125,000. Accordingly, the company shall disclose the loan as below, assuming entire amount is unsecured:

| **Non-current loans** | **Amount** |
|---|---|
| Secured, considered good | - |
| Unsecured, considered good | 260,000 |
| Doubtful | 125,000 |
| | 385,000 |
| Less: Allowance for bad and doubtful debts | 125,000 |
| Total | 260,000 |

**Illustration 6.40: Loans-Non-current: Specimen format**

| | **As at 31st March 2022** | **As at 31st March 2021** |
|---|---|---|
| **Loans – Non-current Secured and considered good**<br>Loans to related parties (giving details thereof);<br>Other loans (specify nature). | | |
| Sub-total (A) | | |
| **Loans – Non-current Unsecured and considered good**<br>Loans to related parties (giving details thereof); | | |

| | As at 31st March 2022 | As at 31st March 2021 |
|---|---|---|
| Other loans (specify nature). | | |
| Sub-total (B) | | |
| **Loans – Non-current Unsecured and considered doubtful**<br>Loans to related parties (giving details thereof);<br>Other loans (specify nature). | | |
| Sub-total (C) | | |
| Total (A)+(B)+(C) = (D) | | |

## 6.19 OTHER FINANCIAL ASSETS

Other Financial Assets would be classified as under:

**Other financial assets**

(i) Security Deposits

(ii) Bank deposits with more than 12 months maturity

(iii) Others (to be specified)

**Bank deposits greater than twelve months maturity**

In accordance with Schedule III – Division II - Ind AS, bank deposits with more than 12 months maturity shall be disclosed under 'Other financial assets'. The maturity should be construed as remaining maturity of more than 12 months. The following disclosures as per Note 6(C) of General Instructions for Preparation of Balance Sheet should be provided for such bank deposits:

(a) Earmarked balances with banks (for e.g., for unpaid dividend) shall be separately stated;

(b) Balances with banks to the extent held as margin money or security against the borrowings, guarantees, other commitments shall be disclosed separately;

(c) Repatriation restrictions, if any, in respect of cash and bank balances shall be separately stated.

**Financial lease receivables**

Ind AS Schedule III does not specify about the presentation of finance lease receivables unlike finance lease obligations which are to be grouped under 'Financial Liabilities'. The scope paragraph of Ind AS 32, Ind AS 109 and Ind AS

107 acknowledges that rights and obligations under leases, to which Ind AS 17 applies, are financial instruments but their measurement is excluded from the scope of these standards. Accordingly, as per ICAI Guidance Note on Schedule III – Division II – Ind AS, the non-current portion of a finance lease receivable shall be presented here under 'Other non-current financial assets' while its current portion shall be presented under 'Other current financial assets'. The disclosure requirements of Ind AS 107 would apply to such receivables.

**Illustration 6.41: Other Financial assets: Specimen format**

| | **As at 31st March 2022** | **As at 31st March 2021** |
|---|---|---|
| Security Deposits<br>Bank deposits with more than 12 months maturity<br>others (to be specified) | | |
| Total | | |

## 6.20 OTHER NON-CURRENT ASSETS

Other non-current assets are classified as under:

(i) Capital Advances.

(ii) Advances other than capital advances.

1. Advances other than capital advances shall be classified as:
   (a) Security Deposits.
   (b) Advances to related parties (giving details thereof),
   (c) Other advances (specify nature).
2. Advances to directors or other officers of the company or any of them either severally or jointly with any other persons or advances to firms or private companies respectively in which any director is a partner or a director or a member should be separately stated.

(iii) Bank deposits with more than 12 months maturity.

(iv) Others (specify nature).

**This is explained diagrammatically in the waterfall chart below.**

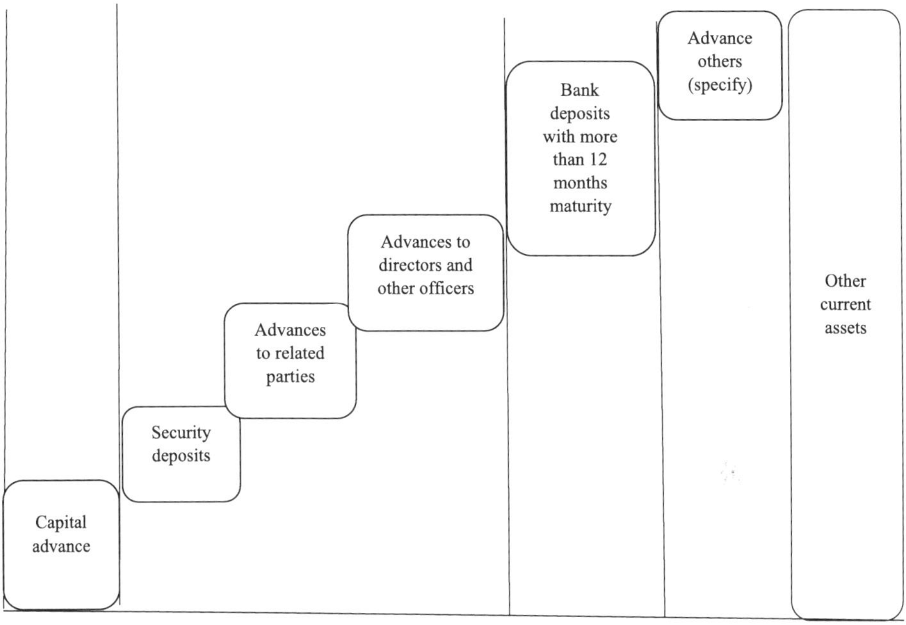


## 6.21 CAPITAL ADVANCE

Capital advances are advances given for procurement of Property, Plant and Equipment including bearer plants, Investment Property, Other Intangible assets or Biological Assets which are non-current assets.

Typically, companies do not expect to realize them in cash, but over a period of time, these get converted into Property, Plant and Equipment including bearer plants, Investment Property, Other Intangible assets or Biological Assets, respectively, which are non-current assets.

Hence, capital advances should be treated as other non-current assets irrespective of when the Property, Plant and Equipment including bearer plants, Investment Property, Other Intangible assets or Biological Assets are expected to be received.

Under Ind AS Schedule III, Capital Advances are not to be classified under Capital Work in Progress, since they are specifically to be disclosed under other non-current assets.

## 6.22 ADVANCE TO DIRECTORS AND OTHER OFFICERS

Advances to directors or other officers of the company or any of them either severally or jointly with any other persons or advances to firms or private companies respectively in which any director is a partner or a director or a member should be separately stated. In case advances are of the nature of a financial asset as per relevant Ind AS, these are to be disclosed under 'other financial assets' separately.

## 6.23 SECURITY DEPOSITS

Security Deposits under other non-current assets should include those deposits which do not meet the definition of a financial asset. Classification of deposits paid into current and non-current depends on the expectation of its realisation, unless an entity expects to recover the same within 12 months after the reporting date.

## 6.24 ADVANCES TO RELATED PARTIES UNDER OTHER NON-CURRENT ASSETS

Details of advances to related parties need to be disclosed. The term "details" should be interpreted to mean the disclosure requirements contained in Ind AS 24.

Other advances include all other items in the nature of advances which do not meet the definition of a financial asset viz., prepaid expenses, CENVAT credit receivable, VAT credit receivable, Service tax credit receivable, etc., which are not expected to be realized within the next twelve months from the Balance Sheet date.

It may be noted that in case advances are of the nature of a financial asset as per Ind AS 32, these are to be disclosed under 'other financial assets' separately. *(Source: ICAI Guidance Note – Schedule III – Division II – Ind AS)*

**Examples of transactions that are disclosed if they are with Related Parties**

The following are examples of transactions that are disclosed if they are with a related party:

(a) purchases or sales of goods (finished or unfinished);

(b) purchases or sales of property and other assets;

(c) rendering or receiving of services;

(d) leases;

(e) transfers of research and development;

(f) transfers under licence agreements;

(g) transfers under finance arrangements (including loans and equity contributions in cash or in kind);

(h) provision of guarantees or collateral;

(i) commitments to do something if a particular event occurs or does not occur in the future, including executory contracts1 (recognised and unrecognised);

(j) settlement of liabilities on behalf of the entity or by the entity on behalf of that related party; and

(k) management contracts including for deputation of employees.

**Illustration 6.42: Other Non-current assets: Specimen format**

| | As at 31st March 2022 | As at 31st March 2021 |
|---|---|---|
| (i) Capital Advances.<br>(ii) Advances other than capital advances.<br>1. Advances other than capital advances shall be classified as:<br>(a) Security Deposits.<br>(b) Advances to related parties (giving details thereof),<br>(c) Other advances (specify nature).<br>2. Advances to directors or other officers of the company or any of them either severally or jointly with any other persons or advances to firms or private companies respectively in which any director is a partner or a director or a member<br>(iii) Bank deposits with more than 12 months maturity.<br>(iv) Others (specify nature). | | |
| Total | | |

**Illustration 6.43: Accounting policy: Financial Instruments (Ind AS 109)**

**1.Financial assets**

**i. Financial Assets**

**A. Initial Recognition and Measurement**

All Financial Assets are initially recognized at fair value. Transaction costs that are directly attributable to the acquisition or issue of Financial Assets, which are not at Fair Value Through Profit or Loss, are adjusted to the fair value on initial recognition. Purchase and sale of Financial Assets are recognized using trade date accounting.

**B. Subsequent Measurement**

**a) Financial Assets measured at Amortized Cost (AC)**

A Financial Asset is measured at Amortized Cost if it is held within a business model whose objective is to hold the asset in order to collect contractual cash flows and the contractual terms of the Financial Asset give rise on specified dates to cash flows that represent solely payments of principal and interest on the principal amount outstanding.

**b) Financial Assets measured at Fair Value Through Other Comprehensive Income (FVTOCI)**

A Financial Asset is measured at FVTOCI if it is held within a business model whose objective is achieved by both collecting contractual cash flows and selling Financial Assets and the contractual terms of the Financial Asset give rise on specified dates to cash flows that represents solely payments of principal and interest on the principal amount outstanding.

**c) Financial Assets measured at Fair Value Through Profit or Loss (FVTPL)**

A Financial Asset which is not classified in any of the above categories are measured at FVTPL. Financial assets are reclassified subsequent to their recognition, if the Company changes its business model for managing those financial assets. Changes in business model are made and applied prospectively from the reclassification date which is the first day of immediately next reporting period following the changes in business model in accordance with principles laid down under Ind AS 109 – Financial Instruments.

**C. Investment in Subsidiaries, Associates and Joint Ventures**

The Company has accounted for its investments in Subsidiaries, associates and joint venture at cost less impairment loss (if any). The investments in preference shares with the right of surplus assets which are in nature equity in accordance with Ind AS 32 are treated as separate category of investment and measured as at FVTOCI.

**D. Other Equity Investments**

All other equity investments are measured at fair value, with value changes recognised in Statement of Profit and Loss, except for those equity investments for which the Company has elected to present the value changes in 'Other Comprehensive Income'. However, dividend on such equity investments are recognised in Statement of Profit and loss when the Company's right to receive payment is established.

**E. Impairment of Financial Assets**

In accordance with Ind AS 109, the Company uses 'Expected Credit Loss' (ECL) model, for evaluating impairment of Financial Assets other than those measured at Fair Value Through Profit and Loss (FVTPL).

Expected Credit Losses are measured through a loss allowance at an amount equal to:

The 12-months expected credit losses (expected credit losses that result from those default events on the financial instrument that are possible within 12 months after the reporting date); or

Full lifetime expected credit losses (expected credit losses that result from all possible default events over the life of the financial instrument).

For Trade Receivables the Company applies 'simplified approach' which requires expected lifetime losses to be recognised from initial recognition of the receivables.

The Company uses historical default rates to determine impairment loss on the portfolio of trade receivables. At every reporting date these historical default rates are reviewed and changes in the forward-looking estimates are analyzed.

For other assets, the Company uses 12 month ECL to provide for impairment loss where there is no significant increase in credit risk. If there is significant increase in credit risk full lifetime ECL is used.

**ii. Financial Liabilities**

**A. Initial Recognition and Measurement**

All Financial Liabilities are recognised at fair value and in case of borrowings, net of directly attributable cost. Fees of recurring nature are directly recognised in the Statement of Profit and Loss as finance cost.

**B. Subsequent Measurement**

Financial Liabilities are carried at amortised cost using the effective interest method. For trade and other payables maturing within one year from the balance sheet date, the carrying amounts approximate fair value due to the short maturity of these instruments.

**iii. Derivative Financial Instruments and Hedge Accounting**

The Company uses various derivative financial instruments such as interest rate swaps, currency swaps, forwards & options and commodity contracts to mitigate the risk of changes in interest rates, exchange rates and commodity prices. At the inception of a hedge relationship, the Company formally designates and documents the hedge relationship to which the Company wishes to apply hedge accounting and the risk management objective and strategy for undertaking the hedge. Such derivative financial instruments are initially recognised at fair value on the date on which a derivative contract is entered into and are also subsequently measured at fair value.

Derivatives are carried as Financial Assets when the fair value is positive and as Financial Liabilities when the fair value is negative. Any gains or losses arising from changes in the fair value of derivatives are taken directly to Statement of

Profit and Loss, except for the effective portion of cash flow hedge which is recognised in Other Comprehensive Income and later to Statement of Profit and Loss when the hedged item affects profit or loss or is treated as basis adjustment if a hedged forecast transaction subsequently results in the recognition of a Non-Financial Assets or Non-Financial liability.

Hedges that meet the criteria for hedge accounting are accounted for as follows:

**A. Cash Flow Hedge**

The Company designates derivative contracts or non-derivative Financial Assets/ Liabilities as hedging instruments to mitigate the risk of movement in interest rates and foreign exchange rates for foreign exchange exposure on highly probable future cash flows attributable to a recognised asset or liability or forecast cash transactions.

When a derivative is designated as a cash flow hedging instrument, the effective portion of changes in the fair value of the derivative is recognised in the cash flow hedging reserve being part of Other Comprehensive Income. Any ineffective portion of changes in the fair value of the derivative is recognised immediately in the Statement of Profit and Loss. If the hedging relationship no longer meets the criteria for hedge accounting, then hedge accounting is discontinued prospectively. If the hedging instrument expires or is sold, terminated or exercised, the cumulative gain or loss on the hedging instrument recognised in cash flow hedging reserve till the period the hedge was effective remains in cash flow hedging reserve until the underlying transaction occurs. The cumulative gain or loss previously recognised in the cash flow hedging reserve is transferred to the Statement of Profit and Loss upon the occurrence of the underlying transaction. If the forecasted transaction is no longer expected to occur, then the amount accumulated in cash flow hedging reserve is reclassified in the Statement of Profit and Loss.

**B. Fair Value Hedge**

The Company designates derivative contracts or non-derivative Financial Assets/Liabilities as hedging instruments to mitigate the risk of change in fair value of hedged item due to movement in interest rates, foreign exchange rates and commodity prices.

Changes in the fair value of hedging instruments and hedged items that are designated and qualify as fair value hedges are recorded in the Statement of Profit and Loss. If the hedging relationship no longer meets the criteria for hedge accounting, the adjustment to the carrying amount of a hedged item for which the effective interest method is used is amortised to Statement of Profit and Loss over the period of maturity.

**iv. Derecognition of Financial Instruments**

The Company derecognizes a Financial Asset when the contractual rights to the cash flows from the Financial Asset expire or it transfers the Financial Asset, and the transfer qualifies for derecognition under Ind AS 109. A Financial liability (or a part of a Financial liability) is derecognized from the Company's Balance Sheet when the obligation specified in the contract is discharged or cancelled or expires.

**v. Offsetting**

Financial Assets and Financial Liabilities are offset, and the net amount is presented in the balance sheet when, and only when, the Company has a legally enforceable right to set off the amount and it intends, either to settle them on a net basis or to realize the asset and settle the liability simultaneously.

**(*Source: Reliance Industries Limited: Annual Report: 2019-20*)**

**Illustration 6.44: Financial Instruments**

**Financial instruments**

Financial assets and financial liabilities are recognised when the Company becomes a party to the contractual provisions of the instrument. Financial assets and liabilities are initially measured at fair value. Transaction costs that are directly attributable to the acquisition or issue of financial assets and financial liabilities (other than financial assets and financial liabilities at fair value through profit and loss) are added to or deducted from the fair value measured on initial recognition of financial asset or financial liability. The transaction costs directly attributable to the acquisition of financial assets and financial liabilities at fair value through profit and loss are immediately recognised in the statement of profit and loss.

**Effective interest method**

The effective interest method is a method of calculating the amortised cost of a financial instrument and of allocating interest income or expense over the relevant period. The effective interest rate is the rate that exactly discounts future cash receipts or payments through the expected life of the financial instrument, or where appropriate, a shorter period.

**(I) Financial assets**

**Cash and bank balances**

Cash and bank balances consist of:

**(i) Cash and cash equivalents** - which includes cash on hand, deposits held at call with banks and other short-term deposits which are readily convertible into known amounts of cash, are subject to an insignificant risk of change in value and have original maturities of less than one year. These balances with banks are unrestricted for withdrawal and usage.

**(ii) Other bank balances** - which includes balances and deposits with banks that are restricted for withdrawal and usage.

**Financial assets at amortized cost**

Financial assets are subsequently measured at amortized cost if these financial assets are held within a business model whose objective is to hold these assets in order to collect contractual cash flows and the contractual terms of the financial asset give rise on specified dates to cash flows that are solely payments of principal and interest on the principal amount outstanding.

**Financial assets measured at fair value**

Financial assets are measured at fair value through other comprehensive income if such financial assets are held within a business model whose objective is to hold these assets in order to collect contractual cash flows or to sell such financial assets and the contractual terms of the financial asset give rise on specified dates to cash flows that are solely payments of principal and interest on the principal amount outstanding.

The Company in respect of equity investments (other than in subsidiaries, associates and joint ventures) which are not held for trading has made an irrevocable election to present in other comprehensive income subsequent changes in the fair value of such equity instruments. Such an election is made by the Company on an instrument by instrument basis at the time of initial recognition of such equity investments. These investments are held for medium or long-term strategic purpose. The Company has chosen to designate these investments in equity instruments as fair value through other comprehensive income as the management believes this provides a more meaningful presentation for medium or long-term strategic investments, than reflecting changes in fair value immediately in the statement of profit and loss.

Financial assets not measured at amortized cost or at fair value through other comprehensive income are carried at fair value through profit and loss.

**Interest income**

Interest income is accrued on a time proportion basis, by reference to the principal outstanding and effective interest rate applicable.

**Dividend income**

Dividend income from investments is recognized when the right to receive payment has been established.

**Impairment of financial assets**

Loss allowance for expected credit losses is recognized for financial assets measured at amortized cost and fair value through other comprehensive income.

The Company recognizes life time expected credit losses for all trade receivables that do not constitute a financing transaction.

For financial assets (apart from trade receivables that do not constitute of financing transaction) whose credit risk has not significantly increased since initial recognition, loss allowance equal to twelve months expected credit losses is recognised. Loss allowance equal to the lifetime expected credit losses is recognised if the credit risk of the financial asset has significantly increased since initial recognition.

**De-recognition of financial assets**

The Company de-recognizes a financial asset only when the contractual rights to the cash flows from the asset expire, or it transfers the financial asset and substantially all risks and rewards of ownership of the asset to another entity.

If the Company neither transfers nor retains substantially all the risks and rewards of ownership and continues to control the transferred asset, the Company recognizes its retained interest in the assets and an associated liability for amounts it may have to pay.

If the Company retains substantially all the risks and rewards of ownership of a transferred financial asset, the Company continues to recognize the financial asset and also recognizes a borrowing for the proceeds received.

**(II) Financial liabilities and equity instruments**

**Classification as debt or equity**

Financial liabilities and equity instruments issued by the Company are classified according to the substance of the contractual arrangements entered into and the definitions of a financial liability and an equity instrument.

**Equity instruments**

An equity instrument is any contract that evidences a residual interest in the assets of the Company after deducting all of its liabilities. Equity instruments are recorded at the proceeds received, net of direct issue costs.

**Financial liabilities**

Trade and other payables are initially measured at fair value, net of transaction costs, and are subsequently measured at amortized cost, using the effective interest rate method where the time value of money is significant.

Interest bearing bank loans, overdrafts and issued debt are initially measured at fair value and are subsequently measured at amortized cost using the effective interest rate method. Any difference between the proceeds (net of transaction costs) and the settlement or redemption of borrowings is recognized over the term of the borrowings in the statement of profit and loss.

**De-recognition of financial liabilities**

The Company de-recognizes financial liabilities when, and only when, the Company's obligations are discharged, cancelled or they expire.

**Derivative financial instruments and hedge accounting**

In the ordinary course of business, the Company uses certain derivative financial instruments to reduce business risks which arise from its exposure to foreign exchange and interest rate fluctuations.

The instruments are confined principally to forward foreign exchange contracts, cross currency swaps, interest rate swaps and collars. The instruments are employed as hedges of transactions included in the financial statements or for highly probable forecast transactions/firm contractual commitments. These derivatives contracts do not generally extend beyond six months, except for certain currency swaps and interest rate derivatives.

Derivatives are initially accounted for and measured at fair value on the date the derivative contract is entered into and are subsequently remeasured to their fair value at the end of each reporting period.

The Company adopts hedge accounting for forward foreign exchange and interest rate contracts wherever possible. At inception of each hedge, there is a formal, documented designation of the hedging relationship. This documentation includes, *inter alia*, items such as identification of the hedged item and transaction and nature of the risk being hedged. At inception, each hedge is expected to be highly effective in achieving an offset of changes in fair value or cash flows attributable to the hedged risk. The effectiveness of hedge instruments to reduce the risk associated with the exposure being hedged is assessed and measured at the inception and on an ongoing basis. The ineffective portion of designated hedges is recognized immediately in the statement of profit and loss.

**When hedge accounting is applied:**

- for fair value hedges of recognized assets and liabilities, changes in fair value of the hedged assets and liabilities attributable to the risk being hedged, are recognized in the statement of profit and loss and compensate for the effective portion of symmetrical changes in the fair value of the derivatives.
- for cash flow hedges, the effective portion of the change in the fair value of the derivative is recognized directly in other comprehensive income and the ineffective portion is recognized in the statement of profit and loss. If the cash flow hedge of a firm commitment or forecasted transaction results in the recognition of a non-financial asset or liability, then, at the time the asset or liability is recognised, the associated gains or losses on the derivative that had previously been recognised in equity are included in the initial measurement of the asset or liability. For hedges that do not result in the recognition of a non-financial asset or a liability, amounts deferred in equity are recognised in the statement of profit and loss in the same period in which the hedged item affects the statement of profit and loss.

In cases where hedge accounting is not applied, changes in the fair value of derivatives are recognised in the statement of profit and loss as and when they arise.

Hedge accounting is discontinued when the hedging instrument expires or is sold, terminated, or exercised, or no longer qualifies for hedge accounting. At that time, any cumulative gain or loss on the hedging instrument recognised in equity is retained in equity until the forecasted transaction occurs. If a hedged transaction is no longer expected to occur, the net cumulative gain or loss recognized in equity is transferred to the statement of profit and loss for the period.

(*Source: Tata Steel: Annual Report 2019-20*)

## 6.25 ACCOUNTING QUALITY OF NON-CURRENT ASSETS

Some of the criteria for evaluation of quality of accounting on non-current assets are highlighted in the table below.

### 6.25.1 Tangible Non-current Assets

| Item |
|---|
| Detailed property records including title deeds and deeds of conveyance |
| Periodic comparison with control accounts |
| Proper authorization of acquisitions |
| Written policies related to acquisitions |
| Insurance cover document related to all acquisitions |
| Internal control over expenses of self-construction |
| Work-orders substantiating the self-construction of assets |
| Individual asset identification plates |
| Written authorization for sale of assets |
| Written authorization for retirement of assets |
| Board resolution for acquisition and sale of major assets/properties |
| Physical existence of assets |
| Policy of valuation of assets whether at cost less depreciation and impairment or under revaluation. |
| Physical safeguard against theft |
| Control over fully depreciated assets |

| Item |
| --- |
| Policy on capitalization of foreign assets and whether the foreign assets have been properly capitalized using the correct exchange rate |
| Policy on capitalization of revenue expenses |
| Policy on depreciation of assets and whether the list of depreciation of assets is available and is matched with assets sub-ledger |
| Whether assets sub-ledger has been reconciled and is in agreement with the general ledger |
| Policy on impairment of assets and whether assets have been impaired as per policy |
| Policy on ascertainment of estimated useful life of each asset and whether technical evaluation has been carried out to ascertain the estimated useful life of the assets |
| Depreciation adjustments for sale and retirement of assets |
| Whether assets have been identified as held for sale and discontinued business and depreciation has been stopped on these assets |
| Whether the assets have been acquired against Government grants |
| Whether borrowing costs have been properly capitalized as per policy and accounting standards |
| Whether assets under finance lease have been correctly reflected in financial statements, |
| Whether assets under finance lease has not been reflected under operating lease |
| Whether there is adequate control on inter company transfer of assets |
| Control over returnable containers |
| Whether investment properties have been reflected as per accounting standards |
| Whether agricultural assets have been valued as per accounting standards |
| Whether all tangible non-current assets have been physically verified and it is in agreement with the asset records in the financial statements |
| Whether there is any policy on discarded assets, and it has been properly disclosed in the financial statement |
| Whether capital work-in-progress has been duly capitalized |
| Whether contingent assets have been disclosed and not capitalized |

### 6.25.2 Intangible Non-current Assets

| Item |
|---|
| Detailed records of all intangible assets |
| Authorization of all intangible assets |
| Process of capitalization of intangible assets |
| Amortization policy of intangible assets and whether it has been adequately reflected in financial statements |
| Whether there is periodic review of amortization of intangible assets |
| Whether goodwill from acquisition has been valued as per accounting standards and internally generated goodwill is not considered in the financial statements |
| Whether goodwill is tested for impairment |

Quality of Accounting of non-current assets need to be evaluated specially with respect to the impact of accelerated depreciation owing to obsolescence, reduction of estimated useful life and impairment owing to business environment, need to be adjusted to the Income Statement. Please refer the chart below which explains our view.

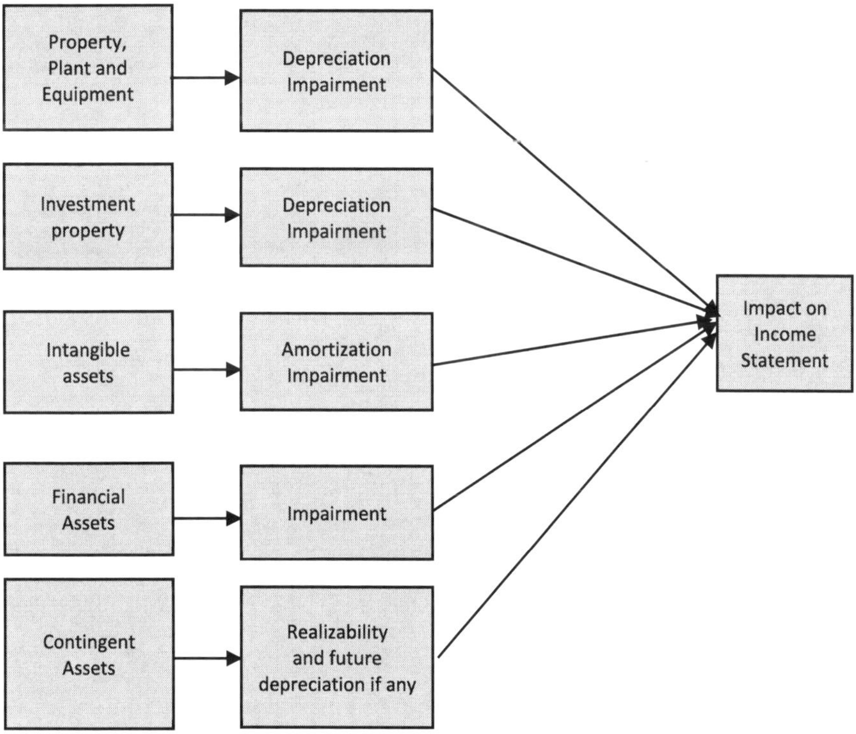

# Chapter 7

# Current Assets

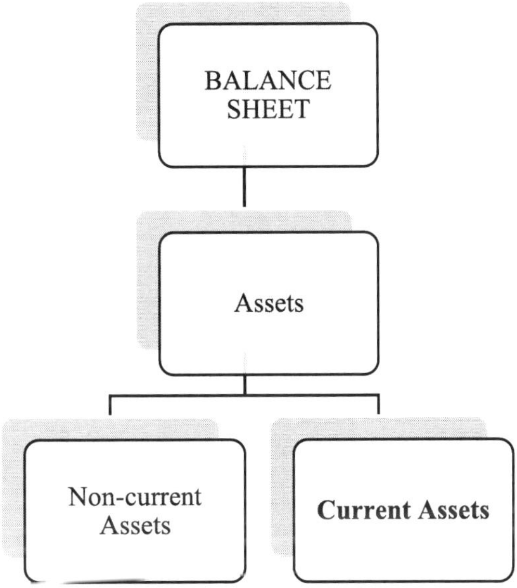


## 7.1 DEFINITION OF CURRENT ASSETS

According to ICAI Guidance Note, Current Asset is defined as under:

"Cash and other assets that are expected to be converted into cash or consumed in the production of goods or rendering of services in the normal course of business."

As explained in Chapter 2, an asset should be classified as a current asset when it:

(a) it expects to realize the asset, or intends to sell or consume it, in its normal ***operating cycle,***

(b) it holds the asset primarily for trading,

(c) it expects to realize the asset within twelve months after the reporting period; or

(d) the asset is cash or a cash equivalent (as defined in Ind AS 7) unless the asset is restricted from being exchanged or used to settle a liability for at least twelve months after the reporting period.

## 7.2 COMPONENTS OF CURRENT ASSETS

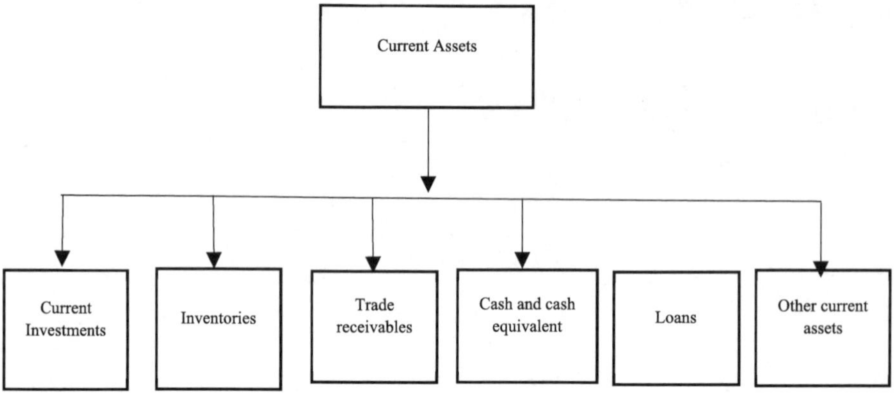


Comparative summary of Current Assets between Schedule III Division I and Division II is summarized as under:

| Under AS | Under Ind AS |
|---|---|
| **N. Current Investments**<br>(i) Current investments shall be classified as:<br>(a) Investments in equity instruments;<br>(b) Investments in Preference Shares;<br>(c) Investment in government or trust securities<br>(d) Investments in debentures or bonds ;<br>(e) Investments in mutual funds ;<br>(f) Investments in partnership firms ;<br>(g) Other investments (specify nature)<br>Under each classifiation, details shall be given of names of the bodies corporate (indicating separately whether such bodies are -<br>(i) subsidiaries,<br>(ii) associates,<br>(iii) joint ventures, or<br>(iv) controlled special purpose entities) in | **II. Investments**<br>(i) Investments shall be classified as:<br>(a) Investments in Equity Instruments;<br>(b) Investment in Preference Shares;<br>(c) Investments in government or trust securities;<br>(d) Investments in debentures or bonds;<br>(e) Investments in Mutual Funds;<br>(f) Investments in partnership firms;<br>(g) Other investments (specify nature).<br>Under each classification, details shall be given of names of the bodies corporate that are-<br>subsidiaries,<br>associates,<br>joint ventures, or<br>structured entities, in whom investments have been made and the nature and extent |

<table>
<tr><th>Under AS</th><th>Under Ind AS</th></tr>
<tr><td>whom investments have been made and the nature and extent of the investment so made in each such body corporate (showing separately investments which are partly-paid). In regard to investments in the capital of partnership firms. The names of the firms (with the names of all their partners, total capital and the shares of each partne) shall be given;<br>(ii) The following shall also be disclosed:<br>(a) basis of valuation of individual investments<br>(b) aggregate amount of quoted investments and market value thereof<br>(c) aggregate amount of unquoted investments<br>(d) aggregate provision made for dimunition in the value of investments.</td><td>of the investment so made in each such body corporate (showing separately investments which are partly-paid).<br>ii) The following shall also be disclosed<br>(a) Aggregate amount of quoted investments and market value thereof;<br>(b) Aggregate amount of unquoted investments;<br>(c) Aggregate amount of impairment in value of investments.</td></tr>
<tr><td>O. Inventories<br>(i) Inventories shall be classified as:<br>(a) Raw materials<br>(b) Work-in-progress<br>(c ) Finished goods<br>(d) Stock-in-trade (in respect of goods acquire for trading)<br>(e) Stores and spares<br>(f) Loose tools<br>(g) Others (specify nature)<br>(ii) Goods-in-transit shall be disclosed under the relevant sub-head of inventories<br>(iii) Mode of valuation shall be stated</td><td>B. Current Assets<br>I. Inventories<br>(i) Inventories shall be classified as:<br>(a) Raw materials;<br>(b) Work-in-progress;<br>(c) Finished goods;<br>(d) Stock-in-trade (in respect of goods acquired for trading);<br>(e) Stores and spares;<br>(f) Loose tools;<br>(g) Others (specify nature).<br>(ii) Goods-in-transit shall be disclosed under the relevant sub-head of inventories.<br>(iii) Mode of valuation shall be stated.</td></tr>
<tr><td>P. Trade Receivables<br>(i) Aggregate amount of trade</td><td>III. Trade Receivables<br>(i) Trade receivables shall be sub-</td></tr>
</table>

| Under AS | Under Ind AS |
|---|---|
| receivables outstanding for a period exceeding six months from the date they are due for payment should be separately stated<br>(ii) Trade receivables shall be sub-classified as<br>(a) secured, considered good<br>(b) unsecured considered good<br>(c ) considered doubtful<br>(iii) Allowance for bad and doubtful debts shall be disclosed under the relevant heads separately<br>(iv) Debts due by directors or other officers of the company or any of them either severally or jointly with any other person or debts due by firms or private companies respectively in which any director or partner or a director or a member should be separately stated | classified as:<br>(a) Secured, considered good;<br>(b) Unsecured considered good;<br>(c) Doubtful.<br>(ii) Allowance for bad and doubtful debts shall be disclosed under the relevant heads separately.<br>(iii) Debts due by directors or other officers of the company or any of them either severally or jointly with any other person or debts due by firms or private companies respectively in which any director is a partner or a director or a member should be separately stated. |
| **Q. Cash and Cash equivalents**<br>Cash and cash equivalents shall be classified as:<br>(a) Balances with banks;<br>(b) Cheques, drafts on hand;<br>(c) Cash in hand;<br>(d) Others (speciy nature)<br>Earmarked balances with banks (e.g. for unpaid dividend) shall be separately stated.<br>Balances with banks to the extent held as margin money or security against borrowings, guarantees, other commitment shall be disclosed separately.<br>Repatriation restrictions, if any, in respect of cash and bank balances shall be separately stated | **IV. Cash and cash equivalents**<br>Cash and cash equivalents shall be classified as:<br>(a) Balances with Banks (of the nature of cash and cash equivalents);<br>(b) Cheques, drafts on hand;<br>(c) Cash on hand;<br>(d) Others (specify nature).<br>**C. Cash and bank balances: The following disclosures with regard to cash and bank balances shall be made:**<br>(a) Earmarked balances with banks (for example, for unpaid dividend) shall be separately stated.<br>(b) Balances with banks to the extent held as margin money or security against the borrowings, guarantees, other commitments |

| Under AS | Under Ind AS |
|---|---|
| Bank deposits with more than 12 months maturity shall be disclosed separately. | shall be disclosed separately.<br>c. Repatriation restrictions, if any, in respect of cash and bank balances shall be separately stated. |
| **R. Short-term loans and advances**<br>(i) Short term loans and advances shall be classified as:<br>(a) Loans and advances to related parties (giving details thereof)<br>(b) Others (specify nature)<br>(ii) The above shall be sub-classified as:<br>(a) secured, considered good<br>(b) unsecured considered good<br>(c) considered doubtful<br>(iii) Allowance for bad and doubtful loans and advances shall be disclosed under the relevant heads separately<br>(iv) Loans and advances due by directors or otherofficers of the company or any of them either severally or jointly with any other person or debts due by firms or private companies respectively in which any director or partner or a director or a member should be separately stated | **V. Loans**<br>(i) Loans shall be classified as:<br>(a) Security deposits;<br>(b) Loans to related parties (giving details thereof);<br>(c) Others (specify nature).<br>(ii) The above shall also be sub-classified as:<br>(a) Secured, considered good;<br>(b) Unsecured, considered good;<br>(c) Doubtful.<br>(iii) Allowance for bad and doubtful loans shall be disclosed under the relevant heads separately.<br>(iv) Loans due by directors or other officers of the company or any of them either severally or jointly with any other person or amounts due by firms or private companies respectively in which any director is a partner or a director or a member shall be separately stated. |
| **S. Other current assets (specify nature)**<br>This is an all-inclusive heading which incorporates current assets that do not fit into other asset categories e.g. unbilled revenue, unamortised premium on forward contracts etc.<br>According to Guidance Note on Revised Schedule VI issued by ICAI, in case any amount classified under this category is doubtful, it is | **VI. Other current assets (specify nature).**<br>This is an all-inclusive heading, which incorporates current assets that do not fit into any other asset categories.<br>Other current assets shall be classified as-<br>(i) Advances other than capital advances<br>1. Advances other than capital |

| Under AS | Under Ind AS |
|---|---|
| advisable that such doubtful amount as well as any provision made against the same should be separately disclosed. It is interpreted that the Guidance Note will be applicable to Schedule III as well. | advances shall be classified as:<br>(a) Security Deposits;<br>(b) Advances to related parties (giving details thereof);<br>(c) Other advances (specify nature).<br>2. Advances to directors or other officers of the company or any of them either severally or jointly with any other persons or advances to firms or private companies respectively in which any director is a partner or a director or a member should be separately stated.<br>(ii) Others (specify nature) |

### 7.2.1 Current Investments

Investments shall be classified as:

| | |
|---|---|
| (a) | Investments in Equity Instruments. |
| (b) | Investment in Preference Shares; |
| (c) | Investments in government or trust securities. |
| (d) | Investments in debentures or bonds. |
| (e) | Investments in Mutual Funds; |
| (f) | Investments in partnership firms; |
| (g) | Other investments (specify nature). |

Under each classification, details shall be given of names of the bodies corporate that are

(i) subsidiaries,

(ii) associates,

(iii) joint ventures, or

(iv) structured entities, in whom investments have been made and the nature and extent of the investment so made in each such body corporate (showing separately investments which are partly-paid).

(ii) The following shall also be disclosed

(a) Aggregate amount of quoted investments and market value thereof;

(b) Aggregate amount of unquoted investments;

(c) Aggregate amount of impairment in value of investments.

ICAI Guidance Notes referred to in Chapter 6 related to Non-current assets will be applicable to current investments as well to the extent applicable.

**Presentation of redemption of debentures**

According to the criteria related to current and non-current disaggregation, if a debenture is to be redeemed partly within twelve months and balance after twelve months, the amount to be redeemed within twelve months should be disclosed as current and balance should be shown as non-current.

**Basis of valuation and classification of current investment**

Schedule III requires basis of valuation of individual investment under current investments as well. It is pertinent to note that there is no requirement to classify investments into trade & non-trade in respect of current investments.

**Provision for diminution of current investments**

The aggregate provision for diminution in the value of current investments that needs to be separately disclosed is the amount written down based on the measurement principles of Current Investments as per AS-13 on a cumulative basis.

**Illustration 7.1: Investments: Current: Specimen format**

| | **As at 31st March 2022** | **As at 31st March 2021** |
|---|---|---|
| **Investments measured at Fair Value through other comprehensive income (FVTOCI)**<br>In Fixed Maturity Plan: Quoted Fully paid-up<br>In Mutual Fund: Quoted<br>In Mutual Fund: Unquoted | | |
| **Total of Investments measured at Fair Value Through Other Comprehensive Income** | xxx | Xxx |
| **Investments measured at Fair Value through Profit & Loss (FVTPL)**<br>In Government securities – Quoted<br>In Debentures or Bonds, Quoted, fully paid-up | | |

| | **As at 31st March 2022** | **As at 31st March 2021** |
|---|---|---|
| In Treasury Bills-Quoted<br>In Mutual Funds-Quoted<br>In Mutual Funds-Unquoted<br>In certificate of deposits-Quoted<br>In Debentures of other companies-Unquoted fully paid-up | | |
| **Total of Investments measured at Fair Value Through Profit and Loss (FVTPL)** | xxx | xxx |
| Aggregate amount of quoted investments<br>Market value of quoted investments<br>Aggregate amount of unquoted investments | | |

### 7.2.2 Inventories

Inventories are classified as under:

(a) Raw materials;
(b) Work-in-progress;
(c) Finished goods;
(d) Stock-in-trade (in respect of goods acquired for trading);
(e) Stores and spares;
(f) Loose tools;
(g) Others (specify nature).

Goods-in-transit shall be disclosed under the relevant sub-head of inventories.
Mode of valuation shall be stated.

**Hence, in accordance with Schedule III, goods in transit should be included under relevant heads with suitable disclosure. Further, mode of valuation for each class of inventories needs to be disclosed. The heading Finished goods should comprise of all finished goods other than those acquired for trading purposes.**

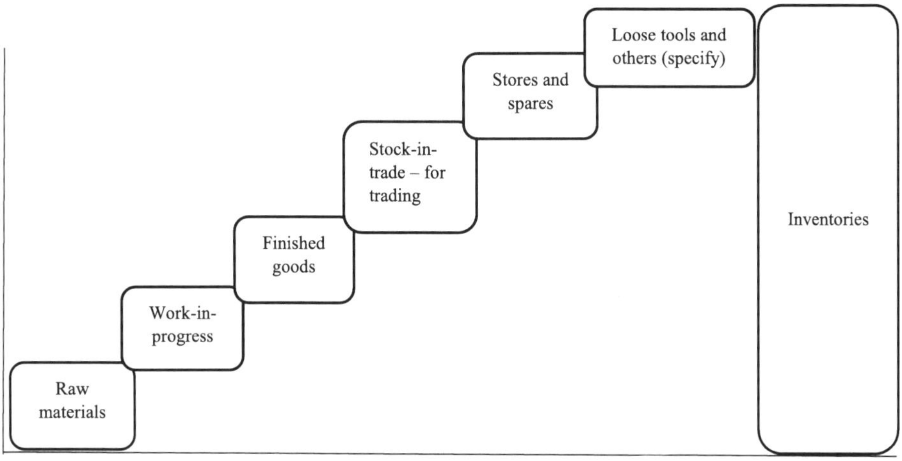


**The waterfall chart above explains the classification of inventories in diagrammatic form.**

**Illustration 7.2: Inventories: Specimen format**

| | As at 31st March 2022 | As at 31st March 2021 |
|---|---|---|
| Raw materials.<br>Work-in-progress;<br>Finished goods;<br>Stock-in-trade (in respect of goods acquired for trading);<br>Stores and spares;<br>Loose tools;<br>Others (specify nature). | | |
| Total | | |

### *7.2.2.1 AS 2: Inventories*

**Inventories are assets:**

(a) held for sale in the ordinary course of business;

(b) in the process of production for such sale; or

(c) in the form of materials or supplies to be consumed in the production process or in the rendering of services.

Net realisable value is the estimated selling price in the ordinary course of business less the estimated costs of completion and the estimated costs necessary to make the sale.

Inventories encompass goods purchased and held for resale, for example, merchandise purchased by a retailer and held for resale, computer software held for resale, or land and other property held for resale.

Inventories also encompass finished goods produced, or work in progress being produced, by the enterprise and include materials, maintenance supplies, consumables and loose tools awaiting use in the production process.

Inventories do not include spare parts, servicing equipment and standby equipment which meet the definition of property, plant and equipment as per AS 10, *Property, Plant and Equipment.* Such items are accounted for in accordance with Accounting Standard (AS) 10, *Property, Plant and Equipment.*

**Measurement of inventories**

Para 5. Inventories should be valued at the lower of cost and net realisable value.

**Cost of Inventories**

The cost of inventories should comprise the following:

**Costs of Purchase**

Para 7. The costs of purchase consist of

| *the purchase price including duties and taxes (other than those subsequently recoverable by the enterprise from the taxing authorities),*<br>*freight inwards and*<br>*other expenditure directly attributable to the acquisition.*<br>*Trade discounts, rebates, duty drawbacks and other similar items are deducted in determining the costs of purchase.* |
|---|

**Costs of Conversion**

| | |
|---|---|
| ***Para 8. The costs of conversion of inventories include*** | costs directly related to the units of production, such as direct labour.<br>They also include a systematic allocation of fixed and variable production overheads that are incurred in converting materials into finished goods. |
| ***Fixed production overheads*** | are those indirect costs of production that remain relatively constant regardless of the volume of production, such as depreciation and maintenance of factory buildings and the cost of factory management and administration. |

| *Variable production overheads* | are those indirect costs of production that vary directly, or nearly directly, with the volume of production, such as indirect materials and indirect labour. |
|---|---|

Para 9. The allocation of fixed production overheads for the purpose of their inclusion in the costs of conversion is based on the normal capacity of the production facilities.

| *Normal capacity is* | the production expected to be achieved on an average over a number of periods or seasons under normal circumstances, taking into account the loss of capacity resulting from planned maintenance. The actual level of production may be used if it approximates normal capacity. |
|---|---|

The amount of fixed production overheads allocated to each unit of production is not increased as a consequence of low production or idle plant. Un allocated overheads are recognised as an expense in the period in which they are incurred. In periods of abnormally high production, the amount of fixed production overheads allocated to each unit of production is decreased so that inventories are not measured above cost.

Variable production overheads are assigned to each unit of production on the basis of the actual use of the production facilities.

## Exclusions from the Cost of Inventories

Para 13. In determining the cost of inventories in accordance with paragraph 6, it is appropriate to exclude certain costs and recognise them as expenses in the period in which they are incurred.

| *Examples of such costs are:* | (a) abnormal amounts of wasted materials, labour, or other production costs;<br>(b) storage costs, unless those costs are necessary in the production process prior to a further production stage;<br>(c) administrative overheads that do not contribute to bringing the inventories to their present location and condition; and<br>(d) selling and distribution costs. |
|---|---|

## Cost formulae used

| *Cost formula applied by the standard constitutes the following:* | *Specific identification method*<br>The cost of inventories of items that are not ordinarily interchangeable and goods or<br>services produced and segregated for specific projects |
|---|---|

| | |
|---|---|
| | should be assigned by specific identification of their individual costs<br>*FIFO (First in first out)*<br>*Weighted Average cost* |

**Techniques for the Measurement of Cost**

Para 18. Techniques for the measurement of the cost of inventories, such as the standard cost method or the retail method, may be used for convenience if the results approximate the actual cost.

| | |
|---|---|
| ***Standard costs method*** | take into account normal levels of consumption of materials and supplies, labour, efficiency and capacity utilisation. They are regularly reviewed and, if necessary, revised in the light of current conditions. |
| ***Para 19. The retail method*** | is often used in the retail trade for measuring inventories of large numbers of rapidly changing items that have similar margins and for which it is impracticable to use other costing methods. The cost of the inventory is determined by reducing from the sales value of the inventory the appropriate percentage gross margin. The percentage used takes into consideration inventory which has been marked down to below its original selling price. An average percentage for each retail department is often used. |

**Net Realisable value**

Para 21. Inventories are usually written down to net realisable value on an item-by-item basis. In some circumstances, however, it may be appropriate to group similar or related items. This may be the case with items of inventory relating to the same product line that have similar purposes or end uses and are produced and marketed in the same geographical area and cannot be practicably evaluated separately from other items in that product line. It is not appropriate to write down inventories based on a classification of inventory, for example, finished goods, or all the inventories in a particular business segment.

Para 22. Estimates of net realisable value are based on the most reliable evidence available at the time the estimates are made as to the amount the inventories are expected to realise. These estimates take into consideration fluctuations of price or cost directly relating to events occurring after the balance sheet date to the extent that such events confirm the conditions existing at the balance sheet date.

Para 23. Estimates of net realisable value also take into consideration the purpose for which the inventory is held. For example, the net realisable value of the quantity of inventory held to satisfy firm sales or service contracts is based on the contract price. If the sales contracts are for less than the inventory quantities held, the net realisable value of the excess inventory is based on general selling prices. Contingent losses on firm sales contracts in excess of inventory quantities held and contingent losses on firm purchase contracts are dealt with in accordance with the principles enunciated in Accounting Standard (AS) 4, Contingencies and Events Occurring After the Balance Sheet Date.

Para 24. Materials and other supplies held for use in the production of inventories are not written down below cost if the finished products in which they will be incorporated are expected to be sold at or above cost. However, when there has been a decline in the price of materials and it is estimated that the cost of the finished products will exceed net realisable value, the materials are written down to net realisable value. In such circumstances, the replacement cost of the materials may be the best available measure of their net realisable value.

Para 25. An assessment is made of net realisable value as at each balance sheet date.

**Disclosure requirements**

Para 26. The financial statements should disclose:

(a) the accounting policies adopted in measuring inventories, including the cost formula used; and

(b) the total carrying amount of inventories and its classification appropriate to the enterprise.

Para 27. Information about the carrying amounts held in different classifications of inventories and the extent of the changes in these assets is useful to financial statement uscrs.

| ***Common classifications of inventories are:*** | (a) Raw materials and components<br>(b) Work-in-progress<br>(c) Finished goods<br>(d) Stock-in-trade (in respect of goods acquired for trading)<br>(e) Stores and spares<br>(f) Loose tools<br>(g) Others (specify nature) |
|---|---|

### 7.2.2.2 Ind AS 2: Inventories

***Inventories*** are assets:

(a) held for sale in the ordinary course of business.

(b) In the process of production for such sale; or

(c) In the form of materials or supplies to be consumed in the production process or in the rendering of services.

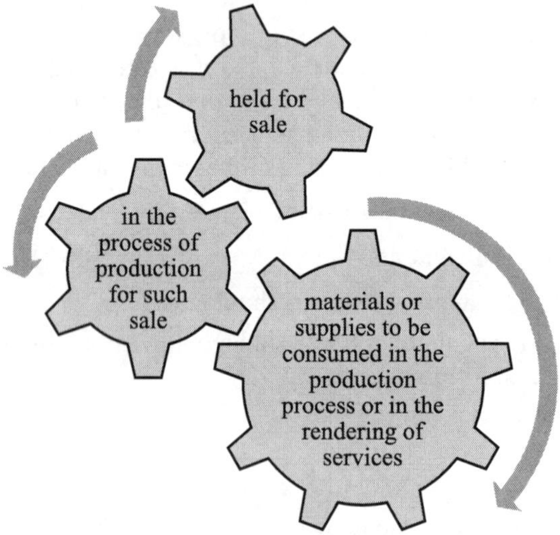


***Net realisable value*** is the estimated selling price in the ordinary course of business less the estimated costs of completion and the estimated costs necessary to make the sale.

***Fair value*** is the price that would be received to sell an asset or paid to transfer a liability in an orderly transaction between market participants at the measurement date. (See Ind AS 113, Fair Value Measurement.)

Recognition principles are depicted as under:

### 7.2.2.3 Measurement of inventories

Inventories shall be measured at lower of cost and net realisable value as shown below.

### 7.2.2.4 Cost of inventories

The cost of inventories shall comprise all costs of purchase, costs of conversion and other costs incurred in bringing the inventories to their present location and condition.

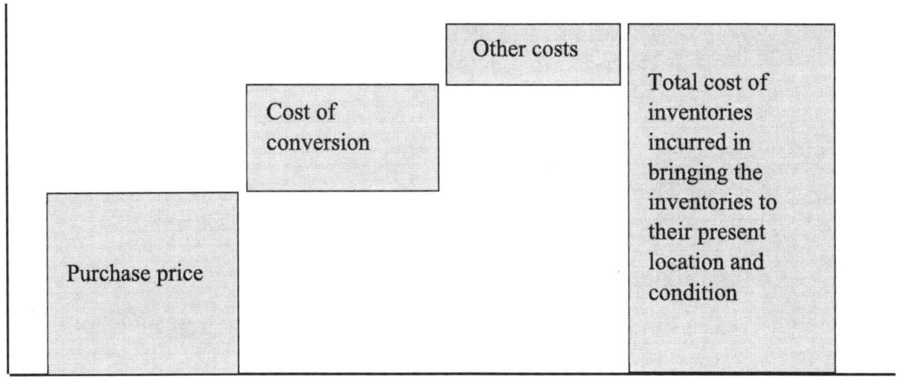


***a) The costs of purchase of inventories comprise***

The purchase price, import duties and other taxes (other than those subsequently recoverable by the entity from the taxing authorities), and transport, handling and other costs directly attributable to the acquisition of finished goods, materials and services.

Trade discounts, rebates and other similar items are deducted in determining the costs of Purchase.

| ***b) The costs of conversion of inventories include*** | Costs directly related to the units of production, such as direct labour.<br>They also include a systematic allocation of fixed and variable production overheads that are incurred in converting materials into finished goods. |
|---|---|
| ***Fixed production overheads*** | those indirect costs of production that remain relatively constant regardless of the volume of production, such as depreciation and maintenance of factory buildings and the cost of factory management and administration.<br>The allocation of fixed production overheads for the purpose of their inclusion in the costs of conversion is based on the normal capacity of the production facilities. |

| ***Normal capacity is*** | the production expected to be achieved on an average over a number of periods or seasons under normal circumstances, taking into account the loss of capacity resulting from planned maintenance. |
|---|---|
| ***Variable production overheads*** | are those indirect costs of production that vary directly,<br>or nearly directly, with the volume of production, such as indirect materials. |

| | |
|---|---|
| | Variable production overheads are assigned to each unit of production on the basis of the actual use of the production facilities. |

***(c) Other costs***

| Other costs are included in the cost of inventories only to the extent that they are incurred in bringing the inventories to their present location and condition. |
|---|

### 7.2.2.5 Costs excluded from valuation of inventories

According to para 16, costs which are excluded from valuation of inventories and recognised as expenses for the period in which they are incurred are:

Abnormal amounts of wasted materials, labour or other production costs

Storage costs, unless those costs are necessary in the production process before a further production stage

Administrative overheads that do not contribute to bringing inventories in their present location and condition and selling costs.

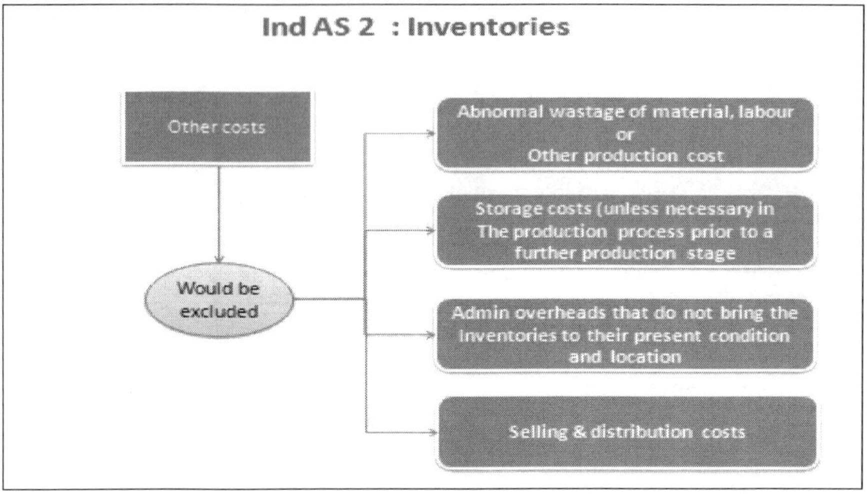


### 7.2.2.6 Borrowing cost and inventories

Ind AS 23, Borrowing Costs, identifies limited circumstances where borrowing costs are included in the cost of inventories.

### 7.2.2.7 Inventories purchased on deferred settlement terms

Para 18: An entity may purchase inventories on deferred settlement terms. When the arrangement effectively contains a financing element, that element, for example a difference between the purchase price for normal credit terms and the amount paid, is recognised as interest expense over the period of the financing.

### 7.2.2.8 Cost of agricultural produce harvested from biological assets

In accordance with Ind AS 41, Agriculture, inventories comprising agricultural produce that an entity has harvested from its biological assets are measured on initial recognition at their fair value less costs to sell at the point of harvest.

This is the cost of the inventories at that date for application of this Standard.

### 7.2.2.9 Techniques for the measurement of cost

Techniques for the measurement of the cost of inventories, such as the standard cost method or the retail method, may be used for convenience if the results approximate cost. Standard costs take into normal levels of materials and supplies, labour, efficiency and capacity utilisation. They are regularly reviewed and revised where necessary.

The retail method is often used in the retail industry for measuring inventories of large numbers of rapidly changing items with similar margins for which it is impracticable to use other costing methods. The cost of the inventory is determined by reducing the sales value of the inventory by the appropriate percentage gross margin. The percentage used takes into consideration inventory that has been marked down to below its original selling price. An average percentage for each retail department is often used.

### 7.2.2.10 Inventories: Cost formulae

The cost of inventories of items that are not ordinarily interchangeable, and goods or services produced and segregated for specific projects shall be assigned by using specific identification of their individual costs.

The cost of inventories, other than those dealt above shall be assigned by using the first-in, first- out (FIFO) or weighted average cost formula. An entity shall use the same cost formula for all inventories having a similar nature and use to the entity. For inventories with a different nature or use, different cost formulas may be justified.

### 7.2.2.11 Net Realisable value

The cost of inventories may not be recoverable if those inventories are damaged, if they have become wholly or partially obsolete, or if their selling prices have declined.

The cost of inventories may also not be recoverable if the estimated costs of completion or the estimated costs to be incurred to make the sale have increased.

The practice of writing inventories down below cost to net realisable value is consistent with the view that assets should not be carried in excess of amounts expected to be realised from their sale or use.

Para 30 stipulates that Estimates of net realisable value are based on the most reliable evidence available at the time the estimates are made, of the amount the inventories are expected to realise. These estimates take into consideration fluctuations of price or cost directly relating to events occurring after the end of the period to the extent that such events confirm conditions existing at the end of the period.

In accordance with para 32, Materials and other supplies held for use in the production of inventories are not written down below cost if the finished products in which they will be incorporated are expected to be sold at or above cost. However, when a decline in the price of materials indicates that the cost of the finished products exceeds net realisable value, the materials are written down to net realisable value. In such circumstances, the replacement cost of the materials may be the best available measure of their net realisable value.

This is summarised below in a table:

| | |
|---|---|
| ***NRV is likely to be less than cost in the following cases:*** | - an increase in costs or a fall in selling price<br>- a physical deterioration in the condition of inventory<br>- Obsolescence of products<br>- Marketing strategy to sell products at a loss<br>- Errors in production or purchasing |
| ***Inventories are usually written down to NRV on the following principles:*** | - items are treated on an item-by-item basis<br>- similar items are normally grouped together<br>- each service is treated as a separate item |

### 7.2.2.12 Recognition as an expense

Para 34 - When inventories are sold, the carrying amount of those inventories shall be recognised as an expense in the period in which the related revenue is recognised.

The amount of any write-down of inventories to net realisable value and all losses of inventories shall be recognised as an expense in the period the write-down or loss occurs.

The amount of any reversal of any write-down of inventories, arising from an increase in net realisable value, shall be recognised as a reduction in the amount of inventories recognised as an expense in the period in which the reversal occurs.

**Illustration 7.3: Accounting policy: Inventories**

**Inventories**

Inventories are stated at the lower of cost and net realisable value.

Cost is ascertained on a weighted average basis. Costs comprise direct materials and, where applicable, direct labour costs and those overheads that have been incurred in bringing the inventories to their present location and condition.

Net realisable value is the price at which the inventories can be realized in the normal course of business after allowing for the cost of conversion from their existing state to a finished condition and for the cost of marketing, selling and distribution.

Provisions are made to cover slow-moving and obsolete items based on historical experience of utilisation on a product category basis, which involves individual businesses considering their product lines and market conditions.

***(Source: Tata Steel: Annual Report 2019-20)***

### 7.2.3 Trade Receivables

Trade Receivables are required to classified as under:

(i) Aggregate amount of Trade Receivables outstanding for a period exceeding six months from the date they are due for payment should be separately stated.

(ii) Trade receivables shall be sub-classified as:

(a) Secured, considered good;

(b) Unsecured considered good;

(c) Doubtful.

(iii) Allowance for bad and doubtful debts shall be disclosed under the relevant heads separately.

This is diagrammatically represented below.

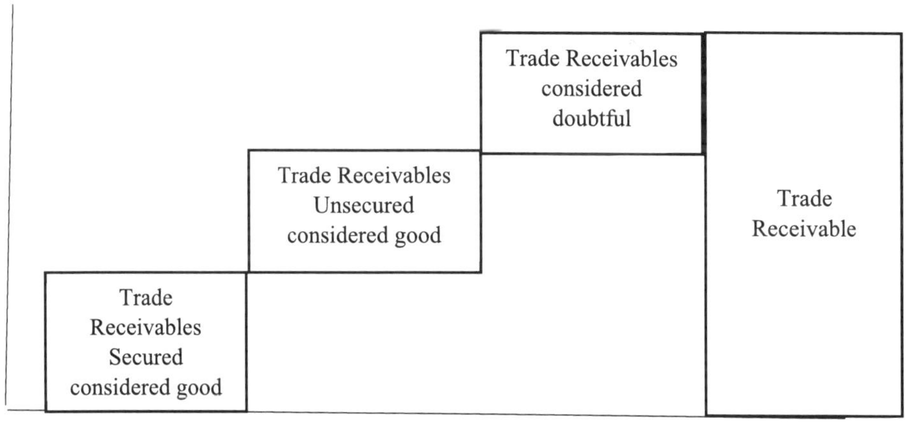


A receivable shall be classified as a "Trade Receivable" if it is in respect of the amount due on account of goods sold or services rendered in the normal course of business.'

A trade receivable will be treated as current, if it is likely to be realised within twelve months from the date of Balance Sheet or within the operating cycle of the business.

Non-Ind AS Schedule III requires separate disclosure of the ageing schedule of "Trade Receivables outstanding" for both viz., the Long-term and the current portion of trade receivables.

According to ICAI Guidance Note on Schedule III, where no due date is specifically agreed upon, normal credit period allowed by the company should be taken into consideration for computing the due date which may vary depending upon the nature of goods or services sold and the type of customers, etc.

Unlike Non-Ind AS Schedule III, Ind AS Schedule III does not require separate presentation of the aggregate amount of Current Trade Receivables outstanding for a period exceeding six months from the date, they are due for payment.

**Illustration 7.4: Trade Receivables: Specimen format**

| | **As at 31st March 2022** | **As at 31st March 2021** |
|---|---|---|
| **Secured and considered good** | | |
| Outstanding for a period exceeding six months from the date they are due for payment | xxx | xxx |
| Other debts. | xxx | xxx |
| Sub-total (A) | Xxx | xxx |
| **Unsecured and considered good** | | |
| Outstanding for a period exceeding six months from the date they are due for payment | xxx | xxx |
| Other debts. | xxx | xxx |
| Sub-total (B) | xxx | xxx |
| **Unsecured and considered doubtful** | | |
| Outstanding for a period exceeding six months from the date they are due for payment | xxx | xxx |
| Other debts. | xxx | xxx |
| Sub-total (C) | xxx | xxx |
| Total (A)+(B)+(C) = (D) | xxx | xxx |

Trade receivables outstanding, ageing schedule shall be given in the following format

**Trade Receivables ageing schedule**

(Amount in Rs.)

| Particulars | Outstanding for following periods from due date of payment# | | | | | |
|---|---|---|---|---|---|---|
| | Less than six months | Six months to one year | One to two years | Two to three years | More than three years | Total |
| (i) Undisputed trade receivable considered good | | | | | | |
| (ii) Undisputed Trade Receivables – which have significant increase in credit risk | | | | | | |
| (iii) Undisputed Trade Receivables – credit impaired | | | | | | |
| (iv) Disputed Trade Receivables– considered good | | | | | | |
| (v) Disputed Trade Receivables – which have significant increase in credit risk | | | | | | |
| (vi) Disputed Trade Receivables – credit impaired | | | | | | |

# similar information shall be given where no due date of payment is specified in that case disclosure shall be from the date of the transaction.

Unbilled dues shall be disclosed separately.

### 7.2.4 Cash and cash equivalents

Cash and cash equivalents shall be classified as:

(a) Balances with Banks (of the nature of cash and cash equivalents);

(b) Cheques, drafts on hand.

(c) Cash on hand.

(d) Others (specify nature).

This is diagrammatically represented below.

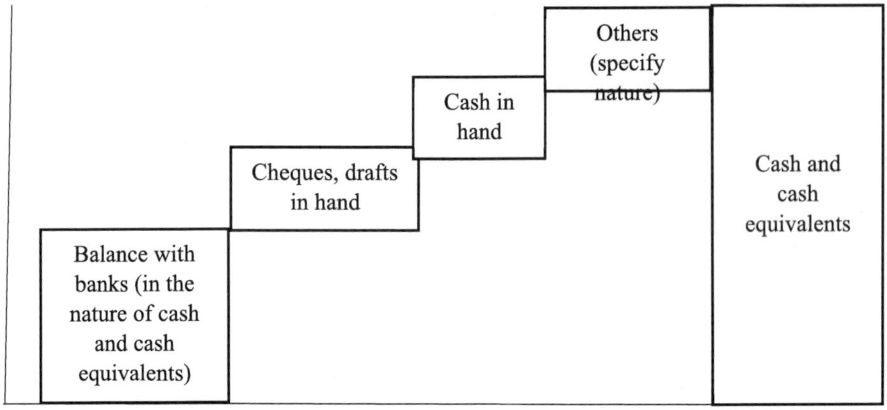


Bank balances other than cash and cash equivalents as above, shall be disclosed below cash and cash equivalents on the face of the Balance Sheet.

Earmarked balances with banks (e.g. for unpaid dividend) shall be separately stated.

Balances with banks to the extent held as margin money or security against borrowings, guarantees, other commitment shall be disclosed separately.

Repatriation restrictions, if any, in respect of cash and bank balances shall be separately stated

Bank deposits with more than 12 months maturity shall be disclosed separately.

"Other bank balances" would comprise of items such as balances with banks to the extent held as margin money or security against borrowings etc. and bank deposits under the sub-head "other bank balances".

The non-current portion of each of the above balances will have to be classified under the head "Other Non-current assets" with separate disclosure thereof.

Cash and cash equivalents is not defined in Ind AS Schedule III however, according to *Ind* According to ICAI Guidance Note on Schedule III, Ind AS, *AS-7 Statement of Cash Flows*, Cash is defined to include cash on hand and demand deposits with banks. Cash Equivalents are defined as short term, highly liquid investments that are readily convertible into known amounts of cash and which are subject to an insignificant risk of changes in value.

Ind AS 7 further explains that an investment normally qualifies as a cash equivalent only when it has a short maturity of, say, three months or less from the date of acquisition. This would include term deposits with banks that have an original maturity of three months or less.

However, bank balances (including term deposits) held as margin money or security against borrowings are neither in the nature of demand deposits, nor readily available for use by the company, and accordingly, do not meet the aforesaid definition of cash equivalents in accordance with the ICAI Guidance Note on Ind AS Schedule III.

Generally, there should not be a difference in the amount of cash and cash equivalent as per Ind AS 1 and as per Ind AS 7. However, as per para 8 of Ind AS 7 "where bank overdrafts which are repayable on demand form an integral part of an entity's cash management, bank overdrafts are included as a component of cash and cash equivalents. A characteristic of such banking arrangements is that the bank balance often fluctuates from being positive to overdrawn." Although Ind AS 7 permits bank overdrafts to be included as cash and cash equivalent, however for the purpose of presentation in the balance sheet, it is not appropriate to include bank overdraft as a component of cash and cash equivalents unless the offset conditions as given in paragraph 42 of Ind AS 32 are complied with. Bank overdraft, in the balance sheet, should be included as 'borrowings' under Financial Liabilities.

**Illustration 7.5: Cash and Cash Equivalents: Specimen format**

| | **As at 31st March 2022** | **As at 31st March 2021** |
|---|---|---|
| Cash on hand<br>Balance with Banks | xxx<br>xxx | xxx<br>xxx |
| **Cash and Cash Equivalents as per Balance Sheet** | xxx | xxx |
| **Cash and Cash Equivalent as per Cash Flows Statement** | xxx | xxx |

## 7.2.5 Loans

Loans are classified as under:

(a) Loans to related parties (giving details thereof);

(b) Others (specify nature).

(ii) The above shall also be sub-classified as:

(a) Secured, considered good;

(b) Unsecured, considered good;

(c) Doubtful.

(iii) Allowance for bad and doubtful loans shall be disclosed under the relevant heads separately.

(iv) Loans due by directors or other officers of the company or any of them either severally or jointly with any other person or amounts due by firms or private companies respectively in which any director is a partner or a director or a member shall be separately stated.

**Illustration 7.6: Loans: Specimen format**

| | As at 31st March 2022 | As at 31st March 2021 |
|---|---|---|
| **Loans – Secured and considered good**<br>Loans to related parties (giving details thereof);<br>Other loans (specify nature). | <br>xxx<br>xxx | <br>xxx<br>xxx |
| Sub-total (A) | xxx | xxx |
| **Loans – Unsecured and considered good**<br>Loans to related parties (giving details thereof);<br>Other loans (specify nature). | <br>xxx<br>xxx | <br>xxx<br>xxx |
| Sub-total (B) | xxx | xxx |
| **Loans – Unsecured and considered doubtful**<br>Loans to related parties (giving details thereof);<br>Other loans (specify nature). | xxx<br>xxx | xxx<br>xxx |
| Sub-total (C) | xxx | xxx |
| Total (A)+(B)+(C) = (D) | xxx | xxx |

This is diagrammatically represented below.

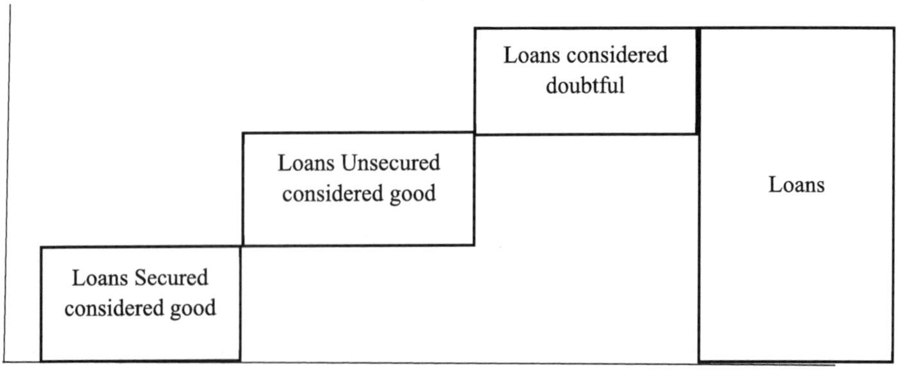

### 7.2.6 Other Financial Assets

According to newly inserted clause VA, of Schedule III Division II related to Ind AS, this is an all-inclusive heading, which incorporates financial assets that do not fit into any other financial asset categories, such as, Security Deposits.

### 7.2.7 Other Current assets (specify nature)

Other current assets (specify nature) related to an all-inclusive heading, which incorporates current assets that do not fit into any other asset categories.

Other current assets shall be classified as-

(i) Advances other than capital advances

1. Advances other than capital advances shall be classified as:
   - (a) Security Deposits;
   - (b) Advances to related parties (giving details thereof);
   - (c) Other advances (specify nature).
2. Advances to directors or other officers of the company or any of them either severally or jointly with any other persons or advances to firms or private companies respectively in which any director is a partner or a director or a member should be separately stated.

(ii) Others (specify nature)

**This is explained diagrammatically in the waterfall chart below.**

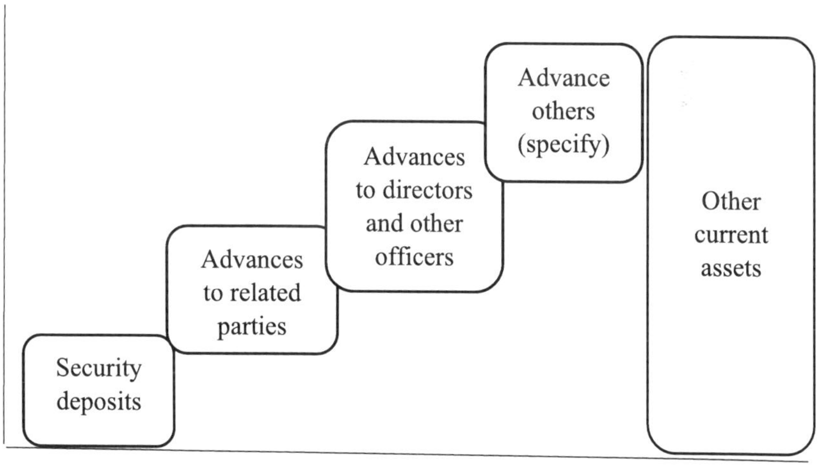

**Illustration 7.7: Other Current assets: Specimen format**

| | As at 31st March 2022 | As at 31st March 2021 |
|---|---|---|
| (i) Advances other than capital advances. | | |
| 1. Advances other than capital advances shall be classified as: | | |
| (a) Security Deposits. | xxx | xxx |
| (b) Advances to related parties (giving details thereof), | xxx | xxx |
| (c) Other advances (specify nature). | xxx | xxx |
| 2. Advances to directors or other officers of the company or any of them either severally or jointly with any other persons or advances to firms or private companies respectively in which any director is a partner or a director or a member | xxx | xxx |
| (ii) Others (specify nature). | xxx | xxx |
| Total | xxx | xxx |

The following disclosures with regard to cash and bank balances shall be made:

(a) Earmarked balances with banks (for example, for unpaid dividend) shall be separately stated.

(b) Balances with banks to the extent held as margin money or security against the borrowings, guarantees, other commitments shall be disclosed separately.

(c) Repatriation restrictions, if any, in respect of cash and bank balances shall be separately stated.

## 7.3 QUALITY OF ACCOUNTING OF CURRENT ASSETS

Quality of Accounting of current assets, especially in areas such as the impact of permanent diminution in value of inventories owing to obsolescence and unserviceability, additional provision on doubtful debts and advances and impairment of short-term financial assets owing to business environment, need to have an impact on Income Statement.

This is explained in the chart below.

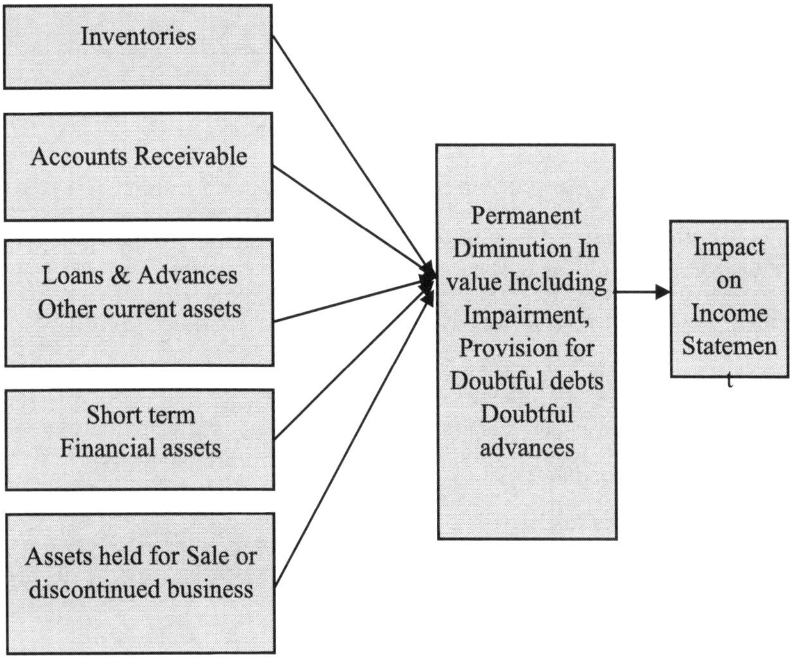


Some of the evaluation criteria for assessing Quality of Accounting of Current Assets are highlighted below.

### 7.3.1 Inventories

| Item |
|---|
| Whether all inventory movements are authorized |
| Whether all inventories included in the financial statements physically exists |
| Whether all purchases and sales of inventories have been recorded in the accounting system |
| Whether all inventory receipts are substantiated through pre-numbered Goods Receipt Notes |
| Whether all inventory issues are substantiated through pre-numbered Stores Issue Slips |
| Whether the inventory cut-off for a particular period is substantiated by last number of Goods Receipts Notes and Stores Issue Slips |
| Whether the ownership of the inventories has been substantiated |
| Whether all inventories quantities have been adequately recorded |

| Item |
|---|
| Whether all inventories items are adequately insured against fire |
| Whether all inventories are adequately covered against theft and pilferage, |
| Whether all inventories are valued at cost or net realizable value whichever is less |
| Whether list of inventories valuation statement ties up with the Inventory ledger, general ledger and the financial statements |
| Whether unserviceable inventories have been adequately provided for |
| Whether insurance spares are adequately valued as per policy |
| Whether all inventories as per valuation statement is reconciled with cost of goods sold break down and both are fairly recorded in the financial statements. |

### 7.3.2 Trade Receivable

| Item |
|---|
| Whether customers are not properly evaluated when sales are made. |
| Whether sales orders are prenumbered and generated from the system |
| Whether there is a process of credit approval in place |
| Whether appropriate credit limits are established for each customer |
| Whether invoices are properly authorized before being sent to customers. |
| Whether billings or invoices sent to customers are complete and accurate. |
| Whether billings or invoices are sent to customers or not sent on a timely basis. |
| Whether billings or invoices are recorded in the accounts receivable system or are recorded on a timely basis. |
| Whether amounts recorded in accounts receivable match invoice amounts. |
| Whether Invoices are linked to the appropriate Trade Receivable account. |
| Whether all Cash receipts or electronic fund transfer receipts on accounts receivable are recorded completely and accurately. |
| Whether amounts received from customers match the invoiced amounts. |
| Whether credit memos are issued to customers without being properly authorized. |
| Whether payments are issued to customers without proper authorization or are not recorded completely and accurately. |

| Item |
|---|
| Whether there is sufficient supporting documentation for sales and accounts receivable transactions. |
| Whether customers are late in remitting payments and the reasons therefor. |
| Whether credit and collection processes are established or are enforced. |
| Whether policies for resolving disputes with customers are established or are enforced. |
| Whether Trade receivable items through invoices and credit memos are recorded to the proper period. |
| Whether receipts or disbursements are recorded to the proper period. |
| Whether Trade receivable detail like invoices and credit memo is properly summarized / posted to the General Ledger.<br>Whether receipts or disbursements are properly summarized / posted to the General Ledger. |
| Whether Trade Receivable duties are effectively segregated to minimize the risk of fraud. |
| Whether there is an audit trail of receivables or billing related activities. |
| Whether Trade receivable balances are not overstated and the amounts reflected under Trade receivable can be realistically collected from customers. |
| Whether Trade receivable balances of foreign subsidiaries are adjusted to reflect currency fluctuations. |
| Whether there is a policy of bad and doubtful debts and basis identified for provision thereof. |
| Whether all trade receivables have been properly aged in respective buckets to assist in recoverability and creation of provisions where these are not recovered beyond six months. |

### 7.3.3 Prepaid expenses, loans and advances and deferred charges

| Item |
|---|
| Whether prepaid expenses are properly authorized |
| Whether prepaid expenses are properly amortized |
| Whether expenses without future benefits have been recorded as prepaid expenses |

| Item |
|---|
| Whether expenses having future benefits have been charged off to revenue |
| Whether all loans and advances have been properly authorized |
| Whether all deferred charges are properly authorized |
| Whether there is sufficient control on all insurance policies in operation |
| Where all loans and advances have been aged and loans and advances not adjusted beyond six months are provided for |
| Whether there is a policy on employee advances and how are these adjusted when they leave the organization |

### 7.3.4 Cash and cash equivalents

| Item |
|---|
| What is the internal control process on all cash receipts and payments? Is it robust enough not to permit any cash leakages? |
| Whether all cash balances are physically counted on a periodic basis if physical cash is maintained |
| Whether there is delegation of authority, and these are built into the systems for adherence, |
| Whether all cash and bank receipts are banked immediately on receipt, |
| Whether trade receivable collections are reconciled with all the invoices raised, |
| Whether all cash and bank receipts are recorded in the correct accounting period, |
| Whether all cash and bank disbursements are properly authorized, |
| Whether all bank payments are through joint authorization process |
| Whether any bearer cheques are permitted for payment |
| Whether employees are permitted to take cash in exchange of signed personal cheques submitted to the cashier |
| Whether there is a system of petty cash and what is the policy of getting these replenished |
| Are all petty cash payments properly scrutinized before providing replenishment |
| Whether all permanent advances are recovered from employees through full and final settlement when they leave the organization |

| Item |
|---|
| Whether bank reconciliations are carried out online real time or at least on a periodic basis such that all bank entries are recorded in the general ledger |
| Whether bank balances of all banks are monitored on a regular basis to evaluate the cash flow situation of the organization |
| Whether there is a process of generating rolling cash forecast to ensure monitoring of fund management in the foreseeable future |

*Chapter 8*

# Statement of Profit and Loss and Other Comprehensive Income

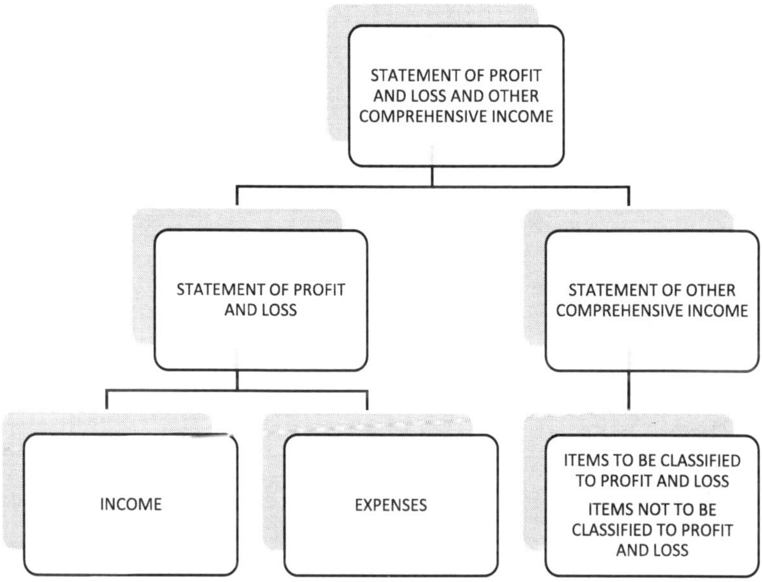


## 8.1 STATEMENT OF PROFIT AND LOSS

According to Glossary on 'Terms Used in Financial Statements', issued by ICAI the phrase 'Profit and Loss statement' is defined as "*the Financial Statement which presents the revenues and expenses of an enterprise for an accounting period and shows the excess of revenues over expenses (or vice versa) It is also known as profit and loss account.*"

**The Statement of Profit and Loss shall include:**

(1) Profit or loss for the period;

(2) Other Comprehensive Income for the period.

The sum of (1) and (2) above is 'Total Comprehensive Income'.

## 8.2 COMPONENTS OF STATEMENT OF PROFIT AND LOSS

Comparative summary of Statement of Profit And Loss between Schedule III Division I and Division II is summarized as under:

| Under AS | Under Ind AS |
|---|---|
| REVENUE FROM OPERATION | Revenue from Operations |
| OTHER INCOME | Other Income |
| (TOTAL INCOME (I + II) | Total Income (I + II) |
| EXPENSES: | EXPENSES: |
| (a) Cost of material consumed | Cost of material consumed |
| (b) Purchase of stock-in-trade | Purchases of stock-in-trade |
| (c) Changes in inventories of finished goods, work-in-progress and stock-in-trade | Changes in inventories of finished goods, stock-in-trade and work-in-progress |
| (d) Employees benefit expenses | Employees benefit expenses |
| (e) Finance cost | Finance cost |
| (f) Depreciation and amortisation expenses | Depreciation and amortisation expenses |
| (h) Other expenses | Other expenses |
| TOTAL EXPENSES | Total expenses (IV) |
| PROFIT BEFORE EXCEPTIONAL AND EXTRA- ORDINARY ITEMS AND TAX (III - IV) | Profit/(loss) before exceptional items and tax (I- IV) |
| EXCEPTIONAL ITEMS | Exceptional items |
| PROFIT BEFORE EXTRAORDINARY ITEMS AND TAX (V-VI) | |
| EXTRAORDINARY ITEMS | |
| PROFIT BEFORE TAX (VII - VIII) | Profit/(loss) before tax (V-VI) |
| TAX EXPENSES: | Tax expenses: |
| (a) Current tax | (a) Current tax |
| (b) Deferred tax | (b) Deferred tax |

| Under AS | Under Ind AS |
|---|---|
| PROFIT/(LOSS) FOR THE PERIOD FROMCONTINUING OPERATIONS (IX - X) | Profit (Loss) for the period from continuing operations (VII-VIII) |
| Profit/(loss) from discontinuing operations | Profit/(loss) from discontinued operations |
| Tax expenses from discontinuing operations | Tax expenses from discontinued operations |
| Profit/(loss) from discontinuing operations (after tax) (XII-XIII) | Profit/(loss) from discontinued operations (X-XI) |
| PROFIT/(LOSS) FOR THE PERIOD (XI + XIV) | Profit/(loss) for the period (IX+XII) |
| | Other Comprehensive Income<br>A (i) Items that will not be reclassified to profit or loss<br>(ii) Income tax relating to items that will not be reclassified to profit or loss<br>B (i) Items that will be reclassified to profit or loss<br>(ii) Income tax relating to items that will be reclassified to profit or loss |
| | Total Comprehensive Income for the period (XIII+XIV)(Comprising Profit (Loss) and Other Comprehensive Income for the period) |
| | Earning per equity share (for continuing operations):<br>(1) Basic<br>(2) Diluted |
| | Earning per equity share (for discontinued operations):<br>(1) Basic<br>(2) Diluted |
| Earning per equity share:<br>(1) Basic<br>(2) Diluted | Earnings per equity share(for discontinued & continuing operations)<br>(1) Basic<br>(2) Diluted |

| Under AS | Under Ind AS |
|---|---|
| General Instructions for preparation of Statement of Profit & Loss in Schedule III.<br>These are summarised as under:<br>1. The provisions of this Part shall apply to the Income and expenditure account referred to in sub-section (2) of Section 210 of the Act, in like manner as they apply to a statement of profit and loss. | GENERAL INSTRUCTIONS FOR PREPARATION OF STATEMENT OF PROFIT AND LOSS<br>1. The provisions of this Part shall apply to the income and expenditure account, in like manner as they apply to a Statement of Profit and Loss. |
| | 2. The Statement of Profit and Loss shall include:<br>(1) Profit or loss for the period;<br>(2) Other Comprehensive Income for the period.<br>The sum of (1) and (2) above is 'Total Comprehensive Income'. |
| 3. Finance costs:<br>Finance costs shall be classified as:<br>(a) Interest expense<br>(b) Other borrowing costs<br>(c) Applicable net gain/loss on foreign currency transactions and translation | 4. Finance Costs<br>Finance costs shall be classified as:<br>(a) interest;<br>(b) dividend on redeemable preference shares;<br>(c) exchange differences regarded as an adjustment to borrowing costs;<br>(d) other borrowing costs (specify nature). |
| 4. Other income shall be classified as:<br>(a) Interest income (in case of a company other than a finance company);<br>(b) Dividend income;<br>(c) Net gain/loss on sale of investments<br>(d) Other non-operating income (net of expenses directly attributable to such income) | 5. Other income<br>Other income shall be classified as:<br>(a) Interest Income;<br>(b) Dividend Income;<br>(c) Other non-operating income (net of expenses directly attributable to such income). |
| | 6. Other Comprehensive Income shall be classified into:<br>(A) Items that will not be reclassified to profit or loss<br>(i) Changes in revaluation surplus; |

| Under AS | Under Ind AS |
|---|---|
| | (ii) Remeasurements of the defined benefit plans;<br>(iii) Equity Instruments through Other<br>(iv) Comprehensive Income;<br>(v) Fair value changes relating to own credit risk;<br>(v) Share of Other Comprehensive Income in Associates and Joint Ventures, to thc extent not to be classified into profit or loss;<br>(vi) Others (specify nature).<br>(B) Items that will be reclassified to profit or loss<br>(i) Exchange differences in translating the financial statements of a foreign operation;<br>(ii) Debt Instruments through Other Comprehensive Income;<br>(iii) The effective portion of gains and loss on hedging instruments in a cash flow hedge;<br>(iv) Share of Other Comprehensive Income in Associates and Joint Ventures, to the extent to be classified into profit or loss;<br>(v) Others (specify nature). |
| | 8. Regulatory Deferral Account Balances shall be presented in the Statement of Profit or Loss in accordance with the relevant Indian Accounting Standards |

## 8.3 REVENUE FROM OPERATIONS

Revenue from Operations have been described separately between non Ind AS entities and Ind AS entities as per table below.

### 8.3.1 Comparative summary: Revenue from operations

| Under AS | Under Ind AS |
|---|---|
| 2. (A) In respect of a company other than a finance company revenue from operations shall disclose separately in the notes revenue from<br>(a) Sale of products;<br>(b) Sale of services;<br>(c) Other operating revenues;<br>(d) Less: excise duty<br>(B) In respect of a finance company, revenue from operations shall include revenue from:<br>(a) Interest<br>(b) Other financial services<br>Revenue from each of the above heads shall be disclosed separately by way of Notes to Accounts to the extent applicable. | 3. Revenue from operations shall disclose separately in the notes<br>(a) sale of products (including Excise Duty);<br>(b) sale of services;<br>(ba) Grants or donations received (relevant in case of section 8 companies only);<br>(c) other operating revenues; |

### 8.3.2 Revenue from operations under non Ind AS entities

Revenue from operations from non Ind AS entities is shown in the chart below:

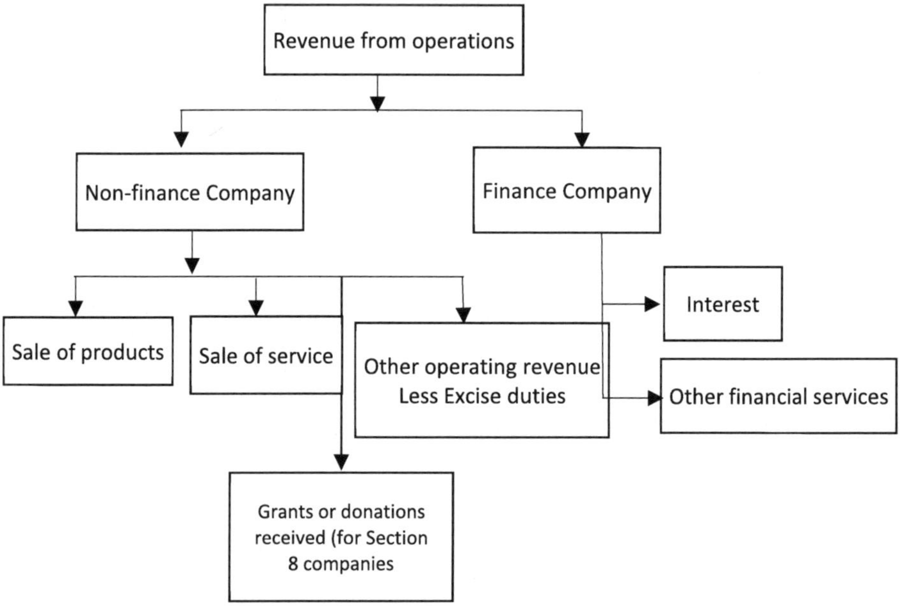

### 8.3.2.1 Revenue from Non-Finance companies

According to Clause 2 (A), in respect of a company other than a finance company revenue from operations shall disclose separately in the notes revenue from—

(a) Sale of products;

(b) Sale of services;

(ba) Grants or donations received (relevant in case of section 8 companies only)

(c) Other operating revenues;

Less:

(d) Excise duty.

The treatment of excise duty, sales tax, service tax, VAT etc. under Schedule III is explained as under:

According to ICAI Guidance Note for non Ind AS entities, AS-9 "Revenue Recognition", prescribes that the above disclosure in respect of Excise Duty needs to be shown on the face of the Statement of Profit and Loss. Since Accounting Standards override Schedule III, the presentation in respect of excise duty will have to be made on the face of the Statement of Profit and Loss.

In doing so, a company may choose to present the elements of revenue from sale of products, sale of services and other operating revenues also on the face of the Statement of Profit and Loss instead of the Notes.

Salient points related to AS- 9 are highlighted in the paragraphs below.

### 8.3.2.2 Presentation of Revenue with indirect taxes

In line with the ICAI Guidance Note on Schedule III on non Ind AS entities, whether revenue should be presented gross or net of taxes would depend on whether the entity is acting as a principal and hence responsible for paying tax on its own account or, whether it is acting as an agent i.e. simply collecting and paying tax on behalf of government authorities.

In the former case, revenue should also be grossed up for the tax billed to the customer and the tax payable should be shown as an expense. However, in cases, where a company collects tax only as an intermediary, revenue should be presented net of taxes.

However, as per the ICAI Guidance Note on Value Added Tax, "Value Added Tax (VAT) is collected from the customers on behalf of the VAT authorities and, therefore, its collection from the customers is not an economic benefit for the enterprise and it does not result in any increase in the equity of the enterprise".

Accordingly, VAT should not be recorded as Revenue of the enterprise. At the same time, the payment of VAT should not be treated as an expense in the Financial Statements of the company.

Further, as per the definition of Revenue in the Guidance Note on Terms Used in Financial Statement, "Revenue excludes amounts collected on behalf of third parties such as certain taxes". The Guidance Note on VAT further states, "Where the enterprise has not charged VAT separately but has made a composite charge, it should segregate the portion of sales which is attributable to tax and should credit the same to 'VAT Payable Account' at periodic intervals".

With the advent of Goods & Services Tax from 1 July 2017 onwards, the collection of GST by an entity would not be an inflow on the entity's own account but it shall be made on behalf of the government authorities. Accordingly, the revenue should be presented net of GST collected.

#### 8.3.2.3 Revenue from Finance company

In accordance with Clause (B) In respect of a finance company, revenue from operations shall include revenue from—

(a) Interest; and

(b) Other financial services.

Revenue under each of the above heads shall be disclosed separately by way of notes to accounts to the extent applicable.

The term "finance company" has neither been defined under the Companies Act 2013 nor under Schedule III. Accordingly, as per Guidance Note of ICAI on Schedule III, the same should be taken to include all companies carrying on activities which are in the nature of "business of non-banking financial institution" as defined under section 45(f) of the Reserve Bank of India Act 1935.

According to the RBI Act 1935, "business of a non-banking financial institution" means carrying on of the business of a financial institution referred to in clause (c) and includes business of a non-banking financial company referred to in clause (f)"

Applying the aforesaid definition, the term "finance company" would include all NBFCs – asset finance companies, investment companies, leasing and hire purchase companies, loan companies, infra finance companies, core investment companies, micro finance companies, housing finance companies regulated by National Housing Bank and so on.

#### 8.3.2.4 AS 9: Revenue Recognition (for non Ind AS entities)

Revenue is the gross inflow of cash, receivables or other consideration arising in the course of the ordinary activities of an enterprise from the following:

- **from sale of goods**
- **from rendering of services**
- **from the use of others of enterprise resources yielding interest, royalty and dividends.**

Revenue is measured by the charges made to customers or clients for goods supplied and services rendered to them and by the charges and rewards arising from the use of the resources by them. In an agency relationship, the revenue is the amount of commission and not the gross inflow of cash, receivables or other consideration.

### 8.3.3 Sale of goods

In a transaction involving the sale of goods, performance should be regarded as being achieved when the following conditions have been fulfilled:

(i) the seller of goods has transferred to the buyer the property in the goods for a price or all significant risks and rewards of ownership have been transferred to the buyer and the seller retains no effective control of the goods transferred to a degree usually associated with ownership; and

(ii) no significant uncertainty exists regarding the amount of the consideration that will be derived from the sale of the goods.

Hence for sale of goods, achievement of performance will centre around the following conditions:

**Illustration 8.1**

Conway Traders, a dealer in air conditioners, sells one unit to Kelly Ltd at Rs.50,000.

In this case the risks and rewards of owning the air conditioners are transferred to Kelly.

The seller has no effective managerial control over the goods.

Also, no significant uncertainty exists regarding the amount of the consideration that will be derived from the sale of goods.

Hence revenue can be recognised in the books of Conway Traders.

**Illustration 8.2**

On 30th September 2021, Gamma sold goods that cost Gamma Rs. 4 million to manufacture at a gross profit margin of 20%. Gamma recognised the sale as revenue when the goods were sent to the customer. The goods were supplied on a sale or return basis, with a right to return up to and including 31st January 2022. The customer returned 50% of the goods by 31$^{st}$ December 2021. It is also uncertain as to how many of the remaining goods will be returned prior to 31st January 2022. Comment on the treatment on Revenue recognition.

**Solution**

Under the stipulations of AS 9– Revenue Recognition the treatment would be as under:

(a) Since the goods are sold on sale or return basis, sales value of goods on sales or return basis should be excluded from revenue and taken back to inventory, where there is uncertainty about the possibility of return. We already know that 50% of the goods have already been returned by 31st December 2021.

(b) Hence the revenue of Rs.5 m (Rs.4 m × 100/80) should be removed from revenue and receivables

(c) Accordingly, Rs.4 m would be added back to inventories and taken out of cost of sales.

### 8.3.4 Rendering of services

In a transaction involving the rendering of services, performance should be measured either under

(a) the complete service contract method or

(b) under the proportionate completion method, whichever relates the revenue to the work accomplished.

Such performance should be regarded as being achieved when no significant uncertainty exists regarding the amount of the consideration that will be derived from rendering the service.

Accordingly, under rendering of services measurement of performance will centre around the following conditions:

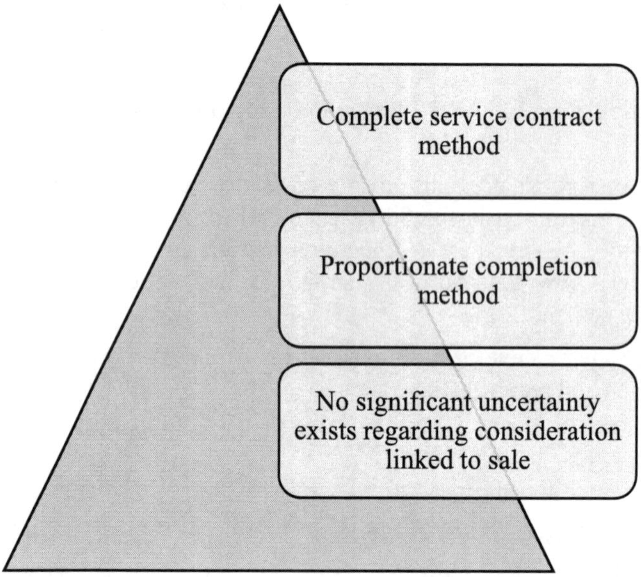


**Illustration 8.3**

Wendy & Chaney is a law firm with its corporate office in Gurgaon. It has recently acquired a high-end client, Keki hotels Ltd having properties in Uttarakhand. The firm would provide professional consulting services related to acquisition of properties for the purposes of building hotels all over South Asia. The duration of the contract would be two years for which a consideration of Rs.2 million would be received. How do we recognise revenue for these services?

**Solution**

As the nature of assignment involves performing continuous services throughout the period of two years, the law firm should recognise revenue on straight line basis at Rs.1 million every year.

**Illustration 8.4**

Dr. Munjal is an ophthalmic surgeon and charges Rs.10,000 for each operation along with pre-operation charges of Rs.5,000. A patient has paid Rs.7,500 before the operation and Rs. 7,500 after the operation. How would be revenue be recognised in this case?

**Solution**

Since this is a specific act of service, revenue can be recognised only after the service has been completed, i.e. after the operation is successfully over. Any payment received before the act would be treated as advance from patient and treated as a liability until the operation is performed.

### 8.3.5 Interest, royalties and dividends

Revenue arising from the use by others of enterprise resources yielding interest, royalties and dividends should only be recognised when no significant uncertainty as to measurability or collectability exists.

These revenues are recognised on the following bases:

| | |
|---|---|
| ***(i) Interest:*** | on a time proportion basis taking into account the amount outstanding and the rate applicable e.g. debenture interest payable on 30th June and 31st December. However, when the books are closed on 31st March, interest for the months of January, February and March will be recognised on time basis though these have not fallen due as yet. |
| ***(ii) Royalties:*** | Are charges for the use of assets such as patents, trademarks and copyrights, know-how and recognised on an accrual basis in accordance with the terms of the relevant agreement. |
| ***(iii) Dividends:*** | These are rewards from the holding of investments in shares and recognised when the owner's right to receive payment is established |

**Illustration 8.5**

On Nov 1 2020, Peter Parker entered into an agreement with the publisher of his book. According to the agreement the royalty would be paid by the publisher on September and March. Financial year ending is on 31st March every year. How the revenue would be recognised.

**Solution**

In the current scenario, Peter Parker would be recognizing royalty between 1st November 2020 till 31st March 2021 i.e. for five months.

**Illustration 8.6**

K bought 70% holding in E Ltd on 30$^{th}$ June 2014 for Rs.50,000. E Ltd declares and pays a dividend of Rs.4,500 to K on 30$^{th}$ November 2021. The dividend was distributed out of profits for the year ended 30th September 2021. Both the entities have a financial year end of 30th September 2021.

Required:

How will this dividend be recognised in the financial statements of K for the year ended 30th September 2021?

**Solution**

The dividend of Rs. 4500 would be split into the following:

(a) Pre-acquisition element of Rs. 4,500 x 9/12 = Rs.3375 representing 9 months to June 2021

(b) Post-acquisition element of Rs.4,500 x 3/12 =Rs.1125 representing 3 months to Sept 2021.

Hence the amount of Rs.3,375 would be deducted from the purchase price of Rs.50,000 while calculating goodwill.

The amount of Rs.1,125 would be recognised as revenue in Profit & Loss Account.

**Illustration 8.7**

Beta Ltd has taken a transit insurance policy. Suddenly in the year 2019-20 the percentage of accident has gone up by 7% and the company wants to recognise Insurance claim as revenue in 2020-21 in accordance with relevant accounting standards.

Do you agree? Explain in brief, as per the relevant accounting standards

**Solution**

When to recognise revenue:

- Revenue recognition is mainly concerned with the timing of recognition of revenue in the profit and loss account
- Where there is no uncertainty as to ultimate collection, revenue is recognised at the time of sale or rendering of services, as the case may be even though payments are made by instalments.
- The amount of revenue is usually determined by agreement between the parties to the transaction.

It may be appropriate to recognise revenue only when it is reasonably certain that the ultimate collection will be made.

In the given case, Beta Limited wants to suddenly recognise insurance claim because it has increased over the previous year. But, there are uncertainties involved in the settlement of the claim. Also the claim does not seem to be in the course of ordinary activity of the company.

Hence Beta Ltd is not advised to recognise the insurance claim as revenue.

**Illustration 8.8**

Victory Ltd purchased goods on credit from Lucky Ltd for Rs.250 crores for export. The Export order was cancelled. Victory Ltd decided to sell the same goods in the local market with a price discount. Lucky Ltd was requested to offer a price discount of 15%. The Chief Accountant of Lucky Ltd wants to adjust the sales figure to the extent of the discount requested by Victory Ltd. Discuss whether this treatment is justified.

**Solution**

Lucky Ltd had sold goods to Victory Ltd on credit worth for Rs.250 crores and the sale was completed in all respects. Victory Ltd.'s decision to sell the same in the domestic market at a discount does not affect the amount recorded as sales by Lucky Ltd. The price discount of 15% offered by Lucky Ltd after request of Victory Ltd was not in the nature of discount given during the ordinary course of trade because otherwise the same would have been given at the time of sale itself. Now as far as Lucky Ltd is concerned, there appears to be uncertainty relating to the collectability of debt which has arisen subsequent to the time of sale.

Therefore, it would be appropriate to make a separate provision to reflect the uncertainty relating collectability rather than to adjust the amount of revenue originally recorded.

Therefore, such discount should be written off to the profit and loss account and not shown as deduction from the sales figure.

**Illustration 8.9**

Bottom Ltd entered into a sale deed for its immovable property before the end of the year. But registration was done with registrar subsequent to Balance Sheet date. But before finalisation is it possible to recognise the sale and the gain at the Balance sheet Date? Give your view with reasons.

**Solution**

Yes, both sales and gain of Bottom Ltd should be recognised. In accordance with AS 9 at the Balance sheet date and what was pending was merely a formality to register the Deed. It is clear that significant risks and rewards of ownership had passed before the Balance sheet date. Further the registration post the balance sheet date confirms the condition of sale at the balance sheet date as per AS 4.

### Illustration 8.10

M/s Prima Co Ltd sold goods worth Rs.50,000 to M/s Y & Co. M/s Y & Co asked for discount of Rs.8,000 which was agreed by M/s Prima Co Ltd. The sale was effected and goods were dispatched. After receiving, goods worth Rs.7,000 was found defective which they returned immediately. They made the payment of Rs.35,000 to M/s Prima Co Ltd. Accountant booked the sales for Rs.35000. Please discuss.

**Solution**

As per AS 9 Revenue Recognition, revenue is the gross inflow of cash, receivables or other consideration arising in the course of the ordinary activities of an enterprise from the sale of goods, from the rendering of services and from the use by others of enterprise resources, yielding interest, royalties and dividends.

In the given case, M/s Prima Co Ltd should record the sale at gross value of Rs.50,000. Discount of Rs. 8,000 in price and goods returned worth Rs.7,000 are to be adjusted by suitable provisions. M/s Prima Co Ltd might have sent the credit note of Rs.15,000 to M/s Y & Co to account for these adjustments. The contention of the accountant to book the sales for Rs.35,000 is not correct.

### Illustration 8.11

Moon Ltd entered into agreement with Sun Ltd for sale of goods of Rs. 8 lakhs at a profit of 20% on cost. The sale transaction took place on 1.2.2021. On the same day Sun Ltd entered into another agreement with Moon Ltd to resell the same goods at Rs.10.80 lakhs on 1st August 2021. State the treatment of this transaction in the financial statements of Moon Ltd as on 31.3.21. The pre-determined re-selling price covers the holding cost of Sun Ltd. Give the journal entries as on 31.3.21 in the books of Moon Ltd

**Solution**

In the given case, Moon Ltd concurrently agreed to repurchase the same goods from Sun Ltd on 1st Feb 2021. Also the re-selling price is predetermined and covers purchasing and holding costs of Sun Ltd. Hence the transaction between Moon Ltd and Sun Ltd on 1st Feb 2021 should be accounted for as financing rather than sale. The resulting cash flow of Rs.9.60 lakhs received by Moon Ltd cannot be considered as revenue as per AS 9 "Revenue Recognition".

Journal entries in the books of Moon Ltd

| Date | Particulars | Rs/Lakhs | Rs/lakhs |
|---|---|---|---|
| 1.02.21 | Bank A/c Dr. | 9.60 | |
| | To Advance from Sun Ltd | | 9.60 |
| | (Being advance received from Sun Ltd amounting to (Rs.8 lakhs + 20% of Rs. 8 lakhs = Rs. 9.60 lakhs) under sale and re-purchase agreement) | | |
| 31.03.21 | Financing charges A/c Dr. | 0.40 | |
| | To Sun Ltd | | 0.40 |
| | (Financing charges for 2 months at Rs.1.20 lakhs (Rs.10.80 – Rs.9.60) i.e. Rs.1.2 lakhs x 2 /6) | | |
| 31.03.21 | Profit & Loss A/c Dr. | 0.40 | |
| | To Financing charges A/c | | 0.40 |
| | (Being amount of finance charges transferred to P&L A/c) | | |

**Illustration 8.12**

Bird Ltd has been successful jewellers for the past 100 years and sales are against cash only. The company diversified into apparels. A young senior executive was put in charge of Apparels business and sales increased 5 times. One of the conditions for sales that dealers can return unsold stocks within one month of the end of the season. Sales return for the year was 25% on sale. Suggest a suitable Revenue recognition policy with reference to AS – 9.

**Solution**

As per AS 9 "Revenue recognition" it is mainly concerned with the timing of recognition of revenue in statement of profit and loss of an enterprise. The amount of revenue arising on a transaction is usually determined by the agreement between parties involved in the transaction. When uncertainties exist regarding the determination of the amount, or its associated costs, these uncertainties may influence the timing of the Revenue recognition.

Effect of uncertainty – in case of the jewellery business the company is selling for cash and the returns are negligible. Hence, revenue can be recognised on sales. On the other hand, in Apparels industry, the dealers have a right to return the unsold goods within one month of the end of the season. In this case, the company is bearing the risk of sales return and therefore, the company should not recognise the revenue to the extent of 25% of its sales. The company may disclose suitable revenue recognition policy in its financial statements separately for both jewellery and Apparels business.

**Illustration 8.13**

Cruise Shipping company is engaged in the business of ship building and ship repair. On completion of the repair work, a work completion certificate is prepared and countersigned by ship owner (customer). Subsequently, invoice is prepared based on the work completion certificate describing the nature of work done together with the amount and the rate. Customer scrutinises the invoice and any variation is informed to the company. Negotiations take place between the company and the customer. Negotiations may result in a deduction being allowed from the invoiced amount either as a lump sum or as a percentage of the invoiced amount. The accounting treatment followed by the company is as follows:

(a) when the invoice is raised, the customer's account is debited and ship repair income account is credited with the invoiced amount

(b) deduction, if any, arrived after negotiation is treated as trade discount by debiting the ship repair income account

(c) at the close of the year, negotiation in respect of certain invoices had not been completed. In such cases, based on past experience, a provision for anticipated loss is created by debiting the Profit and Loss Account. The provision is disclosed in Balance Sheet.

Following two aspects are settled in the negotiations:

(i) Errors in billing arising on account of variation between the quantities as per work Completion certificate and invoice and other clerical errors in preparing the Invoice.

(ii) Disagreement between the company and customer about the rate/cost on which prior agreement has not been reached between them.

Comment:

(a) whether the accounting treatment of deduction as trade discount is correct? If not, state the correct accounting treatment

(b) whether the disclosure of the provision for anticipated loss in Balance Sheet is correct; if not, state correct accounting treatment

**Solution**

(a) In accordance with AS 9 "Revenue Recognition", revenue is recognised at the time when the invoice is raised to the customers; however the treatment of deduction as trade discount is not as per AS 9. Considering the treatment prescribed by AS 4 " Contingencies and events occurring after the Balance

Sheet date" , the correct treatment of the difference between the invoice amount and finally settled amount should be as under:

- The adjustment of the difference between the invoiced amount and the amount finally settled against "ship repair income" account is in order. Events occurring up to the date of approval of the accounts by the Board of Directors should be taken into consideration in determining the amount of adjustment to be made in this regard.
- The description of the difference as "trade discount" is not appropriate.

(b) In respect of ship repair jobs for which negotiations between the ship owners and the company are not over, the accounting treatment is not appropriate. Instead, the amount of difference between the invoiced amount and the amount likely to be settled (as estimated based on past experience) should be adjusted in the "Ship repair income" by a corresponding credit to the accounts of the respective ship owners. Consequently, the figure of sundry debtors included in the Balance Sheet would be net of adjustment for such difference. In other words, the amount of difference would be neither shown under the head provisions nor shown as a deduction from the sundry debtors in the balance sheet.

**Illustration 8.14**

On 25th January 2021, Apollo Advertising Limited obtained advertisement rights for National Games to be held in March/April 2021 for Rs.520 lakhs.

They furnish the following information:

(a) The company obtained the advertisements for 70% of available time for Rs.700 lakhs by 31st January 2021

(b) For the balance time they got bookings in February 2021 for Rs.240 lakhs.

(c) All the advertisers paid the full amount at the time of booking the advertisements.

(d) 40% of the advertisements appeared before the public in March 2021 and balance 60% appeared in the month of April 2021.

You are required to calculate the amount of profit/loss to be recognised in the financial year 2020-21 as per AS 9.

**Solution**

In accordance with para 12 of AS 9 "Revenue Recognition" in a transaction involving the rendering of services, performance should be measured either under the completed service contract method or under the proportionate completion method, whichever relates the revenue to the work accomplished. Further

Appendix B to AS 9 states that revenue from advertising should be recognised when the service is completed. The service as regards advertisement is deemed to be completed when the related advertisement appears before the public.

In the given problem 40% of the advertisement appeared before the public in March 2021 and the balance 60% in April 2021.

Accordingly, the Profit and Loss would be computed as follows:

| | **Rs in lakhs** |
|---|---|
| Advertisement for 70% of available time obtained by 31.1.2021 | 700 |
| Advertisement for balance 30% of available time obtained by Feb 2021 | 240 |
| Total | 940 |
| Less: Cost of advertisement rights | (520) |
| Profit | 420 |

The profit amounting Rs.420 lakhs should be apportioned in the ratio of 40: 60 for the months of March and April 2021. Thus, the company should recognise Rs.168 lakhs.

(Rs.420 lakhs x 40%) in March 2021 i.e. the financial year 2020-21 and the balance of Rs.252 lakhs (RS.420 lakhs x 60%) in April 2021 i.e. the financial year 2021-22.

**Illustration 8.15**

S Ltd. had a plot of land which it sold to K Ltd for Rs.40,00,000 (the prevailing market price of the land). It was decided at the time of sale that S Ltd would repurchase that plot after four years. The purchase price was fixed at Rs. 50,00,000. Comment on Revenue Recognition.

**Solution**

In the given case the legal form of the transaction is that of a sale of land by S Ltd.

However, the substance of the transaction clearly shows that:

- S Ltd has obtained a loan from K Ltd.
- It has handed over the plot of land as security.
- The repurchase price includes an element of interest.

Hence, S Ltd will not recognise this sale as revenue. It will be reflected as loan from K Ltd in the Balance Sheet. The difference between Rs.50,00,000 and Rs.40,00,000 would be treated as Finance charge during the four-year period.

### Illustration 8.16

P's revenue includes a sale of goods on 1 April 20X6 for Rs 100,000. The goods cost P Rs 50,000 to manufacture. The terms of sale gave P an option to repurchase the goods at Rs 110,000 on 31. 3. 20X8. The buyer had an option to repurchase the goods for Rs 110,000 on31.3. 20X8.

Show treatment.

**Solution**

Though the revenue has been booked to the tune of Rs 100,000, since there is an option of repurchase of the goods at Rs 110,000, this does not construe to be a sale. The reason is that the risks and rewards connected with the goods have not been transferred to the buyer from the seller. Hence the following treatment would be as per AS 9 Revenue Recognition:

(a) Reverse sales of Rs 100,000

(b) Reverse cost of sales of Rs 50,000

(c) The amount to be recognised as secured loan under Non-current Liabilities in Balance Sheet (as per Schedule III Part I – format)

(d) Interest @ 5% p.a. (assumed as difference sales and repurchase is Rs.10,000) i.e. Rs.5,000 to be charged as finance cost under Statement of Profit and Loss (a) Amount of inventory to be exceeded by the amount reversed under cost of sales.

### Illustration 8.17

The stages of production and sale of a producer are as under (all in rupees)

| Stage | Activity | Cost to date | Net realisable value |
|---|---|---|---|
| A | Raw materials | 15,000 | 13,500 |
| B | WIP 1 | 17,000 | 18,000 |
| C | WIP 2 | 20,000 | 22,000 |
| D | WIP 3 | 23,000 | 24,000 |
| E | Finished goods | 25,000 | 30,000 |
| F | Ready for sale | 25,000 | 30,000 |
| G | Sale agreed | 25,000 | 30,000 |
| H | Delivered | 25,500 | 30,000 |
| I | Paid for | 27,000 | 30,000 |

Explain the stage at which you think revenue will be recognised and how much would be the gross profit and net profit on a unit of this product?

**Solution**

In accordance with AS 9, revenue will be recognised only when the following two conditions are satisfied:

(a) Sale value is measured reliably – that is fixed and determinable

(b) Title (major risks and rewards) to the goods have been transferred to customer

Both the above conditions are satisfied at stage F when sales are agreed at a price and goods are ready for delivery.

Gross profit is calculated at stage F when goods are ready for sale after all necessary process of production is over = Rs. 5,000 (Rs.30,000 – Rs.25,000)

Net profit is calculated at stage I, when goods are delivered and payment collected i.e.Rs.3,000 (Rs.30,000 – Rs.27,000).

### 8.3.5.1 AS 7: Construction Contracts (for non Ind AS entities)

Construction contracts are categorized as under:

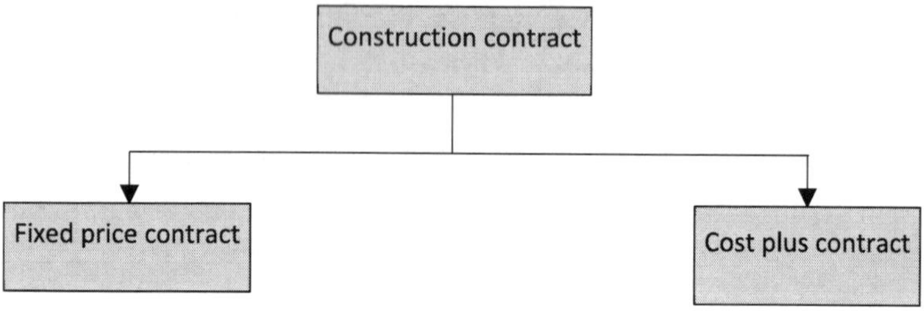


| | |
|---|---|
| ***Construction contract*** | is a contract specifically negotiated for the construction of an asset or a combination of assets that are closely interrelated or interdependent in terms of their design, technology and function or their ultimate purpose or use. |
| ***Fixed price contract*** | is a construction contract in which the contractor agrees to a fixed contract price, or a fixed rate per unit of output, which in some cases is subject to cost escalation clauses. |
| ***Cost plus contract*** | is a construction contract in which the contractor is reimbursed for allowable or otherwise defined costs, plus percentage of these costs or a fixed fee. |

## Contract Revenue

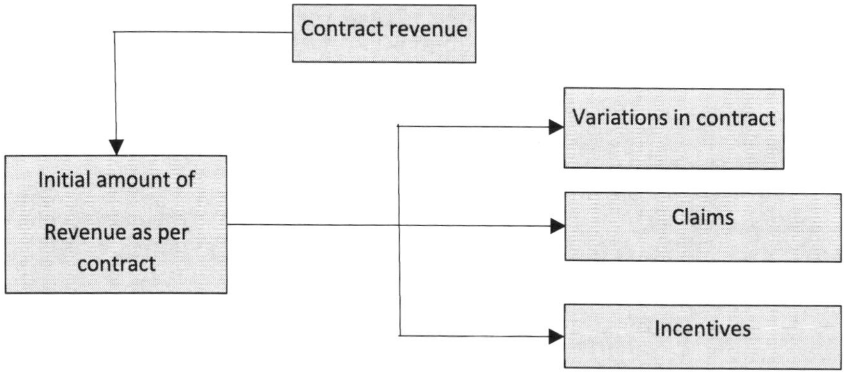


| | |
|---|---|
| ***Contract revenue:*** | (a) the initial amount of revenue agreed in the contract; and<br>(b) variations in contract work, claims and incentive payments:<br>(i) to the extent that it is probable that they will result in revenue; and<br>(ii) they are capable of being reliably measured. |
| ***Variations in contract work*** | Instructions from the customer for changes in the scope of work |
| ***Claims*** | Amounts which the contractor seeks to recover from the customer towards costs not included in the contract price |
| ***Incentives*** | Additional payments by the customer to a contractor who has met or exceeded performance standards. |

## Contract costs

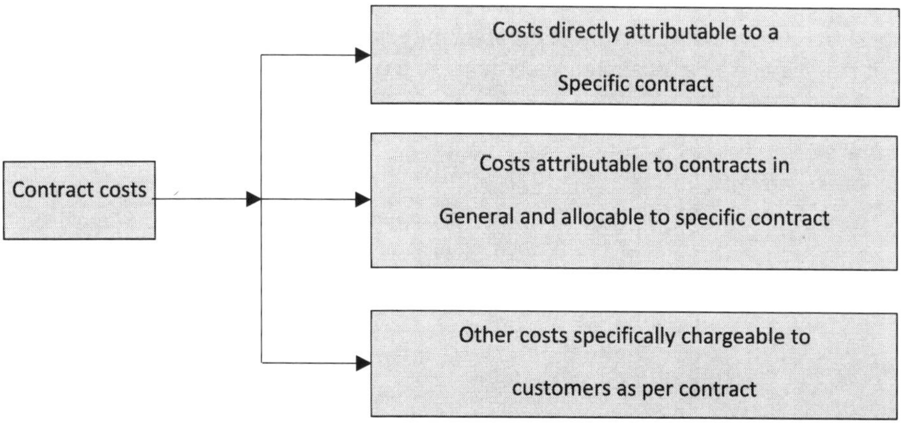

| | |
|---|---|
| ***Contract costs shall comprise:*** | (a) costs that relate directly to the specific contract;<br>(b) costs that are attributable to contract activity in general and can be allocated to the contract; and<br>(c) such other costs as are specifically chargeable to the customer under the terms of the contract. |
| ***Costs that are directly attributable to a specific contract include:*** | (a) site labour costs, including site supervision;<br>(b) costs of materials used in construction;<br>(c) depreciation of plant and equipment used on the contract;<br>(d) costs of moving plant, equipment and materials to and from the contract site<br>(e) costs of hiring plant and equipment;<br>(f) costs of design and technical assistance that is directly related to the contract;<br>(g) the estimated costs of rectification and guarantee work, including expected warranty costs; and<br>(h) claims from third parties. |

These costs may be reduced by any incidental income that is not included in contract revenue, for example income from the sale of surplus materials and the disposal of plant and equipment at the end of the contract.

| | |
|---|---|
| ***Costs that are attributable to contract activity in general and can be allocated to specific contract include:*** | (a) insurance;<br>(b) costs of design and technical assistance that are not directly related to a specific contract; and<br>(c) construction overheads.<br>(d) borrowing costs capitalised under AS 16 borrowing costs |

Such costs are allocated using methods that are systematic and rational and are applied consistently to all costs having similar characteristics. The allocation is based on the normal level of construction activity.

Construction overheads include costs such as the preparation and processing of construction personnel payroll. Costs that may be attributable to contract activity in general and can be allocated to specific contracts also include borrowing costs.

| | |
|---|---|
| ***Costs that cannot be attributed to contract activity:*** | general administration costs for which reimbursement is not specified in the contract;<br>(b) selling costs;<br>(c) research and development costs for which reimbursement is not specified in the contract; and<br>(d) depreciation of idle plant and equipment that is not used on a particular contract. |

**Process of recognition of construction contracts**

The rules of recognition are divided between the following two classes:

| When the outcome of a construction contract can be estimated reliably |
|---|
| Contract revenue and contract costs associated with the construction contract should be recognised as revenue and expenses respectively by reference to the stage of completion of the contract activity at the reporting date. An expected loss on the construction contract should be recognised as an expense immediately. |
| When the outcome of a construction contract cannot be estimated reliably, revenue should be recognised only to the extent of contract costs incurred of which recovery is probable; and contract costs should be recognised as an expense in the period in which they are incurred. |
| An expected loss on the construction contract should be recognised as an expense immediately in accordance with paragraph 35. |

The above schematic is explained diagrammatically as shown below:

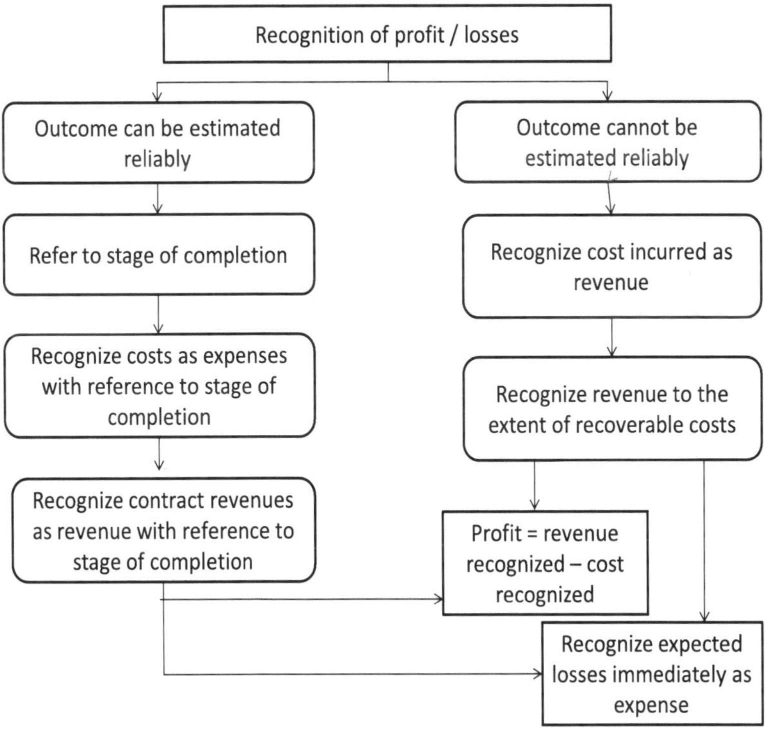

**Percentage completion method**

The recognition of revenue and expenses by reference to the stage of completion of a contract is often referred to as the percentage completion method.

Under this method, contract revenue is matched with the contract costs incurred in reaching the stage of completion, resulting in the reporting of revenue, expenses and profit which can be attributed to the proportion of work completed.

Under the percentage of completion method, contract revenue is recognised as revenue in the statement of profit and loss in the accounting periods in which the work is performed

Contract costs are usually recognised as an expense in the statement of profit and loss in the accounting periods in which the work to which they relate is performed.

Any expected excess of total contract costs over total contract revenue for the contract is recognised as an expense immediately.

The stage of completion of a contract may be determined in a variety of ways. The enterprise uses the method that measures reliably the work performed.

Depending on the nature of the contract, the methods may include:

| | |
|---|---|
| ***Methods of determination of stage of completion*** | (a) the proportion that contract costs incurred for work performed up to the reporting date bear to the estimated total contract costs; or<br>(b) surveys of work performed; or<br>(c) completion of a physical proportion of the contract work. |

Progress payments and advances received from customers may not necessarily reflect the work performed.

When the stage of completion is determined by reference to the contract costs incurred up to the reporting date, only those contract costs that reflect work performed are included in costs incurred up to the reporting date.

**Disclosure requirements**

| | |
|---|---|
| ***An enterprise should disclose: (para 38)*** | (a) the amount of contract revenue recognised as revenue in the period;<br>(b) the methods used to determine the contract revenue recognised in the period; and<br>(c) the methods used to determine the stage of completion of contracts in progress. |
| ***An enterprise should disclose the following for contracts in progress at the reporting date(para 39)*** | The aggregate amount of costs incurred and recognised profits (less recognised losses)<br>up to the reporting date;<br>(b) the amount of advances received; and<br>(c) the amount of retentions. |

| *An enterprise should present: (para 41)* | The gross amount due from customers for contract work as an asset; and the gross amount due to customers for contract work as a liability. |
|---|---|

## 8.3.6 Revenue from operations under Ind AS entities

Revenue from operations shall include the following:

(a) sale of products (including Excise Duty);

(b) sale of services.

(ba) Grants or donations received (relevant in case of section 8 companies only); and

(c) other operating revenues.

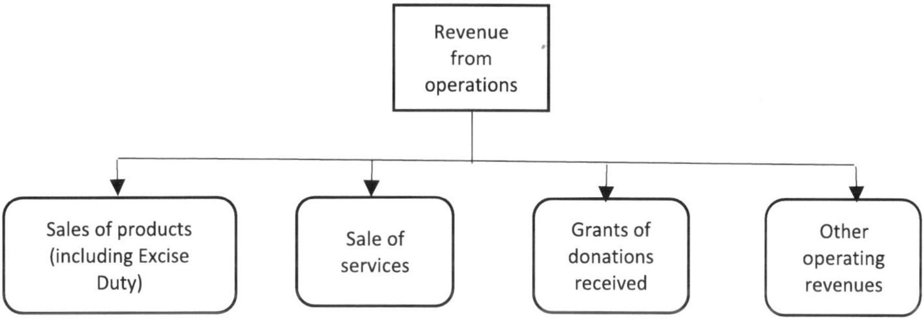


Revenue from each of the above head is presented separately by way of Notes to Accounts to the extent applicable.

In case of company rendering or supplying services, Gross income is derived from services rendered or supplied under broad head.

In case of other companies, gross income is derived from broad heads.

With respect to treatment of indirect taxes on revenue please refer section under Revenue from operations related to non Ind AS related entities explained earlier in this chapter.

### *8.3.6.1 Ind AS 115: Revenue from contract with customers*

#### Core principle

The core principle of this Standard is that an entity shall recognise revenue to depict the transfer of promised goods or services to customers in an amount that reflects the consideration to which the entity expects to be entitled in exchange for those goods or services.

An entity shall consider the terms of the contract and all relevant facts and circumstances when applying this Standard. An entity shall apply this Standard, including the use of any practical expedients, consistently to contracts with similar characteristics and in similar circumstances.

This Standard specifies the accounting for an individual contract with a customer. However, as a practical expedient, an entity may apply this Standard to a portfolio of contracts (or performance obligations) with similar characteristics if the entity reasonably expects that the effects on the financial statements of applying this Standard to the portfolio would not differ materially from applying this Standard to the individual contracts (or performance obligations) within that portfolio. When accounting for a portfolio, an entity shall use estimates and assumptions that reflect the size and composition of the portfolio.

## Recognition

The Ind AS has come up with a five-step model for recognizing revenue from contracts with customers. This is diagrammatically represented as under:

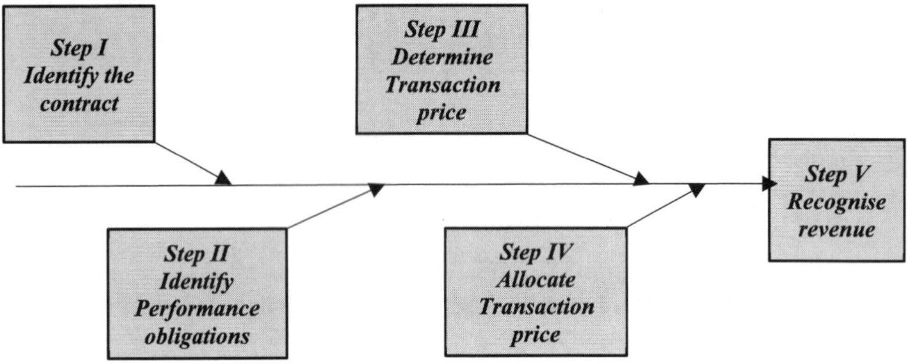


These steps are explained in the paragraphs that follow.

## Identifying the contract

An entity shall account for a contract with a customer that is within the scope of this Standard only when all of the following criteria are met:

(a) The parties to the contract have approved the contract (in writing, orally or in accordance with other customary business practices) and are committed to perform their respective obligations;

(b) The entity can identify each party's rights regarding the goods or services to be transferred;

(c) The entity can identify the payment terms for the goods or services to be transferred;

(d) the contract has commercial substance (i.e. the risk, timing or amount of the entity's future cash flows is expected to change as a result of the contract); and

(e) It is probable that the entity will collect the consideration to which it will be entitled in exchange for the goods or services that will be transferred to the customer. In evaluating whether collectability of an amount of consideration is probable, an entity shall consider only the customer's ability and intention to pay that amount of consideration when it is due. The amount of consideration to which the entity will be entitled may be less than the price stated in the contract if the consideration is variable because the entity may offer the customer a price concession.

Hence an entity shall account for a contract with a customer that is within the scope of this Ind AS only when all of the following criteria are met:

(a) the parties to the contract have approved the contract (in writing, orally or in accordance with other customary business practices) and are committed to perform their respective obligations;

↓

(b) the entity can identify each party's rights regarding the goods or services to be transferred;

↓

(c) the entity can identify the payment terms for the goods or services to be transferred;

↓

(d) the contract has commercial substance (i.e. the risk, timing or amount of the entity's future cash flows is expected to change as a result of the contract); and

↓

(e) it is probable that the entity will collect the consideration to which it will be entitled in exchange for the goods or services that will be transferred to the customer.

A contract is an agreement between two or more parties that creates enforceable rights and obligations. Enforceability of the rights and obligations in a contract is a matter of law. Contracts can be written, oral or implied by an entity's customary business practices. The practices and processes for establishing contracts with customers vary across legal jurisdictions, industries and entities. In addition, they may vary within an entity (for example, they may depend on the class of customer or the nature of the promised goods or services). An entity shall consider those practices and processes in determining whether and when an agreement with a customer creates enforceable rights and obligations.

## Combination of contract

An entity shall combine two or more contracts entered into at or near the same time with the same customer (or related parties of the customer) and account for the contracts as a single contract if one or more of the following criteria are met:

(a) the contracts are negotiated as a package with a single commercial objective;

(b) the amount of consideration to be paid in one contract depends on the price or performance of the other contract; or

(c) the goods or services promised in the contracts (or some goods or services promised in each of the contracts) are a single performance obligation.

## Contract modifications

A contract modification is a change in the scope or price (or both) of a contract that is approved by the parties to the contract. In some industries and jurisdictions, a contract modification may be described as a change order, a variation or an amendment. A contract modification exists when the parties to a contract approve a modification that either creates new or changes existing enforceable rights and obligations of the parties to the contract.

### Illustration 8.18: Revenue based on contract modification

Alpha Construction Co has been awarded a contract for the construction of a large warehouse at Rs. 2 million. The customer added to the original scope of work a generator room and a compound wall and authorised Rs. 0.4 million,

The cost of building material increased by a large margin compared to the estimated cost when the contract was signed, the contractor claimed Rs. 0.5 million separately on this count.

It was agreed by the customer that if the contract is completed within one year, then the contractor would be awarded an incentive of Rs. 0.2 million. The original contract was awarded to Alpha Construction Co on 1st April 2010 and the contractor completed the contract by 28th February 2011. Please calculate the contract revenue based on contract modification.

**Solution**

Original contract value = Rs. 2.0 million.

Variation = Rs. 0.4 million. – additional cost of generator room and compound wall

Claim = Rs. 0.5 million – increased cost of building material claimed by contractor

Incentives = Rs. 0.2 million – As the contract was completed within one year

Total contact revenue = Rs. 3.1 million (2.0 + 0.4+0.5+0.2) based on contract modification.

An entity shall account for a contract modification as a separate contract if both of the following conditions are present:

(a) the scope of the contract increases because of the addition of promised goods or services that are distinct; and

(b) the price of the contract increases by an amount of consideration that reflects the entity's stand-alone selling prices of the additional promised goods or services and any appropriate adjustments to that price to reflect the circumstances of the particular contract.

**Illustration 8.19: Extension of contract**

Speciality Chemicals Co has a 12-month agreement to provide Customer with services for which Customer pays Rs.1,000 per month. The agreement does not include any provisions for automatic extensions, and it expires on November 30, 20X6. The two parties sign a new agreement on February 28, 20X7, which requires Customer to pay Rs.1,250 per month in fees, retroactive to December 1, 20X6.

Customer continued to pay Rs.1,000 per month during December, January, and February, and Speciality Chemicals Co continued to provide services during that period. There are no performance issues being disputed between the parties in the expired period, only negotiation of rates under the new contract.

Does a contract exist in December, January, and February (prior to the new agreement being signed)?

***Analysis***

A contract appears to exist in this situation because Speciality Chemicals Co continued to provide services and Customer continued to pay Rs.1,000 per month according to the previous contract.

However, since the original arrangement expired and did not include any provision for automatic extension, determining whether a contract exists during the intervening period from December to February requires judgment and analysis of the legal enforceability of the arrangement in the relevant jurisdiction. Revenue recognition should not be deferred until the written contract is signed if there are enforceable rights and obligations established prior to the conclusion of the negotiations.

## Identifying performance obligation

At the inception of the contract, an entity shall assess the goods or services promised in a contract with a customer and shall identify as a performance obligation each promise to transfer to the customer either:

(a) a good or service (or a bundle of goods or services) that is distinct; or

(b) a series of distinct goods or services that are substantially the same and that have the same pattern of transfer to the customer.

A series of distinct goods or services has the same pattern of transfer to the customer if both of the following criteria are met:

(a) each distinct good or service in the series that the entity promises to transfer to the customer would meet the performance obligation satisfied over time; and

(b) the same method would be used to measure the entity's progress towards complete satisfaction of the performance obligation to transfer each distinct good or service in the series to the customer.

## Distinct goods and services

| | | |
|---|---|---|
| *According to Para 26 depending on the contract, promised goods or services may include, but are not limited to, the following:* | (a) | sale of goods produced by an entity (for example, inventory of a manufacturer); |
| | (b) | resale of goods purchased by an entity (for example, merchandise of a retailer); |
| | (c) | resale of rights to goods or services purchased by an entity (for example, a ticket resold by an entity acting as a principal, |
| | (d) | performing a contractually agreed-upon task (or tasks) for a customer; |
| | (e) | providing a service of standing ready to provide goods or services (for example, unspecified updates to software that are provided on a when-and-if-available basis) or of making goods or services available for a customer to use as and when the customer decides; |
| | (f) | providing a service of arranging for another party to transfer goods or services to a customer (for example, acting as an agent of another party, |
| | (g) | granting rights to goods or services to be provided in the future that a customer can resell or provide to its customer (for example, an entity selling a product to a retailer promises to transfer an additional good or service to an individual who purchases the product from the retailer), |

(h) constructing, manufacturing or developing an asset on behalf of a customer;

(i) granting licences and

(j) granting options to purchase additional goods or services (when those options provide a customer with a material right).

A good or service that is promised to a customer is distinct if both of the following criteria are met:

a) the customer can benefit from the good or service either on its own or together with other resources that are readily available to the customer (i.e. the good or service is capable of being distinct); and

(b) the entity's promise to transfer the good or service to the customer is separately identifiable from other promises in the contract (i.e. the good or service is distinct within the context of the contract).

**Illustration 8.20: Identifying performance obligations**

ABC Software Co sold a software license to one of its clients. The contract with the client states that ABC is to provide software updates and technical support for the next 3 years from the date of sale. The software remains functional without updates and technical support.

In this case ABC needs to identify distinct performance obligations in order to recognise revenue. The software is delivered to the client before providing updates and technical support and also the customer can benefit from the software distinctly on its own. Also the other parts of the contract requiring technical support and updates are separately identifiable.

On the basis of this evaluation, ABC concludes three performance obligations which are:

- Software license
- Software updates
- Technical support

### Illustration 8.21: Identifying performance obligations

ABC Ltd is a manufacturer of flat screen TV sets. It enters into a contract with a customer to sell ten TV sets. The delivery terms state that legal title and risk of loss passes to the customer when the TV sets are given to carrier. Customer requests ABC Ltd to arrange for delivery of the TV sets. ABC Ltd has a history of replacing TV sets that are damaged during transit at no additional cost to the customer.

The customer has control of the TV sets at the time they are shipped and can sell them to another party. ABC Ltd is precluded from selling the televisions to another customer (for example, redirecting the shipment) once the TV sets are picked up by the carrier at ABC Ltd's shipping dock.

How many performance obligations are in the arrangement?

***Analysis***

There are at least two performance obligations: (1) sale of the TV sets and (2) shipping service. The arrangement may include a performance obligation related to providing risk of loss service during transit of the goods.

ABC Ltd will need to determine if the shipping service and risk of loss service are distinct or if they are a bundle of services.

The shipping and any risk of loss service do not affect when the customer obtains control of the televisions. ABC Ltd's will recognise revenue allocated to the sale of the TV sets when control transfers to the customer (that is, upon shipment) and recognise revenue allocated to the shipping service and/or risk of loss service when performance occurs.

### Bundle of goods and services

If a promised good or service is not distinct, an entity shall combine that good or service with other promised goods or services until it identifies a bundle of goods or services that is distinct. In some cases, that would result in the entity accounting for all the goods or services promised in a contract as a single performance obligation.

### Illustration 8.22: Bundle of goods and service that are combined

XYZ Ltd licences customer relationship management software to a customer. In addition, Persistent promises to provide consulting services to significantly customise the software to the customer's information technology environment for total consideration of Rs.600,000.

XYZ Ltd is providing a significant service of integrating the goods and services (the licence and the consulting services) into the combined item for which the customer has contracted. In addition, the software is significantly customised by Persistent in accordance with the specifications negotiated with the customer.

Hence, XYZ Ltd would account for the licence and consulting services together as one performance obligation. Revenue for that performance obligation would be recognised over time by selecting an appropriate measure of progress towards complete satisfaction of the performance obligation.

### Illustration 8.23: Bundle of goods and services that are combined

Contractor enters into a contract to design and build a house for a new homeowner. Contractor is responsible for the overall management of the project and identifies various goods and services that are provided, including architectural design, site preparation, construction of the home, plumbing and electrical services, and finish carpentry. Contractor regularly sells these goods and services individually to customers.

How many performance obligations are in the contract?

***Analysis***

The bundle of goods and services should be combined into a single performance obligation in this fact pattern. The promised goods and services are capable of being distinct because the homeowner could benefit from the goods or services either on their own or together with other readily available resources. This is because contractor regularly sells the goods or services separately to other homeowners and the homeowner could generate economic benefit from the individual goods and services by using, consuming, or selling them.

## Determining the transaction price

An entity shall consider the terms of the contract and its customary business practices to determine the transaction price. The transaction price is the amount of consideration to which an entity expects to be entitled in exchange for transferring promised goods or services to a customer, excluding amounts collected on behalf of third parties (for example, some sales taxes).

The consideration promised in a contract with a customer may include fixed amounts, variable amounts, or both.

The determinants of transaction price are:

| ***When determining the transaction price, an entity shall consider the effects of all of the following:*** | (a) variable consideration;<br>(b) constraining estimates of variable consideration;<br>(c) the existence of a significant financing component in the contract |
|---|---|

| | |
|---|---|
| | (d) non-cash consideration; and |
| | (e) consideration payable to a customer |

## Variable consideration

(a) If the consideration promised in a contract includes a variable amount, an entity shall estimate the amount of consideration to which the entity will be entitled in exchange for transferring the promised goods or services to a customer.

(b) An amount of consideration can vary because of discounts, rebates, refunds, credits, price concessions, incentives, performance bonuses, or other similar items.

(c) The promised consideration can also vary if an entity's entitlement to the consideration is contingent on the occurrence or non-occurrence of a future event. For example, an amount of consideration would be variable if either a product was sold with a right of return or a fixed amount is promised as a performance bonus on achievement of a specified milestone.

(d) In some contracts penalties are determinants of transfer price.

(e) An entity shall estimate an amount of variable consideration by using either of the following methods, depending on which method the entity expects to better predict the amount of consideration to which it will be entitled:

    (a) The expected value—the expected value is the sum of probability-weighted amounts in a range of possible consideration amounts

    (b) The most likely amount—the most likely amount is the single most likely amount in a range of possible consideration amounts (i.e. the single most likely outcome of the contract).

## Existence of a significant financing component in a contract

In determining the transaction price, an entity shall adjust the promised amount of consideration for the effects of the time value of money if the timing of payments agreed to by the parties to the contract (either explicitly or implicitly) provides the customer or the entity with a significant benefit of financing the transfer of goods or services to the customer.

In those circumstances, the contract contains a significant financing component. A significant financing component may exist regardless of whether the promise of financing is explicitly stated in the contract or implied by the payment terms agreed to by the parties to the contract.

**Illustration 8.24: Financing component in a contract**

On 31st March 2021, Alpha sold goods for a price of Rs.12.1 million. The terms of the sale allowed the customer to extend the credit and the price was payable by the customer in cash as on 31st March 2023. Discount rate appropriate for the risk of this transaction was attributed to 10%. What would be the revenue that would be recognised?

**Solution**

In the instant case, the treatment under Ind AS 115 Revenue from Contracts with Customers would be as under:

(a) On 31st March 2021, Alpha will recognise only Rs.10 m (Rs.12.1 m/(1+10%)2 as credit to revenue and debit to receivables.

(b) On 31st March 2022, it will recognise Rs.1 m (Rs. 10 m x 10%) as finance income and debit to receivables.

(c) On 31st March 2023, it will recognise Rs.1.1 m (Rs.11 X 10%) as finance income and debit to receivables.

However, a contract with a customer would not have a significant financing component if any of the following factors exist:

(a) the customer paid for the goods or services in advance and the timing of the transfer of those goods or services is at the discretion of the customer.

(b) a substantial amount of the consideration promised by the customer is variable and the amount or timing of that consideration varies on the basis of the occurrence or non-occurrence of a future event that is not substantially within the control of the customer or the entity (for example, if the consideration is a sales-based royalty).

(c) the difference between the promised consideration and the cash selling price of the good or service arises for reasons other than the provision of finance to either the customer or the entity, and the difference between those amounts is proportional to the reason for the difference. For example, the payment terms might provide the entity or the customer with protection from the other party failing to adequately complete some or all of its obligations under the contract.

**Non-cash consideration**

(a) To determine the transaction price for contracts in which a customer promises consideration in a form other than cash, an entity shall measure the non-cash consideration (or promise of non-cash consideration) at fair value.

(b) If an entity cannot reasonably estimate the fair value of the non-cash consideration, the entity shall measure the consideration indirectly by reference to the stand-alone selling price of the goods or services promised to the customer (or class of customer) in exchange for the consideration.

**Illustration 8.25: Non-cash consideration**

> Alpha Ltd, a company engaged in manufacturing computers and laptops supplied 150 computers to Beta Ltd under a contract. In accordance with the contract Beta Ltd agreed to pay Alpha Ltd by transferring the rights to one of its patents. This patent will allow Alpha Ltd to improve the display quality of its computer screens. The fair value of patents was estimated at Rs.0.5 million. The stand-alone price of each computer is Rs.2,500.
>
> In this case Alpha Ltd will measure the non-cash consideration i.e. patents at Rs.0.5 million. If the fair value of patent was not available, then in such case, the non-cash consideration would be measured at the stand-alone selling price of computers promised i.e. Rs.2,500 x 150 computers = Rs.0.375 million.
>
> According to the Ind AS non-cash consideration is recorded at fair value.

**Allocating transaction price to performance obligation**

(i) The objective when allocating the transaction price is for an entity to allocate the transaction price to each performance obligation (or distinct good or service) in an amount that depicts the amount of consideration to which the entity expects to be entitled in exchange for transferring the promised goods or services to the customer.

(ii) To meet the allocation objective, an entity shall allocate the transaction price to each performance obligation identified in the contract on a relative stand-alone selling price basis

**Allocation based on stand-alone selling price**

(i) To allocate the transaction price to each performance obligation on a relative stand-alone selling price basis, an entity shall determine the stand-alone selling price at contract inception of the distinct good or service underlying each performance obligation in the contract and allocate the transaction price in proportion to those stand-alone selling prices.

(ii) The stand-alone selling price is the price at which an entity would sell a promised good or service separately to a customer. The best evidence of a stand-alone selling price is the observable price of a good or service when the entity sells that good or service separately in similar circumstances and to similar customers. A contractually stated price or a list price for a good or service may be (but shall not be presumed to be) the stand-alone selling price of that good or service.

(iii) Suitable methods for estimating the stand-alone selling price of a good or service include, but are not limited to, the following:

<table>
<tr><td>(a) Adjusted market assessment approach</td><td>an entity could evaluate the market in which it sells goods or services and estimate the price that a customer in that market would be willing to pay for those goods or services. Factors relevant for this approach are:<br>• Position in the market<br>• Expected profit margin<br>• Customer or geographic segments<br>• Distribution channel<br>• Cost structure</td></tr>
<tr><td>(b) Expected cost plus a margin approach</td><td>an entity could forecast its expected costs of satisfying a performance obligation and then add an appropriate margin for that good or service.<br>Factors to consider when assessing if a margin is reasonable could include:<br>• Margins achieved on standalone sales of similar products<br>• Market data related to historical margins within an industry<br>• Industry sales price averages<br>• Market conditions<br>• Profit objectives</td></tr>
<tr><td>(c) Residual approach</td><td>an entity may estimate the stand-alone selling price by reference to the total transaction price less the sum of the observable stand-alone selling prices of other goods or services promised in the contract.<br>An entity may use a residual approach to estimate … the standalone selling price of a good or service only if one of the following criteria is met:<br>1. The entity sells the same good or service to different customers (at or near the same time) for a broad range of amounts (that is, the selling price is highly variable because a representative standalone selling price is not discernible from past transactions or other observable evidence).<br>2. The entity has not yet established a price for that good or service, and the good or service has not previously been sold on a standalone basis (that is, the selling price is uncertain).</td></tr>
</table>

## Allocation of discount to stand-alone selling price

(i) A customer receives a discount for purchasing a bundle of goods or services if the sum of the stand-alone selling prices of those promised goods or services in the contract exceeds the promised consideration in a contract.

(ii) An entity shall allocate a discount entirely to one or more, but not all, performance obligations in the contract if all of the following criteria are met:

(a) the entity regularly sells each distinct good or service (or each bundle of distinct goods or services) in the contract on a stand-alone basis;

(b) the entity also regularly sells on a stand-alone basis a bundle (or bundles) of some of those distinct goods or services at a discount to the stand-alone selling prices of the goods or services in each bundle; and

(c) the discount attributable to each bundle of goods or services described in (b) above is substantially the same as the discount in the contract and an analysis of the goods or services in each bundle provides observable evidence of the performance obligation (or performance obligations) to which the entire discount in the contract belongs.

**Illustration 8.26: Allocation of stand-alone selling price**

Seagull boat services sells boats and provides mooring facilities for its customers. Seagull boat services sells the boats for Rs.30,000 each and provides mooring facilities for Rs.5,000 per year. Seagull boat services sells these goods and services separately; therefore, they are distinct and accounted for as separate performance obligations. Marine enters into a contract to sell a boat and one year of mooring services to a customer for Rs.32,500.

How should Seagull boat services allocate the transaction price of Rs.32,500 to the performance obligations?

***Analysis***

Seagull boat services should allocate the transaction price of Rs.32,500 to the boat and the mooring services based on their relative standalone selling prices as follows:

Boat: Rs.27,857 (Rs.32,500 x (Rs.30,000/Rs.35,000))

Mooring services: Rs.4,643 (Rs.32,500 x (Rs.5,000/Rs.35,000))

The allocation results in the Rs.2,500 discount being allocated proportionately to the two performance obligations.

**Illustration 8.27: Allocating transaction price – allocating discount**

ABC Ltd enters into an arrangement with its customer to sell product A, B, and C for Rs.5,400. ABC Ltd regularly sells each product on a standalone basis: A for Rs.2,000, B for Rs.3,000, and C for Rs.1,000. The customer receives Rs.600 discount (Rs.6,000 sum of standalone selling prices less Rs.5,400 transaction price) for buying the bundle of products. The product A and B will be delivered on March 28 and product C on April 3. ABC Ltd regularly sells product A and B together as a bundle for Rs.4,400 (that is, at a Rs.600 discount to the standalone selling prices of the two items). Product C is not normally discounted.

How should Retailer allocate the transaction price to the products?

***Analysis***

ABC Ltd has observable evidence that the Rs.600 discount should be allocated to only

Product A and B. The products A and B are regularly sold together for Rs.4,400, and Product C is regularly sold for Rs.1,000.

ABC Ltd therefore allocates the Rs.5,400 transaction price as follows:

Product A and B: Rs.4,400

Product C : Rs.1,000

## Changes in transaction price

(i) After contract inception, the transaction price can change for various reasons, including the resolution of uncertain events or other changes in circumstances that change the amount of consideration to which an entity expects to be entitled in exchange for the promised goods or services.

(ii) An entity shall allocate to the performance obligations in the contract any subsequent changes in the transaction price on the same basis as at contract inception. Consequently, an entity shall not reallocate the transaction price to reflect changes in stand-alone selling prices after contract inception. Amounts allocated to a satisfied performance obligation shall be recognised as revenue, or as a reduction of revenue, in the period in which the transaction price changes.

## Satisfaction of performance obligation

(i) An entity shall recognise revenue when the entity satisfies a performance obligation by transferring a promised good or service (i.e. an asset) to a customer. An asset is transferred when (or as) the customer obtains control of that asset. (Para 31)

For each performance obligation identified in a contract, an entity shall determine at contract inception whether

(a) it satisfies the performance obligation over time or

(b) satisfies the performance obligation

at a point in time (in accordance with paragraph 38). If an entity does not satisfy a performance obligation over time, the performance obligation is satisfied at a point in time.

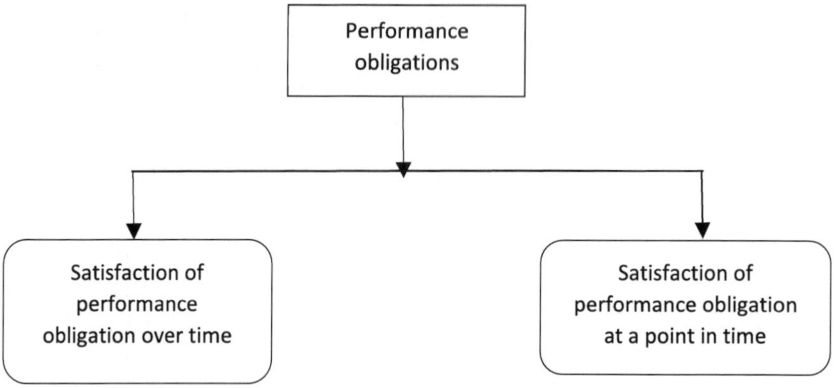


(ii) Goods and services are assets, even if only momentarily, when they are received and used (as in the case of many services). Control of an asset refers to the ability to direct the use of, and obtain substantially all of the remaining benefits from, the asset.

Control includes the ability to prevent other entities from directing the use of, and obtaining the benefits from, an asset. The benefits of an asset are the potential cash flows (inflows or savings in outflows) that can be obtained directly or indirectly in many ways, such as by:

(a) using the asset to produce goods or provide services (including public services);

(b) using the asset to enhance the value of other assets;

(c) using the asset to settle liabilities or reduce expenses;

(d) selling or exchanging the asset;

(e) pledging the asset to secure a loan; and

(f) holding the asset.

Control of an asset represented by:

(a) using the asset to produce goods or Provide services (including public services);
(b) using the asset to enhance the value of other assets,
(c) using the asset to settle liabilities or reduce expenses,
(d) selling or exchanging the asset,
(e) pledging the asset to secure a loan; and
(f) holding the asset.

### Performance obligations satisfied over time

An entity transfers control of a good or service over time and, therefore, satisfies a performance obligation and recognises revenue over time, if one of the following criteria is met:

(a) the customer simultaneously receives and consumes the benefits provided by the entity's performance as the entity performs;

(b) the entity's performance creates or enhances an asset (for example, work in progress) that the customer controls as the asset is created or enhanced or

(c) the entity's performance does not create an asset with an alternative use to the entity and the entity has an enforceable right to payment for performance completed to date (paragraph 35).

### Methods of measuring progress towards complete satisfaction of a performance obligation

Methods that can be used to measure an entity's progress towards complete satisfaction of a performance obligation satisfied over time in accordance with paragraphs 35–37 include the following:

| | |
|---|---|
| (a) output methods; | Output methods recognise revenue on the basis of direct measurements of the value to the customer of the goods or services transferred to date relative to the remaining goods or services promised under the contract |
| (b) input methods; | Input methods recognise revenue on the basis of the entity's efforts or inputs to the satisfaction of a performance obligation (for example, resources consumed, labour hours expended, costs incurred, time elapsed or machine hours used) relative to the total expected inputs to the satisfaction of that performance obligation. If the entity's efforts or inputs are expended evenly throughout the performance period, it may be appropriate for the entity to recognise revenue on a straight-line basis. |

### Performance obligations satisfied at a point in time

To determine the point in time at which a customer obtains control of a promised asset and the entity satisfies a performance obligation, the entity shall consider the requirements for control in paragraphs 31–34. In addition, an entity shall consider indicators of the transfer of control, which include, but are not limited to, the following:

(a) The entity has a present right to payment for the asset

(b) The customer has legal title to the asset

(c) The entity has transferred physical possession of the asset

(d) The customer has the significant risks and rewards of ownership of the asset

(e) The customer has accepted the asset

### Measuring progress towards complete satisfaction of a performance obligation

For each performance obligation satisfied over time, an entity shall recognise revenue over time by measuring the progress towards complete satisfaction of that performance obligation.

An entity shall apply a single method of measuring progress for each performance obligation satisfied over time and the entity shall apply that method consistently to similar performance obligations and in similar circumstances. At the end of each reporting period, an entity shall re-measure its progress towards complete satisfaction of a performance obligation satisfied over time. Appropriate methods of measuring progress include output methods and input methods.

As circumstances change over time, an entity shall update its measure of progress to reflect any changes in the outcome of the performance obligation. Such changes to an entity's measure of progress shall be accounted for as a change in accounting estimate in accordance with Ind AS 8, Accounting Policies, Changes in Accounting Estimates and Errors.

### Contract asset

An entity's right to consideration in exchange for goods or services that the entity has transferred to a customer when that right is conditioned on something other than the passage of time (for example, the entity's future performance).

### Contract liability

An entity's obligation to transfer goods or services to a customer for which the entity has received consideration (or the amount is due) from the customer.

## Costs to fulfil a contract

| | |
|---|---|
| ***Para 95. Contract costs shall comprise:*** | (a) The costs relate directly to a contract or to an anticipated contract that the entity can specifically identify<br>(b) The costs generate or enhance resources of the entity that will be used in satisfying (or in continuing to satisfy) performance obligations in the future; and<br>(c) The costs are expected to be recovered. |
| ***Costs that relate directly to a specific contract include:*** | (a) Direct labour (for example, salaries and wages of employees who provide the promised services directly to the customer);<br>(b) Direct materials (for example, supplies used in providing the promised services to a customer);<br>(c) Allocations of costs that relate directly to the contract or to contract activities (for example, costs of contract management and supervision, insurance and depreciation of tools and equipment used in fulfilling the contract);<br>(d) Costs that are explicitly chargeable to the customer under the contract; and<br>(e) Other costs that are incurred only because an entity entered into the contract (for example, payments to subcontractors). |
| ***An entity shall recognise the following costs as expenses when incurred:*** | (a) General and administrative costs (unless those costs are explicitly chargeable to the customer under the contract, in which case an entity shall evaluate those costs in accordance with paragraph 97);<br>(b) Costs of wasted materials, labour or other resources to fulfil the contract that were not reflected in the price of the contract;<br>(c) Costs that relate to satisfied performance obligations (or partially satisfied performance obligations) in the contract (i.e. costs that relate to past performance); and<br>(d) costs for which an entity cannot distinguish whether the costs relate to unsatisfied performance obligations or to satisfied performance obligations (or partially satisfied performance obligations). |

## Revenue recognition

When (or as) a performance obligation is satisfied, an entity shall recognise as revenue the amount of the transaction price (which excludes estimates of variable consideration that are constrained) that is allocated to that performance obligation.

### Presentation

When either party to a contract has performed, an entity shall present the contract in the balance sheet as a contract asset or a contract liability, depending on the relationship between the entity's performance and the customer's payment. An entity shall present any unconditional rights to consideration separately as a receivable.

### Disaggregation of revenue

(a) An entity shall disaggregate revenue recognised from contracts with customers into categories that depict how the nature, amount, timing and uncertainty of revenue and cash flows are affected by economic factors. An entity shall apply the guidance provided by the Ind AS when selecting the categories to use to disaggregate revenue.

(b) In addition, an entity shall disclose sufficient information to enable users of financial statements to understand the relationship between the disclosure of disaggregated revenue (in accordance with paragraph 114) and revenue information that is disclosed for each reportable segment, if the entity applies Ind AS 108, Operating Segments.

### Contract balance

(i) An entity shall disclose all of the following:

   (a) the opening and closing balances of receivables, contract assets and contract liabilities from contracts with customers, if not otherwise separately presented or disclosed;

   (b) revenue recognised in the reporting period that was included in the contract liability balance at the beginning of the period; and

   (c) revenue recognised in the reporting period from performance obligations satisfied (or partially satisfied) in previous periods (for example, changes in transaction price).

(ii) An entity shall provide an explanation of the significant changes in the contract asset and the contract liability balances during the reporting period. The explanation shall include qualitative and quantitative information.

   Examples of changes in the entity's balances of contract assets and contract liabilities include any of the following:

   (a) changes due to business combinations;

   (b) cumulative catch-up adjustments to revenue that affect the corresponding contract asset or contract liability, including adjustments arising from a change in the measure of progress, a change in an estimate of the transaction price (including any changes in the assessment of whether an estimate of variable consideration is constrained) or a contract modification;

(c) impairment of a contract asset;

(d) a change in the time frame for a right to consideration to become unconditional (i.e. for a contract asset to be reclassified to a receivable); and

(e) a change in the time frame for a performance obligation to be satisfied (i.e. for the recognition of revenue arising from a contract liability).

### Performance Obligation

An entity shall disclose information about its performance obligations in contracts with customers, including a description of all of the following:

(a) when the entity typically satisfies its performance obligations (for example, upon shipment, upon delivery, as services are rendered or upon completion of service), including when performance obligations are satisfied in a bill-and-hold arrangement;

(b) the significant payment terms (for example, when payment is typically due, whether the contract has a significant financing component, whether the consideration amount is variable and whether the estimate of variable consideration is typically constrained in accordance with paragraphs 56–58);

(c) the nature of the goods or services that the entity has promised to transfer, highlighting any performance obligations to arrange for another party to transfer goods or services (i.e. if the entity is acting as an agent);

(d) obligations for returns, refunds and other similar obligations; and

(e) types of warranties and related obligations.

### Transaction price allocated to the remaining performance obligations

An entity shall disclose the following information about its remaining performance obligations:

(a) the aggregate amount of the transaction price allocated to the performance obligations that are unsatisfied (or partially unsatisfied) as of the end of the reporting period; and

(b) an explanation of when the entity expects to recognise as revenue the amount disclosed, which the entity shall disclose in either of the following ways:

    (i) on a quantitative basis using the time bands that would be most appropriate for the duration of the remaining performance obligations; or

    (ii) by using qualitative information.

### Determining the timing of satisfaction of performance obligations

For performance obligations that an entity satisfies over time, an entity shall disclose both of the following:

(a) the methods used to recognise revenue (for example, a description of the output methods or input methods used and how those methods are applied); and

(b) an explanation of why the methods used provide a faithful depiction of the transfer of goods or services.

For performance obligations satisfied at a point in time, an entity shall disclose the significant judgements made in evaluating when a customer obtains control of promised goods or services.

### Determining the transaction price and amounts allocated to performance obligations

(i) An entity shall disclose information about the methods, inputs and assumptions used for all of the following:

  (a) determining the transaction price, which includes, but is not limited to, estimating variable consideration, adjusting the consideration for the effects of the time value of money and measuring non-cash consideration;

  (b) assessing whether an estimate of variable consideration is constrained;

  (c) allocating the transaction price, including estimating stand-alone selling prices of promised goods or services and allocating discounts and variable consideration to a specific part of the contract (if applicable); and

  (d) measuring obligations for returns, refunds and other similar obligations.

(ii) An entity shall reconcile the amount of revenue recognised in the statement of profit and loss with the contracted price showing separately each of the adjustments made to the contract price, for example, on account of discounts, rebates, refunds, credits, price concessions, incentives, performance bonuses, etc., specifying the nature and amount of each such adjustment separately.

### Assets recognized from the costs to obtain or fulfil a contract with customer

(i) An entity shall describe both of the following:

  (a) the judgements made in determining the amount of the costs incurred to obtain or fulfil a contract with a customer; and

  (b) the method it uses to determine the amortisation for each reporting period.

(ii) An entity shall disclose all of the following:

(a) the closing balances of assets recognised from the costs incurred to obtain or fulfil a contract with a customer, by main category of asset (for example, costs to obtain contracts with customers, pre-contract costs and setup costs); and

(b) the amount of amortisation and any impairment losses recognised in the reporting period.

**Illustration 8.28: Accounting policy: Revenue**

The Company manufactures and sells a range of steel and other products.

**Sale of products**

Revenue from sale of products is recognized when control of the products has transferred, being when the products are delivered to the customer. Delivery occurs when the products have been shipped or delivered to the specific location as the case may be, the risks of loss has been transferred, and either the customer has accepted the products in accordance with the sales contract, or the Company has objective evidence that all criteria for acceptance have been satisfied. Sale of products include related ancillary services, if any.

Goods are often sold with volume discounts based on aggregate sales over a 12 months period. Revenue from these sales is recognised based on the price specified in the contract, net of the estimated volume discounts. Accumulated experience is used to estimate and provide for the discounts, using the most likely method, and revenue is only recognised to the extent that it is highly probable that a significant reversal will not occur. A liability is recognized for expected volume discounts payable to customers in relation to sales made until the end of the reporting period. No element of financing is deemed present as the sales are generally made with a credit term of 30-90 days, which is consistent with market practice.

Any obligation to provide a refund is recognized as a provision.

A receivable is recognized when the goods are delivered as this is the point in time that the consideration is unconditional because only the passage of time is required before the payment is due.

The Company does not have any contracts where the period between the transfer of the promised goods or services to the customer and payment by the customer exceeds one year.

As a consequence, the Company does not adjust any of the transaction prices for the time value of money.

**Sale of power**

Revenue from sale of power is recognized when the services are provided to the customer based on approved tariff rates established by the respective regulatory authorities. The Company doesn't recognize revenue and an asset for cost incurred in the past that will be recovered.

(*Source: Tata Steel: Annual Report 2019-20*)

**Illustration 8.29: Accounting policy: Revenue**

**Revenue recognition**

The Company recognises revenue from contracts with customers when it satisfies a performance obligation by transferring promised good or service to a customer. The revenue is recognised to the extent of transaction price allocated to the performance obligation satisfied. Performance obligation is satisfied over time when the transfer of control of asset (good or service) to a customer is done over time and in other cases, performance obligation is satisfied at a point in time. For performance obligation satisfied over time, the revenue recognition is done by measuring the progress towards complete satisfaction of performance obligation. The progress is measured in terms of a proportion of actual cost incurred to-date, to the total estimated cost attributable to the performance obligation.

Transaction price is the amount of consideration to which the Company expects to be entitled in exchange for transferring good or service to a customer excluding amounts collected on behalf of a third party. Variable consideration is estimated using the expected value method or most likely amount as appropriate in a given circumstance. Payment terms agreed with a customer are as per business practice and there is no financing component involved in the transaction price.

Costs to obtain a contract which are incurred regardless of whether the contract was obtained are charged-off in Statement of Profit and Loss immediately in the period in which such costs are incurred. Incremental costs of obtaining a contract, if any, and costs incurred to fulfil a contract are amortised over the period of execution of the contract in proportion to the progress measured in terms of a proportion of actual cost incurred to-date, to the total estimated cost attributable to the performance obligation.

Significant judgments are used in:

1. Determining the revenue to be recognised in case of performance obligation satisfied over a period of time; revenue recognition is done by measuring the progress towards complete satisfaction of performance obligation. The progress is measured in terms of a proportion of actual cost incurred to-date, to the total estimated cost attributable to the performance obligation.
2. Determining the expected losses, which are recognised in the period in which such losses become probable based on the expected total contract cost as at the reporting date.

(i) Revenue from operations Revenue includes adjustments made towards liquidated damages and variation wherever applicable. Escalation and other claims, which are not ascertainable/acknowledged by customers are not taken into account.

A. Revenue from sale of goods including contracts for supply/commissioning of complex plant and equipment is recognised as follows:

Revenue from sale of manufactured and traded goods is recognised when the control of the same is transferred to the customer and it is probable that the Company will collect the consideration to which it is entitled for the exchanged goods.

Performance obligations in respect of contracts for sale of manufactured and traded goods is considered as satisfied at a point in time when the control of the same is transferred to the customer and where there is an alternative use of the asset or the Company does not have either explicit or implicit right of payment for performance completed till date.

In case where there is no alternative use of the asset and the Company has either explicit or implicit right of payment considering legal precedents, performance obligation is considered as satisfied over a period of time and revenue is recognised over time.

B. Revenue from construction/project related activity is recognised as follows:

1. Cost plus contracts: Revenue from cost plus contracts is recognised over time and is determined with reference to the extent performance obligations have been satisfied. The amount of transaction price allocated to the performance obligations satisfied represents the recoverable costs incurred during the period plus the margin as agreed with the customer.

2. Fixed price contracts: Contract revenue is recognised over time to the extent of performance obligation satisfied and control is transferred to the customer. Contract revenue is recognised at allocable transaction price which represents the cost of work performed on the contract plus proportionate margin, using the percentage of completion method. Percentage of completion is the proportion of cost of work performed to-date, to the total estimated contract costs.

Impairment loss (termed as provision for foreseeable losses in the financial statements) is recognised in the Statement of Profit and Loss to the extent the carrying amount of the contract asset exceeds the remaining amount of consideration that the Company expects to receive towards remaining performance obligations (after deducting the costs that relate directly to fulfill such remaining performance obligations). In addition, the Company recognises impairment loss (termed as provision for expected credit loss on contract assets in the financial statements) on account of credit risk in respect of a contract asset using expected credit loss model on similar basis as applicable to trade receivables.

For contracts where the aggregate of contract cost incurred to date plus recognised profits (or minus recognised losses as the case may be) exceeds the progress billing, the surplus is shown as contract asset and termed as "Due from customers". For contracts where progress billing exceeds the aggregate of contract costs incurred to-date plus recognised profits (or minus recognised losses, as the case may be), the surplus is shown as contract liability and termed as "Due to customers". Amounts received before the related work is performed are disclosed in the Balance Sheet as contract liability and termed as "Advances from customer". The amounts billed on customer for work performed and are unconditionally due for payment i.e only passage of time is required before payment falls due, are disclosed in the Balance Sheet as trade receivables. The amount of retention money held by the customers pending completion of performance milestone is disclosed as part of contract asset and is reclassified as trade receivables when it becomes due for payment.

C. Revenue from property development activities is recognised when performance obligation is satisfied, customer obtains control of the property transferred and a reasonable expectation of collection of the sale consideration from the customer exists. The costs incurred on property development activities are carried as "Inventories" till such time the aforesaid conditions are fulfilled.

D. Revenue from rendering of services is recognised over time as and when the customer receives the benefit of the Company's performance and the Company has an enforceable right to payment for services transferred. Unbilled revenue represents value of services performed in accordance with the contract terms but not billed.

E. Revenue from contracts for rendering of engineering design services and other services which are directly related to the construction of an asset is recognised on the same basis as stated in (B) supra.

F. Commission income is recognised as and when the terms of the contract are fulfilled.

G. Other operational revenue represents income earned from the activities incidental to the business and is recognised when the performance obligation is satisfied and right to receive the income is established as per the terms of the contract.

(ii) Other income

A. Interest income on investments and loans is accrued on a time basis by reference to the principal outstanding and the effective interest rate including interest on investments classified as fair value through Profit or Loss or fair value through

Other Comprehensive Income. Interest receivable on customer dues is recognised as income in the Statement of Profit and Loss on accrual basis provided there is no uncertainty towards its realisation.

B. Dividend income is accounted in the period in which the right to receive the same is established.

C. Government grants, which are revenue in nature and are towards compensation for the qualifying costs, incurred by the Company, are recognised as other income in the Statement of Profit and Loss in the period in which such costs are incurred. Government grant receivable in the form of duty credit scrips is recognised as other income in the Statement of Profit and Loss in the period in which the application is made to the government authorities and to the extent there is no uncertainty towards its receipt.

D. Other items of income are accounted as and when the right to receive such income arises and it is probable that the economic benefits will flow to the Company and the amount of income can be measured reliably.

(*Larsen & Toubro Annual Report 2019-20*)

## 8.4 OTHER INCOME

Other income is classified as:

(a) Interest Income;
(b) Dividend Income;
(c) Other non-operating income (net of expenses directly attributable to such income).

### 8.4.1 Presentation of Other Income under non Ind AS entities

- Other income items would include all kinds of interest income, dividend income and net gain on sale of investments separately for Current as well as Long-term Investments as required by AS13 "Accounting for Investments".
- For other non-operating income, income should be disclosed under this head net off expenses directly attributable to such income. However, the expenses so netted off should be separately disclosed

(*Source: ICAI Guidance Note on Schedule III for non Ind AS entities*)

### 8.4.2 Presentation of Other Income under Ind AS entities

- According to Ind AS 107, paragraph 20(b), total interest revenue calculated using the effective interest method for financial assets that are measured at amortized cost and that are measured at FVOCI, to be shown separately.
- Further, Ind AS 107 para B5(e) stipulates an entity to disclose whether interest income on financial assets measured at FVTPL is included as a part of fair value changes.

- According to paragraph 20(a) of Ind AS 107, the fair value gains or losses (net) on financial assets which are measured at FVTPL should be presented under 'Other non-operating income' with the following line items:
  - Investments classified at FVTPL
  - Investments designated at FVTPL
  - Derivatives at FVTPL
  - Other Financial Instruments classified as FVTPL
  - Other Financial Instruments designated at FVTPL
  - Reclassification adjustments
  - Realised gain on debt investments classified as FVOCI
  - Others (to be specified)

  (*Source: ICAI Guidance Note on Schedule III for Ind AS entities*)

**Illustration 8.30: Other income – specimen format**

| | As at 31st March 2022 | As at 31st March 2021 |
|---|---|---|
| Interest Income; | | |
| Bank deposits | | |
| Debt instruments | | |
| Other Financial Assets measured at amortized cost | | |
| Others | | |
| Dividend Income; | | |
| Other non-operating income (net of expenses directly attributable to such income). | | |
| Investment classified at FVTPL | | |
| Investment designated at FVTPL | | |
| Derivatives at FVTPL | | |
| Other Financial Instruments classified at FVTPL | | |
| Other Financial Instruments designated at FVTPL | | |
| Reclassification adjustments | | |
| Realised gain on debt investments classified as FVOCI | | |
| Others (to be specified) | | |
| Gain on Financial Assets | | |
| Realized gain | | |
| Unrealized gain/loss | | |
| Total | xxx | xxx |

## 8.5 OTHER OPERATING REVENUE VIS-À-VIS OTHER INCOME

At the outset it is to be noted that Other Operating Revenue has not been defined by Schedule III. According to Guidance Note on Revised Schedule VI issued by ICAI, Other Operating Revenue would include revenue arising from a company's operating activities, but which is not part of revenue arising from the sale of products or rendering of services.

Whether a particular income in question would be comprised of Other Operating Revenue or Other Income would be decided based on facts of each case and detailed understanding of the company's activities. The classification of income would depend on the purpose for which the particular asset is acquired or held.

**Illustration 8.31: Other Operating Revenue**

| An industrial conglomerate engaged in manufacture and sale of industrial and consumer products also has a real estate vertical. If the real estate vertical is continuously engaged in leasing of real estate properties, the rent arising from leasing of real estate is likely to be "Other Operating Revenue". |
|---|

**Illustration 8.32: Other Income**

| A company owns a building having fifteen stories. The company uses ten stories of the building for its business and corporate use and leases out the balance five floors. The rent received from these five floors would not be a part of Other Operating Revenue but would be included under "Other Income". |
|---|

**Illustration 8.33: Other Operating Revenue**

| Sale of manufacturing scrap arising out of the operations for a manufacturing company should be treated as Other Operating Revenue since the same arises on account of the company's main operating activity. |
|---|

**Illustration 8.34: Other Income**

| Sale of fixed assets is not an operating activity of a company, and hence, profit on sales of fixed assets should be classified as Other Income and not Other Operating Revenue. |
|---|

**Illustration 8.35: Other Income**

| Net gain out of foreign exchange transactions should be classified as Other Income, the reason being the income has not been generated out of the business |
|---|

| operations of the income i.e. sale of products or rendering of services but owing to fluctuation in foreign exchange rates. However, same would not be the case if the company deals in foreign exchange business. |
|---|

Whether an item should be classified as "other operating revenue" or "other income" is a matter of judgment and requires consideration of specific facts. In a number of cases, the dividing line between these two items may be very blur. It requires an exercise of significant judgment.

## 8.6 OTHER COMPREHENSIVE INCOME

Other comprehensive income shall be classified into:

| (A) Items that will not be reclassified to profit or loss | (B) Items that will be reclassified to profit or loss |
|---|---|
| (i) Changes in revaluation surplus;<br>(ii) Re-measurements of the defined benefit plans;<br>(iii) Equity Instruments through Other Comprehensive Income;<br>(iv) Fair value changes relating to own credit risk;<br>(v) Share of Other Comprehensive Income in Associates and Joint Ventures, to the extent not to be classified into profit or loss;<br>(vi) Others (specify nature). | (i) Exchange differences in translating the financial statements of a foreign operation;<br>(ii) Debt Instruments through Other Comprehensive Income;<br>(iii) The effective portion of gains and loss on hedging instruments in a cash flow hedge;<br>(iv) Share of Other Comprehensive Income in Associates and Joint Ventures, to the extent to be classified into profit or loss;<br>(v) Others (specify nature). |

**Illustration 8.36: Other comprehensive income – specimen format**

| | | | As at 31st March 2022 | As at 31st March 2021 |
|---|---|---|---|---|
| (A) | Items that will not be reclassified to profit or loss | | | |
| | (i) | Changes in revaluation surplus; | xxx | xxx |
| | (ii) | Re-measurements of the defined benefit plans; | xxx | xxx |
| | (iii) | Equity Instruments through Other Comprehensive Income; | xxx | xxx |

| | As at 31st March 2022 | As at 31st March 2021 |
|---|---|---|
| (iv) Fair value changes relating to own credit risk; | xxx | xxx |
| (v) Share of Other Comprehensive Income in Associates and Joint Ventures, to the extent not to be classified into profit or loss; | xxx | xxx |
| (vi) Others (specify nature). | xxx | xxx |
| (B) Items that will be reclassified to profit or loss | | |
| (i) Exchange differences in translating the financial statements of a foreign operation; | xxx | xxx |
| (ii) Debt Instruments through Other Comprehensive Income; | xxx | xxx |
| (iii) The effective portion of gains and loss on hedging instruments in a cash flow hedge; | xxx | xxx |
| (iv) Share of Other Comprehensive Income in Associates and Joint Ventures, to the extent to be classified into profit or loss; | xxx | xxx |
| (v) Others (specify nature). | xxx | xxx |
| Total | xxx | Xxx |

## 8.7 EXPENSES

| Constituents of expenses | • Cost of materials consumed<br>• Purchases of stock – in – trade<br>• Changes in inventories of finished goods, work in progress and stock in trade |
|---|---|

| | |
|---|---|
| | • Employee benefits expense<br>• Finance costs<br>• Depreciation and amortisation expenses<br>• Other expenses |

### 8.7.1 Cost of materials consumed

Similar to requirements in Schedule III, Division I, Cost of material consumed (manufacturing companies) would need to be disclosed as under:

– Raw materials under broad heads. In this case, if a company falls under more than one category, it shall be sufficient compliance with the requirements, if purchases, sales and consumption of raw material and gross income from services rendered is shown under broad heads.

### 8.7.2 Purchases of stock-in-trade

Similar to requirements in Schedule III, Division I, Purchases of stock-in-trade (trading companies)

– Goods traded in by the company under the broad heads

**Note:**

(a) In case, if a company falls under more than one category, it shall be sufficient compliance with the requirements, if purchase, sales and consumption of raw materials and gross income from services rendered is shown under broad heads.

(b) In case of Work-in-progress, Work-in-progress under broad heads

### 8.7.3 Changes in inventories of finished goods, work-in-progress and stock-in-trade

According to Guidance Note on Schedule III issued by ICAI, since Schedule III of Companies Act 2013 provides a note stating that, broad heads would be decided taking into account the concept of materiality and presentation of true and fair view of financial statements, a company may consider the following in deciding the disclosures required:

(a) Apparently, there is no need to provide quantitative details for any of the items

(b) Considering ambiguity and on a conservative interpretation, a manufacturing company may disclose the following under broad heads:

– consumption of major items of raw materials (including other items classified as raw material such as intermediates/components/packing materials)

– goods purchased for trading (if any)

- though the Schedule III does not specifically require, it is also suggested to disclosed major items of opening and closing stock, though it is not mandatory
- considering the requirement to disclose gross income in case of a service company and sales in case of a company falling under more than one category, disclosure of sales of finished goods should also be made under broad heads

(c) The term "broad heads" may be interpreted to mean broad categories of raw materials, goods purchased, etc. These categories should be decided based on the nature of each business and other facts and circumstances. Normally, 10 per cent of total value of sales/services, purchases of trading goods and consumption of raw material is considered as an acceptable threshold for determination of broad heads. Any other thresholds can also be considered taking into account the concept of materiality and presentation of true and fair view of financial statements.

(d) Similar principle may be followed to decide disclosure requirement in other cases.

**Illustration 8.37: Cost of materials consumed: Specimen format**

(a) Manufacturing company: Consumption (Amount in Rs.)

| Particulars | For the year ended 31st March 2022 | For the year ended 31st March 2021 |
|---|---|---|
| **Raw materials** | | |
| Raw materials A | XXX | XXX |
| Raw materials B | XXX | XXX |
| Others | XXX | XXX |
| TOTAL | XXX | XXX |

(b) Manufacturing company: Purchases (Amount in Rs.)

| Particulars | For the year ended 31st March 2022 | For the year ended 31st March 2021 |
|---|---|---|
| **Goods purchased** | | |
| Traded item A | XXX | XXX |
| Traded item B | XXX | XXX |
| Others | XXX | XXX |
| TOTAL | XXX | XXX |

(c) Manufacturing company (Amount in Rs.)

| Particulars | Sales value | Closing inventory | Opening inventory |
|---|---|---|---|
| **Manufactured goods** | | | |
| Finished goods A | XXX<br>(XXX) | XXX<br>(XXX) | XXX<br>(XXX) |
| Finished goods B | XXX<br>(XXX) | XXX<br>(XXX) | XXX<br>(XXX) |
| Others | XXX<br>(XXX) | XXX<br>(XXX) | XXX<br>(XXX) |
| TOTAL | XXX<br>(XXX) | XXX<br>(XXX) | XXX<br>(XXX) |

(d) Manufacturing company: Work in progress (Amount in Rs.)

| Particulars | As at 31st March 2022 | As at 31st March 2021 |
|---|---|---|
| **Work in progress** | | |
| Goods A | XXX | XXX |
| Goods B | XXX | XXX |
| Others | XXX | XXX |
| TOTAL | XXX | XXX |

(e) Trading company: (Amount in Rs.)

| Particulars | For the year ended 31st March 2022 | For the year ended 31st March 2021 |
|---|---|---|
| **Traded goods** | | |
| Traded goods A | XXX | XXX |
| Traded goods B | XXX | XXX |
| Others | XXX | XXX |
| TOTAL | XXX | XXX |

(f) Service company: (Amount in Rs.)

| Particulars | For the year ended 31st March 2022 | For the year ended 31st March 2021 |
|---|---|---|
| **Services rendered** | | |
| Service A | | |
| Service B | XXX | XXX |
| Others | XXX | XXX |
| | XXX | XXX |
| TOTAL | XXX | XXX |

## 8.7.4 Employee Benefit expenses

Schedule III, Division I, Part II, Clause (i) (a) Employee Benefits Expense showing separately

(i) salaries and wages,

(ii) contribution to provident and other funds,

(iii) expense on Employee Stock Option Scheme (ESOP) and Employee Stock Purchase Plan (ESPP),

(iv) staff welfare expenses.

### *8.7.4.1 Employee Benefits (for non Ind AS entities)*

**Employee benefits**

(a) Short term benefits e.g. wages, salaries, annual leave and sick leave, profit sharing bonuses etc. (payable within 12 months of the year-end) and non-monetary benefits of current employees

(b) Post-employment benefits (e.g. pension, provident fund, gratuity, post-employment medical care etc.)

(c) Long term employee benefits (e.g. long service awards, long-term disability benefits, bonus not payable within 12 months etc)

(d) Termination benefits (e.g. VRS payments)

**Short term benefits**

Please refer to the chart given below which explains short term employee benefits.

## AS 15 : Employee Benefits

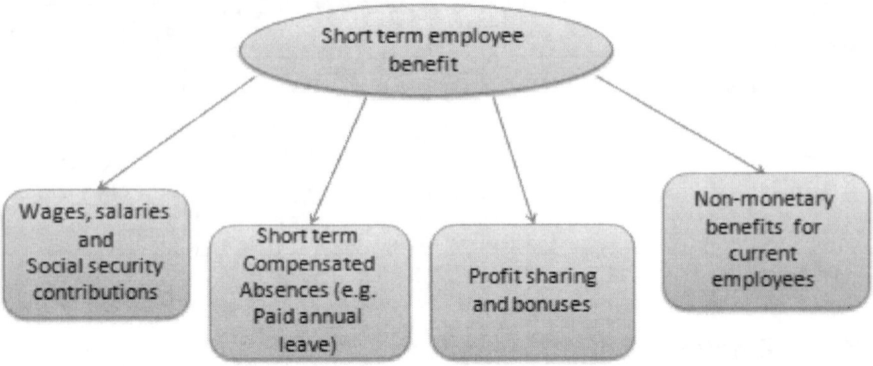


**Accounting for short-term employee benefits is generally straightforward because no actuarial assumptions are required to measure the obligation or the cost and there is no possibility of any actuarial gain or loss. Moreover, short-term employee benefit obligations are measured on an undiscounted basis.**

### Post-employment benefits

Post-employment benefits are payable after completion of employment (e.g. pension, life insurance, medical care etc)

These benefits are classified into either

(a) defined contribution plans or

(b) defined benefit plans

| | |
|---|---|
| (a) Defined contribution plans | are plans where an employer pays fixed contributions to a separate entity and will have no legal or constructive obligations to pay further contributions. Contribution to defined contribution plan to be recognized as expense as the employee renders services to the entity. |

### Recognition and measurement

| | |
|---|---|
| (a) | Contributions to a defined contribution plan should be recognized as an expense in the period they are payable (except to the extent that labour costs may be included within the cost of assets ) |
| (b) | Any liability for unpaid contributions that are due as at the end of the period should be recognized as a liability ( accrued expense) |
| (c) | Any excess contribution paid should be recognized as an asset (prepaid expense) but only to the extent that the prepayment will lead to e.g. a reduction in future payment of cash refund |

| | | |
|---|---|---|
| (b) | Defined benefit plans | are plans where size of post-employment benefits is determined in advance, i.e. the benefits are defined. The employer pays contributions to the plan and the contributions are invested. The size of the contribution is set at an amount that is expected to earn enough investment returns to meet the obligation to pay the post – employment benefits.<br>For a detailed benefit plan, an entity recognizes at the balance sheet date, a net defined benefit asset or liability considering the present value of the defined benefit obligations based on actuarial assumptions net of fair value of any plan assets at the balance sheet date. |

**Recognition and measurement**

(a) The future benefits (arising from employee service in the current or prior years) cannot be estimated exactly, but whatever they are, the employer will have to pay them, and the liability therefore should be recognized now. To estimate these future obligations, it is necessary to use Actuarial assumptions

(b) The obligations payable in future years should be valued, by discounting, on a present value basis. This is because the obligations may be settled in many years' time.

(c) If actuarial assumptions change, the amount of required contributions to the fund will change, and there may be actuarial gains or losses.

Contribution to a fund in any period needs to be adjusted accordingly.

**Other long term employee benefits**

(a) Long-term compensated absences such as long-service awards or sabbatical leave

(b) Jubilee or other long-service benefits

(c) Long-term disability benefits

(d) Profit sharing and bonuses payable twelve months or more after the end of the period in which it is earned

(e) Deferred compensation paid twelve months or more after the end of the period in which it is earned.

**Termination benefits**

These are employee benefits payable as a result of either an enterprise decision to terminate an employee's employment before the normal retirement date or an employee's decision to accept voluntary retirement in exchange for those benefits e.g. VRS payments.

Termination benefits are expensed only when the enterprise has:

(a) A detailed formal plan for the termination which is duly approved and

(b) A reliable estimate can be made of the amount of the obligation.

According to Expert Advisory Committee (EAC), costs related to termination benefits (except gratuity which is provided in the respective accounting period) are to be treated as deferred revenue expenditure since it is construed upon saving in subsequent periods, on some rational basis over a period, preferably over 3 – 5 years.

However, the terminal benefit is, to the extent these are not deferred should be treated as expense in the Statement of Profit and loss with disclosure.

**Disclosure requirements**

(a) In view of varying practices, adequate disclosure of method of accounting for an understanding of the significance of such costs to an employer

(b) Disclosure separately made for statutory compliance or otherwise the retirement benefit costs are treated as an employee remuneration without specific disclosure

(c) Financial statements should disclose whether actuarial valuation is made at the end of the accounting period or earlier (in which case the date of actuarial valuation and the method used for accrual period if not based on actuarial valuation report).

### *8.7.4.2 Employee Benefits Expenses (for Ind AS entities)*

Though Schedule III, Division II does not mention in specific disclosure requirements, in general Employee benefits expense shall disclose information regarding aggregate expenditure on:

(a) Salaries and wages

(b) Contribution to Provident and other funds

(c) Staff welfare expenses

**Illustration 8.38: Employee Benefit Expenses (Specimen format)**

| **Particulars** | **For the year ended 31st March 2022** | **For the year ended 31st March 2021** |
|---|---|---|
| Salaries and Wages | xxx | xxx |
| Contribution to Provident and other funds | xxx | xxx |
| Staff Welfare expenses | xxx | xxx |
| TOTAL | xxx | xxx |

### 8.7.4.3 Employee Benefits (Ind AS 19)

**Types of Employee Benefits**

Employee benefits are all forms of considerations given by an entity in exchange of service rendered by the employees.

These are:

1. Short term benefits:
2. Post-employment benefits:
3. Other long-term benefits:
4. Termination benefits:

| | |
|---|---|
| ***Short term benefits*:** | • Falling due within 12 months of rendering service (e.g. salaries. Bonuses, holiday pay, sick pay).<br>• Recognised as expenses in the period of rendering of services of the employee to the entity.<br>• The expected cost of compensated absences is recognised when<br>- the absences occur for non-accumulating compensated absences and<br>- the service is rendered increasing the employee's entitlement to benefits for accumulating compensated absence<br>• Profit sharing and bonus payments are recognised when the entity has a present legal or constructive obligation as a result of past events and a reliable estimate can be made of the obligation.<br>• Liability is recognised for unpaid short-term benefits |
| ***Post-employment benefits*** | • Payable after completion of employment (e.g. pension, life insurance, medical care etc)<br>• Classified into either<br>(a) defined contribution plans or<br>(b) defined benefit plans |

**Defined contribution plan**

| |
|---|
| These are plans where an employer pays fixed contributions to a separate entity and will have no legal or constructive obligations to pay further contributions if the fund |

does not hold sufficient assets to pay all employee benefits relating to employee service in the current and prior periods. Contribution to defined contribution plan to be recognised as expense as the employee renders services to the entity.

The characteristics of a defined contribution plan are:

(a) The amount of liability of the entity towards post-retirement benefit is restricted to the fixed contributions to a separate entity or fund.

(b) Amount of post-employment benefits received by the employee depends on the contribution paid by the entity and the employee to a post-employment benefit plan or to an insurance company, together with returns from the investment out of the contributions made

(c) Actuarial risk and investment risk rests fully with the employee

(d) In view of the risk of investment returns, participants are interested in knowing whether the contributions have been received and proper control has been exercised to protect the rights of the beneficiaries.

(e) The employer would be interested to know whether the contribution plan is efficiently run

(f) The financial statements of a defined contribution plan shall contain a statement of net assets available for benefits and a description of the funding policy.

**Recognition and measurement of defined contribution plan**

(a) Contributions to a defined contribution plan should be recognised as an expense in the period they are payable (except to the extent that labour costs may be included within the cost of assets)

(b) Any liability for unpaid contributions that are due as at the end of the period should be recognised as a liability (accrued expense)

(c) Any excess contribution paid should be recognised as an asset (prepaid expense) but only to the extent that the prepayment will lead to e.g. a reduction in future payment of cash refund

**Defined Benefit Plan**

These are plans where size of post-employment benefits is determined in advance, i.e. the benefits are defined. The employer pays contributions to the plan and the contributions are invested. The size of the contribution is set at an amount that is expected to earn enough investment returns to meet the obligation to pay the post – employment benefits.

For a detailed benefit plan, an entity recognises at the balance sheet date, a net defined benefit asset or liability considering the present value of the defined benefit obligations based on actuarial assumptions net of fair value of any plan assets at the balance sheet date.

Characteristics of defined benefit plan are:

(a) The entity's obligation is to provide the agreed benefits to current and former employees,

(b) The actuarial risk and investment risk fall, in substance, on the entity.

(c) The amount of retirement benefits is calculated as a formula

- using earnings of the employee and
- the number of years of service of the employee

(d) The amount of promised retirement benefits depend on:

- the financial position of the plan
- ability of contributors to make future contributions
- investment performance and efficiency of the plan

(e) Financial statements shall contain:

- a statement of net assets available for benefits
- the actuarial present value of promised retirement benefit and
- resulting excess or deficit

**Recognition and measurement of defined benefit plan**

(a) The future benefits (arising from employee service in the current or prior years) cannot be estimated exactly, but whatever they are, the employer will have to pay them, and the liability therefore should be recognised now. To estimate these future obligations, it is necessary to use Actuarial assumptions

(b) The obligations payable in future years should be valued, by discounting, on a present value basis. This is because the obligations may be settled in many years' time.

(c) If actuarial assumptions change, the amount of required contributions to the fund will change, and there may be actuarial gains or losses. Contributions to a fund in any period need to be adjusted accordingly.

(i) **Methods of accounting in defined benefit plan**

| Steps | Steps | Activities |
|---|---|---|
| 1 | Actuarial techniques should be used | to make a reliable estimate of the amount of future benefits employees have earned from service in current and previous years.<br>Making estimations about demographic and financial variables |

| Steps | Steps | Activities |
|---|---|---|
| 2 | These future benefits should be attributed to | service performed by employees in the current period, and in prior periods, using Projected Unit Credit Method.<br>This gives a total present value of Future benefit obligations arising from past and current periods of service |
| 3 | The fair value of any plan assets should be established | - |
| 4 | Determination of | Total re-measurements and amount of re-measurements to be recognised in Financial Statements |
| 5 | Determination of past service cost | If the benefits payable under the plan have been improved, the extra cost arising from past services should be determined |
| 6 | Determination of resulting gains/losses | If the benefits payable under the plan have been reduced or cancelled, the resulting gain should be determined |

(ii) **Projected Unit Credit method under defined benefit plan**

(a) With this method it is assumed that each period of service by an employee gives rise to an additional unit of future benefits. The present value of that unit of future benefits can be calculated and attributed to the period in which the service is given.

(b) The units, each measured separately, builds up to the overall obligation.

(c) The accumulated present value of (discounted) future benefits will incur interest over time and an interest expense should be recognised.

According to para 83 of the Standard, the rate used to discount post-employment benefit obligations (both funded and unfunded) shall be determined by reference to market yields at the end of the reporting period on government bonds. However, for currencies other than Indian rupee for which there is deep market in high quality corporate bonds, the market yields (at the end of the reporting period) on such high quality corporate bonds denominated in that currency shall be used. The currency and term of the government bonds or corporate bonds shall be consistent with the currency and estimated term of the post-employment benefit obligations.

Also Para 2 of the Standard prescribes that rate to be used to discount post-employment benefit obligation shall be determined by reference to the market yields on government bonds, whereas under IAS 19, the government bonds can be used only for those currencies where there is no deep market of high quality corporate bonds. However, requirements given in IAS 19 in this regard have been retained with appropriate modifications for currencies other than Indian rupee. (Companies (Indian Accounting Standard) Amendment Rules 2016.

(iii) **Comparison between defined contribution plan and defined benefit plan**

| Defined contribution plan | Defined benefit plan |
|---|---|
| • Defined contribution plans are post-employment benefit plans under which an enterprise pays fixed contribution into a separate fund and will have no obligation to pay further contributions<br>• Under this plan actuarial risk (that benefits will be less than expected) and investment risk (that assets invested will be insufficient to meet expected benefits) fall on the employee.<br>• In defined contribution plans, the contribution is charged to income statement | • Defined benefit plans are post-employment benefit plans other than defined contribution plans.<br>• In defined plans, the actuarial and investment risk fall on the employer.<br>• In defined benefit plans the detailed actuarial calculation is performed to determine the charge<br>• The employer has the liability to make good the shortfall in employee benefit payout and also enjoy contribution holiday if there is any surplus |

(iv) **Actuarial assumptions**

Actuarial assumptions comprise

(a) demographic assumptions and

(b) financial assumptions details of which are enumerated in the table below.

**Ind AS 19: Employee Benefits**

**Defined Benefit Plan**

| Actuarial Assumptions | |
|---|---|
| **Demographic assumptions** | **Financial assumptions** |
| • Mortality rates before and after retirement | • Discount rates to apply |
| • Rate of employee turnover | • Expected return on plan assets |
| • Early retirement | • Future salary levels (allowing for seniority and promotion as well as inflation) |
| • Claim rates under medical plans for former employees | • Future rate of increase in medical costs (not just inflationary cost rises but also cost specific to medical |

| Actuarial Assumptions | |
|---|---|
| **Demographic assumptions** | **Financial assumptions** |
| | treatments - given the expectations of longer average life expectancy) |

(v) **Actuarial Gains and Losses**

These arise because of the following:

(a) Actual events (e.g. employee turnover. Salary increases) differ from the actuarial assumptions that were made to estimate the defined benefit obligations

(b) Actuarial assumptions are revised (e.g. different discount rate is used or a different assumption is made about future employee turnover salary rules etc,)

(c) Actual returns on plan assets differ from expected returns

(vi) **Re-measurement under Ind AS 19**

The concept of re-measurement is a new concept introduced in Ind AS 19 which was issued in June 2011. Re-measurements of net defined liability (asset) comprise:

(a) Actuarial gains and losses on the defined benefit obligation

(b) Return on plan assets, excluding amounts included in net interest on the defined benefits liability (asset)

(c) Any change in the effect of the asset ceiling, excluding amounts included in net interest on the net defined benefit liability (asset).

Please note, asset ceiling is the present value of any economic benefits available in the form of refunds from the plan or reductions in future contributions to the plan.

(vii) **Methods for recognition of re-measurement**

According to Ind AS 19, actuarial gains or losses are now a part of re-measurements. Earlier Ind AS 19 provided three options to defer the actuarial gains or losses using the corridor method, either to SOPL or the OCI.

The amended standard does not provide any option to recognise actuarial losses or gains in profit or loss. Effects of re-measurements are recognised in other comprehensive income and they cannot be recycled through profit or loss in the subsequent periods. Accordingly, the only treatment for re-measurements is to recognise them in other comprehensive income.

Also in accordance with Ind AS 19, the changes in the effect of the asset ceiling are presented both in profit or loss within net interest (for the interest effect on the asset ceiling) and in other comprehensive income as part of the re-measurements for the remainder.

### Illustration 8.39: Defined Benefit Plan

Spice Ltd introduced a pension plan for its employees. Spice accounts for the plan in accordance with defined benefit plan. The amounts recognised in respect of that plan in Spice's financial statements as at 31st December 2019 and 31st December 2020 and their reconciliation are set out below. Spice has determined that the ceiling on recognising a net defined benefit asset in relation to the plan is Rs.150000 at both the start and end of the period.

| Item | Defined benefit obligation (Rs 000) | Fair value of plan asset (Rs 000) | Effect of asset ceiling (Rs 000) | Net defined benefit asset/(liability) (Rs 000) |
|---|---|---|---|---|
| Opening balances determined on 1.1.2020 | (1500) | 1950 | (300) | 150 |
| Service cost | (75) | - | - | (75) |
| Net interest cost based on 10% discount rate | (150) | 195 | (30) | 15 |
| Total amount before computing re-measurements | (1,725) | 2,145 | (330) | 90 |
| Closing balances determined on 31st December 2020 | (1,800) | 2,250 | (300) | 150 |
| Re-measurements | (75) | 105 | 30 | 60 |

Under Ind AS 19, Spice Ltd will recognise a net interest income of Rs.15,000 in SOPL. The re-measurements of Rs.60,000 would be recognised in the Other Comprehensive Income.

(viii) **Net defined benefit liability/(asset) and its treatment in Financial Statements**

| | |
|---|---|
| ***Net defined benefit liability/(asset)*** | Is the deficit or surplus, adjusted for any effect of limiting a net defined benefit asset to the asset ceiling.<br>The deficit or surplus is:<br>(a) The present value of the defined benefit obligation less<br>(b) The fair value of plan assets (if any) Ind AS 19 para 8 |

| | |
|---|---|
| ***Treatment in Balance Sheet*** | Ind AS 19 stipulates that net defined benefit liability (asset) is to be recognised in the statement of financial position. The net defined benefit asset or liability is equal to the amount owed to or from a plan. This is similar to the conventional receivables or payables as we know of.<br>The net defined benefit liability (asset) includes:<br>(a) The present value of defined benefit obligation<br>(b) Less, fair value of any plan assets (including the deficit or surplus in a defined benefit plan) adjusted for<br>(c) Any effect of limiting net defined benefit asset to the asset ceiling |
| ***Treatment in SOPL/OCI*** | Ind AS 19 requires that entities should recognise all changes in the net defined benefit liability (asset) in the period in which those changes occur, and to disaggregate and recognise defined benefit cost as under:<br>Current Service cost – SOPL<br>Past Service cost – SOPL<br>Net interest on the net defined benefit liability (asset) - SOPL<br>Re-measurements – OCI |

(ix) **Past service costs and their measurement by the standard as revised**

| |
|---|
| Past service cost is the change in the present value of the defined benefit obligation for employee service in prior periods, resulting from a plan amendment (the introduction or withdrawal of, or changes to, a defined benefit plan) or a curtailment (a significant reduction by the entity in the number of employees covered by a plan) Ind AS 19 Para 8 |
| According to Ind AS 19, past service cost is to be measured and recognised immediately in the SOPL when any of the following takes place:<br>(a) When restructuring costs (i.e. costs related to restructuring that result in past service costs) arise<br>(b) When termination benefits related to amendments that result in past service costs are recognised<br>(c) When plan amendments that result in past service costs occur |

**Illustration 8.40: Past service cost**

XYZ Ltd provides a pension plan for its employees at 1.5% of final salary for each year of service. The benefits are vested after four years of service. However, on 1st January 2020 the changes the pension to 1.25% of final salary for each year of service starting from 1.1.2010.

The present value of the differential benefits for service from 1.1.2010 to 1.1.2020 at the date of the changes are as under:

| | |
|---|---|
| Employees with more than four years' service on 1/1/2020 | Rs.125,000 |
| Employees with less than four years' service on 1/1/2020 | Rs.121,000 |
| Total | Rs.246,000 |

Determine the amounts recognised in respect of past service costs.

**Solution**

XYZ Ltd needs to recognise the whole amount of past service costs of Rs.246,000 immediately, since Ind AS 19 – states that past service costs are to be recognised immediately, when any of the three events specified occurs:

(a) When restructuring costs (i.e. costs related to restructuring that result in past service costs) arise

(b) When termination benefits related to amendments that result in past service costs are recognised

(c) When plan amendments that result in past service costs occur

**Other long-term benefits**

Not payable within 12 months (long service leave etc)

- An entity recognises a liability for other long term benefits equal to the present value of the defined benefit obligation, minus the fair value of any plan assets at the balance sheet date.
- Recognise immediately any actuarial gains or losses or past service costs as income or expense.

**Termination benefits**

payable when an employee's contract is terminated either voluntarily or involuntarily (e.g. voluntary retirement, redundancy pay)

- An entity recognises the liability and an expense for termination benefits when it is explicitly committed to either

(a) provide termination benefits as a result of an offer made in order to encourage voluntary redundancy or

(b) terminate the employment of employees before the normal retirement date Ind AS 19 provides certain disclosures on employee benefits.

**Other definitions**

| | |
|---|---|
| ***Multi-employer plans are defined contribution plans*** | (a) pool the assets contributed by various entities that are not under common control; and<br>(b) use those assets to provide benefits to employees of |

| | |
|---|---|
| ***(other than state plans) or defined benefit plans (other than state plans) that:*** | more than one entity, on the basis that contribution and benefit levels are determined without regard to the identity of the entity that employs the employees concerned. |
| ***Plan assets comprise:*** | (a) assets held by a long-term employee benefit fund; and<br>(b) qualifying insurance policies. |
| ***Fair value*** | is the amount for which<br>- an asset could be exchanged or a liability settled<br>- between knowledgeable, willing parties<br>- in an arm's length transaction |
| ***Assets held by a long-term employee benefit fund are assets (other than non-transferable financial instruments issued by the reporting entity) that:*** | (a) are held by an entity (a fund) that is legally separate from the reporting entity and exists solely to pay or fund employee benefits; and<br>(b) are available to be used only to pay or fund employee benefits, are not available to the reporting entity's own creditors (even in bankruptcy), and cannot be returned to the reporting entity, unless either:<br>(i) the remaining assets of the fund are sufficient to meet all the related employee benefit obligations of the plan or the reporting entity; or<br>(ii) the assets are returned to the reporting entity to reimburse it for employee benefits already paid. |
| ***A qualifying insurance policy*** | is an insurance policy issued by an insurer that is not a related party (as defined in Ind AS 24 Related Party Disclosures) of the reporting entity, if the proceeds of the policy:<br>(a) can be used only to pay or fund employee benefits under a defined benefit plan; and<br>(b) are not available to the reporting entity's own creditors (even in bankruptcy) and cannot be paid to the reporting entity, unless either:<br>(i) the proceeds represent surplus assets that are not needed for the policy to meet all the related employee benefit obligations; or<br>(ii) the proceeds are returned to the reporting entity to reimburse it for employee benefits already paid. |

**Illustration 8.41: Disclosures under Ind AS 19: Employee Benefits**

**(a) Defined contribution plan (Specimen format)**

| Particulars | For the year ended 31st March 2022 | For the year ended 31st March 2021 |
|---|---|---|
| Employers contribution to Provident Fund | xxx | xxx |
| Employers contribution to Superannuation Fund | xxx | xxx |
| Employers contribution to Pension scheme | xxx | xxx |
| TOTAL | xxx | xxx |

**(b) Defined benefit plan -Reconciliation of defined benefit obligation (Specimen format)**

| Particulars | For the year ended 31st March 2022 | For the year ended 31st March 2021 |
|---|---|---|
| Defined benefit obligation at the beginning of the year | xxx | xxx |
| Add: On acquisition/transfer | xxx | xxx |
| Current service cost | xxx | xxx |
| Actuarial gain/loss | xxx | xxx |
| Benefits paid | xxx | xxx |
| Defined benefit obligation at the end of the year | xxx | xxx |

**(c) Defined benefit plan -Reconciliation of plan assets (Specimen format)**

| Particulars | For the year ended 31st March 2022 | For the year ended 31st March 2021 |
|---|---|---|
| Fair value of Plan assets at the beginning of the year | xxx | xxx |
| Add: On acquisition/transfer | xxx | xxx |
| Return on Plan Assets | xxx | xxx |
| Employer contribution | xxx | xxx |
| Benefits paid | xxx | xxx |
| Fair value of plan assets at the end of the year | xxx | xxx |

**(d) Defined benefit plan -Reconciliation of fair value of assets and obligations (Specimen format)**

| Particulars | For the year ended 31st March 2022 | For the year ended 31st March 2021 |
|---|---|---|
| Fair value of Plan assets | xxx | xxx |
| Present value of obligation | xxx | xxx |
| Amount recognized at Balance Sheet (surplus/(deficit) | xxx | xxx |

**(e) Defined benefit plan – Expenses recognized during the year (Specimen format)**

| Particulars | For the year ended 31st March 2022 | For the year ended 31st March 2021 |
|---|---|---|
| **In income statement** | | |
| Current service cost | xxx | xxx |
| Interest cost | xxx | xxx |
| Return on Plan assets | xxx | xxx |
| **Net cost** | xxx | xxx |
| **In other Comprehensive Income** | | |
| Actuarial (Gain)/Loss | xxx | xxx |
| Return On Plan Assets | xxx | xxx |
| **Net (Income)/Expense for the year recognised in OCI** | xxx | xxx |

**(f) Defined benefit plan – Investment details**

| Particulars | For the year ended 31st March 2022 | | For the year ended 31st March 2021 | |
|---|---|---|---|---|
| | Amount | % invested | Amount | % invested |
| GOI Securities | | | | |
| Insurance policies | | | | |
| Others (including bank balance) | | | | |
| **Total** | | | | |

**(g) Defined benefit plan – Actuarial assumptions (Specimen format)**

| Particulars | For the year ended 31st March 2022 | For the year ended 31st March 2021 |
|---|---|---|
| Discount rate per annum | xxx | xxx |
| Expected rate of return on plan assets per annum | xxx | xxx |
| Rate of escalation in salaries per annum | xxx | xxx |
| Rate of employee turnover per annum | xxx | xxx |

## 8.7.5 Finance Costs

### *8.7.5.1 Schedule III Division I (non Ind AS entities)*

Finance costs shall be classified as:

(a) Interest expense;

(b) Other borrowing costs;

(c) Applicable net gain/loss on foreign currency transactions and translation.

These heads are explained as under:

| | |
|---|---|
| ***Interest expenses*** | This would relate to interest paid on borrowings from banks and others, on debentures, bonds or similar instruments etc. Finance charges on finance leases are in the nature of interest expense and hence should also be classified as interest expense. No bifurcation is required between interest on fixed period loans and other borrowings. |
| ***Other borrowing costs*** | This head would include commitment charges, loan processing charges, guarantee charges, loan facilitation charges, discounts /premiums on borrowings, other ancillary costs incurred in connection with borrowings, or amortisation of such costs. |
| ***Applicable net gain /loss on foreign currency transactions and translations*** | In accordance with para 4(e) of AS 16, borrowing costs also include exchange differences arising from foreign currency borrowings to the extent that they are regarded as an adjustment to interest costs. Any such exchange differences would need to be disclosed under this head. |

**Illustration 8.42: Finance cost: Specimen format (Rs)**

| Particulars | For the year ended 31st March 2021 | For the year ended 31st March 2020 |
|---|---|---|
| Interest Expenses | XXX | XXX |
| Other borrowing costs | XXX | XXX |
| Applicable loss on foreign currency transactions and translation | XXX | XXX |
| TOTAL | XXX | XXX |

### 8.7.5.2 *Schedule III Division II (Ind AS entities)*

Finance costs shall be classified as:

(a) interest;
(b) dividend on redeemable preference shares;
(c) exchange differences regarded as an adjustment to borrowing costs;
(d) other borrowing costs (specify nature).

**Illustration 8.43: Finance costs – specimen format**

| | As at 31st March 2022 | As at 31st March 2021 |
|---|---|---|
| Interest; | XXX | XXX |
| Interest on lease liabilities, | XXX | XXX |
| Dividend on redeemable preference shares; | XXX | XXX |
| Exchange differences regarded as an adjustment to borrowing costs; | XXX | XXX |
| Other borrowing costs (specify nature). | XXX | XXX |
| Total | XXX | XXX |

## 8.7.6 Foreign Currency

### 8.7.6.1 *Schedule III Division I (non Ind AS entities)*

According to sub clause (i) Net gain or loss on foreign currency transaction and translation (other than considered as finance cost) needs to be disclosed.

The treatment of adjustments such as capitalisation of exchange differences where such option has been exercised by the Company as per *AS 11 The effects of changes in foreign exchange rates* and /or adjustments on account of exchange fluctuations for fixed assets in case of non-integral operations as per AS 11 need to be separately disclosed for each class of assets as per Guidance Note of ICAI.

**AS 11: The effects of changes in foreign exchange rates**

Salient features of AS 11 are highlighted below.

**Initial recognition**

A foreign currency transaction should be recorded, on initial recognition in the reporting currency, by applying to the foreign currency amount the exchange rate between the reporting currency and the foreign currency at the date of the transaction.

**Subsequent recognition**

(a) foreign currency monetary items should be reported using the closing rate. However, there may be cases where restrictions on remittances or where the closing rate is unrealistic and it is not possible to effect an exchange of currencies at that rate at the balance sheet date, in such cases, the relevant monetary item should be reported in the reporting currency at the amount which is likely to be realised from or required to disburse, such item at the balance sheet date

(b) non-monetary items which are carried in terms of historical cost denominated in a foreign currency should be reported using the exchange rate at the date of the transaction; and

(c) non-monetary items which are carried at fair value or other similar valuation denominated in a foreign currency should be reported using the exchange rates that existed when the values were determined.

(d) The contingent liability denominated in foreign currency at the balance sheet is disclosed by using the closing rate.

**Recognition principles on exchange difference**

(a) the settlement of monetary items at a date subsequent to initial recognition and

(b) re-measuring an enterprise's monetary items at rates different from those at which they were initially recorded during the period, or reported in previous financial statements, should be recognised as income or as expenses in the period in which they arise.

However, if the transaction is settled in a subsequent accounting period, the exchange difference recognised in each intervening period up to the period of settlement

**Foreign operations are classified as integral and non-integral**

| | |
|---|---|
| ***Integral foreign operations*** | Carries on its business as if it were an extension of the operation of the reporting enterprise e.g. sale of goods imported from the reporting enterprise and remittance of collection proceeds back to the reporting enterprise.<br>In such cases, a change in the exchange rate between reporting currency and the currency of the foreign operation has an immediate impact on the reporting enterprise's cash flows from operations.<br>Therefore, change in exchange rate impacts the individual monetary items held by the foreign operations rather than the reporting enterprise's net investment in that operation |
| ***Non-integral foreign operations*** | Generates income, accumulates cash and other monetary items, incurs expenses, arranges borrowings all substantially in the local currency. It may also enter into transactions in foreign currencies including transactions in the reporting currency.<br>When there is a change in the exchange rate between the reporting currency and the local currency, there is no direct impact on the present and future cash flows from operations of either the non-integral foreign operation or the reporting enterprise.<br>The change in the exchange rate affects the reporting enterprise's net investment in the non-integral foreign operation rather than the individual monetary and non-monetary items held by the non-integral foreign operation. |
| ***Treatment of net investment in a non-integral foreign operation*** | Exchange differences arising on a monetary item that, in substance, forms part of an enterprise's net investment in a non-integral foreign operation should be accumulated in a foreign currency translation reserve in the enterprise's financial statements until the disposal of the net investment, at which time they should be recognised as income or as expenses |
| ***Indications that a foreign operation is a non-integral foreign operation*** | (a) while the reporting enterprise may control the foreign operation, the activities of the foreign operation are carried out with a significant degree of autonomy from those of the reporting enterprise;<br>(b) transactions with the reporting enterprise are not a high proportion of the foreign operation's activities; |

| | |
|---|---|
| | (c) the activities of the foreign operation are financed mainly from its own operations or local borrowings rather than from the reporting enterprise;<br>(d) costs of labour, material and other components of the foreign operation's products or services are primarily paid or settled in the local currency rather than in the reporting currency.<br>(e) the foreign operation's sales are mainly in currencies other than the reporting currency;<br>(f) cash flows of the reporting enterprise are insulated from the day-to-day activities of the foreign operation rather than being directly affected by the activities of the foreign operation;<br>(g) sales prices for the foreign operation's products are not primarily responsive on a short-term basis to changes in exchange rates but are determined more by local competition or local government regulation; and<br>(h) there is an active local sales market for the foreign operation's products, although there also might be significant amounts of exports. |

**How do we translate the following:**

| | |
|---|---|
| (a) Translations of foreign integral operations | • The individual items in the financial statements of the foreign operation are translated as if all its transactions had been entered into by the reporting enterprise itself.<br>• The cost and depreciation of tangible fixed assets is translated using the exchange rate at the date of purchase of the asset, or if at fair value or other similar valuation, using the rate that existed on the date of valuation.<br>• The cost of inventories is translated at the exchange rates that existed when those costs were incurred.<br>• The recoverable amount or realizable value of an asset is translated using the exchange rate applicable on the date the recoverable or net realization value was ascertained usually at the closing rate. |
| (b) Procedure for translation of financial statements of a non-integral foreign operations for incorporation in its financial | (a) the assets and liabilities, both monetary and non-monetary, of the non-integral foreign operation should be translated at the closing rate; |

| | |
|---|---|
| statements | (b) income and expense items of the non-integral foreign operation should be translated at exchange rates at the date of the transactions; and<br>(c) all resulting exchange differences should be accumulated in a foreign currency translation reserve until the disposal of the net investment.<br>(d) For practical reasons, a rate that approximates the actual exchange rates, for example an average rate for the period, is often used to translate income and expense items of a foreign operation<br>(e) Any goodwill or capital reserve arising on the acquisition of a non-integral foreign operation is translated at the closing rate in accordance with paragraph 24.<br>(f) A contingent liability disclosed in the financial statements of a non-integral foreign operation is translated at the closing rate for its disclosure in the financial statements of the reporting enterprise.<br>(g) The incorporation of the financial statements of a non-integral foreign operation in those of the reporting enterprise follows normal consolidation procedures, such as the elimination of intra-group balances and intra-group transactions of a subsidiary (see AS 21, Consolidated Financial Statements, and AS 27, Financial Reporting of Interests in Joint Ventures).<br>However, an exchange difference arising on an intra-group monetary item, whether short-term or long-term, cannot be eliminated against a corresponding amount arising on other intra-group balances because the monetary item represents a commitment to convert one currency into another and exposes the reporting enterprise to a gain or loss through currency fluctuations.<br>(h) When the financial statements of a non-integral foreign operation are drawn up to a different reporting date from that of the reporting enterprise, the non-integral foreign operation often prepares, for purposes of |

| | incorporation in the financial statements of the reporting enterprise, statements as at the same date as the reporting enterprise (AS 21)<br>(i) The exchange differences are not recognised as income or expenses for the period because the changes in the exchange rates have little or no direct effect on the present and future cash flows from operations of either the non-integral foreign operation or the reporting enterprise. When a non-integral foreign operation is consolidated but is not wholly-owned, accumulated exchange differences arising from translation and attributable to minority interests are allocated to and reported as part of the minority interest in the consolidated balance sheet.<br>(j ) An enterprise may dispose of its interest in a non-integral foreign operation through sale, liquidation, repayment of share capital or abandonment of all, or part of , that operation. The payment of a dividend forms part of a disposal only when it constitutes a return on the investment.<br>In the case of a partial disposal, only the proportionate share of the related accumulated exchange difference is included in the gain or loss.<br>(k) A write-down of the carrying amount of a non-integral foreign operation does not constitute a partial disposal. Accordingly no part of the deferred foreign exchange gain or loss is recognised at the time of a write-down. |
|---|---|

**Process of change in classification of foreign operations**

| Integral foreign operation reclassified to non-integral foreign operations | Exchange differences arising on the translation of non-monetary assets at the date of reclassification are accumulated in a foreign currency translation reserve |
|---|---|
| Non-integral foreign operation reclassified to integral foreign operation | The translated amounts for non-monetary items at the date of change are treated as historical cost for those items in the period of change and subsequent periods.<br>Exchange differences which have been deferred are |

| | |
|---|---|
| | not recognised as income or expenses until the disposal of the operation. |

**Forward exchange contracts**

An enterprise may enter into a forward exchange contract or another financial instrument that is in substance a forward exchange contract, which is not intended for trading or speculation purposes, to establish the amount of the reporting currency required or available at the settlement date of a transaction

The premium or discount arising at the inception of such a forward exchange contract should be amortised as expense or income over the life of the contract.

Exchange differences on such a contract should be recognised in the statement of profit and loss in the reporting period in which the exchange rates change.

Any profit or loss arising on cancellation or renewal of such a forward exchange contract should be recognised as income or as expense for the period.

With respect to a forward exchange contract intended for trading or speculation purposes,

- The premium or discount on the contract is ignored
- At each balance sheet date, the value of the contract is marked to its current market value and
- Gains or losses on the contract are charged to Profit and Loss statement.

**Disclosure requirements**

| | |
|---|---|
| An enterprise should disclose | (a) the amount of exchange differences included in the net profit or loss for the period; and<br>(b) net exchange differences accumulated in foreign currency translation reserve as a separate component of shareholders' funds, and a reconciliation of the amount of such exchange differences at the beginning and end of the period.<br>When the reporting currency is different from the currency of the country in which the enterprise is domiciled, the reason for using a different currency should be disclosed. The reason for any change in the reporting currency should also be disclosed. |
| When there is a change in the classification of a significant | (a) the nature of the change in classification;<br>(b) the reason for the change; |

| | |
|---|---|
| foreign operation, an enterprise should disclose: | (c) the impact of the change in classification on shareholders' funds; and<br>(d) the impact on net profit or loss for each prior period presented had the change in classification occurred at the beginning of the earliest period presented. |

### 8.7.6.2 *Schedule III Division II (Ind AS entities)*

**Ind AS 21: The effect of changes in foreign exchange rates**

This Ind AS is applicable as under:

(a) In accounting for transactions and balances in foreign currencies, except for those derivative transactions and balances that are within the scope of Ind AS 109 Financial Instruments,

(b) In translating the results and financial position of foreign operations that are included in the financial statements of the entity by consolidation, proportionate consolidation or the equity method and

(c) In translating an entity's results and financial position into a presentation currency.

**Functional currency**

The primary economic environment in which an entity operates is normally the one in which it primarily generates and expends cash. An entity considers the following factors in determining its functional currency:

(a) the currency:

   (i) that mainly influences sales prices for goods and services (this will often be the currency in which sales prices for its goods and services are denominated and settled); and

   (ii) of the country whose competitive forces and regulations mainly determine the sales prices of its goods and services.

(b) the currency that mainly influences labour, material and other costs of providing goods or services (this will often be the currency in which such costs are denominated and settled).(Para 9)

The following factors may also provide evidence of an entity's functional currency:

(a) the currency in which funds from financing activities (i.e issuing debt and equity instruments) are generated.

(b) the currency in which receipts from operating activities are usually retained. (Para 10)

### Monetary items

The essential feature of a monetary item is a right to receive (or an obligation to deliver) a fixed or determinable number of units of currency.

**Examples include:**

| | |
|---|---|
| (a) | pensions and other employee benefits to be paid in cash; |
| (b) | provisions that are to be settled in cash; and cash dividends that are recognised as a liability. |
| (c) | A contract to receive (or deliver) a variable number of the entity's own equity instruments or a variable amount of assets in which the fair value to be received (or delivered) equals a fixed or determinable number of units of currency is a monetary item. |

### Non-monetary items

Non-monetary items are depicted by the absence of a right to receive (or an obligation to deliver) a fixed or determinable number of units of currency.

**Examples include:**

| | |
|---|---|
| (a) | amounts prepaid for goods and services (e.g. prepaid rent); |
| (b) | goodwill; |
| (c) | intangible assets; |
| (d) | inventories; |
| (e) | property, plant and equipment; and |
| (f) | provisions that are to be settled by the delivery of a nonmonetary asset. |

### Foreign currency transactions:

| | |
|---|---|
| (i) ***Initial recognition*** | According to Para 20 a foreign currency transaction is a transaction that is denominated or requires settlement in a foreign currency, including transactions arising when an entity:<br>(a) buys or sells goods or services whose price is denominated in a foreign currency;<br>(b) borrows or lends funds when the amounts payable or receivable are denominated in a foreign currency; or<br>(c) otherwise acquires or disposes of assets, or incurs or settles liabilities, denominated in a foreign currency.<br>A foreign currency transaction shall be recorded, on initial recognition in the functional currency, by applying to the foreign currency amount the spot exchange rate between the |

| | |
|---|---|
| | functional currency and the foreign currency at the date of the transaction. (Para 21) |
| (ii) ***Subsequent recognition*** | At each balance sheet date:<br>(a) foreign currency monetary items are translated using the closing rate<br>(b) non-monetary items that are measured in terms of historical costs in foreign currencies translated using exchange rate at the date of the transaction – approximate or average rate may be applicable for inventories and<br>(c) non-monetary items are measured at fair value in a foreign currency are translated using the exchange rate at the date when the fair value was measured.<br>Income statement items may be translated using an average rate. |

**Exchange difference**

| | |
|---|---|
| (a) ***Monetary items*** | On settlement of monetary items or on translating monetary items at rates different from those at initial recognition are recognised in profit or loss.<br>Exchange differences arising on a monetary item that forms part of an entity's net investment in foreign operations are recognised as a separate component of equity in the financial statements that include the foreign operation and the reporting entity.<br>(e.g. financial statements in which the foreign operation is consolidated, proportionately consolidated or accounted using the equity method)<br>Such exchange differences are recognised in profit or loss on disposal of net investment. |
| (b) ***Non-monetary items*** | When a gain or loss on a non-monetary item is recognised in other comprehensive income, any exchange component of that gain or loss shall be recognised in other comprehensive income.<br>Conversely, when a gain or loss on a non-monetary item is recognised in profit or loss, any exchange component of that gain or loss shall be recognised in profit or loss. |

### Change in functional currency

When there is a change in an entity's functional currency, the entity shall apply the translation procedures applicable to the new functional currency prospectively from the date of the change.

### Translation to presentation currency

According to para 39, the results and financial position of an entity whose functional currency is not the currency of a hyperinflationary economy shall be translated into a different presentation currency using the following procedure:

(a) Assets and liabilities for each balance sheet presented (i.e. including comparatives) shall be translated at the closing rate at the date of that balance sheet,

(b) Income and expenses for each statement of profit and loss presented (i.e. including comparatives) shall be translated at exchange rates at the dates of the transactions and

(c) All resulting exchange differences shall be recognised in other comprehensive income.

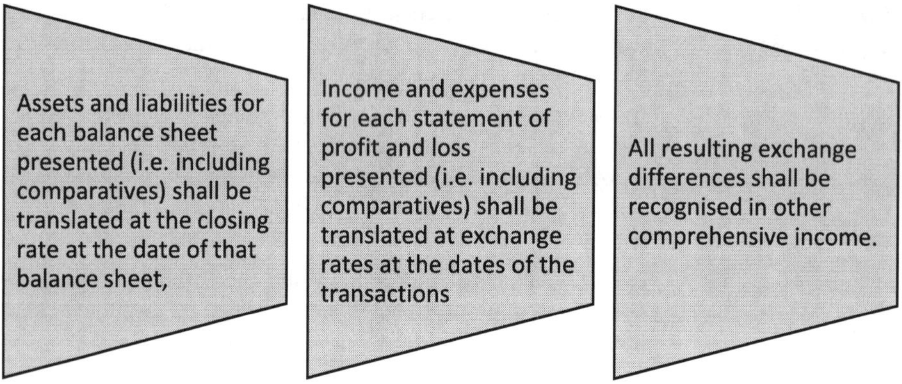


According to para 42, the results and financial position of an entity whose functional currency is the currency of a hyperinflationary economy shall be translated into a different presentation currency using the following procedure:

(a) Assets, liabilities, equity items, income and expenses, including comparatives) shall be translated at the closing rate at the date of that balance sheet, except that

(b) When amounts are translated into the currency of a non-hyperinflationary economy, comparative amounts shall be those that were presented as current year amounts in the relevant prior year financial statements (i.e. not adjusted for subsequent changes in the price level or subsequent changes in exchange rates)

When an entity's functional currency is the currency of a hyperinflationary economy, the entity shall restate its financial statements in accordance with Ind AS 29 before applying the translation method set out as above, except for comparative amounts that are translated into a currency of a non-hyperinflationary economy.

**Translation of a foreign operation**

When translating a foreign operation for inclusion in the reporting entity's financial statements (i.e. translation into presentation currency)

- assets and liabilities are translated at the closing rate
- income and expenses are translated at exchange rates at the date of transaction
- all resulting exchange differences are recognised as separate component of equity

On disposal of foreign operation all exchange differences deferred in separate component of equity related to that operation, are recognised in profit or loss

Goodwill and fair value adjustments arising out of acquisition of foreign operation should be treated as assets and liabilities of foreign operation and expressed in functional currency of foreign operation – and translation would be at closing rate

**Disposal or partial disposal of a foreign operation**

According to para 48, on the disposal of a foreign operation, the cumulative amount of the exchange differences relating to that foreign operation, recognised in other comprehensive income and accumulated in the separate component of equity, shall be reclassified from equity to profit or loss as a reclassification adjustment, when the gain or loss on disposal is recognised.

On the partial disposal of a subsidiary that includes a foreign operation, the entity shall re-attribute the proportionate share of the cumulative amount of the exchange differences recognised in other comprehensive income to the non-controlling interests in that foreign operation. In any other partial disposal of a foreign operation the entity shall reclassify to profit or loss only the proportionate share of the cumulative amount of exchange differences recognised in other comprehensive income.

**Tax effects of all exchange differences**

Gains and losses on foreign currency transactions and exchange differences arising on translating the results and financial position of an entity (including a foreign operation) into a different currency may have tax effects and Ind AS 12 Income Taxes will be applicable to these tax effects.

## Illustration 8.44: Accounting policy: Foreign currency transaction and translation

**Foreign currency transactions and translations**

The financial statements of the Company are presented in Indian Rupees ("₹"), which is the functional currency of the Company and the presentation currency for the financial statements.

In preparing the financial statements, transactions in currencies other than the Company's functional currency are recorded at the rates of exchange prevailing on the date of the transaction. At the end of each reporting period, monetary items denominated in foreign currencies are re-translated at the rates prevailing at the end of the reporting period. Nonmonetary items carried at fair value that are denominated in foreign currencies are re-translated at the rates prevailing on the date when the fair value was determined. Non-monetary items that are measured in terms of historical cost in a foreign currency are not translated.

Exchange differences arising on translation of long-term foreign currency monetary items recognized in the financial statements before the beginning of the first Ind AS financial reporting period in respect of which the Company has elected to recognize such exchange differences in equity or as part of cost of assets as allowed under Ind AS 101 "First-time adoption of Indian Accounting Standards" are added/deducted to/from the cost of assets as the case may be. Such exchange differences recognized as part of cost of assets is recognized in the statement of profit and loss on a systematic basis.

Exchange differences arising on the re-translation or settlement of other monetary items are included in the statement of profit and loss for the period.

*(Source: Tata Steel: Annual Report 2019-20)*

## Illustration 8.45: Accounting policy: Borrowing costs

**Borrowing costs**

Borrowings costs directly attributable to the acquisition, construction, or production of qualifying assets, which are assets that necessarily take a substantial period of time to get ready for their intended use or sale, are added to the cost of those assets, until such time as the assets are substantially ready for the intended use or sale.

Investment income earned on temporary investment of specific borrowings pending their expenditure on qualifying assets is recognized in the statement of profit and loss.

Discounts or premiums and expenses on the issue of debt securities are amortised over the term of the related securities and included within borrowing costs. Premiums payable on early redemptions of debt securities, in lieu of future finance costs, are recognized as borrowing costs.

All other borrowing costs are recognized as expenses in the period in which it is incurred.

**Amendment to Ind AS 23 "Borrowing Costs"**

The amendment clarifies that if any specific borrowing remains outstanding after the related asset is ready for its intended use or sale, that borrowing becomes part of the

funds that an entity borrows generally when calculating the capitalization rate on general borrowings.
The Company has applied the amendments prospectively for annual reporting periods beginning on or after April 1, 2019 There is no material impact on the Company due to the application of the above amendment.
There is no new standard or amendment to the existing standards which would have been applicable from April 1, 2020.
*(Source: Tata Steel: Annual Report 2019-20*

## 8.7.7 Depreciation/amortization

### 8.7.7.1 *Schedule III, Division I: Depreciation and amortization expense (non Ind AS entities)*

The Companies Act, 2013 requires companies to compute the depreciation in accordance with the Schedule II to the Companies Act which provides useful lives to compute the depreciation in accordance with Schedule II to the Companies Act, 2013.

Some of the key changes in Schedule II are summarised as under:

- Schedule II prescribes indicative useful lives of various assets instead of Straight Line
- Method (SLM)/Written Down Value (WDV) rates for calculating depreciation
- Useful lives prescribed for tangible assets only
- No life prescribed for intangible assets. Notified accounting standard to govern the same
- Depreciation is systematic allocation of the depreciable amount of an asset over its useful life.
- The depreciable amount of an assets is the cost of an asset or other amount substituted for cost, less its residual value
- Useful life is the period over which an asset is expected to be available for use by an entity, or the number of production or similar units expected to be obtained from the asset by the entity.
- Companies are allowed to follow different useful lives/residual value if an appropriate
- Justification is given supported by technical advice.
- Component accounting and useful life of a significant part of an asset to be determined separately
- No separate rate for double/triple shift; depreciation to be increased based on the double shift/triple shift use of the assets

- Useful lives of fixed assets prescribed under schedule II of the Act
- No reference to depreciation on low value assets.

**Illustration 8.46: Depreciation and amortization expenses: Specimen format (Rs)**

| Particulars | For the year ended 31st March 2021 | For the year ended 31st March 2020 |
|---|---|---|
| Depreciation and Amortisation | XXX | XXX |
| Less: Transferred from revaluation reserve | XXX | XXX |
| TOTAL | XXX | XXX |

**AS 10: Property, Plant and Equipment (Revised 2016)**

**Depreciation**

Para 45. Each part of an item of property, plant and equipment with a cost that is significant in relation to the total cost of the item should be depreciated separately.

Para 46. An enterprise allocates the amount initially recognised in respect of an item of property, plant and equipment to its significant parts and depreciates each such part separately. For example, it may be appropriate to depreciate separately the airframe and engines of an aircraft, whether owned or subject to a finance lease.

Para 47. A significant part of an item of property, plant and equipment may have a useful life and a depreciation method that are the same as the useful life and the depreciation method of another significant part of that same item. Such parts may be grouped in determining the depreciation charge.

Para 48. To the extent that an enterprise depreciates separately some parts of an item of property, plant and equipment, it also depreciates separately the remainder of the item. The remainder consists of the parts of the item that are individually not significant. If an enterprise has varying expectations for these parts, approximation techniques may be necessary to depreciate the remainder in a manner that faithfully represents the consumption pattern and/or useful life of its parts.

Para 49. An enterprise may choose to depreciate separately the parts of an item that do not have a cost that is significant in relation to the total cost of the item.

Para 50. The depreciation charge for each period should be recognised in the statement of profit and loss unless it is included in the carrying amount of another asset.

Para 51. The depreciation charge for a period is usually recognised in the statement of profit and loss. However, sometimes, the future economic benefits embodied in an asset are absorbed in producing other assets. In this case, the depreciation charge constitutes part of the cost of the other asset and is included in its carrying amount. For example, the depreciation of manufacturing plant and equipment is included in the costs of conversion of inventories (see AS 2). Similarly, the depreciation of property, plant and equipment used for development activities may be included in the cost of an intangible asset recognised in accordance with AS 26, Intangible Assets.

**Depreciation amount and period**

Para 52. The depreciable amount of an asset should be allocated on a systematic basis over its useful life.

Par 53. The residual value and the useful life of an asset should be reviewed at least at each financial year-end and, if expectations differ from previous estimates, the change(s) should be accounted for as a change in an accounting estimate in accordance with AS 5, Net Profit or Loss for the Period, Prior Period Items and Changes in Accounting Policies.

Para 54. Depreciation is recognised even if the fair value of the asset exceeds its carrying amount, as long as the asset's residual value does not exceed its carrying amount. Repair and maintenance of an asset do not negate the need to depreciate it.

Para 55. The depreciable amount of an asset is determined after deducting its residual value.

Para 56. The residual value of an asset may increase to an amount equal to or greater than its carrying amount. If it does, depreciation charge of the asset is zero unless and until its residual value subsequently decreases to an amount below its carrying amount.

Para 57. Depreciation of an asset begins when it is available for use, i.e., when it is in the location and condition necessary for it to be capable of operating in the manner intended by management. Depreciation of an asset ceases at the earlier of the date that the asset is retired from active use and is held for disposal and the date that the asset is derecognised. Therefore, depreciation does not cease when the asset becomes idle or is retired from active use (but not held for disposal) unless the asset is fully depreciated. However, under usage methods of depreciation, the depreciation charge can be zero while there is no production.

Para 58. The future economic benefits embodied in an asset are consumed by an enterprise principally through its use. However, other factors, such as technical or commercial obsolescence and wear and tear while an asset remains idle, often result in the diminution of the economic benefits that might have been obtained from the asset. Consequently, all the following factors are considered in determining the useful life of an asset:

| | |
|---|---|
| **Useful life of an asset** | **(a)** ***expected usage of the asset.*** Usage is assessed by reference to the expected capacity or physical output of the asset.<br>**(b)** ***expected physical wear and tear***, which depends on operational factors such as the number of shifts for which the asset is to be used and the repair and maintenance programme, and the care and maintenance of the asset while idle.<br>**(c)** ***technical or commercial obsolescence*** arising from changes or improvements in production, or from a change in the market demand for the product or service output of the asset. Expected future reductions in the selling price of an item that was produced using an asset could indicate the expectation of technical or commercial obsolescence of the asset, which, in turn, might reflect a reduction of the future economic benefits embodied in the asset.<br>**(d)** legal or similar limits on the use of the asset, such as the expiry dates of related leases. |

Para 59. The useful life of an asset is defined in terms of its expected utility to the enterprise. The asset management policy of the enterprise may involve the disposal of assets after a specified time or after consumption of a specified proportion of the future economic benefits embodied in the asset. Therefore, the useful life of an asset may be shorter than its economic life. The estimation of the useful life of the asset is a matter of judgement based on the experience of the enterprise with similar assets.

Para 60. Land and buildings are separable assets and are accounted for separately, even when they are acquired together. With some exceptions, such as quarries and sites used for landfill, land has an unlimited useful life and therefore is not depreciated. Buildings have a limited useful life and therefore are depreciable assets. An increase in the value of the land on which a building stands does not affect the determination of the depreciable amount of the building.

Para 61. If the cost of land includes the costs of site dismantlement, removal and restoration, that portion of the land asset is depreciated over the period of benefits obtained by incurring those costs. In some cases, the land itself may have a limited useful life, in which case it is depreciated in a manner that reflects the benefits to be derived from it.

**Depreciation Method**

Para 62. The depreciation method used should reflect the pattern in which the future economic benefits of the asset are expected to be consumed by the enterprise.

Para 63. The depreciation method applied to an asset should be reviewed at least at each financial year-end and, if there has been a significant change in the expected pattern of consumption of the future economic benefits embodied in the asset, the method should be changed to reflect the changed pattern. Such a change should be accounted for as a change in an accounting estimate in accordance with AS 5.

Para 64. A variety of depreciation methods can be used to allocate the depreciable amount of an asset on a systematic basis over its useful life. These methods include

| Method | Description |
|---|---|
| the straight-line method | Straight-line depreciation results in a constant charge over the useful life if the residual value of the asset does not change. |
| the diminishing balance method | The diminishing balance method results in a decreasing charge over the useful life. |
| the units of production method | The units of production method results in a charge based on the expected use or output. |

The enterprise selects the method that most closely reflects the expected pattern of consumption of the future economic benefits embodied in the asset. That method is applied consistently from period to period unless there is a change in the expected pattern of consumption of those future economic benefits or that the method is changed in accordance with the statute to best reflect the way the asset is consumed

Para 65. A depreciation method that is based on revenue that is generated by an activity that includes the use of an asset is not appropriate. The revenue generated by an activity that includes the use of an asset generally reflects factors other than the consumption of the economic benefits of the asset. For example, revenue is affected by other inputs and processes, selling activities and changes in sales volumes and prices. The price component of revenue may be affected by inflation, which has no bearing upon the way in which an asset is consumed.

**Illustration 8.47: Component accounting**

(a) A Building may be split up into the following components -
- (i) Structural design
- (ii) Elevators
- (iii) Heating system
- (iv) Water system
- (v) Electrical system

(b) A Ship may be bifurcated into the following components –
- (i) Hull
- (ii) Keel
- (iii) Engine
- (iv) Navigation system

| | |
|---|---|
| (v) | Major overhaul/inspections |
| (vi) | Other fit out assets |

**Illustration 8.48: Determination of useful life of an asset**

| |
|---|
| The useful life of an asset as envisaged under the Schedule II is 10 years. The management has also estimated that the useful life of the principal asset is 10 years. If a component of the asset has useful life of 8 years, AS 10 requires the company to depreciate the component using 8-year life only. However, if the component has 12-year life, the company may depreciate the component using either 10 year life as prescribed in the Schedule II. |

| | |
|---|---|
| Continuous process Plants | Companies can continue to follow the guidance note issued by the ICAI with regard to continuous process plant – "Guidance note on some important issues arising from the amendments to Schedule XIV to the Companies Act, 1956."<br>Concept of component accounting will be applicable for continuous process plants also. |
| Double /triple shift working | Schedule XIV to the 1956 Act prescribed separate rates of depreciation for the single, double and triple shift use of assets. For example, with regard to general plant and machinery, single, double and triple shift depreciation rates applicable under the Schedule XIV were 4.75%, 7.42% and 10.34%, respectively. Under Schedule II to the 2013 Act, no separate rates/lives are prescribed for extra shift working. Rather, it states that for the period of time, an asset is used in double shift depreciation will increase by 50% and by 100% in case of triple shift working.<br>Both under Schedule XIV as well as Schedule II, extra shift depreciation is applicable only for the actual number of days for which the asset has been operated on double/triple shift basis.<br>For example, a company uses an asset for triple shift basis for 100 days in a year. For rest of the year, the asset is used only on single shift basis. In this case, triple shift depreciation rate is applicable only for 100 days. |
| Charging of depreciation in case of revaluation of assets | Pursuant to Companies Act, 1956, depreciation was to be provided on the original cost of an asset. |

| | |
|---|---|
| | Considering this, the ICAI Guidance Note on Treatment of Reserve Created on Revaluation of Fixed Assets allowed an amount equivalent to the additional depreciation on account of the upward revaluation of fixed assets to be transferred from the revaluation reserve to the statement of profit and loss.<br>In contrast, schedule II to Companies Act, 2013 Act requires depreciation to be provided on historical cost or the amount substituted for the historical cost.<br>Therefore, in case of revaluation, a company needs to charge depreciation based on the revalued amount. Consequently, the ICAI Guidance Note, which allows an amount equivalent to the additional depreciation on account of upward revaluation to be recouped from the revaluation reserve, may not apply.<br>AS 10 allows amount standing to the credit of revaluation reserve to be transferred directly to the general reserve on retirement or disposal of revalued asset. A company may transfer the whole of the reserve when the asset is sold or disposed of.<br>However, some of the surplus may be transferred as the asset is used by a Company. In such a case, the amount of the surplus transferred would be the difference between depreciation based on the revalued carrying amount of the asset and depreciation based on its original cost. Transfers from revaluation surplus to the general reserve are not made through the statement of profit and loss. |

### *8.7.7.2 Schedule III, Division II: Depreciation and amortization expense (Ind AS entities)*

**Ind AS 16: Property, Plant and Equipment**

**Depreciation**

According to the Ind AS, each part of an item of property, plant and equipment with a cost that is significant in relation to the total cost of the item shall be depreciated separately.

Depreciation is a systematic allocation of depreciable amount of an asset over useful life.

Depreciation is applied on component basis separately against each item of asset.

**Depreciable amount**

Depreciable amount is allocated on systematic basis over the useful life of the asset Impairment is recognised in accordance with Ind AS 36 on "Impairment of assets".

The residual value and the useful life of an asset shall be reviewed at least at each financial year-end and, if expectations differ from previous estimates, the change(s) shall be accounted for as a change in an accounting estimate in accordance with Ind AS 8, Accounting Policies, Changes in Accounting Estimates and Errors.

Depreciation of an asset begins when it is available for use, i.e when it is in the location and condition necessary for it to be capable of operating in the manner intended by management. Depreciation of an asset ceases at the earlier of the date that the asset is classified as held for sale (or included in a disposal group that is classified as held for sale) in accordance with Ind AS 105 and the date that the asset is derecognised. Therefore, depreciation does not cease when the asset becomes idle or is retired from active use unless the asset is fully depreciated.

However, under usage methods of depreciation the depreciation charge can be zero while there is no production.

The gain or loss on de-recognition of an asset is the difference between

- net disposal proceeds and
- the carrying amount of the item and it is included in P&L account.

If the entity rents some assets and later ceases to rent them, the assets should be transferred to inventories in their carrying amounts as they are now held for sale.

Note: Please refer Ind AS 105 on noncurrent assets held for sale and discontinued operations.

**Depreciation Methods**

The depreciation method used shall reflect the pattern in which the asset's future economic benefits are expected to be consumed by the entity.

The depreciation method applied to an asset shall be reviewed at least at each financial year-end and, if there has been a significant change in the expected pattern of consumption of the future economic benefits embodied in the asset, the method shall be changed to reflect the changed pattern. Such a change shall be accounted for as a change in an accounting estimate in accordance with Ind AS 8.

| ***The methods of depreciation are as under:*** | • ***The straight-line method***: This result is a constant change over the useful life if the asset's residual value does not change<br>• ***The reducing (diminishing) balance method***: This results in decreasing change over the useful life<br>• ***The units of production method***: This results in a change based on expected use or output |
|---|---|

**Depreciation calculation after revaluation**

- Depreciation will be based on revalued amount
- Full depreciation amount charged as expense to Statement of profit or loss
- Difference between depreciation on revalued amount & original cost may be transferred from revaluation reserve to retained earnings. This is further explained in the table below.

| Asset | Treatment |
|---|---|
| ***Sold/no longer used*** | Revaluation surplus transferred to retained earnings. |
| ***Still in use*** | A part of the revaluation surplus can be transferred to retained earnings. It is equal to difference between depreciation based on historical cost and its revalued amount |

**Illustration 8.49: Depreciation on revaluation**

An entity owns a building which originally costs Rs.2,00,000. The property is depreciated over 50 years on a straight-line basis with no residual value. The entity follows revaluation model. At the start of year 2, the building was re-valued at Rs.2,30,000. Show treatment.

**Solution**

Revaluation surplus at start Year 2 = Rs 230,000 - Rs196,000 = Rs.34,000. (Rs.196,000 = Rs.200,000 – Rs.4000)

Depreciation charge for year 1 = Rs.2,00,000/50 years = Rs.4,000

Depreciation charge for year 2 = Rs.2,30,000/49 years = Rs.4,694

The amounts transferred from the revaluation surplus to retained earnings as the revaluation surplus is realised through depreciation are:

Year 1 – nil.

Year 2 – Rs.4,694 – Rs.4,000 = Rs.694.

**Illustration 8.50: Accounting Policy: Depreciation/Amortization**

**Depreciation and Amortisation**

Depreciation on fixed assets is provided to the extent of depreciable amount on written down value method (WDV) at the rates and in the manner prescribed in Schedule XIV to the Companies Act, 1956 over their useful life except:

on fixed assets pertaining to refining segment and SEZ units, depreciation is provided on Straight Line method

(SLM) over their useful life; on fixed bed catalyst with a life of 2 years or more, depreciation is provided over its useful life; on fixed bed catalysts having life of less than 2 years, 100% depreciation is provided in the year of addition; on additions or extensions forming an integral part of existing plants, including incremental cost arising on account of translation of foreign currency liabilities for acquisition of fixed assets and insurance spares, depreciation is provided as aforesaid over the residual life of the respective plants; premium on leasehold land is amortised over the period of lease; technical know-how is amortised over the useful life of the underlying assets and computer software is amortised over a period of 5 years; on intangible assets - development rights, depletion is provided in proportion of oil and gas production achieved vis-a-vis the proved reserves (net of reserves to be retained to cover abandonment costs as per the production sharing contract and the Government of India's share in the reserves) considering the estimated future expenditure on developing the reserves as per technical evaluation; intangible assets - others are amortised over the period of agreement of right to use, provided in case of jetty the aggregate amount amortised to date is not less than the aggregate rebate availed by the Company; on amounts added on revaluation, depreciation is provided as aforesaid over the residual life of the assets as certified by the valuers'; on assets acquired under finance lease from 1st April 2001, depreciation is provided over the lease term.

*(Source: Reliance Industries Limited)*

## 8.7.8 Other Expenses

### *8.7.8.1 Schedule III, Division I: Other expenses (non Ind AS entities)*

All other expenses not classified under other heads will be classified here. For this purpose, any item of expenditure which exceeds one percent of the revenue from operations or Rs. 1,00,000, whichever is higher, needs to be disclosed separately. Further Note 5(vi) requires a separate disclosure of each of the following items, which will also be classified under 'Other expenses'

- Consumption of stores and spare parts;
- Power and fuel;
- Rent;
- Repairs to buildings;
- Repairs to machinery;
- Insurance;
- Rates and taxes, excluding taxes on income;
- Miscellaneous expenses

### 8.7.8.2 Schedule III, Division II: Other expenses (Ind AS entities)

According to ICAI Guidance Note on Schedule III, on Ind AS entities, all other expenses not classified under other heads will be classified here. Net losses on fair value changes should be classified under "Other expenses".

An illustration is provided to highlight this.

**Illustration 8.51: Other expenses (Specimen format)**

| Particulars | For the year ended 31st March 2022 | For the year ended 31st March 2021 |
|---|---|---|
| **Manufacturing expenses** | | |
| Stores, Chemicals and Packing Materials | 3,482 | 3,378 |
| Electric Power, Fuel and Water | 4,094 | 2,255 |
| Labour Processing, Production Royalty and Machinery Hire Charges | 1,829 | 2,284 |
| Repairs to Building | 40 | 29 |
| Repairs to Machinery | 728 | 632 |
| Exchange Difference (Net) | 161 | (368) |
| Excise Duty # | (28) | 34 |
| Lease Rent | 1 | 1 |
| **Sub-total** | 10,307 | 8,245 |
| **Selling and Distribution Expenses** | | |
| Warehousing and Distribution Expenses | 4,380 | 4,195 |
| Goods and Services tax | 821 | 756 |
| Other selling and Distribution Expenses | 192 | 402 |
| **Sub-total** | 5,393 | 5,353 |
| **Establishment Expenses** | | |
| Professional fees | 705 | 666 |
| General Expenses | 255 | 500 |
| Rent | 122 | 103 |
| Insurance | 522 | 529 |
| Rates & Taxes | 83 | 67 |
| Other Repairs | 258 | 243 |
| Travelling Expenses | 82 | 74 |
| Payment to Auditors | 17 | 14 |
| Loss on Sale /Discard of Fixed Assets | 45 | 58 |
| Charity and Donations | 288 | 143 |

| Particulars | For the year ended 31st March 2022 | For the year ended 31st March 2021 |
|---|---|---|
| **Less:** Transferred to Project Development Expenditure<br>TOTAL | 2,377<br>(37)<br>18,040 | 2,397<br>(30)<br>15,965 |

## 8.7.9 Exceptional items

### 8.7.9.1 *Schedule III Division I (Non Ind AS entities)*

The term "exceptional item" has not defined under Schedule III. However, in accordance with AS -5 "Net Profit or Loss for the period, prior period items and changes in accounting policies" there is a reference of such items in paras 12, 13 and 14 of the said standard.

| | |
|---|---|
| Para 12 | When items of income and expenditure within profit or loss from ordinary activities are of such size, nature or incidence that their disclosure is relevant to explain the performance of the enterprise for the period, the nature and amount of such items should be disclosed separately. |
| Para 13 | Although the items of income and expense described in para 12 are not in the nature of extraordinary items, the nature and amount of such items may be relevant to users of Financial Statements in understanding the financial position and performance of an enterprise and in making projections about financial position and performance. Disclosure of such information is sometimes made in the note to the Financial Statements |
| Para 14 | Circumstances which may give rise to the separate disclosure of items of income and expense in accordance with para 12 include;<br>(a) The write down of inventories to net realisable value as well as the reversal of such write-downs<br>(b) A restructuring of the activities of an enterprise and the reversal of any of provisions for the costs of restructuring.<br>(c) disposals of items of fixed assets<br>(d) disposals of long-term investments<br>(e) legislative changes having retrospective application<br>(f) litigation settlements and<br>(g) other reversals of provisions |

In case the company has more than one such item of income or expense of the above nature, the aggregate of such items should be disclosed on the face of the Statement of Profit and Loss.

Detailed break-down of all the individual items should be disclosed in the Notes in accordance with Note 5 (i)(k) to the general instructions for preparation of the Statement of Profit and Loss.

### *8.7.9.2 Schedule III Division II (Ind AS entities)*

The term 'Exceptional items' has neither been defined in Ind AS Schedule III nor in Ind AS. However, Ind AS 1 has reference to such items in paras 85, 86, 97 and 98. This is summarized below.

| | |
|---|---|
| Para 85 | Additional line items, headings and subtotals in the statement of profit and loss shall be presented, when such presentation is relevant to an understanding of the entity's financial performance |
| Para 86 | Disclosure of components of financial performance assists users in understanding the financial performance achieved and in making projections of future financial performance. An entity considers factors including materiality and the nature and function of the items of income and expense. |
| Para 97 | When items of income or expense are material, an entity shall disclose their nature and amount separately |

According to par 98 of Ind AS 1, circumstances that would trigger separate disclosure of items of income and expenses would include:

(a) Write-downs of inventories to net realisable value or of property, plant and equipment to recoverable amount, as well as reversals of such write-downs;

(b) restructurings of the activities of an entity and reversals of any provisions for the costs of restructuring;

(c) disposals of items of property, plant and equipment;

(d) disposals of investments;

(e) discontinued operations;

(f) litigation settlements; and

(g) other reversals of provisions.

In case the company has more than one such item of income /expense of the above nature which is exceptional, then such items need to be disclosed on the face of the Statement of Profit and Loss.

Details of the all individual items need to be disclosed in the Notes.

## 8.7.10 Extraordinary items

### *8.7.10.1 Schedule III Division I (Non Ind AS entities)*

The term "extraordinary items" has not been defined under Schedule III. However, in accordance with para 4.2 of AS 5: Net Profit or Loss for the period, prior period items and changes in accounting policies, extraordinary items are income or expenses that arise from events or transactions that are clearly distinct from the ordinary activities of the enterprise and therefore, are not expected to recur frequently or regularly.

Further para 8 of AS 5 talks about the disclosure requirements of extraordinary items which are explained as under:

Extraordinary items need to be disclosed in the Statement of Profit and Loss as a part of net profit or loss for the period. The nature and the amount of each extraordinary item should be separately disclosed in the Statement of Profit or Loss in a manner that its impact on current profit or loss can be perceived.

In cases where the company has more than one such item of income /expense of the above nature, the aggregate of such items should be disclosed on the face of the Statement of Profit and Loss. Details of all the individual items should be disclosed in the Notes as per Note 5 (i) (k) to the general instructions for preparation of the Statement of Profit and Loss.

### *8.7.10.2 Schedule III Division II (Ind AS entities)*

There is no requirement to present extraordinary items under Schedule III Division II.

## 8.7.11 Discontinuing operations

### *8.7.11.1 Schedule III Division I (Non Ind AS entities)*

The term "Discontinuing Operations" has been defined under AS 24: Discontinuing Operations is shown as under:

| Discontinuing operations as a component of an enterprise | (a) that the enterprise, pursuant to a single plan, is:<br>(i) disposing of substantially in its entirety, such as by selling the component in a single transaction or by demerger or spin-off of ownership of the component to the enterprise's shareholders; or<br>(ii) disposing of piecemeal, such as selling off the component's assets and selling its liabilities individually; or<br>(iii) terminating through abandonment; and<br>(b) that represents a separate major line of business or geographical area of operations; and |
|---|---|

| | |
|---|---|
| | (c) that can be distinguished operationally and for financial reporting purposes |

Profit or loss from discontinuing operations needs to be separately disclosed on the face of Statement of Profit and Loss.

This disclosure is in line with the disclosure requirements prescribed under AS 24: Discontinuing Operations. The disclosure as per 32a requires the amount of pre-tax profit or loss from ordinary activities attributable to the discontinuing operations during the current financial reporting period and related income tax expenses to be disclosed on the face of the Statement of Profit and Loss.

Also, para 32(b) requires the following disclosures on the face of the Statement of Profit and Loss:

> *"The amount of the pre-tax gain or loss recognised on the disposal of assets or settlement of liabilities attributable to the discontinuing operation."*

According to ICAI Guidance Note on Schedule III on non Ind AS entities, in the event of any taxes that may be payable on profits or any tax credits to be availed on losses attributable to the discontinuing operations, the same needs to be disclosed as a separate line item on the Statement of Profit and Loss.

### 8.7.11.2 Schedule III Division II (Ind AS entities)

The term 'discontinued operations' has been defined in Ind AS 105 "Non-current Assets Held for Sale and Discontinued Operations"

| | |
|---|---|
| as a component of an entity that either has been disposed of or is classified as held for sale and: | (a) represents a separate major line of business or geographical area of operations,<br><br>(b) is part of a single co-ordinated plan to dispose of a separate major line of business or geographical area of operations; or<br><br>(c) is a subsidiary acquired exclusively with a view to resale. Profit or loss from Discontinued Operations needs to be separately disclosed on the face of Statement of Profit and Loss.<br><br>This disclosure is in line with the disclosure requirement of Ind AS 105 para 33(a) which requires a single amount in the statement of profit and loss comprising the total of:<br><br>(i) post-tax profit or loss of discontinued operations; and<br><br>(ii) post-tax gain or loss recognized on the measurement to fair value less costs to sell or on the disposal of the assets or disposal group(s) constituting the discontinued operation. |

Further, Ind AS-105 para 33(b) requires an entity to present an analysis of a single amount either in Notes or on the face of the Statement of Profit and Loss:

(i) the revenue, expenses and pre-tax profit or loss of discontinued operations

(ii) the gain or loss recognised on the measurement to fair value less costs to sell or on the disposal of the assets or disposal group(s) constituting the discontinued operation.

(iii) the related income tax expense as required by paragraph 81(h) of Ind AS 12.

According to ICAI Guidance Note on Schedule III on Ind AS, if the above analysis is presented in the Statement of Profit and Loss, then it shall be presented in a section identified as relating to discontinued operations, i.e. separately from continuing operations. Also if there is any taxes payable or tax credit received or receivable from discontinuing operations, it needs to be separately disclosed under Statement of Profit and Loss.

## 8.8 ACCOUNTING QUALITY OF STATEMENT OF PROFIT AND LOSS

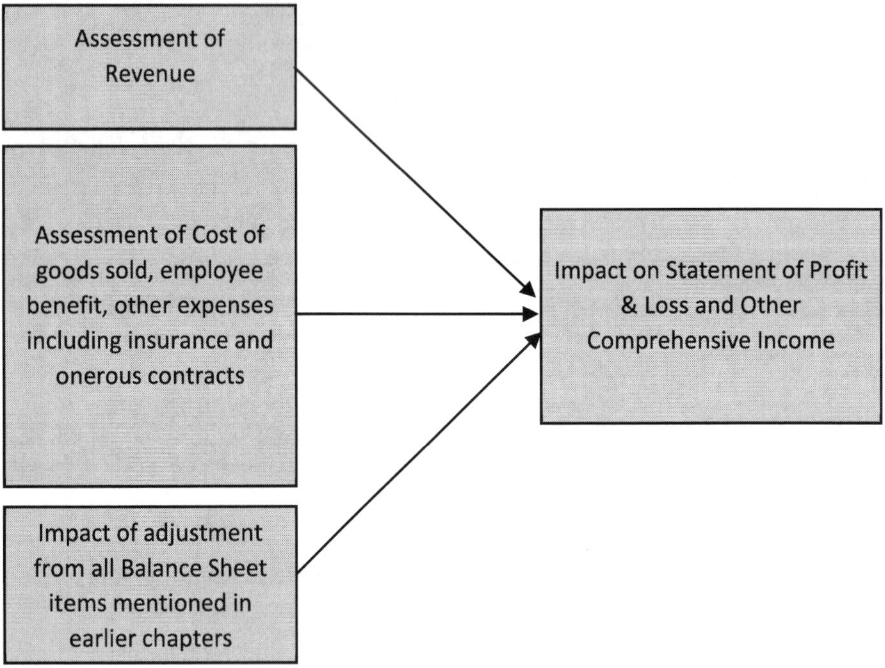


Accounting Quality of Revenue from operations, other Income, cost of goods sold and other expenses are evaluated by going through the following major control areas:

### 8.8.1 Revenue from operations

| Item |
|---|
| Whether one person is not responsible for taking customer orders, recording sales and receiving payment |
| Whether all recorded sales transactions represent goods shipped |
| Whether there is a policy where goods and services are only supplied to customers with good credit rating |
| Whether goods and services are provided at authorized prices and on authorized terms |
| Whether customers are encouraged to pay promptly through progressive discount structure |
| Whether all revenue related to goods dispatched have been recorded. |
| Whether all goods and services dispatched have been correctly invoiced. |
| Whether all sales invoices have been booked through completeness and the revenue is fairly represented in general ledger and financial statements |

### 8.8.2 Cost of goods sold

| Item |
|---|
| Whether existence of robust procure to pay cycle |
| Whether there is a robust ERP system in place to handle inventory and cost of goods sold through the system |
| Whether consumption accounting is properly in place to reconcile opening stock add purchases less closing stock for all items for which revenue is recognised |
| Whether item code masters are regularly cross checked to ensure these are free from errors |
| Whether Goods and services tax is properly accounted |
| Whether the provisions of Schedule III of Companies Act 2013 have been complied with. |

### 8.8.3 Employee benefits

| Item |
|---|
| Whether payments are made to bona fide employees of the organization |
| Whether there is an approved contract issued for each bona fide employee of the organization |

| Item |
|---|
| Whether all payroll costs are substantiated by time sheets of each employee against which the payments are made |
| Whether all benefits and deductions have been computed correctly |
| Whether the tax deduction at source has been accurately done by the deductor based on the provisions of Income Tax Act 1961. |
| Whether all payroll payments have been accurately updated in books of account. |
| Whether all payroll payments have been properly classified in the financial statements. |

### 8.8.4 Depreciation/Amortization

| Item |
|---|
| Whether there is a system of evaluation of useful life of assets |
| Whether depreciation has been charged based on consistency in accounting policy |
| Whether depreciation methods are in line with the relevant accounting standards? |
| Whether depreciation guidelines are as per Schedule II of the Companies Act 2013 |
| Whether amortization of intangible assets have been as per consistent policy |

### 8.8.5 Recording to reporting transactions

| Item |
|---|
| Whether Chart of Accounts adequately represent the operations of the organization |
| Whether there is a comprehensive Finance and Accounts policy manual in vogue |
| Whether there is an updated organization chart so as to define user access rights and responsibilities |
| Whether there is a segregation of duties of recording, checking and approval functions |
| Whether there is proper record retention policy as per local law of the land |
| Whether there is a conflict-of-interest policy, and it is consistently followed |
| Whether all authorized journal vouchers are posted to the general ledger accurately and within the right period. |
| Whether all the authorized journal vouchers are supported by source documents. |
| Whether sales journal is integrated with invoicing in system |
| Whether all receipt and payment entries are updated in cash book to keep the books of accounts up to date |

| Item |
|---|
| Whether Bank Reconciliation statements are completed online for all banks in the system |
| Whether all payroll journals are posted on a monthly basis |
| Whether all documents are generated from the system and no vouchers can be inserted manually |
| Whether the system has functionalities of parking and posting of vouchers, copy journal and reversal journal, in order that the system is not prone to any error owing to manual data entry |
| Whether the system provides workflow for approval to ensure robust internal control |
| Whether all provision related entries are posted with completeness |
| Whether the system has an in-built audit trail to ensure all records and editing of vouchers are well documented |
| Whether there is audit trail of all changes made in general ledger master files and any deviations are reviewed and discussed at Senior Management level. |
| Whether the system generates budget versus actual comparison of financial results |
| Whether all multi-currency postings are done through updated exchange rates and in line with the provisions in the relevant accounting standards. |
| Whether Accounts for some entities (for example, acquired subsidiaries) are properly classified on consolidated financial statements. |
| Whether intercompany adjustments are properly eliminated in the finalization of consolidated financial statements, |
| Whether amounts used in the consolidation for subsidiaries or other business entities agree to the amounts reported by these entities. |
| Whether management is alerted about discrepancies between account balances and amounts that have been budgeted or reflected under forecast. |
| Whether there is a seamless import and export of data to ensure no manual intervention is involved. |
| Whether all Account balances in general ledger are reconciled to amounts in sub-ledger systems on a regular basis. |
| Whether based on all the above functionalities under record to report system, the general ledger and financial statements provide credible financial results which can be relied upon. |

# Chapter 9

# Contingent Liabilities and Assets

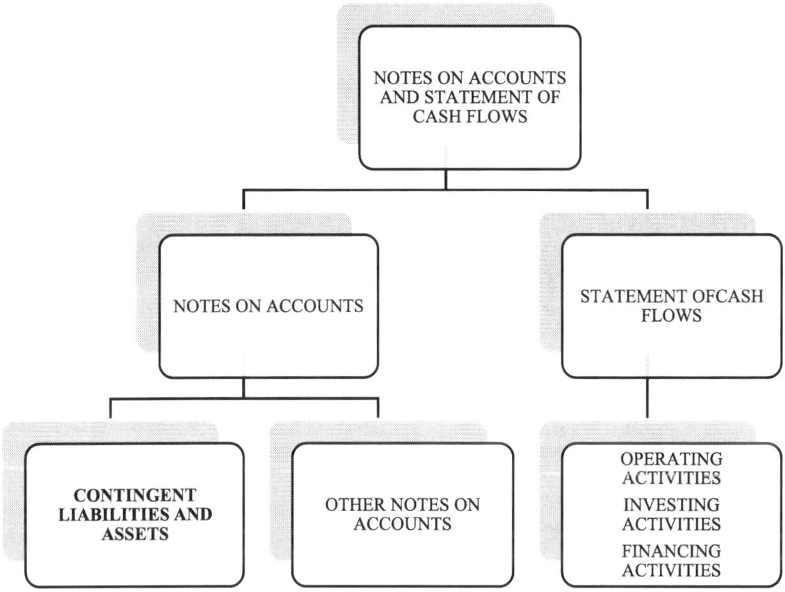


## 9.1 DEFINITION OF CONTINGENT LIABILITIES AND CONTINGENT ASSETS

According to ICAI Guidance Note on Terms used in Financial Statements, the terms Contingent Liabilities and Contingent Assets have been defined as under:

**Contingent Liabilities**

An obligation relating to an existing condition or situation which may arise in future depending on the occurrence or non-occurrence of one or more uncertain future events.

**Contingent Assets**

An asset the existence, ownership or value of which may be known or determined only on the occurrence or non-occurrence of one or more uncertain future events.

## 9.2 COMPONENTS OF CONTINGENT LIABILITIES AND COMMITMENTS

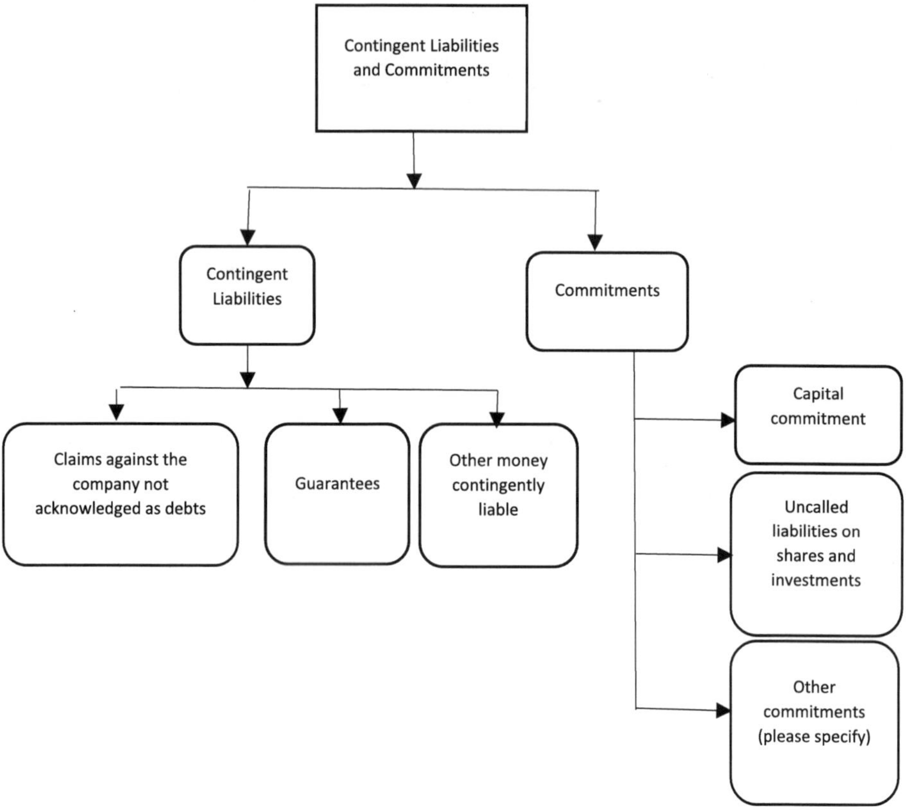


## 9.3 COMPARATIVE SUMMARY

| Under AS[1] | Under Ind AS[2] |
|---|---|
| **T. Contingent liabilities and commitments (to the extent not provided for)**<br>(i) Contingent liabilities shall be classified as:<br>(a) Claims against the company not acknowledged as debt ; | **H. Contingent Liabilities and Commitments (to the extent not provided for)**<br>(i) Contingent Liabilities shall be classified as:<br>(a) Claims against the company not acknowledged as debt; |

1 General Instructions for Preparation of Balance Sheet, Part I of Division I of Schedule III of the Companies Act, 2013.

2 General Instructions for Preparation of Balance Sheet, Part I of Division II of Schedule III of the Companies Act, 2013.

| | |
|---|---|
| (b) Guarantees ;<br>(c) Other money for which the company is contingently liable<br><br>(ii) Commitments shall be classified as:<br>(a) Estimated amount of contracts remaining to be executed on capital account and not provided for ;<br>(b) Uncalled liability on shares and other investments partly paid<br>(c) Other commitments (specify nature) | (b) Guarantees excluding financial guarantees;<br>(c) Other money for which the company is contingently liable.<br>(ii) Commitments shall be classified as:<br>(a) Estimated amount of contracts remaining to be executed on capital account and not provided for;<br>(b) Uncalled liability on shares and other investments partly paid;<br>(c) Other commitments (specify nature). |

## 9.4 GUARANTEES

According to Guidance Note on Schedule III – Division II on Ind AS issued by ICAI, a contingent liability related to guarantees arises when a company issues guarantees to another person on behalf of a third party e.g. when it undertakes to guarantee the loan given to a subsidiary or to another company or gives a guarantee that another company will perform its contractual obligations. However, in certain cases, the company issues a "counter-guarantee" against guarantees given by its bankers. Such "counter-guarantee" is not really a guarantee at all, but is an undertaking to perform the obligation of the company, namely, to pay the insurance premium when demanded or to make deferred payments when due. Hence, such performance guarantees and counter-guarantees should not be disclosed as contingent liabilities. ICAI Guidance Note on Schedule III – Division I for non-Ind AS entities corroborates the same.

Ind AS Schedule III stipulates that guarantees other than financial guarantees are to be disclosed as a part of contingent liabilities, since financial guarantees are recognised on the balance sheet in accordance with Ind AS 109. Ind AS 107 specifies certain disclosure in respect of the exposure to credit risk on financial guarantee contracts as a part of the disclosures on 'credit risk exposures', which an entity should provide in its Notes to Accounts.

## 9.5 COMMITMENTS

The word 'commitment' has not been defined in the Schedule III. The Guidance Note on Terms Used in Financial Statements issued by ICAI defines 'Capital Commitment' as future liability for capital expenditure in respect of which contracts have been made.

Schedule III requires disclosures pertaining to various commitments such as Capital commitments not provided for and Uncalled liability on shares. It also requires disclosures pertaining to 'Other commitments', with specification of nature thereof.

According to ICAI Guidance Note on Schedule III both Division I and Division II, the term 'Other commitments' would include all expenditure related contractual commitments apart from capital commitments such as commitments arising from long-term contracts for purchase of raw material, employee contracts, lease commitments, etc.

Accordingly, the disclosures required to be made for 'other commitments' should include only those non-cancellable contractual commitments (i.e. cancellation of which will result in a penalty disproportionate to the benefits involved).

According to the Guidance Note on Schedule III, the scope of such terminology is very wide and may include contractual commitments for purchase of inventory, services, investments, sales, employee contracts etc. However, to provide disclosure of all contractual commitment would be contrary to the overarching principle under General Instructions that " a balance shall be maintained between providing excessive detail that may not assist users of Financial Statements and not providing important information as a result of too much aggregation".

According to ICAI Guidance Note on Schedule III, entities need to disclose lease commitments for non-cancellable leases are required to be disclosed by AS-19 and Ind AS-116 Leases.

| | |
|---|---|
| ***Examples*** | Commitments in the nature of buy-back arrangements,<br>Commitments to fund subsidiaries and associates,<br>Non-disposal of investments in subsidiaries and undertakings,<br>Derivative related commitments, etc. |

## 9.6 PROPOSED DIVIDEND

The amount of dividend proposed to be distributed to equity and preference shareholders for the period and the related amount per share shall be disclosed separately.

Arrears of fixed cumulative dividends on preference shares shall also be disclosed separately. Though, the Act prohibits issue of irredeemable preference shares, Ind AS Schedule III requires separate disclosure of the arrears of fixed cumulative dividends on irredeemable preference shares.

It may be worthwhile to mention that, Ind AS-10 Events after the Reporting Period requires that dividends in respect of the period covered by the Financial Statements, which are proposed or declared by the enterprise after the Balance Sheet date but before approval of the Financial Statements, should not be adjusted but should be disclosed in accordance with Ind AS-1 Presentation of Financial Statements.

Please refer to Comparative summary of treatment of Proposed Dividend highlighted in Division I and Division II of Schedule III.

### 9.6.1 Comparative Summary

| Under AS[3] | Under Ind AS[4] |
|---|---|
| U. The amount of dividend proposed to be distributed to equity and preference shareholders for the period and the related amount per share shall be disclosed separately. Arrears of fixed cumulative dividends on preference shares shall also be disclosed separately. | I. The amount of dividends proposed to be distributed to equity and preference shareholders for the period and the related amount per share shall be disclosed separately. Arrears of fixed cumulative dividends on irredeemable preference shares shall also be disclosed separately. |

### 9.6.2 Comparative table on treatment of proposed dividend

| Schedule III of Companies Act, 2013 | Ind AS 10 | AS 4 |
|---|---|---|
| Schedule III requires disclosure of the amount of dividends proposed to be distributed to equity and preference shareholders for the period and the related amount per share to be disclosed separately. It also requires separate disclosure of the arrears of fixed cumulative dividends on preference shares. According to Old Schedule VI proposed dividend is to be disclosed under the head "Provisions". In Schedule IIII this needs to be disclosed in the notes. | Para 12 - If an entity declares dividends to holders of equity instruments (as defined in Ind AS 32 *Financial Instruments: Presentation) after the reporting period, the entity shall not recognise those dividends as a liability at the end of the reporting period.* According to para 13, if dividends are declared after the reporting period but before the financial statements are approved for issue, the dividends are not recognised as a liability at the end of the reporting period because no obligation exists at that time. Such dividends are disclosed in the notes in accordance with *Ind AS 1 Presentation of Financial Statements* | In accordance with *AS 4: Contingencies and Events after occurring after the Balance Sheet date (as amended) under Companies (Accounting Standard)Amendment Rules 2016*, dividends stated to be in respect of the period covered by the Financial Statements, which are proposed or declared by the enterprise after the Balance Sheet date but before the approval of the Financial Statements, should be disclosed. Keeping this in view companies will now need to disclose the same during the period covered by the Financial Statements, unless there is a change in statute. |

3 General Instructions for Preparation of Balance Sheet, Part I of Division I of Schedule III of the Companies Act, 2013.

4 General Instructions for Preparation of Balance Sheet, Part I of Division II of Schedule III of the Companies Act, 2013.

## 9.7 ACCOUNTING STANDARDS : AS 29: PROVISIONS, CONTINGENT LIABILITY AND CONTINGENT ASSETS (AS AMENDED)

**Contingent Liabilities and Contingent Assets**

### 9.7.1 Contingent Liabilities

*Para 26. An enterprise should not recognise a contingent liability.*

Para 27. A contingent liability is disclosed, as required by paragraph 68 of the Standard, unless the possibility of an outflow of resources embodying economic benefits is remote.

Para 28. Where an enterprise is jointly and severally liable for an obligation, the part of the obligation that is expected to be met by other parties is treated as a contingent liability. The enterprise recognises a provision for the part of the obligation for which an outflow of resources embodying economic benefits is probable, except in the extremely rare circumstances where no reliable estimate can be made (see paragraph 14).

Para 29. Contingent liabilities may develop in a way not initially expected. Therefore, they are assessed continually to determine whether an outflow of resources embodying economic benefits has become probable. If it becomes probable that an outflow of future economic benefits will be required for an item previously dealt with as a contingent liability, a provision is recognised in accordance with paragraph 14 in the financial statements of the period in which the change in probability occurs (except in the extremely rare circumstances where no reliable estimate can be made).

Under IFRS and Ind AS the decision tree on Contingent liabilities is shown below.

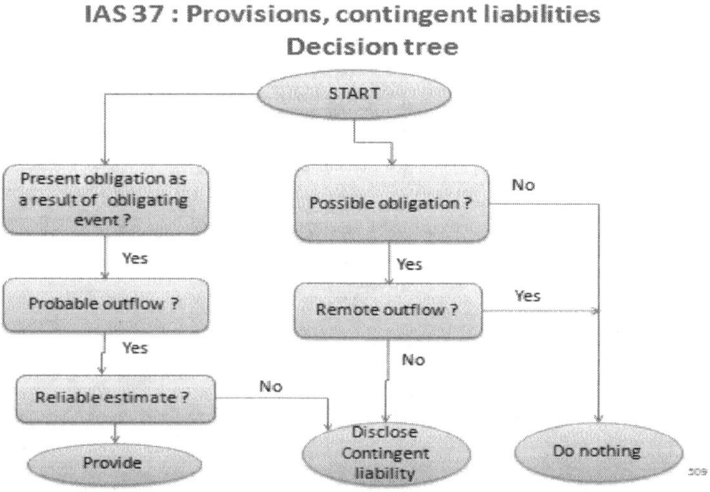

### 9.7.2 Contingent Assets

*Para 30. An enterprise should not recognise a contingent asset.*

Para 31. Contingent assets usually arise from unplanned or other unexpected events that give rise to the possibility of an inflow of economic benefits to the enterprise. An example is a claim that an enterprise is pursuing through legal processes, where the outcome is uncertain.

Para 32. Contingent assets are not recognised in financial statements since this may result in the recognition of income that may never be realised. However, when the realisation of income is virtually certain, then the related asset is not a contingent asset and its recognition is appropriate.

Para 33. A contingent asset is not disclosed in the financial statements. It is usually disclosed in the report of the approving authority (Board of Directors in the case of a company, and, the corresponding approving authority in the case of any other enterprise), where an inflow of economic benefits is probable.

Para 34. Contingent assets are assessed continually and if it has become virtually certain that an inflow of economic benefits will arise, the asset and the related income are recognised in the financial statements of the period in which the change occurs.

## 9.8 INDIAN ACCOUNTING STANDARDS : IND AS 37: PROVISIONS, CONTINGENT LIABILITY AND CONTINGENT ASSETS

**Contingent Liabilities and Contingent Assets**

### 9.8.1 Contingent liabilities

A contingent liability is not recognised but is disclosed unless the possibility of an outflow is resources is remote.

Contingent liabilities are further explained as per the chart below.

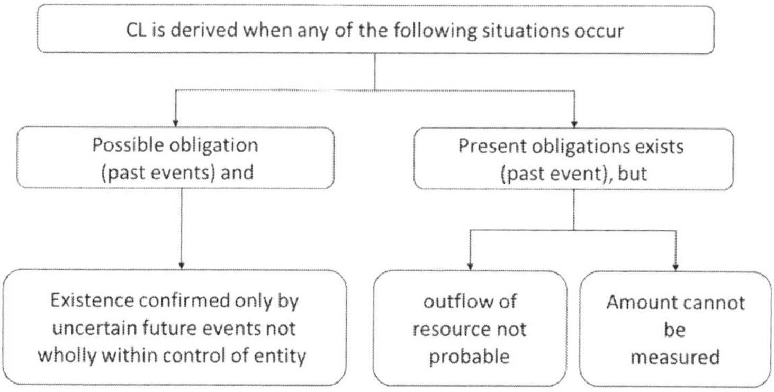

### 9.8.2 Contingent Assets

A contingent asset is not recognized but is disclosed when an inflow of economic benefits is probable.

A contingent asset is a possible asset that arises from past events and whose existence will be confirmed only by the occurrence or non – occurrence of one or more uncertain future events not wholly within the control of the entity.

Contingent assets are assessed continually and when it becomes reasonably certain that inflow of economic benefit will arise, the asset and related income are recognised in the previous year in which the change occurs.

**Illustration 9.1: Specimen format: Contingent liabilities and commitments**

| Particulars | As at 31st March 2022 | As at 31st March 2021 |
|---|---|---|
| (I) Contingent Liabilities | | |
| (A) Claims against the company / disputed liabilities not acknowledged as debts | | |
| (a) In respect of joint ventures | | |
| (b) In respect of others | | |
| (B) Guarantees | | |
| (i) Guarantees to Banks and Financial Institutions against credit facilities extended to third parties | | |
| (a) In respect of joint ventures | | |
| (b) In respect of others | | |
| (ii) Performance Guarantees | | |
| (a) In respect of joint ventures | | |
| (b) In respect of others | | |
| (iii) Outstanding guarantees furnished to Banks and Financial Institutions including in respect of Letters of Credits | | |
| (a) In respect of joint ventures | | |
| (b) In respect of others | | |
| (C) Other Money for which the company is contingently liable | | |
| (i) Liability in respect of bills discounted with Banks (Including third party bills discounting) | | |
| (a) In respect of joint ventures | | |
| (b) In respect of others | | |
| (II) Commitments | | |
| (A) Estimated amount of contracts remaining to be executed on capital account and not provided for: | | |
| (a) In respect of Joint Ventures | | |

| Particulars | As at 31st March 2022 | As at 31st March 2021 |
|---|---|---|
| (b) In respect of others<br>(B) Uncalled Liability on Shares and other investments partly paid<br>(C) Other commitments<br>(a) Sales tax deferral liability assigned<br>(b) Guarantee against future cash calls * | | |
| Total | xxx | xxx |

* The Company has issued guarantees against future cash calls to be made by JV Partners of its wholly owned subsidiary

**Illustration 9.2: Contingent Liabilities and commitments (*Source: ITC Limited*)**

Contingent liabilities and commitments:

(a) Contingent liabilities

Claims against the Company not acknowledged as debts Rs. 287.08 Crores (2011 –Rs. 255.17 Crores). These comprise:

- Excise duty, sales taxes and other indirect taxes claims disputed by the Company relating to issues of applicability and classification aggregating Rs. 199.23 Crores (2011 –Rs. 182.87 Crores).
- Local Authority taxes/cess/royalty on property, utilities etc. claims disputed by the Company relating to issues of applicability and determination aggregating Rs. 47.35 Crores (2011 –Rs. 33.83 Crores).
- Third party claims arising from disputes relating to contracts aggregating Rs. 37.26 Crores (2011 –Rs. 35.08 Crores).
- Other matters Rs. 3.24 Crores (2011 –Rs. 3.39 Crores).

(b) Commitments

- Estimated amount of contracts remaining to be executed on capital accounts and not provided for Rs. 2246.53 Crores (2011 –Rs. 1976.62 Crores).
- Uncalled liability on shares partly paid Rs. 26.40 Crores (2011 –Rs. 26.40 Crores).

# Chapter 10

# Other Notes on Accounts

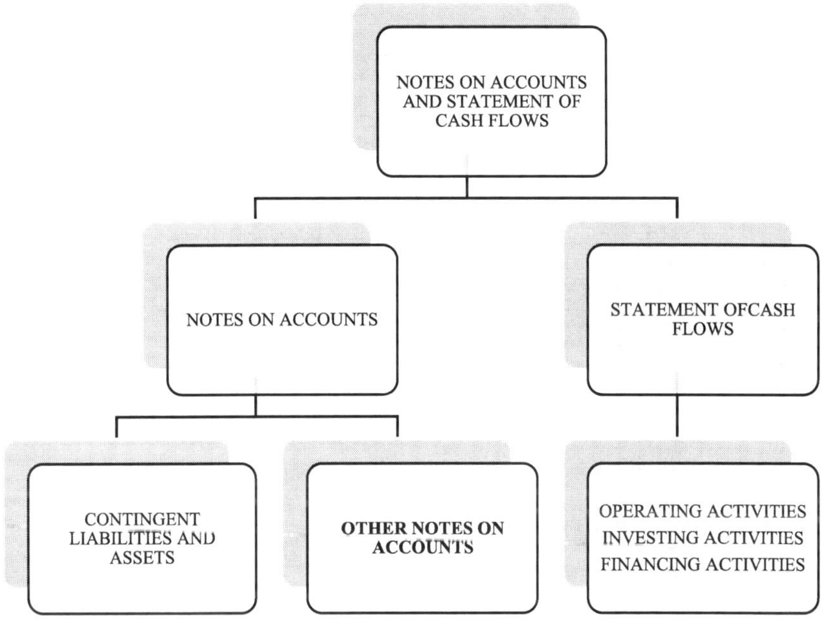


## 10.1 INTRODUCTION

Notes on Accounts is an important section of the Financial Statements, wherein all relevant information related to Balance Sheet and Statement of Profit and Loss are highlighted for the benefit of the shareholders, key stakeholders like banks and financial institutions and prospective investors.

## 10.2 BROAD POINTS COVERED UNDER NOTES TO ACCOUNTS

Notes to be normally presented in the following order:

- A Statement of compliance of all Accounting Standards - AS and Ind AS;
- A summary of significant accounting policies applied;
- The measurement bases used in preparing the financial statements;
- The other accounting policies used that are relevant to an understanding of the financial statements;

- Supporting information for each of the financial statements in the order in which it is presented.

Other disclosures would include-

- contingent liabilities and unrecognized contractual commitments;
- non-financial disclosures – e.g., financial risk management objectives and policies;
- disclosure of judgments;
- disclosure of key sources of estimation uncertainty.

## 10.3 COMPONENTS OF ADDITIONAL INFORMATION

A comparative summary of the information requirement as prescribed by Schedule III of the Companies Act, 2013 is summarized below.

| Under AS (Division I) | Under Ind AS (Division II) |
|---|---|
| **Additional information**<br>A Company shall disclose by way of notes additional information regarding aggregate<br>Expenditure and income on the following items:<br>(i) (a) Employee benefits expense showing separately<br>(i) Salaries and wages<br>(ii) Contribution to Provident and other funds<br>(iii) Expense on employee stock option scheme (ESOP) and Employee Stock Purchase Plan (ESPP)<br>(iv) Staff welfare expenses<br>(b) Depreciation and amortisation expenses<br>(c) Any item of income or expenditure which exceeds one per cent of the revenue from operations or Rs.1,00,000, whichever is higher,<br>(d) Interest income,<br>(e) Interest expense<br>(f) Dividend income<br>(g) Net gain/loss on sale of investments | **Additional Information**<br>A Company shall disclose by way of notes, additional information regarding aggregate expenditure and income on the following items:<br>(a) Employee Benefits expense [showing separately<br>(i) salaries and wages,<br>(ii) contribution to provident and other funds,<br>(iii) share based payments to employees,<br>(iv) staff welfare expenses.<br>(b) Depreciation and amortization expense;<br>(c) Any item of income or expenditure which exceeds one per cent of the revenue from operations or Rs.10,00,000, whichever is higher, in addition to the consideration of 'materiality' as specified in clause 7 of the General Instructions for Preparation of Financial Statements of a Company.<br>(d) Interest Income;<br>(e) Interest Expense;<br>(f) Dividend income;<br>(g) Net gain/loss on sale of investments; |

| Under AS (Division I) | Under Ind AS (Division II) |
|---|---|
| (h) Adjustments to the carrying amount of investments<br>(i) Net gain or loss on foreign currency transaction and translation(other than considered as finance cost)<br>(j) Payments to the auditor as<br>• As auditor<br>• For Taxation matters<br>• For Company Law Matters<br>• For Management services<br>• For other service<br>• For reimbursement of expenses<br>(k) In case of Companies covered under section 135, amount of expenditure incurred on corporate social responsibility activities,<br>(l) Details of items of exceptional and extraordinary nature,<br>(m) Prior period items,<br>(ii) (a) In case of manufacturing companies:<br>(1) Raw materials under broad heads<br>(2) Goods purchased under broad heads<br>(b) In case of trading companies, purchases in respect of goods traded in by the company under broad heads<br>(c) In the case of companies rendering or supplying services, gross income derived from the services rendered or supplied under broad heads<br>(d) In the case of a company, this falls under more than one of the categories mentioned in (a), (b) and (c) above, it shall be sufficient compliance with the requirements herein if purchases, sales and consumption of raw | (h) Net gain/loss on foreign currency transaction and translation (other than considered as finance cost);<br>(i) Payments to the auditor as<br>(a) auditor,<br>(b) for taxation matters,<br>(c) for company law matters,<br>(d) for other services,<br>(e) for reimbursement of expenses;<br>(j) In case of companies covered under section 135, amount of expenditure incurred on corporate social responsibility activities;<br>(k) Details of items of exceptional nature; |

| Under AS (Division I) | Under Ind AS (Division II) |
|---|---|
| material and the gross income from services rendered is shown under broad heads<br>(e) In the case of other companies, gross income derived under the broad heads<br>(iii) In the case of all concerns having works in progress under broad heads<br>(iv) (a) The aggregate, if material, of any amount set aside or proposed to be set aside, to reserve, but not including provisions made to meet any specific liability, contingency or commitment known to exist at the date as to which the balance sheet is made up,<br>(b) The aggregate, if material, of any amounts withdrawn from such reserves,<br>(v) (a) The aggregate, if material, of the amounts set aside to provisions made from meeting specific liabilities, contingencies or commitments<br>(b) The aggregate, if material, of the amounts withdrawn from such provisions, as no longer required<br>(vi) Expenditure incurred on each of the following items, separately for each item:<br>(a) Consumption of stores and spares,<br>(b) Power and fuel<br>(c) Rent<br>(d) Repairs to building<br>(e) Repairs to machinery<br>(f) Insurance<br>(g) Rates & taxes (excluding income tax)<br>(h) Miscellaneous expenditure<br>(vii)(a) Dividends from subsidiary companies<br>(b) Provisions for losses of subsidiary companies | |

| Under AS (Division I) | Under Ind AS (Division II) |
|---|---|
| (viii) The profit and loss account shall also contain by way of a note the following Information namely,<br>(a) Value of imports calculated on C.I.F basis by the company during the Financial year in respect of:<br>(i) Raw materials<br>(ii) Components and spare parts<br>(iii) Capital goods<br>(b) Expenditure in foreign currency during the financial year on account of royalty, know-how, professional and consultation fees, and other matter<br>(c) *Total* value of all imported raw materials, spare parts and components consumed during the financial year and the *total* value of all indigenous raw materials, spare parts and components similarly consumed and the percentage of each to the total consumption<br>(d) The amount remitted during the year in foreign currencies on account of dividends, with a specific mention of the *total* number of non-resident shareholders, the *total* number of shares held by them on which the dividends were due and the year to which the dividends related<br>(e) Earnings in foreign exchange classified under the following heads, namely:<br>(i) Export of goods calculated on FOB basis<br>(ii) Royalty, know-how, professional and consultation fees<br>(iii) Interest and dividends<br>(iv) Other income, indicating the nature thereof | |

| Under AS (Division I) | Under Ind AS (Division II) |
|---|---|
| **Note:** Broad heads shall be decided taking into account the concept of materiality and presentation of true and fair view of financial statement. | |

## 10.4 HIGHLIGHTS OF ADDITIONAL INFORMATION UNDER DIVISION I OF SCHEDULE III (AS)

### 10.4.1 Tax expenses

The disclosure would have to be on the face of the Statement of Profit and Loss and need to be bifurcated as under:

(1) Current tax and

(2) Deferred tax

***Current Tax*** has been defined under AS 22, "Accounting for Taxes" on Income as the amount of income tax determined to be payable (recoverable) in respect of the taxable income (tax loss) for a period. Hence, details of all taxes on income payable under the applicable taxation laws should be disclosed here.

***Deferred Tax*** has been defined under AS 22 as the tax effect of timing differences. Timing differences are defined as "differences between taxable income and accounting income for a period that originate in one period and are capable of reversal in one or more subsequent periods."

#### *10.4.1.1 ICAI Guidance Note on minimum alternative tax under Income Tax Act, 1961*

The Finance Act, 2005, inserted in sub-section (1) to section 115 JAA, to grant tax credit in respect of MAT paid under section 115 JB of the Act with effect from assessment year 2006-07. This Guidance Note deals with various aspects of accounting and presentation of MAT paid and credit available in this regard. The Guidance Note describes the salient features of MAT credit and its accounting treatment.

MAT credit should be recognised as an asset only when there is convincing evidence that the company will pay normal income tax during the specified period. MAT credit is a deferred tax asset for the purposes of AS 22. A company should write down the carrying amount of the MAT credit asset to the extent there is no convincing evidence that the company will pay normal income tax during the specified period.

**Balance Sheet**

Where a company recognises MAT credit as an asset, the same should be presented under "Loans & Advances" since, there is a convincing evidence of realisation of the asset, that it is of the nature of pre-paid tax which would be adjusted against the normal income tax during the specified period. The asset may be reflected as "MAT credit entitlement".

In the year of set-off of credit, the amount of credit availed should be shown as a deduction from the provision for taxation on the liabilities side of the balance sheet.

The unavailed amount of MAT credit entitlement, if any, should continue to be presented under the head "Loans and Advances" if it continues to meet the considerations stated in para 11 of the Guidance Note.

**Profit and Loss Account**

According to para 6 of Accounting Standards Interpretation (ASI) 6, "Accounting for taxes on income in the context of Section 115JB of the Income Tax Act 1961" issued by ICAI, MAT is the current tax. Accordingly, the tax expense arising on account of payment of MAT should be charged at the gross amount, in the normal way, to the profit and loss account in the year of payment of MAT. In the year in which the MAT credit becomes eligible to be recognised as an asset in accordance with the recommendations contained in this Guidance Note, the said asset should be created by way of a credit to the profit and loss account and presented as a separate line item therein.

The disclosure would be as under:

| | |
|---|---|
| Current tax (MAT) | xx |
| Less: MAT credit entitlement | (xx) |
| Net current tax | xx |

Any interest on shortfall in payment of advance income-tax is in the nature of finance cost and hence should not be clubbed with the current tax. This needs to be classified as interest expense under finance costs. However, this needs to be disclosed separately.

Any penalties levied under income tax laws should not be classified as current tax.

Penalties which are compensatory in nature should be treated as interest and disclosed in the manner explained above. Other tax penalties should be classified under Other Expenses.

Wealth tax payable by a company on assets liable for wealth tax should not be included within current tax since the same is not a tax on income. Accordingly, wealth tax should be included in Rates and Taxes under Other Expenses.

Short/excess provision of tax relating to earlier years should be separately disclosed.

### 10.4.1.2 ICAI Guidance Note on Accounting of Corporate Dividend tax

Corporate Dividend Tax (CDT) is in addition to the income tax chargeable in respect of the total income of a domestic company and was introduced under the Finance Act 1997.

Corporate Dividend Tax on dividend, being directly linked to the amount of dividend, should also be reflected in the accounts of the same financial year even though the actual tax liability in respect thereof may arise in a different year.

The liability in respect of CDT arises only if the profits are distributed as dividends whereas the normal income-tax liability arises on the earning of taxable profits.

Since CDT liability relates to distribution of profits as dividends which are disclosed "below the line", it is appropriate that the liability in respect of CDT should also be disclosed "below the line" as a separate item. Such disclosure would give a proper picture regarding payments involved with reference to dividends.

Recommendations of Guidance Note on "Accounting for Corporate Dividend Tax" are as under:

| Item | Description |
|---|---|
| Recognition | Corporate Dividend Tax (CDT) liability should be recognised in the accounts of the same financial year in which the dividend concerned is recognised. |
| Disclosure in Profit & Los A/c | CDT Liability should be disclosed separately in the Profit & Loss A/c below the line as follows:<br>Dividend xxx<br>Corporate Dividend Tax thereon xxx |
| Disclosure in Balance Sheet | Provision for CDT should be disclosed separately under the head "Provisions" in the balance sheet. |

### 10.4.1.3 ICAI Guidance Note on Measurement of Income tax expenses for interim financial reporting in the context of AS 25: Interim Financial Reporting

This Guidance Note deals with measurement of income tax expenses for the purpose of inclusion in the interim financial reports pursuant to AS 25: Interim Financial Reporting.

Accounting for interim period income-tax expense is based on guideline prescribed in AS 25 that the interim period is part of the whole accounting year (often referred to as the "integral approach") and, therefore, the said expense should be worked out on the basis of the estimated weighted average annual effective income-tax rate.

According to this approach, the said rate is determined on the basis of taxable incomc for the whole year, and applied to the accounting income for the interim period in order to determine the amount of tax expense for that interim period.

This approach is in contrast to accounting for certain other expenses such as depreciation which is based on the approach prescribed in AS 25 (often referred to as "discrete approach") that the interim period should be considered on stand-alone basis, because expenses such as depreciation are worked out based on the period for which the fixed asset was available for use.

However, the treatment is consistent with the requirement specified in paragraph 27 of AS 25, whereby an enterprise should apply the same accounting policies in its interim financial statements as are applied in its annual financial statements.

### 10.4.1.4 AS 22: Accounting for taxes

| | |
|---|---|
| ***Current tax*** | The term "current tax" has been defined under AS 22" Accounting for Taxes" on income as the amount of income tax determined to be payable (recoverable) in respect of the taxable income (tax loss) for a period. Hence, details of all taxes on income payable under the applicable taxation laws should be disclosed here.<br>With respect to Minimum Alternative Tax under the Income Tax Act 1961, presentation of Minimum Alternate Tax (MAT) credit should be made as prescribed by the Guidance Note on the subject by ICAI. |
| ***Deferred tax*** | Charge/credit related to deferred taxes needs to be disclosed separately on the face of the Statement of Profit and Loss<br>In accordance with AS 22, Accounting for taxes on income defines "Deferred tax" as the tax effect of timing differences.<br>Timing differences are defined as differences between taxable income and accounting income for a period that originate in one period and are capable of reversal in one or more subsequent periods. |

### 10.4.1.5 Related Party Disclosures

As per ICAI Guidance Note on Schedule III, Accounting Standards will override Schedule III and hence, related party shall be as defined in the Accounting Standard.

**Guidance Note related to remuneration paid to key management personnel – whether a related party transaction**

This Guidance Note deals with the issue whether remuneration paid to key management personnel is a related party transaction. Another related issue dealt by this Guidance Note is whether remuneration paid to nonexecutive directors on the Board of Directors is a related party transaction.

Accounting Standard (AS) 18, Related Party Disclosures, defines "related party transaction" as "a transfer of resources or obligations between related parties, regardless of whether or not a price is charged." Further, paragraph 24 of AS 18 provides as under:

> *"The following are examples of the related party transactions in respect of which disclosures may be made by a reporting enterprise:*
>
> *Remuneration paid to Key Management Personnel - Whether a Related Party,*
>
> - *purchases or sales of goods (finished or unfinished);*
> - *purchases or sales of fixed assets;*
> - *rendering or receiving of services;*
> - *agency arrangements;*
> - *leasing or hire purchase arrangements;*
> - *transfer of research and development;*
> - *licence agreements;*
> - *finance (including loans and equity contributions in cash or in kind); guarantees and collaterals; and*
> - *management contracts including for deputation of employees."*

As per the definition of the expression 'related party transaction', the transaction should be between related parties to qualify as a related party transaction. Since key management personnel are related parties under AS 18, remuneration paid to key management personnel is a related party transaction requiring disclosures under AS 18. Further, in case non-executive directors on the Board of Directors are not related parties, remuneration paid to them is not considered a related party transaction.

The Guidance Note recommends that, remuneration paid to key management personnel should be considered as a related party transaction requiring disclosures under AS 18.

In case non-executive directors on the Board of Directors are not related parties, remuneration paid to them should not be considered a related party transaction.

**Illustration 10.1: Related party disclosures**

As per Accounting Standard 18, the disclosures of transactions with the related parties are given below:

(i) List of related parties where control exists and related parties with whom transactions have taken place and relationships:

| S/l no | Name of related party | Relationship |
|---|---|---|
| | | |

(ii) Transactions during the year with related parties: (Rs. in crore)

| S/l no | Nature of transactions excluding reimbursements | Subsidiaries | Associates | Key managerial personnel | Others | Total |
|---|---|---|---|---|---|---|
| | Current Year<br><br>(Previous Year) | | | | | |

Disclosure in Respect of Material Related Party Transactions during the year:

| S/L no | Description of transaction | Current Year | Previous Year |
|---|---|---|---|
| | | | |

## 10.4.2 Accounting Standards: AS 18: Related Party disclosures

### *10.4.2.1 Objectives*

The objective of this Standard is to establish requirements for disclosure of:

(a) related party relationships; and

(b) transactions between a reporting enterprise and its related parties.

This Standard deals only with related party relationships described in below:

(a) enterprises that directly, or indirectly through one or more intermediaries, control, or are controlled by, or are under common control with, the reporting enterprise (this includes holding companies, subsidiaries and fellow subsidiaries);

(b) associates and joint ventures of the reporting enterprise and the investing party or venturer in respect of which the reporting enterprise is an associate or a joint venture;

(c) individuals owning, directly or indirectly, an interest in the voting power of the reporting enterprise that gives them control or significant influence over the enterprise, and relatives of any such individual;

(d) key management personnel and relatives of such personnel; and

(e) enterprises over which any person described in (c) or (d) is able to exercise significant influence. This includes enterprises owned by directors or major shareholders of the reporting enterprise and enterprises that have a member of key management in common with the reporting enterprise.

### 10.4.2.2 Disclosure requirements

Name of the related party and nature of the related party relationship where control exists should be disclosed irrespective of whether or not there have been transactions between the related parties.

If there have been transactions between related parties, during the existence of a related party relationship, the reporting enterprise should disclose the following:

(i) the name of the transacting related party;

(ii) a description of the relationship between the parties;

(iii) a description of the nature of transactions;

(iv) volume of the transactions either as an amount or as an appropriate proportion;

(v) any other elements of the related party transactions necessary for an understanding of the financial statements;

(vi) the amounts or appropriate proportions of outstanding items pertaining to related parties at the balance sheet date and provisions for doubtful debts due from such parties at that date; and

(vii) amounts written off or written back in the period in respect of debts due from or to related parties.

The following are examples of the related party transactions in respect of which disclosures may be made by a reporting enterprise:

(a) purchases or sales of goods (finished or unfinished);

(b) purchases or sales of fixed assets;

(c) rendering or receiving of services;

(d) agency arrangements;

(e) leasing or hire purchase arrangements;

(f) transfer of research and development;

(g) licence agreements;

(h) finance (including loans and equity contributions in cash or in kind);

(i) guarantees and collaterals; and

(j) management contracts including for deputation of employees.

**Illustration 10.2**

Identify the related parties in the following cases as per AS 18:

(a) A Ltd holds 51% of B Ltd

(b) B Ltd holds 51% of O Ltd

(c) Z Ltd holds 49% of O Ltd

**Solution**

A Ltd, B Ltd and O Ltd are related to each other.

Z Ltd and O Ltd are related to each other by virtue of associate relationship.

However, Z Ltd is not related to A Ltd or B Ltd or vice versa.

**Illustration 10.3**

Kaveri Ltd sold goods worth Rs.90 lakhs to Ganga Ltd during the year ended 31.3.2018. The Managing Director of Kaveri Ltd holds 100% of Ganga Ltd. The sales were made to Ganga Ltd at normal selling price followed by Kaveri Ltd. The Chief Accountant of Kaveri Ltd contends that these sales need not require a different treatment from the other sales made by the company and hence no disclosure is necessary as per the accounting standard. Is the Chief Accountant correct?

**Solution**

As per para 13 of AS 18, enterprises over which a key management personnel is able to exercise significant influence are related parties. This includes enterprises owned by the directors or major shareholders of the reporting enterprise that have a member of key management in common with the reporting enterprise.

In the given case, Kaveri Ltd and Ganga Ltd are related parties and hence disclosure of transaction between them is required irrespective of whether the transaction was done at normal selling price.

Hence the contention of the Chief Accountant of the Kaveri Ltd is incorrect.

**Illustration 10.4**

X Ltd sold goods to its associate company for the 1st quarter ending 30.6.2018. After that the related party relationship ceased to exist. However, goods were supplied as was supplied to other ordinary customers. Decide whether transactions of the entire year have to be disclosed as related party transactions.

**Solution**

As per para 23 of AS 18 transactions of X Ltd with its associate company for the first Quarter ending 30.06.10 only are required to be disclosed as related party transactions. The transactions for the period in which related party relationship did not exist need not be reported.

**Illustration 10.5**

P Ltd has 60% voting right in Q Ltd. Q Ltd has 20% voting right in R Ltd. Also, P Ltd directly enjoys voting right of 14% in R Ltd. R Ltd is a listed company and regularly supplies goods to P Ltd. The management of R Ltd has not disclosed its relationship with P Ltd.

How would you assess the situation from the viewpoint of AS 18 on Related Party disclosures?

**Solution**

P Ltd has direct economic interest in R Ltd to the extent of 14% and through Q Ltd in which it is the majority shareholders, it has further control of 12% in R Ltd (60% of Q Ltd's 20%). These two taken together (14% + 12%) make the total control of 26%.

Para 10 of AS 18 "Related Party Disclosures" defines related party as one that has at any time during the reporting period, the ability to control the other party or exercise significant influence over the other party in financial and/or operating decisions.

Here control is defined as ownership directly or indirectly of more than one-half of the Voting power of an enterprise; and significant influence is defined as participation in the Financial and/or operating policy decisions of an enterprise but not control of those policies.

In the present case, control of P Ltd in R Ltd directly and through Q Ltd does not go beyond 26%. However, as per para 12 of AS 18, significant influence may be exercised as an investing party (P Ltd) holds, directly or indirectly through intermediaries 20% or more of the voting power of R Ltd. As R Ltd is a listed company and regularly supplies goods to P Ltd, therefore, related party disclosure, as per AS 18 is required.

**Illustration 10.6**

"Remuneration paid to key management personnel is not considered as a related party transaction, requiring disclosure under AS 18". Comment on the validity of the statement.

**Solution**

As per Guidance Note on "remuneration paid to key management personnel – whether a related party transaction", the transaction should be between related parties to qualify as a related party transaction. Since key management personnel are related parties under AS 18, remuneration paid to key management personnel is a related party transaction requiring disclosures under AS 18. Further, in case non-executive directors on the board of directors are not related parties, remuneration paid to them is not considered a related party transaction. According to the recommendation given in the Guidance Note, remuneration paid to key management personnel should be considered as a related party transaction requiring disclosures under AS 18. In case of non-executive directors on the Board of Directors are not related parties, remuneration paid to them should not be considered a related party transaction.

**Illustration 10.7**

Mr Kapil a relative of key management personnel received remuneration of Rs.250000 for his services in the company for the period 1.04.2017 till 31.7.2017. On 1.8.2017 he left the service. Should the relative be identified as at the closing date i.e. on 31.3.2018 for the purposes of AS 18?

**Solution**

In accordance with para 10 of AS 18 on Related Party disclosures, parties are considered to be related if at any time during the reporting period one party has the ability to control the other party or exercise significant influence over the other party in making financial and/or operating decisions. Hence Mr. Kapil, a relative of key management personnel should be identified as relative as at the closing date i.e. 31.3.2018.

### *10.4.2.3 Earnings per share*

According to AS 20: Earnings per share, the salient features are as under:

(a) **Presentation requirement of EPS**

An enterprise should present basic and diluted earnings per share on the face of the statement of profit and loss for each class of equity shares that has a different right to share in the net profit for the period. An enterprise should present basic and diluted earnings per share with equal prominence for all periods presented.

This Standard requires an enterprise to present basic and dilute earnings per share, even if the amounts disclosed are negative (a loss per share).

### (b) Basic Earnings Per Share

Calculated by dividing the net profit or loss for the period attributable to equity shareholders by the weighted average number of equity shares outstanding during the period.

For the purpose of calculating basic earnings per share, the net profit or loss for the period attributable to equity shareholders should be the net profit or loss for the period after deducting preference dividends and any attributable tax thereto for the period.

For the purpose of calculating basic earnings per share, the number of equity shares should be the weighted average number of equity shares outstanding during the period.

### (c) Calculation of EPS on bonus shares

**Illustration 10.8: Bonus issue**

**Bonus Issue**

(Accounting year 01-01-20XX to 31-12-20XX)

| | |
|---|---|
| Net profit for the year 20X0 | Rs. 18,00,000 |
| Net profit for the year 20X1 | Rs. 60,00,000 |
| No. of equity shares outstanding until 30th September 20X1 | 20,00,000 |
| Bonus issue 1st October 20X1 | 2 equity shares for each equity share outstanding at 30th September, 20X1<br>20,00,000 x 2 = 40,00,000 |
| Earnings per share for the year 20X1 | Rs. 60,00,000/= Re. 1.00<br>( 20,00,000 + 40,00,000) |
| Adjusted earnings per share for the year 20X0 | Rs. 18,00,000/= Re. 0.30<br>(20,00,000 + 40,00,000) |

Since the bonus issue is an issue without consideration, the issue is treated as if it had occurred prior to the beginning of the year 20X0, the earliest period reported.

### (d) Calculation of Rights issue

**Illustration 10.9: Rights issue**

**Rights Issue**

(Accounting year 01-01-20XX to 31-12-20XX)

| | |
|---|---|
| Net profit | Year 20X0 : Rs. 11,00,000 |

| | Year 20X1 : Rs. 15,00,000 |
|---|---|
| No. of shares outstanding prior to rights issue | 5,00,000 shares |
| Rights issue Outstanding | One new share for each five (i.e. 1,00,000 new shares)<br>Rights issue price: Rs. 15.00<br>Last date to exercise rights:-<br>1st March 20X1 |
| Fair value of one equity share immediately prior to exercise of rights on 1st March 20X1 | Rs. 21.00 |

**Computation of theoretical ex-rights fair value per share**

(Fair value of all outstanding shares immediately prior to exercise of rights + total amount received from exercise)

(Number of shares outstanding prior to exercise + number of shares issued in the exercise)

((Rs. 21.00 x 5,00,000 shares) + (Rs. 15.00 x 1,00,000 shares))/(5,00,000 shares + 1,00,000 shares)

**Theoretical ex-rights fair value per share** = Rs. 20.00

Computation of adjustment factor

Fair value per share prior to exercise of rights Rs. (21.00) = 1.05

Theoretical ex-rights value per share Rs. (20.00)

**Computation of earnings per share**

| EPS for the year 20X0 as originally reported: **Year 20X0** | **Year 20X1** |
|---|---|
| Rs.11,00,000/5,00,000 shares Rs. 2.20 | |
| EPS for the year 20X0 restated for rights issue: Rs.11,00,000/ (5,00,000 shares x 1.05) | Rs. 2.10 |
| EPS for the year 20X1 including effects of rights issue | Rs. 2.55 |
| Rs. 15,00,00<br>(5,00,000 x 1.05 x 2/12) + (6,00,000 x 10/12) | |

## (e) Diluted earnings per share

In calculating diluted earnings per share, effect is given to all dilutive potential equity shares that were outstanding during the period, that is:

(a) the net profit for the period attributable to equity shares is:

(i) increased by the amount of dividends recognised in the period in respect of the dilutive potential equity shares as adjusted for any attributable change in tax expense for the period;

(ii) increased by the amount of interest recognised in the period in respect of the dilutive potential equity shares as adjusted for any attributable change in tax expense for the period; and

(iii) adjusted for the after-tax amount of any other changes in expenses or income that would result from the conversion of the dilutive potential equity shares.

(b) the weighted average number of equity shares outstanding during the period is increased by the weighted average number of additional equity shares which would have been outstanding assuming the conversion of all dilutive potential equity shares.

### Illustration 10.10: Diluted earnings per share

**Computation of Diluted Earnings Per Share**

| | Net Profit Attributable (Rs.) | No. of Equity Shares | Net profit attributable Per Share |
|---|---|---|---|
| (Rs.) | | | |
| As reported | 1,00,00,000 | 20,00,000 | 5.00 |
| Options | 20,000 | | |
| | 1,00,00,000 | 20,20,000 | 4.95 Dil |
| utive | | | |
| 12% Convertible | 84,00,000 | 40,00,000 | |
| Debentures | | | |
| | 1,84,00,000 | 60,20,000 | |
| 3.06 | Dilutive | | |
| Convertible | 70,40,000 | 16,00,000 | |
| Preference | | | |
| Shares | 2,54,40,000 | 76,20,000 | |
| 3.34 | Anti-Dilutive | | |

Since diluted earnings per share is increased when taking the convertible preference shares into account (from Rs. 3.06 to Rs 3.34), the convertible preference shares are anti-dilutive and are ignored in the calculation of diluted earnings per share.

Therefore, a diluted earnings per share is Rs. 3.06.

### *10.4.2.4 Adjustment to the carrying amount of investments*

According to Clause (h) of Note 5(i), adjustments to carrying amount of investments related to diminution in value of the investment (or reversal thereof) in conformity with AS 13 "Accounting for Investments", need to be disclosed.

### *10.4.2.5 Net gains/losses on account of foreign exchange*

Any gains/losses on account of foreign exchange fluctuations need to be disclosed separately as per AS 11. Net exchange loss should be classified under 'other expenses' and the amount so included should be separately disclosed. Under this head, exchange differences to the extent classified as borrowing costs as per Para 4(e) of AS-16 should not be disclosed.

### *10.4.2.6 Payment to auditors*

Expenses incurred towards such auditor's remuneration should be disclosed under each of the following sub-heads as follows:

(a) Auditor,

(b) For taxation matters,

(c) For company law matters,

(d) For management services,

(e) For other services,

(f) For reimbursement of expenses

### *10.4.2.7 Prior period expenses*

The term 'Prior period Items' has not been defined under Schedule III Division I. Accounting Standard *AS 5 "Net Profit or Loss for the period, Prior period items and changes in Accounting Policies*", in para 4.3 defines 'Prior period items' as "*Prior period items are income or expenses which arise in the current period as a result of errors or omissions in the preparation of the Financial Statements of one or more prior periods*".

### 10.4.2.8 Additional information related to Manufacturing and Trading companies

According to ICAI Guidance Note on Schedule III (Revised January, 2022 Edition) for non-Ind AS entities, the additional information related to manufacturing and trading companies have been summarized in the table below.

| Nature of entity | Disclosure requirement |
|---|---|
| Manufacturing companies | Raw materials under broad heads.<br>Goods purchased under broad heads. |
| Trading companies | Purchase of goods traded under broad heads |
| Companies rendering or supplying services | Gross income derived from services rendered under broad heads. |
| Companies falling under more than one category | It will be sufficient compliance with the requirements, if purchases, sales and consumption of raw material and the gross income from services rendered are shown under broad heads. |

### 10.4.2.9 AS 17: Segment Reporting

**Need for Segment Reporting**

We need segment reporting to establish principles for reporting financial information, about the different types of products and services an enterprise produces and the different geographical areas in which it operates. Such information helps users of financial statements:

(a) *better understand the performance of the enterprise;*

(b) *better assess the risks and returns of the enterprise; and*

(c) *make more informed judgements about the enterprise as a whole*

**Business Segment and Reportable Segment**

| | |
|---|---|
| ***(a) A business segment*** | is a distinguishable component of an enterprise that is engaged in providing an individual product or service or a group of related products or services and that is subject to risks and returns that are different from those of other business segments. Factors that should be considered in determining whether products or services are related include:<br>(a) the nature of the products or services;<br>(b) the nature of the production processes;<br>(c) the type or class of customers for the products or services;<br>(d) the methods used to distribute the products or provide the services; and<br>(e) if applicable, the nature of the regulatory environment, for example, banking, insurance, or public utilities. |

| | |
|---|---|
| ***(b) A reportable segment*** | is a business segment or a geographical segment identified on the basis of foregoing definitions for which segment information is required to be disclosed by this Standard. |

**Primary and Secondary reporting formats**

In general, the nature of risks and returns of an enterprise should govern whether its primary segment reporting format will be business segments or geographical segments.

If risks and returns of an enterprise are strongly affected both by differences in the products and services it produces and by differences in the geographical areas in which it operates, as evidenced by "matrix approach", the enterprise should use business segments as its primary segment reporting format and geographical segment as its secondary reporting format.

If internal organization and management structure of an enterprise are based neither on individual products or services or groups of related products/services nor on geographical areas, it should be determined whether the risks and returns of the enterprise are related more to the products or services it produces or to the geographical areas in which it operates and accordingly choose segments.

**Segment (Quantitative Thresholds)**

A business segment or geographical segment should be identified as reportable segment if:

- its reported revenue, both from external customers and inter segment sales and transfers is 10% or more of the combined revenue, internal and external, of all segments or
- its segment results, whether profit or loss is 10% or more of
  - (a) the combined result of all segments in profit or
  - (b) the combined result of all segments in loss, whichever is greater in absolute amount or
    - Its segment assets are 10% or more of the combined assets of all segments
    - If the total external revenue attributable to reportable

segments constitute less than 75 % of the total entity's revenue, additional segments must be identifiable as reportable segments, even if they do not meet the 10 percent thresholds, until at least 75% of the total entity's revenue is included in reportable segments.

**Reporting Requirements:**

**(a) Primary reporting format**

| | |
|---|---|
| ***Disclosure requirements of primary reporting*** | (a) segment revenue, classified into segment revenue from sales to external customers and segment revenue from transactions with other segments; |

| | |
|---|---|
| ***format*** | (b) segment result;<br>(c) total carrying amount of segment assets;<br>(d) total amount of segment liabilities;<br>(e) total cost incurred during the period to acquire segment assets that are expected to be used during more than one period (tangible and intangible fixed assets);<br>(f) total amount of expense included in the segment result for depreciation and amortisation in respect of segment assets for the period; and<br>(g) total amount of significant non-cash expenses, other than depreciation and amortisation in respect of segment assets, that were included in segment expense and, therefore, deducted in measuring segment result. |

## (b) Secondary segment

| | |
|---|---|
| ***Disclosure requirements of secondary segment information***<br>- ***if primary format is business segment*** | If primary format of an enterprise for reporting segment information is business segments, it should also report the following information:<br>(a) segment revenue from external customers by geographical area based on the geographical location of its customers, for each geographical segment whose revenue from sales to external customers is 10 per cent or more of enterprise revenue;<br>(b) the total carrying amount of segment assets by geographical location of assets, for each geographical segment whose segment assets are 10 per cent or more of the total assets of all geographical segments; and<br>(c) the total cost incurred during the period to acquire segment assets that are expected to be used during more than one period (tangible and intangible fixed assets) by geographical location of assets, for each geographical segment whose segment assets are 10 per cent or more of the total assets of all the segments |
| - ***if primary format is geographical segments*** | If primary format of an enterprise for reporting segment information is geographical segments (whether based on location of assets or location of customers), it should also report the following segment information for each business segment whose revenue from sales to external customers is 10 per cent or more of enterprise revenue or whose segment assets are 10 per cent or more of the total assets of all business segments:<br>(a) segment revenue from external customers;<br>(b) the total carrying amount of segment assets; and<br>(c) the total cost incurred during the period to acquire Segment assets that are expected to be used during more than one period (tangible and intangible fixed assets). |

| | |
|---|---|
| - ***If primary format is geographical segment that are based on location of assets, and if location of assets is different from location of its assets*** | then the enterprise should also report revenue from sales to external customers for each customer-based geographical segment whose revenue from sales to external customers is 10 per cent or more of enterprise revenue |
| - ***If primary format is geographical segments that are based on location of customers, and if the assets of the enterprise are located in different geographical areas from its customers*** | then the enterprise should also report the following segment information for each asset-based geographical segment whose revenue from sales to external customers or segment assets are 10 per cent-<br>(a) the total carrying amount of segment assets by geographical location of the assets; and<br>(b) the total cost incurred during the period to acquire segment assets that are expected to be used during more than one period (tangible and intangible fixed assets) by location of the assets. |

### *10.4.2.10 Undisclosed Income*

As per the Income Tax Act, 1961, "undisclosed income" includes any money, bullion, jewellery or other valuable article or thing or any income based on any entry in the books of account or other documents or transactions, where such money, bullion, jewellery, valuable article, thing, entry in the books of account or other document or transaction represents wholly or partly income or property which has not been or would not have been disclosed for the purposes of this Act, or any expense, deduction or allowance claimed under this Act which is found to be false. The meaning of "undisclosed income" shall be considered on the basis of the Income Tax Act, 1961 or basis judicial decisions provided on undisclosed income

The Company shall give details of any transaction not recorded in the books of accounts that has been surrendered or disclosed as income during the year in the tax assessments under the Income Tax Act, 1961 (such as, search or survey or any other relevant provisions of the Income Tax Act, 1961), unless there is immunity for disclosure under any scheme and also shall state whether the previously unrecorded income and related assets have been properly recorded in the books of account during the year

ICAI as per its Guidance Note under Schedule III Division I has recommended a table to facilitate the disclosure related to this.

| S/L No. | Assessment Year | Section of Income Tax Act | Amount disclosed in tax return | Description of transaction along with value treated as income | Status of assessment | Whether transaction is recorded in the books of account | Financial Year in which the transaction was recorded. |
|---|---|---|---|---|---|---|---|
| | | | | | | | |
| | | | | | | | |

In case the company has not recorded/disclosed in the books of accounts – reason for not recording/disclosing needs to be specified.

### 10.4.2.11 Corporate Social Responsibility (CSR)

Where the company covered under section 135 of the companies act, the following shall be disclosed with regard to CSR activities:

(a) amount required to be spent by the company during the year,

(b) amount of expenditure incurred,

(c) shortfall at the end of the year,

(d) total of previous years shortfall,

(e) reason for shortfall,

(f) nature of CSR activities,

(g) details of related party transactions, e.g., contribution to a trust controlled by the company in relation to CSR expenditure as per relevant Accounting Standard,

(h) where a provision is made with respect to a liability incurred by entering into a contractual obligation, the movements in the provision during the year should be shown separately.

### 10.4.2.12 Section 135 (Corporate Social Responsibility) of Companies Act, 2013

The provisions of section 135 of Companies Act, 2013 are depicted below.

(1) Every company having net worth of rupees five hundred crore or more, or turnover of rupees one thousand crore or more or a net profit of rupees five

crore or more during [the immediately preceding financial year] [1] shall constitute a Corporate Social Responsibility Committee of the Board consisting of three or more directors, out of which at least one director shall be an independent director.

[2][**Provided** that where a company is not required to appoint an independent director under sub-section (4) of section 149, it shall have in its Corporate Social Responsibility Committee two or more directors.]

(2) The Board's report under sub-section (3) of section 134 shall disclose the composition of the Corporate Social Responsibility Committee.

(3) The Corporate Social Responsibility Committee shall,—

(a) formulate and recommend to the Board, a Corporate Social Responsibility Policy which shall indicate the activities to be undertaken by the company [in areas or subject, specified in Schedule VII] [3];

(b) recommend the amount of expenditure to be incurred on the activities referred to in clause (a); and

(c) monitor the Corporate Social Responsibility Policy of the company from time to time.

(4) The Board of every company referred to in sub-section (1) shall,—

(a) after taking into account the recommendations made by the Corporate Social Responsibility Committee, approve the Corporate Social Responsibility Policy for the company and disclose contents of such Policy in its report and also place it on the company's website, if any, in such manner as may be prescribed; and

(b) ensure that the activities as are included in Corporate Social Responsibility Policy of the company are undertaken by the company.

(5) The Board of every company referred to in sub-section (1), shall ensure that the company spends, in every financial year, at least two per cent. of the average net profits of the company made during the three immediately preceding financial years, [4][or where the company has not completed the period of three financial years since its incorporation, during such immediately preceding financial years] in pursuance of its Corporate Social Responsibility Policy:

---

1 *Subs.* w.e.f. 19-09-2018 for the words "any financial year" by s 37(i)(a) of the Companies (Amendment) Act, 2017 (1 of 2018) vide Notification SO 4907(E), dt. 19-09-2018.

2 *Ins.* w.e.f. 19-09-2018 by s 37(i)(b) of the Companies (Amendment) Act, 2017 (1 of 2018) vide Notification SO 4907(E), dt. 19-09-2018.

3 *Subs.* w.e.f. 19-09-2018 for "as specified in Schedule VII" by s 37(ii) of the Companies (Amendment) Act, 2017 (1 of 2018) vide Notification SO 4907(E), dt. 19-09-2018.

4 *Ins.*, w.e.f. 22-01-2021, vide SO324(E) dt. 22-01-2021, by the Companies (Amendment) Act, 2019 (22 of 2019), s. 21(a)(i), vide Gazette of India, Extraordinary, No. 41, Part II–Section 1, dt. 31-07-2019.

**Provided** that the company shall give preference to the local area and areas around it where it operates, for spending the amount earmarked for Corporate Social Responsibility activities:

**Provided further** that if the company fails to spend such amount, the Board shall, in its report made under clause (o) of sub-section (3) of section 134, specify the reasons for not spending the amount [5][and, unless the unspent amount relates to any ongoing project referred to in sub-section (6), transfer such unspent amount to a Fund specified in Schedule VII, within a period of six months of the expiry of the financial year].

[6][**Provided also** that if the company spends an amount in excess of the requirements provided under this sub-section, such company may set off such excess amount against the requirement to spend under this sub-section for such number of succeeding financial years and in such manner, as may be prescribed.]

[7][*Explanation.*—For the purposes of this section "net profit" shall not include such sums as may be prescribed, and shall be calculated in accordance with the provisions of section 198.]

[8][(6) Any amount remaining unspent under sub-section (5), pursuant to any ongoing project, fulfilling such conditions as may be prescribed, undertaken by a company in pursuance of its Corporate Social Responsibility Policy, shall be transferred by the company within a period of thirty days from the end of the financial year to a special account to be opened by the company in that behalf for that financial year in any scheduled bank to be called the Unspent Corporate Social Responsibility Account, and such amount shall be spent by the company in pursuance of its obligation towards the Corporate Social Responsibility Policy within a period of three financial years from the date of such transfer, failing which, the company shall transfer the same to a Fund specified in Schedule VII, within a period of thirty days from the date of completion of the third financial year.

[9][(7) If a company is in default in complying with the provisions of sub-section (5) or sub-section (6), the company shall be liable to a penalty of twice the

---

5 *Ins.*, w.e.f. 22-01-2021, vide SO324(E) dt. 22-01-2021, by the Companies (Amendment) Act, 2019 (22 of 2019), s. 21(a)(ii), vide Gazette of India, Extraordinary, No. 41, Part II–Section 1, dt. 31-07-2019.

6 *Ins.*, w.e.f. 22-01-2021, vide SO 325(E), dt. 22-01-2021, third proviso to s 135(5), by The Companies (Amendment) Act, 2020 (29 of 2020), dt. 28-09-2020.

7 *Subs.* w.e.f. 19-09-2018 by s 37(iii) of the Companies (Amendment) Act, 2017 (1 of 2018) vide Notification SO 4907(E), dt. 19-09-2018. Formerly, it read as:

"*Explanation.*— For the purposes of this section "average net profit" shall be calculated in accordance with the provisions of section 198."

8 *Ins.*, w.e.f. 22-01-2021, vide SO324(E) dt. 22-01-2021, sub-sections (6) to (8) by the Companies (Amendment) Act, 2019 (22 of 2019), s. 21(b), vide Gazette of India (Extraordinary), No. 41, Part II–Section 1, dt. 31-07-2019.

9 *Subs.*, w.e.f. 22-01-2021, vide SO 325(E), dt. 22-01-2021, by The Companies (Amendment) Act, 2020 (29 of 2020), dt. 28-09-2020. Formerly, sub-s (7) read:

amount required to be transferred by the company to the Fund specified in Schedule VII or the Unspent Corporate Social Responsibility Account, as the case may be, or one crore rupees, whichever is less, and every officer of the company who is in default shall be liable to a penalty of one-tenth of the amount required to be transferred by the company to such Fund specified in Schedule VII, or the Unspent Corporate Social Responsibility Account, as the case may be, or two lakh rupees, whichever is less.]

(8) The Central Government may give such general or special directions to a company or class of companies as it considers necessary to ensure compliance of provisions of this section and such company or class of companies shall comply with such directions.]

[10][(9) Where the amount to be spent by a company under sub-section (5) does not exceed fifty lakh rupees, the requirement under sub-section (1) for constitution of the Corporate Social Responsibility Committee shall not be applicable and the functions of such Committee provided under this section shall, in such cases, be discharged by the Board of Directors of such company.]

### *10.4.2.13 Schedule VII, Section 135 of Companies Act, 2013*

Activities which may be included by companies in their Corporate Social Responsibility Policies Activities relating to:

(i) Eradicating hunger, poverty, and malnutrition, "promoting health care including preventive health care" and sanitation including contribution to the Swach Bharat Kosh set-up by the Central Government for the promotion of sanitation and making available safe drinking water.

(ii) promoting education, including special education and employment enhancing vocation skills especially among children, women, elderly, and the differently abled and livelihood enhancement projects.

(iii) promoting gender equality, empowering women, setting up homes and hostels for women and orphans; setting up old age homes, day care centres and such other facilities for senior citizens and measures for

---

"(7) If a company contravenes the provisions of sub-section (5) or sub-section (6), the company shall be punishable with fine which shall not be less than fifty thousand rupees but which may extend to twenty-five lakh rupees and every officer of such company who is in default shall be punishable with imprisonment for a term which may extend to three years or with fine which shall not be less than fifty thousand rupees but which may extend to five lakh rupees, or with both"

Earlier, Sub-s (7) was *Ins.*, w.e.f. 22-01-2021, vide SO324(E) dt. 22-01-2021, by the Companies (Amendment) Act, 2019 (22 of 2019), s. 21(b), vide Gazette of India (Extraordinary), No. 41, Part II–Section 1, dt. 31-07-2019.

10 *Ins.*, w.e.f. 22-01-2021, vide SO 325(E), dt. 22-01-2021, sub-s (9), by The Companies (Amendment) Act, 2020 (29 of 2020), dt. 28-09-2020.

reducing inequalities faced by socially and economically backward groups.

(iv) ensuring environmental sustainability, ecological balance, protection of flora and fauna, animal welfare, agroforestry, conservation of natural resources and maintaining quality of soil, air and water [4][including contribution to the Clean Ganga Fund set-up by the Central Government for rejuvenation of river Ganga].

(v) protection of national heritage, art and culture including restoration of buildings and sites of historical importance and works of art; setting up public libraries; promotion and development of traditional art and handicrafts.

(vi) measures for the benefit of armed forces veterans, war widows and their dependents, Central Armed Police Forces (CAPF) and Central Para Military Forces (CPMF) veterans, and their dependents including widows];

(vii) training to promote rural sports, nationally recognized sports, paralympic sports and Olympic sports

(viii) contribution to the prime minister's national relief fund [or Prime Minister's Citizen Assistance and Relief in Emergency Situations Fund (PM CARES Fund)] or any other fund set up by the central govt. for socio economic development and relief and welfare of the schedule caste, tribes, other backward classes, minorities and women;

(ix) (a) Contribution to incubators or research and development projects in the field of science, technology, engineering and medicine, funded by the Central Government or State Government or Public Sector Undertaking or any agency of the Central Government or State Government; and

(b) Contributions to public funded Universities; Indian Institute of Technology (IITs); National Laboratories and autonomous bodies established under Department of Atomic Energy (DAE); Department of Biotechnology (DBT); Department of Science and Technology (DST); Department of Pharmaceuticals; Ministry of Ayurveda, Yoga and Naturopathy, Unani, Siddha and Homoeopathy (AYUSH); Ministry of Electronics and Information Technology and other bodies, namely Defence Research and Development Organization (DRDO); Indian Council of Agricultural Research (ICAR); Indian Council of Medical Research (ICMR) and Council of Scientific and Industrial Research (CSIR), engaged in conducting research in science, technology, engineering and medicine aimed at promoting Sustainable Development Goals (SDGs).]

(x) rural development projects

(xi) slum area development.

Explanation.- For the purposes of this item, the term `slum area' shall mean any area declared as such by the Central Government or any State Government or any other competent authority under any law for the time being in force.

(xii) disaster management, including relief, rehabilitation and reconstruction activities.

### *10.4.2.14 Crypto Currency or Virtual Currency*

According to the ICAI Guidance Note Virtual currency and Crypto currency have been defined as under:

Virtual currency is a digital representation of value, other than a representation of the Indian Rupee (INR) or a foreign currency ("real currency"), that functions as a unit of account, a store of value, and a medium of exchange. Some virtual currencies are convertible, which means that they have an equivalent value in real currency or act as a substitute for real currency.

Crypto currency is a form of digital/virtual currency generated through a series of written computer codes that rely on cryptography which is encryption and is thus independent of any central issuing authority per se.

Where the Company has traded or invested in Crypto currency or Virtual Currency during the financial year, the following shall be disclosed:

(a) profit or loss on transactions involving Crypto currency or Virtual Currency

(b) amount of currency held as at the reporting date,

(c) deposits or advances from any person for the purpose of trading or investing in Crypto Currency/virtual currency.

### *10.4.2.15 Other Disclosures*

The other disclosures are summarized below:

**Value of imports calculated on C.I.F. basis by the company during the financial year [Clause (a) of Note 5(viii)]**

The above disclosure is to be given in respect of –

- Raw materials;
- Components and spare parts;
- Capital goods.

**Expenditure in foreign currency during the financial year [Clause (b) of Note 5 (viii)]** The above needs to be disclosed for expenditure incurred on account of royalty, know-how, professional and consultation fees, interest and other matters.

Total value of all imported raw materials, spare parts and components consumed during the financial year and the total value of all indigenous raw materials, spare parts and components similarly consumed and the percentage of each to the total consumption; [Clause (c) of Note 5(viii)]

Total amount remitted during the year in foreign currencies on account of dividends with a specific mention of the total number of non-resident shareholders, the total number of shares held by them on which the dividends were due and the year to which the dividends related [Clause (d) of Note 5(viii)]

**Earnings in Foreign exchange [Clause (e) of Note 5 (viii)]**

Foreign exchange earnings have to be classified under the following heads:-

(i) export of goods calculated on F.O.B. basis;

(ii) royalty, know-how, professional and consultation fees;

(iii) interest and dividends; and

(iv) other income (indicating the nature thereof)

## 10.5 HIGHLIGHTS OF ADDITIONAL INFORMATION UNDER PART II OF DIVISION II OF SCHEDULE III (IND AS)

Additional Information related to Statement of Profit and Loss are highlighted below.

### 10.5.1 Employee benefits

A Company needs to provide by way of notes, additional information regarding aggregate expenditure and income on the following items:

- (a) Employee Benefits expense showing separately -
  - (i) salaries and wages,
  - (ii) contribution to provident and other funds,
  - (iii) share based payments to employees,
  - (iv) staff welfare expenses.

This has been explained above.

**Illustration 10.11: Share-based payments (Specimen format)**

**(a) Scheme details**

| Financial Year (Year of grant) | Number of options outstanding as at 31st March 2022 | Number of options outstanding as at 31st March 2021 | Financial Year of vesting | Range of exercise price (Rs) | Range of Fair value at grant date (Rs) |
|---|---|---|---|---|---|
| Details of Employee Stock Options granted up to 31st March, 20XX but not vested as on 1st April, 20XX | | | | | |
| Sub-total | | | | | |

**(b) Compensation expenses arising on account of the Share based payments**

| Particulars | For the year ended 31st March 2022 | For the year ended 31st March 2021 |
|---|---|---|
| Expenses arising from equity – settled share-based payment transactions | xxx | xxx |
| Rate of employee turnover per annum | xxx | xxx |

**(c) Fair value at the grant date (specimen data)**

The fair value at grant date is determined using "Black Scholes Model" which takes into account the exercise price, term of the option, share price at grant date and expected price volatility of the underlying shares, expected dividend yield and the risk-free interest rate for the term of the option.

The model inputs for options granted during the year ended March 31, 2019 included as mentioned below. Further no new stock options were granted during Financial Year 2021-22;

(a) Weighted average exercise price

(b) Grant date:

(c) Vesting period:

(d) Share Price at grant date:

(e) Expected price volatility of Company's share:

(f) Expected dividend yield:

(g) Risk free interest rate:

The expected price volatility is based on the historic volatility (based on remaining life of the options).

**(d) Movement of share options during the year (specimen data)**

| | As at 31st March 2022 | | As at 31st March 2021 | |
|---|---|---|---|---|
| Balance at the beginning of the year<br>Exercised during the year<br>Expired/Lapsed during the year | | | | |
| Balance at the end of the year | | | | |

### 10.5.2 Any item of income or expenditure which exceeds one per cent of the revenue from operations or Rs.10,00,000, whichever is higher, in addition to the consideration of 'materiality' as specified in clause 7 of the General Instructions for Preparation of Financial Statements of a Company

In this context it may be pertinent to note that, Ind AS 1 specifies that Information may be purported to material if omitting, misstating or obscuring it could reasonably be expected to influence decisions that the primary users of general-purpose financial statements make on the basis of those financial statements, which provide financial information about a specific reporting entity.

### 10.5.3 Interest Income

'Interest Income' for financial assets measured at amortized cost and for financial assets measured at FVOCI, calculated using effective interest method, should be presented in separate line items under 'Other Income'

### 10.5.4 Finance costs

In accordance with Note 4 of the General Instructions for the Preparation of the Statement of Profit and Loss, disclosure of Finance costs is to be bifurcated under the following:

(A) Interest;

(B) Dividend on redeemable preference shares

(C) Exchange differences regarded as an adjustment to borrowing costs;

(D) Other borrowing costs (specify nature).

### (A) Interest

This would present the following types of finance charges incurred by the Company:

(a) Interest cost on financial liabilities measured at amortized cost such as borrowings from banks and others, on debentures, bonds or similar instruments etc. calculated as per the effective interest method;

(b) Unwinding of the discount that results in an increase in financial liabilities such as security deposits accepted for assets given on lease; GN on Division II - Ind AS Schedule III to the Companies Act 2013;

(c) Increases in the carrying amount of provisions/decommissioning liabilities where such increase reflects the passage of time;

(d) Finance charges on finance leases that are in the nature of interest expense; (e) Net interest on net defined benefit liability which reflects the change in net defined benefit liability that arises from the passage of time.

### (B) Dividend on redeemable preference shares

According to ICAI Guidance Note on Schedule III on Ind AS entities, Dividend on preferences shares, whether redeemable or convertible, is of the nature of 'Interest expense', only where there is no discretion of the issuer over the payment of such dividends. In such case, the portion of dividend as determined by applying the effective interest method should be presented as 'Interest expense' under 'Finance cost'.

At the same time, where there is a discretion of issuer over the payments of dividend on preference shares, whether redeemable or convertible, the entire dividend is in the nature of distribution of profit and accordingly, shall be presented in Statement of Changes in Equity.

### (C) Exchange differences regarded as an adjustment to borrowing costs;

Ind AS 21 and Ind AS 23 deal with foreign exchange differences arising on foreign currency transactions included in the financial statements of an entity. All exchange differences within the purview of Ind AS 21 are recognized as exchange differences and presented accordingly.

However, all exchange differences arising from foreign currency borrowings are within the purview of Ind AS 23 and are regarded as a cost of borrowing irrespective of whether they are capitalized or not as a part of the cost of the asset.

### (D) Other borrowing costs (specify nature).

In accordance with ICAI Guidance Note on Schedule III, Other borrowing costs would include commitment charges, loan processing charges, guarantee charges, loan facilitation charges, discounts/premium on borrowings, other ancillary costs incurred in connection with borrowings, or amortization of such costs, etc. Such finance costs that do not meet the definition of transaction costs directly attributable to issue of a financial liability, shall be presented under 'Other borrowing costs'.

### 10.5.5 Net gain/loss on sale of investments - Schedule III, Division II

Net gain/loss on sale of investments Schedule III, Division II related to Ind AS does not provide a distinction in presenting realized and unrealized gains or losses on fair value changes. An entity shall present "net gain or loss on sale of investments" separately by way of a note below the table on 'Net gains (losses) on fair value changes'.

### 10.5.6 Net gain/loss on foreign currency transaction and translation (other than considered as finance cost)

According to ICAI Guidance Note on Schedule III on Ind AS entities, any gains/losses attributable to foreign exchange fluctuations need to be disclosed separately as per Ind AS 21. Thus, net exchange loss should be classified under other expenses and the amount so included should be separately disclosed. Under this head, net gain or loss on foreign currency transaction and translation to the extent considered as finance costs should not be disclosed.

### 10.5.7 Payments to auditor

Payments to the auditor as -

(a) auditor,

(b) for taxation matters,

(c) for company law matters,

(d) for other services,

(e) for reimbursement of expenses

**Illustration 10.12: Payments to Auditors (Specimen format)**

| Particulars | For the year ended 31st March 2022 | For the year ended 31st March 2021 |
|---|---|---|
| Statutory audit fees | xxx | xxx |
| Tax audit fees | xxx | xxx |
| Certification and consultation fees | xxx | xxx |
| Cost audit fees | xxx | xxx |
| TOTAL | xxx | xxx |

### 10.5.8 Undisclosed income

This is a newly inserted requirement, whereby, the Company shall give details of any transaction not recorded in the books of accounts that has been surrendered or disclosed as income during the year in the tax assessments under the Income Tax Act, 1961 (such as, search or survey or any other relevant provisions of the Income Tax Act, 1961), unless there is immunity for disclosure under any scheme and shall also state whether the previously unrecorded income and related assets have been properly recorded in the books of account during the year. Please refer to paragraph 10.4.2.10 above for further details.

### 10.5.9 Corporate Social Responsibility (CSR)

Please refer paragraph 10.4.2.11 above for details.

### 10.5.10 Details of Crypto Currency or Virtual Currency

Please refer paragraph 10.4.2.14 above for details.

## 10.6 REGULATORY DEFERRAL ACCOUNT BALANCES

### 10.6.1 Regulatory Deferral Account Balances shall be presented in the Statement of Profit or Loss

Loss in accordance with the relevant Indian Accounting Standards (Ind AS 114).

### 10.6.2 Recognition, measurement, impairment and de-recognition of regulatory deferral account balances

An entity that has rate-regulated activities and that is within the scope of, and elects to apply, this Standard shall apply paragraphs 10 and 12 of Ind AS 8 when developing its accounting policies for the recognition, measurement, impairment and de recognition of regulatory deferral account balances.

**This Ind AS has temporary exemption from paragraph 11 of Ind AS 8 *Accounting Policies, Changes in Accounting Estimates and Errors.***

**Continuation of existing accounting policies**

On initial application of this Standard, an entity shall continue to apply previous GAAP accounting policies for the recognition, measurement, impairment and de recognition of regulatory deferral account balances. However, the presentation of such amounts shall comply with the presentation requirements of this Standard, which may require changes to the entity's previous GAAP presentation policies (Para 11)

### 10.6.3 Changes in accounting policies

According to Para 13, an entity shall not change its accounting policies in order to start to recognise regulatory deferral account balances. An entity may only change its accounting policies for the recognition, measurement, impairment and de recognition of regulatory deferral account balances if the change makes the financial statements more relevant to the economic decision-making needs of users and no less reliable, or more reliable and no less relevant to those needs. An entity shall judge relevance and reliability using the criteria in paragraph 10 of Ind AS 8.

### 10.6.4 Presentation

When this Standard is applied, the regulatory deferral account balances are recognised in the balance sheet in addition to the assets and liabilities that are recognised in accordance with other Standards. These presentation requirements separate the impact of recognising regulatory deferral account balances from the financial reporting requirements of other Standards.

### 10.6.5 Classification of regulatory deferral account balances

(i) According to Para 20, an entity shall present separate line items in the balance sheet for:

  (a) the total of all regulatory deferral account debit balances; and

  (b) the total of all regulatory deferral account credit balances.

(ii) Para 21 prescribes that, when an entity presents current and non-current assets, and current and non-current liabilities, as separate classifications in its balance sheet, it shall not classify the totals of regulatory deferral account balances as current or non-current.

  Instead, the separate line items required by paragraph 20 mentioned above shall be distinguished from the assets and liabilities that are presented in accordance with other Standards by the use of sub-totals, which are drawn before the regulatory deferral account balances are presented.

(iii) Classification of movements in regulatory deferral account balances

According to Para 22, an entity shall present, in the other comprehensive income section of the statement of profit and loss , the net movement in all regulatory deferral account balances for the reporting period that relate to items recognised in other comprehensive income.

Separate line items shall be used for the net movement related to items that, in accordance with other Standards:

(a) will not be reclassified subsequently to profit or loss; and

(b) will be reclassified subsequently to profit or loss when specific conditions are met.

Para 23 prescribes that, an entity shall present a separate line item in the profit or loss section of the statement of profit and loss , for the remaining net movement in all regulatory deferral account balances for the reporting period, excluding movements that are not reflected in profit or loss, such as amounts acquired. This separate line item shall be distinguished from the income and expenses that are presented in accordance with other Standards by the use of a sub-total, which is drawn before the net movement in regulatory deferral account balances.

### 10.6.6 Disclosure

According to Para 27 of this Ind AS, an entity that elects to apply this Standard shall disclose information that enables users to assess:

(a) the nature of, and the risks associated with, the rate regulation that establishes the price(s) that the entity can charge customers for the goods or services it provides; and

(b) the effects of that rate regulation on its financial position, financial performance and cash flows.

To meet the disclosure objective in paragraph 27, an entity shall consider all of the following:

(a) the level of detail that is necessary to satisfy the disclosure requirements;

(b) how much emphasis to place on each of the various requirements;

(c) how much aggregation or disaggregation to undertake; and

(d) whether users of financial statements need additional information to evaluate the quantitative information disclosed.

**Illustration 10.13: Rate regulated entity**

XYZ ltd. is an entity engaged in the business of transmission of power. As per the tariff regulations, entities engaged in business of transmission of power are allows certain costs (operating and maintenance) on actual basis for the tariff fixation purpose. However, tariffs for the period are determined at the beginning of the period on the basis of the estimated costs expected to be incurred during the period. In other words, entities engaged in business of transmission of power are allowed to recover the differential of certain estimated costs (O&M) considered for the tariff fixation and the actual cost incurred through a truing up mechanism. As per the truing-up mechanism, once approved by the regulators that the extra cost incurred was justifiable, entities recover the same from its customers who actually consumed the power by raising a separate invoice for the reimbursement of extra cost or by issuing debit or credit note in favour of the customers.

During the year 2020-21, XYZ Ltd. incurred a sum of Rs. 120 crore towards the Operating and Maintenance (O&M) cost against the estimate of Rs. 100 crore for the same considered for the tariff fixation purpose.

XYZ ltd., as permitted by the tariff regulation, has raised an additional invoice to its customers for the differential amount of Rs. 20 Crore (120 crore – 100 crore) plus mark-up.

**Solution**

This Guidance Note covers 'cost of service' type of rate regulation only, where the recovery of excess cost or excess revenue incurred/received in the current period is through adjustment of future tariff to be charged from the customers for the services to be provided in future. In the given case, the recovery of actual cost (O&M) incurred by the entity in excess of the estimate considered for the tariff fixation purpose is not to be adjusted for determining the future tariff rather it is to be recovered by the entity from it past customers without impacting the future tariff to be charged. Accordingly, this type of regulation does not fall within the scope of this Guidance Note.

Paragraph 36 of this Guidance Note requires that regulated entities should comply with the requirements of the Accounting Standards in the same way as other entities. It is observed that in respect of the regulation in this case, the right to reimbursement of actual cost incurred plus mark up on actual basis from the customers who actually consumed the power falls within the scope of Accounting Standard (AS) 9, Revenue Recognition. Accordingly, revenue should be recognised in accordance with the requirements and AS 9. In view of this, in this case, the right of recovery of actual costs does not lead to creation of a regulatory asset.

**Illustration 10.14**

XYZ ltd. is an entity engaged in distribution of power. The relevant tariff regulations permit inclusion of certain expenses for fixing the future tariff.

Such expenses otherwise are required to be recognised in the statement of profit and loss.

During the year 2019-20, XYZ Ltd. incurred a sum of Rs. 100 crore towards additional ex-gratia payment to its employees due to change in the relevant law. As per the regulations governing the tariff charged by the XYZ Ltd. From its customers, the said additional expense is permissible as 'truing up adjustment' in the future tariff. Accordingly, the additional expenditure incurred by XYZ Ltd. is considered to be a regulatory asset by the company.

During the year 2020-21, the regulator in accordance with the tariff regulation adjusts (increase) the tariff to be charged by XYZ Ltd from its customers at by Rs. 10 per unit for increase in employee benefits incurred in the previous year, i.e. 2019-20. During the year 2020-21, XYZ Ltd. billed 56,00,000 units to its customers.

Following accounting entries should be passed by XYZ Ltd. during the period 2019-20 and 2020-21:

**Working Notes:**

**Year 2019-20**

1. At the time when the additional employee benefits expenses are incurred: Rs crores

| | | | |
|---|---|---|---|
| 2019-20 | Employee Benefit expenses Dr.<br>Employee Benefit expenses payable Cr.<br>(Being additional employee benefit expenses incurred) | 100 | 100 |

2. At the end of the reporting period, employee benefit expense is recognised in the statement of profit and loss:

| | | | |
|---|---|---|---|
| 31.03.20 | Profit & Loss Dr.<br>Employee Benefit expenses Cr.<br>(Being additional employee benefit expenses transferred to profit and loss) | 100 | 100 |

3. As the tariff regulations permit inclusion of additional employee benefit expenses in the tariff determination, on the reporting date the same would be recognised as a regulatory asset:

| | | | |
|---|---|---|---|
| 31.03.20 | Regulatory asset A/c Dr.<br>Regulatory income/expenses Cr.<br>(Being regulatory asset recognised) | 100 | 100 |

4. Transfer of Regulatory Income/Expense to Profit and loss A/c.

| | | | |
|---|---|---|---|
| 31.03.20 | Regulatory income/expenses A/c Dr.<br>Profit & Loss Cr.<br>(Being regulatory Income/Expense transferred to Profit and loss) | 100 | 100 |

**Year 2020-21**

5. As during the year, Rs.5.60 crores are recovered by the entity through increased revenue, the following entry for amortisation of regulatory asset is passed by XYZ Ltd:

| 31.03.21 | Regulatory income/expenses A/c Dr.<br>Regulatory assets A/c Cr.<br>(Being increase in revenue adjusted against the regulatory asset) | 5.60 | 5.60 |
|---|---|---|---|

6. Transfer of Regulatory Income/Expense to Profit and loss A/c.

| 31.03.21 | Profit & Loss Dr.<br>Regulatory income/expenses Cr.<br>(Being regulatory Income/Expense transferred to Profit and loss.) | 5.60 | 5.60 |
|---|---|---|---|

XYZ Ltd.

Statement of Profit and Loss the period ended 31.3.2020
(Figures other than the above have been assumed) Rs crore

| Particulars | Amount |
|---|---|
| Sales | 19,900 |
| Other income | 100 |
| Total income | 12,000 |
| Rae materials consumed | 6,800 |
| Increase/decrease of WIP and FG | 1,200 |
| Employee Benefits (including additional expense) | 1,150 |
| Depreciation/Amortization | 750 |
| Other expenses | 100 |
| Total expenses | 10,000 |
| Profit Before Tax (PBT) and Rate Regulated Activities (RRA) | 2,000 |
| Add: Regulatory Income/Expense | 100 |
| PBT | 2,100 |
| Less: Tax Expense* | |
| Current Tax (2000 @35%) | (700) |
| Deferred Tax other than RRA | (100) |
| Deferred Tax expense pertaining to RRA (100@35%) | (35) |

| Profit After Tax (PAT) | 1,265 |
|---|---|

*Tax rate assumed to be 35%.

Extract of Balance Sheet of XYZ Ltd. as on 31.3.2020. Rs crore

| ASSETS | Amount |
|---|---|
| Current Assets | |
| Other Current Assets (Regulatory Asset) | 100 |
| Total | 100 |

Year 2020-21

XYZ Ltd.

Statement of Profit and Loss the period ended 31.3.2021

(Figures other than the above have been assumed) Rs crore

| Particulars | Amount |
|---|---|
| Sales (including increased revenue due to tariff adjustment) | 19,905.6 |
| Other income | 100 |
| Total income | 12,005.6 |
| Rae materials consumed | 6,800 |
| Increase/decrease of WIP and FG | 1,200 |
| Employee Benefits (including additional expense) | 1,150 |
| Depreciation/Amortization | 750 |
| Other expenses | 100 |
| Total expenses | 10,000 |
| Profit Before Tax (PBT) and Rate Regulated Activities (RRA) | 2005.6 |
| Less: Regulatory Income/Expense | 5.6 |
| PBT | 2000 |
| Less: Tax Expense* | |
| Current Tax (2005.6 @35%) | (701.96) |

| | |
|---|---:|
| Deferred Tax other than RRA | (100.00) |
| Deferred Tax expense pertaining to RRA (5.6@35%) | 1.96 |
| Profit After Tax (PAT) | 1,200.0 |

*Tax rate assumed to be 35%.

Extract of Balance Sheet of XYZ Ltd. as on 31.3.2021. Rs crore

| ASSETS | Amount |
|---|---:|
| Current Assets | |
| Other Current Assets (Regulatory Asset) | 94.4 |
| Total | 94.4 |

## 10.7 TAXES

The disclosure would have to be on the face of the Statement of Profit and Loss and need to be bifurcated as under:

**Minimum Alternative Tax under Income Tax Act 1961.**

Please refer ICAI Guidance Note as mentioned above.

**Corporate Dividend Tax**

Please refer ICAI Guidance Note as mentioned above.

**Income taxes**

Recognition of current tax liabilities and current tax assets

- Current tax for current and prior periods shall, to the extent unpaid, be recognised as a liability. If the amount already paid in respect of current and prior periods exceeds the amount due for those periods, the excess shall be recognised as an asset.
- The benefit relating to a tax loss that can be carried back to recover current tax of a previous period shall be recognised as an asset.

## 10.8 EARNINGS PER SHARE (IND AS 33)

Ind AS 33, Earnings per share is similar to AS 20, explained above.

## 10.9 IND AS 24: RELATED PARTY DISCLOSURES

The objective of this Standard is to ensure that an entity's financial statements contain the disclosures necessary to draw attention to the possibility that its financial position and profit or loss may have been affected by the existence of related parties and by transactions and outstanding balances, including commitments with such parties.

### 10.9.1 The Standard shall apply to:

(a) identifying related party relationships and transactions

(b) identifying outstanding balances, including commitments between an entity and its related parties

(c) identifying the circumstances in which disclosure of the items (a) and (b) is required and

(d) determining the disclosures to be made about those items

The Standard also requires disclosure of related party relationships, transactions and outstanding balances, including commitments, in the consolidated and separate financial statements of a parent, venturer or investor presented in accordance with Indian Accounting Standard *(Ind AS 110, Consolidated Financial Statements or Ind AS 27 Separate Financial Statements*). This Standard also applies to individual financial statements.

### 10.9.2 Purpose of related party disclosures

Related party relationships are a normal feature of commerce and business. Entities frequently carry on parts of their activities through subsidiaries, joint ventures and associates. In those circumstances, the entity has the ability to affect the financial and operating policies of the investee through the presence of control, joint control or significant influence.

(a) A related party relationship could have an effect on the profit or loss and financial position of an entity. Related parties may enter into transactions that unrelated parties would not.

(b) The profit or loss and financial position of an entity may be affected by a related party relationship even if related party transactions do not occur. The mere existence of the relationship may be sufficient to affect the transactions of the entity with other parties.

For these reasons, knowledge of an entity's transactions, outstanding balances, including commitments, and relationships with related parties may affect assessments of its operations by users of financial statements, including assessments of the risks and opportunities facing the entity.

### 10.9.3 Definitions

***A related party*** is a person or an entity that is related to the entity that is preparing its financial statements (reporting entity) as under:

(a) A person or a close member of that person's family is related to a reporting entity

 (i) if he has control or joint control over the reporting entity

 (ii) has significant influence over the reporting entity or

 (iii) is a member of key management personnel of the reporting entity or of a parent of the reporting entity

(b) An entity is related to a reporting entity if:

 (i) the entity and reporting entity are members of the same group (i.e. each parent, subsidiary or fellow subsidiary is related to the other)

 (ii) one entity is an associate or joint venture of the other entity or associate or joint venture of a member of a group of which the other entity is a member

 (iii) both entities are joint ventures of the same third party

 (iv) one entity is a joint venture of the third party and the other entity is an associate of the third entity

 (v) the entity is a post-employment defined benefit plan for the benefit of the employees of the reporting entity or an entity related to the reporting entity.

 If reporting entity is itself such a plan then sponsoring employers are also related to the reporting entity

 (vi) the entity is controlled or jointly controlled by a person in (a) above

 (vii) a person identified in a above has significant influence over the entity or is a member of the key management of the entity or its parent

***A related party transaction*** is a transfer of resources, services or obligations between a reporting entity and a related party, regardless of whether a price is charged.

***Close members of the family of a person*** are the persons specified within the meaning of "relative" under the Companies Act 1956 and 2013 and that person's domestic partner, children of that person's domestic partner and dependents of that person's domestic partner.

***Compensation*** includes all employee benefits as defined in *Ind AS 19, Employee Benefits,* including employee benefits to which *Ind AS 102 Share-based payments* applies. Employee benefits are all forms of consideration paid, payable or provided by the entity, or on behalf of the entity, in exchange of services rendered to the entity. It also includes such consideration paid on behalf of a parent of the entity in respect of the entity.

Compensation includes:

(a) short-term employee benefits

(b) post-employment benefits

(c) other long term employee benefits

(d) termination benefits

(e) share-based payments

***Key Management personnel*** are those persons having authority and responsibility for planning, directing and controlling the activities of the entity, directly or indirectly, including any director (whether executive or otherwise) of that entity.

***Government*** refers to government, government agencies and similar bodies whether local, national or international.

**A *Government-related entity*** is an entity that is controlled, jointly controlled or significantly influenced by a government.

The terms '**control**' and '**investment entity**', '**joint control**' and '**significant influence**' are defined in Ind AS 110, Ind AS 111, *Joint Arrangements,* and Ind AS 28, *Investments in Associates and Joint Ventures,* respectively and are used in this Standard with the meanings specified in those Ind ASs.

## 10.9.4 Following are not deemed to be related

- two entities simply because they have a common director or manager
- two venturers who share a joint control over a joint venture
- providers of finance, trade unions, public utilities , and departments and agencies of a Govt that does not control, jointly control or significantly influence the reporting entity simply by virtue of normal dealings with an entity
- a single customer. Vendor, franchiser, distributor, or general agent with whom an entity transacts a significant volume of business merely by virtue of resulting economic dependence

## 10.9.5 Disclosures

**(a) Relationships between parents and subsidiaries**

- an entity must disclose its parent and ultimate controlling entity if applicable
- If neither the parent nor ultimate controlling entity produces a financial statement for public use, then the next most senior parent that does so need to be disclosed

**(b) Management compensation**

Disclose key management compensation in total and with following categories:

- short term employee benefits
- post – employment benefits
- other long term benefits
- Termination benefits
- share based payments benefits

Key management personnel are those persons having authority and responsibility for planning, directing and controlling the activities of the entity whether directly or indirectly including any director (whether executive or otherwise) of the entity

**(c) Related party transactions**

If an entity has had related party transactions during the periods covered by the financial statements, it shall disclose the nature of the related party relationship as well as information about those transactions and outstanding balances, including commitments, necessary for users to understand the potential effect of the relationship on the financial statements. These disclosure requirements are in addition to those in paragraph 17. At a minimum, disclosures shall include:

- nature of related party relationship
- amount of transactions
- amount of outstanding balances, including terms and conditions and guarantees
- provisions for doubtful debts related to outstanding balances
- expense recognized during the period in respect of bad or doubtful debts due from related parties

Amounts incurred by the entity for the provision of key management personnel services that are provided by a separate management entity shall be disclosed.

The disclosures required by paragraph 18 shall be made separately for each of the following categories:

(a) the parent;

(b) entities with joint control of, or significant influence over, the entity;

(c) subsidiaries;

(d) associates;

(e) joint ventures in which the entity is a joint ventures;

(f) key management personnel of the entity or its parent; and

(g) other related parties.

**Examples of transactions that are disclosed if they are with Related Parties**

The following are examples of transactions that are disclosed if they are with a related party:

(a) purchases or sales of goods (finished or unfinished);

(b) purchases or sales of property and other assets;

(c) rendering or receiving of services;

(d) leases;

(e) transfers of research and development;

(f) transfers under licence agreements;

(g) transfers under finance arrangements (including loans and equity contributions in cash or in kind);

(h) provision of guarantees or collateral;

(i) commitments to do something if a particular event occurs or does not occur in the future, including executory contracts (recognised and unrecognised);

(j) settlement of liabilities on behalf of the entity or by the entity on behalf of that related party; and

(k) management contracts including for deputation of employees.

**(d) Government related entities**

According to Para 25 a reporting entity is exempt from the disclosure requirements of paragraph 18 in relation to related party transactions and outstanding balances, including commitments, with:

(a) a government that has control or joint control of, or significant influence over, the reporting entity; and

(b) another entity that is a related party because the same government has control or joint control of, or significant influence over, both the reporting entity and the other entity.

Para 26 stipulates that, if a reporting entity applies the exemption in paragraph 25, it shall disclose the following about the transactions and related outstanding balances referred to in paragraph 25:

(a) the name of the government and the nature of its relationship with the reporting entity (i.e. control, joint control or significant influence);

(b) the following information in sufficient detail to enable users of the entity's financial statements to understand the effect of related party transactions on its financial statements:

(i) the nature and amount of each individually significant transaction; and

(ii) for other transactions that are collectively, but not individually, significant, a qualitative or quantitative indication of their extent. Types of transactions include those listed in paragraph 21.

## 10.10 IND AS 108: OPERATING SEGMENTS

An entity shall present information to enable users of its financial statements to evaluate the nature and financial effects of the business activities in which it engages and the economic environments in which it operates.

This Ind AS shall apply to companies to which Indian Accounting Standards (Ind ASs) notified under the Companies Act apply.

If an entity that is not required to apply this Ind AS chooses to disclose information about segments that does not comply with this Ind AS, it shall not describe the information as segment information.

If a financial report contains both the consolidated financial statements of a parent that is within the scope of this Ind AS as well as the parent's separate financial statements, segment information is required only in the consolidated financial statements.

**Operating segment**

An operating segment is a component of an entity that

**(a)** engages in business activities from which it may earn revenues and incur expenses (including revenues and expenses relating to transactions with other components of the same entity),

**(b)** whose operating results are reviewed regularly by the entity's chief operating decision maker to decide resources to be allocated to the segment and assess its performance and

(c) for which discrete financial information is available.

**Reportable segment**

According to Para 11, an entity shall report separately information about each operating segment that:

(a) has been identified or results from aggregating two or more of those segments in accordance with paragraph 12, and

(b) exceeds the quantitative thresholds highlighted in Paragraph 13

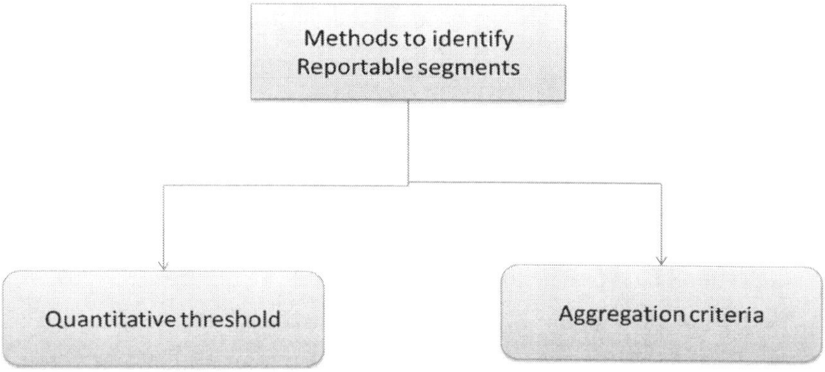


**Quantitative Threshold**

According to Para 13 an entity shall report separately information about an operating segment that meets any of the following quantitative thresholds:

(a) Its reported revenue, including both sales to external customers and intersegment sales or transfers, is **10 per cent or more of the combined revenue**, internal and external, of all operating segments.

(b) The **absolute amount of its reported profit or loss is 10 per cent or more of the greater**, in absolute amount, of

(i) the combined reported profit of all operating segments that did not report a loss and

(ii) the combined reported loss of all operating segments that reported a loss.

(c) Its assets are10 per cent or more of the combined assets of all operating segments.

Reported revenues (both internal and external) are 10% or more of the Combined revenues (internal and external) of all segments

1. Calculate the combined profits of all segments
2. Calculate the combined losses of all segments
3. Identify the greater of the two
4. Reported profit or loss is 10% or more of the amount identified at step 3 above

**Aggregation criteria**

Para 12 prescribes Aggregation criteria wherein operating segments often exhibit similar long-term financial performance if they have similar economic characteristics. For example, similar long-term average gross margins for two operating segments would be expected if their economic characteristics were similar.

Two or more operating segments may be aggregated into a single operating segment if aggregation is consistent with the core principle of this Ind AS, the segments have similar economic characteristics, and the segments are similar in each of the following respects:

(a) the nature of the products and services;

(b) the nature of the production processes;

(c) the type or class of customer for their products and services;

(d) the methods used to distribute their products or provide their services; and

(e) if applicable, the nature of the regulatory environment, for example, banking, insurance or public utilities.

If the total external revenue reported by operating segments constitutes less than 75 % of the entity's revenue. Additional operating segments must be identifiable as reportable segments until at least 75% of the entity's revenue is included in reportable segments.

In certain situations, both the quantitative threshold and the aggregation criteria are used to identify reportable segments.

**Illustration 10.15. Specimen format of operating segment reporting**

| | **Segment 1** | **Segment II** | **Segment II** | **Segment IV** | **Segment V** | **Segment VI** | **TOTAL** |
|---|---|---|---|---|---|---|---|
| Segment revenue External sales Inter-segment sales<br>Total Revenue | | | | | | | |
| Segment results (profit/loss) | 0 | 0 | 0 | 0 | 0 | 0 | 0 |
| Unallocated corporate expenses<br>Profit from operations<br>Investment income<br>Finance cost<br>Income taxes | | | | | | | |
| Net Profit | | | | | | | |

| | Segment 1 | Segment II | Segment II | Segment IV | Segment V | Segment VI | TOTAL |
|---|---|---|---|---|---|---|---|
| Segment assets Unallocated corporate assets<br>Consolidated assets<br>Segment liabilities<br>Unallocated corporate liabilities<br>Consolidated liabilities | | | | | | | |

**Illustration 10.16**

Kilter Ltd has identified the following operating segments

| | Iron | Cement | Steel | Aluminium | Copper | limestone | TOTAL |
|---|---|---|---|---|---|---|---|
| Segment revenue External sales | 25 | 2 | 6 | 20 | s | 23 | 99 |
| Inter segment sales | 12 | 6 | 8 | 2 | 0 | 1 | 29 |
| Total Revenue | 37 | 8 | 14 | 22 | s | 24 | 128 |
| Segment results (profit/loss) | 9 | 15 | 3 | -1 | 6 | 8 | 0<br>35 |
| Segment assets | 81 | 51 | 15 | 16 | 27 | 5 | 196 |

Determine the reportable segments

**Solution**

Using the quantitative threshold mentioned above, reportable segments can be identified as follows:

| Steps | Remarks |
|---|---|
| 1 | Calculate which segments are based on 10% of revenue segments iron, steel, aluminium, copper and limestone have revenue from sales to external customers and from transactions with other segments of more than 10% of the total revenue (external and internal) of all segments |

| | |
|---|---|
| 2 | Calculate which segments are reportable based on 10% of combined profit/loss<br>Segments iron, cement, copper and limestone have segment results, whether profit or loss, at 10% or more of the combined profit of all segments in profit or combined loss of all segments in loss, whichever is greater in absolute amount |
| 3 | Calculate which segments are reportable based on 10% of Total assets.<br>Segments iron, cement and copper have assets which are 10% or more of the total assets of all segments. |

Therefore, segments iron, cement, steel, aluminium, copper and limestone are the reportable segments.

Ascertainment of reportable segments using quantitative threshold

| SA | | Iron | Cement | Steel | Aluminium | Copper | limestone | TOTAL |
|---|---|---|---|---|---|---|---|---|
| 1 | Segment revenue | | | | | | | |
| | External sales | 25 | 2 | 6 | 20 | 23 | 23 | 99 |
| | Inter-segment sales | 12 | 6 | 8 | 2 | 0 | 1 | 29 |
| | Total Revenue | 37 | 8 | 14 | 22 | 23 | 24 | 128 |
| 2 | Total Revenue of each | | | | | | | |
| | segment as a % of | | | | | | | |
| | total revenue (Wl) | 29 | 6 | 11 | 17 | 18 | 19 | 100 |
| 3 | Segment results | | | | | | | |
| | (profit/loss) | 9 | 16 | -3 | -1 | 6 | 8 | 35 |
| 4 | Combined result of | | | | | | | |
| | Segments in profit | 9 | 16 | | | 6 | 8 | 39 |
| 5 | Combined result of | | | | | | | |
| | Segments in loss | | | 3 | 1 | | | -4 |
| 6 | Segment result as a % | | | | | | | |
| | of the greater of the | | | | | | | |
| | totals in 4 and 5 above | 23 | 41 | 8 | 3 | 15 | 21 | |
| 7 | Segment assets | 81 | 51 | 16 | 16 | 27 | 5 | 196 |
| 8 | Segment assets as a % | | | | | | | |
| | of total assets of all | 41 | 26 | 8 | 8 | 14 | 3 | |
| | Segments (W3) | | | | | | | |

## 10.11 DISCLOSURE ON DISTRIBUTION OF DIVIDENDS

The amount of dividends proposed to be distributed to equity and preference shareholders for the period and the related amount per share shall be disclosed separately. Arrears of fixed cumulative dividends on irredeemable preference shares shall also be disclosed separately.

## 10.12 DISCLOSURE OF USE OF UNUTILIZED AMOUNTS FROM ISSUE OF SECURITIES MADE FOR A SPECIFIC PURPOSE

Where in respect of an issue of securities made for a specific purpose the whole or part of amount has not been used for the specific purpose at the Balance Sheet date, there shall be indicated by way of note how such unutilised amounts have been used or invested.

## 10.13 DISCLOSURE OF USE OF UNUTILIZED AMOUNTS ON ACCOUNT OF BORROWINGS FROM BANKS AND FINANCIAL INSTITUTIONS RECEIVED FOR A SPECIFIC PURPOSE

Where the company has not used the borrowings from banks and financial institutions for the specific purpose for which it was taken at the balance sheet date, the company shall disclose the details of where they have been used.

## 10.14 RETROSPECTIVE APPLICATION OF ACCOUNTING POLICY

When a company applies an accounting policy retrospectively or makes a restatement of items in the financial statements or when it reclassifies items in its financial statements, the company shall attach to the Balance Sheet, a "Balance Sheet" as at the beginning of the earliest comparative period from which the above adjustments are made.

## 10.15 SHARE APPLICATION MONEY PENDING ALLOTMENT

Share application money pending allotment shall be classified into equity or liability in accordance with relevant Indian Accounting Standards. Share application money to the extent not refundable shall be shown under the head Equity and share application money to the extent refundable shall be separately shown under 'Other current liabilities'.

## 10.16 PREFERENCE SHARES

Preference shares shall be classified and presented as 'Equity' or 'Liability' in accordance with the requirements of the relevant Indian Accounting Standards. Accordingly, the disclosure and presentation requirements in this regard applicable to the relevant class of equity or liability shall be applicable *mutatis mutandis* to the preference shares. For instance, redeemable preference shares shall be classified and presented under 'non-current liabilities' as "borrowings" and the disclosure requirements in this regard applicable to such borrowings shall be applicable *mutatis mutandis* to redeemable preference shares.

## 10.17 COMPOUND FINANCIAL INSTRUMENTS

Compound financial instruments such as convertible debentures, where split into equity and liability components, as per the requirements of the relevant Indian Accounting Standards, shall be classified and presented under the relevant heads in 'Equity' and 'Liabilities'.

## 10.18 ADDITIONAL REGULATORY INFORMATION (CLAUSE L OF SCHEDULE III, DIVISION II)

### (i) Title deeds of Immovable Properties not held in name of the Company

The company shall provide the details of all the immovable properties (other than properties where the Company is the lessee and the lease agreements are duly executed in favour of the lessee) whose title deeds are not held in the name of the company in following format and where such immovable property is jointly held with others, details are required to be given to the extent of the company's share.

| Relevant line item in the Balance sheet | Description of item of property | Gross carrying value | Title deeds held in the name of | Whether title deed holder is a promoter, director or relative# of promoter*/director or employee of promoter/director | Property held since which date | Reason for not being held in the name of the company** |
|---|---|---|---|---|---|---|
| PPE | Land | - | - | - | - | **also indicate if in dispute |
| Investment property – | Land<br>Building | | | | | |
| Non-current assets held for sale | Land<br>Building | | | | | |
| Others | | | | | | |

#Relative here means relative as defined in the Companies Act, 2013.

*Promoter here means promoter as defined in the Companies Act, 2013.

According to ICAI Guidance Note on Schedule III for Ind AS entities, the Companies Act does not define the term "Immovable Property". However, as per General Clauses Act, 1897, "Immovable Property shall include land, benefits to arise out of land, and things attached to the earth, or permanently fastened to anything attached to the earth". In the absence of any specific guidance, the immovable properties presented under 'property, plant and equipment', 'investment property' or classified as 'non-current assets held for sale' would be covered in the scope of this disclosure but immovable property items presented as inventory by companies carrying on real estate business will not fall under this disclosure.

While making this disclosure in the financial statements, the entity needs to disclose the following information:

(i) *Gross carrying value* – the company shall disclose the gross carrying amount in the financial statements;

(ii) *Title deeds held in the name of* – the company shall disclose the full name of the individual/entity/person holding the title of immovable property;

(iii) *Whether title deed holder is a promoter, director or relative of promoter/director or employee of promoter/director* – the company shall disclose the relationship between itself and the individual/entity/person holding the title of immovable property;

(iv) *Property held since which date* – the company shall disclose the date since the property is held and where the exact date is not available, it shall disclose the month and year since the property is held.

(v) *Reason for not being held in the name of the company, also indicating if there is a dispute* – the company shall state the reason for the immovable property not being held in the name of the company (for example, the documents are under preparation or the registration process of transfer of name is in progress as on the balance sheet date). In case the title deeds of immovable property are not being held in the name of company due to a dispute, the company shall state the nature of dispute.

**(ii) Fair Value of investment property**

The Company shall disclose as to whether the fair value of investment property (as measured for disclosure purposes in the financial statements) is based on the valuation by a registered valuer as defined under rule 2 of Companies (Registered Valuers and Valuation) Rules, 2017.

**(iii) Revaluation of Property, Plant and Equipment (including Right-of-use Assets)**

Where the Company has revalued its Property, Plant and Equipment (including Right-of-Use Assets), the company shall disclose as to whether the revaluation is based on the valuation by a registered valuer as defined under rule 2 of Companies (Registered Valuers and Valuation) Rules, 2017.

### (iv) Revaluation of intangible assets

Where the company has revalued its intangible assets, the company shall disclose as to whether the revaluation is based on the valuation by a registered valuer as defined under rule 2 of Companies (Registered Valuers and Valuation) Rules, 2017.

### (v) Disclosure of Loans or Advances in the nature of loans to promoters, directors, KMPs and other related parties

The following disclosures shall be made where Loans or Advances in the nature of loans are granted to promoters, directors, KMPs and the related parties (as defined under Companies Act, 2013), either severally or jointly with any other person, that are:

(a) repayable on demand; or

(b) without specifying any terms or period of repayment,

| Type of Borrower | Amount of loan or advance in the nature of loan outstanding | Percentage to the total Loans and Advances in the nature of loans |
|---|---|---|
| Promoters | | |
| Directors | | |
| KMPs | | |
| Related Parties | | |

According to ICAI Guidance Note on Schedule III for Ind AS entities, for the purpose of making this disclosure, the relationship should be considered on the date of loan and the amount should be outstanding as at the balance sheet date.

The Guidance Note further opines the following related to the chart above:

(a) The amount outstanding need to represent loan or advance in the nature of loan

(b) It is preferable to add an additional column to the table above reflecting percentage of each category of loans to the total Loans and Advances in the nature of loans.

(c) Further, the amount outstanding should be the gross carrying amount (without netting the provision for doubtful debts or impairment loss allowance) included by the company in its respective balance sheet.

### (vi) Capital-Work-in Progress (CWIP)

**(a) For Capital-work-in progress, following ageing schedule shall be given: CWIP aging schedule**

From the format of disclosure requirement shown below, it is clear that the disclosure needs to be in two parts,

- Projects in progress and

- Progress temporarily suspended.
- Total will tally with Capital Work-in-progress amount shown in the Financial Statements.

The prescribed format is shown in Illustration 10.17 below.

**Illustration 10.17: Capital Work-in-progress: Aging Schedule**

(Amount in Rs.)

| CWIP | Amount in CWIP for a period of | | | | Total* |
|---|---|---|---|---|---|
| | Less than 1 year | 1-2 years | 2-3 years | More than 3 years | |
| Projects in progress<br>Projects temporarily suspended | | | | | |

*Total shall tally with CWIP amount in the balance sheet.

This is further explained in the Illustration 10.18 below.

**Illustration 10.18: Capital Work-in-progress: Aging Schedule**

| Period | Projects in progress | Projects temporarily suspended | Total Capital WIP |
|---|---|---|---|
| 2017 | 100 | - | 100 |
| 2018 | 250 | 100 | 450 |
| 2019 | 150 | - | 600 |
| 2020 | 350 | 100 | 1050 |
| Total | 850 | 200 | 1050 |

It is assumed that the projects commenced at the beginning of 2017 and all payments are made at the beginning of each year. The ageing schedule has been worked out accordingly. The suggested disclosure would be as under:

| CWIP | Amount in CWIP for a period of | | | | Total* |
|---|---|---|---|---|---|
| | Less than 1 year | 1-2 years | 2-3 years | More than 3 years | |
| Projects in progress<br>Projects temporarily | 350 | 150 | 250 | 100 | 850 |

| suspended<br>Total<br>Progressive total | 100<br>450<br>1050 | -<br>150<br>600 | 100<br>350<br>450 | -<br>100<br>100 | 200<br>1050 |
|---|---|---|---|---|---|

(b) For capital-work-in progress, whose completion is overdue or has exceeded its cost compared to its original plan, following **CWIP completion schedule** shall be given**:

**Illustration 10.19: Capital Work-in-progress Completion schedule**

(Amount in Rs.)

| CWIP | To be completed in | | | |
|---|---|---|---|---|
| | Less than 1 year | 1-2 years | 2-3 years | More than 3 years |
| Project 1<br>Project 2" | | | | |

**Details of projects where activity has been suspended shall be given separately.

Neither Schedule III nor Ind AS 16 defines 'project'. According to ICAI Guidance Note on Schedule III related to Ind AS entities, a project may be construed as smallest group of assets having a common intended use. For example, group of assets in an integrated plant may be treated as one project. The identification of project will require judgement and management needs to identify project based on facts of each case. Project identification should be consistent with how management identifies and monitors progress on group of assets internally.

**(vii) Intangible assets under development:**

(a) For Intangible assets under development, following ageing schedule shall be given:

Intangible assets under development aging schedule

**Illustration 10.20: Intangible Assets under development aging schedule**

(Amount in Rs.)

| Intangible assets under development | Amount in CWIP for a period of | | | | Total* |
|---|---|---|---|---|---|
| | Less than 1 year | 1-2 years | 2-3 years | More than 3 years | |
| Projects progress in Projects temporarily suspended | | | | | |

* Total shall tally with the amount of Intangible assets under development in the balance sheet.

(b) For Intangible assets under development, whose completion is overdue or has exceeded its cost compared to its original plan, the following **Intangible assets under development completion schedule** shall be given**

**Illustration 10.21: Intangible Assets under development completion schedule**

(Amount in Rs.)

| Intangible assets under development | To be completed in | | | |
|---|---|---|---|---|
| | Less than 1 year | 1-2 years | 2-3 years | More than 3 years |
| Project 1<br>Project 2 | | | | |

**Details of projects where activity has been suspended shall be given separately.

**(viii) Details of Benami Property held**

Where any proceeding has been initiated or pending against the company for holding any benami property under the Benami Transactions (Prohibition) Act, 1988 (45 of 1988) and rules made thereunder, the company shall disclose the following:

(a) Details of such property,

(b) Amount thereof,

(c) Details of Beneficiaries,

(d) If property is in the books, then reference to the item in the Balance Sheet,

(e) If property is not in the books, then the fact shall be stated with reasons,

(f) Where there are proceedings against the company under this law as an abetter of the transaction or as the transferor then the details shall be provided,

(g) Nature of proceedings, status of same and company's view on same.

**(ix) where the Company has borrowings from banks or financial institutions on the basis of security of current assets, it shall disclose the following:**

(a) whether quarterly returns or statements of current assets filed by the Company with banks or financial institutions are in agreement with the books of accounts.

(b) if not, summary of reconciliation and reasons of material discrepancies, if any to be adequately disclosed.

The ICAI Guidance Note on Schedule III provides a suggested format as shown below.

| Quarter | Name of bank | Nature of securities provided | Amount as per books of account | Amount as reported in quarterly returns | Amount of difference | Reason for material discrepancies |
|---|---|---|---|---|---|---|
| December 20xx | Name of bank | Raw materials | xxx | xxx | | |

**(x) Wilful Defaulter***

Where a company is a declared wilful defaulter by any bank or financial Institution or other lender, following details shall be given:

(a) Date of declaration as wilful defaulter,

(b) Details of defaults (amount and nature of defaults)

* Wilful defaulter" here means a person or an issuer who or which is categorized as a wilful defaulter by any bank or financial institution (as defined under the Companies Act, 2013) or consortium thereof, in accordance with the guidelines on wilful defaulters issued by the Reserve Bank of India.

According to Reserve Bank of India vide its master circular RBI/2014-15/73DBR.No.CID.BC.57/20.16.003/2014-15 dated July 1, 2014 on Wilful Defaulters ("RBI Circular") as updated from time to time has defined that a "wilful default" would be deemed to have occurred if any of the following events is noted:-

(i) The unit has defaulted in meeting its payment/repayment obligations to the lender even when it has the capacity to honour the said obligations.

(ii) The unit has defaulted in meeting its payment/repayment obligations to the lender and has not utilised the finance from the lender for the specific purposes for which finance was availed of but has diverted the funds for other purposes.

(iii) The unit has defaulted in meeting its payment/repayment obligations to the lender and has siphoned off the funds so that the funds have not been utilised for the specific purpose for which finance was availed of, nor are the funds available with the unit in the form of other assets.

(iv) The unit has defaulted in meeting its payment/repayment obligations to the lender and has also disposed off or removed the movable or immovable property given by him or it for the purpose of securing a term loan without the knowledge of the bank/lender.

## (xi) Relationship with Struck off Companies

Where the company has any transactions with companies struck off under section 248 of the Companies Act, 2013 or section 560 of Companies Act, 1956, the Company shall disclose the following details, namely:

| Name of struck off Company | Nature of transactions with struck-off Company | Balance outstanding as at current period | Relationship with the Struck off company, if any, to be disclosed | Balance outstanding as at previous period | Relationship with the Struck off company, if any, to be disclosed |
|---|---|---|---|---|---|
| | Investments in securities | | | | |
| | Receivables | | | | |
| | Payables | | | | |
| | Shares held by stuck off company | | | | |
| | Other outstanding balances (to be specified) | | | | |

According to ICAI Guidance Note on Schedule III, when making this disclosure in the financial statements, the company should provide the following information

(i) Name of the struck off company;

(ii) Nature of transactions with struck off company;

(iii) Balance outstanding

(iv) Relationship with the struck off company, if any,

## (xii) Registration of charges or satisfaction with Registrar of Companies (ROC)

Where any charges or satisfaction yet to be registered with ROC beyond the statutory period, details and reasons thereof shall be disclosed.

## (xiii) Compliance with number of layers of companies

Where the company has not complied with the number of layers prescribed under clause (87) of section 2 of the Act read with the Companies (Restriction on number of Layers) Rules, 2017, the name and CIN of the companies beyond the specified layers and the relationship or extent of holding of the company in such downstream companies shall be disclosed.

**(xiv) Following Ratios to be disclosed:**

(a) Current ratio,
(b) Debt-Equity ratio,
(c) Debt Service Coverage ratio,
(d) Return on Equity ratio,
(e) Inventory turnover ratio,
(f) Trade Receivables turnover ratio,
(g) Trade payables turnover ratio,
(h) Net capital turnover ratio,
(i) Net profit ratio,
(j) Return on Capital employed,
(k) Return on investment.

The company shall explain the items included in numerator and denominator for computing the above ratios. Further explanation shall be provided for any change in the ratio by more than 25% as compared to the preceding year.

**Illustration 10.22: Financial ratios: (specimen format)**

| Ratios | Numerator | Denominator | Current reporting period | Previous reporting period | Variance % | Reasons for variance > 25% |
|---|---|---|---|---|---|---|
| (a) Current Ratio, Current Assets/Current Liabilities | | | | | | |
| (b) Debt-Equity Ratio, Total Debt/Total Equity | | | | | | |
| (c) Debt Service Coverage Ratio, Net operating income/Debt service | | | | | | |
| (d) Return on Equity Ratio, Net | | | | | | |

| Ratios | Numerator | Denominator | Current reporting period | Previous reporting period | Variance % | Reasons for variance > 25% |
|---|---|---|---|---|---|---|
| Income/Shareholders equity | | | | | | |
| (e) Inventory turnover ratio, Cost of goods sold/Average Inventory | | | | | | |
| (f) Trade Receivables turnover ratio, Net credit sales/Average Trade Receivables | | | | | | |
| (g) Trade payables turnover ratio, Total purchase/Average Accounts Payable | | | | | | |
| (h) Net capital turnover ratio, Net Sales/(Total assets – Current liabilities) | | | | | | |
| (i) Net profit ratio, Net profit (after tax)/Net sales | | | | | | |
| (j) Return on Capital employed, Earnings before Interest and Tax/Capital Employed | | | | | | |
| (k) Return on investment (Current value of investment – Initial value of investment)/Initial investment | | | | | | |

### (xv) Compliance with approved Scheme(s) of Arrangements

Where the Scheme of Arrangements has been approved by the Competent Authority in terms of sections 230 to 237 of the Companies Act, 2013, the company shall disclose that the effect of such Scheme of Arrangements have been accounted for in the books of account of the Company 'in accordance with the Scheme' and 'in accordance with accounting standards and any deviation in this regard shall be explained.

### (xvi) Utilization of Borrowed funds and share premium:

(A) Where company has advanced or loaned or invested funds (either borrowed funds or share premium or any other sources or kind of funds) to any other person(s) or entity(ies), including foreign entities (Intermediaries) with the understanding (whether recorded in writing or otherwise) that the Intermediary shall

- (i) directly or indirectly lend or invest in other persons or entities identified in any manner whatsoever by or on behalf of the company (Ultimate Beneficiaries) or
- (ii) provide any guarantee, security or the like to or on behalf of the Ultimate Beneficiaries; the company shall disclose the following:
  - (I) date and amount of fund advanced or loaned or invested in Intermediaries with complete details of each Intermediary.
  - (II) date and amount of fund further advanced or loaned or invested by such Intermediaries to other intermediaries or Ultimate Beneficiaries along with complete details of the ultimate beneficiaries.
  - (III) date and amount of guarantee, security or the like provided to or on behalf of the Ultimate Beneficiaries
  - (IV) declaration that relevant provisions of the Foreign Exchange Management Act, 1999 (42 of 1999) and Companies Act has been complied with for such transactions and the transactions are not violative of the Prevention of Money-Laundering act, 2002 (15 of 2003).

(B) Where a company has received any fund from any person(s) or entity(ies), including foreign entities (Funding Party) with the understanding (whether recorded in writing or otherwise) that the company shall

- (i) directly or indirectly lend or invest in other persons or entities identified in any manner whatsoever by or on behalf of the Funding Party (Ultimate Beneficiaries) or
- (ii) provide any guarantee, security or the like on behalf of the Ultimate Beneficiaries, the company shall disclose the following:

(I) date and amount of fund received from Funding parties with complete details of each Funding party.

(II) date and amount of fund further advanced or loaned or invested other intermediaries or Ultimate Beneficiaries along with complete details of the other intermediaries' or ultimate beneficiaries.

(III) date and amount of guarantee, security or the like provided to or on behalf of the Ultimate Beneficiaries

(IV) declaration that relevant provisions of the Foreign Exchange Management Act, 1999 (42 of 1999) and Companies Act has been complied with for such transactions and the transactions are not violative of the Prevention of Money-Laundering act, 2002 (15 of 2003).

**Illustration 10.23: An extract of Specimen disclosure of Accounting Policies under Notes on Accounts**

**SIGNIFICANT ACCOUNTING POLICIES**

**BASIS OF PREPARATION AND MEASUREMENT**

***Statement of compliance***

The financial statements of the Company have been prepared in accordance with and to comply in all material aspects with the Indian Accounting Standards (Ind AS) as notified under Section 133 of the Companies Act, 2013 and the relevant provisions of the Act, as applicable.

***Basis of measurement***

The financial statements have been prepared on accrual and going concern basis under the historical cost convention except for certain class of financial assets/liabilities, share based payments and net liability for defined benefit plans that are measured at fair value. The accounting policies have been consistently applied by the Company unless stated otherwise.

***Financial Year***

The Company has opted the period of 1st day of January to 31st day of December, each year as its financial year for the purpose of preparation of financial statements under the provisions of Section 2(41) of the Companies Act, 2013, which the Company Law Board has allowed.

***Functional and Presentation Currency***

The financial statements have been prepared and presented in Indian Rupees (`), which is also the Company's functional currency. Rounding off All amounts in the financial statement and accompanying notes are presented in ` million and have been rounded-off to one decimal place unless stated otherwise.

***Current and Non-current Classification***

The Company has ascertained its operating cycle as 12 months for the purpose of current/non-current classification of assets and liabilities. This is based on the nature of products and the time between acquisition of assets for processing and their realisation in cash and cash equivalents.

***Measurement of Profit from Operations***

For better understanding of the financial performance, the Company has chosen to present Profit from Operations as an additional information in the Statement of Profit and Loss. Profit from Operations is derived from Profit before Tax less Other Income and adding back Finance Costs (Including Interest Cost on Employee Benefit Plans) and Corporate Social Responsibility Expense.

***Use of Estimates and Judgement***

The preparation of financial statements requires management to exercise judgement and make estimates and assumptions that affects the reported amounts of revenue, expenses, assets and liabilities. These estimates and assumptions are based on historical experience and various other factors that are believed to be reasonable under the circumstances. Actual results may differ from these estimates. These estimates and underlying assumptions are reviewed on a periodic basis. Revisions to accounting estimates are recognised in the period in which the results are known/materialise. The areas involving significant estimates and judgement include determination of useful life of property, plant and equipment (Refer note 5), measurement of defined benefit obligations (Refer Note 36), recognition and measurement of provisions and contingencies (Refer note 38) and recognition of deferred tax assets/liabilities (Refer Note 40).

***Approval of financial statements***

The financial statements of the Company were approved for issue by the Board of Directors on 16 February 2021.

**REVENUE RECOGNITION**

Revenue from sale of goods is recognised on transfer of control of goods to the buyer. Revenue is measured at the price charged to the customer and are recorded net of returns (if any), trade discounts, rebates, other pricing allowances to trade/consumer, when it is probable that the associated economic benefits will flow to the Company.

The Performance obligation in contracts are considered as fulfilled in accordance with the terms agreed with the respective customers.

Revenue is presented net of Goods and Services Tax (GST).

Interest income is recognised using effective interest rate (EIR) method.

Dividend income on investments is recognized when the right to receive the payment is established.

**GOVERNMENT GRANTS**

Government grants are recognized initially at fair value as Deferred Income for interest free incentives when there is reasonable assurance that they will be received and the Company will comply with the conditions associated with the grant. These are recognized in the statement of profit & loss as a part of other operating revenues on a systematic basis. Government grant in relation to fixed asset is treated as deferred income and is recognised in the statement of profit and loss on a systematic basis over the useful life of the asset. Government grant in relation to investment outlay is recognised as income in the statement of profit & loss on fulfilment of the underlying attached conditions.

**INVENTORIES**

Inventories are stated at cost or net realisable value, whichever is lower. However, raw materials, packing materials and other supplies held for use in the production of inventories are not written down below cost if the finished goods in which they will be included are expected to be sold at or above cost. The bases of determining cost for various categories of inventories are as follows:

Raw and packing material: First-in-first out

Stock-in-trade (Goods purchased for resale): Weighted average

Stores and spare parts: Weighted average

Work-in-progress and finished goods: Material cost plus appropriate share of production overheads, wherever applicable

**EMPLOYEE BENEFITS**

***Employee benefit plans***

The Company makes contributions to Provident Fund, Employee State Insurance, National Pension System etc. for eligible employees and these contributions are charged to statement of profit and loss on accrual basis. Liability for defined benefit plans i.e. gratuity and unfunded pension is determined based on the actuarial valuation carried out by an independent actuary as at the year-end. As these liabilities are relatively long term in nature, the actuarial assumptions take in account the requirements of the relevant Ind AS coupled with a long-term view of the underlying variables/trends, wherever required.

Service cost and net interest cost on the defined benefit liabilities/assets are recognized in the statement of profit and loss as employee benefit expense and finance costs respectively. Gains and losses on remeasurement of defined benefits liabilities/plan assets arising from changes in actuarial assumptions and experience adjustments are recognised in the other comprehensive income and are included in retained earnings in the balance sheet.

Long term employee benefits such as compensated absences and long service awards are charged to statement of profit and loss on the basis of an actuarial valuation carried out by an independent actuary as at the year-end. Actuarial gains and losses are recognised in full in the statement of profit and loss during the year in which they occur.

***Other employee benefits***

Short term employee benefits including performance incentives, are charged to statement of profit and loss on an undiscounted, accrual basis during the period of employment.

**SHARE BASED PAYMENT**

Nestlé Restricted Stock Unit (RSU) Plan/Performance Share Unit (PSU) Plan of Nestlé S.A., whereby select employees of the Company are granted non-tradable units with the right to obtain Nestlé S.A. shares or cash equivalent, is a Cash-Settled Share based payment as per the requirement of Ind AS 102 - Shared based Payment. Liability under the plan is initially measured at the fair value and charged to statement of profit and loss over the vesting period. The Company remeasures the outstanding units at each balance sheet date at their fair values taking into account the Nestlé S.A. share price and exchange rate as at the balance sheet date. The resultant gain/(loss) on remeasurement is recognised in the statement of profit and loss over the vesting period.

**PROPERTY, PLANT AND EQUIPMENT**

Items of property, plant & equipment are stated at cost less accumulated depreciation and accumulated impairment losses, if any. Cost is inclusive of freight, duties, taxes or levies (net of recoverable taxes) and any directly attributable cost of bringing the assets to their working condition for intended use.

Property, plant and equipment which are not ready for intended use as on the date of Balance Sheet are disclosed as “Capital work-in-progress”.

Profit or loss on disposal/scrapping/write off/retirement from active use of an item of property, plant and equipment is recognised in the statement of profit and loss.

**DEPRECIATION/AMORTISATION**

The Company has assessed the useful lives of property, plant and equipment as per Schedule II to the Companies Act, 2013. Accordingly, depreciation has been computed on useful lives based on technical evaluation of relevant class of assets including components thereof. Useful lives and residual values are reviewed annually. Depreciation is provided as per the straight-line method computed basis useful lives of fixed assets as follows:

Buildings: 25 - 40 years

Plant & Machinery: 5 - 25 years

Office Equipments: 5 years

Furniture and fixtures: 5 years

Vehicles: 5 years

Information Technology (IT) equipment: 3 - 5 years

Freehold land is not depreciated.

**IMPAIRMENT OF PROPERTY, PLANT AND EQUIPMENT**

At each balance sheet date, items of property, plant and equipment are reviewed to determine whether there is any indication of impairment. For the purpose of assessing impairment, assets are grouped at the levels for which there are separately identifiable cash flows (cash generating unit). If any impairment indicator exists, estimate of the recoverable amount of the property, plant and equipment/cash generating unit to which the asset belongs is made. An impairment loss is recognised whenever the carrying amount of an asset/cash generating unit exceeds its recoverable amount. The recoverable amount is the greater of the net selling price and value in use. In assessing value in use, the estimated future cash flows are discounted to their present value based on an appropriate discount rate.

Reversal of impairment losses recognised in earlier years is recorded when there is an indication that the impairment losses recognised for the asset/cash generating unit no longer exist or have decreased. However, the increase in carrying amount of an asset due to reversal of an impairment loss is recognised to the extent it does not exceed the carrying amount that would have been determined (net of depreciation) had no impairment loss been recognised for that asset/cash generating unit in earlier years.

**LEASES**

Effective 1 January 2020, the Company has applied Ind AS 116 Leases, using full retrospective approach recognizing the cumulative effect of adopting Ind AS 116 as an adjustment to the retained earnings as on the transition date i.e. 1 January 2019. Accordingly, previous year figures have been restated to make them comparable. Ind AS 116 has replaced the existing leases standard, Ind AS 17 Leases.

The Company assesses whether a contract is or contains a lease, at inception of a contract.

A contract is, or contains a lease if the contract conveys the right to control the use of an identified asset for a period of time in exchange for consideration.

At the date of commencement of the lease, the Company recognises a right-of-use asset ("ROU") and a corresponding lease liability for all lease arrangements in which it is a lessee.

The right-of-use assets are initially recognised at cost, which comprises the initial amount of the lease liability adjusted for any lease payments made at or prior to the commencement date of the lease plus any initial direct costs less any lease incentives. They are subsequently measured at cost less accumulated depreciation and impairment losses, if any. Right-of-use assets are depreciated from the commencement date on a straight-line basis over the shorter of the lease term or useful life of the underlying asset.

The lease liability is initially measured at the present value of the future lease payments. The lease payments are discounted using the interest rate implicit in the lease or, if not readily determinable, using the incremental borrowing rates. The lease liability is subsequently remeasured by increasing the carrying amount to reflect interest on the lease liability, reducing the carrying amount to reflect the lease payments made. A lease liability is remeasured upon the occurrence of certain events such as a change in the lease term or a change in an index or rate used to determine lease payments with a corresponding adjustment to the carrying value of Right-of-use assets.

Lease liability and Right-of-use assets have been separately presented in the Balance Sheet and lease payments have been classified as financing cash flows. The company's leases mainly comprises of land, buildings and vehicles.

The company leases land and buildings primarily for offices, manufacturing facilities and warehouses.

The company recognizes lease payments as operating expense on a straight-line basis over the period of lease for certain short – term (1 month or below) or low value arrangements.

**FOREIGN CURRENCY TRANSACTIONS**

Transactions in foreign currency are initially recorded in the functional currency i.e. Indian Rupees (`) using the exchange rate at the date of transaction.

Monetary items (i.e. receivables, payables, loans etc.) denominated in foreign currency are reported using the closing exchange rate as on each balance sheet date.

The exchange difference arising on the settlement or reporting of monetary items at rates different from rates at which these were initially recorded/reported in previous financial statements, are recognised in the statement of profit and loss in the period in which they arise.

Also refer to accounting policy on 'Derivatives and Hedge accounting'.

**PROVISIONS AND CONTINGENT LIABILITIES**

Provisions for Contingencies/Contingent liabilities are recognised/disclosed after evaluation of facts and legal aspects of the matter involved, in line with Ind AS 37 on Provisions, Contingent Liabilities and Contingent Assets and Ind AS 12 on Income Tax. Provisions are recognised when the Company has a present obligation (legal/constructive) and on management judgement as a result of a past event, for which it is probable that a cash outflow will be required and a reliable estimate can be made of the amount of the obligation. As the timing of outflow of resources is uncertain, being dependent upon the outcome of the future proceedings, these provisions are not discounted to their present value.

A disclosure for a contingent liability is made when there is a possible obligation or a present obligation that may, but probably will not require an outflow of resources. When there is a possible obligation or a present obligation in respect of which likelihood of outflow of resources is remote, no provision or disclosure is made.

Contingent assets are not recognised in the financial statements since this may result in the recognition of income that may never be accrued/realised.

**BORROWING COSTS**

Borrowing costs directly attributable to acquisition or construction of items of property, plant and equipment which take substantial period of time to get ready for their intended use are capitalised as part of the cost of that asset. All other borrowing costs are charged to the statement of profit and loss in the period in which they are incurred.

**FINANCIAL INSTRUMENTS**

***(a) Recognition and Initial measurement***

The Company recognises financial assets and financial liabilities when it becomes a party to the contractual provisions of the instrument. All financial assets and liabilities are measured at fair value on initial recognition. Transaction costs in relation to financial assets and financial liabilities, other than those carried at fair value through profit or loss (FVTPL), are added to the fair value on initial recognition. Transaction costs in relation to financial assets and financial liabilities which are carried at fair value through profit or loss (FVTPL), are charged to the statement of profit and loss.

***(b) Classification and subsequent measurement of financial assets***

***(i) Debt Instruments***

For the purpose of subsequent measurement, financial assets in the nature of debt instruments are classified as follows:

**Amortised cost** - Financial assets that are held within a business model whose objective is to hold the asset in order to collect contractual cash flows that are solely payments of principal and interest are subsequently measured at amortised cost less impairments, if any. Interest income calculated using effective interest rate (EIR) method and impairment loss, if any are recognised in the statement of profit and loss.

**Fair value through other comprehensive income (FVOCI)** - Financial assets that are held within a business model whose objective is achieved by both holding the asset in order to collect contractual cash flows that are solely payments of principal and interest and by selling the financial assets, are subsequently measured at fair value through other comprehensive income.

Changes in fair value are recognized in the other comprehensive income (OCI) and on derecognition, cumulative gain or loss previously recognised in OCI is reclassified to the statement of profit and loss. Interest income calculated using EIR method and impairment loss, if any are recognised in the statement of profit and loss.

**Fair value through profit or loss (FVTPL)** - A financial asset which is not classified in any of the above categories are subsequently measured at fair valued through profit or loss. Changes in fair value and income on these assets are recognised in the statement of profit and loss.

***(ii) Equity Instruments***

The Company has made investment in equity instruments that are initially measured at fair value. These investment are strategic in nature and held on a long-term basis. Accordingly, the company has elected irrevocable option to measure such investments at FVOCI. The Company makes such election on an instrument-by-instrument basis. Pursuant to such irrevocable option, changes in fair value are recognised in the OCI and is subsequently not reclassified to the statement of profit and loss.

***(c) Classification and subsequent measurement of financial liabilities***

For the purpose of subsequent measurement, financial liabilities are classified as follows:

**Amortised cost** - Financial liabilities are classified as financial liabilities at amortised cost by default. Interest expense calculated using EIR method is recognised in the statement of profit and loss.

**Fair value through profit or loss (FVTPL)** - Financial liabilities are classified as FVTPL if it is held for trading, or is designated as such on initial recognition. Changes in fair value and interest expense on these liabilities are recognised in the statement of profit and loss.

***(d) Derecognition of financial assets and financial liabilities***

The Company derecognises a financial asset when the contractual rights to the cash flows from the financial asset expire, or it transfers the rights to receive the contractual cash flows including risks and rewards of ownership. A financial liability is derecognised when the obligation under the liability is discharged or expires.

***(e) Impairment of financial assets***

Financial assets that are carried at amortised cost and fair value through other comprehensive income (FVOCI) are assessed for possible impairments basis expected credit losses taking into account the past history of recovery, risk of default of the counterparty, existing market conditions etc. The impairment methodology applied depends on whether there has been a significant increase in credit risk since initial recognition. For Trade receivables, the Company provides for expected credit losses based on a simplified approach as per Ind AS 109 – Financial Instruments. Under this approach, expected credit losses are computed basis the probability of defaults over the lifetime of the asset.

***(f) Derivatives and hedge accounting***

Derivative instruments used by the company include forward contracts. The Company formally establishes a hedge relationship between such forward contracts ('hedging instrument') and recognized financial asset/liabilities ('hedged item') through a formal documentation at the inception of the hedge. Forward contracts are designated as hedging instruments against changes in fair value of recognised assets and liabilities (fair value hedges) and against highly probable forecast transactions (cash flow hedges). The effectiveness of hedge instruments is assessed at the inception and on an ongoing basis.

Derivatives instruments such as forward contracts are initially measured at fair value. When a forward contract is designated as a cash flow hedge, the effective portion of change in the fair value of the contract is recognised in the other comprehensive income and accumulated in other equity under "effective portion of cash flow hedges". Amount recognised in other equity is subsequently reclassified to the statement of profit and loss upon occurrence of the related forecasted transaction. Any ineffective portion of the change in the fair value of the contract is recognised immediately in the statement of profit and loss.

Changes in fair value of forward contracts designated as fair value hedge are recognised in the statement of profit and loss.

***(g) Fair value measurement***

Fair value of financial assets and liabilities is normally determined by references to the transaction price or market price. If the fair value is not reliably determinable, the company determines the fair value using valuation techniques that are appropriate in the circumstances and for which sufficient data are available, maximising the use of relevant observable inputs and minimising the use of unobservable inputs.

**EARNINGS PER SHARE**

Basic earnings per share is computed by dividing the net profit for the period attributable to the equity shareholders by the weighted average number of equity shares outstanding during the period. For the purpose of calculating diluted earnings per share, the net profit for the period attributable to equity shareholders and the weighted average number of shares outstanding during the period are adjusted for the effects of all dilutive potential equity shares, if any.

**CASH AND CASH EQUIVALENTS**

Cash and cash equivalents for the purpose of Statement of Cash Flows include bank balances, cheques and drafts on hand including remittances in transit, demand deposits with banks where the original maturity is three months or less and other short term highly liquid investments that are readily convertible into cash and which are subject to an insignificant risk of changes in value. Bank overdrafts are included as a component of cash and cash equivalents for the purpose of Statement of Cash flows.

**EVENTS OCCURING AFTER THE BALANCE SHEET DATE**

All material events occurring after the balance sheet date up to the date of approval of financial statements by the Board of Directors on 16 February 2021, have been considered, disclosed and adjusted, wherever applicable, as per the requirements of Ind AS 10 - Events after the Reporting Period.

**(*Source: Nestle' India Annual Report 2020*)**

## 10.19 CHECK LIST ON DISCLOSURE REQUIREMENTS UNDER SCHEDULE III

| Disclosures as per Schedule III | Non Ind AS – Financial Statements | Ind AS – Financial Statements |
|---|---|---|
| *Whether Share capital – authorized, issued, subscribed and paid up need to be disclosed* | Disclosure required | Disclosure required |
| *Whether Goodwill or Capital reserve arising on consolidation need to be disclosed* | As per AS, differing treatment is given to goodwill arising on amalgamation and goodwill arising on consolidation and even SEBI format requires this to be separately disclosed. | IFRS/Ind AS does not require this to be stated separately. |

| Disclosures as per Schedule III | Non Ind AS – Financial Statements | Ind AS – Financial Statements |
|---|---|---|
| *Whether Share Application money received for allotment of securities and due for refund and interest accrued thereon needs to be disclosed separately. Share application money would include advances towards allotment of share capital* | Disclosure required | Disclosure required |
| *Whether excise duty needs to be disclosed separately* | To be disclosed where such information is available.<br>Though AS 9 states excise to be shown separately, where entities are not disclosing it, it would not be practical and also no benefit is derived by disclosure of this. | To be disclosed where such information is available. |
| Whether the period and amount of continuing default as on the Balance Sheet date in repayment of loans and interest, needs to be specified separately in each case. | Disclosure required | Disclosure required |
| Whether loans and advances due by directors or other officers of the company or any of them either severally or jointly with any other persons or amounts due by firms or private companies respectively in which any director is a partner or a director or a member needs to be separately stated | Disclosure required | Disclosure required |
| Whether Debts due by directors or other officers of the company or any of them either severally or jointly with any other person or debts due by firms or private companies respectively in | Disclosure required | Disclosure required |

| **Disclosures as per Schedule III** | **Non Ind AS – Financial Statements** | **Ind AS – Financial Statements** |
|---|---|---|
| which any director is a partner or a director or a member need to be separately stated | | |
| Where in respect of an issue of securities made for a specific purpose, the whole or part of the amount has not been used for the specific purpose at the Balance Sheet date, whether a note needs to be provided indicating how such unutilized amounts have been used or invested. | Disclosure required | Disclosure required |
| *Payments to the auditor as*<br>*(a) auditor,*<br>*(b) for taxation matters,*<br>*(c) for company law matters, (d) for management services, (e) for other services,*<br>*(f) for reimbursement of expense* | Disclosure required | Disclosure required |
| In case of Companies covered under section 135, amount of expenditure incurred on corporate social responsibility activities | Disclosure required | Disclosure required |
| Raw materials under broad heads<br><br>*Goods purchased under broad heads*<br><br>*In the case of trading companies, purchases in respect of goods traded in by the company under broad heads*<br><br>*In the case of companies rendering or supplying services, gross income derived form* | Disclosure required | Not applicable under Ind AS |

| Disclosures as per Schedule III | Non Ind AS – Financial Statements | Ind AS – Financial Statements |
|---|---|---|
| *services rendered or supplied under broad heads*<br><br>*In the case of a company, which falls under more than one of the categories mentioned above it shall be sufficient compliance with the requirements herein if purchases, sales and consumption of raw material and the gross income from services rendered is shown under broad heads*<br><br>*In the case of other companies, gross income derived under broad heads*<br><br>*In the case of all concerns having works in progress, works-in-progress under broad heads* | | |
| *Value of imports calculated on C.I.F basis by the company during the financial year in respect of*<br>*(i) Raw materials*<br>*(ii) Components and spare parts*<br>*(iii)Capital goods* | Disclosure required | Not applicable under Ind AS |
| Expenditure in foreign currency during the financial year on account of royalty, know-how, professional and consultation fees, interest, and other matters | Disclosure required | Not applicable under Ind AS |
| Total value if all imported raw materials, spare parts and components consumed during the financial year and the total value of all indigenous raw materials, spare parts and components similarly consumed | Disclosure required | Not applicable under Ind AS |

| Disclosures as per Schedule III | Non Ind AS – Financial Statements | Ind AS – Financial Statements |
|---|---|---|
| and the percentage of each to the total consumption | | |
| The amount remitted during the year in foreign currencies on account of dividends with a specific mention of<br>(a) the total number of non-resident shareholders,<br>(b) the total number of shares held by them on which the dividends were due and the year to which the dividends related | Disclosure required | Not applicable under Ind AS |
| Earnings in foreign exchange classified under the following heads, namely:<br>(i) Export of goods calculated on F.O.B. basis<br>(ii) Royalty, know-how, professional and consultation fees<br>(iii) Interest and dividend<br>(iv) Other income, indicating the nature thereof | Disclosure required | Not applicable under Ind AS |
| *Disclosure of Shareholding of Promoters* | Disclosure required | Disclosure required |
| *Disclosure related to Trade Payables ageing schedule* | Disclosure required | Disclosure required |
| *Disclosure related to Trade Receivables ageing schedule* | Disclosure required | Disclosure required |
| *Presentation related to Revaluation of Property, Plant and Equipment* | Disclosure required | Disclosure required |
| *Additional disclosures related to Loans or Advances* | Disclosure required | Disclosure required |
| *Disclosure pertaining to details of Benami Property held* | Disclosure required | Disclosure required |
| *Disclosures pertaining to Wilful Defaulter* | Disclosure required | Disclosure required |
| *Presentation and disclosure pertaining relationship with* | Disclosure required | Disclosure required |

| Disclosures as per Schedule III | Non Ind AS – Financial Statements | Ind AS – Financial Statements |
|---|---|---|
| *struck off companies* | | |
| *Disclosure pertaining to Compliance with number of layers of companies* | Disclosure required | Disclosure required |
| *Disclosures pertaining to undisclosed income* | Disclosure required | Disclosure required |
| *Disclosure pertaining to Capital work-in-progress (CWIP) ageing schedule/completion schedule* | Disclosure required | Disclosure required |
| *Disclosure related to Intangible assets under development ageing schedule/completion schedule* | Disclosure required | Disclosure required |
| *Disclosure pertaining to Security of current assets against borrowings* | Disclosure required | Disclosure required |
| *Disclosure pertaining to Compliance with approved Scheme(s) of Arrangements* | Disclosure required | Disclosure required |
| *Disclosure pertaining to Utilization of Borrowed funds and share premium* | Disclosure required | Disclosure required |
| *Disclosure pertaining to 'details of crypto currency or virtual currency'* | Disclosure required | Disclosure required |
| *Disclosure related to Title deeds of Immovable Property not held in the name of the Company* | Disclosure required | Disclosure required |
| *Presentation related to Registration of charges or satisfaction with Registrar of Companies* | Disclosure required | Disclosure required |
| *Presentation of Analytical Ratios* | Disclosure required | Disclosure required |

# Chapter 11

# Statement of Cash Flows

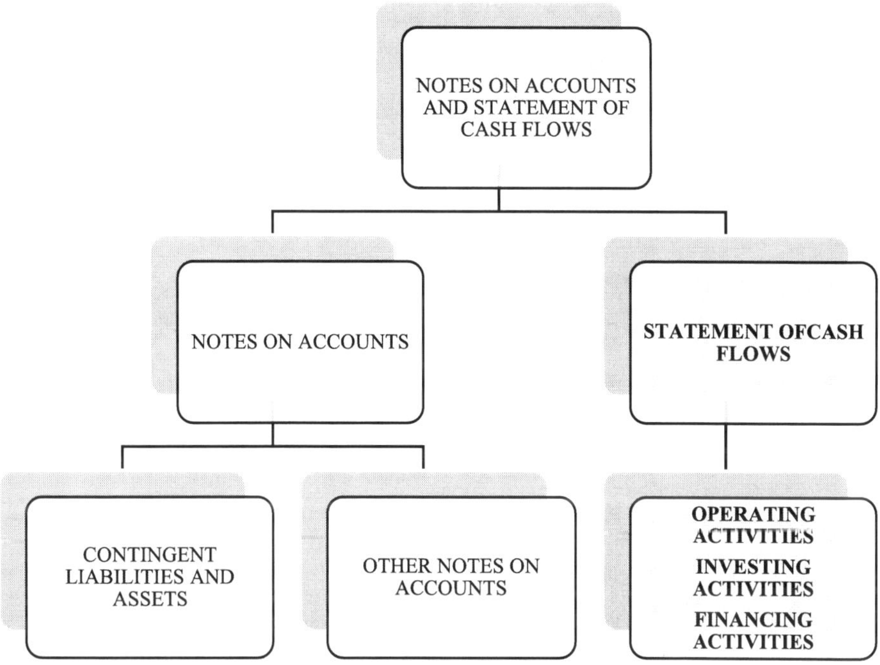


## 11.1 CASH FLOW STATEMENT

The cash flow statement should report cash flows during the period classified by operating, investing and financing activities.

## 11.2 OPERATING ACTIVITIES

Cash flows from operating activities are primarily derived from the principal revenue-producing activities of the enterprise. Therefore, they generally result from the transactions and other events that enter into the determination of net profit or loss.

| *Examples of cash flows from* | (a) | cash receipts from the sale of goods and the rendering of services; |
|---|---|---|

| *operating activities are:* | (b) | cash receipts from royalties, fees, commissions and other revenue; |
|---|---|---|
| | (c) | cash payments to suppliers for goods and services; |
| | (d) | cash payments to and on behalf of employees; |
| | (e) | cash receipts and cash payments of an insurance enterprise for premiums and claims, annuities and other policy benefits; |
| | (f) | cash payments or refunds of income taxes unless they can be specifically identified with financing and investing activities; and |
| | (g) | cash receipts and payments relating to futures contracts, forward contracts, option contracts and swap contracts when the contracts are held for dealing or trading purposes. |

## 11.3 INVESTING ACTIVITIES

The separate disclosure of cash flows arising from investing activities is important because the cash flows represent the extent to which expenditures have been made for resources intended to generate future income and cash flows.

Investing activities fall into two broad categories:

- Investments in long-lived operating assets (which include long-lived tangible assets such as land, buildings, and equipment; intangible assets such as patents, brand names, customer lists, and goodwill; and natural resources such as oil reserves and timberlands).
- Investments in the securities of other firms (including stocks and bonds).

| *Examples of cash flows arising from investing activities are:* | (a) | cash payments to acquire fixed assets (including intangibles). These payments include those relating to capitalised research and development costs and self-constructed fixed assets; |
|---|---|---|
| | (b) | cash receipts from disposal of fixed assets (including intangibles); |
| | (c) | cash payments to acquire shares, warrants or debt instruments of other enterprises and interests in joint ventures (other than payments for those instruments considered to be cash equivalents and those held for dealing or trading purposes); |
| | (d) | cash receipts from disposal of shares, warrants or debt instruments of other enterprises and interests in joint ventures (other than receipts from those instruments |

| | |
|---|---|
| | considered to be cash equivalents and those held for dealing or trading purposes);<br>(e) cash advances and loans made to third parties (other than advances and loans made by a financial enterprise);<br>(f) cash receipts from the repayment of advances and loans made to third parties (other than advances and loans of a financial enterprise);<br>(g) cash payments for futures contracts, forward contracts, option contracts and swap contracts except when the contracts are held for dealing or trading purposes, or the payments are classified as financing activities; and<br>(h) cash receipts from futures contracts, forward contracts, option contracts and swap contracts except when the contracts are held for dealing or trading purposes, or the receipts are classified as financing activities. |

## 11.4 FINANCING ACTIVITIES

The separate disclosure of cash flows arising from financing activities is important because it is useful in predicting claims on future cash flows by providers of funds (both capital and borrowings) to the enterprise. Financing activities cover equity financing from investors and debt financing from creditors.

Equity financing activities include, raising capital by issuing common stock and preferred stock, the return of capital to shareholders via dividends and share repurchases, and the use of equity (and equity appreciation) to compensate employees via stock options, stock appreciation rights, and restricted stock plans.

The three primary events that impact equity financing activities are:

- Investments by shareholders, usually net cash received by the company from equity issuance,
- Distributions to shareholders, usually in the form of periodic cash dividend payments to investors and/or share repurchases,
- Profitable operating and investing activities, primarily consisting of net income as well as "other comprehensive income."

Debt financing activities would include the issue of long-term notes and bonds, debt reduction, accounting for sticky debt, and the issue and conversion of hybrid securities, as well as other financing activities that may or may not result in balance sheet recognition (sales of receivables and operating leases). This also would include lease financing to incorporate off-balance-sheet lease financing in the assessment of financial risk.

| ***Examples of cash flows arising from financing activities are:*** | (a) cash proceeds from issuing shares or other similar instruments;<br>(b) cash proceeds from issuing debentures, loans, notes, bonds, and other short or long-term borrowings; and<br>(c) cash repayments of amounts borrowed. |
|---|---|

### 11.4.1 Reporting Cash Flows from Operating Activities

The results of a firm's operating activities are reported in the operating income section of the income statement (on an accrual basis) and in the operating cash flows section of the statement of cash flows (on a cash basis). Operating activities include:

- revenue recognition and the related balance sheet items created by delayed receipt of cash (accounts receivable) and accelerated receipt of cash (deferred revenues).
- the accounting and reporting for the major income statement expenses, including cost of goods sold (along with inventory and accounts payable);
- selling, general, and administrative (SG&A) expenses (including accounts such as prepaid and accrued expenses);
- income tax expenses (and current and deferred taxes payable); and
- compensation expenses (including pensions and other postemployment benefits obligations).

An enterprise should report cash flows from operating activities using either:

(a) the direct method, whereby major classes of gross cash receipts and gross cash payments are disclosed; or

(b) the indirect method, whereby net profit or loss is adjusted for the effects of transactions of a non-cash nature, any deferrals, or accruals of past or future operating cash receipts or payments, and items of income or expense associated with investing or financing cash flows.

### 11.4.2 Reporting Cash Flows from Investing and Financing Activities

An enterprise should report separately major classes of gross cash receipts and gross cash payments arising from investing and financing activities, except to the extent that cash flows described below which are reported on a net basis.

### 11.4.3 Reporting Cash Flows on a Net Basis

Cash flows arising from the following operating, investing or financing activities may be reported on a net basis:

(a) cash receipts and payments on behalf of customers when the cash flows reflect the activities of the customer rather than those of the enterprise.

Examples of cash receipts and payments referred to above are:

(a) the acceptance and repayment of demand deposits of a bank;

(b) funds held for customers by an investment entity; and

(c) rents collected on behalf of, and paid over to, the owners of properties.

(b) cash receipts and payments for items in which the turnover is quick, the amounts are large, and the maturities are short

Examples of cash receipts and payments referred to above are advances made for, and the repayment of:

(a) principal amounts relating to credit card customers;

(b) the purchase and sale of investments; and

(c) other short-term borrowings, for example, those which have a maturity period of three months or less.

## 11.5 CASH FLOWS FOR FINANCIAL INSTITUTIONS

Cash flows arising from each of the following activities of a financial institution may be reported on a net basis:

(a) cash receipts and payments for the acceptance and repayment of deposits with a fixed maturity date;

(b) the placement of deposits with and withdrawal of deposits from other financial institutions; and

(c) cash advances and loans made to customers and the repayment of those advances and loans.

## 11.6 FOREIGN CURRENCY CASH FLOWS

Cash flows arising from transactions in a foreign currency shall be recorded in an entity's functional currency by applying to the foreign currency amount the exchange rate between the functional currency and the foreign currency at the date of the cash flow.

The cash flows of a foreign subsidiary shall be translated at the exchange rates between the functional currency and the foreign currency at the dates of the cash flows.

## 11.7 INTEREST AND DIVIDENDS

Cash flows from interest and dividends received and paid shall each be disclosed separately.

Cash flows arising from interest paid and interest and dividends received in the case of a financial institution should be classified as cash flows arising from operating activities.

In the case of other entities, cash flows arising from interest paid should be classified as cash flows from financing activities while interest and dividends received should be classified as cash flows from investing activities.

Dividends paid should be classified as cash flows from financing activities.

## 11.8 TAXES ON INCOME

Cash flows arising from taxes on income shall be separately disclosed and shall be classified as cash flows from operating activities unless they can be specifically identified with financing and investing activities.

## 11.9 INVESTMENTS IN SUBSIDIARIES, ASSOCIATES AND JOINT VENTURES

When accounting for an investment in an associate or a subsidiary accounted for by the use of either equity or cost method, an investor restricts its reporting in the statement of cash flows to the cash flows between itself and the investee, for example, cash flows relating to dividends and advances.

An entity which reports its interest in a jointly controlled entity (see Ind AS 31 Interests in Joint Ventures) using proportionate consolidation, includes in its consolidated statement of cash flows its proportionate share of the jointly controlled entity's cash flows. An entity which reports such an interest using the equity method includes in its statement of cash flows the cash flows in respect of its investments in the jointly controlled entity, and distributions and other payments or receipts between it and the jointly controlled entity.

## 11.10 CHANGES IN OWNERSHIP INTERESTS IN SUBSIDIARIES AND OTHER BUSINESSES

The aggregate cash flows arising from obtaining or losing control of subsidiaries or other businesses shall be presented separately and classified as investing activities.

An entity shall disclose, in aggregate, in respect of both obtaining and losing control of subsidiaries and other businesses during the period each of the following:

(a) the total consideration paid or received;

(b) the portion of the consideration consisting of cash and cash equivalents;

(c) the amount of cash and cash equivalents in the subsidiaries or other businesses over which control is obtained or lost; and

(d) the amount of the assets and liabilities other than cash or cash equivalents in the subsidiaries or other businesses over which control is obtained or lost, summarised by each major category.

## 11.11 NON-CASH TRANSACTIONS

Investing and financing transactions that do not require the use of cash or cash equivalents shall be excluded from a statement of cash flows. Such transactions shall be disclosed elsewhere in the financial statements in a way that provides all the relevant information about these investing and financing activities.

## 11.12 SPECIMEN FORMAT

### 11.12.1 Direct Method - Statement of cash flows

| Particulars | Rs.000 | Rs.000 |
|---|---|---|
| Cash flows from operating activities | | |
| Cash receipts from customers | X | |
| Cash paid to suppliers and employees | X | |
| Cash generated from operations | X | |
| Interest paid | X | |
| Income tax paid | X | |
| Net cash from operating activities | | X (A) |
| Cash flows from investing activities | | |
| Purchase of Property, Plant & Equipment | X | |
| Proceeds from sale of equipment | X | |
| Interest received | X | |
| Dividend received | X | |
| Net cash used in investing activities | | X (B) |
| Cash flows from financing activities | | |
| Proceeds from issue of Share capital | X | |
| Proceeds from/repayment of long term borrowings | X | |
| | X | |
| Payment of finance lease liabilities | X | |
| Dividends paid | | |
| Net cash used in financing activities | | X (C ) |

| Particulars | Rs.000 | Rs.000 |
|---|---|---|
| Net increase in cash and cash equivalents (A+B+C)<br>Cash and cash equivalents at beginning of period | | X<br>X |
| Cash and cash equivalents at end of period | | X |

## 11.12.2 Indirect Method - Statement of cash flows

| Particulars | Rs.000 | Rs.000 |
|---|---|---|
| Cash flows from operating activities<br>Profit before taxation<br>Adjustments for<br>Depreciation<br>Loss on sale of current assets<br>Investment income<br>Interest expenses<br>Decrease/(Increase) in trade and other receivables<br>Decrease/(Increase) in inventories<br>Increase/(decrease) in trade payables<br>Cash generated from operations<br>Interest paid<br>Income tax paid | <br>X<br><br>X<br>X<br>X<br>X<br>X<br>X<br>X<br>X<br>X<br>X<br>X | |
| Net cash from operating activities | | X (A) |
| Cash flows from investing activities<br>Purchase of Property, Plant & Equipment<br>Proceeds from sale of equipment<br>Interest received<br>Dividend received | <br>X<br>X<br>X<br>X | |
| Net cash used in investing activities | | X (B) |
| Cash flows from financing activities<br>Proceeds from issue of Share capital<br>Proceeds from/repayment of long term borrowings<br>Payment of finance lease liabilities<br>Dividends paid | <br>X<br>X<br>X<br>X | |

| Particulars | Rs.000 | Rs.000 |
|---|---|---|
| Net cash used in financing activities | | X (C ) |
| Net increase in cash and cash equivalents (A+B+C)<br>Cash and cash equivalents at beginning of period | | X<br>X |
| Cash and cash equivalents at end of period | | X |

# SECTION III

# Financial Statements in Corporate Restructuring and Consolidated Financial Statements

# Chapter 12

# Corporate Restructuring

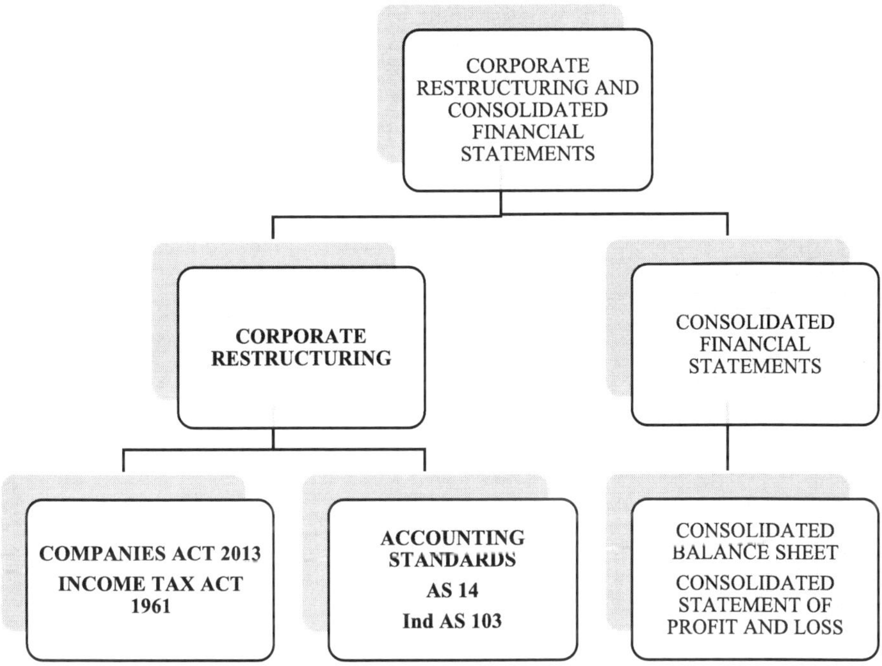


## 12.1 INTRODUCTION

Corporate Restructuring has become an integral part of today's business world, where macro-economic environment is constantly going through metamorphosis of change. As controls and restrictions give way to competition and free trade, restructuring, reorganization, and growth through the inorganic route has become essential. Restructuring usually involves tectonic shift in corporate strategies to meet increased competition or changed market conditions. Furthermore, with the onset of current pandemic which has thrown all kinds of businesses in complete disarray, this has assumed paramount importance to ensure businesses keep the heads above water and not wither way.

This restructuring process takes shape and form through mergers, acquisitions, takeovers, collaborations, consolidation, diversification etc. Domestic firms have taken steps to consolidate their position to face increasing competitive pressures and transnationals have taken this opportunity to enter Indian corporate sector.

The forces that drive corporate restructuring and consequent Merger & Acquisition activities are as under:

(i) Rapid pace of technological change.

(ii) Low costs of communication and transportation.

(iii) Globalization and global markets.

(iv) Nature of competition in terms of forms, sources, and intensity.

(v) Emergence of new types of industries.

(vi) Regulation in some industries and sectors.

(vii) Liberalization in some industries and sectors.

(viii) Growing inequalities in incomes and wealth.

## 12.2 FORMS OF CORPORATE RESTRUCTURING

The forms of corporate restructuring are summarised in the following tables:

### 12.2.1 Expansion

| Expansion |
|---|
| **Amalgamation**<br>This involves fusion of one or more companies where the companies lose their individual identity and a new company comes into existence to take over the business of companies being liquidated. |
| **Absorption**<br>This involves fusion of a small company with a large company where the smaller company ceases to exist after the merger. |
| **Tender offer**<br>This involves making a public offer for acquiring the shares of a target company with a view to acquire management control in that company |
| **Asset acquisition**<br>This involves buying assets of another company. The assets may be tangible assets like manufacturing units or intangible like brands |
| **Joint venture**<br>This involves two companies coming whose ownership is changed |

### 12.2.2 Contraction

| Contraction |
|---|
| **Demerger-spin off**<br>This type of demerger involves division of company into wholly owned subsidiary of parent company by distribution of all its shares of subsidiary company on Pro-rata basis. By this way, both the companies i.e. holding as well as subsidiary company exist |

| **Contraction** |
|---|
| and carry on business. |
| **Demerger - Equity carve out**<br>This is similar to spin offs, except that same part of shareholding of this subsidiary company is offered to public through a public issue and the parent company continues to enjoy control over the subsidiary company by holding controlling interest in it. |
| **Demerger – Split-up**<br>This type of demerger involves the division of parent company into two or more separate companies where parent company ceases to exist after the demerger. |
| **Asset sale**<br>This involves sale of tangible or intangible assets of a company to generate cash. A partial sell off, also called slump sale, involves the sale of a business unit or plant of one firm to another. It is the mirror image of a purchase of a business unit or plant. From the seller's perspective, it is a form of contraction and from the buyer's point of view it is a form of expansion |
| **Divestiture**<br>These are sale of segment of a company for cash or for securities to an outside party. Divestitures, involve contraction. |

## 12.2.3 Corporate control

| **Corporate control** |
|---|
| **Going private**<br>This involves converting a listed company into a private company by buying back all the outstanding shares from the markets |
| **Equity buy back**<br>This involves the company buying its own shares back from the market. This results in reduction in the equity capital of the company. This strengthens the promoter's position by increasing his stake in the equity of the company |
| **Leveraged buy-outs**<br>This involves raising of capital from the market or institutions by the management to acquire a company on the strength of its assets. |
| **Anti – takeover defences**<br>With the incidence of high value of hostile takeover activity in recent years, takeover defences both premature and reactive have been restored by the companies. |

## 12.3 LEGISLATIVE PROVISIONS RELATED TO THE CORPORATE RESTRUCTURING

Legislative provisions related to the corporate restructuring are highlighted in the following paragraphs

(a) Companies Act, 2013.

(b) Income Tax Act, 1961.

(c) Accounting Standards.

In this section, we have not included the provisions of Foreign Exchange Management Act and SEBI guideline, RERA, RBI regulations and labour related laws as this book covers aspects of Financial Due Diligence.

### 12.3.1 Companies Act, 2013

Salient features of the provisions of the Companies Act, 2013 on corporate restructuring are summarised in table below:

| Provisions under Companies Act, 2013 | Description |
|---|---|
| Sec 230 | This corresponds to section 391 of the Companies Act, 1956 and provides for power to Tribunal to make order on the application of the company or any creditor or member or in the case of company being wound up, of liquidator for the proposed compromise or make arrangements with creditors and members. |
| Sec 231 | Corresponding to section 392 of the Companies Act, 1956, this section provides for power of NCLT to supervise the implementation of the compromise or arrangement and enforce the same. The section also provides that if the Tribunal is satisfied that such compromise or arrangement cannot be implemented satisfactorily with or without modifications, and the company is unable to pay its debts as per the scheme, it may make an order for winding up of the company |
| Sec 232 | Corresponding to section 394 of Companies Act 1956, this section seeks to provide powers to NCLT to order for holding meeting of the creditors or the members and to make orders on the proposed reconstruction, merger, or amalgamation of companies. |
| Sec 233 | This is a new section and seeks to provide for merger or amalgamation between two small companies or between a holding company and its wholly owned subsidiary company by giving notice of the proposed scheme inviting objections or suggestions by both the transferor and the transferee company from Registrar, Official liquidator or persons |

| Provisions under Companies Act, 2013 | Description |
|---|---|
| | affected by the scheme. The scheme is to be approved by the respective members at a general meeting holding ninety per cent of total number of shares and also by nine tenth in value of creditors of respective companies. Both the transferor and transferee company has to file declaration of solvency. Transferee company shall file a copy of the approved scheme with the Central Government. On registration of the scheme, the transferor company shall be deemed to be dissolved. The Central Government may make rules for merger and amalgamation of companies. |
| Sec 234 | This is a new section and provides for Merger & Amalgamation of companies registered under the Act of 2013 with foreign company. The Central Government may in consultation with Reserve Bank of India make rules for the purpose of merger or amalgamation provided under this section. |
| Sec 235 | This section corresponds to section 395 of the Companies Act, 1956 and provides the manner in which the transferee company shall acquire shares of the shareholders dissenting from the scheme or contract as approved by the majority shareholders holding not less than nine-tenths in value of the shares whose transfer is involved. |
| Sec 236 | Corresponding to section 395 of Companies Act, 1956, this section provides for the procedure and manner in which the registered holder of at least 90 percent shares of a company shall notify the company of their intention to purchase remaining equity share of minority shareholders by virtue of an amalgamation, share exchange, conversion of securities etc, provision for valuation of shares having been provided by a registered valuer. This section provides for the procedure to be followed for acquisition of shares held by minority shareholders. |
| Sec 237 | Corresponding to section 396 of Companies Act, 1956, this section provides for power of Central Government to provide for amalgamation of Companies in public interest by passing an order to be notified in the Official Gazette. |
| Sec 238 | This section seeks to provide for registration of offer of schemes or contract involving transfer of shares. |
| Sec 239 | Corresponding to section 396A of Companies Act, 1956, this section specifies provisions related to preservation of books and papers of amalgamated companies |

| Provisions under Companies Act, 2013 | Description |
|---|---|
| Sec 240 | This section seeks to provide for liability of officers in respect of offences committed prior to merger, amalgamation etc. |

### 12.3.2 Income Tax Act, 1961

**Merger**

Income-tax Act, 1961 plays a pivotal role among all tax laws which affect the merger of firms from the point view of tax savings/liabilities. Merger has been defined as amalgamation under Sec 2(1B) and it means that the merger of one or more companies with another company or the merger of two or more companies to form one company (the company or companies which so merge being referred to as the amalgamating company or companies and the company with which they merge or which is formed as a result of the merger, as the amalgamated company) in such a manner that:

(i) all the property of the amalgamating company or companies immediately before the amalgamation becomes the property of the amalgamated company by virtue of the amalgamation.

(*ii*) all the liabilities of the amalgamating company or companies immediately before the amalgamation become the liabilities of the amalgamated company by virtue of the amalgamation.

(*iii*) shareholders holding not less than three-fourths in value of the shares in the amalgamating company or companies (other than shares already held therein immediately before the amalgamation by, or by a nominee for, the amalgamated company or its subsidiary) become shareholders of the amalgamated company by virtue of the amalgamation, otherwise than as a result of the acquisition of the property of one company by another company pursuant to the purchase of such property by the other company or as a result of the distribution of such property to the other company after the winding up of the first-mentioned company.

It may be noted that while evaluating the tax implications of restructuring, it is imperative to know the definition of the term 'Amalgamation' as per Income Tax.

**Demerger**

In accordance with section 2(19AA) of the Income Tax Act, 1961, unless the term "demerger", in relation to companies, means the transfer, pursuant to a scheme of arrangement the Companies Act, 2013, by a demerged company of its one or more undertakings to any resulting company in such a manner that-

(*i*) all the property of the undertaking, being transferred by the demerged company, immediately before the demerger, becomes the property of the resulting company by virtue of the demerger;

(*ii*) all the liabilities relatable to the undertaking, being transferred by the demerged company, immediately before the demerger, become the liabilities of the resulting company by virtue of the demerger.

(*iii*) the property and the liabilities of the undertaking or undertakings being transferred by the demerged company are transferred at values appearing in its books of account immediately before the demerger.

However according to proviso inserted vide Finance Act 2019, applicable effective 1 April 2020, the provisions of this sub-clause shall not apply where the resulting company records the value of the property and the liabilities of the undertaking or undertakings at a value different from the value appearing in the books of account of the demerged company, immediately before the demerger, in compliance to the Indian Accounting Standards specified in Annexure to the Companies (Indian Accounting Standards) Rules, 2015.

(*iv*) the resulting company issues, in consideration of the demerger, its shares to the shareholders of the demerged company on a proportionate basis except where the resulting company itself is a shareholder of the demerged company.

(*v*) the shareholders holding not less than three-fourths in value of the shares in the demerged company (other than shares already held therein immediately before the demerger, or by a nominee for, the resulting company or, its subsidiary) become shareholders of the resulting company or companies by virtue of the demerger, otherwise than as a result of the acquisition of the property or assets of the demerged company or any undertaking thereof by the resulting company;

(*vi*) the transfer of the undertaking is on a going concern basis.

(*vii*) the demerger is in accordance with the conditions, if any, notified under sub-section (5) of section 72A by the Central Government in this behalf.

Resulting company, according to section 2(41A) of Income Tax Act,1961 means one or more company, (including a wholly owned subsidiary thereof) to which the undertaking of the demerged company is transferred in a demerger, and the resulting company in consideration of such transfer of undertaking issues shares to the shareholders of the demerged company and include any authority or body or local authority or public sector company or a company established, constituted or formed as a result of demerger.

## 12.3.3 Accounting Standards

The relevant Accounting Standards are as under:

### *12.3.3.1 AS 14: Accounting for Amalgamation*

**Introduction**

This standard deals with accounting for amalgamations and the treatment of any resultant goodwill or reserves. This standard is directed principally to companies although some of its requirements also apply to financial statements of other enterprises.

This standard does not deal with cases of acquisitions which arise when there is a purchase by one company (referred to as the acquiring company) of the whole or part of the shares, or the whole or part of the assets, of another company (referred to as the acquired company) in consideration for payment in cash or by issue of shares or other securities in the acquiring company or partly in one form and partly in the other. The distinguishing feature of an acquisition is that the acquired company is not dissolved and its separate entity continues to exist.

**Definitions**

The following terms are used in this standard with the meanings specified:

(a) ***Amalgamation*** means an amalgamation pursuant to the provisions of the Companies Act, 2013 or any other statute which may be applicable to companies and includes 'merger'.

(b) ***Transferor company*** means the company which is amalgamated into another company.

(c) ***Transferee company*** means the company into which a transferor company is amalgamated.

(d) ***Reserve*** means the portion of earnings, receipts or other surplus of an enterprise (whether capital or revenue) appropriated by the management for a general or a specific purpose other than a provision for depreciation or diminution in the value of assets or for a known liability.

(e) ***Amalgamation in the nature of merger*** is an amalgamation which satisfies all the following conditions:

   (i) All the assets and liabilities of the transferor company become, after amalgamation, the assets and liabilities of the transferee company.

   (ii) Shareholders holding not less than 90% of the face value of the equity shares of the transferor company (other than the equity shares already held therein, immediately before the amalgamation, by the transferee company or its subsidiaries or their nominees) become equity shareholders of the transferee company by virtue of the amalgamation.

   (iii) The consideration for the amalgamation receivable by those equity shareholders of the transferor company who agree to become equity shareholders of the transferee company is discharged by the transferee company wholly by the issue of equity shares in the transferee company, except that cash may be paid in respect of any fractional shares.

(iv) The business of the transferor company is intended to be carried on, after the amalgamation, by the transferee company.

(v) No adjustment is intended to be made to the book values of the assets and liabilities of the transferor company when they are incorporated in the financial statements of the transferee company except to ensure uniformity of accounting policies.

(f) ***Amalgamation in the nature of purchase*** is an amalgamation which does not satisfy any one or more of the conditions specified in sub-paragraph (e) above.

(g) ***Consideration for the amalgamation*** means the aggregate of the shares and other securities issued and the payment made in the form of cash or other assets by the transferee company to the shareholders of the transferor company.

(h) ***Fair value*** is the amount for which an asset could be exchanged between a knowledgeable, willing buyer and a knowledgeable, willing seller in an arm's length transaction.

(i) ***Pooling of interests*** is a method of accounting for amalgamations the object of which is to account for the amalgamation as if the separate businesses of the amalgamating companies were intended to be continued by the transferee company. Accordingly, only minimal changes are made in aggregating the individual financial statements of the amalgamating companies.

**Summary principles**

The Standard summarises the main principles as under:

| | |
|---|---|
| ***Type of amalgamation*** | An amalgamation may be either –<br>(a) an amalgamation in the nature of merger, or<br>(b) an amalgamation in the nature of purchase. |
| ***Amalgamation in the nature of merger*** | Para 29. An amalgamation should be considered to be an amalgamation in the nature of merger when all the following conditions are satisfied:<br>(i) All the assets and liabilities of the transferor company become, after amalgamation, the assets and liabilities of the transferee company.<br>(ii) Shareholders holding not less than 90% of the face value of the equity shares of the transferor company (other than the equity shares already held therein, immediately before the amalgamation, by the transferee company or its subsidiaries or their nominees) become equity shareholders of the transferee company by virtue |

| | |
|---|---|
| | of the amalgamation.<br>(iii) The consideration for the amalgamation receivable by those equity shareholders of the transferor company who agree to become equity shareholders of the transferee company is discharged by the transferee company wholly by the issue of equity shares in the transferee company, except that cash may be paid in respect of any fractional shares.<br>(iv) The business of the transferor company is intended to be carried on, after the amalgamation, by the transferee company.<br>(v) No adjustment is intended to be made to the book values of the assets and liabilities of the transferor company when they are incorporated in the financial statements of the transferee company except to ensure uniformity of accounting policies.<br>Para 31. When an amalgamation is considered to be an amalgamation in the nature of merger, it should be accounted for under the pooling of interests method described in paragraphs 33–35. |
| ***Amalgamation in the nature of purchase*** | Para 30. An amalgamation should be considered to be an amalgamation in the nature of purchase, when any one or more of the conditions specified in paragraph 29 is not satisfied.<br>Para 32. When an amalgamation is considered to be an amalgamation in the nature of purchase, it should be accounted for under the purchase method described in paragraphs 36–39. |
| ***Accounting of the Pooling of Interests Method*** | Para 33. In preparing the transferee company's financial statements, the assets, liabilities and reserves (whether capital or revenue or arising on revaluation) of the transferor company should be recorded at their existing carrying amounts and in the same form as at the date of the amalgamation. The balance of the Profit and Loss Account of the transferor company should be aggregated with the corresponding balance of the transferee company or transferred to the General Reserve, if any.<br>Para 34. If, at the time of the amalgamation, the transferor and the transferee companies have conflicting accounting policies, a uniform set of |

| | |
|---|---|
| | accounting policies should be adopted following the amalgamation. The effects on the financial statements of any changes in accounting policies should be reported in accordance with Accounting Standard (AS) 5 Net Profit or Loss for the Period, Prior Period Items and Changes in Accounting Policies.<br>Para 35. The difference between the amount recorded as share capital issued (plus any additional consideration in the form of cash or other assets) and the amount of share capital of the transferor company should be adjusted in reserves. |
| ***Accounting of the Purchase Method*** | Para 36. In preparing the transferee company's financial statements, the assets and liabilities of the transferor company should be incorporated at their existing carrying amounts or, alternatively, the consideration should be allocated to individual identifiable assets and liabilities on the basis of their fair values at the date of amalgamation. The reserves (whether capital or revenue or arising on revaluation) of the transferor company, other than the statutory reserves, should not be included in the financial statements of the transferee company except as stated in paragraph 39.<br>Para 37. Any excess of the amount of the consideration over the value of the net assets of the transferor company acquired by the transferee company should be recognised in the transferee company's financial statements as goodwill arising on amalgamation. If the amount of the consideration is lower than the value of the net assets acquired, the difference should be treated as Capital Reserve.<br>Para 38. The goodwill arising on amalgamation should be amortised to income on a systematic basis over its useful life. The amortisation period should not exceed five years unless a somewhat longer period can be justified.<br>Para 39. Where the requirements of the relevant statute for recording the statutory reserves in the books of the transferee company are complied with, statutory reserves of the transferor company should be recorded in the financial statements of the transferee company. The corresponding debit should be given to a suitable account head (e.g., 'Amalgamation Adjustment Reserve') which should be presented as a separate line |

| | |
|---|---|
| | item. When the identity of the statutory reserves is no longer required to be maintained, both the reserves and the aforesaid account should be reversed |
| ***Common Procedures*** | Para 40. The consideration for the amalgamation should include any noncash element at fair value. In case of issue of securities, the value fixed by the statutory authorities may be taken to be the fair value. In case of other assets, the fair value may be determined by reference to the market value of the assets given up. Where the market value of the assets given up cannot be reliably assessed, such assets may be valued at their respective net book values.<br>Para 41. Where the scheme of amalgamation provides for an adjustment to the consideration contingent on one or more future events, the amount of the additional payment should be included in the consideration if payment is probable and a reasonable estimate of the amount can be made. In all other cases, the adjustment should be recognised as soon as the amount is determinable [see Accounting Standard (AS) 4, Contingencies and Events Occurring After the Balance Sheet Date]. |
| ***Treatment of Reserves Specified in A Scheme of Amalgamation*** | Para 42. Where the scheme of amalgamation sanctioned under a statute prescribes the treatment to be given to the reserves of the transferor company after amalgamation, the same should be followed. Where the scheme of amalgamation sanctioned under a statute prescribes a different treatment to be given to the reserves of the transferor company after amalgamation as compared to the requirements of this Standard that would have been followed had no treatment been prescribed by the scheme, the following disclosures should be made in the first financial statements following the amalgamation:<br>(a) A description of the accounting treatment given to the reserves and the reasons for following the treatment different from that prescribed in this Standard.<br>(b) Deviations in the accounting treatment given to the reserves as prescribed by the scheme of amalgamation sanctioned under the statute as compared to the requirements of this Standard that would have been followed had no treatment been prescribed by the scheme. |

| | |
|---|---|
| | (c) The financial effect, if any, arising due to such deviation.<br>Paragraph 42 shall not apply to any scheme of amalgamation approved under the Companies Act, 2013. |
| ***Disclosure*** | Para 43. For all amalgamations, the following disclosures should be made in the first financial statements following the amalgamation:<br>(a) names and general nature of business of the amalgamating companies;<br>(b) effective date of amalgamation for accounting purposes;<br>(c) the method of accounting used to reflect the amalgamation; and<br>(d) particulars of the scheme sanctioned under a statute.<br>Para 44. For amalgamations accounted for under the pooling of interests method, the following additional disclosures should be made in the first financial statements following the amalgamation:<br>(a) description and number of shares issued, together with the percentage of each company's equity shares exchanged to effect the amalgamation;<br>(b) the amount of any difference between the consideration and the value of net identifiable assets acquired, and the treatment thereof.<br>Para 45. For amalgamations accounted for under the purchase method, the following additional disclosures should be made in the first financial statements following the amalgamation:<br>(a) consideration for the amalgamation and a description of the consideration paid or contingently payable; and<br>(b) the amount of any difference between the consideration and the value of net identifiable assets acquired, and the treatment thereof including the period of amortisation of any goodwill arising on amalgamation |
| ***Amalgamation after the Balance Sheet Date*** | Para 46. When an amalgamation is effected after the balance sheet date but before the issuance of the financial statements of either party to the amalgamation, disclosure should be made in |

| | |
|---|---|
| | accordance with AS 4, 'Contingencies and Events Occurring After the Balance Sheet Date', but the amalgamation should not be incorporated in the financial statements. In certain circumstances, the amalgamation may also provide additional information affecting the financial statements themselves, for instance, by allowing the going concern assumption to be maintained. |

**Comparative position of two methods**

| Item | Pooling of interest Method | Purchase Method |
|---|---|---|
| ***Discharge of purchase consideration*** | Mainly shares, cash for Settling dues of fractional Shares | Shares or other securities or cash |
| ***Assets and liabilities*** | Recorded at book values | Recorded at fair values |
| ***Reserves*** | Are brought into and Recorded in the books | Only statutory reserves are recorded by debit to Amalgamation adjustment (reversed when statutory conditions are met) |
| ***Difference between consideration and net value of assets*** | Not recorded – difference is adjusted against reserves | Recorded as goodwill or capital reserve |

**Illustration 12.1: Amalgamation in the pooling of interest method**

Alpha Limited and Beta Limited were amalgamated on and from 1st April 2021. A new company Gamma Limited was formed to take over the business of the existing companies. The Balance Sheets of Alpha Limited and Beta Limited as on 31st March 2021 are given below:

(Rs in lakhs)

| Liabilities | Alpha Limited | Beta Limited | Assets | Alpha Limited | Beta Limited |
|---|---|---|---|---|---|
| **Share capital**<br>Equity shares of Rs.100 each | 1000 | 800 | **Non-current Assets** | 1200 | 1000 |

| | | | | | |
|---|---|---|---|---|---|
| 15% preference shares of Rs.100 each | 400 | 300 | **Current Assets, loans and advances** | 880 | 565 |
| **Reserves & surplus** | | | | | |
| Revaluation reserve | 100 | 80 | | | |
| General reserve | 200 | 150 | | | |
| P & L Account | 80 | 60 | | | |
| Secured loan | | | | | |
| 12% debentures of Rs.100 each | 96 | 80 | | | |
| Current liabilities and provisions | 204 | 95 | | | |
| | 2080 | 1565 | | 2080 | 1565 |

Other information:

1. 12% debenture holders of Alpha Limited and Beta Limited are discharged by Gamma Limited by issuing adequate number of 16% debentures of Rs.100 each to ensure that they continue to receive the same amount of interest.
2. Preference shareholders of Alpha Limited and Beta Limited have received same number of 15% preference shares of Rs.100 each of Gamma Limited
3. Gamma Limited has issued 1.5 equity shares for each equity share of Alpha Limited and one equity share for each equity share of Beta Limited. The face value of shares issued by Gamma Limited is Rs.100 each.

Required:

Prepare the Balance Sheet of Gamma Limited as on 1st April 2021 after the amalgamation has been carried out using the "pooling of interest method".

**Solution**

**Working Notes:**

**1. Statement of purchase consideration (Rs in lakhs)**

| **Item** | **Alpha Ltd** | **Beta Ltd** | **Total** |
|---|---|---|---|
| Equity shares<br>Preference shares | 1500<br>400 | 800<br>300 | 2300<br>700 |
| <br>Amount of share capital of transferor companies | 1900<br>1400 | 1100<br>1100 | 3000<br>2500 |
| Difference (A) | 500 | - | 500 |
| Amount of debentures issued<br>Alpha Ltd = 12/16 x 96<br>Beta Ltd = 12 / 16 x 80 | <br>72<br>- | <br>-<br>60 | <br>72<br>60 |

| | | | |
|---|---|---|---|
| Total<br>Amount of debentures of transferor companies | 72<br><br>96 | 60<br><br>80 | 132<br><br>176 |
| Difference (B) | (24) | (20) | (44) |
| Overall difference (A + B) | 476 | (20) | 456 |

**The overall difference of Rs. 456 lakhs to be adjusted first with general reserve and then the balance amount with Profit & Loss A/c as shown below.**

**(Rs in lakhs)**

| **Item** | **Combined amount** | **Adjusted amount** | **Balance Sheet amount** |
|---|---|---|---|
| General reserve (200 + 150)<br>Profit & Loss A/c (80 + 60) | 350<br>140 | 350<br>106 | NIL<br>34 |
| Total | 490 | 456 | 34 |

**Balance Sheet of Gamma Limited**
**As at 1st April 2021**
**(Rs in lakhs)**

| **Particulars** | **Note no.** | **Amount** |
|---|---|---|
| **I. Equity and Liabilities** | | |
| **(1) Shareholders' funds** | | |
| (a) Share capital | 1 | **3000** |
| (b) Reserves and surplus | 2 | **214** |
| **(2) Non-current liabilities** | | |
| Long-term borrowings | 3 | **132** |
| **(3) Current liabilities** (204+95) | | **299** |
| **Total** | | **3645** |
| **II. Assets** | | |
| **(1) Non-current assets** | | |
| (a) Fixed Assets | | |
| Tangible assets (1200 + 1000) | | **2200** |
| (b) Non-current investments | | **nil** |
| (c) Other current assets | | **nil** |
| **(2) Current assets** (880 +565) | | **1445** |
| **Total** | | **3645** |

**Notes on Accounts**

| S/L No | Particulars | Amount (Rs) | Amount (Rs) |
|---|---|---|---|
| 1. | **Share capital** | | |
| | Equity shares of Rs.100 each | **2300** | |
| | 15% preference shares of Rs.100 each | **700** | **3000** |
| 2. | **Reserves and surplus** | | |
| | Revaluation reserve | **180** | |
| | Profit & Loss Account | 34 | **214** |
| 3. | **Long term borrowings** | | |
| | 16% debentures of Rs.100 each | | **132** |

**Illustration 12.2: Amalgamation in the nature of merger and in the nature of purchase**

The following Balance Sheets are presented by X Ltd and Y Ltd as on 31st December 2021 who are amalgamated and form Z Ltd.

| Liabilities | X Ltd Rs. | Y Ltd Rs. | Assets | X Ltd Rs. | Y Ltd Rs. |
|---|---|---|---|---|---|
| Equity shares of Rs.10 each | 100,000 | 150,000 | Goodwill | 40,000 | 50,000 |
| | | | Land | 30,000 | 60,000 |
| General Reserve | 10,000 | 10,000 | Plant & Machinery | 50,000 | 60,000 |
| Profit and Loss A/c | 10,000 | 5,000 | Inventories | 30,000 | 40,000 |
| Capital reserve | 20,000 | - | Trade Receivable | 30,000 | 40,000 |
| Unsecured loans | 20,000 | 65,000 | Cash and bank | 20,000 | 10,000 |
| Trade Payable | 40,000 | 30,000 | | | |
| Total | 200,000 | 260,000 | Total | 200,000 | 260,000 |

**Additional information**

(a) The shareholders of X Ltd be allotted 20000 equity shares of Rs.10 each.

(b) The shareholders of Y Ltd be allotted 10000 equity shares of Rs.10 each.

Prepare the opening Balance Sheet in the books of Z Ltd, assuming that -

(a) the amalgamation is in the nature of Merger and

(b) amalgamation in the nature of purchase.

**Solution**

**(a) Amalgamation in the Nature of Merger:**

**In the books of Z Ltd**

**Balance Sheet**

**As on 31st December 2021**

| Particulars | Note no. | Amount Rs'000 |
|---|---|---|
| **I. Equity and Liabilities** | | |
| **(1) Shareholders' funds** | | |
| (a) Share capital | 1 | 300,000 |
| (b) Reserves and surplus | 2 | 5,000 |
| **(2) Non-current liabilities** | | |
| Unsecured loans (20000+65000) | | 85,000 |
| **(3) Current liabilities** | | |
| (a) Trade payables (40000 + 30000) | | 70,000 |
| **Total** | | **460,000** |
| **II. Assets** | | |
| **(1) Non-current assets** | | |
| (a) Intangible assets Goodwill (40000 + 50000) | | 90,000 |
| (b) Tangible assets | 3 | 200,000 |
| (c) Non-current investments | | Nil |
| **(2) Current assets** | | |
| (a) Inventories (Rs.30000+Rs.40000) | | 70,000 |
| (b) Trade receivables (Rs.30000 + Rs.40000) | | 70,000 |
| (c) Cash and cash equivalents (Rs.20000 + Rs.10000) | | 30,000 |
| **Total** | | **460,000** |

**Notes on Accounts**

| S/L No | Particulars | Amount (Rs'000) | Amount (Rs'000) |
|---|---|---|---|
| 1. | **Share capital**<br>**Issued and paid up**<br>30000 equity shares of Rs.10 each fully | | 300,000 |
| 2. | **Reserves and surplus**<br>Capital reserve | 20,000 | |

| | | | |
|---|---|---|---|
| | Less adjustment (WN1) | **15,000** | **5,000** |
| **3.** | **Tangible asset**<br>- Land (Rs.30000 + Rs.60000)<br>- Plant & Machinery (Rs.50000 + Rs.60000) | **90,000**<br>**110,000** | **200,000** |

**Working Notes:**

**1. Statement of Purchase consideration:**

| Item | Rs. |
|---|---|
| The shareholders of X Ltd allotted 20000 equity shares of Rs.10 each.<br>The shareholders of Y Ltd allotted 10000 equity shares of Rs.10 each | 200,000<br>100,000 |
| Total Purchase consideration<br>Less Share capital - X Ltd Rs.100000<br>Y Ltd Rs.150000<br>Amount to be adjusted | 300,000<br><br>250,000<br>50,000 |
| Adjusted as follows:<br>General Reserve (X Ltd Rs.10000 + Y Ltd Rs.10000) Rs.20000<br>Profit & Loss A/c(X Ltd Rs.10000 + Y Ltd Rs.5000) Rs.15000 | 35,000 |
| Balance to be adjusted against Capital Reserve | 15,000 |

Note: This is on the premise that as per AS 14 Revenue reserves needs to be exhausted first and the balance amount to be adjusted from capital reserve.

**(b) Amalgamation in the nature of purchase:**

**In the books of Z Ltd**

**Balance Sheet**

**As on 31st December 2021**

| Particulars | Note no. | Amount Rs'000 |
|---|---|---|
| **I. Equity and Liabilities** | | |
| **(1) Shareholders' funds** | | |
| (a) Share capital | **1** | **300,000** |
| (b) Reserves and surplus | **2** | **15,000** |
| **(2) Non-current liabilities** | | |
| Unsecured loans (20000+65000) | | **85,000** |
| **(3) Current liabilities** | | |
| (a) Trade payables (40000 + 30000) | | **70,000** |
| **Total** | | **470,000** |

| | | |
|---|---|---|
| **II. Assets** | | |
| **(1) Non-current assets** | | |
| (a) Intangible assets<br>Goodwill (WN1) | | **100,000** |
| (b) Tangible assets | **3** | **200,000** |
| (c) Non-current investments | | **Nil** |
| **(2) Current assets** | | |
| (a) Inventories (Rs.30000+Rs.40000) | | **70,000** |
| (b) Trade receivables (Rs.30000 + Rs.40000) | | **70,000** |
| (c) Cash and cash equivalents (Rs.20000 + Rs.10000) | | **30,000** |
| **Total** | | **470,000** |

Notes on Accounts

| S/L No | Particulars | Amount (Rs'000) | Amount (Rs'000) |
|---|---|---|---|
| 1. | **Share capital**<br>**Issued and Paid up**<br>30000 equity shares of Rs.10 each fully | | **300,000** |
| 2. | **Reserves and surplus**<br>Capital reserve (WN1) | | **15,000** |
| 3. | **Tangible asset**<br>- Land (Rs.30000 + Rs.60000)<br>- Plant & Machinery (Rs.50000 + Rs.60000) | **90,000**<br>**110,000** | **200,000** |

**Working Notes**

1. **Statement of calculation of Goodwill / capital reserve**

| Item | X Ltd Rs | Y Ltd Rs |
|---|---|---|
| Assets taken over: | | |
| Land | 30,000 | 60,000 |
| Plant & Machinery | 50,000 | 60,000 |
| Inventories | 30,000 | 40,000 |
| Sundry debtors | 30,000 | 40,000 |
| Cash & bank | 20,000 | 10,000 |
| Total assets (A) | 160,000 | 210,000 |
| Less: Liabilities taken over | | |

| | | |
|---|---|---|
| Unsecured loans<br>Sundry creditors<br>Total liabilities (B) | 20,000<br>40,000<br>60,000 | 65,000<br>30,000<br>95,000 |
| Net assets taken over (A – B) = (C)<br>Purchase consideration (D) | 100,000<br>200,000 | 115,000<br>100,000 |
| D – C = E | 100,000 | (15,000) |
| **To Balance Sheet above** | Goodwill | Capital reserve |

**Illustration 12.3: Demerger**

Partner Ltd has two divisions A and B and their respective shares of various assets and liabilities in the Company's Balance Sheet as on 31st March 2021 are given below:

(Rs in lakhs)

| | A Division | B Division | Total |
|---|---|---|---|
| Non-current Assets: | | | |
| Cost | 650 | 340 | |
| Less: Depreciation | 225 | 160 | |
| Written down value | 425 | 180 | 605 |
| Investments | | | 115 |
| Current Assets | 350 | 430 | |
| Less: Current liabilities | 185 | 210 | |
| Net current assets | 165 | 220 | 385 |
| | | | 1105 |
| Financed by | | | |
| Loan funds | | | 400 |
| Own funds | | | |
| Equity share capital – shares of Rs.10 each | | | 300 |
| Reserves and surplus | | | 405 |
| | | | 1105 |

Division B has been invariably suffering losses. The company sold this division B along with its assets and liabilities to a newly formed company Carefree Ltd which was incorporated with an Authorized capital of Rs.800 lakhs divided into shares of Rs.10 each. Carefree Ltd allotted to Partner Ltd's shareholders its two fully paid equity shares of Rs.10 each at par for every fully paid equity share of Rs.10 each held in Partner Ltd as discharge of consideration for the division taken over.

Carefree Ltd recorded in its books the non-current assets of Rs.280 lakhs, current assets of Rs.320 lakhs and liabilities at the same value as they appeared in the books of Partner Ltd.

On 1st April 2021 Partner Ltd sold all its investments for Rs.135 lakhs and redeemed debenture liability of Rs.150 lakhs at par, which was included in the loan funds. The cash transaction being recorded in the Bank Account is pertaining to A Division.

You are required to

(a) Show accounting treatment in the books of Partner Ltd

(b) prepare Partner Ltd's balance sheet immediately after demerger and

(c) initial balance sheet of Carefree Ltd.

**Solution**

**(a) Accounting treatment in the books of Partner Ltd**

**(All figures in Rs lakhs)**

| Particulars | Dr. | Cr. |
|---|---|---|
| Bank A/c (current assets) Dr.<br>To Investments A/c<br>To Profit & Loss A/c (Reserves and surplus)<br>(Being sale of investments at a profit of Rs.20 lakhs) | 135 | <br>115<br>20 |
| Debentures A/c (loan funds) Dr.<br>To Bank A/c (current assets)<br>(Being redemption of debentures at par) | 150 | <br>150 |
| Current Liabilities A/c Dr.<br>Provision for depreciation A/c Dr.<br>Reserves and surplus A/c Dr.<br>To Non-current Assets A/c<br>To Current Assets A/c<br>(Being assets and liabilities pertaining to B division taken out of the books on transfer of the division to Carefree Ltd) | 210<br>160<br>400 | <br><br><br>340<br>430 |

**(b) Partner Limited's Balance Sheet (post demerger)**

**As on 1.4.2021**

| | **Rs in lakhs** | **Rs in lakhs** |
|---|---|---|
| **I. Equity & Liabilities**<br>1. Shareholders' funds<br>(1) Share capital<br>(2) Reserves and surplus (W.N.1)<br>2.Long term borrowings (W.N.2)<br>3.Current liabilities | <br><br>300<br>25 | <br><br><br>325<br>250<br>185<br>**760** |
| **II. Assets**<br>Non-current assets: | | |

| | | |
|---|---|---|
| Gross block<br>Less: Depreciation<br>Current assets (W.N.3) | 650<br>225 | <br>425<br>335<br>**760** |

### (c) Initial Balance Sheet of Carefree Ltd

**As on 1.4.2021**

| | Rs in lakhs | Rs in lakhs |
|---|---|---|
| I. **Equity & Liabilities**<br>(1) Shareholders' funds<br>(a)Share capital (issued for acquisition of business)<br>(2) Current liabilities<br>Total | | <br><br>600<br><br>210<br>**810** |
| **II. Assets**<br>(1) Non-current assets<br>(a) Tangible Assets<br>(b) Intangible assets<br>Goodwill (W.N.4)<br>(2) Current assets<br>Total | | <br><br>280<br><br>210<br>320<br>**810** |

**Working Notes:**

1. **Statement of Reserves and surplus of Partner Ltd**

| | Rs in lakhs | Rs in lakhs |
|---|---|---|
| Balance as on 31st March 2021<br>Add: Profit on sale of investments<br><br>Less: Adjustment for difference on demerger | | 405<br>20<br>425<br>400<br>25 |

2. **Statement of Loan funds of Partner Ltd**

| | Rs in lakhs | Rs in lakhs |
|---|---|---|
| Balance as on 31st March 2021<br>Less: Debentures redeemed<br>Balance shown in balance sheet after demerger | | 400<br>150<br>250 |

3. **Statement of Current Assets of Partner Ltd**

| | Rs in lakhs | Rs in lakhs |
|---|---|---|
| Balance as on 31st March 2021<br>Add: Cash received from sale of investments<br>Balance shown in balance sheet after demerger | | 350<br>135<br>485 |

| | | |
|---|---|---|
| Less: Cash paid for redemption of debentures<br>Balance shown in balance sheet after demerger | | 150<br>335 |

4. **Statement of calculation of goodwill of Carefree Ltd**

| | Rs in lakhs | Rs in lakhs |
|---|---|---|
| Purchase consideration (300 x 2) | | 600 |
| Less: Assets sold | | |
| Non-current Assets | 280 | |
| Current Assets | 320 | |
| | 600 | |
| Less: Current liabilities | 210 | 390 |
| Goodwill | | 210 |

### Illustration 12.4: Internal Reconstruction

The Balance Sheet of Alpha Ltd on 31st March 2021 is as under: (Rs)

| Liabilities | Amount | Assets | Amount |
|---|---|---|---|
| Authorised, issued equity share capital: 20000 shares of Rs.100 each | 20,00,000 | Goodwill | 2,00,000 |
| | | Plant & Machinery | 18,00,000 |
| | | Stock | 3,00,000 |
| | | Debtors | 7,50,000 |
| 10000 preference shares (7%) of Rs.100 each | 10,00,000 | Preliminary expenses | 1,00,000 |
| | | Cash | 1,50,000 |
| Sundry creditors | 7,00,000 | Profit & Loss Account | 7,00,000 |
| Bank overdraft | 3,00,000 | | |
| | **40,00,000** | | **40,00,000** |

Two years preference dividends are in arrears. The company had bad time during the last two years and hopes for better business in future, earning profit and paying dividend provided the capital base is reduced.

An internal reconstruction scheme as follows was agreed to by all concerned:

(i) Creditors agreed to forego 50% of the claim.

(ii) Preference shareholders withdrew arrear dividend claim. They also agreed to lower their capital claim by 20% by reducing nominal value in consideration of 9% dividend effective after reorganization in case equity shareholders' losses exceed 50% on the application of the scheme.

(iii) Bank agreed to convert overdraft into term loan to the extent required for making current ratio equal to 2 : 1.

(iv) Revalued figure for plant and machinery was accepted as Rs.1500000.

(v) Debtors to the extent of Rs.400000 were considered good.

(vi) Equity shares shall be exchanged for the same number of equity shares at a revised denomination as required after the reorganization.

Required,

(a) Total loss to be borne by the equity and preference shareholders for the reorganization,

(b) Share of loss to the individual classes of shareholders

(c) New structure of share capital after reorganization

(d) Working capital of the reorganized company and

(e) A proforma balance sheet after reorganization.

**Solution**

**(a) Statement of loss to be borne by Equity and Preference shareholders (Rs.)**

| Item | Amount |
|---|---|
| Profit and loss Account (debit balance) | 7,00,000 |
| Preliminary expenses | 1,00,000 |
| Goodwill | 2,00,000 |
| Plant & Machinery (Rs.1800000 – Rs.1500000) | 3,00,000 |
| Debtors (Rs.750000 – Rs.400000) | 3,50,000 |
| Amount to be written off | 16,50,000 |
| Less: 50% of sundry creditors | 3,50,000 |
| Total loss to be borne by the equity and preference shareholders * | 13,00,000 |

*Two years preference dividend (arrears) have been ignored in the computation of loss to be borne by equity and preference shareholders.

**(b) Share of loss to preference shareholders and equity shareholders (Rs)**

| Item | Amount |
|---|---|
| Total loss as above (A) | 13,00,000 |
| It is more than 50% of the equity share capital i.e.Rs.10 lakhs | |
| Preference shareholders' share of loss = 20% of Rs.1000000 (B) | 2,00,000 |
| Equity shareholders' share of loss (A – B = C) | 11,00,000 |

**(c) Statement of new capital structure after reorganization (Rs)**

| Item | Amount |
|---|---|
| **Equity shares**: 20000 equity shares of Rs.45 each fully paid up (Rs.2000000 – Rs.1100000) | 9,00,000 |
| **Preference shares**: 10000, 9% preference shares of Rs.80 each, fully paid up (Rs.1000000 – Rs.200000) | 8,00,000 |

| | |
|---|---|
| **Total** | **17,00,000** |

**d) Statement of Working capital of the reorganized company**

| Item | Amount |
|---|---:|
| Current Assets:<br>Stock<br>Debtors<br>Cash | <br>3,00,000<br>4,00,000<br>1,50,000 |
| Gross current assets:<br>Less: Current liabilities:<br>Creditors 350000<br>Bank overdraft * 75000 | 8,50,000<br><br><br>4,25,000 |
| Working capital | 4,25,000 |

*Current ratio shall be 2:1 i.e. total current liabilities shall be 50% of Rs.8,50,000 (i.e.Rs.300,000 + Rs.400,000 + 150,000) = Rs.425,000.

Therefore, Bank overdraft = Rs.75,000 (Rs.425,000 less creditors Rs.350,000)

**e) Balance Sheet of Alpha Ltd (and reduced)**

**As on 31st March 2021**

| Particulars | Note no. | Amount |
|---|---|---:|
| **I. Equity and Liabilities** | | |
| **(1) Shareholders' funds** | | |
| (a) Share capital | 1 | **17,00,000** |
| (b) Reserves and surplus | | - |
| **(2) Non-current liabilities** | | |
| Long-term borrowing | | |
| - Term loan with bank | | **2,25,000** |
| **(3) Current liabilities** | | |
| Trade payables | 2 | **4,25,000** |
| **Total** | | **23,50,000** |
| **II. Assets** | | |
| **(1) Non-current assets** | | |
| (a) Fixed Assets | | |
| Tangible assets | 3 | **15,00,000** |
| Intangible assets | | - |
| (b) Non-current investments | | - |
| (c) Other non-current assets | | - |
| **(2) Current assets** | | |
| (a) Inventories | | **3,00,000** |

| | | |
|---|---|---|
| (b) Trade receivables<br>(c) Cash and cash equivalents | | **4,00,000**<br>**1,50,000** |
| **Total** | | **23,50,000** |

**Notes on Accounts**

| S/L No | Particulars | Amount (Rs) | Amount (Rs) |
|---|---|---|---|
| 1. | **Share capital** | | |
| | **Issued, subscribed and paid up** | | |
| | 20000 equity shares of Rs.45 each | 9,00,000 | |
| | 10% preference shares of Rs.80 each | 8,00,000 | 17,00,000 |
| 2. | **Trade payables** | | |
| | Bank overdraft | 75,000 | |
| | Sundry creditors | 3,50,000 | 4,25,000 |
| 3. | **Tangible assets** | | |
| | Plant & Machinery | | 15,00,000 |

### 12.3.3.2 Ind AS 103: Business Combination

This Ind AS is the Indian version of IFRS 3, Business Combination and prescribes only the acquisition method for each business combination.

**Objectives**

According to paragraph 1 of this Ind AS, the objective is to improve the relevance, reliability, and comparability of the information that a reporting entity provides in its financial statements about a business combination and its effects.

To accomplish that, this Ind AS establishes principles and requirements for how the acquirer:

(a) recognizes and measures in its financial statements the identifiable assets acquired, the liabilities assumed and any non-controlling interest in the acquiree.

(b) recognizes and measures the goodwill acquired in the business combination or a gain from a bargain purchase; and

(c) determines what information to disclose to enable users of the financial statements to evaluate the nature and financial effects of the business combination.

## Definitions

| | |
|---|---|
| **Acquiree** | The business or businesses that the acquirer obtains control of in a business combination. |
| **Acquirer** | The entity that obtains control of the acquiree. |
| **Acquisition date** | The date on which the acquirer obtains control of the acquiree. |
| **Business** | An integrated set of activities and assets that is capable of being conducted and managed for the purpose of providing goods or services to customers, generating investment income (such as dividends or interest) or generating other income from ordinary activities. |
| **Business combination** | A transaction or other event in which an acquirer obtains control of one or more businesses. Transactions sometimes referred to as 'true mergers' or 'mergers of equals' are also business combinations as that term is used in this Ind AS. |
| **Contingent consideration** | Usually, an obligation of the acquirer to transfer additional assets or equity interests to the former owners of an acquiree as part of the exchange for control of the acquiree if specified future events occur or conditions are met. However, contingent consideration also may give the acquirer the right to the return of previously transferred consideration if specified conditions are met. |
| **Equity interests** | For the purposes of this Ind AS, equity interests is used broadly to mean ownership interests of investor-owned entities and owner, member or participant interests of mutual entities. |
| **Fair value** | Fair value is the price that would be received to sell an asset or paid to transfer a liability in an orderly transaction between market participants at the measurement date. (See Ind AS 113.) |
| **Goodwill** | An asset representing the future economic benefits arising from other assets acquired in a business combination that are not individually identified and separately recognised. |
| **Identifiable** | An asset is identifiable if it either:<br>(a) is separable, i.e. capable of being separated or divided from the entity and sold, transferred, licensed, rented or exchanged, either individually or together with a related contract, identifiable asset or liability, regardless of whether the entity intends to do so; or<br>(b) arises from contractual or other legal rights, regardless of whether those rights are transferable or separable from the entity or from other rights and obligations. |

| | |
|---|---|
| **Acquiree** | The business or businesses that the acquirer obtains control of in a business combination. |
| **Intangible asset** | An identifiable non-monetary asset without physical substance. |
| **Mutual entity** | An entity, other than an investor-owned entity, that provides dividends, lower costs or other economic benefits directly to its owners, members or participants. For example, a mutual insurance company, a credit union and a co-operative entity are all mutual entities. |
| **Non-controlling interest** | The equity in a subsidiary not attributable, directly or indirectly, to a parent. |
| **Owners** | For the purposes of this Ind AS, owners is used broadly to include holders of equity interests of investor-owned entities and owners or members of, or participants in, mutual entities. |

### Identifying a Business Combination

Paragraph 3. An entity shall determine whether a transaction or other event is a business combination by applying the definition in this Ind AS, which requires that the assets acquired, and liabilities assumed constitute a business. If the assets acquired are not a business, the reporting entity shall account for the transaction or other event as an asset acquisition. Paragraphs B5–B12D provide guidance on identifying a business combination and the definition of a business.

### The Acquisition method

An entity shall account for each business combination by applying the acquisition method. Applying the acquisition method requires:

(a) identifying the acquirer.

(b) determining the acquisition date.

(c) recognizing and measuring the identifiable assets acquired, the liabilities assumed and any non-controlling interest in the acquiree; and

(d) recognizing and measuring goodwill or a gain from a bargain purchase. (para 5).

Paragraph 6. For each business combination, one of the combining entities shall be identified as the acquirer

Paragraph 8. The acquirer shall identify the acquisition date, which is the date on which it obtains control of the acquiree. The date on which the acquirer obtains control of the acquiree is generally the date on which the acquirer legally transfers the consideration, acquires the assets, and assumes the liabilities of the acquiree—the closing date.

## Recognition principle

Paragraph 10. As of the acquisition date, the acquirer shall recognize, separately from goodwill, the identifiable assets acquired, the liabilities assumed and any non-controlling interest in the acquiree.

Paragraph 11. To qualify for recognition as part of applying the acquisition method, the identifiable assets acquired, and liabilities assumed must meet the definitions of assets and liabilities in the Framework for the Preparation and Presentation of Financial Statements in accordance with Indian Accounting Standards issued by the Institute of Chartered Accountants of India at the acquisition date.

Paragraph 12 In addition, to qualify for recognition as part of applying the acquisition method, the identifiable assets acquired and liabilities assumed must be part of what the acquirer and the acquiree (or its former owners) exchanged in the business combination transaction rather than the result of separate transactions.

Paragraph 15. At the acquisition date, the acquirer shall classify or designate the identifiable assets acquired and liabilities assumed as necessary to apply other Ind ASs subsequently. The acquirer shall make those classifications or designations based on the contractual terms, economic conditions, its operating or accounting policies and other pertinent conditions as they exist at the acquisition date.

## Exception to recognition principle

According to Paragraph 22, Ind AS 37, Provisions, Contingent Liabilities and Contingent Assets, defines a contingent liability as:

(a) a possible obligation that arises from past events and whose existence will be confirmed only by the occurrence or non-occurrence of one or more uncertain future events not wholly within the control of the entity; or

(b) a present obligation that arises from past events but is not recognised because:

  (i) it is not probable that an outflow of resources embodying economic benefits will be required to settle the obligation; or

  (ii) the amount of the obligation cannot be measured with sufficient reliability.

Paragraph 23 prescribes that, the requirements in Ind AS 37 do not apply in determining which contingent liabilities to recognize as of the acquisition date.

Instead, the acquirer shall recognize as of the acquisition date a contingent liability assumed in a business combination if it is a present obligation that arises from past events and its fair value can be measured reliably.

Therefore, contrary to Ind AS 37, the acquirer recognizes a contingent liability assumed in a business combination at the acquisition date even if it is not probable that an outflow of resources embodying economic benefits will be required to settle the obligation. Paragraph 56 provides guidance on the subsequent accounting for contingent liabilities.

## Measurement principle

Paragraph 18. The acquirer shall measure the identifiable assets acquired and the liabilities assumed at their acquisition-date fair values.

Paragraph 19. For each business combination, the acquirer shall measure at the acquisition date components of non-controlling interest in the acquiree that are present ownership interests and entitle their holders to a proportionate share of the entity's net assets in the event of liquidation at either:

(a) fair value; or

(b) The present ownership instruments' proportionate share in the recognised amounts of the acquiree's identifiable net assets

All other components of non-controlling interests shall be measured at their acquisition-date fair values, unless another measurement basis is required by Ind AS.

## Exceptions to recognition and measurement principle

These are summarized as under:

| | |
|---|---|
| ***Income taxes*** | Para 24. The acquirer shall recognize and measure a deferred tax asset or liability arising from the assets acquired and liabilities assumed in a business combination in accordance with Ind AS 12, Income Taxes.<br>Para 25. The acquirer shall account for the potential tax effects of temporary differences and carry forwards of an acquiree that exist at the acquisition date or arise because of the acquisition in accordance with Ind AS 12. |
| ***Employee benefits*** | Para 26. The acquirer shall recognize and measure a liability (or asset, if any) related to the acquiree's employee benefit arrangements in accordance with Ind AS 19, Employee Benefits. |
| ***Indemnification assets*** | Para 27. The seller in a business combination may contractually indemnify the acquirer for the outcome of a contingency or uncertainty related to all or part of a specific asset or liability.<br>Para 28 In some cases, the indemnification may relate to an asset or a liability that is an exception to the recognition or measurement principles.<br>For example, an indemnification may relate to a contingent liability that is not recognised at the acquisition date because its fair value is not reliably measurable at that date.<br>Alternatively, an indemnification may relate to an asset or a liability, for example, one that results from an employee benefit, that is |

| | |
|---|---|
| ***Income taxes*** | Para 24. The acquirer shall recognize and measure a deferred tax asset or liability arising from the assets acquired and liabilities assumed in a business combination in accordance with Ind AS 12, Income Taxes.<br>Para 25. The acquirer shall account for the potential tax effects of temporary differences and carry forwards of an acquiree that exist at the acquisition date or arise because of the acquisition in accordance with Ind AS 12. |
| | measured on a basis other than acquisition-date fair value.<br>In those circumstances, the indemnification asset shall be recognised and measured using assumptions consistent with those used to measure the indemnified item, subject to management's assessment of the collectability of the indemnification asset and any contractual limitations on the indemnified amount. |

## Exception to measurement principle

These are summarized in the table below.

| | |
|---|---|
| ***Reacquired rights*** | Para 29. The acquirer shall measure the value of a reacquired right recognised as an intangible asset based on the remaining contractual term of the related contract regardless of whether market participants would consider potential contractual renewals when measuring its fair value. Paragraphs B35 and B36 provide related application guidance. |
| ***Share-based payment transactions*** | Para 30. The acquirer shall measure a liability or an equity instrument related to share-based payment transactions of the acquiree or the replacement of an acquiree's share-based payment transactions with share-based payment transactions of the acquirer in accordance with the method in Ind AS 102,<br>Share-based Payment, at the acquisition date. (This Ind AS refers to the result of that method as the 'market-based measure' of the share-based payment transaction.) |
| **Assets held for sale** | Para 31. The acquirer shall measure an acquired non-current asset (or disposal group) that is classified as held for sale at the acquisition date in accordance with *Ind AS 105, Non-current Assets Held for Sale and Discontinued Operations*, at fair value less costs to sell in accordance with paragraphs 15–18 of that Ind AS. |

## Recognizing and measurement goodwill and bargain purchase

### Goodwill

According to Paragraph 32, the acquirer shall recognize goodwill as of the acquisition date measured as the excess of (a) over (b) below:

(a) the aggregate of:

  (i) the consideration transferred measured in accordance with this Ind AS, which generally, requires acquisition-date fair value (see paragraph 37);

  (ii) the amount of any non-controlling interest in the acquiree measured in accordance with this Ind AS; and

  (iii) in a business combination achieved in stages (see paragraphs 41 and 42), the acquisition-date fair value of the acquirer's previously held equity interest in the acquiree.

(b) the net of the acquisition-date amounts of the identifiable assets acquired and the liabilities assumed measured in accordance with this Ind AS.

### Bargain Purchase

In accordance with Paragraph 34, in extremely rare circumstances, an acquirer will make a bargain purchase in a business combination in which the amount in paragraph 32(b) exceeds the aggregate of the amounts specified in paragraph 32(a).

If that excess remains after applying the requirements in paragraph 36, the acquirer shall recognize the resulting gain in other comprehensive income on the acquisition date and accumulate the same in equity as capital reserve. The gain shall be attributed to the acquirer.

Paragraph 36. Before recognizing a gain on a bargain purchase, the acquirer shall determine whether there exists clear evidence of the underlying reasons for classifying the business combination as a bargain purchase.

If such evidence exists, the acquirer shall reassess whether it has correctly identified all of the assets acquired and all of the liabilities assumed and shall recognize any additional assets or liabilities that are identified in that review.

The acquirer shall then review the procedures used to measure the amounts this Ind AS requires to be recognised at the acquisition date for all of the following:

(a) the identifiable assets acquired, and liabilities assumed.

(b) the non-controlling interest in the acquiree, if any.

(c) for a business combination achieved in stages, the acquirers previously held equity interest in the acquiree; and

(d) the consideration transferred.

The objective of the review is to ensure that the measurements appropriately reflect consideration of all available information as of the acquisition date.

Paragraph 36A. If there does not exist clear evidence of the underlying reasons for classifying the business combination as a bargain purchase, the acquirer shall apply the requirements of reassessment and review described in paragraph 36. The excess, if any, as determined in accordance with paragraph 32 after applying the said requirements of paragraph 36, shall be recognised directly in equity as capital reserve.

### A business combination achieved in stages

Paragraph 41. An acquirer sometimes obtains control of an acquiree in which it held an equity interest immediately before the acquisition date. For example, on 31 December 20X1, Entity A holds a 35 per cent non-controlling equity interest in Entity B. On that date, Entity A purchases an additional 40 per cent interest in Entity B, which gives it control of Entity B. This Ind AS refers to such a transaction as a business combination achieved in stages, sometimes also referred to as a step acquisition.

Paragraph 42. In a business combination achieved in stages, the acquirer shall remeasure its previously held equity interest in the acquiree at its acquisition-date fair value and recognize the resulting gain or loss, if any, in profit or loss or other comprehensive income, as appropriate.

Paragraph 42A. When a party to a joint arrangement (as defined in Ind AS 111, *Joint Arrangements*) obtains control of a business that is a joint operation (as defined in Ind AS 111), and had rights to the assets and obligations for the liabilities relating to that joint operation immediately before the acquisition date, the transaction is a business combination achieved in stages.

The acquirer shall therefore apply the requirements for a business combination achieved in stages, including remeasuring its previously held interest in the joint operation in the manner described in paragraph 42. In doing so, the acquirer shall remeasure its entire previously held interest in the joint operation.

**Illustration 12.5: Steps in calculation of Valuation of Goodwill**

In accordance with the Ind AS, the acquirer shall recognise goodwill as of the acquisition date measured as the excess of:

| | |
|---|---|
| (a) Aggregate of | |
| (i) the consideration transferred measured in accordance with this Ind AS, which generally requires acquisition date fair value | X |
| (ii) the amount of non-controlling interest in the acquiree measured in accordance with this Ind AS and | X |
| (iii) in case of business combination achieved in stages (Ind AS103, para 41 and 42), the acquisition date fair value of the acquirer's previously held equity interest in the acquiree | X |
| TOTAL (A) | X |

| | |
|---|---|
| (a) Aggregate of<br>(i) the consideration transferred measured in accordance with this Ind AS, which generally requires acquisition date fair value<br>(ii) the amount of non-controlling interest in the acquiree measured in accordance with this Ind AS and<br>(iii) in case of business combination achieved in stages (Ind AS103, para 41 and 42), the acquisition date fair value of the acquirer's previously held equity interest in the acquiree | X<br>X<br>X |
| (b) The net of acquisition date amounts of the identifiable assets acquired, and the liabilities assumed measured in terms of this Ind AS | X |
| TOTAL (B) | X |
| Goodwill (A- B) | X |
| Bargain purchase (B – A) | X * |

**Illustration 12.6: Valuation of goodwill**

A Ltd acquired 60% shares of B Ltd @ Rs. 20 per share. Following are the extract of

| Balance Sheet of B Ltd: | Rs |
|---|---|
| 1000000 Equity shares of Rs.10 each | 100,00,000 |
| 10% debentures | 10,00,000 |
| Creditors | 55,00,000 |
| Fixed Assets | 70,00,000 |
| Investments | 45,00,000 |
| Current Assets | 68,00,000 |
| Loans & Advances | 22,00,000 |

On the same day B Ltd declared dividend at 20% and as agreed between both the Companies fixed assets were to be depreciated @ 10% and investment to be taken at market value of Rs.60,00,000. Calculate the goodwill or bargain purchase to be recorded in consolidated financial statement

**Solution**

| Calculation of goodwill/bargain purchase | Rs | Rs |
|---|---|---|
| Net Assets | | |
| Fixed Assets | 70,00,000 | |
| Less Depreciation (70,00,000 x 10%) | 7,00,000 | 63,00,000 |
| Investments at market value | | 60,00,000 |
| Current Assets | | 68,00,000 |

| | | |
|---|---|---|
| Loans & Advances | | 22,00,000 |
| Total Assets | | 213,00,000 |
| Less : Total Liabilities – Creditors | 55,00,000 | |
| 10% debentures | 10,00,000 | 65,00,000 |
| Equity | | 148,00,000 |
| Majority share 60% x Rs.148,00,000 | | 88,80,000 (A) |
| Cost of investment | | |
| Equity - (10,00,000 x 60%) x Rs.20 | 120,00,000 | |
| Less: Dividend (600,000 x 2) | 12,00,000 | 108,00,000 (B) |
| Goodwill (B – A) | | 19,20,000 |

**Illustration 12.7: Valuation of bargain purchase**

A Ltd purchased 40% stake of B Ltd for Rs.12 per share. After two years A Ltd decided to purchase another 40% share in B Ltd. B Ltd has 100,00,000 equity shares of Rs.10 each as fully paid up shares. The purchase deal was finalized in the following terms:

(a) Purchase price per share to be calculated based on average profit of last three years capitalized at 7.5%. Profits for last three years are Rs.3.5 mil, Rs.6.5 mil and Rs.8.9 mil.
(b) Total assets of B Ltd was Rs.115 mil. Assets to be appreciated by Rs.4.0 mil.
(c) Of the external creditors for Rs.25.0 mil one creditor to whom Rs.1.0 mil was due has expired and nothing is to be paid to settle this liability.
(d) B Ltd will declared dividend @ 15%.

Calculate goodwill or bargain purchase for A Ltd in consolidated financial statement.

**Solution**

**Calculation of purchase consideration Rs'000**

| | | |
|---|---|---|
| Profits for last three years | First | 8,900 |
| | Second | 6,500 |
| | Third | 3,500 |
| Total profits for last three years | | 18,900 |
| Average profit (Rs 18,900/3) | | 6,300 |
| Total value of B Ltd (6,300/7.5%) | | 84,000 |
| Number of shares in B Ltd | | 10,000 |
| Value per share | | 8.40 |
| Purchase consideration (100,00,000 x 40%) x 8.4 | | **33,600** |

| **Calculation of goodwill/bargain purchase** | **Rs'000** | **Rs'000** |
|---|---|---|
| Fixed Assets | 115,000 | |
| Add: Appreciation in value | 4,000 | 119,000 |
| Less: Creditors | 25,000 | |

| | | |
|---|---|---|
| Less: amount written back | 1,000 | 24,000 |
| Net Asset | | 95,000 |
| Share in net asset (95,000 x 80%) | | 76,000 (A) |
| Cost of investment: Purchase consideration | 33,600 | |
| Less: Dividend received (10,00,00,000 x 40% x 15%) | 6,000 | |
| | 27,600 | |
| Add: Investment (10000000 x 40% x 12) | 48,000 | 75,600 (B) |
| Bargain purchase (A – B) | | 400 |

## Business Combinations of entities under common control

### Definitions

The following terms are used in this Appendix with the meaning specified:

| | |
|---|---|
| ***Transferor*** | means an entity or business which is combined into another entity because of a business combination. |
| ***Transferee*** | means an entity in which the transferor entity is combined. |
| ***Reserve*** | means the portion of earnings, receipts or other surplus of an entity (whether capital or revenue) appropriated by the management for a general or a specific purpose other than provision for depreciation. |
| ***Common control business combination*** | means a business combination involving entities or businesses in which all the combining entities or businesses are ultimately controlled by the same party or parties both before and after the business combination, and that control is not transitory. |

### Common control business combinations

Common control business combinations will include transactions, such as transfer of subsidiaries or businesses, between entities within a group.

The extent of non-controlling interests in each of the combining entities before and after the business combination is not relevant to determining whether the combination involves entities under common control. This is because a partially owned subsidiary is nevertheless under the control of the parent entity.

The fact that one of the combining entities is a subsidiary that has been excluded from the consolidated financial statements of the group in accordance with Ind AS 27 is not relevant to determining whether a combination involves entities under common control.

An entity can be controlled by an individual, or by a group of individuals acting together under a contractual arrangement, and that individual or group of individuals may not be subject to the financial reporting requirements of Ind ASs. Therefore, it is not necessary for combining entities to be included as part of the same consolidated financial statements for a business combination to be regarded as one having entities under common control.

A group of individuals are regarded as controlling an entity when, because of contractual arrangements, they collectively have the power to govern its financial and operating policies so as to obtain benefits from its activities, and that ultimate collective power is not transitory.

## Method of accounting for common control business combinations

Business combinations involving entities or businesses under common control shall be accounted for using the pooling of interests method.

| | |
|---|---|
| ***The pooling of interest method is considered to involve the following:*** | (i) The assets and liabilities of the combining entities are reflected at their carrying amounts.<br>(ii) No adjustments are made to reflect fair values or recognize any new assets or liabilities. The only adjustments that are made are to harmonize accounting policies.<br>(iii) The financial information in the financial statements in respect of prior periods should be restated as if the business combination had occurred from the beginning of the preceding period in the financial statements, irrespective of the actual date of the combination.<br>However, if business combination had occurred after that date, the prior period information shall be restated only from that date. |

The consideration for the business combination may consist of securities, cash or other assets.

Securities shall be recorded at nominal value. In determining the value of the consideration, assets other than cash shall be considered at their fair values.

The balance of the retained earnings appearing in the financial statements of the transferor is aggregated with the corresponding balance appearing in the financial statements of the transferee.

Alternatively, it is transferred to General Reserve, if any.

The identity of the reserves shall be preserved and shall appear in the financial statements of the transferee in the same form in which they appeared in the financial statements of the transferor.

Thus, for example, the General Reserve of the transferor entity becomes the General Reserve of the transferee, the Capital Reserve of the transferor becomes the Capital Reserve of the transferee and the Revaluation Reserve of the transferor becomes the Revaluation Reserve of the transferee.

As a result of preserving the identity, reserves which are available for distribution as dividend before the business combination would also be available for distribution as dividend after the business combination. The difference, if any, between the amount recorded as share capital issued plus any additional consideration in the form of cash or other assets and the amount of share capital of the transferor shall be transferred to capital reserve and should be presented separately from other capital reserves with disclosure of its nature and purpose in the notes.

### Business combination after the balance sheet date

When a business combination is effected after the balance sheet but before the approval of the financial statements for issue by either party to the business combination, disclosure is made in accordance with Ind AS 10 *Events after the Reporting Period*, but the business combination is not incorporated in the financial statements. In certain circumstances, the business combination may also provide additional information affecting the financial statements themselves, for instance, by allowing the going concern assumption to be maintained.

### Illustration 12.8: Valuation of goodwill

Solomon Ltd has an 80% subsidiary Cox Ltd that it acquired on 31 March 2020 for a cash payment of Rs.80 million. The fair value exercise revealed that the fair value of the identifiable net assets of Cox Ltd at that date was Rs.90 million. The fair value adjustments were incorporated into the individual financial statements of the subsidiary at 31 March 2021.

The summarized balance sheet of Cox Ltd at 31 March 2022 showed the following balances:

| | Rs'000 |
|---|---|
| Non-current assets | 100,000 |
| Current assets | 30,000 |
| | 130,000 |
| Equity | 85,000 |
| Non-current liabilities | 35,000 |
| Current liabilities | 10,000 |
| | 130,000 |

Your assistant is aware that the goodwill of Cox Ltd had not suffered any impairment loss when it was tested for impairment at 31 March 2022. However, he is unsure what this means. He also provides you with the information that the value in use of the non-current assets of Cox Ltd (a single cash-generating unit) is Rs.97 million, and that one of the non-current assets (included in the above balance sheet at a carrying value of Rs. 4 million) has been destroyed and is in fact worthless.

**Solution**

The consolidated balance sheet at 31 March will include the assets and liabilities of Cox Ltd and the consolidated income statement will include its income and expenses. However, the non-current assets of Cox Ltd will need to be reduced by Rs.4 million to reflect the destruction and consequent loss of value. This will lead to a charge of Rs.4 million in the consolidated income statement.

The original goodwill on acquisition of Cox Ltd was Rs.8 million (Rs.80 million

– 80% x Rs.90 million).

Ind AS 103 – *Business combinations – requires that purchased goodwill be reviewed annually for impairment using the principles of Ind AS 36 – Impairment of assets.* This involves computing the recoverable amount of the asset. This is the higher of the net selling price of the asset (not applicable in the case of goodwill since it cannot be sold separately) and its value in use – the present value of the future cash flows derivable from the asset. For many assets – including goodwill – it is not possible to attribute cash flows to individual assets but rather to groups of assets – referred to in Ind AS 36 as cash generating units. In this case the goodwill is located in a cash generating unit together with the non-current assets. The calculation of the impairment loss is as follows:

| | Rs.m |
|---|---|
| Carrying value of non-current assets | 100 |
| Related goodwill – group share | 8 |
| Notionally allocated to minority interest | 2 |
| | 110 |
| Value in use | (97) |
| So total impairment | 13 |

Rs.4 million of this impairment is allocated to the specifically impaired non-current asset and the balance of Rs.9 million to goodwill. Since the goodwill relates to an 80% share the impairment will be 80% x Rs.9 million = Rs.7·2 million.

This means that the new carrying value of the goodwill will be Rs.0·8 million (Rs.8 million – Rs.7·2 million).

**Illustration 12.9: Valuation of goodwill**

On 1st April 20X1, S acquired 100% of ordinary share capital in two subsidiary companies, H and M in separate acquisitions. Consolidated goodwill is as under:

| | H (Rs'000) | M (Rs'000) |
|---|---|---|
| Purchase consideration | 1200 | 4500 |
| Estimated fair value of net assets | (8000) | (3000) |
| Consolidated goodwill | 4000 | 1500 |

A review of fair value of each subsidiary's net assets was undertaken in March 20X2.

Unfortunately, both company's net assets declined in value. Estimated value of its net assets as at 1.4.20X1 was only Rs.7 m. M's net assets were estimated to have a fair value of Rs.500,000 less than the carrying value. The fall is due to some physical damage occurring to its Plant & Machinery. Comment.

**Solution**

Under Ind AS 103 Business Combination, on acquisition of a subsidiary, purchase consideration should be allocated to fair value of net assets and the balance should go to goodwill (or negative goodwill if assets have a greater fair value than purchase consideration). Ind AS 103 recognizes that it is always not possible to assess the value of assets accurately during date of acquisition.

Therefore, provisional accounting can be made within 12 months of acquisition.

Hence in case of H, estimated fair value would be Rs.7 m and goodwill at Rs.5 m respectively, the fall of Rs.1 m is not an impairment loss and should not be charged to Income statement.

In the case of M, since fair value of assets have reduced by Rs.5,00,000, the carrying value owing to some physical damage of the Plant. Plant & Machinery should be written down to Recoverable value and impairment loss charged to Income statement. However, since the Recoverable value of the Company has not fallen, goodwill will not be impaired.

### 12.3.3.3 Comparative position of Accounting Standards

Comparative position of Accounting Standards related to Merger and Acquisition is summarized in the table below:

| S/L No | Ind AS 103<br>Business Combinations | AS 14<br>Accounting for Amalgamations (as amended) |
|---|---|---|
| 1 | Prescribes only the acquisition method for each business combination. | Prescribes two methods:<br>– Pooling of interest method<br>– Purchases method |
| 2. | **Purchase method – values on acquisition**<br>Assets, liabilities, and contingent liabilities of acquired entity are fair valued.<br>If control is obtained in a partial acquisition of a subsidiary the full value of the assets, liabilities and contingent liabilities including portion attributable to the minority (non-controlling) interest is recorded in consolidated business.<br>Goodwill is recognised as the residual between the consideration paid and the percentage of the business acquired.<br>Liabilities for restructuring activities are recognised only when acquiree has an existing liability at acquisition date.<br>Liabilities for future losses or other costs expected to be incurred as a | For an entity acquired and held as a subsidiary, the assets acquired, and liabilities assumed are incorporated in their existing carrying amounts for consolidation purposes.<br>On amalgamation they may be incorporated at their existing carrying amounts or alternatively the consideration is allocated to individual identifiable assets and liabilities at their fair values.<br>On business acquisition they may be incorporated at their fair values or values of surrendered assets.<br>No separate restructuring provision is recognised on acquisition. |

| S/L No | Ind AS 103<br>Business Combinations | AS 14<br>Accounting for Amalgamations (as amended) |
|---|---|---|
| | result of the business combination cannot be recognised. | |
| 3. | **Non-controlling interest**<br>Stated at minority's share of the fair value of acquired identified assets liabilities and contingent liabilities | Stated at minority's share of pre-acquisition carrying value of net assets |
| 4. | **Purchase method – goodwill and intangible assets with indefinite useful lives**<br>Capitalized but not amortized.<br>Goodwill and indefinite intangible assets are reviewed for impairment at least annually at either the Cash Generating Unit (CGU) levels or groups of CGUs as applicable. | Goodwill on consolidation and business acquisitions; no specific guidance – practice varies, between no amortization versus amortization over a period not exceeding 10 years.<br>Goodwill on amalgamation is amortized over a period not exceeding 5 years unless a longer period is justified.<br>Goodwill is reviewed for impairment whenever an indication of impairment exists at CGU level.<br>Intangible assets are not classified into indefinite useful lives category. All intangible assets are amortized over a period not exceeding 10 years. |
| 5. | **Purchase method – capital reserve**<br>The identification and measurement of acquiree's identifiable assets, liabilities and contingent liabilities are reassessed.<br>Any excess remaining after reassessment is recognised in capital reserve in the form of Bargain Purchase. | Negative goodwill is recorded in equity as capital reserve, which is not amortized to income.<br>However, in case of amalgamation, the fair value of intangible assets with no active market is reduced to the extent of capital reserve, if any, arising on the amalgamation. |
| 6. | **Pooling of interest method Prohibited.**<br>However, as per Appendix C of Ind AS 103, Business combinations involving entities or businesses | **Pooling of interest method**<br>Required for certain types of amalgamation when all the conditions are met. |

| S/L No | Ind AS 103 Business Combinations | AS 14 Accounting for Amalgamations (as amended) |
|---|---|---|
| | under common control shall be accounted for using the pooling of interests method. According to this Appendix, pooling of interest method would involve:<br>(i) The assets and liabilities of the combining entities are reflected at their carrying amounts.<br>(ii) No adjustments are made to reflect fair values, or recognise any new assets or liabilities. The only adjustments that are made are to harmonize accounting policies.<br>(iii) The financial information in the financial statements in respect of prior periods should be restated as if the business combination had occurred from the beginning of the preceding period in the financial statements, irrespective of the actual date of the combination. However, if business combination had occurred after that date, the prior period information shall be restated only from that date. | |

## 12.4 COMPARATIVE SUMMARY OF CORPORATE RESTRUCTURING

| AS | IFRS | US GAAP | Ind AS |
|---|---|---|---|
| Business combinations<br>No particular standard has been issued by ICAI till date.<br>However all business acquisitions are business combinations except pooling of interest | All business combinations are combinations as per IFRS 3 Business combinations | Same as IFRS | All business combinations are combinations as per Ind AS 103 Business combinations |

| AS | IFRS | US GAAP | Ind AS |
|---|---|---|---|
| method for certain amalgamations | | | |
| Purchase method – values on acquisition<br>For an entity acquired and held as a subsidiary, the assets acquired and liabilities assumed are incorporated in their existing carrying amounts for consolidation purposes.<br>On amalgamation they may be incorporated at their existing carrying amounts or alternatively the consideration is allocated to individual identifiable assets and liabilities at their fair values.<br>On business acquisition they may be incorporated at their fair values or values of surrendered assets.<br>No separate restructuring provision is recognised on acquisition. | Assets, liabilities and contingent liabilities of acquired entity are fair valued.<br>If control is obtained in a partial acquisition of a subsidiary the full value of the assets, liabilities and contingent liabilities including portion attributable to the minority (non-controlling) interest is recorded in consolidated business.<br>Goodwill is recognised as the residual between the consideration paid and the percentage of the business acquired.<br>Liabilities for restructuring activities are recognised only when acquiree has an existing liability at acquisition date.<br>Liabilities for future losses or other costs expected to be incurred as a result of the business combination cannot be | Similar to IFRS except that minority interest is stated at pre-acquisition carrying value of net assets and contingent liabilities of the acquiree are not recognised at the date of acquisition.<br>Specific rules exist for acquired in process research and development (generally expensed) and contingent liabilities.<br>Some restructuring liabilities relating solely to the acquired entity may be recognised if specific criteria about restructuring plans are met. | Assets, liabilities and contingent liabilities of acquired entity are fair valued.<br>If control is obtained in a partial acquisition of a subsidiary the full value of the assets, liabilities and contingent liabilities including portion attributable to the minority (non-controlling) interest is recorded in consolidated business.<br>Goodwill is recognised as the residual between the consideration paid and the percentage of the business acquired.<br>Liabilities for restructuring activities are recognised only when acquiree has an existing liability at acquisition date.<br>Liabilities for future losses or other costs expected to be incurred as a result of the business combination cannot be recognised. |

| AS | IFRS | US GAAP | Ind AS |
|---|---|---|---|
| | recognised. | | |
| Non-controlling (minority)interest<br>Stated at minority's share of pre-acquisition carrying value of net assets | Stated at minority's share of the fair value of acquired identified assets liabilities and contingent liabilities | Similar to Indian Accounting Standards | Stated at minority's share of the fair value of acquired identified assets liabilities and contingent liabilities |
| Purchase method – goodwill and intangible assets with indefinite useful lives<br>Goodwill on consolidation and business acquisitions; no specific guidance – practice varies, between no amortisation versus amortisation over a period not exceeding 10 years.<br>Goodwill on amalgamation is amortised over a period not exceeding 5 years unless a longer period is justified.<br>Goodwill is reviewed for impairment whenever an indication of impairment exists at CGU level.<br>Intangible assets are not classified into indefinite useful lives category. All intangible assets are amortised over a period not exceeding 10 years. | Capitalised but not amortised.<br>Goodwill and indefinite intangible assets are reviewed for impairment at least annually at either the Cash Generating Unit (CGU) levels or groups of CGUs as applicable. | Similar to IFRS although the level of impairment testing and the impairment test itself are different | Capitalised but not amortised.<br>Goodwill and indefinite intangible assets are reviewed for impairment at least annually at either the Cash Generating Unit (CGU) levels or groups of CGUs as applicable. |

| AS | IFRS | US GAAP | Ind AS |
|---|---|---|---|
| Purchase method – capital reserve<br>Negative goodwill is recorded in equity as capital reserve, which is not amortised to income.<br>However, in case of amalgamation, the fair value of intangible assets with no active market is reduced to the extent of capital reserve, if any, arising on the amalgamation. | The identification and measurement of acquiree's identifiable assets, liabilities and contingent liabilities are reassessed.<br>Any excess remaining after reassessment is recognised in income statement immediately in the form of Bargain Purchase | Any remaining excess after reassessment is used to reduce proportionately the fair values assigned to non-current assets (with certain exceptions)<br>Any excess is recognised in the income statement immediately as an extraordinary gain. | The identification and measurement of acquiree's identifiable assets, liabilities and contingent liabilities are reassessed.<br>Any excess remaining after reassessment is recognised in capital reserve in the form of Bargain Purchase. |
| Pooling of interest method<br>Required for certain types of amalgamation when all the conditions are met. | Prohibited | Prohibited | - |

# *Chapter 13*

# Consolidated Financial Statements

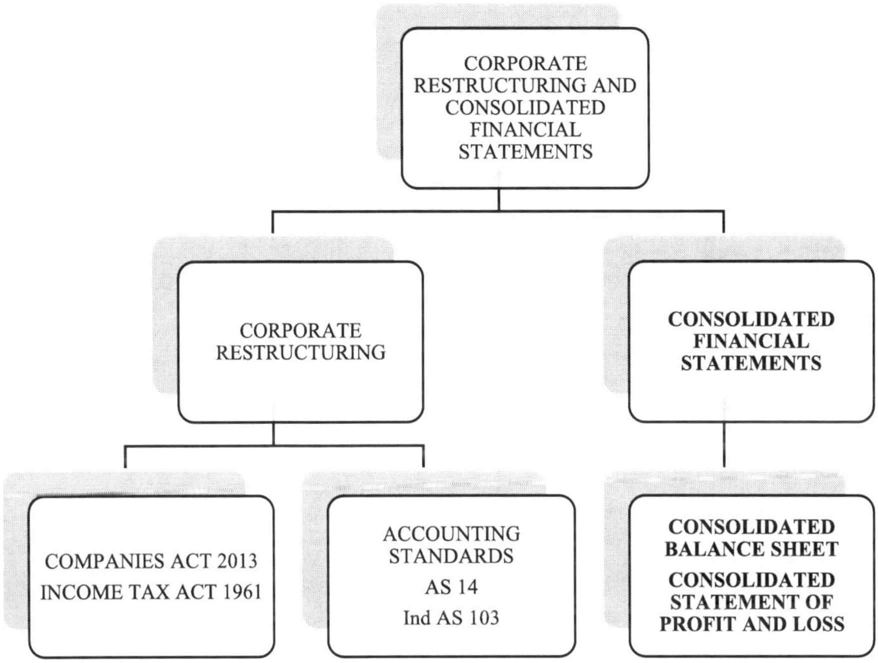


## 13.1 INTRODUCTION

Where a company is required to prepare Consolidated Financial Statements i.e. consolidated balance sheet and consolidated statement of profit and loss, the company shall *mutatis mutandis* follow the requirements as applicable to a company in the preparation of balance sheet and statement of profit & loss. In addition, the consolidated financial statements shall disclose the information as per the requirements specified in the applicable Accounting Standards including the following:

(i) Profit & Loss attributable to "minority or non-controlling interest" and to owners of the parent in the statement of profit & loss shall be presented as allocation for the period.

(ii) "Minority or non-controlling interests" in the balance sheet within equity shall be presented separately from the equity of the owners of the parent.

## 13.2 COMPARATIVE SUMMARY RELATED TO CONSOLIDATED FINANCIAL STATEMENTS

| Under AS[1] | Under Ind AS[2] |
|---|---|
| According to Schedule III, where a company is required to prepare Consolidated Financial Statements i.e. consolidated balance sheet and consolidated statement of profit and loss, the company shall mutatis mutandis follow the requirements of this Schedule as applicable to a company in the preparation of balance sheet and statement of profit & loss. In addition, the consolidated financial statements shall disclose the information as per the requirements specified in the applicable Accounting Standards including the following:<br>(iii) Profit & Loss attributable to "minority interest" and to owners of the parent in the statement of profit & loss shall be presented as allocation for the period.<br>(iv) "Minority interests" in the balance sheet within equity shall be presented separately from the equity of the owners of the parent. | 1. Where a company is required to prepare Consolidated Financial Statements, i.e., consolidated balance sheet, consolidated statement of changes in equity and consolidated statement of profit and loss, the company shall mutatis mutandis follow the requirements of this Schedule as applicable to a company in the preparation of balance sheet, statement of changes in equity and statement of profit and loss. In addition, the consolidated financial statements shall disclose the information as per the requirements specified in the applicable Indian Accounting Standards notified under the Companies (Indian Accounting Standards) Rules 2015, including the following, namely:-<br>(i) Profit or loss attributable to 'non-controlling interest' and to 'owners of the parent' in the statement of profit and loss shall be presented as allocation for the period. Further, 'total comprehensive income' for the period attributable to 'non-controlling interest' and to 'owners of the parent' shall be presented in the statement of profit and loss as allocation for the period. The aforesaid disclosures for 'total comprehensive income' shall also be made in the statement of changes in equity. In addition to the disclosure requirements in the Indian Accounting Standards, the aforesaid |

1 General Instructions for Preparation of Balance Sheet, Part I, Division I of Schedule III of the Companies Act, 2013.

2 General Instructions for Preparation of Balance Sheet, Part I of Division II of Schedule III of the Companies Act, 2013.

| Under AS[1] | Under Ind AS[2] |
|---|---|
| | disclosures shall also be made in respect of 'other comprehensive income'.<br>(ii) 'Non-controlling interests' in the Balance Sheet and in the Statement of Changes in Equity, within equity, shall be presented separately from the equity of the 'owners of the parent'.<br>(iii) Investments accounted for using the equity method. |
| 6.3. All subsidiaries, associates and joint ventures (whether Indian or foreign) will be covered under consolidated financial statements.<br>6.4. All entity shall disclose the list of subsidiaries or associates or joint ventures which have not been consolidated in the consolidated financial statements along with the reasons of not consolidating.<br>6.5. It needs to be clarified that, the requirement of attaching the Balance Sheet, Profit & Loss account, report of Board of Directors, Auditors Report, statement of the Holding Company's interest in the subsidiary and other reports as was required under section 212 of the Companies Act 1956 has been dispensed with.<br>In the consolidated financial statements, the following shall be disclosed by way of additional information:<br>Net Assets, i.e. total assets minus total liabilities<br>As % of consolidated net assets<br>Amount<br>Share in profit or loss<br>As % of consolidated profit or loss<br>Amount | 3. All subsidiaries, associates and joint ventures (whether Indian or foreign) will be covered under consolidated financial statements.<br>4. An entity shall disclose the list of subsidiaries or associates or joint ventures which have not been consolidated in the consolidated financial statements along with the reasons of not consolidating.<br>Specimen format should provide the following information:<br>Net Assets, i.e. total assets minus total liabilities<br>As % of consolidated net assets<br>Amount<br>Share in profit or loss<br>As % of consolidated profit or loss<br>Amount<br>Share in other comprehensive income<br>As % of consolidated other comprehensive income |

| Under AS[1] | Under Ind AS[2] |
|---|---|
| | Amount<br>Share in total comprehensive income<br>As % of total comprehensive income Amount |
| Specimen format should provide the following information as well:<br>Name of the entity in the group<br>Parent<br>Subsidiaries<br>Indian<br>1.<br>2.<br>3.<br>Foreign<br>1.<br>2.<br>3. | Specimen format should provide the following information as well:<br>Name of the entity in the group<br>Parent<br>Subsidiaries<br>Indian<br>1.<br>2.<br>3.<br>Foreign<br>1.<br>2.<br>3. |
| Minority Interests in all subsidiaries | Non-controlling Interests in all subsidiaries |
| Associates (Investment as per the equity method)<br>Indian<br>1.<br>2.<br>3.<br>Foreign<br>1.<br>2.<br>3. | Associates (Investment as per the equity method)<br>Indian<br>1.<br>2.<br>3.<br>Foreign<br>1.<br>2.<br>3. |
| Joint Ventures (as per proportionate consolidation / investment as per the equity method)<br>Indian<br>1.<br>2.<br>3. | Joint Ventures (as per the equity method)<br>Indian<br>1.<br>2.<br>3.<br>Foreign<br>1. |

| Under AS[1] | Under Ind AS[2] |
|---|---|
| Foreign<br>1.<br>2.<br>3. | 2.<br>3. |
| TOTAL | TOTAL |

## 13.3 DISCLOSURE REQUIREMENTS UNDER SCHEDULE III RELATED TO CONSOLIDATED FINANCIAL STATEMENTS

MCA notification dated 24 March 2021 has included certain disclosure requirements in addition to the existing disclosures. The applicability of additional disclosures at Consolidated financial statement (CFS) level with regard to its applicability is summarized below:

| Disclosures as per Schedule III | Non Ind AS – Consolidated Financial Statements | Ind AS – Consolidated Financial Statements |
|---|---|---|
| ***Disclosure of Shareholding of Promoters*** | Company should disclose the promoter shareholding at the CFS level. Generally, the promoter would be same for CFS level and standalone level. | Company should disclose the promoter shareholding at the CFS level. Generally, the promoter would be same for CFS level and standalone level. |
| ***Disclosure related to Trade Payables ageing schedule*** | Trade payable ageing schedule should be disclosed at the CFS level after applying the principles of consolidation. | Trade payable ageing schedule should be disclosed at the CFS level after applying the principles of consolidation. |
| ***Disclosure related to Trade Receivables ageing schedule*** | Trade receivable ageing schedule should be disclosed at the CFS level after applying the principles of consolidation. | Trade receivable ageing schedule should be disclosed at the CFS level after applying the principles of consolidation. |
| ***Presentation related to Revaluation of Property, Plant and Equipment*** | In case of revaluation of property, plant and equipment at CFS level, or for any of the group entity, company may disclose the following:<br>(a) Name of the entity in which revaluation is done; | In case of revaluation of property, plant and equipment at CFS level, or for any of the group entity, company may disclose the following:<br>(a) Name of the entity in which revaluation is done; |

| Disclosures as per Schedule III | Non Ind AS – Consolidated Financial Statements | Ind AS – Consolidated Financial Statements |
|---|---|---|
| | (b) Type & nature of PPE revalued;<br>(c) Indicate whether the revaluation is based on the valuation as per the registered valuer. | (b) Type & nature of PPE revalued;<br>(c) Indicate whether the revaluation is based on the valuation as per the registered valuer. |
| ***Additional disclosures related to Loans or Advances*** | This disclosure needs to be done at the CFS level, on similar lines as the 'Related Party Transactions' are disclosed in CFS. | This disclosure needs to be done at the CFS level, on similar lines as the 'Related Party Transactions' are disclosed in CFS. |
| ***Disclosure pertaining to details of Benami Property held*** | Entity needs to disclose the required details of benami property at CFS level providing the name of each subsidiary / group entity that has such Benami Property. In case if there is any benami proceedings initiated against any associate company, then Company should disclose in case if the proceeding is material to the group. | Entity needs to disclose the required details of benami property at CFS level providing the name of each subsidiary / group entity that has such Benami Property. In case if there is any benami proceedings initiated against any associate company, then Company should disclose in case if the proceeding is material to the group. |
| ***Disclosures pertaining to Wilful Defaulter*** | Entity needs to disclose the required details of wilful defaulter at CFS level providing the name of each subsidiary / group entity that is declared as a wilful defaulter. In case if there is any wilful default by an associate company, then Company should disclose if the default is material to the group. | Entity needs to disclose the required details of wilful defaulter at CFS level providing the name of each subsidiary / group entity that is declared as a wilful defaulter. In case if there is any wilful default by an associate company, then Company should disclose if the default is material to the group. |
| ***Presentation and disclosure pertaining relationship with struck off companies*** | Entity needs to present the required details of relationship with struck off companies at CFS level providing the name of each subsidiary / group entity that has such a relationship. | Entity needs to present the required details of relationship with struck off companies at CFS level providing the name of each subsidiary / group entity that has such a relationship. |

| Disclosures as per Schedule III | Non Ind AS – Consolidated Financial Statements | Ind AS – Consolidated Financial Statements |
|---|---|---|
| | In case if any of the subsidiary is the under the struck off company list, the entity should indicate that fact as a part of disclosure.<br>In case if there is any associate company having relationship with struck off companies, then company should disclose if the transaction is material to the group. | In case if any of the subsidiary is the under the struck off company list, the entity should indicate that fact as a part of disclosure.<br>In case if there is any associate company having relationship with struck off companies, then company should disclose if the transaction is material to the group. |
| ***Disclosure pertaining to Compliance with number of layers of companies*** | Entity needs to disclose this compliance issue for each entity in its group. | Entity needs to disclose this compliance issue for each entity in its group. |
| ***Disclosures pertaining to undisclosed income*** | Entity needs to disclose the required details of undisclosed income at CFS level providing the name of each subsidiary / group entity that has an 'undisclosed income'. In case if there is any associate company having undisclosed income, then Company should disclose if such income is material to the group. | Entity needs to disclose the required details of undisclosed income at CFS level providing the name of each subsidiary / group entity that has an 'undisclosed income'. In case if there is any associate company having undisclosed income, then Company should disclose if such income is material to the group. |

(*Source: ICAI Guidance Note on Schedule III – non Ind AS and Ind AS entities*)

## 13.4 DISCLOSURE REQUIREMENTS UNDER SCHEDULE III RELATED TO CONSOLIDATED FINANCIAL STATEMENTS IF MATERIAL IN NATURE

| Disclosures as per Schedule III | Non Ind AS – Consolidated Financial Statements | Ind AS – Consolidated Financial Statements |
|---|---|---|
| ***Disclosure pertaining to Capital work-in-progress (CWIP) ageing schedule / completion schedule*** | CWIP ageing schedule shall be given at CFS level if it is material to the group i.e. more than 10% of the respective balance sheet item in CFS. | CWIP ageing schedule shall be given at CFS level if it is material to the group i.e. more than 10% of the respective balance sheet item in CFS. |
| ***Disclosure related to Intangible assets under*** | Ageing schedule shall be given at CFS level if it is | Ageing schedule shall be given at CFS level if it is |

| Disclosures as per Schedule III | Non Ind AS – Consolidated Financial Statements | Ind AS – Consolidated Financial Statements |
|---|---|---|
| ***development ageing schedule / completion schedule*** | material to the group i.e. more than 10% of the respective balance sheet item in CFS. | material to the group i.e. more than 10% of the respective balance sheet item in CFS. |
| ***Disclosure pertaining to Security of current assets against borrowings*** | This disclosure shall be provided at CFS level if it is material to the group i.e. more than 10% of the respective balance sheet item in CFS | This disclosure shall be provided at CFS level if it is material to the group i.e. more than 10% of the respective balance sheet item in CFS |
| ***Disclosure pertaining to Compliance with approved Scheme(s) of Arrangements*** | This disclosure shall be provided at CFS level if it is material to the group i.e. more than 10% of the respective financial statement line item in CFS. | This disclosure shall be provided at CFS level if it is material to the group i.e. more than 10% of the respective financial statement line item in CFS. |
| ***Disclosure pertaining to Utilization of Borrowed funds and share premium*** | This disclosure shall be provided at CFS level after applying principles of consolidation i.e. this disclosure would be for funds borrowed / invested outside the group. However, it shall be disclosed only if material i.e. more than 10% of the respective financial statement line item in CFS | This disclosure shall be provided at CFS level after applying principles of consolidation i.e. this disclosure would be for funds borrowed / invested outside the group. However, it shall be disclosed only if material i.e. more than 10% of the respective financial statement line item in CFS |
| ***Disclosure pertaining to 'details of crypto currency or virtual currency'*** | This disclosure shall be provided at CFS level if it is material to the group i.e. more than 10% of the respective financial statement line item in CFS | This disclosure shall be provided at CFS level if it is material to the group i.e. more than 10% of the respective financial statement line item in CFS |
| ***Disclosure related to Title deeds of Immovable Property not held in the name of the Company*** | Not relevant at CFS level | Not relevant at CFS level |
| ***Presentation related to Registration of charges or satisfaction with Registrar of Companies*** | Not relevant at CFS level | Not relevant at CFS level |
| ***Presentation of Analytical Ratios*** | Not relevant at CFS level | Not relevant at CFS level |

(*Source: ICAI Guidance Note on Schedule III – non Ind AS and Ind AS entities*)

## 13.5 REQUIREMENTS OF SCHEDULE III SHALL APPLY TO A CFS, SUBJECT TO THE FOLLOWING EXEMPTIONS / MODIFICATIONS BASED ON THE RELEVANCE TO THE CFS

| Disclosures as per Schedule III | Non Ind AS – Consolidated Financial Statements | Ind AS – Consolidated Financial Statements |
|---|---|---|
| ***Whether Share capital – authorized, issued, subscribed and paid up need to be disclosed*** | It is adequate to present paid up capital and any calls in arrears | It is adequate to present paid up capital and any calls in arrears |
| ***Whether Goodwill or Capital reserve arising on consolidation need to be disclosed*** | Needs to be shown as a separate line item on the face of the Balance Sheet<br>As per AS, differing treatment is given to goodwill arising on amalgamation and goodwill arising on consolidation and even SEBI format requires this to be separately disclosed. | IFRS / Ind AS does not require this to be stated separately. |
| ***Whether Share Application money received for allotment of securities and due for refund and interest accrued thereon needs to be disclosed separately. Share application money would include advances towards allotment of share capital*** | Separate disclosure should be given for such monies due outside the group in respect of entities which are consolidated | Separate disclosure should be given for such monies due outside the group in respect of entities which are consolidated. |
| ***Whether excise duty needs to be disclosed separately*** | To be disclosed where such information is available for the entities consolidated.<br>Note: Though AS 9 states excise to be shown separately, where subsidiaries are not disclosing it, it would not be practical and also no benefit is derived by disclosure of this. | To be disclosed where such information is available for the entities consolidated. |
| ***Whether the period and amount of continuing default as on the Balance Sheet date in repayment of loans and interest, needs to be specified separately in each case.*** | Disclosure can be limited to those which are material to the CFS; materiality could be considered at 10% of the respective balance sheet item | Disclosure can be limited to those which are material to the CFS; materiality could be considered at 10% of the respective balance sheet item |
| ***Whether loans and advances due by directors or other*** | Disclosure can be limited to | Disclosure can be limited to |

| Disclosures as per Schedule III | Non Ind AS – Consolidated Financial Statements | Ind AS – Consolidated Financial Statements |
|---|---|---|
| ***officers of the company or any of them either severally or jointly with any other persons or amounts due by firms or private companies respectively in which any director is a partner or a director or a member needs to be separately stated*** | those which are material to the CFS; materiality could be considered at 10% of the respective balance sheet item | those which are material to the CFS; materiality could be considered at 10% of the respective balance sheet item |
| ***Whether Debts due by directors or other officers of the company or any of them either severally or jointly with any other person or debts due by firms or private companies respectively in which any director is a partner or a director or a member need to be separately stated*** | Disclosure can be limited to those which are material to the CFS; materiality could be considered at 10% of the respective balance sheet item | Disclosure can be limited to those which are material to the CFS; materiality could be considered at 10% of the respective balance sheet item |
| ***Where in respect of an issue of securities made for a specific purpose, the whole or part of the amount has not been used for the specific purpose at the Balance Sheet date, whether a note needs to be provided indicating how such unutilized amounts have been used or invested.*** | Disclosure can be limited to those which are material to the CFS; materiality could be considered at 10% of the respective balance sheet item | Disclosure can be limited to those which are material to the CFS; materiality could be considered at 10% of the respective balance sheet item |
| ***Payments to the auditor as***<br>***(a) auditor,***<br>***(b) for taxation matters,***<br>***(c) for company law matters,***<br>***(d) for management services,***<br>***(e) for other services,***<br>***(f) for reimbursement of expense*** | Not relevant at CFS level and hence, may not be required to be disclosed | Not relevant at CFS level and hence, may not be required to be disclosed |
| ***In case of Companies covered under section 135, amount of expenditure incurred on corporate social responsibility activities*** | | Not relevant at CFS level and hence, may not be required to be disclosed |

| **Disclosures as per Schedule III** | **Non Ind AS – Consolidated Financial Statements** | **Ind AS – Consolidated Financial Statements** |
|---|---|---|
| ***Raw materials under broad heads***<br>***Goods purchased under broad heads***<br>***In the case of trading companies, purchases in respect of goods traded in by the company under broad heads***<br>***In the case of companies rendering or supplying services, gross income derived form services rendered or supplied under broad heads***<br>***In the case of a company, which falls under more than one of the categories mentioned above it shall be sufficient compliance with the requirements herein if purchases, sales and consumption of raw material and the gross income from services rendered is shown under broad heads***<br>***In the case of other companies, gross income derived under broad heads***<br>***In the case of all concerns having works in progress, works-in-progress under broad heads*** | Not relevant at CFS level and hence may not be required to be disclosed | Not applicable under Ind AS |
| ***Value of imports calculated on C.I.F basis by the company during the financial year in respect of***<br>***(i) Raw materials***<br>***(ii) Components and spare parts***<br>***(iii) Capital goods*** | Not relevant at CFS level and hence may not be required to be disclosed | Not applicable under Ind AS |
| ***Expenditure in foreign currency during the financial*** | Not relevant at CFS level and hence may not be required to | Not applicable under Ind AS |

| Disclosures as per Schedule III | Non Ind AS – Consolidated Financial Statements | Ind AS – Consolidated Financial Statements |
|---|---|---|
| ***year on account of royalty, know-how, professional and consultation fees, interest, and other matters*** | be disclosed | |
| ***Total value if all imported raw materials, spare parts and components consumed during the financial year and the total value of all indigenous raw materials, spare parts and components similarly consumed and the percentage of each to the total consumption*** | Not relevant at CFS level and hence may not be required to be disclosed | Not applicable under Ind AS |
| ***The amount remitted during the year in foreign currencies on account of dividends with a specific mention of*** <br> ***(a) the total number of non-resident shareholders,*** <br> ***(b) the total number of shares held by them on which the dividends were due and the year to which the dividends related*** | Not relevant at CFS level and hence may not be required to be disclosed | Not applicable under Ind AS |
| ***Earnings in foreign exchange classified under the following heads, namely:*** <br> ***(i) Export of goods calculated on F.O.B. basis*** <br> ***(ii) Royalty, know-how, professional and consultation fees*** <br> ***(iii) Interest and dividend*** <br> ***(iv) Other income, indicating the nature thereof*** | Not relevant at CFS level and hence may not be required to be disclosed | Not applicable under Ind AS |

(*Source: ICAI Guidance Note on Schedule III – non Ind AS and Ind AS entities*)

## 13.6 CONSOLIDATED FINANCIAL STATEMENTS UNDER DIVISION I OF SCHEDULE III (AS)

In Consolidated Financial Statements, the following details is presented by way of additional information:

| **Name of the entity in the** | **Net assets i.e total assets minus total liabilities** | | **Share in profit and loss** | |
|---|---|---|---|---|
| | **As % of consolidate d net assets** | **Amount** | **As % of consolidated profit and loss** | **Amount** |
| 1 | 2 | 3 | 4 | 5 |
| Parent Subsidiaries | | | | |
| Indian<br>1<br>2<br>3 | | | | |
| Foreign<br>1<br>2<br>3 | | | | |
| Minority Interests in all subsidiaries | | | | |
| Associates (Investment as per the equity method) | | | | |
| Indian<br>1<br>2<br>3 | | | | |
| Foreign<br>1<br>2<br>3 | | | | |
| Joint Ventures (as per proportionate consolidation/ | | | | |

| Name of the entity in the | Net assets i.e total assets minus total liabilities | | Share in profit and loss | |
|---|---|---|---|---|
| | As % of consolidated net assets | Amount | As % of consolidated profit and loss | Amount |
| 1 | 2 | 3 | 4 | 5 |
| investment as per the equity method) | | | | |
| Indian<br>1<br>2<br>3 | | | | |
| Foreign<br>1<br>2<br>3 | | | | |
| Total | | | | |

All subsidiaries, associates, and joint ventures (whether Indian or foreign) will be covered under consolidated financial statements.

An entity shall disclose the list of subsidiaries or associates or joint ventures which have not been consolidated in the consolidated financial statements along with the reasons of not consolidating.

### 13.6.1 AS 21: Consolidated Financial Statements

AS 21 is mandatory if an enterprise presents consolidated financial statements. In other words, the accounting standard does not mandate an enterprise to present consolidated financial statements but, if the enterprise presents consolidated financial statements for complying with the requirements of any statute or otherwise, it should prepare and present consolidated financial statements in accordance with AS 21.

This Standard should be applied in the preparation and presentation of consolidated financial statements for a group of enterprises under the control of a parent.

This Standard should also be applied in accounting for investments in subsidiaries in the separate financial statements of a parent.

In the preparation of consolidated financial statements, other Accounting Standards also apply in the same manner as they apply to the separate statements.

This Standard does not deal with:

(a) methods of accounting for amalgamations and their effects on consolidation, including goodwill arising on amalgamation (see AS 14, Accounting for Amalgamations);

(b) accounting for investments in associates (at present governed by AS 13, Accounting for Investments); and

(c) accounting for investments in joint ventures (at present governed by AS 13, Accounting for Investments).

**Definitions**

For the purpose of this Standard, the following terms are used with the meanings specified:

**Control:**

(a) the ownership, directly or indirectly through subsidiary(ies), of more than one-half of the voting power of an enterprise; or

(b) control of the composition of the board of directors in the case of a company or of the composition of the corresponding governing body in case of any other enterprise so as to obtain economic benefits from its activities.

| | |
|---|---|
| ***Control is presumed*** | when the parent acquires more than half of the voting rights of the entity either directly or indirectly through subsidiaries.<br>Even otherwise control may be evidenced by:<br>control of the composition of board of directors in case of a company or<br>– control of composition of governing body in case of any other enterprise |

A subsidiary is an enterprise that is controlled by another enterprise (known as the parent).

A parent is an enterprise that has one or more subsidiaries.

A group is a parent and all its subsidiaries.

Consolidated financial statements are the financial statements of a group presented as those of a single enterprise.

Equity is the residual interest in the assets of an enterprise after deducting all its liabilities.

Minority interest is that part of the net results of operations and of the net assets of a subsidiary attributable to interests which are not owned, directly or indirectly through subsidiary (ies), by the parent.

| | |
|---|---|
| ***Consolidated financial*** | (a) consolidated balance sheet,<br>(b) consolidated statement of profit and loss, and |

| ***statements normally include*** | (c) notes to accounts,<br>(d) other statements and explanatory material that form an integral part thereof. |
|---|---|

Consolidated cash flow statement is presented in case a parent presents its own cash flow statement. The consolidated financial statements are presented, to the extent possible, in the same format as that adopted by the parent for its separate financial statements.

### Presentation of consolidated financial statements

A parent who presents consolidated financial statements should present these statements in addition to its separate financial statements.

Users of the financial statements of a parent are usually concerned with, and need to be informed about, the financial position and results of operations of not only the enterprise itself but also of the group as a whole. This need is served by providing the users –

(a) separate financial statements of the parent; and

(b) consolidated financial statements, which present financial information about the group as that of a single enterprise without regard to the legal boundaries of the separate legal entities.

### Scope of consolidated financial statements

A parent which presents consolidated financial statements should consolidate all subsidiaries, domestic as well as foreign, other than those referred to in paragraph 11 of the Standard.

Where an enterprise does not have a subsidiary but has an associate and/or a joint venture such an enterprise should also prepare consolidated financial statements in accordance with Accounting Standard (AS) 23, Accounting for Associates in Consolidated Financial Statements, and Accounting Standard (AS) 27, Financial Reporting of Interests in Joint Ventures respectively.

According to Para.10 of the Standard, the consolidated financial statements are prepared on the basis of financial statements of parent and all enterprises that are controlled by the parent, other than those subsidiaries excluded for the reasons set out in paragraph 11. Control exists when the parent owns, directly or indirectly through subsidiary (ies), more than one-half of the voting power of an enterprise. Control also exists when an enterprise controls the composition of the board of directors (in the case of a company) or of the corresponding governing body (in case of an enterprise not being a company) so as to obtain economic benefits from its activities. An enterprise may control the composition of the governing bodies of entities such as gratuity trust, provident fund trust etc. Since the objective of control over such entities is not to obtain economic benefits from their activities, these are not considered for the purpose of preparation of consolidated financial statements.

For the purpose of this Standard, an enterprise is considered to control the composition of:

(i) the board of directors of a company, if it has the power, without the consent or concurrence of any other person, to appoint or remove all or a majority of directors of that company. An enterprise is deemed to have the power to appoint a director, if any of the following conditions is satisfied:

  (a) a person cannot be appointed as director without the exercise in his favour by that enterprise of such a power as aforesaid; or

  (b) a person's appointment as director follows necessarily from his appointment to a position held by him in that enterprise; or

  (c) the director is nominated by that enterprise or a subsidiary thereof.

(ii) the governing body of an enterprise that is not a company, if it has the power, without the consent or the concurrence of any other person, to appoint or remove all or a majority of members of the governing body of that other enterprise. An enterprise is deemed to have the power to appoint a member, if any of the following conditions is satisfied:

  (a) a person cannot be appointed as member of the governing body without the exercise in his favour by that other enterprise of such a power as aforesaid; or

  (b) a person's appointment as member of the governing body follows necessarily from his appointment to a position held by him in that other enterprise; or

  (c) the member of the governing body is nominated by that other enterprise.

**Consolidation when excluded**

According to Para 11 of the Standard, a subsidiary should be excluded from consolidation when:

(a) control is intended to be temporary because the subsidiary is acquired and held exclusively with a view to its subsequent disposal in the near future; or

(b) it operates under severe long-term restrictions which significantly impair its ability to transfer funds to the parent.

In consolidated financial statements, investments in such subsidiaries should be accounted for in accordance with Accounting Standard (AS) 13, Accounting for Investments. The reasons for not consolidating a subsidiary should be disclosed in the consolidated financial statements.

Para 12. Exclusion of a subsidiary from consolidation on the ground that its business activities are dissimilar from those of the other enterprises within the group is not justified because better information is provided by consolidating such subsidiaries and disclosing additional information in the consolidated financial statements about the different business activities of subsidiaries. For example, the disclosures required by Accounting Standard (AS) 17, Segment Reporting, help to explain the significance of different business activities within the group.

## Consolidation process

In accordance with Para 13, in preparing consolidated financial statements, the financial statements of the parent and its subsidiaries should be combined on a line-by-line basis by adding together like items of assets, liabilities, income and expenses. In order that the consolidated financial statements present financial information about the group as that of a single enterprise, the following steps should be taken:

(a) the cost to the parent of its investment in each subsidiary and the parent's portion of equity of each subsidiary, at the date on which investment in each subsidiary is made, should be eliminated;

(b) any excess of the cost to the parent of its investment in a subsidiary over the parent's portion of equity of the subsidiary, at the date on which investment in the subsidiary is made, should be described as goodwill to be recognised as an asset in the consolidated financial statements;

(c) when the cost to the parent of its investment in a subsidiary is less than the parent's portion of equity of the subsidiary, at the date on which investment in the subsidiary is made, the difference should be treated as a capital reserve in the consolidated financial statements;

(d) minority interests in the net income of consolidated subsidiaries for the reporting period should be identified and adjusted against the income of the group in order to arrive at the net income attributable to the owners of the parent; and

(e) minority interests in the net assets of consolidated subsidiaries should be identified and presented in the consolidated balance sheet separately from liabilities and the equity of the parent's shareholders. Minority interests in the net assets consist of:

    (i) the amount of equity attributable to minorities at the date on which investment in a subsidiary is made; and

    (ii) the minorities' share of movements in equity since the date the parent-subsidiary relationship came in existence.

Where the carrying amount of the investment in the subsidiary is different from its cost, the carrying amount is considered for the purpose of above computations.

## Intragroup balances and intragroup transactions

Intragroup balances and intragroup transactions and resulting unrealised profits should be eliminated in full. Unrealised losses resulting from intragroup transactions should also be eliminated unless cost cannot be recovered.

### Reporting date

The financial statements used in the consolidation should be drawn up to the same reporting date. If it is not practicable to draw up the financial statements of one or more subsidiaries to such date and, accordingly, those financial statements are drawn up to different reporting dates, adjustments should be made for the effects of significant transactions or other events that occur between those dates and the date of the parent's financial statements. In any case, the difference between reporting dates should not be more than six months.

### Uniform Accounting policies

Consolidated financial statements should be prepared using uniform accounting policies for like transactions and other events in similar circumstances. If it is not practicable to use uniform accounting policies in preparing the consolidated financial statements, that fact should be disclosed together with the proportions of the items in the consolidated financial statements to which the different accounting policies have been applied.

If a member of the group uses accounting policies other than those adopted in the consolidated financial statements for like transactions and events in similar circumstances, appropriate adjustments are made to its financial statements when they are used in preparing the consolidated financial statements.

### Disposal of investment in subsidiary

The results of operations of a subsidiary are included in the consolidated financial statements as from the date on which parent-subsidiary relationship came in existence. The results of operations of a subsidiary with which parent-subsidiary relationship ceases to exist are included in the consolidated statement of profit and loss until the date of cessation of the relationship. The difference between the proceeds from the disposal of investment in a subsidiary and the carrying amount of its assets less liabilities as of the date of disposal is recognised in the consolidated statement of profit and loss as the profit or loss on the disposal of the investment in the subsidiary.

### Treatment of investment on disposal

An investment in an enterprise should be accounted for in accordance with Accounting Standard (AS) 13, Accounting for Investments, from the date that the enterprise ceases to be a subsidiary and does not become an associate.

### Minority Interest

Minority interests should be presented in the consolidated balance sheet separately from liabilities and the equity of the parent's shareholders. Minority interests in the income of the group should also be separately presented.

### Accounting for investments for subsidiaries in a parent's separate financial statements

In a parent's separate financial statements, investments in subsidiaries should be accounted for in accordance with Accounting Standard (AS) 13, Accounting for Investments.

## 13.6.2 AS 23: Accounting for Associates

### Significant influence

Significant influence does not extend to power to govern the financial and/or operating policies of an enterprise.

Significant influence may be gained by share ownership, statute or agreement.

As regards share ownership, if an investor holds, directly or indirectly through subsidiary (ies), 20% or more of the voting power of the investee, it is presumed that the investor has significant influence.

Conversely, if the investor holds, directly or indirectly through subsidiary (ies), less than 20% of the voting power of the investee, it is presumed that the investor does not have significant influence, unless such influence can be clearly demonstrated.

Significant influence is usually evidenced by:

(a) Representation on the board of directors or corresponding governing body of the investee;

(b) participation in policy making processes;

(c) material transactions between the investor and the investee;

(d) interchange of managerial personnel; or

(e) provision of essential technical information.

Investing Company would have significant influence when the following points are satisfied:

### Equity method

It is a method of accounting whereby

(a) the investment is initially recorded at cost,

(b) any surplus or deficit in cost and net asset to be recorded as goodwill or capital reserve arising at the time of acquisition.

(c) The carrying amount is adjusted for the post-acquisition change in the investor's share of

- net assets of the associate share of profit or loss included in income statement and
- the share of other changes included in equity.

Procedure for the equity method is summarized below.

| | |
|---|---|
| – | Eliminating intra group profits and losses arising from transactions between investor and investee |
| – | identifying the goodwill portion of the purchase price |
| – | amortisation of goodwill |
| – | adjustments for depreciation of depreciable assets, based on their fair values |
| – | adjustments for the effect of cross holdings |
| – | using uniform accounting policies |

### Circumstances under which equity method is followed

An investment in an associate should be accounted for in consolidated financial statements under the equity method except when:

| | |
|---|---|
| (a) | *the investment is acquired and held exclusively with a view to its subsequent disposal in the near future; or* |
| *(b)* | *the associate operates under severe long-term restrictions that significantly impair its ability to transfer funds to the investor.* |

Investments in such associates should be accounted for in accordance with Accounting Standard (AS) 13, Accounting for Investments. The reasons for not applying the equity method in accounting for investments in an associate should be disclosed in the consolidated financial statements.

An investor should discontinue the use of the equity method from the date that:

| | |
|---|---|
| *(a)* | *it ceases to have significant influence in an associate but retains, either in whole or in part, its investment; or* |
| *(b)* | *the use of the equity method is no longer appropriate because the associate operates under severe long-term restrictions that significantly impair its ability to transfer funds to the investor.* |

*From the date of discontinuing the use of the equity method, investments in such associates should be accounted for in accordance with Accounting Standard (AS) 13, Accounting for Investments. For this purpose, the carrying amount of the investment at that date should be regarded as cost thereafter.*

## 13.6.3 AS 27: Financial reporting of interest in Joint ventures

### Characteristics of a Joint Venture

- Where two or more parties undertake an economic activity that is subject to joint control under a contractual arrangement is termed as joint venture.
- The existence of a contract which would contain-
    - the activity, duration and reporting obligations of the joint venture

- the appointment of the board of directors
- the voting rights of the venturers
- capital contribution by the venturers
- the sharing of the venturers of the output, income, expenses, or results of the joint venture

- The parties undertake an economic activity, and the economic activity is subject to joint control.

**Types of Joint Venture**

| |
|---|
| – *jointly controlled operations* |
| – *jointly controlled assets* |
| – *jointly controlled* entities |

Joint control exists only when the strategic, financial and operating decisions related to economic activity require the undisputed consent of the parties sharing control.

A venturer recognises its interest in a jointly controlled operation by recognizing in its financial statements the assets that it controls, the liabilities and expenses it incurs and its share of income from the sale of goods and services of the joint venture.

A venturer recognises its interest in jointly controlled assets on a proportional basis.

The venturer also recognises any liabilities or expenses it incurs, its share of liabilities or expenses incurred jointly, and any income from the sale or use of its share of the output of the joint venture.

General Accounting considerations are summarized in the table below.

| | |
|---|---|
| ***General accounting considerations*** | Transactions between a venturer and joint venture are treated as follows:<br>– the venturer's share of unrealised profits on sales or contribution of assets to a joint venture is eliminated - full unrealised loss on sale or contribution of assets to a joint venture is eliminated<br>– the venturer's share of profits or losses on sales of assets by a joint venture to the venturer is eliminated<br>– An investor in a joint venture that does not have joint control should report its interest in a joint venture in the consolidated financial statements under AS 13 or it has significant influence in terms of AS 23.<br>– Operators or managers of a joint venture should account for any fees as revenue in terms of AS 9. |

**Jointly controlled operations (JCO)**

- each venturer has his own separate business
- there is no separate entity for joint venture business
- all venturers are creating their own assets and maintain them
- each venturer record only his own transactions without any separate set of books maintained for the joint venture business
- there is a common agreement between all of them
- venturers use their assets for the joint venture business
- venturers meet the liabilities created by them for the joint venture business
- venturers meet the expenses of the joint venture business from their funds
- any revenue generated or income earned from the joint venture is shared by the venturers as per the contract

**Jointly controlled assets (JCA)**

- There is no separate legal entity
- There is a common control over the joint assets
- Venturers use these assets to derive some economic benefit to themselves
- Each venturer incurs separate expenses for their transactions
- Expenses on jointly held assets are shared by the venturers as per the contract
- In their financial statement, venturer shows only their share of the asset and total income earned by them along with total expenses incurred by them
- As the assets, liabilities, income and expenses are
- already recognised in the separate financial statements of the venturer and consequently in its consolidated financial statements, no adjustments or other consolidation procedures are required in respect of these items when the venturer presents consolidated financial statements
- Financial statements may not be prepared for the joint venture although the venturers may prepare the accounts for internal use so that they may evaluate the performance of the joint venture.

**Jointly Controlled Entity (JCE)**

- A jointly controlled entity is a joint venture which involves the establishment of a corporation, partnership or other entity in which each venturer has an interest. The entity operates in the same way as other enterprises, except that a contractual arrangement between the venturers establishes joint control over the economic activity of the entity.

- A jointly controlled entity controls the assets of the joint venture, incurs liabilities and expenses and earns income. It may enter into contracts in its own name and raise finance for the purposes of the joint venture activity. Each venturer is entitled a share of the results of the jointly controlled entity, although some jointly controlled entities also involve a sharing of the output of the joint venture.
- An example of a jointly controlled entity is when two enterprises combine their activities in a particular line of business by transferring the relevant assets and liabilities into a jointly controlled entity. Another example is when an enterprise commences a business in a foreign country in conjunction with the government or other agency in that country, by establishing a separate entity which is jointly controlled by the enterprise.

## 13.7 CONSOLIDATED FINANCIAL STATEMENTS UNDER DIVISION II OF SCHEDULE III (IND AS)

Where a company is required to prepare Consolidated Financial Statements, i.e,, consolidated balance sheet, consolidated statement of changes in equity and consolidated statement of profit and loss, the company shall mutatis mutandis follow the requirements of this Schedule as applicable to a company in the preparation of balance sheet, statement of changes in equity and statement of profit and loss .ln addition, the consolidated financial statements shall disclose the information as per the requirements specified in the applicable Indian Accounting Standards notified under the Companies (Indian Accounting Standards) Rules 2015, including the following, namely:

(i) Profit or loss attributable to 'non-controlling interest and to owners of the parent' in the statement of profit and loss shall be presented as allocation for the period Further, 'total comprehensive income for the period attributable to non-controlling interest' and to 'owners of the parent' shall be presented in the statement of profit and loss as allocation for the period. The aforesaid disclosures for 'total comprehensive income' shall also be made in the statement of changes in equity In addition to the disclosure requirements in the Indian Accounting Standards, the aforesaid disclosures shall also be made in respect of 'other comprehensive Income

(ii) 'Non-controlling interests' in the Balance Sheet and in the Statement of Changes in Equity, within equity, shall be presented separately from the equity of the owners of the parent'.

(iii) Investments accounted for using the equity method.

In Consolidated Financial Statement, the following shall be disclosed by the way of additional information.

| Name of the entity in the Group | Net Assets, i.e., total assets minus total liabilities | | Share in profit or loss | | Share in other comprehensive income | | Share in total comprehensive income | |
|---|---|---|---|---|---|---|---|---|
| | As % of consolidated net assets | Amount | As % of consolidated profit or loss | Amount | As % of consolidated other comprehensive income | Amount | As % of total comprehensive income | Amount |
| Parent<br>Subsidiaries<br>Indian<br>1.<br>2.<br>3.<br>.<br>.<br>Foreign<br>1.<br>2<br>3.<br>.<br>.<br>Non-controlling Interests in all subsidiaries<br><br>Associates (Investment as per the equity method)<br>Indian<br>1.<br>2.<br>3.<br>.<br>. | | | | | | | | |
| Foreign<br>1.<br>2.<br>3.<br>.<br>.<br>. | | | | | | | | |

| Name of the entity in the Group | Net Assets, i.e., total assets minus total liabilities | | Share in profit or loss | | Share in other comprehensive income | | Share in total comprehensive income | |
|---|---|---|---|---|---|---|---|---|
| | As % of consolidated net assets | Amount | As % of consolidated profit or loss | Amount | As % of consolidated other comprehensive income | Amount | As % of total comprehensive income | Amount |
| Joint Ventures (investment as per the equity method)<br>Indian<br>1.<br>2.<br>3.<br>.<br>.<br>Foreign<br>1.<br>2.<br>3.<br>.<br>. | | | | | | | | |
| **Total** | | | | | | | | |

All subsidiaries, associates and joint venture (whether Indian or Foreign) will be covered under consolidated financial statement.

An entity shall disclose the list of subsidiaries or associates or joint venture which have been consolidated in the consolidated financial statement along with the reason of not consolidating.

## 13.7.1 Ind AS 27: Separate Financial Statements

The objective of this Ind AS is to prescribe the accounting and disclosure requirements for investments in subsidiaries, joint ventures, and associates when an entity prepares separate financial statements.

This Ind AS shall be applied in accounting for investments in subsidiaries, joint ventures and associates when an entity elects, or is required by law, to present separate financial statements.

This Ind AS does not mandate which entities produce separate financial statements. It applies when an entity prepares separate financial statements that comply with Indian Accounting Standards.

**Definitions**

The following terms are used in this Standard with the meanings specified:

*Consolidated financial statements* are the financial statements of a group in which the assets, liabilities, equity, income, expenses and cash flows of the parent and its subsidiaries are presented as those of a single economic entity.

*Separate financial statements* are those presented by a parent (i.e an investor with control of a subsidiary) or an investor with joint control of, or significant influence over, an investee, in which the investments are accounted for at cost or in accordance with Ind AS 109, *Financial Instruments*.

The following terms are defined in Appendix A of Ind AS 110, *Consolidated Financial Statements*, Appendix A of Ind AS 111, *Joint Arrangements,* and paragraph 3 of Ind AS 28, *Investments in Associates and Joint Ventures*:

- Associate
- control of an investee
- group
- Investment Entity
- joint control
- joint venture
- joint venturer
- parent
- significant influence
- subsidiary.

Separate financial statements are those presented in addition to consolidated financial statements or in addition to financial statements in which investments in associates or joint ventures are accounted for using the equity method. Separate financial statements need not be appended to, or accompany, those statements.

Financial statements in which the equity method is applied are not separate financial statements. These may be termed as 'consolidated financial statements'. Similarly, the financial statements of an entity that does not have a subsidiary, associate or joint venturer's interest in a joint venture are not separate financial statements.

An entity that is exempted in accordance with paragraph 4(a) of Ind AS 110 from consolidation or paragraph 17 of Ind AS 28 from applying the equity method may present separate financial statements as its only financial statements.

An investment entity that is required, throughout the current period and all comparative periods presented, to apply the exception to consolidation for all of its subsidiaries in accordance with paragraph 31 of Ind AS 110 presents separate financial statements as its only financial statements.

**Preparation of Separate Financial Statements**

Separate financial statements shall be prepared in accordance with all applicable Ind AS. When an entity prepares separate financial statements, it shall account for investments in subsidiaries, joint ventures and associates either:

(a) at cost, or

(b) in accordance with Ind AS 109.

The entity shall apply the same accounting for each category of investments. Investments accounted for at cost shall be accounted for in accordance with Ind AS 105, *Non-current Assets Held for Sale and Discontinued Operations,* when they are classified as held for sale (or included in a disposal group that is classified as held for sale). The measurement of investments accounted for in accordance with Ind AS 109 is not changed in such circumstances.

If an entity elects, in accordance with paragraph 18 of Ind AS 28, to measure its investments in associates or joint ventures at fair value through profit or loss in accordance with Ind AS 109, it shall also account for those investments in the same way in its separate financial statements.

If a parent is required, in accordance with paragraph 31 of Ind AS 110, to measure its investment in a subsidiary at fair value through profit or loss in accordance with Ind AS 109, it shall also account for its investment in a subsidiary in the same way in its separate financial statements.

When a parent ceases to be an investment entity, or becomes an investment entity, it shall account for the change from the date when the change in status occurred, as follows:

(a) when an entity ceases to be an investment entity, the entity shall, in accordance with paragraph 10, either:

 (i) account for an investment in a subsidiary at cost. The fair value of the subsidiary at the date of the change of status shall be used as the deemed cost at that date; or

 (ii) continue to account for an investment in a subsidiary in accordance with Ind AS 109.

(b) when an entity becomes an investment entity, it shall account for an investment in a subsidiary at fair value through profit or loss in accordance with Ind AS 109. The difference between the previous carrying amount of the subsidiary and its fair value at the date of the change of status of the investor shall be recognised as a gain or loss in profit or loss. The cumulative amount of any fair value adjustment previously recognised in other comprehensive income in respect of those subsidiaries shall be treated as if the investment entity had disposed of those subsidiaries at the date of change in status.

An entity shall recognise a dividend from a subsidiary, a joint venture or an associate in profit or loss in its separate financial statements when its right to receive the dividend is established.

When a parent reorganises the structure of its group by establishing a new entity as its parent in a manner that satisfies the following criteria:

(a) the new parent obtains control of the original parent by issuing equity instruments in exchange for existing equity instruments of the original parent;

(b) the assets and liabilities of the new group and the original group are the same immediately before and after the reorganisation; and

(c) the owners of the original parent before the reorganisation have the same absolute and relative interests in the net assets of the original group and the new group immediately before and after the reorganisation, and the new parent accounts for its investment in the original parent in accordance with paragraph 10(a) in its separate financial statements, the new parent shall measure cost at the carrying amount of its share of the equity items shown in the separate financial statements of the original parent at the date of the reorganisation.

Similarly, an entity that is not a parent might establish a new entity as its parent in a manner that satisfies the criteria in paragraph 13. The requirements in paragraph 13 apply equally to such reorganisations. In such cases, references to 'original parent' and 'original group' are to the 'original entity'. (Para 14)

## 13.7.2 Ind AS 110: Consolidated Financial Statements

The objective of this Indian Accounting Standard (Ind AS) is to establish principles for the presentation and preparation of consolidated financial statements when an entity controls one or more other entities. To meet the above objective, this Ind AS:

(a) requires an entity (the *parent*) that controls one or more other entities (*subsidiaries*) to present consolidated financial statements;

(b) defines the principle of *control*, and establishes control as the basis for consolidation;

(c) sets out how to apply the principle of control to identify whether an investor controls an investee and therefore must consolidate the investee;

(d) sets out the accounting requirements for the preparation of consolidated financial statements; and

(e) defines an investment entity and sets out an exception to consolidating particular subsidiaries of an investment entity.

This Ind AS does not deal with the accounting requirements for business combinations and their effect on consolidation, including goodwill arising on a business combination (see Ind AS 103, *Business Combinations*).

An entity that is a parent shall present consolidated financial statements. This Ind AS applies to all entities, except as follows:

(a) A parent need not present consolidated financial statements if it meets all the following conditions:

 (i) it is a wholly-owned subsidiary or is a partially-owned subsidiary of another entity and all its other owners, including those not otherwise entitled to vote, have been informed about, and do not object to, the parent not presenting consolidated financial statements;

 (ii) its debt or equity instruments are not traded in a public market (a domestic or foreign stock exchange or an over-the-counter market, including local and regional markets);

 (iii) it did not file, nor is it in the process of filing, its financial statements with a securities commission or other regulatory organisation for the purpose of issuing any class of instruments in a public market; and

 (iv) its ultimate or any intermediate parent produces consolidated financial Statements that are available for public use and comply with Ind ASs.

(b) post-employment benefit plans or other long-term employee benefit plans to which Ind AS19, *Employee Benefits,* applies.

(c) an investment entity need not present consolidated financial statements if it is required, in accordance with paragraph 31 of this Ind AS, to measure all of its subsidiaries at fair value through profit or loss.

**Concept of group**

In today's global economy, most companies operate as a group, in which one main company controls the operations of many other entities. In such situations, it becomes imperative for the shareholders, directors, employees, suppliers, customers, government departments and other stakeholders to know the financial standing of the group as a whole. This is the genesis of consolidated financial statements for a group.

*Ind AS 110 specifies that consolidated financial statements have to be prepared where a group of entities are controlled by a parent.*

*Consolidated financial statements are prepared by combining the financial statements of all the group entities, with a view to determine the financial status of the group as if it were one single entity.*

However, it should be understood that,

(a) Merely preparing consolidated financial statements do not establish a single operating unit,

(b) A group does not have any legal existence, except for accounting purposes.

Hence,

| Group is a parent with all its subsidiaries<br>Parent is an entity that controls one or more entities<br>Subsidiary is an entity that is controlled by another entity (Ind AS 110, Appendix A) |
|---|

The concept of Group is explained based on the chart below.

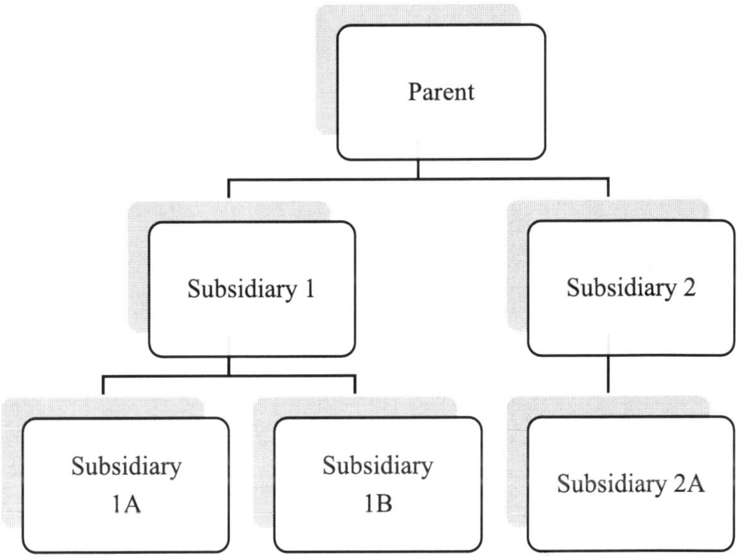


Now the concept of control is explained below.

## Concept of Control

In accordance with Para 7 of Ind AS 110, an investor controls an investee if an only if the investor has ALL of the following characteristics:

(a) Power over the investee

(b) Exposure, or rights, to variable returns from its involvement with the investee and

(c) Ability to use its power over the investee to affect the amount of the investor's returns.

Hence control is:

| = | **Control subsidiaries**<br>Parent is an entity that controls one or more entities<br>Subsidiary is an entity that is controlled by another entity<br>(IFRS 10, Appendix A) | + | **A. Power** | + | **B. Exposure to variability in returns** | + | **C. Link between power and return** |
|---|---|---|---|---|---|---|---|

## A. What is power?

According to Ind AS 110, power of the investor over investee comprises all of the following criteria:

(a) Right to direct the relevant activities of the investee

(b) The way decisions about relevant activities are made

(c) The rights that the investor and other parties have in relation to the investee

(d) Factors to be considered in consolidating a deemed separate entity (SILO)

Constituents of power are enumerated below.

| Constituents of power | Narrative |
|---|---|
| **1. *What are existing rights?*** | To have power over an investee, an investor must have<br>(a) Existing rights that<br>(b) Give the investor current ability to<br>(c) Direct the relevant activities. |
| ***Examples of existing rights*** | (a) rights in the form of voting rights or potential voting rights of an investee<br>(b) rights to appoint, reassign or remove members of an investee's key management personnel who have the right to direct the relevant activities<br>(c) rights to appoint or remove another entity that directs the relevant activities<br>(d) rights to direct the investee to enter into, or veto any changes to, transactions for the benefit of the investor and<br>(e) other rights (such as decision making rights specified in a management contract) that give the holder the ability to direct the relevant activities<br>In order to assess power, only *substantive rights* should be considered. |
| **2. *What are substantive*** | Substantive rights are determined as under:<br>(a) Whether there are any barriers (economic or otherwise) that |

| Constituents of power | Narrative |
|---|---|
| ***rights?*** | prevent holders from exercising rights<br>(b) when the exercise of rights requires the agreement of more than one party, or when the rights are held by more than one party, whether a mechanism is in place that provides those parties with the practical ability to exercise their rights collectively if they choose to do so<br>(c) whether the party or parties that hold the rights would benefit from the exercise of those rights<br>However *Protective rights* do not contribute to power under IFRS 10. |
| **3. *What are protective rights?*** | Protective rights are designed to protect the interest of their holder, but do not give that party power over the investee. Protective rights give the holder protection in exceptional circumstances or prevent fundamental changes from being made to the activities of the investee.<br>*Examples of protective rights include*:<br>(a) a lender's right to restrict the borrower from undertaking activities that could significantly change the credit risk of the borrower to the detriment of the lender<br>(b) the right of a party holding a non-controlling interest in an investee to approve capital expenditure greater than that required in the ordinary course of business, or to approve the issue of debt or equity instruments<br>(c) the right of a lender to seize assets of a borrower if the borrower fail to meet specified loan repayment conditions |
| **4. *What are relevant activities?*** | Relevant activities are activities of the investee that significantly affect the investor's returns. While assessing control over an investee, an investor shall consider the purpose and design of the investee in order to identify the relevant activities.<br>*Examples of relevant activities are:*<br>(a) selling and purchasing of goods and services<br>(b) managing financial assets during their life (including upon default)<br>(c) selecting, acquiring or disposing of assets,<br>(d) researching and developing new products or processes and<br>(e) determining a funding structure or obtaining funding |
| **5.*What are Voting rights?*** | (a) Power with a majority of the voting rights – Control arises when an Investor owns over 50% of the voting rights of an investee. However, voting rights need to be substantive and not protective. |

| **Constituents of power** | **Narrative** |
|---|---|
| | Non-controlling interest – is the equity in a subsidiary not attributable, directly or indirectly to a parent.<br>(b) Majority of the voting rights but no power – Voting rights may be designed in a manner such that they are not the dominant factor in deciding control over an investee. This is possible if the investor cannot direct the relevant activities of the investee or the rights may not be substantive. In such cases the investor does not control the investee<br>(c) Power without a majority of the voting rights – This could be due to<br>– contractual arrangement between the investor and other vote holders<br>– rights arising from other contractual arrangements<br>– the investor's voting rights, referred to as de-facto control (e.g. when the investor holds significantly greater voting rights than any other vote holder or organised group of vote holders<br>– potential voting rights only when they are substantive and not protective,<br>– a combination of above. |
| **6. *What is meant by Control over specified assets?*** | An investor shall consider whether it treats a portion of an investee as a deemed separate entity and, if so, whether it controls the deemed separate entity.<br>The deemed separate entity or the "silo" is a new concept compared to IAS 27, which dealt with only the legal entities. This opens up possibility that only a part of the entity represented by this "silo" may be considered. The conditions are:<br>(a) specified assets of the investee (and related credit enhancements, if any) are the only source of payment for specified liabilities of or specified other interests in, the investee<br>(b) parties other than those with the specified liability do not have rights or obligations related to the specified assets or to residual cash flows from those assets,<br>(c) In substance, none of the returns from the specified assets can be used by the remaining investee and none of the liabilities of the deemed separate entity are payable from the assets of the remaining investee<br>Thus, all the assets, liabilities and equity of that deemed separate entity is "ring fenced" from the overall investee. Such a deemed separate entity is often called "silo". |

| Constituents of power | Narrative |
|---|---|
| **7. *What is meant by design of an investee?*** | While assessing control of an investee, an investor need to consider the purpose and design of the investee in order to identify:<br>The relevant activities<br>How decisions about the relevant activities are made<br>Who has the current ability to direct those activities and<br>Who receives returns from those activities. |
| **B. *What is Exposure to Variability in returns?*** | To control an investee, an investor must be exposed, or have rights to variable returns from its involvement with the investee. This occurs when the investor's returns from its involvement have the potential to vary as a result of the investee's performance.<br>Although only one investor can control an investee, more than one party can share the returns of an investee, e.g. holders of non-controlling interest can share the profits or distributions of an investee, but cannot control the investee. |
| **C. *What is Link between power and returns?*** | The investor does not control the investee in the following circumstances:<br>(a) an investor has power over an investee, but cannot benefit from that power<br>(b) an investor receives return from an investee but cannot use its power to direct the activities that significantly affect the returns of that investee.<br>Therefore, it becomes necessary that the investor should have the ability to use its power over the investee to affect its returns. Hence,<br>(a) when an investor with decision making rights (a decision maker) assesses whether it controls an investee, it shall determine whether it is a principal or an agent.<br>(b) an investor shall also determine whether another entity with decision making rights is acting as an agent for the investor<br>(c) an agent is a party primarily engaged to act on behalf of and for the benefit of another party or parties (i.e. the principals) and therefore does not control the investee when it exercises its decision-making authority. |

**Consolidated Financial Statements**

According to Ind AS 110, consolidated financial statements have to be prepared where a group of entities are controlled by a parent (barring a few exceptional cases highlighted by the standard). So consolidated financial statements are the financial statements of a group presented as those of a single economic entity.

### Objectives of preparing Consolidated Financial Statements

The objectives of preparing consolidated financial statements are:

| | |
|---|---|
| (a) | Determine financial status of group as one single entity |
| (b) | Safeguard interests of ordinary shareholders of parent company |
| (c) | Show full earnings on parent's investments |
| (d) | Show where group as a whole stands |
| (e) | Assist in prevention of malpractices and manipulations in financial statements |

### Circumstances when subsidiaries should be excluded from Consolidated Financial Statements

Ind AS 110 specifies that consolidated financial statements shall include the accounts of ALL the subsidiaries of the parent – both domestic and foreign. The standard has been very strict about exclusions from consolidated financial statements because otherwise companies will indulge in manipulation of their results.

| | |
|---|---|
| ***There are no specific exemptions for the following subsidiaries:*** | 1. Subsidiaries whose business activities are dissimilar from those of the other entities within the group<br>2. Subsidiaries of venture capital organisation, mutual funds, unit trust or any other similar entity<br>3. Subsidiaries held for sale, i.e. investments by a parent in an entity only for the purpose of selling it. In case of such subsidiaries measurement and accounting is done as per Ind AS 105. |
| ***Exemption from preparing consolidated financial statements if all the four conditions are fulfilled:*** | 1. The parent itself is a wholly or partially owned subsidiary of another entity and its owners have been informed and do not object to the parent not presenting consolidated financial statements<br>2. The ultimate or any intermediate parent of the parent produces consolidated financial statements available for public use that comply with Ind ASs<br>3. The parent's debt or equity instruments are not traded in a public market (e.g. a domestic or foreign stock exchange or an over-the-counter market, including local and regional markets<br>4. The parent has not filed, nor in the process of filing, its financial instruments with a securities commission or other regulatory organisation for the purpose of issuing any class of instruments in a public market. |

## Co-terminus year end and uniform accounting policies

| | |
|---|---|
| ***Co-terminus year-ends*** | Means that the financial year ends of two or more entities are identical. It signifies that the financial year used for recording financial statements by two or more entities is the same.<br>If the parent and all its subsidiaries do not have the same year-end, the consolidated financial statements will not reflect a correct picture of the financial status of the group.<br>Hence Ind AS 110 specifies that the financial statements of the parent and its subsidiaries used in the preparation of the consolidated financial statements shall be prepared as of the same date.<br>However, if it is not practicable, then<br>(a) adjustments should be made for the effects of significant transactions or events that occur between the reporting dates of the subsidiary and parent<br>(b) a gap of not more than three months between the reporting date of the parent and subsidiary is allowed. This means if the gap is more than 3 months apart, the subsidiary would need to prepare full financial statements at the parent company's year-end date, to be used for consolidation purposes. |
| ***Uniform accounting policies*** | According to Ind AS 8, Accounting policies are the specific principles, bases, conventions, rules and practices applied by an entity in preparing and presenting financial statements (e.g. valuation of inventories – FIFO or weighted average cost, valuation of Properties, Plant & Equipment – historical cost or revaluation method, valuation of investments – fair value, amortised cost method etc)<br>Ind AS 110 prescribes that consolidated financial statements shall be prepared using uniform accounting policies for similar transactions and events having occurred in similar circumstances.<br>If uniform accounting policies are not followed for all the group entities, the consolidated financial statements will not reflect a correct portrayal of the financial status of the group. |

### Process followed in consolidation of parent with subsidiaries

The consolidation process is summarised as under:

| | |
|---|---|
| **Step I** | Add all items like assets, liabilities, income and expenditure of the parent and the subsidiary line by line. |
| **Step II** | Cancel parent's investment in subsidiary (in parent's books), with parent's portion in subsidiary's ordinary shares (in subsidiary books)<br>Dr. Ordinary share capital (in subsidiary books)<br>Cr. Investment (in parent books |
| **Step III** | Eliminate all intra-group balances, transactions, income and expenses in full from both parent as well as subsidiary books.<br>Some examples are:<br>– Intra group revenue<br>– Intra group inventories<br>– Unrealised profit on intra group inventories (including treatment of deferred tax)<br>– Intra group purchase / sale of tangible assets<br>– Unrealised profit on intra group tangible assets (including treatment of deferred tax)<br>– Intra group loan<br>– Intra group dividends<br>- Make required adjustments for part cancellations |
| **Step IV** | Split profit / loss of subsidiary between pre and post-acquisition portions based on acquisition date |
| **Step V** | Calculate fair value of assets of subsidiary if any on acquisition date |
| **Step VI** | Determine deferred tax on increase in fair value of assets |
| **Step VII** | Calculate value of non-controlling interest (NCI) as on acquisition date |
| **Step VIII** | Calculate goodwill / bargain purchase on the date of acquisition |
| **Step IX** | Calculate parents share in subsidiary's profit = Profit of subsidiary – share of non-controlling interest |
| **Step X** | Calculate parent's reserve |
| **Step XI** | Calculate NCI on SOFP date and show it in consolidated SOFP under Equity |

**Purchase consideration**

Constituents of Purchase consideration is explained in the table below.

| | |
|---|---|
| ***Consideration*** | Consideration is the amount an investor pays to acquire holding in investee company. The consideration transferred in a business combination is to be measured at fair value. The possible variants of considerations may be as under:<br>(a) Cash<br>(b) Share exchange<br>(c) Contingent consideration<br>(d) Deferred consideration |
| ***Cash*** | When consideration is paid in cash it is accounted as under:<br>Dr. Investment x<br>Cr. Cash x |
| ***Share exchange*** | In this case consideration may be in the form of share exchange. |
| ***Contingent consideration*** | This is a consideration that an acquirer commits to the acquiree in cash or additional equity interests or other assets after the acquisition date on the fulfilment of a certain specified event or condition in the future.<br>We need to bear in mind that subsequent measurement of contingent consideration does not affect goodwill. On the date of acquisition, contingent consideration is valued at acquisition date fair value.<br>Subsequent changes in fair value of contingent consideration (post acquisition date) are accounted for as under:<br>(a) If the contingent consideration is classified as equity, then it is not remeasured and is accounted for in equity itself<br>(b) if the contingent consideration is classified as a financial instrument in accordance with Ind AS 109 Financial Instruments: Recognition and Measurement, it is measured at fair value and change in the value is recognised either in profit or loss or equity in accordance with the requirements of Ind AS 109<br>(c) if the contingent consideration is not classified as a financial instrument in accordance with Ind AS 109 and is recognised in line with Ind AS 37 Provisions, contingent liabilities and contingent assets or any other applicable standard, then the change in the value is recognised in the profit or loss.<br>(d) Goodwill is not impacted by the actual outcome of the contingent consideration |
| ***Deferred consideration*** | Deferred consideration is the one which is not payable immediately but is payable in the future and which is not contingent is called a deferred consideration. |

| | |
|---|---|
| | Such consideration is valued at present value of the amount payable. For this, amount payable in future should be multiplied by the present value factor (conventional practice is to use cost of capital of the parent to calculate the present value factor) |

## Non-controlling interest (NCI)

When a subsidiary is not wholly owned (i.e. owned 100% by the parent), a part of the net assets belong to the minority shareholders. This is called the non-controlling interest (NCI) earlier known as Minority Interest.

Ind AS 103 allows an accounting policy choice, available on a transaction-by-transaction basis, to measure NCI either at:

(a) Fair value (sometimes called the full goodwill method) or

(b) The NCI's proportionate share of net assets of the acquiree (option is available on a transaction-by-transaction basis)

**Further,**

(a) Management must elect, for each acquisition, the option to measure the NCI

(b) If NCI is measured at fair value, it can be determined by referring to the market price of shares held by non-controlling shareholders just before the acquisition by the parent.

According to new requirements of Ind AS 103, for each business combination, the acquirer shall measure at the acquisition date components of any non-controlling interests in the acquiree that are present ownership interests and entitle their holders to a proportionate share of the entity's net assets in the event of liquidation at their:

(a) Fair value or

(b) The present ownership instruments' proportionate share in the recognised amounts of the acquiree's identifiable net assets

All other components of non-controlling interests shall be measured at their acquisition date fair values, unless another measurement basis is required by Ind AS.

Thus, the choice to measure NCI using any of the two methods will not be available and these components of non-controlling interests shall be measured at their acquisition date fair values. However, if any other Ind AS requires another basis of measurement it will be measured in accordance with that Ind AS. For example, if a share-based transaction is classified as equity, an entity will be expected to measure it in accordance with Ind AS 2.

Hence non-controlling share is calculated on

(a) Acquisition date for calculation of goodwill and

(b) Reporting date and shown in the consolidated statement of financial position within equity but separately from the parent entity's share in the equity.

## Measurement and recognition of goodwill in Consolidated Financial Statements

Here we revisit the concept of recognition of goodwill in consolidated financial statements. According to Ind AS 103 Appendix A, Goodwill is an asset representing the future economic benefits arising from other assets acquired in a business combination that are not individually identified and separately recognised.

In accordance with Ind AS 103, the acquirer shall recognise goodwill as of the acquisition date measured as the excess of:

| | |
|---|---|
| (a) Aggregate of<br>(i) the consideration transferred measured in accordance with this Ind AS, which generally requires acquisition date fair value<br>(ii) the amount of non-controlling interest in the acquiree measured in accordance with this Ind AS and<br>(iii) in case of business combination achieved in stages, the acquisition date fair value of the acquirer's previously held equity interest in the acquiree | X<br>X<br>X |
| TOTAL (A) | X |
| (b) The net of acquisition date amounts of the identifiable assets acquired and the liabilities assumed measured in terms of this IFRS | X |
| TOTAL (B) | X |
| Goodwill (A- B) | X |
| Bargain purchase (B – A) | X * |

Note: There are two ways of calculating goodwill viz:

(a) Full goodwill method, based on fair value of NCI

(b) Partial goodwill method based on share of NCI in the value of net assets of the company acquired. In this case goodwill shows only the acquirer's share (as the share of non-controlling interest appears in both the sides i.e. value of NCI as well as net assets of subsidiary and therefore does not affect goodwill).

The US standard on business combinations requires goodwill to be calculated on "full" basis.

The underlying principle in IFRS 3 and in Ind AS 103 is that all components of the business acquired are to be recognised at their fair value. This effectively means that the consideration paid, the assets and liabilities of the acquiree as well as the equity attributable to NCI are measured at fair value. This basis was proposed in the exposure draft which preceded the revised standard. However, in view of strong disagreement on the proposed revision regarding recognising NCI at fair value, the IASB introduced a choice as to how NCI is to be measured. Hence this allows goodwill to be measured

| in the same way as depicted in the old standard.<br>Logically, allowing a choice as to the valuation of NCI is driven by the future intentions to acquire the NCI. If such intention is perceived, determining goodwill at "full basis" is likely to be the adopted choice. Standards are supposed to usher in consistency in approach, which unfortunately has been obviated in the IFRS 3. |
|---|
| *In case of bargain purchase the resulting gain has to be recognised by the acquirer in capital reserve on the acquisition date and the gain has to be attributed to the acquirer. |

**Treatment for acquisition related costs**

These are costs the acquirer incurs to effect a business combination. Those costs include finder's fees, advisory, legal, accounting, valuation and other professional or consulting fees, general administrative costs, including the costs of maintaining an internal acquisitions department, and costs of registering and issuing debt and equity securities.

According to Ind AS 103, the acquirer is required to recognise acquisition related costs as expenses in the periods in which the costs are incurred and the services are received.

**Accounting treatment of pre-acquisition and post-acquisition profit**

| | |
|---|---|
| ***Pre-acquisition profit*** | Pre-acquisition profits are made by the subsidiary prior to the date of acquisition by the parent.<br>Formula:<br>Pre-acquisition profit = All the brought forward reserves of the subsidiary + profit for the year in which the subsidiary is acquired, up to acquisition date<br>Pre-acquisition profits are to be deducted from the consideration in the subsidiary when calculating goodwill. |
| ***Post-acquisition profit*** | Post-acquisition profits include profit reflected in the retained earnings in the subsidiary's accounts after the acquisition date.<br>Post-acquisition profits are added to parent entity's retained earnings in the consolidated SOFP<br>Post-acquisition profits of subsidiary =<br>Reserves at the year-end *minus*<br>Pre-acquisition profits. |

**Consolidated Income Statement**

(a) If income consists of post-acquisition profits only (i.e. the subsidiary has been acquired for over one year) and no non-controlling interest exists - add all the items in individual income statement line by line for consolidation up-to the line "profit after tax for the year"

(b) If income consists of post-acquisition profits only (i.e. the subsidiary has been acquired for over one year) and non-controlling interest exists –

| | |
|---|---|
| (i) | add all the items in individual income statement line by line for consolidation up-to the line "profit after tax for the year" |
| (ii) | then show NCI share in subsidiary profit after tax separately as NCI interest in the income statement |
| (iii) | parent share is shown below NCI share and is calculated as (i) less (ii) above |

(c) If the subsidiary is acquired during the year:

| | |
|---|---|
| (i) | The profits for the year of the subsidiary are split to ascertain pre and post-acquisition profits by splitting the income statement |
| (ii) | Pre-acquisition profits- total net assets including pre-acquisition profits are deducted from the total of the consideration, the value of NCI and acquisition date fair value of the previously held equity interests for calculating goodwill. |
| (iii) | Post-acquisition profits – Parent's share added to parent's income for the year and reflected in consolidated statement of comprehensive income |
| (iv) | Post-acquisition profits – NCI share added to non-controlling interest and included in consolidated Balance Sheet |

**Consolidated statement of changes in equity**

Steps are as under:

| | |
|---|---|
| (a) | In parent's equity its share in the subsidiaries' post acquisition equity should be added. |
| (b) | NCI's share in equity needs to be shown separately |
| (c) | Parent's share in the dividend paid by subsidiary should be cancelled out in preparing Consolidated SOPL |
| (d) | NCI's share in the dividend should be shown under the NCI category. |

Ind AS110 does not contain disclosure requirements; these are included in Ind AS 112. Ind AS 112 has greatly increased the amount of disclosures required.

**Treatment of unrealized profit on inventories**

Consolidated financial statements are prepared with the assumption that all group entities are one economic unit. As one economic unit cannot make a profit or a loss from a sale to itself it is imperative to remove the impact of unrealised profit (URP) from inventory as well as from the parent's profit in the consolidated statement of financial position.

The treatment of URP on inventories is twofold:

| Sale by parent to its subsidiary | Sale by subsidiary to its parent |
|---|---|
| URP lies in<br>(a) Inventory in subsidiary books<br>(b) Profit in Parent books | URP lies in<br>(a) Inventory in parent books<br>(b) Profit in subsidiary books |
| Effect:<br>(a) Deduct from inventory<br>(b) Deduct from SOCI of parent | Effect:<br>(c) Deduct from inventory<br>(d) Deduct from SOCI of subsidiary |
| Since profit is in parent books – NCI will not be impacted | Since profit is in subsidiary books, in case of partly owned subsidiary – NCI will be impacted |
| Entry:<br>Dr. Group retained earnings x<br>Cr. Inventories x | Entry:<br>Dr. Group retained earnings (parent share) x<br>Dr. NCI (NCI's share) x<br>Cr. Inventories x |
| Tax effect:<br>Dr. Deferred tax asset x<br>Cr. Group retained earnings x | Tax effect:<br>Dr. Deferred tax asset x<br>Cr. Group retained earnings (parent share) x<br>Cr. Non-controlling interest (NCI share) x |

**Treatment of sale of non-current assets**

Similar to the treatment of unrealised profit in inventories, it is imperative to remove the impact of unrealised profit (URP) from sale of non-current assets in preparation of the consolidated statement of financial position.

The treatment of URP on sale of non-current assets is twofold:

| Sale by parent to its subsidiary | Sale by subsidiary to its parent |
|---|---|
| URP lies in<br>(a) Non-current asset in subsidiary books<br>(b) Effect of depreciation if non-current asset is sold at a profit<br>(c) Profit in Parent books | URP lies in<br>(a) Non-current asset in parent books<br>(b) Effect of depreciation if non-current asset is sold at a profit<br>(c) Profit in subsidiary books |

| Sale by parent to its subsidiary | Sale by subsidiary to its parent |
|---|---|
| Effect:<br>(a) Deduct from non-current asset<br>(b) Adjust depreciation<br>(c) Deduct from SOPL of parent | Effect:<br>(a) Deduct from non-current asset<br>(b) Adjust depreciation<br>(c) Deduct from SOPL of subsidiary |
| Since profit is in parent books – NCI will not be impacted | Since profit is in subsidiary books, in case of partly owned subsidiary – NCI will be impacted |
| Entry on URP on non-current asset reversal<br>Dr. Group retained earnings x<br>Cr. Group Non-current asset x | Entry on URP of non-current asset reversal<br>Dr. Group retained earnings (parent share) x<br>Dr. NCI (NCI's share) x<br>Cr. Group Non-current asset x |
| Tax effect:<br>Dr. Deferred tax asset x<br>Cr. Group retained earnings x | Tax effect:<br>Dr. Deferred tax asset x<br>Cr. Group retained earnings (parent share) x<br>Cr. Non-controlling interest (NCI share) x |
| Entry on additional depreciation charged by subsidiary: (NCI is impacted)<br>Dr. Group Non-current asset x<br>Cr. Group retained earnings x<br>Cr. Non-controlling interest x | Entry on additional depreciation charged by parent: (NCI not impacted)<br>Dr. Group Non-current asset x<br>Cr. Group retained earnings x |
| Tax effect:<br>Dr. Group retained earnings x<br>Dr. Non-controlling interest x<br>Cr. Deferred tax asset x | Tax effect:<br>Dr. Group retained earnings x<br>Cr. Deferred tax asset x |

**Treatment of intra-group interest expenses**

In SOPL the amount of interest expense of one group company is cancelled against the amount of interest income of another group company.

**Treatment of intra-group dividend**

The treatment of intra-group dividends is as under:

| Dividends payable out of post-acquisition profit | Dividend paid out of pre-acquisition profit |
|---|---|
| In the consolidated Balance Sheet:<br>– Dividend payable to parent is not reflected separately. It is cancelled | In the consolidated Balance Sheet:<br>– Dividend payable by the parent is reflected as a liability in the |

| Dividends payable out of post-acquisition profit | Dividend paid out of pre-acquisition profit |
|---|---|
| out with the dividend receivable<br>– Dividend payable to the non-controlling interest is reflected as a current liability (This is because the entire profit of subsidiary has been consolidated. If the dividend received by the parent company was also included, this would lead to double counting) | consolidated Balance Sheet<br>– Dividend payable by the subsidiary is:<br>(a) NCI's share of dividend is reflected as current liability in the consolidated B/S.<br>(b) Parent's share in subsidiary's dividend is deducted from the cost of investment in the subsidiary.<br>(c) This would result in reducing the amount of goodwill.<br>(d) If the subsidiary is acquired during the year then we have to determine how much dividend is paid out of pre-acquisition profits. In the absence of any specific information, the dividend is assumed to have accrued evenly throughout the year. |
| In the consolidated statement of changes in equity:<br>– Dividend payable to NCI is reflected under NCI equity<br>– Under controlling equity, only the amount of dividend by the parent is shown<br>– Dividend payable to parent is not shown | No impact |

**Treatment of fair value in consideration paid for a subsidiary**

We know that conceptual *framework* related to financial statements fulfil two purposes:

(a) the assessment of stewardship or accountability of management and

(b) the provision of information for economic decision making

The assets, liabilities and equity may be recorded at historical cost in the individual Balance Sheet of the acquirer and acquiree.

However, according to Ind AS 103 all business combinations shall be accounted for by applying the acquisition method which states that fair values are to be used while measuring the cost of the business combination (purchase consideration).

The standard goes on to state that acquirer should measure the identifiable assets acquired and the liabilities assumed at their acquisition date fair value and also permits measurement of non-controlling interest at the acquisition date fair value.

This signifies that in any business combination, fair value will be used for the following:

| | |
|---|---|
| (a) | Cost of investment (purchase consideration) |
| (b) | Identifiable assets and liabilities |
| (c) | Non-controlling interest and |
| (d) | Acquirer's previously held investment in acquiree, in the case of step acquisition. |

Hence the acquirer shall measure the cost of a business combination as the aggregate of the fair values, at the date of acquisition, of all the above items in exchange of control of the entity.

Accordingly, applying the acquisition method to business combinations would mean that the cost is viewed from the acquirer's perspective and valued at fair value.

The effect of fair value adjustments to assets are as under:

| **Increase in fair value** | **Decrease in fair value** |
|---|---|
| (a) Dr. Group non-current asset x<br>Cr. Goodwill x<br>(Being non-current asset brought to fair value and the effect considered in goodwill calculation) | (a) Dr. Goodwill x<br>Cr. Group non-current asset x<br>(Being non-current asset brought to fair value and the effect considered in goodwill calculation) |
| Difference between carrying value and fair value will be adjusted in calculating goodwill.<br>NCI's share of fair value adjustments to individual assets / liabilities will be relevant only for calculation of NCI value using proportionate net asset method.<br>If fair value method is used for NCI valuation, this need not be separately considered | Difference between carrying value and fair value will be adjusted in calculating goodwill.<br>NCI's share of fair value adjustments to individual assets / liabilities will be relevant only for calculation of NCI value using proportionate net asset method.<br>If fair value method is used for NCI valuation, this need not be separately considered |
| (b) Increase in depreciation – subsequent to increase in value of assets owing to fair value adjustment on acquisition date:<br>Dr. Group retained earning X<br>(parent share) | (b) decrease in depreciation – subsequent to decrease in value of assets owing to fair value adjustment on acquisition date:<br>Dr. Group non-current asset X<br>Cr. Group retained earning X |

| Increase in fair value | Decrease in fair value |
|---|---|
| Dr. Non-controlling interest (NCI share) X<br>Cr. Group non-current asset X<br>(Being additional depreciation accounted For) | (parent share)<br>Cr. Non-controlling interest (NCI share) X<br>(Being excess depreciation charged earlier written back) |
| (c) Impact on valuation of goodwill:<br>– Increase in fair value of asset = value of goodwill decreases<br>– Increase in fair value of liabilities = value of goodwill increases | (c) Impact on valuation of goodwill:<br>– Decrease in fair value of asset = value of goodwill increases<br>– Decrease in fair value of liabilities = value of goodwill decreases |
| (d) Impact on deferred tax<br>An increase in fair value of asset and decrease in fair value of liabilities would lead to carrying value of net asset being more than tax base.<br>As a result in future taxable profit will be greater than accounting profits and would create a taxable temporary difference and hence a deferred tax liability as under:<br>Dr. Group retained earnings x<br>Cr. Deferred tax liability x<br>(Being deferred tax liability recognised owing to fair value adjustments) | (d) Impact on deferred tax<br>A decrease in fair value of asset and increase in fair value of liabilities would lead to carrying value of net asset being less than tax base.<br>As a result, in future taxable profit will be lower than accounting profits and would create a deductible temporary difference and hence a deferred tax asset as under:<br>Dr. Deferred tax asset x<br>Cr. Group retained earnings x<br>(Being deferred tax asset recognised owing to fair value adjustments) |

**Illustration 13.1: Fair Value Adjustments to Assets**

P Co acquired 60% share in S Co on 1st January 2021. The retained earnings on the date of acquisition were nil. The fair value of the non-controlling interest on the date of acquisition was Rs. 20000.

The Balance Sheets of P Co and S Co as at 31st December 2021 are:

| As at 31st December 2021 | P Co | | S Co | |
|---|---|---|---|---|
| | Rs | Rs | Rs | Rs |
| **Assets** | | | | |
| Non-current assets | | | | |
| Tangible assets | | | | |
| Land | - | | 10,000 | |

| | | | | |
|---|---|---|---|---|
| Property, Plant& Equipment | 33,000 | 33,000 | 15,000 | 25,000 |
| Investments: shares in S Co | | 27,000 | | |
| Current assets | | | | |
| Inventories | 10,500 | | 9,000 | |
| Receivables | 3,000 | | 10,000 | |
| Cash at bank | 1,000 | 14,500 | 3,000 | 22,000 |
| **Total assets** | | 74,500 | | 47,000 |
| Equity and Liabilities | | | | |
| Equity | | | | |
| Ordinary shares | 42,000 | | 25,000 | |
| Retained earnings | 18,500 | 60,500 | 17,000 | 42,000 |
| Current liabilities | | | | |
| Payables | 14,000 | 14,000 | 5,000 | 5,000 |
| Total Liabilities | | 74,500 | | 47,000 |

The directors of P Co carried out a fair value exercise on the net assets of S Co on the date of acquisition. The following matters arose from the exercise:

1. On the date of acquisition, the fair value of S Co's land was Rs 5,000 more than its carrying amount and that of its plant was Rs 10,000 more than its carrying value of Rs 5000. S Co charges depreciation at 10% SLM.

2. Inventories were included at cost to S Co of Rs 7,000. The selling price of the inventories was estimated to be Rs 9,000 and a reasonable allowance for profit on sale was Rs 1,400. All the inventories as at 1 January 2021 had been sold by 31st December 2021.

3. On 1st January 2021, S Co had a brand name that was protected legally but was not included in the Balance Sheet because S Co's directors considered that it did not meet the recognition criteria for internally developed intangible assets. The directors of P Co considered that the brand name had a market value of Rs 4000 on 1st January 2021 and that it would give competitive advantage for 5 years from that date.

4. Fair value adjustments give rise to temporary differences. The rate of taxation to apply to temporary differences is 20%.

**Required:**

Prepare the consolidated financial statements for the group.

**Solution**

Steps

| | |
|---|---|
| Step I | Determine percentage holding of Parent Co and non-controlling interest |
| Step II | Determine purchase consideration |
| Step III | Calculate pre-acquisition reserves |
| Step IV | Calculate fair value of assets on acquisition date. |
| Step V | Calculate deferred tax on fair value changes on acquisition date. |
| Step VI | Calculate goodwill |
| Step VII | Calculate post-acquisition retained earnings. |
| Step VIII | Calculate deferred tax reversal if any on post-acquisition retained earnings on fair value changes e.g. additional depreciation on fair value changes on assets |
| Step IX | Calculate non-controlling interest |
| Step X | Consolidate all items of assets and liabilities line by line. |

**Working Notes:**

**WN1 Statement of fair value changes during the year**

| Item | Carrying value (Rs) 1.1.2021 (A) | Change to goodwill (Rs) 1.1.2021 ((B-A) = C) | Fair value (Rs) 1.1.2021 (B) | Change (Rs) 2021 (D) | Change to B/S date (Rs) 31.12.2021 ((C –D) = E) |
|---|---|---|---|---|---|
| Land | 10,000 | 5,000 | 15,000 | - | 5,000 |
| Plant & Equipment | 5,000 | 10,000 | 15,000 | 1,000 | 9,000 |
| Inventories | 7,000 | 600 | 7,600 | 600 | - |
| Brand name | - | 4,000 | 4,000 | 800 | 3,200 |
| Total | 22,000 | 19,600 | 41,600 | 2,400 | 17,200 |
| Deferred tax 20% | | 3,920 | | (480) | 3,440 |

**WN2 Statement of goodwill**

| Item | Rs | Rs |
|---|---|---|
| Investment in S Co | | 27,000 |
| Fair value of NCI (40%) | | 20,000 |
| Less: Net assets represented by: | | 47,000 |
| Ordinary shares | (25,000) | |
| Fair value adjustments (WN1) | (19,600) | |
| Deferred tax adjustment | 3920 | 40,680 |
| Goodwill | | 6,320 |

WN3 Statement of retained earnings

| Item | P Co Rs | S Co Rs |
|---|---|---|
| Per question above | 18,500 | 17,000 |
| Less: Fair value adjustments | | (2,400) |
| Deferred tax reversal | | 480 |
| | | 15,080 |
| Share of parent (P Co) – 60% | 9,048 | |
| To NCI below – 40% | | 6,032 |
| Total | 27,548 | 6,032 |

**WN4 Statement of Non-controlling interest**

| Item | Rs | Rs |
|---|---|---|
| NCI – Fair value | | 20,000 |
| From retained earnings - NCI above – 40% | | 6,032 |
| Total | | 26,032 |

**Consolidated Balance Sheet as at 31st December 2021**

| | Rs | Rs |
|---|---|---|
| **Assets** | | |
| Non-current assets | | |
| Goodwill (WN2) | | 6,320 |
| Tangible assets | | |
| Land (10,000 + 5,000) | 15,000 | |
| Property, Plant & Equipment (33,000+15,000+9,000) | 57,000 | 72,000 |
| Intangible assets | | 3,200 |
| **Current assets** | | |
| Inventories (10,500+9,000) | 19,500 | |
| Receivables (3,000 + 10,000) | 13,000 | |
| Cash at bank (1,000+3,000) | 4,000 | 36,500 |
| Total assets | | 1,18,020 |
| **Equity and Liabilities** | | |
| Equity | | |
| Ordinary shares | 42,000 | |
| Retained earnings (WN3) | 27,548 | 69,548 |
| Non-controlling interest (WN4) | | 26,032 |
| Non-current liabilities | | |
| Deferred tax | | 3,440 |
| **Current liabilities** | | |
| Payables (14,000 + 5,000) | | 19,000 |
| Total Liabilities | | 1,18,020 |

**Partial disposal of an investment in a subsidiary**

Partial disposal of an investment in a subsidiary while control is retained:

This is accounted as equity transaction with owners, and the gain or loss is not recognised Partial disposal of an investment in a subsidiary that results in loss of control: Loss of control triggers re-measurement of the residual holding to fair value. Any difference between fair value and carrying amount is a gain or loss to be recognised in profit or loss. Thereafter apply Ind AS 28, Ind AS 111 or Ind AS 109, as appropriate, to the remaining holding.

### 13.7.3 Ind AS 28: Investment in Associates and Joint Ventures

The objective of this Standard is to prescribe the accounting for investments in associates and to set out the requirements for the application of the equity method when accounting for investments in associates and joint ventures.

This Standard shall be applied by all entities that are investors with joint control of, or significant influence over, an investee.

**Definitions**

The following terms are used in this Standard with the meanings specified:

**An *associate*** is an entity over which the investor has significant influence.

***Consolidated financial statements*** are the financial statements of a group in which assets, liabilities, equity, income, expenses and cash flows of the parent and its subsidiaries are presented as those of a single economic entity.

**The *equity method*** is a method of accounting whereby the investment is initially recognised at cost and adjusted thereafter for the post-acquisition change in the investor's share of the investee's net assets. The investor's profit or loss includes its share of the investee's profit or loss and the investor's other comprehensive income includes its share of the investee's other comprehensive income.

***A joint arrangement*** is an arrangement of which two or more parties have joint control.

***Joint control*** is the contractually agreed sharing of control of an arrangement, and exists only when the decisions about the relevant activities require the unanimous consent of the parties sharing control.

**A *joint venture*** is a joint arrangement whereby the parties that have joint control of the arrangement have rights to the net assets of the arrangement.

***A joint venturer*** is a party to a joint venture that has joint control of that joint venture
***Significant influence*** is the power to participate in the financial and operating policy decisions of the investee but is not control or joint control of those policies.

The following terms are defined in paragraph 4 of Ind AS 27, *Separate Financial Statements,* and in Appendix A of Ind AS 110, *Consolidated Financial Statements,* and are used in this Standard with the meanings specified in the Ind ASs in which they are defined:

- control of an investee
- group
- parent
- separate financial statements
- subsidiary.

**Significant Influence**

If an entity holds, directly or indirectly (e.g. through subsidiaries), 20% or more of the voting power of the investee, it is presumed that the entity has significant influence unless it can be clearly demonstrated that this is not the case.

Conversely, if the entity holds, directly or indirectly (e.g. through subsidiaries), less than 20% of the voting power of the investee, it is presumed that the entity does not have significant influence, unless such influence can be clearly demonstrated. A substantial or majority ownership by another investor does not necessarily preclude an entity from having significant influence.

The existence of significant influence by an entity is usually evidenced by:

| | |
|---|---|
| (a) | Representation on the board of directors or corresponding governing body of the investee. |
| (b) | participation in policy making processes. |
| (c) | material transactions between the investor and the investee. |
| (d) | interchange of managerial personnel; or |
| (e) | provision of essential technical information. |

The existence and effect of potential voting rights that are currently exercisable or convertible, including potential voting rights held by other entities, are considered when assessing whether an entity has significant influence. Potential voting rights are not currently exercisable or convertible when, for example, they cannot be exercised or converted until a future date or until the occurrence of a future event.

In assessing whether potential voting rights contribute to significant influence, the entity examines all facts and circumstances (including the terms of exercise of the potential voting rights and any other contractual arrangements whether considered individually or in combination) that affect potential rights, except the intentions of management and the financial ability to exercise or convert those potential rights.

An entity loses significant influence over an investee when it loses the power to participate in the financial and operating policy decisions of that investee. The loss of significant influence can occur with or without a change in absolute or relative ownership levels. It could occur, for example, when an associate becomes subject to the control of a government, court, administrator or regulator. It could also occur as a result of a contractual arrangement.

**Equity Method**

Under the equity method, on initial recognition the investment in an associate or a joint venture is recognised at cost, and the carrying amount is increased or decreased to recognise the investor's share of the profit or loss of the investee after the date of acquisition. The investor's share of the investee's profit or loss is recognised in the investor's profit or loss. Hence initial recognition and measurement is applied at cost.

Because the investor has joint control of, or significant influence over, the investee, the investor has an interest in the associate's or joint venture's performance and, as a result, the return on its investment. The investor accounts for this interest by extending the scope of its financial statements to include its share of the profit or loss of such an investee. As a result, application of the equity method provides more informative reporting of the investor's net assets and profit or loss.

When potential voting rights or other derivatives containing potential voting rights exist, an entity's interest in an associate or a joint venture is determined solely on the basis of existing ownership interests and does not reflect the possible exercise or conversion of potential voting rights and other derivative instruments, unless paragraph 13 applies.

Para 13 stipulates that in some circumstances, an entity has, in substance, an existing ownership as a result of a transaction that currently gives it access to the returns associated with an ownership interest.

In such circumstances, the proportion allocated to the entity is determined by taking into account the eventual exercise of those potential voting rights and other derivative instruments that currently give the entity access to the returns.

According to Para 14, Ind AS 109, *Financial Instruments,* does not apply to interests in associates and joint ventures that are accounted for using the equity method. When instruments containing potential voting rights in substance currently give access to the returns associated with an ownership interest in an associate or a joint venture, the instruments are not subject to Ind AS 109. In all other cases, instruments containing potential voting rights in an associate or a joint venture are accounted for in accordance with Ind AS 109.

Unless an investment, or a portion of an investment, in an associate or a joint venture is classified as held for sale in accordance with Ind AS 105, *Non-current Assets Held for Sale and Discontinued Operations*, the investment, or any retained interest in the investment not classified as held for sale, shall be classified as a non-current asset.

**Exemptions to Equity Method**

According to Para 17 an entity need not apply the equity method to its investment in an associate or a joint venture if the entity is a parent that is exempt from preparing consolidated financial statements by the scope exception in paragraph 4(a) of Ind AS 110 or if all the following apply:

(a) The entity is a wholly-owned subsidiary, or is a partially-owned subsidiary of another entity and its other owners, including those not otherwise entitled to vote, have been informed about, and do not object to, the entity not applying the equity method.

(b) The entity's debt or equity instruments are not traded in a public market (a domestic or foreign stock exchange or an over-the-counter market, including local and regional markets).

(c) The entity did not file, nor is it in the process of filing, its financial statements with a securities commission or other regulatory organisation, for the purpose of issuing any class of instruments in a public market.

(d) The ultimate or any intermediate parent of the entity produces financial statements available for public use that comply with Ind ASs, in which subsidiaries are consolidated or are measured at fair value through profit or loss in accordance with Ind AS 110." *(Companies (Indian Accounting Standard) Amendment Rules 2016)*

When an investment in an associate or a joint venture is held by, or is held indirectly through, an entity that is a venture capital organisation, or a mutual fund, unit trust and similar entities including investment-linked insurance funds, the entity may elect to measure that investment at fair value through profit or loss in accordance with Ind AS 109. An entity shall make this election separately for each associate or joint venture, at initial recognition of the associate or joint venture.

When an entity has an investment in an associate, a portion of which is held indirectly through a venture capital organisation, or a mutual fund, unit trust and similar entities including investment-linked insurance funds, the entity may elect to measure that portion of the investment in the associate at fair value through profit or loss in accordance with Ind AS 109 regardless of whether the venture capital organisation has significant influence over that portion of the investment. If the entity makes that election, the entity shall apply the equity method to any remaining portion of its investment in an associate that is not held through a venture capital organisation.

**Procedure of Equity Method**

| | |
|---|---|
| ***In the consolidated Balance Sheet*** | *On date of acquisition:*<br>The investment in the associate company is stated at cost<br>*On reporting date*:<br>The investment in associate company will be reflected in the consolidated Balance Sheet after making the following adjustments:<br>(a) If the associate makes a profit: group share of profit will be added to investment<br>(b) If the associate incurs a loss : group share of loss will be deducted from the investment<br>The procedures used for determining the profit / loss under the equity method are similar to those used for determining profit / loss under the full consolidation method. |
| ***In the consolidated Statement of Profit & Loss*** | *On the date of acquisition:*<br>The pre-acquisition profits have to be revised, to incorporate all fair value adjustments. The group's share in the revised profit |

| | will be deducted from consideration in arriving at goodwill.<br>*On reporting date:*<br>The group's share in the post-acquisition profits of the associate company is included in the consolidated SOPL |
|---|---|

(a) A group's share in an associate or a joint venture is the aggregate of the holdings in that associate or joint venture by the parent and its subsidiaries. The holdings of the group's other associates or joint ventures are ignored for this purpose.

When an associate or a joint venture has subsidiaries, associates or joint ventures,

(1) the profit or loss,

(2) other comprehensive income and

(3) net assets taken into account

in applying the equity method are those recognised in the associate's or joint venture's financial statements (including the associate's or joint venture's share of the profit or loss, other comprehensive income and net assets of its associates and joint ventures), after any adjustments necessary to give effect to uniform accounting policies.''

(b) If an associate or a joint venture uses accounting policies other than those of the entity for like transactions and events in similar circumstances, adjustments shall be made to make the associate's or joint venture's accounting policies conform to those of the entity when the associate's or joint venture's financial statements are used by the entity in applying the equity method.

(c) If an entity that is not itself an investment entity has an interest in an associate or joint venture that is an investment entity, the entity may, when applying the equity method, elect to retain the fair value measurement applied by that investment entity associate or joint venture to the investment entity associate's or joint venture's interests in subsidiaries. This election is made separately for each investment entity associate or joint venture, at the later of the date on which

(a) The investment entity associate or joint venture is initially recognised;

(b) The associate or joint venture becomes an investment entity; and

(c) the investment entity associate or joint venture first becomes a parent.

The Steps for equity method is summarised below:

- Eliminating intra group profits and losses arising from transactions between
- investor and investee

- identifying the goodwill portion of the purchase price
- amortisation of goodwill
- adjustments for depreciation of depreciable assets , based on their fair values
- adjustments for the effect of cross holdings
- using uniform accounting policies

**Illustration 13.2: Equity Method of Accounting**

Day Ltd acquired 40% interest in the ordinary shares of Kay Inc on the date of incorporation January 1 2018 for an amount of Rs. 22,000. This enabled Day Ltd to exercise significant influence over Kay Inc. On December 2021 the shareholders equity of Kay Inc was as follows:

| | Rs |
|---|---|
| Ordinary issued share capital | 55,000 |
| Reserves | 18,000 |
| Accumulated profit | 65,000 |
| TOTAL | 1,38,000 |
| Extract of Income statement and statement of changes in equity: | |
| Income statement | |
| PAT | 22,800 |
| Extraordinary items | (1,200) |
| Net profit for the period | 21,600 |
| Statement of change in equity | |
| Accumulated profit (beginning of the year) | 65,000 |
| Net profit for the period | 21,600 |
| Dividend paid | (8,000) |
| Accumulated profit at the end of the year | 78,600 |

In November 2021 Day Ltd sold inventories to Kay Ltd for the first time at Rs. 5,000 and earned a profit of Rs. 1000. None of the inventories were sold by December 31. Income Tax rate is assumed at 30%

**Solution**

Calculation of equity method Rs

Ordinary cost (Rs.55,000 X 40%) 22,000

Post-acquisition profit beginning of the year{(18,000+65,000)X40%} 33,200

| | |
|---|---|
| Attributable portion of net profit (Schedule I) 8,360 | |
| Dividend received (8,000 X 40%) | (3,200) |
| | 60,360 |
| **Schedule I** | |
| Attributable portion of net profit | |
| Net profit (2,1600 X 40%) 8,640 | |
| After tax effect of unrealised profit {40%X(70%X1,000)} (280) | |
| Total (as above) 8,360 | |

**Treatment of unrealized intra-group profits related to Associates**

Gains and losses resulting from 'upstream' and 'downstream' transactions between an entity (including its consolidated subsidiaries) and its associate or joint venture are recognised in the entity's financial statements only to the extent of unrelated investors' interests in the associate or joint venture. 'Upstream' transactions are, for example, sales of assets from an associate or a joint venture to the investor. 'Downstream' transactions are, for example, sales or contributions of assets from the investor to its associate or its joint venture. The investor's share in the associate's or joint venture's gains or losses resulting from these transactions is eliminated.

Treatment of elimination of unrealised intra-group profits related to associates is shown as under:

| Downstream transactions | Upstream transactions |
|---|---|
| If the sale of goods / assets at profit is made by the investor to the associate, it is known as a downstream transaction. | If the sale of goods / assets at profit is made by the associate to the investor, it is known as upstream transaction. |
| The entry is as under:<br>Dr. Cost of sales (CSOPL) x<br>Cr. Investment in associate (CBS) x<br>(Being the elimination of group's share in unrealised intra-group profits) | The entry is as under:<br>Dr. Cost of sales (CSOCL) x<br>Cr. Inventory (CBS) x<br>(Being elimination of URP on inventory owing to upstream transactions) |
| **Rationale:**<br>In this case, URP is included in the associate's inventory, but associate's inventory is not shown in the investor's financial statements as it does not consolidate the accounts of the associate. | **Rationale:**<br>In this case, URP is included in the investor's inventory which is included in consolidated financial statements.<br>Hence, URP needs to be eliminated from the inventory and corresponding effect will always go to cost of sales / retained earnings |

| Downstream transactions | Upstream transactions |
|---|---|
| Hence URP needs to be eliminated from the investment and not from inventory. | |

**Accounting treatment of goodwill, bargain purchases and losses with respect to Associates**

An investment is accounted for using the equity method from the date on which it becomes an associate or a joint venture. On acquisition of the investment, any difference between the cost of the investment and the entity's share of the net fair value of the investee's identifiable assets and liabilities is accounted for as follows:

(a) Goodwill relating to an associate or a joint venture is included in the carrying amount of the investment. Amortisation of that goodwill is not permitted.

(b) Any excess of the entity's share of the net fair value of the investee's identifiable assets and liabilities over the cost of the investment is recognised directly in equity as capital reserve in the period in which the investment is acquired.

Accounting treatment of goodwill and bargain purchases with respect to associates is shown in table below:

| Goodwill | | Capital reserve | |
|---|---|---|---|
| Cost of investment<br>Less: Investor's share of net fair Value of associate's Identifiable net assets<br>Goodwill (A – B) | x (a)<br><br>x (b)<br>x | Cost of investment<br>Less: Investor's share of net fair Value of associate's Identifiable net assets<br>Capital Reserve (B – A) | x (a)<br><br>x (b)<br>x |
| Positive goodwill is already included in the cost of investment and so needs no further accounting treatment | | The gain on bargain purchase will be recognised directly in equity as capital reserve in the period in which the investment is acquired. | |
| All adjustments made for goodwill impairment and fair value changes in accounting for subsidiaries are also made in accounting for associates | | | |
| If the group's share of losses pertaining to the associate exceeds its investment in the associate, then the investor has to stop accounting for further losses. Hence the cost of investment will be recorded as nil in the consolidated financial statements.<br>After the entity's interest is reduced to zero, additional losses are provided for, and a liability is recognised, only to the extent that the entity has incurred legal or constructive obligations or made payments on behalf of the associate or joint venture. If the associate or joint venture subsequently reports profits, the entity resumes | | | |

| recognising its share of those profits only after its share of the profits equals the share of losses not recognised. |
|---|

**Financial Statements are prepared at different dates**

When the financial statements of an associate or a joint venture used in applying the equity method are prepared as of a date different from that used by the entity, adjustments shall be made for the effects of significant transactions or events that occur between that date and the date of the entity's financial statements. In any case, the difference between the end of the reporting period of the associate or joint venture and that of the entity shall be no more than three months. The length of the reporting periods and any difference between the ends of the reporting periods shall be the same from period to period.

**Classification as held for sale**

An entity shall apply Ind AS 105 to an investment, or a portion of an investment, in an associate or a joint venture that meets the criteria to be classified as held for sale. Any retained portion of an investment in an associate or a joint venture that has not been classified as held for sale shall be accounted for using the equity method until disposal of the portion that is classified as held for sale takes place. After the disposal takes place, an entity shall account for any retained interest in the associate or joint venture in accordance with Ind AS 109 unless the retained interest continues to be an associate or a joint venture, in which case the entity uses the equity method.

When an investment, or a portion of an investment, in an associate or a joint venture previously classified as held for sale no longer meets the criteria to be so classified, it shall be accounted for using the equity method retrospectively as from the date of its classification as held for sale. Financial statements for the periods since classification as held for sale shall be amended accordingly.

**Discontinuance of use of Equity method**

An entity shall discontinue the use of the equity method from the date when its investment ceases to be an associate or a joint venture as follows:

(a) If the investment becomes a subsidiary, the entity shall account for its investment in accordance with Ind AS 103, *Business Combinations,* and Ind AS 110.

(b) If the retained interest in the former associate or joint venture is a financial asset, the entity shall measure the retained interest at fair value. The fair value of the retained interest shall be regarded as its fair value on initial recognition as a financial asset in accordance with Ind AS 109. The entity shall recognise in profit or loss any difference between:

  (i) the fair value of any retained interest and any proceeds from disposing of a part interest in the associate or joint venture; and

  (ii) the carrying amount of the investment at the date the equity method was discontinued.

(c) When an entity discontinues the use of the equity method, the entity shall account for all amounts previously recognised in other comprehensive income in relation to that investment on the same basis as would have been required if the investee had directly disposed of the related assets or liabilities.

Therefore, if a gain or loss previously recognised in other comprehensive income by the investee would be reclassified to profit or loss on the disposal of the related assets or liabilities, the entity reclassifies the gain or loss from equity to profit or loss (as a reclassification adjustment) when the equity method is discontinued.

For example, if an associate or a joint venture has cumulative exchange differences relating to a foreign operation and the entity discontinues the use of the equity method, the entity shall reclassify to profit or loss the gain or loss that had previously been recognised in other comprehensive income in relation to the foreign operation.

The Standard clarifies that, if an investment in an associate becomes an investment in a joint venture or an investment in a joint venture becomes an investment in an associate, the entity continues to apply the equity method and does not re-measure the retained interest.

**Change in ownership interest**

If an entity's ownership interest in an associate or a joint venture is reduced, but the entity continues to apply the equity method, the entity shall reclassify to profit or loss the proportion of the gain or loss that had previously been recognised in other comprehensive income relating to that reduction in ownership interest if that gain or loss would be required to be reclassified to profit or loss on the disposal of the related assets or liabilities.

**Impairment losses**

The net investment in an associate or joint venture is impaired and impairment losses are incurred if, and only if, there is objective evidence of impairment as a result of one or more events that occurred after the initial recognition of the net investment (a 'loss event') and that loss event (or events) has an impact on the estimated future cash flows from the net investment that can be reliably estimated. It may not be possible to identify a single, discrete event that caused the impairment. Rather the combined effect of several events may have caused the impairment. Losses expected as a result of future events, no matter how likely, are not recognised. Objective evidence that the net investment is impaired includes observable data that comes to the attention of the entity about the following loss events:

(a) significant financial difficulty of the associate or joint venture;

(b) a breach of contract, such as a default or delinquency in payments by the associate or joint venture;

(c) the entity, for economic or legal reasons relating to its associate's or joint venture's financial difficulty, granting to the associate or joint venture a concession that the entity would not otherwise consider;

(d) it becoming probable that the associate or joint venture will enter bankruptcy or other financial reorganisation; or

(e) the disappearance of an active market for the net investment because of financial difficulties of the associate or joint venture.

The disappearance of an active market because the associate's or joint venture's equity or financial instruments are no longer publicly traded is not evidence of impairment. A downgrade of an associate's or joint venture's credit rating or a decline in the fair value of the associate or joint venture, is not of itself, evidence of impairment, although it may be evidence of impairment when considered with other available information.

In addition to the types of events mentioned above, objective evidence of impairment for the net investment in the equity instruments of the associate or joint venture includes information about significant changes with an adverse effect that have taken place in the technological, market, economic or legal environment in which the associate or joint venture operates, and indicates that the cost of the investment in the equity instrument may not be recovered. A significant or prolonged decline in the fair value of an investment in an equity instrument below its cost is also objective evidence of impairment.

The carrying amount of the investment is tested for impairment in accordance with Ind AS 36 as a single asset, by comparing its recoverable amount (higher of value in use and fair value less costs of disposal) with its carrying amount, whenever it is indicated that the net investment may be impaired.

An impairment loss recognised in those circumstances is not allocated to any asset, including goodwill that forms part of the carrying amount of the net investment in the associate or joint venture. Accordingly, any reversal of that impairment loss is recognised in accordance with Ind AS 36 to the extent that the recoverable amount of the net investment subsequently increases. In determining the value in use of the net investment, an entity estimates:

(a) its share of the present value of the estimated future cash flows expected to be generated by the associate or joint venture, including the cash flows from the operations of the associate or joint venture and the proceeds from the ultimatc disposal of the investment;

or

(b) the present value of the estimated future cash flows expected to arise from dividends to be received from the investment and from its ultimate disposal.

Using appropriate assumptions, both methods give the same result.

The recoverable amount of an investment in an associate or a joint venture shall be assessed for each associate or joint venture, unless the associate or joint venture does not generate cash inflows from continuing use that are largely independent of those from other assets of the entity.

**Separate financial statements**

An investment in an associate or a joint venture shall be accounted for in the entity's separate financial statements in accordance with paragraph 10 of Ind AS 27.

### 13.6.1.Ind AS 111: Joint Arrangements

The objective of this Indian Accounting Standard (Ind AS) is to establish principles for financial reporting by entities that have an interest in arrangements that are controlled jointly (i.e. *Joint arrangements*).

This Standard defines *joint control* and requires an entity that is a *party to a joint arrangement* to determine the type of joint arrangement in which it is involved by assessing its rights and obligations and to account for those rights and obligations in accordance with that type of joint arrangement.

This Ind AS shall be applied by all entities that are a party to a joint arrangement.

**Definitions**

| Item | Description |
|---|---|
| ***joint arrangement*** | An arrangement of which two or more parties have joint control. |
| ***joint control*** | The contractually agreed sharing of control of an arrangement, which exists only when decisions about the relevant activities require the unanimous consent of the parties sharing control. |
| ***joint operation*** | A joint arrangement whereby the parties that have joint control of the arrangement have rights to the assets, and obligations for the liabilities, relating to the arrangement |
| ***joint operator*** | A party to a joint operation that has joint control of that joint operation. |
| ***joint venture*** | A joint arrangement whereby the parties that have joint control of the arrangement have rights to the net assets of the arrangement. |
| ***joint venturer*** | A party to a joint venture that has joint control of that joint venture. |
| ***party to a joint arrangement*** | An entity that participates in a joint arrangement, regardless of whether that entity has joint control of the arrangement. |
| ***Separate vehicle*** | A separately identifiable financial structure, including separate legal entities or entities recognised by statute, regardless of whether those entities have a legal personality. |

## Joint Arrangement

As defined above, joint arrangement is an arrangement of which two or more parties have joint control.

A joint arrangement has the following characteristics:

(a) The parties are bound by a contractual arrangement

(b) The contractual arrangement gives two or more of those parties joint control of the arrangement

## Types of Joint Arrangement

A joint arrangement is either a *joint operation* or a *joint venture.*

An entity shall determine the type of joint arrangement in which it is involved. The classification of a joint arrangement as a joint operation or a joint venture depends upon the rights and obligations of the parties to the arrangement.

(a) *A joint operation* is a joint arrangement whereby the parties that have joint control of the arrangement have rights to the assets, and obligations for the liabilities, relating to the arrangement. Those parties are called joint operators.

(b) *A joint venture* is a joint arrangement whereby the parties that have joint control of the arrangement has rights to the net assets of the arrangement. Those parties are called joint venturers.

## Comparative treatment of Joint Arrangements

The accounting treatment related to types of joint arrangements is shown in the table below as per classification prescribed under Ind AS 111:

| Joint operations | Joint venture |
|---|---|
| **Characteristic**<br>Each joint operator may:<br>(a) use its own property, plant and equipment<br>(b) carry its own inventories<br>(c) incur own expenses and liabilities<br>(d) raise its own finance, which represents its own obligations<br>Alternatively, each joint operator may have joint control and often joint ownership of one or more assets:<br>(a) contributed to or acquired for the purpose of the joint arrangement, and<br>(b) dedicated to the purposes of the arrangement | **Characteristic**<br>In this type of joint arrangements, the venturers establish a corporation, partnership or other separate entity in order to undertake an economic activity<br>The entities operate in the same way as other entities.<br>The only distinguishing feature is that there exists contract between the venturers in order to establish joint control over the financial and operating decisions related to the activity. |

| Joint operations | Joint venture |
|---|---|
| According to joint venture agreement, each joint operator may take a share of the output from the assets and each bears an agreed share of the revenues earned and expenses incurred | |
| **Accounting treatment**<br>A joint operator would recognise in its books:<br>(a) its assets, including its share of assets held jointly,<br>(b) its liabilities, including its share of assets held jointly,<br>(c) its revenues from the sale of its share of the output of the joint operation,<br>(d) its share of the revenue from the sale of the output by the joint operation, and<br>(e) its expenses, including its share of any expenses incurred jointly<br>A joint operator accounts for the assets, liabilities, revenues and expenses related to its involvement in joint operation in accordance with the relevant IFRSs.<br>A joint arrangement which is not in the form of a separate vehicle e.g. a separate legal entity, would compulsorily be treated as joint operation. | **Accounting treatment**<br>Joint venture has to maintain its own accounting records and prepare and present financial statements in the same way as other entities according to the requirements of the IFRSs.<br>Each venturer usually contributes cash or other resources to the joint venture. These contributions are included in the accounting records of the venturer and recognised in its financial statements as an investment in the joint venture.<br>A venturer needs to recognise its interest in a joint venture using the equity method. |
| **Legal form**<br>If in accordance with the legal form, parties are conferred direct rights to assets and obligation to its liabilities, then it is a joint operation | **Legal form**<br>If the arrangement is structured through a separate vehicle it becomes a joint venture |
| **Contractual arrangement**<br>If in accordance with the contractual arrangement, parties have rights to assets and obligation for liabilities – and not the entity – then the arrangement is a joint operation | **Contractual arrangement**<br>If no such contractual arrangement is there, but is covered by a separate legal entity it is a joint venture |

**Illustration 13.3: Joint Arrangement**

Assume that three parties establish an arrangement: A has 50 per cent of the voting rights in the arrangement, B has 30 per cent and C has 20 per cent. The contractual arrangement between A, B and C specifies that at least 75 per cent of the voting rights are required to make decisions about the relevant activities of the arrangement. Even though A can block any decision, it does not control the arrangement because it needs the agreement of B.

The terms of their contractual arrangement requiring at least 75 per cent of the voting rights to make decisions about the relevant activities imply that A and B have joint control of the arrangement because decisions about the relevant activities of the arrangement cannot be made without both A and B agreeing.

**Illustration 13.4: Joint Arrangement**

Assume an arrangement has three parties: A has 50 per cent of the voting rights in the arrangement and B and C each have 25 per cent. The contractual arrangement between A, B and C specifies that at least 75 per cent of the voting rights are required to make decisions about the relevant activities of the arrangement. Even though A can block any decision, it does not control the arrangement because it needs the agreement of either B or C. In this example, A, B and C collectively control the arrangement. However, there is more than one combination of parties that can agree to reach 75 per cent of the voting rights (i.e. either A and B or A and C). In such a situation, to be a joint arrangement the contractual arrangement between the parties would need to specify which combination of the parties is required to agree unanimously to decisions about the relevant activities of the arrangement.

**Illustration 13.5: Joint Arrangement**

Assume an arrangement in which A and B each have 35 per cent of the voting rights in the arrangement with the remaining 30 per cent being widely dispersed. Decisions about the relevant activities require approval by a majority of the voting rights. A and B have joint control of the arrangement only if the contractual arrangement specifies that decisions about the relevant activities of the arrangement require both A and B agreeing.

### Decision tree on Joint control

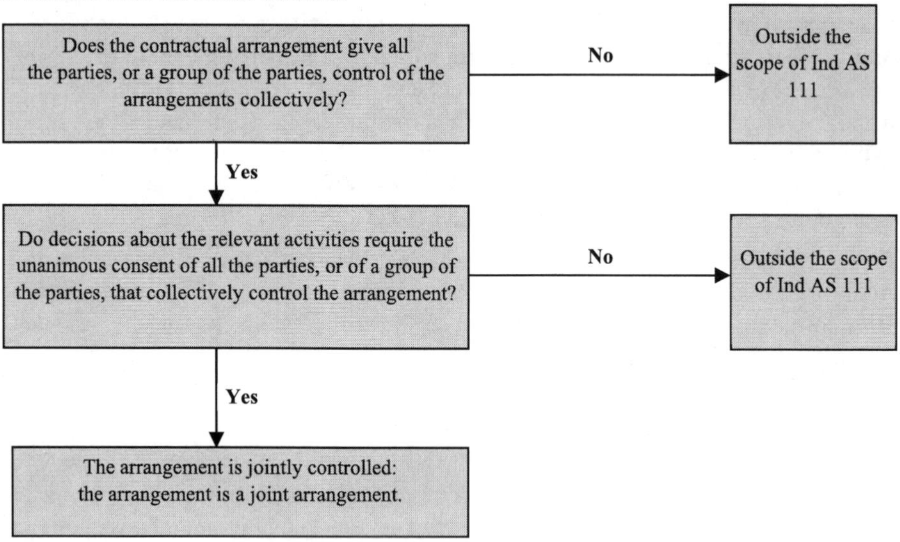


### Comparative analysis of various entities in consolidation of financial statements

| **Investment** | **Nature** | **Accounting treatment** |
|---|---|---|
| Investment > 50% control | Subsidiary | Full consolidation – line by line |
| Significant influence – between > 20% and < 50% | Associate | Equity method |
| In case of joint control | Joint venture | Equity method |
| In case of joint control | Joint operation | Share of assets, liabilities, income and expenses in a joint operation |
| < 20% investment and not a joint venture | None of the above | Treatment in accordance with Ind AS 109 |

The legal form and structure of joint arrangement would like as follows:

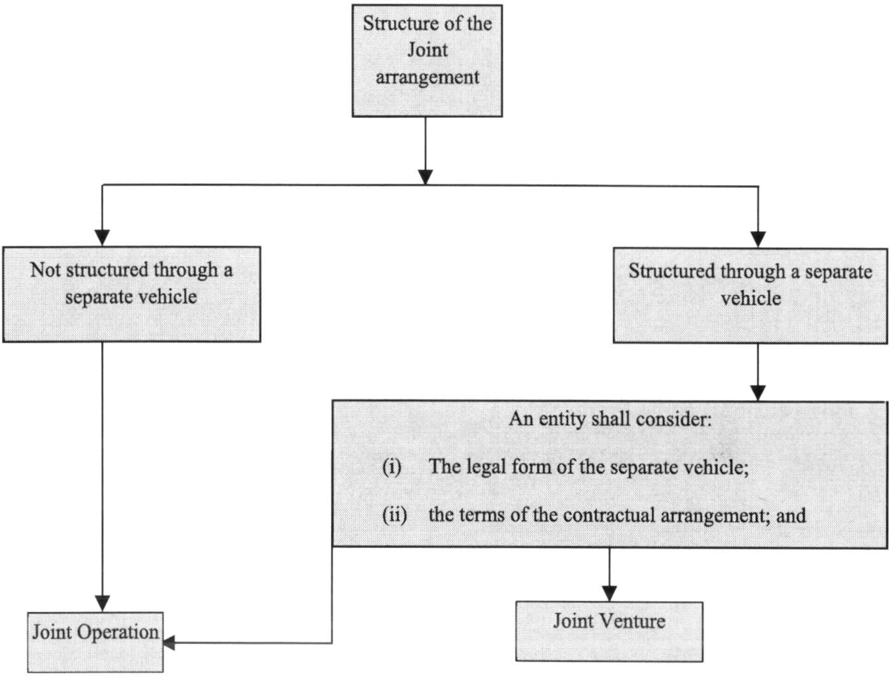


When a joint arrangement is disconnected from the parties and included in a separate entity, it can be either a joint operation or a joint venture. In such cases, further analysis is required of the legal form of the separate entity, the terms and conditions included in the contractual agreement and, sometimes, other facts and circumstances. This is because, in practice, the latter two can override the principles derived from the legal form of the separate vehicle.

Joint operators account for their rights to assets and obligations for liabilities. Joint venturers account for their interest by using the equity method of accounting.

**Illustration 13.6: Consolidated Income Statement**

The income statements and summarised statements of changes in equity of Alpha, Beta and Gamma for the year ended 31 March 2021 are given below:

| **Income Statements** | **Alpha Rs.'000** | **Beta Rs.'000** | **Gamma Rs.'000** |
|---|---|---|---|
| Revenue | 4,70,000 | 4,34,000 | 2,26,000 |
| Cost of sales | (2,56,000) | (2,18,000) | (1,76,000) |

| | | | |
|---|---|---|---|
| Gross profit | 2,14,000 | 2,16,000 | 50,000 |
| Distribution costs | (18,000) | (17,000) | (15,000) |
| Administrative expenses | (19,000) | (16,000) | (17,000) |
| Investment income (Note 5) | 37,300 | Nil | Nil |
| Finance cost (Note 6) | (68,000) | (65,000) | (44,000) |
| Profit/(loss) before tax | 146,300 | 1,18,000 | (26,000) |
| Income tax expense | (41,000) | (33,000) | Nil |
| Profit/(loss) for the year | 1,05,300 | 85,000 | (26,000) |

Summarised Statements of Changes in Equity

| | | | |
|---|---|---|---|
| Balance at 1 April 2020 | 5,40,000 | 3,90,000 | 1,92,000 |
| Comprehensive income for the year | 1,05,300 | 85,000 | (26,000) |
| Dividends paid on 31 December 2020 | (52,000) | (40,000) | Nil |
| Balance at 31 March 2021 | 5,93,300 | 4,35,000 | 1,66,000 |

**Note 1 – purchase of shares in Beta**

On 1 October 2019 Alpha purchased 75 million of the 100 million equity shares in Beta. Details of the share purchase were as follows:

– Alpha issued two new equity shares for every three shares acquired in Beta. On 1 October 2019 the market value of an Alpha share was Rs.6 and the market value of a Beta share was Rs.3·20.

– Alpha agreed to make an additional cash payment of Rs.1 for every share acquired in Beta to be paid on 30 September 2021. This payment is contingent on the profits of Beta exceeding a cumulative target in the two-year period ending 30 September 2021. The fair value of this contingent payment was Rs.55 million on 1 October 2019. The fair value had risen to Rs.58 million by 31 March 2020 and to Rs.64 million by 31 March 2021. The directors of Alpha correctly accounted for this contingent consideration in its financial statements for the year ended 31 March 2020 but no changes have been made to the carrying value of the contingent consideration since 31 March 2020.

– Alpha incurred legal and professional costs of Rs.5 million connected with the acquisition; Rs.2·4 million of these costs related to the cost of issuing shares. Alpha correctly accounted for these acquisition costs in its financial statements for the year ended 31 March 2020.

Alpha decided to value the non-controlling interest in Beta at the date of acquisition at fair value in its consolidated financial statements. The market value of a Beta share at that date was used to calculate the fair value of the non-controlling interest.

The equity of Beta as shown in its own financial statements at 1 October 2019 was Rs.300 million. At that date the property, plant and equipment (PPE) of Beta had a carrying value of Rs.240 million and a fair value of Rs.280 million.

The estimated future useful economic life of the PPE of Beta was four years from 1 October 2019. No disposals of PPE occurred between 1 October 2019 and 31 March 2021.

On 1 October 2019 the directors estimated that the internally generated brand name of Beta had a fair value of Rs.30 million and a future useful economic life of 30 years.

All depreciation and amortisation is charged on a monthly basis and presented in cost of sales.

**Note 2 – impairment review**

On 31 March 2020 and 31 March 2021 the goodwill on consolidation of Beta was reviewed for impairment. No impairment of the goodwill was necessary as a result of the review on 31 March 2020. Beta is regarded as a single cash generating unit for impairment purposes and at 31 March 2021 its recoverable amount was estimated as Rs.550 million. Any impairment of goodwill is charged to cost of sales.

**Note 3 – purchase of shares in Gamma**

On 1 October 2020 Alpha purchased 40% of the equity shares of Gamma for Rs.75 million in cash. This purchase allowed Alpha to exercise a significant influence over Gamma. No material differences between the market value and the book value of the net assets of Gamma were apparent at the date of the share purchase. On 31 March 2021 an impairment review was conducted resulting in an impairment required of Rs.1·8 million.

**Note 4 – inter-company sales**

Beta supplies products to Alpha and Gamma. Sales of the products to Alpha and Gamma during the year ended 31 March 2021 were as follows (all sales were made at a mark-up of 331/3% on cost):

– Sales to Alpha Rs.18 million.

– Sales to Gamma Rs.12 million.

At 31 March 2021 and 31 March 2020 the inventories of Alpha and Gamma included the following amounts in respect of goods purchased from Beta.

Amount in inventory at

| | 31 March 2021<br>Rs.000 | 31 March 2020<br>Rs.000 |
|---|---|---|
| Alpha | 3,600 | 2,100 |
| Gamma | 2,700 | Nil |

**Note 5 – Equity investments**

At 1 April 2020 Alpha had two equity investments that it designated as fair value through other comprehensive income in accordance with Ind AS 109 *Financial Instruments*. At the date of acquisition:

| Name | Original cost<br>Rs.'000 | Fair value at 31st March 2020<br>Rs.'000 | Fair value at 31st March 2021<br>Rs.'000 |
|---|---|---|---|
| Delta | 12,000 | 15,000 | n/a |
| Epsilon | 11,000 | 14,000 | 15,400 |

On 31 January 2021 Alpha disposed of its investment in Delta for Rs.19·5 million and showed a profit on sale of Rs.4·5 million (Rs.19·5 million – Rs.15 million) as part of investment income. Apart from recording the receipt of dividend income no other entries have been made in the financial statements for the year ended 31 March 2021 regarding the investment in Epsilon. Both investments had been correctly treated in the financial statements for the year ended 31 March 2020.

**Note 6 – Convertible notes**

On 1 April 2020 Alpha issued 300 million loan notes of Rs.1 per note at par. The loan notes entitled the holders to an interest payment of 5 paise per note, payable annually in arrears. The loan notes are repayable at par on 31 March 2025. As an alternative to repayment the holders can elect to convert the notes into equity shares in Alpha. On 1 April 2020 investors in non-convertible notes would expect an annual return of 8%. You are given the following discount factors:

| Discount rate | Present value of Rs.1 payable | |
|---|---|---|
| | At the end of year 5 | Cumulatively at the end of years. 1–5 |
| 5%<br>8% | 78·4 paise<br>68·1 paise | Rs.4·33<br>Rs.3·99 |

On 1 April 2020 the directors of Alpha recorded a loan liability of Rs.300 million and in the year ended 31 March 2021 a finance cost of Rs.15 million (300 million x 5 cents) in respect of these notes.

**Note 7 – Environmental damage**

During the year ended 31 March 2021 Alpha began production at three newly acquired factories. The normal production process at each factory results in environmental damage. Alpha has a policy of only rectifying such damage when legally required to do so. Details of the damage caused at the three sites up to and including 31 March 2021 are as follows:

| Factory | Damage caused by 31 March 2021 (Rs.'000) | Clean-up legislation in place at 31 March 2021? |
|---|---|---|
| A | 3,000 | Yes |
| B | 1,000 | No |
| C | 2,000 | No but legislation passed since year end with retrospective effect |

No provision for environmental damage has been made in the financial statements. Any appropriate provision should be reported as part of cost of sales.

Required:

(a) Prepare the consolidated statement of Profit & Loss for Alpha for the year ended 31 March 2021;

(b) Prepare the summarised consolidated statement of changes in equity for Alpha for the year ended 31 March 2021. Your summarised statement should include a column for the non-controlling interest. Ignore deferred tax. (*ACCA UK - Adapted*)

**Solution**

(a) Consolidated statement of Profit & Loss and other comprehensive income for the year ended 31 March 2021

| | Rs.'000 |
|---|---|
| Revenue (W1) | 8,86,000 |
| Cost of sales (balancing figure) | (4,82,145) |

| | |
|---|---|
| Gross profit (W2) | 4,03,855 |
| Distribution costs (18,000 + 17,000) | (35,000) |
| Administrative expenses (19,000 + 16,000) | (35,000) |
| Investment income (W6) | 2,800 |
| Finance cost (W7) | (1,39,132) |
| Share of losses of associate (W9) | (7,000) |
| Profit before tax | 1,90,523 |
| Income tax expense (41,000 + 33,000) | (74,000) |
| Net profit for the year | 1,16,523 |
| Other comprehensive income (W10) | 5,900 |
| Comprehensive income for the year | 1,22,423 |
| Net profit attributable to | |
| Non-controlling interest (W11) | 17,464 |
| Controlling interest | 99,059 |
| Net profit for the year | 1,16,523 |
| Comprehensive income attributable to | |
| Non-controlling interest | 17,464 |
| Controlling interest | 1,04,959 |
| Comprehensive income for the year | 122,423 |

(b) Consolidated statement of changes in equity for the year ended 31 March 2021

| | Controlling interest Rs.'000 | Non-controlling interest Rs.'000 | Total Rs.'000 |
|---|---|---|---|
| Balance at 1 April 2020 (W12 & W13) | 6,02,850 | 1,01,125 | 7,03,975 |
| Comprehensive income for the year | 1,04,959 | 17,464 | 1,22,423 |
| Equity component of convertible bonds (W14) | 35,850 | | 35,850 |
| Dividends | (52.000) | (10,000) | (62,000) |
| Balance at 31 March 2021 | 6,91,659 | 1,08,589 | 8,00,248 |

**WORKINGS**

*Working 1 – revenue*

| | **Rs.000** |
|---|---:|
| Alpha + Beta | 9,04,000 |
| Sales from Alpha – Beta (see note 1) | (18,000) |
| | 8,86,000 |

*Working 2 – gross profit*

| | **Rs.'000** |
|---|---:|
| Alpha + Beta | 4,30,000 |
| Environmental provision (3,000 + 2,000) | (5,000) |
| Unrealised profit adjustments: | |
| Beta: (1/4 (3,600 – 2,100)) | (375) |
| Gamma: (1/4 x 2,700 x 40%) | (270) |
| Extra depreciation (W3) | (11,000) |
| Change in the fair value of contingent consideration (Rs.64 million – Rs.58 million – see note 2) | (6,000) |
| Impairment of goodwill (W4) | (3,500) |
| | 4,03,855 |

***Note 1***

Ind AS 28 – *Investments in associates* – requires partial elimination of unrealised profits on transactions between associates and group entities. Profits can only be included to the extent that they relate to the non-group share. This means that the group share of such profits is eliminated and an adjustment of Rs.270,000 is required to profit in this case (see working 2 above). The Ind AS does not specify exactly how such an adjustment should be reported in the consolidated statement of comprehensive income. The approach taken here is to make no adjustment to revenue whatever. Given the required adjustment to gross profit of Rs.270,000, this would alter cost of sales by an equal and opposite amount.

An alternative approach would be to reduce consolidated revenue by the group share of the revenue that relates to the inventory that is unsold by Gamma at the year-end. Given the required adjustment to gross profit of Rs.210,000, the adjustment to cost of sales follows as the balancing figure.

***Note 2***

The change in fair value of the contingent consideration could have been shown in other sections of the statement of comprehensive income – for example as an administration cost.

*Working 3 – extra depreciation and amortisation*

| | **Rs.000** |
|---|---|
| Depreciation of PPE – ¼ x (Rs.280 million – Rs.240 million)<br>Amortisation of brand – 1/30 x Rs.30 million | 10,000<br>1,000 |
| | 11,000 |

*Working 4 – impairment of goodwill on acquisition of Beta*

| | **Rs.'000** |
|---|---|
| Carrying value of Beta in the consolidated financial statements at 31 March 2021:<br>Per own financial statements<br>Fair value adjustments:<br>PPE – (Rs.280 million – Rs.240 million) x (2·5/4)<br>Brand – Rs.30 million x (28·5/30)<br>Goodwill (W5) | <br><br>4,35,000<br><br>25,000<br>28,500<br>65,000 |
| Recoverable amount | 5,53,500<br>(5,50,000) |
| Impairment of goodwill | 3,500 |

*Working 5 – goodwill on acquisition of Beta*

| | **Rs.'000** | **Rs.'000** |
|---|---|---|
| Fair value of consideration given:<br>Share exchange – 75,000 x 2/3 x Rs.6<br>Contingent consideration<br>Acquisition costs | <br>3,00,000<br>55,000<br>nil | <br><br><br>3,55,000 (a) |
| Fair value of non-controlling interest – 25,000 x Rs.3·20 | | 80,000 (b) |

| | | |
|---|---|---|
| Fair value of net assets of Beta at 1 October 2019:<br>Per own financial statements<br>Fair value adjustment – PPE<br>(Rs.280 million – Rs.240 million)<br>Fair value adjustment – brand | 3,00,000<br><br>40,000<br>30,000 | (3,70,000)(c) |
| Goodwill (A + B – C) | | 65,000 |

*Working 6 – investment income*

| | **Rs.'000** |
|---|---|
| Alpha + Beta | 37,300 |
| Dividend received from Beta (75% x 40,000) | (30,000) |
| Profit on disposal recorded to be treated in accordance with Ind AS.109 | (4,500) |
| In consolidated statement of comprehensive income | 2,800 |

*Working 7 – finance costs*

| | **Rs.000** |
|---|---|
| Alpha + Beta | 1,33,000 |
| Finance cost of convertible loan notes incorrectly recorded by Alpha | (15,000) |
| Correct finance cost of convertible loan notes (W8) | 21,132 |
| In consolidated statement of comprehensive income | 1,39,132 |

*Working 8 – finance costs of convertible loan notes*

| | Rs.000 |
|---|---|
| Liability element of compound financial instrument at 1 April 2020 (15,000 x Rs.3·99) + (300,000 x Rs.0·681) | 2,64,150 |
| So, finance cost at 8% (264,150 x 0·08) | 21,132 |

*Working 9 – share of losses of associate*

| | **Rs.000** |
|---|---|
| Loss after tax of Gamma | (26,000) |
| (26,000) x 40% x 6/12 equals | (5,200) |
| Impairment of investment | (1,800) |
| | (7,000) |

*Working 10 – other comprehensive income*

| | Rs.'000 |
|---|---|
| Gain on revaluation of investment in Epsilon | 1,400 |
| Profit on disposal recorded to be treated in accordance with Ind AS 109 | 4,500 |
| | 5,900 |

Working 11 – *non-controlling interest in Beta*

| | Rs.'000 |
|---|---|
| Net profit of Beta | 85,000 |
| Unrealised profit on intercompany sales (375 + 270) (W2) | (645) |
| Extra depreciation and amortisation (W3) | (11,000) |
| Impairment of goodwill of Beta (W4) | (3,500) |
| | 69,855 |
| Non-controlling interest (25%) | 17,464 |

Working 12 – consolidated equity at 1 April 2020

| | Rs.'000 |
|---|---|
| Alpha | 5,40,000 |
| Beta – post acquisition per own records (390,000 – 300,000) | 90,000 |
| Extra depreciation and amortisation (11,000 (W3) x 0·5) | (5,500) |
| | 84,500 |
| Group share (75%) | 63,375 |
| Unrealised profit on opening inventory (1/4 x 2,100 | (525) |
| | 602,850 |

*Working 13 – non-controlling interest in opening equity of Beta*

| | Rs.'000 | Rs.'000 |
|---|---|---|
| Fair value of non-controlling interest at date of acquisition (W5)<br>Consolidated post-acquisition increase in equity from date of acquisition to start of the period (W12) | 84,500 | 80,000 |

| | | |
|---|---|---|
| Non-controlling interest (25%) | | 21,125 |
| Total | | 1,01,125 |

*Working 14 – equity element of convertible bonds*

| | Rs.'000 |
|---|---|
| Total issue proceeds | 3,00,000 |
| Liability component (W8) | (2,64,150) |
| Equity component | 35,850 |

**Illustration 13.7. Consolidated Financial Statements**

Alpha holds investments in Beta and Gamma. The Balance Sheets of the three entities at 30 September 2021 were as follows:

| | Alpha Rs.'000 | Beta Rs.'000 | Gamma Rs.'000 |
|---|---|---|---|
| **ASSETS** | | | |
| Non-current assets: | | | |
| Property, plant and equipment (Note 1) | 2,10,000 | 1,65,000 | 1,20,000 |
| Investments: | | | |
| – in Beta (Note 1) | 1,80,000 | Nil | Nil |
| – in Gamma (Note 3) | 52,000 | Nil | Nil |
| – in Sigma (Note 6) | 15,000 | nil | nil |
| | 4,57,000 | 1,65,000 | 1,20,000 |
| **Current Assets:** | | | |
| Inventories (Note 4) | 65,000 | 36,000 | 29,000 |
| Trade receivables (Note 5) | 55,000 | 38,000 | 35,000 |
| Cash and cash equivalents | 12,000 | 7,000 | 9,000 |
| Current Assets | 1,32,000 | 81,000 | 73,000 |
| Total Assets | 5,89,000 | 2,46,000 | 1,93,000 |

| EQUITY AND LIABILITIES | | | |
|---|---|---|---|
| Equity | | | |
| Share capital (Rs.1 shares) | 1,80,000 | 1,00,000 | 60,000 |
| Retained earnings | 1,83,000 | 67,000 | 64,000 |
| Other components of equity | 90,000 | 5,000 | Nil |
| Total equity | 4,53,000 | 1,72,000 | 1,24,000 |
| Non-current liabilities: | | | |
| Contingent consideration (Note 1) | 20,000 | Nil | Nil |
| Long-term borrowings (Note 8) | 50,000 | 35,000 | 30,000 |
| Deferred tax | 15,000 | 9,000 | 12,000 |
| Total non-current liabilities | 85,000 | 44,000 | 42,000 |
| Current liabilities: | | | |
| Trade and other payables | 34,000 | 23,000 | 21,000 |
| Short term borrowings | 17,000 | 7,000 | 6,000 |
| Total current liabilities | 51,000 | 30,000 | 27,000 |
| Total equity and liabilities | 5,89,000 | 2,46,000 | 1,93,000 |

***Note 1 – Alpha's investment in Beta***

On 1 April 2020 Alpha acquired 80 million shares in Beta by means of a share exchange. Alpha issued one share for every two shares acquired in Beta. On 1 April 2020 the market value of an Alpha share was Rs.4 and the market value of a Beta share was Rs.1·80. The terms of the business combination provide for an additional cash payment to the former shareholders of Beta on 30 June 2022 based on its post-acquisition financial performance in the first two years. since acquisition. The fair value of this additional payment was Rs.20 million on 1 April 2020. The post-acquisition performance of Beta was such that the fair value of this payment had increased to Rs.22 million by 30 September 2021. The investment in Beta and the non-current liabilities of Alpha at 30 September 2020 include Rs.20 million in respect of the additional payment due to be made on 30 June 2022.

On 1 April 2020 the individual financial statements of Beta showed the following reserves balances:

– Retained earnings Rs.41 million.

– Other components of equity Rs.3 million.

The directors of Alpha carried out a fair value exercise to measure the identifiable assets and liabilities of Beta at 1 April 2020. The following matters. emerged:

- A property, having a carrying amount of Rs.50 million (depreciable amount Rs.30 million), had a fair value of Rs.70 million (depreciable amount Rs.33 million). The estimated future economic life of the depreciable amount of the property at 1 April 2020 was 30 years. This property was still held by Beta at 30 September 2021.
- Plant and equipment, having a carrying amount of Rs.60 million, had an estimated market value of Rs.64 million. The estimated future economic life of the plant at 1 April 2020 was four years. This plant was still held by Beta at 30 September 2021.
- Inventory, having a carrying amount of Rs.30 million, had an estimated market value of Rs.31 million. This entire inventory had been sold since 1 April 2020.

The fair value adjustments have not been reflected in the individual financial statements of Beta. In the consolidated financial statements, the fair value adjustments will be regarded as temporary differences for the purposes of computing deferred tax. The rate of tax to apply to temporary differences (where required but see notes 3, 4, 6 and 7 below) is 20%.

It is the group policy to value the non-controlling interest in subsidiaries at the date of acquisition at fair value. The fair value of an equity share in Beta at 1 April 2020 can be used for this purpose.

***Note 2 – Impairment reviews – Beta***

On 1 April 2020 the directors of Alpha identified that Beta comprised five cash-generating units and allocated the goodwill arising on acquisition equally across each unit. No impairment of goodwill was apparent in the year ended 30 September 2020.

During the year ended 30 September 2021 four of the five cash-generating units performed very satisfactorily and no impairment of the goodwill allocated to these units had occurred. However, the performance of the other unit was below expectations. During the impairment review carried out at 30 September 2021 assets (excluding goodwill) having a carrying amount in the consolidated financial statements of Rs.50 million were allocated to this unit. The recoverable amount of these assets was estimated at Rs.52 million.

***Note 3 – Alpha's investment in Gamma***

On 1 October 2020 Alpha paid Rs.52 million for 40% of the equity shares of Gamma. The retained earnings of Gamma on 1 October 2020 were Rs.60 million. You can ignore any deferred taxation implications of the investment by Alpha in Gamma. The investment in Gamma has not suffered any impairment since 1 October 2020.

***Note 4 – Inter-company sale of inventories***

The inventories of Beta and Gamma at 30 September 2021 included components purchased from Alpha during the year at a cost of Rs.16 million to Beta and Rs.10 million to Gamma. Alpha generated a gross profit margin of 25% on the supply of these components. You can ignore any deferred tax implications of the information in this note.

***Note 5 – Trade receivables and payables***

The trade receivables of Alpha included Rs.5 million receivable from Beta and Rs.4 million receivable from Gamma in respect of the purchase of components (see Note 4). The trade payables of Beta and Gamma included equivalent amounts payable to Alpha.

***Note 6 – Alpha's investment in Sigma***

Alpha's investment in Sigma does not give Alpha sole control, joint control or significant influence. The investment was purchased on 1 January 2021 for Rs.15 million. The investment was classified as fair value through other comprehensive income. The fair value of the investment in Sigma on 30 September 2021 was Rs.16 million. In the tax jurisdiction in which Alpha is located unrealised profits on the revaluation of equity investments are not subject to current tax. Any such profits are taxed only when the investment is sold.

***Note 7 – Employees share option scheme***

On 1 October 2019 Alpha granted 5,000 share options to 1,000 key employees. The options are due to vest on 30 September 2023 provided the employees remain in employment at 30 September 2013. On 1 October 2019 the directors. of Alpha estimated that 90% of the key employees would satisfy the vesting condition. Actual employee turnover was such that this estimate was revised to 92% on 30 September 2020 and 93% on 30 September 2021.

At 1 October 2019 the fair value of each share option was estimated to be Rs.1·20. This estimate was revised to Rs.1·25 on 30 September 2020 and Rs.1·28 on 30 September 2021. You can ignore the deferred tax implications of the information in this note.

Alpha correctly recognised this transaction in the financial statements for the year ended 30 September 2020.

However, they have made no additional adjustments in the financial statements for the year ended 30 September 2021.

***Note 8 – Long-term borrowings***

On 1 October 2020 Alpha issued 50 million loan notes of Rs.1 each at par. The annual interest payable on these notes is 5 cents per note, payable in arrears. The notes are redeemable at par on 30 September 2025 or convertible (at the option of the note-holders.) into equity shares on that date. On 1 October 2020 investors in loan notes with no conversion option would have required an annual rate of return of 8%. On 1 October 2020 the directors. of Alpha included Rs.50 million in long-term borrowings in respect of the loan notes. The actual interest paid of Rs.2·5 million was charged as a finance cost in Alpha's income statement for the year ended 30 September 2021.

Relevant discount factors. are as follows:

| | 5% | 8% |
|---|---|---|
| Present value of Rs.1 payable at the end of year 5 | 78·4 paise | 68·1 paise |
| Cumulative present value of Rs.1 payable at the end of years. 1-5 | Rs.4·33 | Rs.3·99 |

***Note 9 – Modification of vehicles***

On 1 January 2021 legislation was passed requiring Alpha to carry out modifications to its motor vehicles to enable harmful emissions to be reduced. The modifications should have been completed by 30 June 2021 at an estimated cost to Alpha of Rs.3 million. In fact by 30 September 2021 none of the vehicles had been modified although they continued to be used. It is likely that Alpha will be fined Rs.5,00,000 per month for the illegal use of the vehicles. The directors. of Alpha are uncertain exactly when they will carry out the modifications but they intend to do so sometime during the year ended 30 September 2022. They expect that a fine will become payable very shortly as legal action has commenced against Alpha.

**Required:**

Prepare the consolidated Balance Sheet of Alpha at 30 September 2021.

(*ACCA UK - Adapted*)

**Solution**

Consolidated statement of financial position of Alpha at 30 September 2021

| | **Rs.'000** |
|---|---|
| **ASSETS** | |
| **Non-current assets:** | |
| Property, plant and equipment (2,10,000 + 1,65,000 + 19,850 + 2,500 (W1)) | 3,97,350 |
| Goodwill (W2) | 43,600 |
| Investment in associate (W9) | 52,600 |

| | |
|---|---|
| Other investments | 16,000 |
| | 5,09,550 |
| **Current Assets:** | |
| Inventories (65,000 + 36,000 – 4,000 (W5)) | 97,000 |
| Trade receivables (55,000 + 38,000 – 5,000 (inter-company)) | 88,000 |
| Cash and cash equivalents (12,000 + 7,000) | 19,000 |
| | 2,04,000 |
| Total Assets | 713,550 |
| **EQUITY AND LIABILITIES** | |
| Equity attributable to equity holders. of the parent | |
| Share capital | 1,80,000 |
| Retained earnings (W5) | 1,86,052 |
| Other components of equity (W8) | 99,785 |
| | 4,65,837 |
| Non-controlling interest (W4) | 39,496 |
| Total equity | 5,05,333 |
| **Non-current liabilities** | |
| Long-term borrowings (45,047 (W7) + 35,000) | 80,047 |
| Deferred tax (W10) | 28,670 |
| Total non-current liabilities | 1,08,717 |
| **Current liabilities:** | |
| Trade and other payables (34,000 + 23,000 – 5,000 (inter-company)) | 52,000 |
| Contingent consideration | 22,000 |
| Provision for fines | 1,500 |
| Short-term borrowings (17,000 + 7,000) | 24,000 |
| Total current liabilities | 99,500 |
| Total equity and liabilities | 7,13,550 |

## WORKINGS

### Working 1 – Net assets table – Beta:

| | 1 April 2020 Rs.'000 | Change Rs.'000 | 30 Sept 2021 Rs.'000 |
|---|---|---|---|
| Share capital | 1,00,000 | - | 1,00,000 |
| Retained earnings | 41,000 | 26,000 | 67,000 |
| Other components of equity | 3,000 | 2,000 | 5,000 |
| Property adjustment – see below | 20,000 | (150) | 19,850 |
| Plant and equipment adjustment – see below | 4,000 | (1,500) | 2,500 |
| Inventory adjustment | 1,000 | (1,000) | Nil |
| Deferred tax on fair value adjustments | 5,000 | 530 | (4,470) |
| Net assets for the consolidation | 164,000 | 25,880 | 189,880 |

The post-acquisition increase in net assets Rs.25·88 million (Rs.189·88 million – Rs.164 million). Rs.2 million of this increase relates to other components of equity, the balance of Rs.23·88 million relates to retained earnings.

**Note re: post-acquisition depreciation adjustments:**

For the property this is Rs.1,50,000 ((Rs.33 million – Rs.30 million) x 1·5/30). This makes the closing adjustment Rs.19·85 million (Rs.20 million – Rs.150,000).

For the plant and equipment this is Rs.1·5 million ((Rs.64 million – Rs.60 million) x 1·5/4). This makes the closing adjustment Rs.2·5 million (Rs.4 million – Rs.1·5 million).

### Working 2 – Goodwill on consolidation (Beta)

| | Rs.'000 |
|---|---|
| Cost of investment: | |
| Share exchange (80 million x ½ x Rs.4) | 1,60,000 |
| Contingent consideration | 20,000 |
| Fair value of non-controlling interest at date of acquisition (20 million x Rs.1·80) | 36,000 |
| | 2,16,000 |
| Net assets at 1 April 2020 (W1) | (1,64,000) |

| | |
|---|---|
| Goodwill before impairment<br>Impairment (W3) | 52,000<br>(8,400) |
| Goodwill after impairment | 43,600 |

**Working 3 – Impairment of goodwill:**

| | **Rs.'000** |
|---|---|
| Carrying value of assets in cash generating unit | 50,000 |
| Allocated goodwill (20% x Rs.52 million (W2)) | 10,400 |
| | 60,400 |
| Recoverable amount of assets in cash generating unit | (52,000) |
| Goodwill impairment | 8,400 |

**Working 4 – Non-controlling interest in Beta:**

| | Rs.'000 |
|---|---|
| Fair value at date of acquisition (W2) | 36,000 |
| 20% of post-acquisition increase in net assets (Rs.25·88 million (W1) | 5,176 |
| 20% of goodwill impairment (Rs.8·4 million – (W3)) | (1,680) |
| | 39,496 |

**Working 5 – Retained earnings**

| | Rs.'000 |
|---|---|
| Alpha | 1,83,000 |
| Charge for share-based payment for the period (W6) | (1,410) |
| Additional finance cost on loan notes (3,522 – 2,500 (W7)) | (1,022) |
| Provision for fines for illegal operation of vehicles | (1,500) |
| Increase in fair value of contingent consideration (Rs.22 million – Rs.20 million) | (2,000) |
| Beta (80% x Rs.23·88 million (W1)) | 19,104 |
| Gamma (40% x (64,000 – 60,000)) | 1,600 |
| Unrealised profits on sales to Beta (16,000 x 25%) | (4,000) |
| Unrealised profits on sales to Gamma (10,000 x 25% x 40%) | (1,000) |
| 80% of impairment of goodwill on acquisition of Beta (Rs.8·4 million (W3) x 80%) | (6,720) |
| | 186,052 |

**Working 6 – Share based payment charge**

| | Rs.'000 |
|---|---:|
| Expected total cost (5,000 x 1,000 x 93% x Rs.1·20) | 5,580 |
| Amount that should be recognised to date (2/4) | 2,790 |
| Recognised in draft financial statements (5,000 x 1,000 x 92% x Rs.1·20 x ¼) | (1,380) |
| So additional amount to recognise | 1,410 |

**Working 7 – Convertible loan notes**

| | Rs.'000 |
|---|---:|
| Liability element (Rs.2·5 million x 3·99 + Rs.50 million x 0·681) | 44,025 |
| Equity component (balancing figure) | 5,975 |
| | 50,000 |
| Opening liability | 44,025 |
| Finance cost for the period (8%) | 3,522 |
| Actual interest paid | (2,500) |
| Closing liability | 45047 |

**Working 8 – Other components of equity**

| | Rs.'000 |
|---|---:|
| Alpha | 90,000 |
| Addition re: revaluation of investment in Sigma (1,000 – 20% (deferred tax) x 1,000) | 800 |
| Addition re: share based payment (W6) | 1,410 |
| Addition re: convertible loan notes (W7) | 5,975 |
| Beta (80% x Rs.2 million (W1)) | 1,600 |
| | 99,785 |

**Working 9 – Investment in Gamma**

| | **Rs.'000** |
|---|---:|
| Cost | 52,000 |
| Share of post-acquisition profits (W5) | 1,600 |
| Unrealised profits (W5) | (1,000) |
| | 52,600 |

**Working 10 – Deferred tax**

| | Rs.'000 |
|---|---:|
| Alpha + Beta | 24,000 |
| On revaluation of investment in Sigma (W8) | 200 |
| On fair value adjustments (W11) | 4,470 |
| | 28,670 |

**Working 11 – Deferred tax on fair value adjustments:**

Fair value adjustments:

| | 1 April 2020 Rs.'000 | 30 September 2021 Rs.'000 |
|---|---:|---:|
| Land adjustment | 20,000 | 19,850 |
| Plant and equipment adjustment | 4,000 | 2,500 |
| Inventory adjustment | 1,000 | nil |
| Net taxable temporary differences | 25,000 | 22,350 |
| Related deferred tax (20%) | 5,000 | 4,470 |

## 13.8 COMPARATIVE SUMMARY ON CONSOLIDATION OF FINANCIAL STATEMENTS

| AS | IFRS | US GAAP | Ind AS |
|---|---|---|---|
| **Definition of subsidiary** | | | |
| Based on voting control or control over the composition of the board of directors. The existence of currently exercisable potential voting right is not taken into consideration | Control is presumed exist when parent owns directly or indirectly through subsidiaries more than one half of an entity's voting power. Control is defined as combination of power, exposure | Similar to IFRS. However, a bipolar consolidation model is used which distinguishes between a variable interest model and a voting interest model. Control may be direct or indirect | Control is presumed exist when parent owns directly or indirectly through subsidiaries more than one half of an entity's voting power. Control is defined as combination of power, exposure to returns and link between power and returns. |

| AS | IFRS | US GAAP | Ind AS |
|---|---|---|---|
| | to returns and link between power and returns.<br><br>Power arises from rights to direct the relevant activities.<br>Voting rights include substantive voting rights as well as currently exercisable potential voting rights, based on which a parent could have control over an entity in circumstances where it holds less than 50% of the voting rights of an entity | and may exist with a lesser percentage age of ownership voting rights. | Power arises from rights to direct the relevant activities.<br><br>Voting rights include substantive voting rights as well as currently exercisable potential voting rights, based on which a parent could have control over an entity in circumstances where it holds less than 50% of the voting rights of an entity |
| **Definition of associates**<br>Based on significant influence, presumed if 20% or greater interest or participation in entity's affairs | Based on significant influence, presumed if 20% or greater interest or participation in entity's affairs | Similar to IFRS, although the term equity investment is used instead of associate. | Similar to IFRS |
| **Presentation of associate results**<br>In consolidated financial statements equity method is used. Share of post-tax results is shown. In stand-alone financials ; at cost | In consolidated financial statements equity method is used. Share of post-tax results is shown. In stand-alone | In consolidated financial statements similar to IFRS | In consolidated financial statements equity method is used. Share of post-tax results is shown. In stand-alone financials ; at cost or fair value |

| AS | IFRS | US GAAP | Ind AS |
|---|---|---|---|
| less impairment | financials ; at cost or fair value in accordance with IFRS 9 | | in accordance with Ind AS 109 |
| **Joint venture definition**<br>Contractual arrangement whereby two or more parties undertake an economic activity which is subject to joint control<br>Exclusion if it meets the definition of a subsidiary | Contractual arrangement whereby two or more parties are bound by joint control of the arrangement.<br>Exclusion if investment is held for sale.<br>Joint arrangement can be either a<br>Joint operation or<br>Joint venture.<br>Joint control is the contractually agreed sharing of control of an arrangement,<br>which exists only when decisions about the relevant activities require the unanimous<br>consent of the parties sharing control. | A corporation owned and operated by small group of businesses as a separate and specific business or project for the mutual benefit of the members of the group. | Contractual arrangement whereby two or more parties are bound by joint control of the arrangement.<br>Exclusion if investment is held for sale.<br>Joint arrangement can be either a Joint operation or Joint venture.<br>Joint control is the contractually agreed sharing of control of an arrangement,<br>which exists only when decisions about the relevant activities require the unanimous<br>consent of the parties sharing control. |
| **Presentation**<br>In consolidated financial statements proportional consolidation is used;<br>In stand-alone | In consolidated financial statements<br>A joint operator shall account for the assets, | | In consolidated financial statements<br>A joint operator shall account for the assets, liabilities, revenues and expenses relating |

| AS | IFRS | US GAAP | Ind AS |
|---|---|---|---|
| financials; at cost less impairment | liabilities, revenues and expenses relating to its interest in a joint operation in accordance with the IFRSs applicable to the particular assets, liabilities, revenues and expenses.<br>A joint venturer shall recognise its interest in a joint venture as an investment and shall account for that investment using the equity method in accordance with IAS 28, *Investments in Associates and Joint Ventures.* | | to its interest in a joint operation in accordance with the Ind ASs applicable to the particular assets, liabilities, revenues and expenses.<br>A joint venturer shall recognise its interest in a joint venture as an investment and shall account for that investment using the equity method in accordance with Ind AS 28, *Investments in Associates and Joint Ventures* |

# SECTION IV

# Financial Reporting of Non-Banking Financial Companies

*Chapter 14*

# Financial Statements of Non-Banking Finance Companies

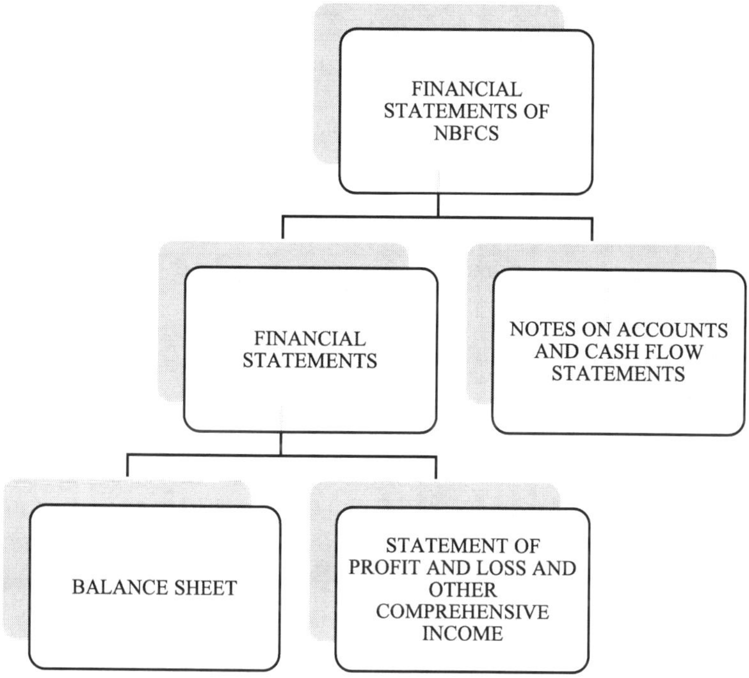


## 14.1 APPLICABILITY

Financial Statements for a Non-Banking Financial Company (NBFC) whose financial statements are drawn up in compliance of the Companies (Indian Accounting Standards) Rules, 2015.

According to rule 4(1),

...

(*iv*) Notwithstanding the requirement of clauses (*i*) to (*iii*), Non-Banking Financial Companies (NBFCs) shall comply with the Indian Accounting Standards (Ind ASs) in preparation of their financial statements and audit respectively, in the following manner, namely:

(*a*) The following NBFCs shall comply with the Indian Accounting Standards (Ind AS) for accounting periods beginning on or after the 1st April, 2018, with comparatives for the periods ending on 31st March, 2018, or thereafter-

(A) NBFCs having net worth of rupees five hundred crore or more;

(B) holding, subsidiary, joint venture or associate companies of companies covered under item (A), other than those already covered under clauses (*i*), (*ii*) and (*iii*) of sub-rule (1) of rule 4.

(*b*) The following NBFCs shall comply with the Indian Accounting Standards (Ind AS) for accounting periods beginning on or after the 1st April, 2019, with comparatives for the periods ending on 31stMarch, 2019, or thereafter-

(A) NBFCs whose equity or debt securities are listed or in the process of listing on any stock exchange in India or outside India and having net worth less than rupees five hundred crore;

(B) NBFCs, that are unlisted companies, having net worth of rupees two-hundred and fifty crore or more but less than rupees five hundred crore; and

(C) holding, subsidiary, joint venture or associate companies of companies covered under item (A) or item (B) of sub-clause (*b*), other than those already covered in clauses (*i*), (*ii*) and (*iii*) of sub-rule (1) or item (B) of sub-clause (*a*) of clause (*iv*).

*Explanation* - For the purposes of clause (*iv*), if in a group of Companies, some entities apply Accounting Standards specified in the Annexure to the Companies (Accounting Standards) Rules, 2006 and others apply accounting standards as specified in the Annexure to these rules, in such cases, for the purpose of individual financial statements, the entities should apply respective standards applicable to them. For preparation of consolidated financial statements, the following conditions are to be followed, namely:

(i) where an NBFC is a parent (at ultimate level or at intermediate level), and prepares consolidated financial statements as per Accounting Standards specified in the Annexure to the Companies (Accounting Standards) Rules, 2006, and its subsidiaries, associates and joint ventures, if covered by clause (i), (ii) and (iii) of sub-rule (1) has to provide the relevant financial statement data in accordance with the accounting policies followed by the parent company for consolidation purposes (until the NBFC is covered under clause (iv) of sub-rule (1).

(ii) where a parent is a company covered under clause (i), (ii) and (iii) of sub-rule (1) and has an NBFC subsidiary, associate or a joint venture, the parent has to prepare Ind AS-compliant consolidated financial statements and the NBFC subsidiary, associate and a joint venture has to provide the relevant financial statement data in accordance with the accounting policies followed by the parent company for consolidation purposes (until the NBFC is covered under clause (*iv*) of sub-rule (1).

## 14.2 STRUCTURE OF FINANCIAL STATEMENTS UNDER COMPANIES ACT, 2013 SCHEDULE III, DIVISION III

The Structure of Division III of Schedule III is shown as under:

A. General Instructions for Preparation of Financial Statements of a Non-Banking Financial Company (NBFC) that is required to comply with Ind AS ('General Instructions for Preparation of Financial Statements')

B. Part I – Form of Balance Sheet and Statement of Changes in Equity

C. Part I Notes – General Instructions for Preparation of Balance Sheet

D. Part II – Form of Statement of Profit and Loss

E. Part II Notes – General Instructions for Preparation of Statement of Profit and Loss

F. Part III – General Instructions for the Preparation of Consolidated Financial Statements

This is further explained in the chart below.

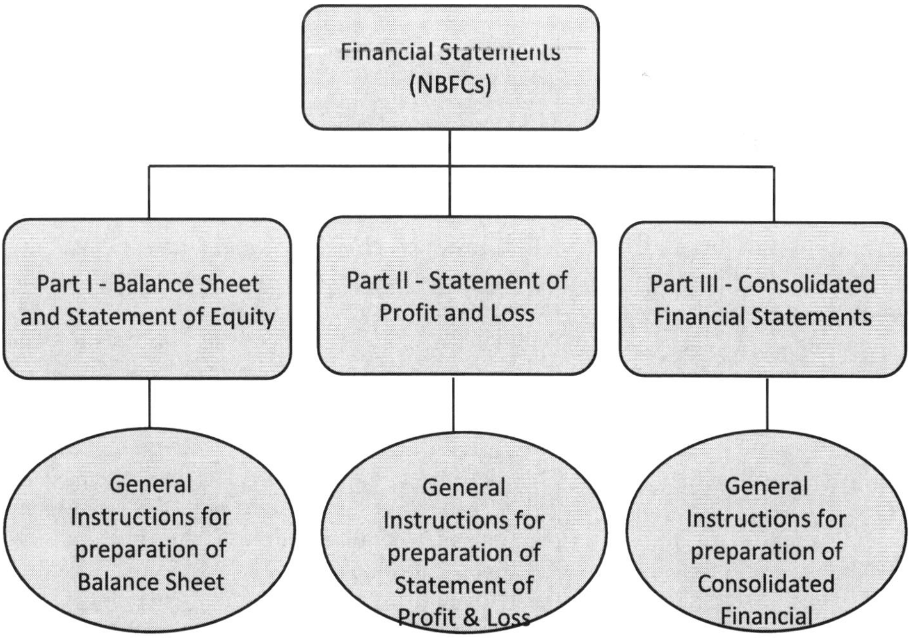

According to paragraph 1 of General Instructions, every Non-Banking Financial company as defined in the Companies (Indian Accounting Standards) (Amendment) Rules, 2016 to which Indian Accounting Standards apply, shall prepare its financial statements in accordance with this Schedule or with such modification as may be required under certain circumstances.

According to ICAI Guidance note (Revised January, 2022 Edition) on Schedule III, Division III, Financial Statements would include the following:

- Balance Sheet,
- Statement of Changes in Equity for the period,
- Statement of Profit and Loss for the period and Notes.
- Cash Flow Statement.

| | |
|---|---|
| ***Balance Sheet*** | • Division III provides a format of the balance sheet and sets out the minimum requirements of disclosure on the face of the balance sheet for NBFCs.<br>• Items presented in the balance sheet are to be classified as financial and non-financial.<br>• It permits NBFCs to avail of the option of presenting assets and liabilities in the order of liquidity, as provided by Ind AS 1, *Presentation of Financial Statements*.<br>• It requires an NBFC to disclose such information that enables users of its financial statements to evaluate the NBFC's objectives, policies and processes for managing capital. |
| ***Statement of changes in Equity*** | • The statement of changes in equity would reconcile opening to closing amounts for each component of equity including reserves and surplus and items of other comprehensive income.<br>• NBFCs are specifically required to disclose the statutory reserves as part of 'other equity' in the statement of changes in equity.<br>• Additionally, the conditions or restrictions for distribution attached to statutory reserves have to be separately disclosed in the notes as stipulated by the relevant statute. |
| ***Statement of Profit & Loss*** | • The division provides a format of the statement of profit and loss and sets out the minimum requirements of disclosure on the face of the statement of profit and loss.<br>• Items comprising 'revenue from operations' and 'other comprehensive income' have to be disclosed on the face of the statement of profit and loss. |

| *Cash flow statement* | • shall be prepared in accordance with the requirements of the relevant Ind AS. |
|---|---|

### 14.2.1 Disclosure Requirements in addition and not in substitution of Disclosure Requirements prescribed in Ind AS

In accordance with paragraph 2 of General Instructions, where compliance with the requirements of relevant Act, Regulations, Guidelines or Circulars issued by the relevant regulator from time to time including Indian Accounting Standards (Ind AS) (**except the option of presenting assets and liabilities in accordance with current, non-current classification as provided by relevant Ind AS**) as applicable to the NBFCs require any change in treatment or disclosure including addition, amendment, substitution or deletion in the head or sub-head or any changes inter se, in the financial statements or statements forming part thereof, the same shall be made and the requirements under this Schedule shall stand modified accordingly.

Here the Guidance Note of ICAI on Schedule III, Division III, highlights the changes related to leases as promulgated under Ind AS 116, Leases. According to the Guidance Note, accounting and disclosure requirements have undergone changes differentiating between lease arrangements as an 'Operating Lease' and 'Finance Lease' for the lessees. It requires recognition of a 'Right-to-use' (ROU) and a corresponding lease liability where the lessee, at the commencement date, has a financial obligation to make lease payments to the lessor for its right to use the underlying asset during the lease term.

While the requirements (including presentation and disclosures) for lessor remains substantially unchanged from Ind AS 17, the requirements for lessee changes significantly as compared to Ind AS 17. An entity shall present and disclose rights and obligations arising from lease arrangements as per Ind AS 116 and the requirements under this schedule stand modified accordingly.

Paragraph 3. The disclosure requirements specified in this Schedule are in addition to and not in substitution of the disclosure requirements specified in the Indian Accounting Standards. Additional disclosures specified in the Indian Accounting Standards shall be made in the Notes or by way of additional statement or statements unless required to be disclosed on the face of the Financial Statements. Similarly, all other disclosures as required by the Companies Act, 2013 shall be made in the Notes in addition to the requirements set out in this Schedule.

### 14.2.2 Current/non-current classification

Paragraph 2 of General Instructions provides an exception related to the option of presenting assets and liabilities in accordance with current, non-current classification as provided in Ind AS 1.

According to Paragraph 60 of Ind AS 1, an entity shall present current and non-current assets, and current and non-current liabilities, as separate classifications in its balance sheet except if a presentation based on liquidity provides information that is reliable and more relevant. The format prescribed by Division III is currently a liquidity-based format. Thus, the assets and liabilities are classified as financial and non-financial instead of current, noncurrent classification as required by Division I and Division II of Schedule III.

However, in line with requirements in Paragraph 61 of Ind AS 1 whichever method of presentation is adopted, an entity shall disclose the amount expected to be recovered or settled after more than twelve months for each asset and liability line item.

Disclosure regarding recovery or settlement within 12 months after the reporting date (current) and more than 12 months after the reporting date (non–current) shall be provided separately in the financial statements.

(*ICAI Guidance Note on Schedule III, Division III*).

### 14.2.3 Information to be provided in Notes to Accounts

(i) Notes shall contain information in addition to that presented in the Financial Statements and shall provide where required-

  (a) narrative descriptions or disaggregation of items recognized in those statements; and

  (b) information about items that do not qualify for recognition in those statements.

(ii) Each item on the face of the Balance Sheet, Statement of Changes in Equity and Statement of Profit and Loss shall be cross-referenced to any related information in the Notes. In preparing the Financial Statements including the Notes, a balance shall be maintained between providing excessive details that may not assist users of Financial Statements and not providing important information as a result of too much aggregation.

According to ICAI Guidance Note, disclosures required under Ind AS (for e.g., fair value measurement reconciliation, fair value hierarchy, risk management and capital management, disclosure of interests in other entities, components of other comprehensive income, reconciliations on first-time adoption of Ind AS, etc.) shall be made in the Notes or by way of additional statement(s) unless required to be disclosed on the face of the Financial Statements.

### 14.2.4 Reporting of comparatives related to immediately preceding reporting period

Financial Statements shall contain the corresponding amounts (comparatives) for the immediately preceding reporting period for all items shown in the Financial

Statements including Notes except in the case of first Financial Statements after incorporation.

### 14.2.5 Materiality

Financial Statements shall disclose all 'material' items, i.e. the items if they could, individually or collectively, influence the economic decisions that users make on the basis of the financial statements. Materiality depends on the size or nature of the item or a combination of both, to be judged in the particular circumstances.

According to ICAI Guidance Note, NBFCs are required to disclose all 'material' items in their financial statements i.e., the items if they could, individually or collectively, influence the economic decisions that users make on the bases of financial statements. Materiality depends on the size and nature of the item judged in particular circumstances. However, while preparing the statement of profit and loss, it specifies that an NBFC should disclose a note for any item of 'other income' or 'other expenditure' which exceeds 1 per cent of the total income, in addition to the consideration of materiality.

### 14.2.6 Definition of terms

With respect to Financial Statements related to NBFCs, the terms used shall have the same meanings assigned to them in Indian Accounting Standards. For example, the terms such as 'associate', 'related parties', etc. will have the same meaning as defined in Ind AS notified under the Companies Ind AS Rules. For any terms which are not specifically defined in Ind AS, attention may also be drawn to the Framework for the Preparation and Presentation of Financial Statements in accordance with Indian Accounting Standards ('Ind AS Framework') issued by ICAI. However, if any term is not defined in the Ind AS Framework, the entity may consider the principles described in provisions of Ind AS 8 for developing and applying an accounting policy.

### 14.2.7 Specific disclosures for NBFCs in addition to requirements of Schedule

Where any Act, Regulation, Guidelines or Circulars issued by the relevant regulators from time to time requires specific disclosures to be made in the standalone financial statements of an NBFC, the said disclosures shall be made in addition to those required under this Schedule.

The NBFCs preparing financial statements as per this Schedule may change the order of presentation of line items on the face of financial statements or order of line items within the schedules in order of liquidity, if appropriate, considering the operations performed by the NBFC.

Note: This Schedule sets out the minimum requirements for disclosure on the face of the Financial Statements, i.e., Balance Sheet, Statement of Changes in Equity for the period, the Statement of Profit and Loss for the period (The term 'Statement of

Profit and Loss' has the same meaning as 'Profit and Loss Account') and Notes. Cash flow statement shall be prepared, where applicable, in accordance with the requirements of the relevant Indian Accounting Standard.

### 14.2.8 Unit of measurement

According to Division III to Schedule III, the same unit of measurement needs to be uniformly used across the Financial Statements. Such requirement should be taken to imply that all figures disclosed in the Financial Statements including Notes should be of the same denomination, except where a different denomination may be required, say for ratios or metrics in order to increase its understandability.

### 14.2.9 Rounding off

Rounding off requirements under Schedule III, Division III are summarized in the table below:

| Item | Narrative |
|---|---|
| ***Total Income less than Rs. 100 crores*** | Round off to the nearest hundreds, thousands, lakhs or millions or decimal thereof. |
| ***Total Income equal to or more than Rs. 100 crores*** | Round off to the nearest lakhs, millions or crores, or decimal thereof. |

## 14.3 PART I — BALANCE SHEET

Name of the Non-Banking Financial Company........................

Balance Sheet as at ..........................

| | Particulars | Note No. | Figures as at the end of current reporting period | Figures as at the end of the previous reporting period |
|---|---|---|---|---|
| | 1 | | 2 | 3 |
| | **ASSETS** | | | |
| (1) | **Financial Assets** | | | |
| (a) | Cash and cash equivalents | | | |
| (b) | Bank Balance other than (a) above | | | |
| (c) | Derivative financial instruments | | | |

| | Particulars | Note No. | Figures as at the end of current reporting period | Figures as at the end of the previous reporting period |
|---|---|---|---|---|
| | 1 | | 2 | 3 |
| (d) | Receivables | | | |
| | (I) Trade Receivables | | | |
| | (II) Other Receivables | | | |
| (e) | Loans | | | |
| (f) | Investments | | | |
| (g) | Other Financial assets (to be specified) | | | |
| | | | | |
| (2) | **Non-financial Assets** | | | |
| (a) | Inventories | | | |
| (b) | Current tax assets (Net) | | | |
| (c) | Deferred tax Assets (Net) | | | |
| (d) | Investment Property | | | |
| (e) | Biological assets other than bearer plants | | | |
| (f) | Property, Plant and Equipment | | | |
| (g) | Capital work-in-progress | | | |
| (h) | Intangible assets under development | | | |
| (i) | Goodwill | | | |
| (j) | Other Intangible assets | | | |
| (k) | Other non - financial assets (to be specified) | | | |

| | Particulars | Note No. | Figures as at the end of current reporting period | Figures as at the end of the previous reporting period |
|---|---|---|---|---|
| | 1 | | 2 | 3 |
| | Total Assets | | | |
| | **LIABILITIES AND EQUITY** | | | |
| | **LIABILITIES** | | | |
| **(1)** | **Financial Liabilities** | | | |
| (a) | Derivative financial instruments | | | |
| (b) | Payables | | | |
| | (I)Trade Payables | | | |
| | (i) total outstanding dues of micro enterprises and small enterprises | | | |
| | (ii) total outstanding dues of creditors other than micro enterprises and small enterprises | | | |
| | (II) Other Payables | | | |
| | (i) total outstanding dues of micro enterprises and small enterprises | | | |
| | (ii) total outstanding dues of creditors other than micro enterprises and small enterprises | | | |
| (c) | Debt Securities | | | |
| (d) | Borrowings (Other than Debt Securities) | | | |

| | Particulars | Note No. | Figures as at the end of current reporting period | Figures as at the end of the previous reporting period |
|---|---|---|---|---|
| | 1 | | 2 | 3 |
| (e) | Deposits | | | |
| (f) | Subordinated Liabilities | | | |
| (g) | Other financial liabilities (to be specified) | | | |
| (2) | Non-Financial Liabilities | | | |
| (a) | Current tax liabilities (Net) | | | |
| (b) | Provisions | | | |
| (c) | Deferred tax liabilities (Net) | | | |
| (d) | Other non-financial liabilities (to be specified) | | | |
| | | | | |
| (3) | EQUITY | | | |
| (a) | Equity Share capital | | | |
| (b) | Other Equity | | | |
| | **Total Liabilities and Equity** | | | |

**See accompanying notes to the financial statements**

## 14.4 STATEMENT OF CHANGES IN EQUITY

**Name of the Non-Banking Financial Company……………………**

**Statement of Changes in Equity for the period ended ……………………**

**(Rupees in…….)**

### A. Equity Share Capital

### (1) Current reporting period

| Balance at the beginning of the current reporting period | Changes in Equity Share Capital due to prior period errors | Restated balance at the beginning of the current reporting period | Changes in equity share capital during the current year | Balance at the end of the current reporting period |
|---|---|---|---|---|
| | | | | |

### (2) Previous reporting period

| Balance at the beginning of the previous reporting period | Changes in Equity Share Capital due to prior period errors | Restated balance at the beginning of the previous reporting period | Changes in equity share capital during the previous year | Balance at the end of the previous reporting period |
|---|---|---|---|---|
| | | | | |

### B. Other Equity

### 1) Current reporting period

| Balance at the beginning of the current reporting period | Changes in Equity Share Capital due to prior period errors | Restated balance at the beginning of the current reporting period | Changes in equity share capital during the current year | Balance at the end of the current reporting period |
|---|---|---|---|---|
| | | | | |

### 2) Previous reporting period

| Balance at the beginning of the previous reporting period | Changes in Equity Share Capital due to prior period errors | Restated balance at the beginning of the previous reporting period | Changes in equity share capital during the previous year | Balance at the end of the previous reporting period |
|---|---|---|---|---|
| | | | | |

B. **Other Equity**

**(1) Current reporting period**

| | **Share application money pending allotment** | **Equity component of compound financial instruments** | **Reserves & surplus - Capital Reserve** | **Reserves & surplus - Securities Premium** | **Reserves & Surplus – Other reserves (specify nature)** | **Reserves & surplus - Retained earnings** |
|---|---|---|---|---|---|---|
| Balance at the beginning of the current reporting period | | | | | | |
| Changes in accounting policy or prior period errors | | | | | | |
| Restated balance at the beginning of the current reporting period | | | | | | |
| Total Comp-rehensive Income for the current year | | | | | | |
| Dividends | | | | | | |
| Transfer to retained earnings | | | | | | |
| Any other | | | | | | |

| | Share application money pending allotment | Equity component of compound financial instruments | Reserves & surplus - Capital Reserve | Reserves & surplus - Securities Premium | Reserves & Surplus – Other reserves (specify nature) | Reserves & surplus - Retained earnings |
|---|---|---|---|---|---|---|
| change (to be specified) | | | | | | |
| Balance at the end of the current reporting period | | | | | | |

| Debt instruments through Other Comp-rehensive Income | Equity Instruments through Other Comp-rehensive Income | Effective portion of Cash Flow Hedges | Reva-luation Surplus | Exchange differences on trans-lating the financial statements of a foreign operation | Other items of Other Compre-hensive Income (specify nature) | Money received against share warrants | Total |
|---|---|---|---|---|---|---|---|
| | | | | | | | |
| | | | | | | | |
| | | | | | | | |
| | | | | | | | |
| | | | | | | | |
| | | | | | | | |
| | | | | | | | |

**(2) Previous reporting period**

| | **Share application money pending allotment** | **Equity component of compound financial instruments** | **Reserves & surplus - Capital Reserve** | **Reserves & surplus - Securities premium** | **Reserves & Surplus – Other reserves (specify nature)** | **Reserves & surplus - Retained earnings** |
|---|---|---|---|---|---|---|
| Balance at the beginning of the current reporting period | | | | | | |
| Changes in accounting policy or prior period errors | | | | | | |
| Restated balance at the beginning of the current reporting period | | | | | | |
| Total Comp-rehensive Income for the current year | | | | | | |
| Dividends | | | | | | |
| Transfer to retained earnings | | | | | | |
| Any other change (to be specified) | | | | | | |
| Balance at the end of the current reporting period | | | | | | |

| Debt instruments through Other Comprehensive Income | Equity Instruments through Other Comprehensive Income | Effective portion of Cash Flow Hedges | Revaluation Surplus | Exchange differences on translating the financial statements of a foreign operation | Other items of Other Comprehensive Income (specify nature) | Money received against share warrants | Total |
|---|---|---|---|---|---|---|---|
| | | | | | | | |
| | | | | | | | |
| | | | | | | | |
| | | | | | | | |
| | | | | | | | |

**Note**: Re-measurement of defined benefit plans and fair value changes relating to own credit risk of financial liabilities designated at fair value through profit or loss shall be recognised as a part of retained earnings with separate disclosure of such items along with the relevant amounts in the Notes or shall be shown as a separate column under Reserves and Surplus.

## 14.5 ACCOUNTING STANDARDS

### 14.5.1 Ind AS 32: Financial Instruments Presentation

It applies to the

(*a*) classification of financial instruments, from the perspective of the issuer, into financial assets, financial liabilities and equity instruments.

(*b*) the classification of related interest, dividends, losses and gains.

(*c*) and the circumstances in which financial assets and financial liabilities should be offset.

*The principles of this Standard complement the principles for recognizing and measuring financial assets and financial liabilities in Ind AS 109 Financial Instruments and for disclosing information about them in Ind AS 107 Financial Instruments: Disclosures.*

The Standard shall be applied to those contracts to buy or sell a non-financial item that can be settled net in cash or another financial instrument, or by exchanging financial instruments, as if the contracts were financial instruments, with the exception of contracts that were entered into and continue to be held for the purpose of the receipt or delivery of a non-financial item in accordance with the entity's expected purchase, sale or usage requirements. However, this standard shall be applied to those contracts that an entity designates as measured at fair value through profit or loss in accordance with the provisions of Ind AS 109.

### 14.5.1.1 Definitions

***A Financial Instrument*** is any contract that gives rise to a financial asset of one entity and a financial liability or equity instrument of another entity.

***A Financial*** *Asset* comprises of the following:

(*a*) cash

(*b*) equity instrument of another entity

(*c*) contractual right to receive cash or another financial assets from an entity

(*d*) contractual right to exchange financial assets or financial liabilities with another entity under the conditions that are potentially favourable to the entity

(*e*) a contract which will be settled with the entity's own equity instruments and is

- (*i*) a derivative that will or may be settled other than by the exchange of a fixed amount of cash or another financial asset for a fixed number of the entity's own equity instrument
- (*ii*) a non-derivative for which the entity is or may be obliged to receive a variable number of its own equity instruments

***A Financial liability*** constitutes the following:

(*a*) Contractual obligation to deliver cash or another financial asset to an entity

(*b*) Contractual obligation to Exchange financial assets or financial liabilities with another entity under conditions that are potentially unfavourable to the entity

(*c*) A contract which will be settled with the entity's own equity instruments and is:

- (*i*) A derivatives that will or may be settled other than by the exchange of a fixed amount of cash or another financial asset for a fixed number of the entity's own equity instruments.
- (*ii*) A non-derivative for which the entity is or may be obliged to deliver a variable number of its own equity instruments

***An equity instrument*** is any contract that evidences a residual interest in the assets of an entity after deducting all of its liabilities

***Fair value*** is the price that would be received to sell an asset or paid to transfer a liability in an orderly transaction between market participants at the measurement date. (See Ind AS 113, *Fair Value Measurement*.)

***A puttable instrument*** is a financial instrument that gives the holder the right to put the instrument back to the issuer for cash or another financial asset or is automatically put back to the issuer on the occurrence of an uncertain future event or the death or retirement of the instrument holder.

#### 14.5.1.2 Presentation

The issuer of a financial instrument shall classify the instrument, or its component parts, on initial recognition as a financial liability, a financial asset or an equity instrument in accordance with the substance of the contractual arrangement and the definitions of a financial liability, a financial asset and an equity instrument.

When an issuer applies the definitions to determine whether a financial instrument is an equity instrument rather than a financial liability, the instrument is an equity instrument if, and only if, both conditions (a) and (b) below are met.

(*a*) The instrument includes no contractual obligation:

(*i*) to deliver cash or another financial asset to another entity; or

(*ii*) to exchange financial assets or financial liabilities with another entity under conditions that are potentially unfavourable to the issuer.

(*b*) If the instrument will or may be settled in the issuer's own equity instruments, it is:

(*i*) a non-derivative that includes no contractual obligation for the issuer to deliver a variable number of its own equity instruments; or

(*ii*) a derivative that will be settled only by the issuer exchanging a fixed amount of cash or another financial asset for a fixed number of its own equity instruments.

For this purpose, rights, options, or warrants to acquire a fixed number of the entity's own equity instruments for a fixed amount of any currency are equity instruments if the entity offers the rights, options, or warrants pro rata to all of its existing owners of the same class of its own non-derivative equity instruments.

#### 14.5.1.3 Puttable Instruments

A puttable financial instrument includes a contractual obligation for the issuer to repurchase or redeem that instrument for cash or another financial asset on exercise of the put. As an exception to the definition of a financial liability, an instrument that includes such an obligation is classified as an equity instrument if it has all the following features:

(*a*) It entitles the holder to a pro rata share of the entity's net assets in the event of the entity's liquidation. The entity's net assets are those assets that remain after deducting all other claims on its assets. A pro rata share is determined by:

(*i*) dividing the entity's net assets on liquidation into units of equal amount; and (*ii*) multiplying that amount by the number of the units held by the financial instrument holder.

(*b*) The instrument is in the class of instruments that is subordinate to all other classes of instruments. To be in such a class the instrument:

  (*i*) has no priority over other claims to the assets of the entity on liquidation, and

  (*ii*) does not need to be converted into another instrument before it is in the class of instruments that is subordinate to all other classes of instruments.

(*c*) All financial instruments in the class of instruments that is subordinate to all other classes of instruments have identical features. For example, they must all be puttable, and the formula or other method used to calculate the repurchase or redemption price is the same for all instruments in that class.

(*d*) Apart from the contractual obligation for the issuer to repurchase or redeem the instrument for cash or another financial asset, the instrument does not include any contractual obligation to deliver cash or another financial asset to another entity, or to exchange financial assets or financial liabilities with another entity under conditions that are potentially unfavourable to the entity, and it is not a contract that will or may be settled in the entity's own equity instruments as set out in sub-paragraph (b) of the definition of a financial liability.

(*e*) The total expected cash flows attributable to the instrument over the life of the instrument are based substantially on the profit or loss, the change in the recognised net assets or the change in the fair value of the recognised and unrecognised net assets of the entity over the life of the instrument (excluding any effects of the instrument)

Also, for an instrument to be classified as an equity instrument, in addition to the instrument having all the above features, the issuer must have no other financial instrument or contract that has:

(*a*) total cash flows based substantially on the profit or loss, the change in the recognised net assets or the change in the fair value of the recognised and unrecognized net assets of the entity (excluding any effects of such instrument or contract) and

(*b*) the effect of substantially restricting or fixing the residual return to the puttable instrument holders.

(*c*) Further, some financial instruments include a contractual obligation for the issuing entity to deliver to another entity a pro rata share of its net assets only on liquidation.

(*d*) The obligation arises because liquidation either is certain to occur and outside the control of the entity (for example, a limited life entity) or is uncertain to occur but is at the option of the instrument holder. As an exception to the definition of a financial liability, an instrument that includes such an obligation is classified as an equity instrument if it has all the following features:

(*a*) It entitles the holder to a pro rata share of the entity's net assets in the event of the entity's liquidation. The entity's net assets are those assets that remain after deducting all other claims on its assets. A pro rata share is determined by:

(*i*) dividing the net assets of the entity on liquidation into units of equal amount; and

(*ii*) multiplying that amount by the number of the units held by the financial instrument holder.

(*b*) The instrument is in the class of instruments that is subordinate to all other classes of instruments. To be in such a class the instrument:

(*i*) has no priority over other claims to the assets of the entity on liquidation, and

(*ii*) does not need to be converted into another instrument before it is in the class of instruments that is subordinate to all other classes of instruments.

(*c*) All financial instruments in the class of instruments that is subordinate to all other classes of instruments must have an identical contractual obligation for the issuing entity to deliver a pro rata share of its net assets on liquidation.

For an instrument to be classified as an equity instrument, in addition to the instrument having all the above features, the issuer must have no other financial instrument or contract that has:

(*a*) total cash flows based substantially on the profit or loss, the change in the recognised net assets or the change in the fair value of the recognised and unrecognized net assets of the entity (excluding any effects of such instrument or contract) and

(*b*) the effect of substantially restricting or fixing the residual return to the instrument holders.

For the purposes of applying this condition, the entity shall not consider non financial contracts with a holder of an instrument described in paragraph 16C that have contractual terms and conditions that are similar to the contractual terms and conditions of an equivalent contract that might occur between a non-instrument holder and the issuing entity. If the entity cannot determine that this condition is met, it shall not classify the instrument as an equity instrument.

#### *14.5.1.4 Substance over legal form*

The substance of a financial instrument, rather than its legal form, governs its classification in the entity's balance sheet. Substance and legal form are commonly consistent, but not always. Some financial instruments take the legal form of equity but are liabilities in substance and others may combine features associated with equity instruments and features associated with financial liabilities.

#### 14.5.1.5 Compound Financial Instruments

The issuer of a non-derivative financial instrument shall evaluate the terms of the financial instrument to determine whether it contains both a liability and an equity component. Such components shall be classified separately as financial liabilities, financial assets or equity instruments.

An entity recognizes separately the components of a financial instrument that

(*a*) creates a financial liability of the entity and

(*b*) grants an option to the holder of the instrument to convert it into an equity instrument of the entity.

For example, a bond or similar instrument convertible by the holder into a fixed number of ordinary shares of the entity is a compound financial instrument. From the perspective of the entity, such an instrument comprises two components: a financial liability (a contractual arrangement to deliver cash or another financial asset) and an equity instrument (a call option granting the holder the right, for a specified period of time, to convert it into a fixed number of ordinary shares of the entity).

Accordingly, in all cases, the entity presents the liability and equity components separately in its balance sheet.

Classification of the liability and equity components of a convertible instrument is not revised as a result of a change in the likelihood that a conversion option will be exercised, even when exercise of the option may appear to have become economically advantageous to some holders. Holders may not always act in the way that might be expected because, for example, the tax consequences resulting from conversion may differ among holders.

Furthermore, the likelihood of conversion will change from time to time. The entity's contractual obligation to make future payments remains outstanding until it is extinguished through conversion, maturity of the instrument or some other transaction.

Ind AS 109 deals with the measurement of financial assets and financial liabilities. Equity instruments are instruments that evidence a residual interest in the assets of an entity after deducting all of its liabilities. Therefore, when the initial carrying amount of a compound financial instrument is allocated to its equity and liability components, the equity component is assigned the residual amount after deducting from the fair value of the instrument as a whole the amount separately determined for the liability component.

The value of any derivative features (such as a call option) embedded in the compound financial instrument other than the equity component (such as an equity conversion option) is included in the liability component. The sum of the carrying amounts assigned to the liability and equity components on initial recognition is always equal to the fair value that would be ascribed to the instrument as a whole.

No gain or loss arises from initially recognising the components of the instrument separately.

Under the approach described in paragraph 31, the issuer of a bond convertible into ordinary shares first determines the carrying amount of the liability component by measuring the fair value of a similar liability (including any embedded non-equity derivative features) that does not have an associated equity component. The carrying amount of the equity instrument represented by the option to convert the instrument into ordinary shares is then determined by deducting the fair value of the financial liability from the fair value of the compound financial instrument as a whole.

#### *14.5.1.6 Treasury Shares*

If an entity re-acquires its own equity instruments, those instruments (treasury shares) shall be deducted from equity. No gain or loss shall be recognised in profit or loss on the purchase, sale, issue or cancellation of an entity's own equity instruments. Such treasury shares may be acquired and held by the entity or by other members of the consolidated group. Consideration paid or received shall be recognized directly in equity.

#### *14.5.1.7 Interest, dividends, losses and gains*

Interest, dividends, losses and gains relating to a financial instrument or a component that is a financial liability shall be recognised as income or expense in profit or loss. Distributions to holders of an equity instrument shall be debited by the entity directly to equity, net of any related income tax benefit. Transaction costs of an equity transaction shall be accounted for as a deduction from equity net of any related income tax benefit

#### *14.5.1.8 Offsetting financial assets with Financial liabilities*

A financial asset and a financial liability shall be offset and the net amount presented in the balance sheet when an entity:

(*a*) Currently has a legally enforceable right to set off the recognised amounts, and

(*b*) Intends either to settle on a net basis, or to realise the asset and settle the liability simultaneously.

In accounting for a transfer of a financial asset that does not qualify for derecognition, the entity shall not offset the transferred asset and the associated liability.

The conditions set out above are generally not satisfied and offsetting is usually inappropriate when:

(*a*) several different financial instruments are used to emulate the features of a single financial instrument (a 'synthetic instrument')

(*b*) financial assets and financial liabilities arise from financial instruments having the same primary risk exposure (for example, assets and liabilities within a portfolio of forward contracts or other derivative instruments) but involve different counterparties;

(*c*) financial or other assets are pledged as collateral for non-recourse financial liabilities;

(*d*) financial assets are set aside in trust by a debtor for the purpose of discharging an obligation without those assets having been accepted by the creditor in settlement of the obligation (for example, a sinking fund arrangement); or

(*e*) obligations incurred as a result of events giving rise to losses are expected to be recovered from a third party by virtue of a claim made under an insurance contract.

## 14.5.2 Ind AS 109: Financial Instruments

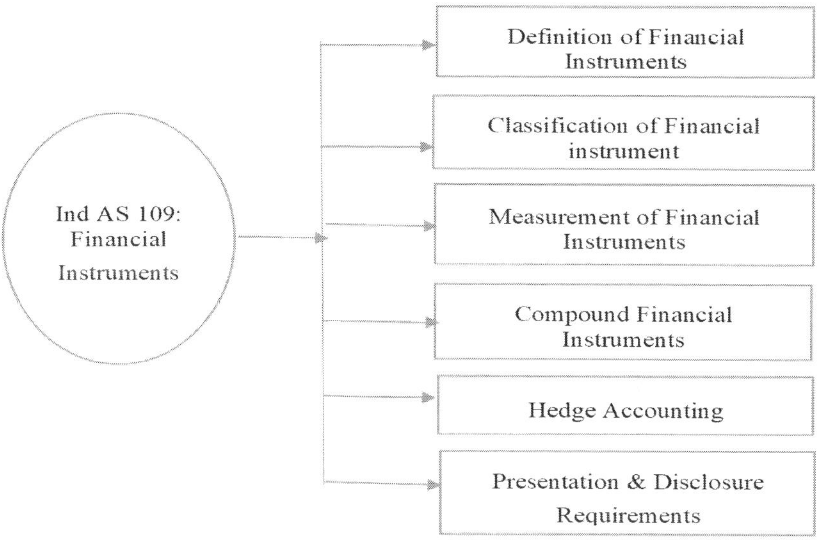


The salient features of the relevant sections of the Standard are summarized below.

### *14.5.2.1 Applicability*

This Standard shall be applicable to all types of financial instruments and applied by all entities except:

(a) those **interests in subsidiaries, associates and joint ventures** that are accounted for in accordance with Ind AS110 *Consolidated Financial Statements*, Ind AS 27 *Separate Financial Statements* or Ind AS 28 *Investments in Associates and Joint Ventures*.

However, in some cases, Ind AS110, Ind AS 27 or Ind AS 28 require or permit an entity to account for an interest in a subsidiary, associate, or joint venture in accordance with some or all of the requirements of this Standard.

Entities shall also apply this Standard to derivatives on an interest in a subsidiary, associate or joint venture unless the derivative meets the definition of an equity instrument of the entity in Ind AS 32 *Financial Instruments: Presentation.*

(b) rights and obligations under leases to which Ind AS 116, *Leases* applies. However:

   (i) finance lease receivables (i.e. net investments in finance leases) and operating lease receivables recognised by a lessor are subject to the derecognition and impairment requirements of this Standard.

   (ii) lease liabilities recognised by a lessee are subject to the derecognition requirements of this Standard; and

   (iii) derivatives that are embedded in leases are subject to the embedded derivatives requirements of this Standard.

(c) employers' rights and obligations under employee benefit plans, to which Ind AS 19 *Employee Benefits* applies.

(d) **financial instruments issued by the entity that meet the definition of an equity instrument in Ind AS 32** (including options and warrants) or that are required to be classified as an equity instrument in accordance with Ind AS 32.

However, the holder of such equity instruments shall apply this Standard to those instruments, unless they meet the exception in (a).

(e) rights and obligations arising under

   (i) an **insurance contract** as defined in Ind AS 104 *Insurance Contracts*, other than an issuer's rights and obligations arising under an insurance contract that meets the definition of a financial guarantee contract, or

   (ii) a contract that is within the scope of Ind AS104 because it contains a discretionary participation feature.

However, this Standard applies to a derivative that is embedded in a contract within the scope of Ind AS104 if the derivative is not itself a contract within the scope of Ind AS 104.

Moreover, if an issuer of financial guarantee contracts has previously asserted explicitly that it regards such contracts as insurance contracts and has used accounting that is applicable to insurance contracts, the issuer may elect to apply either this Standard or Ind AS 104 to such financial guarantee contracts. The issuer may make that election contract by contract, but the election for each contract is irrevocable.

(f) any forward contract between an acquirer and a selling shareholder to buy or sell an acquiree that will result in a business combination within the scope of Ind AS 103 *Business Combinations* at a future acquisition date. The term of the forward contract should not exceed a reasonable period normally necessary to obtain any required approvals and to complete the transaction.

(g) loan commitments other than those loan commitments described in paragraph 2.3. However, an issuer of loan commitments shall apply the impairment requirements of this Standard to loan commitments that are not otherwise within the scope of this Standard. Also, all loan commitments are subject to the derecognition requirements of this Standard.

(h) financial instruments, contracts, and obligations under share-based payment transactions to which Ind AS 102 *Share-based Payment* applies, except for contracts within the scope of paragraphs 2.4–2.7 of this Standard to which this Standard applies.

(i) rights to payments to reimburse the entity for expenditure that it is required to make to settle a liability that it recognises as a provision in accordance with Ind AS 37 *Provisions, Contingent Liabilities and Contingent Assets*, or for which, in an earlier period, it recognised a provision in accordance with Ind AS 37.

(j) rights and obligations within the scope of Ind AS 115 *Revenue from Contracts with Customers* that are financial instruments, except for those that Ind AS115 specifies are accounted for in accordance with this Standard.

### 14.5.2.2 impairment requirements

The impairment requirements of this Standard shall be applied to those rights that Ind AS 115 specifies are accounted for in accordance with this Standard for the purposes of recognising impairment gains or losses.

### 14.5.2.3 Loan commitments

The following loan commitments are within the scope of this Standard:

(a) loan commitments that the entity designates as financial liabilities at fair value through profit or loss. An entity that has a past practice of selling the assets resulting from its loan commitments shortly after origination shall apply this Standard to all its loan commitments in the same class.

(b) loan commitments that can be settled net in cash or by delivering or issuing another financial instrument. These loan commitments are derivatives. A loan commitment is not regarded as settled net merely because the loan is paid out in instalments (for example, a mortgage construction loan that is paid out in instalments in line with the progress of construction).

(c) commitments to provide a loan at a below-market interest rate

This Standard shall be applied to those contracts to buy or sell a non-financial item that can be settled net in cash or another financial instrument, or by exchanging financial instruments, as if the contracts were financial instruments, with the exception of contracts that were entered into and continue to be held for the purpose of the receipt or delivery of a non-financial item in accordance with the entity's expected purchase, sale or usage requirements. However, this Standard shall be applied to those contracts that an entity designates as measured at fair value through profit or loss.

A contract to buy or sell a non-financial item that can be settled net in cash or another financial instrument, or by exchanging financial instruments, as if the contract was a financial instrument, may be **irrevocably designated as measured at fair value through profit or loss** even if it was entered into for the purpose of the receipt or delivery of a non-financial item in accordance with the entity's expected purchase, sale or usage requirements.

This designation is available only at inception of the contract and only if it eliminates or significantly reduces **a recognition inconsistency (sometimes referred to as an 'accounting mismatch')** that would otherwise arise from not recognizing that contract because it is excluded from the scope of this Standard.

Various ways in which a contract to buy or sell a non-financial item can be settled net in cash or another financial instrument or by exchanging financial instruments. These include:

(a) when the terms of the contract permit either party to settle it net in cash or another financial instrument or by exchanging financial instruments

(b) when the ability to settle net in cash or another financial instrument, or by exchanging financial instruments, is not explicit in the terms of the contract, but the entity has a practice of settling similar contracts net in cash or another financial instrument or by exchanging financial instruments (whether with the counterparty, by entering into offsetting contracts or by selling the contract before its exercise or lapse);

(c) when, for similar contracts, the entity has a practice of taking delivery of the underlying and selling it within a short period after delivery for the purpose of generating a profit from short term fluctuations in price or dealer's margin; and

(d) when the non-financial item that is the subject of the contract is readily convertible to cash.

### *14.5.2.4 Recognition and de-recognition*

**Initial recognition**

An entity shall recognize a financial asset or a financial liability in its balance sheet when, and only when, the entity becomes party to the contractual provisions of the instrument. This has been explained in Application Guidance below.

| An entity recognizes all of its contractual rights and obligations under derivatives in its balance sheet as assets and liabilities, respectively, except for derivatives that prevent a transfer of financial assets from being accounted for as a sale. If a transfer of a financial asset does not qualify for derecognition, the transferee does not recognize the transferred asset as its asset |
|---|
| The following are examples of applying the principle:<br>(a) Unconditional receivables and payables are recognised as assets or liabilities when the entity becomes a party to the contract and, as a consequence, has a legal right to receive or a legal obligation to pay cash.<br>(b) Assets to be acquired and liabilities to be incurred because of a firm commitment to purchase or sell goods or services are generally not recognised until at least one of the parties has performed under the agreement. For example, an entity that receives a firm order does not generally recognize an asset (and the entity that places the order does not recognize a liability) at the time of the commitment but, instead, delays recognition until the ordered goods or services have been shipped, delivered or rendered. If a firm commitment to buy or sell non-financial items is within the scope of this Standard, its net fair value is recognised as an asset or a liability on the commitment date. In addition, if a previously unrecognized firm commitment is designated as a hedged item in a fair value hedge, any change in the net fair value attributable to the hedged risk is recognised as an asset or a liability after the inception of the hedge.<br>(c) A forward contract that is within the scope of this Standard is recognised as an asset or a liability on the commitment date, instead of on the date on which settlement takes place. When an entity becomes a party to a forward contract, the fair values of the right and obligation are often equal, so that the net fair value of the forward is zero. If the net fair value of the right and obligation is not zero, the contract is recognised as an asset or liability.<br>(d) Option contracts that are within the scope of this Standard are recognised as assets or liabilities when the holder or writer becomes a party to the contract.<br>(e) Planned future transactions, no matter how likely, are not assets and liabilities because the entity has not become a party to a contract. |

*A regular way purchase or sale* of financial assets shall be recognised and derecognized, as applicable, using trade date accounting or settlement date accounting as per Application Guidance mentioned below.

| A regular way purchase or sale of financial assets is recognised using either trade date accounting or settlement date accounting. An entity shall apply the same method consistently for all purchases and sales of financial assets that are classified in the same way in accordance with this Standard. For this purpose, assets that are mandatorily measured at fair value through profit or loss form a separate classification from assets designated as measured at fair value through profit or loss. |
|---|
| A contract that requires or permits net settlement of the change in the value of the contract is not a regular way contract. Instead, such a contract is accounted for as a derivative in the period between the trade date and the settlement date. |
| The trade date is the date that an entity commits itself to purchase or sell an asset. Trade date accounting refers to<br>(a) the recognition of an asset to be received and the liability to pay for it on the trade date, and<br>(b) derecognition of an asset that is sold, recognition of any gain or loss on disposal and the recognition of a receivable from the buyer for payment on the trade date.<br>Generally, interest does not start to accrue on the asset and corresponding liability until the settlement date when title passes. |
| The settlement date is the date that an asset is delivered to or by an entity.<br>Settlement date accounting refers to<br>(a) the recognition of an asset on the day it is received by the entity, and<br>(b) the derecognition of an asset and recognition of any gain or loss on disposal on the day that it is delivered by the entity.<br>When settlement date accounting is applied an entity accounts for any change in the fair value of the asset to be received during the period between the trade date and the settlement date in the same way as it accounts for the acquired asset.<br>In other words, the change in value is not recognised for assets measured at amortized cost; it is recognised in profit or loss for assets classified as financial assets measured at fair value through profit or loss; and it is recognised in other comprehensive income for financial assets measured at fair value through other comprehensive income and for investments in equity instruments accounted for. |

### De-recognition of Financial assets

i) An entity shall derecognize a financial asset when, and only when

   (a) the contractual rights to the cash flows from the financial asset expire, or

   (b) it transfers the financial asset and the transfer qualifies for de-recognition accordingly.

ii) An entity transfers a financial asset if, and only if, it either:

(a) transfers the contractual rights to receive the cash flows of the financial asset, or

(b) retains the contractual rights to receive the cash flows of the financial asset but assumes a contractual obligation to pay the cash flows to one or more recipients in an arrangement that meets the following conditions according to paragraph 3.2.5. summarized below:

(i) The entity has no obligation to pay amounts to the eventual recipients unless it collects equivalent amounts from the original asset. Short-term advances by the entity with the right of full recovery of the amount lent plus, accrued interest at market rates do not violate this condition.

(ii) The entity is prohibited by the terms of the transfer contract from selling or pledging the original asset other than as security to the eventual recipients for the obligation to pay them cash flows.

(iii) The entity has an obligation to remit any cash flows it collects on behalf of the eventual recipients without material delay. In addition, the entity is not entitled to reinvest such cash flows, except for investments in cash or cash equivalents (as defined in Ind AS 7 *Statement of Cash Flows*) during the short settlement period from the collection date to the date of required remittance to the eventual recipients, and interest earned on such investments is passed to the eventual recipients.

iii) When an entity transfers a financial asset, it shall evaluate the extent to which it retains the risks and rewards of ownership of the financial asset. In this case:

- if the entity transfers substantially all the risks and rewards of ownership of the financial asset, the entity shall derecognize the financial asset and recognize separately as assets or liabilities any rights and obligations created or retained in the transfer.
- if the entity retains substantially all the risks and rewards of ownership of the financial asset, the entity shall continue to recognize the financial asset.
- if the entity neither transfers nor retains substantially all the risks and rewards of ownership of the financial asset, the entity shall determine whether it has retained control of the financial asset.

In this case:

(i) if the entity has not retained control, it shall derecognize the financial asset and recognize separately as assets or liabilities any rights and obligation created or retained in the transfer.

(ii) if the entity has retained control, it shall continue to recognize the Financial asset to the extent of its continuing involvement in the financial asset.

iv) The de-recognition model under Ind AS 109 is to determine whether the asset under consideration for de recognition is an asset in its entirety. On derecognition of a financial asset in its entirety, the difference between:

(a) the carrying amount (measured at the date of derecognition) and

(b) the consideration received (including any new asset obtained less any new liability assumed) shall be recognised in profit or loss. Specifically identified cash flows from an asset (or a group of similar financial assets) or a fully proportionate (pro rata) share of the cash flows from an asset (or a group of similar financial assets) or a fully proportionate (pro rata) share of specifically identified cash flows from a financial asset (or a group of similar financial assets)

**De-recognition of financial liabilities**

i) A financial liability should be removed from the balance sheet when and only when, it is extinguished that is when the obligation specified in the contract is either discharged or cancelled or expires.

ii) Where there has been an exchange between an existing borrower and lender of debt instruments with substantially different terms or there has been a substantial modification of the terms of an existing financial liability, this transaction is accounted for as an extinguishment of the original financial liability and the recognition of a new financial liability.

iii) The difference between the carrying amount of a financial liability (or part of a financial liability) extinguished or transferred to another party and the consideration paid, including any non-cash assets transferred or liabilities assumed, shall be recognised in profit or loss.

iv) If an entity repurchases a part of a financial liability, the entity shall allocate the previous carrying amount of the financial liability between the part that continues to be recognised and the part that is derecognized based on the relative fair values of those parts on the date of the repurchase. The difference between

(a) the carrying amount allocated to the part derecognized and

(b) the consideration paid, including any non-cash assets transferred or liabilities assumed, for the part derecognized shall be recognised in profit or loss.

### *14.5.2.5 Classification and measurement of Financial Instruments*

**Financial Assets**

An entity shall classify financial assets as subsequently measured at

i) amortized cost,

ii) fair value through other comprehensive income or

iii) fair value through profit or loss based on both:

(a) the entity's business model for managing the financial assets and
(b) the contractual cash flow characteristics of the financial asset.

## Financial asset measured at amortized cost

A financial asset shall be measured at amortized cost if both of the following conditions are met:

(a) the financial asset is held within a business model whose objective is to hold financial assets to collect contractual cash flows and

(b) the contractual terms of the financial asset give rise on specified dates to cash flows that are solely payments of principal and interest on the principal amount outstanding.

An entity's business model is determined at a level that reflects how groups of financial assets are managed together to achieve a particular business objective. The entity's business model does not depend on management's intentions for an individual instrument.

Accordingly, this condition is not an instrument-by-instrument approach to classification and should be determined on a higher level of aggregation. However, a single entity may have more than one business model for managing its financial instruments. Consequently, classification need not be determined at the reporting entity level.

*A business model whose objective is to hold assets to collect contractual cash flows*

Financial assets that are held within a business model whose objective is to hold assets in order to collect contractual cash flows are managed to realize cash flows by collecting contractual payments over the life of the instrument. That is, the entity manages the assets held within the portfolio to collect those particular contractual cash flows (instead of managing the overall return on the portfolio by both holding and selling assets). In determining whether cash flows are going to be realized by collecting the financial assets' contractual cash flows, it is necessary to consider the frequency, value and timing of sales in prior periods, the reasons for those sales and expectations about future sales activity.

The following are examples of when the objective of an entity's business model may be to hold financial assets to collect the contractual cash flows.

### Illustration 14.1: Financial Assets and Liabilities

An entity holds investments to collect their contractual cash flows. The funding needs of the entity are predictable, and the maturity of its financial assets is matched to the entity's estimated funding needs.

The entity performs credit risk management activities with the objective of minimizing credit losses. In the past, sales have typically occurred when the financial assets' credit risk has increased such that the assets no longer meet the credit criteria specified in the entity's documented investment policy. In addition, infrequent sales have occurred as a result of unanticipated funding needs. Reports to key management personnel focus on the credit quality of the financial and the contractual return. The entity also monitors fair values of the financial assets, among other information.

**Analysis**

Although the entity considers, among other information, the financial assets' fair values from a liquidity perspective (i.e. the cash amount that would be realized if the entity needs to sell assets), the entity's objective is to hold the financial assets in order to collect the contractual cash flows.

Sales would not contradict that objective if they were in response to an increase in the assets' credit risk, for example if the assets no longer meet the credit criteria specified in the entity's documented investment policy. Infrequent sales resulting from unanticipated funding needs (e.g. in a stress case scenario) also would not contradict that objective, even if such sales are significant in value.

### Illustration 14.2: Financial Assets and Liabilities

An entity's business model is to purchase portfolios of financial assets, such as loans. Those portfolios may or may not include financial assets that are credit impaired. If payment on the loans is not made on a timely basis, the entity attempts to realize the contractual cash flows through various means—for example, by contacting the debtor by mail, telephone, or other methods.

The entity's objective is to collect the contractual cash flows and the entity does not manage any of the loans in this portfolio with an objective of realizing cash flows by selling them.

In some cases, the entity enters into interest rate swaps to change the interest rate on particular financial assets in a portfolio from a floating interest rate to a fixed interest rate.

**Analysis**

The objective of the entity's business model is to hold the financial assets in order to collect the contractual cash flows.

The same analysis would apply even if the entity does not expect to receive all of the contractual cash flows (e.g. some of the financial assets are credit impaired at initial recognition). Moreover, the fact that the entity enters into derivatives to modify the cash flows of the portfolio does not in itself change the entity's business model.

### Illustration 14.3: Financial Assets and Liabilities

An entity has a business model with the objective of originating loans to customers and subsequently selling those loans to a securitization vehicle. The securitization vehicle issues instruments to investors.

The originating entity controls the securitization vehicle and thus consolidates it.

The securitization vehicle collects the contractual cash flows from the loans and passes them on to its investors. It is assumed for the purposes of this example that the loans continue to be recognised in the consolidated balance sheet because they are not derecognized by the securitization vehicle.

**Analysis**

The consolidated group originated the loans with the objective of holding them to collect the contractual cash flows. However, the originating entity has an objective of realizing cash flows on the loan portfolio by selling the loans to the securitization vehicle, so for the purposes of its separate financial statements it would not be considered to be managing this portfolio in order to collect the contractual cash flows.

### Illustration 14.4: Financial Assets and Liabilities

A financial institution holds financial assets to meet liquidity needs in a 'stress case' scenario (e.g, a run on the bank's deposits). The entity does not anticipate selling these assets except in such scenarios.

The entity monitors the credit quality of the financial assets and its objective in managing the financial assets is to collect the contractual cash flows. The entity evaluates the performance of the assets on the basis of interest revenue earned and credit losses realized.

However, the entity also monitors the fair value of the financial assets from a liquidity perspective to ensure that the cash amount that would be realized if the entity needed to sell the assets in a stress case scenario would be sufficient to meet the entity's liquidity needs. Periodically, the entity makes sales that are insignificant in value to demonstrate liquidity.

**Analysis**

The objective of the entity's business model is to hold the financial assets to collect contractual cash flows.

The analysis would not change even if during a previous stress case scenario the entity had sales that were significant in value in order to meet its liquidity needs.

Similarly, recurring sales activity that is insignificant in value is not inconsistent with holding financial assets to collect contractual cash flows.

In contrast, if an entity holds financial assets to meet its everyday liquidity needs and meeting that objective involves frequent sales that are significant in value, the objective of the entity's business model is not to hold the financial assets to collect contractual cash flows.

Similarly, if the entity is required by its regulator to routinely sell financial assets to demonstrate that the assets are liquid, and the value of the assets sold is significant, the entity's business model is not to hold financial assets to collect contractual cash flows. Whether a third party imposes the requirement to sell the financial assets, or that activity is at the entity's discretion, is not relevant to the analysis.

*A business model whose objective is achieved by both collecting contractual cash flows and selling financial assets*

An entity may hold financial assets in a business model whose objective is achieved by both collecting contractual cash flows and selling financial assets. In this type of business model, the entity's key management personnel have decided that both collecting contractual cash flows and selling financial assets are integral to achieving the objective of the business model. There are various objectives that may be consistent with this type of business model. For example, the objective of the business model may be to manage everyday liquidity needs, to maintain a particular interest yield profile or to match the duration of the financial assets to the duration of the liabilities that those assets are funding. To achieve such an objective, the entity will both collect contractual cash flows and sell financial assets.

The following are examples of when the objective of the entity's business model may be achieved by both collecting contractual cash flows and selling financial assets.

**Illustration 14.5: Financial Assets and Liabilities**

An entity anticipates capital expenditure in a few years. The entity invests its excess cash in short and long-term financial assets so that it can fund the expenditure when the need arises. Many of the financial assets have contractual lives that exceed the entity's anticipate disinvestment period.

The entity will hold financial assets to collect the contractual cash flows and, when an opportunity arises, it will sell financial assets to re-invest the cash in financial assets with a higher return.

The managers responsible for the portfolio are remunerated based on the overall return generated by the portfolio.

**Analysis**

The objective of the business model is achieved by both collecting contractual cash flows and selling financial assets. The entity will make decisions on an ongoing basis about whether collecting contractual cash flows or selling financial assets will maximize the return on the portfolio until the need arises for the invested cash.

In contrast, consider an entity that anticipates a cash outflow in five years to fund capital expenditure and invests excess cash in short-term financial assets.

When the investments mature, the entity reinvests the cash in new short-term financial assets. The entity maintains this strategy until the funds are needed, at which time the entity uses the proceeds from the maturing financial assets to fund the capital expenditure. Only sales that are insignificant in value occur before maturity (unless there is an increase in credit risk). The objective of this contrasting business model is to hold financial assets to collect contractual cash flows.

**Illustration 14.6: Financial Assets and Liabilities**

A financial institution holds financial assets to meet its everyday liquidity needs. The entity seeks to minimise the costs of managing those liquidity needs and therefore actively manages the return on the portfolio. That return consists of collecting contractual payments as well as gains and losses from the sale of financial assets.

As a result, the entity holds financial assets to collect contractual cash flows and sells financial assets to reinvest in higher yielding financial assets or to better match the duration of its liabilities. In the past, this strategy has resulted in frequent sales activity and such sales have been significant in value. This activity is expected to continue in the future.

**Analysis**

The objective of the business model is to maximize the return on the portfolio to meet everyday liquidity needs and the entity achieves that objective by both collecting contractual cash flows and selling financial assets. In other words, both collecting contractual cash flows and selling financial assets are integral to achieving the business model's objective.

**Illustration 14.7: Financial Assets and Liabilities**

An insurer holds financial assets in order to fund insurance contract liabilities. The insurer uses the proceeds from the contractual cash flows on the financial assets to settle insurance contract liabilities as they come due. To ensure that the contractual cash flows from the financial assets are sufficient to settle those liabilities, the insurer undertakes significant buying and selling activity on a regular basis to rebalance its portfolio of assets and to meet cash flow needs as they arise.

**Analysis**

The objective of the business model is to fund the insurance contract liabilities. To achieve this objective, the entity collects contractual cash flows as they come due and sells financial assets to maintain the desired profile of the asset portfolio.

Thus, both collecting contractual cash flows and selling financial assets are integral to achieving the business model's objective.

Financial assets are measured at fair value through profit or loss if they are not held within a business model whose objective is to hold assets to collect contractual cash flows or within a business model whose objective is achieved by both collecting contractual cash flows and selling financial assets. One business model that results in measurement at fair value through profit or loss is one in which an entity manages the financial assets with the objective of realizing cash flows through the sale of the assets.

**Contractual cash flows that are solely payments of principal and interest on the principal amount outstanding**

Contractual cash flows that are solely payments of principal and interest on the principal amount outstanding are consistent with a basic lending arrangement. In a basic lending arrangement, consideration for the time value of money and credit risk are typically the most significant elements of interest. However, in such an arrangement, interest can also include consideration for other basic lending risks (for example, liquidity risk) and costs (for example, administrative costs) associated with holding the financial asset for a particular period of time. In addition, interest can include a profit margin that is consistent with a basic lending arrangement.

**Illustration 14.8: Financial Instruments and its contractual cash flows**

The following examples illustrate contractual cash flows that are solely payments of principal and interest on the principal amount outstanding.

| Instrument | Description | Analysis |
|---|---|---|
| ***Instrument A*** | It is a bond with a stated maturity date. Payments of principal and interest on the principal amount outstanding are linked to an inflation index of the currency in which the instrument is issued. The inflation link is not leveraged, and the principal is protected. | The contractual cash flows are solely payments of principal and interest on the principal amount outstanding. Linking payments of principal and interest on the principal amount outstanding to an unleveraged inflation index resets the time value of money to a current level. In other words, the interest rate on the instrument reflects 'real' interest. Thus, the interest amounts are consideration for the time value of money on the principal amount outstanding. |
| ***Instrument B*** | It is a variable interest rate instrument with a stated maturity date that permits the borrower to choose the market interest rate on an ongoing basis.<br>For example, at each interest rate reset date, the borrower can choose to pay three-month LIBOR for a three-month term or one-month LIBOR for a one month term. | The contractual cash flows are solely payments of principal and interest on the principal amount outstanding as long as the interest paid over the life of the instrument reflects consideration for the time value of money, for the credit risk associated with the instrument and for other basic lending risks and costs, as well as a profit margin.<br>The fact that the LIBOR interest rate is reset during the life of the instrument does not in itself disqualify the instrument. |
| ***Instrument C*** | It is a bond with a stated maturity date and pays a variable market interest rate. That variable interest rate is capped. | The contractual cash flows of both:<br>(a) an instrument that has a fixed interest rate and<br>(b) an instrument that has a variable interest rate are payments of principal |

| Instrument | Description | Analysis |
|---|---|---|
| | | and interest on the principal amount outstanding as long as the interest reflects consideration for the time value of money, for the credit risk associated with the instrument during the term of the instrument and for other basic lending risks and costs, as well as a profit margin. |
| ***Instrument D*** | It is a full recourse loan and is secured by collateral. | The fact that a full recourse loan is collateralised does not in itself affect the analysis of whether the contractual cash flows are solely payments of principal and interest on the principal amount outstanding. |
| ***Instrument E*** | It is issued by a regulated bank and has a stated maturity date. The instrument pays a fixed interest rate and all contractual cash flows are nondiscretionary.<br>However, the issuer is subject to legislation that permits or requires a national resolving authority to impose losses on holders of particular instruments, including Instrument E, in particular circumstances. For example, the national resolving authority has the power to write down the par amount of Instrument E or to convert it into a fixed number of the issuer's ordinary shares if the national resolving authority determines that the issuer is having severe financial difficulties, needs additional regulatory capital or is "failing". | The holder would analyse the contractual terms of the financial instrument to determine whether they give rise to cash flows that are solely payments of principal and interest on the principal amount outstanding and thus are consistent with a basic lending arrangement.<br>That analysis would not consider the payments that arise only as a result of the national resolving authority's power to impose losses on the holders of Instrument E.<br>That is because that power, and the resulting payments, are not contractual terms of the financial instrument.<br>In contrast, the contractual cash flows would not be solely payments of principal and interest on the principal amount outstanding if the contractual terms of the financial instrument permit or require the issuer or another entity to impose losses on the holder (e.g. by writing down the par amount or by converting the instrument into a fixed number of the issuer's ordinary shares) as long as those contractual terms are genuine, even if the probability is remote that such a loss will be imposed. |

**Illustration 14.9: Contractual cash flows of Financial Instruments**

The following examples illustrate contractual cash flows that are not solely payments of principal and interest on the principal amount outstanding.

| Instrument | Description | Analysis |
|---|---|---|
| ***Instrument*** F | It is a bond that is convertible into a fixed number of equity instruments of the issuer. | The holder would analyse the convertible bond in its entirety.<br>The contractual cash flows are not payments of principal and interest on the principal amount outstanding because they reflect a return that is inconsistent with a basic lending arrangement; i.e. the return is linked to the value of the equity of the issuer. |
| ***Instrument*** G | Instrument G is a loan that pays an inverse floating interest rate (i.e. the interest rate has an inverse relationship to market interest rates). | The contractual cash flows are not solely payments of principal and interest on the principal amount outstanding.<br>The interest amounts are not consideration for the time value of money on the principal amount outstanding. |
| ***Instrument*** H | It is a perpetual instrument but the issuer may call the instrument at any point and pay the holder the par amount plus accrued interest due.<br>This instrument pays a market interest rate but payment of interest cannot be made unless the issuer is able to remain solvent immediately afterwards.<br>Deferred interest does not accrue additional interest. | The contractual cash flows are not payments of principal and interest on the principal amount outstanding. That is because the issuer may be required to defer interest payments and additional interest does not accrue on those deferred interest amounts. As a result, interest amounts are not consideration for the time value of money on the principal amount outstanding.<br>If interest accrued on the deferred amounts, the contractual cash flows could be payments of principal and interest on the principal amount outstanding.<br>The fact that Instrument H is perpetual does not in itself mean that the contractual cash flows are not payments of principal and interest on the principal amount outstanding. In effect, a perpetual instrument has continuous (multiple) extension options. Such options may result in contractual cash flows that are payments of principal and interest on the principal amount outstanding if interest payments are mandatory and must be paid in perpetuity. |

| Instrument | Description | Analysis |
|---|---|---|
| | | Also, the fact that Instrument H is callable does not mean that the contractual cash flows are not payments of principal and interest on the principal amount outstanding unless it is callable at an amount that does not substantially reflect payment of outstanding principal and interest on that principal amount outstanding. Even if the callable amount includes an amount that reasonably compensates the holder for the early termination of the instrument, the contractual cash flows could be payments of principal and interest on the principal amount outstanding. (See also Paragraph B4.1.12.) |

**Financial asset measured at Option to designate a financial asset or financial liability as at fair value through profit or loss**

| | |
|---|---|
| ***Fair value through other comprehensive income*** | if both of the following conditions are met:<br>(a) the financial asset is held within a business model whose objective is achieved by both collecting contractual cash flows and selling financial assets and<br>(b) the contractual terms of the financial asset give rise on specified dates to cash flows that are solely payments of principal and interest on the principal amount outstanding. |

A financial asset shall be measured at fair value through profit or loss unless it is measured at amortised cost or at fair value through other comprehensive income.

However, an entity may make an irrevocable election at initial recognition for particular investments in *equity instruments* that would otherwise be measured at fair value through profit or loss to present subsequent changes in fair value in other comprehensive income.

| | |
|---|---|
| ***Option to designate a financial asset at fair value through profit or loss*** | An entity may, at initial recognition, irrevocably designate a financial asset as measured at fair value through profit or loss if doing so eliminates or significantly reduces a measurement or recognition inconsistency (sometimes referred to as an '*accounting mismatch'*) that would otherwise arise from measuring assets or liabilities or recognizing the gains and losses on them on different bases. |

**Illustration 14.10: Financial Assets and Liabilities**

Axe Ltd has entered the following transaction involving financial instruments:

(a) Axe Ltd gave loan to Box Ltd during the year. Although Box owes Axe money, this transaction does not give rise to trade receivable. It is part of a portfolio that the company manages in order to collect the contractual cash flows.

(b) Axe made an investment in 500 equity shares at Rs.10 per share to Cox Ltd – which are not held for trading, do not have a quoted price and their fair value cannot be reliably measured.

(c) Axe made an investment of 200 equity shares at Rs.12 per share of Daisy Ltd quoted in an active market. However, this investment was not made or held for trading purposes.

(d) During the year, Axe made a strategic investment in an equity instrument which the company, at the moment, has no intention of selling.

(e) Axe has invested in debt securities, which are not quoted in an active market and are not held for trading.

(f) During the year, Axe purchased debt securities of Ebony Ltd. These debt instruments are quoted in an active market and Axe plans on holding on to them until maturity. However, if market interest rates fall significantly, Axe will consider selling the debt securities to realize the associated gain.

(g) During the year Axe made another investment in Daisy Ltd, which was held for trading purposes.

Please classify these transactions into appropriate category of financial asset or liability.

**Solution**

(a) This would be classified as "at amortized cost" unless Axe take a decision to designate the receivable as a financial asset at fair value through profit or loss to avoid accounting mismatch.

(b) The equity investment in Cox is classified as at fair value since there cannot be any contractual cash flows towards principal and interest and hence amortized cost method cannot be used. The subsequent changes in fair value will be recognised in profit or loss unless an irrecoverable election to classify them as at fair value through other comprehensive income is made.

(c) The equity investment in Daisy Ltd is classified at fair value. According to Ind AS 109, all investments in equity instruments and contracts on those instruments must be measured at fair value which would be determined by applying appropriate valuation technique.

(d) Unless Axe decides to classify the strategic investment as a financial asset held at fair value through profit or loss, the investment should be classified as at fair value through Other Comprehensive Income, through an irrevocable selection.

(e) This investment in debt securities should be classified as at amortized cost

| since it appears that the business model is to hold the assets to collect contractual cash flows of principal and interest.<br>(f) In accordance with Ind AS 109, if an entity holds investments to collect their contractual cash flows but would sell an investment in particular circumstances, the objective of an entity's business model may still be to hold financial assets to collect the contractual cash flows. Hence this item should be classified as "at amortized cost".<br>(g) The second investment in Daisy Ltd would be classified as a financial asset at fair value through profit or loss. |
|---|

### Financial Liabilities

| | |
|---|---|
| ***Financial liabilities measured at amortized cost*** | As mentioned in the Application guidance above, an entity shall classify all financial liabilities as subsequently measured at amortized cost using the effective interest method, except for<br>(a) *financial liabilities at fair value through profit or loss*. Such liabilities, including *derivatives* that are liabilities, shall be subsequently measured at fair value.<br>(b) financial liabilities that arise when a transfer of a financial asset does not qualify for derecognition or when the continuing involvement approach applies.<br>(c) *financial guarantee contracts*. After initial recognition, an issuer of such a contract shall subsequently measure it at the higher of:<br>(i) the amount of the *loss allowance* and<br>(ii) the amount initially recognised less, when appropriate, the cumulative amount of income recognised in accordance with the principles of Ind AS115.<br>(d) commitments to provide a loan at a below-market interest rate. An issuer of such a commitment shall subsequently measure it at the higher of:<br>(i) the amount of the loss allowance and<br>(ii) the amount initially recognised less, when appropriate, the cumulative amount of income recognised in accordance with the principles of Ind AS115.<br>(e) contingent consideration recognised by an acquirer in a business combination to which Ind AS103 applies. Such contingent consideration shall subsequently be measured at fair value with changes recognised in profit or loss. |
| ***Financial liabilities at fair value through profit or loss*** | Ind AS 109 provides for an option to measure financial liability at fair value through profit or loss. This option is exercisable if:<br>(a) using this option recognition inconsistency that would arise on measuring or recognizing gain or loss on financial liability on some different basis is either eliminated or significantly reduced, or |

| | (b) the liability is part or a group of financial liabilities or financial assets and financial liabilities that is managed and its performance is evaluated on a fair value basis, in accordance with a documented risk management or investment strategy, and information about the group is provided internally on that basis to the entity's key management personnel (as defined in Ind AS 24 *Related Party Disclosures*), for example, the entity's board of directors and chief executive officer. |
|---|---|

**Designation eliminating or significantly reducing accounting mismatch**

Measurement of a financial asset or financial liability and classification of recognised changes in its value are determined by the item's classification and whether the item is part of a designated hedging relationship. Those requirements can create a measurement or recognition inconsistency (sometimes referred to as an 'accounting mismatch') when, for example, in the absence of designation as at fair value through profit or loss, a financial asset would be classified as subsequently measured at fair value through profit or loss and a liability the entity considers related would be subsequently measured at amortized cost (with changes in fair value not recognised). In such circumstances, an entity may conclude that its financial statements would provide more relevant information if both the asset and the liability were measured as at fair value through profit or loss.

The following examples show when this condition could be met. In all cases, an entity may use this condition to designate financial assets or financial liabilities as at fair value through profit or loss only if it meets the principle:

(a) an entity has liabilities under insurance contracts whose measurement incorporates current information (as permitted by paragraph 24 of Ind AS104) and financial assets that it considers to be related and that would otherwise be measured at either fair value through other comprehensive income or amortized cost.

(b) an entity has financial assets, financial liabilities or both that share a risk, such as interest rate risk, and that gives rise to opposite changes in fair value that tend to offset each other. However, only some of the instruments would be measured at fair value through profit or loss (for example, those that are derivatives, or are classified as held for trading). It may also be the case that the requirements for hedge accounting are not met because, for example, the requirements for hedge effectiveness are not met.

(c) an entity has financial assets, financial liabilities or both that share a risk, such as interest rate risk, that gives rise to opposite changes in fair value that tend to offset each other and none of the financial assets or financial liabilities qualifies for designation as a hedging instrument because they are not measured at fair value through profit or loss. Furthermore, in the absence of hedge accounting there is a significant inconsistency in the recognition of gains and losses.

For example, the entity has financed a specified group of loans by issuing traded bonds whose changes in fair value tend to offset each other. If, in addition, the entity regularly buys and sells the bonds but rarely, if ever, buys and sells the loans, reporting both the loans and the bonds at fair value through profit or loss eliminates the inconsistency in the timing of the recognition of the gains and losses that would otherwise result from measuring them both at amortized cost and recognizing a gain or loss each time a bond is repurchased.

In cases such as those described in the preceding paragraph, to designate, at initial recognition, the financial assets and financial liabilities not otherwise so measured as at fair value through profit or loss may eliminate or significantly reduce the measurement or recognition inconsistency and produce more relevant information. For practical purposes, the entity need not enter into all of the assets and liabilities giving rise to the measurement or recognition inconsistency at exactly the same time. A reasonable delay is permitted provided that each transaction is designated as at fair value through profit or loss at its initial recognition and, at that time, any remaining transactions are expected to occur.

It would not be acceptable to designate only some of the financial assets and financial liabilities giving rise to the inconsistency as at fair value through profit or loss if to do so would not eliminate or significantly reduce the inconsistency and would therefore not result in more relevant information. However, it would be acceptable to designate only some of a number of similar financial assets or similar financial liabilities if doing so achieves a significant reduction (and possibly a greater reduction than other allowable designations) in the inconsistency.

For example, let us assume an entity has a number of similar financial liabilities that sum to Rs.100 and a number of similar financial assets that sum to Rs.50 but are measured on a different basis. The entity may significantly reduce the measurement inconsistency by designating at initial recognition all of the assets but only some of the liabilities (for example, individual liabilities with a combined total of Rs.45) as at fair value through profit or loss. However, because designation as at fair value through profit or loss can be applied only to the whole of a financial instrument, the entity in this example must designate one or more liabilities in their entirety. It could not designate either a component of a liability (e.g. changes in value attributable to only one risk, such as changes in a benchmark interest rate) or a proportion (ie percentage) of a liability.

### 14.5.2.6 Subsequent measurement of Financial Assets

(a) After initial recognition, an entity shall measure a financial asset in accordance with paragraphs at:

   (a) amortised cost;

   (b) fair value through other comprehensive income; or

(c) fair value through profit or loss.

(b) An entity shall apply the impairment requirements to financial assets that are measured at amortised cost and to financial assets that are measured at fair value through other comprehensive income

(c) An entity shall apply the hedge accounting requirements to a financial asset that is designated as a hedged item.

#### *14.5.2.7 Subsequent measurement of Financial Liabilities*

(a) After initial recognition, an entity shall measure a financial liability as mentioned in paragraphs above.

(b) An entity shall apply the hedge accounting requirements to a financial liability that is designated as a hedged item.

Classification, measurement and subsequent measurement of Financial Assets and liabilities are depicted in the table below.

| Instrument | Ind AS 109 classification | Subsequent Measured | Value Changes | Impairment Testing |
|---|---|---|---|---|
| Debt instruments | Amortized cost | Amortized Cost | Not relevant – unless impaired | Yes |
| | FVTPL | Fair value | Through profit or loss | No |
| Equity instruments | FVTOCI – if irrevocable election made on initial recognition | Fair value | Through OCI | No |
| | FVTPL | Fair value | Through profit or loss | No |
| Financial liabilities | FVTPL | Fair value | Through profit or loss for changes not attributable to changes in credit risk. For changes attributable to credit risk, the change is presented in other comprehensive Income (OCI) | No |
| | Amortized cost | Amortized cost | Not relevant – unless impaired | No |

#### *14.5.2.8 Amortized cost measurement*

**(i) Effective interest method**

Interest revenue shall be calculated by using the *effective interest method.* This shall be calculated by applying the *effective interest rate* to the *gross carrying amount of a financial asset* except for:

(a) purchased or originated credit-impaired financial assets.

For those financial assets, the entity shall apply the *credit adjusted effective interest rate* to the *amortised cost of the financial asset* from initial recognition.

(b) financial assets that are not purchased or originated credit impaired financial assets but subsequently have become *credit-impaired financial assets*. For those financial assets, the entity shall apply the effective interest rate to the amortised cost of the financial asset in subsequent reporting periods.

**(ii) Modification of contractual cash flows**

a) When the contractual cash flows of a financial asset are re-negotiated or otherwise modified and the renegotiation or modification does not result in the derecognition of that financial asset in accordance with this Standard, an entity shall recalculate the gross carrying amount of the financial asset and shall recognise a *modification gain or loss* in profit or loss.

b) The gross carrying amount of the financial asset shall be recalculated as the present value of the renegotiated or modified contractual cash flows that are discounted at the financial asset's original effective interest rate (or credit-adjusted effective interest rate for purchased or originated credit-impaired financial assets) or, when applicable, the revised effective interest rate calculated.

c) Any costs or fees incurred adjust the carrying amount of the modified financial asset and are amortised over the remaining term of the modified financial asset.

**(iii) Write-off**

An entity shall directly reduce the gross carrying amount of a financial asset when the entity has no reasonable expectations of recovering a financial asset in its entirety or a portion thereof. A write-off constitutes a derecognition event.

### *14.5.2.9 Impairment*

***(a) Recognition of expected credit losses***

(i) An entity shall recognise a loss allowance for *expected credit losses* on a financial asset that is measured in accordance with this Standard, a lease receivable, a *contract asset* or a loan commitment and a financial guarantee contract to which the impairment requirements apply.

(ii) An entity shall measure the loss allowance for a financial instrument at an amount equal to the *lifetime expected credit losses* if the credit risk on that financial instrument has increased significantly since initial recognition.

(iii) If, at the reporting date, the credit risk on a financial instrument has not increased significantly since initial recognition, an entity shall measure the loss allowance for that financial instrument at an amount equal to *12-month expected credit losses*.

For loan commitments and financial guarantee contracts, the date that the entity becomes a party to the irrevocable commitment shall be considered to be the date of initial recognition for the purposes of applying the impairment requirements.

(iv) An entity shall recognise in profit or loss, as an *impairment gain* or loss, the amount of expected credit losses (or reversal) that is required to adjust the loss allowance at the reporting date to the amount that is required to be recognised in accordance with this Standard.

***(b) Measurement of expected credit losses***

An entity shall measure expected credit losses of a financial instrument in a way that reflects:

(a) an unbiased and probability-weighted amount that is determined by evaluating a range of possible outcomes.

(b) the time value of money; and

(c) reasonable and supportable information that is available without undue cost or effort at the reporting date about past events, current conditions and forecasts of future economic conditions.

***(c) Determining significant increases in credit risk***

(i) At each reporting date, an entity shall assess whether the credit risk on a financial instrument has increased significantly since initial recognition.

(ii) When making the assessment, an entity shall use the change in the risk of a default occurring over the expected life of the financial instrument instead of the change in the amount of expected credit losses.

(iii) To make that assessment, an entity shall compare the risk of a default occurring on the financial instrument as at the reporting date with the risk of a default occurring on the financial instrument as at the date of initial recognition and consider reasonable and supportable information, that is available without undue cost or effort, that is indicative of significant increases in credit risk since initial recognition.

***(d) Modified financial assets***

If the contractual cash flows on a financial asset have been renegotiated or modified and the financial asset was not derecognised, an entity shall assess whether there has been a significant increase in the credit risk of the financial instrument by comparing:

(a) the risk of a default occurring at the reporting date (based on the modified contractual terms); and

(b) the risk of a default occurring at initial recognition (based on the original, unmodified contractual terms).

***(e) Purchased or originated credit-impaired financial assets***

i) At the reporting date, an entity shall only recognise the cumulative changes in lifetime expected credit losses since initial recognition as a loss allowance for purchased or originated credit-impaired financial assets.

ii) At each reporting date, an entity shall recognise in profit or loss the amount of the change in lifetime expected credit losses as an impairment gain or loss.

iii) An entity shall recognise favourable changes in lifetime expected credit losses as an impairment gain, even if the lifetime expected credit losses are less than the amount of expected credit losses that were included in the estimated cash flows on initial recognition.

***(f) Trade receivables and contract assets***

Trade receivables or contract assets that result from transactions that are within the scope of Ind AS115, and that:

(i) do not contain a significant financing component in accordance with Ind AS 115 (or when the entity applies the practical expedient in accordance with paragraph 63 of Ind AS 115); or

(ii) contain a significant financing component in accordance with Ind AS115, if the entity chooses as its accounting policy to measure the loss allowance at an amount equal to lifetime expected credit losses. That accounting policy shall be applied to all such trade receivables or contract assets but may be applied separately to trade receivables and contract assets.

***(g) Lease receivables***

Lease receivables that result from transactions that are within the scope of Ind AS 116, if the entity chooses as its accounting policy to measure the loss allowance at an amount equal to lifetime expected credit losses. That accounting policy shall be applied to all lease receivables but may be applied separately to finance and operating lease receivables.

### *14.5.2.10 Analysis of Financial instruments – whether debt or equity*

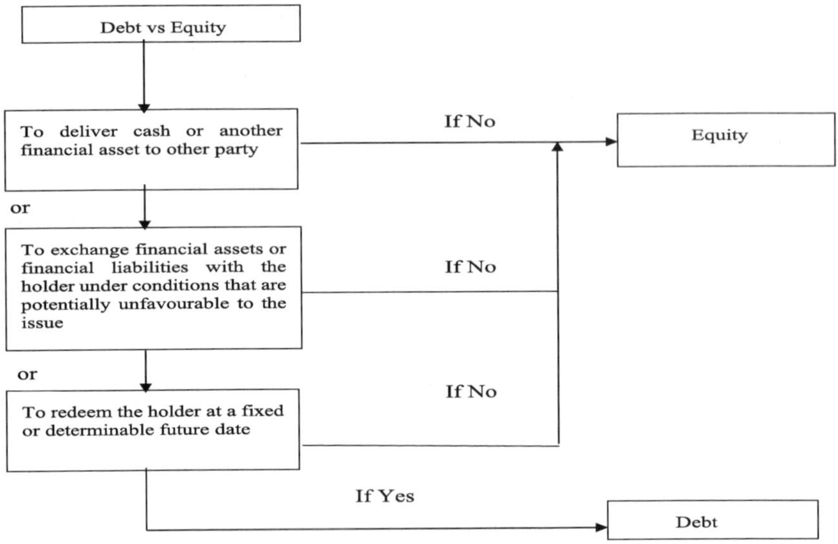


### *14.5.2.11 Derivatives*

| | |
|---|---|
| ***What is a Derivative*** | A derivative is a financial instrument which has all the characteristics as highlighted below<br>(a) its value changes in response to a change in specified interest rate, financial instrument price or other variable<br>(b) no initial net investment or lower initial net investment<br>(c) settled at a future date<br>An example of a derivative is a Forward contract to purchase \$100,000 of Euros at an agreed rate in 3 months' time. |
| ***Characteristics of derivatives are*** | • it creates a contractual right<br>• to exchange financial assets or financial liabilities with another party<br>• under conditions that are potentially favourable or unfavourable<br>• because the instrument's fair value changes in accordance with changes in financial markets.<br>• The basis on which the value of a derivative changes is often referred to as the instruments 'underlying'. |
| ***Examples of derivatives*** | • Forwards – contracts to purchase or sell a specific quantity of a financial instrument with delivery or settlement on pre-agreed future date. These are over-the-counter contracts |

| | |
|---|---|
| | • Futures – similar to forward contracts. These are exchange-traded contracts.<br>• Options – contracts that give the purchaser the right, but not the obligation to buy or sell a specified quantity of a particular financial instrument.<br>• Interest rate swaps – are contracts to exchange cash flows as of specified dates based on a notional amount. |

**Illustration 14.11: Examples of Derivatives and underlying**

Examples of derivatives and underlying as follows:

| *Types of Contract* | *Main Pricing-Settlement variable (Underlying Variable)* |
|---|---|
| Interest Rate Swap | Interest rates |
| Currency Swap (Foreign exchange Swap) | Currency rates |
| Commodity Swap | Commodity prices |
| Equity Swap | Equity prices (equity of another entity) |
| Credit Swap | Credit rating (Credit index or Credit price) |
| Currency futures | Currency rates |
| Commodity futures | Commodity prices |
| Currency forward | Currency rates |
| Commodity forward | Commodity prices |
| Equity forward | Equity prices (equity of another entity) |

### 14.5.2.12 Measurement of derivatives

All derivatives including those linked to unquoted equity investments, are measured at fair value. Value changes are recognized in profit or loss unless the entity has elected to treat the derivative as a hedging instrument in accordance with Ind AS 109, in which case the requirements of Ind AS 109 apply.

### 14.5.2.13 Embedded derivatives

An embedded derivative (sometimes called compound financial instrument) is a component of a hybrid contract that also includes a non-derivative host—with the effect that some of the cash flows of the combined instrument vary in a way similar to a standalone derivative.

An embedded derivative causes some or all of the cash flows that otherwise would be required by the contract to be modified according to a specified interest rate, financial instrument price, commodity price, foreign exchange rate, index of prices or rates, credit rating or credit index, or other variable, provided in the case of a non-financial variable that the variable is not specific to a party to the contract. A derivative that is attached to a *financial instrument* but is contractually transferable independently of that instrument, or has a different counterparty, is not an embedded derivative, but a separate financial instrument.

### 14.5.2.14 Measurement of embedded derivatives

An embedded derivative is a component of a hybrid contract that also includes a non-derivative host, with the effect that some of the cash flows of the combined instrument vary in a way similar to stand-alone derivative.

A derivative that is attached to a financial instrument but is contractually transferable independently of that instrument or has a different counter party is not an embedded derivative but separate financial instrument.

#### Instruments containing embedded derivatives

When an entity becomes a party to a hybrid contract with a host that is not an asset within the scope of this Standard and with one or more embedded derivatives, the Standard requires the entity to identify any such embedded derivative, assess whether it is required to be separated from the host contract and, for those that are required to be separated, measure the derivatives at fair value at initial recognition and subsequently. These requirements can be more complex, or result in less reliable measures, than measuring the entire instrument at fair value through profit or loss. For that reason, this Standard permits the entire hybrid contract to be designated as at fair value through profit or loss.

#### Reassessment of embedded derivatives

An entity shall assess whether an embedded derivative is required to be separated from the host contract and accounted for as a derivative when the entity first becomes a party to the contract. Subsequent reassessment is prohibited unless there is a change in the terms of the contract that significantly modifies the cash flows that otherwise would be required under the contract, in which case reassessment is required. An entity determines whether a modification to cash flows is significant by considering the extent to which the expected future cash flows associated with the embedded derivative, the host contract or both have changed and whether the change is significant relative to the previously expected cash flows on the contract.

The above does not apply to embedded derivatives in contracts acquired in:

(a) a business combination (as defined in Ind AS103 *Business Combinations*);

(b) a combination of entities or businesses under common control as described in provisions of Ind AS103; or

(c) the formation of a joint venture as defined in Ind AS111 *Joint Arrangements* or their possible reassessment at the date of acquisition.

**Illustration 14.12: Compound financial instrument**

Gamma Ltd has issued 10000 convertible debentures with a face value of Rs. 100 per debentures. The interest rate on the debentures is 5%. The debenture holders have the option of converting these debentures into ordinary shares at the end of four years. The prevailing market rate for a similar debt which does not have a conversion right is 7%. Show calculation of compound financial instrument in this transaction.

**Solution**

| *Carrying amount of liability portion* | *Amount (Rs)* |
|---|---|
| Present value (PV) of principal: Rs 10,00,000 at the end of 4 years discounted to PV (10,00,000 X 0.763*) | 7,63,000 |
| PV of interest Rs. 50,000 annually in arrears for 4 years (50,000 X 3.387*) | 1,69,350 |
| Carrying amount of liability | 9,32,350 |

*PV of Rs. 1 at 7% after 4 years (taken from discount value table)

**Annuity of Re. 1 at 7% after 4 years (taken from the annuity tables)

| | *Amount (Rs)* |
|---|---|
| Proceed of the issue (10,000 X 100) | 10,00,000 |
| Less: Carrying amount of liability portion | 9,32,350 |
| Carrying amount of equity portion | 67,650 |

**Note:** *For the calculation of present values, a discount rate of 7% (the prevailing market rate for a similar market rate for a similar debt which does not have a conversion right) is used.*

**Illustration 14.13: Measurement of embedded derivative**

On 1st April 2021, Calahar Ltd issued 6% Convertible Debentures of Face Value of Rs100 per Debenture at par. The Debentures are redeemable at a premium of 10% on 31–03–2015, or these may be converted into Ordinary Shares at the option of the Holder, the interest rate for equivalent debentures without conversion rights would have been 10%. Being a compound financial instrument, you are required to separate Equity and Debt portions as on 01 April 2021. If Equity Portion is Rs.1,85,400, find out the Debt Portion (Debenture Amount). The Present Value of Rs.1 receivable at the end of each year based on discount rates of 6% and 10% can be taken as:

| End of year | 1 | 2 | 3 | 4 |
|---|---|---|---|---|
| 6% | 0.94 | 0.89 | 0.84 | 0.79 |

| 10% | 0.91 | 0.83 | 0.75 | 0.68 |
|---|---|---|---|---|

**Solution**

**Statement of valuation of debt component (based on expectation of 10% p.a.)**

| Nature | Period | Cash flow | DF @ 10% | DCF |
|---|---|---|---|---|
| Annual Interest Payments (Rs100 × 6%) | 1-4 | 6.00 | (0.91+0.83+ 0.75+0.68) = 3.17 | 19.02 |
| Maturity Proceeds: Face Value Rs100 + Premium 10% | 4 | 110.00 | 0.68 | 74.80 |
| | | | | 93.82 |

**Statement of valuation of embedded derivative**

| Particulars | Amount |
|---|---|
| Capital Raised: Rs100 Debenture at Par | 100.00 |
| **Less:** Value of Host (Liability Component) | 93.82 |
| Value of Embedded Derivative (Equity Component) | 6.18 |
| Total value of equity portion (given) | Rs. 1,85,400 |
| No. of debentures (total value Rs 185400/6.18) | 30,000 |
| Total value of debentures (debt portion) (30000 x 93.82) | Rs. 28,14,600 |

### Illustration 14.14: Measurement of embedded derivative

At the beginning of year 1, an enterprise issued 20000 convertible debenture with face value Rs100 per debenture at par. The debentures have six-year term. The interest at annual rate of 9% is paid half-yearly. The bond holders have an option to convert half of the face value of debentures into 2 equity shares at the end of year 3. The bond holders not exercising the conversion option will be repaid at par to the extent of Rs.50 per debenture at the end of the year 3. The non-convertible portion will be repaid at 10% premium at the end of the year 6. At the time of issue, the prevailing market interest rate for similar debt without conversion option was 10%.

Compute the value of embedded derivative.

**Solution**

Computation of value of embedded derivative:

| Half year | Cash flow Rs'000 | DF (5%) | PV Rs'000 |
|---|---|---|---|
| 1- 6 | 90 | 5.076 | 456.84 |
| 7 – 12 | 45 | 3.787 | 170.41 |
| 12 | 1,100 | 0.557 | 612.70 |
| Value of host (liability component) | | | 1239.95 |
| Value of embedded derivative (equity component) | | | 760.05 |
| Issue proceeds | | | 2000.00 |

### 14.5.2.15 Reclassification

**Financial Assets**

(i) When, and only when, an entity changes its business model for managing financial assets it shall reclassify all affected financial assets.

(ii) If an entity reclassifies financial assets, it shall apply the reclassification prospectively from the reclassification date. The entity shall not restate any previously recognised gains, losses (including impairment gains or losses) or interest.

(iii) If an entity reclassifies a financial asset out of the amortized cost measurement category and into the fair value through profit or loss measurement category, its fair value is measured at the reclassification date. Any gain or loss arising from a difference between the previous amortized cost of the financial asset and fair value is recognised in profit or loss.

(iv) If an entity reclassifies a financial asset out of the fair value through profit or loss measurement category and into the amortized cost measurement category, its fair value at the reclassification date becomes its new gross carrying amount.

(v) If an entity reclassifies a financial asset out of the amortized cost measurement category and into the fair value through other comprehensive income measurement category, its fair value is measured at the reclassification date. Any gain or loss arising from a difference between the previous amortized cost of the financial asset and fair value is recognised in other comprehensive income. The effective interest rate and the measurement of expected credit losses are not adjusted because of the reclassification.

(vi) If an entity reclassifies a financial asset out of the fair value through other comprehensive income measurement category and into the amortized cost measurement category, the financial asset is reclassified at its fair value at the reclassification date. However, the cumulative gain or loss previously recognised in other comprehensive income is removed from equity and adjusted against the fair value of the financial asset at the reclassification date. As a result, the financial asset is measured at the reclassification date as if it had always been measured at amortized cost. This adjustment affects other comprehensive income but does not affect profit or loss and therefore is not a reclassification adjustment (see Ind AS 1 *Presentation of Financial Statements*). The effective interest rate and the measurement of expected credit losses are not adjusted because of the reclassification.

(vii) If an entity reclassifies a financial asset out of the fair value through profit or loss measurement category and into the fair value through other comprehensive income measurement category, the financial asset continues to be measured at fair value.

(viii) If an entity reclassifies a financial asset out of the fair value through other comprehensive income measurement category and into the fair value through profit or loss measurement category, the financial asset continues to be measured at fair value. The cumulative gain or loss previously recognised in other comprehensive income is reclassified from equity to profit or loss as a reclassification adjustment (see Ind AS 1) at the reclassification date.

**Financial Liabilities**

An entity shall not reclassify any financial liability.

### *14.5.2.16 Gains and losses on Financial Assets and Liabilities*

**Gains and losses on Financial assets or liabilities that are measured by fair value shall be recognized in profit or loss unless:**

(a) it is part of a hedging relationship

(b) it is an investment in an equity instrument and the entity has elected to present gains and losses on that investment in other comprehensive income in accordance with paragraph

(c) it is a financial liability designated as at fair value through profit or loss and the entity is required to present the effects of changes in the liability's *credit risk* in other comprehensive income or

(d) it is a financial asset measured at fair value through other comprehensive income and the entity is required to recognise some changes in fair value in other comprehensive income.

**Dividends are recognized in Profit & loss only when:**

(a) the entity's right to receive payment of the dividend is established.

(b) it is probable that the economic benefits associated with the dividend will flow to the entity; and

(c) the amount of the dividend can be measured reliably.

**A gain or loss on a financial asset that is measured at amortized cost**

***A gain or loss on a financial asset that is measured at amortised cost*** and is not part of a hedging relationship shall be recognised in profit or loss when the financial asset is derecognised, reclassified, through the amortisation process or in order to recognise impairment gains or losses. A gain or loss on a financial liability that is measured at amortised cost and is not part of a hedging relationship shall be recognised in profit or loss when the financial liability is derecognised and through the amortisation process.

### *14.5.2.17 If an entity recognises financial assets using settlement date accounting*

***If an entity recognises financial assets using settlement date accounting***, any change in the fair value of the asset to be received during the period between the trade date and the settlement date is not recognised for assets measured at amortised cost. For assets measured at fair value, however, the change in fair value shall be recognised in profit or loss or in other comprehensive income, as appropriate. ***The trade date*** shall be considered the date of initial recognition for the purposes of applying the impairment requirements.

### 14.5.2.18 Investment in equity instruments

At initial recognition, an entity may make an irrevocable election to present in other comprehensive income subsequent changes in the fair value of an investment in an equity instrument within the scope of this Standard that is neither *held for trading* nor contingent consideration recognised by an acquirer in a business combination to which Ind AS103 applies.

### 14.5.2.19 Liabilities designated as at fair value through profit or loss

An entity shall present a gain or loss on a financial liability that is designated as at fair value through profit or loss as under:

(a) The amount of change in the fair value of the financial liability that is attributable to changes in the credit risk of that liability shall be presented in other comprehensive income, and

(b) the remaining amount of change in the fair value of the liability shall be presented in profit or loss unless the treatment of the effects of changes in the liability's credit risk described in (a) would create or enlarge an accounting mismatch in profit or loss.

If the requirements would create or enlarge an accounting mismatch in profit or loss, an entity shall present all gains or losses on that liability (including the effects of changes in the credit risk of that liability) in profit or loss.

### 14.5.2.20 Assets measured as at Fair Value through other comprehensive Income

(i) A gain or loss on a financial asset measured at fair value through other comprehensive income, shall be recognised in other comprehensive income, except for impairment gains or losses and foreign exchange gains and losses, until the financial asset is derecognised or reclassified.

(ii) When the financial asset is derecognised the cumulative gain or loss previously recognised in other comprehensive income is reclassified from equity to profit or loss as a reclassification adjustment (see Ind AS 1).

(iii) If the financial asset is reclassified out of the fair value through other comprehensive income measurement category, the entity shall account for the cumulative gain or loss that was previously recognised in other comprehensive income.

(iv) Interest calculated using the effective interest method is recognised in profit or loss.

### *14.5.2.21 Hedge Accounting and Valuation*

**Hedged item**

A 'hedged item' is an asset, liability or transaction that exposes the entity to risks regarding changes in fair value or future cash flows. In order to be classified as a hedged item for accounting purposes, the item should be specifically designated as a hedged item for accounting purposes.

**Hedged instruments**

The hedging instrument is a financial instrument, whose fair value or cash flows is expected to offset changes in the fair value or cash flows of a designated hedged item.

**Hedge Accounting**

Hedge accounting is a technique that changes the normal basis for recognizing gains and losses on associated hedging instruments and hedged items so that both are recognized in earnings in the same accounting period.

This is dissected in the process chart below.

**Classification of Hedges**

Hedging transactions are classified under:

a) Fair value hedges
b) Cash flow hedges
c) Hedges of net investment in an overseas operation

**Classification of hedging relationships**

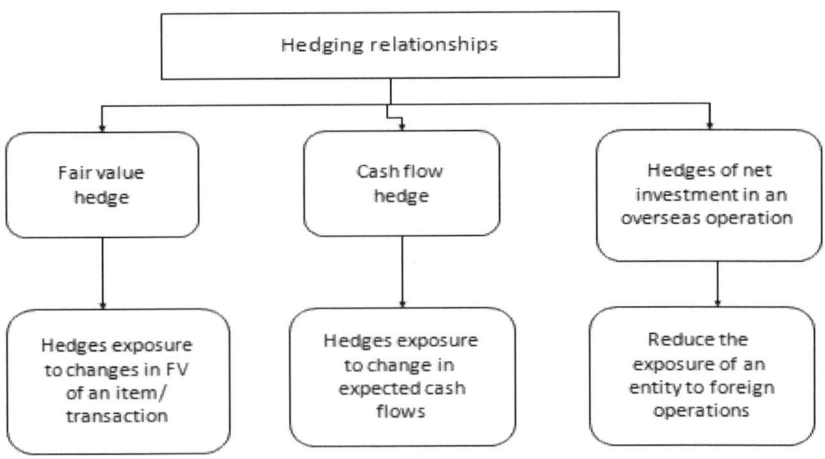

| | |
|---|---|
| ***Fair value hedge*** | Hedging instrument should be re-measured at fair value, with the gain or loss reported in the income statement |
| ***Cash flow hedge*** | Hedging instrument should be split between the proportion which is effective and the proportion which is ineffective |
| ***Hedges of a net investment in a foreign operation*** | Hedges of a net investment in a foreign operation shall be accounted for as the cash flow hedge<br>• The effective proportion should be recognized in equity<br>• The ineffective element should be recognized directly in the income statement. |

## Qualifying Hedging instruments

Derivatives that are embedded in hybrid contracts, but that are not separately accounted for, cannot be designated as separate hedging instruments.

An entity's own equity instruments are not financial assets or financial liabilities of the entity and therefore cannot be designated as hedging instruments.

For hedges of foreign currency risk, the foreign currency risk component of a non-derivative financial instrument is determined in accordance with Ind AS 21.

*Written options*

This Standard does not restrict the circumstances in which a derivative that is measured at fair value through profit or loss may be designated as a hedging instrument, except for some written options. A written option does not qualify as a hedging instrument unless it is designated as an offset to a purchased option, including one that is embedded in another financial instrument (for example, a written call option used to hedge a callable liability).

## Designation of hedging instruments

For hedges other than hedges of foreign currency risk, when an entity designates a non-derivative financial asset or a non-derivative financial liability measured at fair value through profit or loss as a hedging instrument, it may only designate the non-derivative financial instrument in its entirety or a proportion of it.

A single hedging instrument may be designated as a hedging instrument of more than one type of risk, provided that there is a specific designation of the hedging instrument and of the different risk positions as hedged items. Those hedged items can be in different hedging relationships.

## Qualifying hedged items

A firm commitment to acquire a business in a business combination cannot be a hedged item, except for foreign currency risk, because the other risks being hedged cannot be specifically identified and measured. Those other risks are general business risks.

An equity method investment cannot be a hedged item in a fair value hedge. This is because the equity method recognizes in profit or loss the investor's share of the investee's profit or loss, instead of changes in the investment's fair value. For a similar reason, an investment in a consolidated subsidiary cannot be a hedged item in a fair value hedge.

This is because consolidation recognizes in profit or loss the subsidiary's profit or loss, instead of changes in the investment's fair value. A hedge of a net investment in a foreign operation is different because it is a hedge of the foreign currency exposure, not a fair value hedge of the change in the value of the investment.

The Standard permits an entity to designate as hedged items aggregated exposures that are a combination of an exposure and a derivative. When designating such a hedged item, an entity assesses whether the aggregated exposure combines an exposure with a derivative so that it creates a different aggregated exposure that is managed as one exposure for a particular risk (or risks). In that case, the entity may designate the hedged item on the basis of the aggregated exposure. For example:

(a) an entity may hedge a given quantity of highly probable coffee purchases in 15 months' time against price risk (based on US dollars) using a 15-month futures contract for coffee. The highly probable coffee purchases and the futures contract for coffee in combination can be viewed as a 15-month fixed-amount US dollar foreign currency risk exposure for risk management purposes (i.e. like any fixed amount US dollar cash outflow in 15 months' time).

(b) an entity may hedge the foreign currency risk for the entire term of a 10-year fixed rate debt denominated in a foreign currency. However, the entity requires fixed-rate exposure in its functional currency only for a short to medium term (say two years) and floating rate exposure in its functional currency for the remaining term to maturity. At the end of each of the two-year intervals (i.e. on a two-year rolling basis) the entity fixes the next two years' interest rate exposure (if the interest level is such that the entity wants to fix interest rates). In such a situation an entity may enter into a 10-year fixed-to-floating cross-currency interest rate swap that swaps the fixed-rate foreign currency debt into a variable-rate functional currency exposure. This is overlaid with a two-year interest rate swap that—on the basis of the functional currency—swaps variable-rate debt into fixed-rate debt. In effect, the fixed-rate foreign currency debt and the 10-year fixed-to-floating cross-currency interest rate swap in combination are viewed as a 10-year variable-rate debt functional currency exposure for risk management purposes.

When designating the hedged item on the basis of the aggregated exposure, an entity considers the combined effect of the items that constitute the aggregated exposure for the purpose of assessing hedge effectiveness and measuring hedge ineffectiveness. However, the items that constitute the aggregated exposure remain accounted for separately. This means that, for example:

(a) derivatives that are part of an aggregated exposure are recognised as separate assets or liabilities measured at fair value; and

(b) if a hedging relationship is designated between the items that constitute the aggregated exposure, the way in which a derivative is included as part of an aggregated exposure must be consistent with the designation of that derivative as the hedging instrument at the level of the aggregated exposure. For example, if an entity excludes the forward element of a derivative from its designation as the hedging instrument for the hedging relationship between the items that constitute the aggregated exposure, it must also exclude the forward element when including that derivative as a hedged item as part of the aggregated exposure. Otherwise, the aggregated exposure shall include a derivative, either in its entirety or a proportion of it.

The Standard prescribes that in consolidated financial statements the foreign currency risk of a highly probable forecast intragroup transaction may qualify as a hedged item in a cash flow hedge, provided that the transaction is denominated in a currency other than the functional currency of the entity entering into that transaction and that the foreign currency risk will affect consolidated profit or loss.

For this purpose, an entity can be a parent, subsidiary, associate, joint arrangement or branch. If the foreign currency risk of a forecast intragroup transaction does not affect consolidated profit or loss, the intragroup transaction cannot qualify as a hedged item. This is usually the case for royalty payments, interest payments or management charges between members of the same group, unless there is a related external transaction.

However, when the foreign currency risk of a forecast intragroup transaction will affect consolidated profit or loss, the intragroup transaction can qualify as a hedged item. An example is forecast sales or purchases of inventories between members of the same group if there is an onward sale of the inventory to a party external to the group.

Similarly, a forecast intragroup sale of plant and equipment from the group entity that manufactured it to a group entity that will use the plant and equipment in its operations may affect consolidated profit or loss. This could occur, for example, because the plant and equipment will be depreciated by the purchasing entity and the amount initially recognised for the plant and equipment may change if the forecast intragroup transaction is denominated in a currency other than the functional currency of the purchasing entity.

If a hedge of a forecast intragroup transaction qualifies for hedge accounting, any gain or loss is recognised in, and taken out of, other comprehensive income. The relevant period or periods during which the foreign currency risk of the hedged transaction affects profit or loss is when it affects consolidated profit or loss.

## Designation of hedged items

A component is a hedged item that is less than the entire item. Consequently, a component reflects only some of the risks of the item of which it is a part or reflects the risks only to some extent (for example, when designating a proportion of an item).

***Risk components***

To be eligible for designation as a hedged item, a risk component must be a separately identifiable component of the financial or the non-financial item, and the changes in the cash flows or the fair value of the item attributable to changes in that risk component must be reliably measurable.

When identifying what risk components qualify for designation as a hedged item, an entity assesses such risk components within the context of the particular market structure to which the risk or risks relate and in which the hedging activity takes place. Such a determination requires an evaluation of the relevant facts and circumstances, which differ by risk and market.

When designating risk components as hedged items, an entity considers whether the risk components are explicitly specified in a contract (contractually specified risk components) or whether they are implicit in the fair value or the cash flows of an item of which they are a part (non-contractually specified risk components). Non-contractually specified risk components can relate to items that are not a contract (for example, forecast transactions) or contracts that do not explicitly specify the component (for example, a firm commitment that includes only one single price instead of a pricing formula that references different underlying).

### Illustration 14.15: Hedged item

Alpha Limited has a long-term supply contract for natural gas that is priced using a contractually specified formula that references commodities and other factors (for example, gas oil, fuel oil and other components such as transport charges). Alpha Limited hedges the gas oil component in that supply contract using a gas oil forward contract. Because the gas oil component is specified by the terms and conditions of the supply contract it is a contractually specified risk component. Hence, because of the pricing formula, Alpha Limited concludes that the gas oil price exposure is separately identifiable. At the same time, there is a market for gas oil forward contracts.

Hence, Alpha Limited concludes that the gas oil price exposure is reliably measurable. Consequently, the gas oil price exposure in the supply contract is a risk component that is eligible for designation as a hedged item.

**Illustration 14.16: Hedging relationships**

Beta Limited hedges its future coffee purchases based on its production forecast. Hedging starts up to 15 months before delivery for part of the forecast purchase volume. Beta Limited increases the hedged volume over time (as the delivery date approaches). Beta Limited uses two different types of contracts to manage its coffee price risk:

(i) exchange-traded coffee futures contracts; and

(ii) coffee supply contracts for Arabica coffee from Colombia delivered to a specific manufacturing site. These contracts price a tonne of coffee based on the exchange-traded coffee futures contract price plus a fixed price differential plus a variable logistics services charge using a pricing formula.

The coffee supply contract is an executory contract in accordance with which Beta Limited takes actual delivery of coffee.

For deliveries that relate to the current harvest, entering into the coffee supply contracts allows Beta Limited to fix the price differential between the actual coffee quality purchased (Arabica coffee from Colombia) and the benchmark quality that is the underlying of the exchange-traded futures contract.

However, for deliveries that relate to the next harvest, the coffee supply contracts are not yet available, so the price differential cannot be fixed. Beta Limited uses exchange-traded coffee futures contracts to hedge the benchmark quality component of its coffee price risk for deliveries that relate to the current harvest as well as the next harvest. Beta Limited determines that it is exposed to three different risks: coffee price risk reflecting the benchmark quality, coffee price risk reflecting the difference (spread) between the price for the benchmark quality coffee and the particular Arabica coffee from Colombia that it actually receives, and the variable logistics costs. For deliveries related to the current harvest, after Beta Limited enters into a coffee supply contract, the coffee price risk reflecting the benchmark quality is a contractually specified risk component because the pricing formula includes an indexation to the exchange traded coffee futures contract price. Beta Limited concludes that this risk component is separately identifiable and reliably measurable.

For deliveries related to the next harvest, Beta Limited has not yet entered into any coffee supply contracts (i.e. those deliveries are forecast transactions). Hence, the coffee price risk reflecting the benchmark quality is a non-contractually specified risk component. Beta Limited's analysis of the market structure takes into account how eventual deliveries of the particular coffee that it receives are priced. Hence, on the basis of this analysis of the market structure, Beta Limited concludes that the forecast transactions also involve the coffee price risk that reflects the benchmark quality as a risk component that is separately identifiable and reliably measurable even though it is not contractually specified. Consequently, Beta Limited may designate hedging relationships on a risk components basis (for the coffee price risk that reflects the benchmark quality) for coffee supply contracts as well as forecast transactions.

**Illustration 14.17: Hedge effectiveness**

Gamma Limited hedges part of its future jet fuel purchases on the basis of its consumption forecast up to 24 months before delivery and increases the volume that it hedges over time. Gamma Limited hedges this exposure using different types of contracts depending on the time horizon of the hedge, which affects the market liquidity of the derivatives. For the longer time horizons (12–24 months) Gamma Limited uses crude oil contracts because only these have sufficient market liquidity. For time horizons of 6–12 months Gamma Limited uses gas oil derivatives because they are sufficiently liquid. For time horizons up to six months Gamma Limited uses jet fuel contracts. Gamma Limited's analysis of the market structure for oil and oil products and its evaluation of the relevant facts and circumstances is as follows:

(i) Gamma Limited operates in a geographical area in which Brent is the crude oil benchmark. Crude oil is a raw material benchmark that affects the price of various refined oil products as their most basic input. Gas oil is a benchmark for refined oil products, which is used as a pricing reference for oil distillates more generally. This is also reflected in the types of derivative financial instruments for the crude oil and refined oil products markets of the environment in which Gamma Limited operates, such as:
- the benchmark crude oil futures contract, which is for Brent crude oil;
- the benchmark gas oil futures contract, which is used as the pricing reference for distillates—for example, jet fuel spread derivatives cover the price differential between jet fuel and that benchmark gas oil; and
- the benchmark gas oil crack spread derivative (i.e. the derivative for the price differential between crude oil and gas oil—a refining margin), which is indexed to Brent crude oil.

(ii) the pricing of refined oil products does not depend on which particular crude oil is processed by a particular refinery because those refined oil products (such as gas oil or jet fuel) are standardized products.

Hence, Gamma Limited concludes that the price risk of its jet fuel purchases includes a crude oil price risk component based on Brent crude oil and a gas oil price risk component, even though crude oil and gas oil are not specified in any contractual arrangement. Gamma Limited concludes that these two risk components are separately identifiable and reliably measurable even though they are not contractually specified. Consequently, Gamma Limited may designate hedging relationships for forecast jet fuel purchases on a risk components basis (for crude oil or gas oil). This analysis also means that if, for example, Gamma

Limited used crude oil derivatives based on West Texas Intermediate (WTI) crude oil, changes in the price differential between Brent crude oil and WTI crude oil would cause hedge ineffectiveness.

**Illustration 14.18: Designation of hedging relationships**

Delphi Ltd holds a fixed-rate debt instrument. This instrument is issued in an environment with a market in which a large variety of similar debt instruments are compared by their spreads to a benchmark rate (for example, LIBOR) and variable rate instruments in that environment are typically indexed to that benchmark rate.

Interest rate swaps are frequently used to manage interest rate risk on the basis of that benchmark rate, irrespective of the spread of debt instruments to that benchmark rate. The price of fixed-rate debt instruments varies directly in response to changes in the benchmark rate as they happen. Delphi Ltd concludes that the benchmark rate is a component that can be separately identified and reliably measured.

Consequently, Delphi Ltd may designate hedging relationships for the fixed-rate debt instrument on a risk component basis for the benchmark interest rate risk.

### Qualifying criteria for hedge accounting: Hedge effectiveness

Hedge effectiveness is the extent to which changes in the fair value or the cash flows of the hedging instrument offset changes in the fair value or the cash flows of the hedged item (for example, when the hedged item is a risk component, the relevant change in fair value or cash flows of an item is the one that is attributable to the hedged risk). Hedge ineffectiveness is the extent to which the changes in the fair value or the cash flows of the hedging instrument are greater or less than those on the hedged item.

When designating a hedging relationship and on an ongoing basis, an entity shall analyse the sources of hedge ineffectiveness that are expected to affect the hedging relationship during its term.

### Economic relationship between the hedged item and the hedging instrument

The requirement that an economic relationship exists means that the hedging instrument and the hedged item have values that generally move in the opposite direction because of the same risk, which is the hedged risk. Hence, there must be an expectation that the value of the hedging instrument and the value of the hedged item will systematically change in response to movements in either the same underlying or underlying that are economically related in such a way that they respond in a similar way to the risk that is being hedged (for example, Brent and WTI crude oil).

If the underlying are not the same but are economically related, there can be situations in which the values of the hedging instrument and the hedged item move in the same direction, for example, because the price differential between the two related underlying changes while the underlying themselves do not move significantly. That is still consistent with an economic relationship between the hedging instrument and the hedged item if the values of the hedging instrument and the hedged item are still expected to typically move in the opposite direction when the underlying move.

The assessment of whether an economic relationship exists includes an analysis of the possible behaviour of the hedging relationship during its term to ascertain whether it can be expected to meet the risk management objective. The mere existence of a statistical correlation between two variables does not, by itself, support a valid conclusion that an economic relationship exists.

### Hedge ratio

In accordance with the hedge effectiveness requirements, the hedge ratio of the hedging relationship must be the same as that resulting from the quantity of the hedged item that the entity actually hedges and the quantity of the hedging instrument that the entity actually uses to hedge that quantity of hedged item.

**Illustration 14.19: Hedging Effectiveness**

If an entity hedges less than 100 per cent of the exposure on an item, such as 85 per cent, it shall designate the hedging relationship using a hedge ratio that is the same as that resulting from 85 per cent of the exposure and the quantity of the hedging instrument that the entity actually uses to hedge those 85 per cent. Similarly, if, for example, an entity hedges an exposure using a nominal amount of 40 units of a financial instrument, it shall designate the hedging relationship using a hedge ratio that is the same as that resulting from that quantity of 40 units (ie the entity must not use a hedge ratio based on a higher quantity of units that it might hold in total or a lower quantity of units) and the quantity of the hedged item that it actually hedges with those 40 units.

**Illustration 14.20: Designation of hedging relationships**

An entity enters into and designates a quantity of the hedging instrument that is not the quantity that it determined as the best hedge of the hedged item because the standard volume of the hedging instruments does not allow it to enter into that exact quantity of hedging instrument (a 'lot size issue').

An example is an entity that hedges 100 tonnes of coffee purchases with standard coffee futures contracts that have a contract size of 37,500 lbs. (pounds). The entity could only use either five or six contracts (equivalent to 85.0 and 102.1 tonnes respectively) to hedge the purchase volume of 100 tonnes. In that case, the entity designates the hedging relationship using the hedge ratio that results from the number of coffee futures contracts that it actually uses, because the hedge ineffectiveness resulting from the mismatch in the weightings of the hedged item and the hedging instrument would not result in an accounting outcome that is inconsistent with the purpose of hedge accounting.

### *14.5.2.22 Interest rate swap*

Interest rate swap can be defined as a financial contract between two parties (called counter parties) to exchange on a particular date in the future, one series of cash flows (fixed interest) to another series of cash flows (variable or floating interest) in the same currency on the same principal (an agreed amount called notional principal) for an agreed period of time. The contract will specify the interest rates, the benchmark rate to be followed the notional principal amount for the transaction etc.

Interest rates are of two types, fixed interest rates and floating interest rates which vary according to changes in a standard benchmark interest rate.

An investor holding a security which pays a floating interest rate is exposed to interest rate risk.

The investor can manage this risk by entering into a interest rate swap.

**Illustration 14.21: Interest swap on forward contract**

XYZ Ltd needs $ 300000 on May 1 2020 for repayment of loan instalment and interest. As on 1st December 2019 it appears to the company that the dollar may be dearer as compared to the exchange rate prevailing on that date $ 1 = Rs.73.50. Accordingly, the company enters into a forward contract with a banker for $ 300000. Forward rate as on 1 December 2099 was $1 = Rs.74. As on May 1 2020, the banker will have to pay the company $ 300000 at Rs.74. Spot rate as on May 1 2020 was $1 = Rs.74.80. Has the company gained or lost? Had the result been different if the rate would have been $1 = Rs.73.80?

**Solution**

Payment to be made as per forward contract ($300,000 X Rs.74)
= Rs.2,22,00,000 (A)

Amount payable had the forward contract not been in place
($ 300000 x Rs.74.80) = Rs.2,24,40,000 (B)

Gain out of the forward contract (B – A) = Rs.**2,40,000**

In the second scenario the amount payable would have been
($ 300000 x Rs.73.80) = Rs. 2,21,40,000
(C)

Loss out of the forward contract (C – A) = Rs. 60,000

### 14.5.2.23 Definitions used across the Standard

| Item | Definition |
|---|---|
| ***12-month expected credit losses*** | The portion of lifetime expected credit losses that represent the expected credit losses that result from default events on a financial instrument that are possible within the 12 months after the reporting date. |
| ***Amortized cost of a financial asset or financial liability*** | The amount at which the financial asset or financial liability is measured at initial recognition minus the principal repayments, plus or minus the cumulative amortization using the effective interest method of any difference between that initial amount and the maturity amount and, for financial assets, adjusted for any loss allowance. |
| ***Contract assets*** | Those rights that Ind AS 115, *Revenue from Contracts with Customers,* specifies are accounted for in accordance with this Standard for the purposes of recognizing and measuring impairment gains or losses. |
| ***Credit-impaired financial asset*** | A financial asset is credit-impaired when one or more events that have a detrimental impact on the estimated future cash flows of that financial asset have occurred. Evidence that a financial asset is credit-impaired include observable data about the following events:<br>(a) significant financial difficulty of the issuer or the borrower.<br>(b) a breach of contract, such as a default or past due event;<br>(c) the lender(s) of the borrower, for economic or contractual reasons relating to the borrower's financial difficulty, having granted to the borrower a concession(s) that the lender(s) would not otherwise consider;<br>(d) it is becoming probable that the borrower will enter bankruptcy or other financial reorganization.<br>(e) the disappearance of an active market for that financial asset because of financial difficulties; or<br>(f) the purchase or origination of a financial asset at a deep discount that reflects the incurred credit losses.<br>It may not be possible to identify a single discrete event-instead, the combined effect of several events may have caused financial assets to become credit-impaired. |
| ***Credit loss*** | The difference between all contractual cash flows that are due to an entity in accordance with the contract and all the cash flows that the entity expects to receive (i.e. all cash shortfalls), discounted at the original effective interest rate (or credit-adjusted effective interest rate for purchased or originated credit-impaired financial assets). An entity shall estimate cash flows by considering all contractual terms |

| Item | Definition |
|---|---|
| | of the financial instrument (for example, prepayment, extension, call and similar options) through the expected life of that financial instrument. The cash flows that are considered shall include cash flows from the sale of collateral held or other credit enhancements that are integral to the contractual terms. There is a presumption that the expected life of a financial instrument can be estimated reliably. However, in those rare cases when it is not possible to reliably estimate the expected life of a financial instrument, the entity shall use the remaining contractual term of the financial instrument. |
| ***Credit-adjusted effective interest rate*** | The rate that exactly discounts the estimated future cash payments or receipts through the expected life of the financial asset to the amortized cost of a financial asset that is a purchased or originated credit-impaired financial asset.<br>When calculating the credit-adjusted effective interest rate, an entity shall estimate the expected cash flows by considering all contractual terms of the financial asset (for example, prepayment, extension, call and similar options) and expected credit losses. The calculation includes all fees and points paid or received between parties to the contract that are an integral part of the effective interest rate, transaction costs, and all other premiums or discounts. There is a presumption that the cash flows and the expected life of a group of similar financial instruments can be estimated reliably. However, in those rare cases when it is not possible to reliably estimate the cash flows or the remaining life of a financial instrument (or group of financial instruments), the entity shall use the contractual cash flows over the full contractual term of the financial instrument (or group of financial instruments). |
| ***Derecognition*** | The removal of a previously recognised financial asset or financial liability from an entity's balance sheet. |
| ***Derivative*** | A financial instrument or other contract within the scope of this Standard with all three of the following characteristics.<br>(a) its value changes in response to the change in a specified interest rate, financial instrument price, commodity price, foreign exchange rate, index of prices or rates, credit rating or credit index, or other variable, provided in the case of a non-financial variable that the variable is not specific to a party to the contract (sometimes called the 'underlying').<br>(b) it requires no initial net investment or an initial net investment that is smaller than would be required for other types of contracts that would be expected to have a similar response to changes in market factors. |

| Item | Definition |
|---|---|
| | (c) it is settled at a future date. |
| ***Dividends*** | Distributions of profits to holders of equity instruments in proportion to their holdings of a particular class of capital. |
| ***Effective interest method*** | The rate that exactly discounts estimated future cash payments or receipts through the expected life of the financial asset or financial liability to the gross carrying amount of a financial asset or to the amortized cost of a financial liability.<br>When calculating the effective interest rate, an entity shall estimate the expected cash flows by considering all the contractual terms of the financial instrument (for example, prepayment, extension, call and similar options) but shall not consider the expected credit losses. The calculation includes all fees and points paid or received between parties to the contract that are an integral part of the effective interest rate, transaction costs, and all other premiums or discounts.<br>There is a presumption that the cash flows and the expected life of a group of similar financial instruments can be estimated reliably. However, in those rare cases when it is not possible to reliably estimate the cash flows or the expected life of a financial instrument (or group of financial instruments), the entity shall use the contractual cash flows over the full contractual term of the financial instrument (or group of financial instruments). |
| ***Expected credit losses*** | The weighted average of credit losses with the respective risks of a default occurring as the weights. |
| ***Financial guarantee contract*** | A contract that requires the issuer to make specified payments to reimburse the holder for a loss it incurs because a specified debtor fails to make payment when due in accordance with the original or modified terms of a debt instrument. |
| ***Financial liability at fair value through profit or loss*** | A financial liability that meets one of the following conditions:<br>(a) it meets the definition of held for trading.<br>(b) upon initial recognition it is designated by the entity as at fair value through profit or loss.<br>(c) it is designated either upon initial recognition or subsequently as at fair value through profit or loss. |
| ***Firm commitment*** | A binding agreement for the exchange of a specified quantity of resources at a specified price on a specified future date or dates. |
| ***Forecast transaction*** | An uncommitted but anticipated future transaction. |

| Item | Definition |
|---|---|
| ***Gross carrying amount of a financial asset*** | The amortized cost of a financial asset, before adjusting for any loss allowance. |
| ***Hedging instrument*** | a designated derivative or (for a hedge of the risk of changes in foreign currency exchange rates only) a designated non-derivative financial asset or non-derivative financial liability whose fair value or cash flows are expected to offset changes in<br>the fair value or cash flows of a designated hedged item |
| ***Hedge ratio*** | The relationship between the quantity of the hedging instrument and the quantity of the hedged item in terms of their relative weighting. |
| ***Held for trading*** | A financial asset or financial liability that:<br>(a) is acquired or incurred principally for the purpose of selling or repurchasing it in the near term.<br>(b) on initial recognition is part of a portfolio of identified financial instruments that are managed together and for which there is evidence of a recent actual pattern of short-term profit-taking; or<br>(c) is a derivative (except for a derivative that is a financial guarantee contract or a designated and effective hedging instrument). |
| ***Impairment gain or loss*** | Gains or losses that are recognised in profit or loss and that arise from applying the impairment requirements. |
| ***Lifetime expected credit losses*** | The expected credit losses that result from all possible default events over the expected life of a financial instrument. |
| ***Loss allowance*** | The allowance for expected credit losses on financial assets measured in accordance with the provisions of the Standard, lease receivables and contract assets, the accumulated impairment amount for financial assets measured in accordance with the provisions of the Standard and the provision for expected credit losses on loan commitments and financial guarantee contracts. |
| ***Modification gain or loss*** | The amount arising from adjusting the gross carrying amount of a financial asset to reflect the renegotiated or modified contractual cash flows. The entity recalculates the gross carrying amount of a financial asset as the present value of the estimated future cash payments or receipts through the expected life of the negotiated or modified financial asset that are discounted at the financial asset's original effective interest rate (or the Original credit-adjusted |

| Item | Definition |
|---|---|
| | effective interest rate for purchased or originated credit-impaired financial assets) or, when applicable, the revised effective interest rate calculated in accordance with the provisions of the Standard.<br>When estimating the expected cash flows of a financial asset, an entity shall consider all contractual terms of the financial asset (for example, prepayment, call and similar options) but shall not consider the expected credit losses, unless the financial asset is a purchased or originated credit-impaired financial asset, in which case an entity shall also consider the initial expected credit losses that were considered when calculating the original credit adjusted effective interest rate. |
| ***Past due*** | A financial asset is past due when a counterparty has failed to make a payment when that payment was contractually due. |
| ***Purchased or originated credit-impaired financial asset*** | Purchased or originated financial asset(s) that are credit impaired on initial recognition. |
| ***Reclassification date*** | The first day of the first reporting period following the change in business model that results in an entity reclassifying financial assets. |
| ***Regular way purchase or sale*** | A purchase or sale of a financial asset under a contract whose terms require delivery of the asset within the time frame established generally by regulation or convention in the market place concerned. |
| ***Transaction costs*** | Incremental costs that are directly attributable to the acquisition, issue or disposal of a financial asset or financial liability<br>An incremental cost is one that would not have been incurred if the entity had not acquired, issued, or disposed of the financial instrument. |

### 14.5.2.24 Hedges of a net investment in a foreign operation

Many reporting entities have investments in foreign operations. Such foreign operations may be subsidiaries, associates, joint ventures, or branches. Ind AS 21 requires an entity to determine the functional currency of each of its foreign operations as the currency of the primary economic environment of that operation. When translating the results and financial position of a foreign operation into a presentation currency, the entity is required to recognise foreign exchange differences in other comprehensive income until it disposes of the foreign operation.

Hedge accounting of the foreign currency risk arising from a net investment in a foreign operation will apply only when the net assets of that foreign operation are included in the financial statements.

Ind AS 109 requires the designation of an eligible hedged item and eligible hedging instruments in a hedge accounting relationship. If there is a designated hedging relationship, in the case of a net investment hedge, the gain or loss on the hedging instrument that is determined to be an effective hedge of the net investment is recognised in other comprehensive income and is included with the foreign exchange differences arising on translation of the results and financial position of the foreign operation.

**Considerations**

(a) *the nature of the hedged risk and the amount of the hedged item for which a hedging relationship may be designated:*

(b) *where in a group the hedging instrument can be held:*

(c) *what amounts should be reclassified from equity to profit or loss as reclassification adjustments on disposal of the foreign operation:*

**Accounting principles**

**(a) Nature of the hedged risk and amount of the hedged item for which a hedging relationship may be designated**

Hedge accounting may be applied only to the foreign exchange differences arising between the functional currency of the foreign operation and the parent entity's functional currency.

In a hedge of the foreign currency risks arising from a net investment in a foreign operation, the hedged item can be an amount of net assets equal to or less than the carrying amount of the net assets of the foreign operation in the consolidated financial statements of the parent entity.

The hedged risk may be designated as the foreign currency exposure arising between the functional currency of the foreign operation and the functional currency of any parent entity (the immediate, intermediate, or ultimate parent entity) of that foreign operation. The fact that the net investment is held through an intermediate parent does not affect the nature of the economic risk arising from the foreign currency exposure to the ultimate parent entity.

An exposure to foreign currency risk arising from a net investment in a foreign operation may qualify for hedge accounting only once in the consolidated financial statements. Therefore, if the same net assets of a foreign operation are hedged by more than one parent entity within the group (for example, both a direct and an indirect parent entity) for the same risk, only one hedging relationship will qualify for hedge accounting in the consolidated financial statements of the ultimate parent.

**(b) Where the hedging instrument can be held**

A derivative or a non-derivative instrument (or a combination of derivative and non-derivative instruments) may be designated as a hedging instrument in a hedge of a net investment in a foreign operation. The hedging instrument(s) may be held by any entity or entities within the group, as long as the designation, documentation, and effectiveness requirements of Ind AS 109 paragraph 6.4.1 that relate to a net investment hedge are satisfied. In particular, the hedging strategy of the group should be clearly documented because of the possibility of different designations at different levels of the group.

**(c) Disposal of a hedged foreign operation**

When a foreign operation that was hedged is disposed of, the amount reclassified to profit or loss as a reclassification adjustment from the foreign currency translation reserve in the consolidated financial statements of the parent in respect of the hedging instrument is the amount that Ind AS 109 paragraph 6.5.14 requires to be identified. That amount is the cumulative gain or loss on the hedging instrument that was determined to be an effective hedge.

The amount reclassified to profit or loss from the foreign currency translation reserve in the consolidated financial statements of a parent in respect of the net investment in that foreign operation in accordance with Ind AS 21 paragraph 48 is the amount included in that parent's foreign currency translation reserve in respect of that foreign operation.

In the ultimate parent's consolidated financial statements, the aggregate net amount recognised in the foreign currency translation reserve in respect of all foreign operations is not affected by the consolidation method. However, whether the ultimate parent uses the direct or the step-by-step method of consolidation5 may affect the amount included in its foreign currency translation reserve in respect of an individual foreign operation.

The use of the step-by-step method of consolidation may result in the reclassification to profit or loss of an amount different from that used to determine hedge effectiveness. This difference may be eliminated by determining the amount relating to that foreign operation that would have arisen if the direct method of consolidation had been used. Making this adjustment is not required by Ind AS 21. However, it is an accounting policy choice that should be followed consistently for all net investments.

## 14.5.3 Financial Instruments - disclosures

For details of disclosure please refer Ind AS 107: Disclosures

**Illustration 14.22: Accounting Policy: Financial Instruments**

| **Financial Instruments** |
|---|
| Financial assets and financial liabilities are recognised when the Company becomes a party to the contractual provisions of the financial instruments.<br>On initial recognition, financial assets and financial liabilities are recognised at fair value plus/minus transaction cost that is attributable to the acquisition or issue |

of financial assets and financial liabilities. In case of financial assets and financial liabilities which are recognised at fair value through profit and loss (FVTPL), its transaction costs are recognised in Statement of Profit and Loss.
(*Source: Power Finance Corporation*)

**Illustration 14.23: Accounting Policy: Financial Assets and Liabilities**

Financial Assets

All regular way purchases or sales of financial assets are recognised and de-recognised on a settlement date basis. Regular way purchases or sales are purchases or sales of financial assets that require delivery of assets within the time frame established by regulation or convention in the marketplace.

After initial recognition, financial assets are subsequently measured in their entirety at either amortised cost or fair value, depending on the classification of the financial assets.

(i) Classification and Measurement of Financial assets (other than Equity instruments)

a) Financial assets at Amortised Cost:

Financial assets that meet the following conditions are subsequently measured at amortised cost using Effective Interest Rate method (EIR):

- the asset is held within a business model whose objective is to hold assets in order to collect contractual cash flows; and
- the contractual terms of the asset give rise on specified dates to cash flows that are Solely Payments of Principal and Interest (SPPI) on the principal amount outstanding.

Effective Interest Rate (EIR) method

The effective interest rate method is a method of calculating the amortised cost of financial asset and of allocating interest income over the expected life. The Company while applying EIR method, generally amortizes any fees, transaction costs and other premiums or discount that are integral part of the effective interest rate of a financial instrument.

Income is recognised in the Statement of Profit and Loss on an effective interest rate basis for financial assets other than those classified as at FVTPL.

EIR is determined at the initial recognition of the financial asset. EIR is subsequently updated at every reset, in accordance with the terms of the respective contract.

Once the terms of financial assets are renegotiated, other than market driven interest rate movement, any gain/loss measured using the previous EIR as calculated before the modification, is recognised in the Statement of Profit and Loss in period during which such renegotiations occur.

(b) Financial assets at Fair Value through Other Comprehensive Income (FVTOCI)

A financial asset is measured at FVTOCI if both the following conditions are met:

- The objective of the business model is achieved both by collecting contractual cash flows and selling the financial asset; and
- the contractual terms of the asset give rise on specified dates to cash flows that are Solely Payments of Principal and Interest (SPPI) on the principal amount outstanding.

All fair value changes are recognised in Other Comprehensive Income (OCI) and accumulated in Reserve.

(c) Financial assets at fair value through profit or loss (FVTPL)

A financial asset is measured at FVTPL unless it is measured at amortised cost or FVTOCI, with all changes in fair value recognised in Statement of Profit and Loss.

Business Model

An assessment of business model for managing financial assets is fundamental to the classification of a financial asset. The Company determines the business model at a level that reflects how financial assets are managed together to achieve a particular business objective of generating cash flows. The Company's business model assessment is performed at a higher level of aggregation rather than on an instrument-by-instrument basis.

The Company is in the business of lending loans across power sector value chain and such loans are managed to realise the contractual cash flows over the tenure of the loan. Further, other financial assets may also be held by the Company to collect the contractual cash flows.

(ii) Classification and measurement of Equity Instruments

All equity investments other than in subsidiaries, joint ventures and associates are measured at fair value. Equity instruments which are held for trading are classified as at FVTPL. For all other equity instruments, the Company at initial recognition makes an irrevocable election to classify it as either FVTOCI or FVTPL. The Company makes such election on an instrument by instrument basis.

An equity investment classified as FVTOCI is initially measured at fair value plus transaction costs. Subsequently, it is measured at fair value and, all fair value changes are recognised in Other Comprehensive Income (OCI) and accumulated in Reserve. There is no recycling of the amounts from OCI to Statement of Profit and Loss, even on sale of investment. However, the Company transfers the same within equity.

Equity instruments included within the FVTPL category are measured at fair value with all changes recognised in the Statement of Profit and Loss.

(iii) Impairment of financial assets

(a) Subsequent to initial recognition, the Company recognises expected credit loss (ECL) on financial assets measured at amortised cost as required under Ind AS 109 'Financial Instruments'. ECL on such financial assets, other than loans assets, is measured at an amount equal to life time expected losses. The Company presents the ECL charge or reversal (where the net amount is a negative balance for a particular period) in the Statement of Profit and Loss as "Impairment on financial instruments".

The impairment requirements for the recognition and measurement of ECL are equally applied to loan asset at FVTOCI except that ECL is recognised in Other Comprehensive Income and is not reduced from the carrying amount in the Balance Sheet.

(b) Impairment of Loan Assets and commitments under Letter of Comfort (LoC):

The Company measures ECL on loan assets at an amount equal to the lifetime ECL if there is credit impairment or there has been significant increase in credit risk (SICR) since initial recognition. If there is no SICR as compared to initial recognition, the Company measures ECL at an amount equal to 12-month ECL. When making the assessment of whether there has been a SICR since initial recognition, the Company considers reasonable and supportable information, that is available without undue cost or effort. If the Company measured loss allowance as lifetime ECL in the previous period, but determines in a subsequent period that there has been no SICR since initial recognition due to improvement in credit quality, the Company again measures the loss allowance based on 12-month ECL.

ECL is measured on individual basis for credit impaired loan assets, and on other loan assets it is generally measured on collective basis using homogenous groups.

The Company measures impairment on commitments under LoC on similar basis as in case of Loan assets.

(c) The impairment losses and reversals are recognised in Statement of Profit and Loss.

(iv) De-recognition of financial assets

The Company de-recognizes a financial asset when the contractual rights to the cash flows from the asset expire, or when it transfers the financial asset along with all the substantial risks and rewards of ownership of the asset to another party.

On de-recognition of a financial asset in its entirety, the difference between the asset's carrying amount and the sum of the consideration received & receivable, and the cumulative gain or loss that had been recognised in Other Comprehensive Income and accumulated in Equity, is recognised in Statement of Profit and Loss if such gain or loss would have otherwise been recognised in Statement of Profit and Loss on disposal of that financial asset.

Financial Liabilities

(i) All financial liabilities other than derivatives and financial guarantee contracts are subsequently measured at amortised cost using the effective interest rate (EIR) method.

EIR is determined at the initial recognition of the financial liability. EIR is subsequently updated for financial liabilities having floating interest rate, at the respective reset date, in accordance with the terms of the respective contract.

(ii) Financial guarantee

A financial guarantee issued by the Company is initially measured at fair value and, if not designated as at FVTPL, is subsequently measured at the higher of:

- the best estimate of expenditure required to settle any financial obligation arising as a result of the guarantee; and
- the amount initially recognised less, when appropriate, the cumulative amount of income recognised in the Statement of Profit and Loss.

(iii) De-recognition of financial liabilities

The Company de-recognises financial liabilities when, and only when, the Company's obligations are discharged, cancelled or have expired. The difference between the carrying amount of the financial liability de-recognised and the consideration paid & payable is recognised in Statement of Profit and Loss.

*(Source: Power Finance Corporation)*

## 14.6 NOTES ON ACCOUNTS

A Non-Banking Financial company shall disclose the following in the notes to accounts:

### 14.6.1 Cash and cash equivalents:

Cash and cash equivalents shall be classified as:

(i) Cash on hand

(ii) Balances with Banks (of the nature of cash and cash equivalents);

(iii) Cheques, drafts on hand; and

(iv) Others (specify nature).

**Illustration 14.24: Cash and cash equivalents**

| | Current Reporting Period | Previous Reporting Period |
|---|---|---|
| (i) Cash on hand | xxx | xxx |
| (ii) Balances with Banks (of the nature of cash and cash equivalents) | xxx | xxx |
| (iii) Cheques, drafts on hand; and | xxx | xxx |
| (iv) Others (specify nature). | xxx | xxx |
| **Total** | **xxx** | **xxx** |

**Cash and Bank balances**: The following disclosures with regard to cash and bank balances shall be made:

(i) Earmarked balances with banks (for example, for unpaid dividend) shall be separately stated.

(ii) Balances with banks to the extent held as margin money or security against the borrowings, guarantees, other commitments shall be disclosed separately.

(iii) Repatriation restrictions, if any, in respect of cash and bank balances shall be separately stated

**Illustration 14.25: Other balances with banks**

| | Current Reporting Period | Previous Reporting Period |
|---|---|---|
| (a) Balances with banks in current accounts (refer note (i) below) | xxx | xxx |
| (b) Balances with banks in deposit accounts (Refer note (ii) below) | xxx | xxx |
| **Total** | **xxx** | **xxx** |

Note:

(i) Balance with banks in current account includes Rs. xxx lakhs (Previous year Rs.xxx lakhs) towards unclaimed debenture application money and interest accrued thereon.

(ii) Balance with banks in deposit account includes Rs.xxx lakhs (Previous year Rs.xxx lakhs)

comprises deposits that have an original maturity exceeding 3 months and less than 12 months at balance sheet date.

The term 'Cash and cash equivalents' has not defined in Division III to Schedule III. According to *Ind AS-7, Statement of Cash Flows*, Cash is defined to include cash on hand and demand deposits with banks. Cash Equivalents are defined as short term, highly liquid investments that are readily convertible into known amounts of cash and which are subject to an insignificant risk of changes in value.

Further, in accordance with Ind AS 7, an investment normally qualifies as a cash equivalent only when it has a short maturity of, say, three months or less from the date of acquisition. This would include term deposits with banks that have an original maturity of three months or less. However, bank balances (including term deposits) held as margin money or security against borrowings are neither in the nature of demand deposits, nor readily available for use by the company, and accordingly, do not meet the aforesaid definition of cash equivalents. (*Source: ICAI Guidance Note, Schedule III, Division III*)

**Illustration 14.26. Accounting policy: Cash and cash equivalent**

> **Cash, Cash equivalents and bank balances**
>
> Cash, Cash equivalents and bank balances include fixed deposits, (with an original maturity of three months or less from the date of placement), margin money deposits, and earmarked balances with banks are carried at amortised cost. Short term and liquid investments being subject to more than insignificant risk of change in value, are included as part of cash and cash equivalents.
>
> (*Source: Tata Capital Financial Services Ltd*)

### 14.6.2 Derivative financial Instruments

The following should be disclosed in the note for Derivative Financial Instruments.

According to ICAI Guidance Note on Schedule III, Division III, an explanation should be given for the use of derivatives, how the risk is mitigated and for what purpose has the company entered into derivative contracts in accordance with Paragraphs 21A to 24F of Ind AS 107.

Example: To hedge its foreign currency risks, interest rate risks and equity price risks a company may enter into the following kinds of derivative contracts such as:

- interest rate swaps,
- cross-currency swaps,
- forward foreign exchange
- contracts,
- futures and options on interest rates,
- foreign currencies and equities etc.

### 14.6.3 Hedge Accounting

Some illustrations are provided below.

**Illustration 14.27: Derivative Financial Instruments and Cash flow hedges**

> **Derivative Financial Instruments**
>
> The Group holds derivative financial instruments to hedge its foreign currency and interest rate risk exposures. Embedded derivatives are separated from the host contract and accounted for separately if certain criteria are met.
>
> Derivatives are initially measured at fair value; any directly attributed transaction costs are recognised in profit and loss as incurred.
>
> Subsequent to initial recognition derivatives are measured at fair value, and changes therein are generally recognised in profit and loss.
>
> The Group designates certain derivatives as hedging instruments to hedge the variability in cash flows associated with its floating rate borrowings arising from

changes in interest rates and exchange rates.

At inception of designated hedging relationships, the Group documents the risk management objective and strategy for undertaking the hedge. The Group also documents the economic relationship between the hedged item and the hedging instrument, including whether the changes in cash flows of the hedged item and hedging instrument are expected to offset each other.

**Cash flow hedges**

When a derivative is designated as a cash flow hedging instrument, the effective portion of changes in the fair value of the derivative is recognised in OCI and accumulated in the other equity under 'effective portion of cash flows hedges'. The effective portion of changes in the fair value of the derivative that is recognised in OCI is limited to the cumulative change in fair value of the hedged item, determined on a present value basis, from inception of the hedge. Any ineffective portion of changes in fair value of the derivative is recognised immediately in profit or loss.

The Group designates only the change in fair value of the spot element of forward exchange contracts as the hedging instrument in cash flow hedge relationships. The change in fair value of the forward element of the forward exchange contracts ('forward points') is separately accounted for as cost of hedging and recognised separately within equity.

If a hedge no longer meets the criteria for hedge accounting or the hedging instrument is sold, expires, is terminated, or is exercised, then hedge accounting is discontinued prospectively. If the hedged future cash flows are no longer expected to occur, then the amounts that have been accumulated in other equity are immediately reclassified to profit or loss.

*(Source: TCFSL Annual Report: 2020*)

**Illustration 14.28: Derivative Financial Instruments and Cash flow and Fair Value hedges**

**Derivative Financial Instruments**

(i) The Company enters into a variety of derivative financial instruments such as Principal only swaps, Interest rate swaps, Options and forward contracts to manage its exposure to interest rate and foreign exchange rate risks.

(ii) The Company designates certain derivative contracts under hedge relationship either as cash flow hedges or fair value hedges.

**Cash flow hedge**

The effective portion of changes in the fair value of derivatives that are designated and qualify as cash flow hedges is recognised in Other Comprehensive Income. The gain or loss relating to ineffective portion is recognised immediately in Statement of Profit and Loss. Amounts recognised in Other Comprehensive Income (being effective portion) are reclassified to Statement of Profit and Loss in the periods when the hedged item affects profit or loss.

**Fair value hedge**

Changes in fair value of the designated portion of derivatives that qualify as fair value hedges are recognised in Statement of Profit and Loss immediately, together with any changes in the fair value of the hedged item that are attributable to the hedged risk. The change in the fair value of the designated portion of hedging instrument and the change in the hedged item attributable to the hedged risk are recognised in Statement of Profit and Loss in the line item relating to the hedged item.

Hedge accounting is discontinued when the hedging instrument expires, or terminated, or exercised, or when it no longer qualifies for hedge accounting.

(iii) Derivatives, other than those designated under hedge relationship, are initially recognised at fair value at the date the derivative contracts are entered into and are subsequently re-measured to their fair value at the end of each reporting period. The resulting gain or loss is recognised in Statement of Profit and Loss

*(Source: Power Finance Corporation*)

## 14.6.4 Nature and extent of risks arising from Financial Instruments

According to ICAI Guidance Embedded derivative separated from host contract and accounted separately as per Ind AS 109 requirements should be disclosed under the relevant heading, for example, options, etc.

The disclosures under this category are summarized as under:

| Part | Details of disclosures |
|---|---|
| Part I | (i) Currency derivatives<br>- Spot and forwards<br>- Currency futures<br>- Currency swaps<br>- Options purchased<br>- Options sold (written)<br>- Others |
| | Sub-total (i) |
| | (ii) Interest rate derivatives<br>Forward rate agreements and interest rate swaps<br>Options purchased<br>Options sold (written)<br>Futures<br>Others |
| | Sub-total (ii) |

| | |
|---|---|
| | (iii) Credit derivatives<br>(iv) Equity linked derivatives<br>(v) Other derivatives (please specify) |
| | Total Derivative<br>Financial Instruments (i+ii+iii+iv+v) |

| Part | Details of disclosures |
|---|---|
| Part II | Included in above (Part I) are derivatives held for hedging and risk management purposes as follows:<br>**(i) Fair value hedging:**<br>- Currency derivatives<br>- Interest rate derivatives<br>- Credit derivatives<br>- Equity linked derivatives<br>- Others |
| | Sub-total 1 |
| | Cash flow hedging:<br>- Currency derivatives<br>- Interest rate derivatives<br>- Credit derivatives<br>- Equity linked derivatives<br>- Others |
| | Sub-total II |
| | Net investment hedging |
| | (iv) Undesignated derivatives |
| | Total derivatives Financial statements (i+ii+iii+iv) |

**Illustration 14.29: Specimen format related to this section of disclosure has been provided under Schedule III Division III as under:**

| Part I | (Current Year) | | | (Previous Year) | | |
|---|---|---|---|---|---|---|
| | **Notional amounts** | **Fair value - Assets** | **Fair value - liabilities** | **Notional amounts** | **Fair value – Assets** | **Fair value - liabilities** |
| (i) Currency derivatives<br>- Spot and forwards | | | | | | |

| Part I | (Current Year) | | | (Previous Year) | | |
|---|---|---|---|---|---|---|
| | **Notional amounts** | **Fair value - Assets** | **Fair value - liabilities** | **Notional amounts** | **Fair value – Assets** | **Fair value - liabilities** |
| - Currency futures<br>- Currency swaps<br>- Options purchased<br>- Options sold (written)<br>- Others | | | | | | |
| Sub-total (i) | | | | | | |
| (ii) Interest rate derivatives<br>Forward rate agreements and interest rate swaps<br>Options purchased<br>Options sold (written)<br>Futures<br>Others | | | | | | |
| Sub-total (ii) | | | | | | |
| (iii) Credit derivatives<br>(iv) Equity linked derivatives<br>(v) Other derivatives (please specify) | | | | | | |
| Total Derivative Financial Instruments (i+ii+iii+iv+v) | | | | | | |
| Part II | | | | | | |

| Part I | (Current Year) | | | (Previous Year) | | |
|---|---|---|---|---|---|---|
| | **Notional amounts** | **Fair value - Assets** | **Fair value - liabilities** | **Notional amounts** | **Fair value – Assets** | **Fair value - liabilities** |
| Included in above (Part I) are derivatives held for hedging and risk management purposes as follows:<br>(i) Fair value hedging:<br>- Currency derivatives<br>- Interest rate derivatives<br>- Credit derivatives<br>- Equity linked derivatives<br>- Others | | | | | | |
| Sub-total I | | | | | | |
| Cash flow hedging:<br>- Currency derivatives<br>- Interest rate derivatives<br>- Credit derivatives<br>- Equity linked derivatives<br>- Others | | | | | | |
| Sub-total II | | | | | | |
| Net investment hedging | | | | | | |
| (iv) Undesignated derivatives | | | | | | |

| Part I | (Current Year) | | | (Previous Year) | | |
|---|---|---|---|---|---|---|
| | **Notional amounts** | **Fair value - Assets** | **Fair value - liabilities** | **Notional amounts** | **Fair value – Assets** | **Fair value - liabilities** |
| Total derivatives Financial statements (i+ii+iii+iv) | | | | | | |

With respect to hedges and hedge accounting, NBFCs may provide a description in accordance with the requirements of Indian Accounting Standards, of how derivatives are used for hedging, explain types of hedges recognized for accounting purposes and their usage/application by the entity.

### 14.6.5 Receivables

**Receivables shall be sub-classified as:**

(a) Receivables considered good - Secured.

(b) Receivables considered good - Unsecured;

(c) Receivables which have significant increase in Credit Risk; and

(d) Receivables - credit impaired

(ii) Allowance for impairment loss allowance shall be disclosed under the relevant heads separately.

(iii) Debts due by directors or other officers of the NBFC or any of them either severally or jointly with any other person or debts due by firms including limited liability partnerships (LLPs), private companies respectively in which any director is a partner or a director or a member should be separately stated.

**Illustration 14.30: Trade Receivables**

**(Amount in Rs)**

| | **Current Reporting Period** | **Previous Reporting Period** |
|---|---|---|
| (a) Receivables considered good - Secured. | xxx | xxx |
| (b) Receivables considered good - Unsecured; | xxx | xxx |
| (c) Receivables which have significant increase in Credit Risk; and | xxx | xxx |
| (d) Receivables - credit impaired | xxx | xxx |
| **Sub-total** | **xxx** | **xxx** |

| | | |
|---|---|---|
| **Less** Allowance for impairment loss<br>Significant increase in credit risk<br>Credit impaired | <br>xxx<br>xxx | <br>xxx<br>xxx |
| **Total** | xxx | xxx |

## 14.6.6 Impairment of Trade Receivables

### *14.6.6.1 Recognition of expected credit losses - General approach*

An entity shall recognize a loss allowance for expected credit losses on a financial asset that is measured in accordance with the provisions of this Ind AS,

- a lease receivable,
- a contract asset or
- a loan commitment and
- a financial guarantee contract

to which the impairment requirements apply in accordance with the provisions of Ind AS 109.

An entity shall apply the impairment requirements for the recognition and measurement of a loss allowance for financial assets that are measured at fair value through other comprehensive income. However, the loss allowance shall be recognised in other comprehensive income and shall not reduce the carrying amount of the financial asset in the balance sheet.

An entity shall measure the loss allowance for a financial instrument at an amount equal to the lifetime expected credit losses if the credit risk on that financial instrument has increased significantly since initial recognition.

If, at the reporting date, the credit risk on a financial instrument has not increased significantly since initial recognition, an entity shall measure the loss allowance for that financial instrument at an amount equal to 12-month expected credit losses.

For loan commitments and financial guarantee contracts, the date that the entity becomes a party to the irrevocable commitment shall be considered to be the date of initial recognition for the purposes of applying the impairment requirements.

If an entity has measured the loss allowance for a financial instrument at an amount equal to lifetime expected credit losses in the previous reporting period but determines at the current reporting date that it is no longer met, the entity shall measure the loss allowance at an amount equal to 12-month expected credit losses at the current reporting date.

An entity shall recognize in profit or loss, as an impairment gain or loss, the amount of expected credit losses (or reversal) that is required to adjust the loss allowance at the reporting date to the amount that is required to be recognized in accordance with this Standard.

According to ICAI Guidance Note on Schedule III, Division III on NBFCs, if a company chooses to calculate impairment loss under the general approach for trade receivables containing significant financing component, then the disclosures representing the following different categories of Trade Receivables would be provided (amounts are illustrative only):

**Illustration 14.31: Treatment of impairment loss allowance (Rs Lakhs)**

| | Exposure | Impairment loss | Net Amount |
|---|---|---|---|
| (a) Receivables considered good - Secured. | - | - | - |
| (b) Receivables considered good - Unsecured; | 150,000 | 30,000 | 120,000 |
| (c) Receivables which have significant increase in Credit Risk; and | 30,000 | 3,000 | 27,000 |
| (d) Receivables - credit impaired | 15,000 | 3,000 | 12,000 |
| **Total** | **195,000** | **36,000** | **159,000** |

In presentation of 'Trade Receivables which have significant increase in credit risk', the entity shall disclose the amount of trade receivables that have experienced significant increase in credit risk since initial recognition but are not credit-impaired.

In presentation of 'Trade Receivables – credit impaired', the company shall disclose the amount of trade receivables which are credit impaired as defined in Ind AS- 109

The balance amount of trade receivables which have neither experienced significant increase in credit risk nor are credit impaired as per Ind AS 109, needs to be disclosed as 'good'.

For calculating the loss allowance, reference shall be drawn from Ind AS 109.

### 14.6.6.2 *Simplified approach for trade receivables, contract assets and lease receivables*

An entity shall always measure the loss allowance at an amount equal to lifetime expected credit losses for:

(a) trade receivables or contract assets that result from transactions that are within the scope of Ind AS115, and that:

(i) do not contain a significant financing component in accordance with Ind AS 115; or

(ii) contain a significant financing component in accordance with Ind AS 115, if the entity chooses as its accounting policy to measure the loss allowance at an amount equal to lifetime expected credit losses. That accounting policy shall be applied to all such trade receivables or contract assets but may be applied separately to trade receivables and contract assets.

(b) lease receivables that result from transactions that are within the scope of Ind AS 116, if the entity chooses as its accounting policy to measure the loss allowance at an amount equal to lifetime expected credit losses. That accounting policy shall be applied to all lease receivables but may be applied separately to finance and operating lease receivables.

An entity may select its accounting policy for trade receivables, lease receivables and contract assets independently of each other.

### 14.6.6.3 Measurement of expected credit loss

An entity shall measure expected credit losses of a financial instrument in a way that reflects:

(a) an unbiased and probability-weighted amount that is determined by evaluating a range of possible outcomes;

(b) the time value of money; and

(c) reasonable and supportable information that is available

without undue cost or effort at the reporting date about past events, current conditions and forecasts of future economic conditions.

When measuring expected credit losses, an entity need not necessarily identify every possible scenario. However, it shall consider the risk or probability that a credit loss occurs by reflecting the possibility that a credit loss occurs and the possibility that no credit loss occurs, even if the possibility of a credit loss occurring is very low.

The maximum period to consider when measuring expected credit losses is the maximum contractual period (including extension options) over which the entity is exposed to credit risk and not a longer period, even if that longer period is consistent with business practice.

However, some financial instruments include both a loan and an undrawn commitment component and the entity's contractual ability to demand repayment and cancel the undrawn commitment does not limit the entity's exposure to credit losses to the contractual notice period. For such financial instruments, and only those financial instruments, the entity shall measure expected credit losses over the period that the entity is exposed to credit risk and expected credit losses would not be mitigated by credit risk management actions, even if that period extends beyond the maximum contractual period.

### 14.6.6.4 Trade receivables outstanding

This is a new insertion wherein following ageing schedule shall be given:

**Illustration 14.32: Trade Receivables aging schedule**

(Amount in Rs.)

| Particulars | Outstanding for following periods from due date of payment# | | | | | |
|---|---|---|---|---|---|---|
| | Less than 6 months | 6 months – 1 year | 1-2 years | 2-3 years | More than 3 years | Total |
| (i) Undisputed | | | | | | |
| Trade receivables – considered good<br>(ii) Undisputed | | | | | | |
| Trade Receivables – which have significant increase in credit risk<br>(iii) Undisputed | | | | | | |
| Trade Receivables – credit impaired<br>(v) Disputed Trade | | | | | | |
| Receivables– considered good<br>(vi) Disputed Trade | | | | | | |
| Receivables – which have significant | | | | | | |

| Particulars | Outstanding for following periods from due date of payment# | | | | | |
|---|---|---|---|---|---|---|
| | Less than 6 months | 6 months – 1 year | 1-2 years | 2-3 years | More than 3 years | Total |
| increase in credit risk(vii) Disputed Trade | | | | | | |
| Receivables – credit impaired | | | | | | |

# similar information shall be given where no due date of payment is specified in that case disclosure shall be from the date of the transaction.

Unbilled dues shall be disclosed separately.

According to ICAI Guidance Note on Schedule III on NBFCs (Revised January, 2022 Edition), in order to tie-up the amounts presented in the 'total' column with the amounts presented in the financial statements or notes, two additional columns with heading 'Unbilled' and the heading 'Not due' need to be added before the ageing columns to separately disclose the amount for unbilled receivables and the amount of trade receivables which are not due, respectively

The ageing of the trade receivables needs to be determined from the due date of the invoice. Due date is generally considered to be the date on which the payment of an invoice falls due. The due date of an invoice is determined based on terms agreed upon between the buyer and supplier.

Here it may be pertinent to note that, Ind AS 115 requires that an asset arising from contract with customers to be recognized as a receivable when the entity's right to consideration is unconditional and such recognition date can be considered as transaction date for the purpose of ageing disclosure.

The current disclosure under Schedule III requires disaggregation of trade receivables between 'disputed' and 'undisputed'. However, these terms have not been defined in the Schedule III. According to ICAI Guidance Note, a dispute has been defined as s disagreement between two parties demonstrated by some positive evidence which supports or corroborates the fact of disagreement. According to Insolvency and Bankruptcy code 2016, the word "dispute" includes a suit or arbitration proceedings relating to-

(a) the existence of the amount of debt;

(b) the quality of goods or service; or

(c) the breach of a representation or warranty.

### 14.6.7 Loan and Investment

#### *14.6.7.1 Loan*

Under this category, Schedule III, Division III, Clause D, requires that an NBFC shall disclose the following:

| Loans |
|---|
| (A)<br>(i) Bills purchased and bills discounted<br>(ii) Loans repayable on demand<br>(iii) Term loans<br>(iv) Leasing<br>(v) Factoring<br>(vi) Others (to be specified)<br>Total (A)<br>Less: Impairment loss<br>Allowance |
| (B)<br>(i) Secured by tangible assets<br>(ii) Secured by intangible assets<br>(iii) Covered by bank/Government guarantees<br>(iv) Unsecured |
| Total (B) Gross |
| (C)(i) Loans in India<br>(i)Public sector<br>(ii)Others (to be specified) |
| Total (C)-Gross<br>Less: Impairment loss allowance<br>Total (C)(I) Net |
| (C)(ii) Loans outside India<br>Less: Impairment loss allowance<br>Total (C)(ii) Net |
| Total (C)(i) and (C)(ii) |
| Investment<br>Mutual Funds<br>Government securities other approved securities<br>Debt securities |

| Subsidiaries<br>Associates<br>Joint Ventures<br>Others (specify) |
|---|
| Total – Gross (A) |
| (B)<br>(i)Investments outside India<br>(ii)Investments in India |
| Total (B) |
| Total (A) to tally with (B) |
| Less: Impairment loss allowance (C)<br>Total-Net D=(A)-(C) |

A break-up of the total loans should also be disclosed as:

(a) Secured by tangible assets

(b) Secured by intangible assets

(c) Covered by Bank/Government Guarantee

(d) Unsecured

As per ICAI Guidance Note on Terms Used in Financial Statements, 'Secured loan' is defined as loan secured wholly or partly against an asset. The Guidance also explains the category wise disclosures.

The security wise break-up of loans as mentioned above shall additionally disclose as a separate line item of loans secured by book debts, fixed deposits, and other working capital items as applicable.

Loans to the extent they are covered by guarantees of Indian/foreign governments and Indian/foreign banks shall be included in line item (c) above.

Government refers to government, government agencies, and similar bodies whether local, national or international.

All loans or parts thereof that are not classified under the previous sub-heads shall be included in line item (d) above.

For instance, if an advance is secured by tangible assets to the extent of 75 percent, the secured component should be reflected under secured advance, while the balance 25 percent unsecured component would be included under this subhead.

The total of the above line items, after deducting impairment loss allowance in a separate line item, should match with the net loans and advances.

The impairment loss allowance as per Ind AS 109 should be disclosed as a separate line item under the aforesaid measurement categories as applicable.

The above categories of loans need to be categorized into the following both for current year and previous year.

(a) Amortized cost
(b) Fair value through comprehensive income
(c) Fair value through profit or loss
(d) Designated at Fair value through profit or loss.

This is in line with Ind AS 109, wherein. after initial recognition, an entity shall measure a financial liabilities at:

(a) amortized cost;
(b) fair value through other comprehensive income; or
(c) fair value through profit or loss.

In accordance with Ind AS 109, in case of loans measured at fair value through other comprehensive income, the fair value changes shall be presented in other comprehensive income. A company shall estimate a portion of fair value change, if any, attributable to a change in credit risk of such loans, by applying the impairment requirements of Ind AS 109 in recognizing and measuring the loss allowance and disclose the same in the statement of profit and loss with a corresponding impact in other comprehensive income.

In other words, the company shall not reduce/increase the carrying amount of such loans in the balance sheet on account of change in the credit risk as the loan needs to be presented at fair value.

Also, loans need to be disclosed as

(a) Within India and
(b) Outside India

Further, within India, loans should be classified as those from public sector and others (to be specified). According to ICAI Guidance Note on Schedule III, Division III, advances to Central and State Governments and other Government undertakings including Government Companies and statutory corporations are to be included in the category 'Public Sector'. All other loans are included in 'Others' category for example loans to retail or Corporate or industry-wise classification etc. based on the business of the company.

### *14.6.7.2 Investments*

The disclosure requirements related to investments under Schedule III, Division III are:

| Investment |
|---|
| Mutual Funds |

| Government securities other approved securities<br>Debt securities<br>Subsidiaries<br>Associates<br>Joint Ventures<br>Others (specify) |
|---|
| Total – Gross (A) |
| (B)<br>(i)Investments outside India<br>(ii)Investments in India |
| Total (B) |
| Total (A) to tally with (B) |
| Less: Impairment loss allowance (C)<br>Total-Net D=(A)-(C ) |

The above categories of investments need to be categorized into the following both for current year and previous year.

(a) Amortized cost

(b) Fair value through comprehensive income

(c) Fair value through profit or loss

(d) Designated at Fair value through profit or loss.

This is in line with Ind AS 109, wherein after initial recognition, an entity shall measure a financial assets at:

(a) amortized cost;

(b) fair value through other comprehensive income; or

(c) fair value through profit or loss.

In accordance with Ind AS 109, in case of investments measured at fair value through other comprehensive income, the fair value changes shall be presented in other comprehensive income. A company shall estimate a portion of fair value change, if any, attributable to a change in credit risk of such investments, by applying the impairment requirements of Ind AS 109 in recognizing and measuring the loss allowance and disclose the same in the statement of profit and loss with a corresponding impact in other comprehensive income.

In other words, the company shall not reduce/increase the carrying amount of such investments in the balance sheet on account of change in the credit risk as the investment needs to be presented at fair value.

For finance lease receivables, an entity shall apply the presentation and disclosure requirements under Ind AS 116 in addition to the requirements of Division III to Schedule III.

Also, investments need to be disclosed as -

(a) Within India and

(b) Outside India

According to ICAI Guidance Note on Schedule III, Division III, where the NBFC has used a basis other than amortised cost or fair value, the same may be included in column 'Others', with the basis of measurement to be disclosed as a footnote. e.g. Investment in subsidiaries measured at cost under Ind AS 27 shall be classified under 'Others' in the Separate Financial Statements of the NBFC.

The impairment loss allowance as per Ind AS 109 should be disclosed as a separate line item under the aforesaid measurement categories as applicable.

**Aggregate amount of impairment in value of investments**

In accordance with Ind AS 109, the company is required to recognize a loss allowance (i.e. impairment) for expected credit losses on investments measured at amortized cost. Such loss allowance should be presented as an adjustment to the amortized cost of the investment.

In case of debt investments measured at fair value through other comprehensive income, the fair value changes will be presented in other comprehensive income. A company should estimate a portion of fair value change, if any, attributable to a change in credit risk of such investment, by applying the impairment requirements of Ind AS 109 in recognizing and measuring the loss allowance and disclose the same in the statement of profit and loss with a corresponding impact in other comprehensive income.

Disclosure pertaining to impairment shall be disclosed by way of Notes in accordance with the requirements of Ind AS 107.

Also, according to Ind AS 109, equity instruments measured at other than at cost and debt instruments measured at fair value through profit or loss do not require a separate evaluation of impairment amount. Hence, in such cases, the disclosure pertaining to impairment shall not be applicable.

Based on above, for the purpose of disclosing aggregate provision for impairment in the value of investments, an entity shall disclose an amount equal to the aggregate amount of impairment recognized and measured in accordance with Ind AS 109.

**Illustration 14.33: A specimen format related to presentation of loan and investment**

| | (Current Year) | | | | | | (Previous Year) | | | | | |
|---|---|---|---|---|---|---|---|---|---|---|---|---|
| | Amortized cost | Fair value through other comprehensive income | Fair value through profit or loss | Designated at Fair value through profit or loss | Sub-Total | Total | Amortized cost | Fair value through other comprehensive income | Fair value through profit or loss | Designated at Fair value through profit or loss | Sub-total | Total |
| Loans<br>(A)<br>(i) Bills purchased and bills discounted<br>(ii) Loans repayable on demand<br>(iii) Term loans<br>(iv) Leasing<br>(v) Factoring<br>(vi) Others (to be specified)<br>Total (A)<br>Less: Impairment loss<br>Allowance | | | | | | | | | | | | |
| (B)<br>(i) Secured by tangible assets<br>(ii) Secured by intangible assets<br>(iii) Covered by bank/ Government guarantees<br>(iv)Unsecured | | | | | | | | | | | | |
| Total (B) Gross | | | | | | | | | | | | |
| (C)(i) Loans in India<br>(i) Public sector<br>(ii) Others (to be specified) | | | | | | | | | | | | |
| Total (C)-Gross<br>Less: Impairment loss allowance | | | | | | | | | | | | |

| | (Current Year) | | | | | | (Previous Year) | | | | | |
|---|---|---|---|---|---|---|---|---|---|---|---|---|
| | **Amortized cost** | **Fair value through other comprehensive income** | **Fair value through profit or loss** | **Designated at Fair value through profit or loss** | **Sub-Total** | **Total** | **Amortized cost** | **Fair value through other comprehensive income** | **Fair value through profit or loss** | **Designated at Fair value through profit or loss** | **Sub-total** | **Total** |
| Total (C)(I) Net | | | | | | | | | | | | |
| (C)(ii) Loans outside India<br>Less: Impairment loss allowance<br>Total (C)(ii) Net | | | | | | | | | | | | |
| Total (C)(i) and (C)(ii) | | | | | | | | | | | | |
| Investment<br>Mutual Funds<br>Government securities<br>other approved securities<br>Debt securities<br>Subsidiaries<br>Associates<br>Joint Ventures<br>Others (specify) | | | | | | | | | | | | |
| Total – Gross (A) | | | | | | | | | | | | |
| (B)<br>(i) Investments outside India<br>(ii) Investments in India | | | | | | | | | | | | |
| Total (B) | | | | | | | | | | | | |
| Total (A) to tally with (B) | | | | | | | | | | | | |
| Less: Impairment loss allowance (C)<br>Total-Net<br>D=(A)-(C ) | | | | | | | | | | | | |

*Other basis of measurement should be explained as a footnote.

**Structured entities**

It may not be out of place to discuss about structured entities here. Division III to Schedule III does not require an entity to specifically disclose investments in 'structured entities'. However, according to ICAI Guidance Note on Schedule III, Division III (Revised January, 2022 Edition), in case a company has investments in 'structured entities' then the same may be disclosed in addition to investments in subsidiaries, associates, and joint ventures. Where an entity holds investments in subsidiaries, associates and joint ventures which are structured entities, it shall include such investments in the respective line items of investments in subsidiaries, associates and joint ventures. Unconsolidated structured entities shall be disclosed as part of 'others'.

## 14.6.8 Non-current Assets

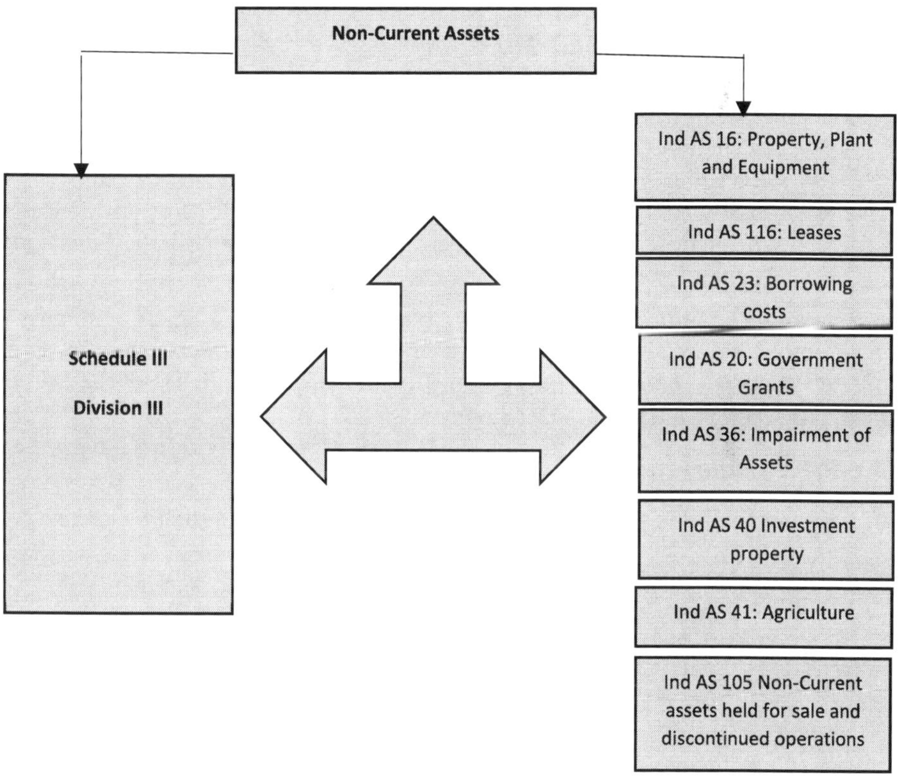


The presentation and disclosure requirements in Financial Statements are similar to the provisions discussed in earlier chapters.

### 14.6.9 Payables

The following details relating to Micro, Small and Medium Enterprises shall be disclosed:

(a) the principal amount and the interest due thereon (to be shown separately) remaining unpaid to any supplier at the end of each accounting year;

(b) the amount of interest paid by the buyer in terms of section 16 of the Micro, Small and Medium Enterprises Development Act, 2006, along with the amount of the payment made to the supplier beyond the appointed day during each accounting year;

(c) the amount of interest due and payable for the period of delay in making payment (which have been paid but beyond the appointed day during the year) but without adding the interest specified under the Micro, Small and Medium Enterprises Development Act, 2006.

(d) the amount of interest accrued and remaining unpaid at the end of each accounting year; and

(e) the amount of further interest remaining due and payable even in the succeeding years, until such date when the interest dues above are actually paid to the small enterprise, for the purpose of disallowance of a deductible expenditure under section 23 of the Micro, Small and Medium Enterprises Development Act, 2006.

Explanation- The terms 'appointed day', 'buyer', 'enterprise', 'micro enterprise', 'small enterprise' and 'supplier', shall have the same meaning assigned to those under clauses (b), (d), (e), (h), (m) and (n) respectively of section 2 of the Micro, Small and Medium Enterprises Development Act, 2006."

#### *14.6.9.1 Trade Payables aging schedule*

For trade payables due for payment, following ageing schedule shall be given:

**Illustration 14.34: Trade Payables aging schedule**

(Amount in Rs.)

| Particulars | Outstanding for following periods from due date of payment# | | | | |
|---|---|---|---|---|---|
| | Less than 1 year | 1-2 years | 2-3 years | More than 3 years | Total |
| (i) MSME<br>(viii) Others<br>(ix) Disputed dues – MSME | | | | | |

| Particulars | Outstanding for following periods from due date of payment# | | | | |
|---|---|---|---|---|---|
| | Less than 1 year | 1-2 years | 2-3 years | More than 3 years | Total |
| (iv) Disputed dues – Others | | | | | |

# similar information shall be given where no due date of payment is specified in that case disclosure shall be from the date of the transaction.

Unbilled dues shall be disclosed separately.

### 14.6.10 Debt Securities

In accordance with the ICAI Guidance Note debt securities **under 'Financial Liabilities'** will include

securities (secured or unsecured) other than those which are classified as 'Subordinated debt'. Debt securities shall comprise of liability component of Compound Financial instruments as per Ind AS and Other such as Bonds and Debentures.

According to Schedule III, Division III, Debt securities will comprise of the following:

| **Debt Securities** |
|---|
| Liability component of compound financial instrument |
| Others (Bonds/Debenture etc.) |
| **Total (A)** |
| Debt securities in India |
| Debt securities outside India |
| **Total (B) to tally with (A)** |

**Illustration 14.35: Debt Securities**

(Rs in crores)

| | As at 31st March 2022 | As at 31st March 2021 |
|---|---|---|
| **Debt securities in India**<br>**At Amortized cost**<br>**Secured** | | |

| | As at 31st March 2022 | As at 31st March 2021 |
|---|---|---|
| Privately placed non-convertible debentures | xxx | xxx |
| Public issue of Non-Convertible Debentures | xxx | xxx |
| **Unsecured** | | |
| (i) Privately Placed Non-Convertible Debentures | xxx | xxx |
| (ii) Commercial paper | xxx | xxx |
| **Debt securities outside India** | | |
| **At Amortized cost** | | |
| **Secured** | | |
| Privately placed non-convertible debentures | xxx | xxx |
| Public issue of Non-Convertible Debentures | xxx | xxx |
| **Unsecured** | | |
| (i) Privately Placed Non-Convertible Debentures | xxx | xxx |
| (ii) Commercial paper | xxx | xxx |
| **Total** | xxx | xxx |

### *14.6.10.1 Compound Financial Instruments*

As discussed earlier in the Chapter, according to Paragraph 28 of Ind AS 32, the issuer of a non-derivative financial instrument shall evaluate the terms of the financial instrument to determine whether it contains both a liability and an equity component. Such components shall be classified separately as financial liabilities, financial assets, or equity instruments.

The issuer of a financial instrument shall classify the instrument, or its component parts, on initial recognition as a financial liability, a financial asset or an equity instrument in accordance with the substance of the contractual arrangement and the definitions of a financial liability, a financial asset and an equity instrument.

Paragraph 29 explains the split. According to this paragraph, an entity recognises separately the components of a financial instrument that

(a) creates a financial liability of the entity and

(b) grants an option to the holder of the instrument to convert it into an equity instrument of the entity.

This is explained with an illustration below.

A bond or similar instrument convertible by the holder into a fixed number of ordinary shares of the entity is a compound financial instrument.

From the perspective of the entity, such an instrument comprises two components:

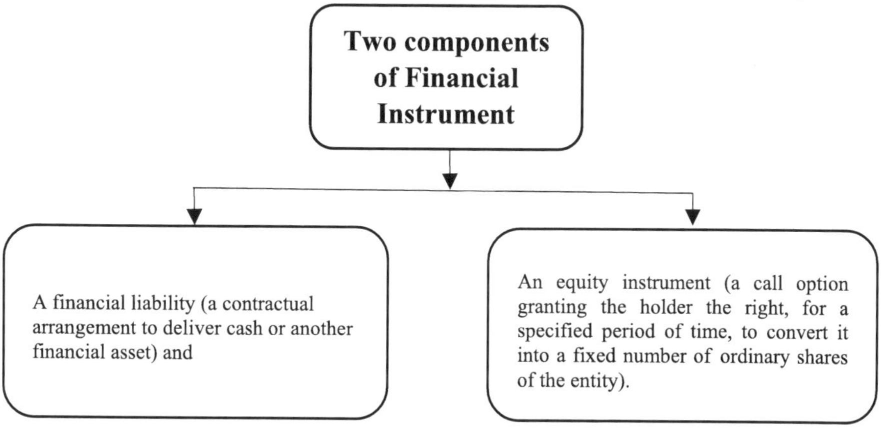


The economic effect of issuing such an instrument is substantially the same as issuing simultaneously a debt instrument with an early settlement provision and warrants to purchase ordinary shares or issuing a debt instrument with detachable share purchase warrants. Accordingly, in all cases, the entity presents the liability and equity components separately in its balance sheet.

Hence, the liability component of the compound financial instrument is disclosed in this section.

**Illustration 14.36: Accounting Policy: Compound Financial Instrument**

**Compound instruments**

The Group has issued financial instruments with equity conversion rights and call options. When establishing the accounting treatment for these non-derivative instruments, the Group first establishes whether the instrument is a compound instrument and classifies such instrument's components separately as financial liabilities or equity instruments in accordance with Ind AS 32. Classification of the liability and equity components of a convertible instrument is not revised as a result of a change in the likelihood that a conversion option will be exercised, even when exercising the option may appear to have become economically advantageous to some holders.

When allocating the initial carrying amount of a compound financial instrument to the equity and liability components, the equity component is assigned as the residual amount after deducting from the entire fair value of the instrument, the amount separately determined for the liability component. The value of any derivative features (such as a call options) embedded in the compound financial instrument, other than the equity component (such as an equity conversion option), is included in the liability component. Once the Group has determined the split between equity and liability, it further evaluates whether the liability component has embedded derivatives that must be separately accounted for. Subsequently the liability is measured as per requirement of IND AS 109.

A Cumulative Compulsorily Convertible Preference Shares (CCCPS), with an option to holder to convert the instrument into variable number of equity shares of the entity upon redemption is classified as a financial liability and dividend including dividend distribution tax is accrued on such instruments and recorded as finance cost. Where the conversion option remains unexercised at the maturity date of the convertible note, the balance recognised in equity will be transferred to retained profits. No gain/loss is recognised in profit or loss upon conversion or expiration of the conversion option.

(*Source: TFSL Annual Report 2020*)

### 14.6.11 Others (Bonds/Debentures etc.)

Schedule III, Division III, provides the following guidance related to disclosures under this category.

(i) bonds or debentures (along with the rate of interest, and particulars of redemption or conversion, as the case may be) shall be stated in descending order of maturity or conversion, starting from earliest redemption or conversion date, as the case may be. Where bonds/debentures are redeemable by instalments, the date of maturity for this purpose must be reckoned as the date on which the first instalment becomes due;

(ii) particulars of any redeemed bonds or debentures which the NBFC has power to reissue shall be disclosed.

According to Guidance Note of ICAI under this section, liabilities arising out of Securitization transactions resulting into issue of debt securities shall be classified as debt securities.

The above disclosures are required in the following categories:

- At amortized cost
- At Fair value through Profit & Loss
- Designated at Fair value through Profit & Loss

Also, the above debt securities need to be bifurcated between:

(a) Within India and

(b) Outside India

**Illustration 14.37: The format provided by Division III of Schedule III:**

| | (Current Year) | | | | (Previous Year) | | | |
|---|---|---|---|---|---|---|---|---|
| | **At amortized cost** | **At fair value through profit & loss** | **Designated at fair value through profit & loss** | **Total** | **At amortized cost** | **At fair value through profit & loss** | **Designated at fair value through profit & loss** | **Total** |
| Liability component of compound financial instrument | | | | | | | | |
| Others (Bonds/Debenture etc.) | | | | | | | | |
| **Total (A)** | | | | | | | | |
| Debt securities in India | | | | | | | | |
| Debt securities outside India | | | | | | | | |
| **Total (B) to tally with (A)** | | | | | | | | |

## 14.6.12 Borrowings (Other than Debt Securities)

This section would include the following:

| Borrowings |
|---|
| (a) Term loans<br>(i) From banks<br>(ii) From other parties |
| (b) Deferred payment liabilities<br>(c) loans from related parties<br>(d) Finance lease obligations<br>(e) Liability component of compound financial instruments<br>(f) Loans repayable on demand |

| |
|---|
| (i) From banks<br>(ii) From other parties<br>(g) Other loans (specify nature) |
| Total (A) |
| Borrowings in India<br>Borrowings outside India |
| Total (B) to tally with (A) |

The above disclosures are required in the following categories:

At amortized cost

At Fair value through Profit & Loss

Designated at Fair value through Profit & Loss

Also, the above debt securities need to be bifurcated between:

(a) Within India and

(b) Outside India

**Illustration 14.38: The format provided by Division III of Schedule III**

| | (Current Year) | | | | (Previous Year) | | | |
|---|---|---|---|---|---|---|---|---|
| | **At amortized cost** | **At fair value through profit & loss** | **Designated at fair value through profit & loss** | **Total** | **At amortized cost** | **At fair value through profit & loss** | **Designated at fair value through profit & loss** | **Total** |
| (a)Term loans<br>(i)From banks<br>(ii)From other parties | | | | | | | | |
| (b)Deferred payment liabilities<br>(c)loans from related parties<br>(d)Finance lease obligations<br>(e)Liability component of compound financial instruments<br>(f)Loans repayable on | | | | | | | | |

| | (Current Year) | | | | (Previous Year) | | | |
|---|---|---|---|---|---|---|---|---|
| | **At amortized cost** | **At fair value through profit & loss** | **Designated at fair value through profit & loss** | **Total** | **At amortized cost** | **At fair value through profit & loss** | **Designated at fair value through profit & loss** | **Total** |
| demand<br>(i)From banks<br>(ii)From other parties<br>(g)Other loans (specify nature) | | | | | | | | |
| Total (A) | | | | | | | | |
| Borrowings in India<br>Borrowings outside India | | | | | | | | |
| Total (B) to tally with (A) | | | | | | | | |

(i) Borrowings shall further be sub-classified as secured and unsecured. Nature of security shall be specified separately in each case.

(ii) Where borrowings have been guaranteed by directors or others, the aggregate amount of such borrowings under each head shall be disclosed.

(iii) terms of repayment of term loans and other loans shall be stated; and

(iv) period and amount of default as on the balance sheet date in repayment of borrowings and interest shall be specified separately in each case.

### Illustration 14.39: Borrowings other than Debt Securities

(Rs in crores)

| | **As at 31st March 2022** | **As at 31st March 2021** |
|---|---|---|
| Debt securities in India | | |
| At Amortized cost | | |
| a) Term loan | | |
| Secured | | |
| From Banks | xxx | xxx |
| From Others | xxx | xxx |
| Unsecured | | |
| From Banks | xxx | xxx |
| From Others | xxx | xxx |
| b) Loans repayable on demand | | |
| Secured | | |
| From Banks | | |
| Working Capital Demand Loan | xxx | xxx |
| Bank Overdraft | xxx | xxx |

| | As at 31st March 2022 | As at 31st March 2021 |
|---|---|---|
| Unsecured | | |
| From Banks | | |
| Working Capital Demand Loan | xxx | xxx |
| Bank Overdraft | xxx | xxx |
| c) Loans from related parties) (unsecured) | | |
| Convertible cumulative preference shares | xxx | xxx |
| Inter-corporate deposits from related parties | xxx | xxx |
| Sub-total | xxx | xxx |
| Debt securities outside India | | |
| At Amortized cost | | |
| a) Term loan | | |
| Secured | | |
| From Banks | xxx | xxx |
| From Others | xxx | xxx |
| Unsecured | | |
| From Banks | xxx | xxx |
| From Others | xxx | xxx |
| b) Loans repayable on demand | | |
| Secured | | |
| From Banks | | |
| Working Capital Demand Loan | xxx | xxx |
| Bank Overdraft | xxx | xxx |
| Unsecured | | |
| From Banks | | |
| Working Capital Demand Loan | xxx | xxx |
| Bank Overdraft | xxx | xxx |
| c) Loans from related parties) (unsecured) | | |
| Convertible cumulative preference shares | xxx | xxx |
| Inter-corporate deposits from related parties | xxx | xxx |
| Sub-total | xxx | xxx |
| Total | xxx | xxx |

Note: The table can be further extended for the following categories (in a columnar form as per specimen provided under Division III of Schedule III.

At Fair value through Profit & Loss

Designated at Fair value through Profit & Loss

### 14.6.13 Deposits

Disclosure requirements under this head has been prescribed as under:

Deposits

(i) Public deposits

(ii) From banks

(iii) From others

The above disclosures are required in the following categories:

- At amortized cost
- At Fair value through Profit & Loss
- Designated at Fair value through Profit & Loss

**Illustration 14.40: The format provided by Division III of Schedule III**

| | (Current Year) | | | | (Previous Year) | | | |
|---|---|---|---|---|---|---|---|---|
| | At amortized cost | At fair value through profit & loss | Designated at fair value through profit & loss | Total | At amortized cost | At fair value through profit & loss | Designated at fair value through profit & loss | Total |
| Deposits<br>(i) Public deposits<br>(ii) From banks<br>(iii) From others | | | | | | | | |
| Total | | | | | | | | |

## 14.6.14 Subordinated liabilities

Disclosure requirements under this head has been prescribed as under:

Perpetual Debt instruments to the extent that do not qualify as Equity.

Preference shares other than those that qualify as Equity.

Others (specifying the nature and type of instruments issued.

The above disclosures are required in the following categories:

At amortized cost

At Fair value through Profit & Loss

Designated at Fair value through Profit & Loss

Also, the above subordinated liabilities need to be bifurcated between:

(a) Within India and

(b) Outside India

## Illustration 14.41: The format provided by Division III of Schedule III

| | (Current Year) | | | | (Previous Year) | | | |
|---|---|---|---|---|---|---|---|---|
| | **At amortized cost** | **At fair value through profit & loss** | **Designated at fair value through profit & loss** | **Total** | **At amortized cost** | **At fair value through profit & loss** | **Designated at fair value through profit & loss** | **Total** |
| Perpetual Debt Instruments to the extent that do not qualify as equity<br>Preference Shares other than those that qualify as Equity<br>Others (specifying the nature and type of instrument issued) | | | | | | | | |
| Total (A) | | | | | | | | |
| Subordinated liabilities in India<br>Subordinated liabilities outside India | | | | | | | | |
| Total (B) to tally with (A) | | | | | | | | |

## Illustration 14.42: Subordinated Liabilities

(Rs in crores)

| | As at 31st March 2021 | As at 31st March 2020 |
|---|---|---|
| **Subordinated liabilities in India** | | |
| **At Amortized cost** | | |
| **Secured** | | |
| **Debentures** | | |
| Non-convertible subordinated debentures | xxx | xxx |
| Non-convertible perpetual debentures | xxx | xxx |
| **Unsecured** | | |
| **Debentures** | | |
| Non-convertible subordinated debentures | xxx | xxx |

| | | |
|---|---|---|
| Non-convertible perpetual debentures | xxx | xxx |
| **Sub-total** | xxx | xxx |
| **Debt securities outside India**<br>**At Amortized cost**<br>**Secured**<br>**Debentures** | | |
| Non-convertible subordinated debentures | xxx | xxx |
| Non-convertible perpetual debentures | xxx | xxx |
| **Unsecured**<br>**Debentures** | | |
| Non-convertible subordinated debentures | xxx | xxx |
| Non-convertible perpetual debentures | xxx | xxx |
| **Sub-total** | xxx | xxx |
| **Total** | xxx | xxx |

Note: The table can be further extended for the following categories (in a columnar form as per specimen provided under Division III of Schedule III.

At Fair value through Profit & Loss

Designated at Fair value through Profit & Loss

### 14.6.15 Other Financial liabilities (to be specified)

Other Financial liabilities shall be classified as:

(a) Interest accrued;

(b) Unpaid dividends;

(c) Application money received for allotment of securities to the extent refundable and interest accrued thereon;

(d) Unpaid matured deposits and interest accrued thereon;

(e) Unpaid matured debentures and interest accrued thereon;

(f) Margin money (to be specified); and

(g) Others (specify nature)

### 14.6.16 Provisions

The amounts shall be classified as-

(a) Provision for employee benefits; and

(b) Others (specify nature)

**Illustration 14.43: Accounting Policy: Provisions, Contingent Liabilities and Contingent Assets**

**Provisions, Contingent Liabilities and Contingent Assets**

(i) Provisions are recognized when the Company has a present legal or constructive obligation as a result of a past event, if it is probable that the Company will be required to settle the obligation and a reliable estimate can be made of the amount of the obligation.

(ii) The amount recognised as a provision is the best estimate of the consideration required to settle the present obligation at the end of the reporting period, taking into account the risks and uncertainties surrounding the obligation.

(iii) When some or all of the economic benefits required to settle a provision are expected to be recovered from a third party, a receivable is recognised as an asset if it is virtually certain that reimbursement will be received and the amount of the receivable can be measured reliably.

(iv) Where it is not probable that an outflow of economic benefits will be required or the amount cannot be estimated reliably, the obligation is disclosed as contingent liability in notes to accounts, unless the probability of outflow of economic benefits is remote.

(v) Contingent assets are not recognised in the financial statements. However, contingent assets are disclosed in the financial statements when inflow of economic benefits is probable.

**(*Source: Power Finance Corporation*)**

## 14.6.17 Other Non-financial liabilities (to be specified)

(a) Revenue received in advance;

(b) Other advances (Specify nature); and

(c) Others (specify nature).

**Contract Liability**

Ind AS 115 stipulates in case of a contract with customer, when either party has performed, to present a contract liability in the balance sheet. Contract liability arises if a customer pays consideration, or an entity has a right to an amount of consideration that is unconditional (for example, a receivable), before the entity transfers a good or service to the customer, the entity shall present the contract as a contract liability when the payment is made or the payment is due (whichever is earlier).

**Liabilities for assets held for sale**

In accordance with paragraph 38 of Ind AS 105, the liabilities of a disposal group classified as held for sale shall be presented separately from other liabilities in the balance sheet. Those assets and liabilities shall not be offset and presented as a single amount. The major classes of assets and liabilities classified as held for sale shall be separately disclosed either in the balance sheet or in the notes.

### 14.6.18 Equity Share Capital

For each class of equity share capital:

(a) the number and amount of shares authorized.

(b) the number of shares issued, subscribed and fully paid, and subscribed but not fully paid;

(c) par value per share;

(d) a reconciliation of the number of shares outstanding at the beginning and at the end of the period;

(e) the rights, preferences and restrictions attaching to each class of shares including restrictions on the distribution of dividends and the repayment of capital;

(f) shares in respect of each class in the company held by its holding company or its ultimate holding company including shares held by or by subsidiaries or associates of the holding company or the ultimate holding company in aggregate;

(g) shares in the company held by each shareholder holding more than five percent shares specifying the number of shares held;

(h) shares reserved for issue under options and contracts/commitments for the sale of shares or disinvestment, including the terms and amounts;

(i) For the period of five years immediately preceding the date at which the Balance Sheet is prepared:

- Aggregate number and class of shares allotted as fully paid up pursuant to contract without payment being received in cash;
- Aggregate number and class of shares allotted as fully paid up by way of bonus shares; and
- Aggregate number and class of shares bought back

(j) terms of any securities convertible into equity shares issued along with the earliest date of conversion in descending order starting from the farthest such date;

(k) calls unpaid (showing aggregate value of calls unpaid by directors and officers);

(l) forfeited shares (amount originally paid up)

(m) An NBFC shall disclose information that enables users of its financial statements to evaluate the NBFC's objectives, policies and processes for managing capital.

"(n) A company shall disclose Shareholding of Promoters* as below:

| Shares held by promoters at the end of the year | | | | % Change during the year*** |
|---|---|---|---|---|
| S. No | Promoter name | No. of Shares** | % of total shares** | |
| Total | | | | |

*Promoter here means promoter as defined in the Companies Act, 2013.

** Details shall be given separately for each class of shares

*** percentage change shall be computed with respect to the number at the beginning of the year or if issued during the year for the first time then with respect to the date of issue."

### 14.6.19 Other Equity

(i) Other Reserves' shall be classified in the notes as:

  (a) Capital Redemption Reserve;

  (b) Debenture Redemption Reserve;

  (c) Share Options Outstanding Account;

  (d) Statutory Reserves; and

  (e) Others – (specify the nature and purpose of each reserve and the amount in respect thereof); (Additions and deductions since last balance sheet to be shown under each of the specified heads)

(ii) Retained Earnings represents surplus i.e. balance of the relevant column in the Statement of Changes in Equity;

(iii) A reserve specifically represented by earmarked investments shall disclose the fact that it is so represented;

(iv) Debit balance of Statement of Profit and Loss shall be shown as a negative figure under the head 'retained earnings'. Similar ly, the balance of 'Other Equity', after adjusting negative balance of retained earnings, if any, shall be shown under the head 'Other Equity' even if the resulting figure is in the negative;

(v) Under the sub-head 'Other Equity', disclosure shall be made for the nature and amount of each item; and

(vi) Under the sub-head 'Other Equity', disclosure shall be made for conditions or restrictions for distribution attached to statutory reserves.

### 14.6.20 Contingent Liabilities and Commitments (to the extent not provided for)

(i) Contingent Liabilities shall be classified as:

| | |
|---|---|
| (a) | Claims against the company not acknowledged as debt; |
| (b) | Guarantees excluding financial guarantees; and |
| (c) | Other money for which the company is contingently liable |

(ii) Commitments shall be classified as:

| | |
|---|---|
| (a) | Estimated amount of contracts remaining to be executed on capital account and not provided for; |
| (b) | Uncalled liability on shares and other investments partly paid; |
| (c) | Other commitments (specify nature). |

**Illustration 14.44: Accounting policy: Contingent liabilities/Contingent Assets and Commitments**

**Contingent Liabilities/Contingent Assets**

A possible obligation that arises from past events and the existence of which will be confirmed only by the occurrence or non-occurrence of one or more uncertain future events not wholly within the control of the Group or; present obligation that arises from past events where it is not probable that an outflow of resources embodying economic benefits will be required to settle the obligation; or the amount of the obligation cannot be measured with sufficient reliability are disclosed as contingent liability and not provided for.

Contingent assets are disclosed where an inflow of economic benefits is probable. Contingent assets are not recognised in the consolidated financial statements.

Provisions, contingent liabilities and contingent assets are reviewed at each Balance Sheet date.

Where the unavoidable costs of meeting the obligations under the contract exceed the economic benefits expected to be received under such contract, the present obligation under the contract is recognised and measured as a provision

**Commitments**

Commitments are future liabilities for contractual expenditure, classified and disclosed as follows:

a) estimated amount of contracts remaining to be executed on capital account and not provided for;
b) uncalled liability on shares and other investments partly paid;
c) funding related commitment to associate; and
d) other non-cancellable commitments, if any, to the extent they are

considered material and relevant in the opinion of management.

e) other commitments related to sales/procurements made in the normal course of business are not disclosed to avoid excessive details.

f) commitments under Loan agreement to disburse Loans

a) lease agreements entered but not executed

(*Source: TCFSL Annual Report 2020*)

## 14.6.21 Dividends

According to clause **(V)** of Schedule III, Division III, the amount of dividends proposed to be distributed to equity and preference shareholders for the period and the related amount per share shall be disclosed separately. Arrears of fixed cumulative dividends on irredeemable preference shares shall also be disclosed separately.

**Illustration 14.45: Accounting policy: Dividend payable**

Interim dividend declared to equity shareholders, if any, is recognised as liability in the period in which the said dividend has been declared by the Board of Directors. Final dividend declared, if any, is recognised in the period in which the said dividend has been approved by the Shareholders.

The dividend payable (including dividend distribution tax) is recognised as a liability with a corresponding amount recognised directly in equity.

(*Source: TCFSL Annual Report 2020*)

## 14.6.22 Disclosure of unutilized amount related to Issue of securities made for a specific purpose

According to clause (W) of Schedule III, Division III, where in respect of an issue of securities made for a specific purpose the whole or part of amount has not been used for the specific purpose at the Balance Sheet date, there shall be indicated by way of note how such unutilized amounts have been used or invested.

## 14.6.23 Disclosure of unutilized amount related to borrowings from banks and financial institutions made for a specific purpose

**(WA)** Where the company has not used the borrowings from banks and financial institutions for the specific purpose for which it was taken at the balance sheet date, the company shall disclose the details of where they have been used.

## 14.6.24 Clause (WB) Additional Regulatory Information

### *14.6.24.1 Title deeds of Immovable Properties not held in name of the Company*

The company shall provide the details of all the immovable property (other than properties where the Company is the lessee and the lease agreements are duly executed in favour of the lessee) whose title deeds are not held in the name of the company in following format and where such immovable property is jointly held with others, details are required to be given to the extent of the company's share.

| Relevant line item in the Balance sheet | Description of item of property | Gross carrying value | Title deeds held in the name of | Whether title deed holder is promoter, director or relative # of promoter/director or employee of promoter/director | Property held since which date | Reason for not being held in the name of the company** |
|---|---|---|---|---|---|---|
| PPE<br>PPE | Land<br>Building | - | — | — | — | **also indicate if in dispute |
| Investment property- | Land<br>Building | | | | | |
| Non-current asset held for sale others | Land<br>Building | | | | | |

#Relative here means relative as defined in the Companies Act, 2013. *Promoter here means promoter as defined in the Companies Act, 2013."

Here it may be pertinent to note, that the Act does not define 'title deeds'. In general, title deeds mean a legal deed or document constituting evidence of a right, (eg. registered sale deed, transfer deed, conveyance deed of land) especially to the legal ownership of the immovable property.

In case of leased assets, title deeds would imply the lease agreements and related documents. Where the Company is the lessee of an immovable property and the lease agreements are not duly executed in favour of the lessee then appropriate disclosure has to be provided for such immovable properties.

Pursuant to ICAI Guidance Note, Schedule III, Division III, while making this disclosure in the financial statements, the entity need to disclose the following information:

(i) *Gross carrying value* – the entity shall disclose the amount in the financial statements;

(ii) *Title deeds held in the name of* – the entity need to disclose the full name of the individual/entity/person holding the title of immovable property;

(iii) *Whether title deed holder is a promoter, director or relative of promoter/director or employee of promoter/director* – the entity needs to disclose the relationship between itself and the individual/entity/person holding the title of immovable property;

(iv) *Property held since which date* – the company needs to disclose the date since the property is held and where the exact date is not available, it shall disclose the month and year since the property is held.

(v) *Reason for not being held in the name of the company, also indicating if there is a dispute* – the entity shall state the reason for the immovable property not being held in the name of the company (for example, the documents are under preparation or the registration process of transfer of name is in progress as on the balance sheet date). In case the title deeds of immovable property are not being held in the name of company due to a dispute, the company shall state the nature of dispute.

#### ***14.6.24.2 Disclosure of fair value of investment property whether carried out by a Registered Valuer***

The company shall disclose as to whether the fair value of investment property (as measured for disclosure purposes in the financial statements) is based on the valuation by a registered valuer as defined under rule 2 of Companies (Registered Valuers and Valuation) Rules, 2017.

#### ***14.6.24.3 Disclosure of revaluation of Property, Plant and Equipment whether carried out by a Registered Valuer***

Where the Company has revalued its **Property, Plant and Equipment** (including Right-of-Use Assets), the company shall disclose as to whether the revaluation is based on valuation by a Registered Valuer as defined under rule 2 of Companies (Registered Valuers and Valuation) Rules, 2017.

#### ***14.6.24.4 Disclosure of revaluation of Intangible Assets whether carried out by a Registered Valuer***

Where the Company has revalued its Intangible assets, the company shall disclose as to whether the revaluation is based on valuation by a Registered Valuer as defined under rule 2 of Companies (Registered Valuers and Valuation) Rules, 2017.

### 14.6.24.5 Disclosure of loans or advances in the nature of loans granted to promoters, directors, KMPSs and other related parties

Following disclosures shall be made where loans or advances in the nature of loans are granted to promoters, directors, KMPs and the related parties (as defined under the Companies Act, 2013), either severally or jointly with any other person that are:

(a) repayable on demand or

(b) without specifying any terms or period of repayment.

| Type of Borrower | Amount of loan or advance in the nature of loan outstanding | Percentage to the total Loans and Advances in the nature of loans |
|---|---|---|
| Promoter | | |
| Directors | | |
| KMPs | | |
| Related parties | | |

### 14.6.24.6 Capital-Work-in Progress (CWIP)

(a) For Capital-work-in progress, following ageing schedule shall be given:

**CWIP aging schedule**

(Amount in Rs.)

| CWIP | Amount in CWIP for a period of | | | | Total* |
|---|---|---|---|---|---|
| | Less than 1 year | 1-2 years | 2-3 years | More than 3 years | |
| Projects in progress<br>Projects temporarily suspended | | | | | |

*Total shall tally with CWIP amount in the balance sheet.

(b) **For capital-work-in progress, whose completion is overdue or has exceeded its cost compared to its original plan, following CWIP completion schedule shall be given**:**

(Amount in Rs.)

| **CWIP** | **To be completed in** | | | |
|---|---|---|---|---|
| | **Less year than1** | **1-2 years** | **2-3 years** | **More years than 3** |
| Project 1<br>Project 2" | | | | |

**Details of projects where activity has been suspended shall be given separately.

Please refer to Paragraph 10.18 in Chapter 10 with respect to details under this section.

### *14.6.24.7 Intangible assets under development*

(a) For Intangible assets under development, following ageing schedule shall be given:

**Intangible assets under development aging schedule**

(Amount in Rs.)

| **Intangible assets under development** | **Amount in CWIP for a period of** | | | | **Total*** |
|---|---|---|---|---|---|
| | **Less than 1 year** | **1-2 years** | **2-3 years** | **More than 3 years** | |
| Projects in progress<br>Projects temporarily suspended | | | | | |

* Total shall tally with the amount of Intangible assets under development in the balance sheet.

(b) For Intangible assets under development, whose completion is overdue or has exceeded its cost compared to its original plan, following **Intangible assets under development completion schedule** shall be given**:

(Amount in Rs.)

| Intangible assets under development | To be completed in | | | |
|---|---|---|---|---|
| | **Less than 1 year** | **1-2 years** | **2-3 years** | **More than 3 years** |
| Project 1<br>Project 2 | | | | |

**Details of projects where activity has been suspended shall be given separately.

### *14.6.24.8 Details of Benami Property held*

Where any proceedings have been initiated or pending against the company for holding any benami property under the Benami Transactions (Prohibition) Act, 1988 (45 of 1988) and rules made thereunder, the company shall disclose the following:-

(a) Details of such property,

(b) Amount thereof,

(c) Details of Beneficiaries,

(d) If property is in the books, then reference to the item in the Balance Sheet,

(e) If property is not in the books, then the fact shall be stated with reasons,

(f) Where there are proceedings against the company under this law as an a better of the transaction or as the transferor then the details shall be provided.

(g) Nature of proceedings, status of same and company's view on same.

### *14.6.24.9 Borrowings from banks or financial institutions based on security of current assets*

Where the Company has borrowings from banks or financial institutions on the basis of security of current assets, it shall disclose the following: -

(a) whether quarterly returns or statements of current assets filed by the Company with banks or financial institutions are in agreement with the books of accounts,

(b) if not, summary of reconciliation and reasons of material discrepancies if any to be adequately disclosed.

Please refer to Paragraph 10.18 in Chapter 10 with respect to details under this section.

### 14.6.24.10 Wilful Defaulter

Where a company is a declared wilful defaulter by any bank or financial Institution or other lender, following details shall be given, namely: -

(a) date of declaration as wilful defaulter,

(b) details of defaults (amount and nature of defaults).

*wilful defaulter" here means a person or an issuer who or which is categorized as a wilful defaulter by any bank or financial institution (as defined under the Companies Act, 2013) or consortium thereof, in accordance with the guidelines on wilful defaulters issued by the Reserve Bank of India.

Please refer to Paragraph 10.18 in Chapter 10 with respect to details under this section.

### 14.6.24.11 Relationship with Struck off Companies

Where the company has any transactions with the companies struck off under section 248 of Companies Act, 2013 or section 560 of Companies Act, 1956, the Company shall disclose the following details, namely:-

| Name of struck off Company | Nature of transactions with struck-off Company | Balance outstanding | Relationship with the Struck off company, if any, to be disclosed |
|---|---|---|---|
| | Investments in securities | | |
| | Receivables | | |
| | Payables | | |
| | Shares held by stuck off company | | |
| | Other outstanding balances (to be specified) | | |

Please refer to Paragraph 10.18 in Chapter 10 with respect to details under this section.

### 14.6.24.12 Registration of charges or satisfaction with Registrar of Companies (ROC)

Where any charges or satisfaction yet to be registered with ROC beyond the statutory period, details and reasons thereof shall be disclosed.

### 14.6.24.13 Compliance with number of layers of companies

Where the company has not complied with the number of layers prescribed under clause (87) of section 2 of the Act read with Companies (Restriction on number of Layers) Rules, 2017, the name and CIN of the companies beyond the specified layers and the relationship/extent of holding of the company in such downstream companies shall be disclosed.

### 14.6.24.14 Following Ratios shall be disclosed

(a) Capital to risk-weighted assets ratio (CRAR)

(b) Tier I CRAR

(c) Tier II CRAR

(d) Liquidity Coverage Ratio

**Illustration 14.46: Disclosure of Ratios: Specimen format**

| Ratios | Numerator | Denominator | Current Reporting period | Previous Reporting period | Variance % | Reasons for Variance > 25% |
|---|---|---|---|---|---|---|
| (a) Capital to risk-weighted assets ratio (CRAR) | | | | | | |
| (b) Tier I CRAR | | | | | | |
| (c) Tier II CRAR | | | | | | |
| (d) Liquidity Coverage Ratio | | | | | | |

**Note:**

**Capital to risk-weighted assets ratio (CRAR)**

CRAR also known as Capital Adequacy Ratio (CAR) is the ratio of a bank's capital to its risk.

The CRAR is computed by dividing the capital of the bank with aggregated risk-weighted assets for credit risk, operational risk, and market risk.

This is calculated by summing a bank's tier 1 capital and tier 2 capitals and dividing the total by its total risk-weighted assets. That is:

Tier 1 CAR = (Eligible Tier 1 capital funds) = (Market Risk RWA + Credit Risk RWA + Operational Risk RWA)

Total CAR = (Eligible Total capital funds) ÷ (Credit Risk RWA + Market Risk RWA + Operational Risk RWA)

CRAR is decided by central banks and bank regulators to prevent commercial banks from taking excess leverage and becoming insolvent in the process.

The Basel III norms stipulated a capital to risk-weighted assets of 8%. n India, scheduled commercial banks are required to maintain a CAR of 9% while Indian public sector banks are emphasized to maintain a CAR of 12% as per RBI norms.

**Liquidity Coverage Ratio**

The liquidity coverage ratio (LCR) represents the proportion of highly liquid assets held by financial institutions, to ensure their ongoing ability to meet short-term obligations.

The formula is as under:

$$\text{LCR} = \frac{\text{High quality liquid asset account}}{\text{Total net cash flow amount}}$$

This ratio is essentially a generic stress test that aims to anticipate market-wide shocks and make sure that financial institutions possess suitable capital preservation, to ride out any short-term liquidity disruptions, that may plague the market.

### *14.6.24.15 Compliance with approved Scheme(s) of Arrangements*

Where any Scheme of Arrangements has been approved by the Competent Authority in terms of sections 230 to 237 of the Companies Act, 2013, the Company shall disclose that the effect of such Scheme of Arrangements have been accounted for in the books of account of the Company 'in accordance with the Scheme' and "in accordance with accounting standards". Any deviation in this regard shall be explained.

### *14.6.24.16 Utilization of Borrowed funds and share premium*

(A) Where company has advanced or loaned or invested funds (either borrowed funds or share premium or any other sources or kind of funds) to any other person(s) or entity(ies), including foreign entities (Intermediaries) with the understanding (whether recorded in writing or otherwise) that the Intermediary shall

- (i) directly or indirectly lend or invest in other persons or entities identified in any manner whatsoever by or on behalf of the company (Ultimate Beneficiaries) or
- (ii) provide any guarantee, security or the like to or on behalf of the Ultimate Beneficiaries; the company shall disclose the following:-
  - (I) date and amount of fund advanced or loaned or invested in Intermediaries with complete details of each Intermediary.
  - (II) date and amount of fund further advanced or loaned or invested by such Intermediaries to other intermediaries or Ultimate Beneficiaries along with complete details of the ultimate beneficiaries.
  - (III) date and amount of guarantee, security or the like provided to or on behalf of the Ultimate Beneficiaries
  - (IV) declaration that relevant provisions of the Foreign Exchange Management Act, 1999 (42 of 1999) and Companies Act has been complied with for such transactions and the transactions are not violative of the Prevention of Money-Laundering act, 2002 (15 of 2003).;

(B) Where a company has received any fund from any person(s) or entity(ies), including foreign entities (Funding Party) with the understanding (whether recorded in writing or otherwise) that the company shall

- (i) directly or indirectly lend or invest in other persons or entities identified in any manner whatsoever by or on behalf of the Funding Party (Ultimate Beneficiaries) or
- (ii) provide any guarantee, security or the like on behalf of the Ultimate Beneficiaries, the company shall disclose the following:
  - (I) date and amount of fund received from Funding parties with complete details of each Funding party.
  - (II) date and amount of fund further advanced or loaned or invested other intermediaries or Ultimate Beneficiaries along with complete details of the other intermediaries' or ultimate beneficiaries.
  - (III) date and amount of guarantee, security or the like provided to or on behalf of the Ultimate Beneficiaries
  - (IV) declaration that relevant provisions of the Foreign Exchange Management Act, 1999 (42 of 1999) and Companies Act has been complied with for such transactions and the transactions are not violative of the Prevention of Money-Laundering act, 2002 (15 of 2003).

### 14.6.24.17 Other Classification related General Instructions

1. When an NBFC applies an accounting policy retrospectively or makes a restatement of items in the financial statements or when it reclassifies items in its financial statements, the NBFC shall attach to the Balance Sheet, a "Balance Sheet" as at the beginning of the earliest comparative period presented.
2. Share application money pending allotment shall be classified into equity or liability in accordance with relevant Indian Accounting Standards. Share application money to the extent not refundable shall be shown under the head Equity and share application money to the extent refundable shall be separately shown under 'Other financial liabilities'.
3. Preference shares including premium received on issue, shall be classified and presented as 'Equity' or 'Liability' in accordance with the requirements of the relevant Indian Accounting Standards. Accordingly, the disclosure and presentation requirements in this regard applicable to the relevant class of equity or liability shall be applicable mutatis mutandis to the preference shares. For instance, plain vanilla redeemable preference shares shall be classified and presented under 'liabilities' as 'borrowings' or 'subordinated liability' and the disclosure requirements in this regard applicable to such borrowings shall be applicable mutatis mutandis to redeemable preference shares.
4. Compound financial instruments such as convertible debentures, where split into equity and liability components, as per the requirements of the relevant Indian Accounting Standards, shall be classified and presented under the relevant heads in ''Liabilities and Equity".
5. Regulatory Deferral Account Balances shall be presented in the Balance Sheet in accordance with the relevant Indian Accounting Standards.

## 14.7 PART II – STATEMENT OF PROFIT AND LOSS

Name of the Non-Banking Financial Company........................

Statement of Profit and Loss for the period ended ..........................

| | Particulars | Note No. | Figures for the current reporting period | Figures for the previous reporting period |
|---|---|---|---|---|
| | **Revenue from operations** | | | |
| (i) | Interest Income | | | |
| (ii) | Dividend Income | | | |
| (iii) | Rental Income | | | |
| (iv) | Fees and commission Income | | | |
| (v) | Net gain on fair value changes | | | |
| (vi) | Net gain on derecognition of financial | | | |

| | Particulars | Note No. | Figures for the current reporting period | Figures for the previous reporting period |
|---|---|---|---|---|
| | instruments<br>under amortised cost category | | | |
| (vii) | Sale of products(including Excise Duty) | | | |
| (viii) | Sale of services | | | |
| (ix) | Others (to be specified) | | | |
| (I) | **Total Revenue from operations** | | | |
| | | | | |
| (II) | Other Income (to be specified) | | | |
| (III) | **Total Income (I+II)** | | | |
| | | | | |
| | **Expenses** | | | |
| (i) | Finance Costs | | | |
| (ii) | Fees and commission expense | | | |
| (iii) | Net loss on fair value changes | | | |
| (iv) | Net loss on de-recognition of financial instruments<br>under amortized cost category | | | |
| (v) | Impairment on financial instruments | | | |
| (vi) | Cost of materials consumed | | | |
| (vii) | Purchases of Stock -in -trade | | | |
| (viii) | Changes in Inventories of finished goods, stock -in - trade and work -in – progress | | | |
| (ix) | Employee Benefits Expenses | | | |
| (x) | Depreciation, amortization and impairment | | | |
| (xi) | Others expenses (to be specified) | | | |
| ( IV ) | **Total Expenses (IV)** | | | |
| | | | | |
| (V) | Profit/(loss) before exceptional items and tax (III - IV) | | | |
| (VI) | Exceptional items | | | |
| (VII) | Profit/(loss) before tax (V -VI) | | | |
| (VIII) | Tax Expense:<br>(1) Current Tax<br>(2) Deferred Tax | | | |
| (IX) | Profit/(loss) for the period from continuing operations(VII-VIII) | | | |
| (X) | Profit/(loss) from discontinued operations | | | |
| (XI) | Tax Expense of discontinued operations | | | |
| (XII) | Profit/(loss) from discontinued operations(After tax) (X-XI) | | | |
| **(XIII)** | **Profit/(loss) for the period (IX+XII)** | | | |
| | | | | |

| | Particulars | Note No. | Figures for the current reporting period | Figures for the previous reporting period |
|---|---|---|---|---|
| (XIV) | **Other Comprehensive Income** | | | |
| | (A) (i) Items that will not be reclassified to profit or loss (specify items and amounts) | | | |
| | (ii) Income tax relating to items that will not be reclassified to profit or loss | | | |
| | **Subtotal (A)** | | | |
| | (B) (i) Items that will be reclassified to profit or loss (specify items and amounts) | | | |
| | (ii) Income tax relating to items that will be reclassified to profit or loss | | | |
| | **Subtotal (B)** | | | |
| | **Other Comprehensive Income (A + B)** | | | |
| | | | | |
| (XV) | **Total Comprehensive Income for the period (XIII+XIV) (Comprising Profit (Loss) and other Comprehensive Income for the period)** | | | |
| | | | | |
| (XVI) | **Earnings per equity share (for continuing operations)** | | | |
| | Basic (Rs.) | | | |
| | Diluted (Rs.) | | | |
| (XVII) | **Earnings per equity share (for discontinued operations)** | | | |
| | Basic (Rs.) | | | |
| | Diluted (Rs.) | | | |
| (XVIII) | **Earnings per equity share (for continuing and discontinued operations)** | | | |
| | Basic (Rs.) | | | |
| | Diluted (Rs.) | | | |

See accompanying notes to the financial statements

## 14.8 NOTES ON ACCOUNTS

The provisions of this Part shall apply to the income and expenditure account, in like manner as they apply to a Statement of Profit and Loss.

### 14.8.1 Components of Statement of Profit and Loss include:

The Statement of Profit and Loss shall include:

(A) Profit or loss for the period;

(B) Other Comprehensive Income for the period. The sum of (A) and (B) above is 'Total Comprehensive Income'.

| Particulars | Current Year | | | Previous Year | | |
|---|---|---|---|---|---|---|
| | On Financial Assets measured at fair value through OCI | On financial assets measured at Amortized cost | Interest income on financial assets classified at fair value through profit or loss | On Financial Assets measured at fair value through OCI | On financial assets measured at Amortized cost | Interest income on financial assets classified at fair value through profit or loss |
| Interest on loans<br>Interest income from investments<br>Interest on deposits with banks<br>Subordinated liabilities in India<br>Other interest income | | | | | | |
| Total | | | | | | |

## Illustration 14.47: Accounting policy: Recognition of Income and expenses

(i) Interest income, on financial assets subsequently measured at amortised cost, is recognised using the Effective Interest Rate (EIR) method. The Effective Interest Rate (EIR) is the rate that exactly discounts estimated future cash receipts through expected life of the financial asset to that asset's net carrying amount on initial recognition.

(ii) Interest on financial assets subsequently measured at fair value through profit and loss, is recognised on accrual basis in accordance with the terms of the respective contract.

(iii) Rebate on account of timely payment of dues by borrowers is recognised on receipt of entire dues in time, in accordance with the terms of the respective contract and is presented against the corresponding interest income.

(iv) Income from services rendered is recognised based on the terms of agreements/arrangements with reference to the stage of completion of contract at the reporting date.

(v) Dividend income from investments is recognised in Statement of Profit and Loss when the Company's right to receive dividend is established, which in the case of quoted securities is the ex-dividend date.

(vi) Interest expense on borrowings subsequently measured at amortised cost is recognised using Effective Interest Rate (EIR) method.

(vii) Other income and expenses are accounted on accrual basis, in accordance with terms of the respective contract.

(viii) A Prepaid expense up to Rs. 1,00,000/- is recognised as expense upon initial recognition.

(*Source: Power Finance Corporation Annual Report 2020*)

### 14.8.2 Net gain/(loss) on fair value changes*

| Particulars | (Current Year) | (Previous Year) |
|---|---|---|
| (A) Net gain/(loss) on financial instruments at fair value through profit or loss | | |
| (i) On trading portfolio | | |
| - Investments | | |
| - Derivatives | | |
| - Others | | |
| (ii) On financial instruments designated at fair value through profit or loss | | |
| (B) Others (to be specified) | | |
| Total Net gain/(loss) on fair value changes (C) | | |
| Fair Value changes:<br>- Realized<br>- Unrealised | | |
| Total Net gain/(loss) on fair value changes(D) to tally with (C) | | |

*Fair value changes in this schedule are other than those arising on account of accrued interest income/expense.

### 14.8.3 Other Income (to be specified)

| Particulars | (Current Year) | (Previous Year) |
|---|---|---|
| Net gain/(loss) on ineffective portion of hedges | | |
| Net gain/(loss) on de-recognition of property, plant and equipment | | |
| Net gain or loss on foreign currency transaction and translation (other than considered as finance cost)( to be specified) | | |
| Others (to be specified)* | | |
| Total | | |

* Any item under the subhead 'Others' which exceeds one per cent of the total income to be presented separately.

**Illustration 14.48: Accounting policy: Foreign currency transaction**

**Foreign currency transactions**

Transactions in currencies other than the Group's functional currency are recorded on initial recognition using the exchange rate at the transaction date. At each Balance Sheet date, foreign currency monetary items are reported at the rates prevailing at the year end. Nonmonetary items that are measured in terms of historical cost in foreign currency are not retranslated.

Exchange differences that arise on settlement of monetary items or on reporting of monetary items at each Balance Sheet date at the closing spot rate are recognised in the Statement of Profit and Loss in the period in which they arise.

*(Source: TSFL Annual Report 2020)*

### 14.8.4 Finance Costs

| Particulars | (Current Year) | | (Previous Year) | |
|---|---|---|---|---|
| | On Financial liabilities measured at fair value through profit or loss | On Financial liabilities measured at Amortised Cost | On Financial liabilities measured at fair value through profit or loss | On Financial liabilities measured at Amortised Cost |
| Interest on deposits | | | | |
| Interest on borrowings | | | | |
| Interest on debt securities | | | | |
| Interest on subordinated liabilities | | | | |
| Other interest expense | | | | |
| Total | | | | |

**Illustration 14.49: Accounting policy: Leases**

**Leasing**

For recognition, measurement and presentation of lease contracts, the Company applies the principles of Ind AS 116 'Leases'.

**The Company as a lessee**

The Company at inception of a contract assesses, whether the contract is, or contains, a lease. A contract is, or contains, a lease if the contract conveys the right to control the use of an identified asset for a period of time in exchange for consideration. To assess whether a contract conveys the right to control the use of an identified asset, the Company assesses whether (a) the Company has substantially all of the economic benefits from use of the asset through the period of the lease, and (b) the Company has the right to direct the use of the identified asset.

The Company at inception of a lease contract recognizes a Right-of-Use (RoU) asset at cost and a corresponding lease liability, except for leases with term of less than twelve months (short-term) and low-value assets which are recognised as an operating expense on a straight-line basis over the term of the lease.

Certain lease arrangements include the options to extend or terminate the lease before the end of the lease term. RoU assets and lease liabilities includes these options when it is reasonably certain that they will be exercised.

The right-of-use (RoU) assets are initially recognised at cost, which comprise the initial amount of the lease liability adjusted for any lease payments made at or before the inception date of the lease plus any initial direct costs, less any lease incentives received. They are subsequently measured at cost less any accumulated depreciation and accumulated impairment losses. The right-of-use assets is depreciated using the straight-line method from the commencement date over the shorter of lease term or useful life of right-of-use assets.

The lease liability is initially measured at amortised cost at the present value of future lease payments. The lease payments are discounted using the interest rate implicit in the lease or, if not readily determinable, using the Company's incremental borrowing rates in the country of domicile of the leases.

Lease liabilities are re-measured with a corresponding adjustment to the related right-of-use (RoU) asset if the Company changes its assessment if whether it will exercise an extension or a termination option.

Lease liability and RoU asset is separately presented in the Balance Sheet. Interest expense on lease liability is presented separately from depreciation on right of use asset as a component of finance cost in the Statement of Profit and Loss. Lease payments are classified as Cash flow used in financing activities.

**The Company as a lessor**

Leases for which the Company is a lessor is classified as a finance or operating lease. Contracts in which all the risks and rewards of the lease are substantially transferred to the lessee are classified as a finance lease. All other leases are classified as operating leases. For operating leases, rental income is recognised on a straight-line basis over the term of the relevant lease.

Amount due from lessee under finance leases is recognised as receivable at an amount equal to the net investment of the Company in the lease. Finance income on the lease is allocated to accounting periods so as to reflect a constant periodic rate of return on the Company's net investment outstanding in respect of lease at the reporting date.

*(Source: Power Finance Corporation Annual Report 2020)*

### 14.8.5 Employee Benefits Expenses

| Particulars | (Current Year) | (Previous Year) |
|---|---|---|
| Salaries and wages | | |
| Contribution to provident and other funds | | |

| Particulars | (Current Year) | (Previous Year) |
|---|---|---|
| Share Based Payments to employees | | |
| Staff welfare expenses | | |
| Others (to be specified) | | |
| Total | | |

**Illustration 14.50: Employee Benefit Expenses**

(i) Defined Contribution Plan

Company's contribution paid/payable during the reporting period towards provident fund and pension are charged in the Statement of Profit and Loss when employees have rendered service entitling them to the contributions.

(ii) Defined Benefit Plan

The Company's obligation towards gratuity to employees and post-retirement benefits such as medical benefit, economic rehabilitation benefit, and settlement allowance after retirement are determined using the projected unit credit method, with actuarial valuations being carried out at the end of each annual reporting period. Actuarial gain/loss on re-measurement of gratuity and other post-employment defined benefit plans is recognised in Other Comprehensive Income (OCI). Past service cost is recognised in the Statement of Profit and Loss in the period of a plan amendment.

(iii) Other long-term employee benefits

The Company's obligation towards leave encashment, service award scheme is determined using the projected unit credit method, with actuarial valuations being carried out at the end of each annual reporting period. These obligations are recognised in the Statement of Profit and Loss.

(iv) Short-term employee benefits

Short-term employee benefits such as salaries and wages are recognised in the Statement of Profit and Loss, in the period in which the related service is rendered at the undiscounted amount of the benefits expected to be paid in exchange for that service.

(v) Loan to employees at concessional rate

Loans given to employees at concessional rate are initially recognised at fair value and subsequently measured at amortised cost. The difference between the initial fair value of such loans and transaction value is recognised as deferred employee cost upon issuance of Loan, which is amortised on a straight-line basis over the expected remaining period of the loan. In case of change in expected remaining period of the loan, the un-amortised deferred employee cost on the date of change is amortised over the updated expected remaining period of the Loan on a prospective basis.

*(Source: Power Finance Corporation Annual Report 2020*

### 14.8.6 Impairment on financial instruments

| Particulars | (Current Year) | | (Previous Year) | |
|---|---|---|---|---|
| | On Financial instruments measured at fair value through OCI | On Financial instruments measured at Amortised Cost | On Financial instruments measured at fair value through OCI | On Financial instruments measured at Amortised Cost |
| Loans | | | | |
| Investments | | | | |
| Others (to be specified) | | | | |
| Total | | | | |

### 14.8.7 Other expenses (to be specified)

| Particulars | (Current Year) | (Previous Year) |
|---|---|---|
| Rent, taxes and energy costs | | |
| Repairs and maintenance | | |
| Communication Costs | | |
| Printing and stationery | | |
| Advertisement and publicity | | |
| Director's fees, allowances and expenses | | |
| Auditor's fees and expenses | | |
| Legal and Professional charges | | |
| Insurance | | |
| Other expenditure | | |
| Total | | |

* Any item under the subhead 'Others expenditure' which exceeds one per cent of the total income to be presented separately

### 14.8.8 Other Comprehensive Income shall be classified into-

(A) Items that will not be reclassified to profit or loss

- (i) Changes in revaluation surplus;
- (ii) Remeasurements of the defined benefit plans;
- (iii) Equity Instruments through Other Comprehensive Income;

(iv) Fair value changes relating to own credit risk of financial liabilities designated at fair value through profit or loss;

(v) Share of Other Comprehensive Income in Associates and Joint Ventures, to the extent not to be classified into profit or loss; and

(vi) Others (specify nature).

(B) Items that will be reclassified to profit or loss;

(i) Exchange differences in translating the financial statements of a foreign operation;

(ii) Debt Instruments through Other Comprehensive Income;

(iii) The effective portion of gains and loss on hedging instruments in a cash flow hedge;

(iv) Share of Other Comprehensive Income in Associates and Joint Ventures, to the extent to be classified into profit or loss; and

(v) Others (specify nature).

**Illustration 14.51: Accounting policy: Income Taxes**

**Income Taxes**

Income Tax expense comprises of current and deferred tax. It is recognised in Statement of Profit and Loss, except when it relates to an item that is recognised in OCI or directly in equity, in which case, tax is also recognised in OCI or directly in equity.

(i) Current Tax

Current tax is the expected tax payable on taxable income for the year, using tax rates enacted or substantively enacted and as applicable at the reporting date, and any adjustments to tax payable in respect of previous years.

Current tax assets and liabilities are offset when there is a legally enforceable right to set off the recognised amounts and there is an intention to settle the asset and liability on a net basis.

(ii) Deferred Tax

Deferred tax is recognised on temporary differences between the carrying amounts of assets and liabilities in the financial statements and the corresponding tax bases used in the computation of taxable income. Deferred tax is measured at the tax rates based on the laws that have been enacted or substantively enacted by the reporting date, based on the expected manner of realization or settlement of the carrying amount of assets/liabilities. Deferred tax assets and liabilities are offset when there is a legally enforceable right to set off current tax assets against liabilities, and they relate to income taxes levied by the same tax authority.

A deferred tax liability is recognised for all taxable temporary differences. A deferred tax asset is recognised for all deductible temporary differences to the extent that it is probable that future taxable profits will be available against which the deductible temporary difference can be utilized. Deferred tax assets are reviewed at each reporting date and are reduced to the extent that it is no longer probable that the related tax benefit will be realized.

(iii) Additional Income Tax that arises from distribution of dividend is recognised at the same time when the liability to pay dividend is recognised.

(*Source: Power Finance Corporation*)

### 14.8.9 Additional Information

An NBFC shall disclose by way of notes, additional information regarding aggregate expenditure and income on the following items:

#### *14.8.9.1 Depreciation, Amortization and impairment*

**Illustration 14.52: Depreciation, Amortization**

**Depreciation and Amortization**

Depreciable amount for tangible property, plant and equipment is the cost of an asset, or other amount substituted for cost, less its estimated residual value. The residual value of each asset given on Operating lease is determined at the time of recording of the lease asset. If the residual value of the Operating lease asset is higher than 5%, the Group has a justification in place for considering the same.

Depreciation on tangible property, plant and equipment deployed for own use has been provided on the straight-line method as per the useful life prescribed in Schedule II to the Companies Act, 2013 except in respect of buildings, computer equipment, electrical installation and equipment and vehicles, in whose case the life of the assets has been assessed based on the nature of the asset, the estimated usage of the asset, the operating conditions of the asset, past history of replacement, etc.

Depreciation on tangible property, plant and equipment deployed on operating lease has been provided on the straight-line method over the primary lease period of the asset. Depreciation method is reviewed at each financial year end to reflect expected pattern of consumption of the future economic benefits embodied in the asset. The estimated useful life and residual values are also reviewed at each financial year end with the effect of any change in the estimates of useful life/residual value is accounted on prospective basis. Depreciation for additions to/deductions from owned assets is calculated pro rata to the remaining period of use.

Depreciation charge for impaired assets is adjusted in future periods in such a manner that the revised carrying amount of the asset is allocated over its remaining useful life. All capital assets with individual value less than Rs. 5,000 are depreciated fully in the year in which they are purchased.

Purchased software/licenses are amortised over the estimated useful life during which the benefits are expected to accrue, while Goodwill if any is tested for impairment at each Balance Sheet date. The method of Amortisation, residual value and useful life are reviewed at the end of each accounting year with the effect of any changes in the estimate being accounted for on a prospective basis.

Amortisation on impaired assets is provided by adjusting the Amortisation charge in the remaining periods so as to allocate the asset's revised carrying amount over its remaining useful life.

(*Source: TCFSL Annual Report 2020*)

#### 14.8.9.2 Payments to the auditor as

Payments to the auditor as:

(a) auditor,

(b) for taxation matters,

(c) for company law matters,

(d) for other services,

(e) for reimbursement of expenses.

#### 14.8.9.3 NBFCs covered under section 135, amount of expenditure incurred on corporate social responsibility activities

#### 14.8.9.4 Details of items of exceptional nature

#### 14.8.9.5 Undisclosed income

The Company shall give details of any transactions not recorded in the books of accounts that has been surrendered or disclosed as income during the year in the tax assessments under the Income Tax Act, 1961 (such as, search or survey or any other relevant provisions of the Income Tax Act, 1961), unless there is immunity for disclosure under any scheme. Also, state whether the previously unrecorded income and related assets have been properly recorded in the books of account during the year.

#### 14.8.9.6 Corporate Social Responsibility (CSR)

Where the company (NBFC) covered under section 135 of the Companies Act, the following shall be disclosed with regard to CSR activities:

(a) amount required to be spent by the company during the year,

(b) amount of expenditure incurred,

(c) shortfall at the end of the year,

(d) total of previous years shortfall,

(e) reason for shortfall,

(f) nature of CSR activities,

(g) details of related party transactions, e.g., contribution to a trust controlled by the company in relation to CSR expenditure as per relevant Accounting Standard,

(h) where a provision is made with respect to a liability incurred by entering into a contractual obligation, the movements in the provision during the year shall be shown separately.

### *14.8.9.7 Details of Crypto Currency or Virtual Currency*

Where the Company has traded or invested in Crypto currency or Virtual Currency during the financial year, the following shall be disclosed:-

(a) profit or loss on transactions involving Crypto currency or Virtual Currency,

(b) amount of currency held as at the reporting date,

(c) deposits or advances from any person for the purpose of trading or investing in Crypto Currency or virtual currency."

## 14.9 CHECK LIST ON DISCLOSURE REQUIREMENTS UNDER SCHEDULE III

| **Disclosures as per Schedule III** | **Ind AS – Financial Statements related to NBFCs** |
|---|---|
| ***Whether Share capital – authorized, issued, subscribed and paid up need to be disclosed*** | Disclosure required |
| ***Sources from which bonus shares are issued, e.g., capitalisation of profits or Reserves or from Securities Premium Account.*** | Disclosure required |
| ***Whether Share Application money received for allotment of securities and due for refund and interest accrued thereon needs to be disclosed separately. Share application money would include advances towards allotment of share capital*** | Disclosure required |

| Disclosures as per Schedule III | Ind AS – Financial Statements related to NBFCs |
|---|---|
| ***Whether the period and amount of continuing default as on the Balance Sheet date in repayment of loans and interest, needs to be specified separately in each case.*** | Disclosure required |
| ***Whether loans and advances due by directors or other officers of the company or any of them either severally or jointly with any other persons or amounts due by firms or private companies respectively in which any director is a partner or a director or a member needs to be separately stated*** | Disclosure required |
| ***Whether Debts due by directors or other officers of the company or any of them either severally or jointly with any other person or debts due by firms or private companies respectively in which any director is a partner or a director or a member need to be separately stated*** | Disclosure required |
| ***Where in respect of an issue of securities made for a specific purpose, the whole or part of the amount has not been used for the specific purpose at the Balance Sheet date, whether a note needs to be provided indicating how such unutilized amounts have been used or invested.*** | Disclosure required |
| ***Payments to the auditor as***<br>***(a) auditor,***<br>***(b) for taxation matters,***<br>***(c) for company law matters,***<br>***(d) for management services,***<br>***(e) for other services,***<br>***(d) for reimbursement of expense*** | Disclosure required |
| ***In case of Companies covered under section 135, amount of expenditure incurred on corporate social responsibility activities*** | Disclosure required |

| **Disclosures as per Schedule III** | **Ind AS – Financial Statements related to NBFCs** |
|---|---|
| ***Disclosure of Shareholding of Promoters*** | Disclosure required |
| ***Disclosure related to Trade Payables ageing schedule*** | Disclosure required |
| ***Disclosure related to Trade Receivables ageing schedule*** | Disclosure required |
| ***Presentation related to Revaluation of Property, Plant and Equipment*** | Disclosure required |
| ***Additional disclosures related to Loans or Advances*** | Disclosure required |
| ***Disclosure pertaining to details of Benami Property held*** | Disclosure required |
| ***Disclosures pertaining to Wilful Defaulter*** | Disclosure required |
| ***Presentation and disclosure pertaining relationship with struck off companies*** | Disclosure required |
| ***Disclosure pertaining to Compliance with number of layers of companies*** | Disclosure required |
| ***Disclosures pertaining to undisclosed income*** | Disclosure required |
| ***Disclosure pertaining to Capital work-in-progress (CWIP) ageing schedule/completion schedule*** | Disclosure required |
| ***Disclosure related to Intangible assets under development ageing schedule/completion schedule*** | Disclosure required |
| ***Disclosure pertaining to Security of current assets against borrowings*** | Disclosure required |
| ***Disclosure pertaining to Compliance with approved Scheme(s) of Arrangements*** | Disclosure required |
| ***Disclosure pertaining to Utilization of Borrowed funds and share premium*** | Disclosure required |
| ***Disclosure pertaining to 'details of crypto currency or virtual currency'*** | Disclosure required |
| ***Disclosure related to Title deeds of Immovable Property not held in the name*** | Disclosure required |

| Disclosures as per Schedule III | Ind AS – Financial Statements related to NBFCs |
|---|---|
| *of the Company* | |
| ***Presentation related to Registration of charges or satisfaction with Registrar of Companies*** | Disclosure required |
| ***Presentation of Analytical Ratios*** | Disclosure required |

## 14.10 CONSOLIDATED FINANCIAL STATEMENTS

Where a Non-Banking Financial Company (NBFC) is required to prepare Consolidated Financial Statements, i.e., consolidated balance sheet, consolidated statement of changes in equity and consolidated statement of profit and loss, the NBFC shall mutatis mutandis follow the requirements of this Schedule as applicable to an NBFC in the preparation of balance sheet, statement of changes in equity and statement of profit and loss. However, where the consolidated financial statements contains elements pertaining to NBFCs and other than NBFCs, mixed basis of presentation may be followed for consolidated financial statements where both kinds of operations are significant. In addition, the consolidated financial statements shall disclose the information as per the requirements specified in the applicable Indian Accounting Standards notified under the Companies (Indian Accounting Standards) Rules 2015, including the following, namely:-

(i) Profit or loss attributable to 'non-controlling interest' and to 'owners of the parent' in the statement of profit and loss shall be presented as allocation for the period. Further, 'total comprehensive income' for the period attributable to 'non-controlling interest' and to 'owners of the parent' shall be presented in the statement of profit and loss as allocation for the period. The aforesaid disclosures for 'total comprehensive income' shall also be made in the statement of changes in equity. In addition to the disclosure requirements in the Indian Accounting Standards, the aforesaid disclosures shall also be made in respect of 'other comprehensive income'

(ii) 'Non-controlling interests' in the Balance Sheet and in the Statement of Changes in Equity, within equity, shall be presented separately from the equity of the 'owners of the parent'.

(iii) Investments accounted for using the equity method.

For provisions related to consolidation of financial statements please refer Chapter 13.

## Illustration 14.53: Accounting policy: Consolidated Financial Statements

**Presentation of consolidated financial statements**

The Balance Sheet, Statement of Profit and Loss and Statement of Changes in Equity are prepared and presented in the format prescribed in the Division III of Schedule III of the Companies Act, 2013 (the 'Act'). The Statement of Cash Flows has been prepared and presented as per the requirements of Ind AS.

A summary of the significant accounting policies and other explanatory information is in accordance with the Companies (Indian

Accounting Standards) Rules, 2015 as specified under Section 133 of the Companies Act, 2013 (the 'Act') including applicable Indian Accounting Standards (Ind AS) and accounting principles generally accepted in India.

Amounts in the consolidated financial statements are presented in Indian Rupees in Lakh, which is also the Group's functional currency, and all amounts have been rounded off to the nearest lakhs unless otherwise indicated.

**Basis of measurement**

The consolidated financial statements have been prepared on the historical cost basis except for certain financial instruments that are measured at fair values at the end of each reporting period as explained in the accounting policies below.

Historical cost is generally based on the fair value of the consideration given in exchange for goods and services at the time of entering into the transaction.

**Investment in Associates**

The financial statements of the associates used in the consolidation are drawn up to the same reporting date as that of the Group i.e., March 31, 2020, except for certain associates for which financial statements as on the reporting date are not available. These have been consolidated based on their latest available financial statements. Necessary adjustments have been made for the effects of significant transactions and other events between the reporting dates of such financial statements and the consolidated Financial Statements.

The Consolidated Financial Statements include the share of profit/(loss) of associates, which have been accounted for using the equity method as per Ind AS 28- (Accounting for Investments in Associates in Consolidated Financial Statements). Accordingly, the share of profit/(loss) of the associates (the loss being restricted to the cost of the investment) have been added/deducted to the costs of investments.

The difference between the cost of investment in the associate and the share of net assets at the time of acquisition of shares in the associate is identified in the Consolidated Financial Statements as Goodwill or Capital Reserve as the case may be and adjusted against the carrying amount of investment in the associate

The carrying amount of investment in associates is reduced to recognise impairment, if any, when there is objective evidence of impairment.

(*Source: TCFSL Annual Report 2020)*

**Illustration 14.54: Accounting policy: Business Combination under common control**

A business combination involving entities or businesses under common control is a business combination in which all of the combining entities or businesses are ultimately controlled by the same party or parties both before and after the business combination and that control is not transitory.

Business combinations involving entities or businesses under common control are accounted for using the pooling of interest method as follows:

- The assets and liabilities of the combining entities are reflected at their carrying amounts.
- No adjustments are made to reflect fair values or recognize new assets or liabilities. Adjustments are made only to harmonize significant accounting policies.
- The financial information in the financial statements in respect of prior periods is restated as if the business combination has occurred from the beginning of the preceding period in the financial statements, irrespective of the actual date of the combination.

The balance of the retained earnings appearing in the financial statements of the transferor is aggregated with the corresponding balance appearing in the financial statements of the transferee. The identity of the reserves is preserved, and the reserves of the transferor become the reserves of the transferee.

The difference, if any, between the amounts recorded as share capital issued plus any additional consideration in the form of cash or other assets and the amount of share capital of the transferor is transferred to capital reserve and is presented separately from other capital reserves.

(*Source: Power Finance Corporation Annual Report 2020*)

### 14.10.1 Summary of Disclosure requirements under Schedule III related to Consolidated Financial Statements for NBFCs

MCA notification dated 24 March 2021 has included certain disclosure requirements in addition to the existing disclosures. The applicability of additional disclosures at Consolidated Financial Statement (CFS) level with regard to its applicability is summarized below:

| Disclosures as per Schedule III | Ind AS – Consolidated Financial Statements related to NBFCs |
|---|---|
| ***Disclosure of Shareholding of Promoters*** | Company should disclose the promoter shareholding at the CFS level. Generally, the promoter would be same for CFS level and standalone level. |
| ***Disclosure related to Trade Payables ageing schedule*** | Trade payable ageing schedule should be disclosed at the CFS level after applying the principles of consolidation. |
| ***Disclosure related to Trade Receivables ageing schedule*** | Trade receivable ageing schedule should be disclosed at the CFS level after applying the principles of consolidation. |
| ***Presentation related to Revaluation of Property, Plant and Equipment*** | In case of revaluation of property, plant and equipment at CFS level, or for any of the group entity, company may disclose the following:<br>(a) of the entity in which revaluation is done;<br>(b) Type & nature of PPE revalued;<br>(c) Indicate whether the revaluation is based on the valuation as per the registered valuer. |
| ***Additional disclosures related to Loans or Advances*** | This disclosure needs to be done at the CFS level, on similar lines as the 'Related Party Transactions' are disclosed in CFS. |
| ***Disclosure pertaining to details of Benami Property held*** | Entity needs to disclose the required details of benami property at CFS level providing the name of each subsidiary/group entity that has such Benami Property. In case if there is any benami proceedings initiated against any associate company, then Company should disclose in case if the proceeding is material to the group. |
| ***Disclosures pertaining to Wilful Defaulter*** | Entity needs to disclose the required details of wilful defaulter at CFS level providing the name of each subsidiary/group entity that is declared as a wilful defaulter. In case |

| Disclosures as per Schedule III | Ind AS – Consolidated Financial Statements related to NBFCs |
|---|---|
| | if there is any wilful default by an associate company, then Company should disclose if the default is material to the group. |
| ***Presentation and disclosure pertaining relationship with struck off companies*** | Entity needs to present the required details of relationship with struck off companies at CFS level providing the name of each subsidiary/group entity that has such a relationship.<br>In case if any of the subsidiary is the under the struck off company list, the entity should indicate that fact as a part of disclosure.<br>In case if there is any associate company having relationship with struck off companies, then company should disclose if the transaction is material to the group. |
| ***Disclosure pertaining to Compliance with number of layers of companies*** | Entity needs to disclose this compliance issue for each entity in its group. |
| ***Disclosures pertaining to undisclosed income*** | Entity needs to disclose the required details of undisclosed income at CFS level providing the name of each subsidiary/group entity that has an 'undisclosed income'. In case if there is any associate company having undisclosed income, then Company should disclose if such income is material to the group. |

*(Source: ICAI Guidance Note on Schedule III – Ind AS entities related to NBFCs)*

### 14.10.2 Summary of Disclosure requirements under Schedule III related to Consolidated Financial Statements if material in nature

| Disclosures as per Schedule III | Ind AS – Consolidated Financial Statements related to NBFCs |
|---|---|
| ***Disclosure pertaining to Capital work-in-progress (CWIP) ageing schedule/completion schedule*** | CWIP ageing schedule shall be given at CFS level if it is material to the group i.e. more than 10% of the respective balance sheet item in CFS. |
| ***Disclosure related to Intangible assets under development ageing schedule/completion schedule*** | Ageing schedule shall be given at CFS level if it is material to the group i.e. more than |

| Disclosures as per Schedule III | Ind AS – Consolidated Financial Statements related to NBFCs |
|---|---|
| | 10% of the respective balance sheet item in CFS. |
| *Disclosure pertaining to Security of current assets against borrowings* | This disclosure shall be provided at CFS level if it is material to the group i.e. more than 10% of the respective balance sheet item in CFS |
| *Disclosure pertaining to Compliance with approved Scheme(s) of Arrangements* | This disclosure shall be provided at CFS level if it is material to the group i.e. more than 10% of the respective financial statement line item in CFS. |
| *Disclosure pertaining to Utilization of Borrowed funds and share premium* | This disclosure shall be provided at CFS level after applying principles of consolidation i.e. this disclosure would be for funds borrowed/invested outside the group. However, it shall be disclosed only if material i.e. more than 10% of the respective financial statement line item in CFS |
| *Disclosure pertaining to 'details of crypto currency or virtual currency'* | This disclosure shall be provided at CFS level if it is material to the group i.e. more than 10% of the respective financial statement line item in CFS |
| *Disclosure related to Title deeds of Immovable Property not held in the name of the Company* | Not relevant at CFS level |
| *Presentation related to Registration of charges or satisfaction with Registrar of Companies* | Not relevant at CFS level |
| *Presentation of Analytical Ratios* | Not relevant at CFS level |

(*Source: ICAI Guidance Note on Schedule III – Non Ind AS and Ind AS entities, (Revised January, 2022 Edition)*)

### 14.10.3 Summary of Requirements of Schedule III shall apply to a CFS, subject to the following exemptions/modifications based on the relevance to the CFS

| Disclosures as per Schedule III | Ind AS – Consolidated Financial Statements related to NBFCs |
|---|---|
| *Whether Share capital – authorized,* | It is adequate to present paid up capital and |

| Disclosures as per Schedule III | Ind AS – Consolidated Financial Statements related to NBFCs |
|---|---|
| ***issued, subscribed and paid up need to be disclosed*** | any calls in arrears |
| ***Sources from which bonus shares are issued, e.g., capitalisation of profits or Reserves or from Securities Premium Account.*** | Not relevant at CFS level and hence, may be dispensed with. |
| ***Whether Share Application money received for allotment of securities and due for refund and interest accrued thereon needs to be disclosed separately. Share application money would include advances towards allotment of share capital*** | Separate disclosure should be given for such monies due outside the group in respect of entities which are consolidated. |
| ***Whether excise duty needs to be disclosed separately*** | To be disclosed where such information is available for the entities consolidated. |
| ***Whether the period and amount of continuing default as on the Balance Sheet date in repayment of loans and interest, needs to be specified separately in each case.*** | Disclosure can be limited to those which are material to the CFS; materiality could be considered at 10% of the respective balance sheet item |
| ***Whether loans and advances due by directors or other officers of the company or any of them either severally or jointly with any other persons or amounts due by firms or private companies respectively in which any director is a partner or a director or a member needs to be separately stated*** | Disclosure can be limited to those which are material to the CFS; materiality could be considered at 10% of the respective balance sheet item |
| ***Whether Debts due by directors or other officers of the company or any of them either severally or jointly with any other person or debts due by firms or private companies respectively in which any director is a partner or a director or a member need to be separately stated*** | Disclosure can be limited to those which are material to the CFS; materiality could be considered at 10% of the respective balance sheet item |
| ***Where in respect of an issue of securities made for a specific purpose, the whole or part of the amount has not been used for the specific purpose*** | Disclosure can be limited to those which are material to the CFS; materiality could be considered at 10% of the respective balance sheet item |

| Disclosures as per Schedule III | Ind AS – Consolidated Financial Statements related to NBFCs |
|---|---|
| ***at the Balance Sheet date, whether a note needs to be provided indicating how such unutilized amounts have been used or invested.*** | |
| ***Payments to the auditor as***<br>***(a) auditor,***<br>***(b) for taxation matters,***<br>***(c) for company law matters, (d) for management services, (e) for other services,***<br>***(f) for reimbursement of expense*** | Not relevant at CFS level and hence, may not be required to be disclosed |
| ***In case of Companies covered under section 135, amount of expenditure incurred on corporate social responsibility activities*** | Not relevant at CFS level and hence, may not be required to be disclosed |

*(Source: ICAI Guidance Note on Schedule III – Ind AS entities related to NBFCs, Revised January, 2022 Edition).*

# SECTION V

## Health and Hygiene of the Businesses Emanating from Financial Statements

# Chapter 15

# Financial Health and Hygiene Analysis

## 15.1 FINANCIAL ANALYSIS

Financial analysis is the art and science of analysis of statutory financial statements and come up with deterministic and predictive inferences for management decision making. Financial analysis is professed to provide the users of financial statements the following:

(a) understanding of the strengths and weaknesses of the business;

(b) highlight the possible pitfalls and business risks that may hit the business in the foreseeable future;

(c) come up with clear action plan how to redress the financial weaknesses and avoid the pitfalls and business risks.

The other term for it is business analytics (both financial and non-financial) and this is supposed to work as a lighthouse function, to ensure the business ship is guided safely through hostile business waters and moored to safe havens.

Financial statement analysis is one of the principal techniques regularly used in analysis of financial statements and financial due diligence. It is used extensively used in all merger and acquisition related exercise both from buy as well sell side.

Areas where business/financial analysis have major impact on business decision making have been listed below. This list is by no means exhaustive and can be extended according to business needs.

## 15.2 TYPES OF BUSINESS/FINANCIAL ANALYSIS

To summarize the areas of business/financial analysis we have created a simple dash board below.

| **Capacity Utilization Analysis** | **Cost and Contribution Analysis** | **Working Capital Analysis** |
|---|---|---|
| **Productivity Analysis** | **Product / service profitability Analysis** | **Inventory Analysis** |
| **Utilities / energy efficiency Analysis** | **Market / customer profitability Analysis** | **Manpower Analysis** |

### 15.2.1 Capacity utilization analysis

Product-wise, Product Group-wise and Unit-wise:

- Under-utilization of Capacities
- Idle Capacities
- Non-Productive Assets
- Trend Analysis
- opportunity Analysis
- Outsourcing/Sub-Contracting Vs. Internal Capacities
- Plant Break-down hours with impact on productivity, costs, and profitability
- Scope of Expansion and likely cost-benefit analysis

### 15.2.2 Productivity analysis

**Productivity Analysis** along with estimated impact on costs and profitability (Product-wise, Product Group-wise and Unit-wise):

- Production/Operations/Process Cycle Time and Productivity
- Input-Output Analysis compared with Budgets or Standards or Industry Norms
- Conversion Efficiency Analysis
- Cost of wastages in operations

### 15.2.3 Utilities/energy efficiency analysis

**Utilities/Energy Efficiency Analysis** (Utility-wise, Unit-wise, Product-wise, and Product Group-wise)

- Utility Productivity compared with Budgets or Standards or Industry Norms
- Input-Output Efficiency – impact on costs and profitability
- Energy Conversion Ratio highlighting wastage & inefficiency
- Energy Consumption Ratio for each product/operation and each product/activity group compared with Budgets or Standards or Industry Norms

### 15.2.4 Cost and Contribution analysis

**Key-Expense Ratios** vs. Cost of Production/Cost of Sales

- Abnormal & Non-Recurring Costs – impact on profitability
- Key Costs Trend Analysis indicating estimated impact on future profitability
- Cost-effectiveness Analysis: Cost of Operation/Process vs. Benefits
- Cost of Management vs. Net Turnover or Gross Margin or Net Margin
- Cost Variance Analysis vs. Standards or Budgets – impact on profitability
- Volume Variance Analysis vs. Standards or Budgets – impact on profitability
- Marginal Cost and Contribution Analysis for each product/activity, each product/activity group, each market segment, each customer segment, etc.
- Service Department-wise cost trends (elementwise)

### 15.2.5 Product/service profitability

**Product/Service Profitability** (for key products/services only)

- Product profitability, as % of total profitability,
- Turnover, % to Total,
- Capital Employed, % to Total CE,
- Gross Margin, % to Total,
- Gross Margin as % of Turnover,
- Gross Margin as % of Capital Employed,
- Net Margin, % to Total Net Margin,
- Net Margin as % to Turnover,
- Net Margin as % to Capital Employed,

### 15.2.6 Market/customer profitability

**Market/Customer Profitability** – similar analysis as above

- Market Distribution – Indigenous vs. Overseas broken into smaller geographical divisions/segments
- Customer Distribution – in order of percentage share in each product/ activity and in each product/activity group
- Indicate cost of servicing each market/customer and its efficiency in terms of business, contributions, gross/net margins, scope of sustainability, etc.
- Indicate cost of each supply chain vs. benefits
- Indicate impact of FTAs and Dumping on each product, product-group or each market/customer.

### 15.2.7 Working capital analysis

*Movement of Debtors* vs. *Credit Sales*

- Days Debtors Analysis – impact on cash flow and profitability
- Overseas Debtors – impact of likely FE Variations
- Movement of Creditors vs. Credit Purchases
- Days Creditors Analysis – impact on supplies and product-line
- Inventory Turnover
- Cash Flow Turnover – impact on profitability

### 15.2.8 Inventory analysis

**Inventory Analysis** - Basis of valuation & Consistency

- Turnover efficiency: Cost of Goods Sold/Average Inventory
- Return on Inventory: GM/Average Inventory, NM/Average Inventory
- Slow-moving or dead inventory
- ABC analysis; Period holding analysis
- Policy for Insurance Spares; Inventory Holding due to changes in technology, changes in production process, obsolescence, etc

### 15.2.9 Manpower analysis

**Manpower Analysis** (Function-wise, Unit-wise, Product-wise, and Product Group-wise)

- Manpower Productivity vs. Returns compared with Budgets or Standards or Industry Norms
- Manpower Pyramid – Ratio of Top Management to Middle Management to Officers to Workmen to Contract Labour
- Idle Man-hours to Total Man-hours with reason-wise analysis and impact on productivity, costs, and profitability
- Manpower Absenteeism Vs. Total paid Man-days
- Cost of Manpower Pyramid Analysis – broken into broad categories (including contract labour)
- Cost of Training to Total Employee Cost

### 15.2.10 Application of management accounting tools

**Management Accounting Tools** – use of modern management accounting tools and techniques such as:-

- Activity Based Costing,
- Target Costing
- Lifecycle Costing
- Quality Costing
- Value Engineering
- Supply Chain Management
- Balanced Scorecard
- Performance Pyramid
- Lean Accounting
- Theory of Constraints
- Throughput Accounting
- Kaizen Costing
- Customer Valuation
- Strategic Cost Management, etc. and benefits availed, if any

In this Chapter we have discussed relatively simpler financial analytics linked to Financial Statements and these are depicted as under:

(a) Comparative financial statements

(b) Common size statements

(c) Trend ratios

(d) Forecasting techniques

## 15.3 COMPARATIVE FINANCIAL STATEMENTS

When the financial statements of current year and previous year are recast for comparison of all the elements of financial statements and the comparison is in absolute numbers as well as in percentages, it is called comparative financial statement. This is considered as the first step in carrying out Financial Analysis.

The statement is constructed by:

(a) using absolute numbers represented by monetary values in the years/periods under consideration and

(b) calculating the increase or decrease in monetary values in absolute numbers

(c) calculating percentage increase of the monetary values by using the following formula:

$$\text{Percentage increase of the monetary values} = \frac{(\text{Current period figures} - \text{Previous period figures})}{\text{Previous period figures}} \times 100$$

(d) the results of the aforesaid comparison are then analysed and interpreted

**Merits**

1. Comparison of numbers related to two corresponding periods is simple to calculate as well as comprehend
2. This can be used in inter firm comparisons of entities belonging to similar industry
3. It brings out the source and deployment of funds at a high level, one can understand and interpret which way the funds have moved
4. It also brings out whether the funds generated out of source of funds are getting utilised or blocked-in working capital like debtors, inventories and cash and bank balances
5. It can also broadly depict the pattern of source of funds, whether the funds have been internally generated out of profits/reserves or from external sources through infusion of equity or additional debt either through secured or unsecured route
6. In broad terms the comparison throws insight in apparent weaknesses in operating cycle, financial liquidity, and solvency of the business.

**Demerits**

1. The comparison does not highlight interpretation through ratios like current ratio, debt equity ratio etc
2. Without the knowledge of internal dynamics of the business, the conclusions may be misleading
3. Proper comparison between two or more entities is not possible by this analysis because there is no common base of comparison.

### Illustration 15.1: Comparative Balance Sheet

Following are the Balance Sheet of Mayfair Ltd as on 31.3.2020 and 31.3.2021 and interpret the results.

| Particulars | 31.03.2020 INR crores | 31.03.2021 INR crores |
|---|---|---|
| **Share capital and liabilities** | | |
| Share capital | 6393.21 | 6453.39 |
| Equity share suspense | 60.14 | - |

| | | |
|---|---|---|
| Equity share warrant | - | 1,682.40 |
| Reserves and surplus | 57.513.78 | 73,312.81 |
| Secured loans | 9,569.12 | 6,600.17 |
| Unsecured loans | 18.256.61 | 29.879.51 |
| Current liabilities | 16,865.53 | 21,045.47 |
| Provisions | 1,712.87 | 2,992.62 |
| Deferred tax liability | 6,982.02 | 7,872.54 |
| | **1,17,353.28** | **1,49,838.91** |
| **Assets** | | |
| Net Fixed Assets | 63,660.46 | 61,883.63 |
| Capital work-in-progress | 9,528.13 | 25,005.84 |
| Investments | 16,251.34 | 22,063.60 |
| Current Assets | | |
| Inventories | 10,136.51 | 12,247.54 |
| Sundry debtors | 3,732.42 | 6,227.58 |
| Cash & bank | 1,835.35 | 4,280.05 |
| Other current assets | 3.07 | 72.54 |
| Loans and advances | 12,206.00 | 18,058.13 |
| | **1,17,353.28** | **1,49,838.91** |

**Solution**

**Comparative Balance Sheet of Mayfair Ltd (INR crores)**

| | **31.03.2020** | **31.03.2021** | **Absolute change** | **% change** |
|---|---|---|---|---|
| **Share capital and liabilities** | | | | |
| Share capital | 6393.21 | 6453.39 | 60.18 | 0.941 |
| Equity share suspense | 60.14 | - | (60.14) | (100.00) |
| Equity share warrant | - | 1,682.40 | 1,682.40 | 100.00 |
| Reserves and surplus | 57.513.78 | 73,312.81 | 15,799.03 | 27.469 |
| Secured loans | 9,569.12 | 6,600.17 | (2,968.95) | (31.026) |
| Unsecured loans | 18.256.61 | 29.879.51 | 11,622.90 | 63.664 |
| Current liabilities | 16,865.53 | 21,045.47 | 4,179.94 | 24.784 |
| Provisions | 1,712.87 | 2,992.62 | 1,279.75 | 74.714 |
| Deferred tax liability | 6,982.02 | 7,872.54 | 890.52 | 12.754 |
| **Total** | **1,17,353.28** | **1,49,838.91** | **32,485.63** | **27.682** |

| **Assets** | | | | |
|---|---|---|---|---|
| Net Fixed Assets | 63,660.46 | 61,883.63 | 1,776.83 | (2.791) |
| Capital work-in-progress | 9,528.13 | 25,005.84 | 15,477.71 | 162.442 |
| Investments | 16,251.34 | 22,063.60 | 5,812.26 | 35.765 |
| Current Assets | 10,136.51 | 12,247.54 | 2,111.03 | 20.826 |
| Inventories | 3,732.42 | 6,227.58 | 2,495.16 | 66.851 |
| Sundry debtors | 1,835.35 | 4,280.05 | 2,444.70 | 133.200 |
| Cash & bank | 3.07 | 72.54 | 69.47 | 2262.866 |
| Other current assets and Loans and advances | 12,206.00 | 18,058.13 | 5,852.13 | 47.944 |
| **Total** | **1,17,353.28** | **1,49,838.91** | **32,485.63** | **27.682** |

Interpretation of the aforesaid comparison is as under:

(a) The share capital has increased by INR 60.18 crores, owing to transfer of equity share suspense account into share capital

(b) During the current year equity share warrant of INR 1,682.40 has been issued

(c) Reserves and surplus has shown a significant increase of INR 15,799.03 crores (27.469%) in the current year over the previous year.

(d) Secured loan has reduced by INR 2,968.95 crores over previous year (31.026%)

(e) The entity has raised unsecured loans to the tune of INR 11,622.90 an increase of 63.664%.

(f) Current liabilities and provisions have increased to the tune of 24.784% and 74.714% respectively.

(g) Net Fixed Assets of the entity has reduced by 2.791% whereas capital work-in-progress has gone up by INR 15,477.71 crores which is evidence to investment by the entity on its upcoming projects which have not been capitalized.

(h) On the other hand investments have increased by INR 5, 812.26 crores, which is an increase of 35.765%.

(i) Gross current assets have increased significantly as substantiated by increase in inventories by 20.82%, sundry debtors by 66.851%, cash & bank balances by 133.2 % and loans and advances by 47.944%.

## 15.4 COMMON SIZE STATEMENTS

Common size financial statements are restated financial statement showing percentage of total items with common base for comparison.

**The steps followed are as under:**

**Assets**

(a) Assets side is classified in fixed assets, investments, current assets (CA), fictitious assets showing individually and its total.

(b) Then total assets are taken as common base of 100 and the calculation is made as shown below:

- Tangible assets/Total assets × 100
- Investments/Total assets ×100
- Fictitious assets/Total assets × 100 etc

**Liabilities**

(c) Similarly, liabilities side of the Balance Sheet is classified into owners' equity, long term borrowings, current liabilities showing individually and its total.

(d) The total liabilities are taken as common base of 100 and the calculation is made as shown below:

- Owners' equity/Total Liabilities × 100
- Long term borrowings/Total liabilities × 100

**Income statement**

(e) Income statement is classified in sales, cost of goods sold, operating expenses, net profit, interest, tax, earnings after tax etc. Percentage of each element to sales is calculated.

**Merits**

1. It helps in inter-firm comparison having a common base and this is used in Financial Due Diligence exercise.
2. It shows the changes over the years in relation to total assets, total liabilities etc
3. It helps in vertical analysis of figures
4. It assists in understanding financial strategy of the firms in comparison
5. It shows the relative efficiency of each cost item of two firms

**Demerits**

1. Does not show changes of each item from period to period
2. The observations are not very useful because there are more definite approaches for the proportion of each item to total
3. If there is no uniform costing system, no similar accounting policy among all the firms of an industry, it is meaningless for studying the comparative position of two entities.

**Illustration 15.2: Common size analysis**

From the following Balance Sheet, prepare a common size statement:

| | 31.03.2020 INR | 31.03.2021 INR |
|---|---|---|
| Equity share capital (INR 10 each) | 7,00,000 | 7,50,000 |
| Reserves and surplus | 3,00,000 | 5,00,000 |
| Long term debt | 5,00,000 | 4,50,000 |
| Current liabilities | 3,00,000 | 2,00,000 |
| Total | 18,00,000 | 19,00,000 |
| Tangible assets | 12,00,000 | 11,50,000 |
| Inventories | 3,00,000 | 3,50,000 |
| Trade receivables | 2,00,000 | 2,50,000 |
| Cash & bank | 1,00,000 | 1,50,000 |
| Total | 18,00,000 | 19,00,000 |

**Solution**

Common size statement is shown as under:

| | On 31.03.2020 % of total | On 31.03.2021 % of total |
|---|---|---|
| **Assets** | | |
| Tangible assets | 67% | 61% |
| (Tangible assets/Total assets) × 100 | | |
| Inventories | 17% | 18% |
| (Inventories/Total assets) × 100 | | |
| Trade receivables | 11% | 13% |
| (Trade receivables/Total assets) × 100 | | |
| Cash & bank | 5% | 8% |
| (Cash & bank/Total assets × 100) | | |
| | 100% | 100% |
| **Liabilities** | | |
| Equity share capital | 39% | 39% |
| (Equity share capital/Total liabilities) × 100 | | |
| Reserves and surplus | 17% | 26% |
| (Reserves and surplus/Total liabilities) × 100 | | |
| Long term debt | 28% | 24% |
| (Long term debt/Total liabilities) × 100 | | |
| Current liabilities | 16% | 11% |

| (Current liabilities/Total liabilities) × 100 | | |
|---|---|---|
| | 100% | 100% |

**Observations**

(a) It shows that shareholders' funds of the organisation have improved from 56% (39% + 17%) to 65% (39% + 26%). Conversely, long term debt has shrunk from 28% to 24%. This reflects that the degree of riskiness of the entity's financial solvency have reduced with less dependency on the outside borrowing and more internal generation of funds ploughed back to business (reserves and surplus going up from 17% to 26%).

(b) Current Assets as a percentage of total assets have gone up from 33% to 39% whereas current liabilities have gone down from 16% to 11%. This reflects that liquidity position of the entity has improved.

(c) Tangible assets as % of total assets have gone down from 67% to 61%. It signifies that the entity believes in more short-term measures and need to invest more on long term projects to ensure further growth and long-term stability rather than short term profitability.

## 15.5 TREND RATIOS

Another financial modelling tool used in Financial Analysis is called Trend Ratios.

Trend ratios are calculated in the form of index no. of each financial item in the financial statement of different periods. The method presupposes percentage relation of items with the similar item in the base year. The formula is as under:

$$\textbf{Trend ratio} = \frac{\textbf{Value of each item in financial statement of any period}}{\textbf{Value of same item in financial statement of base period}} \times 100$$

In order to ensure that trend ratios are meaningful following care needs to be taken:

(a) There must be uniform accounting policies followed year on year to make this analysis meaningful

(b) Consistency convention is a pre-requisite for this type of analysis

(c) Trend percentages need to be calculated only for items having logical relationship with one another

(d) Care should be taken to select the base year. This must be a normal year and be adequately representative of the performance trend

(e) Trend percentages should be studied after considering the absolute numbers on which they are based, otherwise they may give misleading and skewed results.

(f) The figures of the current year should be adjusted in the light of price level changes as compared to the base year before calculating the trend analysis, otherwise comparison may not be meaningful.

**Merits**

(a) It depicts trend of items with passage of time

(b) It shows the manner and rate of improvement or decline of various financial parameters

(c) Keeping everything constant, it estimates and predicts the financial parameters of the foreseeable future

(d) It also shows horizontal and vertical analysis to reflect behaviour of various financial items with the passage of time.

**Demerits**

(a) Without uniform accounting policies this analysis is meaningless

(b) This analysis does not consider inflation accounting. So in case of inflation figures of base year may be widely differing from the figures of the current year.

(c) In today's dynamic business environment where things change very quickly, it would be difficult to use the premise that everything will continue to remain the same going forward in the foreseeable future

(d) Trend ratios must be read based on absolute data; otherwise the analysis and conclusion may not be practical in approach.

**Illustration 15.3: Trend ratios**

Compute the trend ratios from the following data and comment (INR)

| | 2017 | 2018 | 2019 | 2020 |
|---|---|---|---|---|
| Cost of material consumed | 2,00,000 | 2,50,000 | 2,00,000 | 1,80,000 |
| Labour cost | 1,50,000 | 1,50,000 | 2,00,000 | 1,25,000 |
| Other expenses | 1,50,000 | 2,00,000 | 1,00,000 | 1,50,000 |
| Cost of sales | 5,00,000 | 6,00,000 | 5,00,000 | 4,55,000 |
| Profit | 3,00,000 | 3,00,000 | 2,50,000 | 3,45,000 |
| Sales | 8,00,000 | 9,00,000 | 7,50,000 | 8,00,000 |

**Solution**

**Statement of computation of trend ratio (%)**

| | **2017** | **2018 (2018/2017 × 100)** | **2019 (2019/2017 × 100)** | **2020 (2020/2017 × 100)** |
|---|---|---|---|---|
| Cost of material consumed | 100 | 125 | 100 | 90 |
| Labour cost | 100 | 100 | 133.3 | 83.3 |
| Other expenses | 100 | 133.3 | 66.7 | 100 |
| Cost of sales | 100 | 120 | 100 | 91 |
| Profit | 100 | 100 | 83.3 | 115 |
| Sales | 100 | 112.5 | 93.8 | 100 |

**Conclusion**

From the above numbers, it is evident that the numbers do not show any clear trend except those costs of sales have been showing a downward trend, whereas sales growth remained flat.

## 15.6 HANDLING FORECASTING TECHNIQUES

Forecasting is a prediction about a condition or situation at some future time. Business decisions and especially financially related business decisions depend heavily on forecasts of future events. Decisions related to future investments, borrowing and lending funds depend heavily on forecasts of future business events. Even the valuation of enterprise or business verticals or projects also heavily depends on future forecasts. Hence this happens to be one of the principal tools of the CFO to gauge the future of the organization and raise alarm bells if he senses a storm brewing in the horizon.

## 15.7 NEED FOR FORECASTING TECHNIQUES

Most enterprises use significant senior management time and sophisticated forecasting tools to map uncertain future events. Budgeting and forecasting are used to do the following:

(a) Build yardsticks and benchmarks for future performance
(b) Monitor actual performance and compare with budget and forecasts
(c) Handle uncertainty of the future.

Three critical questions to answer are:

(a) estimate the future forecast with accuracy as much as possible
(b) the cost-benefit trade-off and what efforts need to be put in to generate reasonably accurate forecast

(c) Meet the criteria for timeliness. The annual forecast must be before the commencement of the financial year. Monthly or quarterly forecasts must be before the commencement of the respective periods.

## 15.8 Types of forecasts

(a) Judgement forecast – where forecasts are made based on experience and information available instead of any mathematical and statistical models

(b) Time series forecast – where a pattern of a time series based on experience is used to create a model that will predict the future movement

(c) Casual forecast – based on the casual relationship which is expected to be stable over time and casual variables are relatively easy to predict.

## 15.9 Essential attributes of a good forecast

(a) Robust assumptions of the internal factors driving the business and external macro-economic factors- like CPI and WPI for forecasting inflation, the market size of the product/services

(b) Identification of variables that can swing results of forecasts e.g. prediction of sales prices, raw material costs, exchange rates for imports etc.

(c) sensitivity analysis, where results of assumptions are adjusted linking possible changes in key variables driving the business

**Illustration 15.4: Specimen revenue forecast**

| Activity | Actual Jan 2021 | Feb-21 | Mar-21 | Apr-21 | May-21 | Jun-21 | Jul-21 | Aug-21 | Sep-21 | Oct-21 | Nov-21 | Dec-21 | Forecast Jan - December 2021 |
|---|---|---|---|---|---|---|---|---|---|---|---|---|---|
| Gates Foundation - Digital Health | - | 1,288,131 | | - | - | | - | - | | - | - | - | 1,288,131 |
| Gates Foundation - State engagement | - | | | | | | | 1,250,028 | | | | | 1,250,028 |
| Gates Foundation - HSTP | | | | | | | | | | 1,442,592 | | | 1,442,592 |
| Gates Foundation - Capacity Building | | | | | 1,023,288 | - | | | | | | | 1,023,288 |
| Gates Foundation - Financing Health Reform - Supplementary | | | | | | | 741,042 | | | | | | 741,042 |
| President's Development Fund | 3,063 | 3,063 | 3,063 | 3,063 | 3,063 | 3,063 | 3,063 | 3,063 | | | | | 24,504 |
| IPE Global | 82,463 | - | - | 28,044 | - | - | - | - | - | - | - | - | 110,508 |
| Management Sciences for Health | - | - | 25,000 | - | - | 40,000 | - | - | 55,000 | - | - | - | 120,000 |
| Fintech for Health- Singapore | - | - | - | 13,438 | - | 13,438 | - | - | - | 10,750 | - | - | 37,625 |
| ADL Project | - | 10,000 | - | - | - | - | - | 114,000 | - | - | 500,000 | - | 624,000 |
| GIZ Project | - | 25,639 | - | - | - | 38,459 | - | - | - | - | - | - | 64,099 |
| Total | 85,526 | 1,326,833 | 28,063 | 44,545 | 1,026,351 | 94,960 | 744,105 | 1,367,091 | 55,000 | 1,453,342 | 500,000 | - | 6,725,816 |

### Illustration 15.5: Specimen format of cash forecast

| Activity | Actual Jan 2021 | Feb-21 | Mar-21 | Apr-21 | May-21 | Jun-21 | Jul-21 | Aug-21 | Sep-21 | Oct-21 | Nov-21 | Dec-21 | Forecast Jan-December 2021 |
|---|---|---|---|---|---|---|---|---|---|---|---|---|---|
| Opening Balance | 47,960 | 56,608 | 43,451 | 67,033 | 74,099 | 60,943 | 104,928 | 119,771 | 106,614 | 80,958 | 67,801 | 54,644 | 47,960 |
| Confirmed income | 14,290 | - | 49,238 | 20,224 | - | 72,359 | 28,000 | - | - | - | - | - | 184,110 |
| Total Revenue | 14,290 | - | 49,238 | 20,224 | - | 72,359 | 28,000 | - | - | - | - | - | 184,110 |
| Staff related expenses | 5,433 | 5,433 | 5,433 | 5,433 | 5,433 | 8,149 | 5,433 | 5,433 | 5,433 | 5,433 | 5,433 | 8,149 | 70,628 |
| Employee Benefits | - | 491 | 491 | 491 | 491 | 491 | 491 | 491 | 491 | 491 | 491 | 491 | 5,400 |
| Travel | - | 327 | 327 | 327 | 327 | 327 | 327 | 327 | 327 | 327 | 327 | 327 | 3,600 |
| Office Related Expenses | 52 | 759 | 759 | 759 | 759 | 759 | 759 | 759 | 759 | 759 | 759 | 759 | 8,400 |
| Service Fees-Financial, Audit, Accounting | - | 709 | 709 | 709 | 709 | 709 | 709 | 709 | 709 | 709 | 709 | 709 | 7,800 |
| Publications and Communications | - | 327 | 327 | 327 | 327 | 327 | 327 | 327 | 327 | 327 | 327 | 327 | 3,600 |
| Other Program expenses | 171 | 5,000 | 5,000 | 5,000 | 5,000 | 5,000 | 5,000 | 5,000 | 5,000 | 5,000 | 5,000 | 5,000 | 55,171 |
| Exchange gain / loss | (14) | 110 | 110 | 110 | 110 | 110 | 110 | 110 | 110 | 110 | 110 | 110 | 1,200 |
| Central Overhead | - | - | 12,500 | - | - | 12,500 | - | - | 12,500 | - | - | 12,500 | 50,000 |
| TOTAL | 5,642 | 13,157 | 25,657 | 13,157 | 13,157 | 28,373 | 13,157 | 13,157 | 25,657 | 13,157 | 13,157 | 28,373 | 205,800 |
| Surplus/Deficit | 56,608 | 43,451 | 67,033 | 74,099 | 60,943 | 104,928 | 119,771 | 106,614 | 80,958 | 67,801 | 54,644 | 26,271 | 26,271 |

This financial model considers week/month-wise revenue and expenses of foreseeable future and predicts possible surplus or shortfall if any. If it shows a shortfall, then the organization needs to plan action to either introduce more revenue or cut costs to ensure that there is no deficit at the end of the financial year.

So for any target entity, the potential buyer may like to ask for a month-wise cash forecast to fully comprehend month-wise revenue and expenses trends and possible deficit if any and if so during which period.

## 15.10 RATIO ANALYSIS

They say, figures always tell the truth. This is true for the use of Ratio Analysis. This is a very important tool used by professionals in Financial Due Diligence. Ratio Analysis combined with trend analysis go a long way in evaluating the financial health and hygiene of an organization and the possible direction the Organization as a going concern is headed towards, whether a dismal future or a bright one.

The major financial ratios emanating from Financial Statements are categorised as under:

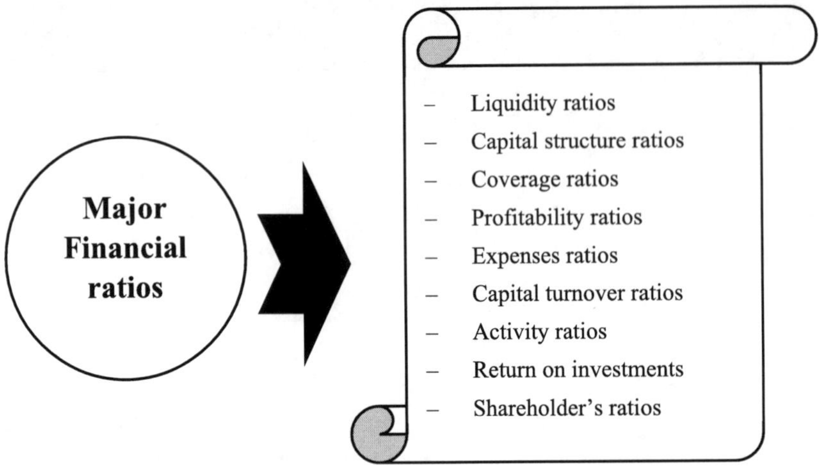


## 15.10.1 Liquidity ratios

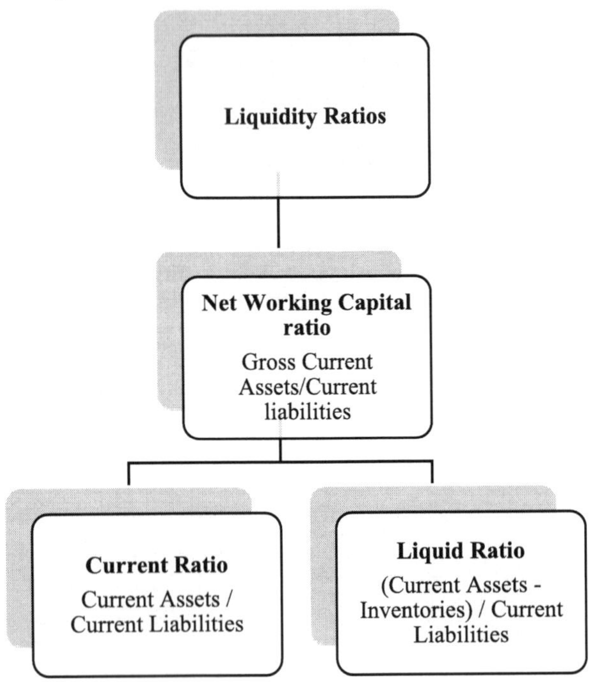

| Ratio | Rationale |
|---|---|
| **Net working capital** $= \frac{\text{Gross Current assets}}{\text{Current liabilities}}$ | It measures the liquidity of an enterprise |
| **Current ratio** $= \frac{\text{Current assets}}{\text{Current liabilities}}$ | It reflects the short-term liquidity position of the enterprise. In general ratio of 2:1 is considered adequate. If it is lower, then it depicts tightness in liquidity. If it is higher, then there is adequate liquidity, but it may also be possible that funds are tied up in obsolete/slow moving inventories and overdue debts |
| **Liquid ratio/Acid test ratio** $= \frac{\text{Quick assets}}{\text{Current liabilities}}$ | Quick assets are current assets less inventories, and this ratio is a measure of the liquidity position of the enterprise. In general, a ratio of 1: 1 would be considered adequate, as it would signify that the enterprise has enough cash to pay off all its current liabilities |

## 15.10.2 Capital structure ratios

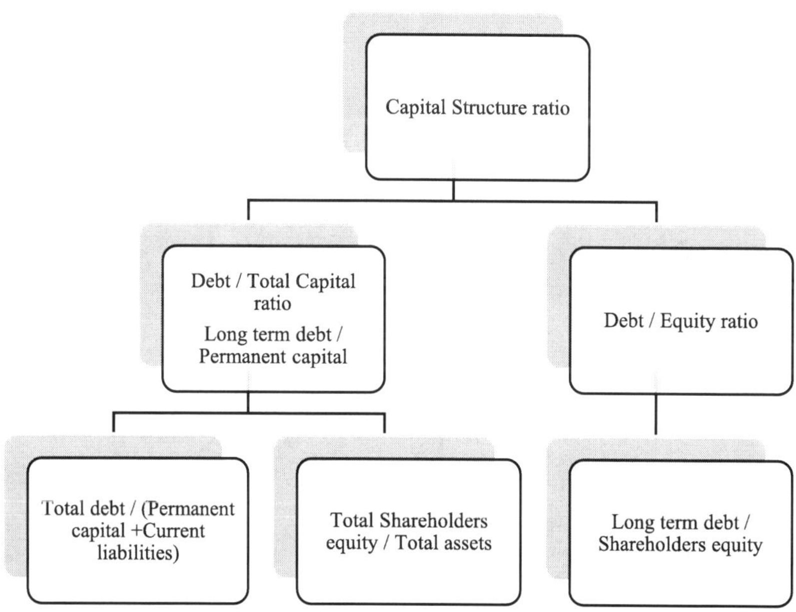


| Ratio | Rationale |
|---|---|
| **Debt equity ratio** $= \frac{\text{Long term debt}}{\text{Shareholders' equity}}$ | This is a very important ratio which depicts the relative proportion of debt and equity in financing the assets of an enterprise. A ratio of 1:1 is |

| Ratio | Rationale |
|---|---|
| | considered adequate.<br>If the debt content is higher the enterprise is considered highly geared and if the equity content is higher, then the enterprise is considered low geared. |
| **Debt to total capital ratio**<br>$= \frac{\text{Long term debt}}{\text{Permanent capital}}$ | This ratio is also a determinant based on which weighted average cost of capital is calculated. (WACC)<br>This ratio indicates what proportion of the permanent capital of the enterprise is funded out of long-term debt. |
| Or<br>$= \frac{\text{Total debt}}{\text{Permanent capital + Current liabilities}}$ | A ratio of 1:2 is considered adequate<br>It measures the proportion of total assets financed by outside funds. A low ratio is low risk specially for outsiders like creditors |
| Or<br>$= \frac{\text{Total Shareholders' equity}}{\text{Total assets}}$ | It depicts the proportion of total assets funded by owners' equity. |

## 15.10.3 Coverage ratios

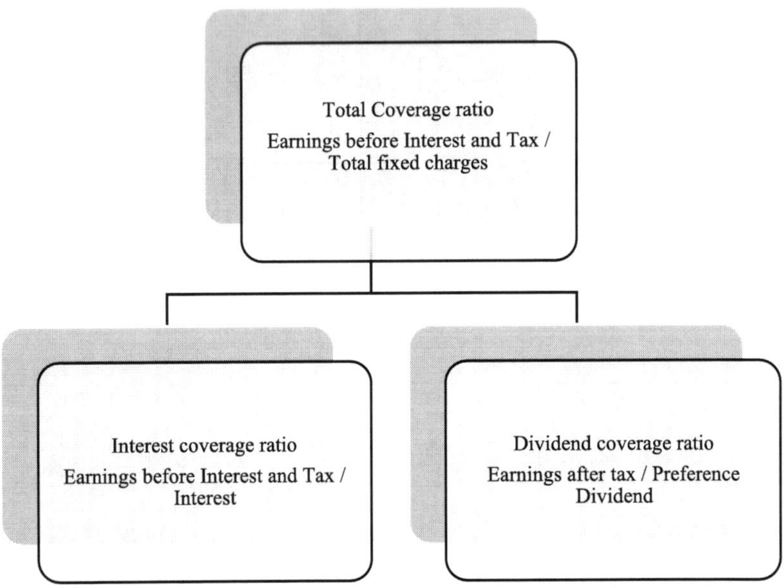

| Rat | Rationale |
|---|---|
| **Interest coverage** $= \frac{\text{Earnings before interest and tax}}{\text{Interest}}$ | This is a ratio used to ascertain how easily an enterprise can pay its outstanding dues.<br>A ratio of 1:5 is considered satisfactory. |
| **Dividend coverage** $= \frac{\text{Earnings after tax}}{\text{Preference dividend}}$ | This ratio measures the ability of the enterprise to pay dividend on preference shares.<br>A high ratio indicates better ability. |
| **Total coverage** $= \frac{\text{Earnings before interest and tax}}{\text{Total fixed charges}}$ | It shows the overall ability of the enterprise to fulfil the liabilities.<br>A high ratio is better for creditors. |

## 15.10.4 Profitability ratios

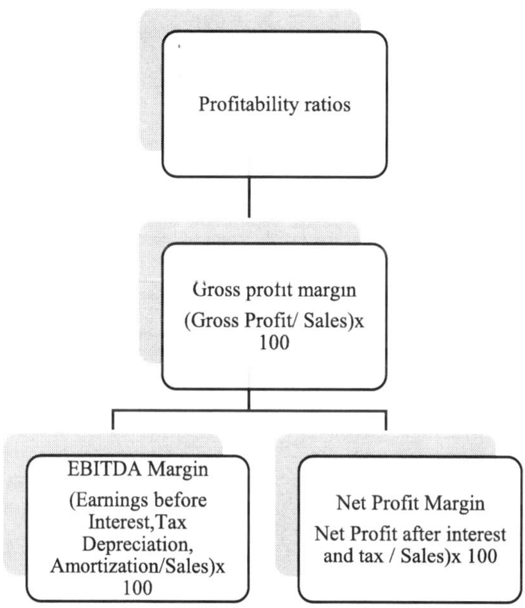


| Ratio | Rationale |
|---|---|
| **Gross profit margin** $= \frac{\text{Gross Profit} \times 100}{\text{Sales}}$ | This ratio measures the profit in relation to sales. This ratio is measured with the benchmark ratio prevalent in the industry for inter-firm comparison purposes. |
| **EBITDA margin** $= \frac{\text{Earnings before Interest depreciation, amortisation and tax} \times 100}{\text{Sales}}$ | This is a very critical ratio which is looked at by the outside world including bankers to measure |

| Ratio | Rationale |
|---|---|
| | the profitability of the enterprise in the short term and also used as a benchmark for valuation for the medium to long term. |
| **Net Profit margin**<br>$= \frac{\text{Net Profit after interest and tax} \times 100}{\text{Sales}}$ | This ratio measures the net profit of the enterprise with respect to sale. |
| Or,<br>$= \frac{\text{Net Profit after tax before interest} \times 100}{\text{Sales}}$ | This ratio measures the net profit of the enterprise with respect to sale.<br><br>Both these ratios are used to compare with benchmark industry average to evaluate the profitability of the enterprise. |

## 15.10.5 Expense ratios

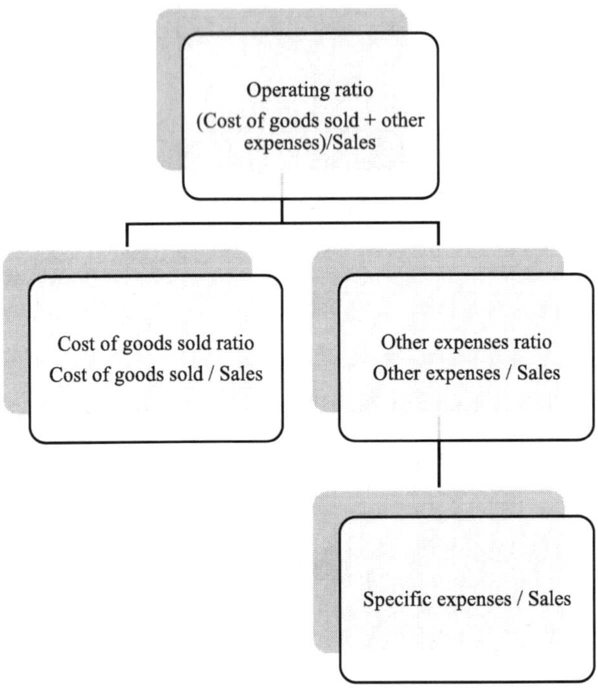

| Ratio | Rationale |
|---|---|
| **Operating ratio** $= \frac{\text{Cost of goods sold + other expenses}}{\text{Sales}}$ | This ratio is an effective measure to depict the operational efficiency of the business. |
| **Cost of goods sold ratio** $= \frac{\text{Cost of goods sold}}{\text{Sales}}$ | Lower operating ratio would depict higher profitability and higher operating ratio would signify lower profitability. It measures the cost of goods sold per sale. |
| **Specific expenses ratio** $= \frac{\text{Specific expenses}}{\text{Sales}}$ | It measures specific expenses per sale. |

## 15.10.6 Capital turnover ratios

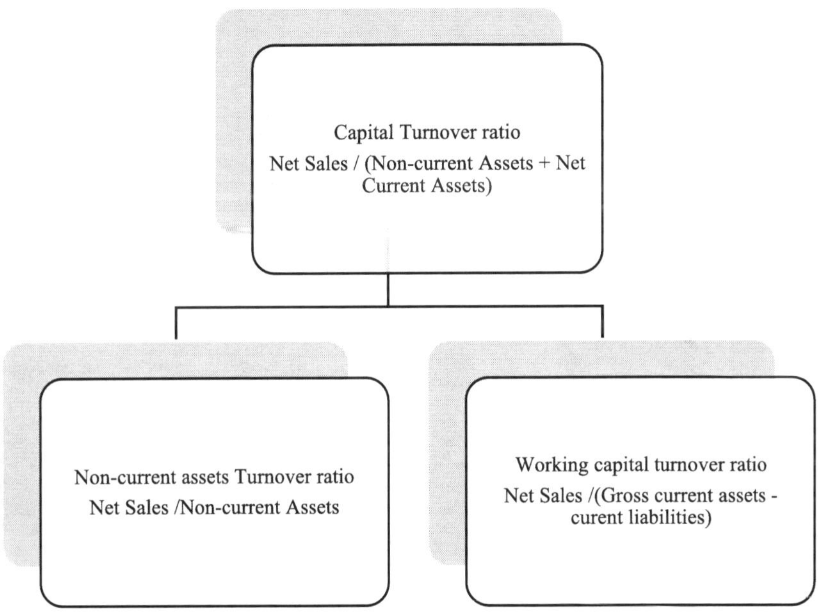


| Ratio | Rationale |
|---|---|
| **Total Assets turnover ratio** $= \frac{\text{Net Sales}}{\text{Total assets}}$ | It measures the degree of efficiency of an enterprise in utilising its assets during the operations of the enterprise.<br><br>The higher the ratio, better is the efficiency and effectiveness of the enterprise in managing its |

| Ratio | Rationale |
|---|---|
| **Capital turnover ratio** $= \frac{\text{Net Sales}}{\text{Capital employed}}$<br><br>**Non – current Assets turnover ratio** $= \frac{\text{Net Sales}}{\text{Non} - \text{current assets}}$<br><br>**Current Assets turnover ratio** $= \frac{\text{Net Sales}}{\text{Current assets}}$<br><br>**Working capital turnover ratio** $= \frac{\text{Net Sales}}{\text{Net current assets}}$ | assets. |

## 15.10.7 Activity ratios

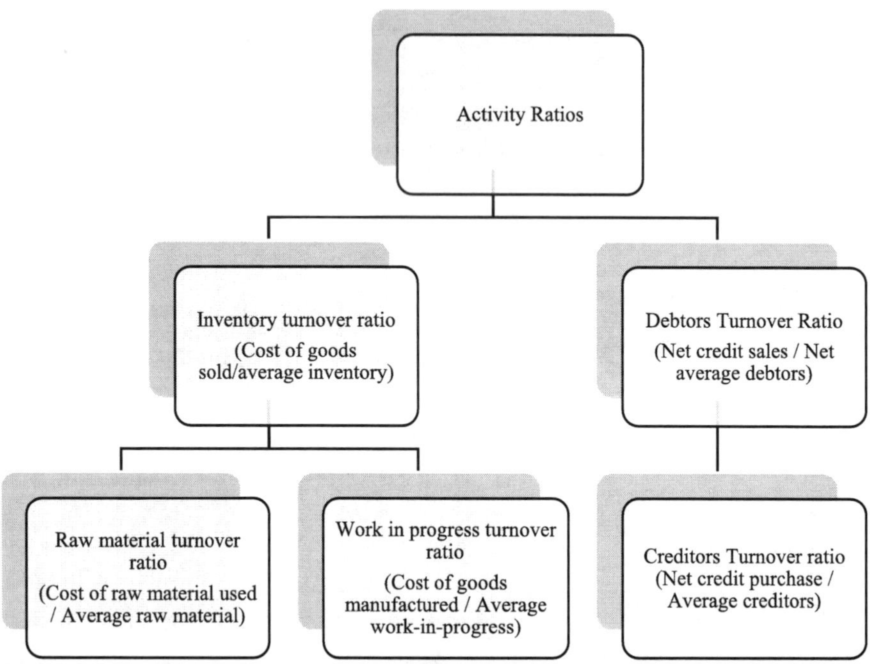


| Ratio | Rationale |
|---|---|
| **Debtors turnover ratio** $= \frac{\text{Net credit Sales}}{\text{Average net debtors}}$ | This reflects how quickly receivables are converted into cash. |

| Ratio | Rationale |
|---|---|
| **Inventory turnover ratio** $= \frac{\text{Cost of goods sold}}{\text{Average inventories}}$ | This reflects how quickly inventories are sold a converted into cash. This would depend on the nature of industry and can be benchmarked accordingly. |
| **Raw material turnover ratio** $= \frac{\text{Cost of raw material used}}{\text{Average raw material inventory}}$ | This reflects how quickly raw material inventories are converted into finished goods. If the ratio is high, it would be mean that the enterprise is converting raw material into finished goods very efficiently. If it is other way round, it would mean there are inefficiencies in the production process which needs to be weeded out. The yard stick is the benchmark ratio of the industry in which the enterprise belongs. |
| **Work in progress turnover ratio** $= \frac{\text{Cost of goods manufactured}}{\text{Average work in progress inventory}}$ | Same as above |
| **Creditors turnover ratio** $= \frac{\text{Net credit purchase}}{\text{Average creditors}}$ | This reflects how quickly the enterprise settles its trade payables. Higher the ratio, it would be indication that the enterprise has enough liquidity to pay off its trade payables. |

## 15.10.8 Return on investment ratios

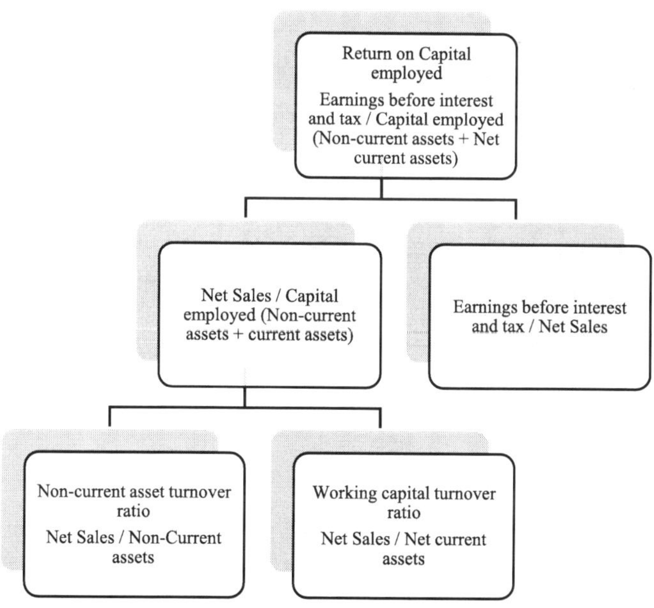

| Ratio | Rationale |
|---|---|
| **Return on Assets (ROA)**<br>$= \frac{\text{(Net Profit after tax)} \times 100}{\text{Total assets}}$<br>Or,<br>$= \frac{\text{(Net Profit after tax + Interest)} \times 100}{\text{Tangible assets}}$<br>$= \frac{\text{(Net Profit after tax + Interest)} \times 100}{\text{Tangible assets}}$<br>Or,<br>$= \frac{\text{(Net Profit after tax + Interest)} \times 100}{\text{Fixed assets}}$ | This ratio is a measure of return on the funds invested in the total assets of the enterprise.<br>The higher the ratio, it signifies more efficient use of the total assets. |
| **Return on capital employed (ROCE)**<br>$= \frac{\text{(Net Profit after tax)} \times 100}{\text{Total capital employed}}$<br>Or,<br>$= \frac{\text{(Net Profit after tax + Interest)} \times 100}{\text{Total capital employed}}$<br>Or,<br>$= \frac{\text{(Net Profit after tax + Interest)} \times 100}{\text{Total capital employed} - \text{Intangible assets}}$ | This ratio is a measure of return on the funds invested in the capital employed of the enterprise.<br>The higher the ratio, it signifies more efficient use of the total capital employed. |

## 15.10.9 Shareholders' ratios

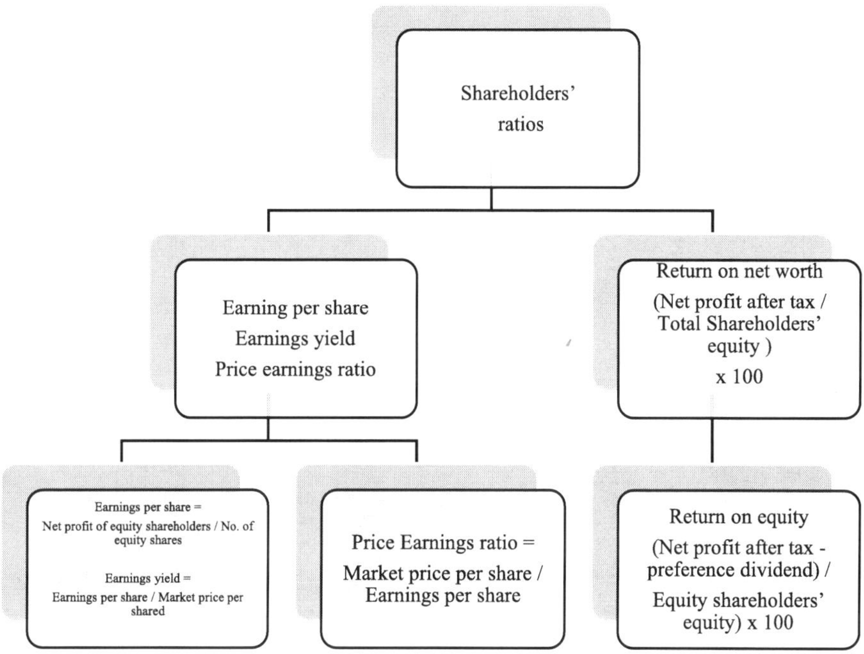


| Ratio | Rationale |
|---|---|
| **Return on total shareholders' Equity** $= \frac{\text{(Net Profit after tax)} \times 100}{\text{Total shareholders' equity}}$ | This ratio depicts the return on total shareholders' fund deployed in the enterprise. Higher the return, it would signify better return on total shareholders' fund. |
| **Return on total ordinary shareholders' Equity** $= \frac{\text{(Net Profit after tax)} \times 100}{\text{Total shareholders' equity}}$ $= \frac{\text{(Net Profit after tax and preference dividend)}}{\text{Ordinary shareholders' equity}}$ | This ratio depicts the return on ordinary shareholders' fund deployed in the enterprise. Higher the return, it would signify better return on equity from ordinary shareholders. |
| **Earnings per share (EPS)** $= \frac{\text{Net Profit of equity holders}}{\text{Number of Ordinary shares}}$ | The ratio measures the profit available to the equity holders on a per share basis. |

| Ratio | Rationale |
|---|---|
| **Dividend per share (DPS)** $= \dfrac{\text{Net Profit after interest and preference dividend paid to ordinary shareholders}}{\text{Number of Ordinary Share outstanding}}$ | The ratio measures the profit distributed as dividend to the equity holders on a per share basis. |
| **Dividend pay – out ratio (D/P)** $= \dfrac{\text{Total dividend to equity holders}}{\text{Total net profit of equity Holders}}$ Or, $= \dfrac{\text{Dividend per ordinary share}}{\text{Earnings per share}}$ | This ratio is a measure of percentage share of net profit paid out as dividend to equity shareholders The higher the D/P ratio, more attractive it is for the investor. |
| **Earnings yield** $= \dfrac{\text{Earnings per share}}{\text{Market value per share}}$ | This ratio is a measure of percentage of each rupee invested in the stock that has been earned by the enterprise |
| **Dividend yield** $= \dfrac{\text{Dividend per share}}{\text{Market value per share}}$ | This ratio is a measure of percentage dividend paid out by the enterprise each year in relation to its share price |
| **Price earnings ratio (P/E)** $= \dfrac{\text{Market value per share}}{\text{Earnings per share}}$ | This ratio is a measure which signifies the price currently paid by the investor for each rupee of EPS. Higher the ratio more expensive is the stock price and more market capitalization for the owners. |
| **Earning power** $= \dfrac{\text{Net profit after tax}}{\text{Total assets}}$ | The ratio is a measure of the earning power of the enterprise as it depicts overall profitability and operational efficiency of an enterprise. |

To work out the above financial ratios, basic numbers are picked up from the financial statements. A specimen format of the financial statements is enumerated below.

## 15.11 SPECIMEN FORMATS

### 15.11.1 Specimen format of Financial Statements used as base for computation of financial ratios

**Illustration 15.6: Balance Sheet (specimen format) (INR Million)**

| Sl No. | Particulars | Note. No. | As at 31.03.21 | As at 31.03.20 | As at 31.03.19 |
|---|---|---|---|---|---|
| | | | | | |
| | **EQUITY & LIABILITIES** | | | | |
| 1 | **Shareholders' funds** | | | | |
| | (a) Share capital | | | | |
| | (b) Reserves and surplus | | | | |
| | (c) Money received against share warrants | | | | |
| 2 | **Share application money pending allotment** | | | | |
| 3 | **Non-current liabilities** | | | | |
| | (a) Long term borrowings | | | | |
| | (b) Deferred tax liabilities (net) | | | | |
| | (c) Other long term liabilities | | | | |
| | (d) Long-term provisions | | | | |
| 4 | **Current liabilities** | | | | |
| | (a) Short term borrowings | | | | |
| | (b) Trade payables | | | | |
| | (c) Other current liabilities | | | | |
| | (d) Short term provisions | | | | |
| | **TOTAL** | | | | |
| | **ASSETS** | | | | |
| 1 | **Non-current Assets** | | | | |
| | (a) Property, Plant and Equipment | | | | |

| Sl No. | Particulars | Note. No. | As at 31.03.21 | As at 31.03.20 | As at 31.03.19 |
|---|---|---|---|---|---|
| | (i) Tangible assets | | | | |
| | (ii) Intangible assets | | | | |
| | (iii) Capital work-in-progress | | | | |
| | (iv) Intangible assets under development | | | | |
| | (b) Non-current investments | | | | |
| | (c) Deferred tax assets (net) | | | | |
| | (d) Long term loans & advances | | | | |
| | (e) Other non-current assets | | | | |
| 2 | **Current Assets** | | | | |
| | (a) Current investments | | | | |
| | (b) Inventories | | | | |
| | (c) Trade receivables | | | | |
| | (d) Cash & cash equivalents | | | | |
| | (e) Short-term loan and advances | | | | |
| | (f) Other current assets | | | | |
| | **TOTAL** | | | | |

**Illustration 15.7: Statement of Profit & Loss (specimen format) (INR Million)**

| Sl No. | Particulars | Note no. | As at 31.03.21 | As at 31.03.20 | As at 31.03.19 |
|---|---|---|---|---|---|
| | | | | | |
| I | REVENUE FROM OPERATION | | | | |
| II | OTHER INCOME | | | | |
| **III** | **(TOTAL REVENUE (I + II)** | | | | |
| IV | EXPENSES: | | | | |
| | (a) Cost of material consumed | | | | |
| | (b) Purchase of products for sale | | | | |

| Sl No. | Particulars | Note no. | As at 31.03.21 | As at 31.03.20 | As at 31.03.19 |
|---|---|---|---|---|---|
| | (c) Changes in inventories of finished goods, work-in-progress and products for sale | | | | |
| | (d) Employees cost benefit expenses | | | | |
| | (e) Finance cost | | | | |
| | (f) Depreciation and amortisation expenses | | | | |
| | (g) Product development expenses | | | | |
| | (h) Other expenses | | | | |
| | (i) Expenditure transfer to capital and other Account | | | | |
| | **TOTAL EXPENSES** | | | | |
| V | PROFIT BEFORE EXCEPTIONAL AND EXTRA- | | | | |
| | ORDINARY ITEMS AND TAX (III - IV) | | | | |
| VI | EXCEPTIONAL ITEMS | | | | |
| VII | PROFIT BEFORE EXTRAORDINARY ITEMS AND TAX (V-VI) | | | | |
| VIII | EXTRAORDINARY ITEMS | | | | |
| IX | PROFIT BEFORE TAX AND CONTINUING OPERATIONS (VII - VIII) | | | | |
| X | TAX EXPENSES: | | | | |
| | (a) Current tax | | | | |
| | (b) Deferred tax | | | | |
| XI | PROFIT AFTER TAX FOR THE YEAR FROM | | | | |
| | CONTINUING OPERATION | | | | |

| Sl No. | Particulars | Note no. | As at 31.03.21 | As at 31.03.20 | As at 31.03.19 |
|---|---|---|---|---|---|
| | (IX - X) | | | | |
| XII | Profit/(loss) from discontinuing operations | | | | |
| XIII | Tax expenses from discontinuing operations | | | | |
| XIV | Profit/(loss) from discontinuing operations (after tax) (XII-XIII) | | | | |
| XV | PROFIT/(LOSS) FOR THE PERIOD (XI + XIV) | | | | |
| | Balance brought forward from previous year | | | | |
| | Profit available for appropriation: | | | | |
| | Proposed dividend | | | | |
| | Transfer to General Reserve | | | | |
| | Distribution tax | | | | |
| | Total | | | | |
| | Balance carried forward | | | | |
| XVI | Earning per equity share: | | | | |
| | (1) Basic | | | | |
| | (2) Diluted | | | | |

**Illustration 15.8: Specimen Notes to Balance Sheet** **(INR Million)**

| Sl No. | Particulars | | As at 31.03.21 | As at 31.03.20 | As at 31.03.19 |
|---|---|---|---|---|---|
| | | | | | |
| 1 | Long term borrowings | | | | |
| | Secured loans | | | | |
| | Unsecured loans | | | | |
| | Total | | | | |
| 2 | Tangible assets | | | | |

| Sl No. | Particulars | | As at 31.03.21 | As at 31.03.20 | As at 31.03.19 |
|---|---|---|---|---|---|
| | Gross block | | | | |
| | Less: Accumulated depreciation | | | | |
| | Total | | | | |

**Illustration 15.9: Specimen Notes to Statement of Profit & loss (INR Million)**

| Sl No. | Particulars | | As at 31.03.21 | As at 31.03.20 | As at 31.03.19 |
|---|---|---|---|---|---|
| | | | | | |
| 1 | **Cost of material consumed** | | | | |
| | Raw material cost | | | | |
| | Goods and service tax | | | | |
| | Total | | | | |
| 2 | **Finance cost** | | | | |
| | Interest expenses | | | | |
| | Total | | | | |
| 3 | **Depreciation and amortisation expenses** | | | | |
| | Depreciation | | | | |
| | Total | | | | |

## 15.11.2 Specimen format for definitions

**(INR Million)**

| Sl No. | Particulars | | As at 31.03.21 | As at 31.03.20 | As at 31.03.19 |
|---|---|---|---|---|---|
| **1** | **Operating Profit** | | | | |
| | Revenue | | | | |
| | Less: Raw material cost | | | | |
| | Goods and service tax | | | | |
| | Other expenses | | | | |

| Sl No. | Particulars | | As at 31.03.21 | As at 31.03.20 | As at 31.03.19 |
|---|---|---|---|---|---|
| | Total | | | | |
| 2 | **Gross Profit** | | | | |
| | Operating profit | | | | |
| | Less: Interest expenses | | | | |
| | Total | | | | |
| 3 | **Net Profit (Profit After Tax : PAT)** | | | | |
| | Gross Profit | | | | |
| | Add: Other income | | | | |
| | Other non-recurring income | | | | |
| | Less Depreciation | | | | |
| | Tax expenses | | | | |
| | Total | | | | |
| 4 | **Profit before tax (PBT)** | | | | |
| | Net Profit | | | | |
| | Less: Non-recurring income | | | | |
| | Add: Tax expenses | | | | |
| | Total | | | | |
| 5 | **Non-current assets** | | | | |
| | Net tangible assets | | | | |
| | Add: Capital work-in-progress | | | | |
| | Investments | | | | |
| | Total | | | | |
| 6 | **Net Worth** | | | | |
| | Share capital | | | | |
| | Reserves & surplus | | | | |

| Sl No. | Particulars | | As at 31.03.21 | As at 31.03.20 | As at 31.03.19 |
|---|---|---|---|---|---|
| | Total | | | | |
| 7 | **Capital employed** | | | | |
| | Total assets | | | | |
| | Less: Current liabilities | | | | |
| | Capital employed | | | | |

**Illustration 15.10: Specimen format for Trend Analysis**

**Balance Sheet (specimen format)**

**INR Million**

| Sl No. | Particulars | | As at 31.03.21 | As at 31.03.20 | As at 31.03.19 | Remarks |
|---|---|---|---|---|---|---|
| | | | | | | |
| 1 | Current Assets | | | | | |
| | | | | | | |
| | | | | | | |
| 2 | Fixed Assets | | | | | |
| | | | | | | |
| | | | | | | |
| 3 | Current liabilities | | | | | |
| | | | | | | |
| | | | | | | |
| 4 | Long term liabilities | | | | | |
| | | | | | | |
| | | | | | | |

**Trend Analysis:**

**Statement of Profit & Loss (specimen format)**

**INR Million**

| Sl No. | Particulars | | As at 31.03.21 | As at 31.03.20 | As at 31.03.19 | Remarks |
|---|---|---|---|---|---|---|
| 1 | Sales | | | | | |
| | | | | | | |
| | | | | | | |
| 2 | Raw material cost | | | | | |
| | | | | | | |
| | | | | | | |
| 3 | Operating profit | | | | | |
| | | | | | | |
| | | | | | | |
| 4 | Profit before tax (PBT) | | | | | |
| | | | | | | |
| | | | | | | |
| 5 | Net profit | | | | | |
| | | | | | | |

**Illustration 15.11: Specimen format for Ratio Analysis**

**Ratio Analysis: (Specimen format)**

**INR Million**

| Sl No. | Particulars | | As at 31.03.21 | As at 31.03.20 | As at 31.03.19 | Remarks |
|---|---|---|---|---|---|---|
| **1** | **Net working capital** | | | | | |
| | (Current Asset - Current liabilities) | | | | | |
| **2** | **Current ratio** | | | | | |
| | (Current Asset/Current | | | | | |

| Sl No. | Particulars | | As at 31.03.21 | As at 31.03.20 | As at 31.03.19 | Remarks |
|---|---|---|---|---|---|---|
| | liabilities) | | | | | |
| **3** | **Quick ratio/Acid test ratio** | | | | | |
| | (Quick Asset/Current liabilities) | | | | | |
| **4** | **Debt - Equity ratio** | | | | | |
| | (Long term debt/ Shareholders' equity) | | | | | |
| **5** | **Interest coverage ratio** | | | | | |
| | (Operating profit/Interest) | | | | | |
| **6** | **Operating Profit margin** | | | | | |
| | (Operating profit × 100)/ Sales | | | | | |
| **7** | **Gross Profit margin** | | | | | |
| | (Gross profit × 100)/Sales | | | | | |
| **8** | **Net Profit margin** | | | | | |
| | (Net profit × 100)/Sales | | | | | |
| **9** | **Return on Assets** | | | | | |
| | (Operating profit/Average assets) | | | | | |
| **10** | **Return on investments** | | | | | |
| | (Net profit before tax × 100)/ Net worth | | | | | |
| **11** | **Return on net worth** | | | | | |
| | (Net profit × 100)/Average Net worth | | | | | |
| 12 | Return on capital employed | | | | | |
| | (Net profit after tax × 100)/ Total capital employed) | | | | | |

| Sl No. | Particulars | | As at 31.03.21 | As at 31.03.20 | As at 31.03.19 | Remarks |
|---|---|---|---|---|---|---|
| 13 | **Cost of goods sold ratio** | | | | | |
| | (Cost of goods sold/Sales) | | | | | |
| 14 | **Operating ratio** | | | | | |
| | (Cost of goods sold + other expenses/Sales) | | | | | |
| 15 | **Fixed Assets turnover** | | | | | |
| | (Sales/Fixed assets) | | | | | |
| | | | | | | |

## 15.12 RETURN ON INVESTMENT

Short term and long-term profitability of shareholders' investments in an entity is evaluated through Return on Equity (ROE) and growth in investment. Growth in earnings also is determined by growth in investment and the profitability of that investment. For forecasting profitability of an entity, we need understand both profitability and growth and the factors which drive them. The analysis of drivers of ROE is often called Profitability Analysis and the analysis of drivers of growth is called growth analysis.

As we have seen in our earlier chapters, building blocks of financial statements is the corner stone on which the edifice of profitability analysis and growth analysis rests.

## 15.13 ANALYSIS OF PROFITABILITY

Profitability analysis determines the state of viability of the firm as of today. In its practical approach it carries out the following:

(a) Calculate the ROE of the enterprise based on current performance

(b) Identify the value drivers which would build up to the current ROE.

(c) Based on these drivers, assess the forecast and predict the future ROE, which in turn talks about the overall growth of the enterprise.

Because of these attributes, profitability analysis becomes an effective tool to carry out:

(a) Management planning as to how to survive and grow with the current businesses

(b) Strategy analysis as to retain, grow or dispose of verticals which are not profitable

(c) Decision analysis related to future of the business based on business vision, mission and strategic intent

(d) Enterprise valuation, which is always required for future growth through inorganic route

## 15.14 RETURN ON EQUITY (ROE)

As we have seen before Return on Equity (ROE) is calculated as under:

$$\textbf{Return on Equity (ROE)} = \frac{\textbf{Comprehensive Income}}{\textbf{Average Shareholders' Equity (SE)}}$$

Return on Equity is cascaded into three levels of drivers. These are:

(a) Level 1 identifies the effect of financing and operating liability leverage.

(b) Level 2 identifies effect of profit margins and asset turnovers on operative profitability, and

(c) Level 3 identifies the drivers of profit margins, asset turnovers and the borrowing cost.

Before we get into this drill down, let us understand the nomenclatures:

**Financial statements line items**

- Earnings = Comprehensive income
- SE = Shareholders' equity
- OI = Operating Income
- NOA = Net Operating Assets
- NFE = Net Financial expenses
- NFO = Net Financial obligations

**Ratios used for drill down**

- ROE = Return on Equity
- RNOA = Return on net operating assets
- ROOA = Return on operating assets
- NBC = Net borrowing cost
- OLLEV = Operating liability leverage
- OLSPREAD = Operating liability leverage spread

- FLEV = Financial leverage
- SPREAD = Operating spread
- PM = Operating profit margin
- ATO = Asset turnover

### 15.14.1 Level I: Drill down

This is determined by operating profitability, financial leverage and the operating spread.

Operating profitability is defined by the definition of ROE which as mentioned above is

$$\textbf{Return on Equity (ROE)} = \frac{\textbf{Comprehensive Income}}{\textbf{Average Shareholders' Equity (SE)}}$$

Comprehensive income is the numerator of ROE and aggregates operating income (OI) and net financial expense (NFE) as depicted in a reformulated income statement. Shareholders' Equity (SE) in the denominator is net operating assets (NOA) less net financial obligations (NFO). Hence, ROE is broken down to the following:

$$\textbf{Return on Equity (ROE)} = \frac{\textbf{OI} - \textbf{NFE}}{\textbf{NOA} - \textbf{NFE}}$$

Operating Income (OI) is calculated by the net operating assets (NOA) and the operating profitability measure, Return on net operating assets (RNOA) expressed in percentage terms.

The net financial expense (NFE) on the other hand is calculated by the net financial obligations (NFO) and the rate at which the NFE is incurred is the net borrowing cost (NBC) expressed in percentage terms. Accordingly, the ROE is expressed as under:

$$\textbf{Return on Equity (ROE)} = \frac{\textbf{NOA}}{\textbf{SE}} \times \textbf{RNOA} \; \frac{\textbf{NFO}}{\textbf{SE}} \times \textbf{NBC}$$

**Where, RNOA = Operating Income (OI)/Net Operating Assets (NOA) and**

**NBC = Net financial expenses (NFE)/Net Financial Obligation (NFO)**

The ratio above is further rearranged as under:

**NFO**

$$\textbf{Return on Equity (ROE)} = \frac{\textbf{RNOA}}{\textbf{SE}} \times (\textbf{RNOA} - \textbf{NBC})$$

**= RNOA + (Financial leverage x operating spread)**

**= RNOA + (FLEV X SPREAD)**

**Hence, first level drivers of ROE are:**

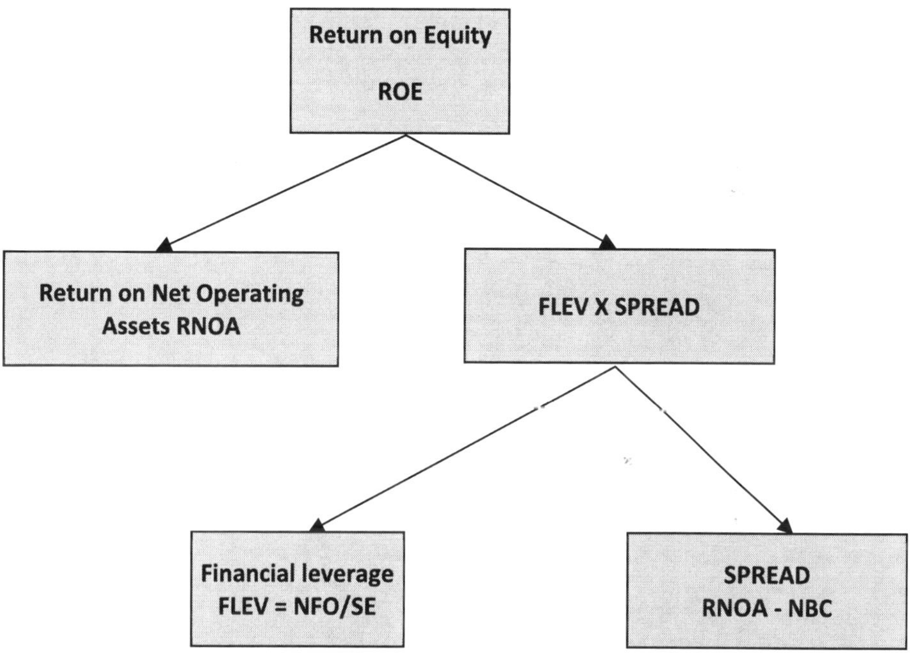


### *15.14.1.1 Financial leverage*

Financial leverage is the degree to which net operating assets are financed by borrowing with net financial obligations (NFO) or by equity. The measure FLEV = NFO/SE captures financial leverage. To the extent that net operating assets are financed by net financial obligations rather than equity, the return on equity is affected. A typical FLEV is around 0.4, but there would considerable variation between industries and enterprises at large.

### 15.14.1.2 Operating spread

Operating Spread is the difference between the return on net operating assets and the net borrowing cost and represented as:

**SPREAD = Return on Net Operating Assets (RNOA) –**
**Net Borrowing Cost (NBC)**

This formula says that the ROE is levered up over the return from operations if the enterprise has financial leverage and the return from operations is greater than the borrowing cost. The enterprise earns more on its equity if the net operating assets are financed by net debt, provided those assets earn more than the cost of debt.

### 15.14.1.3 Net Borrowing cost

The net borrowing cost (NBC) is a weighted average of the cost for the different sources of net financing. It can be calculated as under:

$$\text{NBC} = \frac{\text{NFE}}{\text{NFO}}$$

**Where, NFE = Net Financial Expenses**
**NFO = Net Financial Obligations**

The drivers of Net Borrowing cost are:

$$\text{NBC} = \frac{\text{FO}}{\text{NFO}} \times \frac{\text{After tax interest on financial obligations (FO)}}{\text{FO}}$$

**Minus**

$$\frac{\text{FO}}{\text{NFO}} \times \frac{\text{After tax interest on financial assets (FA)}}{\text{FO}}$$

**Minus**

$$\frac{\textbf{FA}}{\textbf{NFO}} \times \frac{\textbf{Unrealised gains on financial assets (FA)}}{\textbf{FA}}$$

**Plus**

$$\frac{\textbf{Preference shares}}{\textbf{NFO}} \times \frac{\textbf{Preference dividend}}{\textbf{Preference shares}}$$

**Where,**

**FO = Financial obligations**

**NFO = Net Financial Obligations**

**FA = Financial Assets**

Hence, from the above, the drivers of Net Borrowing Cost (NBC) are:

(a) After tax interest on Financial obligations

(b) After tax interest on financial assets

(c) Unrealised gains on financial assets

(d) Preference dividend

#### *15.14.1.4 Operating liability leverage*

Similar to financial leverage, just as financial liabilities can lever up the ROE, so can operating liabilities lever up the return on net operating assets. Operating liabilities are obligations incurred during operations and are distinct from financial obligations incurred to finance the operations. The operating liability leverage is expressed as under:

$$\textbf{Operating liabilities leverage (OLLEV)} = \frac{\textbf{OI}}{\textbf{NOA}}$$

The typical OLLEV is about 0.4. We know, operating liabilities reduce the net operating assets that are employed and so lever the return on net operating assets. To the extent a firm can get credit in its operations with no explicit interest, it reduces its investment in net operating assets and levers its RNOA. On the other hand vendors who provide credit without interest also charge higher prices for the goods and services they supply than would be the case if the firm paid cash. Hence, operating leverage, like financial leverage, can be unfavourable as well as favourable.

To conclude, ROE is affected by both financial leverage and operating liability leverage. Without either type of leverage, ROE would be equal to ROOA, the rate of return on operating assets. Operating liability leverage levers RNOA over ROOA and financial leverage levers ROE over RNOA.

**Hence, ROE = ROOA + (RNOA – ROOA) + (ROE – RNOA)**

Hence, in overall profitability analysis the ratios stack up as under:

| | Year 1 | Year 2 | Year 3 | Year 4 | Year 5 |
|---|---|---|---|---|---|
| Sales Revenue (INR Million) | | | | | |
| Profitability: | | | | | |
| EBITDA/Sales % | | | | | |
| Net profit margin % | | | | | |
| Asset turnover | | | | | |
| Return on Equity % | | | | | |
| Return on Net Operating Assets % | | | | | |
| Financial leverage | | | | | |
| Operating Spread | | | | | |
| Net borrowing cost % | | | | | |
| Operating Liability Leverage | | | | | |

### 15.14.2 Level II: Drill Down: Drivers of operating profitability

We have seen above

**ROE = RNOA + (FLEV X SPREAD), which is**
**ROE = RNOA + (FLEV X (RNOA – NBC)**
**ROE = (PM X ATO) + (FLEV X (RNOA – NBC))**

The two drivers of RNOA are:

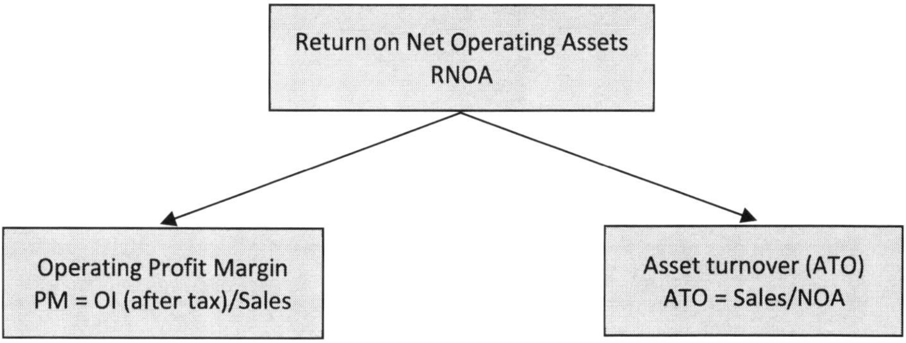


Operating Profit Margin depicts profitability of the entity towards each rupee of sales.

Asset Turnover ratio depicts the sales revenue per rupee of net operating assets. It measures the ability of the NOA to generate sales and to what degree. For example if ATO is say 4.0, it signifies that the entity is using 25 paise of net operating assets to generate a rupee of sales.

The decomposition of operating profitability is known as the **DuPont financial model**. It states that profitability in operations arises from two sources, namely,

(a) Operating income as a percentage of sales, which means higher the earning per rupee of sales, it will push up the RNOA and

(b) Turnover of Net operating assets to sales, which means higher the turnover of net operating assets, higher would be the sales as well as RNOA as a resultant.

This signifies that an enterprise can optimise Return on Net Operating Assets (RNOA) by increasing profit margins as well as by levering up margins by using operating assets and operating liabilities more efficiently to generate sales.

### 15.14.3 Level III: Drill down: Drivers of ROE

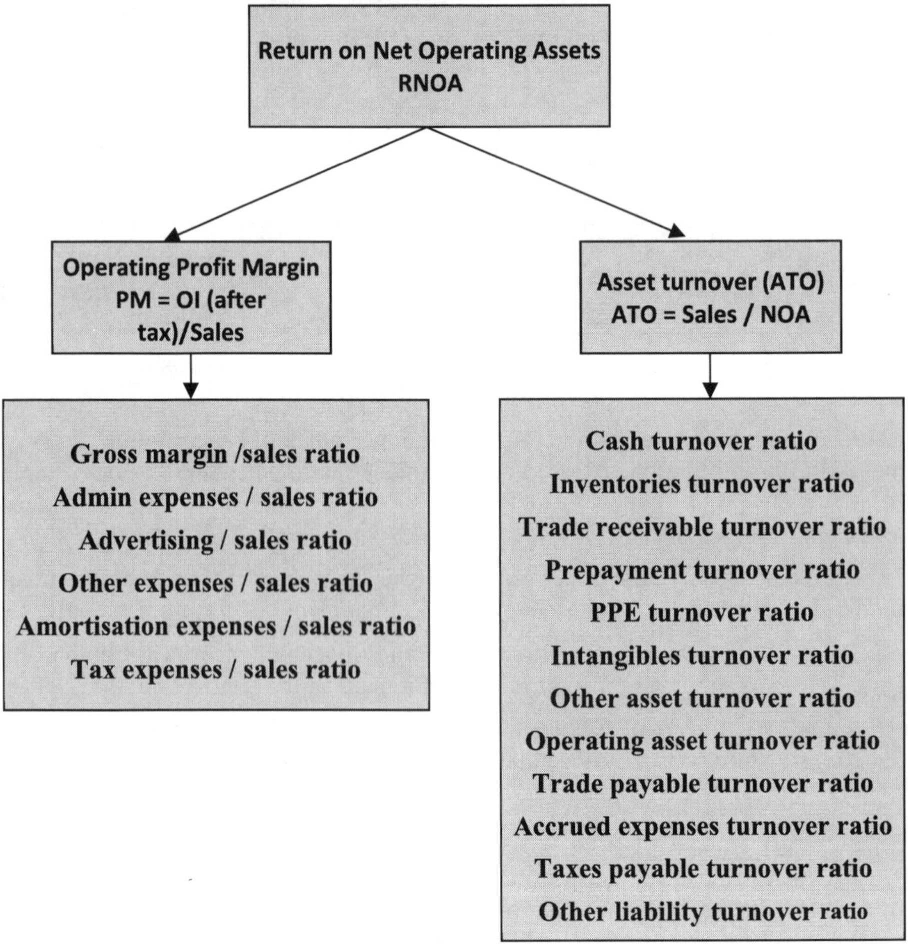


#### *15.14.3.1 Operating profit margin drivers*

| Items | Ratios |
|---|---|
| Gross margin /sales ratio | $= \frac{\text{Gross margin}}{\text{Sales}}$ |
| Admin expenses/sales ratio | $= \frac{\text{Administration expenses}}{\text{Sales}}$ |
| Advertising/sales ratio | $= \frac{\text{Advertising expenses}}{\text{Sales}}$ |

| | |
|---|---|
| Other expenses/sales ratio | $= \frac{\text{Other expenses}}{\text{Sales}}$ |
| Amortisation expenses/sales ratio | $= \frac{\text{Amortisation expenses}}{\text{Sales}}$ |
| Tax expenses/sales ratio | $= \frac{\text{Tax expenses}}{\text{Sales}}$ |
| Net margin/sales ratio<br>(resultant of all of above) | $= \frac{\text{Net margin}}{\text{Sales}}$ |

### 15.14.3.2 Turnover drivers

| Items | Ratios |
|---|---|
| Cash turnover ratio | $= \frac{\text{Sales}}{\text{Cash}}$ |
| Inventories turnover ratio<br>Inventories days sales (IDS) | $= \frac{\text{Cost of goods sold}}{\text{Inventory}}$<br>$= \frac{365}{\text{Inventory turnover}}$ |
| Trade receivable turnover ratio<br>Days sales Outstanding (DSO) | $= \frac{\text{Sales}}{\text{Trade Receivable}}$<br>$= \frac{365}{\text{Trade receivable turnover}}$ |
| Trade payable turnover ratio | $= \frac{\text{Purchases}}{\text{Trade Payable}}$<br>$= \frac{365}{\text{Trade payable turnover}}$ |
| PPE turnover ratio | $= \frac{\text{Sales}}{\text{Property, Plant \& Equipment}}$ |
| Intangibles turnover ratio | $= \frac{\text{Sales}}{\text{Intangible properties}}$ |
| Prepayment turnover ratio | $= \frac{\text{Sales}}{\text{Prepayments}}$ |

| Items | Ratios |
|---|---|
| Accrued expenses turnover ratio | $= \frac{\text{Cost of goods sold}}{\text{Accrued expenses}}$ |
| Other liabilities turnover ratio | $= \frac{\text{Cost of goods sold}}{\text{Other liabilities}}$ |
| Tax payable turnover ratio | $= \frac{\text{Sales}}{\text{Tax payable}}$ |

## 15.15 DUPONT ANALYSIS

In line with the above analysis and as discussed above, students would also like to go through the DuPont Financial Analysis. Similar to above, in this matrix, the following metrics would be considered:

### 15.15.1 Return on Assets (ROA)

This is expressed as under:

$$\textbf{ROA} = \frac{\textbf{Net Income}}{\textbf{Total Assets}} \times \textbf{100}$$

This ratio is then broken into:

ROA = Net profit margin x Asset turnover ratio

$$= \frac{\textbf{Net profit margin}}{\textbf{Sales}} \times \frac{\textbf{Sales}}{\textbf{Total Assets}}$$

From the above it is evident that the drivers of ROA are:

(a) Profit margin and

(b) Asset turnover ratio

These ratios can be further cascaded down to elements in both the streams under profit margin as well as turnover ratios similar to the ratios highlighted above.

### 15.15.2 Return on Equity (ROE)

This is expressed as under:

$$\text{ROE} = \frac{\textbf{Net Income}}{\textbf{Owners' equity}} \times 100$$

This ratio is then sub-divided into:

ROE = Net Income x Asset turnover ratio

$$= \frac{\textbf{Net Income}}{\textbf{Sales}} \times \frac{\textbf{Sales}}{\textbf{Owners' Equity}}$$

From the above it is evident that the drivers of ROA are:

(a) Profit margin and

(b) Asset turnover ratio

## 15.16 FINANCIAL ANALYSIS

After having gone through the financial ratios in the earlier paragraphs of this Chapter, we now come to applying these ratios in working out a comprehensive financial analysis to comprehend the financial health and hygiene of the target organizations under study.

These measures are enumerated as under:

(a) Financial Analysis

(b) Sales Summary

(c) Cost trend

(d) Profitability Analysis

(e) Working Capital trend

### 15.16.1 Financial analysis

(a) Key Financials

(b) Profitability Analysis

(c) Solvency Analysis

(d) Liquidity Analysis

(e) Return on Investment

### 15.16.2 Sales summary

| | |
|---|---|
| (a) | Sales volume trend |
| (b) | Sales price trend |
| (c) | Sales value trend |
| (d) | Comparison of sales volume and value with budget |

### 15.16.3 Cost trend

| | |
|---|---|
| (a) | Costs by functional cost centres |
| (b) | Product cost trend |
| (c) | Cost by facilities |
| (d) | Cost by job/activity |
| (e) | Variances with budget and previous year |

### 15.16.4 Profitability analysis

| | |
|---|---|
| (a) | Product profitability analysis |
| (b) | Customer profitability analysis |
| (c) | Market segment wise profitability analysis |
| (d) | Distribution Channel wise profitability analysis |

### 15.16.5 Working capital trend

| | |
|---|---|
| (a) | Working capital trend |
| (b) | Debtors trend |
| (c) | Inventories trend |
| (d) | Creditors trend |
| (e) | Variances with budget and previous year |

Some of these measures are highlighted below with examples. This will provide a fair idea to the reader as to the power of the numbers generated and the indicative interpretations each such measure provide.

## 15.17 FINANCIAL ANALYSIS

### 15.17.1 Key financials

In this section we have included a series of illustrations to explain how the financial ratios with the help of trend analysis help us in analysing the health and hygiene of an organization in real life scenario. We need to remember that the source of all the base information is our yearly audited financial statements.

## Illustration 15.12. Financial Summary

This is a comparative financial summary for multiple years and assists us in understanding the financial trend of the organization under review.

| Year | 2014-15 | % | 2015-16 | % | YTD July 2016 | % |
|---|---|---|---|---|---|---|
| Sales | 13,637.2 | | 15,264.0 | | 3,576.7 | |
| Other income | 96.3 | | 65.8 | | 18.6 | |
| **Sales and other income** | 13,733.5 | | 15329.83 | | 3595.34 | |
| Raw material consumed / Traded goods | 3,980.7 | 29.0% | 4,590.4 | 29.9% | 1,172.6 | 32.6% |
| Purchase of carpets | 2,226.6 | 16.2% | 1,800.2 | 11.7% | 354.0 | 9.8% |
| Materials purchased for resale | 159.1 | 1.2% | 34.6 | 0.2% | 11.9 | 0.3% |
| Changes in inventories | (648.3) | -4.7% | (536.7) | -3.5% | (381.3) | -10.6% |
| Manufacturing and other direct expenses | 4,078.3 | 29.7% | 4,870.5 | 31.8% | 1,341.9 | 37.3% |
| Contribution | 3937.1 | 28.7% | 4570.9 | 29.8% | 1096.2 | 30.5% |
| Employee benefit expenses | 582.6 | 4.2% | 723.1 | 4.7% | 321.8 | 9.0% |
| Other Expenses (Admin and selling) | 1,409.7 | 10.3% | 1,581.1 | 10.3% | 494.7 | 13.8% |
| CSR Expenses | 11.5 | 0.1% | 16.5 | 0.1% | 5.5 | 0.2% |
| **Other Expenses** | 2003.9 | 14.6% | 2320.7 | 15.1% | 822.0 | 22.9% |
| **Operating Profit ( EBIDTA)** | 1933.2 | 14.1% | 2250.2 | 14.7% | 274.3 | 7.6% |
| EBITDA / Sales % | 14.1% | | 14.7% | | 7.6% | |
| Depreciation | 171.1 | 1.2% | 226.4 | 1.5% | 80.0 | 2.2% |
| EBIT | 1762.2 | 12.8% | 2023.82 | 13.2% | 194.25 | 5.4% |
| EBIT / Sales % | 12.8% | | 13.2% | | 5.4% | |
| Finance cost | 550.7 | 4.0% | 518.1 | 3.4% | 221.1 | 6.2% |
| Prior period charges | - | | - | | - | |
| PBT | 1211.4 | 8.8% | 1505.8 | 9.8% | -26.9 | -0.7% |
| Tax | 326.7 | 2.4% | 435.1 | 2.8% | - | 0.0% |
| Net Profit (PAT) | 884.8 | 6.4% | 1070.7 | 7.0% | -26.9 | -0.7% |
| Net Profit /Sales % | 6.4% | | 7.0% | | -0.7% | |
| Cash Accrual (NP+ DEP) | 1055.8 | | 1297.1 | | 53.1 | |

## Illustration 15.13: Month-wise key financials

| Year | 2014-15 | 2015-16 | Apr-16 | May-16 | Jun 16 | Jul-16 | YTD July 2016 |
|---|---|---|---|---|---|---|---|
| Sales and other income | 13,733 | 15,330 | 814 | 887 | 1,007 | 887 | 3,595 |
| Raw material consumed / Traded goods | 3,981 | 4,590 | 255 | 359 | 319 | 240 | 1,173 |
| Purchase of carpets | 2,227 | 1,800 | 96 | 100 | 78 | 80 | 354 |
| Materials purchased for resale | 159 | 35 | 0 | 7 | 1 | 4 | 12 |
| Changes in inventory | -648 | -537 | 81 | -379 | 68 | -152 | -381 |
| Manufacturing and direct expenses | 4,078 | 4,870 | 236 | 352 | 368 | 385 | 1,342 |
| Employee benefit expenses | 583 | 723 | 75 | 79 | 78 | 90 | 322 |
| Other expenses | 1,410 | 1,581 | 91 | 127 | 134 | 142 | 495 |
| CSR Expenses | 12 | 17 | 0 | 0 | 5 | 1 | 6 |
| Expenses | 11,800 | 13,080 | 836 | 643 | 1,051 | 791 | 3,321 |
| EBITDA | 1,933 | 2,250 | -21 | 244 | -44 | 96 | 274 |
| EBITDA / Sales % | **14.1%** | **14.7%** | -2.6% | **27.5%** | -4.4% | **10.8%** | **7.6%** |
| Depreciation | 171 | 226 | 20 | 20 | 20 | 20 | 80 |
| EBIT | 1,762 | 2,024 | -41 | 224 | -64 | 76 | 194 |
| Finance charges | 551 | 518 | 57 | 51 | 54 | 60 | 221 |
| PBT | 1,211 | 1,506 | -98 | 173 | -118 | 16 | -27 |
| Tax | 327 | 435 | 0 | 45 | -45.0 | 0.0 | 0 |
| PAT | 885 | 1,071 | -98 | 128 | -73 | 16 | -27 |

## 15.17.2 Profitability analysis

### Illustration 15.14: Margin analysis

The chart below depicts a trend analysis of EBITDA margin, EBIT, PBT and PAT margins. The chart shows the EBITDA margin has dropped in June and started slowly picking up in July 2021. It also shows the widening gap between EBIT and PBT margins, which signifies that the interest component may have been increasing owing to additional borrowing.

| Year | 2014-15 | 2015-16 | YTD May 2016 | YTD June 2016 | YTD July 2016 |
|---|---|---|---|---|---|
| EBITDA as a % of Sales & other income | 14.1% | 14.7% | 13.1% | 6.6% | 7.6% |
| EBIT as % of Sales & other income | 12.8% | 13.2% | 10.7% | 4.4% | 5.4% |
| PBT as % of Sales & other income | 8.8% | 9.8% | 4.4% | -1.6% | -0.7% |
| PAT as % of Sales & other income | 6.4% | 7.0% | 1.8% | -1.6% | -0.7% |

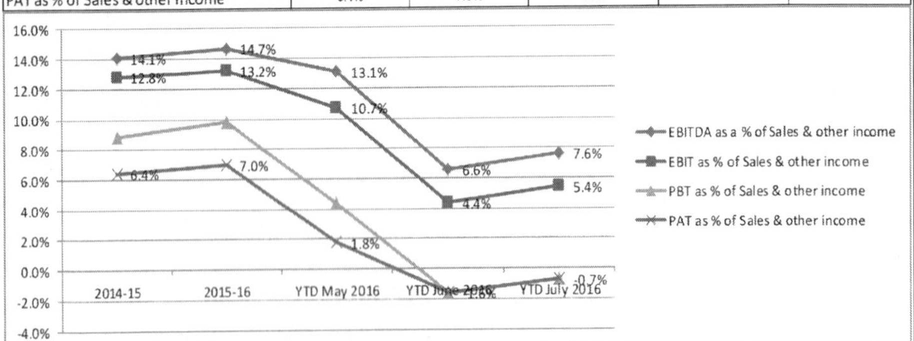


### Illustration 15.15: Revenue trend

| Year | 2014-15 | 2015-16 | YTD June 2016 | YTD July 2016 |
|---|---|---|---|---|
| Revenue | 13637 | 15264 | 2699 | 3577 |
| Break-even sales | 9508 | 10280 | 2859 | 3683 |

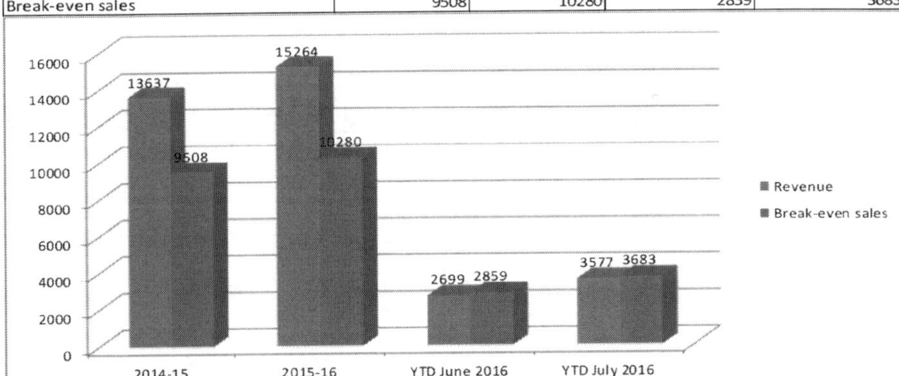

The above chart shows a trend analysis of Revenue and also break-even sales. The difference between actual sales and breakeven sales shows the margin of safety.

### Illustration 15.16: Expenditure trend

| Year | 2014-15 | 2015-16 | Apr-16 | May-16 | Jun-16 | Jul-16 |
|---|---|---|---|---|---|---|
| Raw material / traded products | 3981 | 4590 | 255 | 359 | 319 | 240 |
| Purchase of goods | 2227 | 1800 | 96 | 100 | 78 | 80 |
| Materials purchased for resale | 159 | 35 | 0 | 7 | 1 | 4 |
| Changes in inventory | -648 | -537 | 81 | -379 | 68 | -152 |
| Manufacturing and direct expenses | 4078 | 4870 | 236 | 352 | 368 | 385 |
| Employee benefit expenses | 583 | 723 | 75 | 79 | 78 | 90 |
| Other expenses | 1410 | 1581 | 91 | 127 | 134 | 142 |
| CSR Expenses | 12 | 17 | 0 | 0 | 5 | 1 |
| Depreciation | 171 | 226 | 20 | 20 | 20 | 20 |
| Finance charges | 551 | 518 | 57 | 51 | 54 | 60 |
| Total | 12522 | 13824 | 912 | 714 | 1124 | 871 |

The above table shows a trend analysis of elements of expenses.

### Illustration 15.17: Expenditure trend as a percentage of sales

| Year | 2014-15 | 2015-16 | Apr-16 | May-16 | Jun-16 | Jul-16 |
|---|---|---|---|---|---|---|
| Raw material / traded products | 29.0% | 29.9% | 31.3% | 40.4% | 31.7% | 27.1% |
| Purchase of goods | 16.2% | 11.7% | 11.8% | 11.2% | 7.8% | 9.0% |
| Materials purchased for resale | 1.2% | 0.2% | 0.0% | 0.8% | 0.1% | 0.4% |
| Changes in inventory | -4.7% | -3.5% | 10.0% | -42.7% | 6.8% | -17.1% |
| Manufacturing and direct expenses | 29.7% | 31.8% | 29.0% | 39.6% | 36.6% | 43.5% |
| Employee benefit expenses | 4.2% | 4.7% | 9.2% | 8.9% | 7.7% | 10.2% |
| Other expenses | 10.3% | 10.3% | 11.2% | 14.3% | 13.3% | 16.1% |
| CSR Expenses | 0.1% | 0.1% | 0.0% | 0.0% | 0.4% | 0.1% |
| Depreciation | 1.2% | 1.5% | 2.5% | 2.3% | 2.0% | 2.3% |
| Finance charges | 4.0% | 3.4% | 7.0% | 5.7% | 5.3% | 6.8% |
| Expenses as % of Revenue | 91.2% | 90.2% | 112.0% | 80.5% | 111.7% | 98.2% |

The above table shows a trend analysis of elements of expenses as a percentage of sales. The percentage will either go up or go down depending on whether the revenue goes up or goes down, or elements of expenses go up or down as well. It may also provide a broad understanding of the nature of expenses, whether variable or fixed. For instance, variable expenses percentage on sales will relatively remain constant with growth in Sales, whereas fixed expenses percentage will reduce with increase in sales.

### Illustration 15.18: EBITDA trend

The chart below shows EBITDA trend and movement from period to period, with and without stock difference. If the delta between the two ratios is significantly high then it will be clear that the EBITDA margin is reflecting more a stock related profit owing to difference in opening and closing stock rather than normal profit which generates as a surplus of revenue over expenses in general.

| Year | 2014-15 | 2015-16 | YTD May 2016 | YTD June 2016 | YTD July 2016 |
|---|---|---|---|---|---|
| Sales and other income | 13,733 | 15,330 | 1,702 | 2,708 | 3,595 |
| Expenses | 11,800 | 13,080 | 1,479 | 2,530 | 3,321 |
| Operating Profit ( EBIDTA) | 1,933 | 2,250 | 223 | 178 | 274 |
| EBITDA / Sales % | 14.1% | 14.7% | 13.1% | 6.6% | 7.6% |

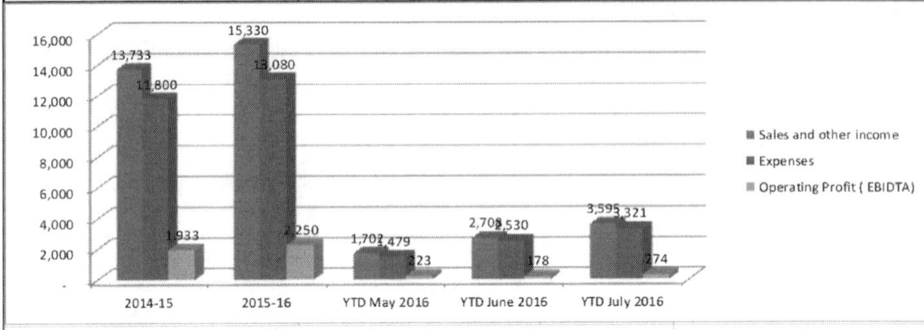


**EBITDA Trend w/o Stock Difference**

| Year | 2014-15 | 2015-16 | YTD May 2016 | YTD June 2016 | YTD July 2016 |
|---|---|---|---|---|---|
| Income | 13,733 | 15,330 | 1,702 | 2,708 | 3,595 |
| Expenses | 12,449 | 13,616 | 1,777 | 2,760 | 3,702 |
| Operating Profit ( EBIDTA) | 1,285 | 1,713 | -75 | -51 | -107 |
| EBITDA / Sales % | 9.4% | 11.2% | -4.4% | -1.9% | -3.0% |

## Illustration 15.19: Contribution analysis

| Year | 2014-15 | 2015-16 | YTD June 2016 | YTD July 2016 |
|---|---|---|---|---|
| Sales and other income | 13,733 | 15,330 | 2,708 | 3,595 |
| Total | 13,733 | 15,330 | 2,708 | 3,595 |
| Raw material / traded products | 3,981 | 4,590 | 933 | 1,173 |
| Purchase of carpets | 2,227 | 1,800 | 274 | 354 |
| Materials purchased for resale | 159 | 35 | 8 | 12 |
| Manufacturing and direct expenses | 4,078 | 4,870 | 956 | 1,342 |
| Changes in inventory | -648 | -537 | -230 | -381 |
| Variable cost total | 9,796 | 10,759 | 1,942 | 2,499 |
| Contribution | 3,937 | 4,571 | 767 | 1,096 |
| Contribution / revenue % | 28.7% | 29.8% | 28.3% | 30.5% |
| Employee benefit expenses | 583 | 723 | 231 | 322 |
| Other expenses | 1,410 | 1,581 | 352 | 495 |
| CSR Expenses | 12 | 17 | 5 | 6 |
| Depreciation | 171 | 226 | 60 | 80 |
| Finance charges | 551 | 518 | 161 | 221 |
| Fixed cost total | 2,726 | 3,065 | 809 | 1,123 |
| Fixed Expenses as % of revenue | 19.8% | 20.0% | 29.9% | 31.2% |
| PBT | 1,211 | 1,506 | -43 | -27 |
| PBT as % of revenue | 8.8% | 9.8% | -1.6% | -0.7% |
| Break even sales | 9,508 | 10,280 | 2,859 | 3,683 |

Contribution analysis is a very important chart which depicts the contribution margin, the fixed expenses as percentage of sales and breakeven sales which is worked out as Fixed expenses total divided by contribution margin. This chart clearly explains the Profit and loss position, especially whether,

(a) variable expenses are growing more than the revenue thereby showing deteriorating contribution margin,

(b) whether fixed expenses as a percentage of revenue is increasing significantly,

(c) whether revenue growth is adequate to ensure recovery of fixed expenses and leave enough margin of safety to hedge against uncertainties in future revenue generation.

## 15.17.3 Solvency analysis

### Illustration 15.20: Source and application of funds

**Capital Employed - Source** — Rs lakhs

| Year | 2013-14 | 2014-15 | 2015-16 | YTD Jun 2016 | YTD July 2016 |
|---|---|---|---|---|---|
| Shareholders funds | 2930 | 3806 | 4876 | 4833 | 4849 |
| Long term borrowings | 212 | 94 | 173 | 159 | 159 |
| Deferred tax Liabilities | 0 | 5 | 40 | 40 | 40 |
| Other long term liabilities | 57 | 57 | 10 | 10 | 10 |
| Long term provisions | 21 | 29 | 38 | 38 | 38 |
| Short term borrowings | 3513 | 4231 | 6086 | 6331 | 6332 |
| Capital employed | 6733 | 8222 | 11222 | 11411 | 11427 |

**Capital Employed - Application** — Rs lakhs

| Year | 2013-14 | 2014-15 | 2015-16 | YTD Jun 2016 | YTD July 2016 |
|---|---|---|---|---|---|
| Net tangible assets | 1,036 | 1,347 | 3,291 | 3,329 | 3,381 |
| Intangible assets | 42 | 28 | 9 | 10 | 10 |
| Capital work-in-progress | 25 | 625 | 190 | 255 | 364 |
| Deferred tax assets | 1 | 0 | 0 | 0 | 0 |
| Non-current investments | 86 | 91 | 81 | 81 | 81 |
| Long term loans and advance | 32 | 93 | 41 | 136 | 71 |
| Net current assets | 5,511 | 6,037 | 7,610 | 7,600 | 7,520 |
| Capital employed | 6,733 | 8,222 | 11,222 | 11,411 | 11,427 |

### Illustration 15.21: Debt equity ratio

| Year | 2011-12 | 2012-13 | 2013-14 | 2014-15 | 2015-16 | YTD June 2016 | YTD June 2016 |
|---|---|---|---|---|---|---|---|
| Debt equity ratio | 0.11 | 0.13 | 0.07 | 0.02 | 0.04 | 0.03 | 0.03 |
| Debt Equity Ratio (including short term) | 1.72 | 1.79 | 1.27 | 1.14 | 1.28 | 1.34 | 1.34 |

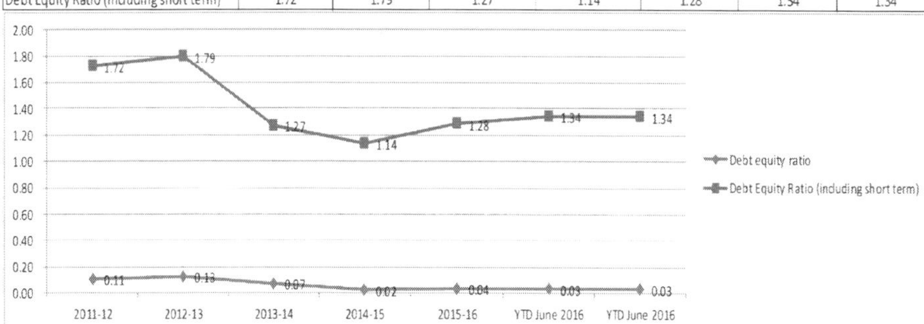

**Illustration 15.22: Financial cost trend**

| Year | 2013-14 | 2014-15 | 2015-16 | YTD July 2016 |
|---|---|---|---|---|
| Interest cost | 384 | 551 | 518 | 221 |
| Interest cost as % of revenue | 3.2% | 4.0% | 3.4% | 6.2% |
| Interest coverage ratio | 3.26 | 3.20 | 3.91 | 0.88 |

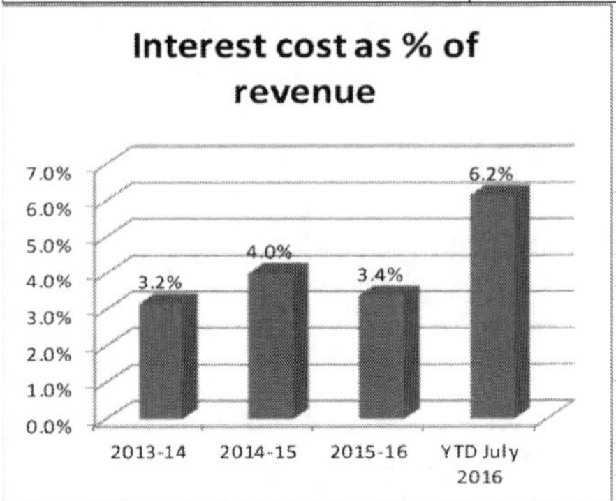


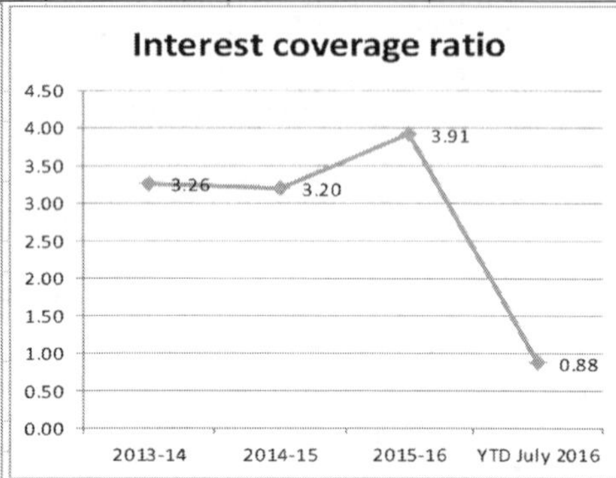


The above charts give a reasonable understanding of the solvency position of the organization, the extent debt in the capital structure as will be evident through the debt equity ratio and increasing component of interest.

## 15.17.4 Liquidity analysis

**Illustration 15.23: Working capital jaw**

| Year | 2013-14 | 2014-15 | 2015-16 | YTD Jun 2015 | YTD July 2015 |
|---|---|---|---|---|---|
| Gross current assets | 7,785 | 9,126 | 10,920 | 10,985 | 11,101 |
| Current liabilities & provisions | 2,274 | 3,089 | 3,310 | 3,385 | 3,582 |
| Working capital | 5,511 | 6,037 | 7,610 | 7,600 | 7,520 |

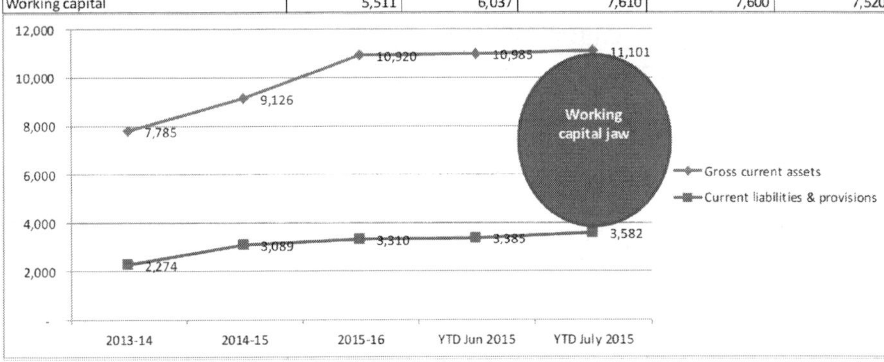

## Illustration 15.24: Current Assets trend

| Year | 2013-14 | 2014-15 | 2015-16 | YTD June 2016 | YTD July 2016 |
|---|---|---|---|---|---|
| Current Investments | 88 | 70 | 115 | 115 | 115 |
| Inventories | 2,814 | 4,761 | 5,544 | 5,793 | 5,897 |
| Sundry debtors | 3,461 | 3,088 | 4,214 | 3,868 | 3,893 |
| Cash & bank balances | 65 | 54 | 35 | 53 | 40 |
| Loans & Advances | 1,357 | 1,153 | 1,013 | 1,156 | 1,157 |
| **Gross current assets** | **7,785** | **9,126** | **10,920** | **10,985** | **11,101** |

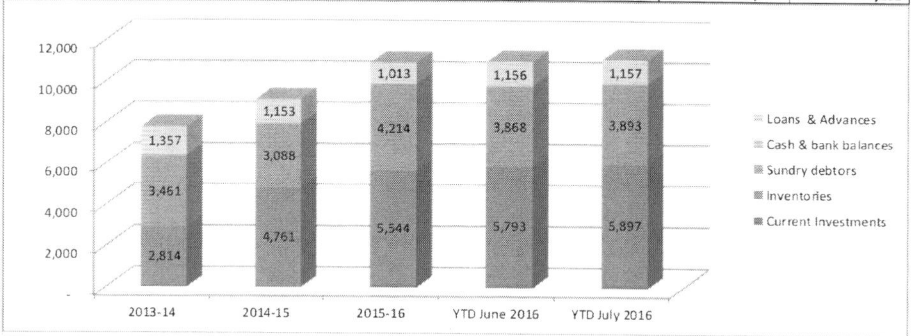


## Illustration 15.25: Current Liabilities trend

| Year | 2013-14 | 2014-15 | 2015-16 | YTD June 2016 | YTD July 2016 |
|---|---|---|---|---|---|
| Trade payable | 1,714 | 2,527 | 2,558 | 2,749 | 2,907 |
| Other current liabilities | 534 | 556 | 746 | 629 | 668 |
| Provisions | 26 | 6 | 6 | 6 | 6 |
| **Current Liabilities** | **2,274** | **3,089** | **3,310** | **3,385** | **3,582** |

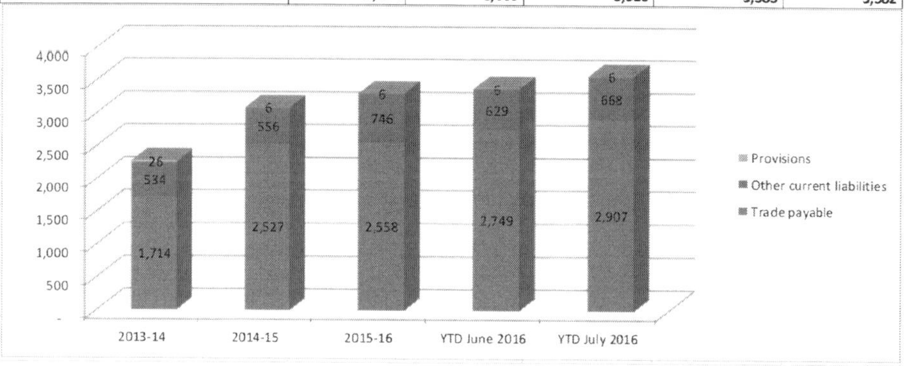

## Illustration 15.26: Current Ratio

| Year | 2013-14 | 2014-15 | 2015-16 | YTD Jun 2016 | YTD July 2016 |
|---|---|---|---|---|---|
| Current ratio | 3.4 | 3.0 | 3.3 | 3.2 | 3.1 |
| Liquid ratio | 2.2 | 1.4 | 1.3 | 1.5 | 1.5 |

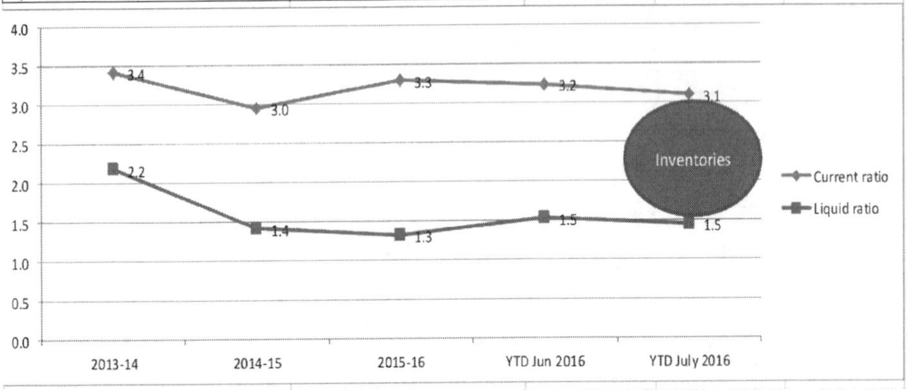


## Illustration 15.27: Inventory trend

| Year | 2013-14 | 2014-15 | 2015-16 | YTD June 2016 | YTD July 2016 |
|---|---|---|---|---|---|
| Raw material and components | 1909 | 3208 | 3454 | 3473 | 3425 |
| Work-in-progress | 298 | 367 | 606 | 816 | 905 |
| Finished goods - traded goods | 141 | 220 | 273 | 351 | 345 |
| Finished goods | 466 | 966 | 1211 | 1153 | 1222 |
| Total inventories | 2814 | 4761 | 5544 | 5793 | 5897 |

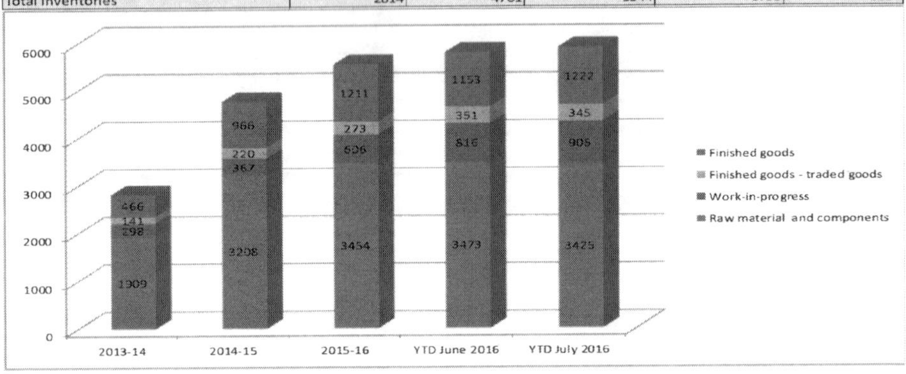

### Illustration 15.28: Days Sales Outstanding (DSO)

| Year | 2013-14 | 2014-15 | 2015-16 | YTD June 2016 | YTD July 2016 |
|---|---|---|---|---|---|
| Days Sales Outstanding (DSO) | 104.06 | 82.06 | 100.33 | 128.52 | 129.93 |

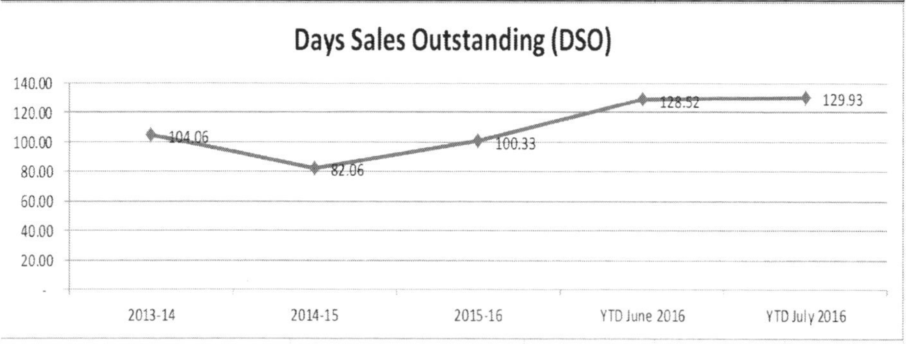


### Illustration 15.29: Inventories Days Sales (IDS)

| Year | 2013-14 | 2014-15 | 2015-16 | YTD June 2016 | YTD July 2016 |
|---|---|---|---|---|---|
| Total inventory | 114.76 | 177.38 | 188.07 | 268.53 | 283.14 |
| Raw material and components | 195.38 | 294.11 | 274.61 | 335.21 | 350.52 |
| Work-in-progress | 20.58 | 23.43 | 37.56 | 74.52 | 93.81 |
| Finished goods - traded goods | 33.06 | 36.10 | 55.40 | 114.99 | 116.84 |
| Finished goods | 32.35 | 36.00 | 41.08 | 53.47 | 58.68 |

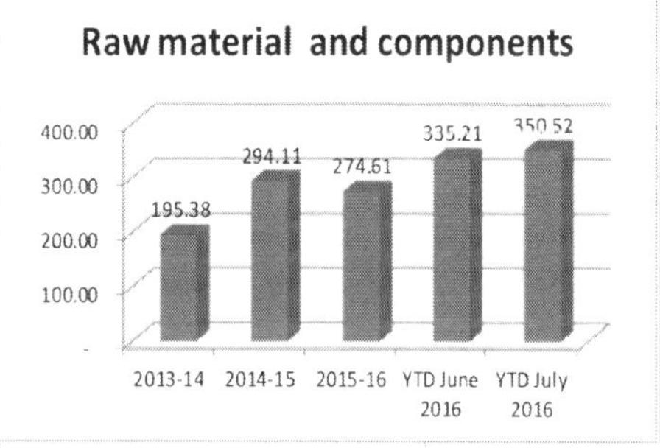


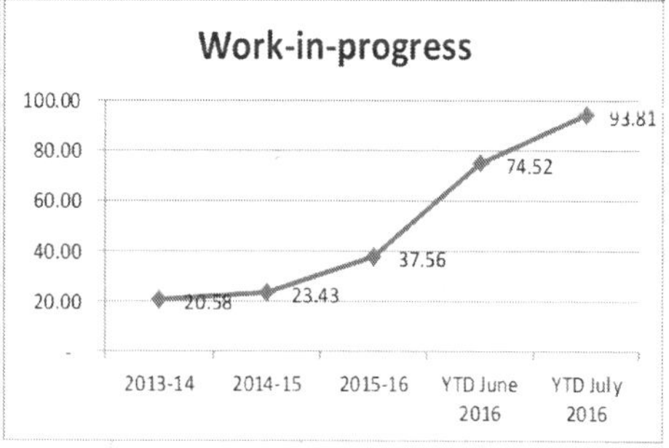

## Illustration 15.30: Creditors Days Outstanding (CDO)

| Year | 2013-14 | 2014-15 | 2015-16 | YTD June 2016 | YTD July 2016 |
|---|---|---|---|---|---|
| Creditors days outstanding | 77.06 | 95.53 | 92.37 | 120.41 | 129.42 |

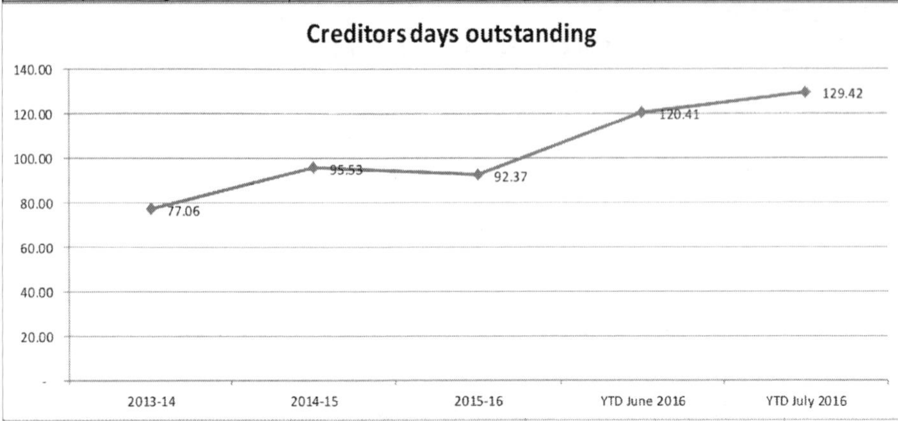


The above trend analysis provides a clear understanding of the condition of working capital and highlight the following areas:

**(a)** Whether the inventory levels are increasing and the working capital jaw is widening,

**(b)** Whether trade receivables and inventories as number of days sales and cost of goods sold respectively are increasing to show the working capital being blocked up in these elements, leading to incremental short term borrowing and high incremental interest cost.

**(c)** The difference between current ratio and liquid ratio provides us a broad understanding of the condition of inventories and whether all the inventories are current and serviceable and whether incidence of obsolete or unserviceable inventories are effectively controlled.

## Illustration 15.31: Cash flow summary

The cash flow summary below, shows an effective way to depict what are the total available funds and how these are being utilized in the operations of the business.

| Year | 2013-14 | 2014-15 | 2015-16 | YTD July 2016 |
|---|---|---|---|---|
| **Sources of Funds** | | | | |
| **Increase in Shareholders funds** | 341.72 | 875.86 | 1,070.04 | -26.86 |
| Long term borrowings | 78.17 | -118.15 | 79.00 | -14.60 |
| Deferred tax Liabilities | - | 4.90 | 34.82 | -0.00 |
| Other long term liabilities | 57.49 | - | -47.98 | -0.00 |
| Long term provisions | 9.16 | 8.12 | 9.67 | - |
| Short term borrowings | 673.39 | 718.20 | 1,854.44 | 246.62 |
| Opening Balance - Cash in hand | 93.72 | 65.41 | 54.26 | 34.64 |
| **Total Available Funds** | 1,253.65 | 1,554.35 | 3,054.27 | 239.80 |
| **Utilization of Funds** | | | | |
| Net fixed assets | -38.08 | 311.35 | 1,943.54 | 90.33 |
| Intangible assets | -8.34 | -13.62 | -19.39 | 0.94 |
| Capital work-in-progress | 53.25 | 600.37 | -435.34 | 174.23 |
| Deferred tax assets | -0.82 | -1.19 | - | - |
| Non-current investments | 5.72 | 4.50 | -9.55 | - |
| Long term loans and advances | -2.87 | 60.77 | -52.22 | 30.49 |
| Current investments | 1.50 | -17.54 | 45.00 | - |
| Inventories | 265.82 | 1,946.92 | 782.87 | 352.77 |
| Debtors | 1,205.39 | -373.75 | 1,126.01 | -320.85 |
| Other current assets Loans & Advances | 622.51 | -203.54 | -139.80 | 143.63 |
| Current assets | 2,095.22 | 1,352.09 | 1,814.08 | 175.55 |
| Trade payables | 995.49 | 812.82 | 30.82 | 349.73 |
| Other current liabilities | -55.16 | 21.54 | 190.26 | -78.04 |
| Provisions | -45.92 | -20.19 | 0.43 | - |
| Current liabilities & provisions | 894.41 | 814.17 | 221.51 | 271.68 |
| Net current assets | 1,200.81 | 537.93 | 1,592.56 | -96.13 |
| **Total Utilization of Funds** | 1,209.67 | 1,500.09 | 3,019.62 | 199.86 |
| | | | | |
| **Closing cash balance** | 43.98 | 54.25 | 34.65 | 39.94 |
| | | | | |
| **Reconcilition of cash surplus / deficit** | | | | |
| Opening balance | 93.72 | 65.41 | 54.26 | 34.64 |
| Closing balance | 43.98 | 54.26 | 34.64 | 39.94 |
| **(Surplus) / deficit** | 49.74 | 11.14 | 19.62 | -5.30 |

## 15.17.5 Return on Investment

### Illustration 15.32: Return on capital employed and capital turnover ratio

| Year | 2011-12 | 2012-13 | 2013-14 | 2014-15 | 2015-16 | YTD July 2016 |
|---|---|---|---|---|---|---|
| EBIT / Sales % | 9.3% | 8.7% | 10.3% | 12.8% | 13.2% | 5.4% |
| Capital turnover ratio | 1.50 | 1.56 | 1.80 | 1.67 | 1.37 | 0.94 |
| Return on capital employed % | 13.9% | 13.5% | 18.6% | 21.4% | 18.0% | 5.1% |

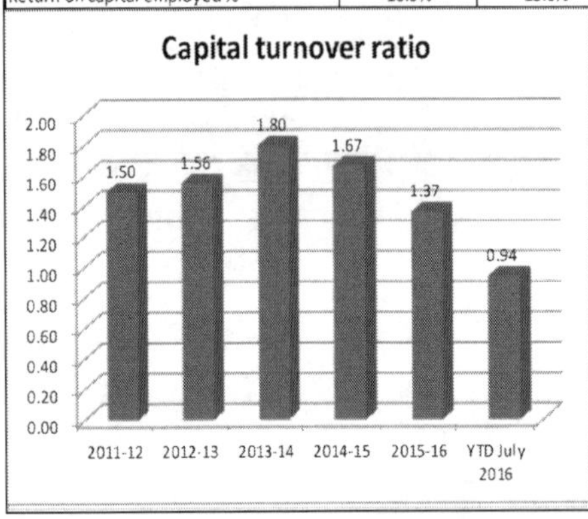


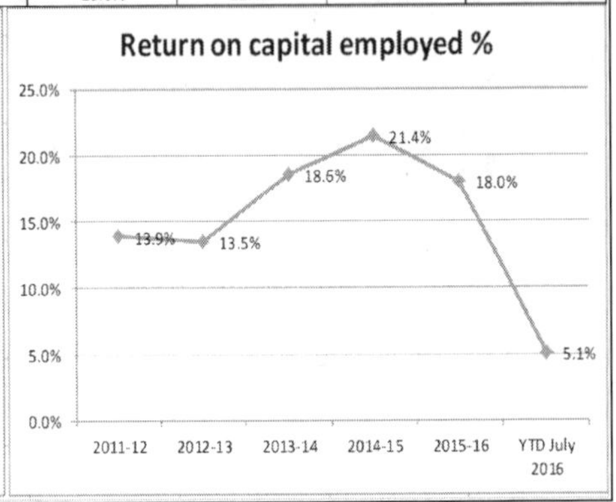


### Illustration 15.33: Shareholders Return

| Year | 2011-12 | 2012-13 | 2013-14 | 2014-15 | 2015-16 | YTD July 2016 |
|---|---|---|---|---|---|---|
| Return on net worth % | 15.0% | 14.9% | 21.6% | 23.2% | 22.0% | -1.7% |

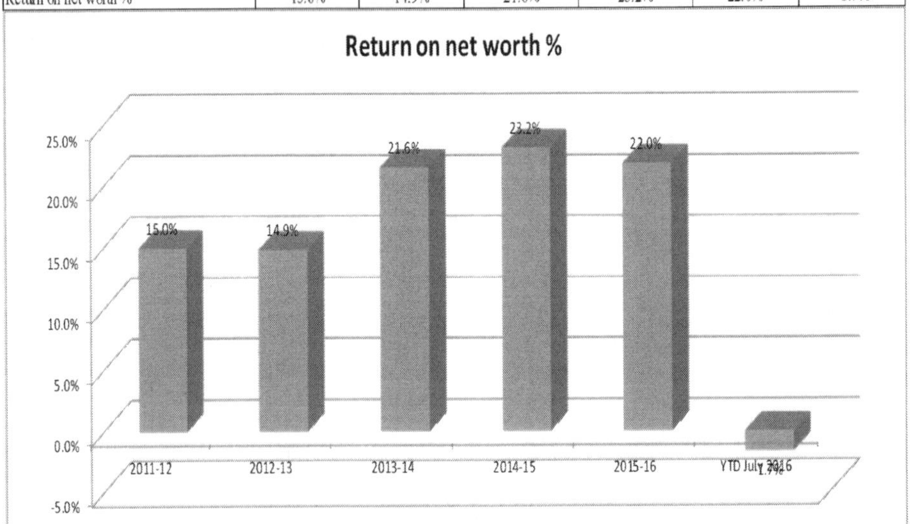


These are two very important charts which shows whether the organization has adequate return on capital employed, and whether the capital employed both non-current and current are effectively utilized and rotated to generate enough revenue and there is no ideal capacity in the system. Hence if the capital turnover ratio increases it would show better utilization of existing resources, and if is the other way round, it would show that existing resources are not being effectively utilized to generate adequate revenue.

The results of the above will have a direct impact on the Shareholder returns as eventually the efficient running of the organization will result in increase in Shareholder returns.

**Conclusion**

The analysis derived out of the data extracted from the Financial Statements help us to understand the basic strengths of the organization. At the same time it helps us understand the basis problems we have in the system which need to be addressed by the promoters of the organization and the leadership engaged by them to run the operations of the business.

We have used these parameters in reviewing some of the case studies which are analyzed in the next chapter.

# *Chapter 16*

# Case Studies

## 16.1 CALCULATION OF FINANCIAL RATIOS

Financial performance summary of Company A is provided as under: (INR lakhs)

| Sr. No. | Subject | 2012-13 | 2011-12 | 2010-11 | 2009-10 | 2008-09 |
|---|---|---|---|---|---|---|
| 1 | Share Capital | 39.90 | 39.90 | 39.90 | 39.90 | 39.90 |
| 2 | Reserves | 317.98 | 306.91 | 296.31 | 291.72 | 258.09 |
| 3 | Accumulated losses if any | - | - | - | - | - |
| 4 | Net Worth | 357.88 | 346.81 | 336.21 | 331.62 | 297.99 |
| 5 | Term Loans | 240.15 | 12.19 | 26.87 | 44.24 | 34.36 |
| 6 | Deferred Payment Liabilities | - | - | - | - | - |
| 7 | Working Capital Borrowings | - | - | - | - | 6.08 |
| 8 | Capital employed | 598.03 | 359.00 | 363.08 | 375.86 | 338.43 |
| 9 | Gross Block | 179.26 | 193.68 | 121.49 | 76.89 | 72.01 |
| 10 | Depreciation | 15.96 | 27.42 | 27.50 | 13.63 | 15.36 |
| 11 | Net Block | 163.30 | 166.26 | 93.99 | 63.26 | 56.65 |
| 12 | Investments | 434.47 | 354.47 | 254.47 | 208.47 | 63.22 |
| 13 | Other non-current assets | - | - | - | - | - |
| 14 | Current Assets | 1,289.31 | 364.88 | 887.49 | 776.19 | 946.33 |
| 15 | Current Liability ( Inc W.C Loan) | 1,289.05 | 526.61 | 872.86 | 672.06 | 727.77 |
| 16 | Net working capital | 0.26 | -161.73 | 14.63 | 104.13 | 218.56 |
| 17 | Capital employed | 598.03 | 359.00 | 363.09 | 375.86 | 338.43 |
| 18 | Income | 1,447.44 | 1,430.89 | 1,327.38 | 1,396.46 | 1,208.75 |
| 19 | Expenses | 1,416.45 | 1,388.22 | 1,276.87 | 1,346.02 | 868.80 |
| 20 | Operating Profit ( EBIDTA) | 30.99 | 42.67 | 50.51 | 50.44 | 339.95 |
| 21 | Depreciation | 15.96 | 27.42 | 27.51 | 13.63 | 15.35 |
| 22 | EBIT | 15.03 | 15.25 | 23.00 | 36.81 | 324.60 |
| 23 | Tax | 4.62 | 4.69 | 7.11 | - | 118.64 |
| 24 | Net Profit (PAT) | 10.41 | 10.56 | 15.89 | 36.81 | 205.96 |

Please calculate the following financial ratios and carry out an interpretation of the same:

(a) Debt equity ratio

(b) Current ratio

(c) EBITDA as a % of sales

(d) PAT as a % of sales

(e) Capital turnover ratio

(f) Return on capital employed

(g) Return on Equity

**Solution**

Based on the financial summary provided in the question the financial ratios have been worked out which is enumerated in the table as under:

**Financial Performance Summary**

**INR Lakhs**

| SR.NO. | SUBJECT | 2012-13 | 2011-12 | 2010-11 | 2009-10 | 2008-09 |
|---|---|---|---|---|---|---|
| | | | | | | |
| 1 | Capital | 39.90 | 39.90 | 39.90 | 39.90 | 39.90 |
| 2 | Reserves | 317.98 | 306.91 | 296.31 | 291.72 | 258.09 |
| 3 | Accumulated losses if any | - | - | - | - | - |
| 4 | Net Worth | 357.88 | 346.81 | 336.21 | 331.62 | 297.99 |
| 5 | Term Loans | 240.15 | 12.19 | 26.87 | 44.24 | 34.36 |
| 6 | Deferred Payment Liabilities | - | - | - | - | - |
| 7 | Working Capital Borrowings | - | - | - | - | 6.08 |
| 8 | Capital employed | 598.03 | 359.00 | 363.08 | 375.86 | 338.43 |
| 9 | Gross Block | 179.26 | 193.68 | 121.49 | 76.89 | 72.01 |
| 10 | Depreciation | 15.96 | 27.42 | 27.50 | 13.63 | 15.36 |
| 11 | Net Block | 163.30 | 166.26 | 93.99 | 63.26 | 56.65 |
| 12 | Investments | 434.47 | 354.47 | 254.47 | 208.47 | 63.22 |
| 13 | Other non-current assets | - | - | - | - | - |
| 14 | Cutrrent Assets | 1,289.31 | 364.88 | 887.49 | 776.19 | 946.33 |
| 15 | Current Liability ( Inc W.C Loan) | 1,289.05 | 526.61 | 872.86 | 672.06 | 727.77 |
| 16 | Net working capital | 0.26 | -161.73 | 14.63 | 104.13 | 218.56 |
| 17 | Capital employed | 598.03 | 359.00 | 363.09 | 375.86 | 338.43 |
| 18 | Debt equity ratio | 0.67 | 0.04 | 0.08 | 0.13 | 0.12 |
| 19 | Current Ratio | 1.00 | 0.69 | 1.02 | 1.15 | 1.30 |
| 20 | Income | 1,447.44 | 1,430.89 | 1,327.38 | 1,396.46 | 1,208.75 |
| 21 | Expenses | 1,416.45 | 1,388.22 | 1,276.87 | 1,346.02 | 868.80 |
| 22 | Operating Profit ( PBIDT) | 30.99 | 42.67 | 50.51 | 50.44 | 339.95 |
| 23 | EBITDA / Sales % | 2.1% | 3.0% | 3.8% | 3.6% | 28.1% |
| 24 | Depreciation | 15.96 | 27.42 | 27.51 | 13.63 | 15.35 |
| 25 | EBIT | 15.03 | 15.25 | 23.00 | 36.81 | 324.60 |
| 26 | Tax | 4.62 | 4.69 | 7.11 | - | 118.64 |
| 27 | Net Profit (PAT) | 10.41 | 10.56 | 15.89 | 36.81 | 205.96 |
| 28 | Net Profit /Sales % | 0.7% | 0.7% | 1.2% | 2.6% | 17.0% |
| 29 | Cash Accrual (NP+ DEP) | 26.37 | 37.98 | 43.40 | 50.44 | 221.31 |
| 30 | Capital turnover ratio | 2.42 | 3.99 | 3.66 | 3.72 | 3.57 |
| 31 | Return on capital employed % | 2.5% | 4.2% | 6.3% | 9.8% | 95.9% |
| 32 | Return on net worth % | 4.2% | 4.4% | 6.8% | 11.1% | 108.9% |

The financial analysis is highlighted in the form of charts and interpretations have been provided below each of these charts in the form of a comments under the following categories:

- Source of funds
- Application of funds
- Income Trend
- Expenditure Trend
- EBITDA Trend
- Net Cash Accrual
- Shareholder's return

**Source of funds**

**Balance Sheet summary**

| SUBJECT | 2012-13 | 2011-12 | 2010-11 | 2009-10 | 2008-09 |
|---|---|---|---|---|---|
| | | | | | |
| Capital | 39.90 | 39.90 | 39.90 | 39.90 | 39.90 |
| Reserves | 317.98 | 306.91 | 296.31 | 291.72 | 258.09 |
| Accumulated losses if any | - | - | - | - | - |
| Net Worth | 357.88 | 346.81 | 336.21 | 331.62 | 297.99 |
| Term Loans | 240.15 | 12.19 | 26.87 | 44.24 | 34.36 |
| Deferred Payment Liabilities | - | - | - | - | - |
| Working Capital Borrowings | - | - | - | - | 6.08 |
| Capital employed | 598.03 | 359.00 | 363.08 | 375.86 | 338.43 |
| | | | | | |
| Debt equity ratio | 0.67 | 0.04 | 0.08 | 0.13 | 0.12 |

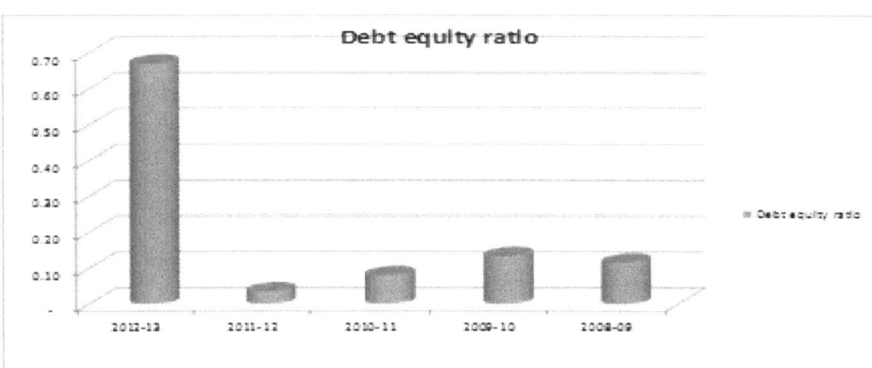


The chart shows that company A had minimal debt till 2011-12. Thereafter in 2012-13 the term loan has gone up showing a skewed debt equity ratio (percentage of debt to equity). This indicates that the company is slowly going ahead and depending on debt. May be its internal cash generation is not as good as it was earlier.

The trend related to application of funds in the table related to Application of funds will help understand the situation better.

**Application of funds**

## Balance Sheet summary

| SUBJECT | 2012-13 | 2011-12 | 2010-11 | 2009-10 | 2008-09 |
|---|---|---|---|---|---|
| Net Block | 163.30 | 166.26 | 93.99 | 63.26 | 56.65 |
| Investments | 434.47 | 354.47 | 254.47 | 208.47 | 63.22 |
| Other non-current assets | - | - | - | - | - |
| Current Assets | 1,289.31 | 364.88 | 887.49 | 776.19 | 946.33 |
| Current Liability ( Inc W.C Loan) | 1,289.05 | 526.61 | 872.86 | 672.06 | 727.77 |
| Net working capital | 0.26 | -161.73 | 14.63 | 104.13 | 218.56 |
| Capital employed | 598.03 | 359.00 | 363.09 | 375.86 | 338.43 |

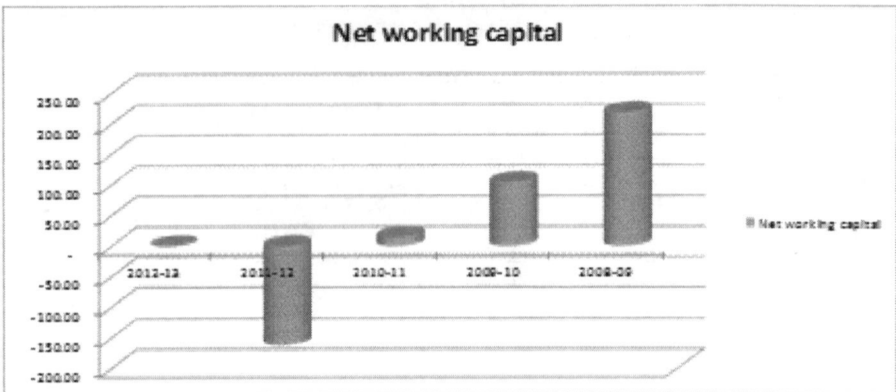


As expected, the situation shows that net working capital has become negative in 2011-12, which shows that the company is going through acute shortage of working capital. Though the situation has slightly revived in 2012-13, still it is quite alarming that the company is running short of liquidity.

## Income trend

### Income Trend

| Year | 2012-13 | 2011-12 | 2010-11 | 2009-10 | 2008-09 |
|---|---|---|---|---|---|
| Income | 1,447.44 | 1,430.89 | 1,327.38 | 1,396.46 | 1,208.75 |

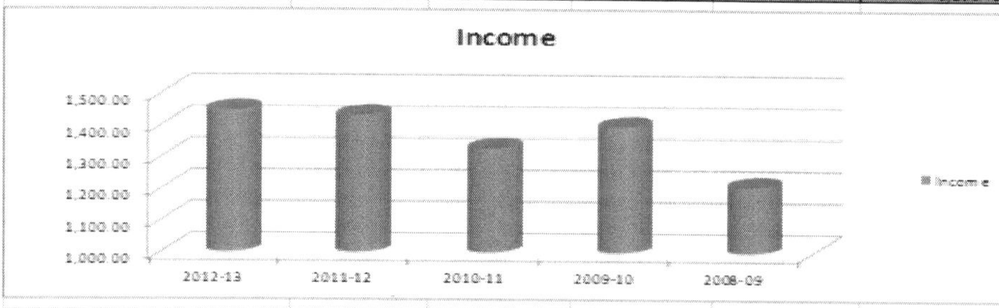


The income trend according to table above shows an upward trend though there has been a dip in 2010-11.

## EBITDA trend

### EBITDA Trend

Rs lakhs

| Year | 2012-13 | 2011-12 | 2010-11 | 2009-10 | 2008-09 |
|---|---|---|---|---|---|
| Income | 1,447.44 | 1,430.89 | 1,327.38 | 1,396.46 | 1,208.75 |
| Expenses | 1,416.45 | 1,388.22 | 1,276.87 | 1,346.02 | 868.80 |
| Operating Profit ( PBIDT) | 30.99 | 42.67 | 50.51 | 50.44 | 339.95 |
| EBITDA / Sales % | 2.1% | 3.0% | 3.8% | 3.6% | 28.1% |

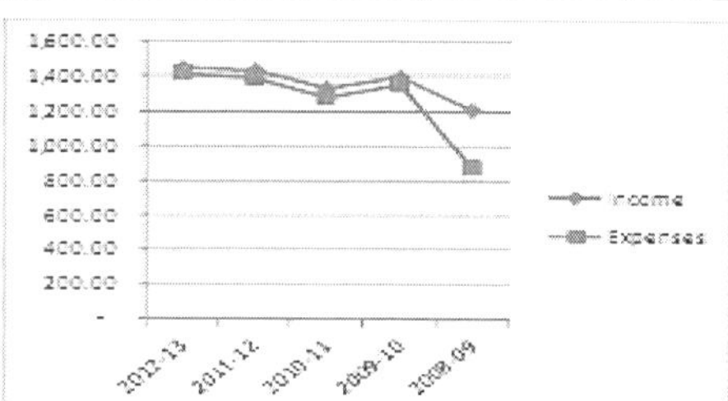


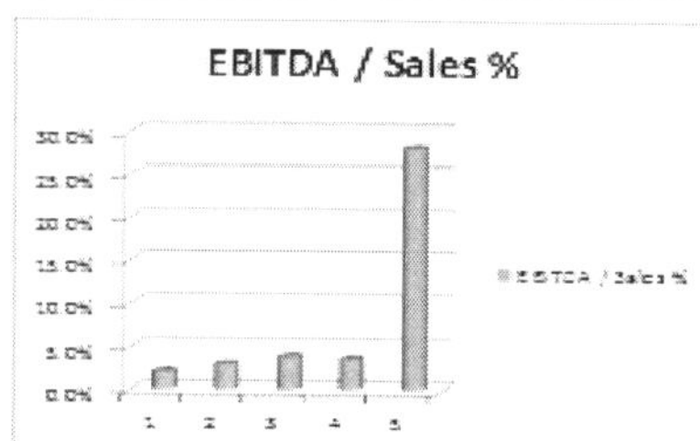


Table above states that, owing to increase in expenditure trend more than revenue trend the EBITDA level has started to drop significantly reflecting eroding profitability.

## Expenditure trend

**Expenditure trend**

| Year | 2012-13 | 2011-12 | 2010-11 | 2009-10 | 2008-09 |
|---|---|---|---|---|---|
| Employee benefit expenses | 610.86 | 531.38 | 414.02 | 418.35 | 254.9 |
| Finance costs | 11.27 | 22.59 | 11.13 | 11.13 | 6.95 |
| Other expenses | 794.32 | 834.19 | 851.67 | 916.48 | 606.88 |
| Total | 1416.45 | 1388.16 | 1276.82 | 1345.96 | 868.73 |
| Expenses as % of Income | 98% | 97% | 96% | 96% | 72% |

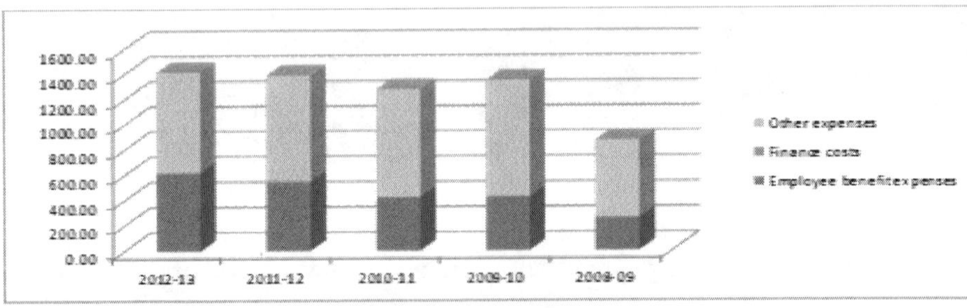


Table above corroborates the fact that expenditure especially other expenses and employee benefit expenses have significantly increased.

The above tables show that the profitability of Company A has reduced significantly leading to huge cash crunch.

## Net cash accrual

| Year | 2012-13 | 2011-12 | 2010-11 | 2009-10 | 2008-09 |
|---|---|---|---|---|---|
| Cash Accrual (NP+ DEP) | 26.37 | 37.98 | 43.40 | 50.44 | 221.31 |

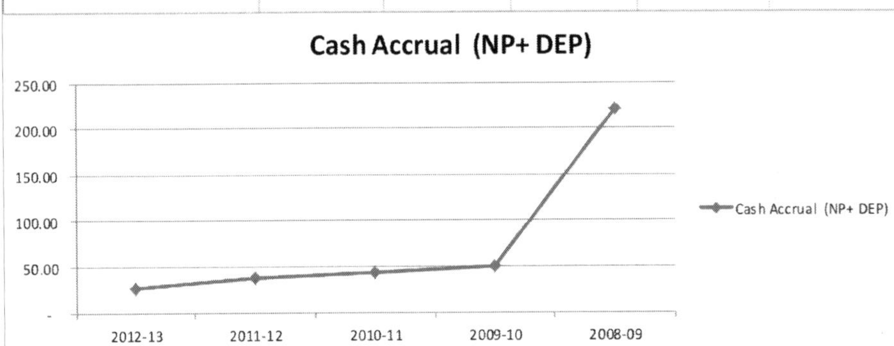


The table above shows net cash accrual, which is the sum of Profit after tax plus depreciation, going down regularly resulting in the cash crunch. The net cash accrual position confirms the cash crunch as depicted by declining working capital trend highlighted in table 2 above.

### Shareholder's return

| Year | 2012-13 | 2011-12 | 2010-11 | 2009-10 | 2008-09 |
|---|---|---|---|---|---|
| Return on capital employed % | 2.5% | 4.2% | 6.3% | 9.8% | 95.9% |
| Return on net worth % | 2.9% | 3.0% | 4.7% | 11.1% | 69.1% |

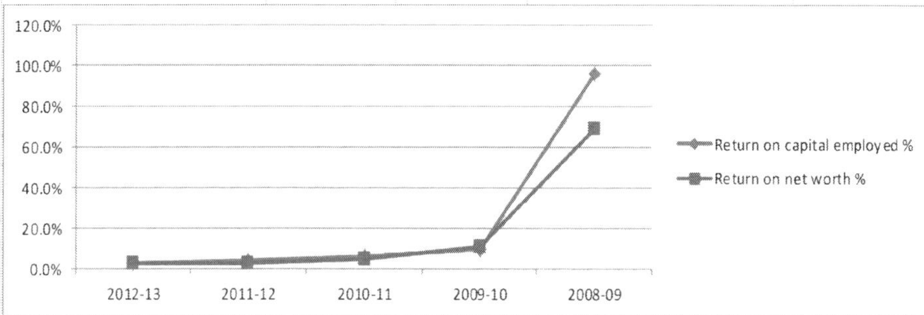


At the same time Return on capital employed (EBIT/Capital Employed %) has been dropping from 2008-09 onwards till 2012-13, which reveals that along with liquidity crunch, profitability has also eroded over the years.

The organization has to have a fresh look at its business model and the business and financial plan to try and fix the bottleneck if it has to successfully turn around the business.

## 16.2 CALCULATION OF FINANCIAL RATIOS

Comparative financial results of ABC Ltd are shown as under:

**Comparative Balance Sheet *(INR lakhs)***

| Sr. No. | Particulars | 2012-13 | 2011-12 | 2010-11 | 2009-10 | 2008-09 |
|---|---|---|---|---|---|---|
| 1 | Capital | 539.90 | 539.90 | 539.90 | 539.90 | 539.90 |
| 2 | Reserves | 304.44 | 306.91 | 296.31 | 291.72 | 258.09 |
| 3 | Accumulated losses if any | - | - | - | - | - |
| 4 | Net Worth | 844.34 | 846.81 | 836.21 | 831.62 | 797.99 |
| 5 | Term Loans | 640.15 | 512.19 | 226.87 | 144.24 | 34.36 |
| 6 | Deferred Payment Liabilities | - | - | - | - | - |
| 7 | Working Capital Borrowings | - | - | - | - | 6.08 |
| 8 | Capital employed | 1,484.49 | 1,359.00 | 1,063.08 | 975.86 | 838.43 |
| 9 | Gross Block | 679.26 | 693.68 | 621.49 | 576.89 | 572.01 |
| 10 | Depreciation | 29.50 | 27.42 | 27.50 | 13.63 | 15.36 |

| Sr. No. | Particulars | 2012-13 | 2011-12 | 2010-11 | 2009-10 | 2008-09 |
|---|---|---|---|---|---|---|
| 11 | Net Block | 649.76 | 666.26 | 593.99 | 563.26 | 556.65 |
| 12 | Investments | 434.47 | 354.47 | 254.47 | 208.47 | 63.22 |
| 13 | Other non-current assets | - | - | - | - | - |
| 14 | Current Assets | 1,689.31 | 864.88 | 887.49 | 876.19 | 946.33 |
| 15 | Current Liability ( Inc W.C Loan) | 1,289.05 | 526.61 | 672.87 | 672.06 | 727.77 |
| 16 | Net working capital | 400.26 | 338.27 | 214.62 | 204.13 | 218.56 |
| 17 | Capital employed | 1,484.49 | 1,359.00 | 1,063.08 | 975.86 | 838.43 |

**Comparative Statement of Profit & Loss *(INR Lakhs)***

| Sr. No. | Particulars | 2012-13 | 2011-12 | 2010-11 | 2009-10 | 2008-09 |
|---|---|---|---|---|---|---|
| 1 | Income | 6,447.44 | 4,830.89 | 4,327.38 | 3,396.46 | 2,408.75 |
| 2 | Employee benefit expenses | 2610.86 | 2531.38 | 2414.02 | 2418.35 | 1654.9 |
| 3 | Finance costs | 111.27 | 122.59 | 111.13 | 111.13 | 106.95 |
| 4 | Other expenses | 2994.32 | 1634.25 | 1351.72 | 516.54 | 401.90 |
| 5 | Expenses | 5,716.45 | 4,288.22 | 3,876.87 | 3,046.02 | 2,163.75 |
| 6 | Operating Profit (EBIDTA) | 730.99 | 542.67 | 450.51 | 350.44 | 245.00 |
| 7 | Depreciation | 15.96 | 27.42 | 27.51 | 13.63 | 15.35 |
| 8 | EBIT | 715.03 | 515.25 | 423.00 | 336.81 | 229.65 |
| 9 | Tax | 235.96 | 170.03 | 139.59 | 111.15 | 75.78 |
| 10 | Net Profit (PAT) | 479.07 | 345.22 | 283.41 | 225.66 | 153.87 |

Please calculate the following ratios and provide your analysis of the same:

(a) Profitability ratios

(b) Expense ratios

(c) Liquidity ratios

(d) Turnover ratios

(e) Solvency ratios

(f) Return on investment

## Solution

### (a) Profitability ratios

| Sr. No. | Particulars | 2012-13 | 2011-12 | 2010-11 | 2009-10 | 2008-09 |
|---|---|---|---|---|---|---|
| 1 | EBITDA/Income % | 11.3% | 11.2% | 10.4% | 10.3% | 10.2% |
| 2 | EBIT/Income % | 11.1% | 10.7% | 9.8% | 9.9% | 9.5% |
| 3 | PAT/Income % | 7.4% | 7.1% | 6.5% | 6.6% | 6.4% |

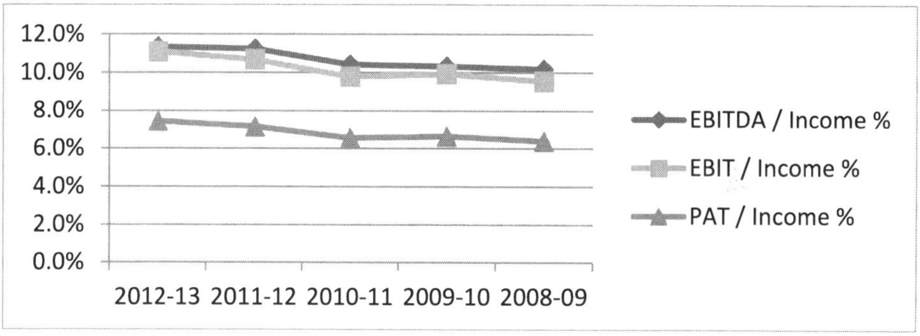


Profitability ratios as above show a clear trend of improvement showing that the profitability position of the company is quite healthy and look promising going forward.

### (b) Expense ratios

| Sr. No. | Particulars | 2012-13 | 2011-12 | 2010-11 | 2009-10 | 2008-09 |
|---|---|---|---|---|---|---|
| 1 | Total expense/Income % | 88.7% | 88.8% | 89.6% | 89.7% | 89.8% |
| 2 | Other expense/Income % | 46.4% | 33.8% | 31.2% | 15.2% | 16.7% |
| 3 | Employee cost/Income % | 40.5% | 52.4% | 55.8% | 71.2% | 68.7% |

The above ratios show that there has been a reduction of employee cost to income ratio. However, other expenses to income trend shows a significant increase. However, overall expenses to income ratio remains in reigned in showing proper expenditure control.

### (c) Liquidity ratio

| Sr. No. | Particulars | 2012-13 | 2011-12 | 2010-11 | 2009-10 | 2008-09 |
|---|---|---|---|---|---|---|
| 1 | Current ratio | 1.31 | 1.64 | 1.32 | 1.30 | 1.30 |

Current ratio has been dropping below zero, showing effective working capital management. However, there remains a risk of working capital tightness in the foreseeable if not managed properly.

### (d) Turnover ratios

| Sr. No. | Particulars | 2012-13 | 2011-12 | 2010-11 | 2009-10 | 2008-09 |
|---|---|---|---|---|---|---|
| 1 | Total assets turnover ratio | 2.32 | 2.56 | 2.49 | 2.06 | 1.54 |
| 2 | Capital turnover ratio | 4.34 | 3.55 | 4.07 | 3.48 | 2.87 |
| 3 | Fixed Assets turnover ratio | 9.92 | 7.25 | 7.29 | 6.03 | 4.33 |
| 4 | Current Asset turnover ratio | 3.82 | 5.59 | 4.88 | 3.88 | 2.55 |
| 5 | Working capital turnover ratio | 16.11 | 14.28 | 20.16 | 16.64 | 11.02 |

On an overall basis turnover ratios have shown an increasing trend, depicting effective utilisation of the assets of the enterprise.

### (e) Solvency ratios

| Sr. No. | Particulars | 2012-13 | 2011-12 | 2010-11 | 2009-10 | 2008-09 |
|---|---|---|---|---|---|---|
| 1 | Debt equity ratio | 0.76 | 0.60 | 0.27 | 0.17 | 0.04 |
| 2 | Total debt to total assets | 0.34 | 0.30 | 0.18 | 0.12 | 0.03 |
| 3 | Shareholders' funds/total assets | 0.45 | 0.50 | 0.65 | 0.70 | 0.75 |

The various trends shown in the above ratios depict that debt to equity ratio have been increasing, which signify that the enterprise has started going for increasing debt vis-à-vis equity.

### (f) Return on investment

| Sr. No. | Particulars | 2012-13 | 2011-12 | 2010-11 | 2009-10 | 2008-09 |
|---|---|---|---|---|---|---|
| 1 | Return on assets (ROA) | 25.4% | 20.3% | 22.2% | 19.1% | 14.6% |
| 2 | Return on capital employed (ROCE) | 48.2% | 37.9% | 39.8% | 34.5% | 27.4% |
| 3 | Return on Equity (ROE) | 56.7% | 40.8% | 33.9% | 27.1% | 19.3% |

The return on investment has been showing positive trend, which shows that the enterprise has high profitability with growth and there is enough room for ploughing back these profits in the enterprise for generating future growth potential. Overall the enterprise shows quite a healthy returns with profitability and would always be the target for investment for the prospective investor, if its shares are traded in stock exchange.

## 16.3 ANALYSIS OF FINANCIAL RATIOS

An analyst is comparing the non-current asset turnover ratios of two listed enterprises A Ltd and B Ltd engaged in similar businesses. The non-current asset turnover ratio of A Ltd is almost 50% higher than that of B Ltd. The analyst concludes that A Ltd having higher asset turnover ratio is utilising the non-current assets far more effectively. Please give your reasons why this conclusion may not be valid.

**Solution**

The observation of the analyst may be incorrect based on the following reasons:

(a) B Ltd having lower non-current asset turnover ratio, may have a policy of revaluing non-current assets, in which case the revalued assets will be much higher than the carrying value of the non-current assets. Hence, comparing two enterprises A Ltd valuing non-current assets in cost model and B Ltd in revaluation model, may lead to incongruous conclusions.

(b) It may also be possible that the A Ltd has non-current assets which have been commissioned much earlier compared to that of B Ltd. Accordingly, the carrying value of the non-current assets in A Ltd are considerably lesser than B Ltd. Hence, this can also result in an anomaly where the conclusion derived from apparent results may not be correct.

## 16.4 COMPUTATION OF FINANCIAL RATIOS AND WRITING A REPORT ON PERFORMANCE

Alpha Ltd operates a number of retail outlets across India. In recent years, the company has found it necessary to provide credit facilities to its customers with the objective of achieving growth in revenue. As a result of this the liability of the bankers of this enterprise has increased substantially.

The financial statements of the last three years are appended below.

## Balance Sheet of Vespa Ltd as at 31.3. 2021

**INR Million**

| Sl No. | Particulars | Note No. | As at 31.03.19 | As at 31.03.20 | As at 31.03.21 |
|---|---|---|---|---|---|
| | EQUITY & LIABILITIES | | | | |
| 1 | **Shareholders' funds** | | | | |
| | (a) Share capital | | 90.0 | 90.0 | 90.0 |
| | (b) Reserves and surplus | | 252.0 | 262.0 | 262.0 |
| | (c) Money received against share warrants | | | | |
| 2 | **Share application money pending allotment** | | | | |
| 3 | **Non-current liabilities** | | | | |
| | (a) Long term borrowings | | | | |
| | (b) Deferred tax liabilities (net) | | | | |
| | (c) Other long-term liabilities | | | | |
| | (d) Long-term provisions | | | | |
| 4 | **Current liabilities** | | | | |
| | (a) Short term borrowings | | 200.0 | 200.0 | 320.0 |
| | (b) Trade payables | | | | |
| | (c) Other current liabilities | 1 | 640.0 | 840.0 | 928.0 |
| | (d) Short term provisions | | | | |
| | **TOTAL** | | **1182.0** | **1392.0** | **1600.0** |
| | **ASSETS** | | | | |
| 1 | **Non-current Assets** | | | | |
| | (a) Property, Plant & Equipment | | | | |
| | (i) Tangible assets | | 278.0 | 290.0 | 332.0 |
| | (ii) Intangible assets | | | | |
| | (iii) Capital work-in-progress | | | | |

| Sl No. | Particulars | Note No. | As at 31.03.19 | As at 31.03.20 | As at 31.03.21 |
|---|---|---|---|---|---|
| | (iv) Intangible assets under development | | | | |
| | (b) Non-current investments | | | | |
| | (c) Deferred tax assets (net) | | | | |
| | (d) Long term loans & advances | | | | |
| | (e) Other non-current assets | | | | |
| **2** | **Current Assets** | | | | |
| | (a) Current investments | | | | |
| | (b) Inventories | | 400.0 | 540.0 | 620.0 |
| | (c) Trade receivables | | 492.0 | 550.0 | 633.0 |
| | (d) Cash & cash equivalents | | 12.0 | 12 | 15.0 |
| | (e) Short-term loan and advances | | | | |
| | (f) Other current assets | | | | |
| | **TOTAL** | | **1182.0** | **1392.0** | **1600.0** |

**Notes to Balance Sheet**

| Sl No. | Particulars | | As at 31.03.19 | As at 31.03.20 | As at 31.03.21 |
|---|---|---|---|---|---|
| 1 | Other current liabilities | | | | |
| | Payable | | 300.0 | 300.0 | 310.0 |
| | Taxation | | 20.0 | 20.0 | 8.0 |
| | Overdraft | | 320.0 | 520.0 | 610.0 |
| | Total | | 640.0 | 840.0 | 928.0 |

**Statement of Profit & Loss of Vespa Ltd as at 31.3. 2021**

**INR Million**

| Sl No. | Particulars | Note No. | As at 31.03.19 | As at 31.03.20 | As at 31.03.21 |
|---|---|---|---|---|---|
| I | REVENUE FROM OPERATION | | 1850.0 | 2200.0 | 2500.0 |

| Sl No. | Particulars | Note No. | As at 31.03.19 | As at 31.03.20 | As at 31.03.21 |
|---|---|---|---|---|---|
| II | OTHER INCOME | | 0 | 0 | 0 |
| **III** | **(TOTAL REVENUE (I + II)** | | **1850.0** | **2200.0** | **2500.0** |
| IV | EXPENSES: | | | | |
| | (a) Cost of material consumed | | | | |
| | (b) Purchase of products for sale | | | | |
| | (c) Changes in inventories of finished goods, work-in-progress and products for sale | | | | |
| | (d) Employees cost benefit expenses | | | | |
| | (e) Finance cost | 1 | -20.0 | 0.0 | 20.0 |
| | (f) Depreciation and amortisation expenses | | | | |
| | (g) Product development expenses | | | | |
| | (h) Other expenses | 2 | 1800.0 | 2140.0 | 2450.0 |
| | (i) Expenditure transfer to capital and other Account | | | | |
| | **TOTAL EXPENSES** | | **1780.0** | **2140.0** | **2470.0** |
| V | PROFIT BEFORE EXCEPTIONAL AND EXTRA-ORDINARY ITEMS AND TAX (III - IV) | | 70.0 | 60.0 | 30.0 |
| VI | EXCEPTIONAL ITEMS | | 0.00 | 0.00 | 0.00 |
| VII | PROFIT BEFORE EXTRAORDINARY ITEMS AND TAX (V-VI) | | 70.00 | 60.00 | 30.00 |
| VIII | EXTRAORDINARY ITEMS | | 0.00 | 0.00 | 0.00 |
| IX | PROFIT BEFORE TAX AND CONTINUING OPERATIONS (VII - VIII) | | 70.00 | 60.00 | 30.00 |
| X | TAX EXPENSES: | | | | |

| Sl No. | Particulars | Note No. | As at 31.03.19 | As at 31.03.20 | As at 31.03.21 |
|---|---|---|---|---|---|
| | (a) Current tax | | 23.00 | 20.00 | 10.00 |
| | (b) Deferred tax | | | | |
| XI | PROFIT AFTER TAX FOR THE YEAR FROM CONTINUING OPERATION (IX - X) | | 47.00 | 40.00 | 20.00 |
| XII | Profit/(loss) from discontinuing operations | | | | |
| XIII | Tax expenses from discontinuing operations | | | | |
| XIV | Profit/(loss) from discontinuing operations (after tax) (XII-XIII) | | | | |
| XV | PROFIT/(LOSS) FOR THE PERIOD (XI + XIV) | | | | |
| | Balance brought forward from previous year | | | | |
| | Profit available for appropriation: | | 47.00 | 40.00 | 20.00 |
| | Proposed dividend | | 30.00 | 30.00 | 20.00 |
| | Transfer to General Reserve | | | | |
| | Distribution tax | | | | |
| | Total | | | | |
| | Balance carried forward | | 17.0 | 10.0 | 0.0 |
| XVI | Earning per equity share: | | | | |
| | (1) Basic | | | | |
| | (2) Diluted | | | | |

**Notes to Statement of Profit & loss**

**INR Million**

| Sl No. | Particulars | | As at 31.03.19 | As at 31.03.20 | As at 31.03.21 |
|---|---|---|---|---|---|
| **1** | **Finance cost** | | | | |

| Sl No. | Particulars | | As at 31.03.19 | As at 31.03.20 | As at 31.03.21 |
|---|---|---|---|---|---|
| | Interest from credit sales | | 45.0 | 60.0 | 90.0 |
| | Interest payable | | -25.0 | -60.0 | -110.0 |
| | **Total** | | **20.0** | **0.0** | **-20.0** |
| 2 | **Other expenses** | | | | |
| | Cost of sales | | 1250.0 | 1500.0 | 1750.0 |
| | Operating cost | | 550.0 | 640.0 | 700.0 |
| | **Total** | | **1800.0** | **2140.0** | **2450.0** |

**Other information**

**INR Million**

| Sl No. | Particulars | | As at 31.03.19 | As at 31.03.20 | As at 31.03.21 |
|---|---|---|---|---|---|
| 1 | Level of credit sales | | 375.0 | 263.0 | 213.0 |
| 2 | Depreciation | | 70.0 | 60.0 | 55.0 |

The loans are secured by a floating charge over the assets of Alpha. They are due for repayment on 31st March 2021.

The bank overdraft is unsecured. The bank has set a limit of INR 630 million on the overdraft.

Owing to the steady increase in bank overdraft the company has sent a request to the bankers to increase the limit. The request was received by the bank on 15th May 2021, two weeks after the financial statements for the year ended 31st March 2021 were published.

Required:

Write a report to the regional manager of the bank analysing the financial performance and position of the enterprise for the period covered by the financial statements.

**Solution**

The report to regional manager would be as under:

To: The Regional Manager

XYZ Bank

From: Management Accountant

Dated: 17.12.2021

Sub: Financial performance of Alpha Ltd

**Executive Summary**

As requested, I have carried out a financial analysis of the financial statements of Alpha Ltd for the last three years in order to identify reasons for increase in overdraft facilities for the entity. My observations are as under:

**1. Revenue**

Revenue of the entity has improved by around 19% in 2019-20 over 2018-19 and by around 13.6% in 2020-21 over 2019-20 (Table 2)

**2. Profitability**

Net profit of the entity has dropped significantly by 14.9% in 2019-20 over 2018-19 and by 50% in 2020-21 over 2019-20. (Table 2). The reason for this drop has been explained by drop in profit margins - gross margin of 30% in 2020-21, getting reduced to operating margin of only 2% in 2020-21 – the reason for this drop being attributable to interest charges of 28% on sales during this period. Interest charges have increased by 140% in 2019-20 and 83.3% in 2020-21 (Table 2).

This had an overall impact on Return on Capital Employed which dropped from 13.74% in 2019 to 5.68% in 2021(Table 4).

The decline in profitability of Alpha Ltd has led to significant decline of the cash position of the entity.

**3. Capital structure**

The gearing ratio of the entity showed a marked increase from 0.5848 in 2018-19 to 0.9091 in 2020-21. This has resulted in the increase in interest charges as highlighted above. This has also led to significant deterioration in interest cover from 2.0 in 2018-19 to 0.45 in 2020-21(Table 3).

**4. Liquidity**

The current ratio of the entity has been hovering around 1.08 to 1.02 in the last three years. This has been further compounded by weak acid test ratio of 0.60 to 0.52. This clearly shows that the entity is currently going through a severe liquidity crunch. (Table 3)

**5. Conclusion**

The entity's performance has significantly deteriorated over the last three years despite a healthy increase in revenue. Accordingly, it may not be appropriate to go for an expansion of overdraft facility currently. Instead, a strategy of going for long term sources of financing at a comparatively lower rate of interest may be much sounder at this stage of the enterprise. Hence, proposed increase of overdraft limit needs to be carefully considered.

Thanks & Regards,
Management Accountant

**Table 1: Trend Analysis: Balance Sheet**

**INR Million**

| Sl No. | Particulars | | As at 31.03.19 | As at 31.03.20 | As at 31.03.21 | Remarks |
|---|---|---|---|---|---|---|
| 1 | Current Assets | | 904.0 | 1102.0 | 1268.0 | Current assets have increased by |
| | % increase over previous year | | | 21.9% | 15.1% | 22% in 2019-20 and 15% in 2020-21 |
| 2 | Non-current assets | | 278.0 | 290.0 | 332.0 | Showed increasing trend in fixed assets, |
| | % increase over previous year | | | 4.3% | 14.5% | marginal investments made in 2020-21 |
| 3 | Current liabilities | | 840.0 | 1040.0 | 1248.0 | Current liabilities have increased by 24% in |
| | % increase over previous year | | | 23.8% | 20.0% | 2019-20 and 20% in 2020-21, |

**Table 2: Trend Analysis: Statement of Profit & Loss**

**INR Million**

| Sl No. | Particulars | | As at 31.03.19 | As at 31.03.20 | As at 31.03.21 | Remarks |
|---|---|---|---|---|---|---|
| 1 | Revenue | | 1850 | 2200 | 2500 | Sales position has improved by around 18.9% in 2019-20, and by 13.6% in 2020-21 |
| | % increase over previous year | | | 18.9% | 13.6% | |
| 2 | Cost of sales | | 1250 | 1500 | 1750 | Cost of sales have increased by 20% |
| | % increase over previous year | | | 20.0% | 16.7% | in 2019-20 and 16.7% in 2020-21 |
| 3 | Operating profit | | 600 | 700 | 750 | Operating profit has shown increasing trend |
| | % increase over previous year | | | 16.7% | 7.1% | over two years |

| Sl No. | Particulars | | As at 31.03.19 | As at 31.03.20 | As at 31.03.21 | Remarks |
|---|---|---|---|---|---|---|
| 4 | Interest | | 25.0 | 60.0 | 110.0 | Interest payable has increased by 140% |
| | % increase over previous year | | | 140.0% | 83.3% | in 2019-20 and 83.3% in 2020-21 |
| 5 | Net profit | | 47.0 | 40.0 | 20.0 | Net profit has dropped significantly in 2020-21 by 50% |
| | % increase/decrease over previous year | | | -14.9% | -50.0% | |

### Table 3: Ratio Analysis: Liquidity and solvency ratios

| Sl No. | Particulars | | As at 31.03.19 | As at 31.03.20 | As at 31.03.21 | Remarks |
|---|---|---|---|---|---|---|
| 1 | **Net working capital** (Current Asset - Current liabilities) | | 64.0 | 62.0 | 20.0 | Liquidity position has reduced over 2019-20 and 2020-21 |
| 2 | **Current ratio** (Current Asset/Current liabilities) | | 1.08 | 1.06 | 1.02 | Liquidity position has remained unsatisfactory |
| 3 | **Quick ratio/Acid test ratio** (Quick Asset/Current liabilities) | | 0.60 | 0.54 | 0.52 | Liquidity position has remained unsatisfactory |
| 4 | **Debt - Equity ratio** (Debt/Shareholders' equity) | | 0.5848 | 0.5682 | 0.9091 | The company's gearing ratio has shown an increasing trend and is currently at 0.91. This has resulted in high interest charges |
| 5 | **Interest coverage ratio** (Operating profit/Interest) | | 2.00 | 1.00 | 0.45 | This ratio has significantly dropped from 2018-19 showing exposure on debt servicing |

**Table 4: Ratio Analysis: Profitability and turnover ratios**

| Sl No. | Particulars | | As at 31.03.19 | As at 31.03.20 | As at 31.03.21 | Remarks |
|---|---|---|---|---|---|---|
| **1** | **Margin ratios** | | | | | |
| 1.1. | **Gross Profit margin** (Operating profit x 100)/Sales | | 32.43% | 31.82% | 30.00% | Operating margin trend has dropped marginally |
| 1.2. | **Interest expenses/sales %** | | 29.73% | 29.09% | 28.00% | This ratio has dropped marginally |
| 1.3. | **Operating profit/sales %** (gross profit x 100)/Sales | | 2.70% | 2.73% | 2.00% | Gross margin ratio has dropped compared to 2019-20 but not satisfactory |
| 1.4 | **Net Profit margin** (Net profit x 100)/Sales | | 2.54% | 1.82% | 0.80% | This shows a deteriorating trend and net margin has significantly dropped over the years |
| **2** | **Turnover ratios** | | | | | |
| 2.1. | **Fixed Assets turnover** (Sales/Fixed assets) | | 6.655 | 7.586 | 7.530 | Shows marginal improvement |
| 2.2. | **Working capital turnover** (Sales/Net current assets) | | 28.91 | 35.48 | 125.00 | Showed an upward trend over 2018-19 and 2019-20 |
| 2.3. | **Assets turnover ratio** (Sales/total assets) | | 1.57 | 1.58 | 1.56 | Remained at same levels |
| 3 | **Return on assets (ROA)** (Net profit margin x Assets turnover ratio) | | 3.98% | 2.87% | 1.25% | Showed significant drop over 2018-19 and 2019-20 and is not satisfactory |
| 4 | **Equity multiplier** (Sales/Net worth) | | 5.409 | 6.250 | 7.102 | Showed reasonable improvement over 2018-19 but still lot of room for improvement |
| 5 | **Return on Equity (ROE)** (ROA X Equity multiplier) | | 21.51% | 17.96% | 8.88% | Showed significant drop over 2018-19 and 2019-20 and is not satisfactory |

| Sl No. | Particulars | | As at 31.03.19 | As at 31.03.20 | As at 31.03.21 | Remarks |
|---|---|---|---|---|---|---|
| 6 | **Return on capital employed** (Net profit after tax x 100)/Total capital employed) | | 13.74% | 11.36% | 5.68% | Trend not satisfactory and has dropped significantly |

**Working Notes:**

**INR Million**

| Sl No. | Particulars | | As at 31.03.19 | As at 31.03.20 | As at 31.03.21 |
|---|---|---|---|---|---|
| 1 | **Gross Profit** | | | | |
| | Revenue | | 1850.0 | 2200.0 | 2500.0 |
| | Less: Cost of sales | | 1250.0 | 1500.0 | 1750.0 |
| | **Total** | | **600.0** | **700.0** | **750.0** |
| | **Gross Profit margin on revenue** | | **32.4%** | **31.8%** | **30.0%** |
| 2 | **Operating profit** | | | | |
| | Gross profit | | 600.0 | 700.0 | 750.0 |
| | Less: Operating cost | | 550.0 | 640.0 | 700.0 |
| | Total | | 50.0 | 60.0 | 50.0 |
| | **Operating profit margin on revenue** | | **2.7%** | **2.7%** | **2.0%** |
| 3 | **Net Profit** | | | | |
| | Gross Profit | | 50.0 | 60.0 | 50.0 |
| | Add: Other income | | 0 | 0 | 0 |
| | Other non-recurring income | | 0.0 | 0.0 | 0.0 |
| | Add/Less: Interest Income/Expenses | | -20.0 | 0.0 | 20.0 |
| | Less: Tax expenses | | 23 | 20 | 10 |
| | Total | | 47.0 | 40.0 | 20.0 |
| | **Net Profit to Revenue %** | | **2.5%** | **1.8%** | **0.8%** |

| Sl No. | Particulars | | As at 31.03.19 | As at 31.03.20 | As at 31.03.21 |
|---|---|---|---|---|---|
| **4** | **Fixed Assets** | | | | |
| | Net tangible assets | | 278.0 | 290.0 | 332.0 |
| | Add: Capital work-in-progress | | | | |
| | Investments | | | | |
| | Total | | 278.0 | 290.0 | 332.0 |
| | **Fixed Asset turnover ratio** | | **6.65** | **7.59** | **7.53** |
| **5** | **Net Worth** | | | | |
| | Share capital | | 90.0 | 90.0 | 90.0 |
| | Reserves & surplus | | 252.0 | 262.0 | 262.0 |
| | **Total** | | **342.0** | **352.0** | **352.0** |
| **6** | **Capital employed** | | | | |
| | **Total assets** | | **1182.0** | **1392.0** | **1600.0** |
| | **Less: Current liabilities** | | **840.0** | **1040.0** | **1248.0** |
| | **Capital employed** | | **342.0** | **352.0** | **352.0** |

## 16.5 COMPUTATION OF FINANCIAL RATIOS

The following are the financial statements of Scala Ltd.

**Balance Sheet of Scala Ltd as at 31.3. 2021**

**INR Million**

| Sl No. | Particulars | Note no. | As at 31.03.21 | As at 31.03.20 |
|---|---|---|---|---|
| | **EQUITY & LIABILITIES** | | | |
| 1 | **Shareholders' funds** | | | |
| | (a) Share capital | 1 | 120.0 | 120.0 |
| | (b) Reserves and surplus | 2 | 116.0 | 118.0 |
| | (c) Money received against share warrants | | | |

| Sl No. | Particulars | Note no. | As at 31.03.21 | As at 31.03.20 |
|---|---|---|---|---|
| 2 | **Share application money pending allotment** | | | |
| 3 | **Non-current liabilities** | | | |
| | (a) Long term borrowings | | 80.0 | 80.0 |
| | (b) Deferred tax liabilities (net) | | | |
| | (c) Other long-term liabilities | | | |
| | (d) Long-term provisions | | | |
| 4 | **Current liabilities** | | | |
| | (a) Short term borrowings | | | |
| | (b) Trade payables | | 72 | 110 |
| | (c) Other current liabilities | | | |
| | (d) Short term provisions (tax) | | 20 | 20 |
| | **TOTAL** | | **408.0** | **448.0** |
| | **ASSETS** | | | |
| 1 | **Non-current Assets** | | | |
| | (a) Fixed Assets | | | |
| | (i) Tangible assets | | 260.0 | 278.0 |
| | (ii) Intangible assets | | | |
| | (iii) Capital work-in-progress | | | |
| | (iv) Intangible assets under development | | | |
| | (b) Non-current investments | | | |
| | (c) Deferred tax assets (net) | | | |
| | (d) Long term loans & advances | | | |
| | (e) Other non-current assets | | | |
| 2 | **Current Assets** | | | |
| | (a) Current investments | | | |

| Sl No. | Particulars | Note no. | As at 31.03.21 | As at 31.03.20 |
|---|---|---|---|---|
| | (b) Inventories | | 84.0 | 74.0 |
| | (c) Trade receivables | | 58.0 | 46.0 |
| | (d) Cash & cash equivalents | | 6.0 | 50 |
| | (e) Short-term loan and advances | | | |
| | (f) Other current assets | | | |
| | **TOTAL** | | **408.0** | **448.0** |

**Notes to Balance Sheet:**

| Sl No. | Particulars | | As at 31.03.21 | As at 31.03.20 |
|---|---|---|---|---|
| 1 | **Share capital** | | | |
| | Ordinary share capital of Re.1 each | | 70 | 70 |
| | 8% Preference share capital | | 50 | 50 |
| | | | 120 | 120 |
| 2 | **Reserves and surplus** | | | |
| | Securities premium | | 34.0 | 34.0 |
| | Revaluation reserve | | 20.0 | 0.0 |
| | Profit & loss account | | 62.0 | 84.0 |
| | Total | | 116.0 | 118.0 |

**Statement of Profit & Loss of Scala Ltd as at 31.3. 2021**

**INR Million**

| Sl No. | Particulars | Note no. | As at 31.03.21 | As at 31.03.20 |
|---|---|---|---|---|
| I | REVENUE FROM OPERATION | | 418.0 | 392.0 |
| II | OTHER INCOME | | 0 | 0 |
| **III** | **(TOTAL REVENUE (I + II)** | | **418.0** | **392.0** |
| IV | EXPENSES: | | | |

| Sl No. | Particulars | Note no. | As at 31.03.21 | As at 31.03.20 |
|---|---|---|---|---|
| | (a) Cost of material consumed | 1 | 314.0 | 302.0 |
| | (b) Purchase of products for sale | | | |
| | (c) Changes in inventories of finished goods, work-in-progress and products for sale | | | |
| | (d) Employees cost benefit expenses | | | |
| | (e) Finance cost | | 4.0 | 4.0 |
| | (f) Depreciation and amortisation expenses | | 18.0 | 18.0 |
| | (g) Product development expenses | | | |
| | (h) Other expenses | | 28.0 | 22.0 |
| | (i) Expenditure transfer to capital and other Account | | | |
| | **TOTAL EXPENSES** | | **364.0** | **346.0** |
| V | PROFIT BEFORE EXCEPTIONAL AND EXTRA-ORDINARY ITEMS AND TAX (III - IV) | | 54.0 | 46.0 |
| VI | EXCEPTIONAL ITEMS | | 0.00 | 0.00 |
| VII | PROFIT BEFORE EXTRAORDINARY ITEMS AND TAX (V-VI) | | 54.00 | 46.00 |
| VIII | EXTRAORDINARY ITEMS | | 0.00 | 0.00 |
| IX | PROFIT BEFORE TAX AND CONTINUING OPERATIONS (VII - VIII) | | 54.00 | 46.00 |
| X | TAX EXPENSES: | | | |
| | (a) Current tax | | 20.00 | 20.00 |
| | (b) Deferred tax | | | |
| XI | PROFIT AFTER TAX FOR THE YEAR FROM CONTINUING OPERATION (IX - X) | | 34.00 | 26.00 |
| XII | Profit/(loss) from discontinuing operations | | | |
| XIII | Tax expenses from discontinuing operations | | | |
| XIV | Profit/(loss) from discontinuing operations (after tax) (XII-XIII) | | | |
| XV | PROFIT/(LOSS) FOR THE PERIOD (XI + XIV) | | | |
| | Balance brought forward from previous year | | | |

| Sl No. | Particulars | Note no. | As at 31.03.21 | As at 31.03.20 |
|---|---|---|---|---|
| | Profit available for appropriation: | | 34.00 | 26.00 |
| | Proposed dividend –Equity | | 12.00 | 10.00 |
| | - preference | | 4.00 | 4.00 |
| | Transfer to General Reserve | | | |
| | Distribution tax | | | |
| | Total | | | |
| | Balance carried forward | | 18.0 | 12.0 |
| XVI | Earning per equity share: | | | |
| | (1) Basic | | | |
| | (2) Diluted | | | |

**Notes to Statement of Profit & loss**

**INR Million**

| Sl No. | Particulars | | As at 31.03.21 | As at 31.03.20 |
|---|---|---|---|---|
| 1 | Cost of material consumed | | | |
| | Opening inventory | | 74.0 | 58.0 |
| | Purchases | | 324.0 | 318.0 |
| | | | 398.0 | 376.0 |
| | Less: Closing inventory | | 84.0 | 74.0 |
| | Total | | 314.0 | 302.0 |
| | | | | |

Calculate and comment on the following ratios for Scala Ltd:

(1) ROCE

(2) All liquidity and solvency ratios

(3) All profitability and turnover ratios

(4) Equity gearing

(5) Total gearing

(6) Interest coverage

(7) Dividend coverage

(8) EPS

(9) PE if market value of ordinary shares is INR 2.40.

**Solution: Ratio Analysis: Liquidity and solvency ratios**

| Sl No | Particulars | | As at 31.03.21 | As at 31.03.20 | Remarks |
|---|---|---|---|---|---|
| 1 | **Net working capital (INR million)** (Current Asset - Current liabilities) | | 56.0 | 40.0 | Liquidity position has increased over 2020-21 over 2019-20 |
| 2 | **Current ratio** (Current Asset/Current liabilities) | | 1.61 | 1.31 | Liquidity position has improved but still unsatisfactory |
| 3 | **Quick ratio/Acid test ratio** (Quick Asset/Current liabilities) | | 0.70 | 0.74 | Liquidity position has remained unsatisfactory |
| 4 | **Total gearing ratio** (Debt/Shareholders' funds) | | 0.411 | 0.409 | The company's gearing ratio has been constant and low, the company can borrow more |
| 5 | **Equity gearing ratio** (Debt/Shareholders' equity) | | 0.699 | 0.691 | Equity gearing has been constant and is low geared by less than 100 |
| 6 | **Interest coverage ratio** (Operating profit/Interest) | | 14.50 | 12.50 | This ratio has improved over 2019-20 and shows satisfactory position on debt servicing |
| 7 | **Dividend coverage ratio** (Operating profit/dividend) | | 2.13 | 1.86 | This ratio has improved over 2019-20 |
| 8 | **Cost of goods sold ratio** (Cost of goods sold/Sales) | | 0.75 | 0.77 | Deteriorating trend is not satisfactory |
| 9 | **Operating ratio** (Cost of goods sold + other expenses /Sales) | | 0.82 | 0.83 | Trend not satisfactory |

**Ratio analysis - Profitability and turnover ratios**

| Sl No. | Particulars | | As at 31.03.21 | As at 31.03.20 | Remarks |
|---|---|---|---|---|---|
| 1 | **Margin ratios** | | | | |
| 1.1 | **Gross Profit margin** | | 24.88% | 22.96% | Gross margin trend has increased |

| Sl No. | Particulars | | As at 31.03.21 | As at 31.03.20 | Remarks |
|---|---|---|---|---|---|
| | (Gross profit x 100)/Sales | | | | marginally |
| 1.2 | **Interest expenses/sales %** | | 0.96% | 1.02% | This ratio has dropped marginally |
| 1.3 | **Operating profit/sales %**<br>(operating profit x 100)/Sales | | 13.88% | 12.76% | Operating margin ratio has increased compared to 2019-20 but not satisfactory |
| 1.4 | **Net Profit margin**<br>(Net profit x 100)/Sales | | 8.13% | 6.63% | This has increasing trend and net margin has improved over the years |
| 2 | **Turnover ratios** | | | | |
| 2.1 | **Debtors turnover ratio**<br>(Sales/Receivables) | | 7.207 | 8.522 | Shows deteriorating trend where receivables are turned over less |
| 2.2 | **Days sales outstanding (DSO)**<br>(Receivables/Sales per day) | | 50.65 | 42.83 | Corroborated by increase in DSO |
| 2.3 | **Inventory turnover ratio**<br>(Cost of goods sold/Inventories) | | 3.74 | 4.08 | Shows deteriorating trend where inventories are turned over have reduced |
| 2.4 | **Inventories days sales (IDS)**<br>(Inventories/Cost of goods sold per day) | | 97.64 | 89.44 | Corroborated by increase in IDS |
| 2.5 | **Creditors turnover ratio**<br>(Cost of goods sold + other expenses)/creditors) | | 4.8 | 2.9 | Creditors management has improved |
| 2.6 | **Creditors days outstanding**<br>(Creditors/Cost of goods sold per day) | | 76.84 | 123.92 | Creditors pay-out has improved |
| 2.7 | **Working capital turnover**<br>(Sales/Net current assets) | | 7.46 | 9.80 | Showed an downward trend over 2019-20 |
| 2.8 | **Fixed Assets turnover** | | 1.608 | 1.410 | Trend improved marginally but |

| Sl No. | Particulars | | As at 31.03.21 | As at 31.03.20 | Remarks |
|---|---|---|---|---|---|
| | (Sales/Fixed assets) | | | | needs to improve further |
| 2.9 | **Assets turnover ratio** (Sales/total assets) | | 1.02 | 0.88 | Improved over previous year |
| 3 | **Return on assets (ROA)** (Net profit margin x Assets turnover ratio) | | 8.33% | 5.80% | Showed significant improvement over 2019-20 but is not satisfactory |
| 4 | **Equity multiplier** (Sales/Net worth) | | 1.771 | 1.647 | Showed reasonable improvement over 2019-20 but still lot of room for improvement |
| 5 | **Return on Equity (ROE)** (ROA X Equity multiplier) | | 14.76% | 9.56% | Showed significant improvement over 2019-20 but needs to improve |
| 6 | **Return on capital employed** (Net profit after tax x 100)/Total capital employed) | | 18.35% | 15.72% | Trend not satisfactory and has dropped significantly |
| 7 | **Earnings per share (EPS)** (Net profit after tax - preference dividend) /no. of shares) | | INR 21.4 | INR 15.7 | Showed significant improvement |
| 8 | **Price earnings ratio** (Market price/ EPS) | | 11.21 | | Quite high which indicates the market has confidence in the performance of the company |

**Working Notes:**

**INR Million**

| Sl No. | Particulars | | As at 31.03.21 | As at 31.03.20 |
|---|---|---|---|---|
| 1 | **Gross Profit** | | | |
| | Revenue | | 418.0 | 392.0 |
| | Less: Cost of sales | | 314.0 | 302.0 |

| Sl No. | Particulars | | As at 31.03.21 | As at 31.03.20 |
|---|---|---|---|---|
| | **Total** | | **104.0** | **90.0** |
| | **Gross Profit margin on revenue** | | **24.9%** | **23.0%** |
| 2 | **Operating profit** | | | |
| | Gross Profit | | 104.0 | 90.0 |
| | Less: Depreciation | | 18.0 | 18.0 |
| | Other expenses | | 28.0 | 22.0 |
| | **Operating profit** | | **58.0** | **50.0** |
| | **Operating Profit margin on revenue** | | **13.9%** | **12.8%** |
| 3 | **Total Assets** | | | |
| | Net tangible assets | | 260.0 | 278.0 |
| | Add: Net Current Assets | | 56.0 | 40.0 |
| | **Total** | | **316.0** | **318.0** |
| | **Asset turnover ratio** | | **1.32** | **1.23** |
| 4 | **Net Worth** | | | |
| | Share capital | | 120.0 | 120.0 |
| | Reserves & surplus | | 116.0 | 118.0 |
| | **Total** | | **236.0** | **238.0** |
| | **Return on equity** | | **12.7%** | **9.2%** |
| 5 | **Capital employed** | | | |
| | **Total assets** | | **408.0** | **448.0** |
| | **Less: Current liabilities** | | **92.0** | **130.0** |
| | **Capital employed** | | **316.0** | **318.0** |
| | **Return on capital employed** | | **18.4%** | **15.7%** |

## 16.6 DUPONT ANALYSIS

Calculate ratios in line with DuPont analysis based on the following numbers: (INR lakhs)

| Item | 2021 | 2020 | 2019 | 2018 |
|---|---|---|---|---|
| Net Income | 6068 | 6945 | 5157 | 3566 |
| Revenue | 26273 | 25070 | 20847 | 16202 |
| Assets | 31471 | 28880 | 23735 | 17504 |
| Owners' equity | 23377 | 19295 | 16872 | 12140 |

Also provide your observations on the health of the enterprise based on the analysis.

**Solution**

The ratios based on DuPont analysis are as under:

| Item | 2021 | 2020 | 2019 | 2018 | Remarks |
|---|---|---|---|---|---|
| Net Income | 6068 | 6945 | 5157 | 3566 | |
| Revenue | 26273 | 25070 | 20847 | 16202 | |
| Assets | 31471 | 28880 | 23735 | 17504 | |
| Owners' equity | 23377 | 19295 | 16872 | 12140 | |
| Ratios | | | | | |
| Profit margin (net income/sales %) | 23.1% | 27.7% | 24.7% | 22.0% | Profitability has dropped in 2021 |
| Asset turnover ratio (Assets/Sales) | 0.835 | 0.868 | 0.878 | 0.926 | Similarly, there appears to be lower efficiency in utilisation of assets |
| Return on assets % Profit margin × asset turnover | 19.3% | 24% | 21.7% | 20.4% | Has resulted in drop in Return on Assets |
| Equity multiplier (Sales/Equity) | 1.35 | 1.50 | 1.41 | 1.44 | Decrease in leverage in 2021 |
| Return on Equity % (ROA X Equity multiplier) | 26.0 | 36.0 | 30.6 | 29.4 | There is sharp decline in ROE in 2021, lowest in the last four years. |

On an overall analysis it shows that there is a significant negative trend on profitability margin as well as return on assets and return on equity in 2021 and this is wake-up call of the management of the enterprise to take note of this, analyse the reasons of this decline and take remedial measures.

## 16.7 DUPONT ANALYSIS

Using the Balance Sheet and Statement of Profit & loss of LMN Ltd please carry out a DuPont Analysis for three years and provide your interpretations.

**Balance Sheet of LMN Ltd as at 31.3. 2021**

**INR Million**

| Sl No. | Particulars | Note No. | As at 31.03.21 | As at 31.03.20 | As at 31.03.19 |
|---|---|---|---|---|---|
| | **EQUITY & LIABILITIES** | | | | |
| 1 | **Shareholders' funds** | | | | |
| | (a) Share capital | | 636.0 | 318.0 | 318.0 |
| | (b) Reserves and surplus | | 11551.1 | 10298.97 | 8069.33 |
| | (c) Money received against share warrants | | | | |
| 2 | **Share application money pending allotment** | | | | |
| 3 | **Non-current liabilities** | | | | |
| | (a) Long term borrowings | 1 | 4785.7 | 6642.9 | 9598.3 |
| | (b) Deferred tax liabilities (net) | | | | |
| | (c) Other long term liabilities | | | | |
| | (d) Long-term provisions | | | | |
| 4 | **Current liabilities** | | | | |
| | (a) Short term borrowings | | | | |
| | (b) Trade payables | | | | |
| | (c) Other current liabilities | | 4374.2 | 4438.04 | 4042.8 |
| | (d) Short term provisions | | 7540.26 | 6096.85 | 4936.49 |
| | **TOTAL** | | **28887.2** | **27794.7** | **26964.9** |

| Sl No. | Particulars | Note No. | As at 31.03.21 | As at 31.03.20 | As at 31.03.19 |
|---|---|---|---|---|---|
| | **ASSETS** | | | | |
| 1 | **Non-current Assets** | | | | |
| | (a) Fixed Assets | | | | |
| | (i) Tangible assets | 2 | 13082.0 | 13428.3 | 13713.6 |
| | (ii) Intangible assets | | | | |
| | (iii) Capital work-in-progress | | 19.5 | 134.08 | 329.02 |
| | (iv) Intangible assets under development | | | | |
| | (b) Non-current investments | | | | |
| | (c) Deferred tax assets (net) | | | | |
| | (d) Long term loans & advances | | | | |
| | (e) Other non-current assets | | | | |
| 2 | **Current Assets** | | | | |
| | (a) Current investments | | 585.6 | 607.38 | 613.9 |
| | (b) Inventories | | 591.87 | 482.5 | 293.59 |
| | (c) Trade receivables | | 926.2 | 807.7 | 933.52 |
| | (d) Cash & cash equivalents | | 946.3 | 1280.66 | 745.5 |
| | (e) Short-term loan and advances | | 12625.6 | 11021.89 | 9980.44 |
| | (f) Other current assets | | 110.08 | 32.21 | 355.41 |
| | **TOTAL** | | **28887.21** | **27794.7** | **26964.9** |

**Notes to Balance Sheet:**

| Sl No. | Particulars | | As at 31.03.21 | As at 31.03.20 | As at 31.03.19 |
|---|---|---|---|---|---|
| 1 | **Long term borrowings** | | | | |
| | Secured loans | | 0.0 | 2000.0 | 9598.29 |
| | Unsecured loans | | 4785.71 | 4642.86 | 0 |
| | Total | | 4785.7 | 6642.9 | 9598.3 |

| Sl No. | Particulars | | As at 31.03.21 | As at 31.03.20 | As at 31.03.19 |
|---|---|---|---|---|---|
| 2 | **Tangible assets** | | | | |
| | Gross block | | 18864.1 | 18465.34 | 17917.84 |
| | Less: Accumulated depreciation | | 5782.0 | 5037.03 | 4204.29 |
| | Total | | 13082.0 | 13428.31 | 13713.6 |

**Statement of Profit & Loss of LMN Ltd as at 31.3. 2021**

**INR Million**

| Sl No. | Particulars | Note No. | As at 31.03.21 | As at 31.03.20 | As at 31.03.19 |
|---|---|---|---|---|---|
| I | REVENUE FROM OPERATION | | 9772.79 | 9801.22 | 5889.49 |
| II | OTHER INCOME | | 452.01 | 556.07 | 338.74 |
| **III** | **(TOTAL REVENUE (I + II)** | | **10224.8** | **10357.29** | **6228.2** |
| IV | EXPENSES: | | | | |
| | (a) Cost of material consumed | 1 | 957.1 | 324.92 | 297.7 |
| | (b) Purchase of products for sale | | | | |
| | (c) Changes in inventories of finished goods, work-in-progress and products for sale | | | | |
| | (d) Employees cost benefit expenses | | | | |
| | (e) Finance cost | 2 | 583.5 | 718.7 | 745.0 |
| | (f) Depreciation and amortisation expenses | 3 | 777.8 | 955.37 | 1293.2 |
| | (g) Product development expenses | | | | |
| | (h) Other expenses | | 4107.7 | 3882.86 | 2622.84 |
| | (i) Expenditure transfer to capital and other Account | | | | |
| | **TOTAL EXPENSES** | | **6426.1** | **5881.82** | **4958.7** |
| V | PROFIT BEFORE EXCEPTIONAL AND EXTRA- | | 3798.7 | 4475.47 | 1269.53 |

| Sl No. | Particulars | Note No. | As at 31.03.21 | As at 31.03.20 | As at 31.03.19 |
|---|---|---|---|---|---|
| | ORDINARY ITEMS AND TAX (III - IV) | | | | |
| VI | EXCEPTIONAL ITEMS | | 125.0 | 68.8 | -296.1 |
| VII | PROFIT BEFORE EXTRAORDINARY ITEMS TAX (V-VI) | | 3673.66 | 4406.64 | 1565.59 |
| VIII | EXTRAORDINARY ITEMS | | 0 | 0 | 0 |
| IX | PROFIT BEFORE TAX AND CONTINUING OPERATIONS (VII - VIII) | | 3673.66 | 4406.64 | 1565.59 |
| X | TAX EXPENSES: | | | | |
| | (a) Current tax | | 1336.0 | 1444.6 | 590.7 |
| | (b) Deferred tax | | | | |
| XI | PROFIT AFTER TAX FOR THE YEAR FROM | | | | |
| | CONTINUING OPERATION (IX - X) | | 2337.67 | 2962.0 | 974.85 |
| XII | Profit/(loss) from discontinuing operations | | | | |
| XIII | Tax expenses from discontinuing operations | | | | |
| XIV | Profit/(loss) from discontinuing operations (after tax) (XII-XIII) | | | | |
| | | | | | |
| | Balance brought forward from previous year | | | | |
| | Profit available for appropriation: | | 2337.67 | 2962.0 | 974.85 |
| | Proposed dividend | | 636.0 | 318.0 | 318.0 |
| | Transfer to General Reserve | | | | |
| | Distribution tax | | | | |

| Sl No. | Particulars | Note No. | As at 31.03.21 | As at 31.03.20 | As at 31.03.19 |
|---|---|---|---|---|---|
| | Total | | | | |
| | Balance carried forward | | 1701.7 | 2644 | 656.8 |
| XVI | Earning per equity share: | | | | |
| | (1) Basic | | | | |
| | (2) Diluted | | | | |

**Notes to Statement of Profit & loss**

**INR Million**

| Sl No. | Particulars | | As at 31.03.21 | As at 31.03.20 | As at 31.03.19 |
|---|---|---|---|---|---|
| 1 | **Cost of material consumed** | | | | |
| | Raw material cost | | 917.77 | 315.6 | 296.9 |
| | Excise | | 39.33 | 9.34 | 0.78 |
| | Total | | 957.1 | 324.92 | 297.7 |
| 2 | **Finance cost** | | | | |
| | Interest expenses | | 583.5 | 718.67 | 744.96 |
| | **Total** | | **583.5** | **718.7** | **745.0** |
| 3 | **Depreciation and amortisation expenses** | | | | |
| | Depreciation | | 777.8 | 955.37 | 1293.2 |
| | **Total** | | **777.8** | **955.37** | **1293.2** |
| 4 | **Exceptional items** | | | | |
| | **Other non-recurring income** | | **125.0** | **68.83** | **-296.06** |
| | **Total** | | **125.0** | **68.8** | **-296.1** |

**Solution**

**Working Notes**

**INR Million**

| Sl No. | Particulars | | As at 31.03.21 | As at 31.03.20 | As at 31.03.19 |
|---|---|---|---|---|---|
| 1 | **Operating Profit** | | | | |
| | Revenue | | 9772.79 | 9801.22 | 5889.49 |
| | Less: Raw material cost | | 917.77 | 315.58 | 296.92 |
| | Excise | | 39.33 | 9.34 | 0.78 |
| | Other expenses | | 4107.7 | 3882.86 | 2622.84 |
| | **Total** | | **4707.99** | **5593.44** | **2968.95** |
| 2 | **Gross Profit** | | | | |
| | Operating profit | | 4707.99 | 5593.44 | 2968.95 |
| | Less: Interest expenses | | 583.5 | 718.7 | 745.0 |
| | **Total** | | **4124.5** | **4874.8** | **2224.0** |
| 3 | **Net Profit** | | | | |
| | Gross Profit | | 4124.5 | 4874.8 | 2224.0 |
| | Add: Other income | | 452.01 | 556.07 | 338.74 |
| | Other non-recurring income | | -125.0 | -68.8 | 296.1 |
| | Less Depreciation | | 777.8 | 955.37 | 1293.2 |
| | Tax expenses | | 1335.99 | 1444.64 | 590.74 |
| | **Total** | | **2337.7** | **2962.0** | **974.8** |
| 4 | **Fixed Assets** | | | | |
| | Net tangible assets | | 13082.04 | 13428.31 | 13713.55 |
| | Add: Capital work-in-progress | | 19.5 | 134.08 | 329.02 |
| | Investments | | 585.59 | 607.38 | 613.9 |
| | **Total** | | **13687.13** | **14169.77** | **14656.47** |
| 5 | **Net Worth** | | | | |

| Sl No. | Particulars | | As at 31.03.21 | As at 31.03.20 | As at 31.03.19 |
|---|---|---|---|---|---|
| | Share capital | | 636 | 318 | 318 |
| | Reserves & surplus | | 11551.1 | 10299.0 | 8069.3 |
| | **Total** | | **12187.1** | **10616.97** | **8387.33** |

**Statement of DuPont Analysis**

| Sl No. | Particulars | | As at 31.03.21 | As at 31.03.20 | As at 31.03.19 | Remarks |
|---|---|---|---|---|---|---|
| 1 | **Margin ratios** | | | | | |
| 1.1. | **Operating Profit margin** | | | | | |
| | (Operating profit × 100)/ Sales | | 48.17% | 57.07% | 50.41% | Operating margin trend has dropped marginally |
| 1.2. | **Interest expenses/sales %** | | 5.97% | 7.33% | 12.65% | This ratio has dropped sharply owing sales going up and interest remaining at same levels |
| 1.3. | **Gross margin/sales %** (gross profit x 100)/Sales | | 42.20% | 49.74% | 37.76% | Gross margin ratio has dropped compared to 2019-20. |
| 1.4 | **Net Profit margin** | | | | | |
| | (Net profit × 100)/Sales | | 23.92% | 30.22% | 16.55% | Shows an upward trend compared 2018-19 but dropped from previous year |
| 2 | **Turnover ratios** | | | | | |
| 2.1. | **Fixed Assets turnover** | | | | | |
| | (Sales/Fixed assets) | | 0.714 | 0.692 | 0.402 | Shows marginal improvement |
| 2.2. | **Working capital turnover** | | | | | |
| | (Sales/Net current assets) | | 3.08 | 3.21 | 1.98 | Showed an upward trend over 2018-19 but has reduced from 2019-20 |

| Sl No. | Particulars | | As at 31.03.21 | As at 31.03.20 | As at 31.03.19 | Remarks |
|---|---|---|---|---|---|---|
| 2.3. | **Assets turnover ratio** | | | | | |
| | (Sales/total assets) | | 0.34 | 0.35 | 0.22 | Shows reasonable improvement |
| 3 | **Return on assets (ROA)** | | | | | |
| | (Net profit margin x Assets turnover ratio) | | 8.09% | 10.66% | 3.62% | Showed reasonable improvement over 2018-19 but still lot of room for Improvement |
| 4 | **Equity multiplier** | | | | | |
| | (Sales/Net worth) | | 0.802 | 0.923 | 0.702 | Showed reasonable improvement over 2018-19 but still lot of room for improvement |
| | | | | | | |
| 5 | **Return on Equity (ROE)** (ROA X Equity multiplier) | | 6.49% | 9.84% | 2.54% | Showed reasonable improvement over 2018-19 but still lot of room for improvement |

## 16.8 DUPONT ANALYSIS

Using the Balance Sheet and Statement of Profit & loss of DEF Ltd please carry out a DuPont Analysis for three years and provide your interpretations.

**Balance Sheet of DEF Ltd as at 31.3. 2021**

**INR Million**

| Sl No. | Particulars | Note No. | As at 31.03.21 | As at 31.03.20 | As at 31.03.19 |
|---|---|---|---|---|---|
| | **EQUITY & LIABILITIES** | | | | |
| 1 | **Shareholders' funds** | | | | |
| | (a) Share capital | | 4225.3 | 4225.3 | 4225.3 |
| | (b) Reserves and surplus | | 139350.5 | 114256.6 | 72045.3 |
| | (c) Money received against share | | | | |

| Sl No. | Particulars | Note No. | As at 31.03.21 | As at 31.03.20 | As at 31.03.19 |
|---|---|---|---|---|---|
| | warrants | | | | |
| 2 | **Share application money pending allotment** | | | | |
| 3 | **Non-current liabilities** | | | | |
| | (a) Long term borrowings | 1 | 86.9 | 3.9 | 3.9 |
| | (b) Deferred tax liabilities (net) | | | | |
| | (c) Other long term liabilities | | | | |
| | (d) Long-term provisions | | | | |
| 4 | **Current liabilities** | | | | |
| | (a) Short term borrowings | | | | |
| | (b) Trade payables | | | | |
| | (c) Other current liabilities | | 13742.0 | 12377.8 | 9478.0 |
| | (d) Short term provisions | | 1981.3 | 1235.8 | 1849.5 |
| | **TOTAL** | | **159386.0** | **132099.4** | **87602.0** |
| | **ASSETS** | | | | |
| 1 | **Non-current Assets** | | | | |
| | (a) Fixed Assets | | | | |
| | (i) Tangible assets | 2 | 41049.2 | 36372.8 | 22356.0 |
| | (ii) Intangible assets | | | | |
| | (iii) Capital work-in-progress | | 11083.9 | 5253.4 | 6349.9 |
| | (iv) Intangible assets under development | | | | |
| | (b) Non-current investments | | | | |
| | (c) Deferred tax assets (net) | | | | |
| | (d) Long term loans & advances | | | | |
| | (e) Other non-current assets | | | | |
| 2 | **Current Assets** | | | | |

| Sl No. | Particulars | Note No. | As at 31.03.21 | As at 31.03.20 | As at 31.03.19 |
|---|---|---|---|---|---|
| | (a) Current investments | | 69288.7 | 63324.5 | 44033 |
| | (b) Inventories | | 5456.6 | 5181.0 | 4992.8 |
| | (c) Trade receivables | | 1649.4 | 4436.6 | 5566.2 |
| | (d) Cash & cash equivalents | | 27191.5 | 13627.8 | 1197.0 |
| | (e) Short-term loan and advances | | 3666.7 | 3903.3 | 3107.1 |
| | (f) Other current assets | | 0 | 0 | 0 |
| | **TOTAL** | | **159386** | **132099.4** | **87602.0** |

**Notes to Balance Sheet:**

| Sl No. | Particulars | | As at 31.03.21 | As at 31.03.20 | As at 31.03.19 |
|---|---|---|---|---|---|
| **1** | **Long term borrowings** | | | | |
| | Secured loans | | 83.0 | 0.0 | 0 |
| | Unsecured loans | | 3.9 | 3.9 | 3.9 |
| | **Total** | | **86.9** | **3.9** | **3.9** |
| **2** | **Tangible assets** | | | | |
| | Gross block | | 58555.1 | 51219.2 | 34997.9 |
| | Less: Accumulated depreciation | | 17505.9 | 14846.4 | 12641.9 |
| | Total | | 41049.2 | 36372.8 | 22356.0 |

**Statement of Profit & Loss of DEF Ltd as at 31.3. 2021**

**INR Million**

| Sl No. | Particulars | Note No. | As at 31.03.21 | As at 31.03.20 | As at 31.03.19 |
|---|---|---|---|---|---|
| I | REVENUE FROM OPERATION | | 56885.1 | 78954.7 | 85474.2 |
| II | OTHER INCOME | | 8320.3 | 5316.5 | 1139.5 |
| **III** | **(TOTAL REVENUE (I + II)** | | **65205.4** | **84271.2** | **86613.7** |
| IV | EXPENSES: | | | | |

| Sl No. | Particulars | Note No. | As at 31.03.21 | As at 31.03.20 | As at 31.03.19 |
|---|---|---|---|---|---|
| | (a) Cost of material consumed | 1 | 11055.4 | 13752.6 | 9448.5 |
| | (b) Purchase of products for sale | | | | |
| | (c) Changes in inventories of finished goods, work-in-progress and products for sale | | | | |
| | (d) Employees cost benefit expenses | | | | |
| | (e) Finance cost | 2 | 218.8 | 230.5 | 284.4 |
| | (f) Depreciation and amortisation expenses | 3 | 2852.7 | 2205.1 | 1560.8 |
| | (g) Product development expenses | | | | |
| | (h) Other expenses | | 18488.1 | 11222.3 | 11779.1 |
| | (i) Expenditure transfer to capital and Other account | | | | |
| | TOTAL EXPENSES | | 32615.0 | 27410.5 | 23072.8 |
| V | PROFIT BEFORE EXCEPTIONAL AND EXTRA-ORDINARY ITEMS AND TAX (III - IV) | | 32590.4 | 56860.7 | 63540.9 |
| VI | EXCEPTIONAL ITEMS | | -1316.2 | -3804.9 | -1247.6 |
| VII | PROFIT BEFORE EXTRAORDINARY ITEMS AND TAX (V-VI) | | 33906.6 | 60665.6 | 64788.5 |
| VIII | EXTRAORDINARY ITEMS | | 0 | 0 | 0 |
| IX | PROFIT BEFORE TAX AND CONTINUING OPERATIONS (VII - VIII) | | 33906.6 | 60665.6 | 64788.5 |
| X | TAX EXPENSES: | | | | |
| | (a) Current tax | | 6630.5 | 16689.6 | 20365.3 |
| | (b) Deferred tax | | | | |
| XI | PROFIT AFTER TAX FOR THE YEAR FROM CONTINUING OPERATION (IX - X) | | 27276.1 | 43976 | 44423.2 |
| XII | Profit/(loss) from discontinuing | | | | |

| Sl No. | Particulars | Note No. | As at 31.03.21 | As at 31.03.20 | As at 31.03.19 |
|---|---|---|---|---|---|
| | operations | | | | |
| XIII | Tax expenses from discontinuing operations | | | | |
| XIV | Profit/(loss) from discontinuing operations (after tax) (XII-XIII) | | | | |
| XV | PROFIT/(LOSS) FOR THE PERIOD (XI + XIV) | | | | |
| | Balance brought forward from previous year | | | | |
| | Profit available for appropriation: | | 27276.1 | 43976.0 | 44423.2 |
| | Proposed dividend | | 1690.1 | 2112.6 | 2112.6 |
| | Transfer to General Reserve | | | | |
| | Distribution tax | | | | |
| | Total | | | | |
| | Balance carried forward | | 25586.0 | 41863.4 | 42310.6 |
| XVI | Earning per equity share: | | | | |
| | (1) Basic | | | | |
| | (2) Diluted | | | | |

## Notes to Statement of Profit & loss

**INR Million**

| Sl No. | Particulars | | As at 31.03.21 | As at 31.03.20 | As at 31.03.19 |
|---|---|---|---|---|---|
| 1 | **Cost of material consumed** | | | | |
| | Raw material cost | | 6525.8 | 5338.2 | 2718.2 |
| | Excise | | 4529.6 | 8414.4 | 6730.3 |
| | **Total** | | **11055.4** | **13752.6** | **9448.5** |
| 2 | **Finance cost** | | | | |
| | Interest expenses | | 218.8 | 230.5 | 284.4 |
| | **Total** | | **218.8** | **230.5** | **284.4** |

| Sl No. | Particulars | | As at 31.03.21 | As at 31.03.20 | As at 31.03.19 |
|---|---|---|---|---|---|
| 3 | **Depreciation and amortisation expenses** | | | | |
| | Depreciation | | 2852.7 | 2205.1 | 1560.8 |
| | **Total** | | **2852.7** | **2205.1** | **1560.8** |
| 4 | **Exceptional items** | | | | |
| | Other non-recurring income | | 1316.2 | 3804.9 | 1247.6 |
| | **Total** | | **1316.2** | **3804.9** | **1247.6** |

## Solution

## Working Notes

**INR Million**

| Sl No. | Particulars | | As at 31.03.21 | As at 31.03.20 | As at 31.03.19 |
|---|---|---|---|---|---|
| 1 | **Operating Profit** | | | | |
| | Revenue | | 56885.1 | 78954.7 | 85474.2 |
| | Less: Raw material cost | | 6525.8 | 5338.2 | 2718.2 |
| | Excise | | 4529.6 | 8414.4 | 6730.3 |
| | Other expenses | | 18488.1 | 11222.3 | 11779.1 |
| | **Total** | | **27341.6** | **53979.8** | **64246.6** |
| 2 | **Gross Profit** | | | | |
| | Operating profit | | 27341.6 | 53979.8 | 64246.6 |
| | Less: Interest expenses | | 218.8 | 230.5 | 284.4 |
| | **Total** | | **27122.8** | **53749.3** | **63962.2** |
| 3 | Net Profit | | | | |
| | Gross Profit | | 27122.8 | 53749.3 | 63962.2 |
| | Add: Other income | | 8320.3 | 5316.5 | 1139.5 |
| | Other non-recurring income | | 1316.2 | 3804.9 | 1247.6 |
| | Less Depreciation | | 2852.7 | 2205.1 | 1560.8 |
| | Tax expenses | | 6630.5 | 16689.6 | 20365.3 |

| Sl No. | Particulars | | As at 31.03.21 | As at 31.03.20 | As at 31.03.19 |
|---|---|---|---|---|---|
| | **Total** | | **27276.1** | **43976.0** | **44423.2** |
| 4 | **Fixed Assets** | | | | |
| | Net tangible assets | | 41049.2 | 36372.8 | 22356 |
| | Add: Capital work-in-progress | | 11083.9 | 5253.4 | 6349.9 |
| | Investments | | 69288.7 | 63324.5 | 44033 |
| | **Total** | | **121421.8** | **104950.7** | **72738.9** |
| 5 | **Net Worth** | | | | |
| | Share capital | | 4225.3 | 4225.3 | 4225.3 |
| | Reserves & surplus | | 139350.5 | 114256.6 | 72045.3 |
| | **Total** | | **143575.8** | **118481.9** | **76270.6** |

## DuPont Analysis

| Sl No. | Particulars | | As at 31.03.21 | As at 31.03.20 | As at 31.03.19 | Remarks |
|---|---|---|---|---|---|---|
| 1 | **Margin ratios** | | | | | |
| 1.1. | **Operating Profit margin** | | | | | |
| | (Operating profit × 100)/Sales | | 48.06% | 68.37% | 75.16% | Operating margin trend has dropped significantly |
| 1.2. | **Interest expenses/sales %** | | 0.38% | 0.29% | 0.33% | Remained more or less constant across three years |
| 1.3. | **Gross margin/sales %** (gross profit × 100)/Sales | | 47.68% | 68.08% | 74.83% | Gross margin ratio has dropped significantly compare to 2018-19 and 2019-20 |
| 1.4 | **Net Profit margin** (Net profit × 100)/Sales | | 47.95% | 55.70% | 51.97% | Shows an upward trend compared 2018-19 but dropped from previous year |
| 2 | **Turnover ratios** | | | | | |
| 2.1. | **Fixed Assets turnover** (Sales/Fixed assets) | | 0.468 | 0.752 | 1.175 | Shows major decline in the turnover of assets to turnover |
| 2.2. | **Working capital turnover** (Sales/Net current assets) | | 2.56 | 5.83 | 24.18 | Shows major decline in the turnover of assets to turnover |

| Sl No. | Particulars | | As at 31.03.21 | As at 31.03.20 | As at 31.03.19 | Remarks |
|---|---|---|---|---|---|---|
| 2.3. | **Assets turnover ratio** (Sales/total assets) | | 0.36 | 0.60 | 0.98 | Shows major decline in the turnover of assets to turnover |
| 3 | **Return on assets (ROA)** (Net profit margin x Assets turnover ratio) | | 17.11% | 33.29% | 50.71% | Showed significant deterioration over 2018-19 and 2019-20 |
| 4 | **Equity multiplier** (Sales/Net worth) | | 0.396 | 0.666 | 1.121 | Showed significant deterioration over 2018-19 and 2019-20 |
| 5 | **Return on Equity (ROE)** (ROA × Equity multiplier) | | 6.78% | 22.18% | 56.83% | Showed significant deterioration over 2018-19 and 2019-20 |

## 16.9 FINANCIAL ANALYSIS OF A HEAVY MACHINERY MANUFACTURING COMPANY

**Please find below the Financial Summary of previous five years of a Heavy Machinery manufacturing company.**

**All figures are in Rs. Lakhs**

**Financial Summary**

| SR.NO. | SUBJECT | 2020-21 | 2019-20 | 2018-19 | 2017-18 | 2016-17 |
|---|---|---|---|---|---|---|
| | | | | | | |
| 1 | Capital | 600.00 | 600.00 | 600.00 | 600.00 | 600.00 |
| 2 | Reserves | (124.04) | (166.15) | (199.18) | (240.79) | (574.33) |
| 3 | Share application pending allotment | - | | - | - | - |
| 4 | Net Worth | 475.96 | 433.85 | 400.82 | 359.21 | 25.67 |
| 5 | Long term borrowings | 772.48 | 763.66 | 718.03 | 846.03 | 679.17 |
| 6 | Deferred tax Liabilities | - | - | - | - | - |
| 7 | Long term provisions | 0.00 | 0.00 | - | - | - |
| 8 | Short term borrowings | 165.98 | 156.11 | 160.58 | 113.33 | 90.45 |
| 9 | Capital employed | 1,414.42 | 1,353.62 | 1,279.43 | 1,318.57 | 795.29 |
| 10 | Net Block | 127.17 | 120.99 | 123.84 | 128.44 | 139.25 |
| 11 | Non-current investments | - | - | 13.00 | 13.03 | 13.03 |
| 12 | Other non-current assets | 487.14 | 44.31 | 263.50 | 202.32 | 35.84 |
| 13 | Long term loans and advance | 29.89 | 17.84 | 28.29 | 7.74 | 21.13 |
| 14 | Inventories | 724.31 | 536.87 | 123.00 | 86.29 | 79.29 |
| 15 | Sundry debtors | 1.344.80 | 1,265.19 | 1,616.82 | 1,126.99 | 1,194.86 |
| 16 | Cash & bank balances | 8.02 | 136.92 | 88.77 | 307.51 | 241.59 |
| 17 | Other current assets, Loans & advances | 123.49 | 188.11 | 124.63 | 142.92 | 106.29 |
| 18 | Current Assets | 2,200.62 | 2.127.09 | 1,953.22 | 1,663.71 | 1,622.03 |
| 19 | Current Liability | 1,412.76 | 939.61 | 1,082.94 | 678.50 | 1,035.99 |
| 20 | Provisions | 17.64 | 17.00 | 19.48 | 18.17 | - |
| 21 | Current Liability & provisions | 1,430.40 | 956.61 | 1.102.42 | 696.67 | 1,035.99 |
| 22 | Net working capital | 770.22 | 1,170.48 | 850.80 | 967.04 | 586.04 |
| 23 | Pre-operative expenses | | | | | |
| 24 | Capital employed | 1,414.42 | 1,353.62 | 1,279.43 | 1,318.57 | 795.29 |
| 25 | Debt equity ratio | 1.62 | 1.76 | 1.79 | 2.36 | 26.46 |
| 26 | Current Ratio | 1.54 | 2.22 | 1.77 | 2.39 | 1.57 |
| 27 | Liquid ratio | 1.03 | 1.66 | 1.66 | 2.26 | 1.49 |
| 28 | Sales | 2.013.63 | 1,428.11 | 2,043.80 | 2,011.24 | 1,838.53 |
| 29 | Other income | 31.52 | 17.30 | 12.86 | 35.30 | 18.82 |
| 30 | Income | 2,045.15 | 1,445.41 | 2,056.66 | 2,046.54 | 1,857.35 |
| 31 | Raw material consumed / Traded goods | 1.647.10 | 1,321.34 | 1,639.76 | 1,584.38 | 1,413.67 |
| 32 | Changes in inventory | (187.43) | (413.87) | (36.71) | (7.01) | 25.79 |
| 33 | Personnel expenses | 130.64 | 145.89 | 117.51 | 90.02 | 79.83 |
| 34 | Other expenses | 347.33 | 291.63 | 235.66 | 268.13 | 196.08 |
| 35 | Expenses | 1,937.64 | 1,344.99 | 1,956.22 | 1,935.52 | 1,715.37 |
| 36 | Operating Profit ( PBIDT) | 107.51 | 100.42 | 100.44 | 111.02 | 141.98 |
| 37 | EBITDA / Sales % | 5.3% | 6.9% | 4.9% | 5.4% | 7.6% |
| 38 | Depreciation | 13.38 | 18.45 | 18.80 | 18.02 | 17.28 |
| 39 | EBIT | 94.13 | 81.97 | 81.64 | 93.00 | 124.70 |
| 40 | EBIT / Sales % | 4.6% | 5.7% | 4.0% | 4.5% | 6.7% |
| 41 | Finance cost | 34.38 | 31.89 | 20.55 | 35.90 | 19.63 |
| 42 | PBT | 59.75 | 50.08 | 61.09 | 57.10 | 105.07 |
| 43 | Extra-ordinary item | - | - | - | 310.14 | |
| 44 | Tax | 17.64 | 17.05 | 19.48 | 33.70 | 44.33 |
| 45 | Net Profit (PAT) | 42.11 | 33.03 | 41.61 | 333.54 | 60.74 |
| 46 | Net Profit /Sales % | 2.1% | 2.3% | 2.0% | 1.1% | 3.3% |
| 47 | Cash Accrual (NP+DEP) | 55.49 | 51.48 | 60.41 | 351.56 | 78.02 |
| 48 | Fixed Assets turnover ratio | 3.17 | 7.89 | 4.80 | 5.82 | 8.88 |
| 49 | Working capital turnover ratio | 2.66 | 1.23 | 2.42 | 2.12 | 3.17 |
| 48 | Capital turnover ratio | 1.45 | 1.07 | 1.61 | 1.55 | 2.34 |
| 49 | Return on capital employed % | 6.7% | 6.1% | 6.4% | 7.1% | 15.7% |
| 50 | Return on net worth % | 8.8% | 7.6% | 10.4% | 6.5% | 236.6% |

Based on the above numbers a financial analysis has been carried out which would bring out the financial health of the organization. Please refer to the analysis below.

## Profitability Analysis

| Year | 2020-21 | 2019-20 | 2018-19 | 2017-18 | 2016-17 |
|---|---|---|---|---|---|
| Sales and other income | 2,045.15 | 1,445.41 | 2,056.66 | 2,046.54 | 1,857.35 |
| Raw material consumed / Traded goods | 1,647.10 | 1,321.34 | 1,639.76 | 1,584.38 | 1,413.67 |
| Changes in inventory | (187.43) | (413.87) | (36.71) | (7.01) | 25.79 |
| Personnel expenses | 130.64 | 145.89 | 117.51 | 90.02 | 79.83 |
| Other expenses | 347.33 | 291.63 | 235.66 | 268.13 | 196.08 |
| Expenses | 1,937.64 | 1,344.99 | 1,956.22 | 1,935.52 | 1,715.37 |
| EBITDA | 107.51 | 100.42 | 100.44 | 111.02 | 141.98 |
| EBITDA / Sales % | 5.3% | 6.9% | 4.9% | 5.4% | 7.6% |
| Depreciation | 13.38 | 18.45 | 18.80 | 18.02 | 17.28 |
| EBIT | 94.13 | 81.97 | 81.64 | 93.00 | 124.70 |
| Finance charges | 34.38 | 31.89 | 20.55 | 35.90 | 19.63 |
| PBT | **59.75** | **50.08** | 61.09 | 57.10 | 105.07 |
| Extra-ordinary item | 0 | 0 | 0 | 310.14 | 0 |
| Tax | 17.64 | 17.05 | 19.48 | 33.70 | 44.33 |
| PAT | **42.11** | **33.03** | 41.61 | 333.54 | 60.74 |

## PBT and PAT as percentage of sales

| Year | 2020-21 | 2019-20 | 2018-19 | 2017-18 | 2016-17 |
|---|---|---|---|---|---|
| EBITDA as a % of Revenue | 5.3% | 6.9% | 4.9% | 5.4% | 7.6% |
| EBIT as % of Revenue | 4.6% | 5.7% | 4.0% | 4.5% | 6.7% |
| PAT as % of Revenue | 2.1% | 2.3% | 2.0% | 1.1% | 3.3% |

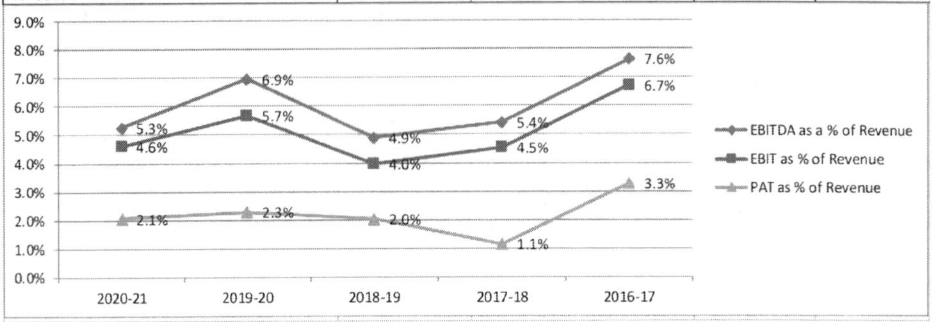


## Revenue Trend

| Year | 2020-21 | 2019-20 | 2018-19 | 2017-18 | 2016-17 |
|---|---|---|---|---|---|
| Revenue | 2014 | 1428 | 2044 | 2011 | 1839 |
| Break-even sales | 1836 | 1311 | 1780 | 1797 | 1390 |

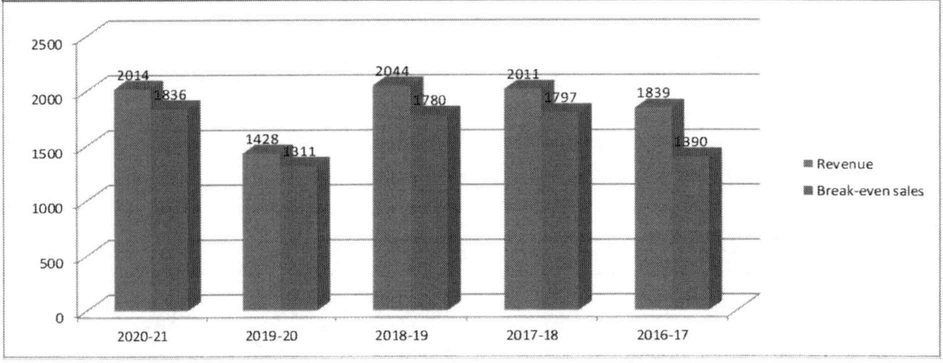

## Expenditure Trend

| Year | 2020-21 | 2019-20 | 2018-19 | 2017-18 | 2016-17 |
|---|---|---|---|---|---|
| Raw material / traded products | 1647.10 | 1321.34 | 1639.76 | 1584.38 | 1413.67 |
| Personnel expenses | 130.64 | 145.89 | 117.51 | 90.02 | 79.83 |
| Other expenses | 347.33 | 291.63 | 235.66 | 268.13 | 196.08 |
| Total | 2125.07 | 1758.86 | 1992.93 | 1942.53 | 1689.58 |

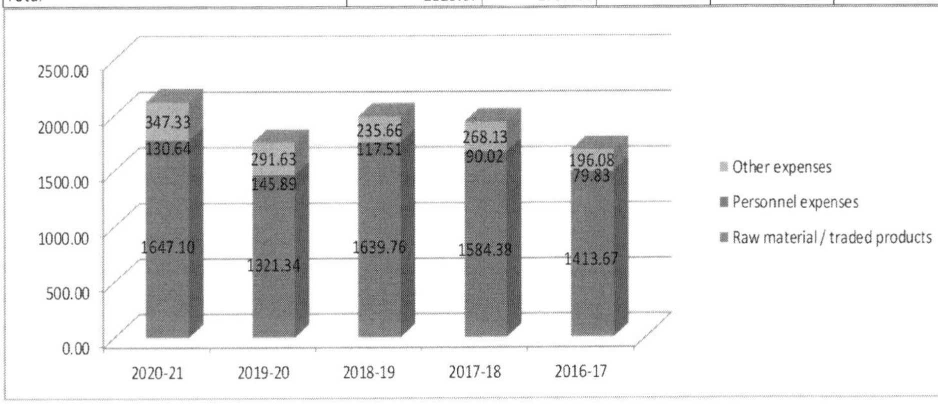


## Expenditure as a percentage of sales

| Year | 2020-21 | 2019-20 | 2018-19 | 2017-18 | 2016-17 |
|---|---|---|---|---|---|
| Raw material as % of Revenue | 80.5% | 91.4% | 79.7% | 77.4% | 76.1% |
| Personnel expenses as % of Revenue | 6.4% | 10.1% | 5.7% | 4.4% | 4.3% |
| Other expenses /Revenue % | 17.0% | 20.2% | 11.5% | 13.1% | 10.6% |
| Expenses as % of Revenue | 94.7% | 121.7% | 96.9% | 94.9% | 91.0% |

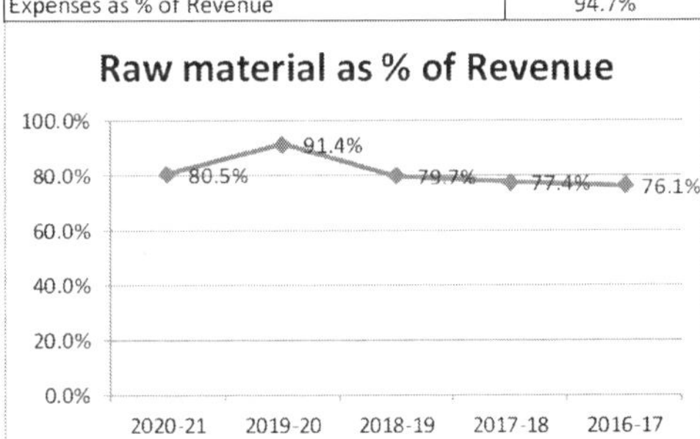


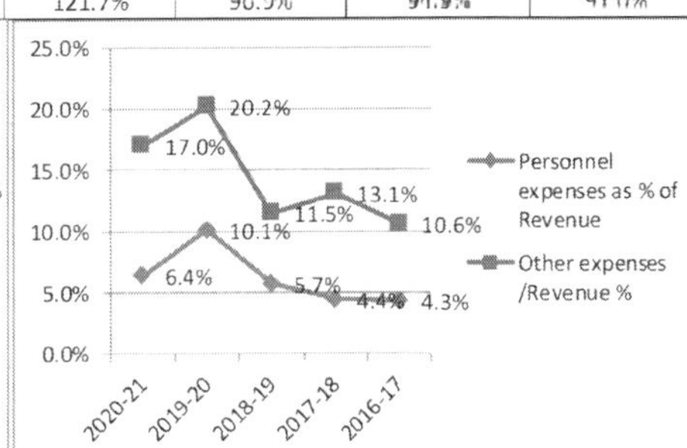

## EBITDA Trend

| Year | 2020-21 | 2019-20 | 2018-19 | 2017-18 | 2016-17 |
|---|---|---|---|---|---|
| Income | 2,045 | 1,445 | 2,057 | 2,047 | 1,857 |
| Expenses | 1,938 | 1,345 | 1,956 | 1,936 | 1,715 |
| Operating Profit ( EBIDT A) | 108 | 100 | 100 | 111 | 142 |
| EBITDA / Sales % | 5.3% | 6.9% | 4.9% | 5.4% | 7.6% |

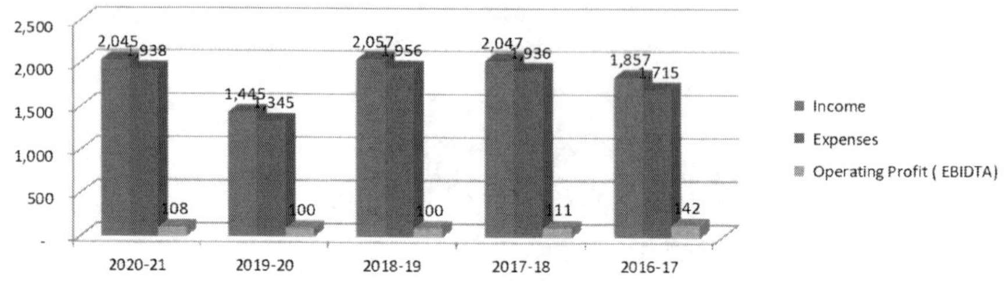


**Without stock difference**

| Year | 2020-21 | 2019-20 | 2018-19 | 2017-18 | 2016-17 |
|---|---|---|---|---|---|
| Income | 2,045 | 1,445 | 2,057 | 2,047 | 1,857 |
| Expenses | 2,125 | 1,759 | 1,993 | 1,943 | 1,690 |
| Operating Profit ( EBIDT A) | -80 | -313 | 64 | 104 | 168 |
| EBITDA / Sales % | -3.9% | -21.7% | 3.1% | 5.1% | 9.0% |

## Contribution Analysis

| Year | 2020-21 | 2019-20 | 2018-19 | 2017-18 | 2016-17 |
|---|---|---|---|---|---|
| Revenue | 2,045 | 1,445 | 2,057 | 2,047 | 1,857 |
| Total | 2,045 | 1,445 | 2,057 | 2,047 | 1,857 |
| Raw material | 1,647 | 1,321 | 1,640 | 1,584 | 1,414 |
| Stock difference | -187 | -414 | -37 | -7 | 26 |
| Variable cost total | 1,460 | 907 | 1,603 | 1,577 | 1,439 |
| Contribution | 585 | 538 | 454 | 469 | 418 |
| Contribution / revenue % | 28.6% | 37.2% | 22.1% | 22.9% | 22.5% |
| Personnel expenses | 131 | 146 | 118 | 90 | 80 |
| Other expenses | 347 | 292 | 236 | 268 | 196 |
| Depreciation | 13 | 18 | 19 | 18 | 17 |
| Finance charges | 34 | 32 | 21 | 36 | 20 |
| Fixed cost total | 526 | 488 | 393 | 412 | 313 |
| Fixed Expenses as % of revenue | 25.7% | 33.8% | 19.1% | 20.1% | 16.8% |
| PBT | 60 | 50 | 61 | 57 | 105 |
| PBT as % of revenue | 2.9% | 3.5% | 3.0% | 2.8% | 5.7% |
| Break even sales | 1,836 | 1,311 | 1,780 | 1,797 | 1,390 |

## Debt Equity Ratio

| Year | 2020-21 | 2019-20 | 2018-19 | 2017-18 |
|---|---|---|---|---|
| Debt equity ratio | 1.62 | 1.76 | 1.79 | 2.36 |

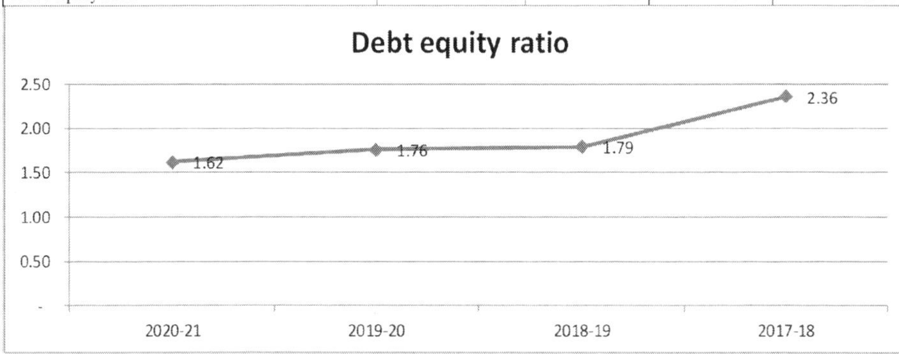


## Capital Employed Source

| Year | 2020-21 | 2019-20 | 2018-19 | 2017-18 | 2016-17 |
|---|---|---|---|---|---|
| Share capital | 600.00 | 600.00 | 600.00 | 600.00 | 600.00 |
| Reserves and surplus | (124.04) | (166.15) | (199.18) | (240.79) | (574.33) |
| Shareholders funds | 475.96 | 433.85 | 400.82 | 359.21 | 25.67 |
| Long term borrowings | 772.48 | 763.66 | 718.03 | 846.03 | 679.17 |
| Short term borrowings | 165.98 | 156.11 | 160.58 | 113.33 | 90.45 |
| **Capital employed** | **1,414.42** | **1,353.62** | **1,279.43** | **1,318.57** | **795.29** |

## Capital Employed Application

| Year | 2020-21 | 2019-20 | 2018-19 | 2017-18 | 2016-17 |
|---|---|---|---|---|---|
| Net block (including capital WIP) | 127.17 | 120.99 | 123.84 | 128.44 | 139.25 |
| Other non-current assets | 487.14 | 44.31 | 263.50 | 202.32 | 35.84 |
| Long term loans and advances | 29.89 | 17.84 | 28.29 | 7.74 | 21.13 |
| Non-current investments | - | - | 13.00 | 13.03 | 13.03 |
| Net current assets | 770.22 | 1,170.48 | 850.80 | 967.04 | 586.04 |
| **Capital employed** | **1,414.42** | **1,353.62** | **1,279.43** | **1,318.57** | **795.29** |

## Working Capital Trend

| Year | 2020-21 | 2019-20 | 2018-19 | 2017-18 | 2016-17 |
|---|---|---|---|---|---|
| Gross current assets | 2,200.62 | 2,127.09 | 1,953.22 | 1,663.71 | 1,622.03 |
| Current liabilities & provisions | 1,430.40 | 956.61 | 1,102.42 | 696.67 | 1,035.99 |
| **Working capital** | **770.22** | **1,170.48** | **850.80** | **967.04** | **586.04** |

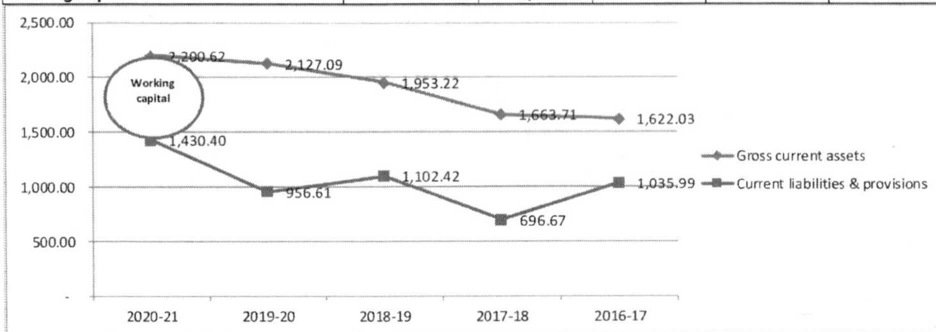


## Gross Current Assets and Liabilities

| Year | 2020-21 | 2019-20 | 2018-19 | 2017-18 | 2016-17 |
|---|---|---|---|---|---|
| Inventories | 724.31 | 536.87 | 123.00 | 86.29 | 79.29 |
| Sundry debtors | 1,344.80 | 1,265.19 | 1,616.82 | 1,126.99 | 1,194.86 |
| Cash & bank balances | 8.02 | 136.92 | 88.77 | 307.51 | 241.59 |
| Loans & Advances | 123.49 | 188.11 | 124.63 | 142.92 | 106.29 |
| **Gross current assets** | **2,200.62** | **2,127.09** | **1,953.22** | **1,663.71** | **1,622.03** |

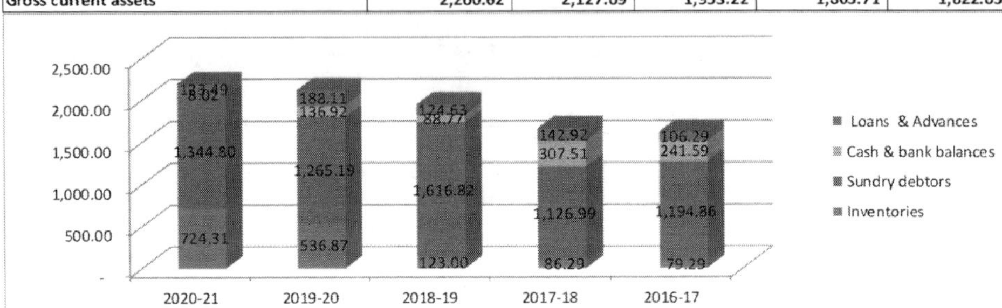


## Current liabilities

| Year | 2020-21 | 2019-20 | 2018-19 | 2017-18 | 2016-17 |
|---|---|---|---|---|---|
| Current liabilities | 1,412.76 | 939.61 | 1,082.94 | 678.50 | 1,035.99 |
| Provisions | 17.64 | 17.00 | 19.48 | 18.17 | - |
| **Total** | **1,430.40** | **956.61** | **1,102.42** | **696.67** | **1,035.99** |

## Current Ratio and Liquid Ratio

| Year | 2020-21 | 2019-20 | 2018-19 | 2017-18 | 2016-17 |
|---|---|---|---|---|---|
| Current ratio | 1.54 | 2.22 | 1.77 | 2.39 | 1.57 |
| Liquid ratio | 1.03 | 1.66 | 1.66 | 2.26 | 1.49 |

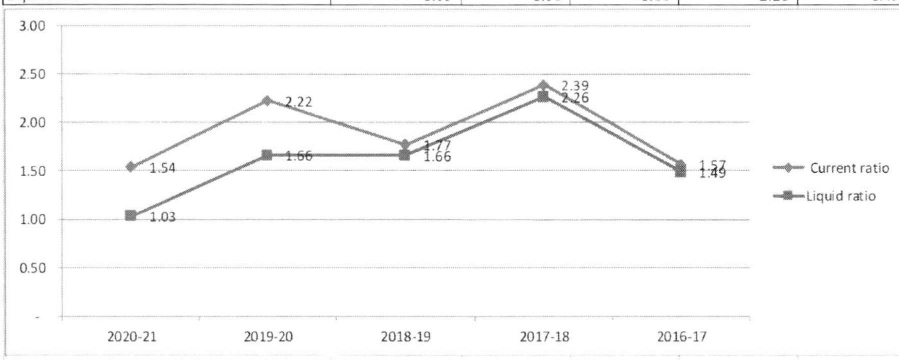


## Days Sales Outstanding (DSO)

| Year | 2020-21 | 2019-20 | 2018-19 | 2017-18 | 2016-17 |
|---|---|---|---|---|---|
| Days Sales Outstanding (DSO) | **236.72** | **315.11** | **283.01** | **198.25** | **231.59** |

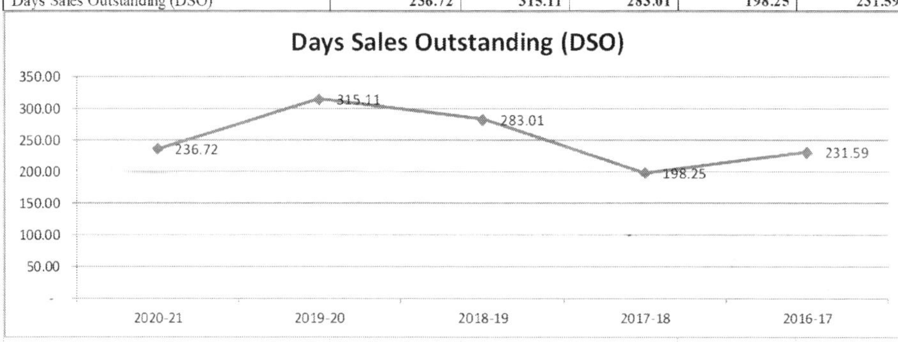


## Inventory Days Sales (IDS)

| Year | 2020-21 | 2019-20 | 2018-19 | 2017-18 | 2016-17 |
|---|---|---|---|---|---|
| Inventory days sales (IDS) | **158.31** | **146.27** | **27.00** | **19.61** | **20.19** |

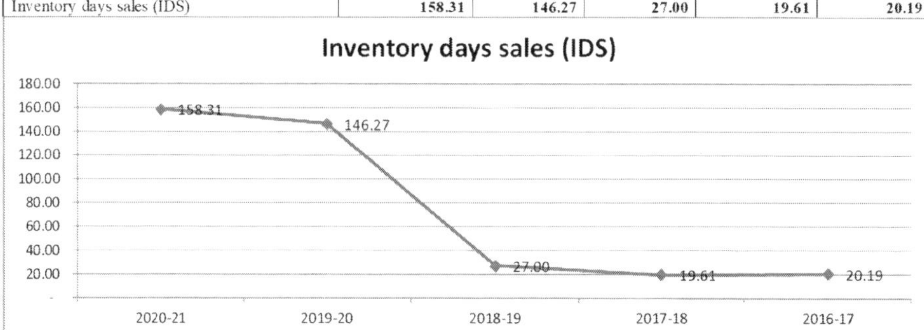

## Creditors Days Outstanding (CDO)

| Year | 2020-21 | 2019-20 | 2018-19 | 2017-18 | 2016-17 |
|---|---|---|---|---|---|
| Creditors days outstanding | 265.76 | 256.05 | 202.88 | 129.58 | 217.42 |

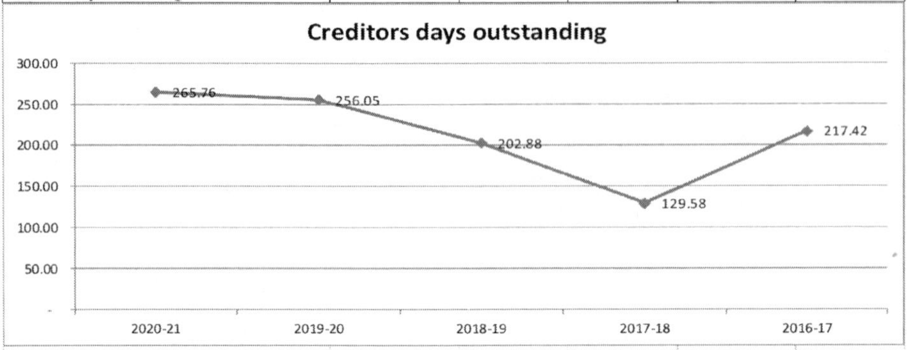


## Return on Capital Employed

| Year | 2020-21 | 2019-20 | 2018-19 | 2017-18 | 2016-17 |
|---|---|---|---|---|---|
| EBIT / Sales % | 4.6% | 5.7% | 4.0% | 4.5% | 6.7% |
| Capital turnover ratio | 1.45 | 1.07 | 1.61 | 1.55 | 2.34 |
| Return on capital employed % | 6.7% | 6.1% | 6.4% | 7.1% | 15.7% |

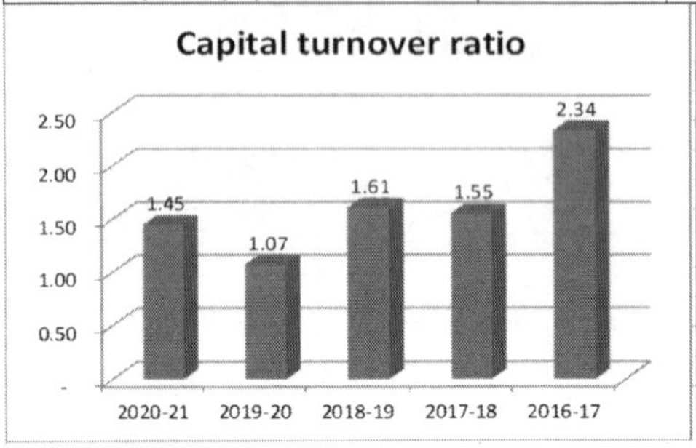


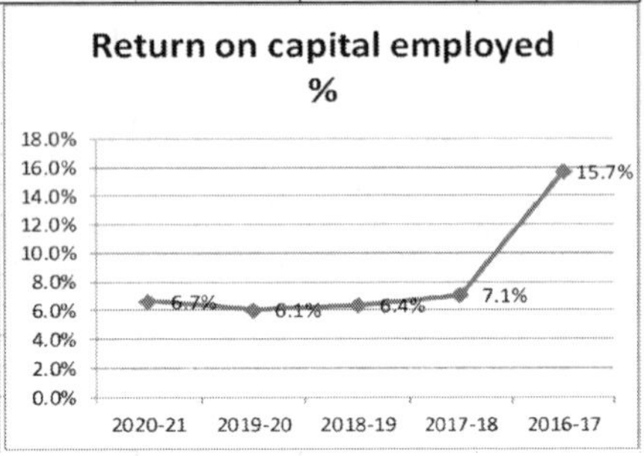


## Return on Net Worth

| Year | 2020-21 | 2019-20 | 2018-19 | 2017-18 |
|---|---|---|---|---|
| Return on net worth % | 8.8% | 7.6% | 10.4% | 6.5% |

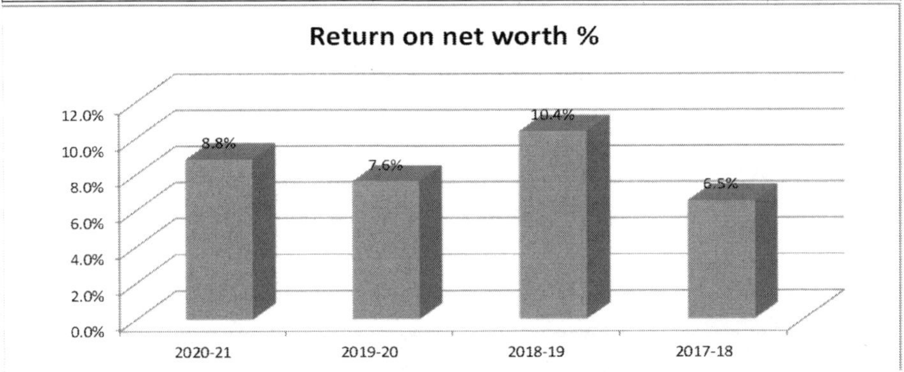

## Source and Application of Funds

| Year | 2020-21 | 2019-20 | 2018-19 | 2017-18 |
|---|---|---|---|---|
| | | | | |
| **Sources of Funds** | | | | |
| **Increase in Shareholders funds** | 42.11 | 33.03 | 41.61 | 333.54 |
| Long term borrowings | 8.82 | 45.63 | -128.00 | 166.86 |
| Deferred tax Liabilities | - | - | - | - |
| Long term provisions | - | - | - | - |
| Short term borrowings | 9.87 | -4.47 | 47.25 | 22.88 |
| Opening Balance - Cash in hand | 136.92 | 88.77 | 307.51 | 241.59 |
| **Total Available Funds** | 197.72 | 162.96 | 268.37 | 764.87 |
| **Utilization of Funds** | | | | |
| Net fixed assets | 6.18 | -2.85 | -4.60 | -10.81 |
| Non-current investments | - | -13.00 | -0.03 | - |
| Other non-current assets | 442.83 | -219.19 | 61.18 | 166.48 |
| Long term loans and advances | 12.05 | -10.45 | 20.55 | -13.39 |
| Inventories | 187.44 | 413.87 | 36.71 | 7.00 |
| Debtors | 79.61 | -351.63 | 489.83 | -67.87 |
| Loans & Advances | -64.62 | 63.48 | -18.29 | 36.63 |
| Current assets | 202.43 | 125.72 | 508.25 | -24.24 |
| Creditors | 473.15 | -143.33 | 404.44 | -357.49 |
| Provisions | 0.64 | -2.48 | 1.31 | 18.17 |
| Current liabilities & provisions | 473.79 | -145.81 | 405.75 | -339.32 |
| Net current assets | -271.36 | 271.53 | 102.50 | 315.08 |
| **Total Utilization of Funds** | 189.70 | 26.04 | 179.60 | 457.36 |
| | | | | |
| **Closing cash balance** | 8.02 | 136.92 | 88.77 | 307.51 |
| | | | | |
| **Reconcilition of cash surplus / deficit** | | | | |
| Opening balance | 136.92 | 88.77 | 307.51 | 241.59 |
| Closing balance | 8.02 | 136.92 | 88.77 | 307.51 |
| **(Surplus) / deficit** | 128.90 | (48.15) | 218.74 | (65.92) |

## Conclusions from the above analysis

### Profitability Analysis

Though Contribution as a percentage on sales has been growing, the EBITDA margin along with PBT and PAT has been dropping. Also it appears whatever, profit that has been reflected is primarily owing to stock difference. Between closing and opening inventories. This signifies some of the inventories lying unsold have increased over opening inventories.

### Liquidity Analysis

This is corroborated by liquidity ratios where gross current assets, especially inventories are increasing significantly. This is also double checked with the increase in Inventories days sales.

### Return on capital employed

On an overall basis, return on capital employed as dropped owing to reduced profitability and capital turnover ratio. It also shows that there is significant idle capacity sitting in the system and activities need to be improved to push for higher revenue.

## 16.10 FINANCIAL ANALYSIS OF A RETAIL ORGANIZATION

| SR.NO. | SUBJECT | 2020-21 | 2019-20 | 2018-19 | 2017-18 |
|---|---|---|---|---|---|
| | | | | | |
| 1 | Capital | 15,277,220 | 14,382,183 | 11,135,352 | 5,646,198 |
| 2 | Reserves | 3,300,544 | 1,421,753 | 705,160 | 109,483 |
| 3 | Share application pending allotment | - | - | - | |
| 4 | Net Worth | 18,577,764 | 15,803,935 | 11,840,512 | 5,755,680 |
| 5 | Long term borrowings | 23,795,904 | 34,162,431 | 23,441,379 | 26,330,837 |
| 6 | Deferred tax Liabilities | - | - | - | - |
| 7 | Long term provisions | - | - | - | - |
| 8 | Short term borrowings | 10,188,070 | - | - | - |
| 9 | Capital employed | 52,561,739 | 49,966,367 | 35,281,891 | 32,086,518 |
| 10 | Opening WDV | 3,957,676 | 2,108,899 | 2,172,720 | 997,680 |
| 11 | Add: Capex | 1,387,756 | 2,531,501 | 326,852 | 1,535,924 |
| 12 | Closing WDV | 5,345,432 | 4,640,400 | 2,499,572 | 2,533,604 |
| 13 | Less: Depreciation | 773,740 | 682,724 | 390,674 | 360,884 |
| 14 | Net Block | 4,571,692 | 3,957,676 | 2,108,898 | 2,172,720 |
| 15 | Deferred tax assets | - | - | - | - |
| 16 | Long term loans and advance | - | 3,822,907 | 3,354,457 | 3,026,132 |
| 17 | Inventories | 94,296,904 | 72,568,745 | 44,632,871 | 46,914,174 |
| 18 | Sundry debtors | - | 380,712 | 272,250 | 895,500 |
| 19 | Cash & bank balances | 1,913,302 | 1,587,961 | 1,672,524 | 2,683,868 |
| 20 | Other current assets, Loans & advances | 4,450,846 | 177,583 | 259,965 | 51,628 |
| 21 | Current Assets | 100,661,052 | 74,715,001 | 46,837,610 | 50,545,170 |
| 22 | Current Liability | 52,671,005 | 32,444,166 | 16,771,531 | 23,627,382 |
| 23 | Provisions | - | 85,051 | 247,543 | 30,122 |
| 24 | Current Liability & provisions | 52,671,005 | 32,529,217 | 17,019,074 | 23,627,382 |
| 25 | Net working capital | 47,990,047 | 42,185,784 | 29,818,536 | 26,917,788 |
| 26 | Pre-operative expenses | | | | |
| 27 | Capital employed | 52,561,739 | 49,966,367 | 35,281,891 | 32,116,640 |
| 28 | Debt equity ratio | 1.28 | 2.16 | 1.98 | 4.57 |
| 29 | Current Ratio | 1.91 | 2.30 | 2.75 | 2.14 |
| 30 | Liquid ratio | 0.12 | 0.07 | 0.13 | 0.15 |
| 32 | Sales | 115,790,557 | 85,301,424 | 74,083,597 | 56,768,796 |
| 33 | Other income | - | - | - | - |
| 34 | Income | 115,790,557 | 85,301,424 | 74,083,597 | 56,768,796 |
| 35 | Raw material consumed / Traded goods | 110,221,581 | 92,713,505 | 55,350,017 | 67,505,825 |
| 36 | Changes in inventory | (21,728,159) | (27,935,874) | 2,281,303 | (18,903,032) |
| 38 | Personnel expenses | 4,636,336 | 2,968,147 | 2,552,743 | 737,985 |
| 39 | Other expenses | 12,753,339 | 10,273,167 | 12,063,547 | 4,509,032 |
| 41 | Expenses | 105,883,097 | 78,018,945 | 72,247,610 | 53,849,810 |
| 42 | Operating Profit ( PBIDT) | 9,907,460 | 7,282,479 | 1,835,987 | 2,918,986 |
| 43 | EBITDA / Sales % | 9% | 9% | 2% | 5% |
| 44 | Depreciation | 773,740 | 682,724 | 390,674 | 360,884 |
| 45 | EBIT | 9,133,720 | 6,599,755 | 1,445,313 | 2,558,102 |
| 46 | EBIT / Sales % | 8% | 8% | 2% | 5% |
| 47 | Finance cost | 3,988,895 | 3,595,542 | 2,945,666 | 1,919,909 |
| 48 | PBT | 5,144,824 | 3,004,213 | (1,500,353) | 638,193 |
| 49 | Tax | 1,697,792 | 472,820 | 228,895 | 40,130 |
| 50 | Net Profit (PAT) | 3,447,032.34 | 2,531,393.00 | (1,729,248.00) | 598,062.83 |
| 51 | Net Profit /Sales % | 3.0% | 3.0% | -2.3% | 1.1% |
| 52 | Cash Accrual (NP+ DEP) | 4,220,772 | 3,214,117 | (1,338,574) | 958,947 |
| 53 | Capital turnover ratio | 2.20 | 1.71 | 2.10 | 1.77 |
| 54 | Return on capital employed % | 17.4% | 13.2% | 4.1% | 8.0% |
| 55 | Return on net worth % | 18.6% | 16.0% | -14.6% | 10.4% |

Enterprise ratio analysis based on the above numbers are highlighted in the respective tables below.

## SALES AND PROFITABILITY ANALYSIS

**(RS LAKHS)**

| Year | 2020-21 | % | 2019-20 | % | 2018-19 | % |
|---|---|---|---|---|---|---|
| **Sales** | 1,157.9 | | 853.01 | | 740.84 | |
| Other income | - | | - | | - | |
| **Sales and other income** | 1,157.9 | | 853.01 | | 740.84 | |
| Raw material consumed / Traded goods | 884.9 | 76.4% | 647.8 | 75.9% | 576.3 | 77.8% |
| Gross Margin | 273.0 | 32.0% | 205.2 | 24.1% | 164.5 | 22.2% |
| Personnel expenses | 46.4 | 4.0% | 29.7 | 3.5% | 25.5 | 3.4% |
| Other Expenses | 127.5 | 11.0% | 102.7 | 12.0% | 120.6 | 16.3% |
| **Other Expenses** | 173.9 | 15.0% | 132.4 | 15.5% | 146.2 | 19.7% |
| **Operating Profit ( EBIDTA)** | 99.1 | 8.6% | 72.8 | 8.5% | 18.4 | 2.5% |
| EBITDA / Sales % | 8.6% | | 8.5% | | 2.5% | |
| Depreciation | 7.7 | 0.7% | 6.8 | 0.8% | 3.9 | 0.5% |
| EBIT | 91.3 | 7.9% | 66.0 | 7.7% | 14.5 | 2.0% |
| EBIT / Sales % | 7.9% | | 7.7% | | 2.0% | |
| Finance cost | 39.9 | 3.4% | 36.0 | 4.2% | 29.5 | 4.0% |
| PBT | 51.4 | 4.4% | 30.0 | 3.5% | (15.0) | -2.0% |
| Tax | 17.0 | 1.5% | 4.7 | 0.6% | 2.3 | 0.3% |
| Net Profit (PAT) | 34.5 | 3.0% | 25.3 | 3.0% | -17.3 | -2.3% |
| Net Profit /Sales % | 3.0% | | 3.0% | | -2.3% | |
| Cash Accrual (NP+DEP) | 42.2 | | 32.1 | | (13.4) | |

## REVENUE TREND (RS LAKHS)

| Year | 2020-21 | 2019-20 | 2018-19 | 2017-18 |
|---|---|---|---|---|
| Revenue | 1,158 | 853 | 741 | 568 |
| Break-even sales | 940 | 728 | 808 | 523 |

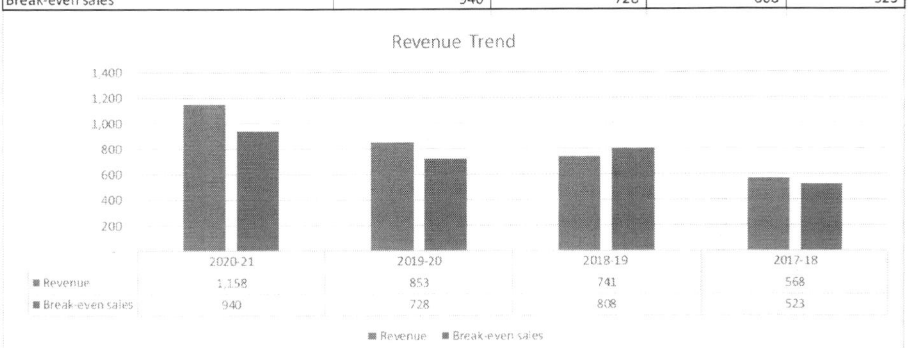


## EXPENDITURE AS PERCENTAGE OF SALES

| Year | 2020-21 | 2019-20 | 2018-19 | 2017-18 |
|---|---|---|---|---|
| Raw material as % of Revenue | 95.2% | 108.7% | 74.7% | 118.9% |
| Changes in inventory | -18.8% | -32.7% | 3.1% | -33.3% |
| Personnel expenses as % of Revenue | 4.0% | 3.5% | 3.4% | 1.3% |
| Other expenses /Revenue % | 11.0% | 12.0% | 16.3% | 7.9% |
| Expenses as % of Revenue | 91.4% | 91.5% | 97.5% | 94.9% |

## CONTRIBUTION ANALYSIS (RS LAKHS)

| Year | 2020-21 | 2019-20 | 2018-19 | 2017-18 |
|---|---|---|---|---|
| Revenue | 1,158 | 853 | 741 | 568 |
| Total | 1,158 | 853 | 741 | 568 |
| Raw material | 1,102 | 927 | 554 | 675 |
| Stock difference | (217) | (279) | 23 | (189) |
| Variable cost total | 885 | 648 | 576 | 486 |
| Contribution | 273 | 205 | 165 | 82 |
| Contribution / revenue % | 23.6% | 24.1% | 22.2% | 14.4% |
| Personnel expenses | 46 | 30 | 26 | 7 |
| Other expenses | 128 | 103 | 121 | 45 |
| Depreciation | 8 | 7 | 4 | 4 |
| Finance charges | 40 | 36 | 29 | 19 |
| Fixed cost total | 221.5 | 175.2 | 179.5 | 75.3 |
| Fixed Expenses as % of revenue | 19.1% | 20.5% | 24.2% | 13.3% |
| PBT | 51 | 30 | -15 | 6 |
| PBT as % of revenue | 4.4% | 3.5% | -2.0% | 1.1% |
| Break even sales | 939.7 | 728.2 | 808.4 | 523.3 |

## EBITDA TREND

| Year | 2015-16 | 2014-15 | 2013-14 | 2012-13 |
|---|---|---|---|---|
| Income | 1,158 | 853 | 741 | 568 |
| Expenses | 1,059 | 780 | 722 | 538 |
| Operating Profit ( EBIDTA) | 99 | 73 | 18 | 29 |
| EBITDA / Sales % | 8.6% | 8.5% | 2.5% | 5.1% |

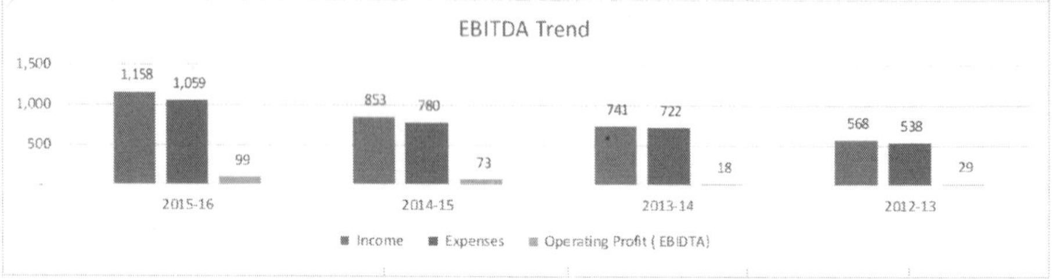


## PBT & PAT AS PERCENTAGE OF SALES

| Year | 2020-21 | 2019-20 | 2018-19 | 2017-18 |
|---|---|---|---|---|
| EBITDA as a % of Revenue | 8.6% | 8.5% | 2.5% | 5.1% |
| EBIT as % of Revenue | 7.9% | 7.7% | 2.0% | 4.5% |
| PAT as % of Revenue | 3.0% | 3.0% | -2.3% | 1.1% |

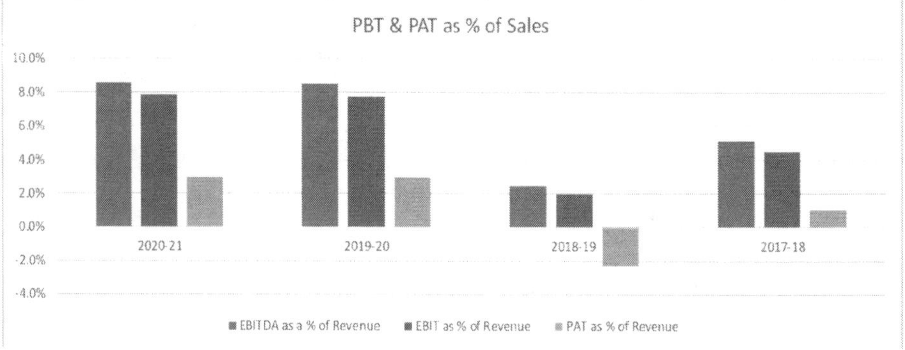

## SOLVENCY ANALYSIS

## CAPITAL EMPLOYED – SOURCE

| Year | 2020-21 | 2019-20 | 2018-19 | 2017-18 |
|---|---|---|---|---|
| Shareholders funds | 186 | 158 | 118 | 58 |
| Long term borrowings | 238 | 342 | 234 | 263 |
| Short term borrowings | 102 | - | - | - |
| **Capital employed** | **526** | **500** | **353** | **321** |

## CAPITAL EMPLOYED – APPLICATION

| Year | 2020-21 | 2019-20 | 2018-19 | 2017-18 |
|---|---|---|---|---|
| Net block | 46 | 40 | 21 | 22 |
| Long term loans and advances | - | 38 | 34 | 30 |
| Net current assets | 480 | 422 | 298 | 269 |
| **Capital employed** | **526** | **500** | **353** | **321** |

## DEBT EQUITY RATIO

| Year | 2020-21 | 2019-20 | 2018-19 | 2017-18 |
|---|---|---|---|---|
| Debt equity ratio | 1.28 | 2.16 | 1.98 | 4.57 |

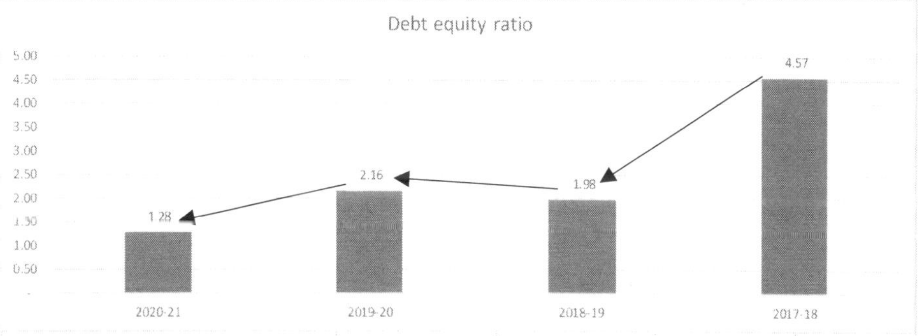


## LIQUIDITY ANALYSIS (RS LAKHS)

| Year | 2020-21 | 2019-20 | 2018-19 | 2017-18 |
|---|---|---|---|---|
| Gross current assets | 1,007 | 747 | 468 | 505 |
| Current liabilities & provisions | 527 | 325 | 170 | 236 |
| Working capital | 480 | 422 | 298 | 269 |

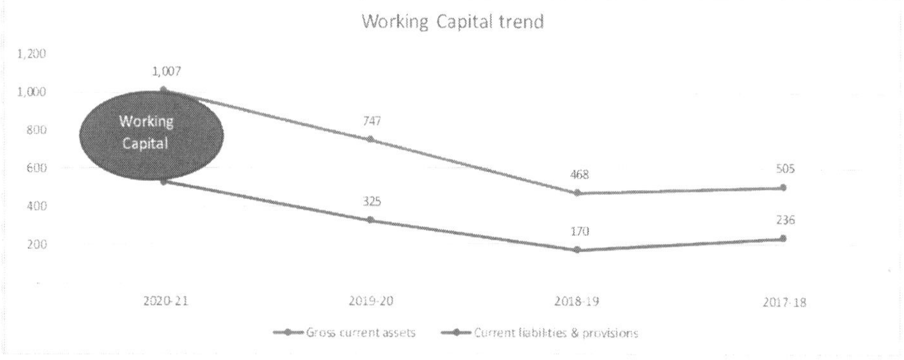

## CURRENT RATIO AND LIQUID RATIO

| Year | 2020-21 | 2019-20 | 2018-19 | 2017-18 |
|---|---|---|---|---|
| Current ratio | 1.91 | 2.30 | 2.75 | 2.14 |
| Liquid ratio | 0.12 | 0.07 | 0.13 | 0.15 |

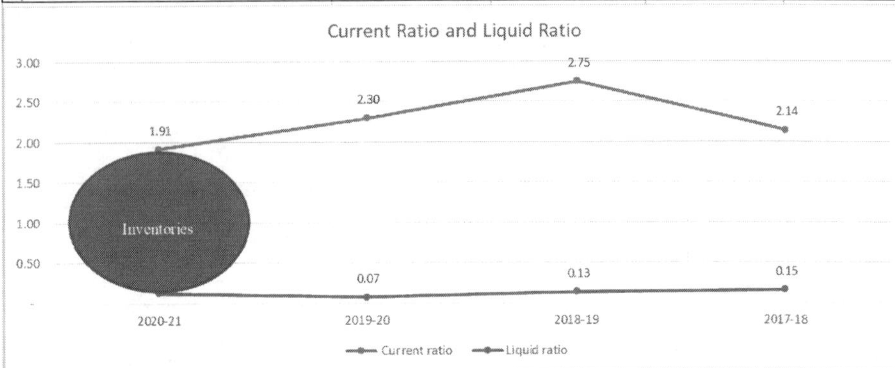


## GROSS CURRENT ASSET TREND

| Year | 2020-21 | 2019-20 | 2018-19 | 2017-18 |
|---|---|---|---|---|
| Inventories | 943 | 726 | 446 | 469 |
| Sundry debtors | - | 4 | 3 | 9 |
| Cash & bank balances | 19 | 16 | 17 | 27 |
| Loans & Advances | 45 | 2 | 3 | 1 |
| **Gross current assets** | 1,007 | 747 | 468 | 505 |

## CURRENT LIABILITIES TREND

| Year | 2020-21 | 2019-20 | 2018-19 | 2017-18 |
|---|---|---|---|---|
| Current Liabilities | 527 | 324 | 168 | 236 |
| Provisions | - | 1 | 2 | 0 |
| **Total** | **527** | **325** | **170** | **237** |

## INVENTORIES DAYS SALES (IDS)

| Year | 2020-21 | 2019-20 | 2018-19 | 2017-18 |
|---|---|---|---|---|
| Inventory days sales (IDS) | 312.27 | 285.69 | 294.33 | 253.66 |

## CREDITORS DAYS OUTSTANDING (CDO)

| Year | 2015-16 | 2014-15 | 2013-14 | 2012-13 |
|---|---|---|---|---|
| Creditors days outstanding | 181.57 | 152.18 | 85.98 | 160.15 |

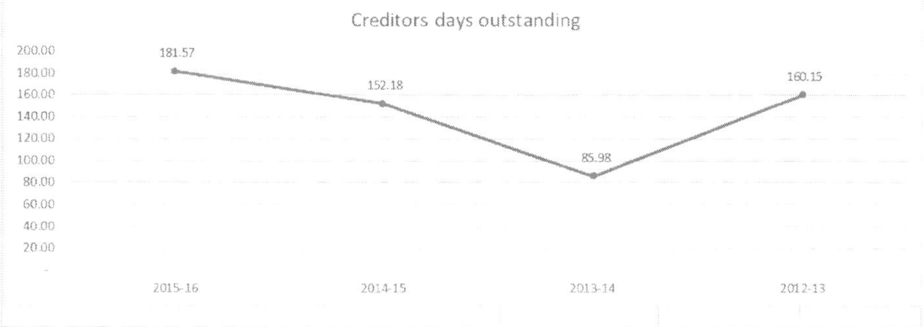


## RETURN ON CAPITAL EMPLOYED

| Year | 2020-21 | 2019-20 | 2018-19 | 2017-18 |
|---|---|---|---|---|
| EBIT / Sales % | 7.9% | 7.7% | 2.0% | 4.5% |
| Capital turnover ratio | 2.20 | 1.71 | 2.10 | 1.77 |
| Return on capital employed % | 17.4% | 13.2% | 4.1% | 8.0% |

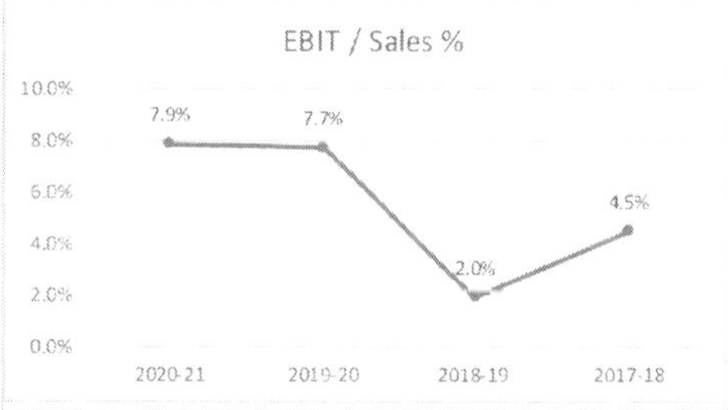


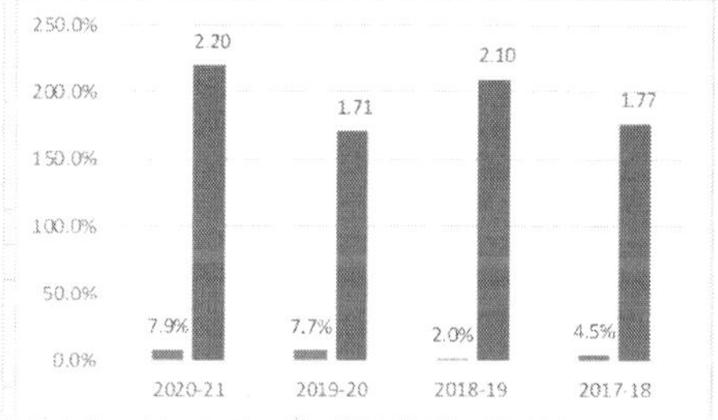


## RETURN ON NET WORTH

| Year | 2020-21 | 2019-20 | 2018-19 | 2017-18 |
|---|---|---|---|---|
| Return on net worth % | 18.6% | 16.0% | -14.6% | 10.4% |

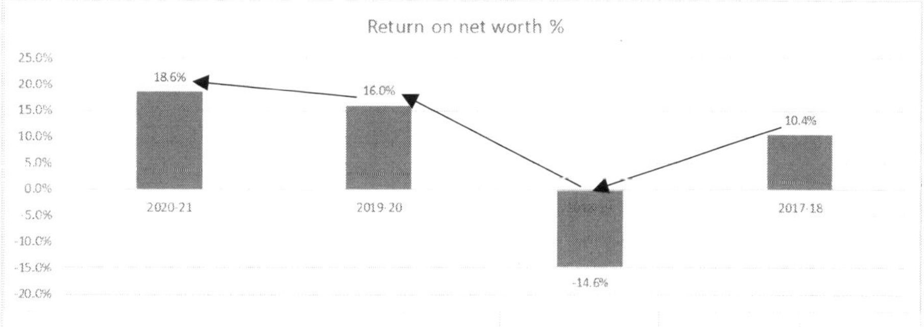


## CONCLUDING REMARKS

Enterprise ratio analysis highlighted above shows that, profitability of the organization is not very high, as being in the retail space, the competition appears to be quite high. However, with respect to Solvency analysis the debt equity ratio appears to be improving with low interest cost. With respect to liquidity analysis the Inventory days sales (IDS) appears to be very high at 312 days, though Creditor's days outstanding (CDO) also appears to be high at 182 days.

Overall, the capital turnover ratio is high and improving leading to reasonably high Return on capital employed (ROCE) and Return on Net Worth.

## 16.11 ANALYTICS AND FINANCIAL RE-ENGINEERING OF A CARPET MANUFACTURING COMPANY BASED ON FINANCIAL STATEMENTS

At the request of the promoters of this organization, a study of Health and Hygiene of the organization was carried out. Based on latest audited financials, the organization was profitable, but carried a very high level of working capital in the form of inventories and these have been funded by mounting short term debt. The primary objectives of the promoters were to enhance the profitability of the organization, make it debt free and improve the return of equity of the family shareholders.

So our work commenced by articulating the objectives and do a drill down of the current financial status of the organization. The results of the study and action recommended are summarized below.

### Objectives of the exercise

- Review and analyse the current financial status and cash flow situation of the organization.
- Identify *high risk* areas through which there has been apparent erosion of cash flows.
- Recommend areas where Financial Re-engineering needs to be carried out.
- Produce indicative results post Financial Re-engineering initiatives and its impact on financial health of the organization, especially in:
  - converting it into a debt free organization and
  - generate enough free cash flows to maintain operations without working capital support.

### Analysis of Current Financial Status

The table below depicts the Financial Summary of the organization with a budget as well as two future projection years.

| Ratio | 2017-18 Actual | 2018-19 Actual | 2019-20 Actual | 2020-21 Budget | 2021-22 Projection | 2022-23 Projection | % Increase |
|---|---|---|---|---|---|---|---|
| Revenue | 12,537 | 15,505 | 14,337 | 14,623 | 15,351 | 16,116 | 5.7% |
| Direct cost | 7,383 | 9,401 | 8,177 | 8,644 | 9,077 | 9,531 | 5.8% |
| Gross Margin | 5,154 | 6,103 | 6,160 | 5,978 | 6,275 | 6,586 | 5.6% |
| Gross Margin % on sales | 41% | 39% | 43% | 41% | 41% | 41% | |
| Indirect cost | 3,000 | 3,713 | 4,292 | 4,721 | 5,193 | 5,713 | 18.1% |
| EBITDA | 2,153 | 2,390 | 1,868 | 1,257 | 1,081 | 873 | -11.9% |
| EBITDA Margin % on sales | 17% | 15% | 13% | 9% | 7% | 5% | |
| Depreciation | 431 | 428 | 482 | 506 | 516 | 527 | 4.4% |
| Interest | 366 | 446 | 340 | 340 | 374 | 412 | 2.5% |
| PBT | 1,356 | 1,516 | 1,046 | 411 | 190 | (66) | (0) |
| Tax | 396 | 386 | 242 | 123 | 57 | 0 | |
| Profit after tax | 960 | 1,130 | 803 | 287 | 133 | (66) | -21.4% |
| Net Operating Profit after tax (NOPAT) | 1,757 | 2,005 | 1,626 | 1,134 | 1,024 | 873 | -10.1% |

Note: 2020-21 budget, 2021-22 and 2022-23 projections have been worked out based on past trend and best judgement.

## Sales and Profitability

Turnover for the previous three years did not show any significant growth. With the uncertainty in business environment on the onset of the Pandemic, there may be an adverse impact on revenue in the next two years.

Gross Margin percentage has been maintained at 41% uniformly over the years.

Employee benefit expenses has been increasing at 26% year on year.

Administration and selling expenses have been increasing at 20% year on year.

EBITDA Margin has been dropping from 17% in 2017-18 to 13% in 2019-20 and there may be significant drop further in the next couple of years.

With the onset of global Pandemic maintaining the sales growth is a big risk.

Hence the increasing direct cost and indirect cost lines need to be controlled.

- Financial Re-engineering – Recommended Initiatives
- Impact analysis of Financial Re-engineering Initiatives
- Concluding Remarks

| Item | 2017-18 Actual | 2018-19 Actual | 2019-20 Actual | 2020-21 Budget | 2021-22 Projection | 2022-23 Projection |
|---|---|---|---|---|---|---|
| Revenue | 12,537 | 15,505 | 14,337 | 14,623 | 15,351 | 16,116 |
| Gross Margin | 5,154 | 6,103 | 6,160 | 5,978 | 6,275 | 6,586 |
| EBITDA | 2,153 | 2,390 | 1,868 | 1,257 | 1,081 | 873 |

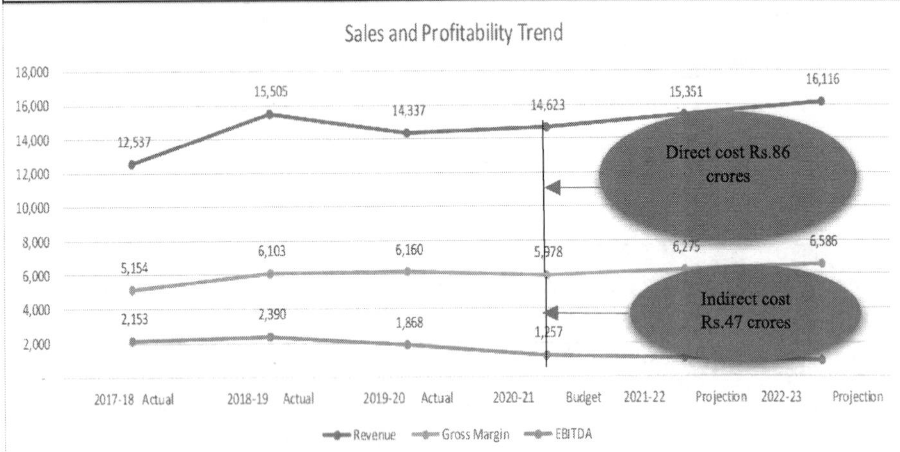


## Net Working Capital Summary

This is shown in the table below.

| Item | 2016-17 Actual | 2017-18 Actual | 2018-19 Actual | 2019-20 Actual | 2020-21 Budget | 2021-22 Projection | 2022-23 Projection | % Increase |
|---|---|---|---|---|---|---|---|---|
| Current Investments | 91 | 139 | 161 | 172 | 172 | 172 | 172 | 14.8% |
| Inventories | 4,969 | 5,859 | 6,362 | 6,913 | 6,913 | 7,258 | 7,621 | 8.9% |
| Trade receivables | 4,303 | 3,283 | 4,151 | 4,022 | 3,620 | 4,344 | 5,213 | 3.5% |
| Loans and advances | 899 | 1,295 | 1,433 | 1,863 | 1,900 | 2,090 | 2,299 | 26.0% |
| Cash and Bank Balances | 67 | 223 | 691 | 499 | 1,081 | 716 | 671 | 150.2% |
| Gross Current Assets | 10,329 | 10,799 | 12,798 | 13,469 | 13,686 | 14,580 | 15,976 | 9.1% |
| Current Liabilities and provisions | 3,010 | 2,320 | 1,928 | 2,737 | 2,463 | 2,710 | 2,981 | -0.2% |
| Net Working Capital | 7,319 | 8,479 | 10,870 | 10,732 | 11,222 | 11,871 | 12,995 | |
| Net Working Capital change | | (1,160) | (2,391) | 138 | (490) | (648) | (1,125) | |
| Short term debt | 4472 | 5,767 | 7,108 | 6,428 | 6,299 | 6,394 | 7,270 | 10.4% |
| Short term debt as % of working capital | 61% | 68% | 65% | 60% | 56% | 54% | 56% | |

## Net Working Capital and Short-term debt

Net Working Capital has increased from Rs.73 crores in 2016-17 to Rs.107 crores in 2019-20 (an increase of 15% year on year).

Inventories has increased from Rs. 50 crores in 2016-17 to Rs.69 crores in 2019-20 (an increase of 13% year on year).

Loans and Advances has increased from Rs.9 crores in 2016-17 to Rs.19 crores in 2019-20 (an increase of 35% year on year).

To fund the above increase, the short-term debt has increased by Rs.20 crores (an increase of 15% year on year).

Short term debt has been used to fund capex of Rs.3.70 crores. Interest pay out for the previous three years have been around Rs.3.8 crores.

## Net Working Capital Trend

| Item | 2016-17 Actual | 2017-18 Actual | 2018-19 Actual | 2019-20 Actual | 2020-21 Budget | 2021-22 Projection | 2022-23 Projection |
|---|---|---|---|---|---|---|---|
| Gross Current Assets | 10,329 | 10,799 | 12,798 | 13,469 | 13,686 | 14,580 | 15,976 |
| Current Liabilities and Provisions | 3,010 | 2,320 | 1,928 | 2,737 | 2,463 | 2,710 | 2,981 |

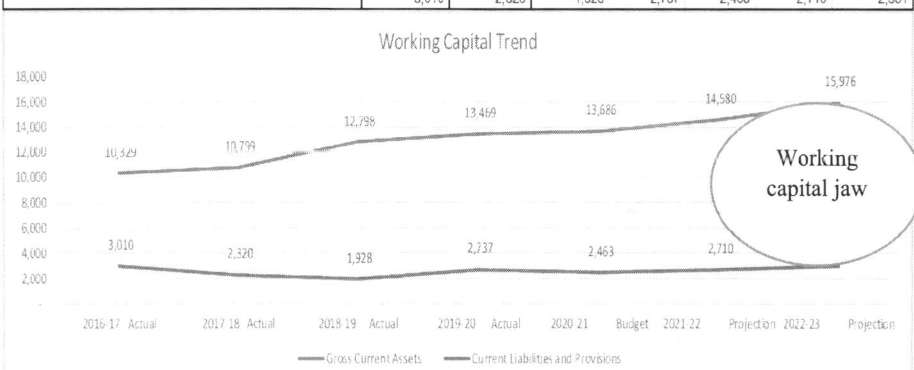


The working capital jaw is getting bigger by the day.

## Inventories versus short term debt

| Item | 2016-17 Actual | 2017-18 Actual | 2018-19 Actual | 2019-20 Actual | 2020-21 Budget | 2021-22 Projection | 2022-23 Projection |
|---|---|---|---|---|---|---|---|
| Inventories | **4,969** | **5,859** | **6,362** | **6,913** | **6,913** | **7,258** | **7,621** |
| Short term debt | 4,472 | 5,767 | 7,108 | 6,428 | 6,299 | 6,394 | 7,270 |

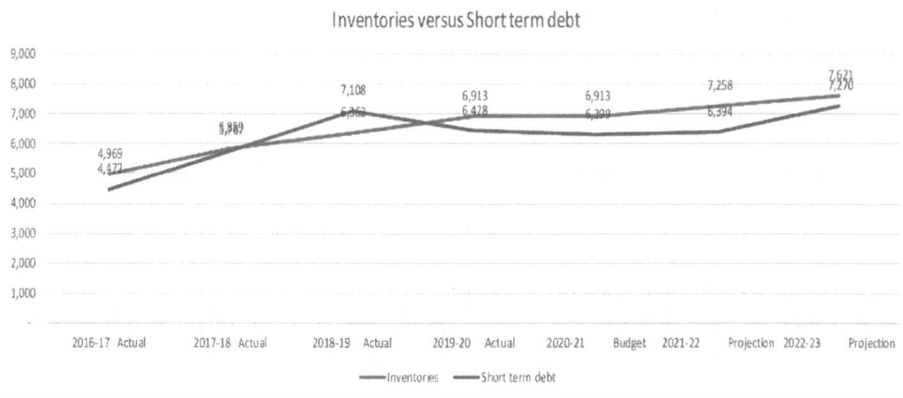


The above chart shows that we have been borrowing to fund our increasing Inventories with high interest cost.

## Free cash flow trend

Based on above numbers, the free cash flow trend looks as under:

| Item | 2016-17 Actual | 2017-18 Actual | 2018-19 Actual | 2019-20 Actual | 2020-21 Budget | 2021-22 Projection | 2022-23 Projection | Terminal value |
|---|---|---|---|---|---|---|---|---|
| Net Operating profit after tax (NOPAT) | | 1,757 | 2,005 | 1,626 | 1,134 | 1,024 | 873 | |
| Capex | | (330) | (514) | (816) | (568) | (400) | (400) | |
| Net working capital change | | (1,160) | (2,391) | 138 | (490) | (648) | (1,125) | |
| Free cash flow | | 267 | (900) | 1,764 | 76 | (24) | (652) | (4,345) |
| Cumulative free cash flow | | 267 | (633) | 1,131 | 1,206 | 1,182 | 530 | |
| WACC | | 15% | | | | | | |
| NPV | | (1,173) | | | | | | |
| NPV(Without terminal value) | | 461 | | | | | | |
| IRR | | -20% | | | | | | |

| Item | 2017-18 Actual | 2018-19 Actual | 2019-20 Actual | 2020-21 Budget | 2021-22 Projection | 2022-23 Projection |
|---|---|---|---|---|---|---|
| Free Cash Flow Trend | 267 | (900) | 1,764 | 76 | (24) | (652) |

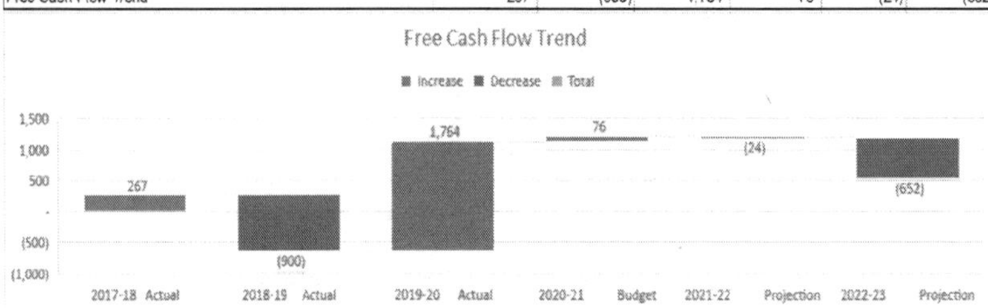


In 2018-19 there has been a negative free cash flow owing to increase in inventories.

There has been significant improvement in free cash flows in 2019-20.

Owing to the onset of Pandemic and consequent economic downturn there is very high risk of significant depletion of free cash flow for the organization in the next few years.

### Risk Analysis

The Risk map is shown below.

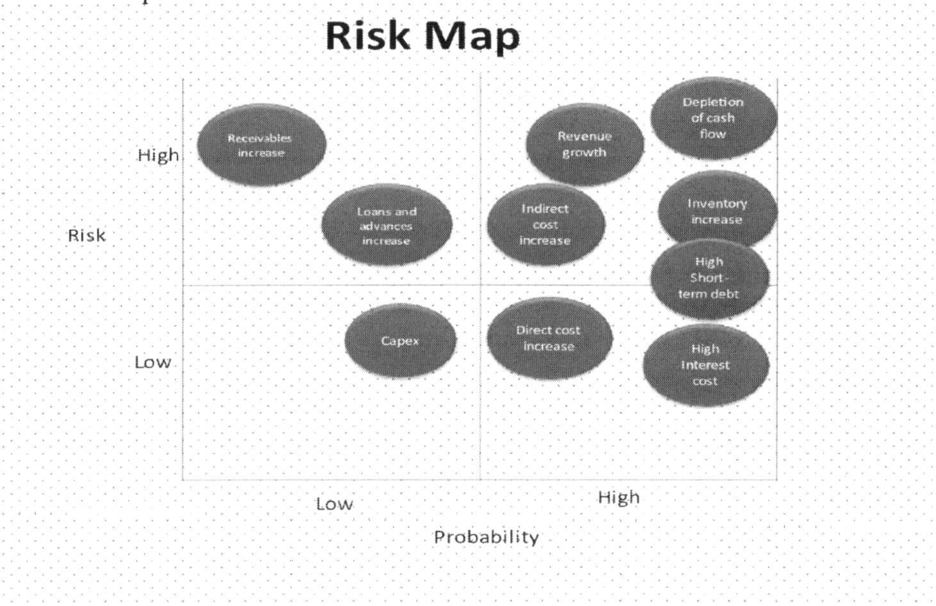


### High Risk areas

Sales growth owing to uncertainty in economy triggered by Pandemic

Progressive decline of EBITDA Margin owing to high incidence of direct and indirect costs

Very high inventories – may include a significant portion of unserviceable raw materials, semi-finished and finished goods

Increase of short-term debt hand in hand with increase in inventories leading into a potential debt trap. All the above may lead to erosion of free cash flows in the foreseeable future.

### Financial Re-engineering Initiatives

Based on the above study, the shortcomings came to light, and these were evident from the risk map shown above. Then the team moved to come up with financial re-engineering initiatives which are highlighted below.

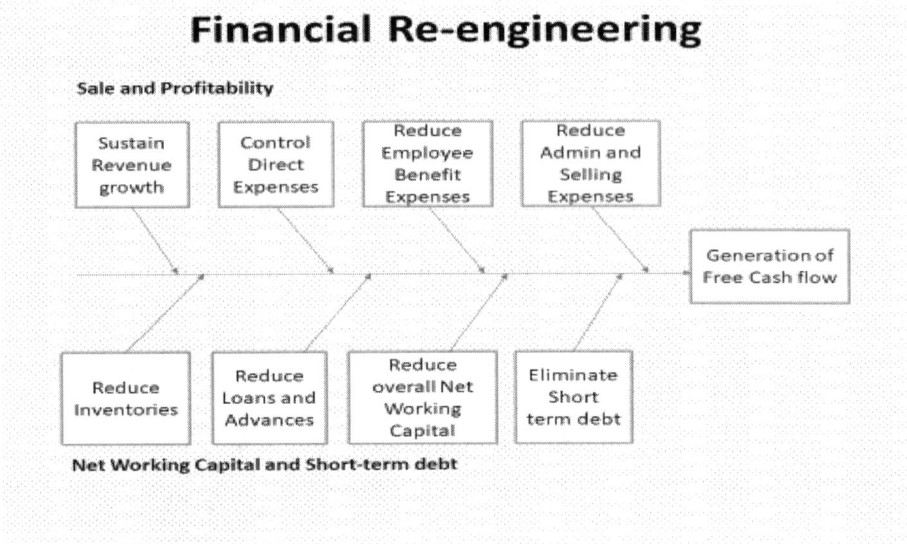


The initiatives depicted in the chart above are explained below.

### Sustain sales growth

Create an updated market analysis both in domestic and export market (specially in EU and the US) to get a fair understanding of the market demand related to our product under the current scenario.

Create a robust and credible month-wise sales forecast in line with the market study of export and domestic market in view of the uncertainty involved with the continuance of the Pandemic.

Produce innovative pricing strategy including attractive volume and price discount.

Develop attractive schemes connected with sales both for export and domestic market.

### Control direct expenses

Once we have a fair understanding of the volume forecast, we need to have detailed sales and operating plan for the next three quarters.

We would need to plan the sales from our inventories first and adjust the production process according to ensuing market demand.

We need to ensure we do not generate fresh inventories which may not have immediate market and hence will add to the already increased inventories going forward.

Review thoroughly the direct operating cost and close down production units which may not be viable in the current scenario.

### Reduce Employee Benefit expenses

Review the list of employees and rework the employee payout between variable and fixed.

For the sales team 60% of the existing payout should be fixed and balance 40% need to be linked to revenue generation.

For the rest of the staff members 75% of the existing payout should be fixed and balance 25% need to be linked to revenue.

The leadership team including the directors need to take a cut in the salaries at least by 25% for the coming three quarters of 2020-21.

### Reduce Administration and selling expenses

Review the Admin and Selling Expenses line by line and make efforts to reduce these expenses.

Advertising and Sales Promotion expenses need to be scrutinized and linked to incremental revenue.

Rent and other expenses attributable to the showrooms in various cities need to be evaluated with the revenue each of these showrooms generate.

All consultancy expenses need to be reviewed rigorously and minimized wherever possible.

Owing to continuance of Pandemic, traveling and local conveyance like motor car running expenses need to be reduced.

Directors' remuneration to the tune of Rs.2.76 crores per annum need to be brought down and linked to incremental revenue generated in the organization.

### Net working capital

**Inventories**

Carry out a financial due diligence of physical inventories across locations by an independent organization.

Segregate physical inventories between serviceable and unserviceable items.

Consider a onetime write down of the unserviceable inventories.

Push the sales team to sell the serviceable inventories within specific timeline.

Work on reducing the operating cycle of conversion of raw materials to finished goods in order that inventory carrying cost is brought down.

Commence strategy of funding inventories through operating cash flows rather than the easier route of initiating short term borrowing.

### Target reduction

Consider target reduction of components of working capital as follows:

Reduce the current level of inventories at Rs.69 crores as under:

2020-21: 20%

2021-22: 5%

2022-23: 10%

Reduce the current level of Trade receivables at Rs.40 crores as under:

2020-21: 10%

Reduce the current level of loans and advances at Rs. Rs.17.70 crores as under:

2020-21: 5%

Reduce the current level of current liabilities at Rs. 27 crores as under:

2020-21: 10%

### Target reduction in short term debt

Additional cash generation from above will ensure reduction of short-term debt as under:

2020-21: 35%

2021-22: 50% (of reducing balance)

2022-23: balance 50% (to make it nil).

In similar traction interest pay out would also be reduced and would eventually become nil as well.

### Impact analysis of Financial Re-engineering initiatives

**Sales and Profitability Analysis**

| Ratio | 2017-18 Actual | 2018-19 Actual | 2019-20 Actual | 2020-21 Budget | 2021-22 Projection | 2022-23 Projection | % Increase |
|---|---|---|---|---|---|---|---|
| Revenue | 12,537 | 15,505 | 14,337 | 14,628 | 15,356 | 16,121 | 5.7% |
| Direct cost | 7,383 | 9,401 | 8,177 | 8,644 | 9,077 | 9,531 | 5.8% |
| Gross Margin | 5,154 | 6,103 | 6,160 | 5,983 | 6,279 | 6,590 | 5.6% |
| Gross Margin % on sales | 41% | 39% | 43% | 41% | 41% | 41% | |
| Indirect cost | 3,000 | 3,713 | 4,292 | 3,442 | 3,614 | 3,794 | 5.3% |
| EBITDA | 2,153 | 2,390 | 1,868 | 2,541 | 2,666 | 2,796 | 6.0% |
| EBITDA Margin % on sales | 17% | 15% | 13% | 17% | 17% | 17% | |
| Depreciation | 431 | 428 | 482 | 506 | 516 | 527 | 4.4% |
| Interest | 366 | 446 | 340 | 340 | 170 | - | -20.0% |
| Profit before tax | 1,356 | 1,516 | 1,046 | 1,695 | 1,979 | 2,269 | 13.5% |
| Tax | 396 | 386 | 242 | 508 | 594 | 681 | |
| Profit after tax | 960 | 1,130 | 803 | 1,186 | 1,385 | 1,588 | 13.1% |
| Net Operating Profit after tax (NOPAT) | 1,757 | 2,005 | 1,626 | 2,033 | 2,072 | 2,115 | 4.1% |

## Working Capital Analysis

| Item | 2016-17 Actual | 2017-18 Actual | 2018-19 Actual | 2019-20 Actual | 2020-21 Budget | 2021-22 Projection | 2022-23 Projection | % Increase |
|---|---|---|---|---|---|---|---|---|
| Current Investments | 91 | 139 | 161 | 172 | 172 | 172 | 172 | 14.8% |
| Inventories | 4,969 | 5,859 | 6,362 | 6,913 | 5,530 | 5,254 | 4,728 | -0.8% |
| Trade receivables | 4303 | 3,283 | 4,151 | 4,022 | 3,620 | 3,801 | 3,991 | -1.2% |
| Loans and advances | 899 | 1,295 | 1,433 | 1,863 | 1,770 | 1,682 | 1,682 | 14.5% |
| Cash and Bank Balances | 67 | 223 | 691 | 499 | 1,371 | 1,558 | 1,705 | |
| Gross Current Assets | 10,329 | 10,799 | 12,798 | 13,469 | 12,463 | 12,466 | 12,278 | 3.1% |
| Current Liabilities and provisions | 3,010 | 2,320 | 1,928 | 2,737 | 2,463 | 2,587 | 2,716 | -1.6% |
| Net Working Capital | 7,319 | 8,479 | 10,870 | 10,732 | 10,000 | 9,880 | 9,562 | |
| Net Working Capital change | | (1,160) | (2,391) | 138 | 732 | 120 | 318 | |
| Short term debt | 4472 | 5,767 | 7,108 | 6,428 | 4,178 | 2,175 | - | -16.7% |
| Short term debt as % of working capital | 61% | 68% | 65% | 60% | 42% | 22% | 0% | |

## Generation of Free Cash Flows

The above financial re-engineering would generate additional free cash flows as under:

| | | |
|---|---|---|
| 2020-21 | : | Rs. 22 crores |
| 2021-22 | : | Rs. 18 crores |
| 2022-23 | : | Rs. 20 crores |

Net present value would work out to Rs. 88 crores discounted at 15% weighted average cost of capital.

This additional cash flow will be used to extinguish the long term and short-term debt.

## Free Cash Flow Trend (To be state)

| Item | 2016-17 Actual | 2017-18 Actual | 2018-19 Actual | 2019-20 Actual | 2020-21 Budget | 2021-22 Projection | 2022-23 Projection | Terminal value |
|---|---|---|---|---|---|---|---|---|
| Net Operating profit after tax (NOPAT) | | 1,757 | 2,005 | 1,626 | 2,033 | 2,072 | 2,115 | |
| Capex | | (330) | (514) | (816) | (568) | (400) | (400) | |
| Net working capital change | | (1,160) | (2,391) | 138 | 732 | 120 | 318 | |
| Free cash flow | | 267 | (900) | 1,764 | 2,197 | 1,792 | 2,033 | 13,552 |
| Cumulative free cash flow | | 267 | (633) | 1,131 | 3,328 | 5,120 | 7,152 | |
| WACC | | 15% | | | | | | |
| NPV | | 8,832 | | | | | | |
| NPV(Without terminal value) | | 3,737 | | | | | | |

The numbers are depicted in graphical mode.

| Item | 2017-18 Actual | 2018-19 Actual | 2019-20 Actual | 2020-21 Budget | 2021-22 Projection | 2022-23 Projection |
|---|---|---|---|---|---|---|
| Free cash flow trend | 267 | (900) | 1,764 | 2,197 | 1,792 | 2,033 |

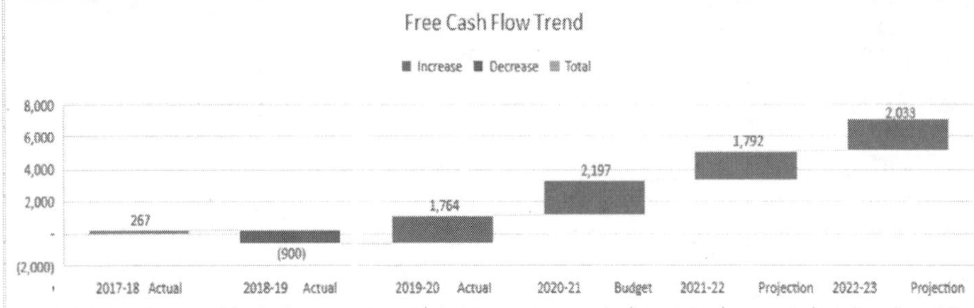


**Impact of Cash generation based on Financial Reengineering initiatives**

| Item | 2017-18 Actual | 2018-19 Actual | 2019-20 Actual | 2020-21 Budget | 2021-22 Projection | 2022-23 Projection |
|---|---|---|---|---|---|---|
| Cumulative Free Cash Flow (buyer side) | 267 | (633) | 1,131 | 1,206 | 1,182 | 530 |
| Cumulative Free Cash Flow (seller side) | 267 | (633) | 1,131 | 3,328 | 5,120 | 7,152 |

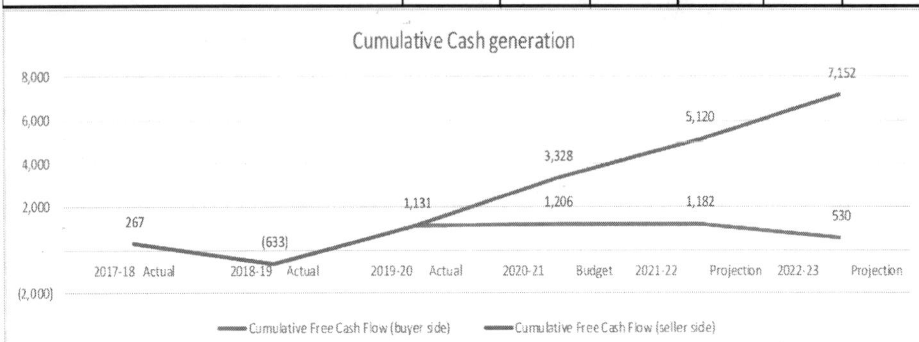


## Concluding remarks

The organization needs to achieve at least nominal sales growth during uncertainty in economy triggered by Pandemic.

EBITDA Margin needs to be restored back to 17% by implementing stringent measures in controlling direct and indirect costs.

Effective initiatives need to be implemented to reduce existing level of inventories by at least 20%, one of the major initiatives may include removal of unserviceable raw materials, semi- finished and finished goods.

Based on the above initiatives, generate additional free cash flows which may be used to repay short term debt and come out of potential debt trap.